CME PROJECT

Geometry

COMMON CORE

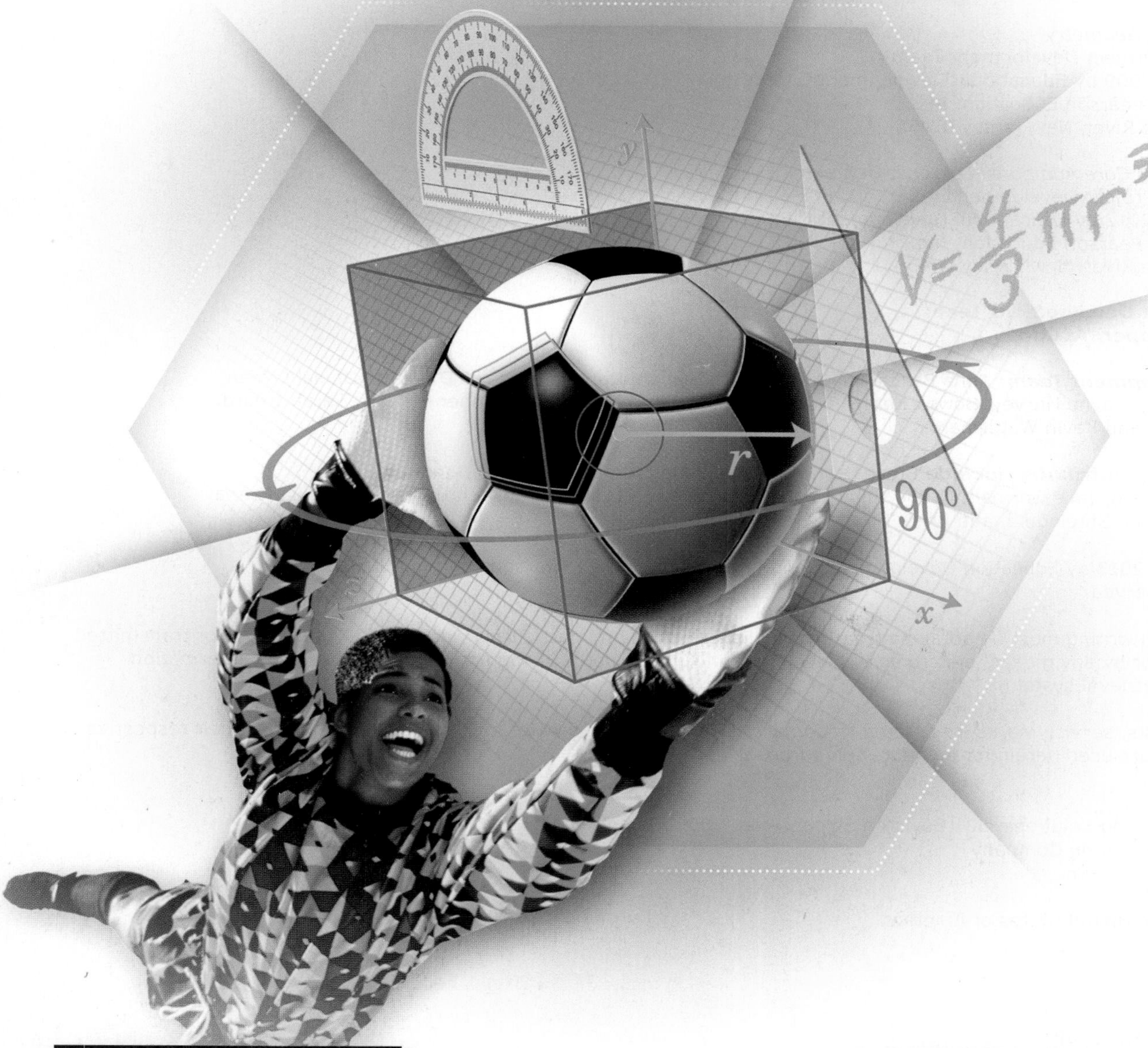

PEARSON

The Center for Mathematics Education Project was developed at Education Development Center, Inc. (EDC) within the Center for Mathematics Education (CME), with partial support from the National Science Foundation.

Education Development Center, Inc.
Center for Mathematics Education
Newton, Massachusetts

This material is based upon work supported by the National Science Foundation under Grant No. ESI-0242476, Grant No. MDR-9252952, and Grant No. ESI-9617369. Any opinions, findings, and conclusions or recommendations expressed in this material are those of the author(s) and do not necessarily reflect the views of the National Science Foundation.

Cover Art: 9 Surf Studios; Jim Cummins/Corbis; Stockbyte/Getty Images, Inc.

Taken from:
CME Project: Geometry
By the CME Project Development Team
Copyright ©2009 by Educational Development Center, Inc.
Published by Pearson Education, Inc.
Upper Saddle River, New Jersey 07458

CME Common Core Additional Lessons: Geometry
By the CME Project Development Team
Copyright ©2012 by Educational Development Center, Inc.
Published by Pearson Education, Inc.
Upper Saddle River, New Jersey 07458

CME Project Development Team
***Lead Developer:* Al Cuoco**

Core Development Team: Anna Baccaglini-Frank, Jean Benson, Nancy Antonellis D'Amato, Daniel Erman, Brian Harvey, Wayne Harvey, Bowen Kerins, Doreen Kilday, Ryota Matsuura, Stephen Maurer, Sarah Sword, Audrey Ting, and Kevin Waterman.

Others who contributed include Steve Benson, Paul D'Amato, Robert Devaney, Andrew Golay, Paul Goldenberg, Jane Gorman, C. Jud Hill, Eric Karnowski, Helen Lebowitz, Joseph Leverich, Melanie Palma, Mark Saul, Nina Shteingold, and Brett Thomas.

Pearson Learning Solutions, 501 Boylston Street, Suite 900, Boston, MA 02116
A Pearson Education Company
www.pearsoned.com

Printed in the United States of America

5 16

000200010271661109

MD

ISBN 10: 1-256-74148-5
ISBN 13: 978-1-256-74148-0

Contents in Brief

Introduction to the CME Project

The CME Project, developed by EDC's Center for Mathematics Education, is a new NSF-funded high school program, organized around the familiar courses of algebra 1, geometry, algebra 2, and precalculus. The CME Project provides teachers and schools with a third alternative to the choice between traditional texts driven by basic skill development and more progressive texts that have unfamiliar organizations. This program gives teachers the option of a problem-based, student-centered program, organized around the mathematical themes with which teachers and parents are familiar. Furthermore, the tremendous success of NSF-funded middle school programs has left a need for a high school program with similar rigor and pedagogy. The CME Project fills this need.

The goal of the CME Project is to help students acquire a deep understanding of mathematics. Therefore, the mathematics here is rigorous. We took great care to create lesson plans that, while challenging, will capture and engage students of all abilities and improve their mathematical achievement.

The Program's Approach

The organization of the CME Project provides students the time and focus they need to develop fundamental mathematical ways of thinking. Its primary goal is to develop in students robust mathematical proficiency.

- The program employs innovative instructional methods, developed over decades of classroom experience and informed by research, that help students master mathematical topics.
- One of the core tenets of the CME Project is to focus on developing students' Habits of Mind, or ways in which students approach and solve mathematical challenges.
- The program builds on lessons learned from high-performing countries: develop an idea thoroughly and then revisit it only to deepen it; organize ideas in a way that is faithful to how they are organized in mathematics; and reduce clutter and extraneous topics.
- It also employs the best American models that call for grappling with ideas and problems as preparation for instruction, moving from concrete problems to abstractions and general theories, and situating mathematics in engaging contexts.
- The CME Project is a comprehensive curriculum that meets the dual goals of mathematical rigor and accessibility for a broad range of students.

About CME

EDC's Center for Mathematics Education, led by mathematician and teacher **Al Cuoco,** brings together an eclectic staff of mathematicians, teachers, cognitive scientists, education researchers, curriculum developers, specialists in educational technology, and teacher educators, internationally known for leadership across the entire range of K–16 mathematics education. We aim to help students and teachers in this country experience the thrill of solving problems and building theories, understand the history of ideas behind the evolution of mathematical disciplines, and appreciate the standards of rigor that are central to mathematical culture.

Contributors to the CME Project

National Advisory Board The National Advisory Board met early in the project, providing critical feedback on the instructional design and the overall organization. Members include

Richard Askey, University of Wisconsin
Edward Barbeau, University of Toronto
Hyman Bass, University of Michigan
Carol Findell, Boston University
Arthur Heinricher, Worcester Polytechnic Institute
Roger Howe, Yale University
Barbara Janson, Janson Associates
Kenneth Levasseur, University of Massachusetts, Lowell
James Madden, Louisiana State University, Baton Rouge
Jacqueline Miller, Education Development Center
James Newton, University of Maryland
Robert Segall, Greater Hartford Academy of Mathematics and Science
Glenn Stevens, Boston University
Herbert Wilf, University of Pennsylvania
Hung-Hsi Wu, University of California, Berkeley

Core Mathematical Consultants **Dick Askey, Ed Barbeau,** and **Roger Howe** have been involved in an even more substantial way, reviewing chapters and providing detailed and critical advice on every aspect of the program. Dick and Roger spent many hours reading and criticizing drafts, brainstorming with the writing team, and offering advice on everything from the logical organization to the actual numbers used in problems. We can't thank them enough.

Teacher Advisory Board The Teacher Advisory Board for the CME Project was essential in helping us create an effective format for our lessons that embodies the philosophy and goals of the program. Their debates about pedagogical issues and how to develop mathematical topics helped to shape the distinguishing features of the curriculum so that our lessons work effectively in the classroom. The advisory board includes

Jayne Abbas, Richard Coffey, Charles Garabedian, Dennis Geller, Eileen Herlihy, Doreen Kilday, Gayle Masse, Hugh McLaughlin, Nancy McLaughlin, Allen Olsen, Kimberly Osborne, Brian Shoemaker, and **Benjamin Sinwell**

Field-Test Teachers Our field-test teachers gave us the benefit of their classroom experience by teaching from our draft lessons and giving us extensive, critical feedback that shaped the drafts into realistic, teachable lessons. They shared their concerns, questions, challenges, and successes and kept us focused on the real world. Some of them even welcomed us into their classrooms as co-teachers to give us the direct experience with students that we needed to hone our lessons. Working with these expert professionals has been one of the most gratifying parts of the development—they are "highly qualified" in the most profound sense.

California **Barney Martinez,** Jefferson High School, Daly City; **Calvin Baylon** and **Jaime Lao,** Bell Junior High School, San Diego; **Colorado** **Rocky Cundiff,** Ignacio High School, Ignacio; **Illinois** **Jeremy Kahan, Tammy Nguyen,** and **Stephanie Pederson,** Ida Crown Jewish Academy, Chicago; **Massachusetts** **Carol Martignette, Chris Martino,** and **Kent Werst,** Arlington High School, Arlington; **Larry Davidson,** Boston University Academy, Boston; **Joe Bishop** and **Carol Rosen,** Lawrence High School, Lawrence; **Maureen Mulryan,** Lowell High School, Lowell; **Felisa Honeyman,** Newton South High School, Newton Centre; **Jim Barnes** and **Carol Haney,** Revere High School, Revere; **New Hampshire** **Jayne Abbas** and **Terin Voisine,** Cawley Middle School, Hooksett; **New Mexico** **Mary Andrews,** Las Cruces High School, Las Cruces; **Ohio** **James Stallworth,** Hughes Center, Cincinnati; **Texas** **Arnell Crayton,** Bellaire High School, Bellaire; **Utah** **Troy Jones,** Waterford School, Sandy; **Washington** **Dale Erz, Kathy Greer, Karena Hanscom,** and **John Henry,** Port Angeles High School, Port Angeles; **Wisconsin** **Annette Roskam,** Rice Lake High School, Rice Lake.

Special thanks go to our colleagues at Pearson, most notably Elizabeth Lehnertz, Joe Will, and Stewart Wood. The program benefits from their expertise in every way, from the actual mathematics to the design of the printed page.

1 An Informal Introduction to Geometry

2 Congruence and Proof

3 Dissections and Area

Similarity

5 Circles

6 Using Similarity

Coordinates and Vectors

8 Optimization

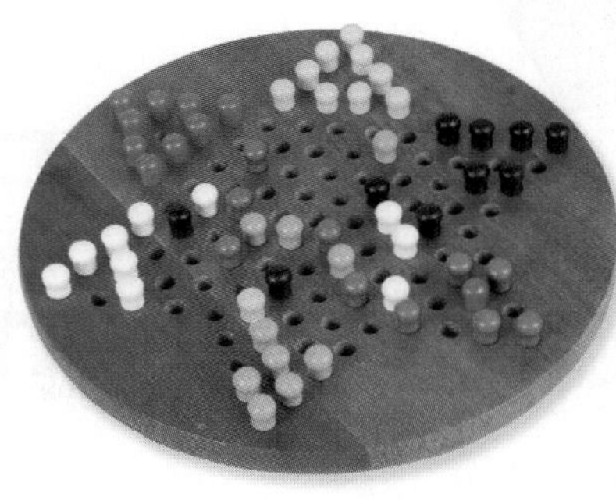

CME Project Student Handbook

What Makes CME Different

Welcome to the CME Project! The goal of this program is to help you develop a deep understanding of mathematics. Throughout this book, you will engage in many different activities to help you develop that deep understanding. Some of these instructional activities may be different from ones you are used to. Below is an overview of some of these elements and why they are an important part of the CME Project.

The Habits of Mind Experience

Mathematical Habits of Mind are the foundation for serious questioning, solid thinking, good problem solving, and critical analysis. These Habits of Mind are what will help you become a mathematical thinker. Throughout the CME Project, you will focus on developing and refining these Habits of Mind.

Lesson 1.0 is an introduction to Habits of Mind. This lesson consists of experiments that allow you to tinker with the mathematical ideas that you will formalize throughout the course.

Developing Habits of Mind

Develop thinking skills. This feature provides you with various methods and approaches to solving problems.

You will develop, use, and revisit specific Habits of Mind throughout the course. These include

- **Process** (how you work through problems)
- **Visualization** (how you "picture" problems)
- **Representation** (what you write down)
- **Patterns** (what you find)
- **Relationships** (what you find or use)

Developing good habits will help you as problems become more complicated.

Habits of Mind

Think. These special margin notes highlight key thinking skills and prompt you to apply your developing Habits of Mind.

You can find Developing Habits of Mind **on pages** 45, 55, 91, 106, 153, 198, 241, 243, 291, 325, 331, 332, 340, 440, 442, 462, 504, 562, 583, 603, 613, 617, 631, 661, 678, 694, and 727.

Minds in Action

Discussion of mathematical ideas is an effective method of learning. The Minds in Action feature exposes you to ways of communicating about mathematics.

Join Sasha, Tony, Derman, and others as they think, calculate, predict, and discuss their way towards understanding.

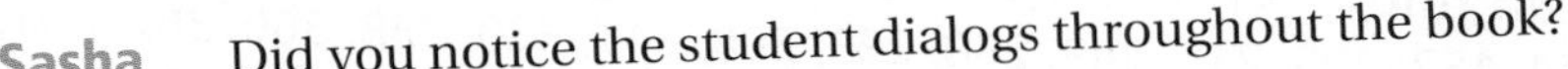

Minds in Action **prologue**

Sasha, Tony, and Derman have just skimmed through their CME Project Geometry *book.*

Sasha Did you notice the student dialogs throughout the book?

Derman Sure did!

Tony They talk and think just the way we do.

Sasha I know! And they even make mistakes sometimes, just the way we do.

Tony But I like how they help each other to learn from those mistakes. I bet they use the Habits of Mind I saw all over the book, too.

Sasha That's great! They should help a lot.

You can find Minds in Action **on pages** 27, 75, 92, 148, 175, 181, 206, 240, 266, 269, 275, 281, 310, 338, 358, 401, 415, 421, 428, 438, 442, 468, 483, 495, 518, 526, 534, 570, 580, 595, 603, 608, 628, 636, 675, 695, 699 and 701.

Exploring Mathematics

Throughout the CME Project, you will engage in activities that extend your learning and allow you to explore the concepts you learn in greater depth. Two of these activities are In-Class Experiments and Chapter Projects.

In-Class Experiment

In-Class Experiments allow you to explore new concepts and apply the Habits of Mind.

You will explore math as mathematicians do. You start with a question and develop answers through experimentation.

Chapter Projects

Chapter Projects allow you to apply your Habits of Mind to the content of the chapter. These projects cover many different topics and allow you to explore and engage in greater depth.

Chapter Projects
Using Mathematical Habits

Here is a list of the Chapter Projects and page numbers.

Using your CME Book

To help you make the most of your CME experience, we are providing the following overview of the organization of your book.

Focusing your Learning

In *Geometry*, there are 8 chapters, with each chapter devoted to a mathematical concept. With only 8 chapters, your class will be able to focus on these core concepts and develop a deep understanding of them.

Within each chapter, you will explore a series of Investigations. Each Investigation focuses on an important aspect of the mathematical concept for that chapter.

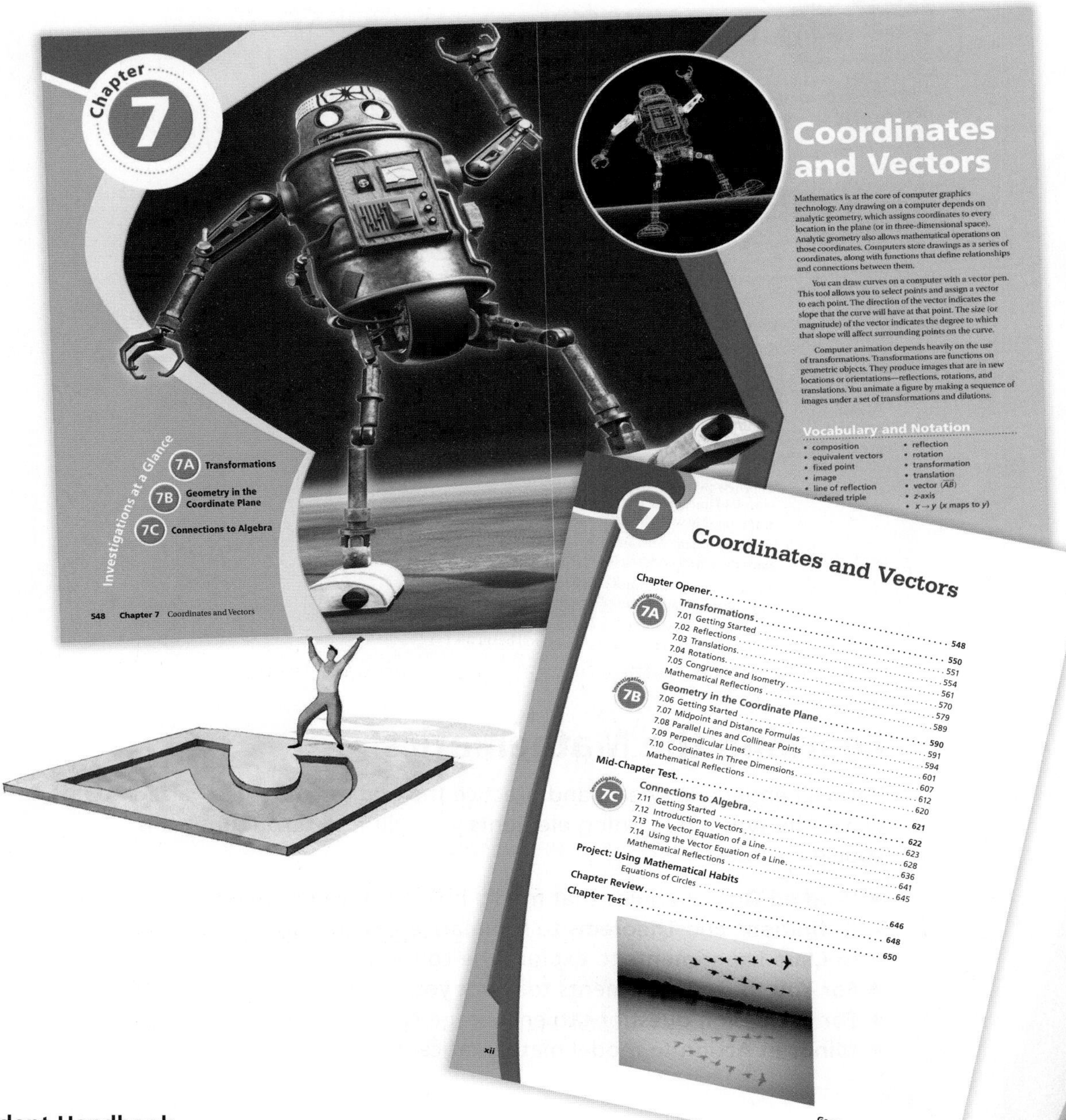

Chapter 7

Investigations at a Glance

7A Transformations

7B Geometry in the Coordinate Plane

7C Connections to Algebra

548 Chapter 7 Coordinates and Vectors

Coordinates and Vectors

Mathematics is at the core of computer graphics technology. Any drawing on a computer depends on analytic geometry, which assigns coordinates to every location in the plane (or in three-dimensional space). Analytic geometry also allows mathematical operations on those coordinates. Computers store drawings as a series of coordinates, along with functions that define relationships and connections between them.

You can draw curves on a computer with a vector pen. This tool allows you to select points and assign a vector to each point. The direction of the vector indicates the slope that the curve will have at that point. The size (or magnitude) of the vector indicates the degree to which that slope will affect surrounding points on the curve.

Computer animation depends heavily on the use of transformations. Transformations are functions on geometric objects. They produce images that are in new locations or orientations—reflections, rotations, and translations. You animate a figure by making a sequence of images under a set of transformations and dilations.

Vocabulary and Notation

- composition
- equivalent vectors
- fixed point
- image
- line of reflection
- ordered triple
- reflection
- rotation
- transformation
- translation
- vector ($\overline{AB}$)
- z-axis
- $x \rightarrow y$ (x maps to y)

7 Coordinates and Vectors

xii

Geometry

The CME Investigation

The goal of each mathematical Investigation is for you to formalize your understanding of the mathematics being taught. There are some common instructional features in each Investigation.

Getting Started

You will launch into each Investigation with a Getting Started lesson that activates prior knowledge and explores new ideas. This lesson provides you the opportunity to grapple with ideas and problems. The goal of these lessons is for you to explore—not all your questions will be answered in these lessons.

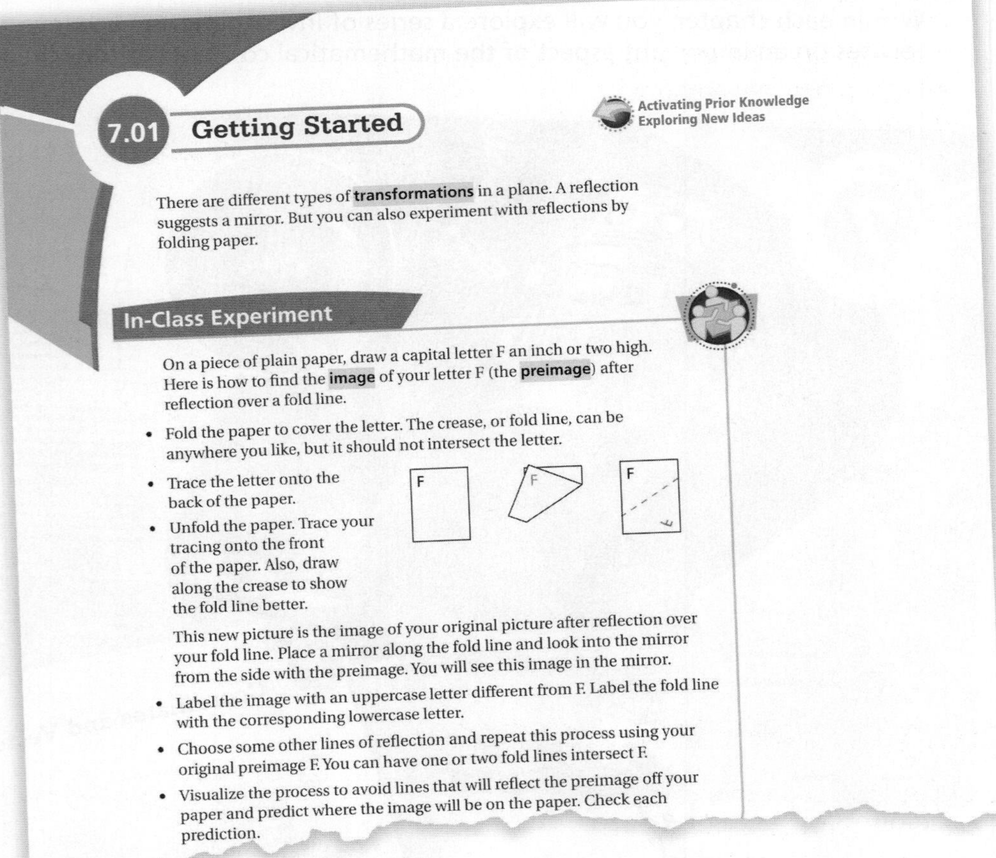

7.01 Getting Started

Activating Prior Knowledge
Exploring New Ideas

There are different types of **transformations** in a plane. A reflection suggests a mirror. But you can also experiment with reflections by folding paper.

In-Class Experiment

On a piece of plain paper, draw a capital letter F an inch or two high. Here is how to find the **image** of your letter F (the **preimage**) after reflection over a fold line.

- Fold the paper to cover the letter. The crease, or fold line, can be anywhere you like, but it should not intersect the letter.
- Trace the letter onto the back of the paper.
- Unfold the paper. Trace your tracing onto the front of the paper. Also, draw along the crease to show the fold line better.

This new picture is the image of your original picture after reflection over your fold line. Place a mirror along the fold line and look into the mirror from the side with the preimage. You will see this image in the mirror.

- Label the image with an uppercase letter different from F. Label the fold line with the corresponding lowercase letter.
- Choose some other lines of reflection and repeat this process using your original preimage F. You can have one or two fold lines intersect F.
- Visualize the process to avoid lines that will reflect the preimage off your paper and predict where the image will be on the paper. Check each prediction.

Learning the Mathematics

You will engage in, learn, and practice the mathematics in a variety of ways. The types of learning elements you will find throughout this course include

- **Worked-Out Examples** that model how to solve problems
- **Definitions and Theorems** to summarize key concepts
- **In-Class Experiments** to explore the concepts
- **For You to Do** assignments to check your understanding
- **For Discussion** questions to encourage communication
- **Minds in Action** to model mathematical discussion

Communicating the Mathematics

Minds in Action

Student dialogs
By featuring dialogs between characters, the CME Project exposes you to a way of communicating about mathematics. These dialogs will then become a real part of your classroom!

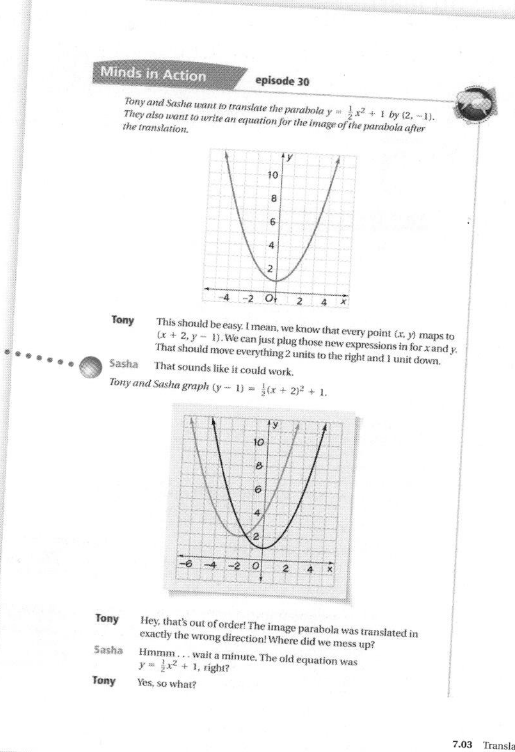

Minds in Action episode 30

Tony and Sasha want to translate the parabola $y = \frac{1}{2}x^2 + 1$ by $(2, -1)$. They also want to write an equation for the image of the parabola after the translation.

Tony This should be easy. I mean, we know that every point (x, y) maps to $(x + 2, y - 1)$. We can just plug those new expressions in for x and y. That should move everything 2 units to the right and 1 unit down.

Sasha That sounds like it could work.

Tony and Sasha graph $(y - 1) = \frac{1}{2}(x + 2)^2 + 1$.

Tony Hey, that's out of order! The image parabola was translated in exactly the wrong direction! Where did we mess up?

Sasha Hmmm . . . wait a minute. The old equation was $y = \frac{1}{2}x^2 + 1$, right?

Tony Yes, so what?

7.03 Translations 563

Reflecting on the Mathematics

At the end of each Investigation, Mathematical Reflections give you an opportunity to put ideas together. This feature allows you to demonstrate your understanding of the Investigation and reflect on what you learn.

Practice

The CME Project views extensive practice as a critical component of a mathematics curriculum. You will have daily opportunities to practice what you learn.

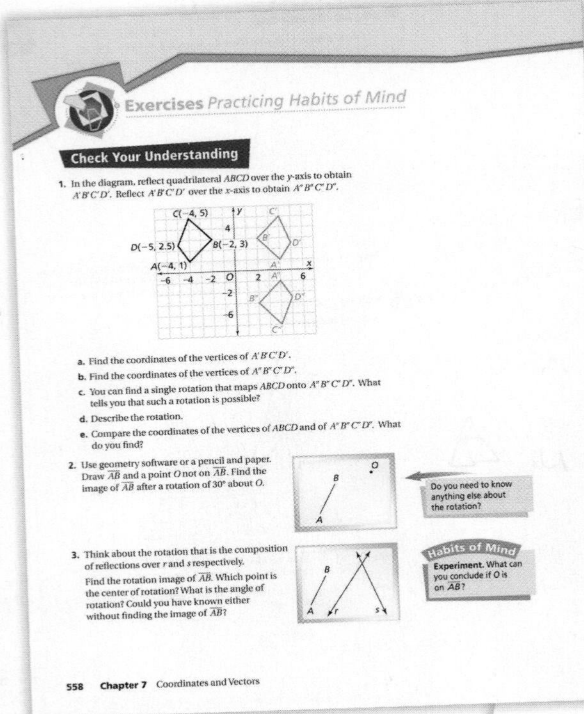

Exercises *Practicing Habits of Mind*

Check Your Understanding

1. In the diagram, reflect quadrilateral $ABCD$ over the y-axis to obtain $A'B'C'D'$. Reflect $A'B'C'D'$ over the x-axis to obtain $A''B''C''D''$.

   a. Find the coordinates of the vertices of $A'B'C'D'$.
   b. Find the coordinates of the vertices of $A''B''C''D''$.
   c. You can find a single rotation that maps $ABCD$ onto $A''B''C''D''$. What tells you that such a rotation is possible?
   d. Describe the rotation.
   e. Compare the coordinates of the vertices of $ABCD$ and of $A''B''C''D''$. What do you find?

2. Use geometry software or a pencil and paper. Draw $\overline{AB}$ and a point O not on $\overline{AB}$. Find the image of $\overline{AB}$ after a rotation of 30° about O.

Do you need to know anything else about the rotation?

3. Think about the rotation that is the composition of reflections over r and s respectively. Find the rotation image of $\overline{AB}$. Which point is the center of rotation? What is the angle of rotation? Could you have known either without finding the image of $\overline{AB}$?

Habits of Mind
Experiment. What can you conclude if O is on $\overline{AB}$?

558 **Chapter 7** Coordinates and Vectors

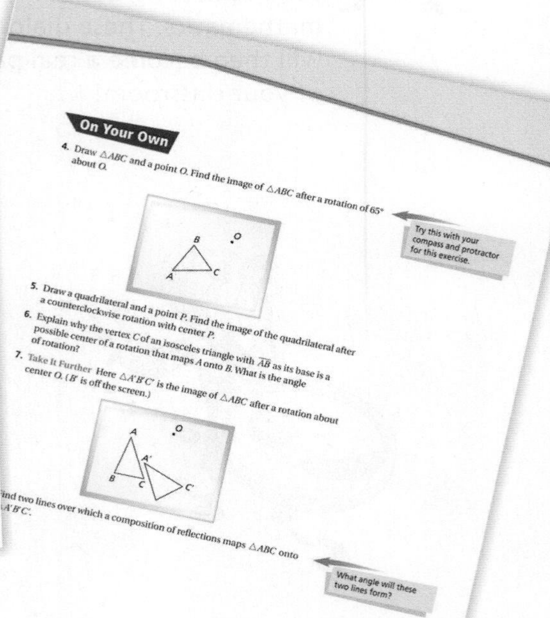

On Your Own

4. Draw $\triangle ABC$ and a point O. Find the image of $\triangle ABC$ after a rotation of 65° about O.

Try this with your compass and protractor for this exercise.

5. Draw a quadrilateral and a point P. Find the image of the quadrilateral after a counterclockwise rotation with center P.
6. Explain why the vertex C of an isosceles triangle with $\overline{AB}$ as its base is a possible center of a rotation that maps A onto B. What is the angle of rotation?
7. Take It Further Here $\triangle A'B'C'$ is the image of $\triangle ABC$ after a rotation about center O. (B' is off the screen.)

ind two lines over which a composition of reflections maps $\triangle ABC$ onto $\triangle A'B'C'$.

What angle will these two lines form?

7.04 Rotations 577

Check Your Understanding

Assess your readiness for independent practice by working through these problems in class.

On Your Own

Practice and continue developing the mathematical understanding you learn in each lesson.

Maintain Your Skills

Review and reinforce skills from previous lessons.

Also Available

An additional Practice Workbook is available separately.

Go Online

With PearsonSuccessNet your teachers have selected the best tools and features to help you succeed in your classes.

Log-in to www.pearsonsuccessnet.com to find:

- **an online Pearson eText version of your textbook**
- **extra practice and assessments**
- **worksheets and activities**
- **multimedia**

Check out PearsonSuccessNet

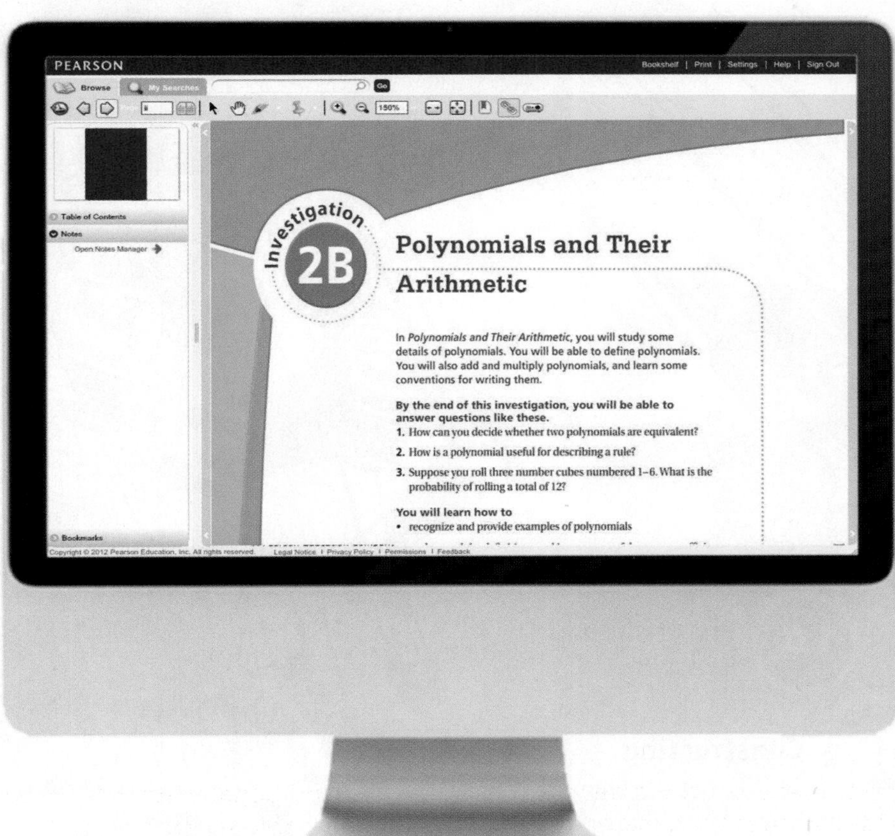

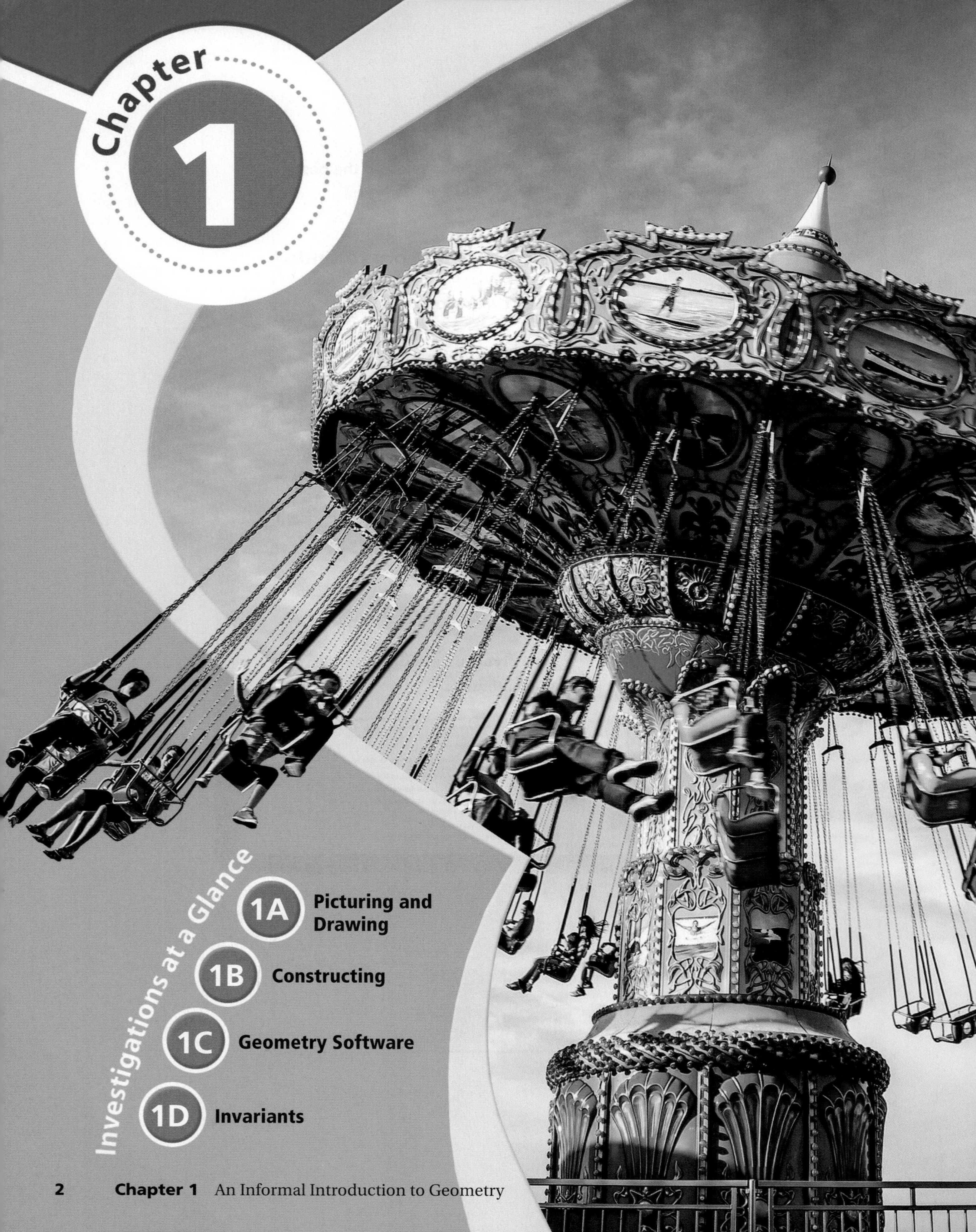
Chapter
1
Investigations at a Glance
1A Picturing and Drawing
1B Constructing
1C Geometry Software
1D Invariants

An Informal Introduction to Geometry

A valuable geometry skill is being able to recognize what relationships between the parts or the measures of geometric figures stay the same while other elements associated with the figures change.

Here are some simple examples:

- The radius of a circle stays the same while you turn the circle about its center.
- The height of a triangle stays the same while you move a vertex of the triangle parallel to the triangle's base.
- The diagonals of a parallelogram bisect each other while you move the sides of the parallelogram.

Recognizing such invariants is a mathematical *habit of mind*. There are many others. And they are a focus of this book. The ways you think about mathematics—your habits of mind—are among the invaluable life applications that you will take from this course.

Vocabulary and Notation

- altitude
- angle bisector
- collinear points
- concurrent lines
- congruent
- constant
- construction
- disc
- equidistant
- equilateral
- invariant
- line of symmetry
- line segment
- median
- midline
- midpoint
- parallel lines
- parallel planes
- perpendicular bisector
- prism
- symmetric
- theorem
- $\angle ACB$ (angle ACB)
- $\overleftrightarrow{CD}$ (line CD)
- $\overline{AB}$ (segment AB)

1.0 Habits of Mind

If you watch college sports on television, you may have seen this message from the National Collegiate Athletic Association (NCAA).

> There are over 380,000 student-athletes, and just about every one of them will go pro in something other than sports.

For practitioners of mathematics (mathletes), a similar message could say

> There are over 30,000,000 student-mathletes in this country, and just about every one of them will go pro in something other than mathematics.

So, why play sports? Why study mathematics? Simple. In either venture, the habits you learn have value for the rest of your life. Compare these lists.

Habits of Body	Habits of Mind
Athletics	**Mathematics**
Take care of the body.	Take care of the mind.
Think ahead.	Think ahead.
Build strength.	Build mental agility.
Take a chance.	Take a chance.
Develop conditioning.	Develop persistence.
Respect the rules.	Respect the rules.
Practice mental toughness.	Practice mental discipline.
Visualize perfection.	Visualize relationships.
Plan strategies.	Plan strategies.
Have confidence.	Have confidence.
Model the opponent.	Model the problem.
Study styles.	Look for patterns.
Work as a team.	Work with others.
and many more . . .	**and many more . . .**

To get you started this year, try some of the following activities. As you proceed (and throughout the course), think about how you are thinking. Pay attention to your habits of mind!

Good habits of body will help you on and off the court. Good habits of mind will help you inside and outside the classroom.

In-Class Experiment

Look for Patterns

1. Since this is early in the class year, it is time for introductions. If everyone in a class shakes hands with everyone else, how many handshakes will there be?
2. How many diagonals are in a square? In a pentagon? In a hexagon? In a heptagon? In an octagon? Write a formula that relates the number of diagonals of *any* regular polygon to the number of sides.

If *penta-*, *hexa-*, *hepta-*, and *octa-* mean 5, 6, 7, and 8, and *poly-* means "many," what does *-gon* mean?

Definitions

A regular polygon is a closed figure with sides all equal in length and angles all equal in measure. A diagonal of a polygon is a segment that joins two nonconsecutive vertices.

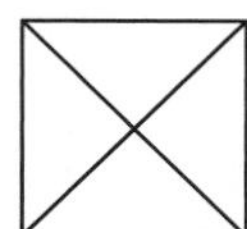
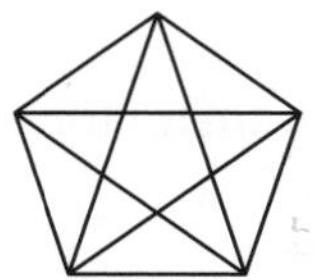
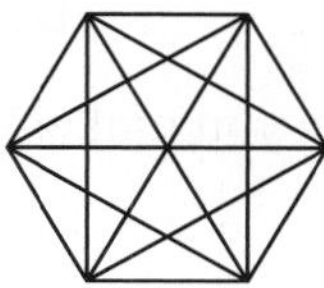

3. How is counting handshakes similar to counting diagonals? Explain.

In-Class Experiment

Build Mental Agility

Consider the question "How many squares are in the figure at the right?"

Many people would quickly answer "four," but, in fact, there are five squares in the figure, four small squares and one large square.

4. How many squares are in the figure at the left below? Explain how you got your answer.
5. Copy the dot pattern at the right below. How many squares can you make using the dots for vertices? Draw diagrams to support your answer.

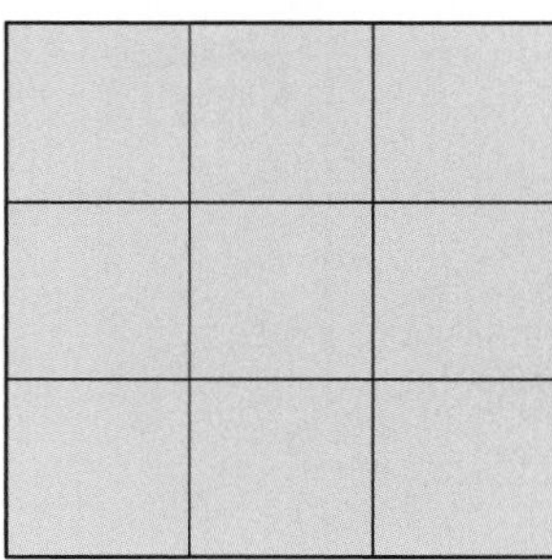

In-Class Experiment

Plan Strategies

Think about unfolding a cube and laying out its faces as a set of squares attached at their edges. The figure that results from unfolding a three-dimensional solid is called a **net.** There are many nets for a cube.

6. Which of the following are nets for cubes? How do you know?

a.

b.

c.

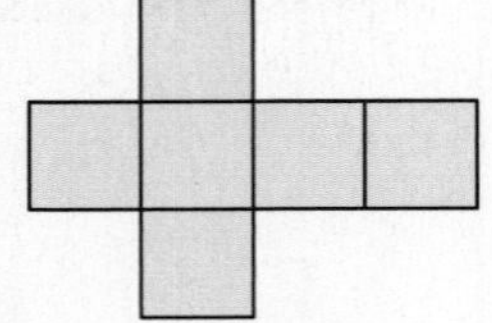

d.

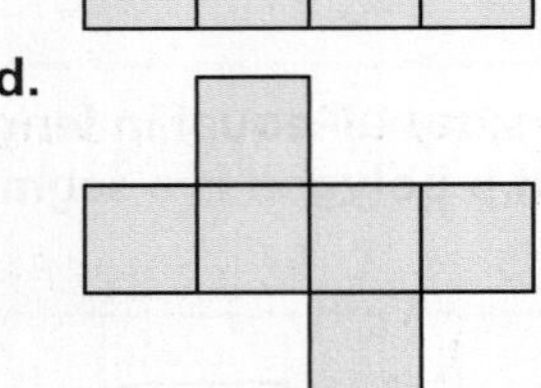

7. How many *different* nets for a cube can you make? What does it mean for nets to be different?

8. Find all the possible nets for a regular tetrahedron.

9. Draw a net for a cylinder. It should include the top and bottom circular faces. In your drawing, what lengths should be the same?

10. The three-dimensional figure made from eight triangular faces is an **octahedron.** Here are four drawings of eight congruent triangles connected in some way. Decide whether each is a net for a regular octahedron. What other nets can you find for regular octahedrons?

a.

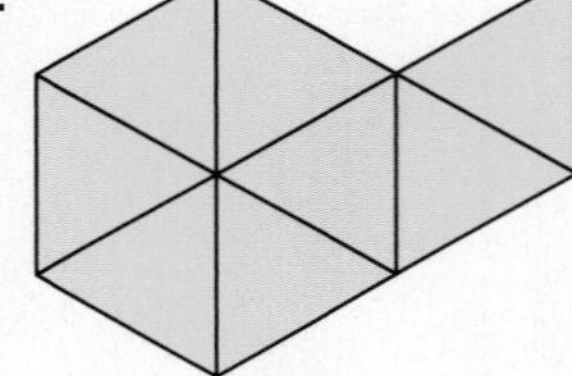

b.

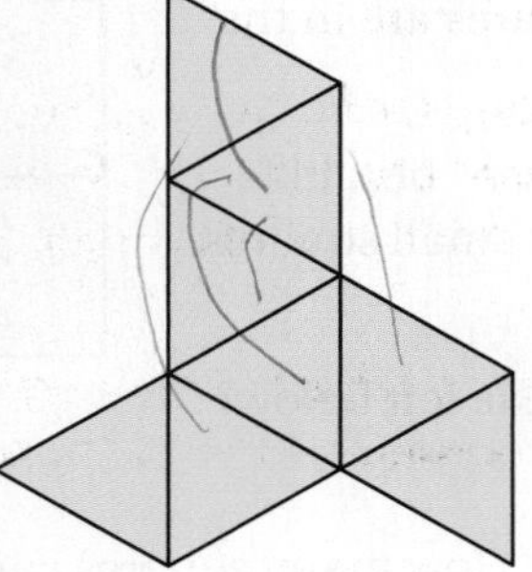

c.

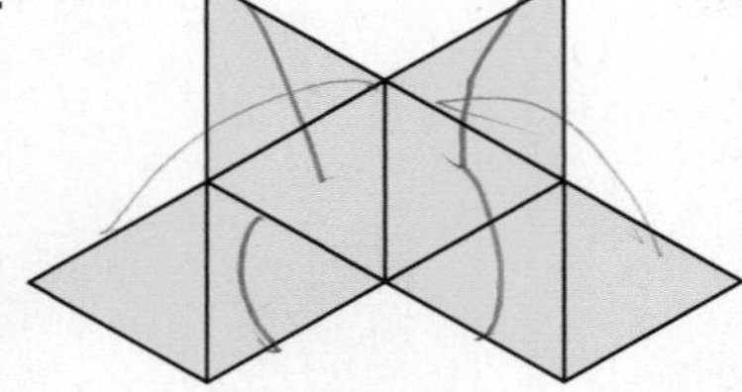

d.

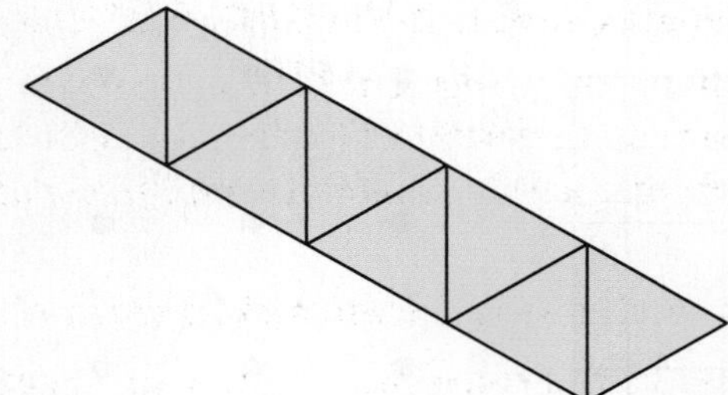

Habits of Mind

Visualize. Continue to unfold the cube in your mind.

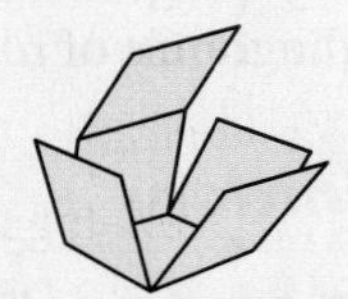

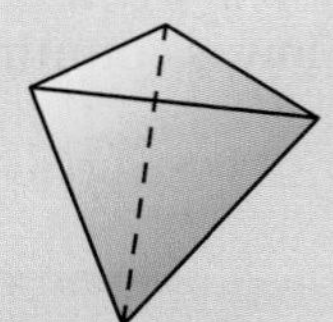

A **tetrahedron** is a three-dimensional solid with four triangular faces.

In-Class Experiment

Visualize Relationships

A **cross section** is the face you get when you make one slice through an object. These questions ask you to visualize the insides of solid objects.

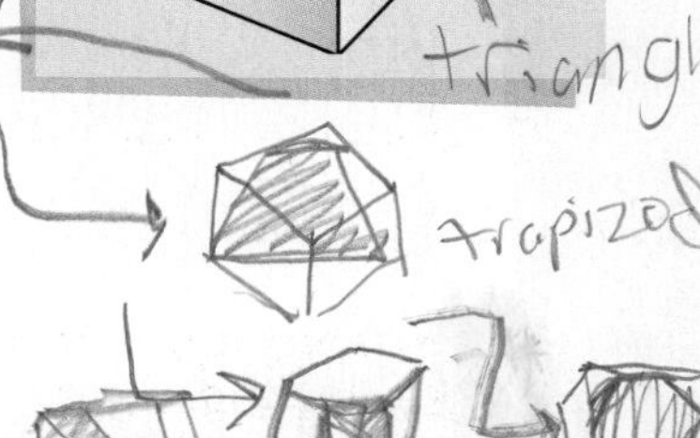

Here is an example of a cross section of a prism, showing one possible shape.

a square	an equilateral triangle
a rectangle that is not a square	a triangle that is not equilateral
a pentagon	a hexagon
an octagon	a trapezoid
a parallelogram that is not a rectangle	

11. What cross sections can you make by slicing a cube? Record which shapes above you can make, and describe how to make them.

12. Can you produce any shapes that are not listed above? Draw and name any other cross sections you can make.

13. If you think any of the shapes on the list above are impossible to make by slicing a cube, explain what makes them impossible.

14. What cross sections can you construct from the following shapes?

a. a sphere **b.** a cylinder

In-Class Experiment

Model the Problem

For this experiment, you need three number cubes and eighteen rods—three rods of each length, 1 unit through 6 units.

Roll the number cubes and pick three corresponding rods. For example, if you roll 5, 3, 5, pick two rods of size 5 and one of size 3. Try to make a triangle using the three rods as the sides of the triangle. Some sets of three rods will work, and others will not.

15. Repeat the experiment several times. Keep a table of your results. For the combinations that do not work, write an explanation of what went wrong when you tried to make a triangle.

16. **Write About It** Your experiments dealt only with side lengths from 1 to 6 and not with noninteger lengths, such as $4\frac{1}{2}$ or 3.14159. Write a rule that explains how you can tell if *any* three segments will actually fit together to make a triangle. Some sets of three lengths just do not work. Explain why they do not and how to predict which ones do not from the lengths involved.

17. Which of the following sets of three lengths will make a triangle? Explain.

a. 1 cm, 6 cm, 6 cm **b.** 2 cm, 4 cm, 6 cm **c.** 1 cm, 1 cm, 1 cm

d. 2.1 cm, 4 cm, 6 cm **e.** 0.99 cm, 0.99 cm, 2 cm

Picturing and Drawing

In *Picturing and Drawing,* you will learn the importance of pictures. Many problems are solved or made easier by drawing pictures. The pictures can be on paper, on a computer, or in your head. Even when your goal is to draw a picture on paper, mental pictures are important. Visualizing clear and detailed pictures in your head can help you draw better.

By the end of this investigation, you will be able to answer questions like these.

1. What is a line of symmetry?
2. What is a prism?
3. What should you keep in mind when you give traveling directions to someone or tell someone how to draw a figure or complete a task?

You will learn how to

- visualize mental images in order to analyze their parts
- analyze visual scenes in order to draw them
- develop clear language to describe shapes

You will develop these habits and skills:

- Write and follow careful directions.
- Identify and represent parallels.
- Use names, features, and algorithms to describe shapes accurately and precisely.

The roof of the Pantheon in Rome is a dome with a round opening (oculus) 29 ft in diameter. Describe the shadow cast by the roof of the Pantheon on the inside of the building.

1.01 Getting Started

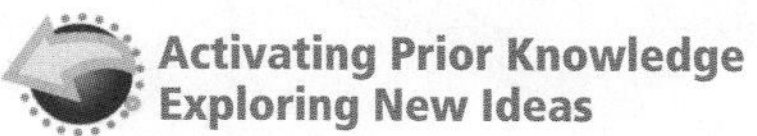

For artists to draw realistic scenes, they must be able to draw shadows.

For You to Explore

1. Visualize a square casting a shadow on a floor or wall. Can the shadow be nonsquare? Nonrectangular? In other words, can the measures of the shadow's angles be other than 90°?
2. What kinds of shadows can an equilateral triangle cast? Can its shadow be circular?

Definition

When you can fold a figure in half so that the two halves fit exactly on top of each other, the shape is symmetric. The line that contains the fold is a line of symmetry.

For example, the vertical line through the first letter T below is a line of symmetry. The horizontal line through the second T is not a line of symmetry even though it divides the T into two identical parts. If you fold the T along the horizontal line, the two halves will not fit exactly on top of each other.

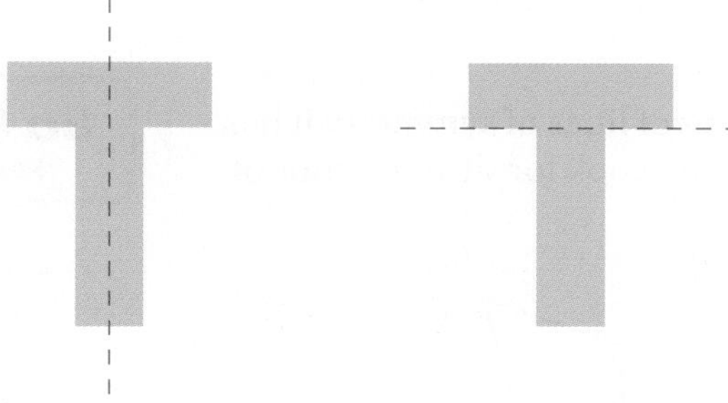

vertical line of symmetry

3. Which other letters are symmetric? Which letters are both horizontally symmetric and vertically symmetric?
4. Describe the lines of symmetry of a circle.

Exercises *Practicing Habits of Mind*

On Your Own

5. Which of the shapes below can cast a square shadow? Which ones cannot? Explain.

6. Classify each quadrilateral below by the number of lines of symmetry it has. Draw the lines of symmetry of each quadrilateral. Look for various kinds of lines of symmetry.

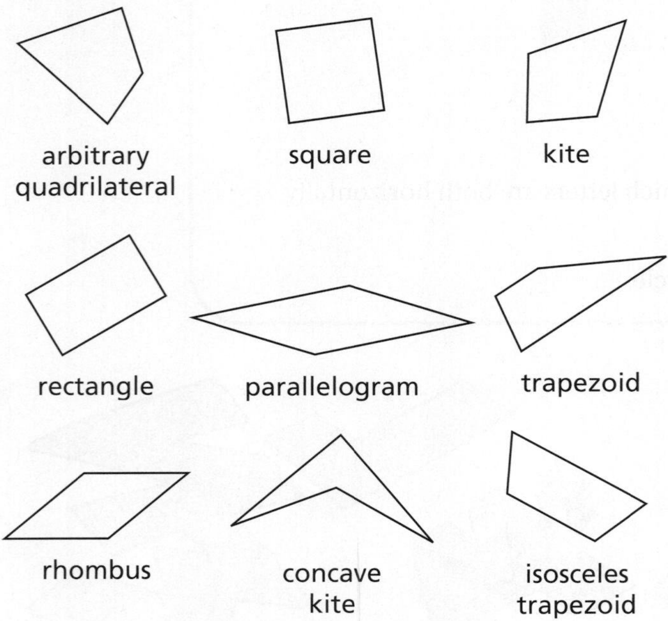

Go Online
Pearsonsuccessnet.com

7. Suppose a light shines directly down on a triangle that is parallel to the ground. What properties of the triangle and its shadow are the same? What properties are different?

Maintain Your Skills

A grid polygon is a polygon that has all of its sides on the grid lines of graph paper. Three of the four figures below are grid polygons. Two of the grid polygons, B and D, are the same except for their positions.

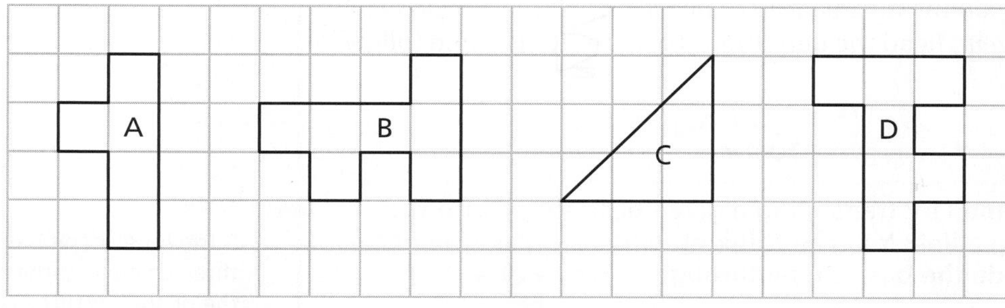

grid polygon (encloses 5 grid squares) | grid polygon (encloses 7 grid squares) | not a grid polygon | same polygon as polygon B

For Exercises 8–11, draw as many different grid polygons as you can that

- enclose the given number of grid squares
- have at least two lines of symmetry

Show all the lines of symmetry in each polygon.

8. 4 grid squares
9. 5 grid squares
10. 6 grid squares
11. 7 grid squares

1.02 Drawing 3-D Objects

Have you ever tried to write your name in letters that have a three-dimensional look?

You can use the recipe on the next page to turn "flat" letters like these

into "solid" letters like these

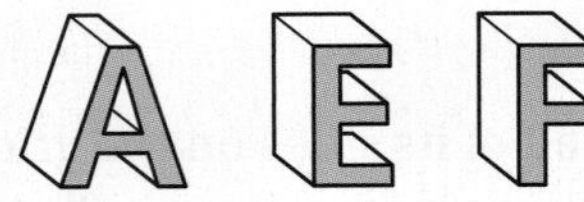

For You to Do

1. The steps of the recipe on the next page use special terms, such as *prism*, *parallel*, and *line segment*. Read the definitions of these terms. Then follow the steps of the recipe.

Definitions

A prism is a solid formed by translating a given base shape into the third dimension along a line. You can think of a prism as the trail of the base shape as you slide the base shape through space.

If the base shape has three or more corners, the prism has three or more edges that are parallel.

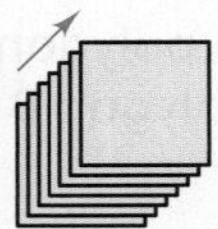

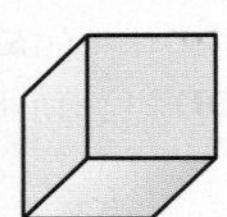

A line segment is part of a line that contains two endpoints and all the points between the two endpoints.

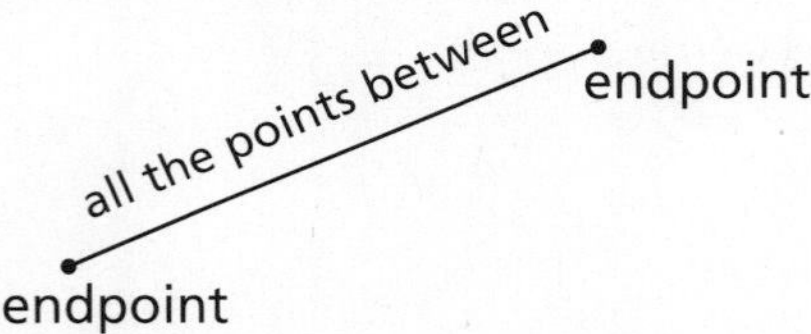

Parallel lines are lines in the same plane that do not intersect.

Parallel planes are planes in space that do not intersect.

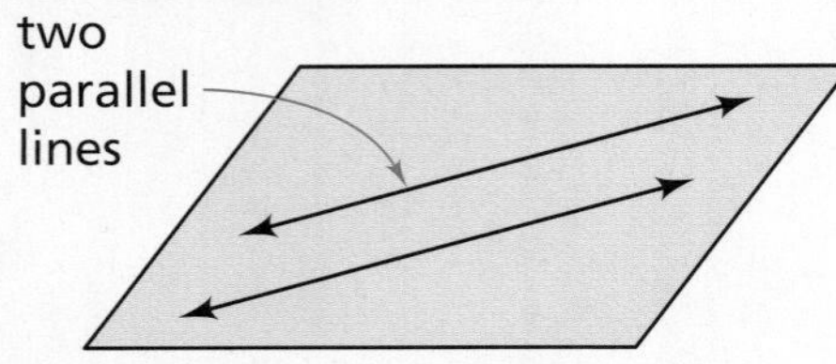

a plane (for example, a piece of paper)

two parallel planes

Unlike a piece of paper, a plane has no edges. A plane extends without end in the directions of the lines it contains.

Sample Recipe

Step 1 Choose a letter or other shape. Draw it in your notebook. This shape is the base of the prism that you will draw. The example at the right shows two bases. One is an L-shaped hexagon and the other is a house-shaped pentagon. If you like, you can rotate the base of your prism into the third dimension, as shown at the right.

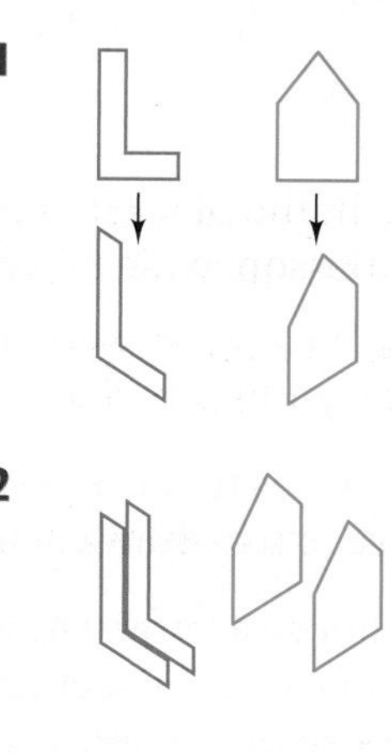

Step 2 A prism needs two parallel bases, so draw a copy of your base shape near the first. Take care to make the line segments of the copy parallel to (and the same size as) the corresponding line segments of the first base. Note that the word *base* does not necessarily mean the bottom or the top of the solid. It can mean the front or the back, as shown at the right.

Step 3 Now connect the corresponding corners of the two bases. The result is called a wire-frame drawing.

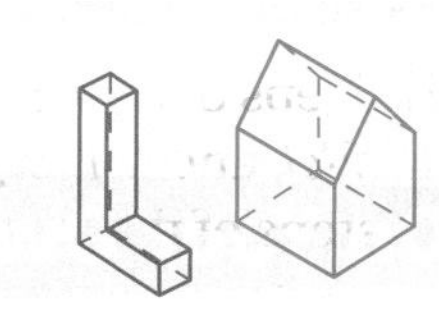

Step 4 Wire-frame drawings can be visually confusing. Erasing the back lines may help the eye make sense of the picture. (It is usually easier to start with the wire-frame drawing and then erase the back lines, than it is to draw the correct view from scratch.) Go ahead and erase the appropriate lines in your picture.

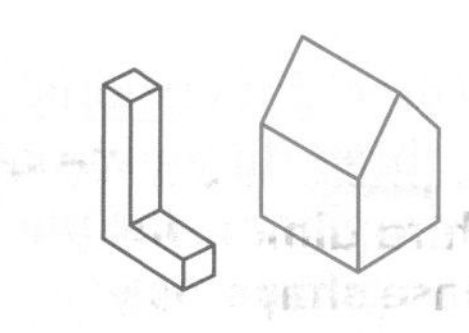

Step 5 Shading can also help the eye make sense of the drawing. Shade all the visible parallel faces in your drawing. In general, you should shade the visible parallel faces in the same way.

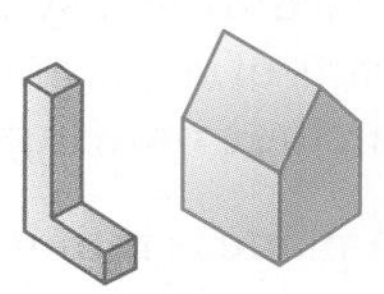

Now that the pentagonal prism looks like a house, the term *base* may be especially confusing. The *house's* base is the bottom rectangular face of the solid. The *prism's* bases are the front and back faces of the house.

Exercises *Practicing Habits of Mind*

Check Your Understanding

1. **Write About It** In each wire-frame drawing above, the segments that connect the two bases are parallel. Convince yourself that this is true. Then write a convincing argument to explain why.

2. a. In the block letters that you can draw by following the recipe in the lesson, which faces are parallel?

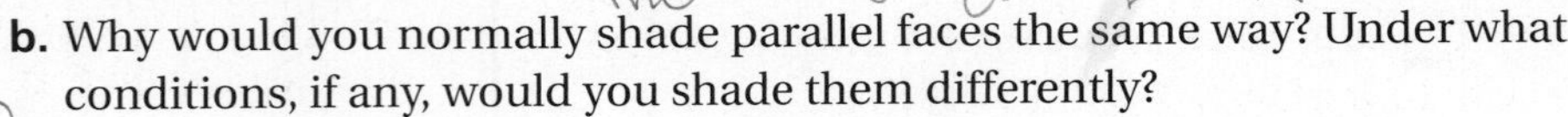

b. Why would you normally shade parallel faces the same way? Under what conditions, if any, would you shade them differently?

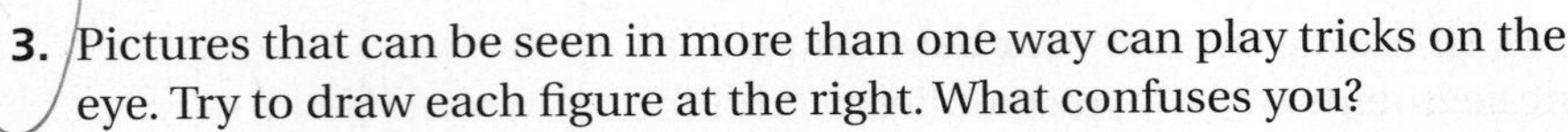

3. Pictures that can be seen in more than one way can play tricks on the eye. Try to draw each figure at the right. What confuses you?

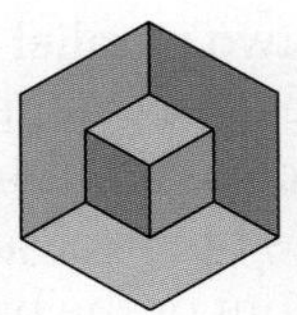

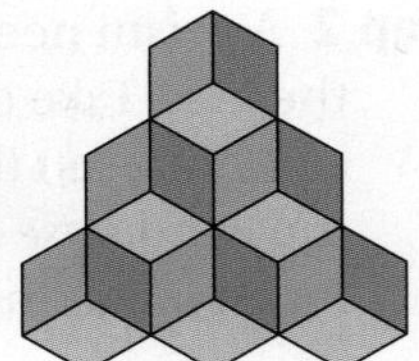

4. Choose a letter. Draw a 2-in. block version of it. Use the technique shown in this section. Shade a base of the prism. Explain why you chose this shape as the base.

On Your Own

5. Three-dimensional solids can also have symmetry. A *plane of symmetry* of a three-dimensional figure divides it into two identical pieces. If you think of replacing the plane with a mirror, the half of the figure that is reflected in the mirror looks the same as the half that is hidden behind the mirror. Find five different symmetrical objects around your house, such as tissue boxes, cans of soup, and so on. Describe the planes of symmetry of each. You may include drawings of your descriptions.

Remember...

What does the term *infinite* mean?

6. A plane is infinite. Any line in a plane divides the plane into two regions.

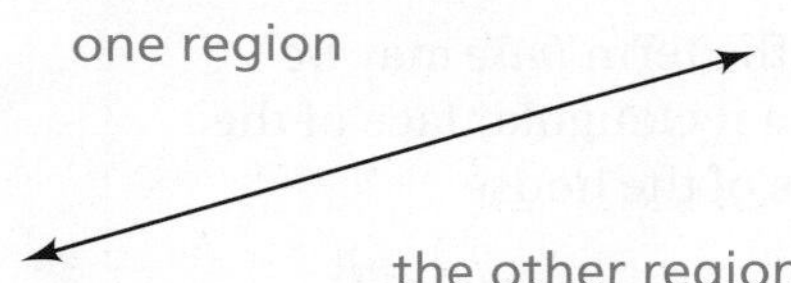

Two lines may divide a plane into three or four regions, depending on how you place the lines.

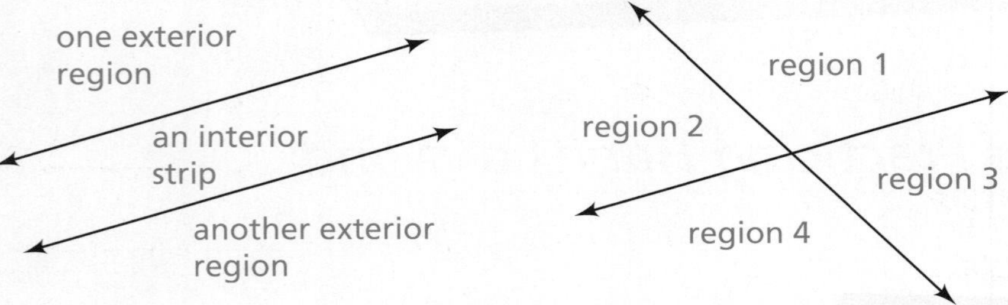

With five lines, what is the maximum number of regions into which you can divide a plane?

7. **Take It Further** Space is infinite. Any plane in space divides space into two regions. Two planes may divide space into three or four regions, depending on how you place the planes. Three planes divide space into as few as four or as many as eight regions. What is the maximum number of regions into which you can divide space with four planes? With five planes?

This is the three-dimensional version of Exercise 6, but it is hard to picture. Experienced mathematicians can puzzle for weeks over the questions asked here.

8. **Standardized Test Prep** The Soma Cube is a cube with side length three units. You can construct the cube 240 different ways from six shapes called tetracubes and one shape called a tricube. One of the tetracubes, shown at the right, is a branch or corner piece that is made of four cubes. One cube is hidden in the drawing at the right. (The Soma Cube was invented by Piet Hein. www.piethein.com)

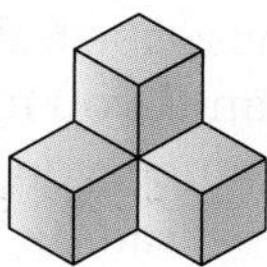

How many planes of symmetry does this tetracube have?

A. 1 **B.** 2 **C.** 3 **D.** 4

Sometimes pictures help you visualize and understand quantities or relationships between quantities.

9. **Write About It** What does each picture below tell you about the multiplication of binomials? Give reasons for each answer.

	a	b
a	a^2	ab
b	ab	b^2

$(a + b)^2 = a^2 + 2ab + b^2$

	c	d
a	ac	ad
b	bc	bd

$(a + b)(c + d) = ac + ad + bc + bd$

10. **Write About It** The first figure above shows $(a + b)^2 = a^2 + 2ab + b^2$. Explain how the figure at the right shows a similar equation involving $(a + b)^2$.

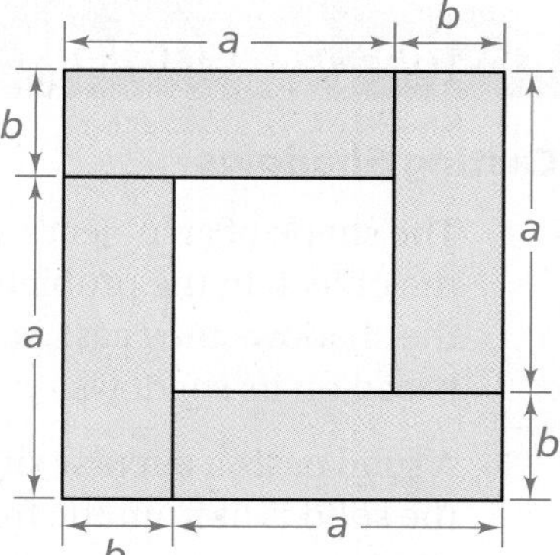

11. Draw a picture that illustrates the equation $d(c + f) = dc + df$.

Maintain Your Skills

12. Make a list of all capital block letters that have lines of symmetry. Draw a three-dimensional representation of each capital letter. What kinds of symmetry do you see?

1.03 Drawing and Describing Shapes

It is often important to describe shape and other spatial information accurately with words.

You can describe shapes in many ways.

Names Some shapes have special names, such as *circle* or *square*. One name may be enough to describe a shape. When a shape looks like another shape that has a special name, you may use some extra words to describe the original shape. For instance, you may say, "like an upside-down L," "like a house lying on its side," or "saddle-shaped."

Features Often you may not know the shape of a figure or solid. You must determine the shape from some set of features. Scientists face this situation when they try to deduce the shape of a molecule from what they know about the atoms that form the molecule or from how the molecule scatters light or X-rays.

Recipes Sometimes, describing how a picture looks is not as helpful as describing how to draw it. For example, suppose you give someone traveling directions. You would more likely say to walk two blocks north, turn left, and walk another block than describe the path as an upside-down L. The recipes you use in mathematics are often called *algorithms* or *constructions*.

You will practice using each of these three ways to describe shapes. Then you will be better prepared to combine them in whatever manner best suits your purpose.

As you proceed, try to notice whether you use *names*, *features*, or *recipes* to describe pictures or to draw pictures from descriptions.

In-Class Experiment

Casting Shadows

The shape of an object's shadow usually depends on how light hits the object. In the problems below, you will think about solids and the shadows they cast. You will also deduce the properties of a solid based on its shadows.

Objects under the midday sun on a clear day generally cast the most distinct and least-distorted shadows.

1. A solid casts a circular shadow on the floor. When the solid is lit from the front, it casts a square shadow on the back wall. What solid might it be? Try to make a model out of clay, sponge, dough, or other material. Describe the solid in words as well as you can. Then try to draw a picture of it.

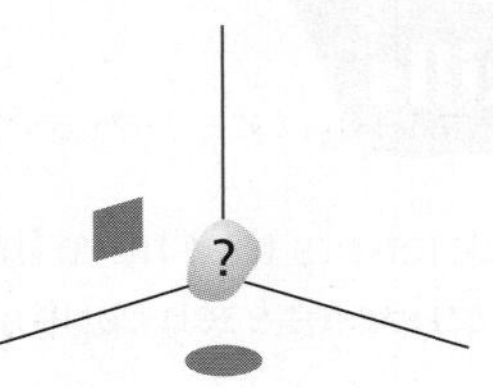

2. A solid casts a circular shadow on the floor. When the solid is lit from the left, it casts a triangular shadow on the right wall. What solid might it be? Try to make a model out of clay, sponge, dough, or other material. Describe the solid in words as well as you can. Then try to draw a picture of it.

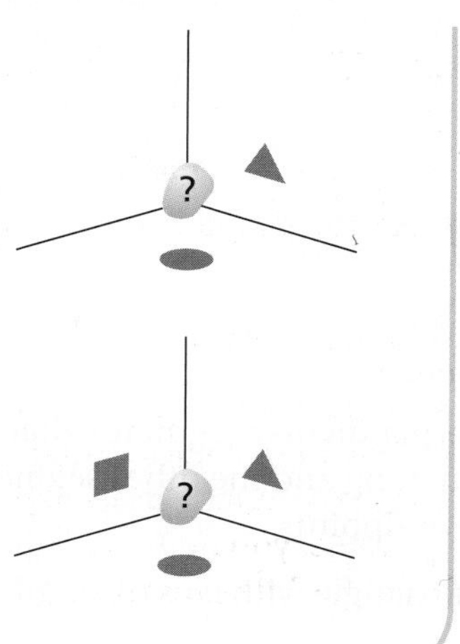

3. Suppose a solid casts a circular shadow on the floor, a triangular shadow when lit from the left, and a square shadow when lit from the front. What solid might it be? Try to make a model out of clay, sponge, dough, or other material. Describe the solid in words as well as you can. Then try to draw a picture of it.

Exercises *Practicing Habits of Mind*

Check Your Understanding

1. Suppose you follow these directions.

   Face north. Walk four feet. Turn right. Walk six feet. Turn right again. Walk four feet. Turn right again and walk six feet. Turn right again.

   a. What shape will your path form?

   b. In what direction will you be facing when you finish?

   c. The direction *turn right* does not specify how far to turn. Yet you probably made an assumption. What was your assumption? What makes it seem reasonable?

2. Pick a simple shape.

   a. Describe it by name.

   b. Describe it with a recipe that you can use to draw it.

3. Read the following recipe.

   Draw two segments that are perpendicular at their midpoints. Connect the four endpoints in order.

   a. Draw a shape that the recipe above describes.

   b. Does the recipe describe only one shape? Explain.

On Your Own

4. Read the two recipes below.

   Recipe 1: Draw two perpendicular segments that share one endpoint. Make one segment 3 cm long and the other segment 6 cm long. Connect the other two endpoints.

   Recipe 2: Draw a right triangle with legs of length 3 cm and 6 cm.

   a. Do the two recipes describe the same shape?

   b. Draw the shapes that each recipe describes.

5. A quadrilateral has horizontal, vertical, and diagonal lines of symmetry.

   a. Draw a quadrilateral that fits this description.

   b. Is there only one quadrilateral that fits the description? Explain.

6. What three-dimensional solid has a circle as every cross section?

Maintain Your Skills

The exercises below use commands from Turtle Geometry. Turtle Geometry is a computer language that moves a cursor (the turtle) forward or backward. The programmer tells the cursor how many steps to move and in what direction. The command *FD 2* means "move forward 2 steps." *RT 90* means "turn to the right 90°." *Repeat 6* means "repeat the given command 6 times."

Follow the commands below. Use a computer or a pencil and protractor to trace out a path.

7. FD 2 RT 90, FD 2 RT 90, FD 2 RT 90, FD 2 RT 90
8. Repeat 6 [FD 2 RT 45]
9. Repeat 6 [FD 2 RT 60]
10. Repeat 8 [FD 2 RT 45]
11. Repeat 8 [FD 2 RT 30]
12. Repeat 12 [FD 2 RT 30]
13. **Standardized Test Prep** Amina entered the following commands into her Turtle Geometry program.

    RT 30 FD 20, RT 60 FD 30, RT 60 FD 20, RT 120 FD 50, RT 120 FD 20

    Which figure did the program draw for her?

    A. an irregular pentagon **B.** an open figure

    C. a triangle **D.** an isosceles trapezoid

1.04 Drawing From a Recipe

As you translate words into drawings and drawings into words, you will meet more geometry ideas. Many of them will be familiar to you. You may want to talk about others with classmates or your teacher. To talk about the new ideas, you will need to recall more terminology.

If you carefully follow the instructions in the recipe below, you will get a certain picture. Compare your picture to your classmates' pictures. Are they they same?

In-Class Experiment

Drawing From a Recipe

Step 1 Draw a horizontal line segment.

Step 2 Above the segment, draw two circles that are the same size and tangent to the segment. *Tangent* means "just touching." Leave some space between the two circles—a space roughly the size of the circles' diameter.

Step 3 Draw a line segment above the two circles and tangent to them. It should extend slightly beyond the two circles. Label this segment's left endpoint L and its right endpoint R.

Step 4 From L, draw a segment upward that is perpendicular to $\overline{LR}$ and about half the length of $\overline{LR}$. Label its top endpoint B. From R, draw another segment in the same way. Label its top endpoint F.

Step 5 Draw $\overline{BF}$.

Step 6 Use a pencil to lightly extend $\overline{BF}$ about two thirds of its length to the right. Label the endpoint of the new segment X.

Step 7 Use a pencil to lightly draw a segment downward from X that is perpendicular to $\overleftrightarrow{LR}$. This segment should be roughly the length of $\overline{FR}$. Find the midpoint of this new segment. Label it M.

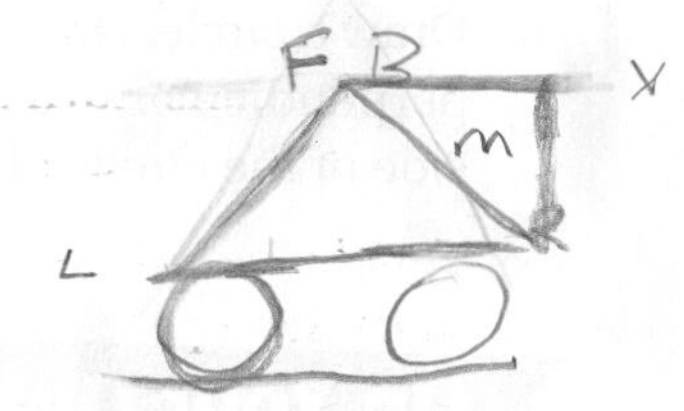

Step 8 Draw $\overline{MR}$. Then erase the construction lines from Steps 6 and 7. What does your picture look like?

Exercises *Practicing Habits of Mind*

Check Your Understanding

1. Use a pencil and straightedge to draw a large triangle. Find and label the midpoint of each side. Connect each midpoint to the opposite vertex. Label the points where these three segments intersect.

Exercises 2–4 describe how to draw certain letters of the alphabet. Use the descriptions to draw the letters. The descriptions are fairly good, but you may have to guess what some parts of the descriptions mean. Check whether your results make sense.

2. Draw an equilateral triangle with 2-inch sides and a horizontal base. Find and connect the midpoints of the two nonhorizontal sides. Erase the base of the original triangle. What letter did you draw?

> The prefix *equi-* means "equal." *Lateral* means "side." **Equilateral** means "sides with equal length."

3. Draw a circle with a $\frac{1}{2}$-inch radius. Draw a slightly larger circle directly below and tangent to the first circle. Draw the vertical segment that connects the centers of the circles. Draw the horizontal diameter of each circle. In the top circle, erase the bottom right 90° section of the circle. In the bottom circle, erase the top left 90° section of the circle. Then erase the vertical and horizontal segments that you sketched. What letter did you draw?

4. Draw a circle. Draw two diameters that are about 45° from vertical and are perpendicular to each other. Erase the 90° section of the circle on the right side of the circle. Then erase the diameters. What letter did you draw?

On Your Own

5. Write directions that describe how to draw your initials. Use precise language. Some letters are complicated to draw, so take advantage of any geometry terms that will make your directions more clear.

6. Write careful directions that describe how to walk from the door of your math classroom to the main office of your school.

7. Write directions that describe how to draw the figure at the right. Then have three classmates draw the figure following your directions. If any of the three pictures differs from the figure at the right, explain what you think caused the difference.

8. Standardized Test Prep Enrique has a system he uses to draw regular polygons inscribed in a circle.

Step 1 He draws a large circle. Then he draws a line tangent to the circle.

Step 2 For a polygon with m congruent sides, he divides 360° by $2m$ to get y.

Step 3 He then draws an angle with measure $y°$ such that the following statements are true.

- The point of tangency is the vertex of the angle.
- The tangent line is one side of the angle.
- The other side of the angle passes through the circle.

Step 4 Next, he draws a line segment from the point of tangency to the point where the other side of the angle intersects the circle.

Step 5 Finally, he uses a compass to construct $(m - 1)$ segments with endpoints on the circle such that the following are true:

- The $(m - 1)$ segments are congruent to the first segment.
- The m segments form a regular polygon.

If Enrique wants to draw a regular nonagon, or nine-sided polygon, inscribed in a circle, what number of degrees will he use for his angle with the tangent?

A. 10° **B.** 20° **C.** 40° **D.** 80°

The more difficult the task, the clearer the directions must be.

9. Carefully read and follow the recipe below.

Step 1 Draw a circle. Label the center of the circle point *A*.

Step 2 Draw a radius of the circle. Label its endpoint on the circle point *B*.

Step 3 Draw a segment that is tangent to the circle at *B*. The segment should be longer than the diameter of the circle.

Step 4 Draw a second radius of the circle that is perpendicular to $\overline{AB}$. Label the point where it touches the circle point *D*.

Step 5 Draw a segment that is tangent to the circle at *D*. The segment should intersect the other tangent segment.

Step 6 Label the intersection of the two tangent segments point *C*.

a. What kind of quadrilateral is *ABCD*?

b. Make a conjecture. In a circle, what is the measure of the angle formed by a radius and a line that is tangent to the circle at the endpoint of the radius?

Maintain Your Skills

Write directions that describe how to draw each figure.

10.

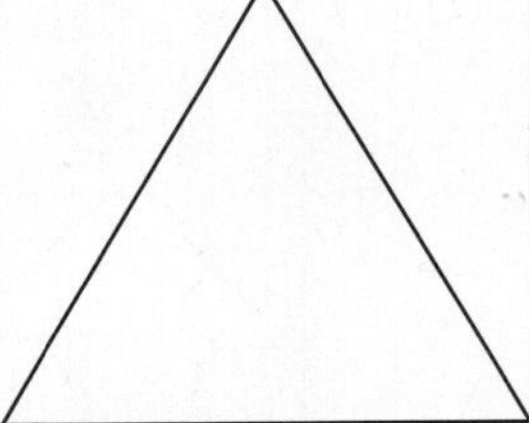

11.

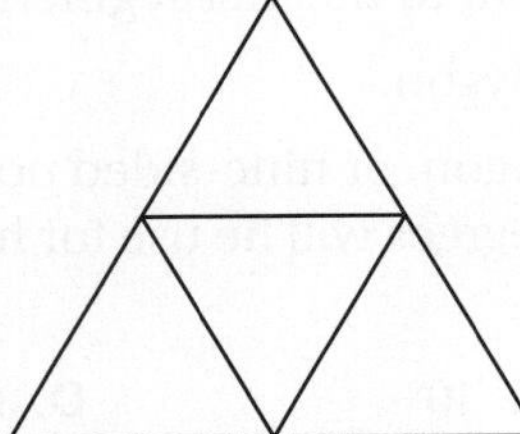

12.

13.

Go Online
Pearsonsuccessnet.com

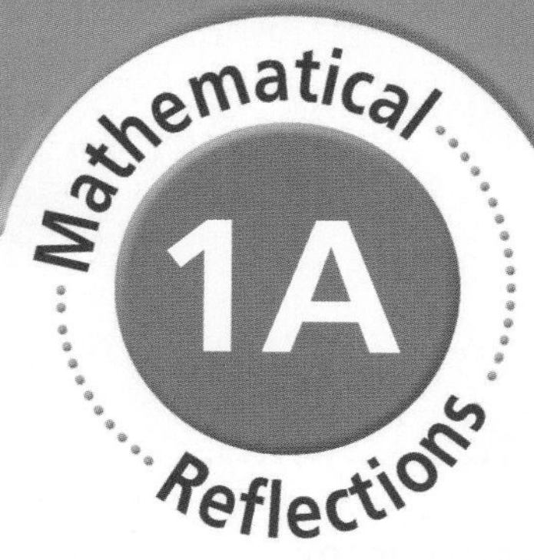

In this investigation, you learned the importance of pictures. You found lines of symmetry. You also learned to draw three-dimensional solids. The following questions will help you summarize what you have learned.

1. Name three kinds of shapes that can cast a circular shadow. Name a shape that cannot cast a circular shadow. Explain your reasoning.
2. Draw a three-dimensional block version of the figure at right. Label the base. Shade any visible parallel faces.
3. How many lines of symmetry does a square have? How many lines of symmetry does a rectangle have? Can a rectangle ever have the same number of lines of symmetry as a square? Explain.
4. Read the following recipe.

   Draw two horizontal parallel segments that are the same length. Connect the two left endpoints. Connect the two right endpoints.

   a. Draw a shape described by this recipe.

   b. Does this recipe describe only one shape? Explain.
5. Write careful directions that describe how to draw the number 5. Use any geometry terms that might make your directions more clear.
6. What is a line of symmetry?
7. What is a prism?
8. What should you keep in mind when you give traveling directions to someone or tell someone how to draw a figure or complete a task?

Vocabulary

In this investigation, you learned these terms. Make sure you understand what each one means and how to use it.

- **equilateral**
- **line of symmetry**
- **line segment**
- **parallel lines**
- **parallel planes**
- **prism**
- **symmetric**

The shadow of the roof of the Pantheon covers the entire inside of the building except for one spot of sunlight.

Investigation 1B Constructing

In *Constructing,* you will construct geometric figures. For many figures, you will have to deduce the recipes—how to construct each figure—on your own. Life often presents problems in this way. You know what you need, but not how to make it. Such problems have always inspired creative, inventive thinking. The solutions—the how-to parts—always depend on what tools are available.

By the end of this investigation, you will be able to answer questions like these.

1. What is the difference between drawing a figure and constructing a figure?
2. What is invariant about the measures of the angles in a triangle?
3. How can you construct the perpendicular bisector of a segment?

You will learn

- to use hand construction tools
- that points on the perpendicular bisector of a line segment are equidistant from its endpoints
- about special segments that are associated with triangles

You will develop these habits and skills:

- Use hand construction tools.
- Choose the right tool for a construction (including paper folding).
- Identify invariants—values or relationships that stay the same while other values or relationships change.

Follow construction steps carefully and you get the desired result.

1.05 Getting Started

Measurements are approximations. However, very careful measurements can suggest exact relationships.

For You to Explore

For the problems below, use whatever tools seem best. Keep track of your answers, as well as *how* you solved each problem—what tools you used and how you used them.

Use these sets of lengths for Problems 1–4.

3 in., 5 in., 7 in.   3 in., 5 in., 4 in.

3 in., 8 in., 4 in.   2 in., 3 in., 3 in.

1. For each set of lengths given above, construct a triangle with those side lengths. If a triangle is not possible, explain why.

2. For each triangle you constructed in Problem 1, do the following.

a. Measure the angles.

b. Compare your triangle to someone else's triangle. Are the two triangles identical? Do the angles of the two triangles match exactly?

c. Summarize and explain what you observe.

3. For each triangle you constructed in Problem 1, find the sum of the measures of its angles. Are the sums invariant?

4. The triangles you constructed in Problem 1 may have an invariant, but you only tested a few triangles.

a. Do you believe that your invariant holds for all triangles or only for some triangles? Explain.

b. What will convince you that the sum of the measures of the angles of any triangle is invariant?

Use these sets of angle measures for Problems 5 and 6.

40°, 60°, 80°   60°, 70°, 80°   120°, 30°, 30°

30°, 60°, 90°   90°, 90°, 90°

5. For each set of angle measures given above, construct a triangle with those angle measures. If a triangle is not possible, explain why.

6. For each triangle you constructed in Problem 5, do the following.

a. Measure the lengths of the sides (in inches or centimeters, whichever is more convenient).

b. Find the ratio of the longest side to the shortest side (divide the longest side by the shortest side).

c. Compare your triangle to someone else's triangle. Are the two triangles identical? Are the ratios from part (b) equal?

d. Summarize and explain what you observe.

Habits of Mind

Look for a relationship. In one of the triangles you constructed, exactly two sides are the same length. Why do you think this is true?

Exercises *Practicing Habits of Mind*

On Your Own

7. Choose a triangle you constructed for Problem 1. Without measuring, construct a new triangle with sides that are half the length of each side of your original triangle.

8. In Problems 1 and 5, some of the triangles were impossible to construct. Which ones were they? Explain what went wrong when you tried to construct each triangle.

9. In Problems 2 and 6, you used given side lengths and angle measures to construct triangles. Then you compared your results with those of classmates. Now compare the two experiments. In what ways, if any, are the results different?

After you completed Problems 1–3, you probably came to the following conclusion:

Conjecture 1.1 ***Triangle Angle-Sum Conjecture***

The sum of the measures of the angles of a triangle is an invariant. Regardless of the triangle, the angle sum is 180°.

You will prove this later.

10. Assume that the Triangle Angle-Sum Conjecture is true. Explain whether it is possible to construct a triangle with each of the given angle measures.

a. 50°, 50°, 50°
b. 60°, 60°, 60°
c. 45°, 45°, 90°
d. 72°, 72°, 36°
e. two 90° angles and a third angle

Maintain Your Skills

In each exercise below, construct three different triangles that meet the given condition.

11. one 30° angle and one 60° angle

12. one 40° angle and one 50° angle

13. one 20° angle and one 70° angle

1.06 Compasses, Angles, and Circles

Geometers distinguish between a drawing and a construction. You make a drawing to aid memory, thought, or communication. A rough sketch serves this purpose quite well. On the other hand, a **construction** is a guaranteed recipe. A construction shows how, in principle, to accurately draw a figure with a specified set of tools.

Drawings are aids to problem solving. Constructions are solutions to problems.

In your study of geometry you will probably use both hand construction tools and computer tools. The computer tools are introduced in the next investigation.

Hand Construction Tools

Compass A compass is any device—even a knotted piece of string—that allows you to move a pencil a fixed distance around a certain point. A compass allows you to copy distances and to construct circles of any size that you can place anywhere.

Straightedge An object with a straight edge—even a piece of paper—helps you draw a segment to look straight. In general, a straightedge is unmarked and you cannot use it to measure distances. You can use a straightedge to draw a line through, or a segment between, two points. You can also use a straightedge to extend a drawing of a line.

Remember...

You use a ruler to draw straight segments and to measure distances. You can also use a ruler as a straightedge, ignoring its markings.

Measuring devices Rulers and protractors are measuring devices. You can use a ruler to measure the length of a segment or the distance between two points. You can use a protractor to measure an angle.

Paper Paper is not just a surface on which to write and draw. You can use the symmetries formed by folding paper to construct geometric figures creatively. You can also use dissection—the process of cutting paper figures and rearranging their parts—as a powerful aid to reasoning.

String You can use string and tacks to build devices that you can use to construct circles, ellipses, spirals, and other curves.

Minds in Action episode 1

Sasha and Tony are trying to draw a triangle with side lengths 3 in., 4 in., and 5 in.

Sasha I'm going to use three rulers to draw this triangle.

Tony Why *three* rulers?

Sasha Watch and learn, Tony. First, I'll draw a segment that is one of the given lengths, say the 5-inch segment. Then I'll use the other two rulers to represent the other two sides of the triangle and swing them toward each other until they meet. I'll connect the point where the two rulers meet to each end of the 5-inch segment. That gives me my triangle.

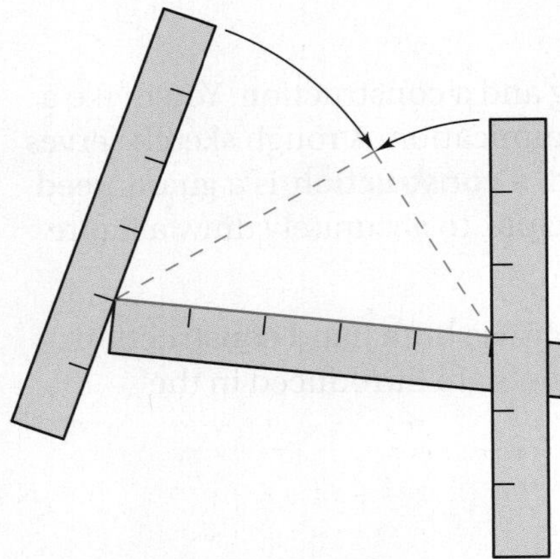

Tony Very nice, but I bet I can do the same thing with only one ruler.

Sasha Let's see!

Tony Okay. First I'll start just like you did and draw the 5-inch segment. Then I'll put the ruler at one end of the 5-inch segment, mark off 4 inches, and swing the ruler around with my pencil to sketch an arc.

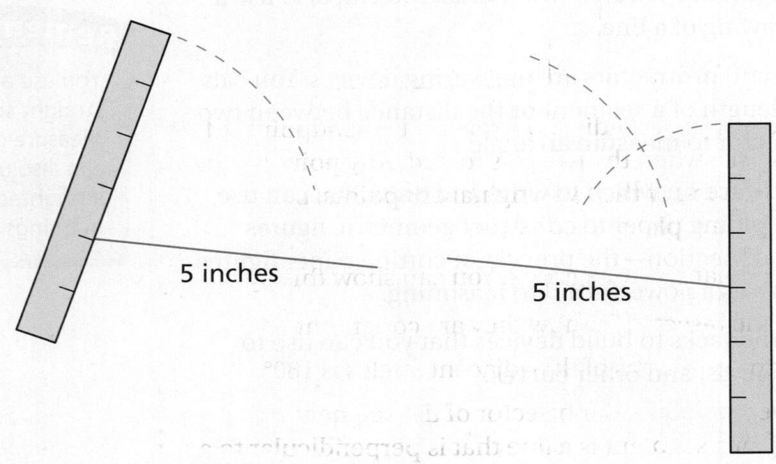

Then I'll put the ruler at the other end of the 5-inch segment, mark off the 3-inch side, and swing the ruler around to make another arc. And, voilà, there's my triangle!

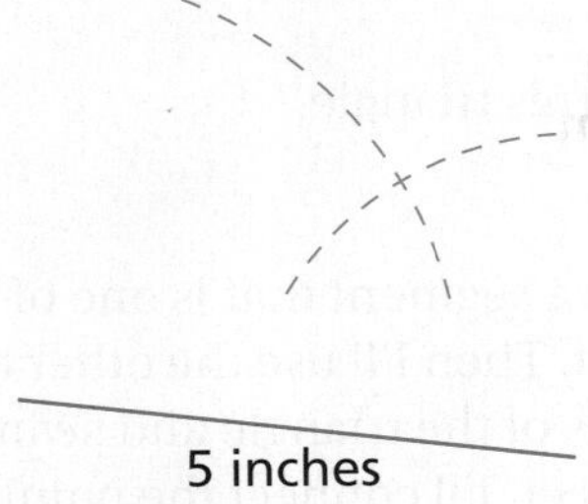

For Discussion

1. Do you see Tony's triangle? Explain how you know his triangle has the correct side lengths.
2. The title of this lesson is *Compasses, Angles, and Circles*, but this lesson has not yet mentioned compasses, angles, and circles. How do Sasha's and Tony's ruler tricks both imitate a compass?
3. How can a compass make a geometric construction easier?

Example

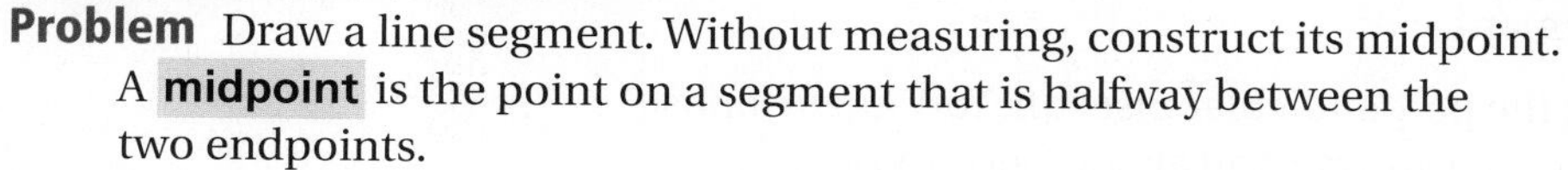

Problem Draw a line segment. Without measuring, construct its midpoint. A **midpoint** is the point on a segment that is halfway between the two endpoints.

Solution The simplest approach is to use symmetry by folding. Fold the segment so that its endpoints lie on top of each other. This matches its two halves exactly. The point that separates the two halves is the midpoint.

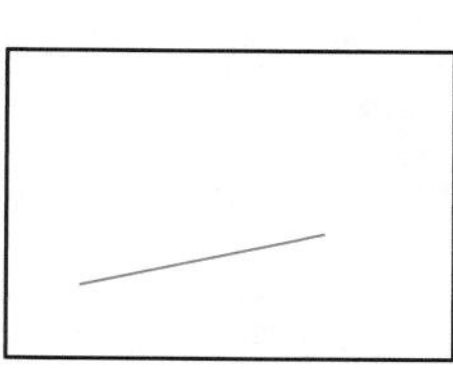

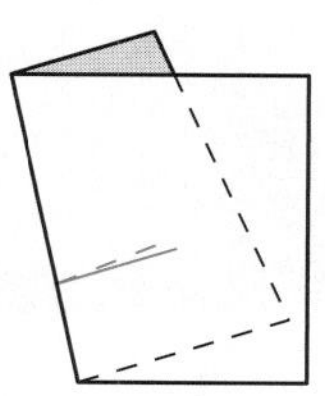

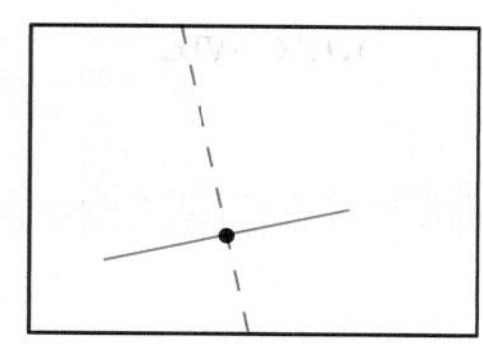

In fact, all points on the fold line are equidistant from the two endpoints of the segment. This is easier to see when the paper is folded. Any point on the fold is the same distance from each of the two original endpoints, because the endpoints are now at the same place.

Equidistant means "the same distance."

The fold line is also perpendicular to the segment. You can show this by

- matching angles around the bisector to show they are congruent
- showing that the sum of the measures of the adjacent angles is 180°

Therefore, the fold line is the perpendicular bisector of the segment. The **perpendicular bisector** of a segment is a line that is perpendicular to a segment at the segment's midpoint.

Theorem 1.1 Perpendicular Bisector Theorem

Each point on the perpendicular bisector of a segment is equidistant from the two endpoints of the segment.

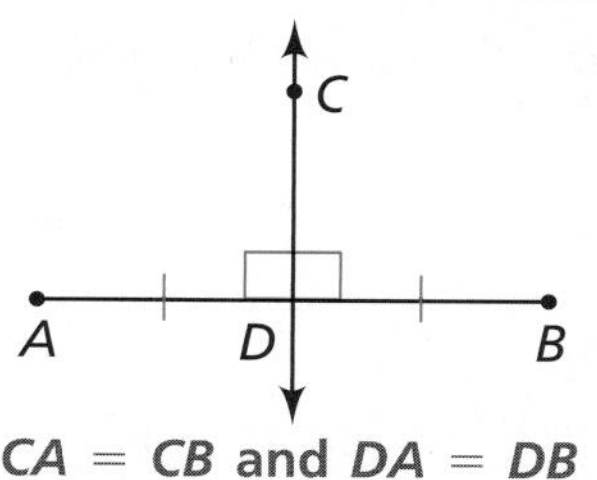

$CA = CB$ and $DA = DB$

A **theorem** is a statement that has been proven. Although you will not prove the Perpendicular Bisector Theorem or its converse until Chapter 2, you can use both as theorems now.

The converse of the Perpendicular Bisector Theorem is also true. Each point that is equidistant from the two endpoints of a segment is on the perpendicular bisector of the segment.

You can use the converse of the Perpendicular Bisector Theorem to find the midpoint of a segment using a compass and a straightedge. From each segment endpoint, swing an arc with radius *r*. Make sure that *r* is greater than half the length of the original segment.

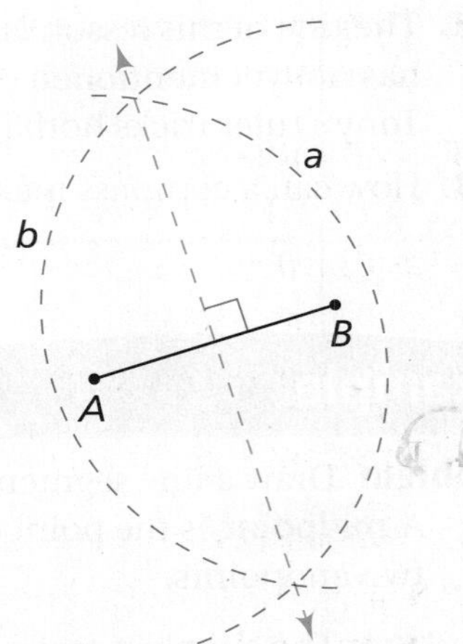

The two points of intersection of the arcs are both *r* units from each endpoint of the segment. The line through the two points is the perpendicular bisector of the segment. All points on the perpendicular bisector are equidistant from the endpoints of the segment. This includes the point of intersection of the perpendicular bisector and the segment, namely the midpoint of the segment.

To see this, fold the paper along the perpendicular bisector. You superimpose the two endpoints of the segment in this way. You also superimpose the two line segments from any point on the fold to each endpoint of the segment. This means that the distances from any point on the perpendicular bisector to the endpoints of the segment must be the same.

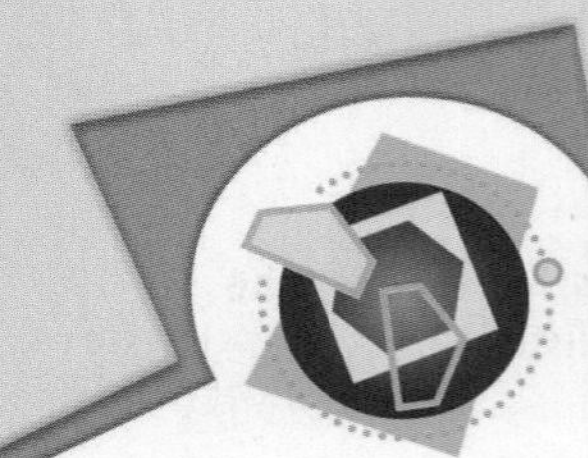

Exercises *Practicing Habits of Mind*

Check Your Understanding

For each construction described, do the construction and then tell how you did it. Use any hand construction tools *except* rulers, protractors, or other measurement tools. Do not forget paper folding. Some exercises are harder than others. If you have trouble with an exercise, skip it. Come back to it later. When you return to it, you will have more experience and knowledge.

1. Draw a line. Then construct a line with the given property.

a. perpendicular to the given line

b. parallel to the given line

Habits of Mind

Use standard notation. To distinguish a line from a segment, show an arrowhead at each end of a line. Show a small dot at each end of a segment.

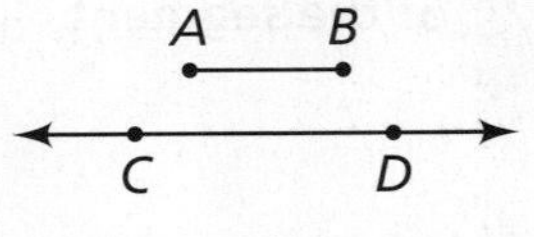

$\overline{AB}$ is a segment.
$\overleftrightarrow{CD}$ is a line.

2. Start with a sheet of paper ($8\frac{1}{2}$ in. by 11 in.). Use paper folding and scissors to construct the largest square possible.

3. Start with the largest square you can construct from an $8\frac{1}{2}$ in.-by-11 in. sheet of paper (you may want to make a few of them). Then do the following:

   a. Construct a square with exactly one fourth the area of your original square.

   b. Construct a square with exactly one half the area of your original square.

4. Draw an angle. Then construct its bisector.

An **angle bisector** is a ray that divides an angle exactly in half, making two congruent angles.

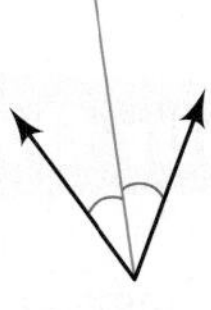

5. For each construction below, start with a new segment. Then use the segment to construct the given shape.

   a. an isosceles triangle with each congruent side also congruent to your segment

   b. an isosceles triangle with base congruent to your segment

   c. an equilateral triangle with each side congruent to your segment

   d. a square with each side congruent to your segment

6. Illustrate each definition below with a sketch. The first is done for you as an example.

Definitions

a. A triangle has three *altitudes.*

An altitude is a perpendicular segment from a vertex of a triangle to the line that contains the opposite side.

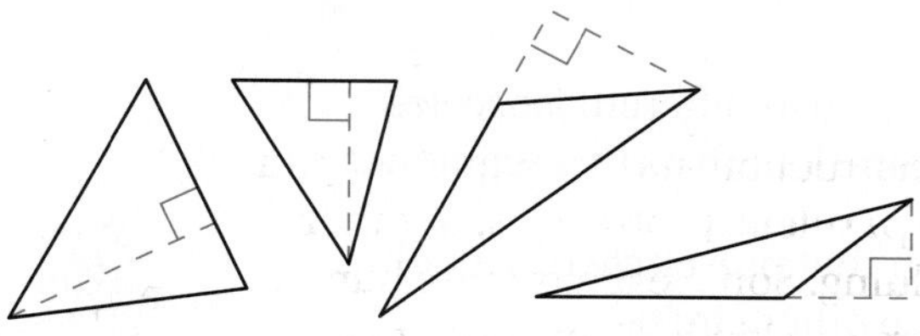

b. A triangle has three medians.

A median is a segment that connects a vertex of a triangle to the midpoint of the opposite side.

c. A triangle has three *midlines.*

A midline is a segment that connects the midpoints of two sides of a triangle.

7. Draw four triangles. Use one triangle for each construction below.

   a. Construct the three medians of the triangle.

   b. Construct the three midlines of the triangle.

   c. Construct the three angle bisectors of the triangle.

   d. **Take It Further** Construct the three altitudes of the triangle.

   e. Compare your constructions in parts (a)–(d) to other students' constructions. What are the similarities and differences? Write any conjectures you have.

Construct—do not draw.

8. Start with a square. Construct its diagonals. Study the resulting figure. Write what you observe about the diagonals (lengths, angles formed, regions formed, and so on).

9. Start with an equilateral triangle. Construct a circle that passes through the three vertices of the triangle.

On Your Own

10. Copy this segment onto a sheet of paper.

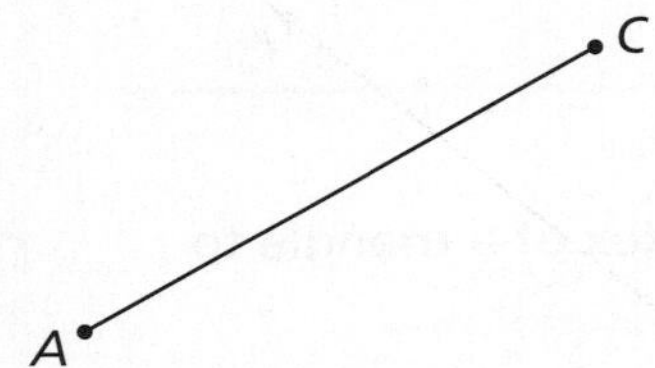

Use a straightedge and a compass to construct two different isosceles triangles, each with two sides that are the same length as this segment.

11. Use a compass to construct two circles, such that one circle has a radius that is the same length as the diameter of the other circle.

12. Construct a quadrilateral with at least one 60° angle and all sides that are the same length.

13. Draw several different triangles. For each triangle, construct a circle that passes through all three vertices. For what kinds of triangles is the circle's center in the following locations?

   a. inside the triangle

   b. on the triangle

   c. outside the triangle

14. **Standardized Test Prep** Mr. Mendoza's geometry class came up with four conjectures about the medians and the altitudes of triangles. Which of the following conjectures is NOT correct?

A. A median of a triangle divides the triangle into two smaller triangles of equal area.

B. The intersection of the three medians of a triangle is always inside the triangle.

C. In a right triangle, the altitudes intersect at the vertex of the largest angle.

D. In an obtuse triangle, exactly one of the altitudes lies outside the triangle.

15. Salim planted three new saplings. He wants to install a rotating sprinkler to water the three saplings. Where should he install the sprinkler to make sure that all three saplings get the same amount of water?

a. Trace the saplings onto your paper.

b. Show where Salim should install the sprinkler.

c. Explain your answer.

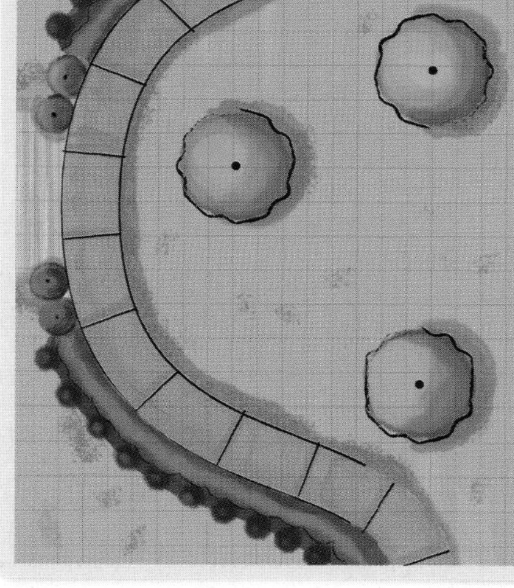

This is Salim's garden.

16. To reflect a point over a line, do the following:

- Construct a perpendicular line from the given point A to the given line ℓ.
- On the perpendicular, mark point A' on the other side of ℓ from A so that A' and A are the same distance from ℓ.

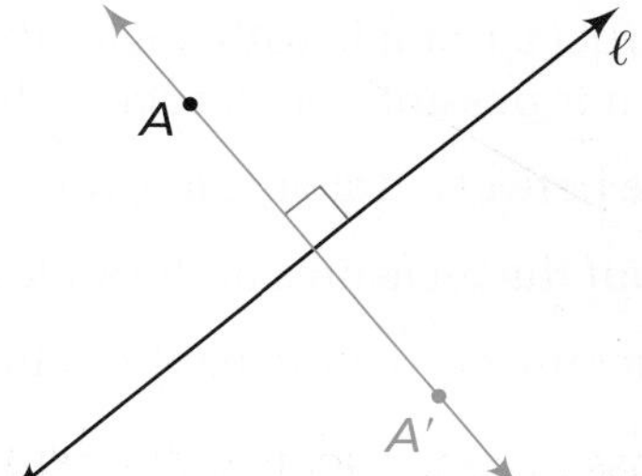

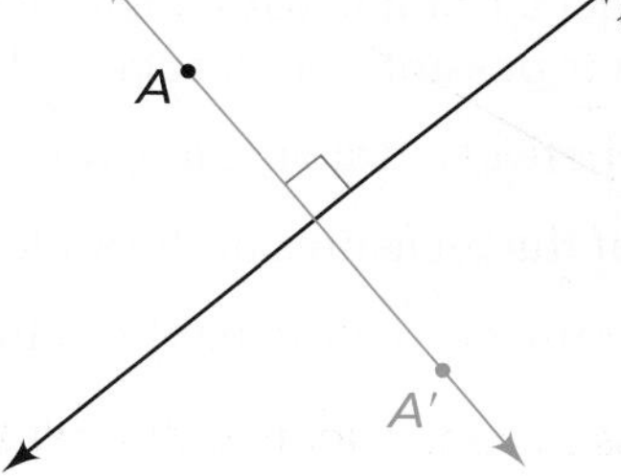

a. On your own, draw a point and then draw a line that does not pass through that point.

b. Follow the directions above to reflect the point over the line. Think of the line as a mirror. In the figure above, A' is the reflection of A in the mirror. A and A' are the same distance from and in the same position relative to the mirror.

Maintain Your Skills

17. Copy points A and B onto a sheet of paper. Then construct 15 different points that are equidistant from A and B.

A $\qquad\qquad\qquad$ B

In this investigation, you learned the difference between a rough drawing or sketch and a geometric construction. The following questions will help you summarize what you have learned.

1. Describe each shape below using its features. Each description should be specific enough that no other shape can be confused with the given shape.

   a. isosceles trapezoid **b.** isosceles triangle

   c. rhombus **d.** regular octagon

2. Draw an angle and construct its bisector. Describe each step.

3. Copy $\overline{AC}$ at the right onto a sheet of paper. Then construct a square such that $\overline{AC}$ is one of its diagonals.

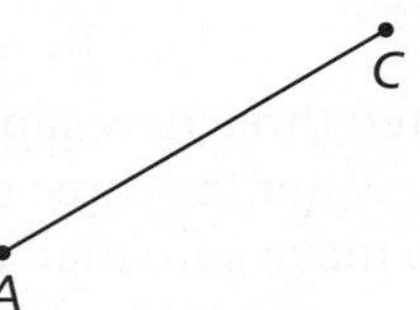

4. Write the steps that describe how to construct the circle that passes through points A, B, and C below.

C

A

B

5. Is it possible to construct a triangle with angles that measure 30°, 60°, and 90°? If you think it is possible, construct such a triangle.

6. What is the difference between drawing a figure and constructing a figure?

7. What is invariant about the measures of the angles in a triangle?

8. How can you construct the perpendicular bisector of a segment?

Vocabulary and Notation

In this investigation, you learned these terms and symbols. Make sure you understand what each one means and how to use it.

- **altitude**
- **angle bisector**
- **construction**
- **equidistant**
- **median**
- **midline**
- **midpoint**
- **perpendicular bisector**
- **theorem**
- $\overleftrightarrow{CD}$ **(line *CD*)**
- $\overline{AB}$ **(segment *AB*)**

Chapter 1

Mid-Chapter Test

Multiple Choice

1. How many lines of symmetry does the figure have?

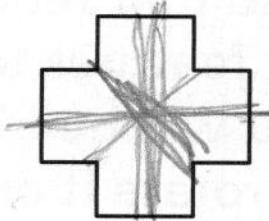

A. 1 B. 2
C. 3 D. 4

2. The plane is horizontal. What best describes the shape of the cross section?

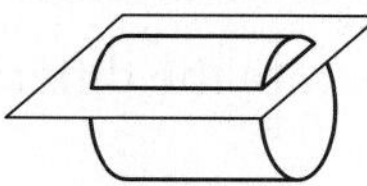

A. rectangle
B. rhombus
C. square
D. trapezoid

3. The following directions describe how to draw a certain letter of the alphabet.

Draw a 2-in. vertical segment. Construct the midpoint of the segment. From the midpoint, draw a $\frac{3}{4}$-in. horizontal segment to the right. From each endpoint of the vertical segment, draw a 1-in. horizontal segment to the right.

If you follow the directions, which letter of the alphabet will you draw?

A. B B. E
C. F D. H

Open Response

4. Construct each shape that is described below. Then name the shape.
   a. a quadrilateral with four 90° angles
   b. a closed figure with three sides, each 5 centimeters long
   c. a quadrilateral with two pairs of congruent sides
   d. the set of points that are equidistant from a given point

5. Fifty chalkboard designers attend the National Chalkboard Designers meeting in St. Johnsbury, Vermont. Each designer greets and exchanges business cards with each of the other designers. How many business card exchanges are there?

6. Tell whether each statement below is true. If a statement is not true, explain why.
   a. A square can cast a square shadow.
   b. A square can cast a circular shadow.
   c. A circle can only cast a circular shadow.
   d. All sides of a figure are shown by its shadow.

7. Use a compass and straightedge to construct an equilateral triangle. Describe each step of your construction.

8. Construct a triangle that meets each of the following specifications. If a triangle cannot be constructed, explain why.
   a. side lengths: 3 cm, 4 cm, 6 cm
   b. side lengths: 3 cm, 3 cm, 6 cm
   c. angle measures: 40°, 40°, 110°
   d. angle measures: 30°, 60°, 90°

9. Copy $\overline{AB}$ onto a sheet of paper. Then construct three different isosceles triangles such that $\overline{AB}$ is one of the congruent sides of each triangle.

Geometry Software

In *Geometry Software*, you will make moving pictures of geometric figures. You will construct figures so that required features are built in. Then you will vary other features to experiment with the figures. For instance, you will build a square so that it will stay a square while you rotate it or resize it in any way you please.

By the end of this investigation, you will be able to answer questions like these.

1. How can you use geometry software to construct figures with specific features?
2. How can you use geometry software to test for invariants?
3. How can you use geometry software to illustrate the difference between *drawing* a figure and *constructing* a figure?

You will learn how to

- use geometry software to construct figures
- explain the difference between a construction and a drawing

You will develop these habits and skills:

- Use geometry software to construct figures.
- Choose the right tool for a construction.
- Use geometry software to find invariants in familiar figures.

What changes when you drag any of the star tips *A*, *B*, *C*, *D*, or *E*?

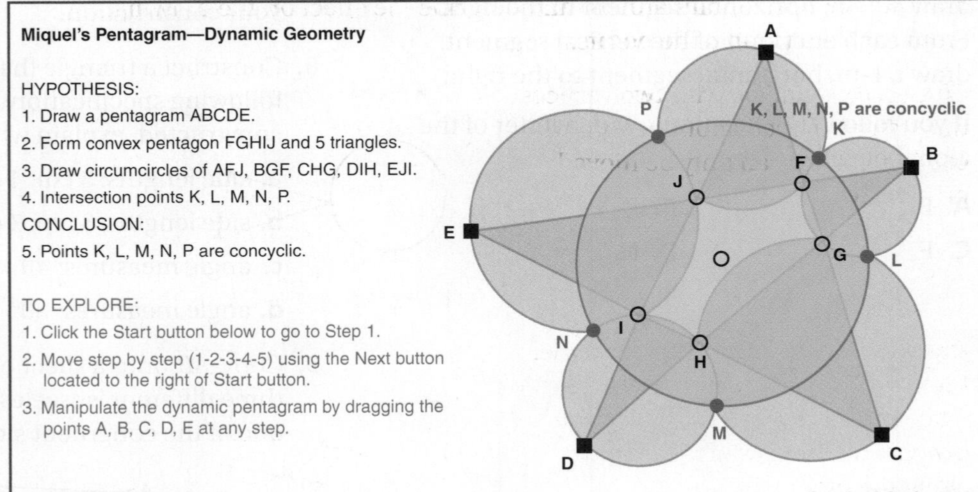

1.07 Getting Started

Activating Prior Knowledge
Exploring New Ideas

Every geometry software program has geometric construction tools, labeling tools, and movement tools.

For You to Explore

1. Use geometry software. Explore and ask questions until you can do the following.
   - Use line segments to draw a triangle.
   - Draw two circles. Connect them with a line segment. The segment's endpoints should be on the circles.
   - Move a point, segment, or circle in each of the first two drawings.
   - Draw a ray.
   - Draw a line.
   - Draw a point that travels *only* along a segment.

2. a. Use the point tool to place two points on your screen as shown below on the left. Then use only the circle tool to complete the picture below on the right. Make sure that your picture does not contain more than four points.

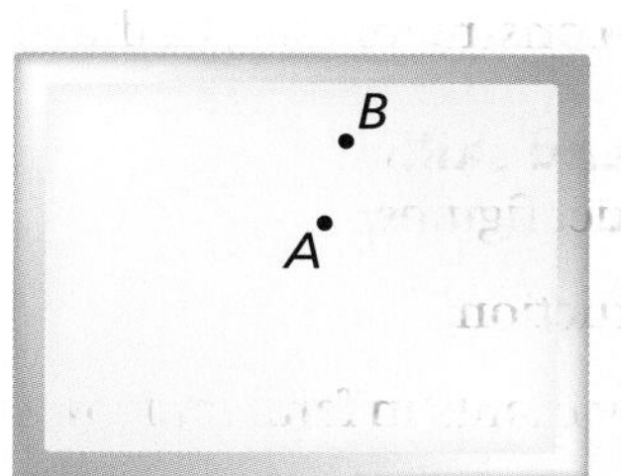

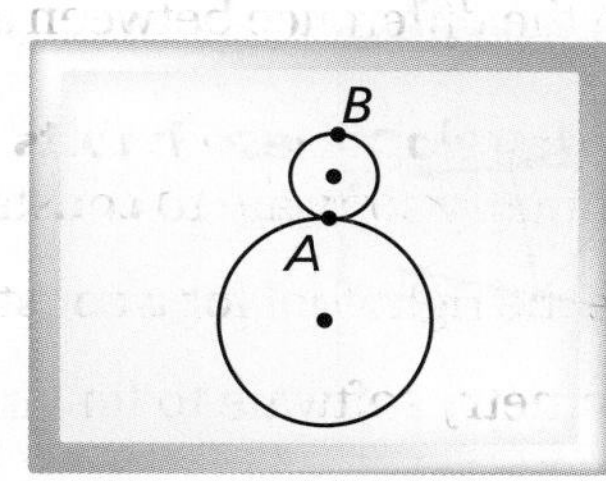

   b. Now move each point around and describe the effect on the drawing. It may help to label the points.

3. Construct a triangle with two vertices that can be moved about freely and one vertex that can only be moved on a circle.

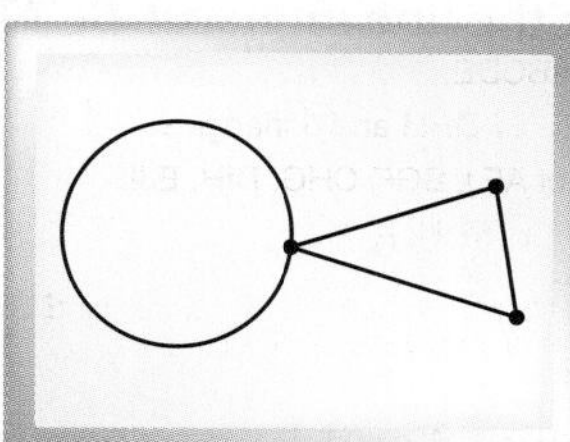

4. Draw two lines. Construct a triangle. Fix one vertex on one of the lines. Place the other vertices so that you can move both of them, but only along the other line.

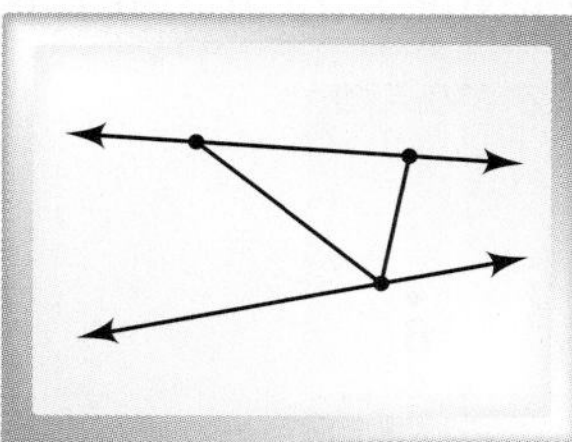

A bit of everything

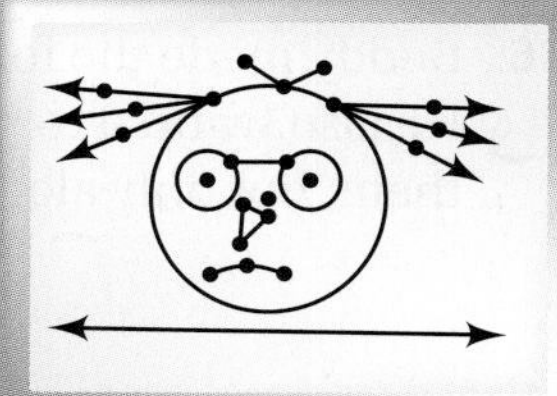

For help constructing a ray or a line, see the TI-Nspire™ Handbook, p. 712.

Exercises *Practicing Habits of Mind*

On Your Own

5. **Write About It** Write directions for drawing the figures in Problems 2–4. Include directions for how to get a point to "stick" to a line or circle.
6. Buddy made the following sketch. He intended to fix one vertex on one line. He also wanted to place the other vertices so that he could move both of them, but only along the other line.

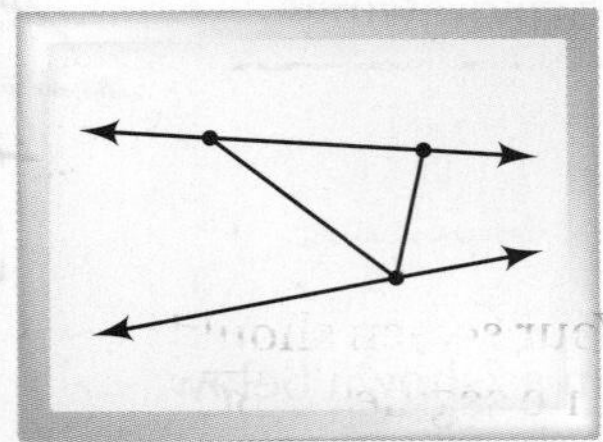

When the teacher checked Buddy's sketch, she selected a point and moved it to a new position, as shown below.

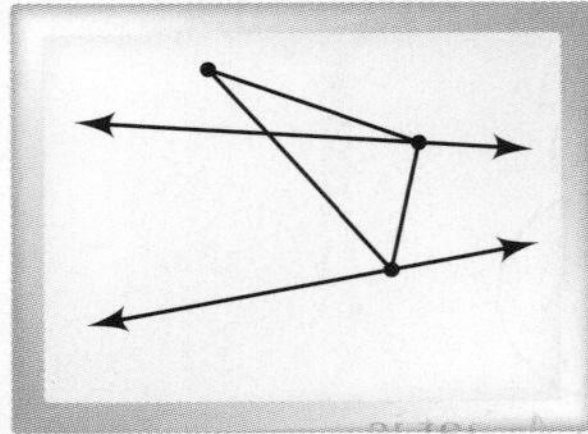

a. What mistake did Buddy make?

b. How can he fix his mistake?

7. If a line is perpendicular to $\overline{BC}$, must the line intersect $\overline{BC}$? Explain.

Maintain Your Skills

8. Use geometry software. Place two points A and B on your screen, as shown. Find positions for point C such that the measure of $\angle ACB$ is 90°.

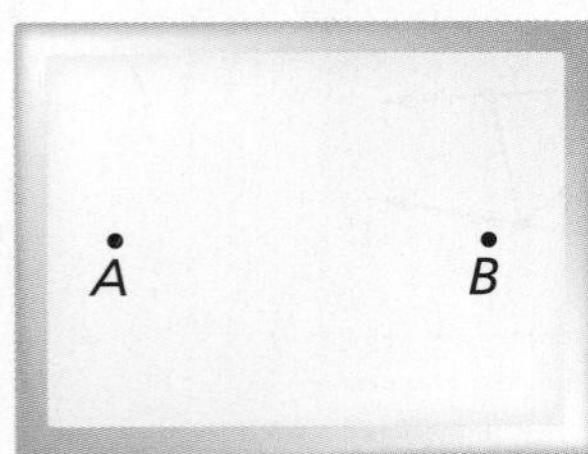

The notation $\angle ACB$ ("angle ACB") means the angle formed by $\overline{CA}$ and $\overline{CB}$.

1.08 Drawings vs. Constructions

To construct a figure that stays the way you want when you move one of its parts, you must build in the required features. If a point must be on a line or circle, you cannot place the point first and then adjust it to look right. You must actually place the point *on* the line or *on* the circle.

When you build in the required properties with geometry software, you can move one part of a figure and all the other parts will adjust accordingly. For instance, parallel lines will remain parallel. The midpoint of a segment will remain the midpoint.

Example

Constructing a Windmill

Step 1 Open a new sketch page on your computer.

Step 2 Place point A on your screen. Then construct $\overline{BC}$. Your screen should now show four objects: three points, A, B, and C, and one segment, $\overline{BC}$.

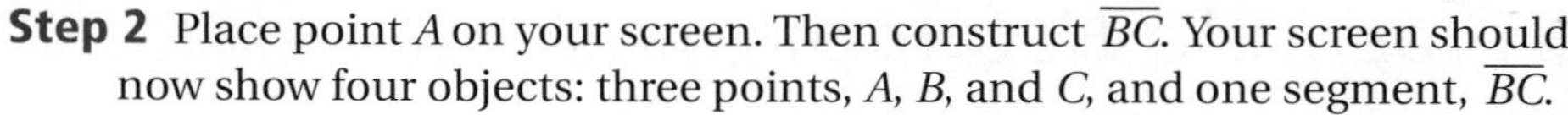

> Due to software settings, labels for points may not appear automatically. Also, the labels for your points may be different from the labels shown here. Labels for points depend on the order in which you place the points. For help constructing a perpendicular or parallel line through a given point, see the TI-Nspire Handbook, p. 712.

Step 3 Use the appropriate tool to construct a line through A that is perpendicular to the line containing $\overline{BC}$. The line should stay perpendicular to $\overline{BC}$ no matter how you move A, B, or C.

Step 4 Construct a line through A that is parallel to $\overline{BC}$.

Step 5 Construct a circle centered at A with radius the same length as $\overline{BC}$. If you stretch or shrink $\overline{BC}$, the circle should stretch or shrink, accordingly. Again, you need a special tool for this construction. (Keep this sketch for Exercise 1.)

> *Radius of a circle* usually refers to a segment from the circle's center to a point on the circle. *Radius of the circle* usually refers to the length of a radius.

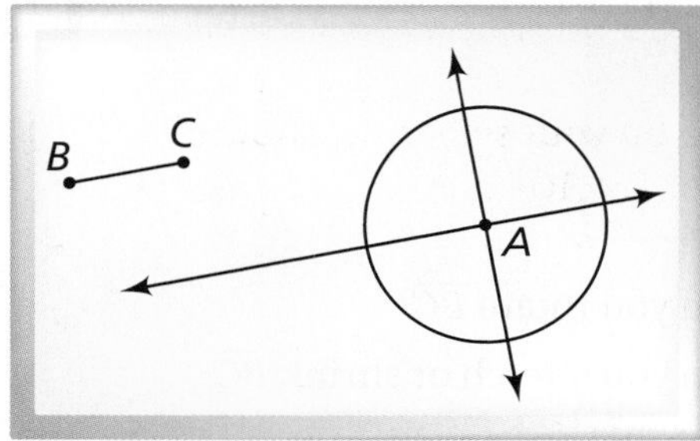

For Discussion

1. What happens when you use the selection tool to move *A*, *B*, and *C*?

Sometimes you need to use a line or a circle to construct a figure, but you may not want to see these construction lines in the finished product.

When you used construction lines to construct a figure by hand, you later erased them. When you use geometry software to construct a figure, you must not erase, or delete, the construction lines. You can, however, *hide* them. Find out how to use your software to hide parts of a construction.

Exercises *Practicing Habits of Mind*

Check Your Understanding

In the Example you constructed a windmill. Follow Steps 1–3 below to clean up the construction. Refer to the diagram in Step 5 of the Example. You will use the windmill in Exercises 1 and 2.

Step 1 Place points where the circle intersects the two lines.

Step 2 Construct segments from the center of the circle to each intersection point.

Step 3 Hide (do not delete) the circle and the lines. Do not hide the segments.

Sometimes you may want to hide a construction line or delete a mistake. See the TI-Nspire Handbook, p. 712.

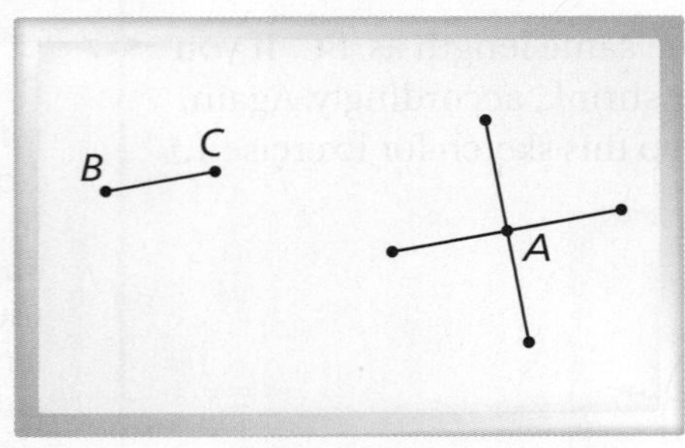

1. **a.** Describe what happens to the segments when you rotate $\overline{BC}$.

   b. Describe what happens to the segments when you stretch or shrink $\overline{BC}$.

2. Most geometry software allows you to trace the position of an object as you move it. Activate the Trace feature for the four points at the end of your windmill. Then move point *B* and watch what happens. Describe the effect.

3. Use geometry software to draw two intersecting segments. Move them until they look about the same length and perpendicular to each other at their midpoints. Move one of the endpoints. How is your sketch affected when you move this point, compared to how your construction is affected when you move point B?

On Your Own

4. **Write About It** Compare the tools used for hand constructions (paperfolding, compass, straightedge) to the basic tools of geometry software. How are they similar? How are they different? Do you think you can do more with one set of tools than with the other? Explain.
5. In Step 4 of the windmill construction (see the Example), why was it necessary to *construct* the line parallel to $\overline{BC}$ rather than *draw* it parallel to $\overline{BC}$?
6. Why did you need the circle to construct the windmill?
7. **Standardized Test Prep** Naima is frustrated. Her geometry software does not have a command that constructs a line tangent to a given circle. Which of the following methods can Naima use to construct a line that is tangent to a circle with center O so that point P on the circle is the point of tangency?

   A. Construct the perpendicular bisector of $\overline{OP}$.

   B. Construct the line that is perpendicular to $\overline{OP}$ at point O. Let Q be one point where this line intersects the circle. Construct $\overleftrightarrow{PQ}$.

   C. Construct a line through P that is parallel to a diameter of the circle and that intersects the circle in two points.

   D. Construct the line through P that is perpendicular to $\overline{OP}$.

Use geometry software.

8. **a.** Draw any triangle. Label it $\triangle ABC$.

   b. Construct M, the midpoint of $\overline{AB}$.

   c. Through M, construct a line parallel to $\overline{AC}$. Let N be the point where this line intersects $\overline{BC}$.

   d. Hide the line. Then draw $\overline{MN}$.

   e. Drag one of the vertices of $\triangle ABC$. Then compare the lengths of $\overline{MN}$ and $\overline{AC}$.

1.09 Drawing UnMessUpable Figures

Here is one way to think about the difference between a construction and a drawing. Think about which properties of a figure remain unchanged when you move a point or other part of the figure.

If you *draw* (not *construct*) a square, you are guaranteed to have a quadrilateral at best. The figure may happen to look like a square at certain moments, but you can change it into a nonsquare quadrilateral by dragging a vertex or side. Its squareness is not guaranteed—it is not UnMessUpable, you could say.

Example

Problem Construct a square.

Solution Below are two possible solutions. Other solutions are possible as well.

Two adjacent congruent sides, four right angles Construct $\overline{AB}$. Construct a perpendicular to $\overline{AB}$ at each of points *A* and *B*. Construct the circle centered at *A* with radius $\overline{AB}$ to locate point *C*. Construct the line through *C* that is perpendicular to $\overline{AC}$ (or parallel to $\overline{AB}$) to locate point *D*. *ABDC* is the constructed square.

Congruent sides are sides that are equal in length.

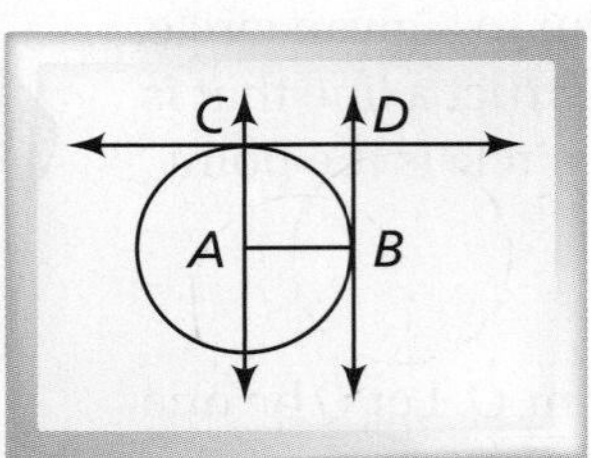

Three congruent sides with right angles between them Construct $\overline{AB}$. Construct a perpendicular to $\overline{AB}$ at each of points *A* and *B*. Construct two circles—one centered at *A* and one centered at *B*, each with radius $\overline{AB}$—to locate points *C* and *D*. *ABDC* is the constructed square.

Measure the length of the segment and use it as the radius in constructing the circles. See the TI-Nspire Handbook, p. 712.

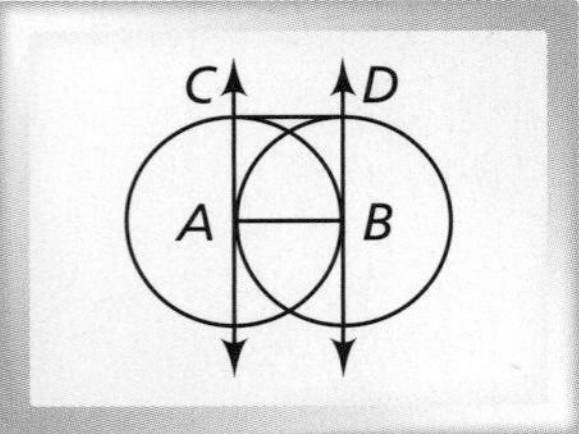

For Discussion

1. Describe other ways to construct a square.

Exercises *Practicing Habits of Mind*

Check Your Understanding

In the exercises below, your mission is to construct figures that are guaranteed UnMessUpable. No one should be able to change what is required for your figure by dragging a point or moving a segment. Work to construct the figure that is specified, not just a figure that looks like it.

1. Construct a parallelogram that will remain a parallelogram even if you move its vertices.

A *parallelogram* is a quadrilateral with two pairs of parallel sides. Note that rectangles, rhombuses, and squares are all special types of parallelograms.

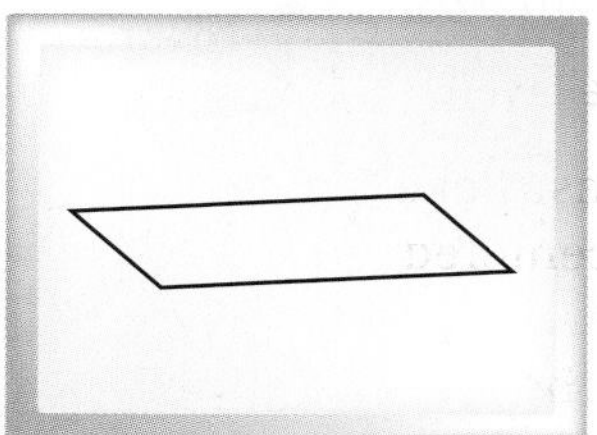

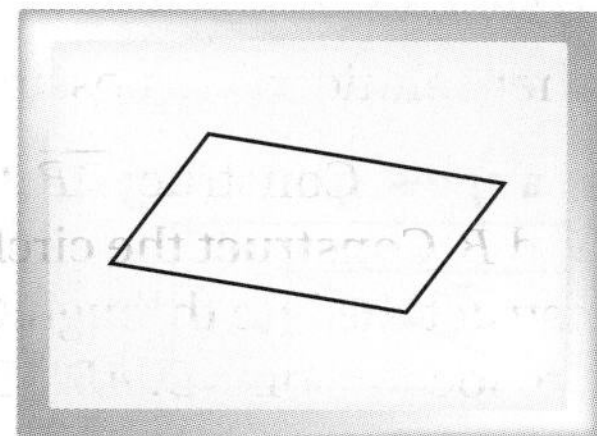

2. Construct two circles so that each circle passes through the center of the other circle. If you change the size of one circle, the size of the other circle should change with it.

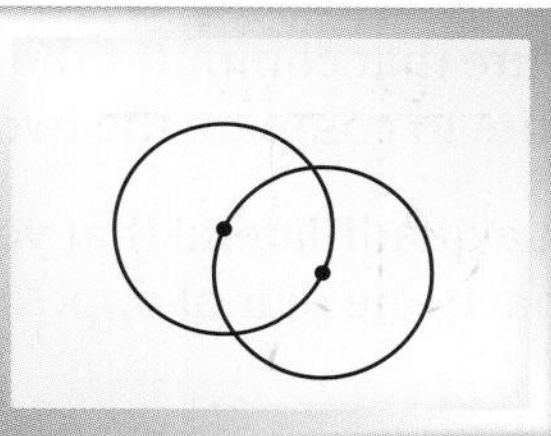

For help constructing a circle with a given center through a given point, see the TI-Nspire Handbook, p. 712.

3. Construct three circles so that each circle passes through the centers of the other two circles. As you change the size of one circle, the sizes of the other two circles should also change.

Why are the three points in this figure exactly the same distance from one another?

4. Construct an equilateral triangle that remains an equilateral triangle when you change its size and orientation.

5. Construct the letter T with the following requirements. The top of the T is to remain perpendicular to and centered on the stem when you move points or segments of the T.

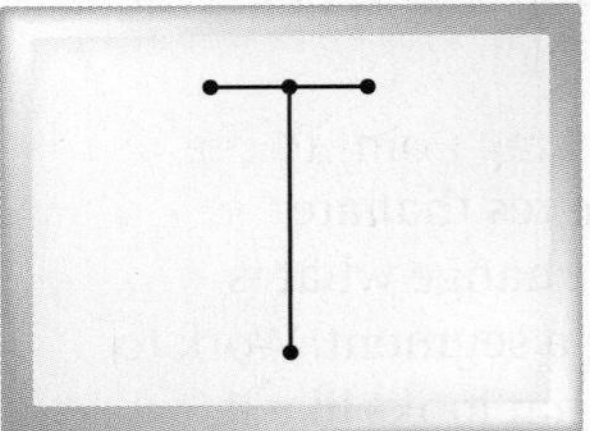

Can you construct your T so it always stays upright?

6. Find two different ways to construct a guaranteed UnMessUpable rhombus with geometry software. Write clear directions for each construction. If either construction guarantees only a certain type of rhombus, explain why.

A *rhombus* is a quadrilateral with four congruent sides.

7. **a.** Construct two rectangles that
   - share one vertex
   - have two sides lined up
   - have one diagonal lined up, as shown, no matter how you move the vertices or sides

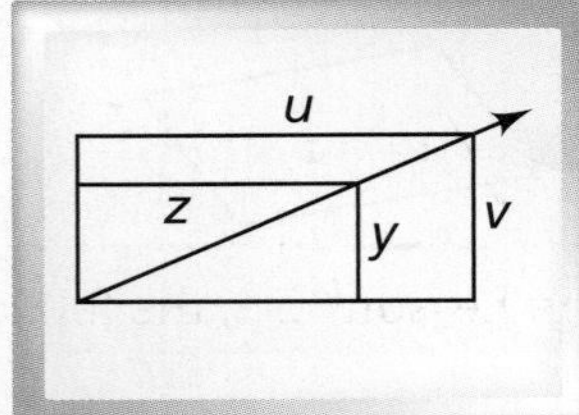

   b. Your software has a feature that computes the ratio of the lengths of two segments. Use that feature to compare the two ratios $\frac{z}{y}$ and $\frac{u}{v}$.

8. **Take It Further** Construct a quadrilateral that you can distort in all sorts of ways but that will *always* have one pair of opposite sides equal in length.

9. **Take It Further** Use geometry software to construct a house in perspective. When you are done, your construction should have these features:

- You should be able to adjust the points on its near end so that the corresponding points on its far end adjust automatically.
- Your picture should include a *drag* point. Move the drag point to see what the house looks like from different perspectives.

Drag the point to change the perspective. See the TI-Nspire Handbook, p. 712.

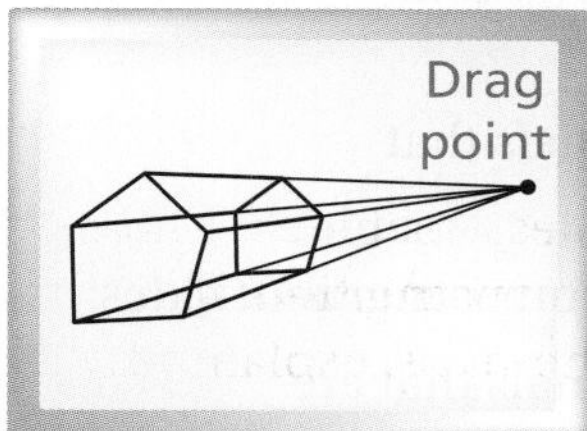

Developing Habits of Mind

Make a model. For the house you drew in Lesson 1.02, the following statements are true.

- Its two bases are identical.
- The segments that connect the bases are all parallel.
- The corresponding sides of the bases are parallel.

On the other hand, in the perspective construction of the house above, the following statements are true.

- The bases of the house are not identical (what mathematicians call "congruent"). They are, however, the same shape (what mathematicians call "similar").
- The segments that connect the bases are not parallel. Instead, they converge to a single point.
- The corresponding sides of the bases are parallel.

These facts suggest one way to construct a house in perspective. Sketch the near end of the house. Place a drag point (also called a vanishing point in both mathematics and art) on your screen. Connect the vertices of the house's near end to the vanishing point. Then construct the house's far end. Make sure each segment of the house's far end is parallel to the corresponding segment of the near end.

On Your Own

10. **Standardized Test Prep** The students in Ms. Lau's class used geometry software to construct a specific type of quadrilateral that keeps its required features if someone drags one of the vertices.

- Jeremy's group constructed a parallelogram with congruent adjacent sides.
- Amy's group constructed a quadrilateral with diagonals that bisect the quadrilateral's angles.
- Alexandra's group constructed a quadrilateral with four congruent sides.
- Sang's group constructed a quadrilateral with diagonals that are perpendicular and intersect each other at their midpoints.

Which type of quadrilateral did each group construct?

A. a rectangle **B.** a square **C.** a rhombus **D.** a trapezoid

11. **Write About It** As you learned to use geometry software, you probably also did some geometric thinking. List some geometric ideas, terminology, or techniques that you learned, relearned, polished up, or invented.

12. No geometry software allows you to construct a line that is perpendicular to another line or segment unless you first identify both a line (or a segment) *and* a point. Why is this a sensible restriction?

13. **Write About It** Select one of the UnMessUpable figures you constructed in Exercises 1–8. Write detailed directions that describe the construction process. To test your directions, switch with a partner. Do you both get the predicted results?

14. Look back at Exercise 4. How do you make sure that the triangle you construct is equilateral? Describe what features of the construction or the resulting figure guarantee that the triangle has three congruent sides.

Maintain Your Skills

Use geometry software to construct the following figures. Describe required features that remain unchanged if you drag a vertex.

15.

16.

17.

In this investigation, you learned the difference between drawing and constructing with geometry software. You used software to construct figures that retained specific features no matter how you moved around their parts. The following questions will help you summarize what you have learned.

1. Tony had to construct a triangle inscribed in a circle. He drew the picture on the left. Sasha selected a vertex. She moved it and made the picture on the right. Explain Tony's mistake.

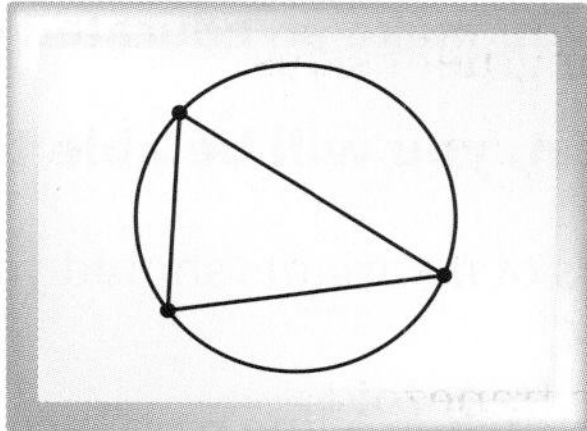
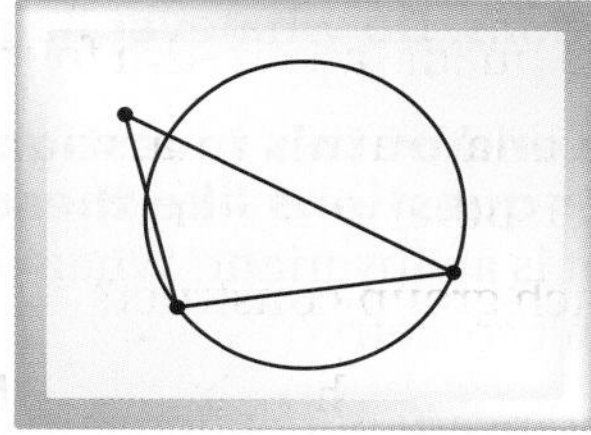

2. Construct an UnMessUpable square with a side length of 5 cm.
3. List steps that tell how to construct a rectangle with geometry software. The figure must remain a rectangle for any movement of its vertices.
4. Use geometry software to construct an equilateral triangle with side lengths that vary when you drag a point of the construction.
5. What feature do you have to make invariant in a parallelogram so that it is always a rhombus, no matter how you drag its vertices?
6. How can you use geometry software to construct figures with specific features?
7. How can you use geometry software to test for invariants?
8. How can you use geometry software to illustrate the difference between *drawing* a figure and *constructing* a figure?

Vocabulary and Notation

In this investigation, you learned this term and this symbol. Make sure you understand what each one means and how to use it.

- **congruent**
- **$\angle ACB$ (angle *ACB*)**

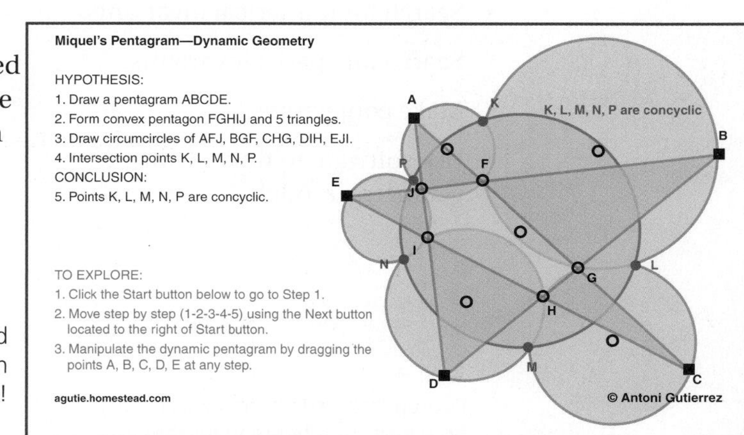

Drag any of the vertices *A*, *B*, or *C*, and the points *D*, *E*, *F*, *G*, *H*, or *I* remain concyclic (on the same circle)!

Invariants

In *Invariants*, you will use geometry software to experiment with figures. You will stretch and squash parts of a figure to get a feel for how the parts work together, which patterns exist, and which values or relationships stay the same, even when others change.

Some of the invariants that you discover will lead to useful theorems. As you proceed, visualize, draw pictures, and make calculations. Do whatever helps you make an educated guess.

By the end of this investigation, you will be able to answer questions like these.

1. What is an invariant? What kinds of invariants should you look for in geometry?
2. What invariant relationship exists when a line parallel to the base of a triangle intersects the other sides of that triangle?
3. What shape do you form when you connect the consecutive midpoints of a quadrilateral?

You will learn how to

- describe various types of invariants in geometry
- identify the invariant relationships for the sums of the measures of the angles of polygons
- identify the invariant relationship that exists when a line parallel to one side of a triangle cuts the other two sides of the triangle proportionally
- search for geometric invariants, such as points of concurrency and collinearity of points

You will develop these habits and skills:

- Search for numerical invariants.
- Search for spatial invariants.
- Make conjectures.
- Use software to tinker with geometric models.

Pop-up book artists are experts on how parts of a figure work together.

1.10 Getting Started

Something that is true for each member of a collection is an **invariant** for the collection.

For You to Explore

1. Study the three different collections below.

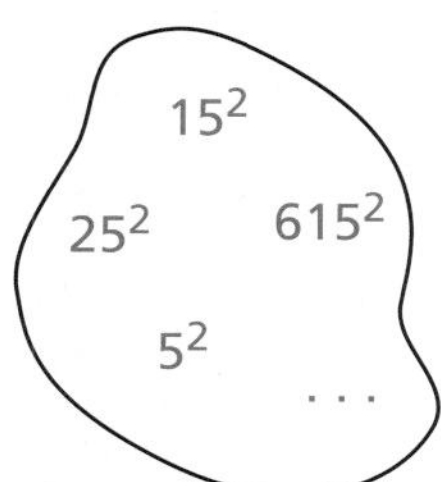

$(27^2, 103^2)$ $(31^2, 39^2)$ $(14^2, 6^2)$ $(34^2, 6^2)$ $(16^2, 254^2)$ . . .

55 1 22 34 37 10 43 58 88 28 64 25 49 52 31 70 7 46 13 67 19 91 61 100 16 4 76 40 . . .

a. In the first set, each number before squaring ends in 5. Evaluate the squares. What invariants do you find?

b. The second set contains pairs of square numbers. In each pair, the two numbers before squaring end in digits that add to 10. Evaluate all the squares. What invariants do you find?

c. The third set contains 1, 4, 7, 10, 13, and so on. Decide whether 301 is in the set. Choose pairs of numbers from the set and find their products. What seems to be true about their products? What seems to be true about the sums of four numbers chosen from the set? What seems to be true about the differences of any two numbers chosen from the set?

Remember...

An invariant over a set is something that is the same for every member of the set.

2. Draw two polygons like quadrilateral $ABCD$ and $\triangle EFG$ below. On each side, draw two points that roughly divide the sides into thirds. Connect each vertex to two points on different sides to form the largest angle possible. The connecting segments surround a region. The two diagrams here suggest

- the region has eight sides when the original shape has four sides
- the region has six sides when the original shape has three sides

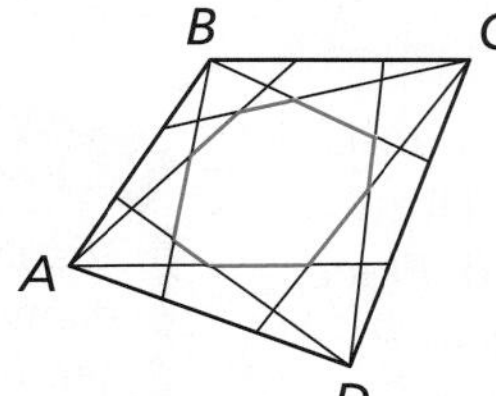

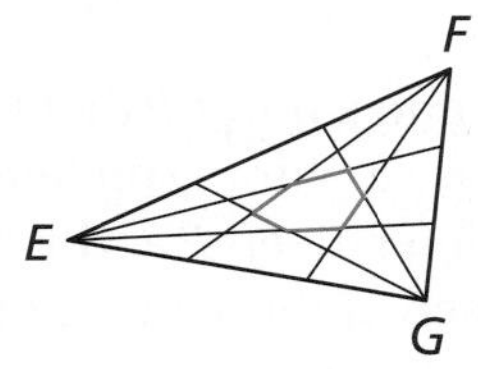

Is this a reliable pattern? In other words, does the inside region always have twice the number of sides as the original shape when you connect vertices to "third points" in this way? Explain.

To make the angle with vertex at B, connect B to the point on $\overline{AD}$ that is closer to A, and to the point on $\overline{CD}$ that is closer to C.

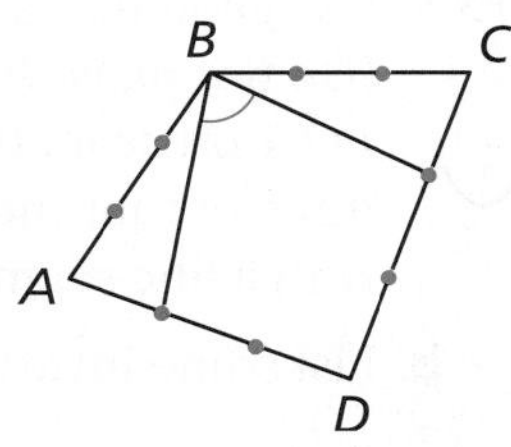

Exercises *Practicing Habits of Mind*

On Your Own

3. The table at the right shows pairs of numbers. An invariant for the table is 4 because $\frac{r}{q} = 4$ for each pair. Make three different tables like the one at the right so that the invariant for each table is 8. Use a different operation to build each table.

q	*r*
$\frac{1}{8}$	$\frac{1}{2}$
4	16
8	32
100	400

4. Draw a quadrilateral. Construct the midpoints of its sides. Then connect the consecutive midpoints.

a. Explain why the figure formed must be a quadrilateral.

b. Can the figure formed be *any* kind of quadrilateral, or are certain kinds of quadrilaterals not possible? Explain.

In other words, besides the number of sides, what other invariants, if any, exist?

Maintain Your Skills

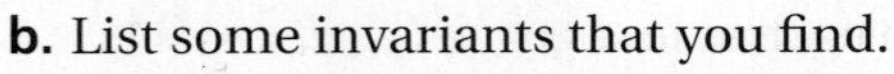

5. a. Use geometry software to construct a figure like the one at the right, in which lines ℓ and m are parallel. Then drag a point or one of the lines to change the appearance of the figure. Lines ℓ and m should remain parallel.

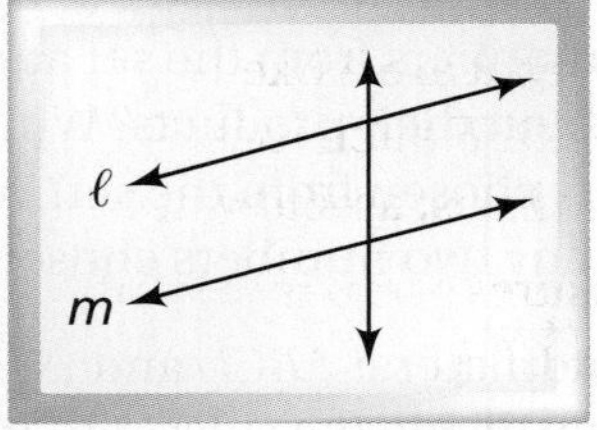

b. List some invariants that you find.

6. a. Use geometry software to construct a square like the one at the right.

b. Drag some points. List some invariants that you find.

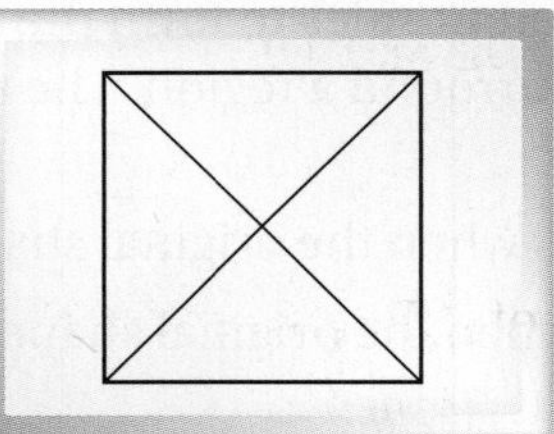

A square is a regular polygon. For help, see the TI-Nspire Handbook, p. 712.

7. a. Use geometry software. Construct a line ℓ and a point P that is not on ℓ. (Do not place P too far away from ℓ.) Choose a point Q on line ℓ. Draw $\overline{PQ}$. Construct the circle with $\overline{PQ}$ as a diameter. Keep P and ℓ fixed. Place three or four more points on ℓ. Connect each of these new points to P with a line segment. Draw a circle with this segment as its diameter.

b. List some invariants that you find.

Habits of Mind

Visualize. If $\overline{PQ}$ is a diameter, where is the center of the circle?

1.11 Numerical Invariants in Geometry

Positions of points, intersections of lines, lengths of segments, measures of angles, and even sums or ratios of these measurements may be invariant.

A numerical invariant is called a **constant.** In this section, *invariant* and *constant* mean the same thing.

For the problems in the following In-Class Experiments, do each of the following tasks.

- Draw and measure the objects with geometry software.
- Drag parts of the figure. Watch what changes and what remains the same.
- Make conjectures that seem likely. Then find a way to test them.
- Organize and record your results.

In-Class Experiment

Geometric Objects

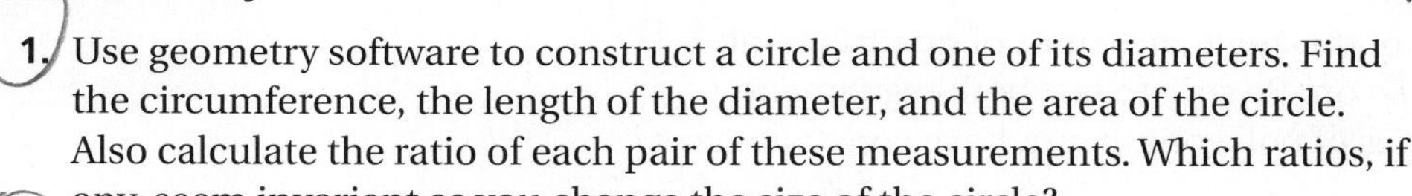

1. Use geometry software to construct a circle and one of its diameters. Find the circumference, the length of the diameter, and the area of the circle. Also calculate the ratio of each pair of these measurements. Which ratios, if any, seem invariant as you change the size of the circle?

2. Construct two parallel lines that are a fixed distance apart. Construct $\triangle DEF$ such that points D, E, and F are on the lines, as shown.

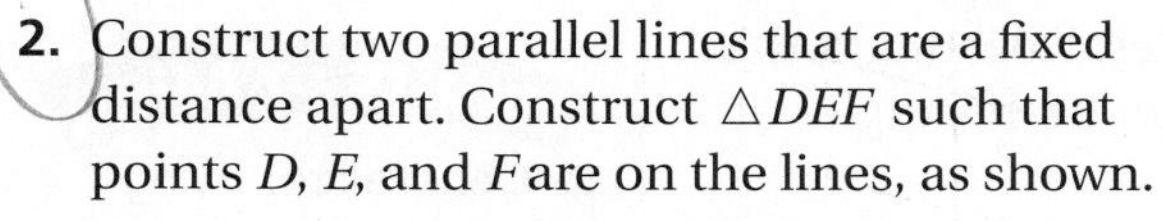

   In parts (a)–(e), which measures seem invariant in $\triangle DEF$ as D moves along $\overleftrightarrow{CD}$?

   a. the measure of $\angle EDF$

   b. the sum of the lengths of $\overline{DE}$ and $\overline{DF}$

   c. the perimeter of $\triangle DEF$

   d. the area of $\triangle DEF$

   e. the sum of the measures of $\angle D$, $\angle E$, and $\angle F$

   f. Can you find any other invariants?

For help finding the area of the triangle, see the TI-Nspire Handbook, p. 712.

3. Study your construction from Problem 2 as D moves along $\overleftrightarrow{CD}$.

   a. Find two angles that have equal measure, no matter where D is located on $\overleftrightarrow{CD}$.

   b. Find pairs or groups of angles that have an invariant sum of 180°.

   c. Can you find two angles such that the measure of one is always greater than the measure of the other? Explain.

4. Draw $\triangle ABC$. Construct the midpoint D of $\overline{BC}$. Construct median $\overline{AD}$. As you stretch and distort $\triangle ABC$, what is invariant? (Be sure that D remains the midpoint of $\overline{BC}$!)

a. Find two segments such that their lengths are a constant ratio.

b. Are there any invariant areas? Invariant ratios of areas?

c. Find at least one other invariant. Provide a chart or table of measurements and some sketches to show the measures or ratios that do not change.

Remember...

A median of a triangle is a line segment that connects one of the triangle's vertices to the midpoint of the opposite side.

In-Class Experiment

Constant Sum and Difference

You may be convinced that the sum of the angle measures of a triangle is invariably 180°. What do you think about the sums of the angle measures of other kinds of polygons? Are they also 180°? Or do different kinds of polygons—quadrilaterals, pentagons, hexagons, and so on—have their own special fixed numbers? If so, is it possible to predict the sum of the angle measures of a given polygon?

5. Experiment with the sums of the angle measures of quadrilaterals, pentagons, hexagons, and so on. Be sure to test both regular and irregular shapes. Which types of polygons, if any, have constant sums of angle measures?

6. You can divide a polygon with n sides into $(n - 2)$ triangles. How might this help you find a rule that describes the sum of the measures of the angles of a polygon?

Habits of Mind

Generalize. Trying this for a few simple polygons may suggest what you can do for any polygon. Once you get the general idea, try to make a convincing argument that applies to every polygon.

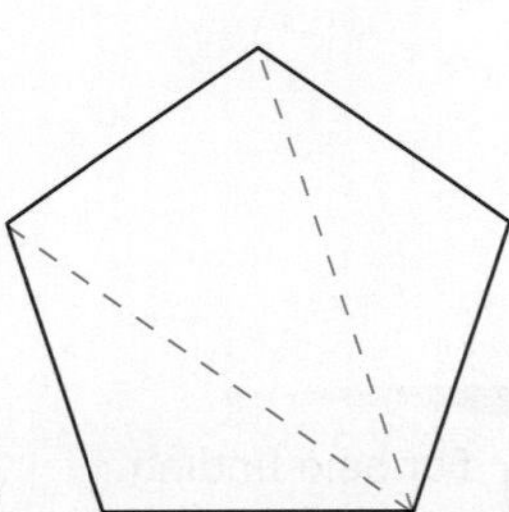

Three triangles form a pentagon.

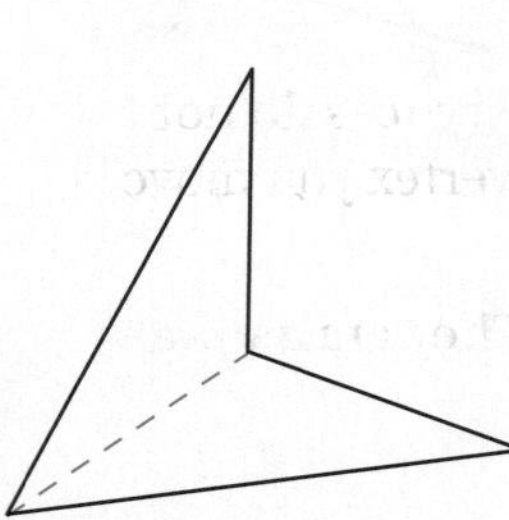

Two triangles form a quadrilateral.

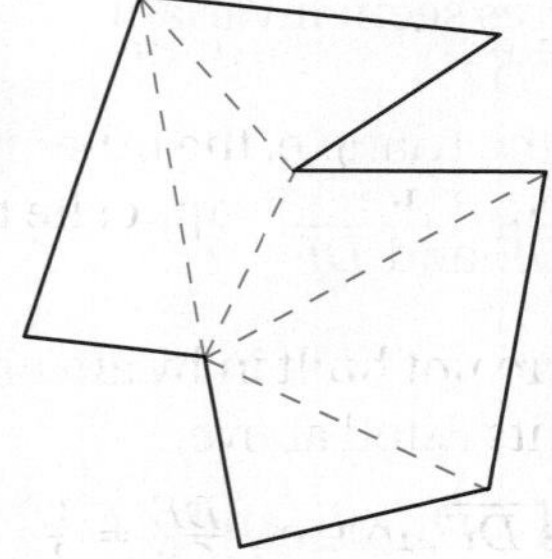

Six triangles form an octagon.

7. Assume that the sum of the angle measures of a triangle is invariant. Write an argument that shows that the sum of the angle measures of an n-sided polygon is also invariant. Find a rule that will tell you the angle sum if you know n, the number of sides.

In-Class Experiment

Constant Product and Ratio

Use geometry software to draw a triangle. Construct and connect the midpoints of two sides. Your construction will look something like the construction below. Point D is the midpoint of $\overline{AC}$, and E is the midpoint of $\overline{AB}$.

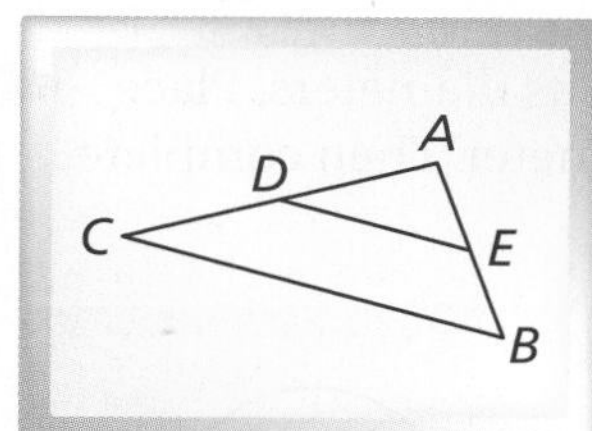

Go Online
Pearsonsuccessnet.com

8. Move one of the triangle's vertices. As you distort the triangle, look for invariants.

9. Measure the lengths of $\overline{DE}$ and $\overline{BC}$. Compare these lengths as you drag one of the vertices.

You know about the following invariants because you deliberately built them into your triangle.

- $CD = DA$ (because D is the midpoint of $\overline{AC}$)
- $AE = EB$ (because E is the midpoint of $\overline{AB}$)
- $\frac{AD}{AC} = \frac{1}{2}$
- $\frac{AE}{AB} = \frac{1}{2}$

CD, without the overbar, represents the length of segment $\overline{CD}$.

You may not have listed this next invariant because it is almost too obvious. It is built into the software, and it is important.

- As you drag one vertex of the triangle, the other two vertices do not move. Therefore, the length of the side opposite the vertex you move does not change.

The remaining invariants were not built in by anyone. They are natural consequences of the invariants listed above.

- As $\overline{CB}$ gets longer, so does $\overline{DE}$. In fact, $\frac{DE}{CB} = \frac{1}{2}$.
- $\frac{\text{area}(\triangle ABC)}{\text{area}(\triangle AED)} = 4$
- $\overline{DE}$ is parallel to $\overline{CB}$.

The results of the In-Class Experiment suggest the following conjecture.

Conjecture 1.2 Midline Conjecture

A segment connecting the midpoints of two sides of a triangle is parallel to the third side and is half its length.

You will prove the Midline Conjecture in Chapter 2.

Exercises *Practicing Habits of Mind*

Check Your Understanding

For help placing a point on the circle, see the TI-Nspire Handbook, p. 712.

1. Use geometry software to construct a circle and one of its diameters. Place a point on the circle away from an endpoint of the diameter. Then complete the triangle as shown in the third figure below.

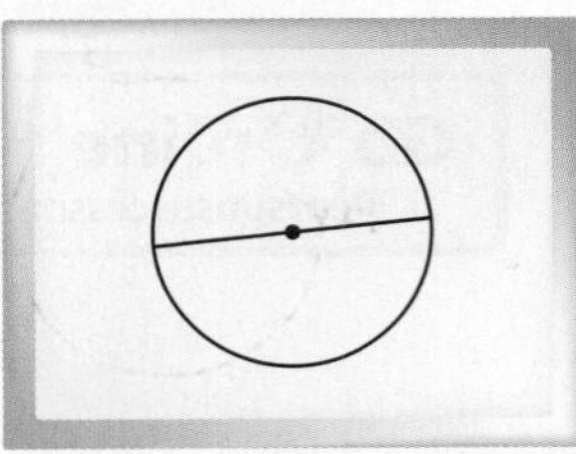

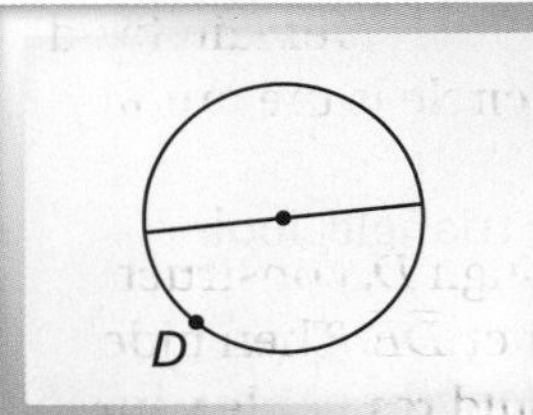

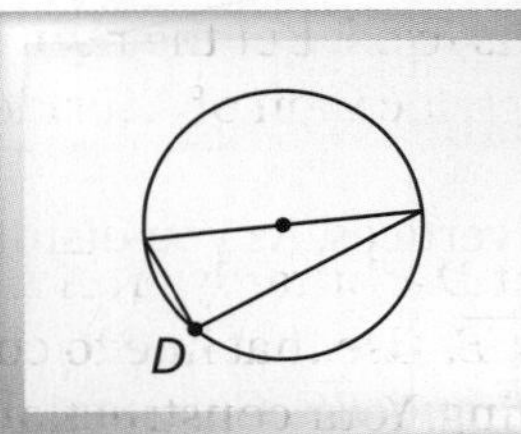

a. Move D around the circle. What measures or relationships are invariant as D moves? Look at angles, lengths, sums, and ratios.

b. Leave D in one place and stretch the circle. What measures or relationships are invariant as the size of the circle changes?

2. Construct a rectangle $ABCD$ so that you can stretch its length and width. Which of the following are invariants?

a. the length-to-width ratio: $\frac{AB}{AD}$

b. the ratio of the lengths of the opposite sides: $\frac{AB}{DC}$

c. the perimeter of rectangle $ABCD$

d. the ratio of the lengths of the diagonals: $\frac{AC}{BD}$

e. the ratio of the perimeter of rectangle $ABCD$ to its area

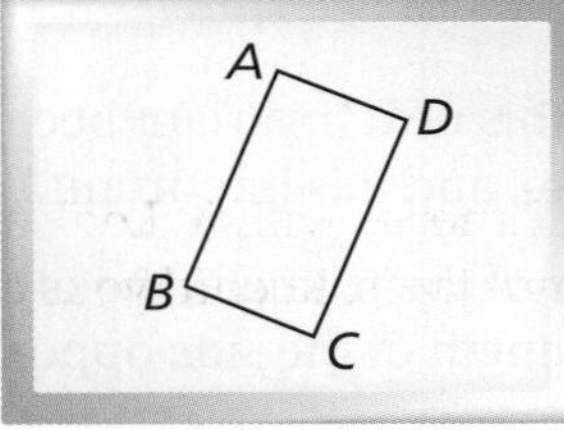

3. In the figure below, C is fixed on $\overline{AB}$, but D is not fixed. Move D. Find two sums related to the figure that are constant.

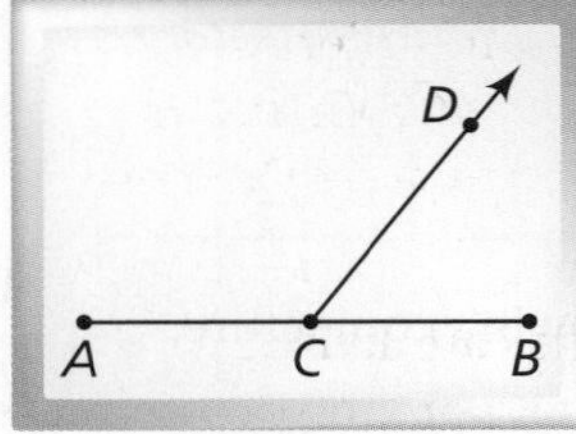

4. Use geometry software to draw two parallel lines m and n. Fix points A and B on line m. Place point C on line n. Draw $\triangle ABC$. Now move point C along n. Look at the area and perimeter of the triangle. What invariants do you notice?

Use geometry software to construct a circle. Place a point C anywhere inside the circle. Place point D on the circle. Construct the line through D and C to meet the circle a second time at point E. Then hide $\overleftrightarrow{DC}$. Construct $\overline{DC}$, $\overline{EC}$, and $\overline{DE}$. As you move D along the circle, $\overline{DE}$ will pivot about C.

5. Measure $\overline{CE}$ and $\overline{CD}$. When the chord pivots about C, do CE and CD change in opposite ways (one increases while the other decreases) or in the same way? Use that information to help you find a numerical invariant.

A *chord* of a circle is a segment with endpoints that are on the circle.

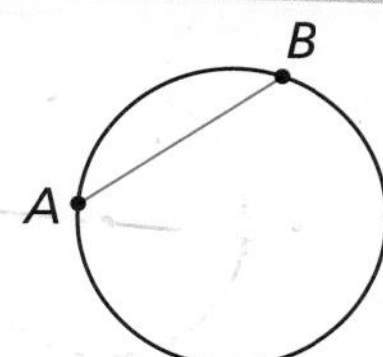

$\overline{AB}$ is a chord of the circle.

6. The number you found does not depend on the location of D. You can move D, and the number remains fixed. But the number does *not* remain fixed when C is moved. For which location of C inside the circle is the number greatest? Explain.

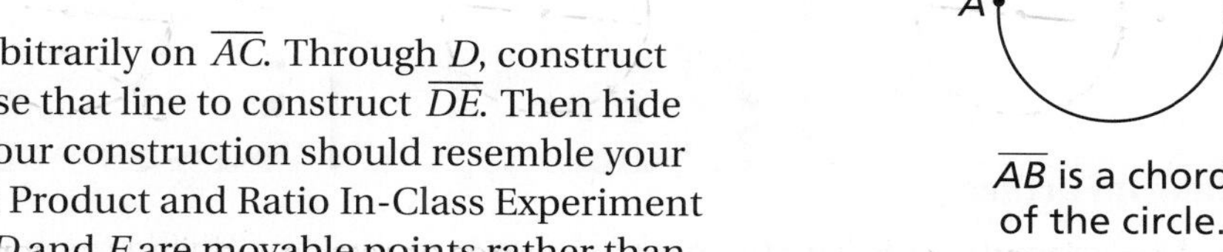

7. Draw $\triangle ABC$. Place a point D arbitrarily on $\overline{AC}$. Through D, construct the line that is parallel to $\overline{CB}$. Use that line to construct $\overline{DE}$. Then hide $\overleftrightarrow{DE}$, leaving just $\overline{DE}$ showing. Your construction should resemble your construction from the Constant Product and Ratio In-Class Experiment earlier in the lesson. This time, D and E are movable points rather than midpoints.

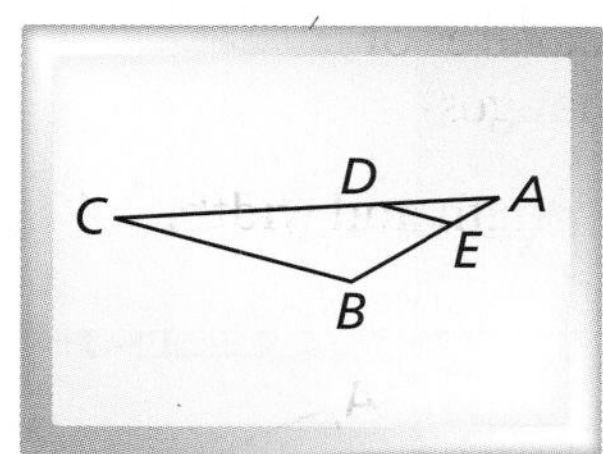

As D moves along $\overline{AC}$, $\overline{DE}$ moves with it. Look at different lengths and areas. Try to find some invariants. Record your conjectures and appropriate supporting evidence.

Developing Habits of Mind

Experiment. Exercise 7 is a good example of how you get different results when you slightly change a problem. You know from earlier work that certain ratios are invariant when D is the midpoint of $\overline{AC}$. When D is fixed on $\overline{AC}$ but is *not* its midpoint, are those ratios still invariant? Or does their invariance depend on D being the midpoint?

When you move D, are the ratios constant? If so, the ratios are again invariant. If not, perhaps a relationship exists between two or more of the ratios.

On Your Own

8. Tennis balls are sold in cans of three stacked balls. Which is greater—the height of the can or the circumference of the can?

9. In the figure below, $\overleftrightarrow{CD} \parallel \overleftrightarrow{AB}$. How can you construct a right triangle that has the same area as $\triangle EFG$?

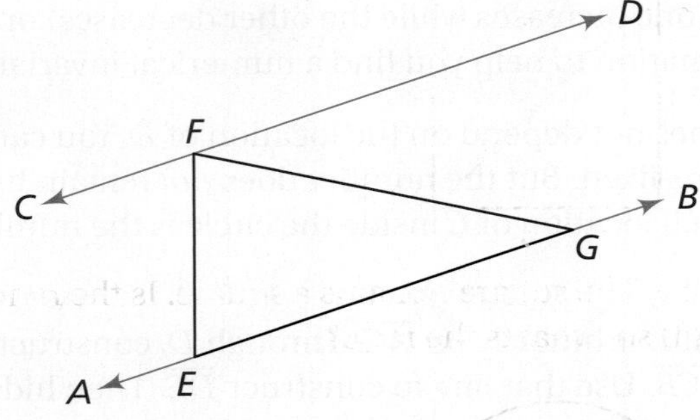

10. **Take It Further**

a. Use geometry software to construct a rectangle. Then divide the rectangle into a square and a smaller rectangle.

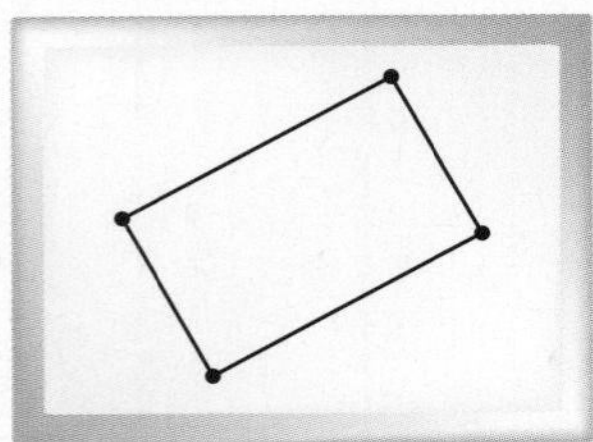
a rectangle

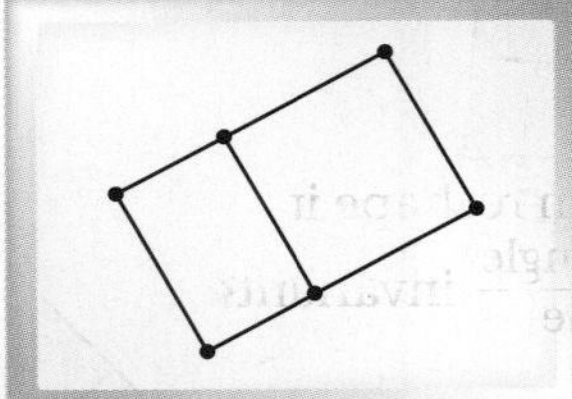
the rectangle divided into a square and a smaller rectangle

Find the length-to-width ratio in each nonsquare rectangle. Are the two ratios equal?

b. The figure at the right illustrates a special ratio for a particular type of rectangle. If you divide this type of rectangle into a square and a smaller rectangle, as shown, the length-to-width ratios of the large and small nonsquare rectangles are equal. In fact, you can divide the smaller rectangle into a square and an even smaller rectangle. The length-to-width ratio of the smaller rectangle is the same as the length-to-width ratio of the first two rectangles. What is the numerical value of this length-to-width ratio?

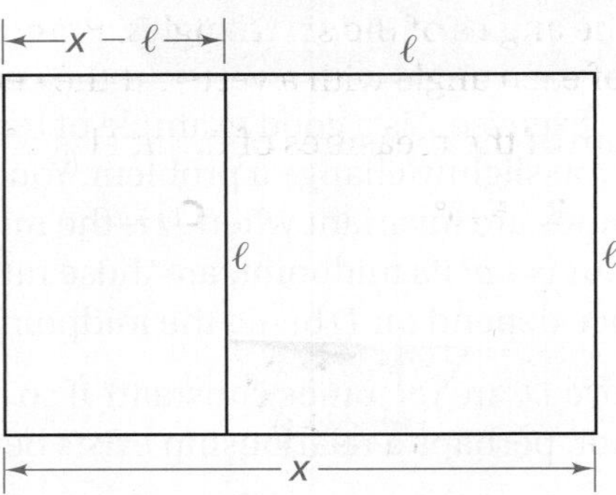

11. Decide whether each ratio in parts (a)–(c) is constant, even if you stretch the given figure with the given restrictions. Justify each answer.

a. The square remains square. Is the ratio $\frac{\text{area of triangle}}{\text{area of square}}$ invariant? If so, what is the ratio?

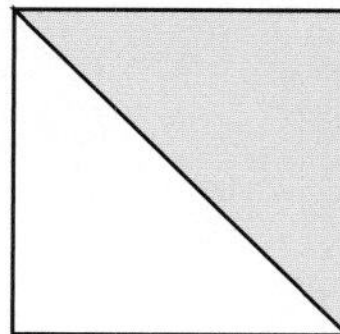

b. The circle remains a circle. The square remains a square. Is the ratio $\frac{\text{area of circle}}{\text{area of square}}$ invariant? If so, what is the ratio?

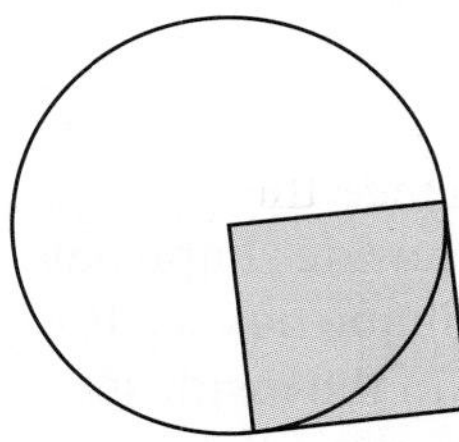

c. The triangle remains a triangle. You can reshape it in any way. Is the ratio $\frac{\text{perimeter of triangle}}{\text{area of triangle}}$ invariant? If so, what is the ratio?

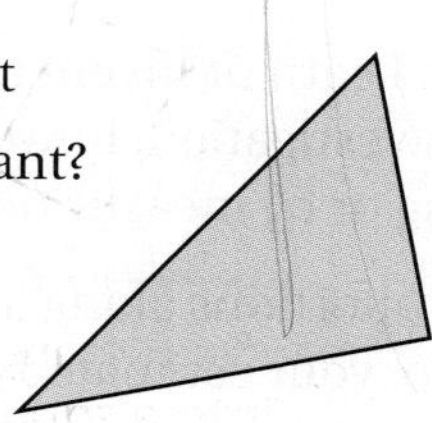

12. **Standardized Test Prep** Maya constructed a regular hexagon inside a circle. The hexagon consists of six equilateral triangles. To compute the sum of the measures of the angles of the regular hexagon, she found the sum of the measures of the angles of the six triangles. From that sum, she subtracted the measure of each angle with a vertex at the center of the circle.

What is the sum of the measures of the angles of Maya's regular hexagon?

A. 360° **B.** 540° **C.** 720° **D.** 1080°

Go Online
Pearsonsuccessnet.com

Maintain Your Skills

13. Find five cylindrical objects. Measure the diameter and the circumference of each. What is the $\frac{\text{circumference}}{\text{diameter}}$ ratio for each object?

1.12 Spatial Invariants

Shape: A Geometric Invariant

Invariants do not have to be numbers or relationships between numbers. Invariants can be shapes or relationships between shapes, as well. In Lesson 1.10, you searched for shape invariants in the figures below.

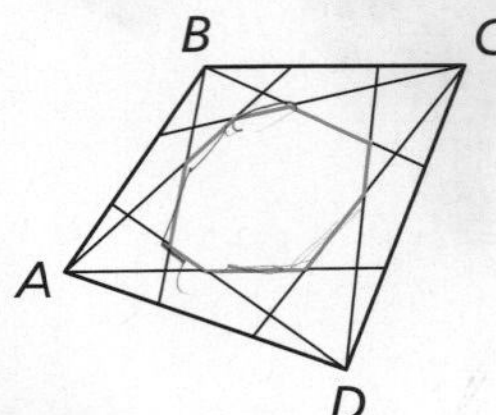

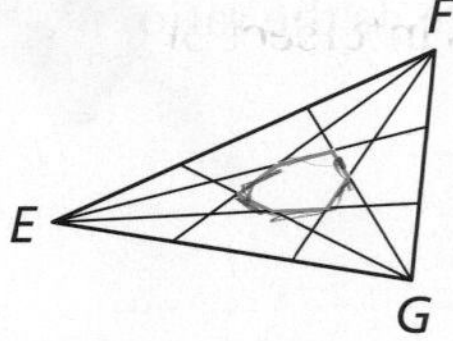

It appears that when the outside shape has four sides, the inside shape has eight. When the outside shape has three sides, the inside shape has six. It turns out that, in the case of a triangle, the figure formed on the inside is always a hexagon. Otherwise, the strict doubling pattern is not reliable.

Investigate these figures further. Learn or invent a way to divide a segment accurately into thirds. For this investigation, however, it is acceptable to divide the segment by estimating or by measuring.

Geometry software preserves proportions along a segment when you stretch or shrink the segment. So, your estimated thirds will stay fixed throughout the experiment, unless you deliberately change them.

For Discussion

What *can* happen is often as useful as what *must* happen.

1. If the outside polygon has n sides, can the inside polygon ever have more than $2n$ sides? If so, what is the greatest number of sides the inside polygon can have?
2. Can the inside polygon ever have fewer than $2n$ sides? If so, what is the fewest number of sides the inside polygon can have?
3. Can the inside polygon ever be regular? Explain.

Concurrence: A Geometric Invariant

You may recognize the picture below from one of the experiments you performed earlier.

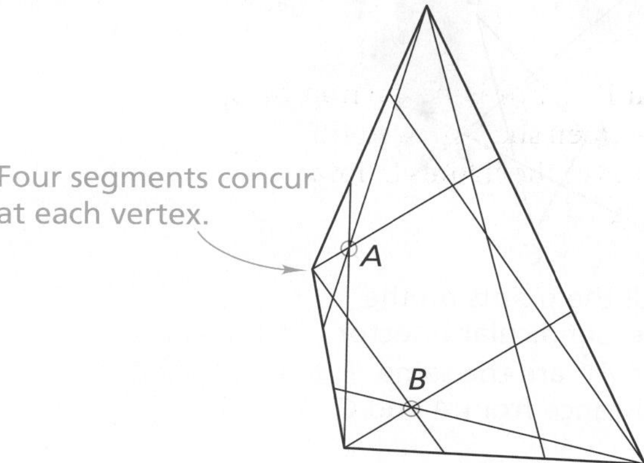

At each vertex of the outside quadrilateral, four segments intersect or concur. That is no surprise. It was intentional.

Definition

Three or more lines that meet or intersect at one point are concurrent lines.

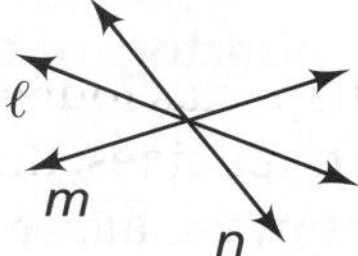

Lines ℓ, m, and n are concurrent lines.

In the first figure above, three *inside* segments are also concurrent. Two such concurrences are at points A and B. These concurrences were not deliberately built in. They are something of a surprise. If you move the vertices of the quadrilateral, you will see that these concurrences are not invariant.

When concurrence is an invariant for a given figure, a special relationship exists.

For You to Do

4. Use geometry software to draw a triangle. Construct the perpendicular bisector of each side. Can you adjust the triangle so that the three perpendicular bisectors are concurrent?

5. Hide the perpendicular bisectors. Construct the angle bisectors of your triangle. Can you adjust the triangle so that the three angle bisectors are concurrent?

6. Under which circumstances, if any, are the three perpendicular bisectors and the three angle bisectors of a triangle all concurrent?

For help constructing the perpendicular bisectors, see the TI-Nspire Handbook, p. 712.

It may surprise you that the perpendicular bisectors in a triangle are concurrent. If you analyze the situation, though, it becomes less surprising.

Refer to Theorem 1.1 in Lesson 1.06.

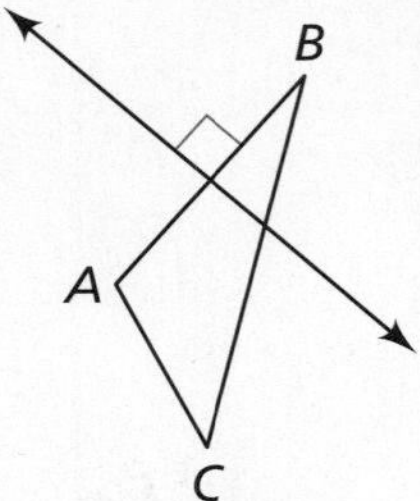

All the points on the perpendicular bisector of $\overline{AB}$ are the same distance from A and B.

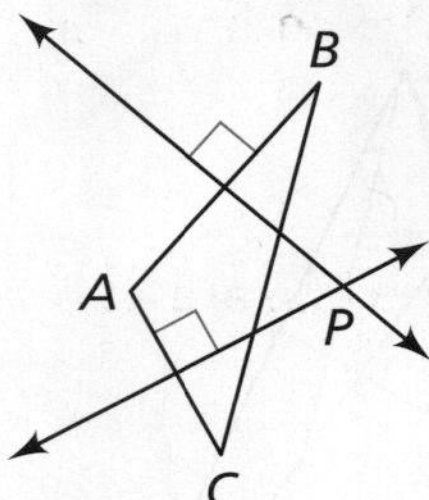

All the points on the perpendicular bisector of $\overline{AC}$ are the same distance from A and C.

Point P is constructed so that it is equidistant from A and B and equidistant from A and C. So P is also equidistant from B and C. P must lie on the perpendicular bisector of $\overline{BC}$.

Theorem 1.2 Concurrence of Perpendicular Bisectors

In any triangle, the perpendicular bisectors of the sides are concurrent.

In $\triangle ABC$, the perpendicular bisectors of $\overline{AB}$, $\overline{BC}$, and $\overline{AC}$ are concurrent at G.

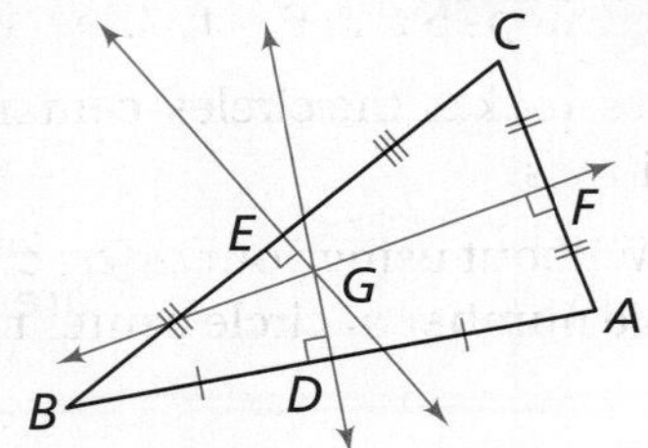

You can make a similar argument for the angle bisectors of a triangle. Any point on the bisector of $\angle ABC$ is the same distance from $\overline{AB}$ and $\overline{BC}$. Any point on the bisector of $\angle CAB$ is the same distance from $\overline{AC}$ and $\overline{AB}$. The point of intersection of the two angle bisectors is the same distance from $\overline{AC}$ and $\overline{BC}$. That puts it on the bisector of $\angle ACB$ as well.

Theorem 1.3 Concurrence of Angle Bisectors

In any triangle, the angle bisectors are concurrent.

In $\triangle XYZ$, the angle bisectors of $\angle X$, $\angle Y$, and $\angle Z$ are concurrent at K.

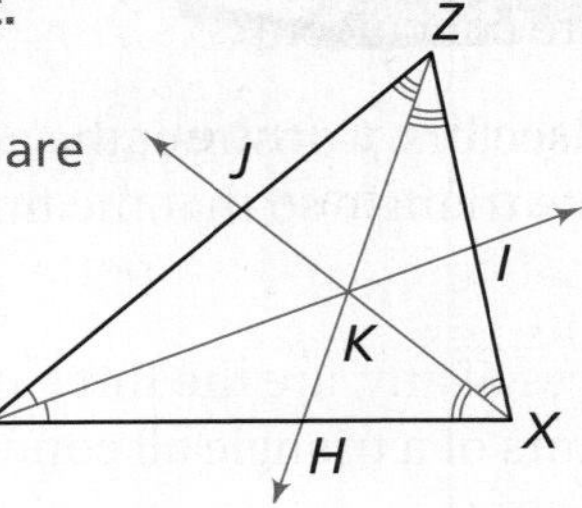

Collinearity

It is noteworthy when three lines intersect at the same point. It is also noteworthy when three apparently unrelated points lie on the same line.

Definition

Three or more points that are on the same line are collinear points.

For You to Do

Step 1 Trace a circle onto a sheet of paper.

Step 2 Poke a small hole through the paper at the center of the circle.

Step 3 Carefully cut out your **disc** (the circle and its interior).

Step 4 Work with three or four classmates who made discs of different sizes. Draw two points on a large sheet of paper. Place them close enough together that the smallest disc can touch both.

Step 5 Place one of your discs on the large sheet. Move it so that the edge of the disc touches both points.

Step 6 Mark the center of the circle on the large sheet.

Step 7 Remove the disc. Repeat Steps 5 and 6 with the other discs.

Step 8 After using all your discs, look at the circles' center marks. What is invariant about their positions?

Step 9 Draw two new points. Without using your discs, draw the figure that would be formed by a large number of circle center marks.

Exercises *Practicing Habits of Mind*

Check Your Understanding

1. Use geometry software. Place five points on your screen. Connect them with segments so that you have an arbitrary convex pentagon. Construct the perpendicular bisector of each side of your pentagon. See the diagrams and answer the questions on the next page.

a. In the diagram at the left below, is there a point at which three or more perpendicular bisectors are concurrent?

b. If not, is it possible to adjust the vertices of the pentagon so that at least three bisectors are concurrent?

c. Is it possible to adjust the vertices of the pentagon so that all five bisectors are concurrent?

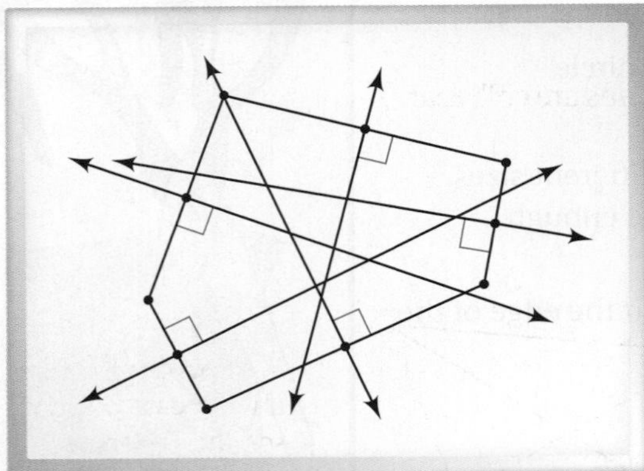

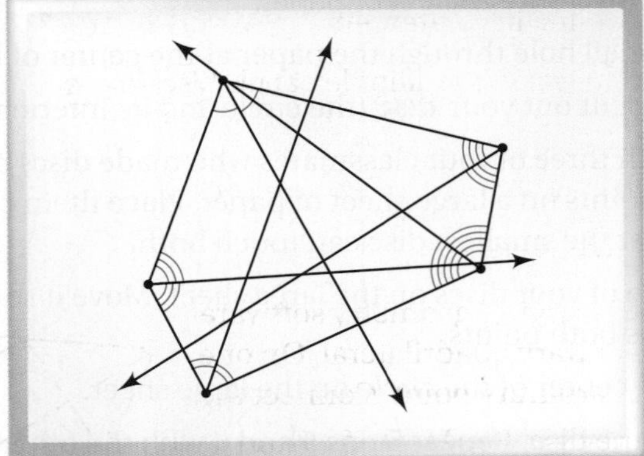

2. Try the same kind of experiment with the angle bisectors of a pentagon. See the diagram at the right above. Start with an arbitrary pentagon. Construct the angle bisector of each angle. Is it possible to adjust the vertices of the pentagon so that all five angle bisectors are concurrent?

It is a good habit to start an investigation with a special case. It simplifies what you have to look at. It can also suggest what to look for in other cases. Among polygons, the triangle is special because it is the simplest. Exercises 3–6 suggest other special cases.

3. Regular polygons are a very special case. Is concurrence of perpendicular bisectors an invariant for regular polygons? Experiment. Be sure to experiment with regular quadrilaterals (squares), regular pentagons, and regular hexagons. What do your experiments suggest? Explain.

4. Is concurrence of angle bisectors an invariant for regular polygons? Experiment, describe a conjecture, and explain the result.

5. Use geometry software to construct a circle. Place five points on the circle. Connect the points to form an irregular pentagon. Check the angle bisectors and perpendicular bisectors of the pentagon for concurrence. Do you observe any invariants? Explain.

6. Draw a circle. Construct an irregular polygon outside the circle so that all the sides of the polygon are tangent to the circle. Perform the two concurrence experiments. Do you observe any invariants? Explain.

On Your Own

7. Construct several different triangles. Then construct their medians. Describe any concurrence or collinearity you find.

8. **Standardized Test Prep** Triangle ABC is an isosceles triangle. $\overline{AD}$, $\overline{BE}$, and $\overline{CF}$ are altitudes. $\overline{AD}$, $\overline{BG}$, and $\overline{CH}$ are angle bisectors. Points D, I, and J are the midpoints of $\overline{BC}$, $\overline{AC}$, and $\overline{AB}$, respectively.

Which of the following statements may NOT be true?

A. The concurrences of the altitudes, angle bisectors, and medians are collinear.

B. $\overline{CI} \cong \overline{CD}$

C. $\overline{AD}$ is a median.

D. $\angle BCH \cong \angle HCA$

9. Use a piece of paper or geometry software to build an arbitrary quadrilateral. On one side, place an arbitrary point. Connect the point to the two opposite vertices of the quadrilateral. Do the same on the opposite side.

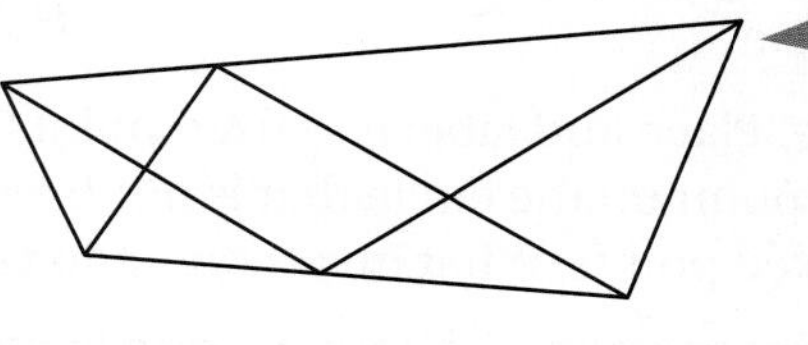

For help constructing an irregular polygon, see the TI-Nspire Handbook, p. 712.

Finally, draw the diagonals of the quadrilateral. Find two obvious collinearities. Find one surprising collinearity.

10. **Take It Further** Consider this statement: In any hexagon, there can be at most one concurrence of three diagonals. Is this statement true or false? Explain your reasoning.

Maintain Your Skills

11. Construct trapezoid $ABCD$ such that you can drag its vertices and sides.

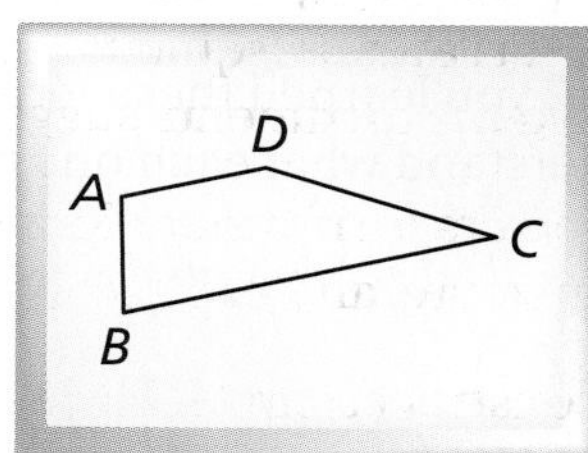

a. Construct the diagonals and their point of intersection. Then construct the midpoints of the two parallel sides.

b. Find two collinearities that are intentionally built in. Find one collinearity that is not intentionally built in. Experiment to determine whether that collinearity is invariant.

In this investigation you studied invariants—things that are the same for every member of a collection. You explored numerical invariants and spatial invariants, including concurrence and collinearity. The following questions will help you summarize what you have learned.

1. What is the sum of the measures of the angles of a pentagon? Of a hexagon?
2. In $\triangle ABC$, D and E are the midpoints of $\overline{BC}$ and $\overline{AC}$, respectively. The lengths of some segments are marked. Find $\frac{CD}{CB}$ and $\frac{CF}{CH}$. Explain your reasoning.

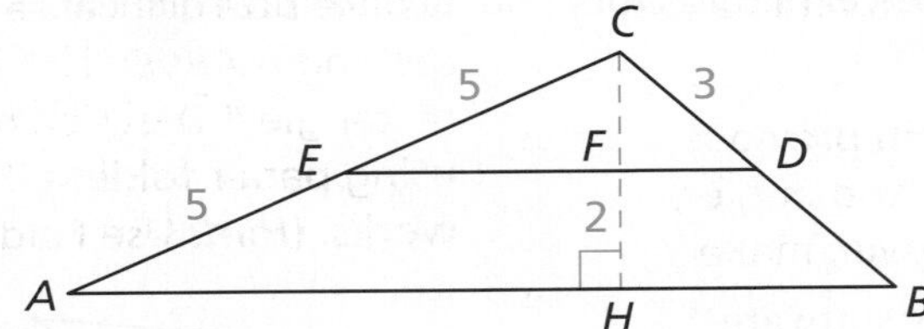

3. Draw a circle. Place and label two fixed points on the circle. Then place and label a third point on the circle that is not fixed. Build segments from it to each of the two fixed points. What invariant(s) do you notice in your construction?
4. Are the medians of an equilateral triangle concurrent? Explain.
5. What invariants can you think of for a regular hexagon? List as many as you can.
6. What is an invariant? What kinds of invariants should you look for in geometry?
7. What invariant relationship exists when a line parallel to the base of a triangle intersects the other sides of that triangle?
8. What shape do you form when you connect the consecutive midpoints of a quadrilateral?

Vocabulary

In this investigation, you learned these terms. Make sure you understand what each one means and how to use it.

- **collinear points**
- **concurrent lines**
- **constant**
- **disc**
- **invariant**

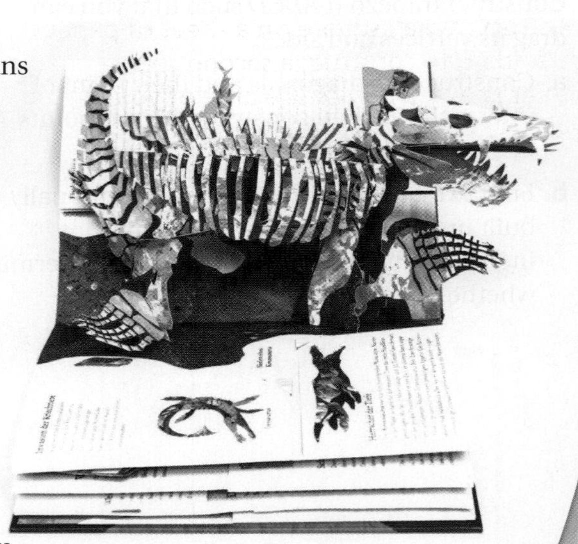

What remains invariant when you open the pop-up book?

Project: Using Mathematical Habits

Folding Squares

The good news is that there are several ways to use paper folding to solve each problem below. The challenge is to find one way!

You can use all that you know from previous courses about squares, their sides and angles, and their areas. You cannot, however, make any measurements with a ruler.

Materials:

square sheets of paper

Begin with several sheets of square paper.

1. Select a square. Use folding to construct a square with area $\frac{3}{4}$ the area of your original square. Remember, no rulers are allowed. Explain your construction.

2. Select another square and another fraction of the form $\frac{m}{n}$. Use folding. Try to construct a square with area $\frac{m}{n}$ times the area of the original square. For what fractions $\frac{m}{n}$ can you do this? Explain.

3. Construct a small square on a sheet of paper. Use folding to construct a second square with area exactly twice the area of your small square. Explain how you did it.

4. The paper below has been folded so that square *BGJH* has area equal to that of rectangle *ABCD*. This is called "squaring the rectangle." Describe how to square a rectangle using paper folding. Explain why the folding works. (*Hint:* Use Fold 0 to make rectangle *ABCD*.)

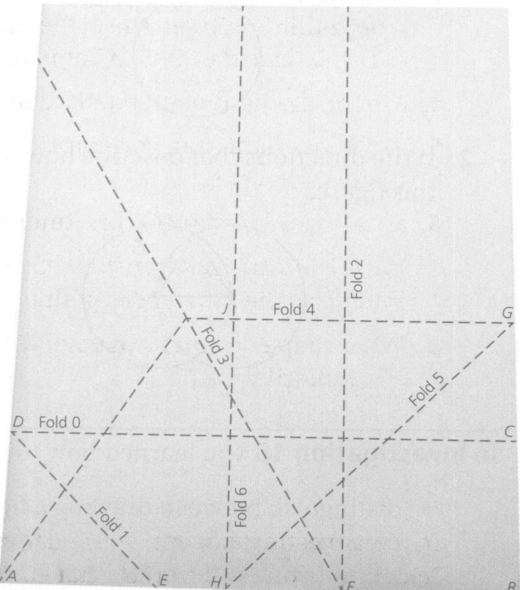

Chapter 1 Review

Go Online
Pearsonsuccessnet.com

In **Investigation 1A** you learned how to

- visualize geometric objects well enough to draw them
- use clear language to describe shapes
- write and follow careful directions

The following questions will help you check your understanding.

1. Copy the figure. Draw all of its lines of symmetry.

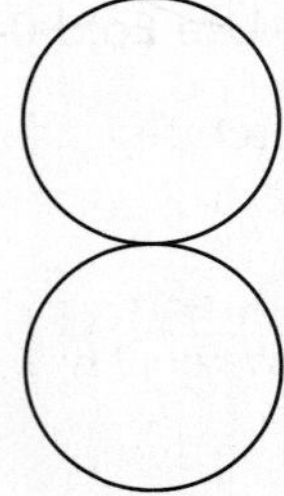

2. Write directions that describe how to draw this figure.

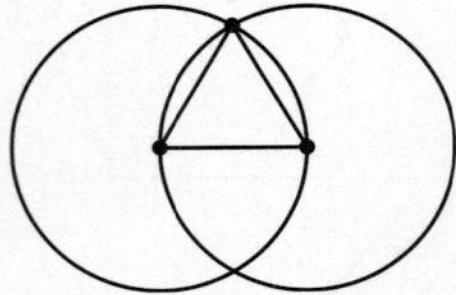

In **Investigation 1B** you learned how to

- distinguish between drawing a figure and constructing a figure
- use hand construction tools, including paper folding
- recognize invariants

The following questions will help you check your understanding.

3. If possible, construct a triangle with the given angle measures.

   a. 60°, 40°, 80° **b.** 100°, 20°, 45°

4. If possible, construct a triangle with the given side lengths.

   a. 4 cm, 5 cm, 6 cm **b.** 3 in., 2 in., 6 in.

5. What is invariant about the angles of a quadrilateral? About a polygon with n sides?

In **Investigation 1C** you learned how to

- use geometry software tools to construct UnMessUpable figures
- use geometry software to test for invariants

The following questions will help you check your understanding.

6. Construct an UnMessUpable square with side length 4 cm.

7. Use geometry software. Construct an UnMessUpable rectangle. Which invariant would you have to build into your rectangle to make the figure an UnMessUpable square?

8. The two lines below are parallel. If you choose any four points on the lines and connect them, will the result be a parallelogram? To get a parallelogram, which points can you choose randomly, and how do you have to choose the others?

In **Investigation 1D** you learned how to

- apply the Midline Conjecture
- search for numerical and spatial invariants
- make conjectures and use software to experiment with geometric models

The following questions will help you check your understanding.

9. What is the definition of a perpendicular bisector? Explain why the three perpendicular bisectors of the sides of a triangle are concurrent.

10. Decide whether each ratio below is constant, even if the given figure is stretched, with the given restrictions. Justify each answer.

a. The rectangle remains a rectangle. Points E and F remain the midpoints of $\overline{AB}$ and $\overline{DC}$, respectively. Is the ratio

$$\frac{\text{area of } AEFD}{\text{area of } ABCD}$$

invariant? If so, what is the ratio?

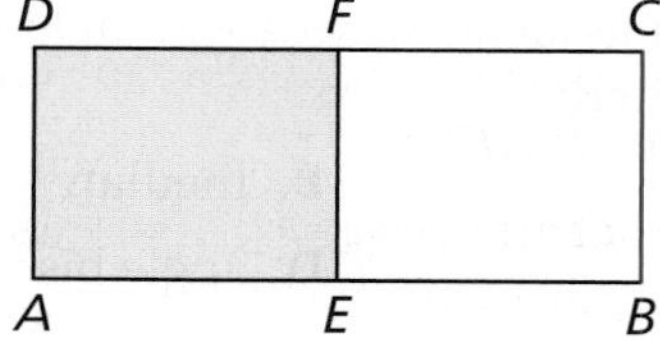

b. The two circles below remain centered at A and B and have radius AB. You can stretch $\overline{AB}$. Is the ratio

$$\frac{\text{area of } AEBF}{\text{area of circle centered at } A}$$

invariant? If so, what is the ratio? (Recall, the area of a circle is πr^2, where r is the radius of the circle.)

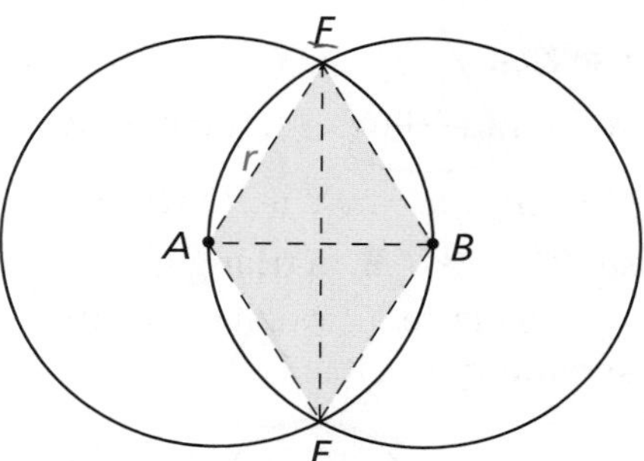

c. You can stretch the sides of the regular hexagon below. Is the ratio

$$\frac{\text{area of hexagon}}{\text{perimeter of hexagon}}$$

invariant? If so, what is the ratio?

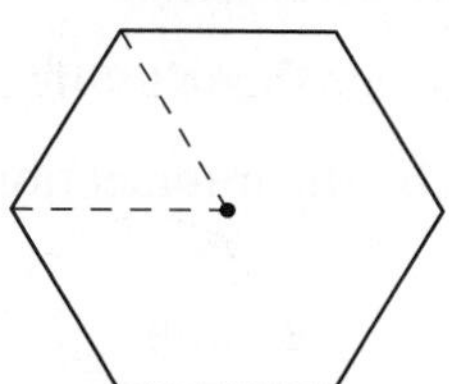

Chapter 1 Test

Multiple Choice

1. Which type of cross section can you NOT form by intersecting a plane and a right circular cone?

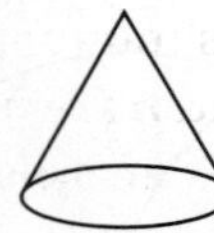

A. an ellipse

B. a triangle

C. a rectangle
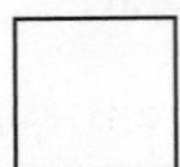

D. a circle

2. Which figure has exactly two lines of symmetry?

A. regular pentagon B. circle
C. square D. rectangle

3. Which figure could be the intersection of two different planes?

A. point B. line
C. line segment D. plane

4. Which block letter has a vertical line of symmetry?

A. 
B. 
C. 
D. 

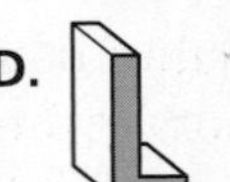

5. Which name best describes a parallelogram with four right angles?

A. square B. rectangle
C. trapezoid D. rhombus

6. Which method describes how to divide a segment into four congruent segments?

A. Construct the midpoint of the segment.
B. Construct the perpendicular bisector of the segment.
C. Construct a square with each side congruent to the original segment.
D. Construct the perpendicular bisector of the segment. Then construct the perpendicular bisector of each of the new segments.

7. Which word or phrase best completes the following sentence?

The point of concurrency of the medians of a triangle is always __?__ the triangle.

A. inside B. on a vertex of
C. on a side of D. outside

8. The figures below show how to construct a type of segment associated with a triangle. What is constructed?

A. altitude B. median
C. midline D. angle bisector

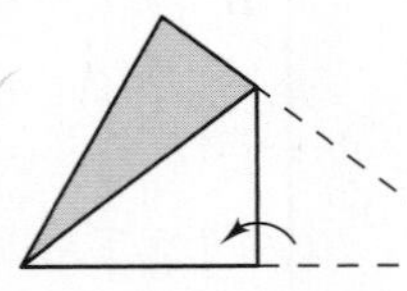
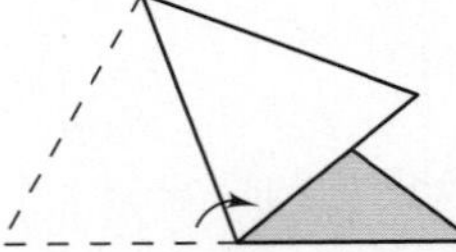

9. Which method describes how to construct an altitude of a triangle?

A. Construct the midpoint of one side of the triangle. Then construct the segment from that midpoint to the opposite vertex.
B. Construct the perpendicular from a vertex to the opposite side.
C. Construct the midpoint of two sides of the triangle. Then construct the segment connecting those two midpoints.
D. Construct the angle bisector of one angle of the triangle.

Open Response

You will need a compass and straightedge to complete these problems.

10. Give three examples of geometric invariants that you learned in this chapter. Think about lengths, angle measures, areas (and ratios of those quantities), collinearity, concurrence, shape, and so on. Describe each invariant carefully. Include pictures with each descriptions.

11. Which of the figures below can you fold into a closed solid? For each one, name the solid or describe its features.

a.

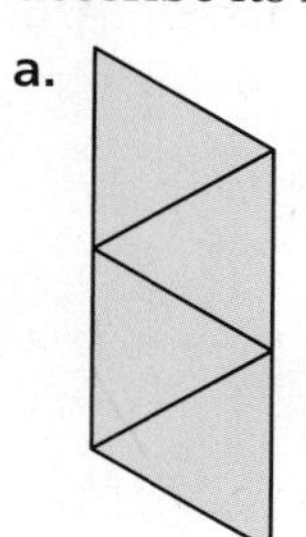

b.

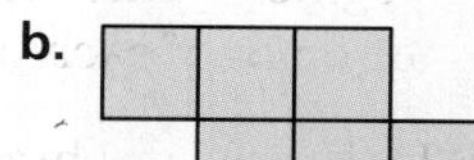

c.

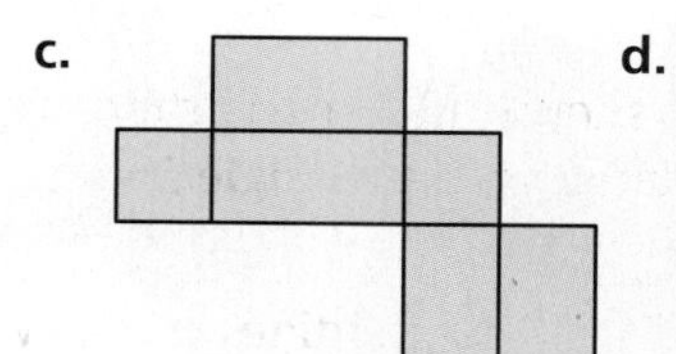

d.

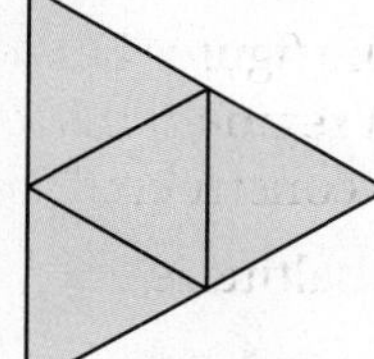

e.

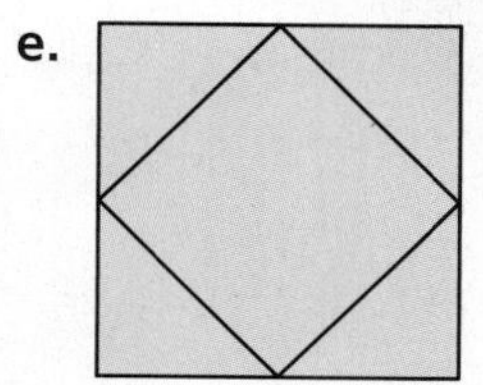

f.

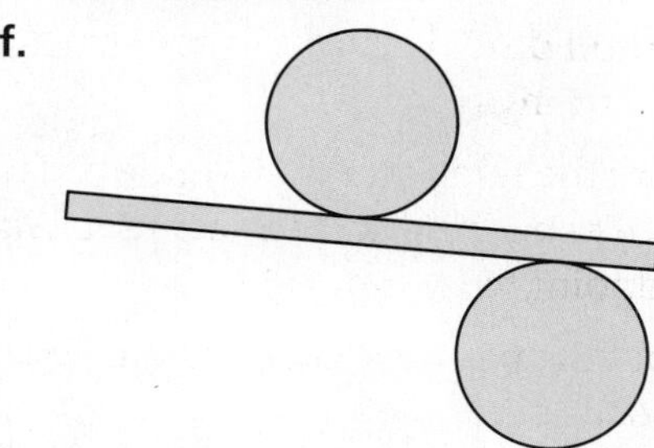

g.

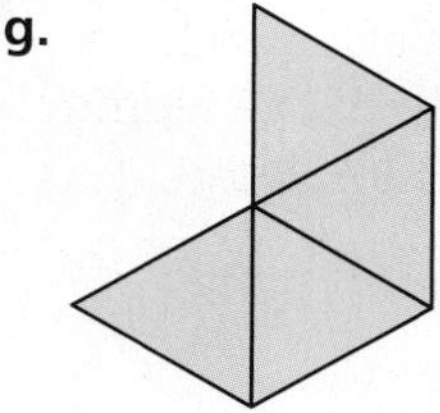

12. Describe what the term *concurrence* means. Then give three examples of concurrences in triangles. Draw a figure to represent each. Explain which segments in each drawing are concurrent.

13. Use a compass and straightedge to construct an equilateral triangle. Describe how you completed this construction.

14. Make a table that shows the following invariant relationship: m and n are numbers such that their product mn is invariant. (Choose a specific value of mn.)

15. a. To construct a parallel line with geometry software, which two pieces of information do you need? Explain.

b. To construct a circle with geometry software, which two pieces of information do you need? Explain.

16. Explain why the angle bisectors of a triangle are concurrent.

17. Imagine that you construct $\triangle ABC$ using geometry software so that A and B are fixed. You can move C, but $\overline{AC}$ remains congruent to $\overline{BC}$. (*Hint:* Along what path can you move C?)

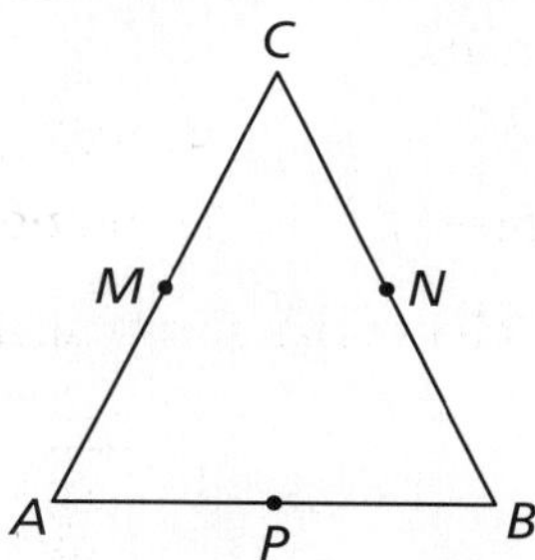

The midpoints of the sides of $\triangle ABC$ are M, N, and P. Connect them and shade $\triangle MNP$. Find the ratio $\frac{\text{area } \triangle MNP}{\text{area } \triangle ABC}$. Is this ratio invariant?

Chapter
2
Investigations at a Glance
2A The Congruence Relationship
2B Proof and Parallel Lines
2C Writing Proofs
2D Quadrilaterals and Their Properties

Congruence and Proof

You may have heard the saying, "Red sky at night, sailor's delight. Red sky at morning, sailors take warning." Through years of experience, sailors learned that they can use this saying, within limits, to predict the weather. You can use your own experiences, as well, to make predictions or conjectures. After you complete the following activity, you will be able to make a conjecture about the sum of the measures of the angles of a triangle.

Draw a large triangle on paper and cut it out. Tear off the angles. Place the vertices of the three angles together. Arrange the sides of the angles edge to edge, so there are no gaps. One edge of your new figure should appear to form a straight angle, which measures 180°. But how can you be sure? You can measure the three angles with a protractor, but measurement is not exact.

For problems like this, you can use mathematical proof to verify your results. Mathematical proof is a method that relies on certain assumptions, precise definitions, and logical deductions to prove new facts. In this chapter, you will prove, among many other results, that the sum of the measures of the angles of a triangle is 180°.

Vocabulary and Notation

- **alternate interior angles**
- **consecutive angles**
- **corresponding angles**
- **equiangular**
- **exterior angle**
- **isosceles trapezoid**
- **isosceles triangle**
- **kite**
- **parallelogram**
- **quadrilateral**
- **rhombus**
- **scalene triangle**
- **supplementary angles**
- **transversal**
- **trapezoid**
- **vertical angles**
- **$\cong$ (is congruent to)**
- **$\parallel$ (is parallel to)**
- **$\perp$ (is perpendicular to)**
- **AB (the length of $\overline{AB}$)**

The Congruence Relationship

In *The Congruence Relationship*, you will study congruent figures—figures that are the same shape and the same size. To understand mathematics or the arts, history or psychology, science or social relationships, you look at how things differ and also at how they are the same. Mathematics looks at quantities, relationships in space, ways to classify items, and certain processes that are used. The focus of this investigation is shape and what it means when two shapes are the same.

By the end of this investigation, you will be able to answer questions like these.

1. What does it mean to say that two figures are congruent?
2. Why is it important to keep track of corresponding parts in congruent figures?
3. What are some ways to prove that two triangles are congruent?

You will learn how to

- define congruence
- interpret statements about congruent figures and use the correct notation to write statements
- test for congruence in triangles

You will develop these habits and skills:

- Name corresponding parts of congruent figures.
- Use triangle congruence postulates to show that two triangles are congruent.
- Make logical inferences to draw conclusions about congruence.

Some houses in master-planned developments are the same shape and size.

2.01 Getting Started

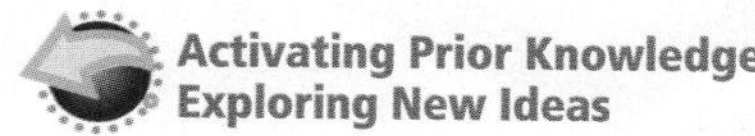

Mathematical language is clear and precise. Each word has exactly one meaning. Sometimes you invent new words. Sometimes you modify the meanings of familiar words. In either case, everyone must agree on which words to use and what those words mean.

For You to Explore

1. As a class, decide what you will mean by this statement: "These two figures are the same."

   To make a wise decision about the meaning of the statement, you might consider some specific cases. For example, look at the four figures below. Decide which figures you would call the same.

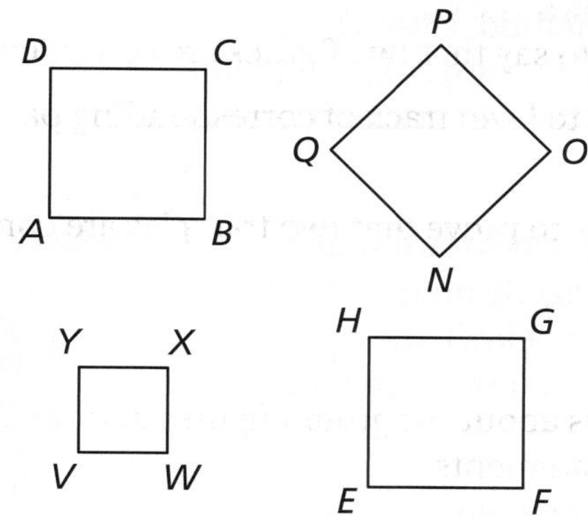

2. In some ways, all of the objects above are the same. Explain.

3. In some ways, they are all different. Explain.

   Mathematical language uses several words to describe two figures that are the same. For a start, we say that two figures are congruent if they have the same shape and the same size, regardless of location or orientation. But size and shape are not very precise terms, so we will develop a better definition.

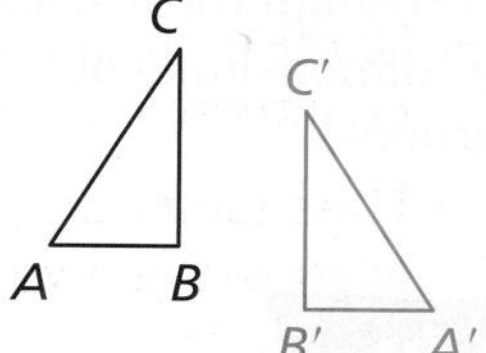

$\triangle ABC$ is congruent to $\triangle A'B'C'$, but they have different orientations. If you walk from A to B to C to A, you turn *left* twice. If you walk from A' to B' to C' to A', you turn *right* twice.

   Congruence is such an important mathematical relationship that it has its own symbol, $\cong$. In Problem 1 above, squares *ABCD* and *EFGH* are congruent. You write $\square ABCD \cong \square EFGH$.

4. You can think of the congruence symbol as composed of two parts: $=$ and $\sim$. What aspects of congruence might these two parts represent?

Exercises *Practicing Habits of Mind*

On Your Own

Go Online
Pearsonsuccessnet.com

You can use *congruent* to describe figures in any number of dimensions. Here are some examples.

- 1 dimension: two line segments that are the same length
- 2 dimensions: two triangles that are the same shape and same size
- 3 dimensions: two spheres with the same radius, or two tetrahedrons that are the same shape and same size

5. **Write About It** Assume you can use any tool or method. Describe how you can decide whether a pair of each of the following are congruent: line segments; angles; triangles; rectangular solids (boxes); cones; and cylinders.

One class chose the following test for congruence. Given two shapes drawn on paper, if you can cut out one and fit it exactly on top of the other shape (nothing hanging over above or sticking out below), then the two shapes are congruent. Or, two figures are congruent if they differ only in position.

The word *congruence* comes from the Latin word *congruens,* which means "to meet together." If you superimpose one figure on another and they meet edge to edge, then they are congruent.

6. Can you use this test to determine whether two line segments are congruent? Explain.

7. **Take It Further** How can you adapt the test so that you can use it to determine whether three-dimensional objects such as spheres or rectangular boxes are congruent?

Maintain Your Skills

Translate these congruence statements into English sentences.

8. $\triangle TRL \cong \triangle MTV$

9. $\overline{TO} \cong \overline{BE}$

10. $\square BARK \cong \square MEOW$

11. $\triangle LMO \cong \triangle L'M'O'$

12. $\angle ABC \cong \angle ABD$

Are these two gloves congruent?

2.02 Length, Measure, and Congruence

You can describe a single geometric object in more than one way. For example, you can refer to a line segment by its name or by its length. In the coordinate plane, you can also refer to a line segment by its slope. In geometry, it is important to make the distinction between a geometric object, such as a point or a segment or a circle, and a numerical value that describes it.

Symbols are designed to help make these distinctions. For example, the symbol $\overline{JK}$, with an overbar, represents the line segment with endpoints J and K. The symbol JK, without the overbar, represents the length of $\overline{JK}$.

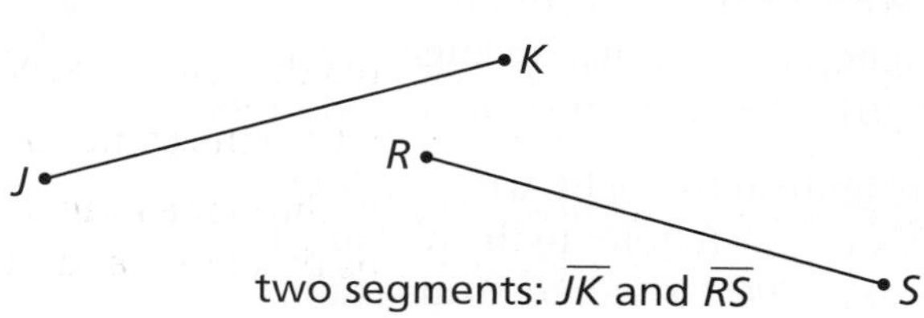

two segments: $\overline{JK}$ and $\overline{RS}$

You can compare two shapes to determine whether they are congruent. You can also compare two numbers to determine whether they are equal. You cannot, however, compare a shape to a number.

Minds in Action episode 2

Sasha and Tony discuss the seven statements below that seem to describe the two segments at the right.

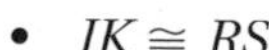

- $JK \cong RS$
- $\overline{JK} \cong \overline{RS}$
- $JK = RS$
- $\overline{JK} = \overline{RS}$
- $JK = 1$ inch
- $\overline{JK} = 1$
- $\overline{JK} \cong 1$ inch

Sasha The sentence $JK \cong RS$ makes no sense!

Tony What do you mean?

Sasha Well, $\cong$ is the symbol for *congruent,* right?

Tony Yes.

Sasha So, when you use that symbol you're supposed to be comparing objects. Without the little line over them, JK and RS aren't segments. They're just lengths.

Tony That's being a little picky, don't you think?

Sasha No, not really. You have to make a distinction between things that are *equal,* like the lengths JK and RS, and things that are *congruent,* like $\overline{JK}$ and $\overline{RS}$.

Tony So, the statement $JK = RS$ is correct, right? Because it says that the two *measurements* are equal, and numbers can be equal.

Sasha Yes.

For Discussion

1. Determine whether each of the statements that Sasha and Tony discussed in the dialog is correct. If a statement is *not* correct, explain why.
2. If two segments are the same length, are they congruent? Explain.
3. If two segments are congruent, are they the same length? Explain.

The symbols for an angle and its measure are different from the symbols for a segment and its length, but the distinction is the same. An angle is a geometric object. Its measure is a number.

In the figure at the right, write $\angle NPQ$, $\angle QPN$, or $\angle P$ to refer to the first angle. Write $m\angle NPQ$ to refer to its measure.

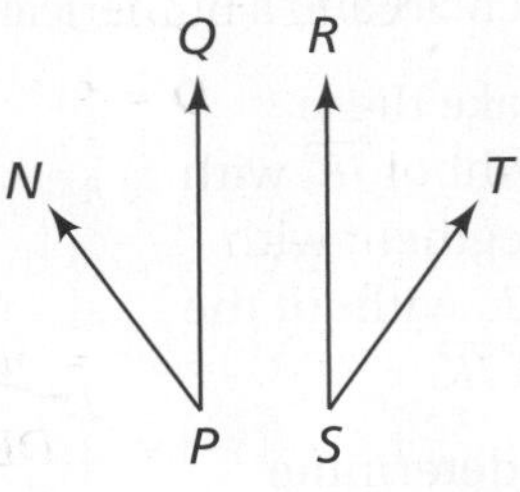

$\angle NPQ \cong \angle RST$
or
$m\angle NPQ = m\angle RST$

Remember...

In this course, angles are measured in degrees. A *right* angle measures 90°. A *straight* angle measures 180°.

Exercises *Practicing Habits of Mind*

Check Your Understanding

1. Decide whether each statement below describes geometric objects or numbers. If a statement describes geometric objects, state whether points, segments, or other objects are explicitly mentioned.
   a. $JK = RS$
   b. $\overline{JK} \cong \overline{RS}$
   c. $\overline{JK}$ and $\overline{RS}$ are the same length.
   d. The distance from *J* to *K* is the same as the distance from *R* to *S*.
2. a. Explain why the following statement is incorrect: $\angle NPQ = 56.6°$
   b. Write the following statement symbolically: Angle *NPQ* has a measure of 56.6 degrees.
3. If $m\angle NPQ = m\angle RST$, are the two angles congruent? Explain.
4. If $\angle NPQ \cong \angle RST$, are the measures of the two angles equal? Explain.
5. Explain whether the following statement is true or false: If two triangles are both congruent to the same triangle, then they are congruent to each other.

6. In $\triangle ABD$ at the right, $AD = BD$, $\overline{DC}$ is an altitude (that is, $\overline{DC} \perp \overline{AB}$), and F and E are midpoints. Decide whether each of the following statements is *true, false,* or *nonsensical.* Justify your answers. You may use measuring tools if you want.

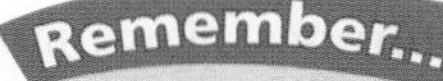

The symbol $\perp$ means "is perpendicular to."

a. $FD = DE$

b. $\overline{FD} = \overline{DE}$

c. $\overline{FD} = 1.5$ cm

d. $\angle ACD = 90°$

e. $\triangle DFB = \triangle DEA$

f. $\angle ACD$ is a right angle.

g. $\overline{FA} \cong \overline{BE}$

h. $\overline{FA} \cong \overline{BD}$

i. $\angle ADC = \angle BDC$

j. $m\angle ADC = m\angle BDC$

k. $m\angle DFB \cong m\angle DEA$

l. $\angle DFB \cong \angle DEA$

m. $\triangle DCA \cong \angle DCB$

n. $\triangle DCA \cong \overline{DC}$

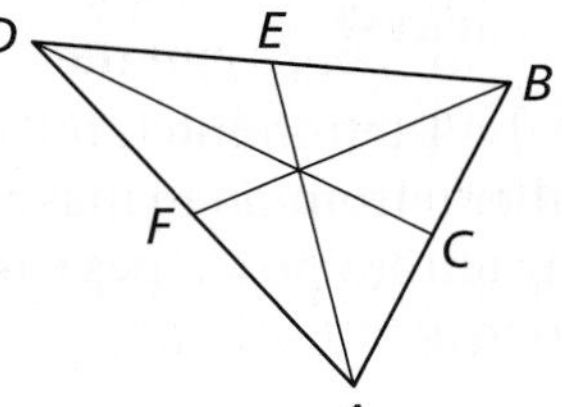

On Your Own

7. Define the following words or symbols.

a. congruent **b.** $\cong$ **c.** $\perp$

8. **Standardized Test Prep** Anna has a simple rule for deciding which symbol to use.

Objects are congruent. Measurements of objects are equal.

Which of the following statements is NOT written correctly according to Anna's rule?

A. $\overline{DF} \cong \overline{RT}$

B. $m\angle CSD \cong m\angle BSL$

C. $\angle ADF \cong \angle WZM$

D. $AC = FH$

9. Are all equilateral triangles congruent? Explain.

Polyominoes are shapes that are made of squares. The sides of polyominoes meet edge to edge with no gaps or overlaps. The three shapes on the left are polyominoes. The three shapes on the right are not polyominoes, because the squares do not meet edge to edge.

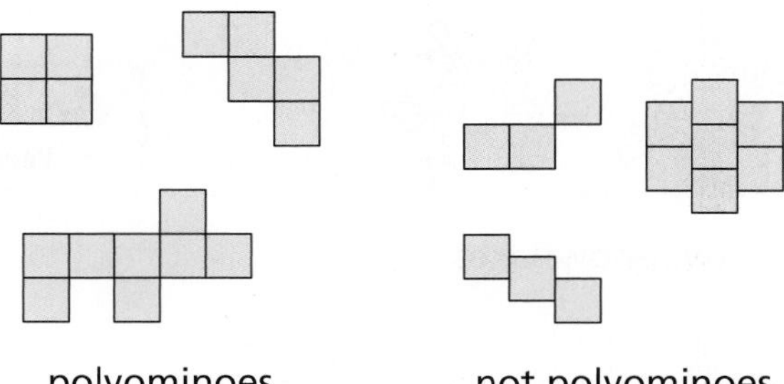

Congruent polyominoes that have different orientations are not different polyominoes.

10. **Dominoes:** How many different polyominoes can you make with two squares?

11. **Trominoes:** How many different polyominoes can you make with three squares?

12. **Tetrominoes:** How many different polyominoes can you make with four squares?

13. Combine the T tetromino (polyomino with 4 squares) at the right with another tetromino to make an eight-square polyomino. How many tetromino shapes can you combine with the T tetromino to get this shape?

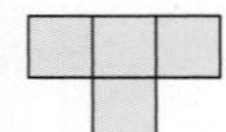

Maintain Your Skills

14. Assume you can use any tool or method. Describe how you can decide whether the figures in each pair are congruent.

a.

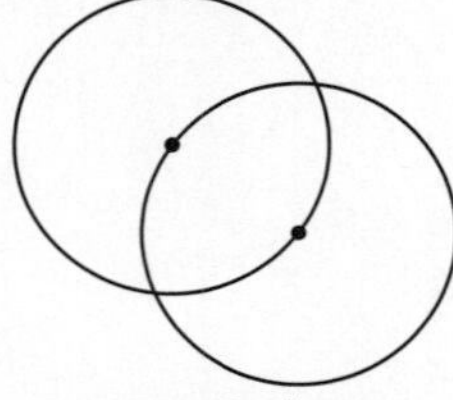

two circles

b.

two artists

c.

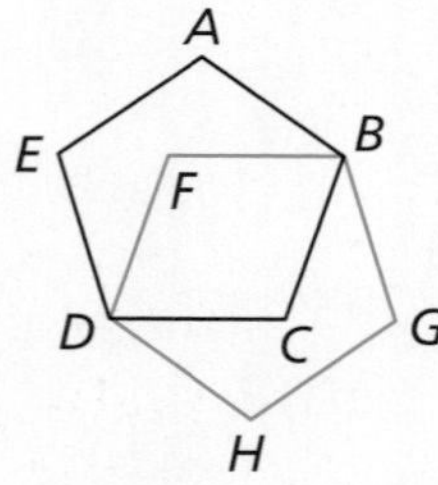

two pentagons, *ABCDE* and *BGHDF*

d.

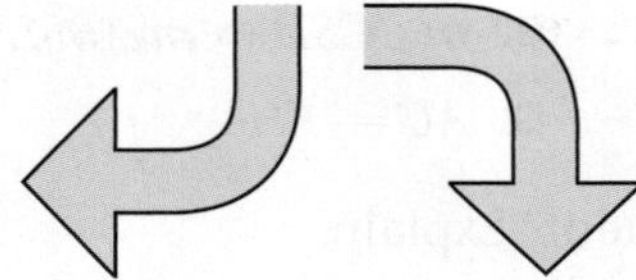

two bent arrows

e.

two stars

f.

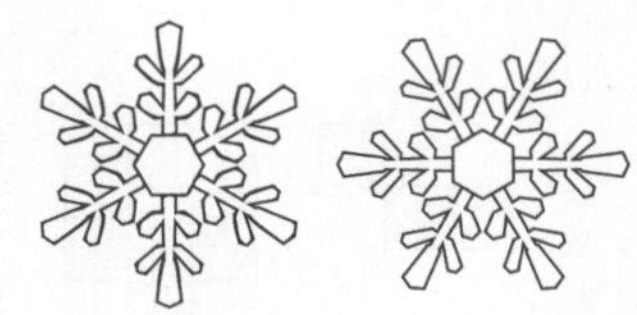

two snowflakes

2.03 Corresponding Parts

It is difficult to draw congruent figures by hand. It is also difficult to decide whether two given figures are congruent. You may not have the tools necessary. Or you may not want to take the time to use those tools. For these reasons, tick marks are very useful.

The picture below shows nine segments, with eight of the segments forming four angles. Like markings indicate which segments are congruent and which angles are congruent. For example, $\overline{ON} \cong \overline{BC}$ and $\angle GHI \cong \angle ABC$.

The small box that marks $\angle DEF$ indicates that $\angle DEF$ is a right angle.

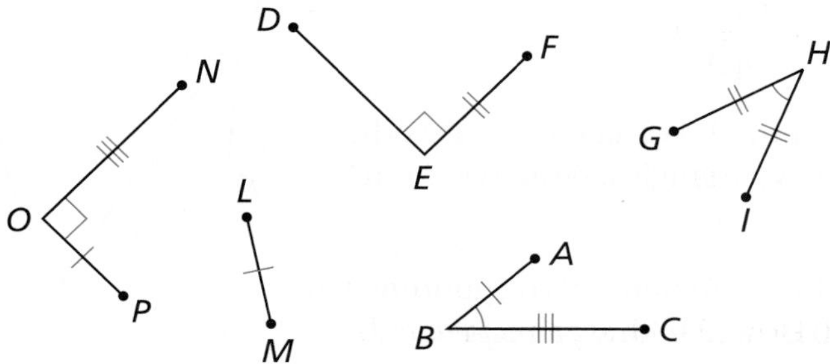

Habits of Mind

Compare. Are two segments that have different numbers of tick marks not congruent?

For You to Do

1. What other relationships are indicated in the above diagram?

A congruence statement communicates a large amount of information. The congruence statement $\triangle QRS \cong \triangle XYZ$ tells you that the two triangles are congruent. The orders in which the vertices are written also tells you that

$$\overline{QR} \cong \overline{XY}, \overline{RS} \cong \overline{YZ}, \text{ and } \overline{QS} \cong \overline{XZ},$$

and that

$$\angle Q \cong \angle X, \angle R \cong \angle Y, \text{ and } \angle S \cong \angle Z.$$

You can summarize this matching of parts in a congruence statement by saying that corresponding parts of congruent figures are congruent.

Remember...

For triangles, *parts* means "sides" and "angles".

The sails are congruent.
So are their corresponding parts.

Exercises *Practicing Habits of Mind*

Check Your Understanding

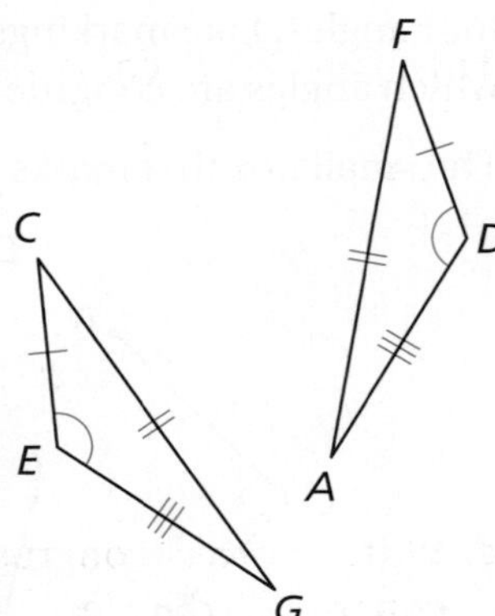

1. The two triangles at the right are congruent. Decide whether each congruence statement below is correct. Explain your reasoning.

a. $\triangle DFA \cong \triangle GCE$ **b.** $\triangle DFA \cong \triangle EGC$

c. $\triangle DFA \cong \triangle CEG$ **d.** $\triangle DFA \cong \triangle ECG$

e. $\triangle DFA \cong \triangle GEC$ **f.** $\triangle DFA \cong \triangle CGE$

2. Even though only one of the statements above is correct, there are other correct congruence statements for these two triangles. Write two more triangle congruence statements.

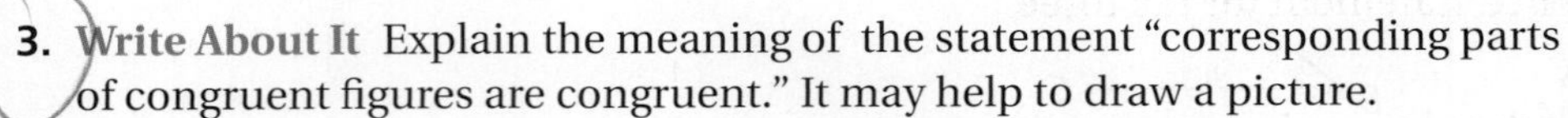

3. **Write About It** Explain the meaning of the statement "corresponding parts of congruent figures are congruent." It may help to draw a picture.

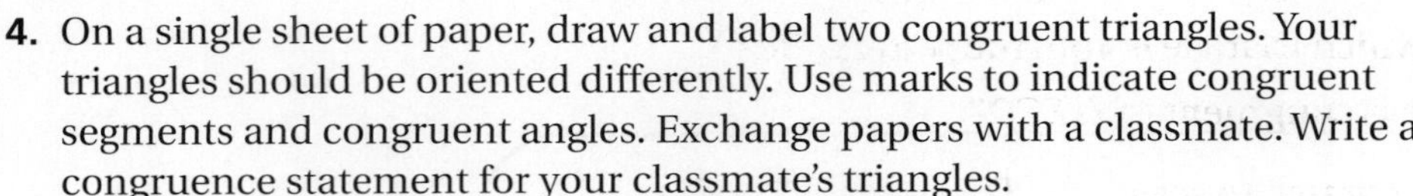

4. On a single sheet of paper, draw and label two congruent triangles. Your triangles should be oriented differently. Use marks to indicate congruent segments and congruent angles. Exchange papers with a classmate. Write a congruence statement for your classmate's triangles.

On Your Own

5. Assume $\triangle CAT \cong \triangle DOG$. List all the corresponding parts.

6. **Standardized Test Prep** You are given that $\triangle DFG \cong \triangle CHK$. Which of the following statements is true by "corresponding parts of congruent figures are congruent"?

A. $m\angle FGD = m\angle CKH$ **B.** $\overline{CH} \cong \overline{DG}$

C. $DF = HK$ **D.** $\angle FGD \cong \angle KCH$

7. Use the figure below. Some pairs of triangles are *certainly not* congruent. List any pairs of triangles that appear to be congruent.

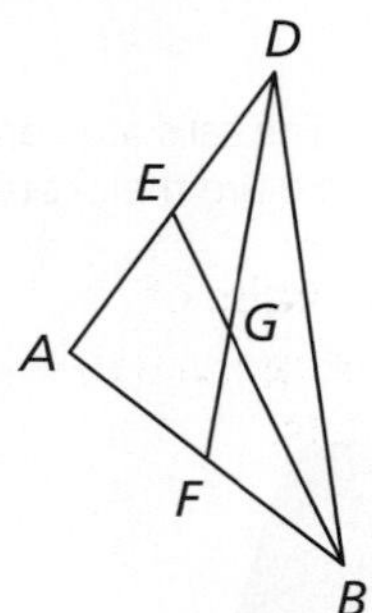

8. You can compare figures in many different ways. Congruence is a *shape* comparison. Area is a *quantitative* comparison. Use what you know about area to answer the following questions.

   a. If two polygons are congruent, must they have the same area? Explain.

   b. If two polygons have the same area, must they be congruent? Explain.

Similarity is another shape comparison. Perimeter is another quantitative comparison.

9. The figure below contains three congruent triangles.

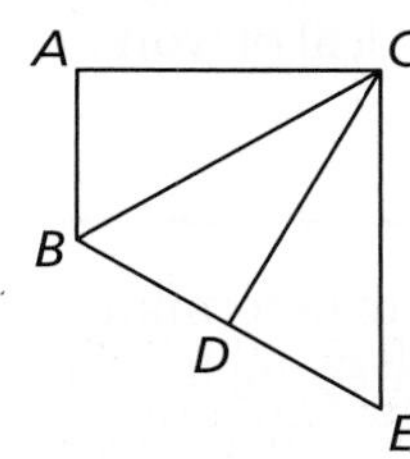

   a. Write a correct congruence statement for the three congruent triangles.

   b. On your own sketch, mark congruent corresponding parts.

   c. In quadrilateral *ABDC*, which triangle is congruent to $\triangle ABC$?

   d. In $\triangle BCE$, which triangle is congruent to $\triangle ECD$?

10. The figure at the right is not drawn to scale. The markings indicate which pairs of segments and which pairs of angles are congruent. Segments that appear to be straight are meant to be.

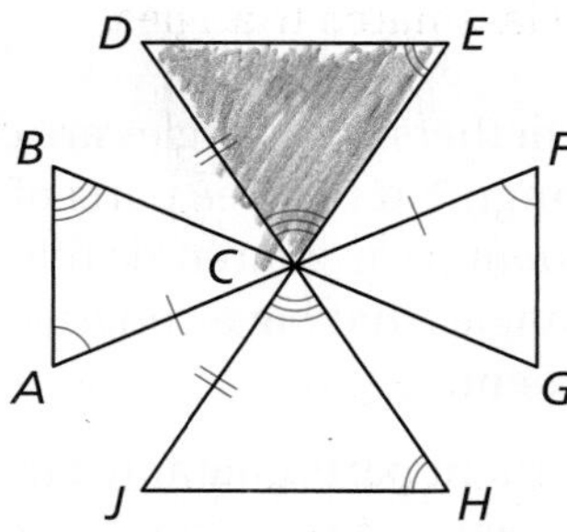

   a. Assume $m\angle F = 80°$, $m\angle H = 50°$, and $m\angle B = 40°$. What are the measures of $\angle A$, $\angle E$, and $\angle D$?

   b. Use a ruler and protractor to draw the figure to scale. Draw each angle with the correct angle measure. Draw congruent segments so that they are actually congruent.

Maintain Your Skills

11. Think about two congruent irregular pentagons. How many pairs of corresponding parts do they have? Draw and label your pentagons. Write a congruence statement. List all corresponding congruent parts.

2.04 Triangle Congruence

You know that corresponding parts of congruent figures are congruent. For triangles, you say that corresponding parts of congruent triangles are congruent. In other words, if two triangles are congruent, then their corresponding sides and corresponding angles are also congruent.

You can abbreviate *corresponding parts of congruent triangles are congruent* as CPCTC.

The converse of this statement is also true. If the corresponding sides and corresponding angles of two triangles are congruent, then the triangles are congruent. This gives an exact method for proving triangles are congruent, but checking the six pairs of corresponding parts is a great deal of work.

For Discussion

1. Can you check fewer than six pairs of corresponding parts to determine whether two triangles are congruent? For instance, if the three angles in one triangle are congruent to the three angles in another triangle, are the two triangles congruent? Or if the three sides in one triangle are congruent to the three sides of another triangle, are the two triangles congruent?

2. Discuss the meaning of the following statement. *Information that is enough to specify one triangle is also enough to ensure that two triangles are congruent.* Is the statement true? Explain.

Classifying Your Information

You can *sometimes* determine whether two triangles are congruent when three parts of one triangle are congruent to three parts of another triangle. But not any three pairs of congruent parts guarantee that two triangles are congruent. For example, two triangles that have congruent corresponding angles are not necessarily congruent.

Which sets of three pairs of congruent parts guarantee that two triangles are congruent? To answer that question, first make a list of the possible combinations of three parts in one triangle. For example, $\triangle ABC$ has six parts: three sides and three angles.

three sides: $\overline{AB}$, $\overline{BC}$, and $\overline{AC}$
three angles: $\angle A$, $\angle B$, and $\angle C$

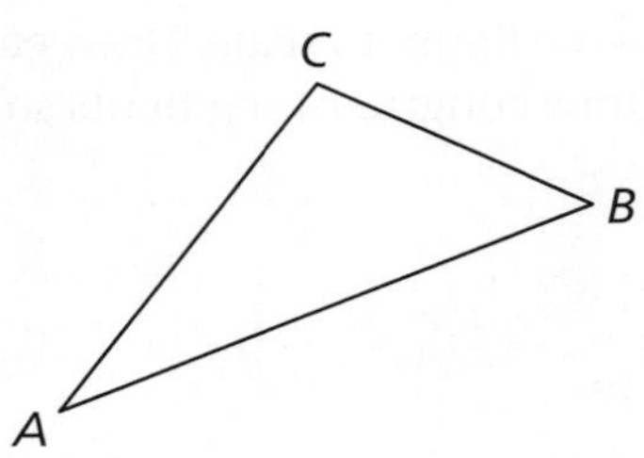

For You to Do

3. List the possible combinations of three parts of $\triangle ABC$.
Here are two examples.

- $\angle A$, $\angle B$, $\angle C$
- $\overline{AB}$, $\angle A$, $\angle B$

You can classify your combinations in many ways. Here is a scheme that people have found useful. Note that this is *not* a list of ways to show two triangles are congruent.

Three Parts	Abbreviation Triplet	Meaning for a Triangle	Example for $\triangle ABC$
Three angles	AAA	Three angles of the triangle	$\angle A, \angle B, \angle C$
Two angles, one side	ASA	Two angles and the side between them	$\angle A, \overline{AB}, \angle B$
	AAS	Two angles and a side not between the angles	$\angle A, \angle B, \overline{BC}$
Two sides, one angle	SAS	Two sides and the angle between them	$\overline{AC}, \angle A, \overline{AB}$
	SSA	Two sides and an angle not between the sides	$\overline{AC}, \overline{AB}, \angle B$
Three sides	SSS	Three sides of the triangle	$\overline{AC}, \overline{AB}, \overline{BC}$

You read *ASA* as "angle-side-angle."

Order is important. SAS is not the same as SSA.

Which of these triplets can you use to prove that two triangles are congruent? You can investigate this question. Try to build two noncongruent triangles that share a given triplet. If you can, then the triplet does not guarantee triangle congruence. If you cannot, then there is a good chance that the triplet does guarantee congruence.

In-Class Experiment

Work with a partner or in a small group to determine which of the triplets below guarantee triangle congruence. For each triplet, try to build two noncongruent triangles with the given angle measures and side lengths.

4. ASA $m\angle A = 40°, AB = 2$ in., $m\angle B = 70°$

5. AAS $m\angle A = 40°, m\angle B = 70°, BC = 2$ in.

6. SAS $AC = 2$ in., $m\angle A = 60°, AB = 3$ in.

7. SSA $AC = 2$ in., $AB = 4$ in., $m\angle B = 20°$

8. SSS $AC = 2$ in., $AB = 3$ in., $BC = 4$ in.

The results of the In-Class Experiment suggest the following assumption.

Postulate 2.1 *The Triangle Congruence Postulates*

If two triangles share the following triplets of congruent corresponding parts, then the triangles are congruent.

- **ASA**
- **SAS**
- **SSS**

Remember...

Another word for assumption is *postulate*. A **postulate** is a statement that is accepted without proof.

What can you do with the AAS triplet? You can prove that this triplet guarantees triangle congruence if you assume that the other triangle congruence postulates are true. You also have to assume that the sum of the measures of the angles of a triangle is 180°.

Mathematicians like to make as few assumptions and to prove as many theorems as possible.

And what can you do with the SSA triplet? In Exercise 7, you will show why this triplet does not guarantee triangle congruence.

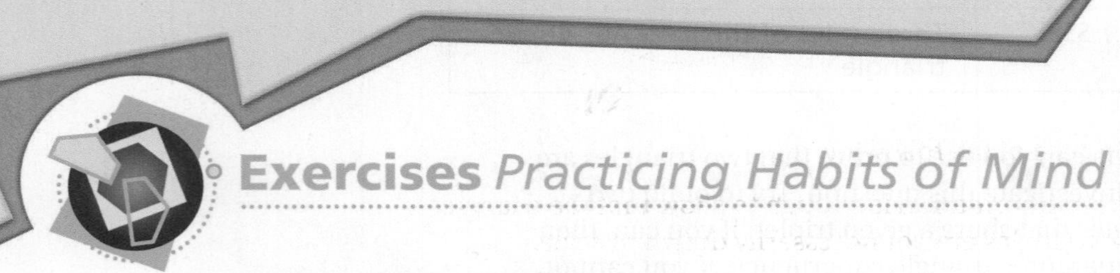

Exercises *Practicing Habits of Mind*

Check Your Understanding

For Exercises 1 and 2, do each of the following:

a. Construct $\triangle ABC$ with the given angle measures and given side lengths.

b. Compare results with a classmate. Are your triangles congruent?

c. If your triangles are not congruent, what additional information will guarantee that the triangles are congruent?

1. $m\angle A = 36°, m\angle B = 72°, m\angle C = 72°$

2. $m\angle A = 60°, AB = 8 \text{ cm}, BC = 7 \text{ cm}$

In Exercises 3 and 4, is $\triangle ABC \cong \triangle ADC$? If the two triangles are congruent, state which triangle congruence postulate helped you decide.

3.

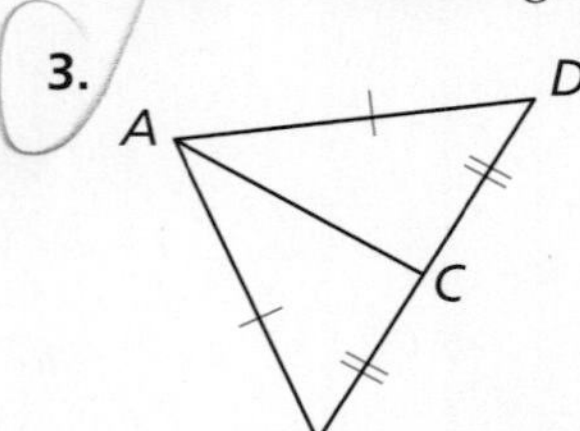

4.

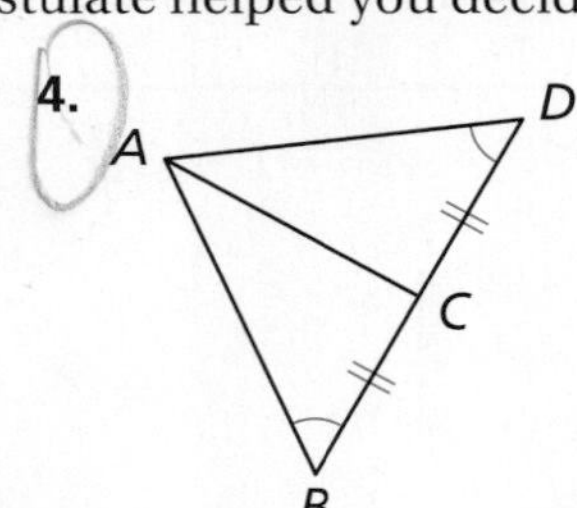

5. Show in two different ways that a diagonal of a square divides the square into two congruent triangles. Use a different triangle congruence postulate each time.

6. You and a friend are making triangular pennants. Your friend says that each pennant should have a 30° angle, a 14-inch side, and an 8-inch side. Explain why this information does not guarantee that all the pennants will be congruent.

7. The diagram at the right proves, without words, that the SSA triplet does not guarantee triangle congruence. Explain the proof.

> **Remember...**
> A *square* is a quadrilateral with four congruent sides and four right angles.

> Note that point O is the center of the circle. Why use a circle in this proof without words?

On Your Own

For Exercises 8–12, do each of the following:

a. Tell whether the given information is enough to show that the triangles are congruent. The triangles are not necessarily drawn to scale.

b. If the given information is enough, list the pairs of corresponding vertices of the two triangles. Then state which triangle congruence postulate guarantees that the triangles are congruent.

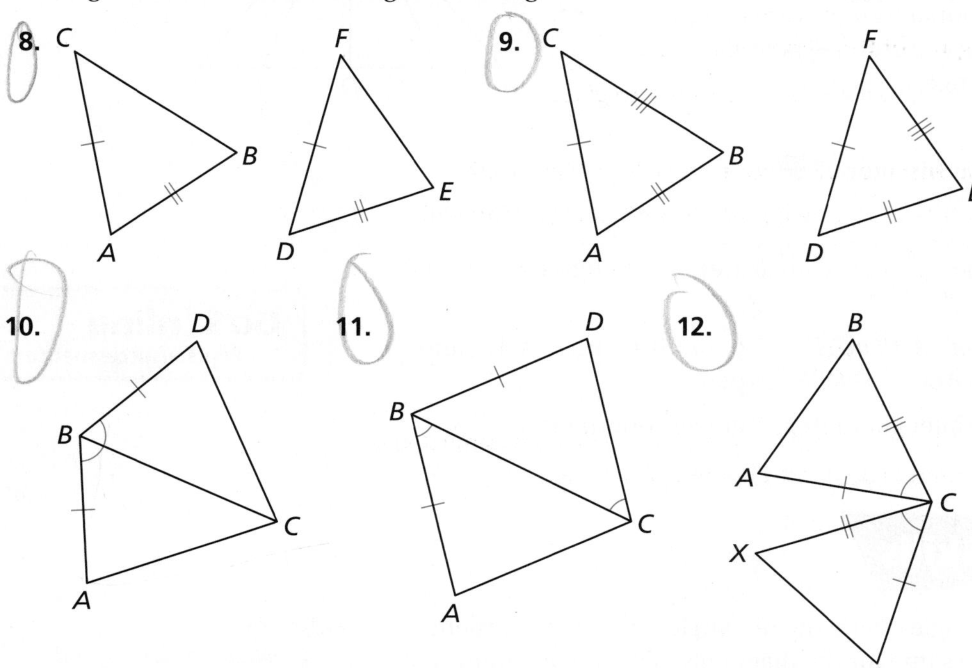

13. **Standardized Test Prep** In $\triangle ABC$, $\overline{CD}$ is the bisector of $\angle ACB$. Which of the following conjectures is true?

A. There is not sufficient evidence to prove that $\triangle ACD \cong \triangle BCD$.

B. $\triangle ACD \cong \triangle BCD$ is true by the Angle-Side-Angle postulate. In each triangle, the side between the two angles is $\overline{CD}$.

C. $\triangle ACD \cong \triangle BCD$ is true by the Side-Angle-Side postulate. Angle ACD and $\angle BCD$ are the congruent angles that are between the two pairs of congruent sides.

D. $\triangle ACD \cong \triangle BCD$ is true by the Side-Side-Side postulate.

14. In the figure at the right, $\overline{BD}$ is the perpendicular bisector of $\overline{AC}$. Based on this statement, which two triangles are congruent? Prove that they are congruent.

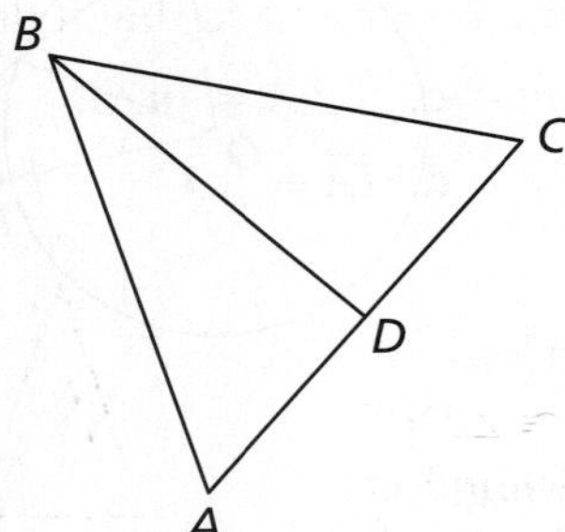

15. **Take It Further** In the figure at the right, $\overline{AD}$ is the perpendicular bisector of $\overline{BC}$. Based on this information, two triangles in the figure are congruent.

For each part, does the given piece of information help you determine that any additional triangles are congruent? If so, state the triangles and the congruence postulate that guarantees their congruence.

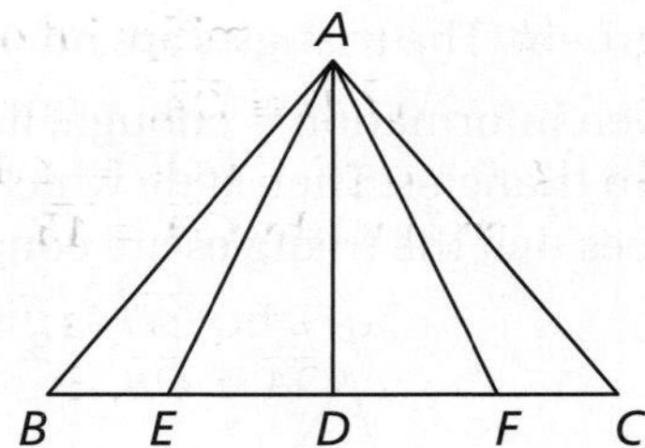

a. $AB = AC$

b. $\overline{AD}$ is the perpendicular bisector of $\overline{EF}$.

c. $\angle EAD \cong \angle FAD$

16. Assume you know that the sum of the measures of the angles in a triangle is 180°.

a. In $\triangle ABC$ and $\triangle DEF$, $m\angle A = m\angle D = 72°$, $m\angle B = m\angle E = 47°$, and $AC = DF = 10$ in. Is $\triangle ABC \cong \triangle DEF$? Explain.

b. Explain why the AAS triplet guarantees triangle congruence.

Maintain Your Skills

17. Does a diagonal of a rectangle divide the rectangle into two congruent triangles? Can you say the same for the diagonals of a parallelogram? For the diagonals of a trapezoid? For the diagonals of a kite? Explain.

What are some good definitions for *rectangle, parallelogram, trapezoid,* and *kite*?

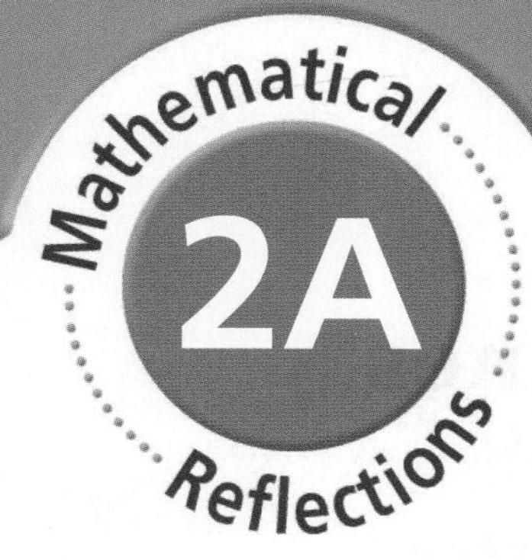

In this investigation, you studied congruent figures—figures that are the same shape and size. You determined whether two figures were congruent based on relationships between their parts. You also learned postulates that you can use to prove two triangles are congruent.

1. **a.** Name the triangle congruence postulates.

b. Explain what each one means.

c. Draw a picture to illustrate each postulate.

2. Tell whether each statement below makes sense. If a statement does not make sense, explain why. Then rewrite the statement so that it does make sense.

a. $MA \cong FL$ **b.** $m\angle A = m\angle L$

c. $MT = FO$ **d.** $\overline{TA} \cong \overline{LO}$

e. $\angle AMT = \angle LFO$

3. Triangle ABC and $\triangle DEF$ are isosceles. $\overline{AC} \cong \overline{BC}$ and $\overline{DF} \cong \overline{EF}$. If $\angle ACB \cong \angle DFE$ and $\overline{CB} \cong \overline{FD}$, can you determine whether the two triangles are congruent? Explain.

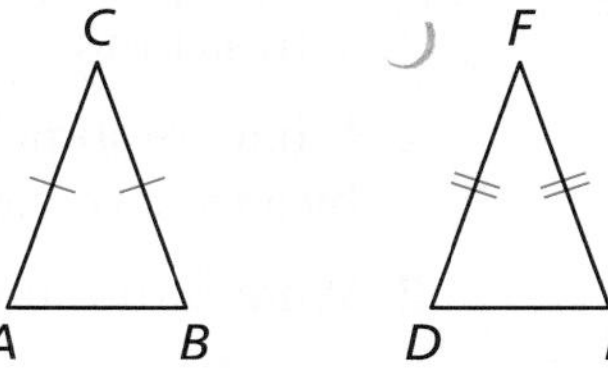

4. Draw $\triangle ABC$. Find the midpoint of $\overline{BC}$. Call it point O. Draw $\overrightarrow{AO}$. Mark point D on $\overrightarrow{AO}$ so that $\overline{OD} \cong \overline{OA}$. Draw $\overline{BD}$ and $\overline{CD}$. Look for congruent triangles in your figure. (*Hint:* $\angle DOB \cong \angle AOC$ and $\angle AOB \cong \angle DOC$.) Explain why $\overline{BD} \cong \overline{AC}$. Explain why $\overline{CD} \cong \overline{AB}$.

5. In the figure at the right, $\overrightarrow{OD}$ is the angle bisector of $\angle AOB$. $\overline{OA} \cong \overline{OB}$. Explain why $\overline{AD} \cong \overline{BD}$.

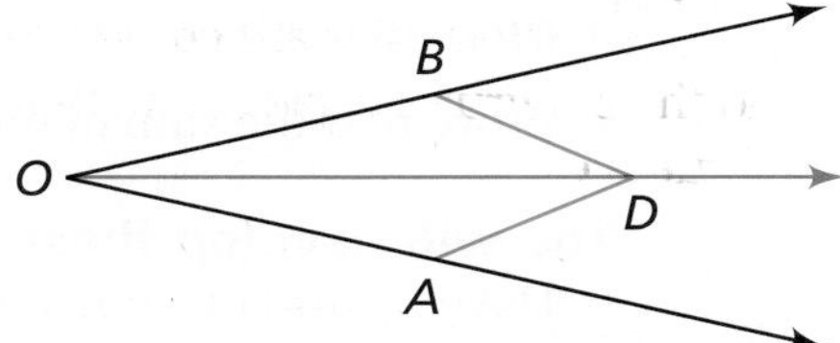

6. What does it mean to say that two figures are congruent?

7. Why is it important to keep track of corresponding parts in congruent figures?

8. What are some ways to prove that two triangles are congruent?

Vocabulary and Notation

In this investigation, you learned this term and these symbols. Make sure you understand what each one means, and how to use it.

- **postulate**
- **≅ (is congruent to)**
- ***JK* (length of $\overline{JK}$)**
- **⊥ (is perpendicular to)**

These two houses are the same shape and size.

Proof and Parallel Lines

In *Proof and Parallel Lines,* you will study one of the basic objects in geometry, the line. Some distinct lines in a plane intersect, while others do not. When lines intersect, they form angles. These angles have special relationships. You will prove some of these relationships in this investigation. When lines do not intersect, there are also provable consequences. As you investigate parallel lines and angle measures, you will gather what you need to prove that the sum of the angle measures in a triangle is 180 degrees.

By the end of this investigation, you will be able to answer questions like these.

1. Why is proof so important in mathematics?
2. What are some invariant angle relationships when parallel lines are cut by a transversal?
3. What is the sum of the measures of the interior angles of any triangle?

You will learn how to

- identify pairs of congruent angles when parallel lines are cut by a transversal
- make assumptions and write proofs in order to understand the need for proof in mathematics
- prove that the sum of the angle measures in any triangle is 180°

You will develop these habits and skills:

- Develop and present a deductive proof.
- Search for invariants.
- Visualize key elements of a problem situation.

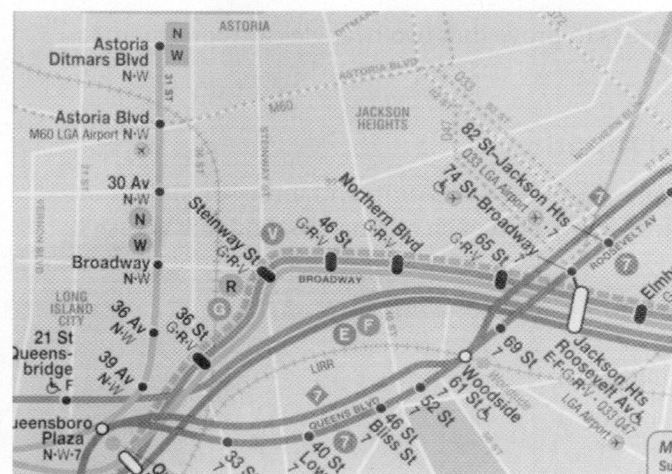

As parallel lines, the E, F, G, R, and V routes form congruent alternate exterior angles with the 7 route.

2.05 Getting Started

Activating Prior Knowledge
Exploring New Ideas

You can use geometry software to discover important geometric relationships.

For You to Explore

Use geometry software to complete Problems 1 and 2.

1. Construct two parallel lines cut by a transversal. Measure the angles.
   a. Move the transversal while the parallel lines remain fixed. Which angles remain congruent? Move one of the parallel lines while keeping remain parallel. Which angles remain congruent?
   b. Which sums of angle measures are invariant?

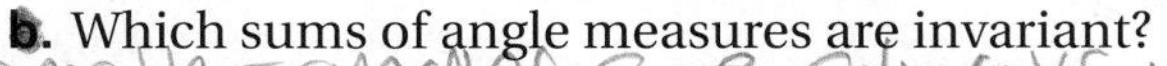

2. Construct a pair of intersecting lines cut by a transversal. Measure the angles.
   a. Move the transversal while the intersecting lines remain fixed. What invariants can you find? Move one of the intersecting lines while the transversal remains fixed. What invariants can you find?
   b. How do the angle measures compare to the angle measures in Problem 1? How do the sums of angle measures compare to the sums of angle measures in Problem 1?

A **transversal** is a line that intersects two or more lines.

Find the measure of each angle in degrees. See the TI–Nspire™ Handbook, p. 712.

Exercises *Practicing Habits of Mind*

On Your Own

3. Construct a triangle. Draw its three midlines. Consider the side lengths, angle measures, and areas of the figures formed. If you know each of the following, what else can you determine about the triangle?
   a. the length of one midline
   b. the area of the original triangle

Remember...

A midline (or midsegment) connects the midpoints of two sides of a triangle.

4. In this figure, M is the midpoint of $\overline{BC}$, and $AM = MR$. Prove that $m\angle C = m\angle CBR$.

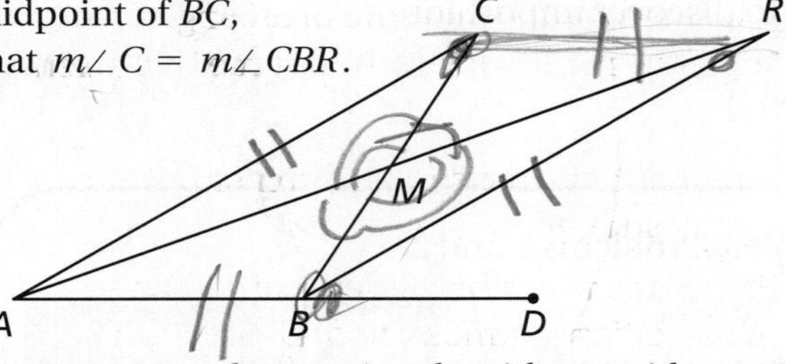

5. A common problem in geometry involves a triangle with one side extended. In the figure below, $\angle CBD$ is an **exterior angle** of $\triangle ABC$.

One form of the Exterior Angle Theorem states that the measure of a triangle's exterior angle is greater than the measures of either of the triangle's two remote interior angles. The remote interior angles are nonadjacent to the exterior angle. In this case, $m\angle CBD$ is greater than either $m\angle A$ or $m\angle C$. How can you prove the Exterior Angle Theorem?

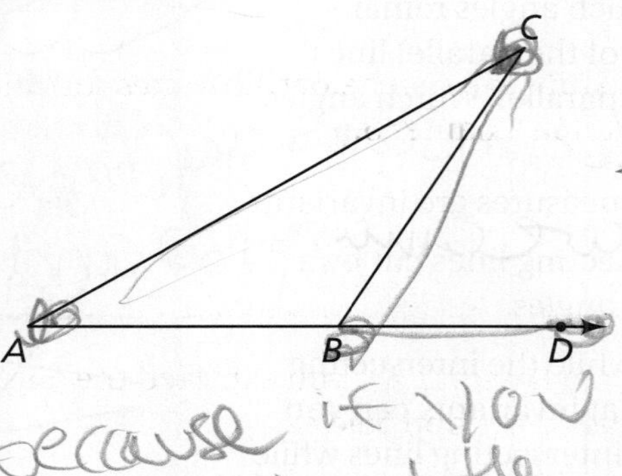

In order to actually *prove* the Exterior Angle Theorem, you must show that the measure of any exterior angle is greater than the measures of either remote interior angle in any triangle.

6. Use the figure at the right. Find the measures of $\angle BDA$, $\angle ADQ$, and $\angle CDQ$ for the following conditions.

   a. $m\angle BDC = 62°$
   b. $m\angle BDC = 72°$
   c. $m\angle BDC = 55°$
   d. $m\angle BDC = x°$

Maintain Your Skills

Use geometry software. Draw a line ℓ. Draw a point P not on line ℓ.

7. How many lines will the software allow you to construct parallel to ℓ through P? How many lines exist that are parallel to ℓ through P?

8. How many lines will the software allow you to construct perpendicular to ℓ through P? How many lines exist that are perpendicular to ℓ through P?

For help constructing the parallel and perpendicular lines, see the TI-Nspire Handbook, p. 712.

9. a. Construct a line through P that is perpendicular to ℓ. Label it n.

   b. Construct a line through P that is perpendicular to n. Label it m.

   c. What happens when you use the software to determine the intersection of ℓ and m?

2.06 Deduction and Proof

How do you know the length of a segment or the measure of an angle? One way is to measure using a ruler or protractor, respectively. But measurement has some drawbacks.

- Measurement is not exact. No matter how precise your ruler or protractor is, neither will provide an exact measurement.
- Certain measurements are difficult or impossible to determine. For instance, the distance between two cities is difficult to find directly. The distance between Earth and the moon is impossible to measure directly.
- A measurement is only reliable if it holds true for an infinite number of cases.

In many real-life cases, estimation is sufficient. In mathematics, however, exactness is necessary to eliminate error.

The Developing Habits of Mind section below illustrates the third point. You will also learn more about it in Chapter 5.

Developing Habits of Mind

Use a Deductive Process. In Lesson 1.11, you explored the angle measures in a figure similar to the one below.

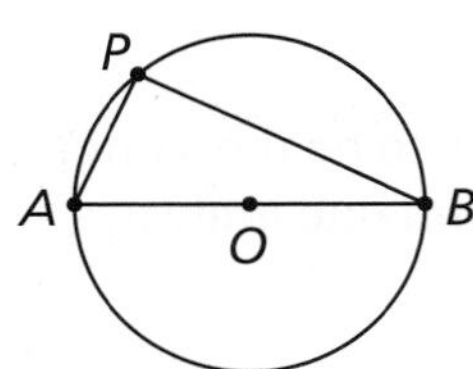

You may have noticed that, no matter where P is on the circle, the measure of $\angle P$ seems to be 90°. How can you prove that this is true? You can measure $\angle P$ when P is at various points until you grow tired of it. Suppose you do this 100 times. Will you know for sure that $m\angle P$ is always 90°? You may be very convinced, but you cannot be certain. Mathematicians establish certainty by proving a statement is true using the deductive method.

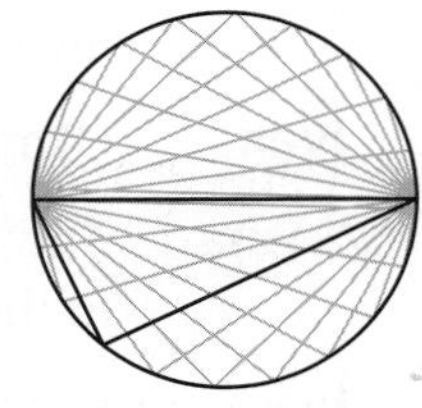

You could check all these angles.

You can prove statements using the deductive method by showing that a simple statement leads to a desired conclusion based on logical reasoning. Important conclusions are called theorems. Conclusions that are accepted without proof are called postulates, axioms, or assumptions. Once you prove a theorem, you can use it as an assumption to prove other theorems.

You may wonder where ideas for new theorems come from or who gets to decide what statements are assumed without proof. Ideas from theorems often come from experiments. The postulates that are assumed depend on what information is necessary and what is already known.

One reason to prove results in geometry is to check measurements. For example, if you know from a theorem that two segments should be equal, then the measurements of those segments should be the same. Measurements are subject to error in a way that logical deduction is not.

Habits of Mind

Reason logically. New results come from reasoning about things that must follow logically from what is already known or assumed. The mixing of deduction and experiment is one of the distinguishing features of mathematical research.

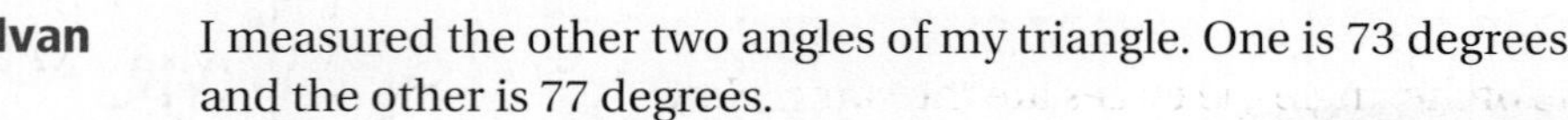

Minds in Action episode 3

Sasha and Ivan are making triangular pennants for the school's sports teams. Ivan made a pennant with two 14-in. sides and a 30° angle between those two sides.

Ivan I measured the other two angles of my triangle. One is 73 degrees and the other is 77 degrees.

Sasha But they should both be the same. Measure more carefully.

So Ivan did.

Ivan This time, I got 74 degrees and 76 degrees.

Sasha Close. But they have to be the same.

Ivan What do you mean? How do you know they have to be the same? My protractor says they are a little off. The bottom one is always a little bigger than the top one.

Sasha They have to be the same. Draw a median. The two triangles are congruent.

Ivan Okay, I see.

Sasha And the two angles you are measuring are corresponding angles in the congruent triangles. So they have to be congruent.

Ivan I guess I'll get a better protractor.

Remember...

A *median* of a triangle is a line segment drawn from one of the triangle's vertices to the midpoint of the opposite side.

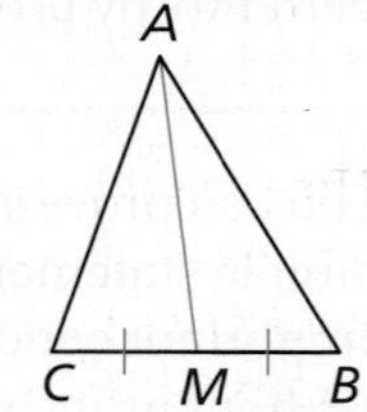

$\overline{AM}$ is a median of $\triangle ABC$.

For Discussion

1. Ivan agrees that the two triangles formed by Sasha's median are congruent. Do you? Explain.
2. How do you know that the two angles that Ivan measured are corresponding parts of the two triangles formed by the median?

For You to Do

The result of the experiment below may lead to a theorem.

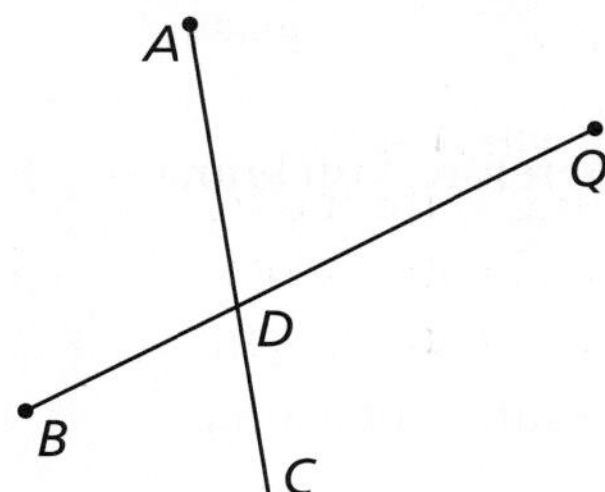

two intersecting segments

Suppose that $\overline{AC}$ and $\overline{BQ}$ intersect so that $m\angle BDC = 72°$. What is the measure of each angle below?

3. $m\angle BDA$ **4.** $m\angle ADQ$ **5.** $m\angle QDC$

Angles such as $\angle ADB$ and $\angle CDQ$ are called *vertical angles.*

You may find it helpful to look back at Exercise 6 in Lesson 2.5.

You should notice that some of the angle measures are the same. Now suppose that $m\angle ADB = 125°$. What are the measures of the other angles?

Each time you repeat this experiment, you should find that two pairs of angles have the same measure. Your measurements may lead you to believe that the statement below is true.

Theorem 2.1 The Vertical Angles Theorem

In the figure below, $m\angle ADB = m\angle CDQ$ and $m\angle BDC = m\angle ADQ$.

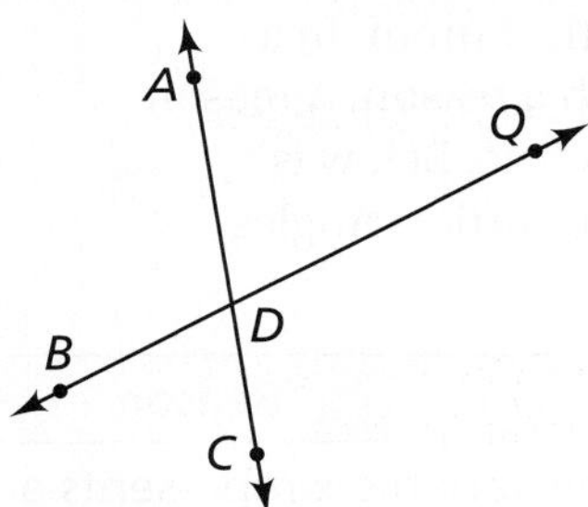

How can you prove this theorem true without using measurement? Since angle measures are numbers, you can use algebra. Use guess-check-generalize to show that the theorem is true for certain angle measures. Do not forget to keep track of your steps. For instance, the steps shown on the following page are for the case in which $m\angle ADB = 125°$.

Step 1 Suppose that $m\angle ADB = 125°$.

Step 2 You know that $m\angle ADB + m\angle ADQ = 180°$. Therefore, you know that $125° + m\angle ADQ = 180°$.

Step 3 So, $m\angle ADQ = 180° - 125° = 55°$.

Step 4 You also know that $m\angle ADQ + m\angle CDQ = 180°$. Therefore, you know that $55° + m\angle CDQ = 180°$.

Step 5 Then, $m\angle CDQ = 180° - 55° = 125°$.

Step 6 So, $m\angle ADB = m\angle CDQ$ because they both have the same measure, 125°.

Habits of Mind

Generalize. The idea is to get into the rhythm of the steps.

If you repeat this process with several different angle measures, you may convince yourself that the steps will always work. To present a more convincing argument, repeat this process with a generic value for the measure of $\angle ADB$. Simply use a variable to represent $m\angle ADB$.

Step 1 Suppose that $m\angle ADB = x°$.

Step 2 You know that $m\angle ADB + m\angle ADQ = 180°$. Therefore, $x° + m\angle ADQ = 180°$.

Step 3 So, $m\angle ADQ = 180° - x°$.

Step 4 You also know that $m\angle ADQ + m\angle CDQ = 180°$. Therefore, $(180° - x°) + m\angle CDQ = 180°$.

Step 5 So $m\angle CDQ = 180° - (180° - x°) = 180° - 180° + x° = x°$.

Step 6 Then $m\angle ADB = m\angle CDQ$ because they both measure $x°$.

This argument is convincing, but it is not a mathematical proof. In a mathematical proof, each statement is supported with a reason. A reason is an assumption or theorem that you already know is true. Below is an incomplete two-column mathematical proof of the Vertical Angles Theorem.

Statement	Reason
1. Let $m\angle ADB = x°$.	The variable x represents any number.
2. $m\angle ADB + m\angle ADQ = 180°$, so $x° + m\angle ADQ = 180°$.	
3. $m\angle ADQ = 180° - x°$	basic rules of algebra
4. $m\angle ADQ + m\angle CDQ = 180°$, so $(180° - x°) + m\angle CDQ = 180°$.	
5. $m\angle CDQ = 180° - (180° - x°) = 180° - 180° + x° = x°$	basic moves and rules of algebra
6. $m\angle ADB = m\angle CDQ$	If the measures of two angles are equal to the same value, then the measures of the two angles are equal to each other.

For Discussion

6. As a class, choose a reason to support statements 2 and 4 in the proof. Your reason should be an assumption or theorem that you can accept without proof.
7. The reasons for statements 3 and 5 in the proof on the previous page come from algebraic reasoning. What basic rules of algebra are used in these steps?

Exercises *Practicing Habits of Mind*

Check Your Understanding

1. Use the figure below. $\angle COA$ and $\angle DOB$ are right angles.

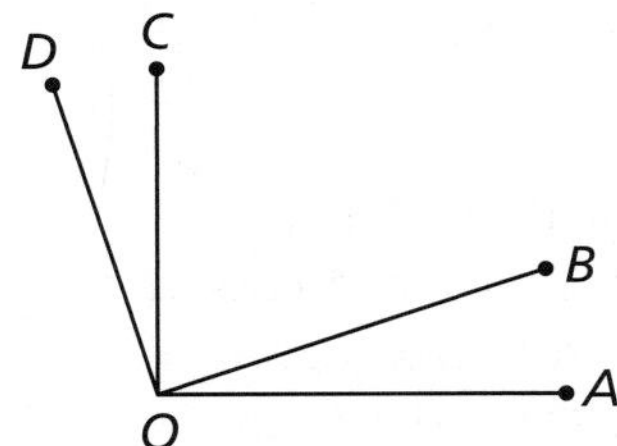

a. If $m\angle BOA = 25°$, find $m\angle COB$ and $m\angle COD$.

b. If $m\angle COB = 63°$, find $m\angle BOA$ and $m\angle COD$.

c. If $m\angle DOC = 31°$, find $m\angle COB$ and $m\angle BOA$.

d. If $m\angle DOC = 31°$, find $m\angle DOA$.

e. If $m\angle AOB = x°$, find $m\angle COB$ and $m\angle COD$.

2. Use the figure below. $\angle COA$ and $\angle DOB$ are right angles. Prove that $m\angle BOA = m\angle COD$.

When you write a proof, be sure to state explicitly any assumptions you make.

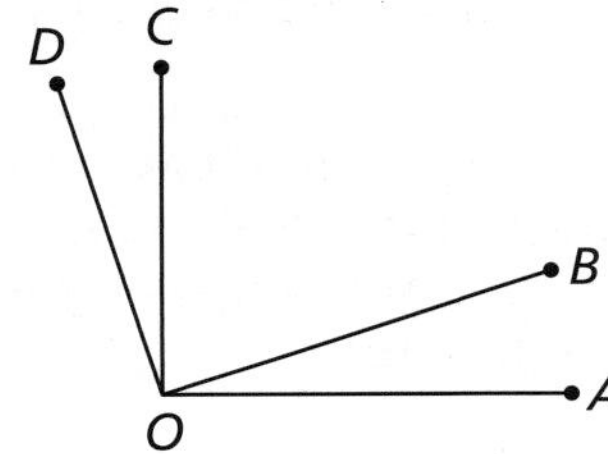

On Your Own

3. **Standardized Test Prep** $\overline{BE}$ bisects $\overline{AD}$ at C. Point C is the midpoint of $\overline{BE}$. Choose the correct reason for step 4 in the following proof.

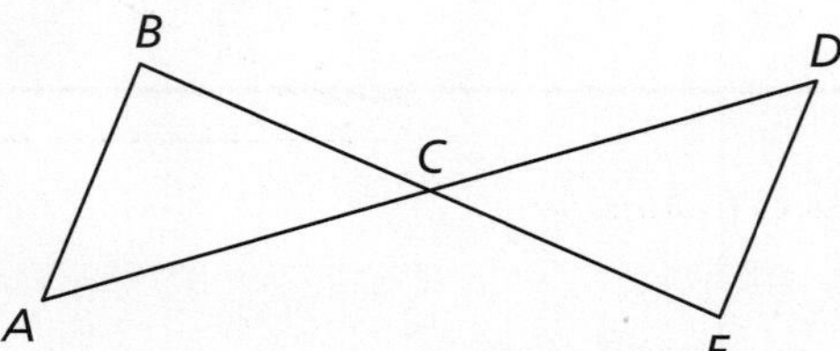

Statements	**Reasons**
1. $\overline{BE}$ bisects $\overline{AD}$ at C. Point C is the midpoint of $\overline{BE}$.	**1.** Given
2. $\overline{AC} \cong \overline{DC}$	**2.** Definition of bisects
3. $\overline{BC} \cong \overline{EC}$	**3.** Definition of midpoint
4. $\angle BCA \cong \angle ECD$	**4.** $\underline{\ ?\ }$
5. $\triangle ABC \cong \triangle DEC$	**5.** SAS triangle congruence postulate

A. Straight angles are congruent.

B. Corresponding angles are congruent.

C. Opposite angles are congruent.

D. Vertical angles are congruent.

4. Use the figure below. $\overline{AB} \cong \overline{DB}$ and $m\angle ABC = m\angle DBC$.

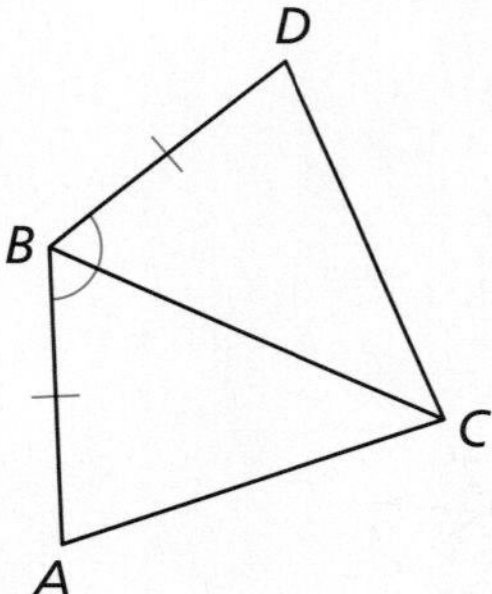

Provide the missing reasons in the proof to show that $\overline{AC} \cong \overline{DC}$.

Statements	**Reasons**
a. $\overline{AB} \cong \overline{BD}$	Given
b. $m\angle ABC = m\angle DBC$	$\underline{\ ?\ }$
c. $\overline{BC} \cong \overline{BC}$	$\underline{\ ?\ }$
d. $\triangle ABC \cong \triangle DBC$	$\underline{\ ?\ }$
e. $\overline{AC} \cong \overline{DC}$	$\underline{\ ?\ }$

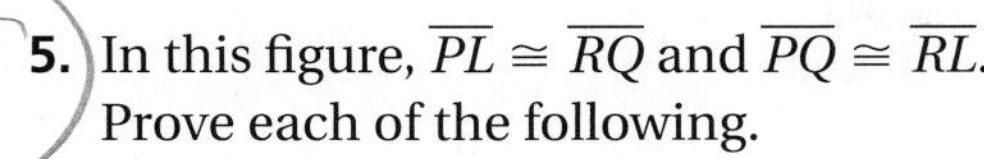

5. In this figure, $\overline{PL} \cong \overline{RQ}$ and $\overline{PQ} \cong \overline{RL}$. Prove each of the following.

a. $\triangle QPL \cong \triangle LRQ$

b. $\angle P \cong \angle R$

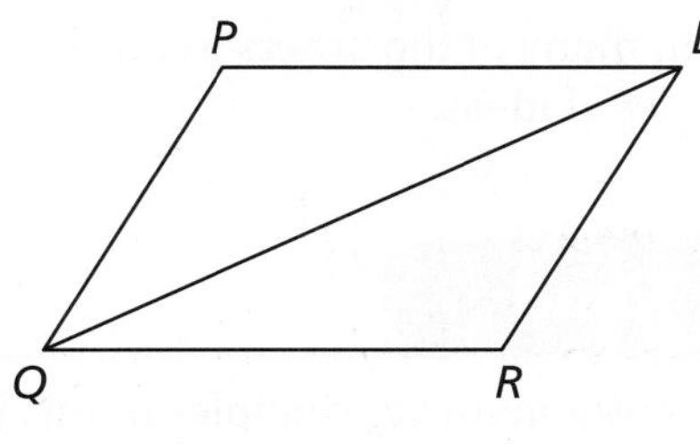

6. Use the figure below. $m\angle DCB = m\angle ECA$. Points E, C, and D are collinear. $\overline{FC} \perp \overline{ED}$.

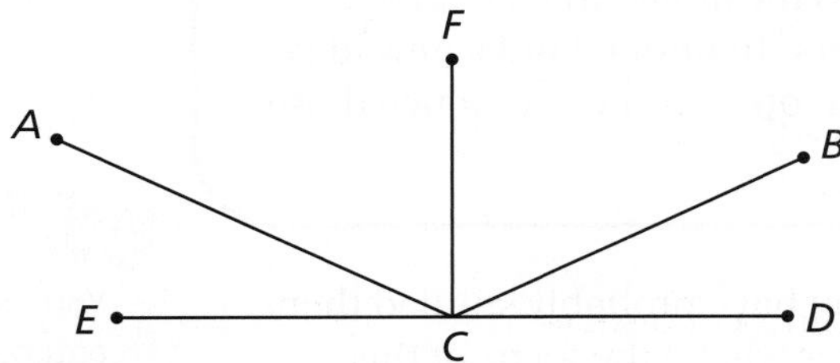

a. Based on the given information, what can you prove?

b. Prove your conjecture from part (a).

Maintain Your Skills

7. Use the figure below. Suppose that $m\angle 1 + m\angle 6 = 90^\circ$ and $m\angle 7 = 140^\circ$.

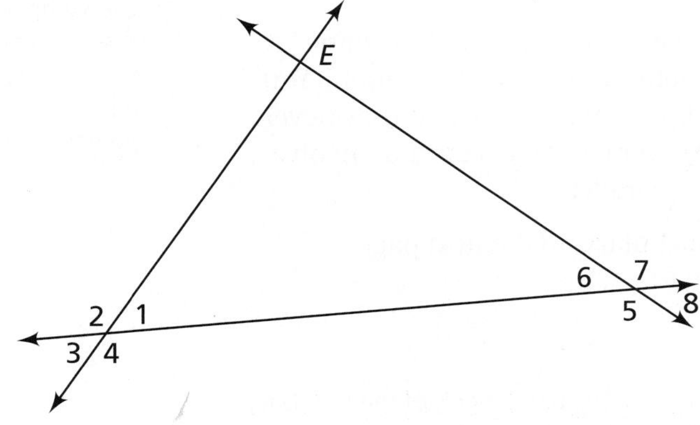

a. Find the measure of each numbered angle.

b. Assume you know that the sum of the measures of the angles in a triangle is 180°. Find the measure of each angle around point E.

Go Online
Pearsonsuccessnet.com

In Lesson 2.8, you will prove that the sum of the measures of the angles in a triangle is 180°.

2.07 Parallel Lines

This lesson is different from many of the others in this book. You will need to read and comprehend a set of ideas.

Developing Habits of Mind

Read to understand. The mathematical principles in this lesson have been studied for centuries. Some of them took generations to solve or prove. An important part of mathematics is the ability to read and understand the mathematical writing of others. To understand a new idea, sometimes you may need to read it more than once. You will practice these skills in this lesson.

Remember...

You have studied the equations of parallel lines. How can you determine whether two lines are parallel from their equations?

You see parallel lines in your everyday life. You have probably studied them in previous mathematics courses. Parallel lines will be the focus of this lesson and the following lesson. You will address these questions.

1. How can you determine whether two lines are parallel?
2. What information can you draw from parallel lines?

Here is the definition of parallel lines given in Chapter 1.

Definition

Parallel lines are lines in the same plane that do not intersect.

Remember...

You can also say that parallel lines are everywhere equidistant. *Everywhere equidistant* means "the same distance apart at every point."

This seems like a simple definition. However, if you need to determine whether two given lines are parallel, the definition is not very helpful. You cannot graph both lines forever in each direction to check that they never intersect. In this lesson, you will develop several simple tests that involve measuring angles to determine if lines are parallel.

First, you need to be familiar with the vocabulary on the next page.

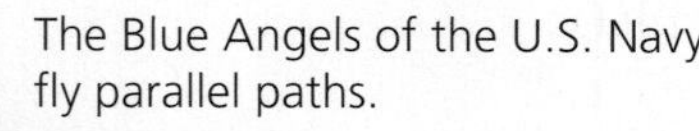

The Blue Angels of the U.S. Navy fly parallel paths.

Facts and Notation

The pairs of angles that are formed when a transversal intersects two lines have special names based on their positions.

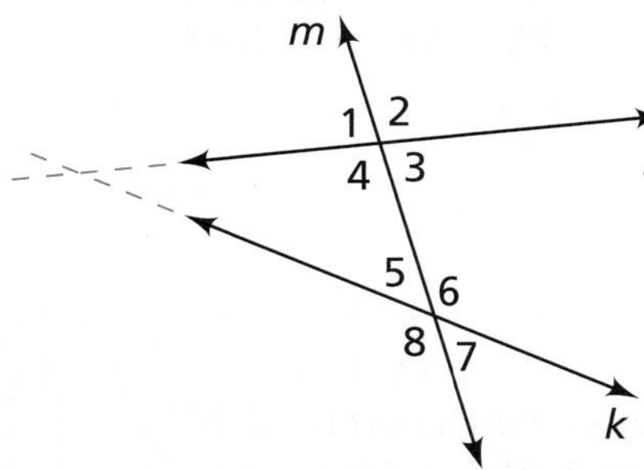

- **Pairs of angles such as $\angle 3$ and $\angle 5$, or $\angle 4$ and $\angle 6$, are alternate interior angles.**
- **Pairs of angles such as $\angle 1$ and $\angle 5$, or $\angle 4$ and $\angle 8$, are corresponding angles.**
- **Pairs of angles such as $\angle 2$ and $\angle 4$, or $\angle 5$ and $\angle 7$, are vertical angles.**
- **Angles on the same side of the transversal and between the lines (for example, $\angle 3$ and $\angle 6$) are consecutive angles.**

Pairs of angles such as $\angle 1$ and $\angle 7$, or $\angle 2$ and $\angle 8$, are **alternate exterior angles.**

For You to Do

1. Use the figure at the right. Suppose you have three sticks. The sticks represent lines ℓ, m, and n. The sticks ℓ and n are fixed together to form a 62° angle at point A. The sticks representing m and n intersect at P. You can pivot the stick representing m about point P.

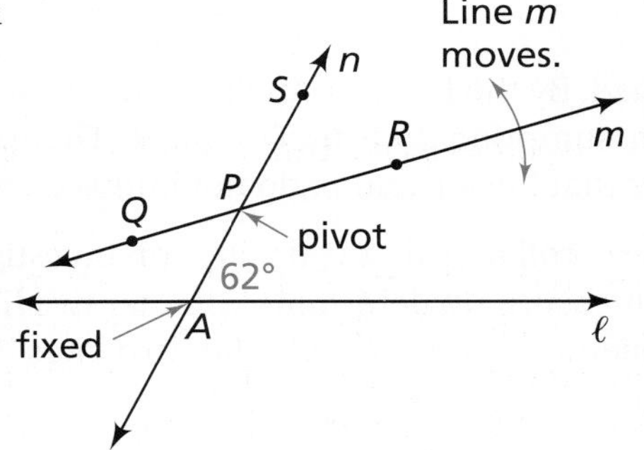

How can you adjust the angles at P to ensure that line ℓ is parallel to line m ($\ell \parallel m$)? Explain.

Habits of Mind

Experiment. This is a thought experiment. You can turn it into a physical experiment by building a model with sticks.

The result of the experiment above suggests several theorems that allow you to say that two lines are parallel.

Theorem 2.2 The AIP Theorem

If two lines form congruent alternate interior angles with a transversal, then the two lines are parallel.

AIP stands for "alternate interiors parallel." You can think of the *AI* as the hypothesis of the theorem, and the *P* as the conclusion.

The AIP Theorem on the previous page is illustrated in the figure below.

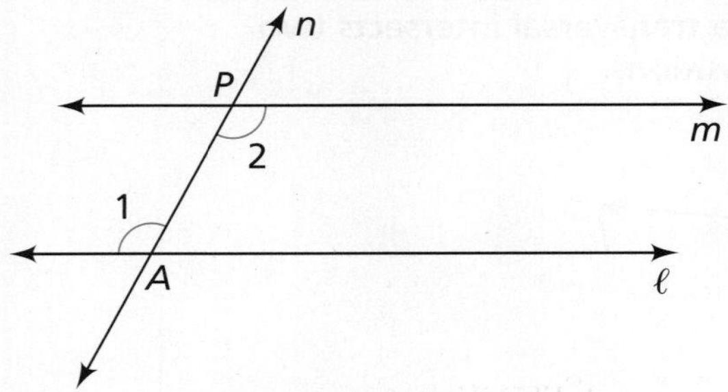

Proof Assume that $m\angle 1 = m\angle 2$. You need to show that $\ell \parallel m$. The proof of this fact is indirect. Begin by supposing the lines are not parallel and then prove the theorem by contradiction.

Suppose lines ℓ and m are not parallel. Then they must intersect somewhere. Suppose they intersect at a point R like this.

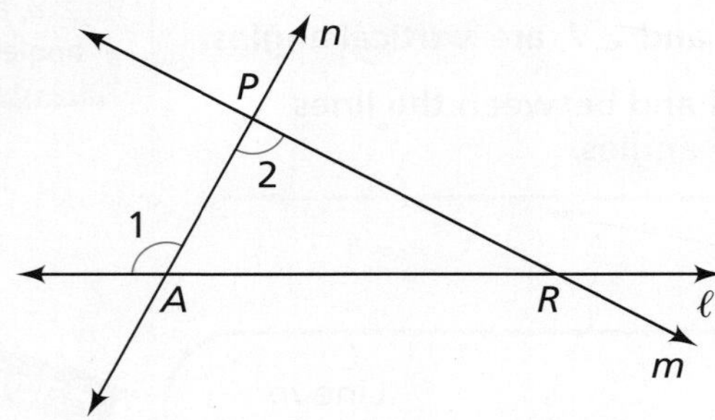

A triangle, $\triangle ARP$, is formed. By the Exterior Angle Theorem, $m\angle 1 > m\angle 2$. But this contradicts our assumption that $m\angle 1 = m\angle 2$. Therefore, point R cannot exist. This implies that lines ℓ and m do not intersect. So, $\ell \parallel m$.

The AIP Theorem and the corollaries that you will soon investigate allow you to use certain angle measures to determine whether two lines are parallel. This is much easier than checking whether two lines intersect.

Remember...

Congruent angles have the same measure and vice versa.

A **corollary** is a consequence that logically follows from a theorem.

For Discussion

2. The proof of the AIP Theorem depends on the Exterior Angle Theorem shown here.

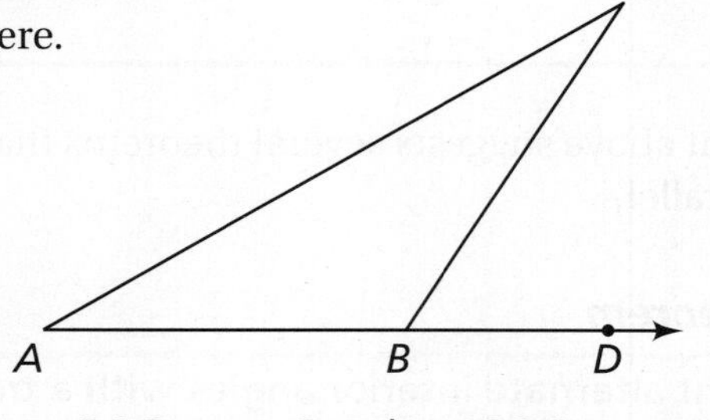

$m\angle DBC > m\angle C$ and $m\angle DBC > m\angle A$

The Exterior Angle Theorem also depends on some basic assumptions. Discuss these assumptions.

Exercises *Practicing Habits of Mind*

Check Your Understanding

1. Give a precise definition for each term listed below. Illustrate each with a diagram.

a. alternate interior angles
b. alternate exterior angles
c. corresponding angles
d. consecutive angles

These types of angles are formed when two lines are cut by a transversal. The two lines may or may not be parallel.

2. Use the figure below. The tick marks indicate congruent segments.

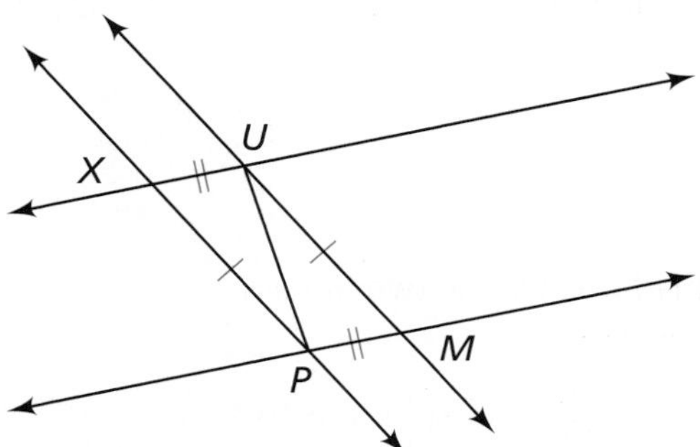

a. Which triangles, if any, are congruent? Explain.
b. Which angles, if any, are congruent? Explain.
c. Which lines, if any, are parallel? Explain.

3. Use the figure below. The tick marks indicate congruent segments.

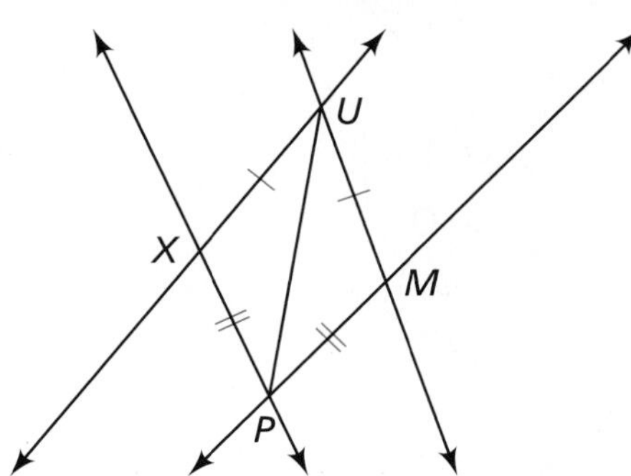

a. Which triangles, if any, are congruent? Explain.
b. Which angles, if any, are congruent? Explain.
c. Which lines, if any, are parallel? Explain.

4. Decide whether each statement below is true. Prove why or why not.

   a. If two lines form congruent corresponding angles with a transversal, then the two lines are parallel.

   b. If two lines form congruent alternate exterior angles with a transversal, then the two lines are parallel.

   c. If two lines form congruent consecutive angles with a transversal, then the two lines are parallel.

   d. If two lines form supplementary alternate exterior angles with a transversal, then the two lines are parallel.

   e. If two lines form supplementary consecutive angles with a transversal, then the two lines are parallel.

Each statement that is true is a corollary of the AIP Theorem.

Remember...

Two angles are **supplementary angles** if the sum of their measures is 180°.

On Your Own

5. Suppose two lines are perpendicular to the same line. Are the two lines parallel? Explain.

6. Two lines in the same plane either intersect or are parallel. Explain. Is the statement true of two lines in space? Explain.

In Exercises 7 and 8, use the given information to determine which segments in each figure must be parallel. For each exercise, provide a proof to support your answer.

7. Point O is the midpoint of both $\overline{NP}$ and $\overline{MQ}$.

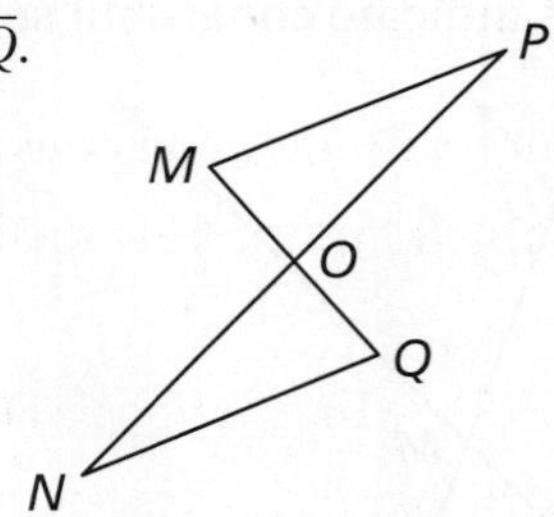

8. The diagonals of quadrilateral $MPQN$ intersect at point O. $MO = PO$ and $NO = QO$.

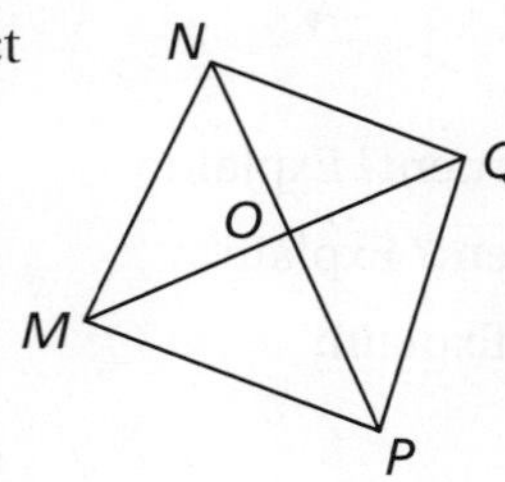

9. Standardized Test Prep In the figure at the right, $\overrightarrow{BG}$ intersects $\overline{AC}$ at point B. $\overrightarrow{BG}$ intersects $\overline{DF}$ at point E. Angle ABG and $\angle GEF$ are supplementary.

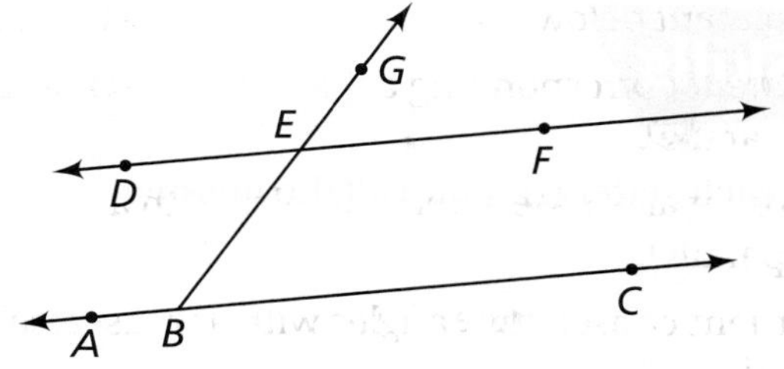

Choose the correct reason for step number 8 in the following proof that $\overleftrightarrow{AC} \parallel \overleftrightarrow{DF}$.

Statements	**Reasons**
1. $\overline{BG}$ intersects $\overline{AC}$ and $\overline{DF}$ at points B and E, respectively.	**1.** Given
2. $\angle ABG$ and $\angle GEF$ are supplementary.	**2.** Given
3. $m\angle ABG + m\angle GEF = 180°$	**3.** definition of supplementary angles
4. $\angle GEF \cong \angle DEB$	**4.** Vertical angles are congruent.
5. $m\angle GEF = m\angle DEB$	**5.** definition of congruent angles
6. $m\angle ABG + m\angle DEB = 180°$	**6.** substitution property of equality
7. $\angle ABG$ and $\angle DEB$ are supplementary angles.	**7.** definition of supplementary angles
8. $\overleftrightarrow{AC} \parallel \overleftrightarrow{DF}$	**8.** __?__

A. If corresponding angles are congruent, then the lines are parallel.

B. If consecutive angles are supplementary, then the lines are parallel.

C. If alternate interior angles are congruent, then the lines are parallel.

D. If alternate exterior angles are supplementary, then the lines are parallel.

10. In the figure below, $m\angle DEG + m\angle HFI = 180°$, and $m\angle FGE = m\angle HFI$.

Find the lines in the figure that must be parallel, if there are any. Prove what you find.

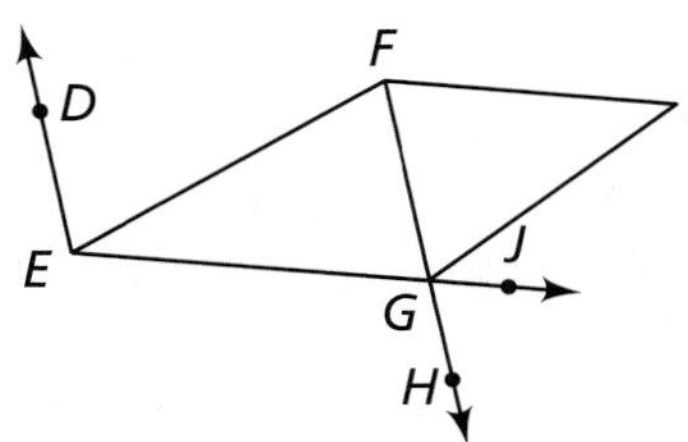

Keep going

Maintain Your Skills

11. Use the figure below. For each statement, find all the missing angle measures.

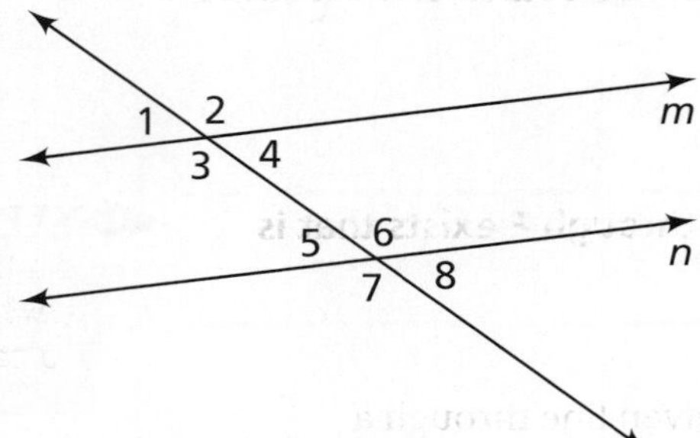

a. $m\angle 1 = 58°$ and $m\angle 5 = 58°$
b. $m\angle 1 = 58°$ and $m\angle 6 = 125°$
c. $m\angle 4 = 55°$ and $m\angle 6 = 125°$
d. $m\angle 7 = 125°$ and $m\angle 3 = 125°$
e. $m\angle 7 = 125°$ and $m\angle 1 = 55°$

Go Online
Pearsonsuccessnet.com

12. Decide whether each statement below guarantees that $m \parallel n$. If so, explain.

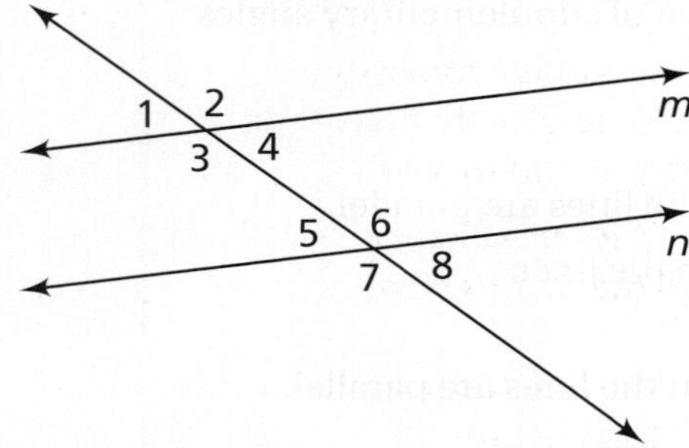

a. $m\angle 1 = 58°$ and $m\angle 5 = 58°$
b. $m\angle 1 = 58°$ and $m\angle 6 = 125°$
c. $m\angle 4 = 55°$ and $m\angle 6 = 125°$
d. $m\angle 7 = 125°$ and $m\angle 3 = 125°$
e. $m\angle 7 = 125°$ and $m\angle 1 = 55°$
f. $m\angle 7 = m\angle 6$
g. $m\angle 7 = m\angle 2$
h. $m\angle 7 + m\angle 3 = 180°$
i. $m\angle 4 + m\angle 6 = 180°$

2.08 The Parallel Postulate

Suppose you have a line ℓ and a point P that is not on ℓ. How many lines through P can you draw that are parallel to ℓ? The experiments in this book and your common sense suggest that there is only one. People tried for centuries to prove this from simpler statements, and they had no success. The concept that there exists only one line parallel to a given line through a point not on the given line cannot be proved. In this course, it is accepted that no proof exists, and it is assumed true.

Postulate 2.2 The Parallel Postulate

If a point P is not on a line ℓ, exactly one line through P exists that is parallel to ℓ.

In this case, the word *exists* means that there is a parallel line.

Now that you have assumed that a parallel to a given line through a point exists and is unique, you can answer the second question from the beginning of Lesson 2.7: What information can you draw from parallel lines? In Lesson 2.7, you used certain angle measures to determine whether lines were parallel. Now you can work in the other direction and determine the measures of certain angles when two parallel lines are cut by a transversal.

For You to Do

1. Use geometry software to construct two parallel lines and a moveable transversal. Measure all the angles and note any two angles that have the same measure and any two angles with measures that add to $180°$.

   Move the transversal. Check which of the equalities found above is invariant. Is there a state of the sketch in which all the angles have the same measure?

This activity leads to the converse of the AIP Theorem.

To form the **converse** of an *if-then* statement, interchange the *if* and *then* clauses. So the PAI Theorem is the converse of the AIP Theorem.

Theorem 2.3 The PAI Theorem

If two parallel lines are cut by a transversal, then the alternate interior angles are congruent.

You can prove the PAI Theorem with an indirect proof.

Proof Suppose parallel lines n and ℓ are cut by a transversal t, as shown in the figure below.

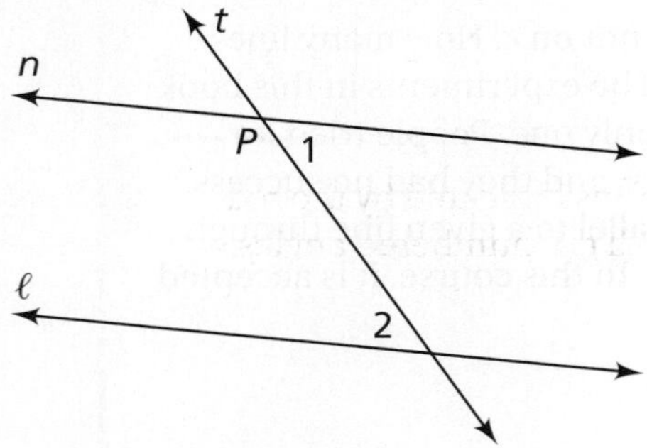

You want to prove that $\angle 1 \cong \angle 2$. Since this is an indirect proof, suppose that $\angle 1 \ncong \angle 2$ and show that this leads to something that is impossible. Construct a line m through P so that the intersection of m and t form an $\angle 3$ that is congruent to $\angle 2$.

The symbol $\ncong$ means "is not congruent to."

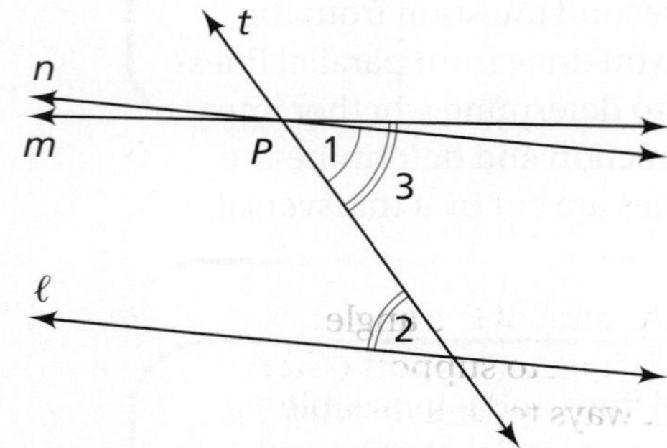

By the AIP Theorem, you can conclude that $m \parallel \ell$. However, you originally assumed that $n \parallel \ell$. So there are two distinct lines through P that are parallel to ℓ. This contradicts the Parallel Postulate. So you can conclude that $\angle 1 \cong \angle 2$. Therefore, if two parallel lines are cut by a transversal, then the alternate interior angles are congruent.

Developing Habits of Mind

Use a different process to get the same result. You can prove the PAI Theorem in a more direct way. Without assuming that $\angle 1 \ncong \angle 2$, construct line m as you did above so that $\angle 3 \cong \angle 2$. By the AIP Theorem, $m \parallel \ell$. Since there is only one line parallel to ℓ through P, m and n must be the same line. Therefore, $\angle 1$ and $\angle 3$ must be the same angle, so $\angle 1 \cong \angle 2$.

For Discussion

2. What assumptions do you need to make in this argument?

For You to Do

3. Use the figure below. Lines n and m are parallel, as indicated by the red arrowhead on each line. Find the measures of all the numbered angles.
4. Explain how you found each angle measure.

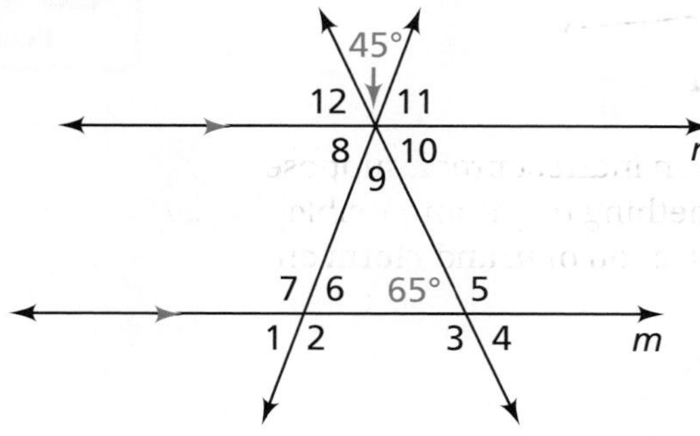

For Discussion

5. You already have overwhelming evidence that the sum of the angle measures in a triangle is $180°$. You have used this idea to support other arguments. You may even know several different ways to explain why it is true. Use the diagram below to write an argument that proves that the sum of the angle measures in any triangle is $180°$.

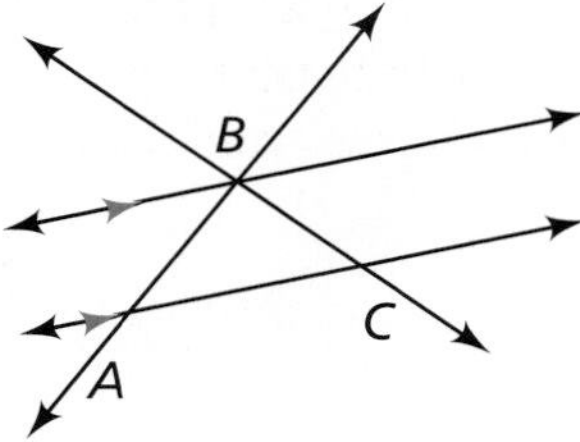

You can state the result of this discussion as a theorem.

Theorem 2.4 The Triangle Angle-Sum Theorem

The sum of the measures of the angles of a triangle is 180°.

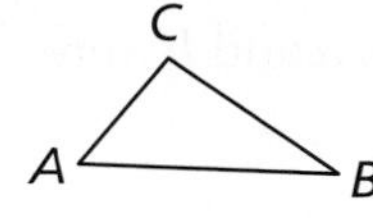

$$m\angle A + m\angle B + m\angle C = 180°$$

Exercises *Practicing Habits of Mind*

Check Your Understanding

Go Online
Pearsonsuccessnet.com

1. Use the figure below. Assume $m \parallel n$.

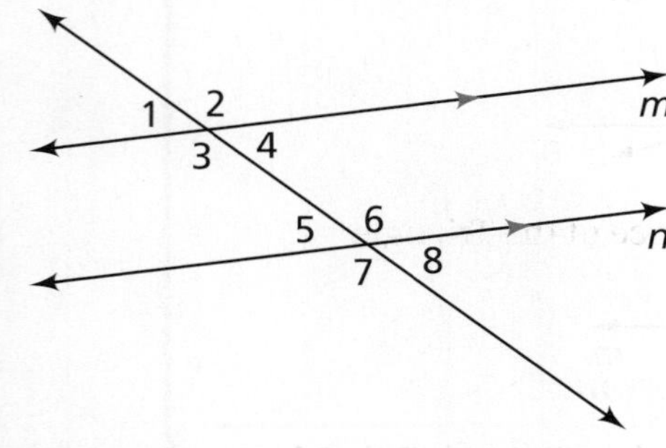

Find the measure of each numbered angle for each of the following conditions.

a. $m\angle 6 = 108°$

b. $m\angle 8 = 46°$

c. $m\angle 4 = x°$

d. $2m\angle 4 = m\angle 7$

e. $m\angle 7 = 2x°$ and $m\angle 4 = x°$

2. Use geometry software to construct two parallel lines a and b. Then construct two transversals c and d that each intersect a and b. See the figure below.

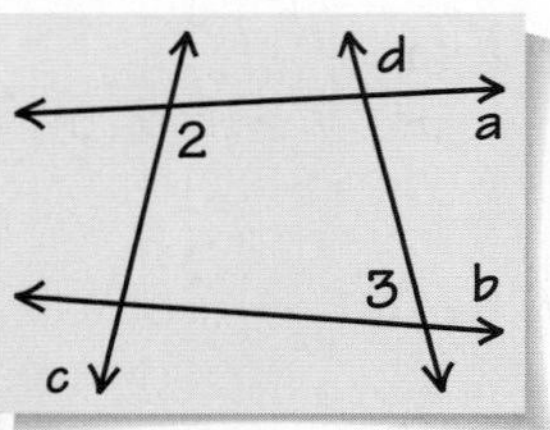

In this figure, lines *a* and *b* were drawn carelessly. They are clearly *not* parallel.

a. Move the lines so that $\angle 2 \cong \angle 3$. Do lines c and d have any special relationship? Is this relationship invariant or is it dependent on the congruence of $\angle 2$ and $\angle 3$?

b. Move the lines so that $c \parallel d$. What is the relationship between $\angle 2$ and $\angle 3$?

c. How would your answers to parts (a) and (b) differ if lines a and b were not parallel?

3. Use geometry software to construct a pair of parallel lines so that point A is on one line and point B is on the other. Place a moveable point P between the parallel lines. Construct $\overline{PA}$ and $\overline{PB}$, as shown in the figure below. What invariants can you find?

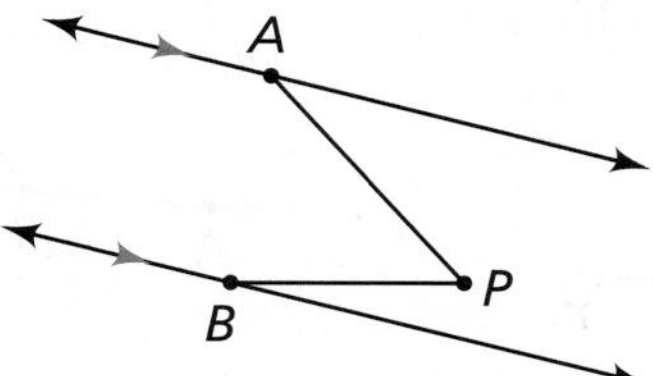

4. The following theorem is an important consequence of the Triangle Angle-Sum Theorem.

Theorem 2.5 The Unique Perpendicular Theorem

If a point P is not on line ℓ, there is exactly one line through P that is perpendicular to ℓ.

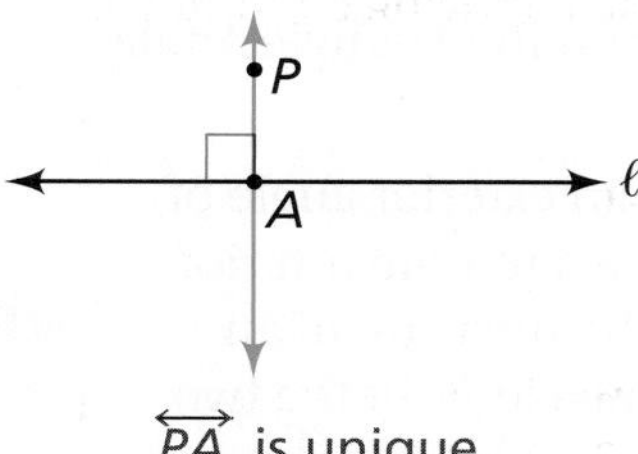

$\overleftrightarrow{PA}$ is unique.

Prove this theorem. (*Hint:* You may want to prove the theorem by contradiction. What would happen if there were more than one line through P that was perpendicular to ℓ?)

5. Is the sum of the measures of the angles of a quadrilateral invariant? Explain.

6. **Write About It** Explain the difference between the AIP and PAI Theorems.

7. Use geometry software to construct $\overrightarrow{AD}$ and $\overrightarrow{AE}$. Place point B on $\overrightarrow{AD}$ and point C on $\overrightarrow{AE}$. Then construct $\overline{BC}$, $\overline{CD}$, and $\overline{DE}$, as shown in the figure below. Move the parts so that $\overline{BC} \cong \overline{CD} \cong \overline{DE}$.

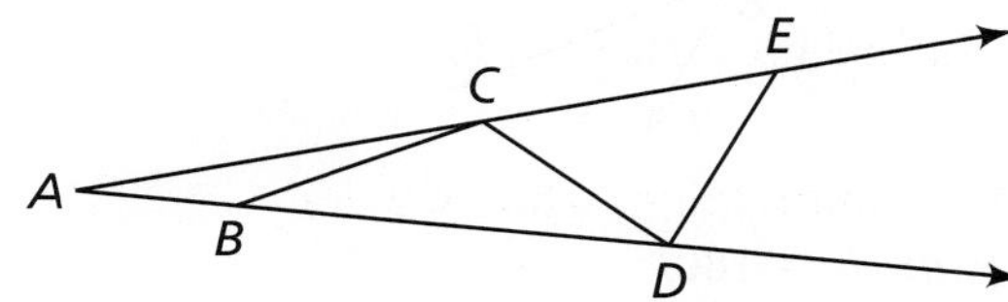

a. What conjectures can you make about the angles in the figure? Describe any invariant relationships you find.

b. Is it possible to make $\overline{BC}$ and $\overline{DE}$ parallel *and* congruent? Explain.

On Your Own

8. **Standardized Test Prep** In the figure at the right, $\overleftrightarrow{AB} \parallel \overleftrightarrow{EF}$. The measure of $\angle BCD$ is 25°. The measure of $\angle ABD$ is 125°. What is the measure of $\angle BDC$?

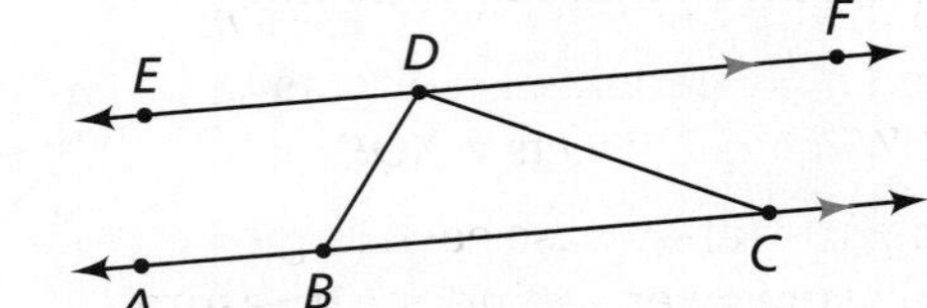

A. 55° B. 80°

C. 100° D. 125°

9. In the figure at the right, lines p and t are parallel.

a. Why is $\angle 1 \cong \angle 2$?

b. Why is $\angle 2 \cong \angle 3$?

c. Why is $\angle 1 \cong \angle 3$?

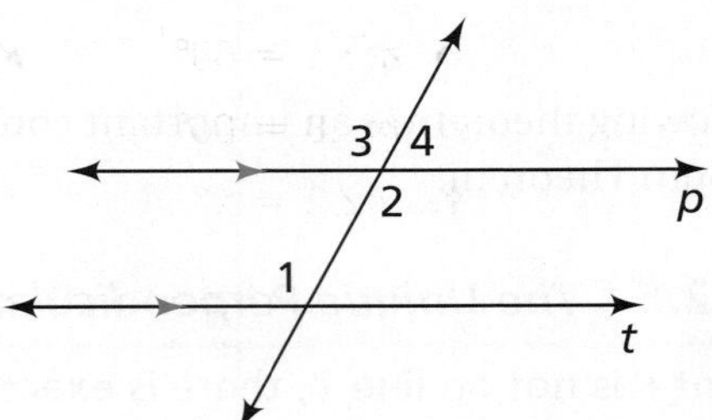

10. **Take It Further** Prove that, in a plane, two lines that are both parallel to a third line are parallel to each other.

11. Prove that the AAS triplet guarantees triangle congruence. Use the triangle congruence postulates and the Triangle Angle-Sum Theorem in your proof.

12. The Exterior Angle Theorem says that the measure of an exterior angle of a triangle is greater than the measure of either of the two remote interior angles. You can take this one step further. Prove that the measure of an exterior angle of a triangle is equal to the sum of the measures of the two remote interior angles.

Why do you think we did not prove this originally?

13. For each polygon listed below, prove that the sum of the measures of its angles is invariant. Then find the sum of the measures of the angles for each polygon. Justify your answers.

a. pentagon (five-sided polygon) b. hexagon (six-sided polygon)

14. **Take It Further** Use your knowledge of parallel lines. Decide whether each of the constructions (a)–(d) is possible. Explain.

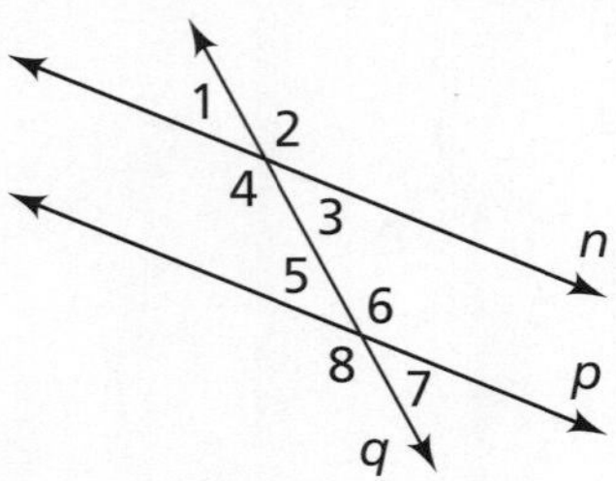

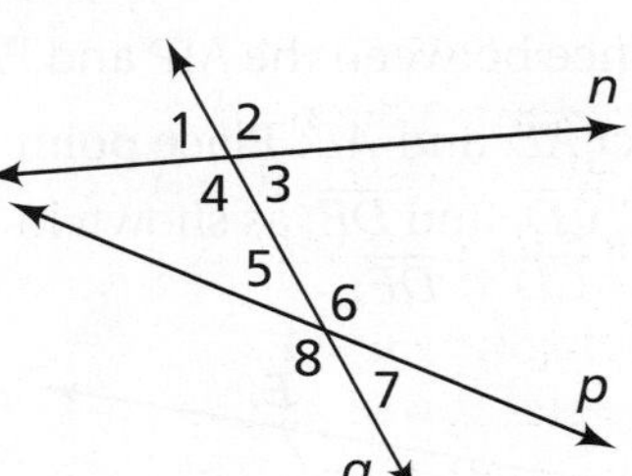

a. Lines n and p are not parallel and $m\angle 3 + m\angle 6 = 180°$.

b. Line n is parallel to line p and $m\angle 4 = m\angle 6$.

c. Line n is parallel to line p and $m\angle 2 = m\angle 5$.

d. $m\angle 4 + m\angle 5 > m\angle 2 + m\angle 7$

Maintain Your Skills

15. In the figure at the right, lines m and n are parallel. $\overline{PR}$ bisects $\angle WPQ$. $\overline{QR}$ bisects $\angle XQP$.

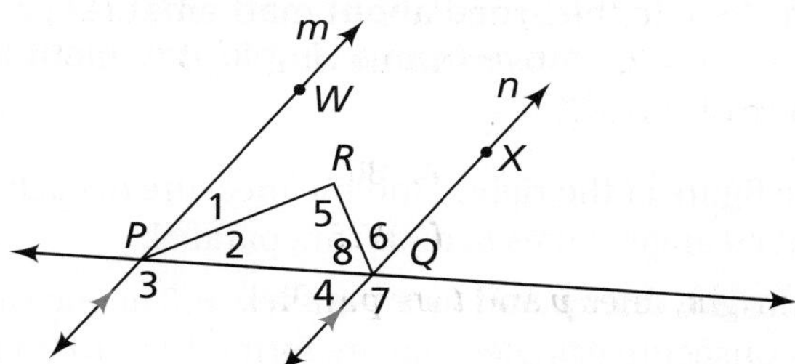

In parts (a)–(f), use each angle measure given to find the measure of the remaining numbered angles.

a. $m\angle 1 = 64°$ **b.** $m\angle 1 = 68°$

c. $m\angle 3 = 130°$ **d.** $m\angle 8 = 60°$

e. $m\angle 7 = 140°$ **f.** $m\angle 2 = x°$

Habits of Mind

Look for invariants. Which angle measures are invariant? What conjecture, if any, can you make?

Historical Perspective

Around 300 B.C., Euclid and other Greek mathematicians tried to formalize the system of mathematical proof. They wanted to start with a few basic facts that everyone agreed were true. These facts allowed them to derive statements that were not as obvious and that could not be checked by physical experiment. These mathematicians wrote a series of books called *Elements.*

Much of *Elements* is about numbers, arithmetic, and what we now call algebra. There is also a detailed treatment of geometry. *Elements* formed the basis of how geometry has been taught and learned for centuries.

The Euclidean tradition of deducing new results from simple assumptions and other established results is the "gold standard" in mathematics. Mathematicians discover results, solve problems, and get insights in a variety of ways. Many of these methods are very complex. But when mathematicians present their results to others, their claims are accepted only when they can justify them with a logical deductive proof.

In this investigation, you studied lines and angles. You learned about the types of angles formed when two lines intersect and the types of angles formed when two parallel lines are intersected by a transversal. You also learned about mathematical proof—a logical way to move from a simple statement to a desired conclusion.

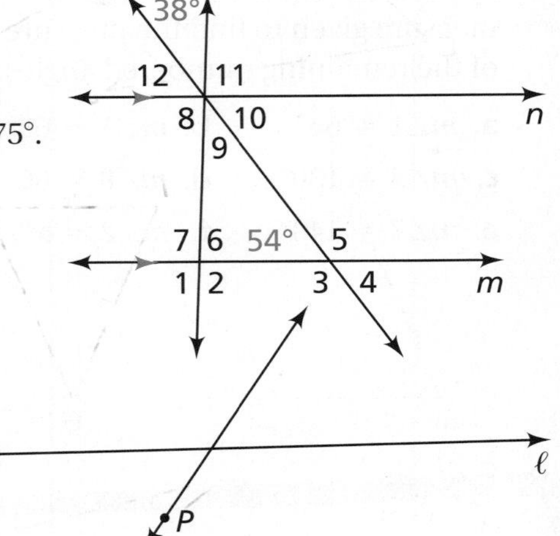

1. Use the figure at the right. Find the measure of each numbered angle. Lines m and n are parallel.
2. Two lines are intersected by a transversal. The measures of the consecutive angles that are formed are 103° and 75°. Are the two lines parallel? Explain.
3. Draw two segments $\overline{AB}$ and $\overline{CD}$ that intersect at point O so that $\overline{AO} \cong \overline{OB}$ and $\overline{CO} \cong \overline{OD}$. Prove that $\overline{AC} \cong \overline{BD}$.
4. Use the figure at the right. Explain how to construct a line through P that is parallel to ℓ.
5. Why is proof so important in mathematics?
6. What are some invariant angle relationships when parallel lines are cut by a transversal?
7. What is the sum of the measures of the interior angles of any triangle?

Vocabulary and Notation

In this investigation, you learned these terms and symbols. Make sure you understand what each one means and how to use it.

- **alternate exterior angles**
- **alternate interior angles**
- **consecutive angles**
- **converse**
- **corollary**
- **corresponding angles**
- **exterior angle**
- **parallel lines**
- **supplementary angles**
- **transversal**
- **vertical angles**
- **$\not\cong$ (is not congruent to)**
- **$\|$ (is parallel to)**

The G train forms congruent vertical angles with the L and J, M, and Z trains.

Mid-Chapter Test

1. The triangles in each pair below are congruent. Use the tick marks to write correct congruence statements.

   a.

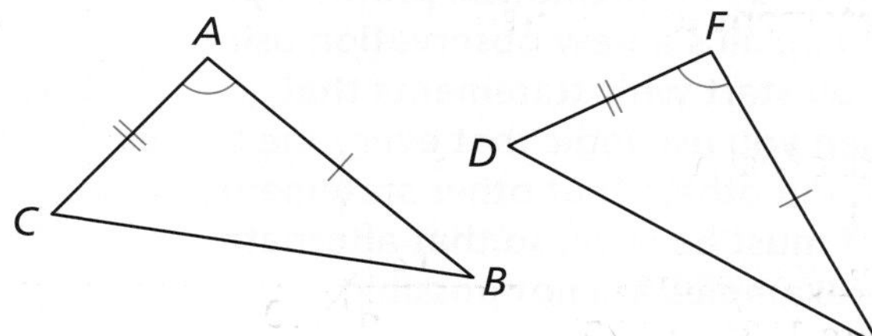

   b.

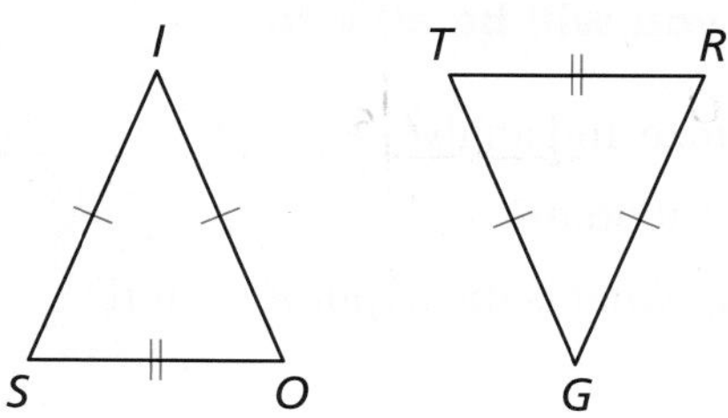

   c.

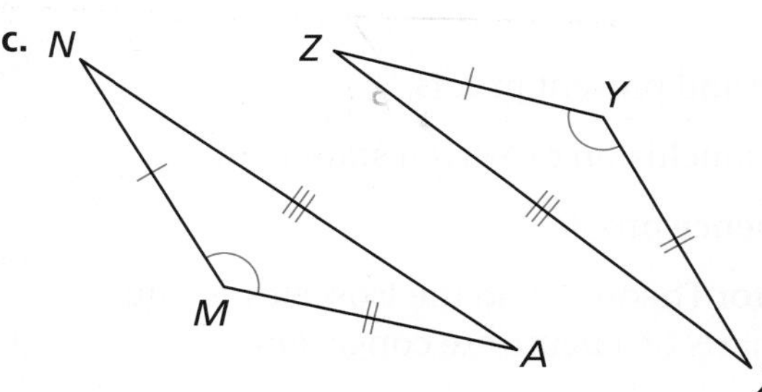

2. In the figure below, lines m and n are parallel. Find the measure of each numbered angle.

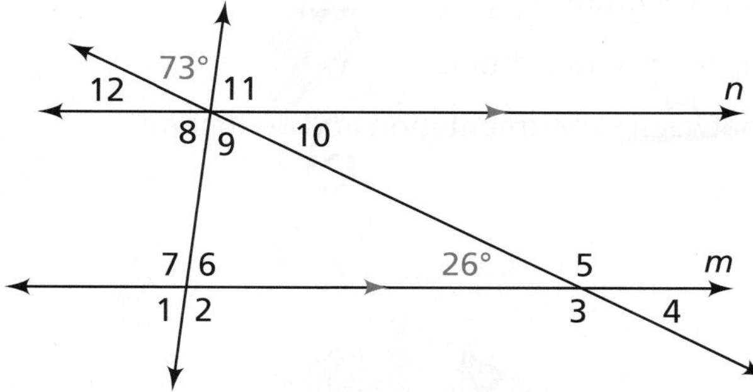

3. Suppose $\triangle CAT \cong \triangle PIG$.

   a. Name five pairs of congruent parts.

   b. Construct two such triangles. Use tick marks to mark the corresponding congruent parts.

4. Suppose that two students both construct a triangle based on the information given. Can you be sure that the students' triangles are congruent? Explain.

   a. $AB = 3$ cm, $BC = 4$ cm, $m\angle C = 40°$

   b. $XY = 1$ cm, $YZ = 2$ cm, $XZ = 1.5$ cm

   c. $m\angle T = 30°$, $m\angle O = 20°$, $m\angle M = 130°$

5. Determine whether you have enough information to prove that the triangles in each pair are congruent. If you do have enough information, state which triangle congruence theorem or postulate guarantees that they are congruent. The triangles are not necessarily drawn to scale.

   a.

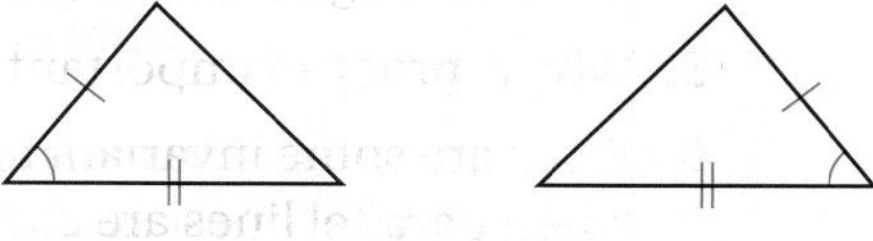

   b.

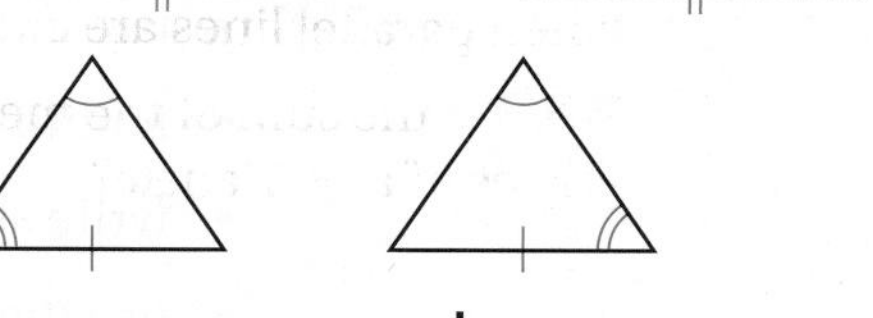

   c. d.

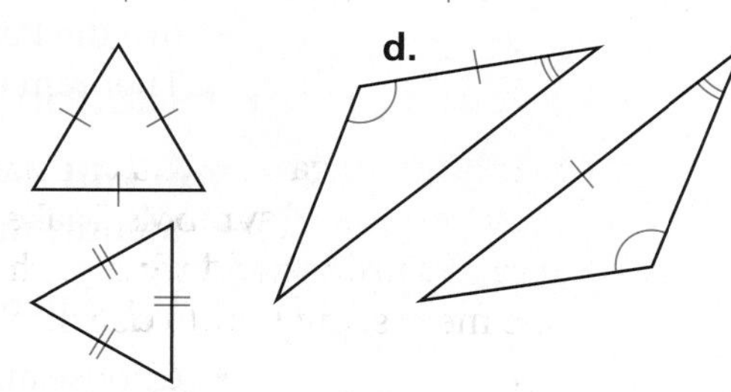

6. In the figure below, $\overline{AD}$ bisects $\angle CAB$ and $\overline{PM} \parallel \overline{AD}$. Prove that $\triangle APM$ is isosceles.

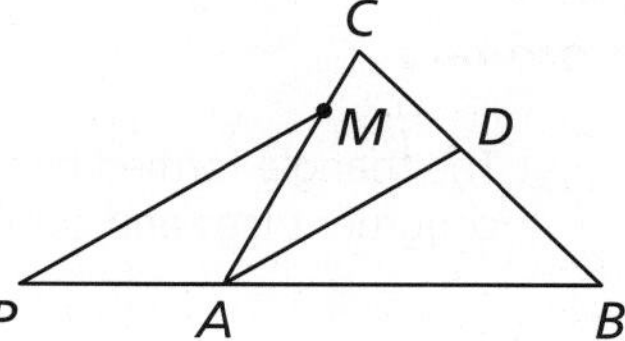

7. Find x, y, and z.

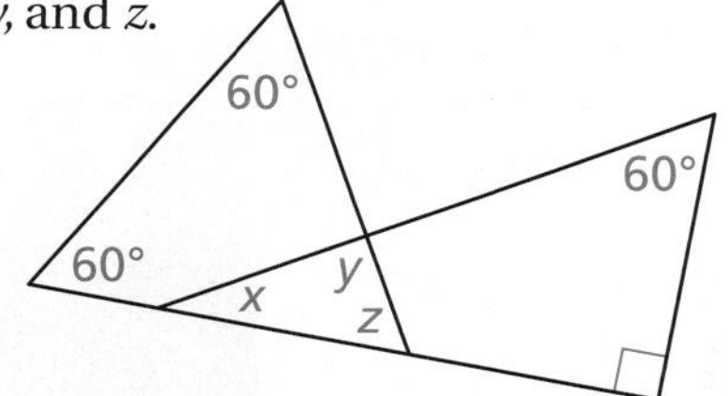

Writing Proofs

In *Writing Proofs,* you will study mathematical proof. A proof is a logical argument that explains a new observation using facts you already know. You start with statements that everyone agrees with. Then you use logic that everyone agrees with to convince yourself and others that other statements have to follow. Your proof must be clear, so that alternate interpretations or counterexamples are not possible.

By the end of this investigation, you will be able to answer questions like these.

1. What are the different ways to organize and analyze a proof?
2. What is the Perpendicular Bisector Theorem?
3. In the statement "All trees are green," what is the hypothesis and what is the conclusion?

You will learn how to

- use a variety of ways to write and present proofs
- identify the hypothesis and conclusion of a given statement
- write simple triangle congruence proofs
- use the Perpendicular Bisector Theorem and the Isosceles Triangle Theorem to prove that two parts of a figure are congruent

You will develop these habits and skills:

- Identify the hypothesis and conclusion of a statement.
- Use different methods to write a proof.
- Choose an appropriate way to present a proof.
- Recognize the difference between experimentation and deduction.

The triangle formed by this ski bridge has congruent legs and congruent base angles.

2.09 Getting Started

In previous lessons, you used assumptions and theorems to informally prove that triangles are congruent and lines are parallel. In this lesson, you will write more informal **proofs,** or convincing arguments, in preparation for writing formal mathematical proofs.

How is the term *argument* used differently in mathematics than in everyday language?

For You to Explore

1. Draw a square and divide it into four equal parts. Write an argument that convinces a classmate that each part has the same area. Share your argument with a classmate. Is your argument convincing?
2. Draw a square and divide it into five equal parts. Write an argument that shows that each of the five parts has the same area. Make sure that your argument is convincing.
3. If you find the sum of an odd number and an even number, is the result an odd number or an even number? Write a convincing argument to prove that your result is correct for each of the following audiences.
   a. fourth graders
   b. algebra students
4. You know that the sum of the measures of the angles in a triangle is 180°. Use this fact to show that the sum of the measures of the angles in a quadrilateral is 360°.

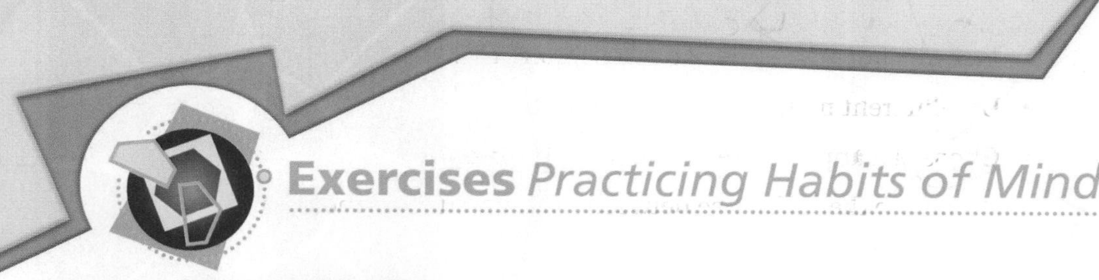

On Your Own

5. Use the figure at the right. Ruth claims that $\triangle ABC \cong \triangle DBC$.

   Her argument states the following.
   - The triangles share side $\overline{BC}$.
   - $\angle ACB \cong \angle DCB$ because they are both right angles.
   - The diagram tells us that $\overline{AC} \cong \overline{DC}$.

   Does Ruth's argument support her claim? What triangle congruence postulate should she use to conclude that $\triangle ABC \cong \triangle DBC$? Explain.

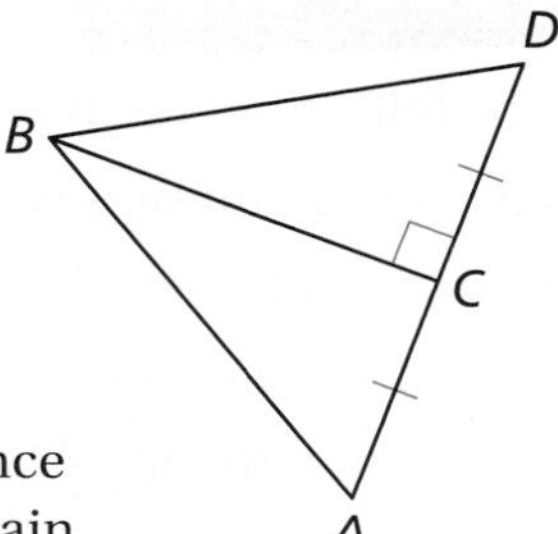

6. **What's Wrong Here?** Ruth was asked to make a conjecture about the figure below and then prove it. The given information is $\angle ABC \cong \angle ACB$ and $\overline{BE} \cong \overline{CD}$.

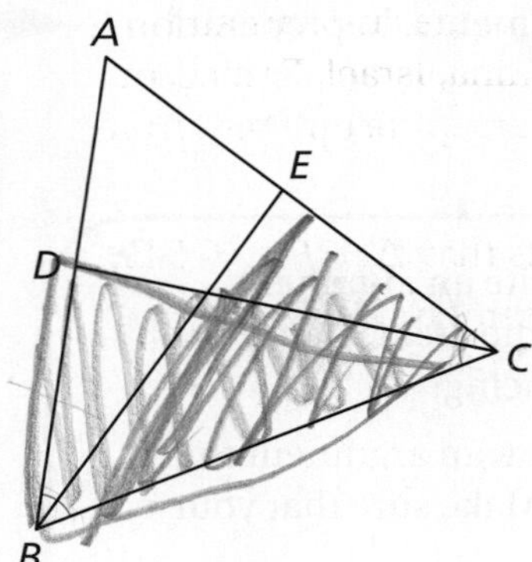

Ruth decided that $\triangle BDC \cong \triangle CEB$. She used the following argument.

- The triangles share side $\overline{BC}$.
- This, with the given information, shows that $\triangle BDC \cong \triangle CEB$ by SAS.

Explain what is wrong with Ruth's argument.

7. Write an argument to show that the measure of one of a triangle's exterior angles is equal to the sum of the measures of the two remote interior angles. Use the figure below to show that $m\angle DAB = m\angle B + m\angle C$.

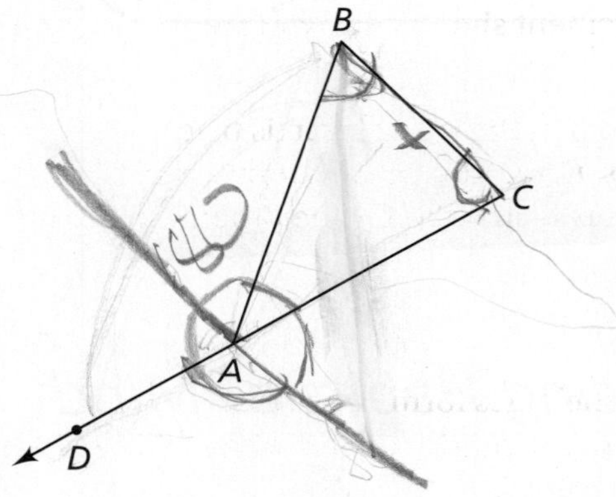

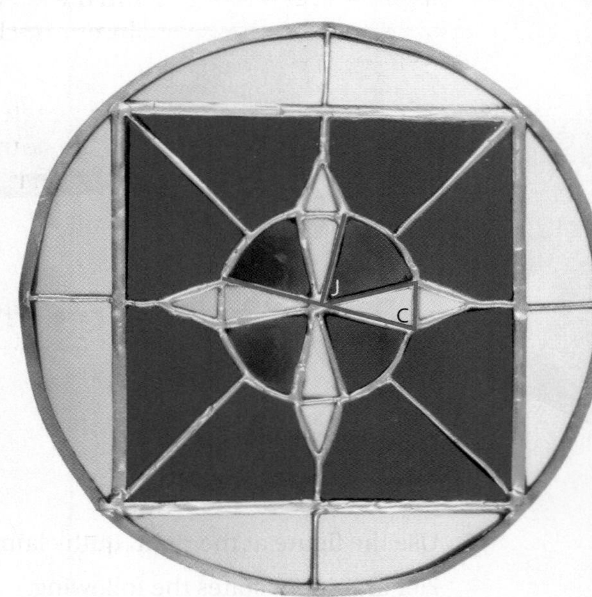

In this stained glass suncatcher, which is greater, $m\angle C$ or $m\angle J$? Give a convincing argument.

Maintain Your Skills

8. Prove each of the following statements using algebra.

   a. The sum of two even numbers is even.

   b. The sum of two odd numbers is even.

   c. The product of an even number and another integer is even.

   d. **Take It Further** The product of two odd numbers is odd.

2.10 What Does a Proof Look Like?

As you might imagine, the way that you make your argument in a proof can vary. The rules of reasoning govern the logic of the proof, no matter who writes it. However, the way the proof looks depends on the customs and culture of the country where you study. Schools in China, Israel, France, or Russia sometimes teach ways to present proofs that are quite different from the methods taught in most American schools.

Following the diagram below are four different proofs that $\triangle ABE \cong \triangle DCE$. The given information is $\overline{AB} \parallel \overline{CD}$, and E is the midpoint of $\overline{AD}$.

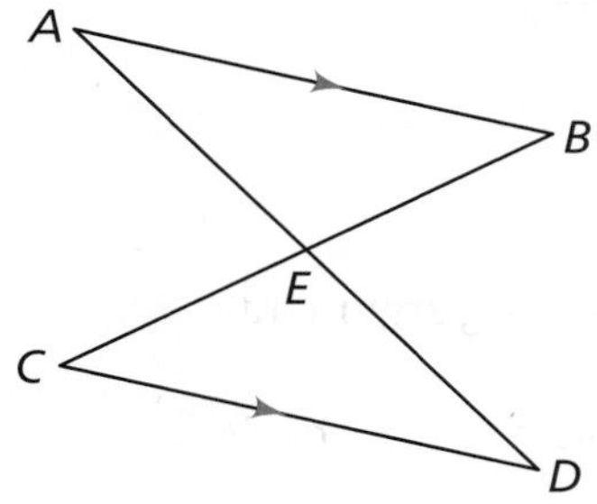

Two-Column Statement-Reason Proof

In the two-column statement-reason proof below, a set of true statements, logically ordered, appears in the left column. The given information usually appears first in the left column. The last statement shows what you are trying to prove.

The right column explains why each statement in the left column is true. You usually state the reasons as assumptions, theorems, or definitions, or as "givens." Givens are statements that one assumes are true for the proof.

Statements	**Reasons**
1. $\overline{AB} \parallel \overline{CD}$	1. given
2. $\angle ABE \cong \angle DCE$	2. Parallel lines form congruent alternate interior angles with a transversal.
3. $\angle BAE \cong \angle CDE$	3. Parallel lines form congruent alternate interior angles with a transversal.
4. E is the midpoint of $\overline{AD}$.	4. given
5. $\overline{AE} \cong \overline{DE}$	5. The midpoint is defined as the point that divides a segment into two congruent parts.
6. $\triangle ABE \cong \triangle DCE$	6. AAS

Paragraph Proof

In the paragraph proof below, a series of sentences fit together logically to establish that the two triangles are congruent. The sentences are written in paragraph form.

> Because $\overline{AB} \parallel \overline{CD}$, the alternate interior angles are congruent. So $\angle ABE \cong \angle DCE$ and $\angle BAE \cong \angle CDE$. Also, because E is the midpoint of $\overline{AD}$, $\overline{AE} \cong \overline{DE}$. Therefore, $\triangle ABE \cong \triangle DCE$ by AAS.

Notice that a paragraph proof consists of several sentences that contain both words and mathematical symbols.

Outline-Style Proof

Students who study in China may use an outline-style proof. You can use the symbol $\because$ meaning *because* to indicate the given information. The symbol $\therefore$ means *therefore*. It indicates that the information follows from the given information. You write the important reasons inside the parentheses.

$\because$ $\overline{AB}$ is parallel to $\overline{CD}$.

$\therefore$ $\angle ABE \cong \angle DCE$ (alternate interior angles)

$\therefore$ $\angle BAE \cong \angle CDE$ (alternate interior angles)

$\because$ E is the midpoint of $\overline{AD}$.

$\therefore$ $\overline{AE} \cong \overline{ED}$ (definition of midpoint)

$\therefore$ $\triangle ABE \cong \triangle DCE$ (AAS)

Students who study in Russia may use another type of outline-style proof. The proof below illustrates this type of proof. You make an outline of the written statements and justify each statement.

Given that $\overline{AB}$ is parallel to $\overline{CD}$ and E is the midpoint of $\overline{AD}$, $\triangle ABE \cong \triangle DCE$ by AAS because

1. $\angle ABE \cong \angle DCE$ (PAI Theorem)
2. $\angle BAE \cong \angle CDE$ (PAI Theorem)
3. $\overline{AE} \cong \overline{DE}$ (definition of midpoint)

For Discussion

1. Each of the four proofs above uses the AAS triangle congruence postulate to show that $\triangle ABE \cong \triangle DCE$. What else do the four proofs have in common?
2. What are the advantages and disadvantages of each type of proof?

You have just learned several different ways to present a mathematical proof. However, you may still be wondering, "Why bother doing a proof at all?" This is a surprisingly complex question. The need for proof is a result of tradition, necessity, and culture.

Mathematicians are experimenters performing thought experiments. They build models, gather data, and use data to make conjectures. To reach a valid conclusion, mathematicians rely on deduction and proof. New insights, or results, come from reasoning about things that must follow logically from what they already know or assume.

The combination of deduction and experimentation is one of the distinguishing characteristics of mathematical research. The results of mathematical research do not hold true because they are *observed* to hold true. Instead, mathematicians derive results logically from some very simple assumptions.

Early in your geometry course, you prove that two triangles are congruent for two reasons. Triangle concepts are important, and the structure of these proofs is relatively simple. In most of the proofs that follow, you can follow a straightforward plan.

- Determine which parts of the two triangles are congruent.
- Determine whether you have enough information to prove that the triangles are congruent. Which set of congruent parts (SSS, SAS, ASA, or AAS) can you use to prove that they are congruent?
- Organize the information. Then write the proof.

Exercises *Practicing Habits of Mind*

Check Your Understanding

1. Use the following conjecture to answer parts (a) and (b). The sum of the measures of the interior angles of an n-gon is $(n - 2)180°$.

a. Describe an experiment you can perform to test this conjecture.

b. Write a deductive proof to prove the conjecture.

An n-gon is a polygon with n sides, where n is a whole number greater than or equal to 3.

For Exercises 2–4, use each figure and the given information to write a proof. Use a proof style described in this lesson.

2. Given $\overline{AB} \cong \overline{CB}$ and $\overline{BD} \cong \overline{BE}$

Prove $\triangle ABD \cong \triangle CBE$

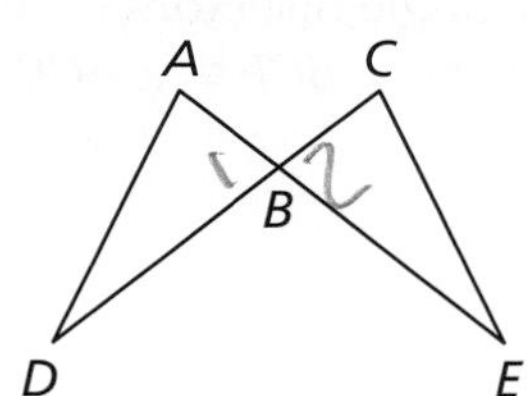

3. **Given** $\overline{SV} \cong \overline{UT}$ and $\overline{ST} \cong \overline{UV}$

Prove $\triangle STV \cong \triangle UVT$

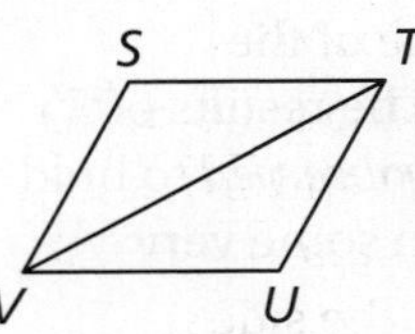

4. **Given** $SEBW$ is a square.

Prove $\triangle SWB \cong \triangle EBW$

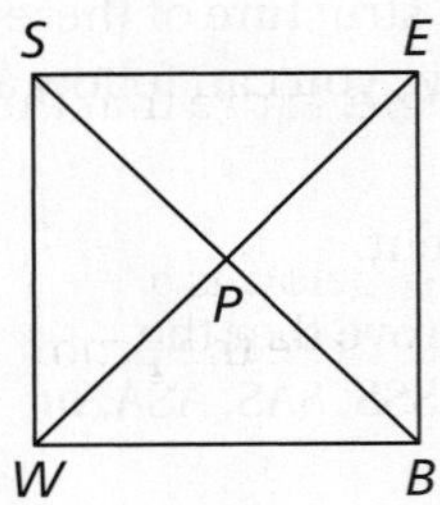

On Your Own

5. **Standardized Test Prep** In the figure below, $\triangle ABC$ is an isosceles triangle with $\overline{AC} \cong \overline{BC}$. $\overline{CD}$ is a median of $\triangle ABC$. $\overline{CE}$ bisects $\angle ACD$. $\overline{CF}$ bisects $\angle BCD$. Which of the following is a correct way to prove that $\triangle ACE \cong \triangle BCF$?

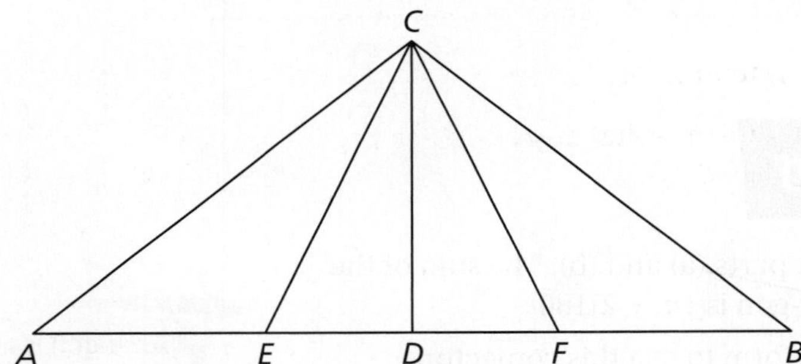

A. It is *not* possible to prove that $\triangle ACE \cong \triangle BCF$ based on the information given.

B. $\overline{AD} \cong \overline{BD}$, since D is the midpoint of $\overline{AB}$. So $\triangle ACD \cong \triangle BCD$ by SSS. This implies $\angle A \cong \angle B$ and $\angle ACD \cong \angle BCD$ by CPCTC. So $m\angle ACD = m\angle BCD$. Because $\overline{CE}$ and $\overline{CF}$ are angle bisectors, $m\angle BCF = \frac{1}{2}m\angle BCD = \frac{1}{2}m\angle ACD = m\angle ACE$. So $\angle BCF \cong \angle ACE$. Then $\triangle ACE \cong \triangle BCF$ by ASA.

Remember...

An **isosceles triangle** is a triangle with at least two congruent sides. You call the congruent sides **legs.** The **vertex angle** is the angle formed by the two legs. You call the third side the **base.** The angles on either side of the base are the **base angles.**

C. Point D is the midpoint of $\overline{AB}$, so $\overline{AD} \cong \overline{BD}$. Then $\triangle ACD \cong \triangle BCD$ by SSS and $\overline{AE} \cong \overline{FB}$ by CPCTC. This implies $\triangle ACE \cong \triangle BCF$ by SAS.

D. Since $\overline{CD}$ is a median of $\triangle ABC$, D is the midpoint of $\overline{AB}$. So $\overline{AD} \cong \overline{BD}$. Because $\overline{CE}$ and $\overline{CF}$ are angle bisectors, they divide $\overline{AD}$ and $\overline{BD}$, respectively, into two congruent segments. So $\overline{AE} \cong \overline{ED}$ and $\overline{BF} \cong \overline{FD}$. Because $\triangle ABC$ is an isosceles triangle with $\angle A \cong \angle B$, the sides opposite those angles are congruent. So $\overline{AC} \cong \overline{BC}$. Since $\overline{AE} \cong \overline{BF}$, $\triangle ACE \cong \triangle BCF$ by SAS.

6. Draw an isosceles triangle and the bisector of its vertex angle. Prove that the two smaller triangles formed are congruent.

7. In $\triangle XMY$, $\overline{XE}$ is a median, and $\overline{XY} \cong \overline{XM}$. The bulleted list below is a sketch of a proof that $\triangle XEM \cong \triangle XEY$. Study the list. Then write the proof in either two-column, paragraph, or outline style.

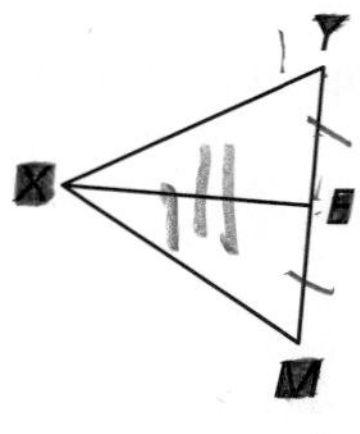

- $\overline{XE}$ is a median, so E is the midpoint of $\overline{MY}$. Then $\overline{ME} \cong \overline{EY}$.
- $\overline{XY} \cong \overline{XM}$ is given.
- The two triangles share $\overline{XE}$.
- The triangles have three pairs of congruent sides.

8. What's Wrong Here? Below is a proof that shows that any two lines are parallel. Explain what is wrong with the proof.

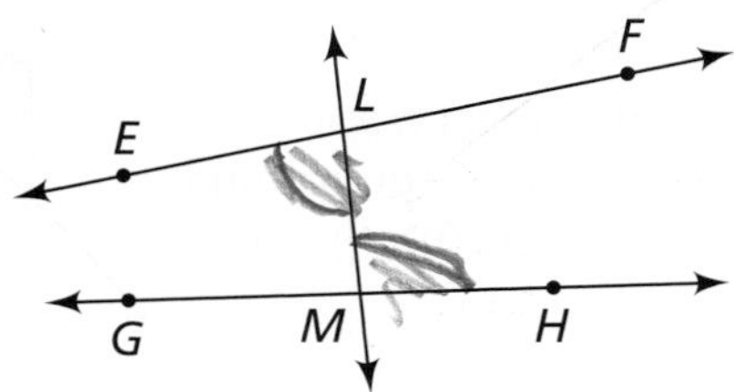

Suppose $\overleftrightarrow{EF}$ and $\overleftrightarrow{GH}$ are lines. Draw transversal $\overleftrightarrow{LM}$.

$\because \angle ELM$ and $\angle HML$ are alternate interior angles.

$\therefore \angle ELM \cong \angle HML$

$\therefore \overleftrightarrow{EF} \parallel \overleftrightarrow{GH}$ (AIP Theorem)

9. In the figure at the right, $\overleftrightarrow{AB} \parallel \overleftrightarrow{ED}$ and $\overline{AB} \cong \overline{ED}$.

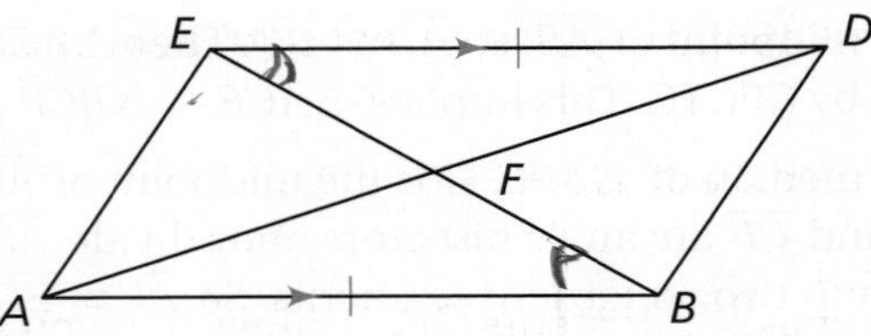

a. Timothy uses this information to prove that $\triangle ABF \cong \triangle DEF$. Explain why his paragraph proof is incorrect.

It is given that $\overleftrightarrow{AB} \parallel \overleftrightarrow{ED}$, so $\angle DEB \cong \angle ABE$ because parallel lines form congruent alternate interior angles with a transversal. And $\angle AFB \cong \angle DFE$ because they are vertical angles, and vertical angles are congruent. It is also given that $\overline{AB} \cong \overline{ED}$, so $\triangle ABF \cong \triangle DEF$ by ASA.

b. Is it possible to prove that $\triangle ABF \cong \triangle DEF$? If so, write a correct proof.

10. To show that a statement is true, mathematicians require deductive proof. Explain how you can convince someone that the statement "All horses are the same color" is *not* true.

11. Use circle P below to prove that the three triangles are congruent. Point P is the center of the circle.

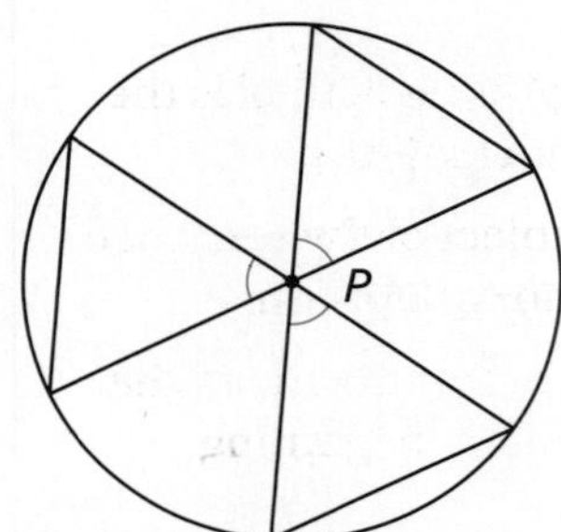

Maintain Your Skills

12. Use this conjecture about prime numbers. "Choose an integer n and square it. Then find the sum of the original whole number, its square, and 41. The sum is a prime number." For each value of n in parts (b)–(i) below, determine whether the sum is a prime number.

a. What is a prime number?

b. $n = 1$	c. $n = 2$	d. $n = 3$	e. $n = -1$
f. $n = -2$	g. $n = -10$	h. $n = 15$	i. $n = 100$

j. Determine whether the conjecture is true. If it is true, prove it. If it is not true, find a counterexample.

Remember...

A counterexample is an example that makes the statement false.

2.11 Analyzing the Statement to Prove

Usually, statements that you prove are not expressed in the following Given-Prove form.

Given isosceles triangle ABC with $AB = BC$
Prove $\angle A \cong \angle C$

Instead, you may make statements about things that you suspect are true, such as the results of an experiment. Most likely, you use English sentences to make these statements. For instance, you might say, "Vertical angles are congruent," or "Base angles of an isosceles triangle are congruent," or "If it rains this afternoon, then practice will be canceled."

In the above statements, how do you know what to prove? You can break each sentence into two parts, a hypothesis and a conclusion. In the sentence "Vertical angles are congruent," the hypothesis is "The angles are vertical angles." The conclusion is "The angles are congruent." Then you can rewrite the sentence "Vertical angles are congruent." You can write, "If two angles are vertical angles, then they are congruent."

Remember...

The **hypothesis** is what you are assuming is true. The **conclusion** states what you need to prove.

Here are two rules of thumb that may help you recognize each part of a sentence.

- If a sentence appears in *if-then* form, the clause beginning with *if* is the hypothesis. The clause beginning with *then* is the conclusion.
- If a sentence does not appear in *if-then* form, the subject of the sentence is the hypothesis. The predicate of the sentence is the conclusion.

Sometimes the word *then* is not stated. For example, "If it is raining this afternoon, practice will be canceled."

The fact that a sentence states a conclusion does not necessarily mean that the conclusion is true. Carefully read the table below before beginning the exercises.

Sentence	Hypothesis	Conclusion
If two parallel lines are cut by a transversal, the alternate interior angles are congruent.	Two parallel lines are cut by a transversal.	The alternate interior angles are congruent.
The base angles of an isosceles triangle are congruent.	Two angles are base angles of an isosceles triangle.	These two angles are congruent.
Two triangles with the same area are congruent.	Two triangles have the same area.	The two triangles are congruent.
Congruent triangles have the same area.	Two triangles are congruent.	They have the same area.
People with large hands have large feet.	Certain people have large hands.	These people have large feet.
Out of sight, out of mind.	Something is out of sight.	It is also out of mind.

Exercises *Practicing Habits of Mind*

Check Your Understanding

1. Which of the statements in the table on the previous page are not necessarily true? Explain.

2. In each sentence below, identify the hypothesis and conclusion.

   a. If two lines form congruent alternate interior angles with a transversal, then the lines are parallel.

   b. If n is any whole number, $n^2 + n + 41$ is prime.

   c. Two triangles are congruent if three sides of one triangle are congruent to three sides of the other triangle.

   d. Two lines that are parallel to a third line are also parallel to each other.

On Your Own

3. **Standardized Test Prep** Which is the hypothesis of the following statement? If two angles are congruent, then they have the same measure.

   A. Two angles are congruent. **B.** They have the same measure.
   C. Two angles are not congruent. **D.** They do not have the same measure.

For Exercises 4–9, draw a picture that illustrates the hypothesis. Then determine whether the statement is true. If a statement is true, give a proof. If a statement is not true, give a counterexample.

4. In a plane, two lines that are perpendicular to the same line are parallel to each other.
5. A line that bisects an angle of a triangle also bisects the side that is opposite the angle.
6. Equilateral quadrilaterals are **equiangular** (all angles congruent).
7. If a triangle has two congruent angles, it is isosceles.
8. Equiangular triangles are equilateral.
9. Equiangular quadrilaterals are equilateral.

Maintain Your Skills

10. In a right $\triangle ABC$ with hypotenuse $\overline{CB}$, $AB = \frac{1}{2}AC$. Prove that $(CB)^2 = 5(AB)^2$. Then write this result as a statement in if-then form.

2.12 Analysis of a Proof

You have had some practice writing proofs. However, the real question is, how do you come up with a proof in the first place? Coming up with a proof is sometimes called the "analysis of the proof."

Analysis is always necessary before writing a proof. Sometimes analysis is very brief and occurs almost without you noticing it. If you readily find the logic underlying the proof, then writing the proof is just a matter of expressing the logic clearly.

How can you begin a proof if you do not yet understand the logic? Suppose that you have many facts and clues, but none of them points to a solution. In this chapter, you will learn three techniques for analyzing proofs.

- visual scan
- flowchart
- reverse list

You may find that a single method makes the most sense to you and becomes your main tool for analysis. However, to be skilled at analysis, you will need to use all three techniques. In fact, if you are having trouble understanding a proof using one method, it can be quite helpful to switch from one technique to another.

The Visual Scan

A visual scan is a strategy that involves careful examination of the figures in the proof. First, you can mark a sketch of the figure to show all of the known congruent parts. Next, you can mark additional parts that you can conclude are congruent. Finally, study the figure and a strategy for writing the proof may become clear.

The visual-scan strategy may be the simplest way to analyze a proof. The strategy is similar to doing mental math. You simply see what you have to do.

A basketball player visually scans the court before passing the ball.

Example 1

Given E is the midpoint of $\overline{HF}$. $\overline{EG} \perp \overline{HF}$.

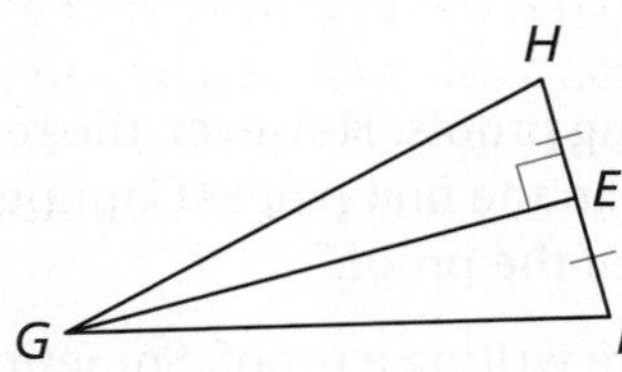

Prove $\overline{HG} \cong \overline{FG}$

First, sketch $\triangle FGH$. Then mark the triangle showing the given information. The marked triangle may suggest the following proof.

- Show that $\triangle HEG \cong \triangle FEG$ by SAS.
- Then conclude that $\overline{HG} \cong \overline{FG}$ because they are corresponding parts of congruent triangles.

You can use this strategy to write the proof below.

Proof Point E is the midpoint of $\overline{HF}$. So $\overline{HE} \cong \overline{FE}$. $\overline{EG} \perp \overline{HF}$. So $m\angle GEF = m\angle GEH = 90°$. It follows that $\angle GEF \cong \angle GEH$. Triangle HEG and $\triangle FEG$ share $\overline{EG}$. So $\triangle HEG \cong \triangle FEG$ by SAS. Since corresponding parts of congruent triangles are congruent, $\overline{HG} \cong \overline{FG}$.

For You to Do

1. Use the visual-scan strategy. Prove that the base angles of an isosceles triangle are congruent. Below is an outline for your proof.
   - First sketch an isosceles triangle. Label its vertices.
   - Construct the bisector of the vertex angle. Label the point where the bisector intersects the base of the triangle.
   - Show that the two triangles formed by the bisector are congruent.
   - Conclude that the base angles of the isosceles triangle are congruent.

For Discussion

2. How can you use a proof like the one above to prove that an equilateral triangle is equiangular?

In the proofs above, you used the CPCTC strategy to prove that corresponding sides or corresponding angles of two triangles are congruent. To show that two segments or angles are congruent, you can use this strategy:

- First, find two triangles that contain the segments or the angles that you are trying to prove congruent. Prove that the triangles are congruent.
- Then, conclude that the segments or the angles are congruent, because they are corresponding parts of congruent triangles.

This strategy is simple and direct. Can you only use it with triangles, though?

Keep the CPCTC strategy in mind as you work on this lesson. Notice how often you use it.

The Flowchart

The flowchart strategy is a "top-down" analysis technique. For instance, at the top of the flowchart you write statements about what you know is true. Below each statement you write conclusions based on the statement. You continue to write statements, moving down in the flowchart, until you reach the desired conclusion. An example of a flowchart is shown in Example 2.

Example 2

Make a flowchart for the following proof.

Given isosceles $\triangle ABC$ with $\overline{AB} \cong \overline{CB}$ and $\overline{AE} \cong \overline{CD}$

Prove $\angle BDE \cong \angle BED$

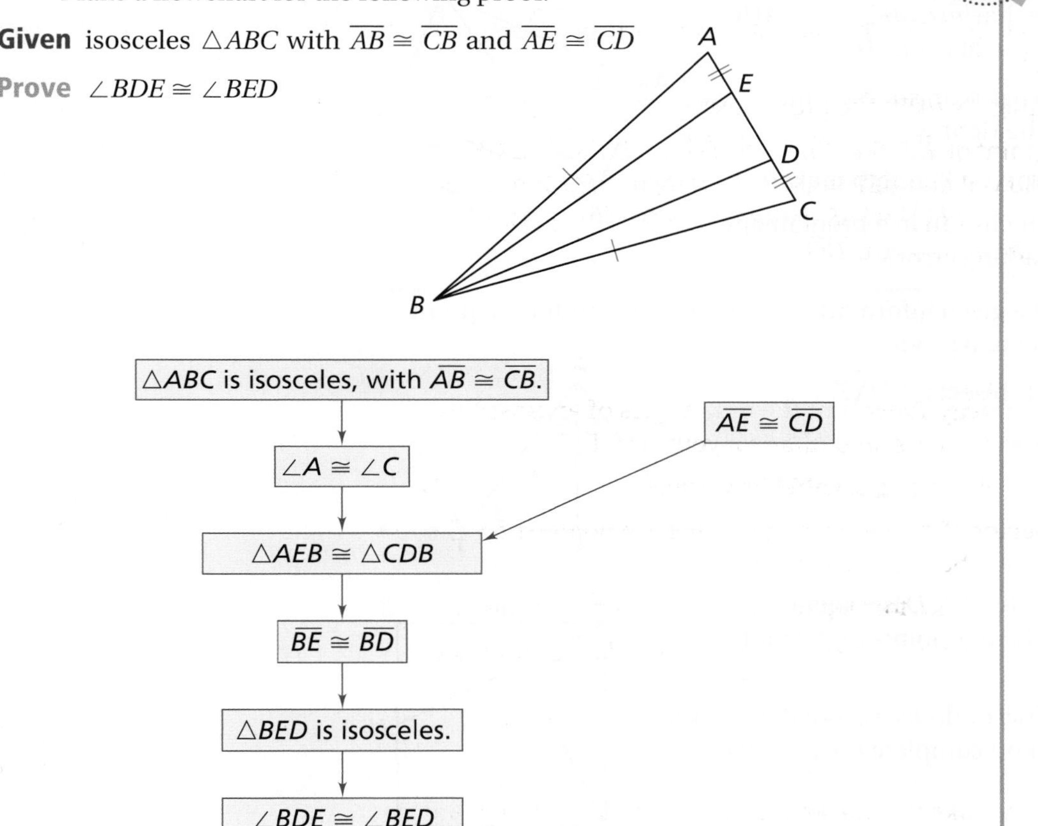

For You to Do

3. Write the proof that is outlined in the flowchart above.

A flowchart strategy has several advantages. When a flowchart is complete, it forms an outline for writing the actual proof. A flowchart also gives you a way to investigate and organize what you know, even if the entire proof is still unclear. You may also write any extra information in the flowchart. This information may help you generate alternate ways to write the proof.

Habits of Mind

Be concise. When you write a proof, leave out any unnecessary information. A well-written proof takes the most direct route through the flowchart.

Exercises *Practicing Habits of Mind*

Check Your Understanding

1. What's Wrong Here? Kenneth is given the following problem.

Given that $\overline{AC}$ and $\overline{BH}$ bisect each other and that $\overline{AB} \cong \overline{CH}$, show that $m\angle ABC = m\angle AHC$. What type of quadrilateral is $ABCH$?

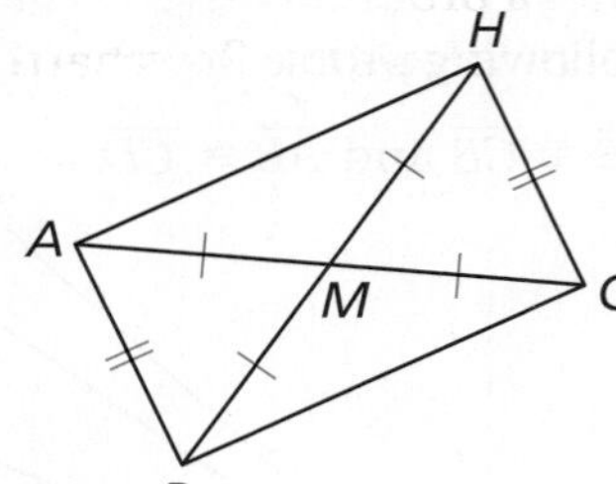

Kenneth uses the visual-scan strategy and marks the figure at the right.

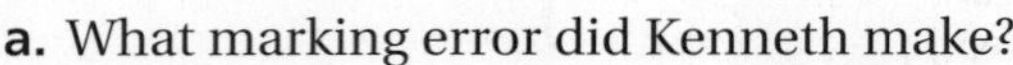

a. What marking error did Kenneth make?

b. What incorrect conclusion in a proof might result from his marking error?

2. Use the figure and the given information. Make a flowchart for the proof without writing the actual proof.

Given $\angle 1 \cong \angle 2$. $\overline{XY}$ bisects $\angle MXT$.

Prove $\overline{MY} \cong \overline{YT}$

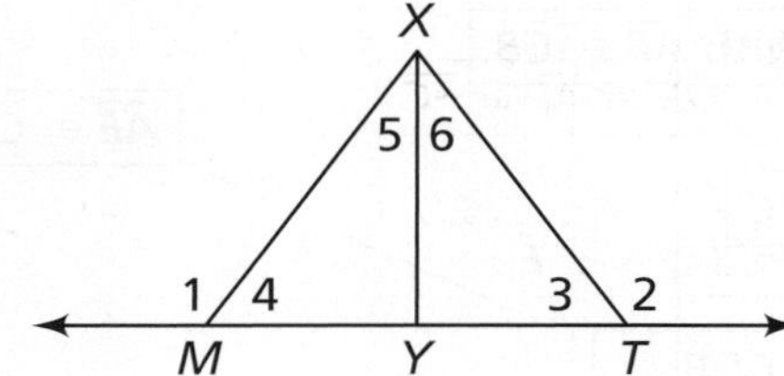

3. In the figure at the right, $ABCD$ is a square. Points M and N are the midpoints of $\overline{AB}$ and $\overline{BC}$, respectively.

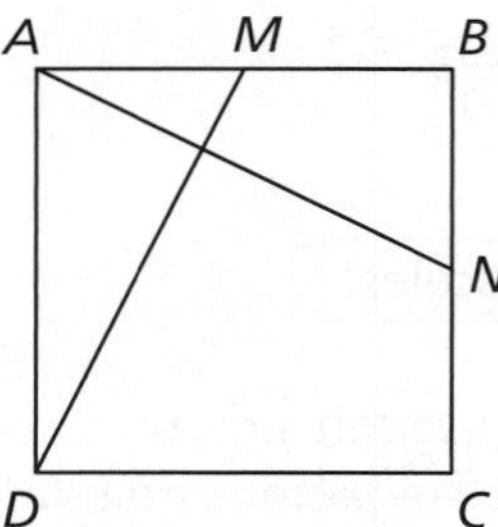

a. The flowchart below outlines a proof that shows $\overline{AN} \cong \overline{DM}$. Copy and complete the flowchart.

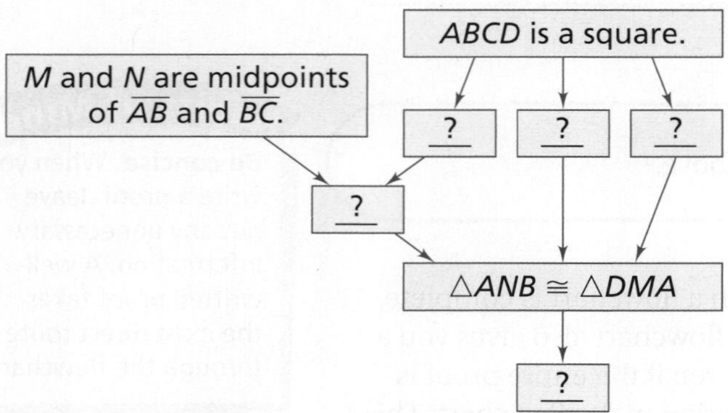

b. Use the completed flowchart to write the proof.

On Your Own

4. **Standardized Test Prep** $\triangle ABC$ is an isosceles triangle with $\overline{AB} \cong \overline{AC}$. $\overline{AE}$, $\overline{BF}$, and $\overline{CD}$ are medians.

The flowchart below outlines a proof that shows that $\overline{FB} \cong \overline{DC}$. Which of the statements below best completes the flowchart?

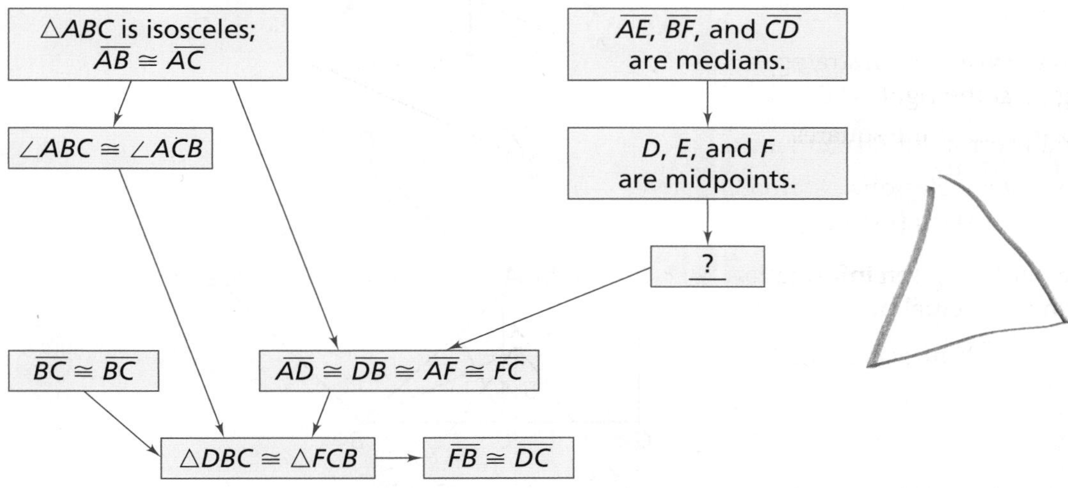

A. $\angle ABF \cong \angle FBC$

B. $\overline{AD} \cong \overline{DB}$; $\overline{AF} \cong \overline{FC}$; $\overline{BE} \cong \overline{EC}$

C. $\overline{AE} \cong \overline{AE}$

D. $\triangle ABE \cong \triangle ACE$

For Exercise 5, use the visual scan strategy to analyze the proof. Copy the figure onto a separate piece of paper, and mark the given information. Then write an outline for the proof.

5. **Given** $\overline{HJ} \cong \overline{HL}$ and $\overline{JK} \cong \overline{LK}$
Prove $\triangle HJM \cong \triangle HLM$

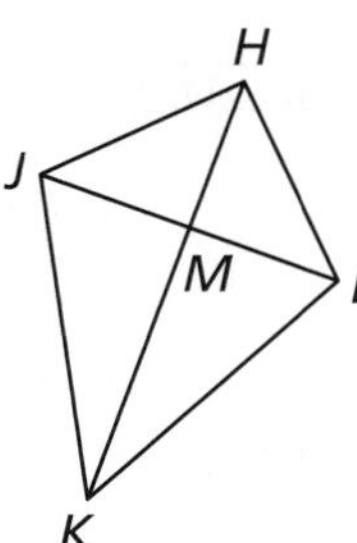

6. **Given** $\overleftrightarrow{GF} \perp \overleftrightarrow{GH}$ and $\overleftrightarrow{GJ} \perp \overleftrightarrow{GK}$
Prove $\angle JGF \cong \angle KGH$

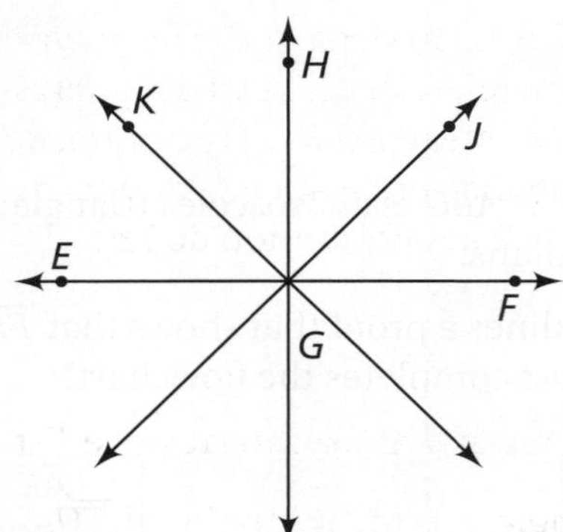

7. **Given** $FACG$ and $DABE$ are squares.
Prove $\triangle FAB \cong \triangle CAD$

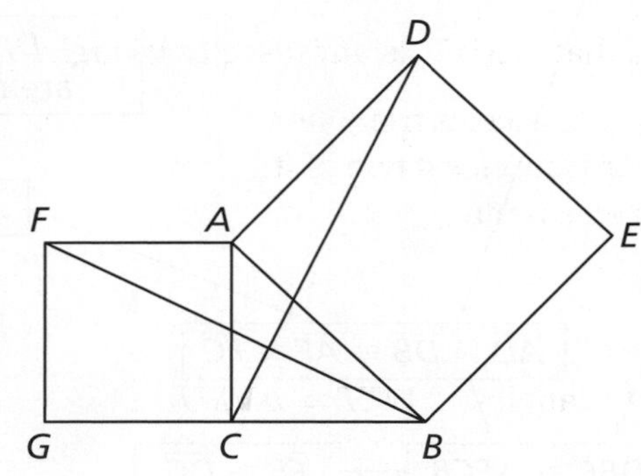

8. **Given** $\triangle LJM$ and $\triangle LKN$ are equilateral.
Prove $\overline{MK} \cong \overline{NJ}$

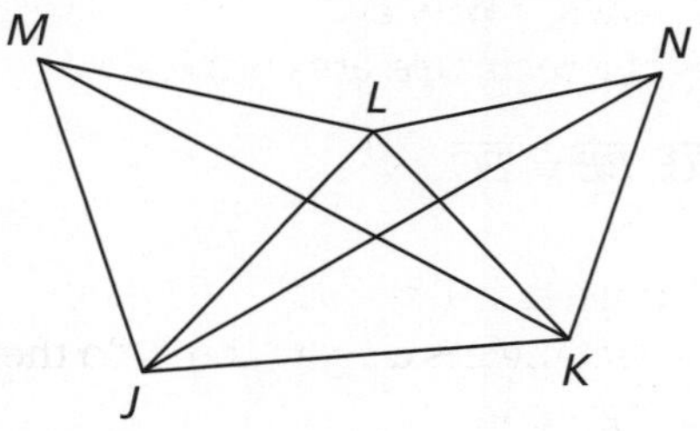

9. **Given** $\triangle QRT$ is an isosceles triangle. $\overline{QT} \cong \overline{TR}$. $\overline{VR}$ and $\overline{UQ}$ are medians.
Prove $VR = UQ$

Go Online
Pearsonsuccessnet.com

10. **Given** Point P is on the perpendicular bisector of $\overline{LM}$.
Prove $PL = PM$

Maintain Your Skills

11. Draw a coordinate plane. Plot points $O(0, 0)$ and $A(6, 0)$. Choose and label point B on the line $x = 3$ such that B is *not* on the x-axis. Prove that $\triangle AOB$ is an isosceles triangle.

Habits of Mind

Visualize. Before you write the proof, sketch a coordinate plane. Draw $\triangle AOB$ and the line $x = 3$. Then use the visual-scan strategy.

2.13 The Reverse List

When you use the visual-scan strategy or the flowchart strategy, you start with what you know and work toward the final conclusion that you want to prove. The reverse-list strategy works in the opposite direction. You start with the information that you want to prove and work backward. You repeatedly ask yourself, "What information do I need?" and "What strategy can I use to prove that?"

> **Habits of Mind**
>
> **Different Approaches** The reverse-list strategy is a bottom-up strategy rather than a top-down strategy.

Make a reverse list.

Below is an analysis of a proof that uses the reverse-list strategy.

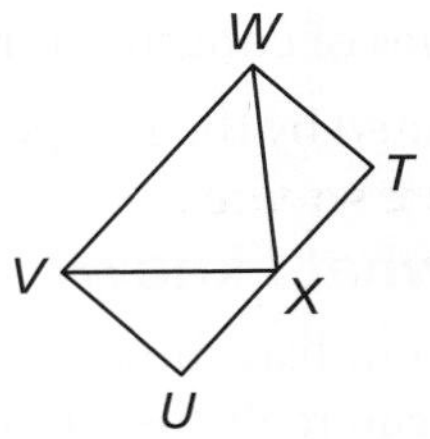

Given $TUVW$ is a rectangle. X is the midpoint of $\overline{TU}$.

Prove $\triangle XWV$ is isosceles.

You need to prove that $\triangle XWV$ is an isosceles triangle.

Need $\triangle XWV$ is an isosceles triangle.
Use A triangle is isosceles if two of its sides are congruent.

Need $\overline{VX} \cong \overline{WX}$
Use CPCTC

Need congruent triangles: $\triangle WXT \cong \triangle VXU$
Use SAS

Need two congruent sides: $\overline{TW} \cong \overline{UV}$
Use Opposite sides of a rectangle are congruent.

Need $TUVW$ is a rectangle.
Use given information

Need two congruent angles: $\angle T \cong \angle U$
Use Each angle in a rectangle is a right angle. So the four angles in a rectangle are congruent.

Need $TUVW$ is a rectangle.
Use given information

Need two congruent sides: $\overline{TX} \cong \overline{UX}$
Use The midpoint of a segment divides the segment into two congruent segments.

Need X is the midpoint of $\overline{TU}$.
Use given information

> **Habits of Mind**
>
> **Draw a diagram.** When you use the reverse-list strategy, how do you know which sides, angles, or triangles to try to prove congruent? A careful sketch often helps.

A complete reverse-list analysis outlines the proof in reverse order. Below is the proof that is outlined in the reverse list above.

Proof Point X is the midpoint of $\overline{TU}$. So $\overline{TX} \cong \overline{UX}$. $TUVW$ is a rectangle. So its opposite sides are congruent, and its four right angles are congruent. So $\overline{TW} \cong \overline{UV}$ and $\angle T \cong \angle U$. Therefore $\triangle WXT \cong \triangle VXU$ by SAS. So $\overline{VX} \cong \overline{WX}$ by CPCTC. This tells us that $\triangle XWV$ is an isosceles triangle.

How do you decide which strategies to use when you write a reverse list? There is no foolproof method. However, there is a straightforward way to narrow down the number of strategies.

What results prove the needed conclusion?

Look back through your notes or back in your book. Find all the previously established results that you have used to prove a needed conclusion. For example, in the reverse list above, you needed to show that $\overline{TX} \cong \overline{UX}$. This is your needed conclusion. So you should look for previously established results with the conclusion "congruent segments." At this point, you have only used a few.

- The legs of an isosceles triangle are congruent.
- The corresponding sides of congruent triangles are congruent.
- The two segments formed by the midpoint of a segment are congruent.

Which results relate to what I know?

Once you narrow down your list, you go through the results one by one. Decide which result you can really use to prove your conclusion. How do you choose? You decide whether a relationship exists between the conclusion you need and each result. In this case, you can go down the list of results and ask a question for each one.

- Are $\overline{TX}$ and $\overline{UX}$ the sides of an isosceles triangle? No; $\overline{TX}$ and $\overline{UX}$ are not sides of the same triangle.
- Are $\overline{TX}$ and $\overline{UX}$ the corresponding sides of two congruent triangles? $\overline{TX}$ and $\overline{UX}$ are the corresponding sides of $\triangle WXT$ and $\triangle VXU$. The reason you want to prove that $\overline{TX} \cong \overline{UX}$ in the first place is so you can prove that $\triangle WXT \cong \triangle VXU$.
- Are $\overline{TX}$ and $\overline{UX}$ two segments that are formed by the midpoint of a segment? Yes; you know from the given information that X is the midpoint of $\overline{TU}$.

When you use the reverse-list strategy to analyze a proof, here are some points to remember:

- Use the given information to prove a needed result when possible.
- Use CPCTC to prove that corresponding sides or corresponding angles of congruent triangles are congruent.
- Right now, you have four ways to prove that two triangles are congruent: SSS, SAS, ASA, and AAS.
- The reverse-list strategy almost always works.

You may go down some dead ends before you hit the right path.

Exercises Practicing Habits of Mind

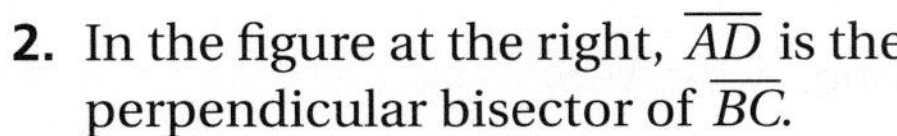

Check Your Understanding

1. In the figure at the right, P is a point on the perpendicular bisector of $\overline{AB}$.
   a. Make a reverse list that you can use to prove that $\triangle APB$ is an isosceles triangle.
   b. Write a proof that shows $\triangle APB$ is an isosceles triangle. Use your reverse list from part (a).

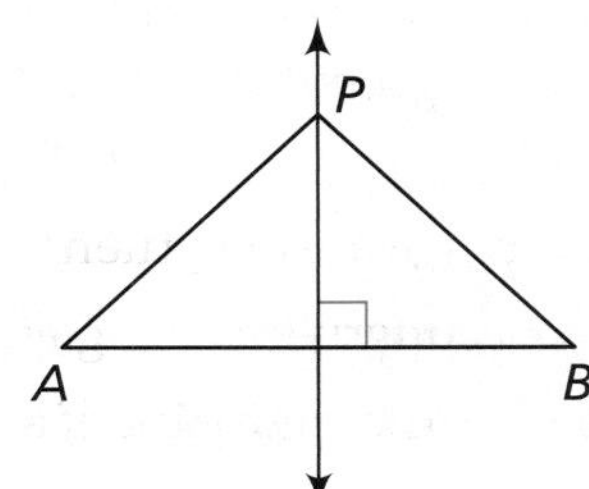

2. In the figure at the right, $\overline{AD}$ is the perpendicular bisector of $\overline{BC}$.
   a. Which triangles must be congruent?
   b. Write a proof that shows that the two triangles in part (a) are congruent.

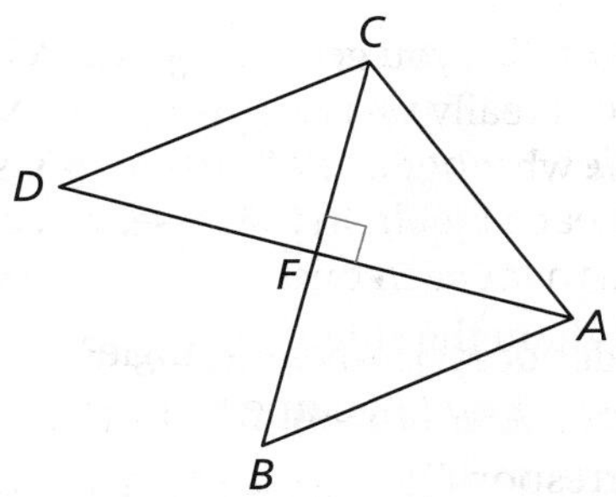

On Your Own

In Exercises 3–8, prove each statement. Use a reverse list to write each proof.

3. If a triangle is isosceles, then the medians from its legs to the vertices of its base angles are congruent.
4. If a triangle is isosceles, then the bisectors of its base angles are congruent.
5. If two altitudes of a triangle are congruent, then the triangle is isosceles.
6. If a triangle is isosceles, then the altitudes drawn to its legs are congruent.
7. In isosceles triangle ABC, $\overline{AC} \cong \overline{BC}$. Point M is the midpoint of $\overline{AC}$. Point N is the midpoint of $\overline{CB}$. Prove that $\triangle CMN$ is an isosceles triangle.
8. **Take It Further** In the two triangles below, $\overline{AC} \cong \overline{DF}$ and $\overline{CB} \cong \overline{FE}$. $\overline{AM}$ and $\overline{DN}$ are congruent medians. Show that $\triangle ABC \cong \triangle DEF$.

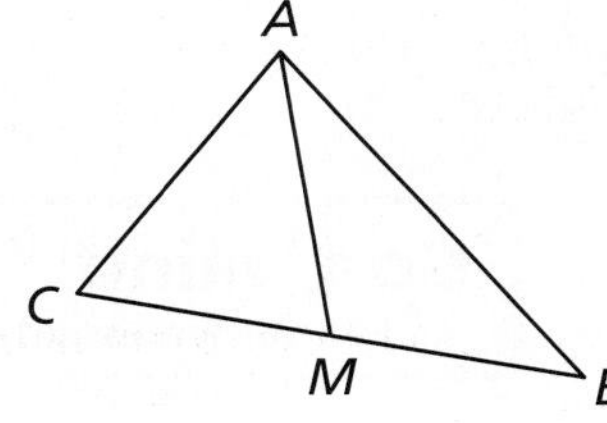

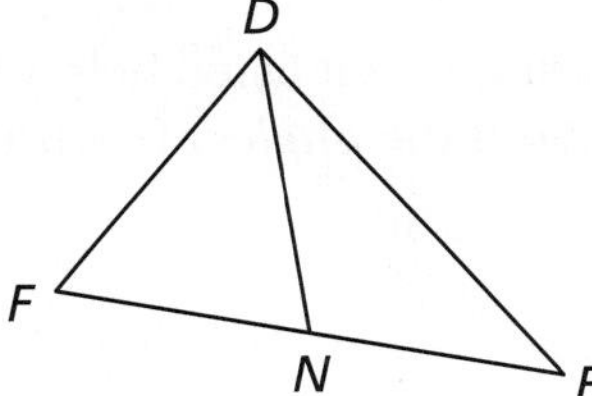

9. **Standardized Test Prep** Triangle ABC at the right is an isosceles triangle with $\overline{AB} \cong \overline{AC}$ and $\angle ABC \cong \angle ACB$. $\overline{CD}$ is the bisector of $\angle ACB$. $\overline{BE}$ is the bisector of $\angle ABC$. Suppose you want to prove that $\overline{EF} \cong \overline{DF}$.

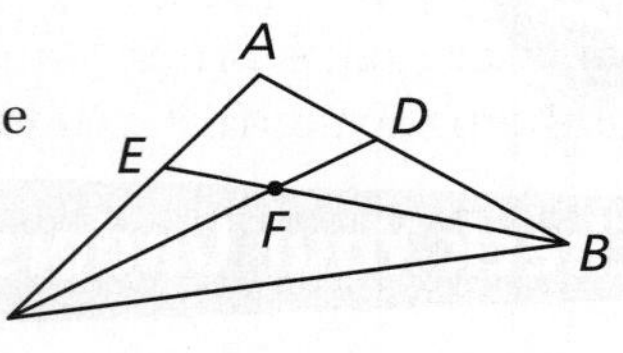

Which of the statements and reasons below complete the following reverse list?

Need $\overline{EF} \cong \overline{DF}$
Use CPCTC

Need I
Use I

Need II
Use II

Need III
Use III

Need $\triangle BCE \cong \triangle CBD$
Use ASA

Need $\overline{BC} \cong \overline{BC}$
Use The two triangles share the side.

Need $\angle ACD \cong \angle DCB \cong \angle ABE \cong \angle EBC$
Use definition of congruent angles

Need $m\angle ACD = m\angle DCB = m\angle ABE = m\angle EBC$
Use definition of angle bisector

Need $\overline{CD}$ is the bisector of $\angle ACB$. $\overline{BE}$ is the bisector of $\angle ABC$.
Use given

Need $\frac{1}{2} m\angle ABC = \frac{1}{2} m\angle ACB$
Use multiplication property of equality

Need $m\angle ABC = m\angle ACB$
Use definition of congruent angles

Need $\angle ABC \cong \angle ACB$
Use given

A. I. $\triangle BDF \cong \triangle CEF$; AAS
II. $\angle CFE \cong \angle BFD$; the Vertical Angles Theorem
III. $\overline{CE} \cong \overline{BD}$; CPCTC

B. I. $\triangle ADC \cong \triangle AEB$; SAS
II. $\overline{AB} \cong \overline{AC}$; given
III. $\overline{BE} \cong \overline{CD}$; CPCTC

C. I. $\triangle ADC \cong \triangle AEB$; AAS
II. $\overline{AB} \cong \overline{AC}$; given
III. $\angle A \cong \angle A$; the two triangles share this angle.

D. I. $\triangle BDF \cong \triangle CEF$; ASA
II. $\angle BDF \cong \angle CEF$; CPCTC
III. $\overline{BE} \cong \overline{CD}$; CPCTC

Maintain Your Skills

10. In $\triangle ABC$, $m\angle CAB = 90°$. To conclude that each statement listed below is true, what additional information do you need about the *angles* of $\triangle ABC$? About the *sides*?

   a. $\triangle ABC$ is half of an equilateral triangle.

   b. $\triangle ABC$ is half of a square.

   c. $\triangle ABC$ is half of an isosceles triangle.

2.14 Practicing Your Proof-Writing Skills

Below are some general guidelines for you to follow as you work on a mathematical investigation.

- *Explore* the problem. Use hand or computer drawings to help you understand the statement of the problem.
- *Explain* what you observe. If you can, justify your observations with a proof. If you cannot write a complete proof, describe the information you have. Then say what information is missing from your proof.
- *Summarize* your work. Include drawings, conjectures that you made, a list of important vocabulary words, theorems, rules or ideas that you discovered, and questions that require further exploration.

Below is the Perpendicular Bisector Theorem again, along with its proof.

Theorem 1.1 Perpendicular Bisector Theorem

Each point on the perpendicular bisector of a segment is equidistant from the two endpoints of the segment.

Proof Suppose $\overline{PC}$ is the perpendicular bisector of $\overline{AB}$. Then C is the midpoint of $\overline{AB}$. So $\overline{AC} \cong \overline{BC}$.

Also, because $\overline{PC}$ is the perpendicular bisector of $\overline{AB}$, $m\angle PCA = m\angle PCB = 90°$.

Triangle PCA and $\triangle PCB$ share $\overline{PC}$, so $\triangle PCA \cong \triangle PCB$ by SAS.

Since $\triangle PCA \cong \triangle PCB$, $\overline{AP} \cong \overline{BP}$ by CPCTC.

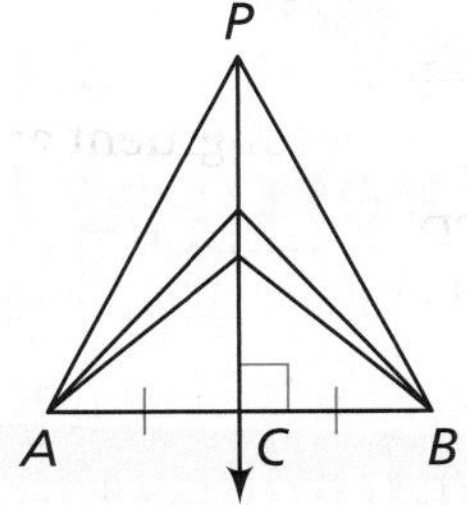

A similar argument proves that $\overline{AP} \cong \overline{BP}$ for any point P on $\overline{PC}$.

Therefore, any point on the perpendicular bisector of a line segment is equidistant from the endpoints of the line segment.

For You to Do

1. State and prove the converse of the Perpendicular Bisector Theorem.

Remember...

Where have you seen this proof before?

B
D
A
C

The measures of the angles in a triangle are related to the lengths of the triangle's sides. For example, suppose a triangle has two congruent sides. Then it must also have two congruent angles.

Proof Suppose $\triangle ABC$ is an isosceles triangle, with $\overline{AB} \cong \overline{AC}$. Construct the median from A. Call the point where the median intersects $\overline{BC}$ point D. Point D is the midpoint of $\overline{BC}$. So $\overline{BD} \cong \overline{CD}$.

Triangle ADB and $\triangle ADC$ share side $\overline{AD}$. So $\triangle ADB \cong \triangle ADC$ by SSS. Then, by CPCTC, $\angle B \cong \angle C$.

You proved the following theorem in Lesson 2.12.

Theorem 2.6 Isosceles Triangle Theorem

The base angles of an isosceles triangle are congruent.

If $\overline{AB} \cong \overline{BC}$, then $\angle A \cong \angle C$.

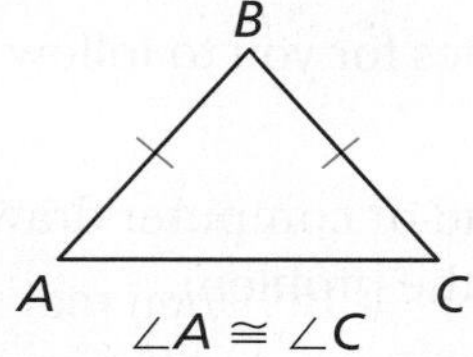

For You to Do

2. State and prove the converse of the Isosceles Triangle Theorem.
3. Can a scalene triangle have two angles the same size? Develop a conjecture that you can use to identify the largest, smallest, and middle-sized angles in a triangle. How can you prove your conjecture?

Remember...

A **scalene triangle** has no sides that are the same length.

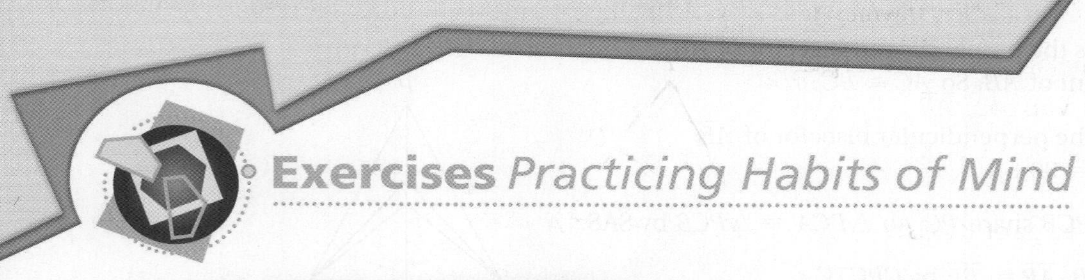

Exercises *Practicing Habits of Mind*

Check Your Understanding

1. Use the figure at the right. $\overleftrightarrow{ST}$ is the perpendicular bisector of $\overline{RQ}$. Prove that $\angle SRT \cong \angle SQT$.

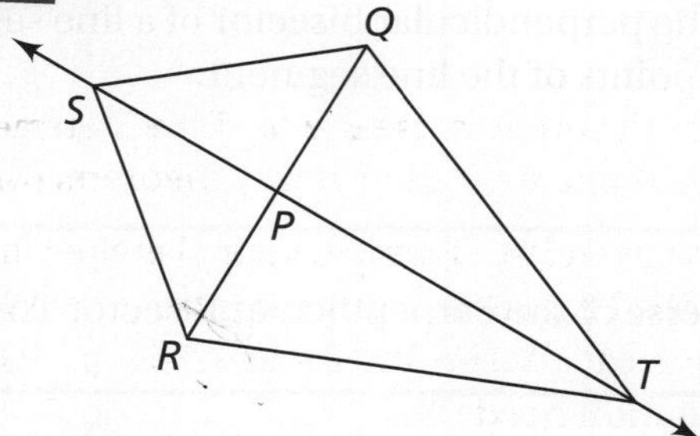

2. The SAS postulate implies that if two sides and the included angle of one triangle are congruent to two sides and the included angle of another triangle, then the third sides of the two triangles are also congruent.

   Suppose, instead, that two sides of one triangle are congruent to two sides of another, but that the included angle in the first triangle is larger than the included angle in the second triangle. What can you conclude about the third sides of the two triangles?

This result is sometimes called the Hinge Theorem. Can you think of a reason why?

For Exercises 3–5, do each of the following.

- Draw the figure described.
- Use your drawing. Explain what the statement says about the figure.
- Write what you know about the figure. Then make and explain conjectures about what you think might be true.
- Try to prove the last sentence. Use any method.

3. Draw square *ABCD*. Construct rays $\overrightarrow{AB}$, $\overrightarrow{BC}$, $\overrightarrow{CD}$, and $\overrightarrow{DA}$. Choose point *E* on $\overrightarrow{AB}$, point *F* on $\overrightarrow{BC}$, point *G* on $\overrightarrow{CD}$, and point *H* on $\overrightarrow{DA}$ such that the points are not on the sides of square *ABCD* and $\overline{BE} \cong \overline{CF} \cong \overline{DG} \cong \overline{AH}$. Quadrilateral *EFGH* is a square.

Remember...

In order to *prove* that a quadrilateral is a square, you need to show that its sides are all congruent and its angles are all congruent.

4. Draw a quadrilateral with congruent diagonals and one pair of opposite sides that are congruent. At least one of the four triangles into which the quadrilateral is divided is isosceles.

5. Draw an isosceles triangle. Pick any point along the base. From this point, draw lines parallel to the congruent sides, forming a parallelogram. The perimeter of the parallelogram is fixed, regardless of which point you pick along the base.

You can do this exercise with geometry software.

6. The four statements below describe this figure.

- $\triangle ABC$ is isosceles with base $\overline{AB}$.
- $\overline{CD}$ is a median.
- $\overline{CD}$ is an altitude.
- $\overline{CD}$ is the angle bisector of $\angle ACB$.

B
D
A
C

Show that if any two of the statements are given, you can prove the other two statements. For example,

Given statements 1 and 2
Prove statements 3 and 4

Continue writing proofs until you have used two of the statements to prove the remaining two for all but one case. How many theorems do you have?

Write up your work for this exercise. Organize your sketches, notes, questions, ideas, and proofs. Prepare a page on which you will write the proof for the one remaining case. Write and hand in that proof when you know you have the information needed.

On Your Own

7. Refer to the diagram for Exercise 6. Write one new statement, either about $\triangle ABC$ or about $\triangle ADC$ and $\triangle BDC$, that guarantees that all four of the statements in Exercise 6 are true.

8. Describe the set of triangles that meets each of the following conditions.

   a. The perpendicular bisector of exactly one side passes through the opposite vertex.

   b. The perpendicular bisector of each of exactly two of the sides passes through the opposite vertex.

   c. The perpendicular bisector of each of the sides passes through the opposite vertex.

   You may find it helpful to construct some triangles that meet each condition and some triangles that do not. Explain what you find.

9. Use a cup or glass to trace a circle on a sheet of paper. Explain how to find the center of the circle.

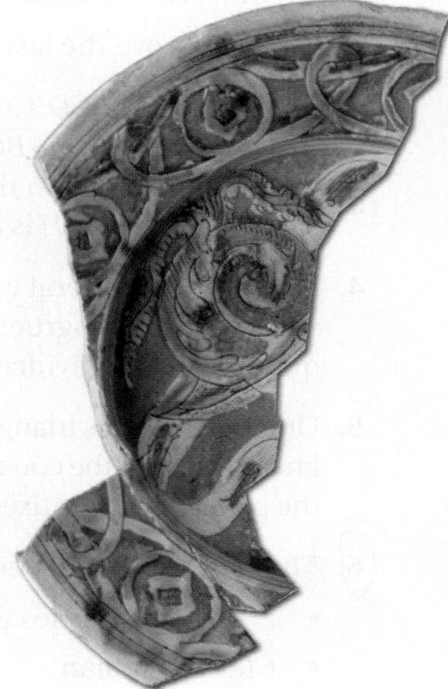

How can you make a model of the original plate if you find only this piece?

10. **Standardized Test Prep** Brittany found a piece of broken pottery that looks like part of a circular dinner plate. She wants to determine the radius of the plate, but she has less than half of the plate. First, she traces the outline of the outer edge of the pottery on a sheet of paper. Then she draws two line segments with endpoints that are on different parts of the curve. Next, she constructs the perpendicular bisector of each line segment. She extends the perpendicular bisectors until they intersect. Finally, she measures the distance from the point of intersection of the perpendicular bisectors to a point on the curve. Why does this procedure guarantee that she has found the radius of the plate?

   A. A line that is perpendicular to a tangent of a circle will always go through the center of the circle. Each bisected line segment is tangent to the circle.

   B. The perpendicular bisector of a chord divides the arc associated with the chord into two congruent arcs. The length of each arc is equal to the radius of the circle.

   C. A point on the perpendicular bisector of a segment is equidistant from the endpoints of the segment. The distance from the intersection of the perpendicular bisectors to a point on a circle is the radius of the circle.

   D. The point of intersection of the perpendicular bisectors, along with the midpoints of the bisected segments, determine an isosceles triangle. The segment that connects the midpoints of bisected segments is the base of the isosceles triangle. The radius of the circle is the length of one of the legs of the isosceles triangle.

11. Describe an algorithm that you can use to construct a circle that passes through the vertices of a given triangle.

Remember...

What does the term *algorithm* mean?

12. A circular saw blade shattered. All you can find is a piece that looks like the figure at the right. Explain how to find the diameter of the blade so you can buy a new one.

13. Show that if the hypotenuse and a leg of one right triangle are congruent to the hypotenuse and a leg of another right triangle, then the triangles are congruent.

This test for right-triangle congruence is sometimes called "hypotenuse-leg" and is abbreviated HL.

14. Draw several triangles. In each triangle, construct the perpendicular bisector of each side. Notice that the perpendicular bisectors in each triangle intersect in one point. Is this true for all triangles? Provide a proof or a counterexample.

Habits of Mind

Be efficient. If you use geometry software, you can make one construction and just drag it around.

15. Perform the paper-folding construction shown at the right. Start with a rectangular sheet of paper.

Fold A onto B and crease along the dotted line.

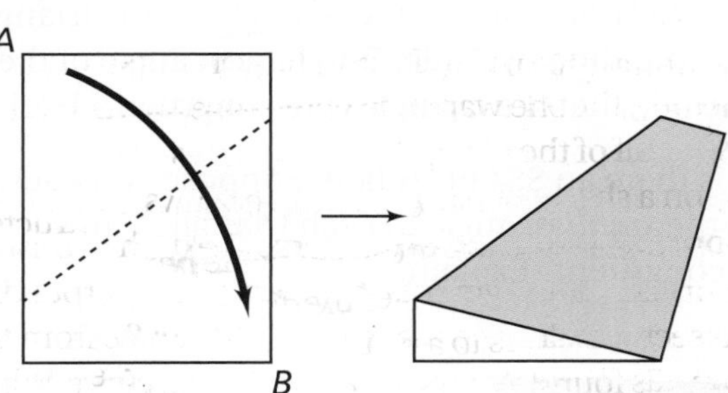

Then fold C onto D, and crease along the dotted line.

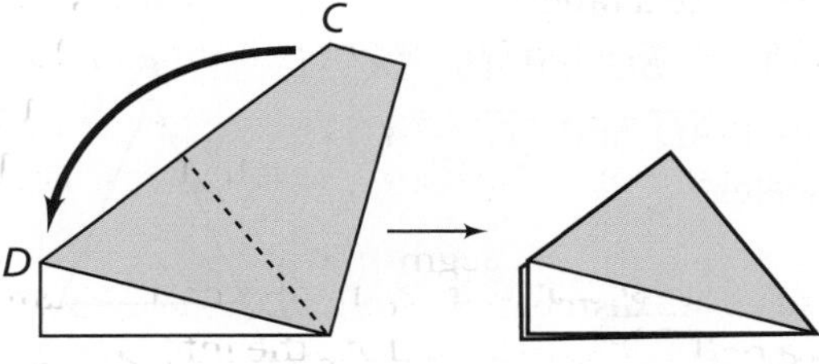

Unfold the paper. The creases should look like this.

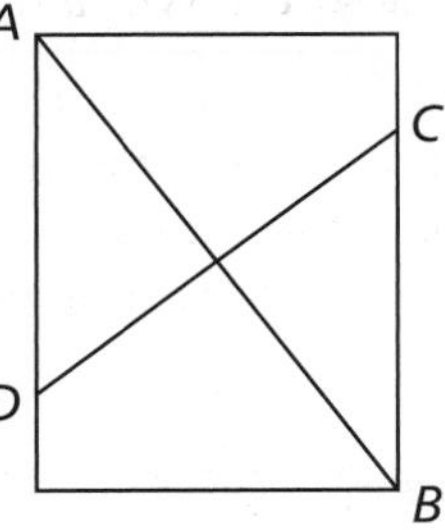

Prove that any point on $\overline{CD}$ is the same distance from A as from B.

There is no SSA triangle postulate. Two sides and a nonincluded angle of one triangle can be congruent to two sides and the corresponding nonincluded angle of another triangle without the two triangles being congruent.

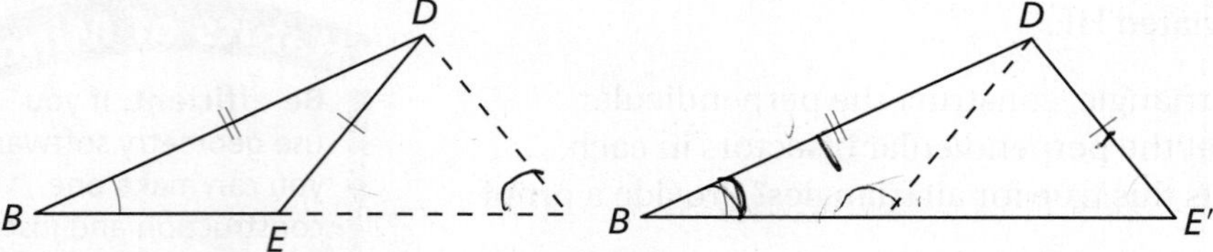

16. **Take It Further** Could there be an SSA postulate? Suppose you know that the nonincluded angle is the *largest* angle in each triangle. That is, suppose that the two sides and the largest nonincluded angle of one triangle are congruent to the corresponding two sides and largest angle of the other triangle. Can you conclude that the triangles are congruent? Explain.

If SSA does guarantee triangle congruence, it is a generalization of HL. Explain.

17. **Take It Further** And is there an SSa postulate? Suppose you know that the nonincluded angle is the *smallest* angle in each triangle. Can you conclude that the triangles are congruent? Explain.

Maintain Your Skills

18. In the figure at the right, $\overline{AD} \cong \overline{BC}$ and $\overline{AB} \parallel \overline{DC}$. Point E is the intersection of $\overleftrightarrow{AD}$ and $\overleftrightarrow{BC}$. Prove that $\triangle ABE$ is isosceles.

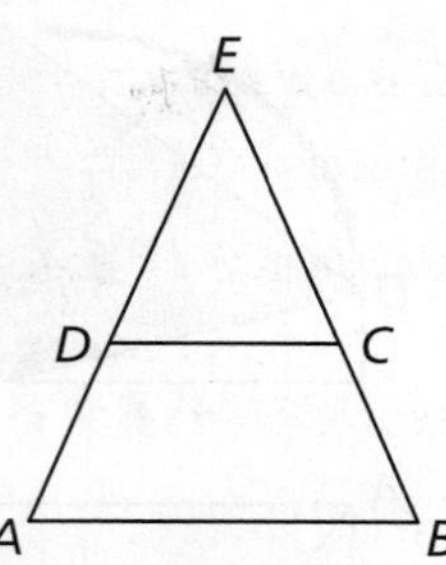

19. Here are two quite plausible statements.

In a triangle,

- the longest side is opposite the largest angle
- the shortest side is opposite the smallest angle

You may assume that both statements are theorems. Use one or both of the statements to help you prove the Triangle Inequality Theorem:

In a triangle, the length of one side is less than the sum of the lengths of the other two sides.

In other words, in $\triangle ABC$, prove that $AB < AC + CB$. (*Hint:* Use the figure at the right to write a reverse list.)

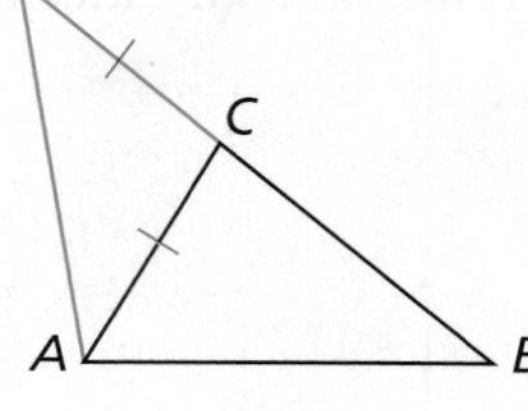

Go Online
Pearsonsuccessnet.com

In this investigation, you studied mathematical proof. You learned different ways to think about and analyze the proof-writing process. You also learned several ways to write and organize a mathematical proof. You used these skills to practice and improve your own proof-writing techniques.

1. In the figure at the right, $\triangle ABC$ is isosceles with $\overline{AC} \cong \overline{BC}$. $\overleftrightarrow{CP}$ is the bisector of $\angle ACB$. Point P is on this angle bisector.

   Prove that $\triangle APB$ is isosceles.

2. The hypotenuse and one of the acute angles of a right triangle are congruent to the hypotenuse and one of the acute angles of another right triangle. Prove that the two triangles are congruent or give a counterexample.

3. In the figure at the right, $\triangle ABC$ is isosceles with $\overline{AC} \cong \overline{BC}$. $\overline{EA} \cong \overline{FB}$ and $\overline{AS} \cong \overline{BT}$. Prove that $\triangle AES \cong \triangle BFT$.

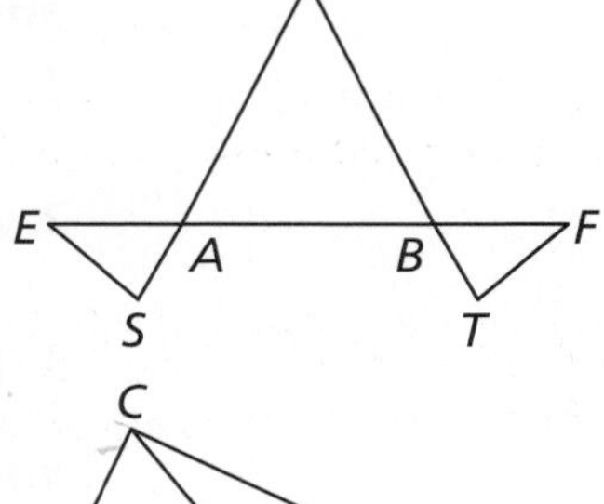

4. The base and the angle opposite the base in one isosceles triangle are congruent to the base and the angle opposite the base in another isosceles triangle. Prove that the two triangles are congruent or provide a counterexample.

5. Write a reverse list for this statement about the figure at the right.

   If $\overline{TA} \cong \overline{TC} \cong \overline{TB}$, then $\triangle ABC$ is a right triangle.

   Then use the list to prove the statement.

6. What are the different ways to organize and analyze a proof?

7. What is the Perpendicular Bisector Theorem?

8. In the statement "All trees are green," what is the hypothesis and what is the conclusion?

The steel cables form congruent angles with the roadway, so the triangle is isosceles.

Vocabulary

In this investigation, you learned these terms. Make sure you understand what each one means and how to use it.

- **base angle**
- **base of an isosceles triangle**
- **conclusion**
- **equiangular**
- **hypothesis**
- **isosceles triangle**
- **leg**
- **proof**
- **scalene triangle**
- **vertex angle**

Quadrilaterals and Their Properties

In *Quadrilaterals and Their Properties*, you will explore four-sided figures. Chances are you already know a great deal about quadrilaterals. From the earliest elementary grades, you have constructed, measured, cut, and folded squares and rectangles. Now you will use this practical experience as you begin a more formal study of quadrilaterals. All of the properties of these shapes are important in understanding what makes each one unique.

By the end of this investigation, you will be able to answer questions like these.

1. What are some special properties of parallelograms? Of kites? Of trapezoids?
2. Are all squares also considered parallelograms? Are all parallelograms also considered squares? Explain.
3. If a statement is true, must its converse also be true?

You will learn how to

- define and classify quadrilaterals
- write the converse of a conditional statement
- understand the meaning of *always, never,* and *sometimes* in mathematics

You will develop these habits and skills:

- Characterize sets in a given class.
- Understand that the converse of a statement is not automatically true when the initial statement is true.
- Reason by continuity.

A nonconformist use of quadrilaterals

2.15 Getting Started

You will use your basic knowledge of squares and rectangles to discover additional properties and characteristics of quadrilaterals.

For You to Explore

1. Use any method you choose to construct a square and a rectangle.
2. List as many properties as you can of the sides, angles, and diagonals of the square and of the rectangle.
3. Can you find a property of the rectangle that is not a property of the square?

Remember...

A diagonal is a segment that connects two non-consecutive vertices of a polygon.

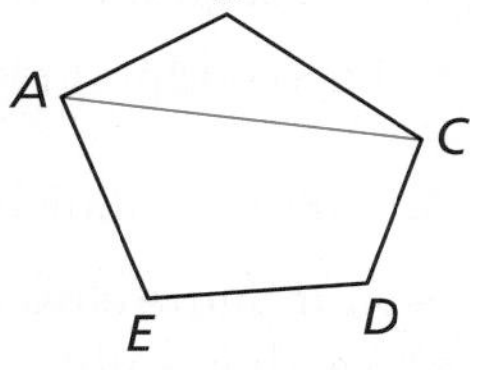

Exercises *Practicing Habits of Mind*

On Your Own

4. Draw a quadrilateral with four congruent sides that is not a square. What do you call this type of quadrilateral?
5. Draw a quadrilateral with two congruent diagonals that is not a rectangle.
6. Draw a quadrilateral with four congruent angles. Must it be a rectangle?
7. Construct a rectangle with perpendicular diagonals that are 4 cm.
8. Write another description for the figure you constructed in Exercise 7. Use a different name for the quadrilateral.
9. **Take It Further** Without using a ruler to measure, fold a nonsquare sheet of paper into a square. How do you know that the figure you folded is a square?

Remember...

A polygon with exactly four sides is called a *quadrilateral*.

Maintain Your Skills

Find the area of each figure.

10. $\frac{1}{2}$ in., 8 in., not to scale

11. 4 cm

12. 10 ft, 2 ft

Go Online
Pearsonsuccessnet.com

2.16 General Quadrilaterals

You have already explored some properties and characteristics of familiar quadrilaterals, such as squares and rectangles. Now, you are going to take a look at some less-common quadrilaterals.

In-Class Experiment

On a separate sheet of paper, sketch several figures that each have the following properties.

- The figure is made of four segments.
- The segments intersect at their endpoints.
- Each endpoint is shared by exactly two segments.

Answer the following questions about each of your figures.

1. Is your figure closed? Can you draw a figure with the three properties listed above that is not closed?
2. Must your figure lie on a plane? Can you show a figure with the three properties listed above that does not lie on a plane?
3. Does your figure intersect itself? Explain.

A figure is **closed** if you can "walk" its outer edges and get back to where you started.

The following definition is not new to you, but here it is stated formally.

Definition

A quadrilateral is a figure that consists of four segments called its sides. The sides intersect at their endpoints, called the quadrilateral's vertices, so that each vertex is the endpoint of exactly two sides.

Vertices is the plural of *vertex*.

Are these figures quadrilaterals?

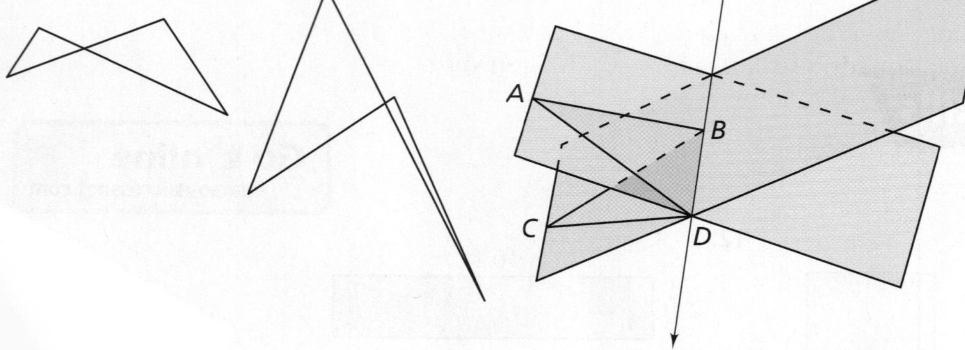

The definition of quadrilateral does not say that the sides of a quadrilateral are only connected to each other at their endpoints. The first two figures on the previous page have points in common in addition to their endpoints. You call such figures self-intersecting quadrilaterals.

> A figure is **self-intersecting** if you "walk" its outer edges and go through the same point more than once before you get back to where you started.

The definition of a quadrilateral also does not say that the quadrilateral must lie in one plane. The last figure on the previous page does not. You call it a **skew quadrilateral.**

The two figures below are also quadrilaterals, but it is often inconvenient to include them in a discussion. You call them **concave** (or nonconvex) quadrilaterals. A concave quadrilateral has at least one diagonal outside the quadrilateral.

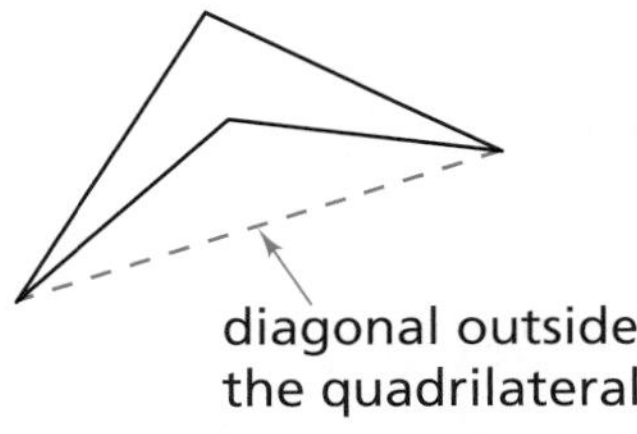

diagonal outside the quadrilateral

In this book, the term *quadrilateral* does not include self-intersecting, skew, or concave quadrilaterals, unless mentioned specifically.

Exercises *Practicing Habits of Mind*

Check Your Understanding

1. A figure is closed if you can walk its outer edges and get back to where you started. The definition of *quadrilateral* does not say that a quadrilateral must be closed. Can you draw a quadrilateral that satisfies the definition, but is not closed?
2. A figure is *planar* if all its points lie in the same plane. The definition of *quadrilateral* does not say that a quadrilateral must be planar. Can you draw a quadrilateral that satisfies the definition but is not planar?
3. Explain why each figure below is not a quadrilateral.

a. 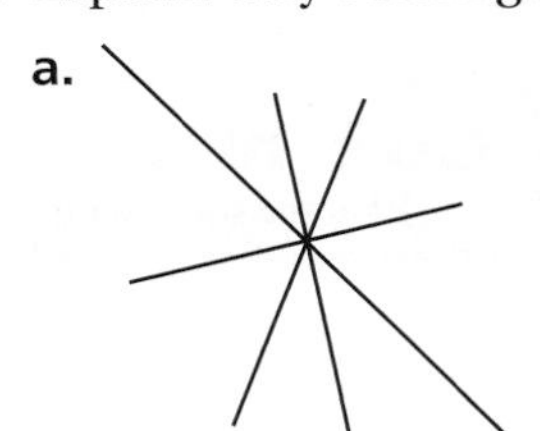

b. 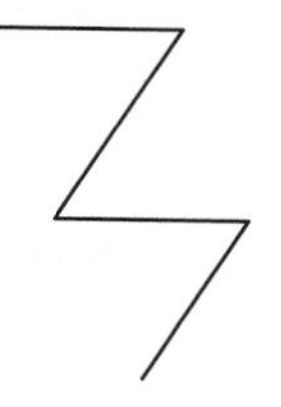

c. 

d. 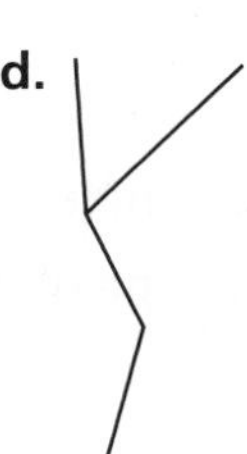

On Your Own

4. **Standardized Test Prep** Which of the following statements is NOT true about a quadrilateral in a plane?

   A. Except for its endpoints, all the points on at least one of a quadrilateral's diagonals lie in the interior of the quadrilateral.

   B. At least one diagonal of a quadrilateral divides the quadrilateral into two triangles.

   C. The sum of the measures of the interior angles of a quadrilateral is 360°.

   D. The four vertices of every quadrilateral lie on a unique circle.

Review the following triangle theorems. Then complete Exercises 5–8.

- The sum of the measures of the angles of a triangle is 180°.
- The sum of the lengths of any two sides of a triangle is greater than the length of the third side.

5. The sum of the measures of the angles of a quadrilateral is always 360°. Explain why this is true.

6. Is the sum of the measures of the angles of a self-intersecting quadrilateral always 360°? Explain.

How would you define the angles of a self-intersecting quadrilateral?

7. Is the sum of the measures of the angles of a skew quadrilateral always 360°? Explain.

8. **Take It Further** Prove that the sum of the lengths of any three sides of a quadrilateral is greater than the length of the fourth side. Determine whether your proof works for each type of quadrilateral listed below.

   - concave
   - self-intersecting
   - skew

   If your proof does not work for one or more types of the quadrilaterals listed above, can you write a different proof that will hold? Or does the proof fail because the property is not a characteristic of that type of quadrilateral?

Maintain Your Skills

9. Two angles of a quadrilateral both measure $x°$. The other two angles both measure $2x°$.

   a. Find the value of x.

   b. Find the measure of each angle.

   c. Can you determine the shape of the quadrilateral? Is more than one type of quadrilateral possible?

2.17 Properties of Quadrilaterals

Certain quadrilaterals have properties and characteristics that distinguish them from other quadrilaterals. For example, a square is the only quadrilateral that has four congruent sides and four congruent angles.

You can use the special properties of certain quadrilaterals to prove additional properties. You will do this in the exercises.

Below are the definitions of two special types of quadrilaterals.

Definition

A trapezoid is a quadrilateral with exactly one pair of parallel sides. The two parallel sides are called the bases of the trapezoid.

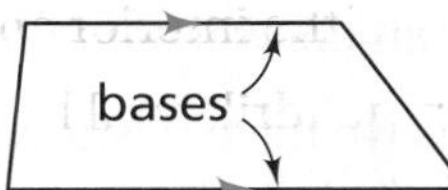

Definition

A kite is a quadrilateral in which two adjacent sides are congruent, and the other two adjacent sides are congruent as well.

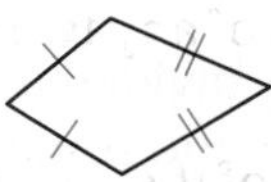

Habits of Mind

Understand more than one meaning. A trapezoid is sometimes defined as a quadrilateral with *at least* one pair of parallel sides. According to this definition, a parallelogram is a special type of trapezoid.

Example

Prove that one of the diagonals of a kite divides it into two congruent triangles.

First you must determine which diagonal appears to divide the kite into two congruent triangles. Unless your kite is a square, only one of its diagonals will divide the kite into two congruent triangles. This diagonal is sometimes called the *symmetry diagonal.*

What is so special about the diagonals of a square?

Given kite $ABCD$ with diagonal $\overline{BD}$

Prove $\triangle DAB \cong \triangle DCB$

Proof Because $ABCD$ is a kite, $\overline{AB} \cong \overline{CB}$ and $\overline{AD} \cong \overline{CD}$. $\triangle DAB$ and $\triangle DCB$ share $\overline{BD}$. So $\triangle DAB \cong \triangle DCB$ by SSS.

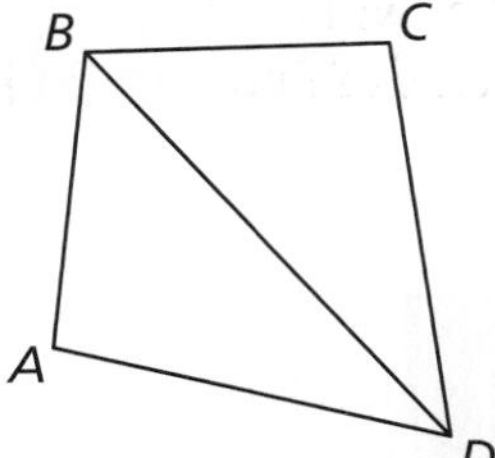

Minds in Action episode 4

Sasha and Tony are working on Exercises 2–8 in the Check Your Understanding section of this lesson.

Tony Here are the directions: Complete each sentence with *always, sometimes,* or *never* to make the statement true.

Sasha *Always* means you can prove it. So if we choose *always,* we have to be ready to write a proof.

Tony Proofs mean work. Let's try to answer *never.*

Sasha But for *never* we have to give a proof also—a proof that shows that the statement cannot be true.

Tony Well, maybe we can answer *sometimes.*

Sasha *Sometimes* means we have to show an example when the statement is true, and another example when the statement is false. We need two different examples!

Tony So these kinds of questions are like true-or-false questions. *Always* is the same as *true.*

Sasha Yeah, but *false* is divided into *sometimes* statements, which are sometimes true (and sometimes false), and *never* statements, which are never true.

Tony That's terrible—whatever we answer, we have to prove something!

Sasha Come on—proofs are fun!

Exercises *Practicing Habits of Mind*

Check Your Understanding

1. Which of the figures A–L, here and on the next page, appear to be trapezoids? Explain.

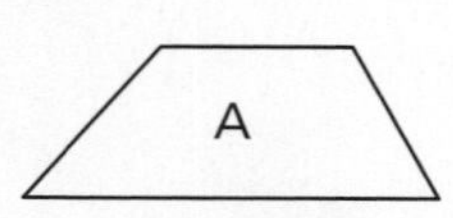

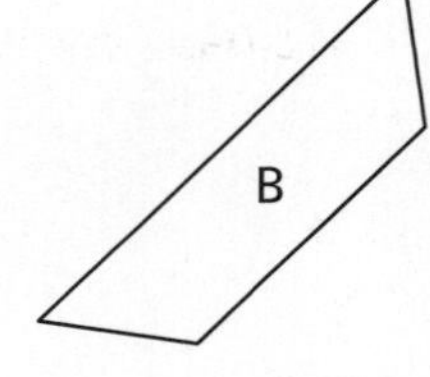

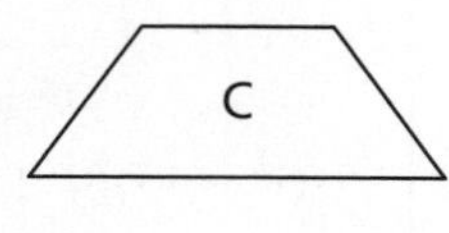

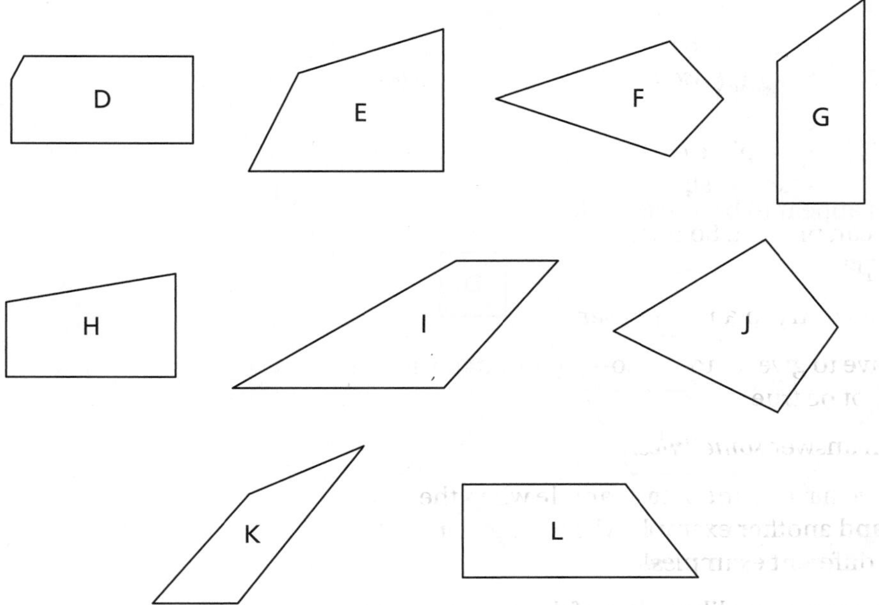

For Exercises 2–8, complete each sentence with *always, sometimes,* or *never* to make the statement true. Justify your answer with a proof or some examples.

2. The sum of the measures of the angles of a trapezoid is __?__ 360°.
3. The diagonals of a trapezoid are __?__ congruent.
4. Two sides of a trapezoid are __?__ congruent.
5. Three sides of a trapezoid are __?__ congruent.
6. One diagonal of a trapezoid __?__ bisects one of the trapezoid's angles.
7. Two angles of a trapezoid are __?__ right angles.
8. A trapezoid __?__ has exactly one right angle.
9. Two parallel lines can be close to each other or far apart. So it is natural to refer to the distance between two parallel lines. Write a definition that describes the distance between parallel lines.
10. Read the following definition. Then prove that the base angles of an isosceles trapezoid are congruent.

Definition

An isosceles trapezoid is a trapezoid with opposite nonparallel sides that are congruent. Each pair of angles with vertices that are the endpoints of the same base are called base angles.

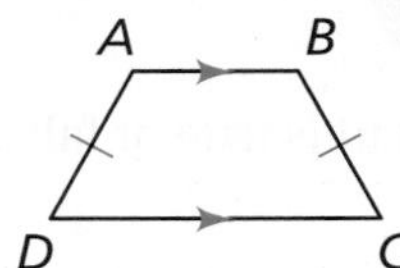

$\angle A$ and $\angle B$ are base angles.
$\angle D$ and $\angle C$ are base angles.

11. Prove that the diagonals of an isosceles trapezoid are congruent.

On Your Own

12. Which of the following figures appear to be kites? Explain.

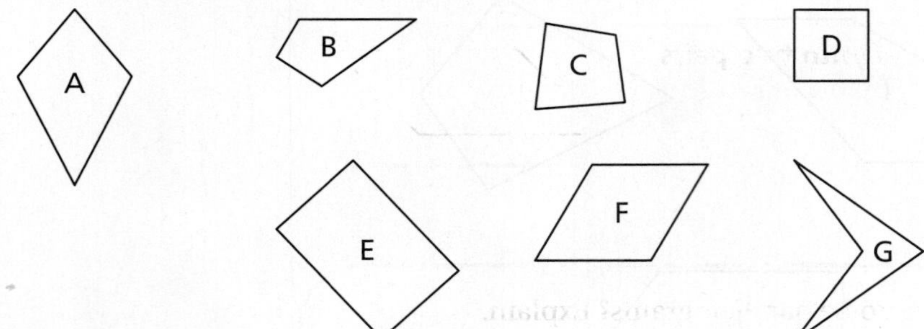

For Exercises 13–17, complete each sentence with *always, sometimes,* or *never* to make the statement true.

13. The sum of the measures of the angles of a kite is __?__ 360°.
14. The diagonals of a kite are __?__ perpendicular.
15. A kite __?__ has two congruent angles.
16. A kite __?__ has a right angle.
17. One diagonal of a kite __?__ bisects one of its angles.
18. **Standardized Test Prep** Which of the following statements is always true?
    I. A kite has at least one pair of congruent adjacent sides.
    II. A kite has at least one pair of congruent opposite angles.
    III. The diagonals of an isosceles trapezoid are congruent.
    A. I only **B.** I and II only **C.** I and III only **D.** I, II, and III
19. Prove that the symmetry diagonal of a kite bisects two angles of the kite.
20. Prove that the diagonals of a kite are perpendicular.

Maintain Your Skills

Determine whether each statement is true or false. Provide a counterexample if the statement is false.

21. If you live in Canada, then you live in Montreal.
22. If you live in Montreal, then you live in Canada.
23. If a figure has an area of 16 square units, then it is a square.
24. All telephone numbers in Vermont have an area code of 802.
25. If your home telephone number area code is 802, then you live in Vermont.

2.18 Parallelograms

You define special quadrilaterals, such as parallelograms, by their characteristics. You can probably guess the defining characteristic of a parallelogram, just from its name.

Definition

A parallelogram is a quadrilateral with two pairs of opposite parallel sides.

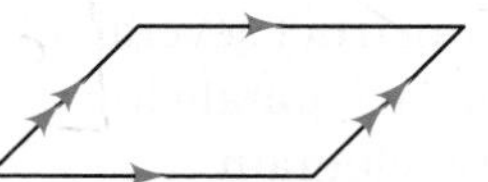

For You to Do

1. Which of the figures below appear to be parallelograms? Explain.

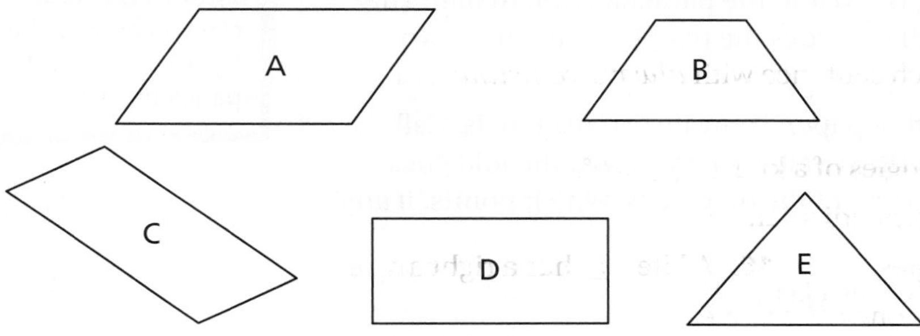

2. Notice that a rectangle is a parallelogram, according to the definition of *parallelogram* above. Which other common quadrilaterals fit the definition of *parallelogram*?

When you study any kind of quadrilateral, it is often useful to draw its diagonals. The following is an important theorem about the diagonals of a parallelogram.

Theorem 2.7

Each diagonal of a parallelogram divides the parallelogram into two congruent triangles.

Given Parallelogram $ABCD$ with diagonal $\overline{AC}$

Prove $\triangle ABC \cong \triangle CDA$

Proof $ABCD$ is a parallelogram. By definition, $\overline{BC} \parallel \overline{AD}$ and $\overline{BA} \parallel \overline{CD}$. From the PAI Theorem, it follows that $\angle BCA \cong \angle DAC$ and $\angle BAC \cong \angle DCA$. Triangle ABC and $\triangle CDA$ share $\overline{AC}$. So $\triangle ABC \cong \triangle CDA$ by ASA.

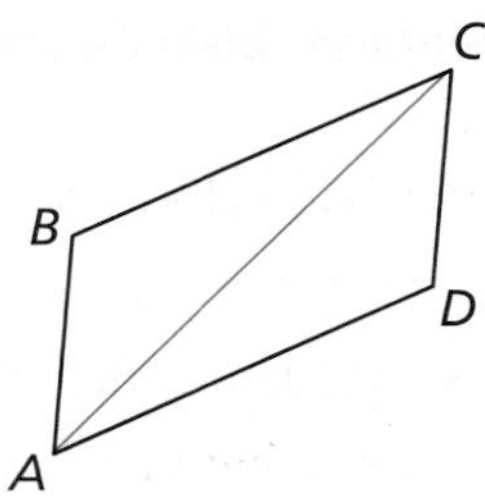

For Discussion

3. Prove that $\overline{BD}$ also divides parallelogram *ABCD* into two congruent triangles.

In-Class Experiment

4. Use geometry software. Construct several different parallelograms. Then construct the diagonals of each parallelogram. Compare the lengths of the two diagonals of each parallelogram.
5. The diagonals of a parallelogram divide each of the parallelogram's four angles into a pair of smaller angles. Find the measure of each angle in each pair. What invariant relationship, if any, exists between the measures of the two angles in each pair?
6. Cut a parallelogram out of paper. Try to fold the parallelogram in half. That is, try to find a line of symmetry that divides the parallelogram into two congruent pieces.
7. Use the parallelogram you cut out of paper. Draw its two diagonals. Call their point of intersection *P*. Fold the parallelogram so that the fold goes through *P* and is perpendicular to one of the diagonals. Which points, if any, coincide after you make the fold?

Discuss your results with the rest of the class.

Habits of Mind

Check your work. How can you be sure that the figure you cut out is a parallelogram?

For Discussion

8. Do you think the statement below is true or false?

The intersection point of the diagonals of a parallelogram is the midpoint of each diagonal.

Give a proof or find a counterexample.

You can prove that the statement is true. This important fact leads to the theorem below.

Theorem 2.8

The diagonals of a parallelogram bisect each other.

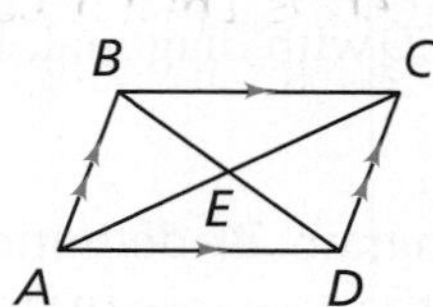

$AE = EC$ and $BE = ED$

You now know several things about parallelograms. If you know that a figure is a parallelogram, then all of the following statements are true:

1. Its opposite sides are parallel. (definition of *parallelogram*)
2. Its opposite sides are congruent. (See Exercise 7 part (a).)
3. Its opposite angles are congruent. (See Exercise 7 part (b).)
4. Its consecutive angles are supplementary. (See Exercise 6.)
5. Either diagonal divides the figure into two congruent triangles. (Theorem 2.7.)
6. Its diagonals bisect each other. (Theorem 2.8.)

Converses

Later you will investigate the converses of the statements listed above. What will the converses tell you? Well, for example, here is the converse of statement 6:

> If the diagonals of a quadrilateral bisect each other, then the quadrilateral is a parallelogram.

You can use converse statements that are true to classify quadrilaterals as parallelograms.

Developing Habits of Mind

Communicate a conditional situation. Statements of the form "if A, then B" are sometimes called conditional statements. One or more conditions are implied by the *if* part.

Some *if-then* statements are descriptions of elements of sets. You may see a statement like this one: "If an object belongs to set A, then it also belongs to set B."

For example, you can restate one of the corollaries to Theorem 2.7 this way:

> If a quadrilateral belongs to the set of parallelograms, then it also belongs to the set of quadrilaterals with opposite sides congruent.

The converse of this statement, also a conditional statement, is the following:

> If a quadrilateral belongs to the set of quadrilaterals with opposite sides congruent, then it also belongs to the set of parallelograms.

You can prove that the converse of the statement is also true. Start with a quadrilateral with opposite sides that are congruent. Draw the diagonals of the quadrilateral. By SSS, there is a pair of congruent triangles. Then by CPCTC, the alternate interior angles are congruent. By AIP, the sides of the figure are parallel.

In this example, the statement and its converse are both true, but this is not always the case. Sometimes the converse of a true conditional statement is false. For example, consider this statement: "If a person lives in Dallas, then that person lives in Texas." The converse of this statement is "If a person lives in Texas, then that person lives in Dallas." You can easily find a counterexample to the converse, such as "the person lives in Austin."

Remember...

A corollary is a consequence of a main theorem.

Exercises *Practicing Habits of Mind*

Check Your Understanding

For Exercises 1–5, do the following.

- Write the converse of the statement.
- Decide whether the converse is true or false.
- If the converse is true, provide a proof.
- If the converse is false, give a counterexample.

1. If a quadrilateral is a parallelogram, then its opposite sides are congruent.

2. If a quadrilateral is a parallelogram, then its consecutive angles are supplementary.

3. If a quadrilateral is a parallelogram, then its opposite angles are congruent.

4. If a quadrilateral is a parallelogram, then each diagonal divides the parallelogram into two congruent triangles.

5. If a quadrilateral is a parallelogram, then its diagonals bisect each other.

6. The two angles at either end of a side in a parallelogram are called *consecutive angles.* State and prove a theorem about the consecutive angles of a parallelogram.

7. Prove the following corollaries of Theorem 2.7.

a. Both pairs of opposite sides of a parallelogram are congruent.

b. Both pairs of opposite angles of a parallelogram are congruent.

8. Take It Further A line that passes through the intersection point of a parallelogram's diagonals intersects the parallelogram in two points. Prove that the intersection point of the parallelogram's diagonals is the midpoint of the line segment that connects these points.

On Your Own

For Exercises 9–28, complete each sentence with *always, sometimes,* or *never* to make the statement true.

9. A parallelogram __?__ has two congruent sides.

10. A parallelogram __?__ has three congruent sides.

11. A parallelogram __?__ has exactly three congruent sides.

12. A parallelogram __?__ has four congruent sides.

13. A parallelogram __?__ has congruent diagonals.

14. A quadrilateral with congruent diagonals is __?__ a parallelogram.

15. If one diagonal of a quadrilateral divides it into two congruent triangles, then the quadrilateral is __?__ a parallelogram.

16. If two consecutive angles of a quadrilateral are supplementary, then the quadrilateral is __?__ a parallelogram.

17. A quadrilateral with one right angle is __?__ a parallelogram.

18. A quadrilateral with exactly one right angle is __?__ a parallelogram.

19. A quadrilateral with two right angles is __?__ a parallelogram.

20. A quadrilateral with exactly two right angles is __?__ a parallelogram.

21. A quadrilateral with exactly two right angles opposite each other is __?__ a parallelogram.

22. A quadrilateral with three right angles is __?__ a parallelogram.

Hint: Can a quadrilateral have exactly three right angles?

23. A quadrilateral with diagonals that bisect each other is __?__ a parallelogram.

24. If the longer diagonal of a quadrilateral bisects the shorter diagonal, then the quadrilateral is __?__ a parallelogram.

25. A quadrilateral with two congruent sides is __?__ a parallelogram.

26. A quadrilateral with three congruent sides is __?__ a parallelogram.

27. A quadrilateral with exactly three congruent sides is __?__ a parallelogram.

28. A quadrilateral with four congruent sides is __?__ a parallelogram.

29. **Standardized Test Prep** Which of the following statements is NOT true?

A. Every parallelogram has at least one line of symmetry.

B. The diagonals of a parallelogram always bisect each other.

C. Opposite angles of a parallelogram are congruent.

D. Consecutive angles of a parallelogram are supplementary.

30. **Take It Further** In the figure at the right, the sides of parallelogram *MNPQ* are trisected. Four of the trisection points form quadrilateral *STWX*.

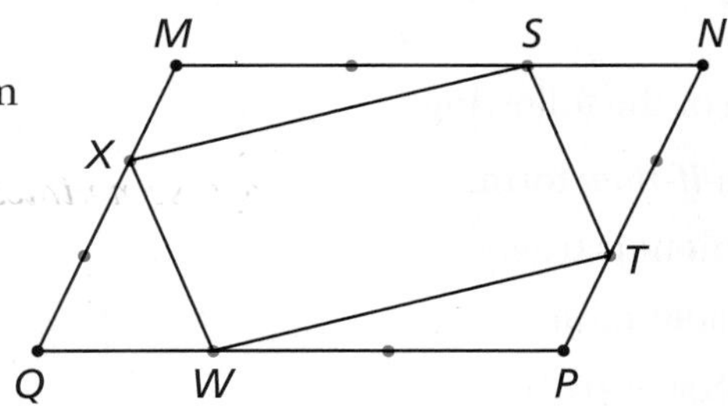

A segment is **trisected** if it is divided into three congruent parts.

a. List some facts that you can prove about quadrilateral *STWX*.

b. What type of quadrilateral is *STWX*? Prove your conjecture.

c. Suppose you draw $\overline{SW}$ and $\overline{TX}$. What can you say about these two segments?

31. Prove the theorem below.

Theorem 2.9

If two opposite sides of a quadrilateral are congruent and parallel, then the figure is a parallelogram.

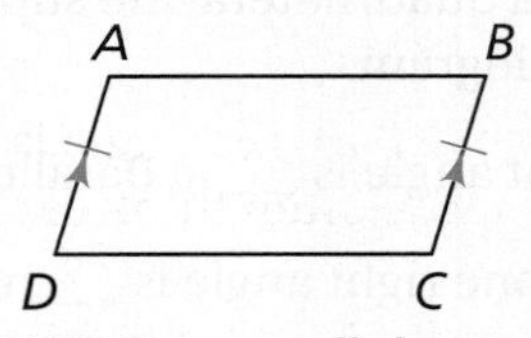

ABCD is a parallelogram.

32. In the figure at the right, *M* and *N* are midpoints of $\overline{AB}$ and $\overline{AC}$, respectively. Point *P* lies on the same line as *M* and *N*, and $\overline{MN} \cong \overline{NP}$.

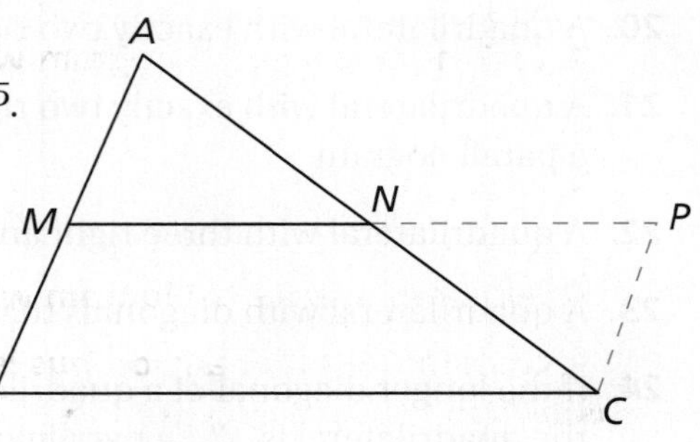

a. Prove that $\triangle AMN \cong \triangle CPN$.

b. What can you conclude about quadrilateral *MPCB*? Explain.

c. Show that $MN = \frac{1}{2}BC$.

d. What else can you conclude about the relationship between $\overline{MN}$ and $\overline{BC}$? Explain.

You can state the results of Exercise 32 as a theorem.

Theorem 2.10 Midline Theorem

The segment that joins the midpoints of two sides of a triangle is parallel to the third side and half the length of the third side.

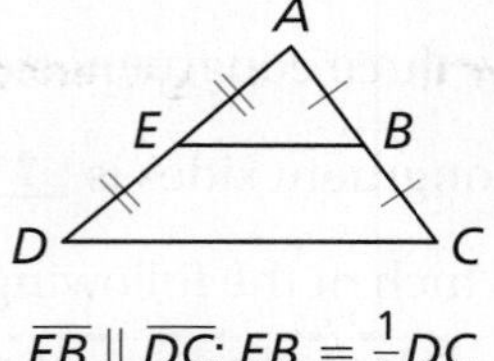

$\overline{EB} \parallel \overline{DC}$; $EB = \frac{1}{2}DC$

Remember...

You first saw this statement as Conjecture 1.2 in Chapter 1.

Maintain Your Skills

For Exercises 33–37, do each of the following.

a. Rewrite each statement in *if-then* form.

b. Decide whether the statement is true.

c. Write the converse of the statement.

d. Decide whether the converse is true.

33. People who live in New York City also live in New York State.

34. Every lizard is a reptile.

35. A bird is an animal with feathers.

36. All cowboys are from Texas.

37. Every piece of fruit is an apple.

2.19 Classifying Parallelograms

The different types of parallelograms are ordinary parallelograms, rectangles, rhombuses, and squares. Rectangles and rhombuses are special types of parallelograms. Squares are a special type of rectangle and a special type of rhombus.

You may be surprised that an ordinary rectangle is a type of parallelogram. This is probably because you more often think of a rectangle's four right angles than of its parallel sides.

Definitions

A rectangle is a parallelogram with four right angles.

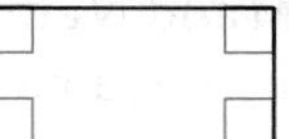

A rhombus is a parallelogram with four congruent sides.

A common term for a rhombus is *diamond.*

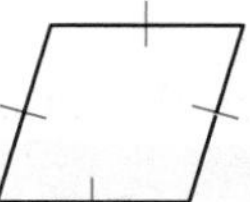

A square is a special kind of rectangle with four congruent sides. A square is also a special kind of rhombus, with four congruent angles.

The definition for a square is given below.

A square is a rectangle with four congruent sides.

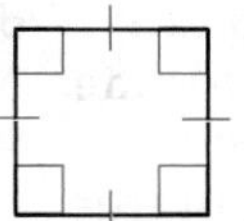

A square has all the properties of both a rectangle and a rhombus. Of course, a square also has the properties of a parallelogram and of a quadrilateral.

- The diagonals of a square are congruent because a square is a rectangle. (See Exercise 1.)
- The diagonals of a square are perpendicular because a square is a rhombus. (See Exercise 21.)
- The diagonals of a square bisect each other because a square is a parallelogram.
- The sum of the measures of the angles of a square is 360° because a square is a quadrilateral.

For You to Do

Decide whether each statement is true.

1. All rectangles are parallelograms.
2. Some parallelograms are rhombuses.
3. All rectangles are squares.
4. Some squares are rectangles.

The word *some* means "at least one."

Exercises *Practicing Habits of Mind*

Check Your Understanding

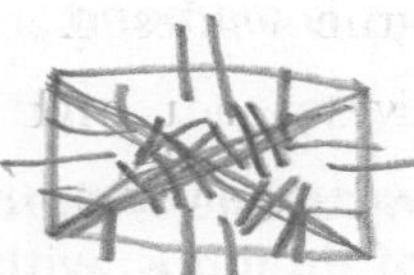

1. Prove that the diagonals of a rectangle are congruent.
2. Prove that a parallelogram with two congruent adjacent sides is a rhombus.

For Exercises 3–13, complete each sentence with *always, sometimes,* or *never* to make the statement true.

3. A rhombus is __?__ a rectangle.
4. A square is __?__ a parallelogram.
5. A rectangle is __?__ a rhombus.
6. A square is __?__ a rectangle.
7. The opposite sides of a rectangle are __?__ congruent.
8. The diagonals of a rectangle are __?__ congruent.
9. If the diagonals of a quadrilateral are congruent, then the quadrilateral is __?__ a rectangle.
10. Two adjacent sides of a rectangle are __?__ congruent.
11. The diagonals of a rectangle __?__ bisect its angles.
12. A rhombus __?__ has a right angle.
13. Opposite sides of a rhombus are __?__ congruent.

On Your Own

14. **Standardized Test Prep** Which of the following statements is NOT true?

    A. A square is different from a rhombus because a square has four congruent sides.

    B. A rectangle is a parallelogram with four congruent angles.

    C. A square is a rectangle with four congruent sides.

    D. A rhombus is a parallelogram with four congruent sides.

15. Prove that a parallelogram with one right angle is a rectangle.
16. Prove that if the diagonals of a parallelogram are congruent, then the parallelogram is a rectangle.
17. What type of quadrilateral do you form when you connect the midpoints of a rectangle's sides? Prove your conjecture.

In Exercises 17 and 18, make sure you do not assume that the quadrilateral is a parallelogram.

For Exercises 18–23, prove each statement.

18. If a quadrilateral has four congruent sides, then it is a rhombus.
19. Either diagonal of a rhombus divides the rhombus into two isosceles triangles.
20. The diagonals of a rhombus bisect the vertex angles of the rhombus.
21. The diagonals of a rhombus are perpendicular.
22. If the diagonals of a parallelogram are perpendicular, then the parallelogram is a rhombus.
23. If one diagonal of a parallelogram bisects two opposite angles of the parallelogram, then the parallelogram is a rhombus.
24. Draw a square and connect the midpoints of its sides. Prove that the figure formed is also a square.

Habits of Mind

Think it through. To prove that a quadrilateral is a square, can you just prove that its four sides are congruent?

Maintain Your Skills

Rectangles, rhombuses, and squares are special types of quadrilaterals. You can show the relationships among these quadrilaterals with a Venn diagram. In a Venn diagram, a circle represents a set.

25. Copy and complete each Venn diagram with the correct type of quadrilateral.

a.

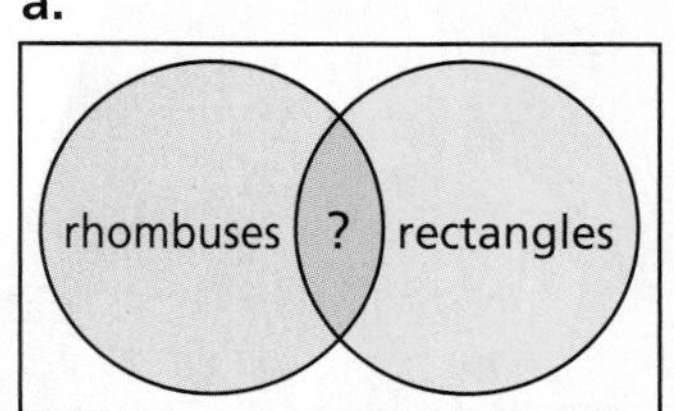

b.

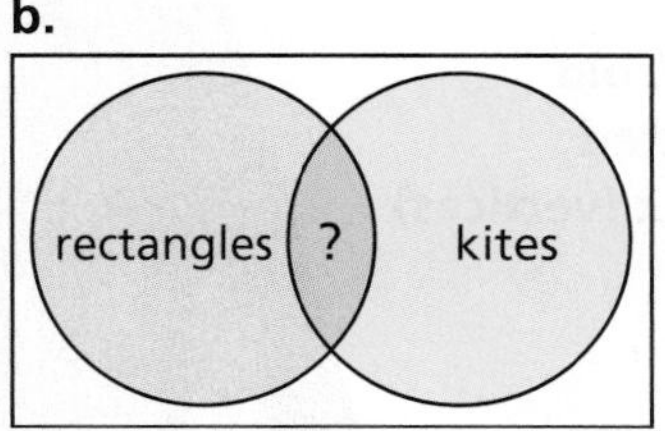

c.

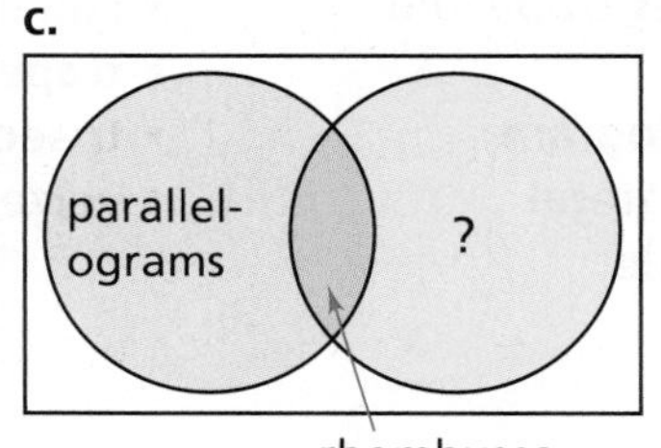

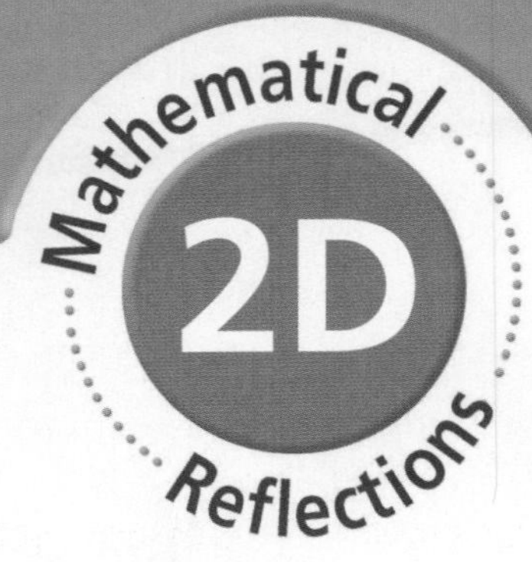

In this investigation, you studied different types of quadrilaterals, such as kites and trapezoids. You also studied the characteristics of the special types of parallelograms—rectangles, rhombuses, and squares.

1. Is a quadrilateral with perpendicular diagonals always a kite? Explain.
2. In the figure below, $\overline{ST} \cong \overline{RT}$, but the segments are not congruent to $\overline{TQ}$. All angles of $\triangle PTS$ and $\angle RTQ$ measure 60°. Prove that $PQRS$ is a trapezoid.

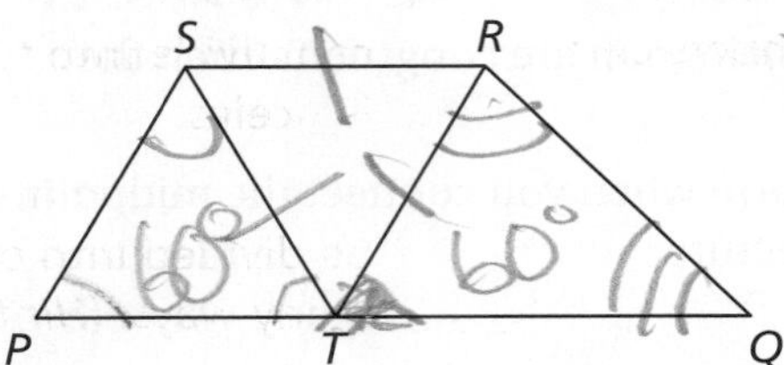

3. Describe the difference between a parallelogram and a rectangle.
4. Can a kite ever be a parallelogram? Explain.
5. Prove that a kite can be divided into two isosceles triangles by a single segment. Can this be done in more than one way? Explain.
6. List some special properties of each quadrilateral below.
   - parallelogram
   - kite
   - trapezoid
7. Are all squares also parallelograms? Are all parallelograms also squares? Explain.
8. If a statement is true, must its converse also be true?

Vocabulary

In this investigation, you learned these terms. Make sure you understand what each one means and how to use it.

- **base angle**
- **base of a trapezoid**
- **closed figure**
- **concave**
- **isosceles trapezoid**
- **kite**
- **parallelogram**
- **quadrilateral**
- **rectangle**
- **rhombus**
- **self-intersecting figure**
- **side**
- **skew quadrilateral**
- **square**
- **trapezoid**
- **trisected**
- **vertex (vertices)**

Nonconformity stands out.

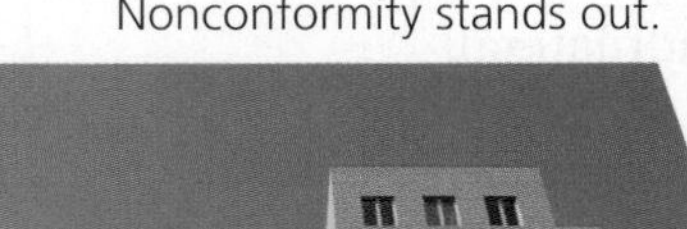

Project: Using Mathematical Habits

Dividing Into Congruent Pieces

Draw several different triangles. Try to divide your triangles into the following numbers of congruent triangles.

- two
- three
- four
- five

Margaret divided this triangle into two congruent triangles.

1. Into how many of the above numbers of congruent triangles can you always divide any triangle? Explain.
2. Dividing a triangle into certain of the above numbers of congruent triangles is possible only if you begin with a special type of triangle. How is it special?
3. For which of the above numbers, if any, is it *impossible* to find a triangle that can be divided into that number of congruent triangles?
4. **Write About It** Explain why a triangle that you can divide into two congruent triangles must be isosceles.
5. **Write About It** Explain why any triangle can be divided into congruent triangles in infinitely many ways. (*Hint:* See Exercise 1.)
6. Draw five different squares. Try to divide the squares into the following numbers of congruent triangles.
   - two
   - three
   - four
   - five
   - six
7. For what values of n is it easy to divide a square into n congruent triangles? Explain.
8. Give a convincing argument that it is impossible to divide a square into 3 congruent triangles.

A Noncongruent Challenge

9. Show how to divide an 11-by-15 rectangle into nine squares so that no two of the squares have a side completely in common. The squares are not necessarily congruent.

Chapter Review

In **Investigation 2A** you learned how to

- define congruence
- test for congruence in triangles
- use the correct language and notation to read and write statements about congruent figures

The following questions will help you check your understanding.

1. Use $\triangle ABC$. Draw point D so that $\overline{BC}$ is the angle bisector of $\angle ACD$ and of $\angle ABD$. Prove that $\triangle ABC \cong \triangle DBC$.

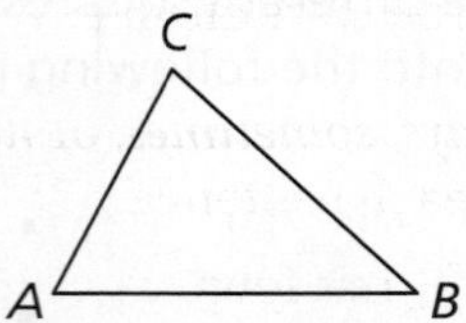

2. Use your drawing from Exercise 1. Choose a point P on $\overline{BC}$. Prove that $\overline{AP} \cong \overline{DP}$.

In **Investigation 2B** you learned how to

- identify parallel lines by looking at pairs of angles that are formed when the lines are cut by transversals
- identify pairs of congruent angles when parallel lines are cut by transversals
- write and present a deductive proof
- prove that the sum of the angle measures of a triangle is 180°

The following questions will help you check your understanding.

3. Draw $\overline{AB}$. Draw two parallel lines—one through A and one through B. Choose a point C on the line through A. Choose a point D on the line through B. Choose C and D so that they are on opposite sides of $\overline{AB}$ and $\overline{AC} \cong \overline{BD}$. Draw $\overline{CD}$. Let E name the point where $\overline{AB}$ and $\overline{CD}$ intersect. Prove that E is the midpoint of $\overline{AB}$.

4. What is the sum of the measures of the angles of a quadrilateral?

5. Use the figure below. Suppose $\angle 1 \cong \angle 5$. What can you conclude about lines ℓ and m? Explain.

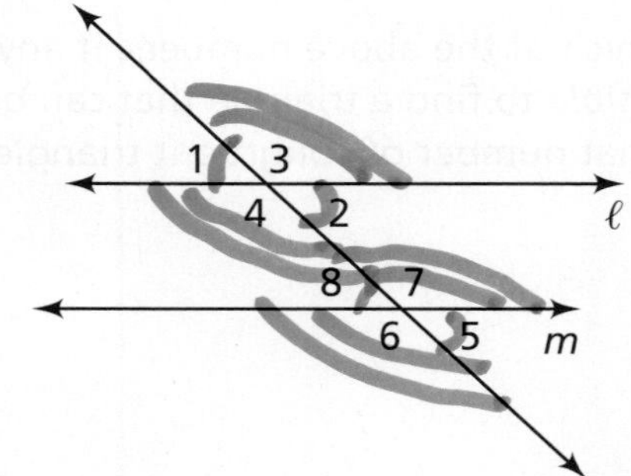

In **Investigation 2C** you learned how to

- recognize the difference between experimentation and deduction
- write and present triangle congruence proofs
- use the Perpendicular Bisector Theorem
- apply the Isosceles Triangle Theorem to prove parts of a figure are congruent

The following questions will help you check your understanding.

6. Draw $\overline{AB}$ that is less than 4 cm long. Find a point R that is 2 cm from both A and B. Find a point S that is 3 cm from both A and B. Draw $\overleftrightarrow{RS}$. Prove that $\overleftrightarrow{RS} \perp \overline{AB}$.

7. Describe the type of triangle that has the given property.

a. The bisector of exactly one angle of the triangle contains the midpoint of the opposite side.

b. Each altitude of the triangle coincides with a perpendicular bisector of a side.

8. Use the figure below. $\triangle ABC \cong \triangle DCB$. Prove that $\triangle CTB$ is isosceles.

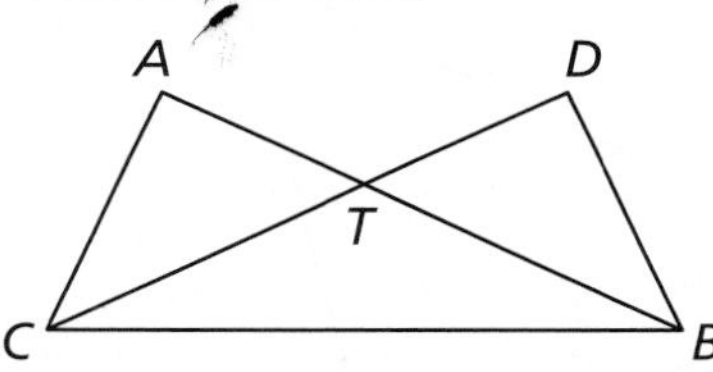

In **Investigation 2D** you learned how to

- classify quadrilaterals
- understand the meaning of *converse*
- reason by continuity
- understand the meaning of *always, never,* and *sometimes* in mathematics

The following questions will help you check your understanding.

9. Write the converse of the following statement.

If a quadrilateral is a kite, then the diagonals of the quadrilateral intersect to form right angles.

Determine whether the converse is true. If it is true, provide a written proof. If it is not, provide a counterexample.

10. Write *always, sometimes,* or *never* to best complete each sentence.

a. A kite __?__ has four congruent sides.

b. The diagonals of a parallelogram __?__ bisect each other.

c. The diagonals of a rectangle are __?__ perpendicular.

d. A kite __?__ has exactly one pair of parallel sides.

Chapter 2 Test

1. If $\triangle DEF \cong \triangle LMN$, which of the following must be a correct congruence statement?

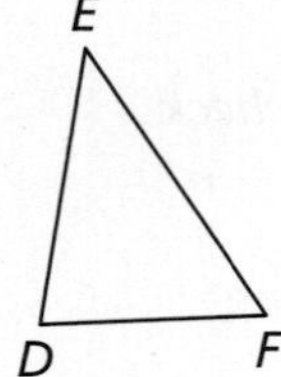
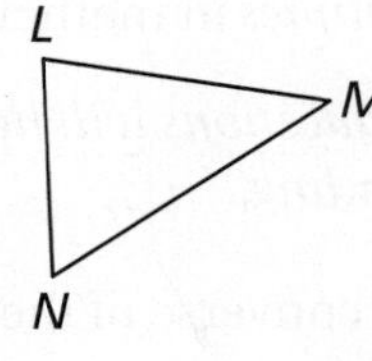

A. $\angle D \cong \angle N$ **B.** $\angle F \cong \angle L$
C. $\overline{EF} \cong \overline{MN}$ **D.** $\overline{DE} \cong \overline{NM}$

2. What other information do you need to prove that the two triangles are congruent by SSS?

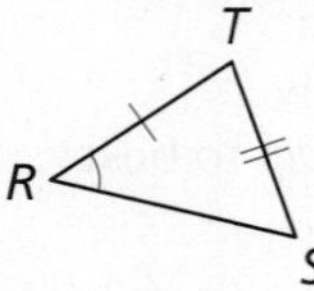
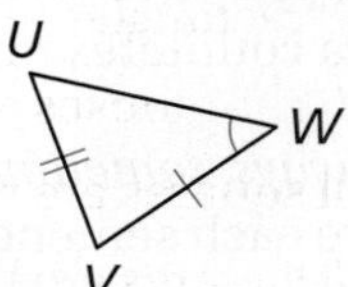

A. $\overline{RS} \cong \overline{WU}$
B. $\angle T \cong \angle V$
C. $\angle S \cong \angle U$
D. no additional information needed

3. Lines *f* and *g* are parallel. Which statement can you deduce from this information?

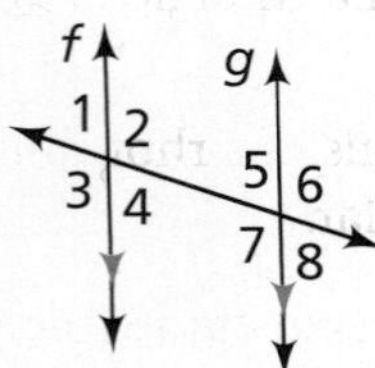

A. $\angle 3 \cong \angle 8$ **B.** $\angle 3 \cong \angle 4$
C. $\angle 3 \cong \angle 7$ **D.** $\angle 3 \cong \angle 5$

4. The diagonals of a certain quadrilateral bisect each other and are perpendicular. What kind of quadrilateral must the figure be?

A. parallelogram **B.** rhombus
C. rectangle **D.** square

5. For each pair, decide whether the two figures are congruent. Explain your reasoning.

a.

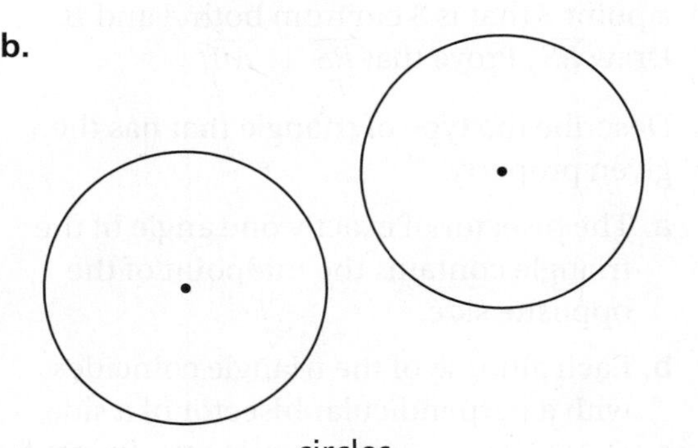

b.

circles

c.

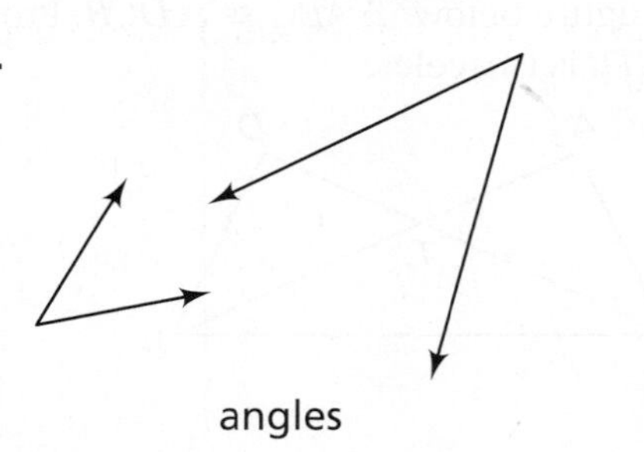

angles

d.

e.

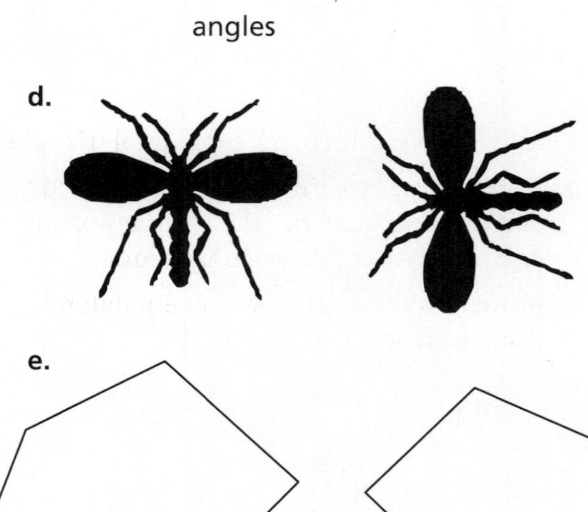

pentagons

6. For each diagram, use the given information. Determine whether the two triangles are congruent. If they are congruent, prove it using the triangle congruence postulates.

a. $ABCD$ is a parallelogram. Is $\triangle ABC \cong \triangle CDA$?

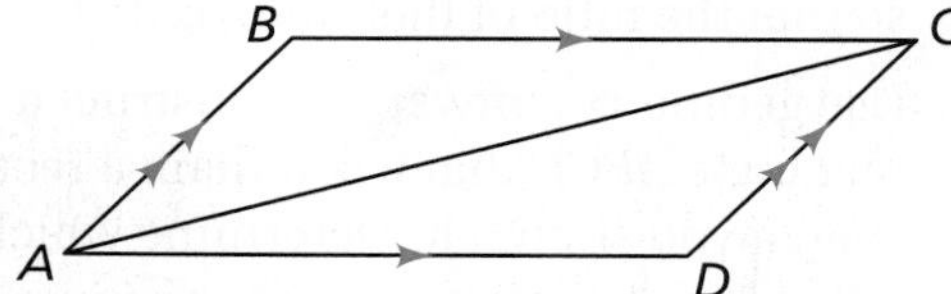

b. $\angle ADE \cong \angle B$ and $\angle AED \cong \angle C$. Is $\triangle ABC \cong \triangle ADE$?

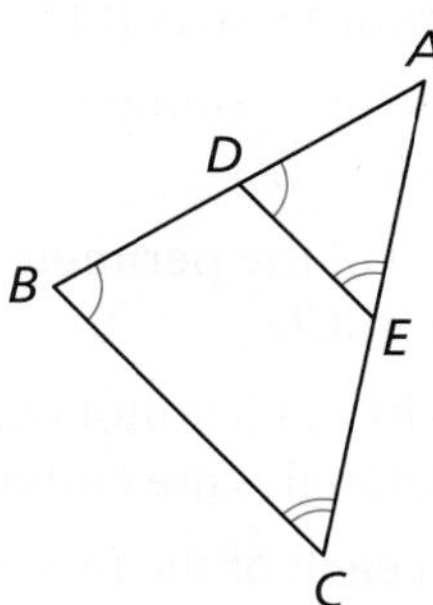

c. $\triangle ABC$ is an equilateral triangle. Points E and F are the midpoints of $\overline{AB}$ and $\overline{CB}$, respectively. Is $\triangle EAC \cong \triangle FCA$?

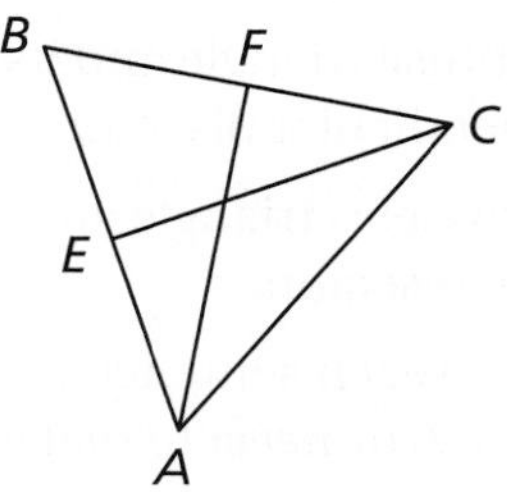

7. Recall the definition of an equilateral triangle.

a. Describe an experiment that would lead you to conjecture that the altitudes of an equilateral triangle are congruent.

b. Prove that the altitudes of an equilateral triangle are congruent.

8. Use the figure below. Lines m and n are parallel. Prove that $m\angle 1 = m\angle 2$.

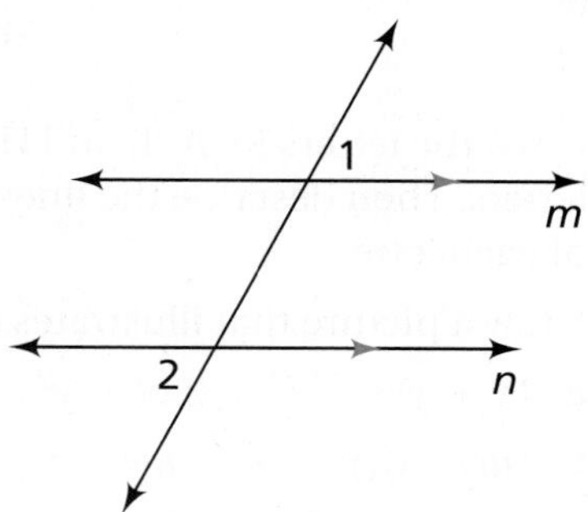

9. Decide whether each statement is true. If a statement is not true, provide a counterexample.

a. All rectangles are squares.

b. All trapezoids are parallelograms.

c. All rectangles are parallelograms.

d. All rhombuses are squares.

e. All squares are rhombuses.

f. All squares are kites.

g. All parallelograms are kites.

10. Write *always, sometimes,* or *never* to best complete each sentence.

a. The diagonals of a kite _?_ bisect each other.

b. The diagonals of a parallelogram _?_ bisect each other.

c. A median of a triangle is _?_ an altitude of the triangle.

d. The diagonals of a rhombus are _?_ perpendicular.

11. Write the converse of the following statement.

If an altitude of a triangle is the perpendicular bisector of one side of the triangle, then the triangle is equilateral.

If the statement is true, provide a written proof.

If the converse is true, provide a written proof.

Chapter 2

Cumulative Review

1. Draw the letters M, A, T, and H as block letters. Then describe the lines of symmetry of each letter.

2. Draw a picture that illustrates each equation.

   a. $(x + y)^2 = x^2 + 2xy + y^2$

   b. $(w + x)(y + z) = wy + wz + xy + xz$

3. Describe each shape by name. Then write directions that describe how to draw each shape.

   a. 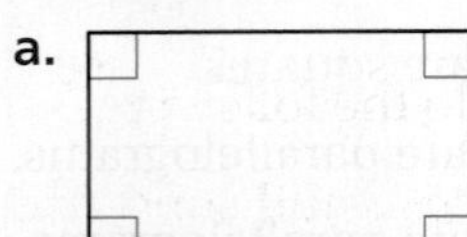

   b. 

4. Describe how to construct a midline of a triangle.

5. On a sheet of paper, copy line ℓ and point P. Then construct the line through P that is parallel to ℓ.

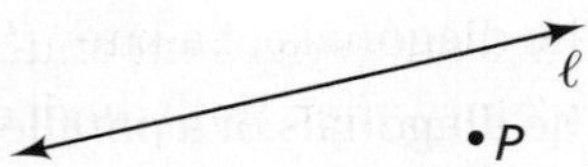

6. Construct an equilateral triangle with 2-in. sides.

7. Copy the angle onto a sheet of paper. Then construct its bisector.

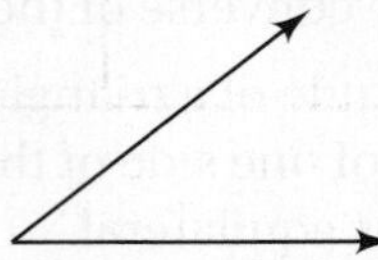

8. Use geometry software to draw a triangle. Then construct one of its altitudes.

9. Construct each figure so that it is UnMessUpable. Write clear directions that describe each construction.

   a. a square

   b. a right triangle

   c. two congruent circles that pass through each other's centers

10. Construct two circles that share a center so that the ratio of their radii is 3 : 1.

11. Use geometry software to construct a rectangle $ABCD$ that will remain a rectangle, even if you stretch it. Determine which of the following measures, if any, is an invariant.

    a. the ratio of the lengths of the opposite sides, $\frac{AB}{CD}$

    b. the perimeter of $ABCD$

    c. the ratio of the lengths of the diagonals, $\frac{AC}{BD}$

    d. the ratio of the perimeter of $ABCD$ to the area of $ABCD$

12. Explain why you cannot use SSA to prove that two triangles are congruent.

13. Construct each of the following. Label each point of concurrency.

    a. an equilateral triangle and its three altitudes

    b. a right triangle and its three medians

    c. an obtuse triangle and its three perpendicular bisectors

    d. an isosceles triangle and its three angle bisectors

14. Complete each sentence with *always, sometimes,* or *never* to make the statement true.

    a. The altitudes of a regular polygon with an odd number of sides are __?__ concurrent.

    b. The medians of a regular polygon with an odd number of sides are __?__ concurrent.

    c. The angle bisectors of a regular polygon are __?__ concurrent.

15. Explain the difference between the terms *congruent* and *equal.*

16. Are all right isosceles triangles congruent? Explain.

For Exercises 17 and 18, do the following. The triangles in each pair are congruent.

a. Write a congruence statement.

b. Tell which congruence postulate or theorem helped you decide.

17.

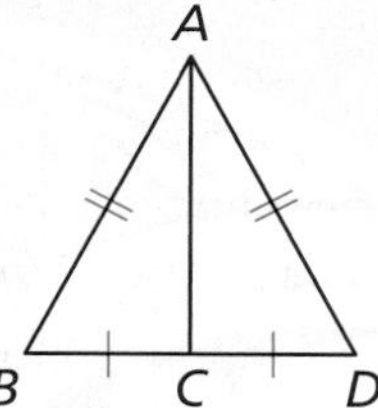

18.

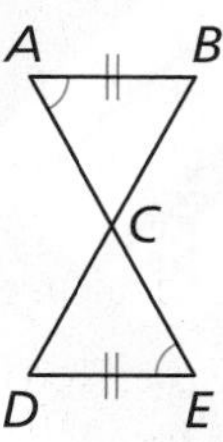

19. In the figure below, M is the midpoint of $\overline{AB}$ and $\overline{CD}$. Prove that $\triangle ADM \cong \triangle BCM$.

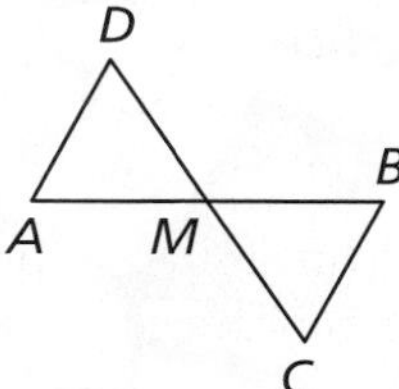

20. If you and a classmate both construct $\triangle ABC$ so that $m\angle A = 53°$, $m\angle B = 39°$, and $m\angle C = 88°$, will your two triangles be congruent? Explain.

21. In the figure below, $f \parallel g$. Classify each pair of angles as *alternate interior angles, consecutive angles,* or *corresponding angles.*

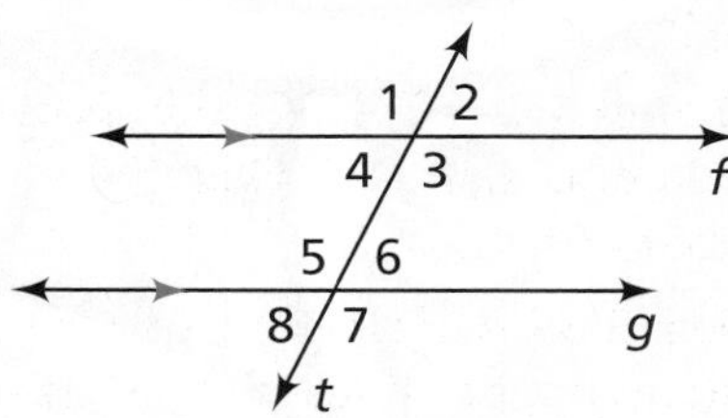

a. $\angle 4$ and $\angle 6$ **b.** $\angle 5$ and $\angle 4$

c. $\angle 3$ and $\angle 7$ **d.** $\angle 5$ and $\angle 1$

22. In the figure below, $m \parallel n$. Find $m\angle 1$ and $m\angle 2$.

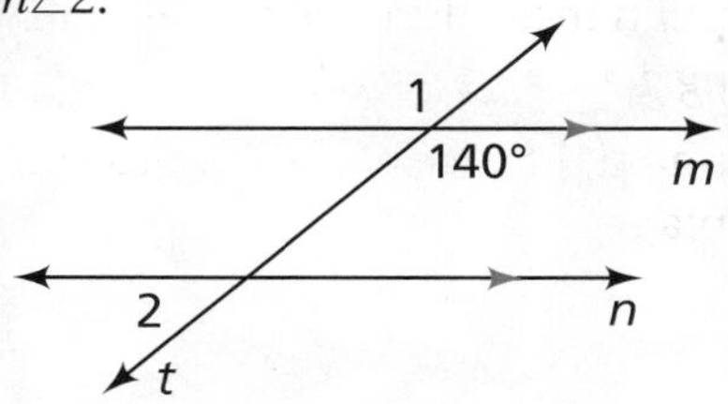

23. In the figure, H is the midpoint of $\overline{GI}$ and K is the midpoint of $\overline{GL}$. Prove that $\overleftrightarrow{HK} \parallel \overleftrightarrow{IL}$.

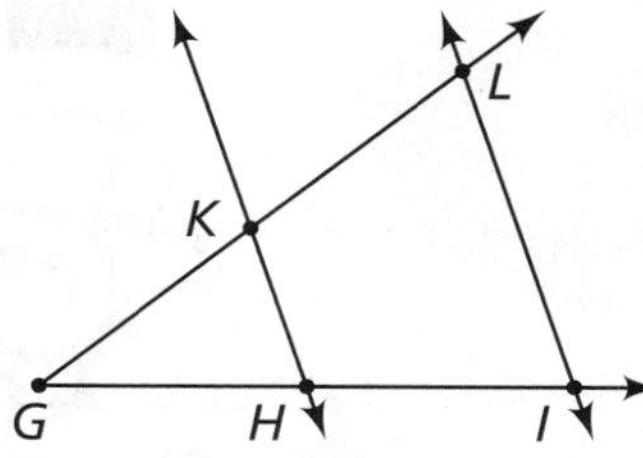

24. Given $\overline{AB} \parallel \overline{CD}$ and $\overline{AB} \cong \overline{CD}$

Prove $\triangle ABC \cong \triangle CDA$

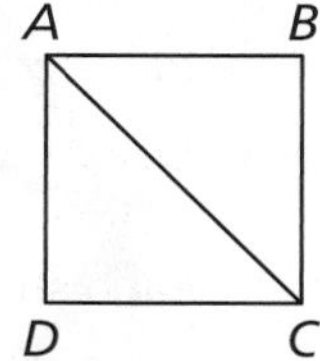

For Exercises 25–27, do the following.

a. Identify the hypothesis and conclusion.

b. Draw a picture that illustrates the hypothesis.

c. Decide whether the statement is true.

d. If the statement is true, give a proof. If the statement is false, give a counterexample.

25. Two lines that are parallel to a third line are parallel to each other.

26. An equiangular parallelogram is a square.

27. If two angles are congruent and supplementary, then both angles are right angles.

28. Make a flowchart for the proof without writing the actual proof.

Given $\ell \perp \overline{AB}$, ℓ bisects $\overline{AB}$ at C, and P is on ℓ.

Prove $\overline{PA} \cong \overline{PB}$

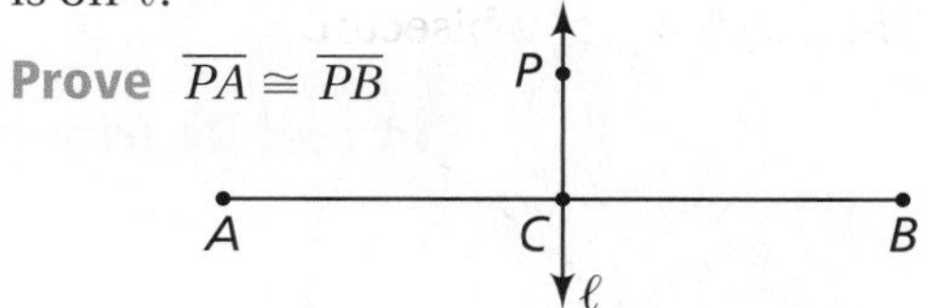

For Exercises 29 and 30, write a reverse list. Then prove each statement.

29. If a point is on the bisector of an angle, then the point is equidistant from the sides of the angle.

30. If a point is equidistant from the sides of an angle, then that point is on the bisector of the angle.

Chapter
3
Investigations at a Glance
3A Cut and Rearrange
3B Area Formulas
3C Proof by Dissection
3D Measuring Solids

Dissections and Area

"Who has more?" has been an important question ever since people started sharing.

To compare two pieces of string, for example, it is enough to see which is longer. You can stretch them out together, or you can measure the strings with a ruler.

But suppose you are comparing pieces of glass. If the pieces are congruent, they are obviously the same size. But if the shapes are different, how can you tell which is larger? You might be able to compare them directly. For example, if one piece fits completely inside the other, then you know it is smaller.

Unfortunately, there is not a tool like a ruler to measure area. For some shapes, however, there are some measurements you can make with a ruler to help you find the areas. This chapter is about knowing which measurements to make, how to calculate with them, and why the calculations work.

Vocabulary

- algorithm
- apex
- base
- circumference
- cone
- cylinder
- face
- frustum
- height
- hypotenuse
- lateral face
- lateral surface
- lateral surface area
- oblique
- perimeter
- polyhedron
- pyramid
- Pythagorean triple
- right prism
- right pyramid
- scissors-congruent
- slant height
- surface area
- volume

Cut and Rearrange

In *Cut and Rearrange,* you will cut a given shape into parts. Then you will rearrange the parts to form a second shape. Cutting and rearranging will not convert a given shape into just any other imaginable shape. For example, you would not expect the resulting shape to have greater or lesser area. Chih-Han Sah was a mathematician who specialized in dissections of this sort. He called two figures that can be cut into each other scissors-congruent.

By the end of this investigation, you will be able to answer questions like these.

1. What is an algorithm?
2. Why is it important to justify each step in an algorithm?
3. What does the Midline Theorem say about the relationship between a midline and the sides of a triangle?

You will learn how to

- devise and follow algorithms to dissect and rearrange one figure into an equal-area figure
- justify each cut in a dissection
- write general algorithms for dissections
- test algorithms with standard and extreme cases

You will develop these habits and skills:

- Visualize ways to make equal-area figures through dissection.
- Write clear and precise algorithms.
- Reason by continuity to identify extreme cases.

The total area remains the same no matter how you arrange the pieces.

3.01 Getting Started

Geometric language helps you clearly describe how to move pieces to change one shape to another. Assume that you have a shape made of two congruent right triangles. You can use three types of moves to change the shape into another.

In the figure at the upper left, the two right triangles form a parallelogram. Moving clockwise, you can

- slide the gold triangle parallel to a base of the parallelogram to form a rectangle
- reflect the gold triangle across the dashed line to form a kite
- rotate the gold triangle about a vertex to form a triangle
- reflect the gold triangle across the dashed line to form the original parallelogram

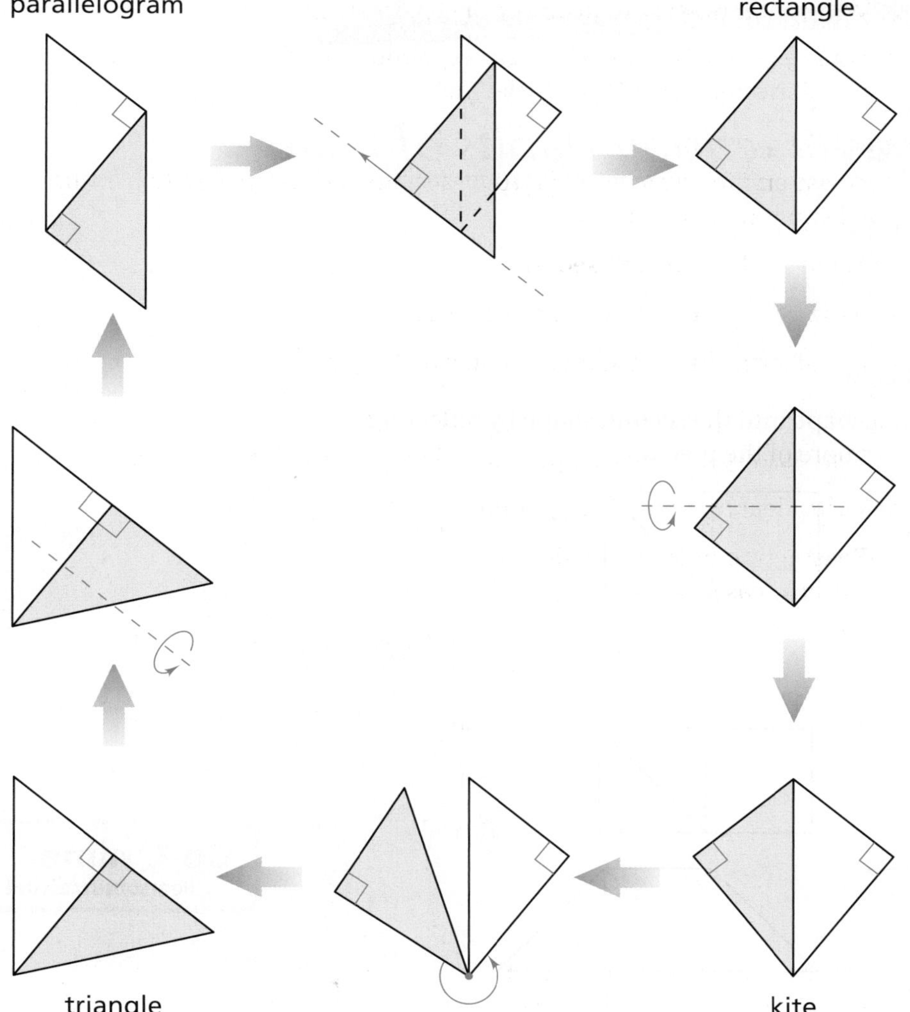

For You to Explore

For Problems 1–5, start with the shape described. (Your teacher may give you copies of shapes to work with.) Cut this shape into pieces that you can rearrange to form the second shape described in the problem. The two shapes are **scissors-congruent.** Write a complete description of the cuts you made and how you moved the pieces.

1. Start with a parallelogram. Cut and rearrange to form a rectangle.
2. Start with a right triangle. Cut and rearrange to form a rectangle.
3. Start with a (not right) scalene triangle. Cut and form a parallelogram.
4. Start with a (not right) scalene triangle. Cut and form a rectangle.
5. Start with a trapezoid. Cut the trapezoid and form a rectangle.

Each problem can be solved in more than one way. Work with classmates to find a few solutions. Then pick one that you like best. Save your written work. You will need it later.

Remember...

A scalene triangle has no two sides the same length.

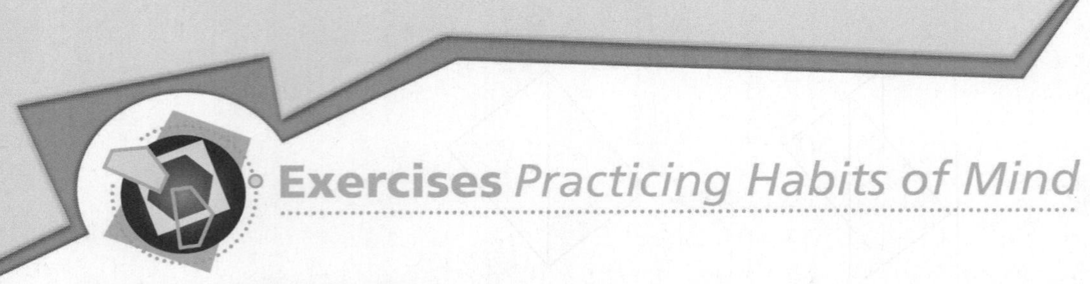

Exercises *Practicing Habits of Mind*

On Your Own

6. Study each pair of figures below.

Describe how to turn the first shape into the second shape by reflecting, rotating, or translating one or more of the pieces.

a.

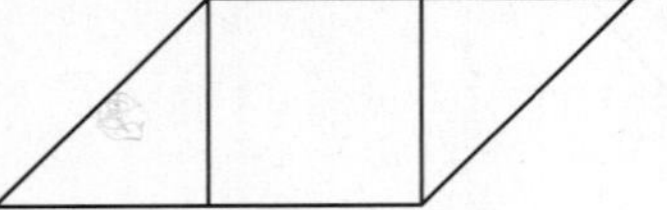

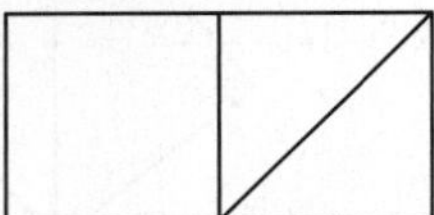

b.

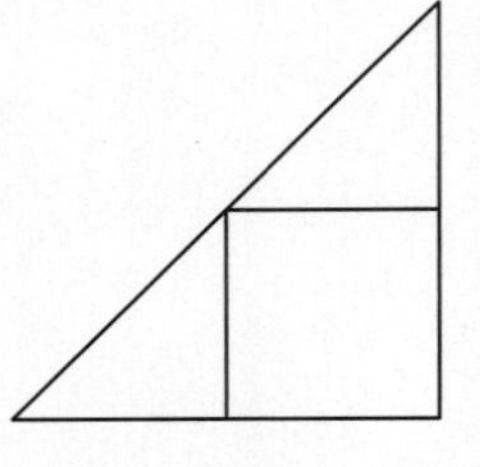

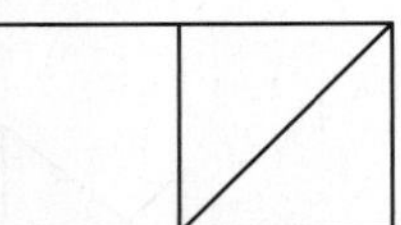

c.

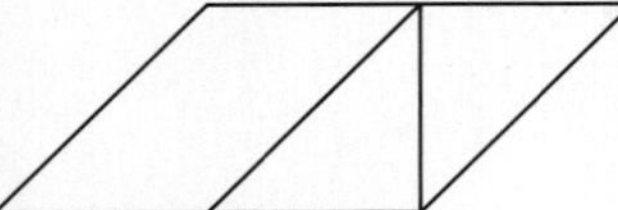

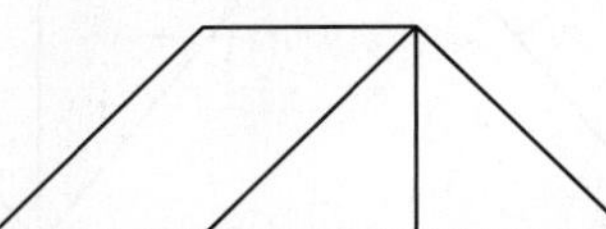

7. Here is one definition of congruence.

Two polygons are congruent if there is a transformation (reflection, rotation, translation, or combination of these) that maps one of the polygons onto the other.

"Translation" is another way of saying *slide*.

For example, polygons A and B are congruent. If you move A to the right and rotate it 90° clockwise, it will fit exactly on B.

Decide whether the polygons in each pair below are congruent. If they are, describe a transformation that maps A onto B. If they are not, explain how you know.

a.

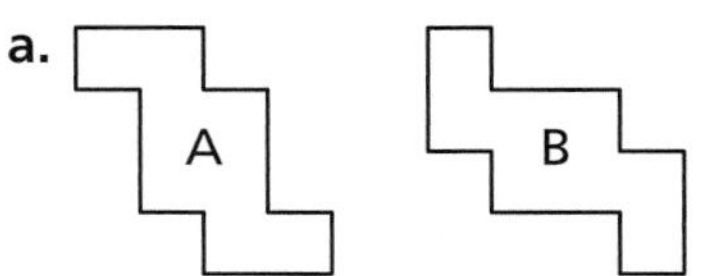

b.

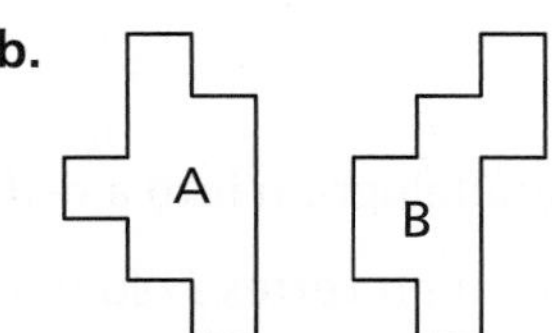

c.

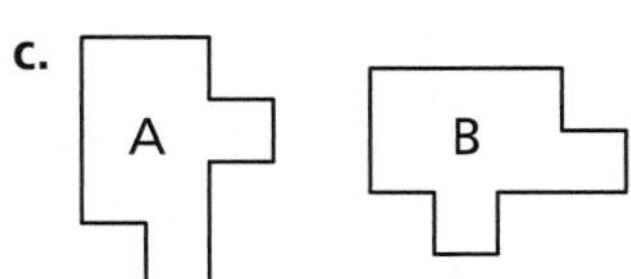

8. Combine two polygons shaped like the polygon at the right to form new polygons. For example, you can make a polygon like the one below.

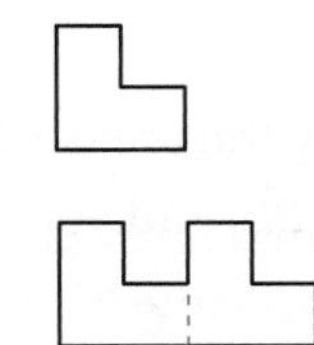

Form as many *different* polygons as you can. Polygons that are reflections, rotations, or translations of polygons you already have do not count as different. You may want to use graph paper.

Maintain Your Skills

9. Start with two congruent isosceles right triangles and a square. The sides of the square have the same length as each leg of the triangles. Put all three pieces together to form each figure.

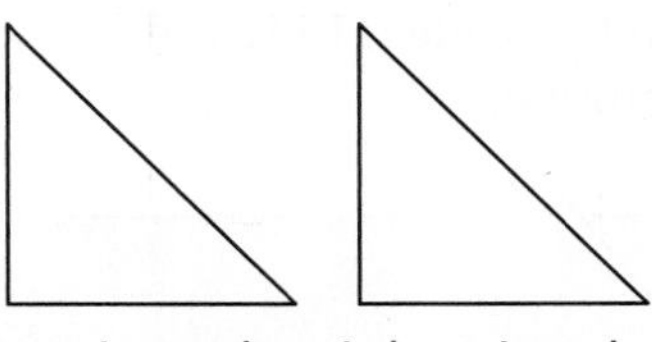

two isosceles right triangles

a. a trapezoid

b. a right triangle

c. a parallelogram that is not a rectangle

d. a rectangle

3.02 Do the Cuts Really Work?

Have you ever expected a dissection to work, but then discovered that the pieces did not quite fit? Or perhaps the pieces looked like they fit, but you found it difficult to be sure?

A dissection involves cutting something into pieces. In this book, a dissection also involves rearranging those pieces.

To understand why a dissection works, you must know properties of the shapes you are cutting. Here are some properties of parallelograms that you learned in Chapter 2.

- Parallelograms have exactly four sides.
- Opposite sides are parallel.
- Opposite sides are congruent.
- Opposite angles are congruent.
- Consecutive angles are supplementary.
- The diagonals bisect each other.

Here is Tony's method for dissecting a parallelogram into a rectangle.

Cut out the parallelogram. Make a fold through vertex D so that A lines up on the bottom, on $\overline{AB}$.

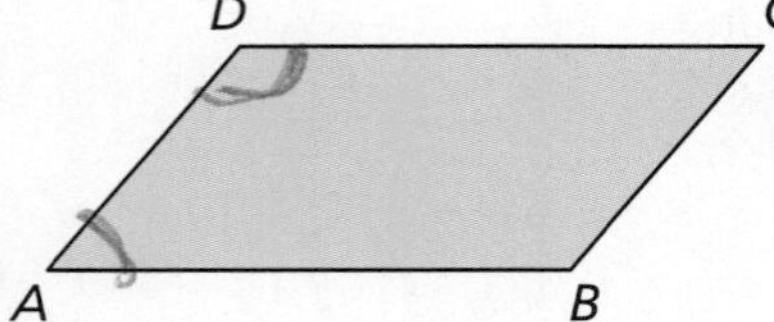

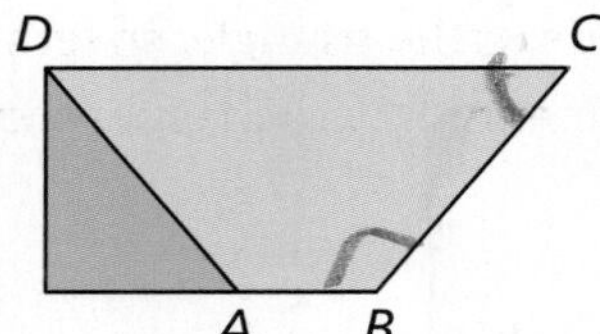

Then unfold and cut along the crease. Slide the triangular piece along $\overline{AB}$ so that $\overline{AD}$ matches up with $\overline{BC}$ and you have a rectangle.

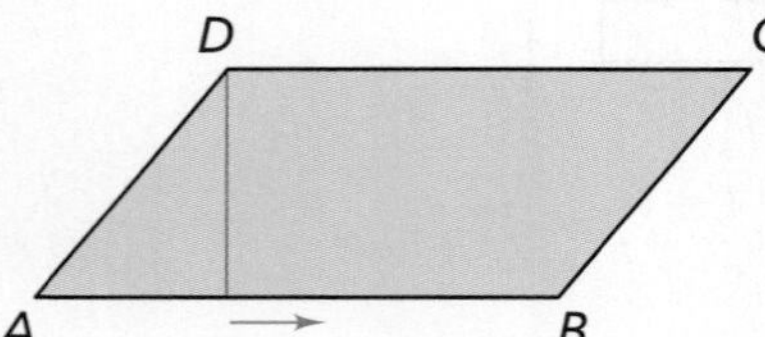

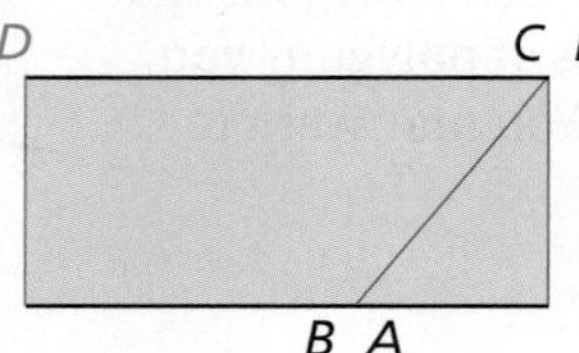

Tony cut two pieces: a triangle and a trapezoid. He then rearranged those pieces. But what guaranteed that the rearrangement had four sides? Here are two ways that his dissection might fail.

The newly glued edges might not match.

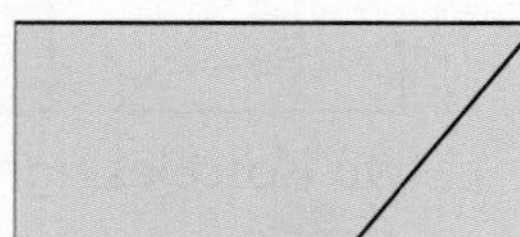

The new bottom edge might be crooked.

For Discussion

In Tony's method on the previous page, you slide the triangle to the opposite side of the trapezoid. Explain how the properties of parallelograms guarantee each of the following.

1. The two pieces fit together exactly.
2. The new bottom edge is straight.

Minds in Action episode 5

Sasha and Derman are trying to dissect $\triangle ABC$ into a parallelogram.

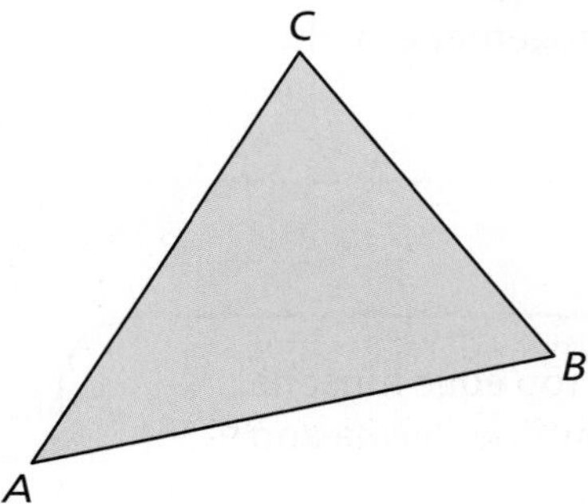

Sasha A midline is parallel to one side of the triangle, so let's make one. Find the midpoint of $\overline{AC}$. Name it M. Find the midpoint of $\overline{BC}$. Name it N. Cut along $\overline{MN}$.

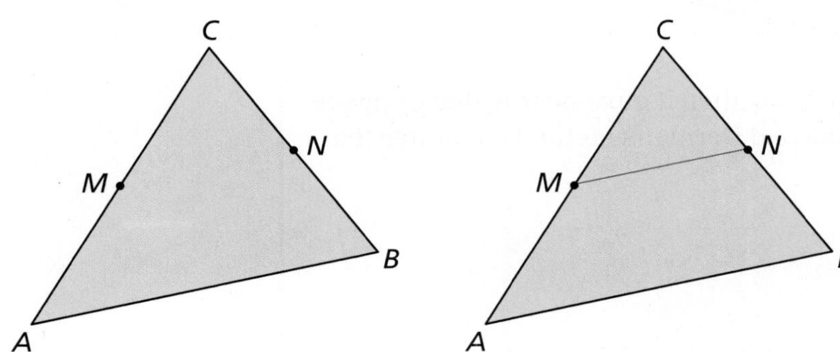

Derman I see where you're going with this. You can rotate $\triangle MCN$—the triangle you just cut off—around M, until $\overline{MC}$ matches up with $\overline{MA}$.

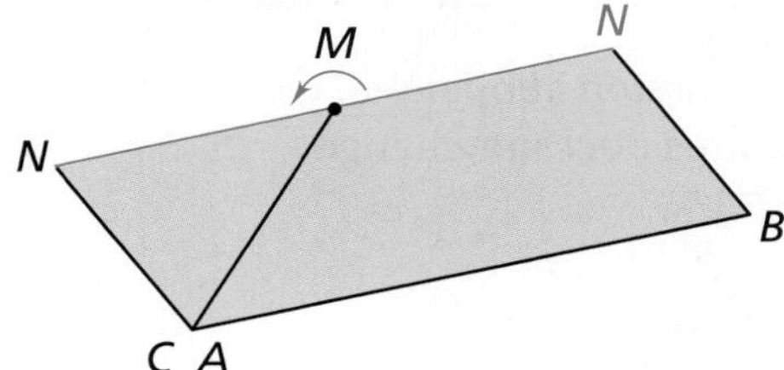

Sasha Now we have a parallelogram, right?

Derman I guess we do, but what if it just *looks* like a parallelogram? What if our scissors techniques aren't accurate and the picture should really look like this?

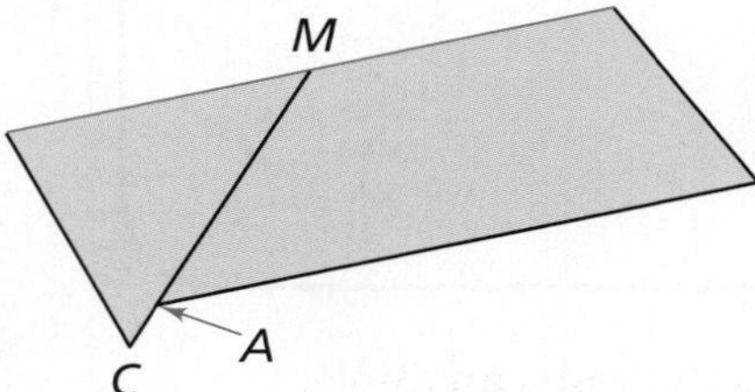

Sasha Good try Derman. But the steps we took *guarantee* that we can stick those pieces together.

See, since M is the midpoint of $\overline{AC}$ in the original triangle, MC must equal MA. So, sides $\overline{MC}$ and $\overline{MA}$ fit together exactly.

Derman Aaaahhh. It's a proof!

For Discussion

3. If the final figure is really a parallelogram, then the top edge must be straight. It must not look like the picture below. How does Sasha and Derman's method guarantee that it will be straight?

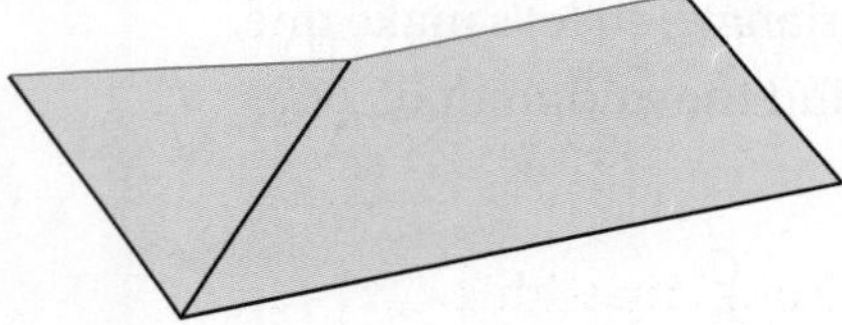

4. If the final figure is really a parallelogram, then it must be true that opposite sides are congruent. How does Sasha and Derman's method guarantee that $\overline{CN} \cong \overline{BN}$? That $\overline{AB} \cong \overline{NN}$?

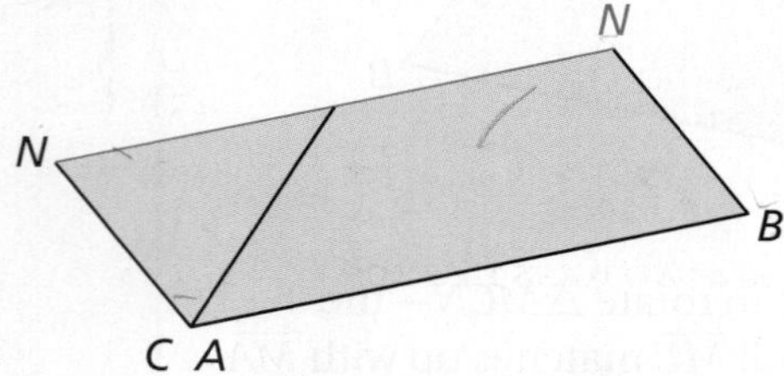

Later in this chapter you will see a more formal discussion about area. For now, assume that a polygon has area and that the area does not change when you dissect the polygon.

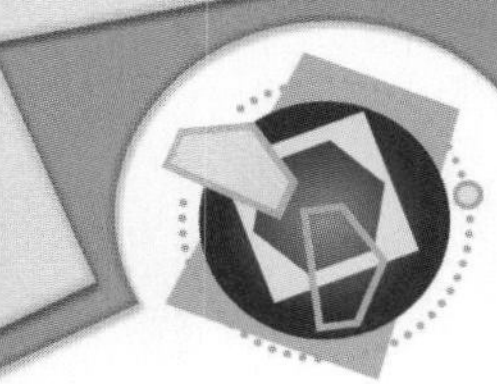

Exercises *Practicing Habits of Mind*

Check Your Understanding

1. Write About It List all the properties of rectangles that you can think of. Here is a start.

- Rectangles are parallelograms.
- Rectangles have exactly four sides.
- All angles measure 90°.

Habits of Mind

Make a list. Listing all properties—even obvious or redundant ones—can help you notice things you might otherwise overlook.

Here is Diego's method for turning a rectangle into an isosceles triangle. Use this for Exercises 2 and 3.

Start with a rectangle. Cut along a diagonal.

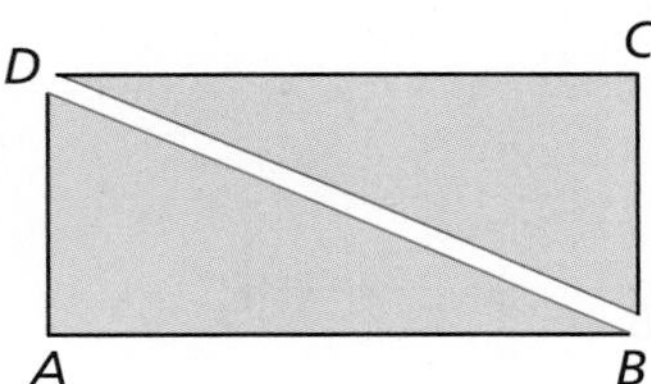

Slide $\triangle ABD$ to the right, along the bottom, so $\overline{AD}$ lines up with $\overline{BC}$. Then flip $\triangle ABD$ so you have a triangle instead of a parallelogram.

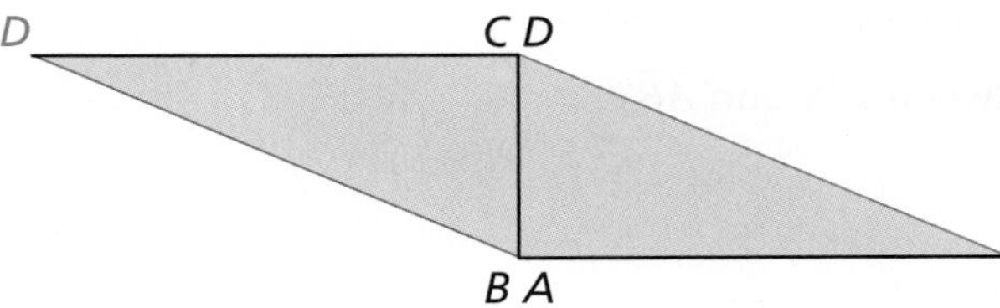

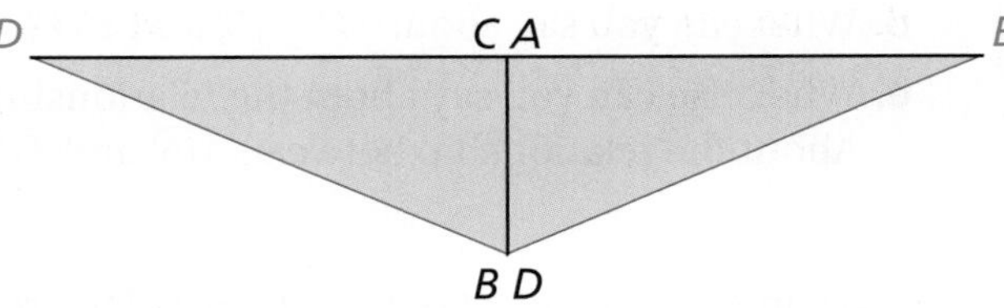

Diego's diagonal cut makes two triangles. Below are two ways that the dissection might fail.

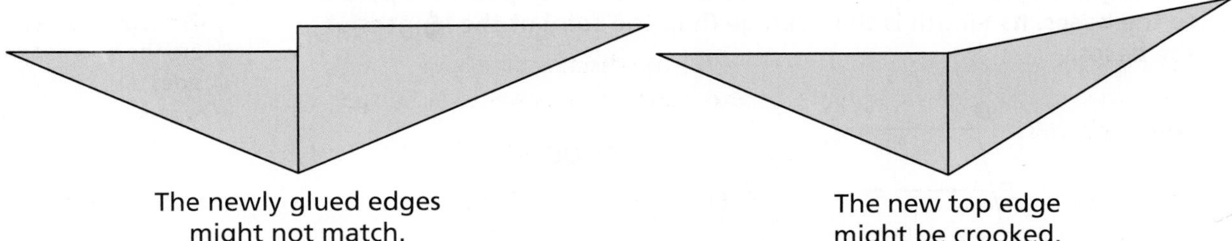

The newly glued edges might not match.

The new top edge might be crooked.

2. For Diego's method on the previous page, explain how the properties of rectangles guarantee the following.

a. $\overline{AD}$ fits $\overline{BC}$ exactly.

b. The new top edge is straight.

3. If Diego cuts along the other diagonal, will he get a different triangle? Explain. Be sure to use what you know about rectangles.

4. Can you reverse a dissection process? Choose three shapes from the list below. For each shape, start with a rectangle and dissect it into pieces you can rearrange to form that shape.

a. an isosceles triangle

b. a right triangle

c. a nonrectangular parallelogram

d. a scalene triangle

e. a trapezoid

5. For trapezoid $ABCD$, $\overline{MN}$ connects midpoint M of $\overline{AD}$ and midpoint N of $\overline{BC}$. Draw segment $\overline{DN}$. Then show the line through D and N and the line through A and B meeting at point P.

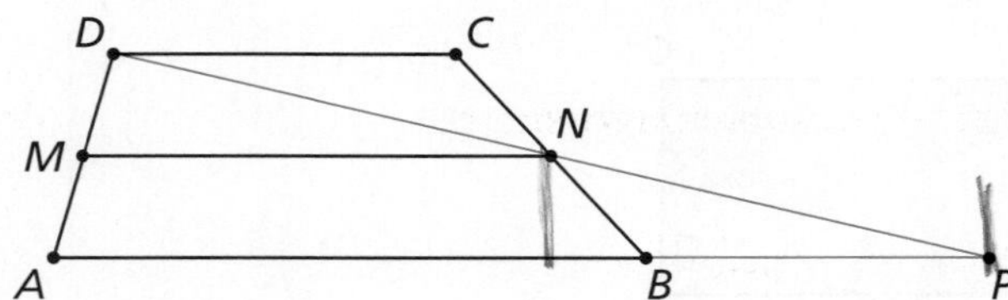

a. Find two congruent triangles in the diagram. Prove they are congruent.

b. Use these triangles to show that $\overline{CD} \cong \overline{BP}$.

c. What does Theorem 2.10 (the Midline Theorem) say about $\overline{MN}$ and $\overline{AP}$?

d. What can you say about $\overline{MN}$, $\overline{AB}$, and $\overline{CD}$?

e. What else can you say about the relationship between $\overline{MN}$ and $\overline{AB}$? About the relationship between $\overline{MN}$ and $\overline{DC}$?

You can state the result of Exercise 5 as Theorem 3.1.

Theorem 3.1

The segment joining the midpoints of the legs of a trapezoid is parallel to the bases. Its length is the average (half the sum) of the lengths of the bases.

The legs of a trapezoid are the two nonparallel sides.

D C E F A B

$\overline{AB} \parallel \overline{EF} \parallel \overline{DC}$

$EF = \frac{1}{2}(AB + DC)$

6. **Take It Further** Show how to dissect a parallelogram and rearrange the parts to form a rectangle that has one base that is congruent to a diagonal of the parallelogram.

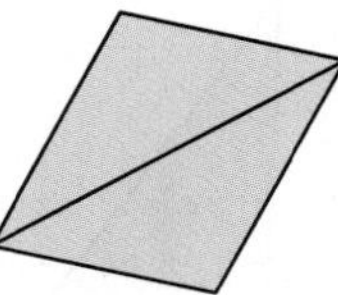

7. **Take It Further** Start with a rectangle. Use dissection to make a rectangle with no sides congruent to the sides of the original figure.

On Your Own

8. Make a second copy of the trapezoid you used for Problem 5 in Lesson 3.1. Dissect it so that the pieces form a triangle.

9. Use a dissection argument. Show that $\triangle ABC$ is scissors-congruent to a right triangle.

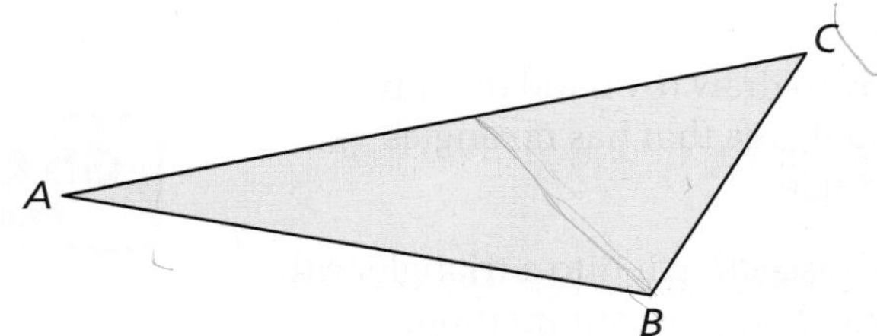

10. Cut a square into a rectangle that has a base congruent to one of the square's diagonals. Describe your steps.

11. **Take It Further** Start with an isosceles triangle with two sides of length *s*. Dissect it into two parts that you can rearrange to form a new isosceles triangle with two sides of length *s*. Are the two isosceles triangles congruent? Explain.

12. **Standardized Test Prep** *ACDF* is a trapezoid. *B* is the midpoint of $\overline{AC}$, and *E* is the midpoint of $\overline{DF}$. *CD* is 1.00 m. *BE* is 2.75 m. What is *AF*?

A. 1.875 m **B.** 3.75 m

C. 4.50 m **D.** 5.50 m

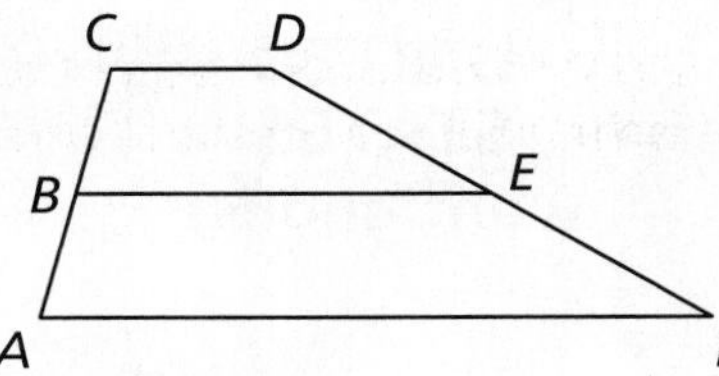

13. **Take It Further** Can you dissect any quadrilateral into a rectangle? Trace each figure. Then try to cut and rearrange it into a rectangle.

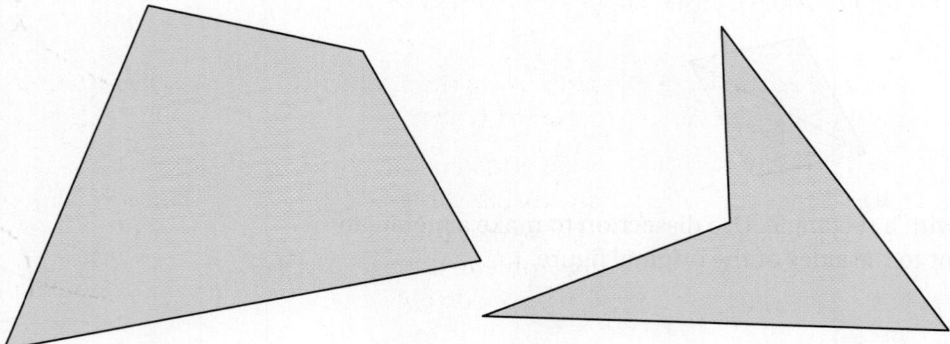

14. **Take It Further** If you suspect that two shapes have unequal areas, how could you show that one has greater area than the other?

Maintain Your Skills

15. Start with a scalene triangle. Think of a way to draw (by hand or with geometry software) another triangle of equal area that has no angles congruent to the angles of the original triangle.

16. Start with a scalene triangle. Find a way of dissecting it into a triangle with no sides congruent to the sides of the original. Justify your method.

Go Online
Pearsonsuccessnet.com

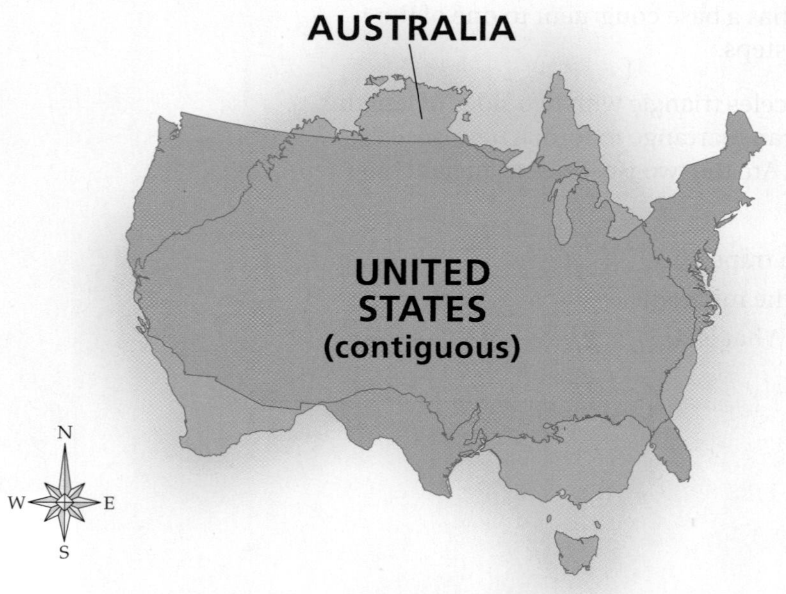

You can compare areas of irregular shapes by placing one shape over the other.

3.03 Cutting Algorithms

An **algorithm** is a process—a set of steps—that is completely determined. There is no unpredictability, no doubt what the steps will do each time you apply them. Many computer programs are algorithms, with every step precisely detailed.

The word *algorithm* is a distorted transliteration of the name of a well-known mathematician. Abu Ja'far Muhammad ibn Musa al-Khwarizmi lived in Baghdad about 850. The Latin attempt at spelling al-Khwarizmi was Algorismi, which later became algorism and then algorithm.

In Lesson 3.1, Problems 1–5 asked you to write a description of the cuts you made and how you moved the pieces. You may have written your descriptions as algorithms.

Now you will develop algorithms for successfully dissecting any triangle, trapezoid, or parallelogram into a rectangle. You will prove that your algorithms will always work. Remember that, for each problem, there may be many algorithms that work. However, there are others that do not work, or work only for special cases.

Later, you will use successful algorithms to develop formulas for the areas of triangles, parallelograms, and trapezoids.

Minds in Action episode 6

Sasha draws the pictures below to show how to dissect a triangle into a rectangle. Tony studies her pictures. Then he tries to write complete and precise instructions for the cuts and rearrangements.

Sasha Tony, here's how I dissected a triangle into a rectangle.

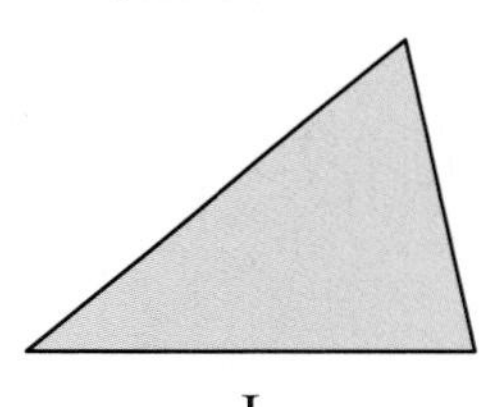

I

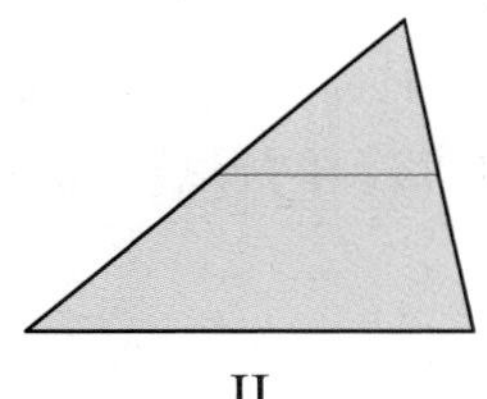

II

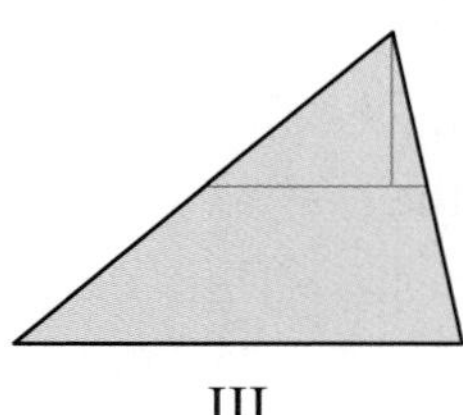

III

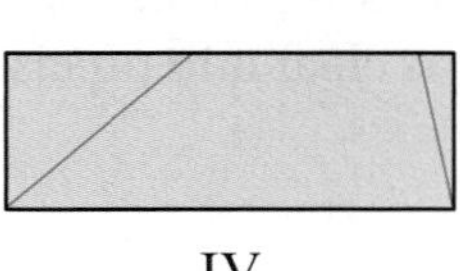

IV

Tony Okay, let me see if I can figure out what you did. It looks like you first cut the triangle into two pieces.

Sasha Well, yes, but where did I make the cut? Be specific.

Tony Picky, picky. I guess you found the midpoints of the two sides of the triangle and connected them. That guarantees that you have congruent edges when you move the pieces around.

Sasha Good. What did I do next?

Tony You drew this little segment to make two triangles.

I know, I need to be specific.

The segment must be the altitude from the vertex of the triangle to the midline. An altitude forms 90° angles, which you want for a rectangle.

Then you rotated each little right triangle around a midpoint. The hypotenuse of each lined up with the lower half of the side of the original triangle. Now you have a rectangle!

In a right triangle, the **hypotenuse** is the side opposite the right angle.

For Discussion

1. Why is it important for Tony to "be specific" when he describes the cuts that Sasha made? What might happen if he were not as specific as Sasha insisted?

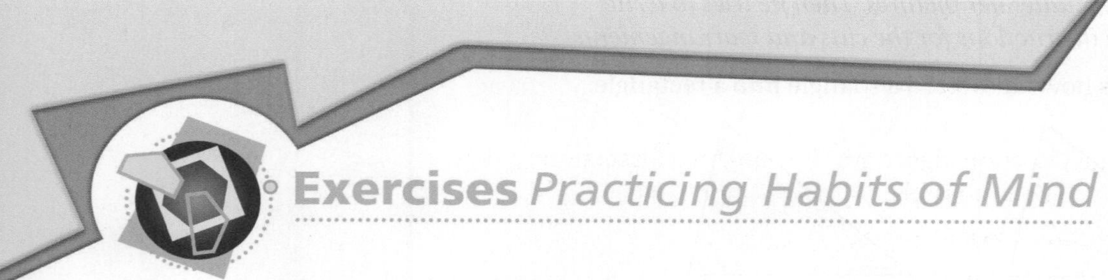

Exercises *Practicing Habits of Mind*

Check Your Understanding

In Lesson 3.1, you wrote about how you dissected a parallelogram, a triangle, and a trapezoid into rectangles. Exercises 1–3 below ask you to edit these old descriptions (or write new ones). Be as clear and precise about the steps as you now can be.

1. Rewrite your algorithm for each dissection.
   - parallelogram to rectangle
   - triangle to rectangle
   - trapezoid to rectangle

   a. Draw pictures that show your steps.

   b. Describe the same steps precisely using words only.

2. Find a partner. Exchange the steps you wrote in Exercise 1 (but not the pictures) on how to dissect a parallelogram into a scissors-congruent rectangle.

   a. Follow your partner's directions exactly as written. Does the algorithm work? Are the directions clear? Are any directions confusing?

   b. Give your partner feedback on the algorithm you tried. Listen to your partner's feedback on yours. How can you refine the directions?

3. Work with a partner again in the same way. Refine your algorithm for dissecting a trapezoid into a rectangle.

On Your Own

4. **Standardized Test Prep** In $\triangle ABC$, E and F are midpoints. The area of $\triangle ABC$ is 30 cm^2. What is the area of parallelogram $ABIF$?

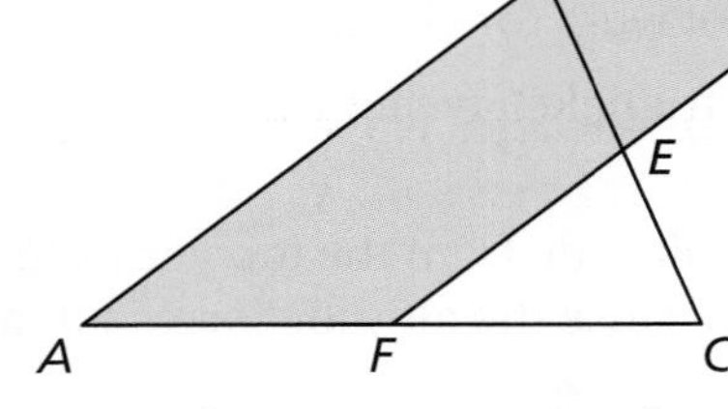

   A. 15 cm^2 B. 20 cm^2 C. 30 cm^2 D. 60 cm^2

5. Write an algorithm for tying your shoelace. Be precise. Do not leave out any steps.

6. Write an algorithm for multiplying a three-digit number by a two-digit number.

Assume you know how to multiply two one-digit numbers.

7. Write final versions of dissection algorithms for the three dissections below. (See Exercise 1.) Be as clear as possible.

   a. Dissect a parallelogram into a rectangle.

   b. Dissect a triangle into a rectangle.

   c. Dissect a trapezoid into a rectangle.

Maintain Your Skills

8. Describe a way to dissect each triangle into a rectangle that has the same base as the triangle.

   a. 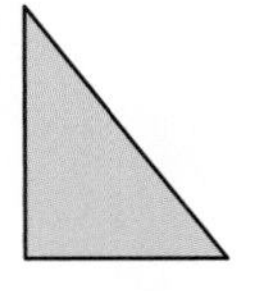

   b. 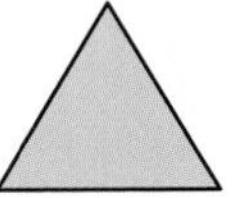

   c. 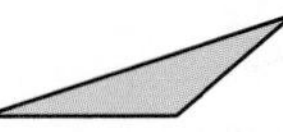

   d. 

   e. 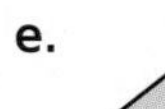

3.04 Checking an Algorithm

How can you know whether an algorithm works?

- You can check that it works for all possible cases. (Why will this not work for the algorithms you just wrote?)
- You can check the justification for each step.
- You can look for a single counterexample—a case for which the algorithm fails.

For Discussion

1. **What's Wrong Here?** Steps 1–3 below dissect a triangle into a rectangle. Study the pictures and justifications for each step.
   a. Show why this method will not work for all triangles.
   b. What special features must a triangle have for this method to work? Explain.

Step 1 Cut out the triangle. Draw an altitude from the top vertex to the base. This makes two right triangles because the altitude forms 90° angles.

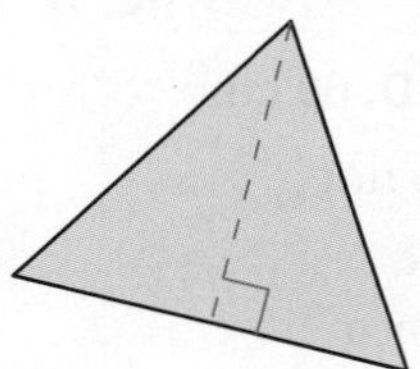

Step 2 Slide one of the triangles along the base.

Step 3 Flip one of the triangles. Now two of the sides of the original triangle match up.

The final shape is a rectangle because

- the two vertical sides are congruent. They were made by the same cut.
- two opposite angles are right angles. They were made by an altitude cut.

For You to Do

2. Here is another algorithm. This one is for cutting a parallelogram into a rectangle. It also has a flaw, but the flaw is quite subtle. Although it seems to work perfectly, there are parallelograms for which it fails. Fix it.

Step 1 Draw the perpendicular bisector of one side of the parallelogram.

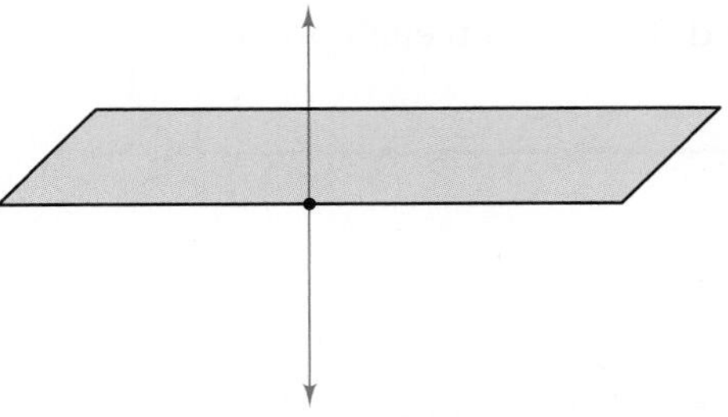

Step 2 Cut along the perpendicular bisector. This perpendicular cut guarantees right angles.

Step 3 Slide one piece parallel to the bisected side until the uncut ends match.

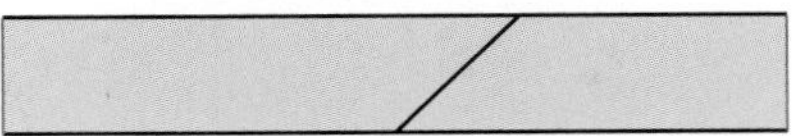

The sides *will* match. The properties of parallelograms guarantee that opposite sides are congruent. They also guarantee that the sum of measures of two consecutive angles is 180°.

There is a very natural pitfall in writing an algorithm. You may base the algorithm on a drawing or a situation that is too typical.

For example, most people tend to picture fairly symmetric figures, such as the first figure below.

But a less-symmetric figure is less special.

Most people also tend to picture a figure with one side horizontal, such as the second figure below, so that it looks as if it will not fall over. That can also be a pitfall. A rule that works well for an apparently stable figure may not work so well for a figure that looks "unbalanced," such as the third figure below.

This is why it is so important to have good strategies for checking and debugging a process.

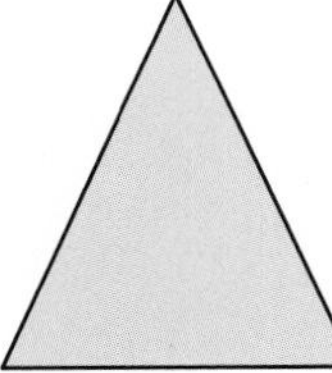

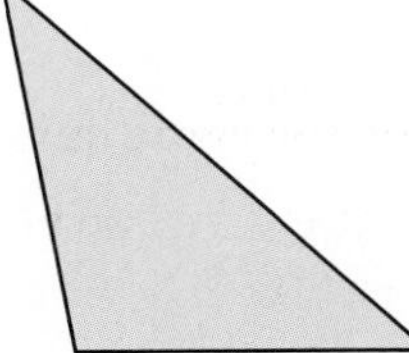

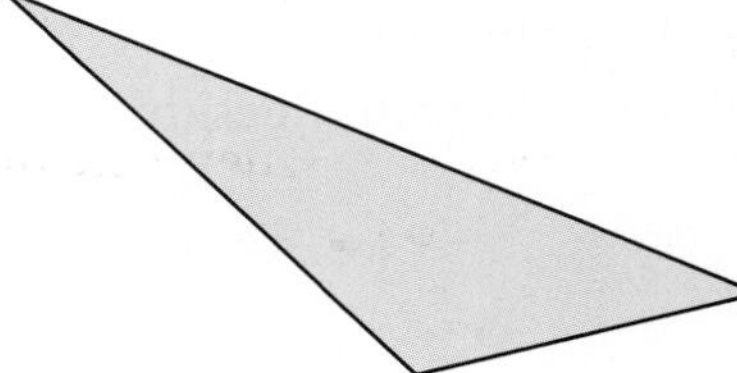

For Discussion

Here is one way to find important special cases to test an algorithm. Stretch a definition to its extreme.

3. Discuss the difference between the definition of a trapezoid and your usual mental picture of a trapezoid.

4. With other students, find four trapezoids, quite different from each other, that are very atypical.

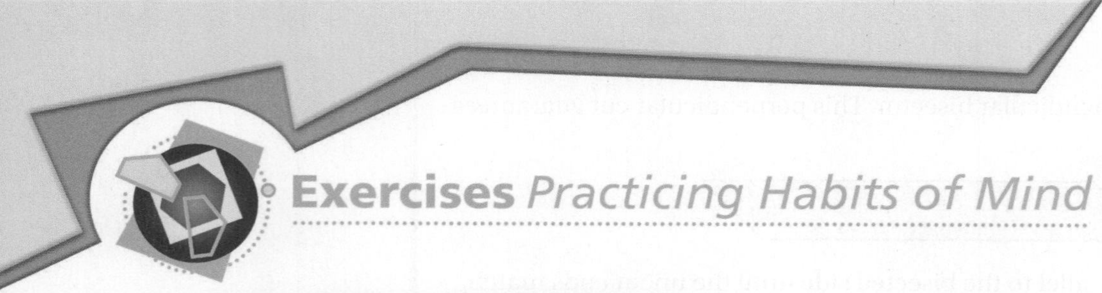

Exercises *Practicing Habits of Mind*

Check Your Understanding

1. **Write About It** Study your algorithms for dissecting parallelograms, triangles, and trapezoids into rectangles. Check some nonstandard figures for each algorithm. If there *are* figures for which your algorithm does not work, explain what features caused your algorithm to fail. Then revise the method and test it again.

2. **What's Wrong Here?** A student was asked to dissect a parallelogram and rearrange the pieces into a rectangle. The student gave the following argument.

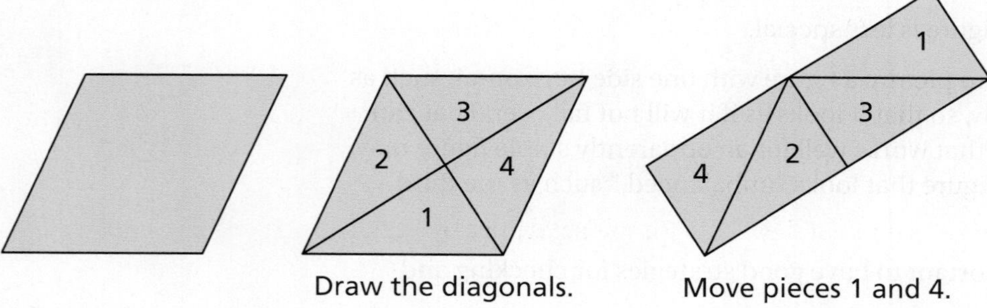

Draw the diagonals. Move pieces 1 and 4.

a. What is wrong with this argument?

b. For which type(s) of parallelograms does this dissection work?

3. Choose one of your algorithms for dissecting parallelograms, scalene triangles, and trapezoids into rectangles. Justify each step to show why your algorithm reliably produces the desired result.

   a. Why do pieces match?

   b. Why are line segments straight?

   c. Why are angles right angles?

   d. Once more, pay close attention to whether your justification works in general, or only in certain cases.

4. Here is an algorithm for turning a scalene triangle into a right triangle. Justify each step.

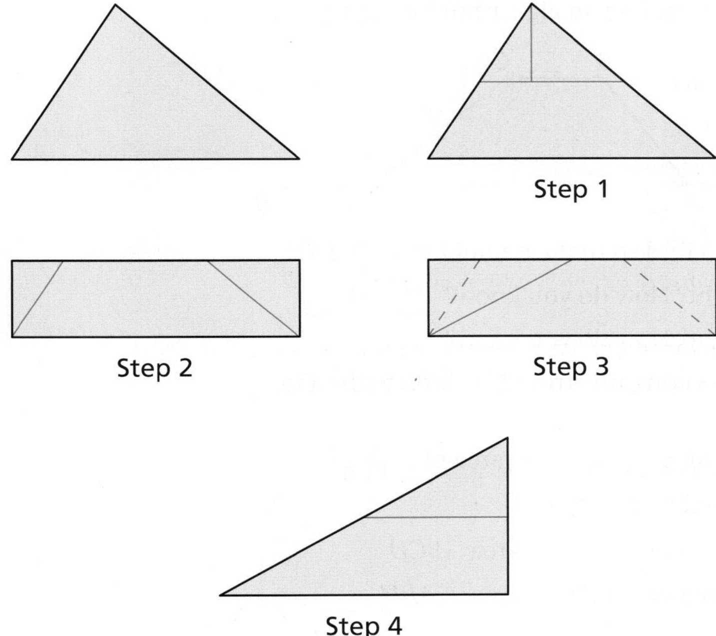

   a. Why do pieces match up?

   b. Are segments straight?

   c. Why are there right angles?

   d. Is this a specific case, or is it general enough for the algorithm to work for all scalene triangles?

On Your Own

5. Write an algorithm for dissecting a parallelogram into a triangle.

6. Justify each step you used in the dissection of the parallelogram into a triangle.

7. Write an algorithm for dissecting a triangle that is isosceles (but not equilateral) and rearranging it into a scalene triangle.

8. Justify each step you can use in the dissection of an isosceles triangle into a scalene triangle.

9. Suppose that Jane has an algorithm for dissecting a trapezoid into a rectangle. Explain how you could use Jane's steps to dissect a rectangle into a trapezoid.

10. Use your algorithms for dissecting a trapezoid into a rectangle and dissecting a rectangle into a nonrectangular parallelogram. Describe an algorithm for dissecting a trapezoid into a nonrectangular parallelogram.

11. Use your algorithms for dissecting a trapezoid into a rectangle and dissecting a triangle into a rectangle. Describe an algorithm for dissecting a trapezoid into a triangle.

12. The diagram suggests Noriko's method for cutting a trapezoid into a triangle.

    Answer the questions to help her justify her method.

    a. What point on $\overline{CD}$ does she need to find so that $\overline{CF}$ matches with $\overline{DF}$?

    b. Will the edge from B to B' be straight? How do you know?

    c. Will the edge from A to B' be straight? How do you know?

13. **Standardized Test Prep** What can you conclude from Noriko's method for dissection in Exercise 12?

    A. area of $\triangle ABB'$ + area of $\triangle BCF$ + area of $\triangle FDB$ = area of $\triangle BCD$

    B. area of $\triangle ABB'$ = area of $ABCD$

    C. area of $\triangle BCF$ + area of $ABFD$ − area of $\triangle FB'D$ = area $ABCD$

    D. area of $\triangle BCF$ + area of $ABFD$ − area of $\triangle FB'D$ = area $\triangle ABB'$

Maintain Your Skills

14. For each trapezoid below, apply Noriko's method (Exercise 12) for cutting a trapezoid into a triangle.

a.

b.

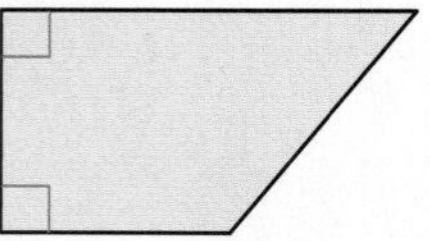

c.

3.05 The Midline Theorem

In Lesson 3.2, Sasha used the following method to dissect a triangle into a parallelogram.

Start with a triangle. Cut between the midpoints of two sides.

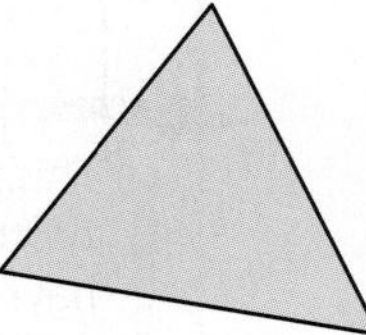

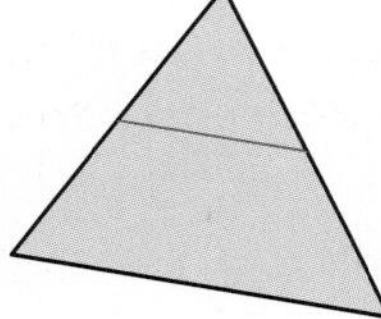

Rotate the top triangle around one of the midpoints. The two segments will match because you cut at a midpoint.

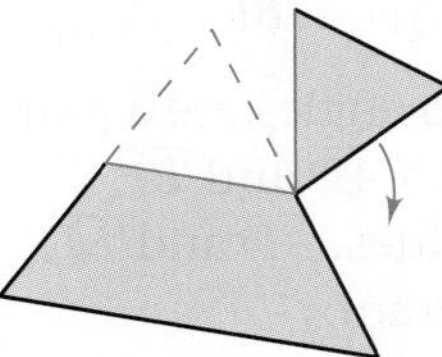

Quadrilateral *ABCD* is a parallelogram because the opposite sides are congruent. $\overline{AD} \cong \overline{BC}$ because they were made by cutting at a midpoint. $\overline{AB} \cong \overline{DC}$ because a midline cut makes a segment half as long as the base.

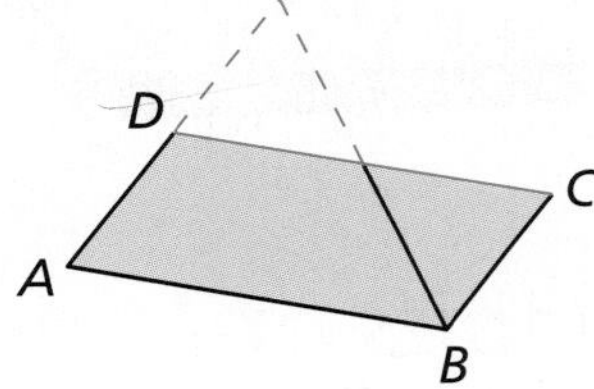

This proof uses the Midline Theorem, which you studied in Lesson 2.18.

Theorem 2.10 The Midline Theorem

The segment joining the midpoints of two sides of a triangle is parallel to the third side and is half as long as the third side.

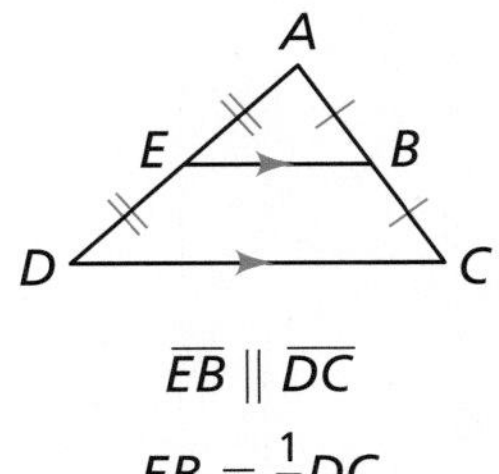

$\overline{EB} \parallel \overline{DC}$

$EB = \frac{1}{2}DC$

Four horizontal cards form the base of this house of cards, so two horizontal cards are needed halfway up.

Example

Problem To prove the midline cut works, you need a slightly different construction. In $\triangle ABC$ below, D is the midpoint of $\overline{AC}$. E is the midpoint of $\overline{BC}$. You locate point F such that D, E, and F are collinear and $\overline{DE} \cong \overline{EF}$. Prove that $ABFD$ is a parallelogram.

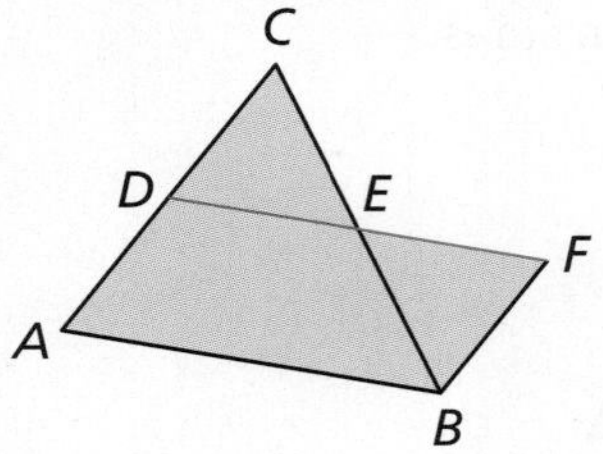

This setup makes DF twice DE. That is why you have to show only that $ABFD$ is a parallelogram.

Solution $\angle CED \cong \angle BEF$ because they are vertical angles. So, $\triangle DEC \cong \triangle FEB$ because of SAS. You can use CPCTC to conclude that $CD = BF$. Since D is the midpoint of $\overline{AC}$, you know that $CD = AD$. Therefore $AD = BF$.

Apply CPCTC again to see that $\angle CDE \cong \angle BFE$. These two angles are a pair of alternate interior angles formed by the transversal $\overline{DF}$ to $\overline{AD}$ and $\overline{BF}$. Therefore, $\overline{AD}$ and $\overline{BF}$ are parallel. Since $ABFD$ has two sides, $\overline{AD}$ and $\overline{BF}$, that are both congruent and parallel, $ABFD$ is a parallelogram.

Exercises *Practicing Habits of Mind*

Check Your Understanding

1. Find x, y, and z in the picture below. Assume segments that appear parallel are parallel.

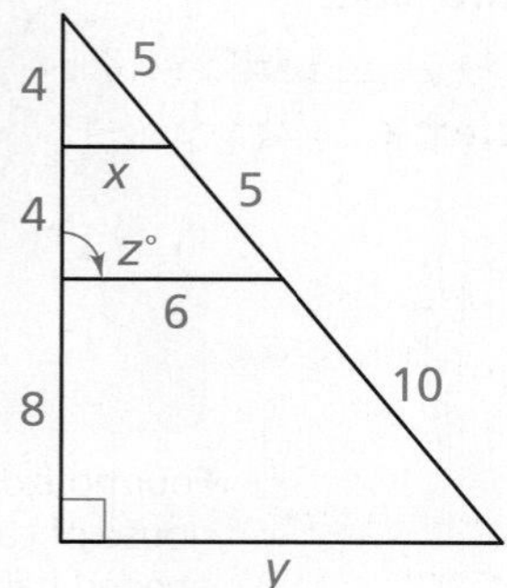

For Exercises 2–4 use quadrilateral *ABCD*. The midpoints of the sides, points *E*, *F*, *G*, and *H*, are connected in order.

2. Explain why $\overline{EF}$ is congruent to $\overline{GH}$.

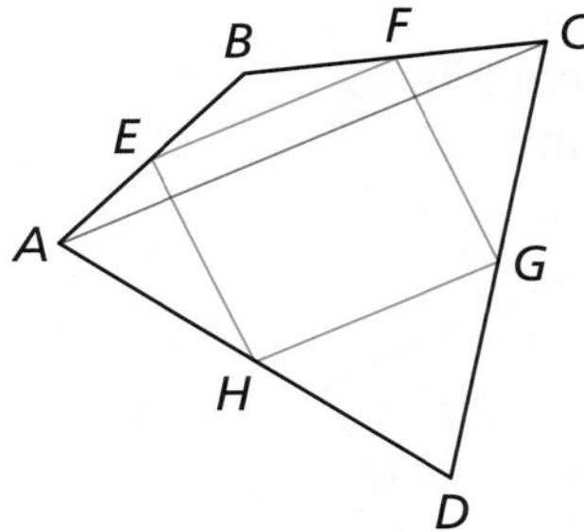

3. Explain why two other segments are congruent. (See Exercise 2.)

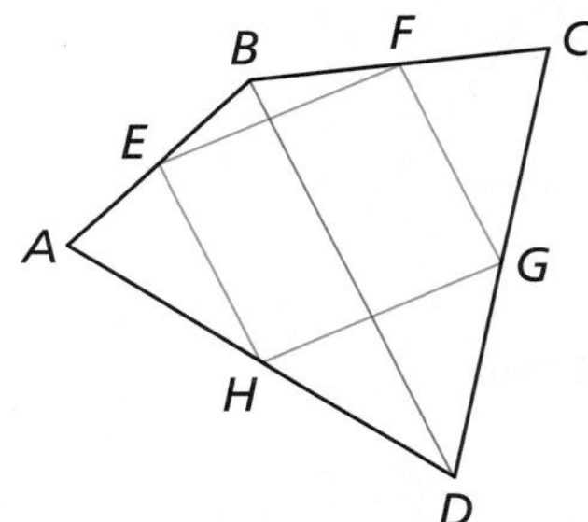

4. What kind of shape is *EFGH*? Prove it.

On Your Own

5. One side of a triangle has length 12.

a. How long is the segment that joins the midpoints of the other two sides?

b. How long would the segment joining the midpoints be if the side of the triangle had length 10? Length 18? Length 19?

6. A kite has diagonals with lengths 5 and 8. You form an inner quadrilateral by joining the midpoints of the kite's sides. What is the perimeter of the inner quadrilateral? Describe its angles.

7. The diagonals of a quadrilateral measure 12 and 8. You form an inner quadrilateral by joining the midpoints of the sides of the given quadrilateral. What is the perimeter of the inner quadrilateral?

8. What kind of quadrilateral do you get when you connect the midpoints of a kite? You may want to use geometry software to experiment.

9. **Standardized Test Prep** The lengths of the diagonals of a quadrilateral are 30 cm and 40 cm. What is the perimeter of the polygon you get when you connect the midpoints of the adjacent sides of this quadrilateral?

A. 25 cm **B.** 50 cm **C.** 70 cm **D.** 100 cm

10. **Take It Further** You can generalize the idea of a midline (a segment joining midpoints of two sides of a triangle) to quadrilaterals. Here are some possible midlines for quadrilaterals.

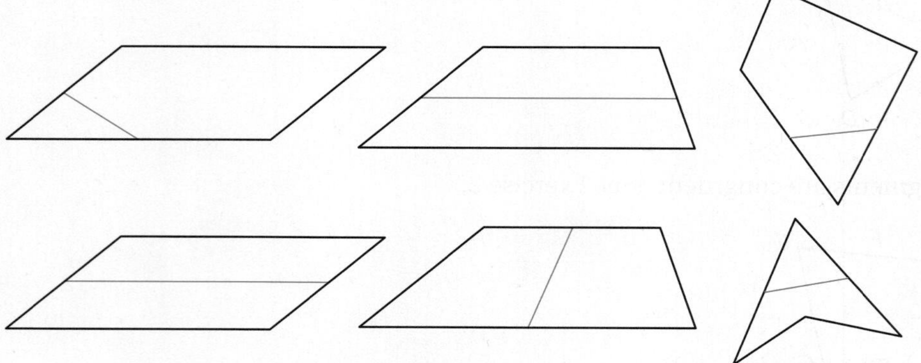

Experiment with the possible meanings of *midline* for a quadrilateral. Can you find any relationship between a midline and the sides of a quadrilateral? Between a midline and a diagonal? Answer the following questions.

a. How do you define *midline* for a quadrilateral? Does it join any two midpoints? Two opposite midpoints? Two consecutive midpoints?

b. With what kinds of quadrilaterals did you experiment?

c. What did you find? Are there any special properties of a midline of a quadrilateral? Can you make any conjectures?

Maintain Your Skills

11. Draw a few quadrilaterals such that when you connect the midpoints of adjacent sides you get a rhombus. Is there some way to tell whether a particular type of quadrilateral will have a midpoint quadrilateral that is a rhombus? Explain.

In this investigation, you used dissection to make scissors-congruent shapes. You also used the Midline Theorem. These questions will help you summarize what you have learned.

1. Describe and justify each step in the dissection that turns any parallelogram into a rectangle.
2. Describe how you would dissect this rectangle into a right triangle. Justify each step. Draw pictures as needed.

3. Is it possible to dissect each of these triangles into a parallelogram? If you think it is possible in either or both of the cases, describe the steps.

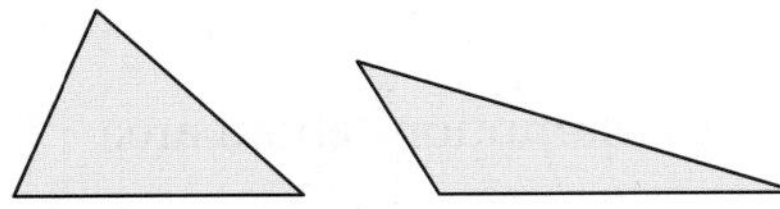

4. Copy and dissect the trapezoid at the right into a triangle.
5. Draw $\triangle ABC$. Join the midpoints of its three sides to form $\triangle DEF$. What is the ratio of the perimeter of $\triangle DEF$ to the perimeter of $\triangle ABC$?
6. What is an algorithm?
7. Why is it important to justify each step in an algorithm?
8. What does the Midline Theorem say about the relationship between a midline and the sides of a triangle?

Vocabulary

In this investigation, you learned these terms. Make sure you understand what each one means and how to use it.

- **algorithm**
- **hypotenuse**
- **scissors-congruent**

Some arrangements of parts make more sense than others.

Area Formulas

In *Area Formulas*, you will formalize the ideas of cutting and rearranging. You will derive and prove the area formulas for triangles, parallelograms, and trapezoids.

By the end of this investigation, you will be able to answer questions like these.

1. If two figures are scissors-congruent, do they have the same area? Explain.
2. Are all squares with the same area congruent?
3. What is the area formula for a parallelogram? For a triangle? For a trapezoid?

You will learn how to

- understand and apply basic assumptions about area
- identify critical measurements that can be used to find the areas of different types of polygons
- use dissection algorithms to develop area formulas for parallelograms, triangles, and trapezoids

You will develop these habits and skills:

- Understand what area is and what kinds of transformations preserve area.
- Calculate areas of rectangles, parallelograms, triangles, and trapezoids.
- Reason by continuity to relate different area formulas and polygons.

You can disassemble the tabletop and the table leaves. The total area remains the same.

3.06 Getting Started

When you think of measurement, you probably think of feet or inches, or maybe centimeters or miles. These all are measures of length. Sometimes it is more important to know how much area a figure covers rather than how long or wide it is.

For You to Explore

1. a. What is the area formula for a rectangle?

   b. Draw several pictures of rectangles that have area 12 square units. How many are there in all?

2. Use half sheets of standard $8\frac{1}{2}$ in.-by-11 in. paper as your starting rectangle. Cut that rectangle into the following number of equal-area rectangles.

   a. two b. four c. five

3. Suppose you want to cut a rectangle into pieces having equal areas. Is there any number of pieces that is *not* possible? Explain your answer.

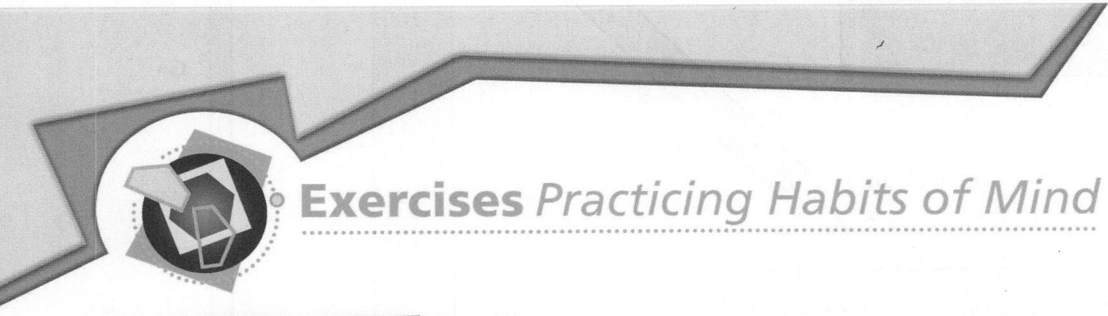

On Your Own

4. Make a parallelogram. Dissect it into a rectangle. Use an algorithm that you know will work with any parallelogram.

   a. Measure and record the length and width of the rectangle.

   b. Carefully rearrange your pieces into your original parallelogram. Note the measurements of the parallelogram that correspond to the rectangle's length and width.

5. Draw a triangle. Dissect it into a rectangle. Use an algorithm that you know will work with any triangle.

   a. Record the length and width of the rectangle.

   b. Carefully rearrange your pieces into your original triangle. Note how the rectangle's length and width relate to measurements of the triangle.

Maintain Your Skills

6. Use the rectangles shown below.
   a. Which of the rectangles have equal areas?
   b. Of the rectangles with equal areas, are any two congruent?

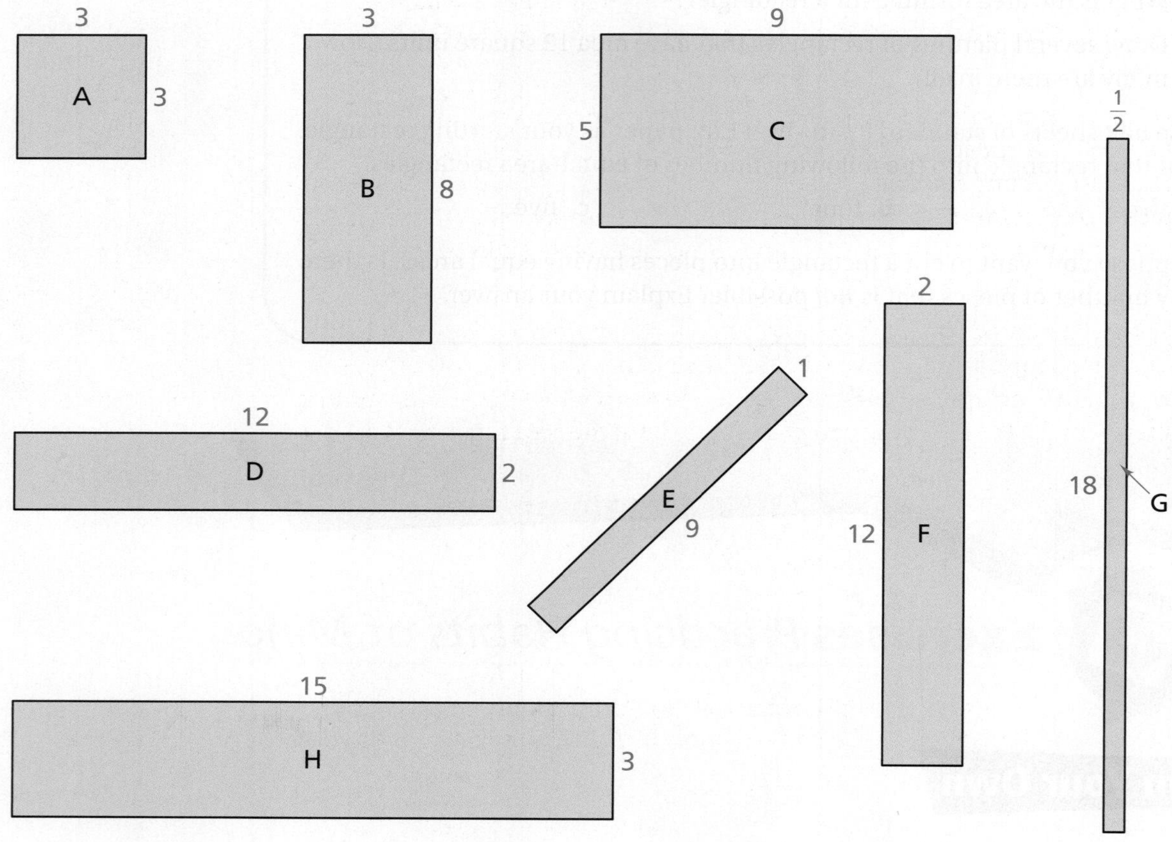

3.07 What Is Area, Anyway?

What is area? Someone might answer, "Area is what is inside a figure."

Attempts to make this answer more precise lead to statements such as "The area of a figure is the number of square units it contains." Square units could be square inches or square feet or square meters.

You choose a unit length (say, 1 inch) and construct a square with that side length—a square inch. Then you see how many of these squares fill the figure. A square that is 5 inches on a side will contain 25 square inches. A rectangle that is 5 feet by 3 feet will contain 15 square feet. (Why is that true?)

For areas of more complicated figures, counting squares gets out of hand. You cannot tile most shapes evenly with square units. You end up counting partial squares and making estimates. Sometimes an estimate is the best you can do. But for triangles, parallelograms, trapezoids, and other familiar figures, you can get exact formulas for area. They are given in terms of lengths and they are easy to calculate.

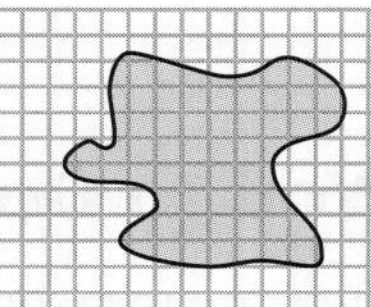

blob covered by unit squares

To get the formulas, you need to build a theory of area. Start with some basic assumptions that describe how you want area to behave. First, you assume that area is a function that assigns to each polygon a nonnegative real number. Then you make the following two postulates about the area function.

Postulate 3.1 The Congruence Postulate

Congruent figures have the same area.

Postulate 3.2 The Additivity Postulate

If two polygons *P* and *Q* do not intersect (except possibly at a point or along an edge), then the area of the union of *P* and *Q* is the sum of the areas of *P* and *Q*.

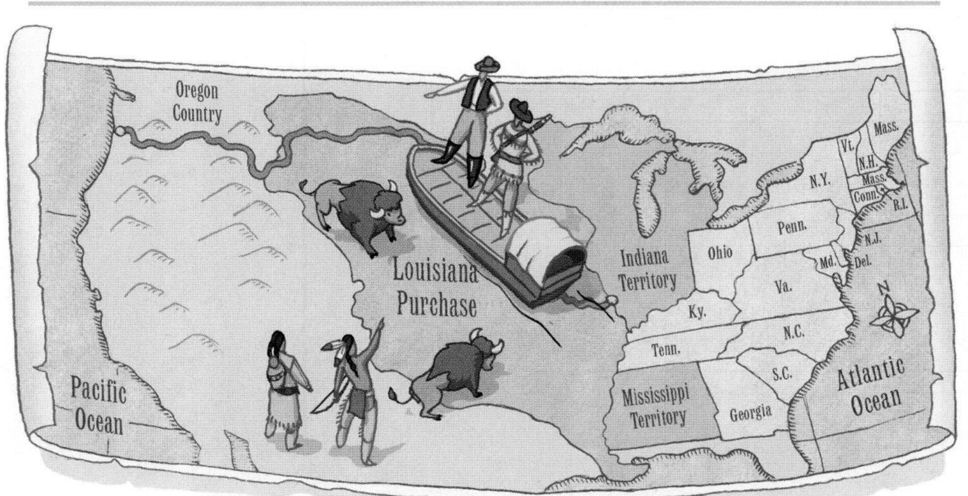

The Louisiana Purchase, in 1803, doubled the area of the United States.

Example 1

Problem What is the area of a square that measures $\frac{1}{3}$ on a side?

Solution A square that is $\frac{1}{3}$ on a side is the shaded portion of the unit square, or $\frac{1}{9}$ square unit.

The area of the small square is $\frac{1}{9}$ square unit.

$\frac{1}{3}$ $\frac{1}{3}$ $\frac{1}{3}$

$\frac{1}{3}$ $\frac{1}{3}$ $\frac{1}{3}$

For You to Do

Here are measurements for four rectangles. Find the area of each rectangle using only the definition of area and the area assumptions.

1. base 5 in. and height 2 in.
2. length 5 in. and width 1 in.
3. length 5.5 cm and width 2 cm
4. base $5\frac{1}{2}$ ft and width $2\frac{1}{4}$ ft

You may know a formula for the area of a rectangle. Do not use it.

Developing Habits of Mind

Use Multiplication to Count. If you can divide the sides of a unit square and the sides of a rectangle into congruent segments, you can tile the rectangle with squares and find the area.

For example, you can fill a rectangle that measures $5\frac{1}{2}$ in. by $2\frac{1}{4}$ in. with squares $\frac{1}{4}$ in. on a side.

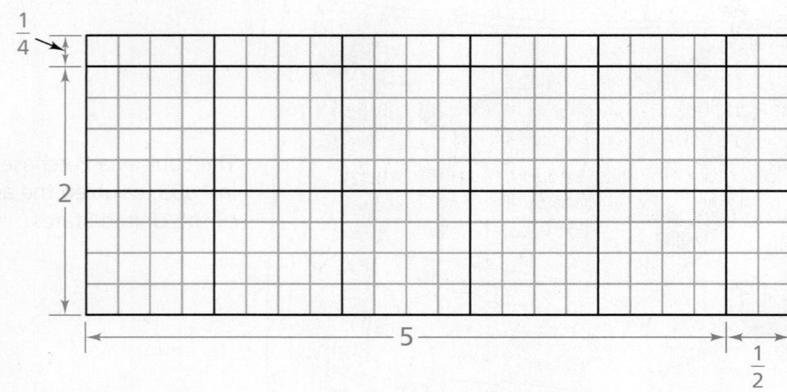

There will be 22 of these squares along the $5\frac{1}{2}$-in. side. There will be 9 such rows, so the rectangle contains

$$22 \cdot 9 = 198$$

squares, each $\frac{1}{4}$ in. on a side. But the area of each of these small squares is $\frac{1}{16}$ square inch. (Why?) So the area of the rectangle is

$$\frac{198}{16} = \frac{99}{8} = 12\frac{3}{8}$$

square inches.

But wait—there is another way to think about it: You have $2\frac{1}{4}$ rows of $5\frac{1}{2}$ squares. So you have

$$2\frac{1}{4} \cdot 5\frac{1}{2} = \frac{9}{4} \cdot \frac{11}{2} = \frac{99}{8} = 12\frac{3}{8}$$

unit squares altogether. To count the unit squares, you have only to multiply the dimensions—base times height—as you probably learned in previous courses.

The area model described above works for any rectangle with sides that you can divide into segments congruent to segments of a unit square. There are rectangles for which this cannot be done—one with side length $\sqrt{2}$, for example. The branch of mathematics called *analysis* shows that the method of multiplying length and width (or base and height) to find area works for all lengths. For now, you will assume that this is true.

Remember...

The fact that you cannot evenly divide the lengths 1 and $\sqrt{2}$ by the same number is the same as saying that $\sqrt{2}$ is irrational. You prove this fact in algebra.

Postulate 3.3 The Rectangle Postulate

The area of a rectangle with dimensions *b* and *h* (expressed in the same unit) is *bh*.

You need one more assumption about area that gets to the heart of this chapter. Dissecting one figure into another by cutting and rearranging the parts does not change what is inside the figure.

Postulate 3.4 The Scissors-Congruence Postulate

Two figures that are scissors-congruent have the same area.

This is all you will need to calculate areas of familiar shapes. By dissecting figures into rectangles and keeping track of the dimensions, you can find how many square units are in parallelograms, triangles, and trapezoids.

Example 2

Problem Find the area of this triangle.

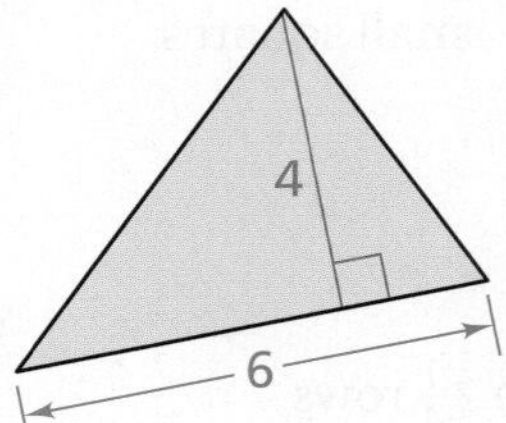

Solution You can cut the triangle into a parallelogram.

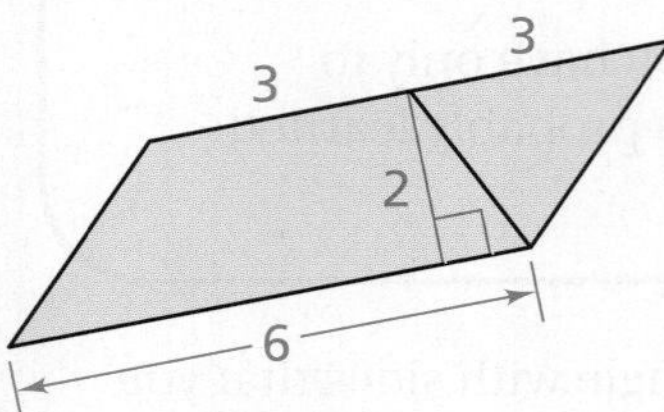

Then you can cut the parallelogram into a rectangle.

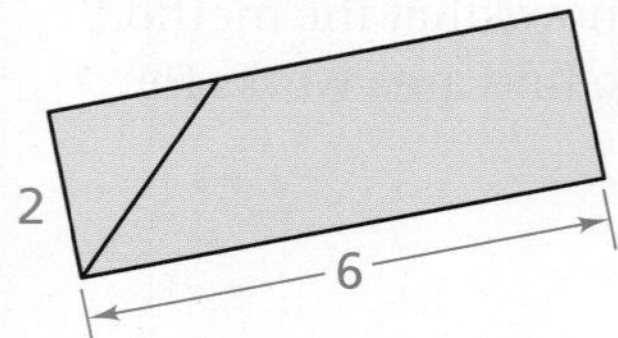

The area of the rectangle is 12. All of these dissections preserve area. So the area of the triangle is 12.

Habits of Mind

Be intuitive. It seems plausible that the midline bisects the altitude. You use that idea here, but you have yet to justify it. See Exercise 1.

For You to Do

5. Find the area of this triangle by dissecting it into a rectangle.

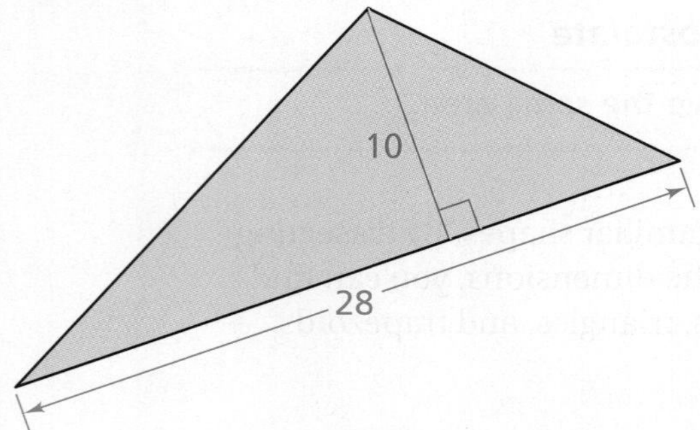

Exercises *Practicing Habits of Mind*

Check Your Understanding

1. Here is a proof that a midline of a triangle cuts an altitude into two congruent parts. Supply the missing reasons.

Given $\triangle ABC$ with midline $\overline{DE}$ and altitude $\overline{AF}$

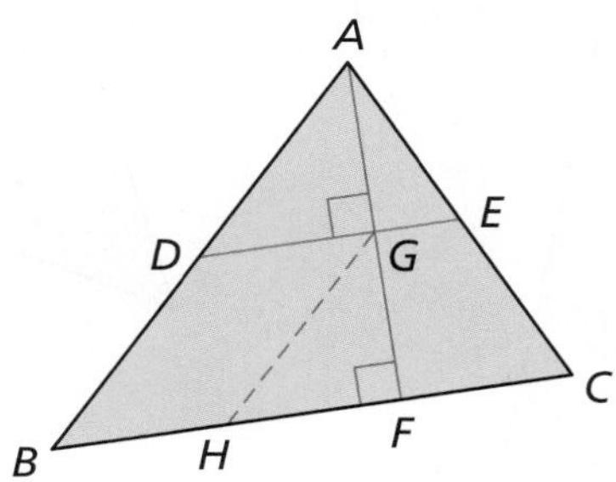

No matter how you climb, the line shows that you are halfway to the top.

Prove $\overline{AG} \cong \overline{GF}$

Proof

Statement	Reason
Draw $\overline{HG} \parallel \overline{BA}$.	Parallel Postulate
$\overline{DE} \parallel \overline{BC}$	?
$BDGH$ is a parallelogram.	?
$\overline{BD} \cong \overline{DA}$	?
$\overline{HG} \cong \overline{BD}$	?
$\overline{HG} \cong \overline{DA}$	?
$\angle AGD \cong \angle GFH$	?
$\angle BAG \cong \angle HGF$	?
$\triangle DAG \cong \triangle HGF$	?
$\overline{AG} \cong \overline{GF}$	?

2. Use the triangles shown below.

   a. Which of the triangles have equal areas?

   b. Are any two of the triangles congruent?

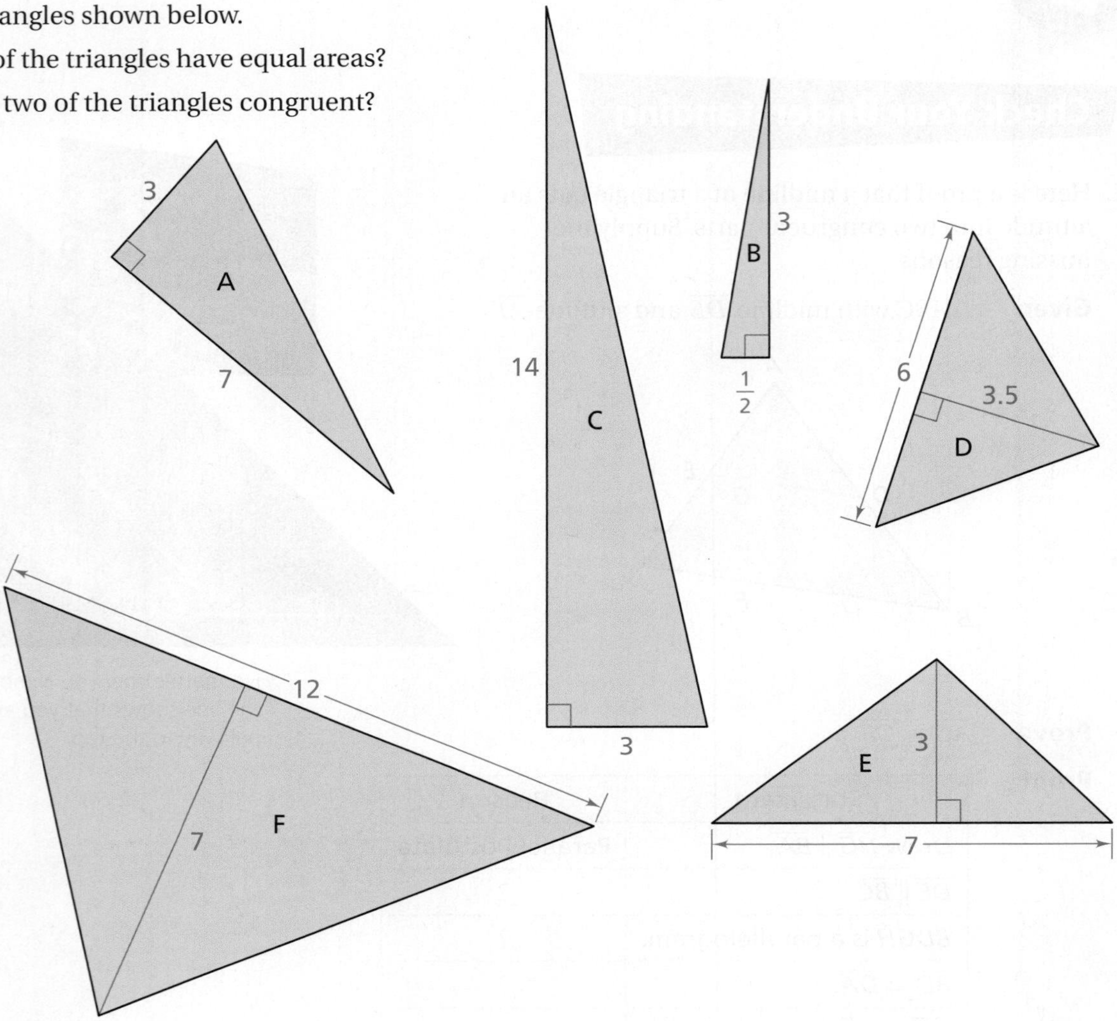

On Your Own

For Exercises 3–8, find the area of each figure. Assume that sides that look parallel are parallel and angles that appear to be right angles are right angles.

3.

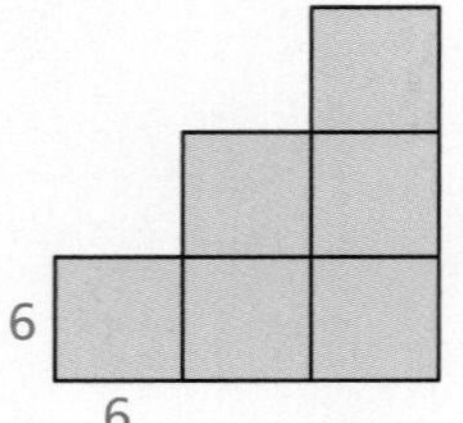

4.

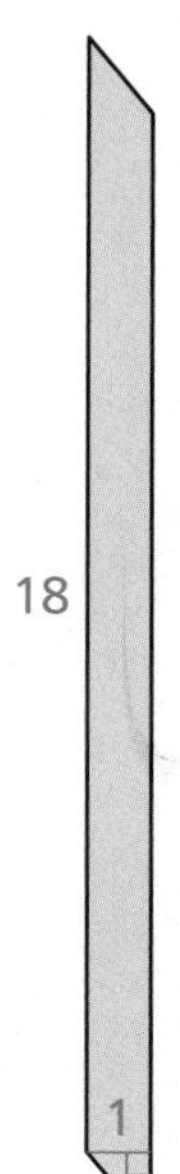

5.

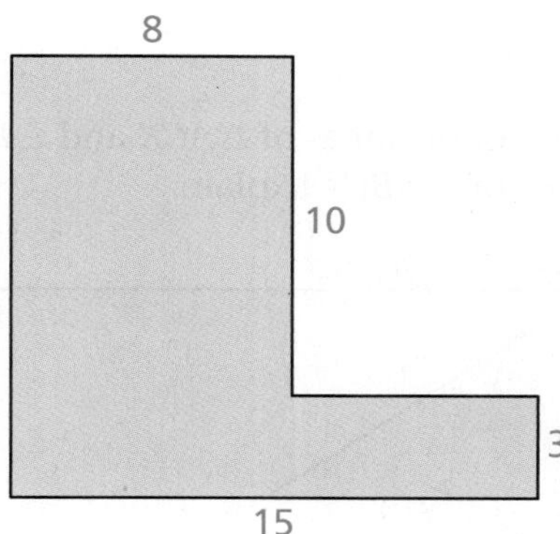

6.

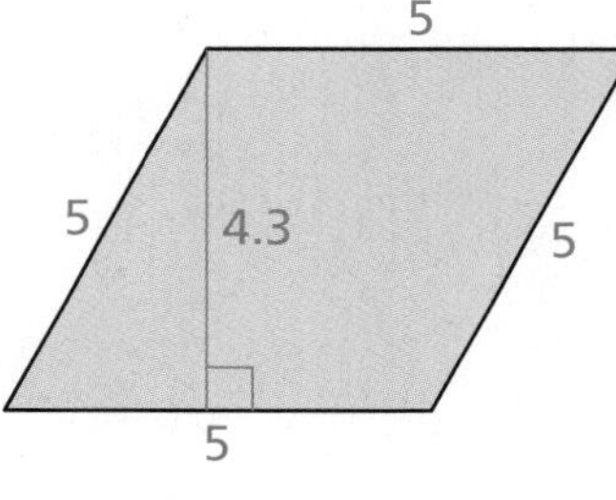

7.

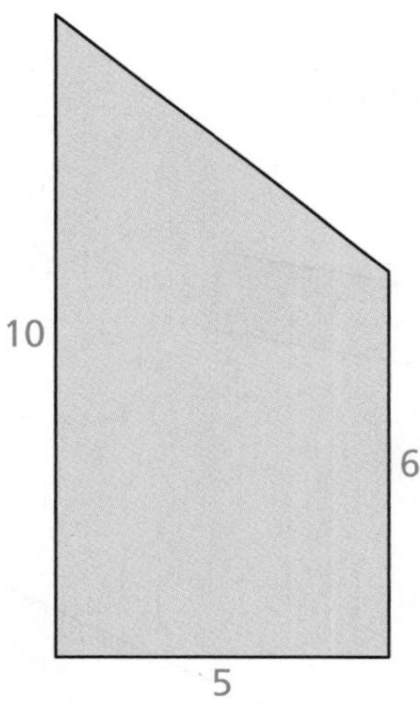

8.

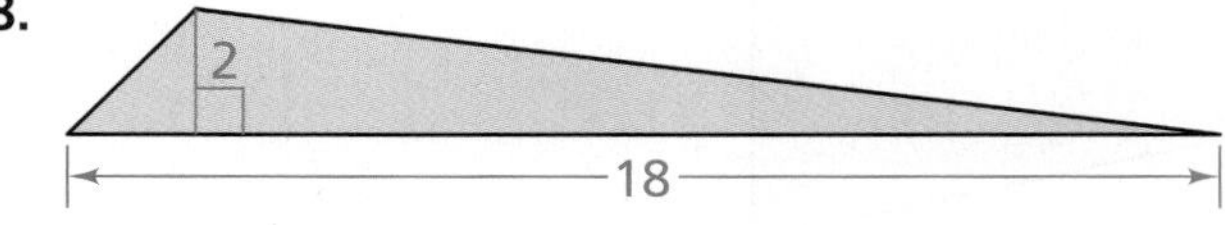

9. **Standardized Test Prep** What is the area of the shaded portion of the figure at the right?

A. 69 square units

B. 87 square units

C. 90 square units

D. 108 square units

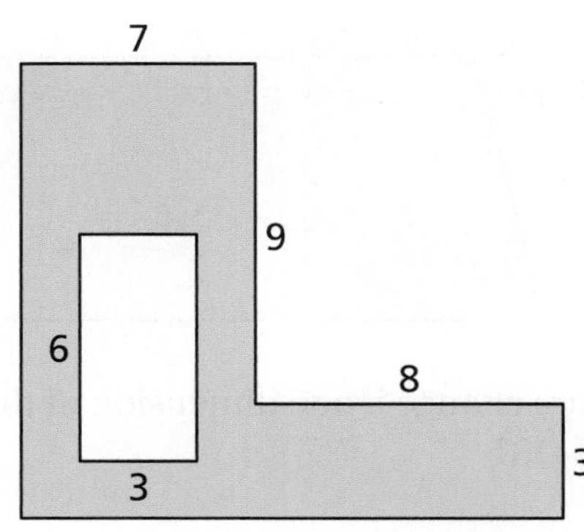

10. In rectangle $ABYX$, is the sum of the areas of $\triangle ACX$ and $\triangle BCY$ greater than, less than, or equal to the area of $\triangle ABC$? Explain.

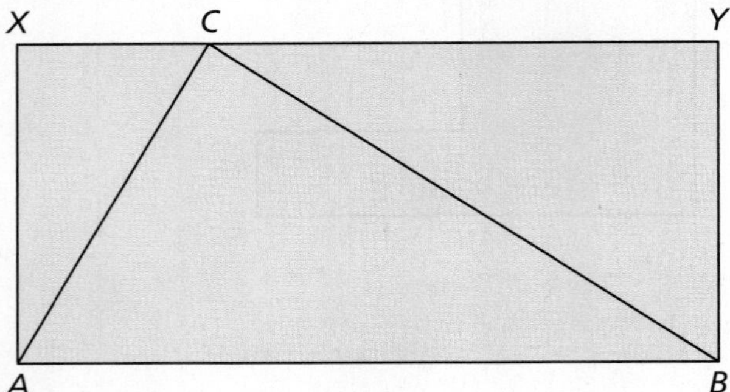

Maintain Your Skills

Find the areas of the two figures in each pair.

11.

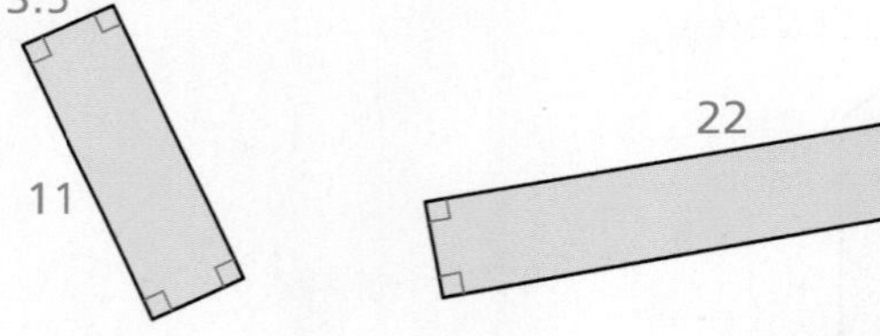

12.

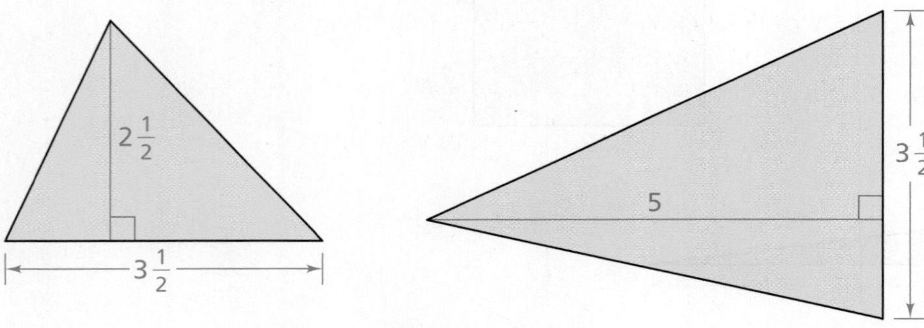

13.

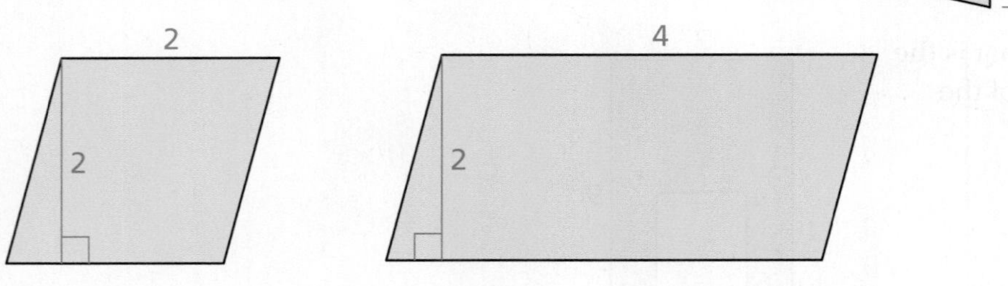

14. How does the area of a figure change if one dimension of the figure is doubled, as in Exercises 11–13?

3.08 Area by Dissection

Sometimes you will need to find areas of figures that are not rectangles. If you can take these figures apart and rearrange them into rectangles you can use what you already know to find their areas.

In-Class Experiment

1. Discuss your answer to Exercise 4 from Lesson 3.7 with others. What conjectures can you make about measurements of a parallelogram compared with the dimensions of a scissors-congruent rectangle?
2. Discuss your answer to Exercise 8 from Lesson 3.7 with others. Write a conjecture about how measurements of a triangle compare with the dimensions of a scissors-congruent rectangle.
3. Draw a trapezoid (the more unusual its shape, the better). Trace at least two copies of it to dissect.
   a. Dissect the trapezoid into another figure—one with an area you know how to compute.
   b. Measure and record the dimensions that you will use to find its area.
   c. Carefully rearrange the parts into the original trapezoid.
   d. How do the measurements of the trapezoid compare to the dimensions of the new figure?

Name a pair of opposite sides of a parallelogram as its bases. The **height** of the parallelogram corresponding to the bases is the length of a perpendicular segment joining the lines that contain the bases.

Does this definition agree with the image you have of the "height of a parallelogram"?

In each of the following figures, the length of the dashed red segment is the height corresponding to the bases shown in blue.

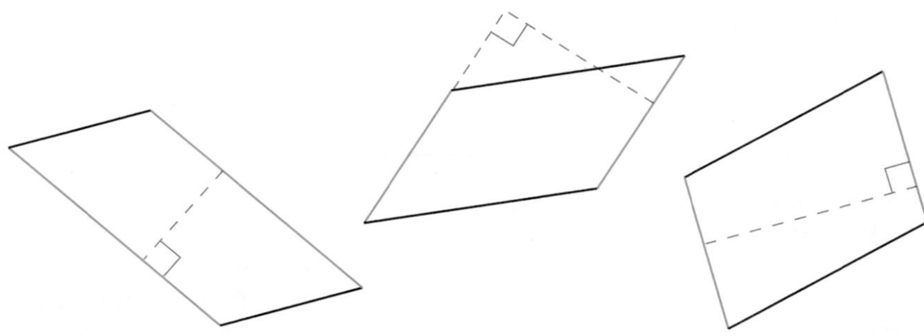

The height is not the same as the length of the other two sides, unless the parallelogram happens to be rectangular. Depending on your choice of the bases, you will sometimes have to measure the height outside, or partly outside, the parallelogram.

Minds in Action episode 7

Derman sees a connection.

Derman Tony, it seems that parallelograms and rectangles have something in common.

Tony Well, they both have four sides.

Derman Okay, that's true. But I think that they have the same area formula, too. Look what happens when I dissect this parallelogram into a rectangle.

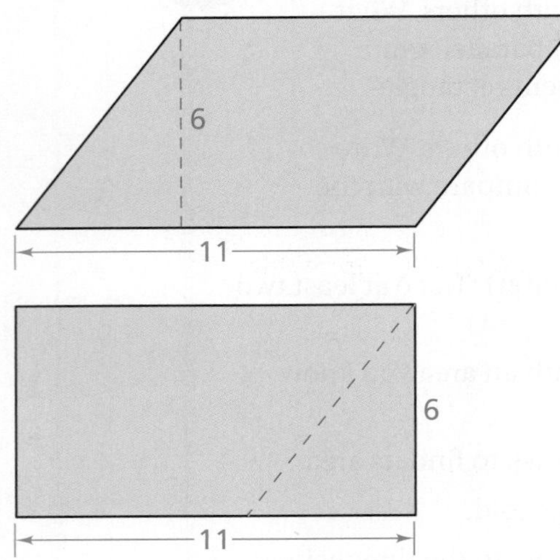

Slide the lower right triangular section to the left and up to form a rectangle.

First I cut along the height of the parallelogram. Then I slide that piece over to make a rectangle.

Tony So, how does that show that they have the same area formula?

Derman Can't you see? I didn't throw away any part. Each figure has all of the same stuff. The rectangle has dimensions 6 by 11. Its area is 66. That means that the parallelogram's area is 66, too.

Tony So the formula for the area of a parallelogram is *base* × *height*? Will that work for any parallelogram?

For Discussion

Will Derman's method work for any parallelogram? Draw a new parallelogram. Label the base b and the corresponding height h.

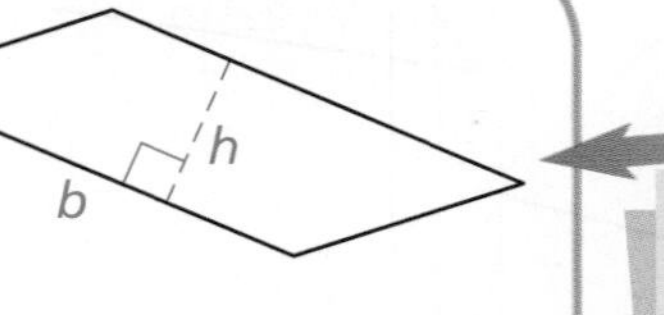

Does it matter which side of the parallelogram you call the base?

4. Dissect the parallelogram and rearrange the parts into a rectangle.
5. Explain how your dissection ensures that the base and height of the rectangle are b and h.

Name a side of a triangle as its base. The altitude of the triangle corresponding to the base is the perpendicular segment from the line containing the base to the opposite vertex. The **height** of the triangle corresponding to the base is the length of the altitude.

Does this agree with how you normally picture the height of a triangle?

In each of the following figures, the dashed red segment is the altitude corresponding to the base shown in blue. Depending on your choice of base, you may sometimes have to measure a height of a triangle outside the triangle.

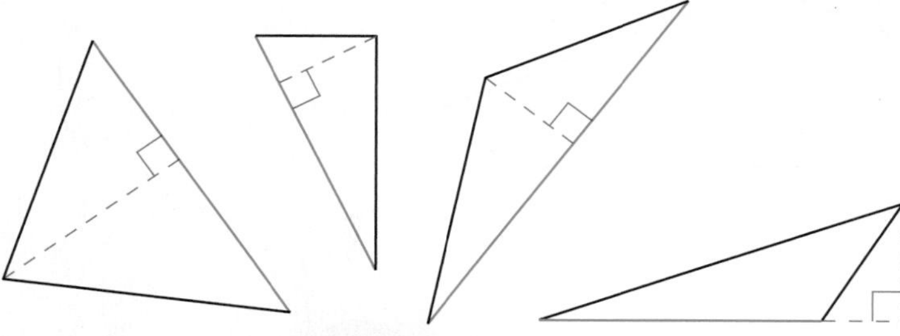

You already know that one way to dissect a triangle into a rectangle is to cut at a midline and rotate one part to form a parallelogram. The parallelogram then has base b and height $\frac{1}{2}h$.

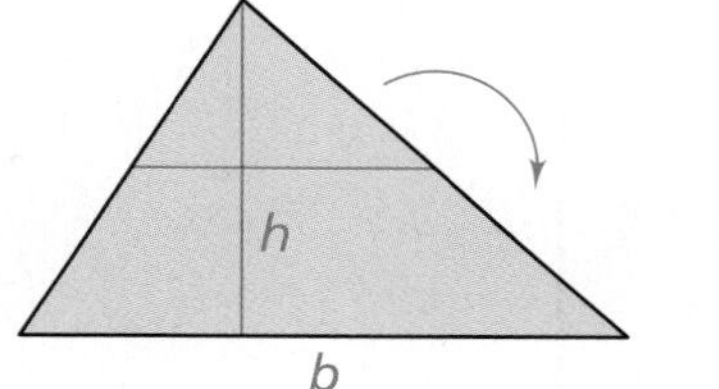

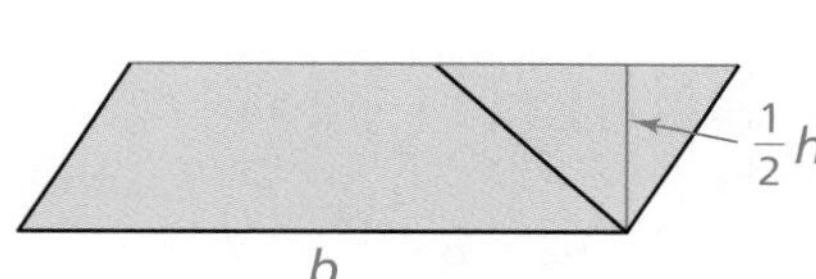

Next, you cut from a vertex of the parallelogram perpendicular to the opposite side as shown below. You slide one part to the opposite end of the parallelogram to form a rectangle. The rectangle has base b and height $\frac{1}{2}h$.

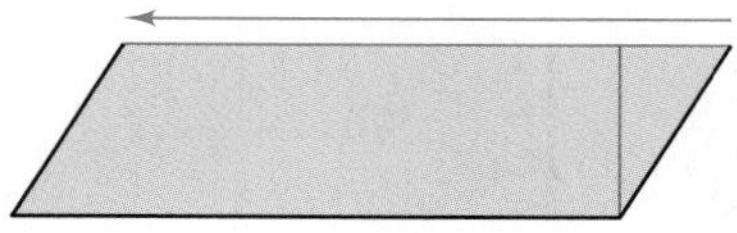

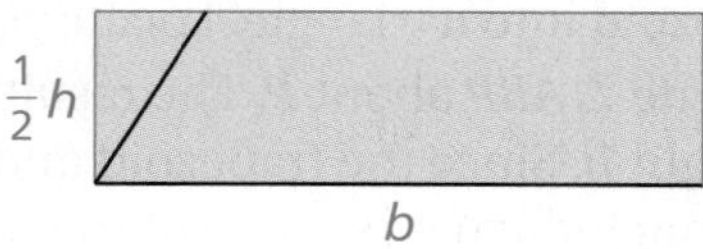

The original triangle and the rectangle are scissors-congruent. So the area of this rectangle, $\frac{1}{2}bh$, is the same as the area of the triangle.

The area formula for a triangle is

$$\text{area} = \frac{1}{2}(\text{base} \times \text{height})$$

Definitions

The two parallel sides (blue) of a trapezoid are its bases. The height of a trapezoid is the length of a perpendicular segment (red) between the lines containing the bases.

How do you normally picture the bases and height of a trapezoid?

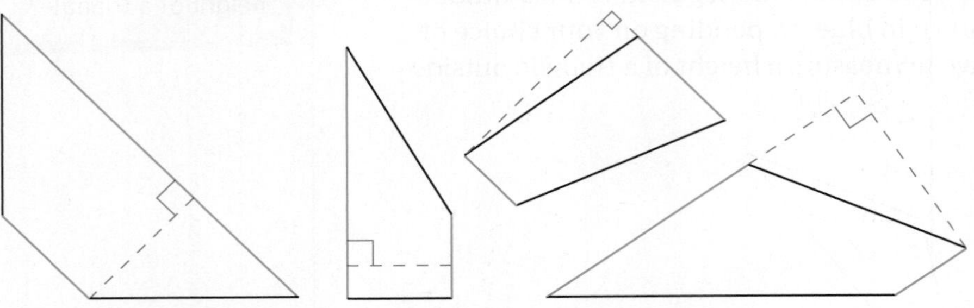

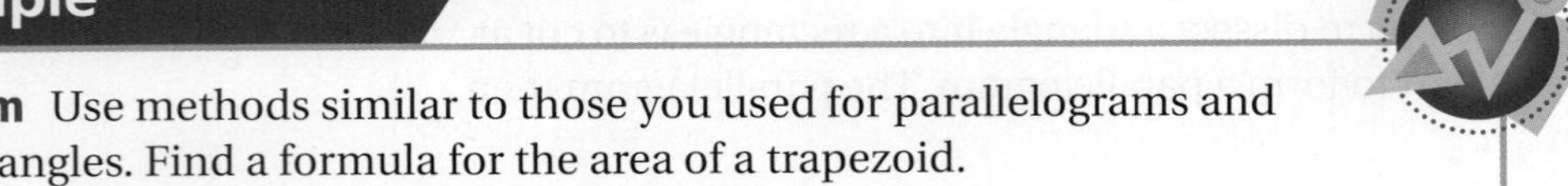

Example

Problem Use methods similar to those you used for parallelograms and triangles. Find a formula for the area of a trapezoid.

Solution Let a and b be the lengths of the bases of the trapezoid. Let h be the height of the trapezoid.

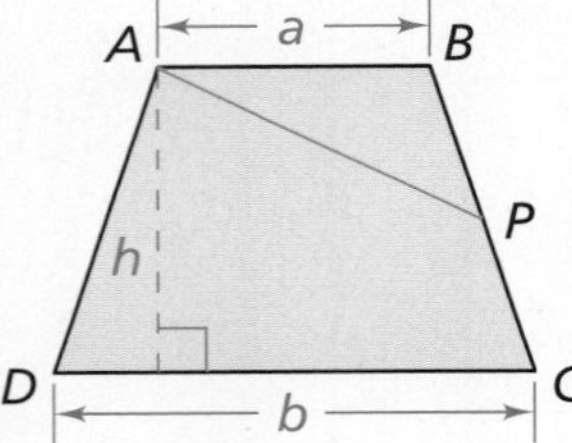

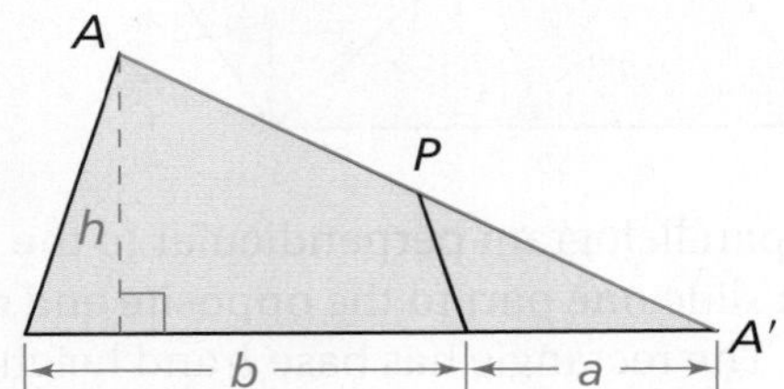

Use your method for dissecting a trapezoid into a triangle. Locate P, the midpoint of side $\overline{BC}$. Draw $\overline{AP}$ and rotate $\triangle ABP$ about P. The resulting triangle has base length $a + b$ and height h. Since the trapezoid and the triangle have the same area, you can conclude that the area of the trapezoid is given by

$$\text{area} = \frac{1}{2}(a + b)h = \frac{1}{2}h(a + b)$$

Notice that the area of the trapezoid is its height times the average of its base lengths.

For Discussion

6. As a class, review the area formulas presented in this section. Make a poster or a special page in your notebook for the formulas and figures. Represent each formula using words and using symbols. Also show two diagrams representing different cases.

Exercises *Practicing Habits of Mind*

Check Your Understanding

1. Find the area of each parallelogram.

a.

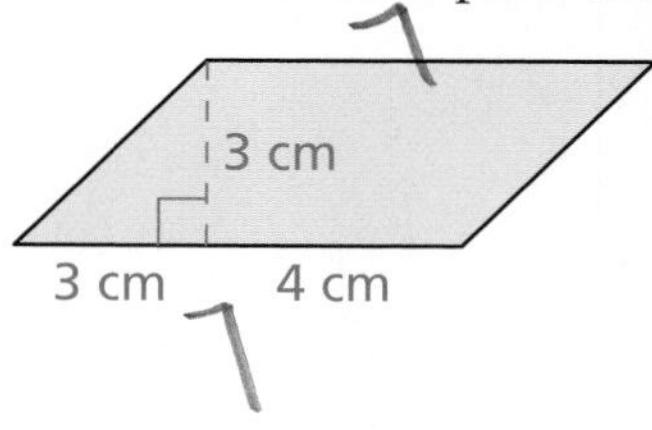

b.

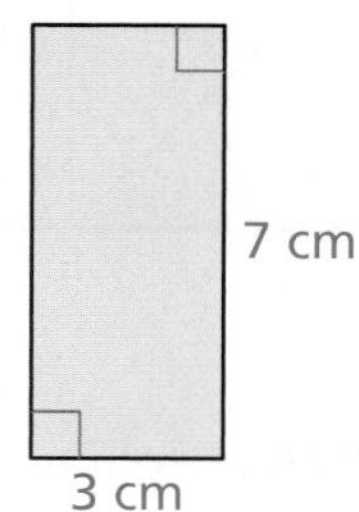

c.

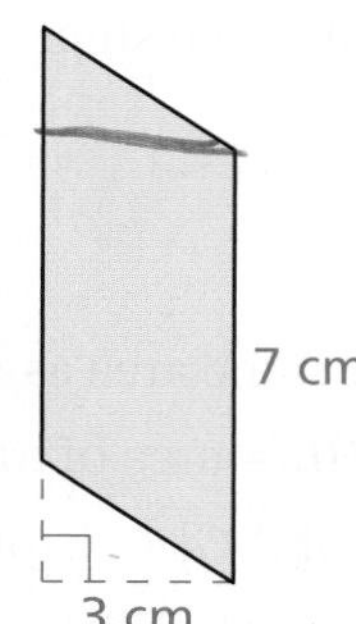

2. Find the area of the given triangle.

a. $\triangle LAU$

b. $\triangle LUE$

c. $\triangle LAE$

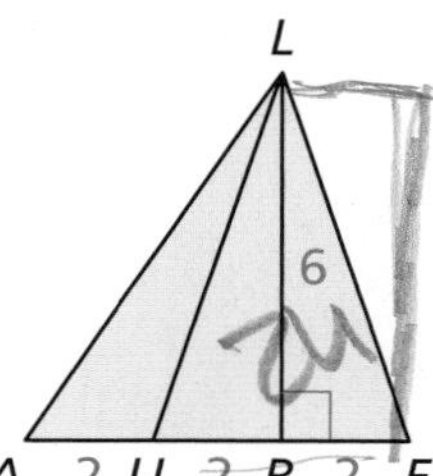

3. Find the area of each trapezoid.

a.

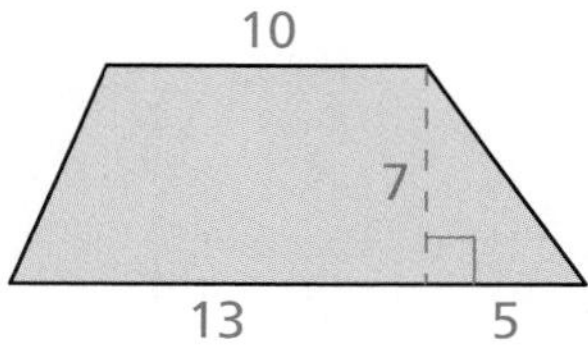

b.

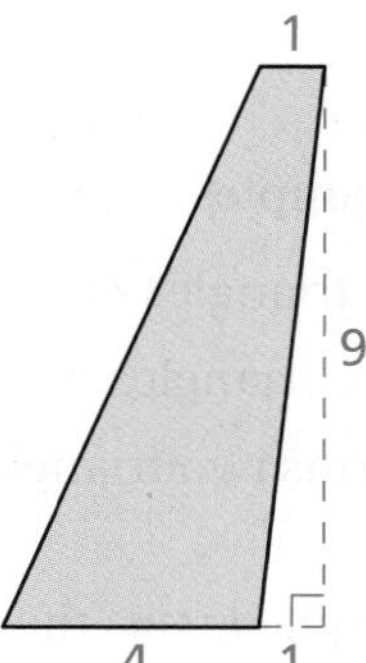

c.

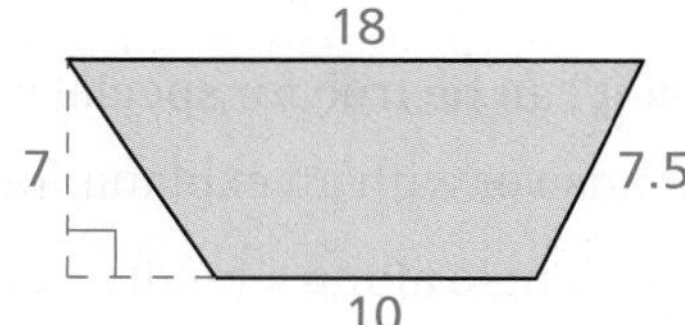

ABCD is a square. *EHGD* is a square. *E, F,* and *G* are midpoints. In Exercises 4–6, show that two indicated areas are equal as follows. Find two large congruent shapes that have equal areas. Then subtract the same amount from each large area to end up with the desired smaller equal areas. Justify each step.

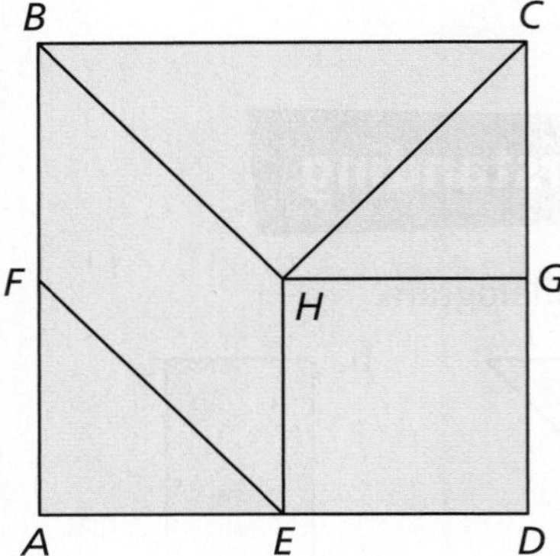

4. Show that *DEHG* has the same area as *EFBH*.

a. Area of trapezoid $ABHE$ = area of trapezoid $DEHC$. Explain.

b. Area of $\triangle AFE$ = area of $\triangle GHC$. Explain.

c. So, area of $DEHG$ = area of $EFBH$.

5. Show that $\triangle BCH$ has the same area as *EHGD*.

6. Show that $\triangle BCH$ has the same area as *EFBH*.

On Your Own

7. Decide whether each statement below is true for all cases. If you decide it is *not* generally true, do one of the following.

- State that it is never true.
- State that it can be true for special cases.

Justify your answer with an explanation and examples.

a. Cutting a triangle along a median forms two triangles of equal area.

b. Cutting a triangle along an altitude forms two triangles of equal area.

c. Cutting a triangle along an angle bisector forms two triangles of equal area.

d. If two triangles have congruent angles and equal areas, they are congruent.

e. If two triangles have equal side lengths, they have equal areas.

f. If two triangles have equal areas, then they have equal side lengths.

g. If two triangles have congruent angles, then they have equal areas.

8. Refer to the seven shapes below. Use a ruler to measure for parts (a)–(h). Give reasons for your responses.

   a. Find two shapes with equal areas.

   b. Group the shapes by area.

   c. Is the area of shape A greater than, less than, or equal to the area of shape D?

   Compare the areas of the following pairs of shapes as you did for shapes A and D.

   d. A and C   e. B and C   f. B and E   g. F and G   h. B and G

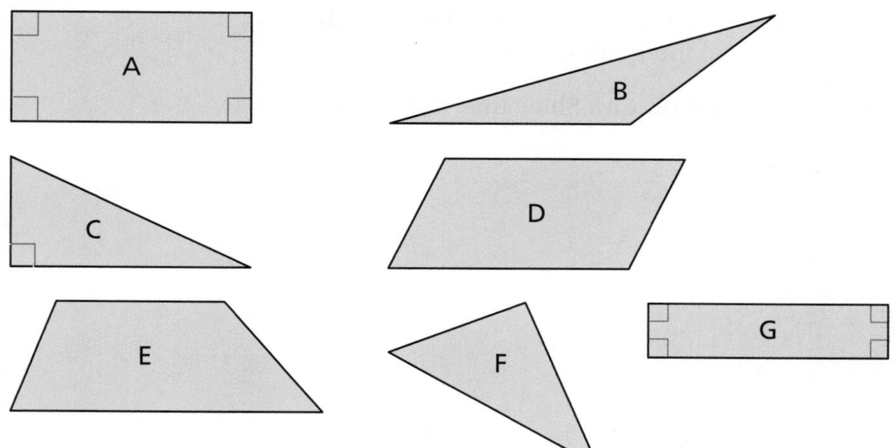

9. Give each value for the right triangle shown.

   a. the height from vertex A to base $\overline{BC}$

   b. the area of the triangle

   c. **Take It Further** the height from vertex C to base $\overline{AB}$

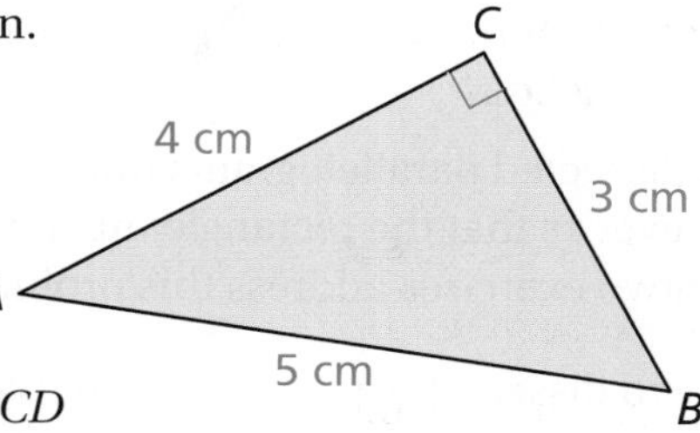

10. **Standardized Test Prep** Parallelogram $ABCD$ and $\triangle XYZ$ have the same area. What is the height h of parallelogram $ABCD$ relative to $\overline{AB}$?

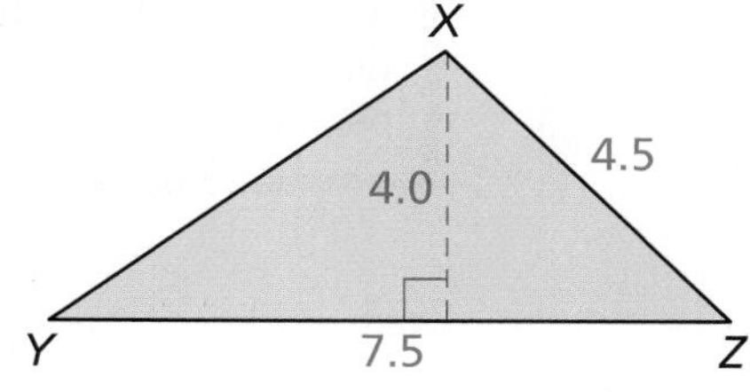

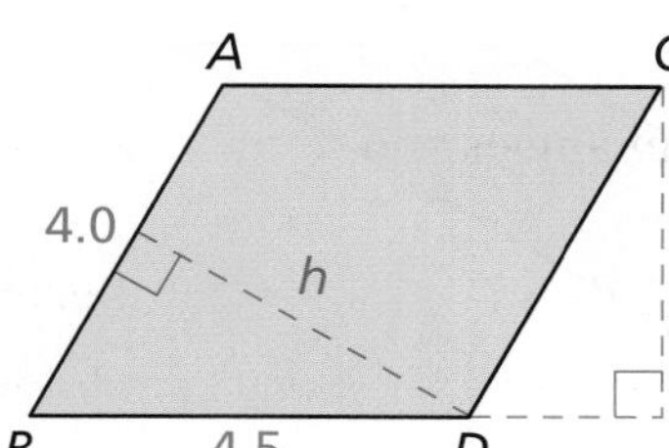

A. $3\frac{1}{3}$ B. $3\frac{1}{2}$ C. $3\frac{3}{4}$ D. $7\frac{1}{2}$

11. In $\triangle ABC$, $m\angle ABC = 90°$ and h is the altitude to base $\overline{AC}$. Compare the quantities $AC \cdot h$ and $AB \cdot BC$.

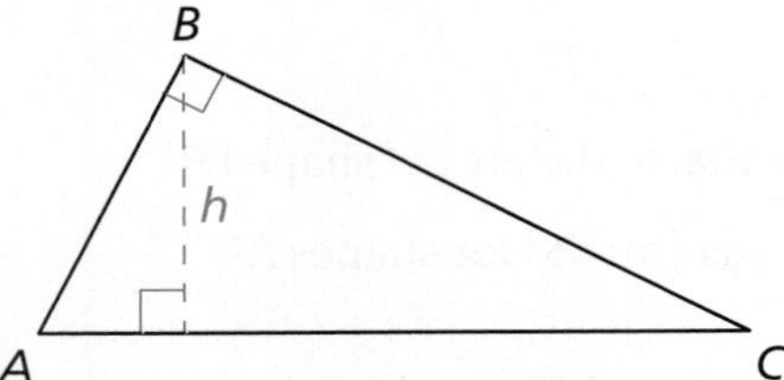

12. Show that for any triangle, the product of the length of a side and the length of the altitude to that side is the same for all three sides.

13. **Take It Further** $\overline{CM}$ is a median. P is a point on $\overline{CM}$. Show that $\triangle APC$ has the same area as $\triangle PBC$.

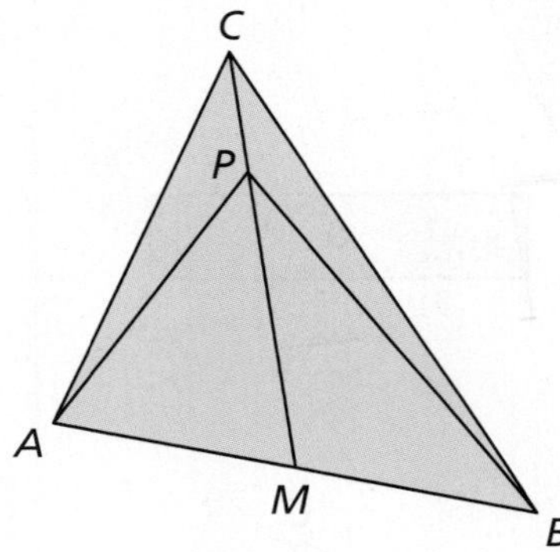

In previous exercises, you dissected parallelograms into rectangles without restrictions. Suppose, however as that the rectangle must have a specific base length. The following two exercises address this problem.

14. **Take It Further** Show how to dissect this parallelogram into a rectangle with the same base and height as shown. Trace the figures and cut them out, or use geometry software.

Habits of Mind

Represent the result. You may find it helpful to draw the desired rectangle. Then try to fill it with pieces of the parallelogram.

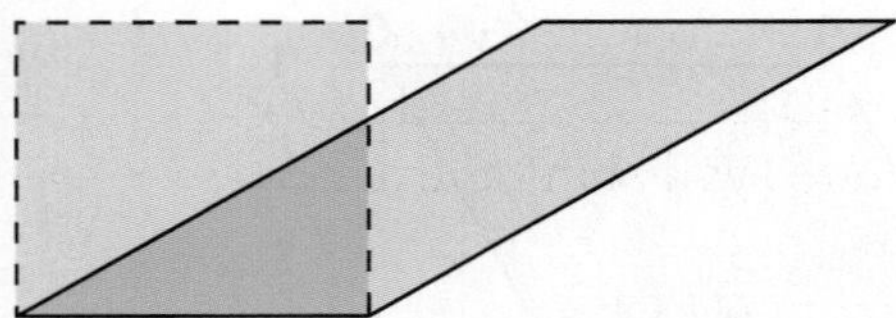

15. Take It Further The parallelogram at the right is an extreme example of the one in Exercise 14. Trace and copy it. Then figure out how to dissect it into a rectangle with one side congruent to the shorter side of the parallelogram.

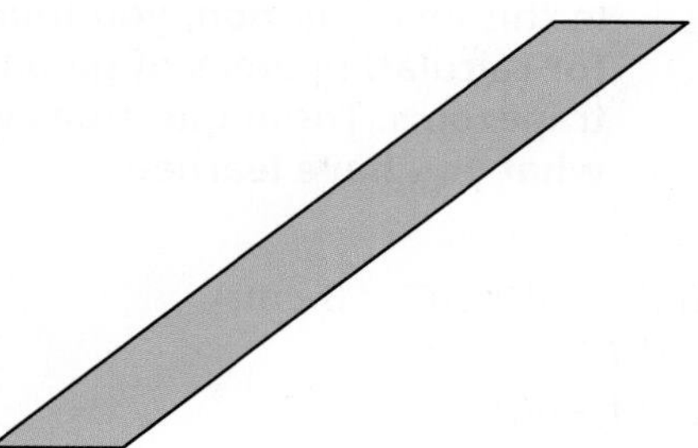

Maintain Your Skills

Exercises 16–18 ask you to think about how the area formulas for triangles, trapezoids, and parallelograms are related. The diagrams below show one way you can dissect a trapezoid into a parallelogram.

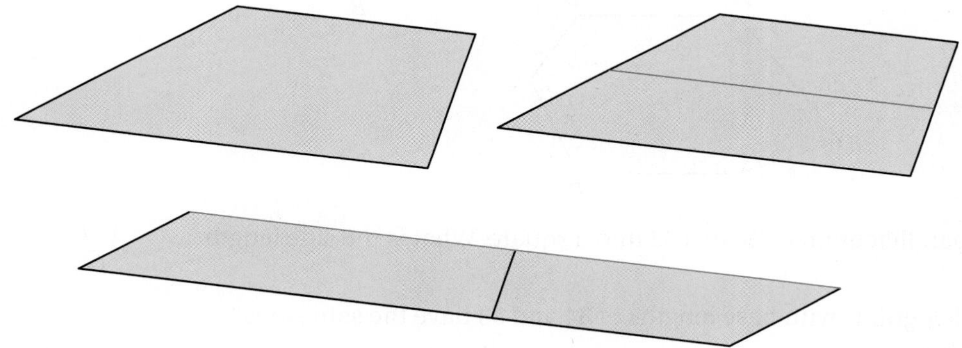

16. a. Describe the dimensions of the parallelogram in terms of the dimensions of the original trapezoid.

b. Describe the area of the parallelogram in terms of the area of the original trapezoid.

c. Derive an area formula for trapezoids from this relationship.

17. a. In your head, imagine redoing Exercise 16 with a trapezoid in which one base is a few centimeters in length, but the other is so small that it can hardly be seen. What does such a situation tell you about the area formula for triangles?

b. What does the area formula for trapezoids suggest if one of the bases is extremely small—practically a single point—compared to the other?

18. What happens to the area formula for trapezoids if you let both bases be the same size? What kind of figure is this?

Habits of Mind

Represent the extreme. For Exercise 17a, picture a trapezoid like this one,

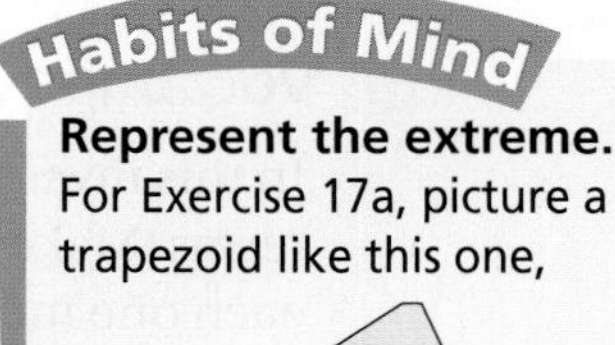

only with an even smaller base on top—"infinitesimally small," a mathematician might say.

In this investigation, you found and proved formulas for calculating areas of parallelograms, triangles, and trapezoids. These questions will help you summarize what you have learned.

1. In kite $ABCD$ at the right, $AC = 3$ cm, $DH = 2$ cm, and $BH = 5$ cm. What is the area of $ABCD$?
2. Two triangles have equal areas. Does this mean that they are congruent? Explain with an example.
3. In hexagon $ABCDEF$, $\overline{AB}$ and $\overline{DE}$ are congruent and parallel. Also, $\overline{AE} \perp \overline{DE}$. Is hexagon $ABCDEF$ scissors-congruent to a rectangle? If you think so, write down the steps that are necessary for dissecting it into a rectangle.

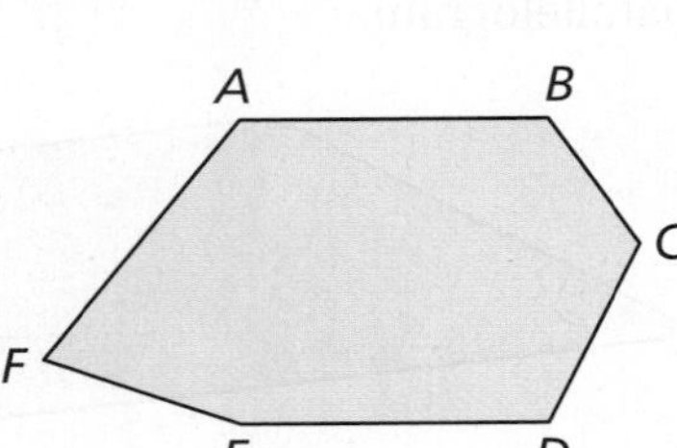

4. You dissect a parallelogram with area 32 into a square. What is the side length of the square?
5. Can two parallelograms with base lengths of 34 and 53 have the same area? If so, describe how.
6. If two figures are scissors-congruent, do they have the same area? Explain.
7. Are all squares with the same area congruent?
8. What is the area formula for a parallelogram? For a triangle? For a trapezoid?

Vocabulary

In this investigation, you learned these terms. Make sure you understand what each one means and how to use it.

- **base**
- **height**

You can assemble the table leaves and the tabletop. The total area remains the same.

Mid-Chapter Test

1. Copy and dissect each figure into a rectangle. Draw diagrams to illustrate the algorithm you use. Justify each step of the algorithm.

   a.

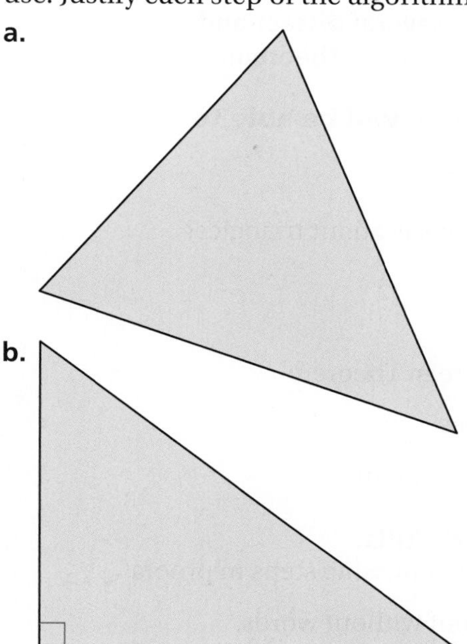

   b.

   c.

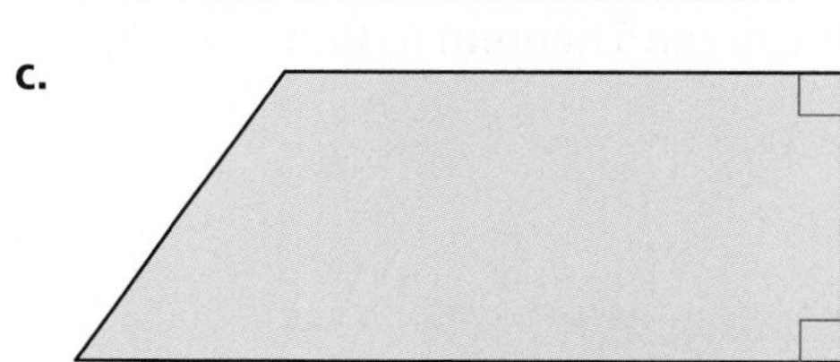

2. Quadrilateral *KITE* is a kite. *A, B, C,* and *D* are midpoints of the sides of *KITE*. $IE = 12$ and $KT = 17$. Find the perimeter of *ABCD*.

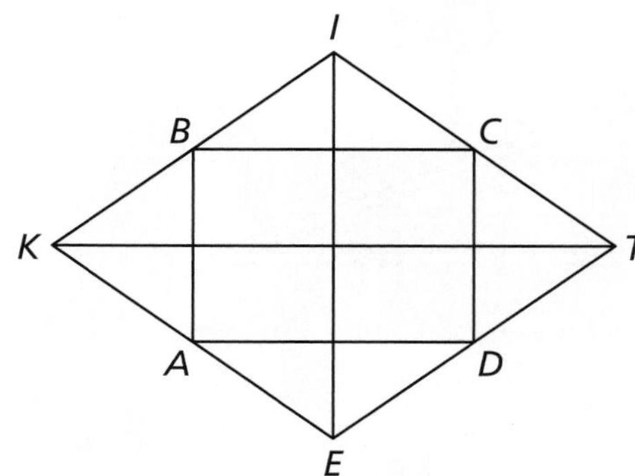

3. The following questions refer to Exercise 1. Justify each answer.

   a. Will your dissection in part (a) work for any triangle?

   b. Will your dissection in part (b) work for any right triangle?

   c. Will your dissection in part (c) work for any trapezoid?

4. Find the area of each figure.

   a.

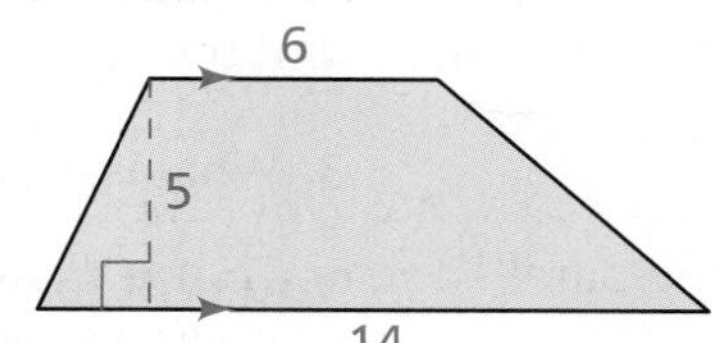

   b.

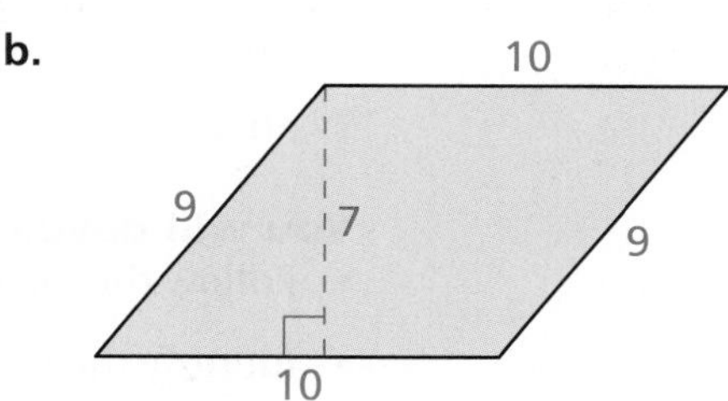

   c.

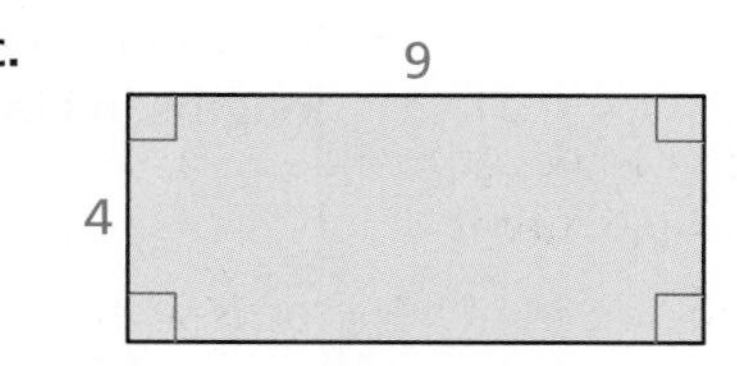

   d.

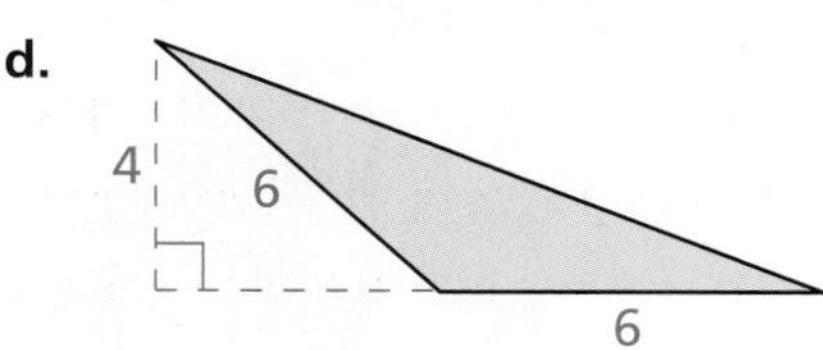

5. Tom is making a picture frame that will hold a 5 in.-by-7 in. picture centered in a 10 in.-by-12 in. frame. He wants to cover each trapezoidal piece of wood with gold leaf before putting the frame together. What is the area of each trapezoid?

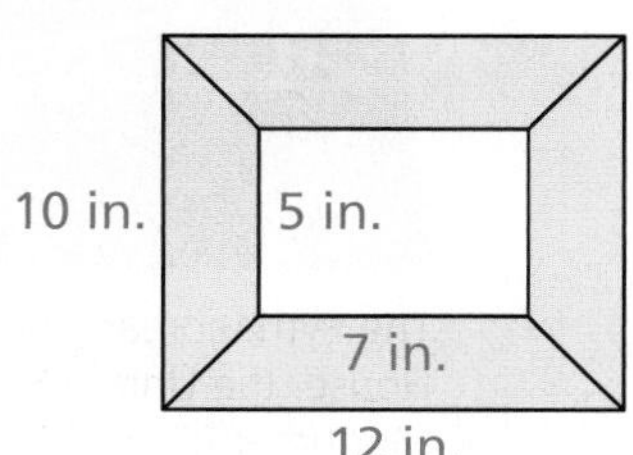

Proof by Dissection

In *Proof by Dissection*, you will study several dissect-and-rearrange proofs of the famous Pythagorean Theorem.

By the end of this investigation, you will be able to answer questions like these.

1. What is a proof without words?
2. What does the Pythagorean Theorem say about triangles?
3. What is a Pythagorean triple?

You will learn how to

- build a formal proof of the Pythagorean Theorem
- find lengths of sides of right triangles
- analyze proofs of the Pythagorean Theorem

You will develop these habits and skills:

- Follow the logical reasoning and fill in missing steps in proofs.
- Identify the critical features in a proof without words.
- See where and how to use the Pythagorean Theorem to find missing lengths in figures.

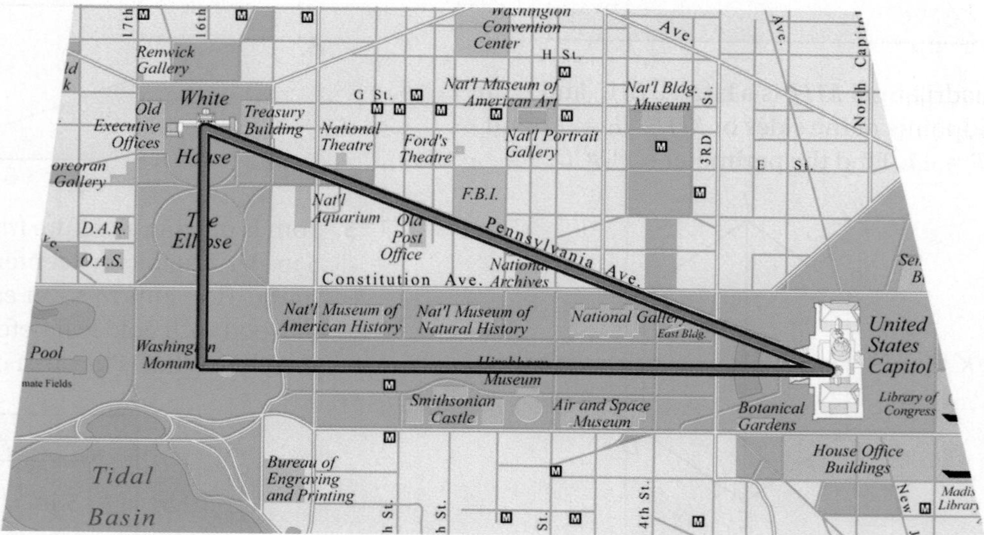

The Pythagorean Theorem relates the distances between the White House, the United States Capitol, and the grounds of the Washington Monument.

3.09 Getting Started

Reasoning about dissection and rearrangement has been useful throughout mathematics. Many proofs of the Pythagorean Theorem, a famous and valuable fact about right triangles, use dissection. Euclid's classic text, *Elements*, states the theorem this way:

Theorem 3.2 Pythagorean Theorem

In a right triangle, the square built on the longest side has area equal to the sum of the areas of the squares built on the other two sides.

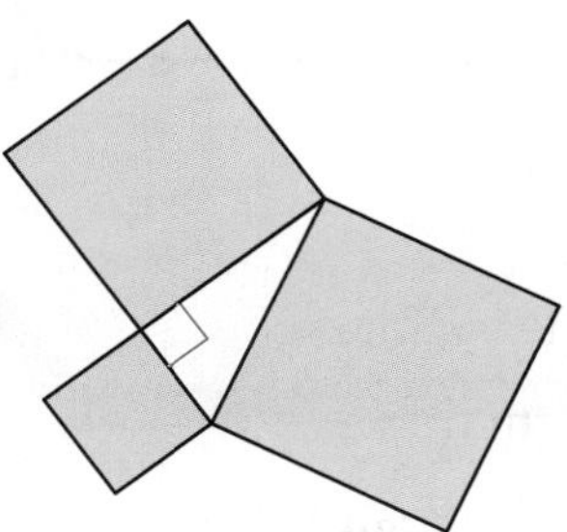

As worded, the theorem is about a relationship involving three squares. That is how Euclid meant it.

Euclid viewed the Pythagorean Theorem differently than we do today.

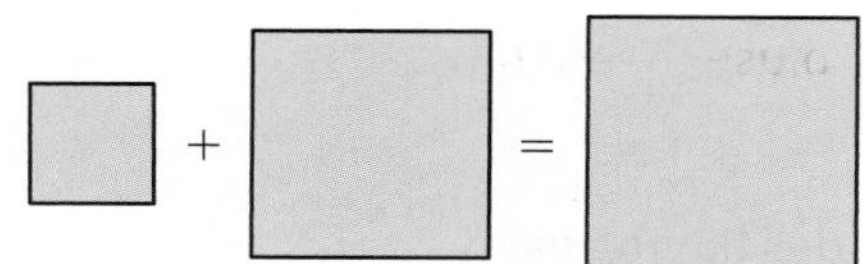

Today, most people think of the theorem as stating a relationship involving three numbers, a, b, and c, that represent the side lengths of a right triangle.

If c is the length of the hypotenuse (the longest side), then c^2 is the area of the square on the hypotenuse. The theorem states that the area of that square is equal to the combined area of the other two squares: $c^2 = a^2 + b^2$.

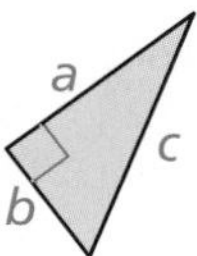

For You to Explore

1. Many people have written proofs of the Pythagorean Theorem. Below is a famous one-word proof by Bhāskara Acharya (1114–1185), an Indian mathematician. Study this proof and explain each step.

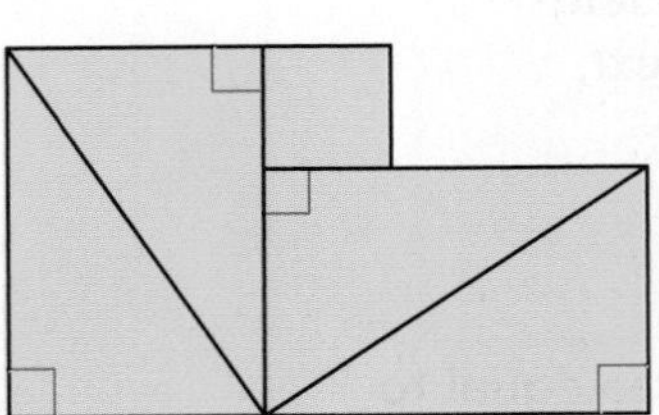

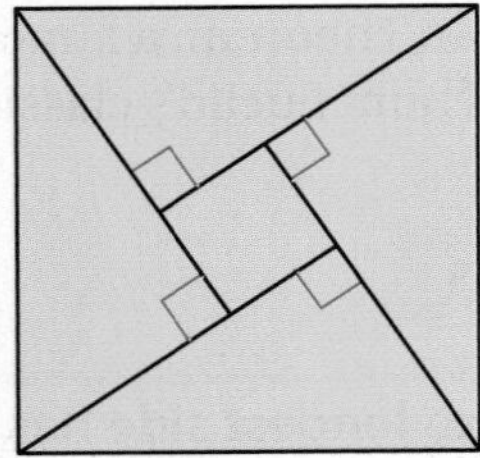

Behold!

Acharya published a book, *Lilavati*, named after his daughter. His focus was algebra, and the book included work with Pythagorean triples. Three positive integers a, b, and c form a **Pythagorean triple** if $a^2 + b^2 = c^2$. Keep an eye out for Pythagorean triples throughout this Investigation.

Exercises *Practicing Habits of Mind*

On Your Own

2. Find the length of the diagonal of a square with sides having each given length.

   a. 1 foot
   b. 2 feet
   c. 4 feet
   d. 10 feet
   e. 100 feet

3. Find a pattern in the lengths of the diagonals of the squares in Exercise 2. Write a simple rule relating a square's diagonal length to its side length.

Maintain Your Skills

4. A baseball diamond is a square 90 ft on a side. How far is second base from home plate?

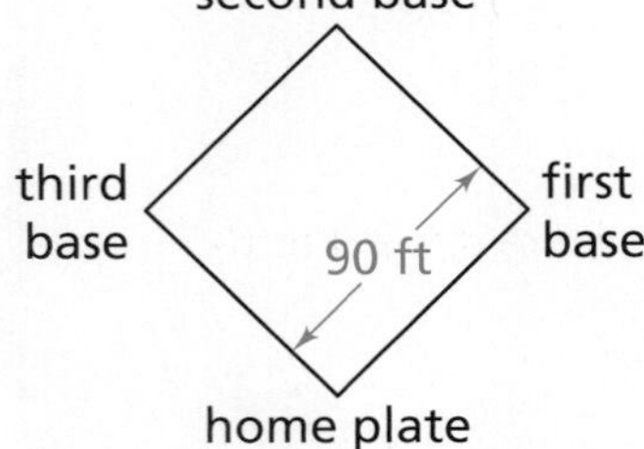

3.10 The Pythagorean Theorem

The proof outlined below is probably from China, about 200 B.C. Most likely, the author of the proof developed the theorem statement independently, rather than learning of it from another mathematician.

In-Class Experiment

For the proof outline, follow the directions at each step and answer the questions as you work. When you are finished, you will have constructed a proof of the Pythagorean Theorem.

Step 1 Construct an arbitrary (scalene) right triangle. Label the short leg a, the long leg b, and the hypotenuse c.

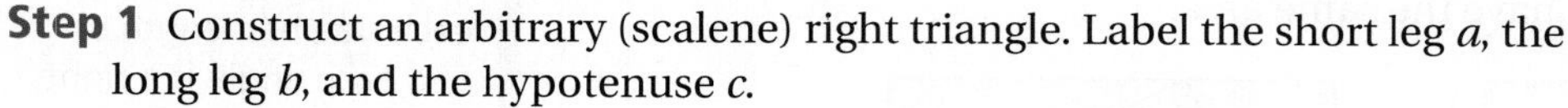

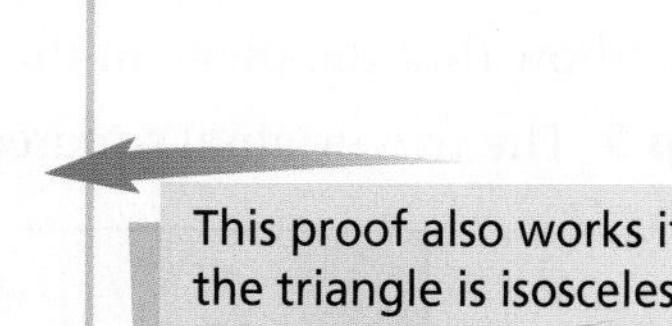

This proof also works if the triangle is isosceles, but in that case, you cannot talk about a "short leg" and a "long leg."

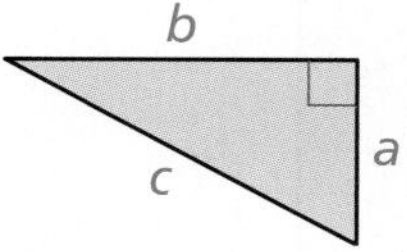

Step 2 Construct two squares with sides of length $a + b$.

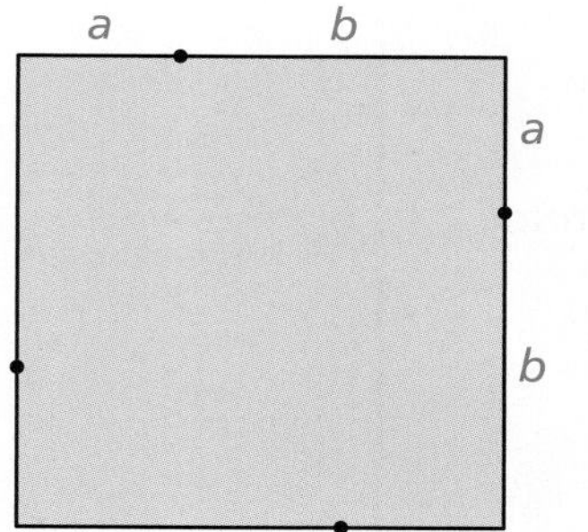

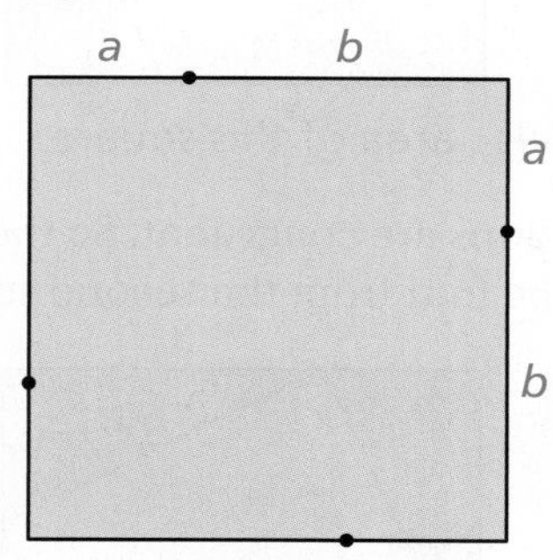

Step 3 Dissect one of the squares into six parts as shown below.

- a square with side length b in one corner
- a square with side length a in the opposite corner
- two rectangles cut at their diagonals into two triangles each

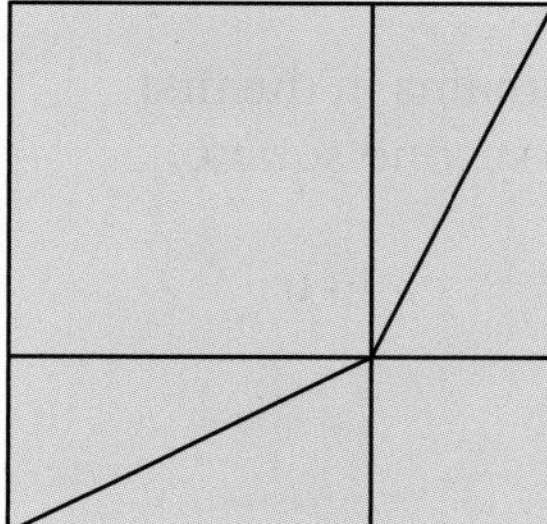

1. Show that each of the four triangles you have just cut is congruent to the original right triangle.

Step 4 Dissect the other square into five parts as shown below.

- four triangles congruent to the original right triangle
- a remaining piece in the center

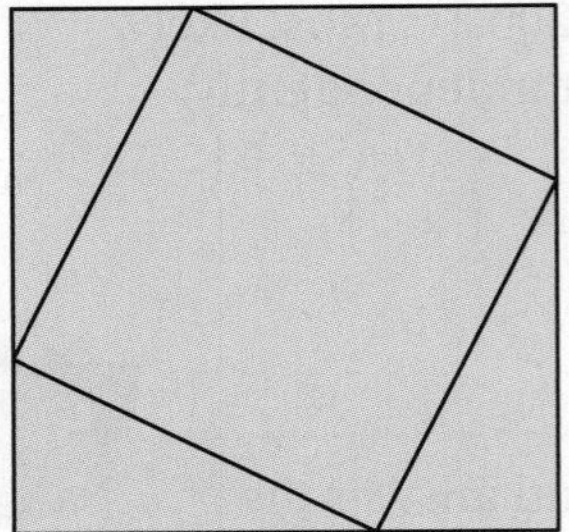

2. Show that the piece in the center is a square with side length c.

Step 5 The two original squares have the same area.

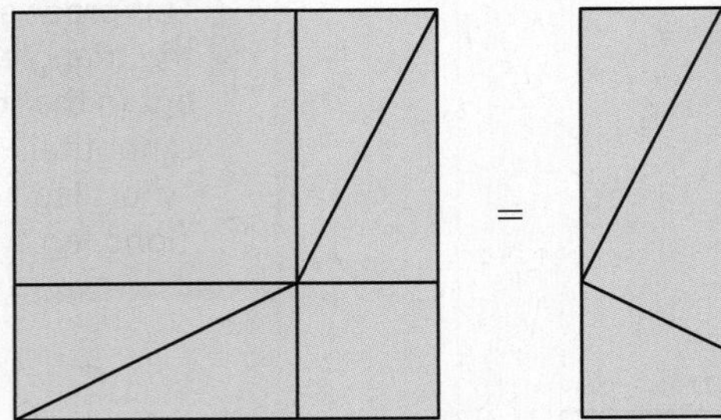

Area of this square equals area of this square.

The eight triangles in the two dissections are congruent. So the four from the first square are equal in area to the four from the second square.

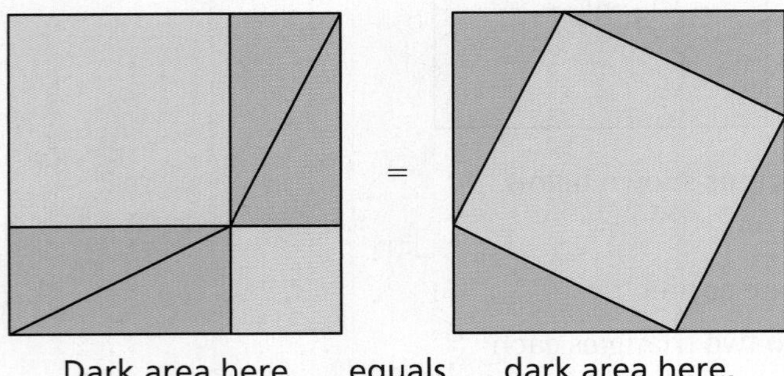

Dark area here equals dark area here.

Step 6 Remove the four triangles from each square. What remains in the first square must have the same area as what remains in the second square.

Habits of Mind

Simplify the process. You need to prove that each side has length c and each angle is a right angle. The symmetry of the situation lets you prove all cases by proving just one. Do you see why?

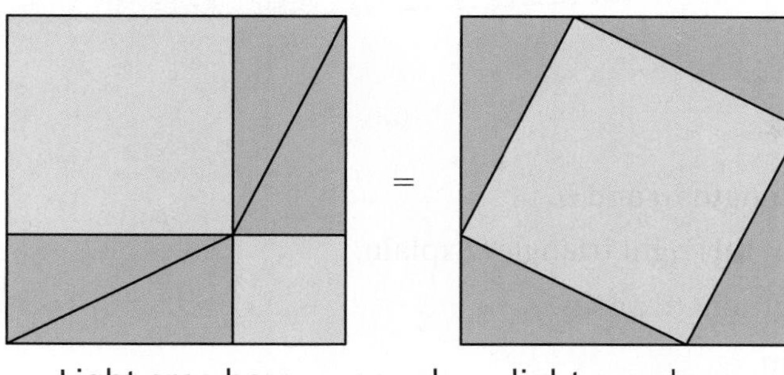

Light area here equals light area here.

You have proved the Pythagorean Theorem as Euclid knew it!

The modern algebraic statement

$$a^2 + b^2 = c^2$$

follows from the formula for the area of a square. The areas of the two squares on the left above are a^2 and b^2. The area of the square on the right is c^2. Geometric reasoning tells us that the areas on the left $(a^2 + b^2)$ and on the right (c^2), are equal: $a^2 + b^2 = c^2$.

You can state the Pythagorean Theorem this way: If $\triangle ABC$ is a right triangle, then the sum of the squares on the legs equals the square on the hypotenuse.

You can also use the *converse* of this theorem: If the sum of the squares on two sides of a triangle equals the square on the third side, then the triangle is a right triangle.

You now have the tools you need to prove the converse of the Pythagorean Theorem. You must use what you know about triangle congruence.

Exercises *Practicing Habits of Mind*

Check Your Understanding

1. An outline for a proof of the converse of the Pythagorean Theorem follows. Do parts (*a*)–(*d*) to complete the proof.

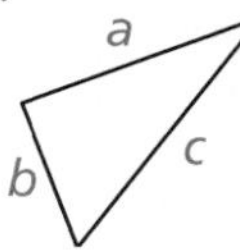

Given $\triangle ABC$, where the lengths of the sides satisfy $a^2 + b^2 = c^2$

Prove $\triangle ABC$ is a right triangle.

a. Construct a right triangle with legs of lengths a and b.

b. What is the length of the hypotenuse of this right triangle? Explain.

c. Your new triangle and $\triangle ABC$ are congruent. Explain.

d. $\triangle ABC$ must be a right triangle. Explain.

2. Write a formal proof for the following: If a triangle has sides with lengths that satisfy the equation $a^2 + b^2 = c^2$, then the triangle is a right triangle.

3. Verify the Pythagorean Theorem numerically by testing a specific case.

a. Construct a right triangle with one leg 3 inches long and the other leg 4 inches long. What is the area of your triangle?

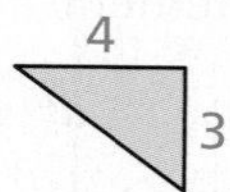

b. Construct a square with sides of length 7 inches ($a + b = 3 + 4$). What is the area of your square?

c. Dissect the square into five pieces as shown at the right.

- four right triangles congruent to the original one
- one square in the middle

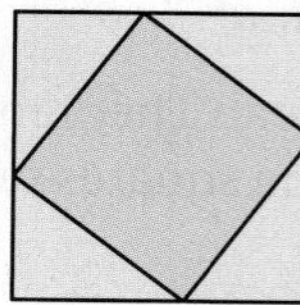

Find the area of the square in the middle by subtracting the areas of the four right triangles.

d. Calculate $a^2 + b^2 = 3^2 + 4^2$. Is the sum equal to the area of the middle square in part (c)?

4. How long is one side of the middle square in Exercise 3?

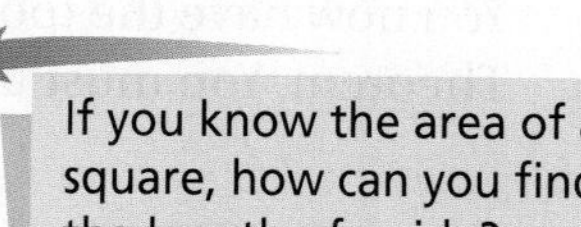

On Your Own

5. Draw a right triangle with legs 5 cm and 12 cm. Draw a square with one side that is the hypotenuse of this triangle.

a. Use the Pythagorean Theorem to find the area of this square.

b. What is the perimeter of this square?

6. The diagram shows squares on the sides of a right triangle. It gives the areas of two of the squares.

a. Find the area of the third square.

b. Find the lengths of the three sides of the triangle.

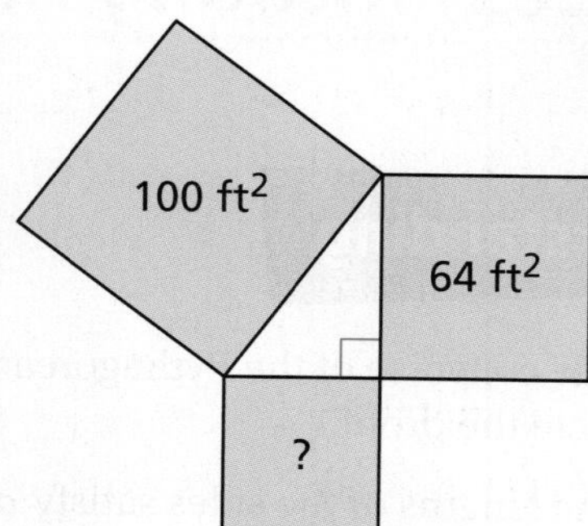

How long is one side?

7. Construct a right triangle with a 17-cm hypotenuse and a leg of length 8 cm. Draw a square on the other leg of the triangle.

   a. What is the area of the square you have drawn?

   b. What is the length of the other leg of the triangle?

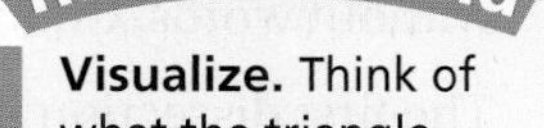

Visualize. Think of what the triangle must look like. In your "picture," think of what you are given. Then plan how to use what you know to do the construction.

8. You are standing at one corner of a rectangular parking lot. The lot measures 100 feet by 300 feet.

   a. You walk along the sides of the parking lot to the opposite corner. How far do you walk?

   b. You walk diagonally across the parking lot back to your starting point. How far do you walk? How much shorter or longer is this path?

   c. There might be cars in the parking lot. This could block you from walking directly on the diagonal. How might a path along the sides of the whole parking lot differ in length from a zig-zag path through the lot? Explain.

Walk to here.

parking lot

You are here.

9. You have seen square ABCD before. Suppose $AE = BF = CG = DH = 3$, and $EB = FC = GD = HA = 1$. Find each of the following.

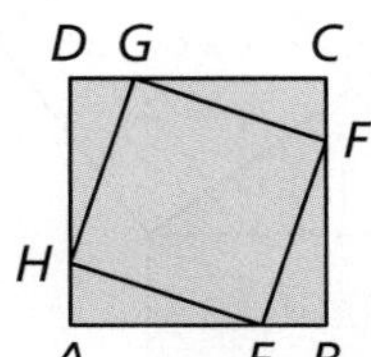

   a. EF b. perimeter of $ABCD$ c. area of $ABCD$

10. Standardized Test Prep Three squares are arranged so that they meet at their vertices to determine a right triangle. Which are possible areas of the three squares?

   A. (3, 4, 5) B. (5, 12, 13) C. (25, 16, 51) D. (9, 16, 25)

Maintain Your Skills

11. In this familiar figure, two smaller squares $CGEF$ and $AHEJ$ are inside the large square $ABCD$. Suppose $CF = 1$ and $BF = 3$. Find each of the following.

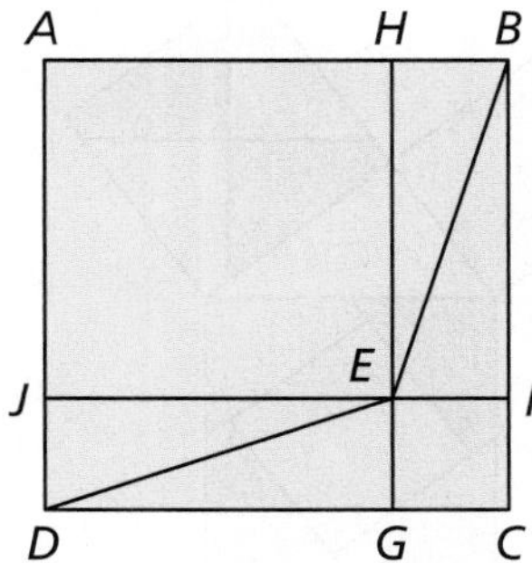

   a. AB b. BE

   c. BJ (not drawn) d. HJ (not drawn)

   e. CE (not drawn) f. area of $AHEJ$

   g. area of $CGEF$ h. area of $\triangle BEF$

3.11 Pick a Proof

The following famous proofs of the Pythagorean Theorem are proofs without words. Choose one of them to study and explain.

The first dissection proof is based on Euclid's proof of the Pythagorean Theorem. It is Proposition 47 in Book 1 of *Elements*.

Euclid's *Elements* is a collection of 13 books.

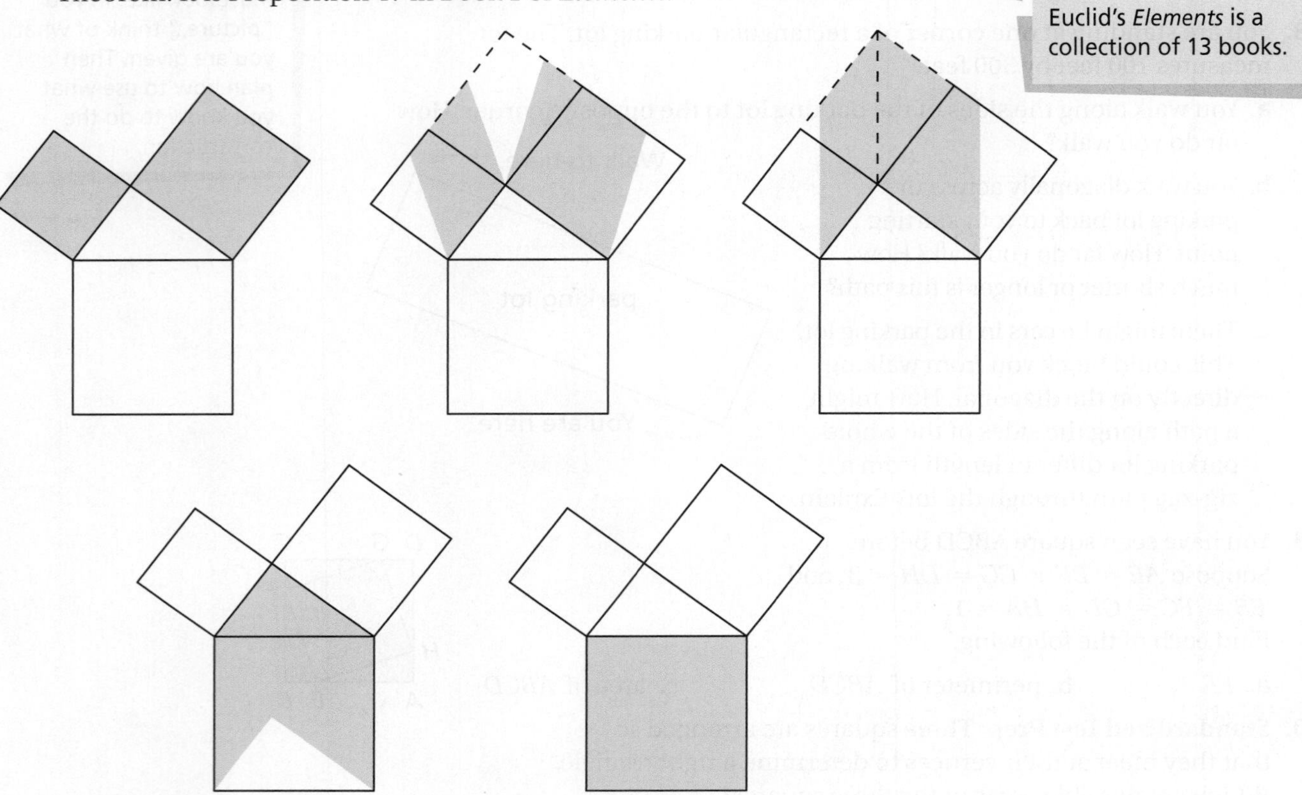

The second proof is by Henry Perigal (1801–1898). Henry Perigal was a stockbroker who lived in London. He discovered this dissection proof of the Pythagorean Theorem around 1830. He liked it so much that he had the diagram printed on his business cards.

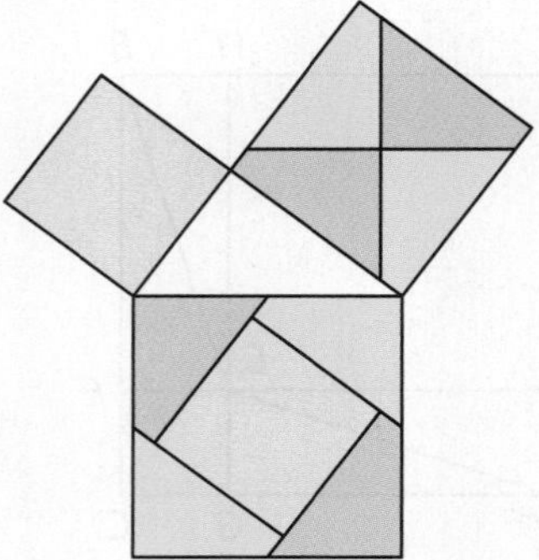

James Garfield (1831–1881) was the 20th President of the United States. Five years before becoming president, he discovered this proof of the Pythagorean Theorem.

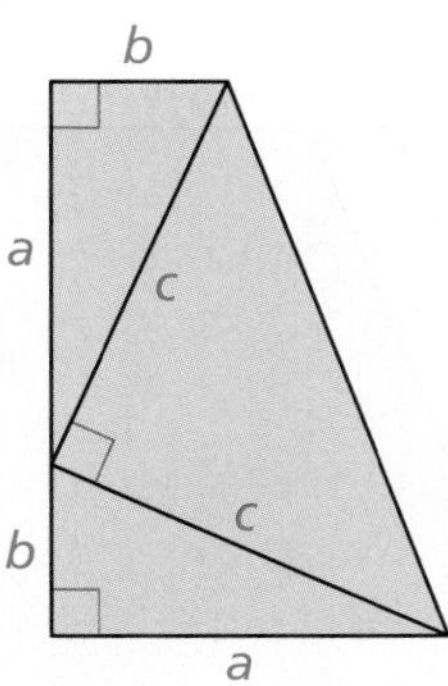

$$\frac{1}{2}(a + b)(a + b) = \frac{1}{2}(ab) + \frac{1}{2}(ab) + \frac{1}{2}c^2$$

$$a^2 + 2ab + b^2 = 2ab + c^2$$

$$a^2 + b^2 = c^2$$

Exercises *Practicing Habits of Mind*

Check Your Understanding

Your earlier proofs all showed that things were what they seemed to be. In Exercise 1 on the next page, proof is essential, but in an upside-down kind of way. You *do not* want to believe the result. You want to show that something is *not* what it seems to be.

When something is not what it seems, you usually want to explain why.

1. Carefully copy the square at the right onto a separate sheet of paper. It is eight units on a side. (You may want to use graph paper.) Then cut your copy into four pieces as indicated by the sketch.

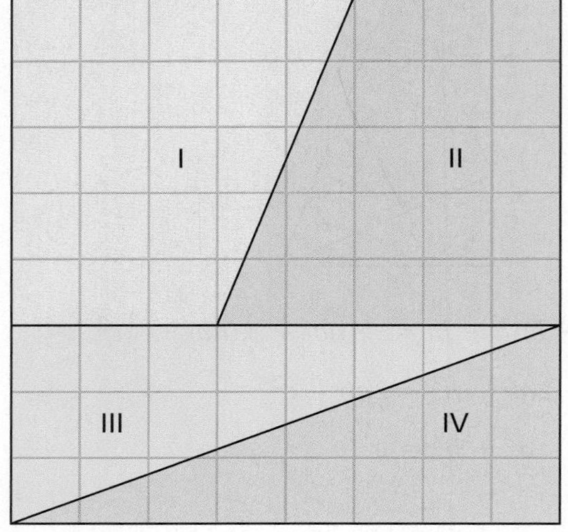

a. What is the area of an 8×8 square?

Now rearrange the pieces into the following figure.

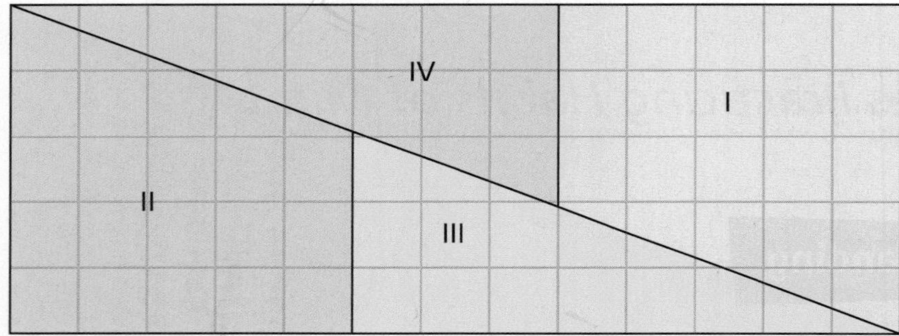

b. What is the area of a 5-by-13 rectangle?

c. **What's Wrong Here?** The same four pieces seem to make both a square and a rectangle. Yet, if you find the two areas by using the area formula, the areas are not the same! Explain.

On Your Own

2. Find the height of an equilateral triangle with sides of the given length.

a. 1 cm **b.** 2 cm **c.** 3 cm **d.** 10 cm **e.** 100 in.

3. Find a pattern in the heights you found in Exercise 2. Write a rule that relates the height of an equilateral triangle to the length of its sides.

4. An equilateral triangle has side length *s*. Find a formula for its area in terms of *s*.

5. Find the length of each segment shown in blue. Describe a pattern in the lengths.

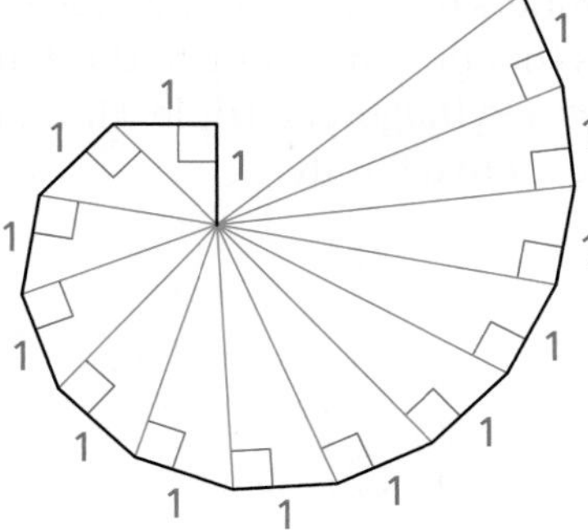

6. The diagram below shows a cube and one of its diagonals. The edges of the cube are 10 inches long. How long is the diagonal?

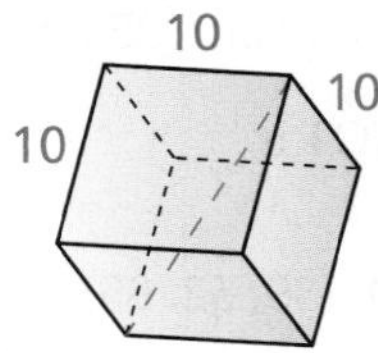

7. An airplane leaves Los Angeles. It flies 100 miles north. It turns due east and flies 600 miles. Then it turns north again and flies 350 miles. About how far is the airplane from its starting point?

Why does the Pythagorean Theorem not give the precise distance here?

8. What is the area of the plot of land shown in the diagram? (State any assumptions you make.)

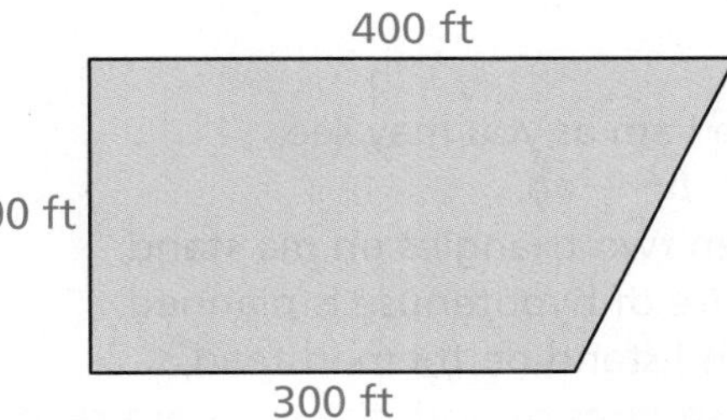

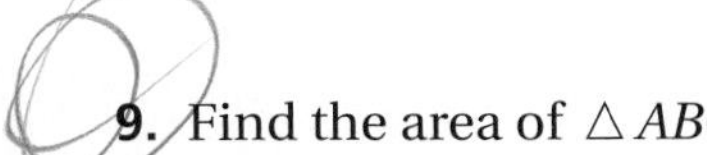

9. Find the area of $\triangle ABC$.

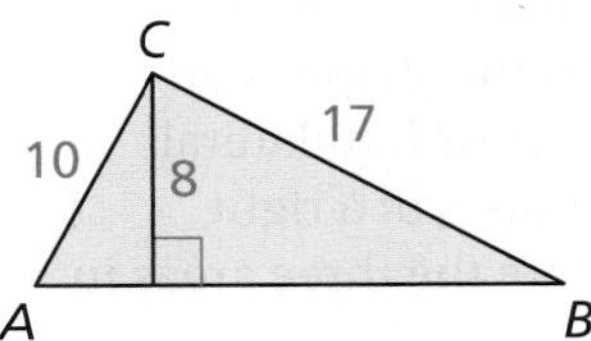

Habits of Mind

Be critical. Do you think the measure of $\angle ACB$ is less than 90°, equal to 90°, or greater than 90°?

A Pythagorean triple is a set of three positive integers (a, b, c), such as (3, 4, 5), that satisfy the equation $a^2 + b^2 = c^2$. If you have a Pythagorean triple (a, b, c), you can build a right triangle with side lengths a, b, and c.

However, not all right triangles have integer side lengths.

10. Look back through your work in this section. Find two other Pythagorean triples.

11. The following triples are members of a family of Pythagorean triples. (There are other Pythagorean triples that do not belong to this family.) Check that each triple listed below is a Pythagorean triple. How are these triples enough alike to justify calling them a family?

- (3, 4, 5)
- (6, 8, 10)
- (30, 40, 50)
- (45, 60, 75)
- (300, 400, 500)

12. Draw triangles with the following side lengths. What do the triangles have in common?

a. 6 cm, 8 cm, 10 cm **b.** 3 in., 4 in., 5 in. **c.** 15 cm, 20 cm, 25 cm

13. **Standardized Test Prep** Which of the following triples is NOT a Pythagorean triple?

A. (21, 28, 35) **B.** (42, 56, 98) **C.** (9, 40, 41) **D.** (39, 52, 65)

14. **Take It Further** Explain the following pictorial proof of the Pythagorean Theorem. It was probably devised by George Biddel Airy (1801–1892), an astronomer. It is more difficult than the ones already shown in this investigation, but the poem to the right of the diagram may help you explain the proof.

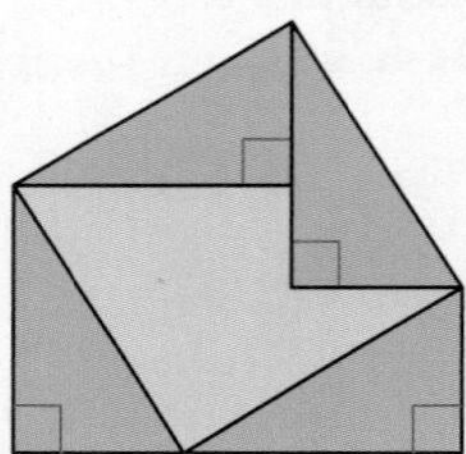

Here I am as you may see,
$a^2 + b^2 - ab$.
When two triangles on me stand,
Square of hypotenuse is planned.
But if I stand on them instead,
The squares of both the sides are read.

15. **Take It Further** The Pythagorean Theorem makes a statement about the areas of squares built on the sides of a right triangle. What can you say if the shapes built are not squares? What would you find if the shapes you constructed on the sides of a right triangle were semicircles? Equilateral triangles? Rectangles? Construct various shapes on the sides of a right triangle. Explore the cases for which it is possible to relate the three areas in some way.

Maintain Your Skills

16. Use at least 5 pairs of numbers to verify the following identity.

$$(x^2 + y^2)^2 = (x^2 - y^2)^2 + (2xy)^2$$

In this investigation, you studied several dissect-and-rearrange proofs of the Pythagorean Theorem. You also applied the Pythagorean Theorem. These questions will help you summarize what you have learned.

1. **a.** State the Pythagorean Theorem in terms of side lengths.

   b. State the Pythagorean Theorem in terms of areas.

2. Find the length of a diagonal of a square that has a side length of 4 cm.

3. What is the area of the parallelogram below?

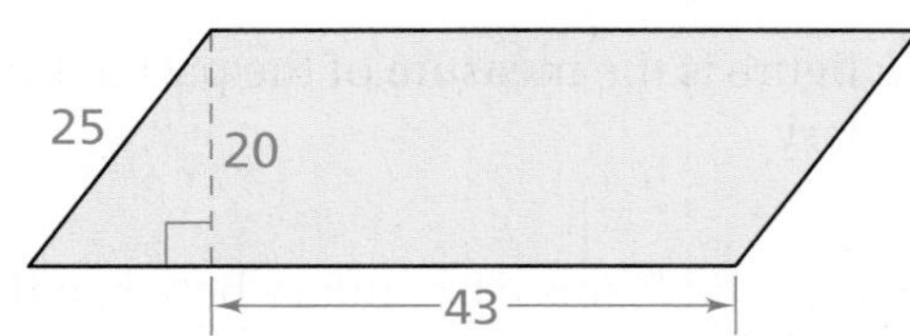

4. Find the height of an isosceles triangle with a base that is 120 cm long and congruent sides that are 100 cm long.

5. Suppose you need to divide a rectangular pool into an area for adults to swim and an area for children to swim. How much rope would you need to divide the pool as shown?

23 m
12 m
rope
18 m

6. What is a proof without words?

7. What does the Pythagorean Theorem say about triangles?

8. What is a Pythagorean triple?

Vocabulary

In this investigation, you learned this term. Make sure you understand what it means and how to use it.

- **Pythagorean triple**

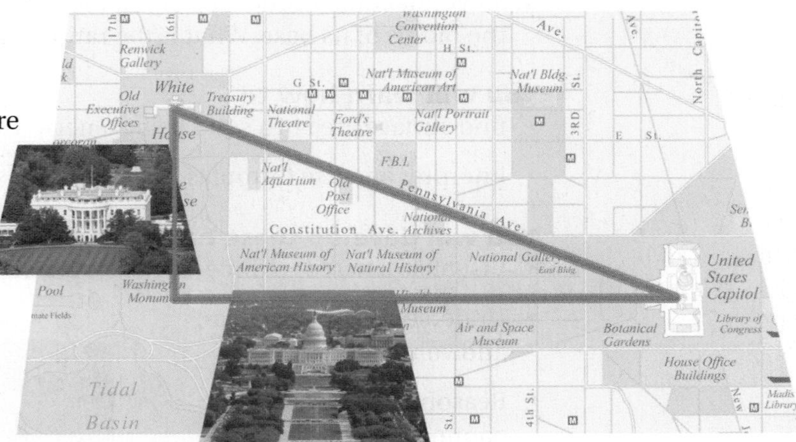

The ground was too marshy at the vertex of the right angle, so builders moved the Washington Monument site a bit to the east.

Measuring Solids

In *Measuring Solids*, you will learn some similarities between plane figures and space figures.

In a plane,
- a polygon or a circle forms a boundary between the inside and the outside of the figure
- the perimeter of a figure is the total length of the figure's boundary
- the area of a figure is the measure of the part of the plane enclosed by the boundary

In space,
- the surface of a solid forms a boundary between the inside and the outside of the solid
- the surface area of a solid is the total area of the solid's boundary
- the volume of a solid is the measure of the part of space enclosed by the boundary

By the end of this investigation, you will be able to answer questions like these.

1. How can you use perimeter and area of two-dimensional shapes to find surface area and volume of three-dimensional solids?
2. What is the relationship between a prism and a cylinder? Between a pyramid and a cone?
3. A cylinder and a cone have the same base. The height of each is equal to the radius of its base. What is the ratio of their lateral surface areas?

You will learn how to
- find surface area of a solid using a net
- interpret and use formulas for lateral and surface areas and for volume

You will develop these habits and skills:
- Visualize a net for a three-dimensional object.
- Understand surface area and volume.
- Reason by continuity to connect formulas.

This diamond mine in Russia suggests a cone. It is about 525 m deep and 1250 m across.

3.12 Getting Started

In Chapter 1, you made nets of three-dimensional objects. Now you can use the net of a three-dimensional solid to find the **surface area** of the solid.

Example

Problem Draw a net for this cube. Use the net to find the surface area of the cube.

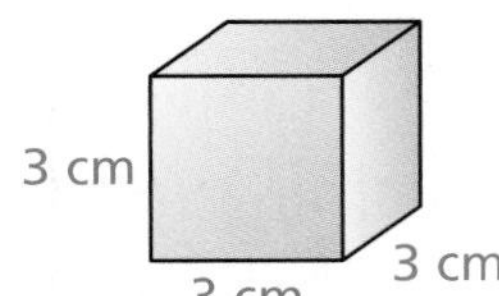

Solution Think of cutting the cube along some edges and opening the cube to lie flat. Here is a possible net.

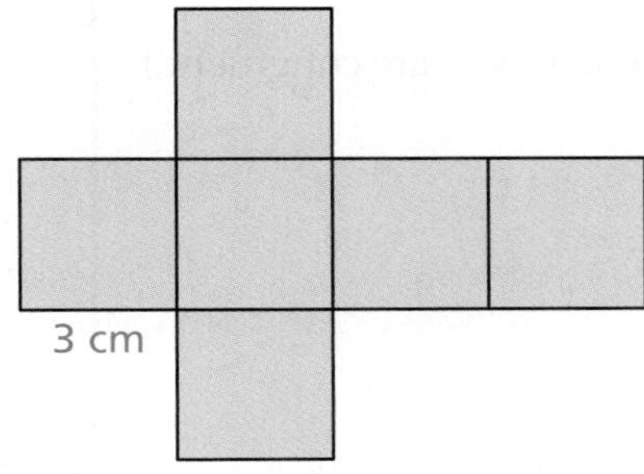

The surface area of the cube is the total area of the six squares.

$$\begin{aligned} \text{Surface Area} &= 6 \cdot \text{Area of Square} \\ &= 6 \cdot 3^2 \\ &= 6 \cdot 9 \\ &= 54 \end{aligned}$$

The surface area of the cube is 54 cm^2.

Habits of Mind

Visualize. You can cut different edges to make different nets. It is easy to see, however, that all of the nets are scissors-congruent.

For You to Explore

For Problems 1–4, sketch a net of the solid. Use the net to find the surface area of the solid.

1. a right rectangular prism (All six faces are rectangles.)

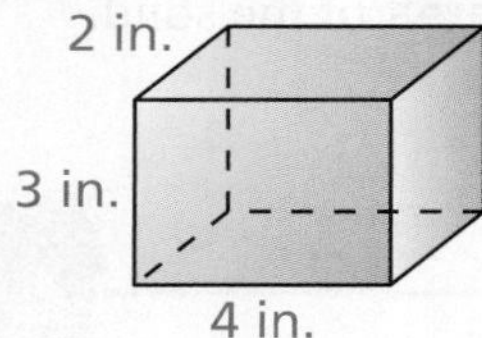

2. a tetrahedron (All four faces are equilateral triangles.)

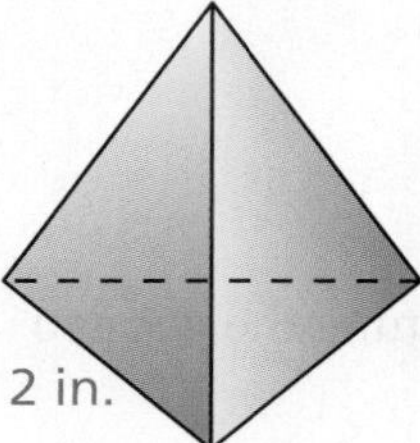

3. a right square pyramid (The base is square; the triangular faces are congruent.)

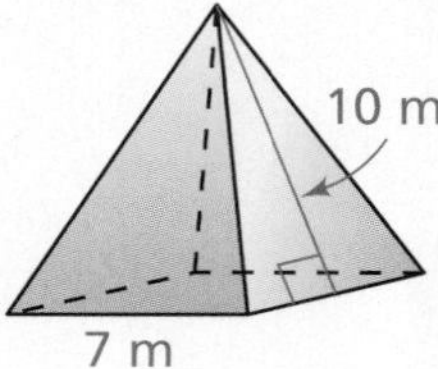

4. a parallelepiped (Here, faces *ABCD* and *EFGH* are parallelograms; the other faces are rectangles.)

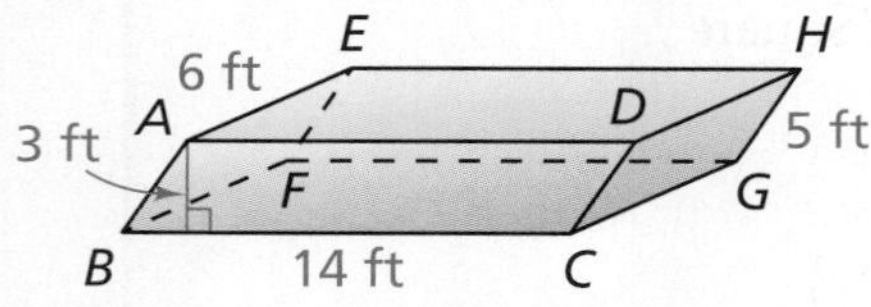

A parallelepiped is a kind of prism that can be "slanty." Opposite faces are congruent parallelograms.

When you assemble the box, the surface area of its faces . . .

Exercises *Practicing Habits of Mind*

On Your Own

5. **Write About It** The three triangles are drawn to scale.

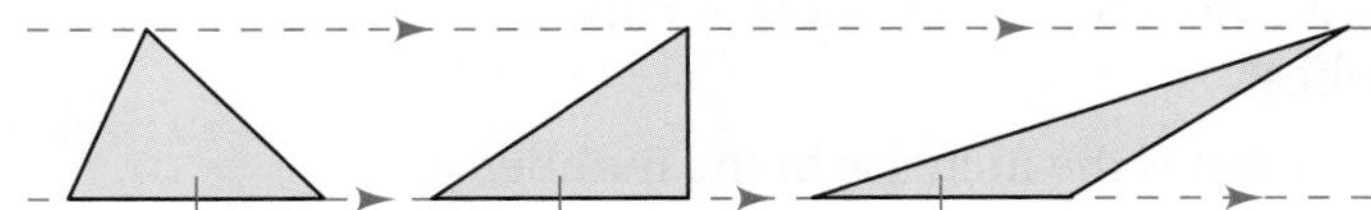

a. Does knowing the area of one triangle help you find the areas of the other two? Explain.

b. Does knowing the perimeter of one triangle help you find the perimeters of the other two? Explain.

6. **Write About It** The three parallelograms are drawn to scale.

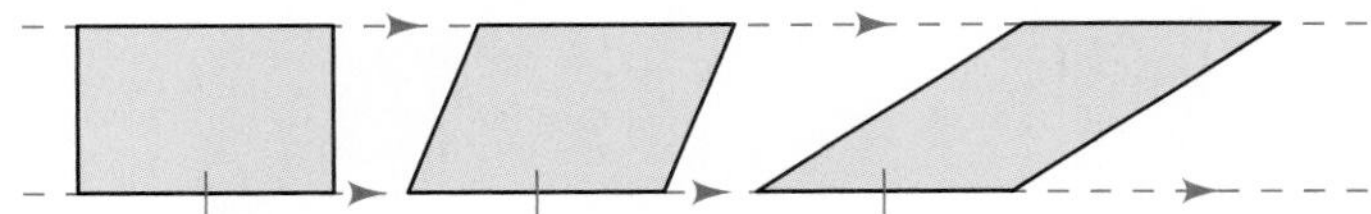

a. Does knowing the area of one parallelogram help you find the areas of the other two?

b. Does knowing the perimeter of one parallelogram help you find the perimeters of the other two? Explain.

7. **a.** You have a rectangular box that measures 1 in. by 3 in. by 5 in. What is the surface area of the box?

b. Suppose you have another box with length, width, and height that are all twice those of your original box. How does the surface area of the larger box compare to the surface area of the smaller box?

8. **a.** Write a formula for the surface area of a right rectangular prism (a box) in terms of its length ℓ, width w, and height h.

Surface area is the sum of the face areas.

b. Write a formula for the surface area of a cube in terms of its side length s.

c. Explain how you can use the first formula to find the second.

. . . remains the same.

9. Suppose you connect small cubes face to face in the manner suggested here.

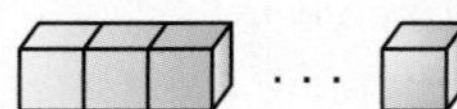

a. How many of the original cube faces are covered by another cube when you use 4 cubes? 8 cubes? n cubes?

b. How many of the original cube faces are not covered by another cube when you use 4 cubes? 8 cubes? n cubes?

c. When you add a new cube at the end, what is the increase in the number of noncovered faces? In the number of covered faces?

10. You build each structure shown below from six 1-in. cubes. Find the surface area of each structure by counting the visible faces.

a. 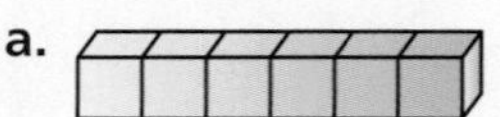

b. 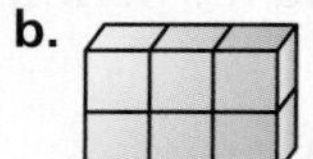

c. 

Maintain Your Skills

In Exercises 11–13, find the surface area of the indicated solid for the side lengths given.

11. right rectangular prism

a. 1 cm by 5 cm by 4 cm
b. 2 cm by 4 cm by 4 cm
c. 3 cm by 3 cm by 4 cm
d. 1 cm by 5 cm by 6 cm
e. 2 cm by 4 cm by 6 cm
f. 3 cm by 3 cm by 6 cm

12. right triangular prism

a. 1 cm by 2 cm by $\sqrt{5}$ cm, height 4 cm
b. 1 cm by 3 cm by $\sqrt{10}$ cm, height 4 cm
c. 2 cm by 2 cm by $2\sqrt{2}$ cm, height 4 cm

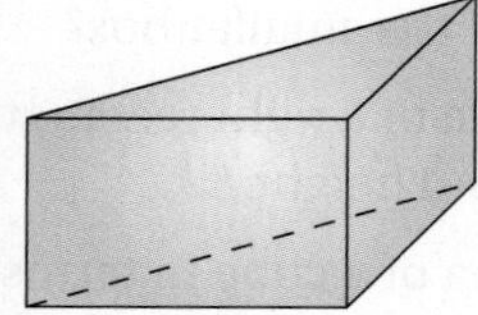

13. **Take It Further** right square pyramid

a. 4 cm by 4 cm, height 1 cm
b. 4 cm by 4 cm, height 2 cm
c. 4 cm by 4 cm, height 3 cm

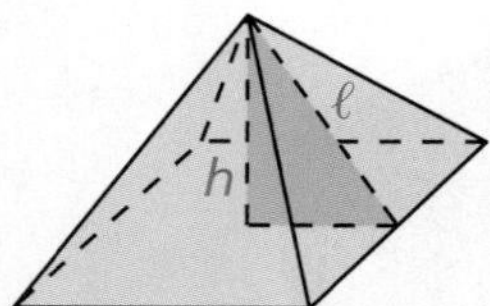

Habits of Mind

Visualize. Use this right triangle inside the pyramid to help you find the *slant height* ℓ. (The **slant height** is the height of each triangular face.)

3.13 Surface Area: Prisms and Pyramids

To measure perimeter and area of two-dimensional figures, you first classify them (squares, rectangles, triangles, and so on). Then you sort them according to properties that help you find their measurements. You do the same to measure solids.

For Discussion

Here are some solids.

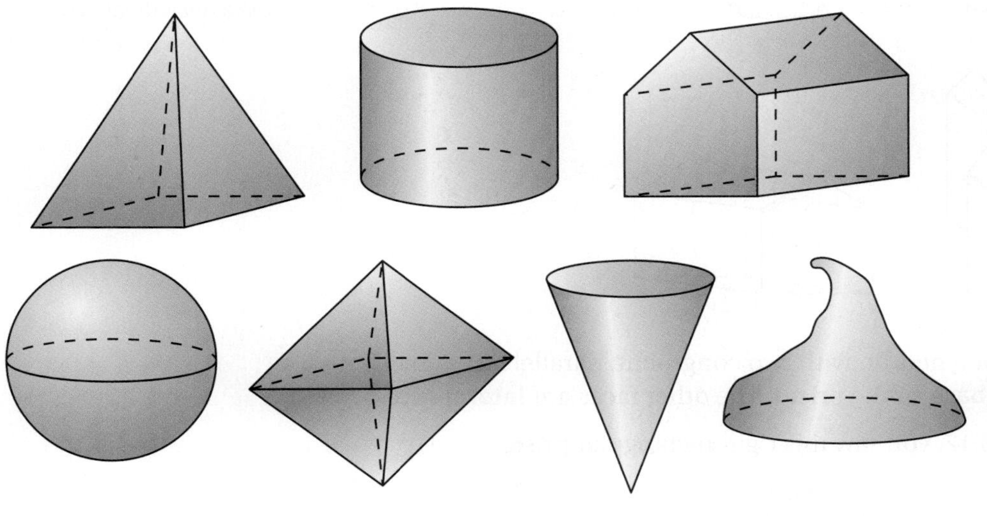

1. How are these solids alike? How are they different?

You may have noticed that some solids have all flat surfaces and all straight edges. If these surfaces are polygons, the solid is a **polyhedron.** Each polygon on the surface of a polyhedron is a **face.**

Poly- is from the Greek word for "many." What do you think *hedron* means?

In Lesson 3.12, you found the surface area of a polyhedron by adding the areas of the polygons in its net. This method works for any polyhedron, but finding the net can be cumbersome. Now you will develop faster methods for two special special types of polyhedrons: prisms and pyramids.

Prisms

You may have used a glass object, called a prism, to separate light into the entire color spectrum. Here is an example of a triangular prism.

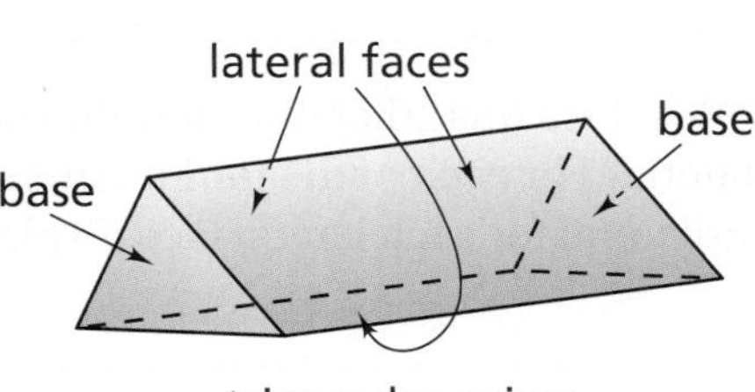

A triangular prism has two congruent triangular faces, one on each end. The other faces are quadrilaterals. (Are the lateral faces a special kind of quadrilateral? How do you know?) It is classified as a prism because the two triangles are in parallel planes. Each solid pictured below is also a prism. As you can see, the term *prism* identifies a wider range of solids than just those with triangles on the ends.

A prism base can have any shape or number of sides. A triskaidecagonal prism has a base with 13 sides. The third prism shown here is a triskaidecagonal prism.

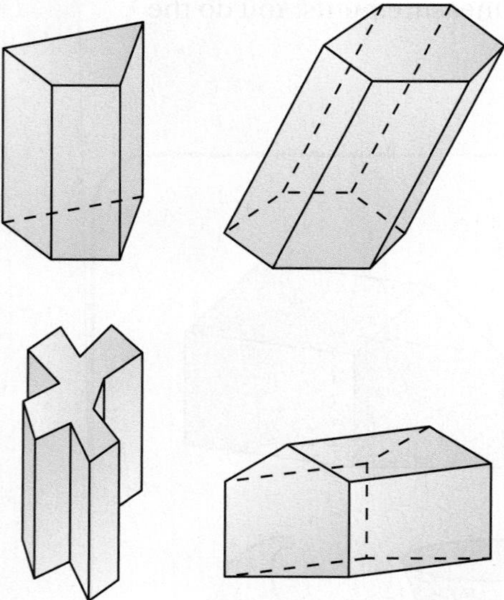

Recall that a prism is a polyhedron with two congruent, parallel faces. Each of the parallel faces is a **base** of the prism. The other faces are **lateral faces.**

In Problem 1 of Lesson 3.12, you saw this right rectangular prism.

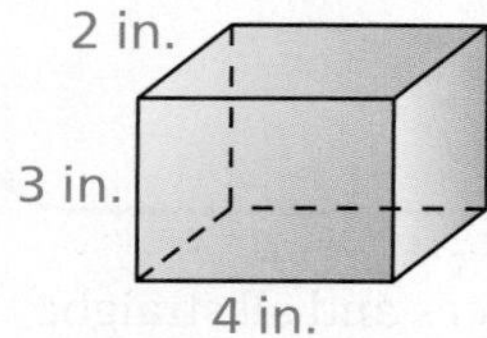

The prism is rectangular because the bases are congruent rectangles. It is a **right prism** because its lateral edges (the edges that are not sides of the bases) are perpendicular to the bases. The bases are also congruent to each other. So all of the lateral faces of any right prism are rectangles.

Which pairs of faces can be the bases in a right rectangular prism?

If the lateral edges are not perpendicular to the bases, the prism is called an **oblique prism.** The hexagonal prism shown above is oblique.

For Discussion

2. A lateral face of any prism must be a quadrilateral. How do you know? Is it any special kind of quadrilateral? For each of the four prisms shown above, determine the type of quadrilateral for each lateral face. Explain your answers.

Pyramids

The pyramid is another special type of polyhedron.

The Pyramid of Khufu in Giza, Egypt

Definitions

A pyramid is a polyhedron with one base that can be any polygon. The lateral faces are triangles that have a common vertex, the apex of the pyramid.

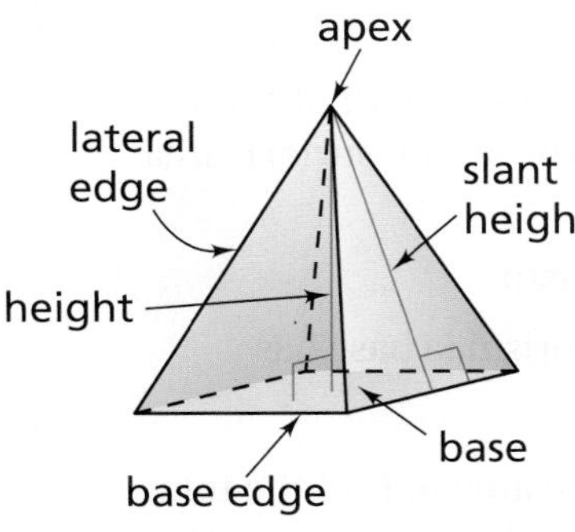

The pyramids at Giza in Egypt are regular pyramids. They have a regular polygon (a square) for the base. These pyramids are also **right pyramids** because the line through the apex and the center of the base is perpendicular to the base.

In a regular polygon, all sides are the same length. All angles of a regular polygon are congruent.

In an **oblique pyramid,** the line through the apex and the center of the base is not perpendicular to the base. Unless otherwise stated, you can assume in this book that a pyramid is a right regular pyramid.

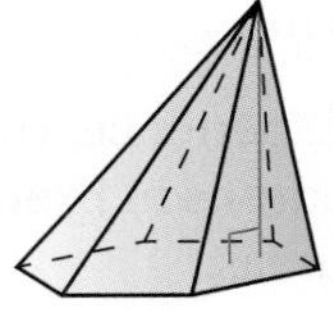

oblique hexagonal pyramid

For Discussion

3. Show that the lateral faces of a right square pyramid are congruent isosceles triangles.
4. Show that the lateral faces of an oblique square pyramid are not congruent triangles and are not all isosceles.

Facts and Notation

Total surface area and lateral surface area are distinct ideas. To find total surface area of a polyhedron, include the area of every face. To find the lateral surface area, include the area of every lateral face but not the area of any base.

Why do we make this distinction? As you will soon see, the surface area formulas can be simplified more easily if you focus on just the lateral surface area.

Exercises *Practicing Habits of Mind*

Check Your Understanding

1. Each of the following prisms is right and regular. The side length of each base is 5 cm. The height of each prism is 3 cm. Find the lateral surface area of each prism.

   a. a triangular prism

   b. a square prism

   c. a pentagonal prism

   d. an n-gonal prism (a base has n sides)

2. With your current knowledge and experience, you are able to find the total surface area for some of the polyhedrons in Exercise 1. Figure out which ones. Then find their total surface areas.

3. Each pyramid described below has a base with side length 6 cm. Find the lateral surface area of each pyramid.

   a. a triangular pyramid with slant height 4 cm

   b. a square pyramid with slant height 4 cm

   c. a square pyramid with height 4 cm

4. With your current knowledge and experience, you are able to find the total surface area for some of the polyhedrons in Exercise 3. Figure out which ones. Then find their total surface areas.

On Your Own

5. The Pyramid of Kukulcán at Chichén Itzá in Mexico (shown here) is a square pyramid. To the nearest foot, its base has side length 180 feet. Its height is 98 feet.

   a. What is the slant height of a square pyramid with base length 180 ft and height 98 ft?

   b. What is the lateral surface area of such a pyramid?

   c. If the pyramid is made from blocks 1 ft by 1 ft by 3 ft, estimate how many blocks are on the outside of the pyramid. Assume that the side of a block facing outward measures 1 ft by 3 ft.

6. Write a formula you can use to find the total surface area of a square pyramid if you know the length of a side of the base square and each of the following.

   a. the slant height
   b. the height
   c. the length of each edge

7. a. The total surface area of a right rectangular prism is 119 square feet. Its base measures 5 feet by 8 feet. What is its height?

   b. Another right rectangular prism has total surface area 160 cm^2. It has a square base and is twice as tall as it is wide. What are its dimensions?

   c. **Take It Further** A right, regular hexagonal prism has height 4 in. Its base has side length 1 in. What is its total surface area?

8. a. The total surface area of a square pyramid is 84 m^2. It has a slant height of 4 m. How wide is its base?

   b. Another square pyramid has total surface area 160 cm^2. It has a slant height equal to twice the side length of its base. What are its dimensions?

   c. **Take It Further** A hexagonal pyramid has height 4 in. Its base has side length 1 in. What is its total surface area?

9. Write a formula for the total surface area of each given solid. Let s be the length of an edge.

   a. tetrahedron
   b. cube
   c. octahedron
   d. icosahedron

An octahedron has 8 triangular faces. An icosahedron has 20 triangular faces.

10. **Standardized Test Prep** What is the lateral surface area of a right square pyramid with base edge length 12 cm and height 8 cm?

    A. 192 cm^2 B. 240 cm^2 C. 346.13 cm^2 D. 384 cm^2

Maintain Your Skills

In Exercises 11–13, assume that each cube is 1 inch on a side.

11. If you connect two cubes face to face, all the polyhedrons you can form will be congruent. Sketch the resulting polyhedron. Find its surface area. Is it a prism? A pyramid?

12. If you connect three cubes face to face, you can form two different polyhedrons. Sketch both polyhedrons. Find their total surface areas. Is either a prism? A pyramid?

Any other polyhedron you make will be congruent to one of these two.

13. If you connect four cubes face to face, you can form six different polyhedrons. Sketch the polyhedrons. Find their total surface areas. Identify any prisms or pyramids.

3.14 Surface Area: Cylinders and Cones

You started this investigation by looking at polyhedrons—solids with polygonal faces. Now you will look at some common solids that have rounded edges.

Cylinders

Definitions

A cylinder is a solid with two congruent parallel circles as its bases, joined by a curved, smooth lateral surface.

Like prisms or pyramids, cylinders can be either right or oblique, as shown below.

The cylinders in this book are right cylinders unless stated otherwise.

A cylinder is like a prism, in that it has two congruent, parallel bases. But those bases are circles. Also, the lateral surface is curved. So a cylinder is not a polyhedron.

How do you find the surface area of a cylinder?

Minds in Action — episode 8

Derman and Tony are trying to figure out the lateral surface area of a cylinder.

Derman I only know how to find the lateral surface area of a polyhedron. You add the areas of the faces that aren't bases. But a cylinder isn't a polyhedron. So how am I supposed to start?

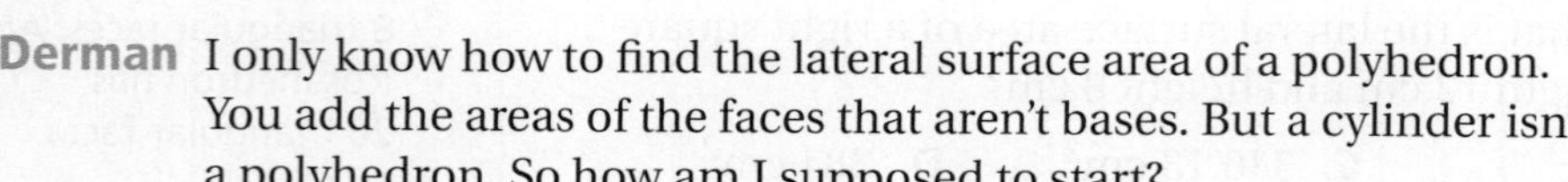

Tony Remember when we started talking about surface area? We started with nets. We talked about unfolding a cube into a net, and looking at the faces? Well, what happens if we unfold a cylinder?

Derman Unfold? I think we did this before.

Tony Yes, back in Chapter 1. When we made a net for a cylinder, the curved sides made a rectangle.

Derman Right! You don't unfold the cylinder, you *unroll* it. So it just comes down to finding the area of that unrolled rectangle: length times width.

Tony But what are the length and the width?

For Discussion

1. What are the length and width of the rectangle that is formed when you unroll the lateral surface of a cylinder?

Developing Habits of Mind

Generalize. When you unroll a cylinder, you see a net like the one on the left. You can unfold a right prism in the same way—keeping all the lateral faces together. For a triangular prism, you get the net on the right.

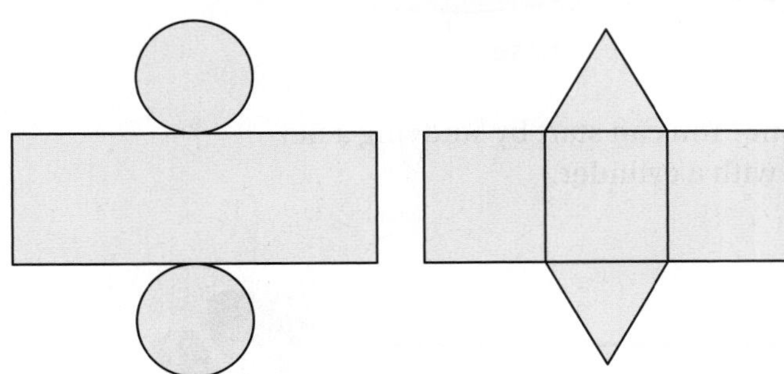

The lateral surfaces look alike—one large rectangle. You should be able to make a general formula that works for both types of solids.

The width of each rectangle is the same as the *height* of the solid before you unfolded it. The top and bottom edges of the rectangle went around the base of the solid. For the triangular prism, the length of the rectangle is the perimeter of the triangle. For the cylinder, the length of the rectangle is the circumference of the circle.

With this in mind, you can write one formula for the lateral surface area of both a prism and a cylinder.

lateral surface area $(LA) = Ph$,

where P is the perimeter (or circumference) of the base, and h is the height of the solid.

Remember...

Even though they are different words, **perimeter** and **circumference** measure the same thing—the length of the border of a two-dimensional shape.

To find the total surface area for a cylinder (or a prism), add the area of the bases to the lateral surface area.

For You to Do

Sketch each solid. Find its lateral surface area. Find its total surface area.

2. a right square prism with base edge length 5 cm and lateral edge length 9 cm
3. a cylinder with base radius 4 in. and height 7 in.
4. A right triangular prism has bases that are isosceles triangles. The base of each triangle is 6 feet. The corresponding height of each triangle is 4 feet. A lateral edge of the prism is 20 feet.

Remember...

The circumference of a circle is $2\pi r$. The area of a circle is πr^2. In both of these formulas, r is the radius of the circle. Pi (π) is the infinite nonrepeating decimal constant that begins 3.14159. . . .

Cones

Definitions

A cone is a solid with one base that is a circle and a curved, smooth lateral surface that comes to a point, the apex.

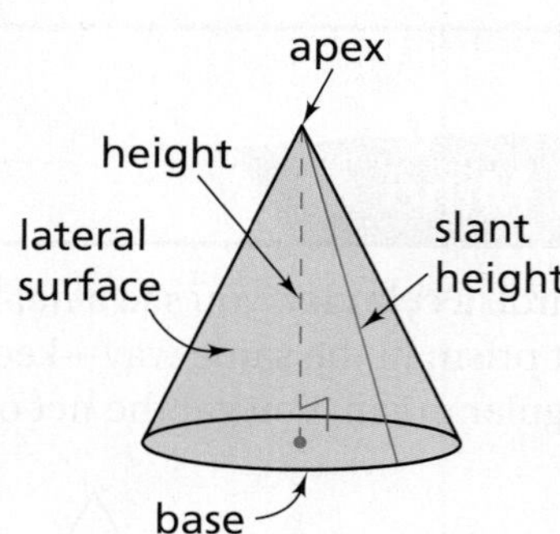

A cone has a curved lateral surface, so it is not a polyhedron. Even so, a cone is like a pyramid because it has a single base, and the lateral surface comes to a point at a vertex opposite the base. The difference is that the base is a circle.

How do you find the surface area of a cone? You can start by studying a net for a cone, just as Tony and Derman did with a cylinder.

Example

Problem Find the lateral surface area of this cone.

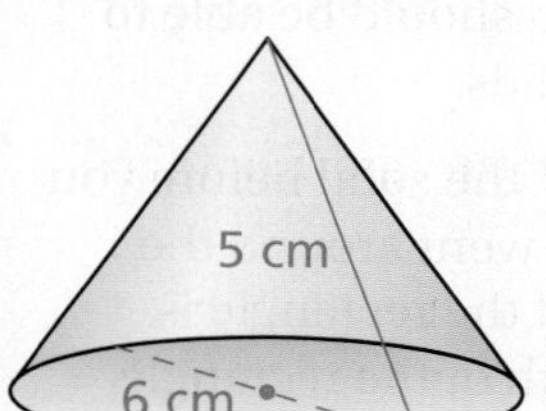

Solution First, slice the cone from the apex to the base. Lay out the lateral surface to get a net. The edge of the cone's base becomes the curved edge shown here. (The base of the cone is omitted from this diagram.)

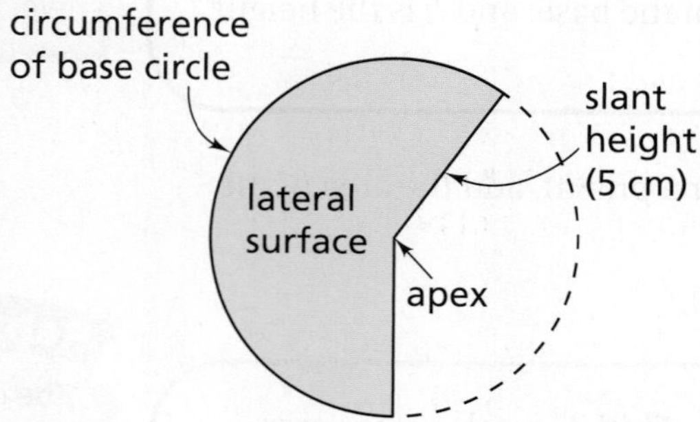

The lateral surface area of the cone is the area of the portion of the circle shown above.

The circumference of the base circle is 6π cm. A complete circle with radius 5 cm has circumference 10π cm.

You have

$$\frac{\text{lateral surface area of cone}}{\text{area of circle}} = \frac{\text{edge length of portion of circle}}{\text{circumference of circle}}$$

The edge length of the portion of the circle is the circumference of the base of the cone. Therefore,

$$\frac{\text{lateral suface area of cone}}{(\pi 5^2)} = \frac{\text{circumference of base of cone}}{2\pi(5)} = \frac{2\pi(3)}{2\pi(5)}$$

$$\text{lateral surface area of cone} = \frac{3}{5}\pi(5^2)$$

$$= 15\pi$$

The area of the green portion of the circle is $\frac{3}{5}$ the area of the complete circle.

For Discussion

5. A cone has base radius r and slant height ℓ. Find a formula for the lateral surface area.

6. A cone has base circumference C and slant height ℓ. Find a formula for the lateral surface area.

For You to Do

Use either formula you found in Problems 5 and 6. Find the lateral surface area of the cone with the given measurements.

7. base diameter 5 m, slant height 12 m

8. base radius 3 mm, slant height 5 mm

9. base circumference 4π in., slant height 3 in.

Developing Habits of Mind

Make and verify a conjecture. Earlier in this lesson, you used the idea that the perimeter of a polygon and the circumference of a circle measure the same thing. You found that for the lateral surface area of both a prism and a cylinder,

$$LA = Ph$$

where P is the perimeter (or circumference) of the base and h is the height of the solid.

In the For Discussion above, you found a formula for the lateral surface area of a cone based on its circumference and slant height. What conjecture can you make about a possible formula for the lateral surface area of a pyramid based on its base perimeter and slant height?

For a triangular pyramid with slant height ℓ and a base with side length s,

$$\begin{aligned} LA &= \frac{1}{2}s\ell + \frac{1}{2}s\ell + \frac{1}{2}s\ell \\ &= \frac{1}{2}(3s)\ell \\ &= \frac{1}{2}P\ell \end{aligned}$$

where P is the perimeter of the base. You can use the same formula to find the lateral surface area of any kind of pyramid. The formula also works for cones.

For Discussion

10. Explain how the formula $LA = \frac{1}{2}P\ell$ extends to any kind of pyramid.

In this book, you can assume that a pyramid is a right regular pyramid.

Facts and Notation

Here are the simplified formulas for lateral surface area of special solids. P is the perimeter or circumference of the base, h is the height of the prism or cylinder, and ℓ is the slant height of the pyramid or cone.

Right prisms and cylinders: $LA = Ph$

Right pyramids and cones: $LA = \frac{1}{2}P\ell$

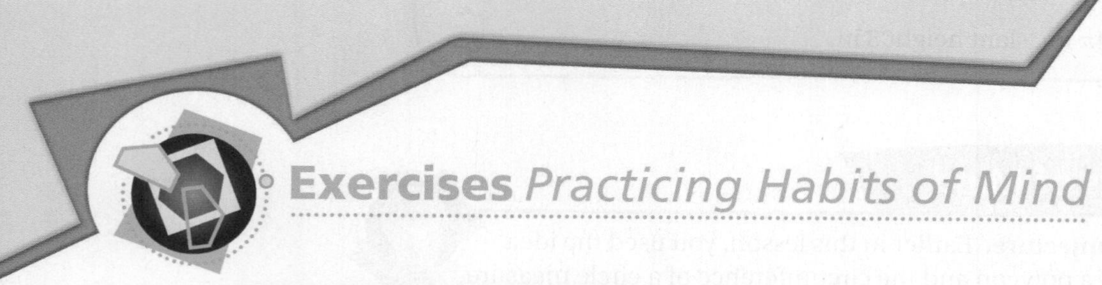

Exercises *Practicing Habits of Mind*

Check Your Understanding

1. Right square prism A has a base edge length 2 m. Right square prism B has a base edge length $\sqrt{2}$ m. Cylinder C has base radius 1 m. Each shape has height 4 m.

a. Find the lateral surface area of each shape.

b. Which shape has the least lateral surface area? The greatest lateral surface area?

c. Draw three bases for the shapes so that they all have the same center. How are they related? Does this agree with your results for part (b)?

2. In Exercise 1, replace "prism" with "pyramid." Replace "cylinder" with "cone." Do part (a).

3. Cylinder A has a height of 8 cm. Cone B has a slant height of 8 cm. Cone C has a height of 8 cm. Each shape has a base radius of 6 cm.

   a. Find the total surface area of each shape.

   b. Which shape has the least total surface area? The greatest total surface area?

On Your Own

4. Find the lateral and total surface areas for the solids described.

   a. a right cylinder: radius 7 ft, height 12 ft

   b. a right cylinder: radius 12 ft, height 7 ft

   c. a right cone: diameter 12 cm, slant height 13 cm

   d. a right cone: diameter 13 cm, slant height 12 cm

5. You can make two different cylinders by taping together opposite edges of a standard $8\frac{1}{2}$ in.-by-11 in. sheet of paper. (You tape together either the two short edges or the two long edges.) For each cylinder, find the radius, height, lateral surface area, and total surface area (including bases).

6. A cone has base radius 15 cm and height 20 cm. A cylinder has the same height and the same lateral surface area as the cone. What is the radius of the cylinder?

7. A cylinder has base radius 10 cm and height 20 cm. A cone has a base congruent to that of the cylinder and the same lateral surface area as the cylinder. What is the height of the cone?

8. **What's Wrong Here?** Tony and Sasha were making up problems so they could practice finding surface area. They made up one problem that asked for the lateral surface area of a cone with radius 13 cm and slant height 5 cm.

   a. Sasha said, "Hey! Wait a minute! This cone isn't possible!" Draw a picture to show why.

   b. Tony said, "You're right. But I think we *can* have a cone with radius 13 cm and height 5 cm." Find the slant height of this cone. Then find its lateral surface area.

   c. What does this exercise tell you about how the slant height and the radius of a cone are related?

9. **Standardized Test Prep** What is the lateral surface area of an ice cream cone with diameter 3 in. and height 4 in.?

   A. 18.85 in.^{2} **B.** 20.13 in.^{2} **C.** 40.26 in.^{2} **D.** 47.12 in.^{2}

Cut a cone parallel to its base to get two pieces as in the diagram. The top piece is a new, smaller cone. The bottom piece is a **frustum.**

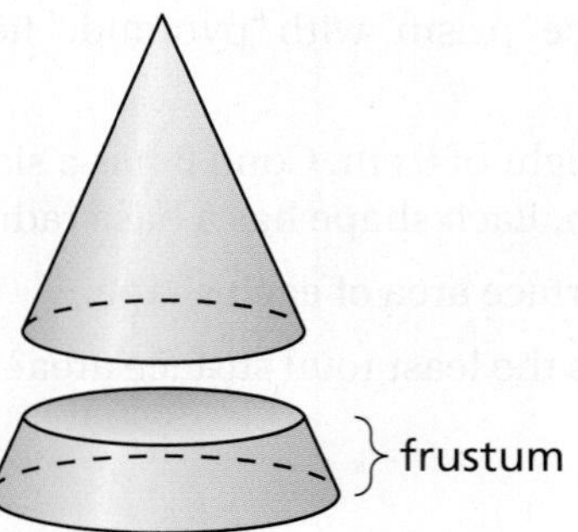

10. **Take It Further** A frustum has bottom radius 12 cm, top radius 9 cm, and height 4 cm.

a. What is the slant height of the frustum?

b. What was the slant height of the original cone before the cut? (*Hint:* Draw a cross section of the original cone. Think about the slope of a line.)

c. What is the lateral surface area of the smaller cone formed by the cut?

d. What is the lateral surface area of the frustum?

e. What is the total surface area of the frustum?

11. **Take It Further** Many different frustums have a bottom radius of 13 cm and a slant height of 5 cm. The radius of the top of these frustums must fall within a certain range of values.

a. How small can the radius of the top circle be?

b. How large can the radius of the top circle be? (Remember that even though the bottom circle has radius 13 cm, that does not necessarily mean that it is the larger circular end of the frustum.)

c. Think of a frustum with its top circle halfway between the two extremes. There is a special name for this frustum. What is it?

12. **Take It Further** If you had a frustum with one of the circles having radius 0, what else could you call this shape?

Maintain Your Skills

A cylinder and a cone have the same radius. What is the ratio of the lateral surface area of the cylinder to the lateral surface area of the cone for each given condition?

13. The height of the cylinder and the slant height of the cone are the same.

14. The cylinder and cone have the same height.

15. The cylinder and the cone have the same base and the same lateral surface area. What is the ratio of the height of the cylinder to the slant height of the cone?

3.15 Volumes of Solids

Now you will explore the **volumes** of some special solids.

Prisms and Cylinders

The first volume you encountered was probably that of a box (a right rectangular prism). You likely think of volume as the following formula.

$$\text{volume} = \text{length} \times \text{width} \times \text{height}$$

This formula works well for a right rectangular prism. But will it work for other solids?

Volume is measured in cubic units, such as cubic meters (m^3), cubic centimeters (cm^3), cubic feet (ft^3), and cubic inches ($in.^3$). When you measure the volume of a solid, you are trying to determine how many cubes of a particular size would fit inside the solid. The process is similar to how you measure area in Lesson 3.7.

> You sometimes see the abbreviation "cc" for cubic centimeter (cm^3), often for medicine and motorcycles.

Suppose you have a box that is 4 in. long, 3 in. wide, and 2 in. tall.

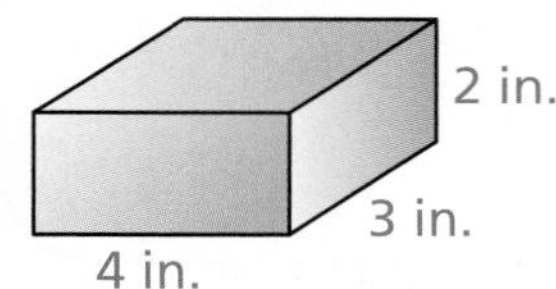

You can draw a number of cubes inside the box, each with a side length of 1 in. Then you can count how many cubes fill the box.

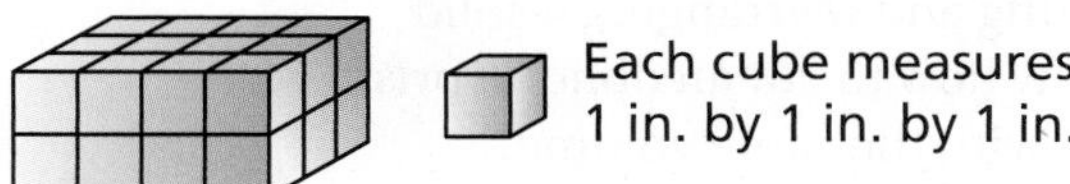

When you say the volume of the box is 24 cubic inches, you mean that you can fit 24 cubes, each with side length 1 inch, inside the box.

24 cubes fill the box.

Example

Problem Find the volume of this right triangular prism. The base is a right triangle.

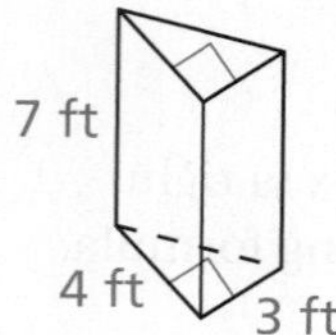

Solution The base of the prism is a right triangle. So you can take a copy of the prism and place it next to the original to make a box. And you know how to find the volume of the box! So all you have to do is find the volume of the box and divide by 2.

The volume of the box is length × width × height.

$$\begin{aligned} V_B &= 3 \times 4 \times 7 \\ &= 84\,\text{ft}^3 \end{aligned}$$

The volume of the original triangular prism is half of that.

$$\begin{aligned} V_P &= \frac{84}{2} \\ &= 42\,\text{ft}^3 \end{aligned}$$

Is it possible that the rules and formulas you learned earlier in this chapter will help you compute volume? Indeed, it is! Just as cutting a polygon and rearranging it leaves area unchanged, so cutting and rearranging a solid leaves volume unchanged. The diagrams show how to cut an oblique prism, rearrange the pieces, and make a right prism with the same volume.

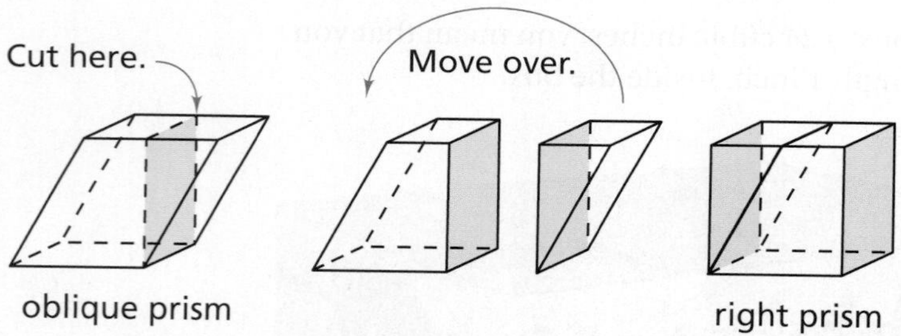

When you find volume, you can use the same view of cylinders that helped you find surface area. Visualize a cylinder as a prism with many, many sides.

Here is a general formula for volume of prisms and cylinders.

Facts and Notation *Volume of a Prism or Cylinder*

$V = Bh$

where B is the area of a base and h is the height.

For You to Do

Find the volume of each right prism.

1. a right square prism with base side length 4 cm and height 100 cm
2. a right octagonal prism with base area 145 cm^2 and height 2 cm
3. a cube with side length 3 ft
4. a cylinder with base radius 1 in. and height 1 ft

Facts and Notation

There are other units (besides cubic units) used to measure volume. These include fluid ounces, gallons, liters, and milliliters. You can define these units to be equal to specific cubic measurements. For example, a milliliter is the same amount as a cubic centimeter (1 mL = 1 cm^3). A gallon is exactly 231 cubic inches.

Pyramids and Cones

There is a relationship between the volumes of a pyramid and a prism when the two figures have the same height and base area.

In-Class Experiment

Estimating volume. In this experiment, you compare the volumes of a pyramid and a prism with the same base and height.

You will need rice or dry sand, 1 hollow square prism, and 1 hollow square pyramid. Both must have the same base area and height as well as an open base.

Fill the pyramid completely with the rice or sand. Then pour the contents of the pyramid into the prism. Continue to fill the pyramid and pour into the prism until the prism is full. Keep track of how many times you pour.

5. How many pyramids full of rice does the prism hold? How many times can you fill the pyramid from a full prism? Explain why your results suggest that a formula for the volume of a pyramid is

$$V = \frac{1}{3}Bh$$

Here is another way to make sense of the formula for the volume of a pyramid. Take a cube and dissect it along its diagonals. You get 6 identical square pyramids.

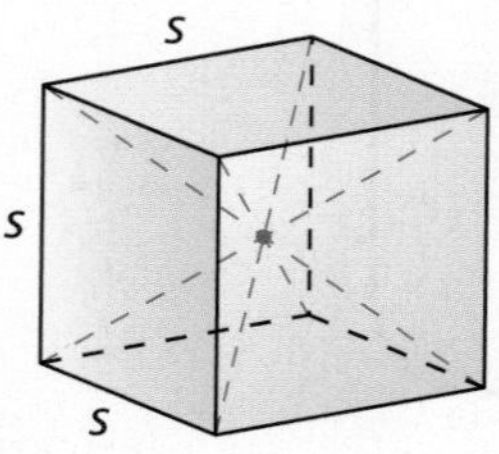

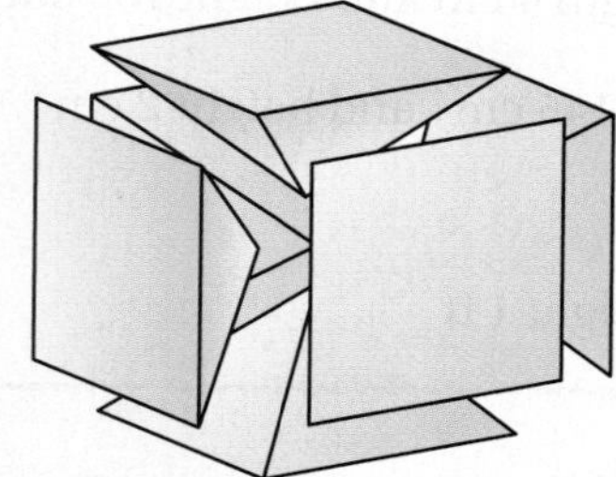

Since the pyramids are identical, they all have a volume that is $\frac{1}{6}$ that of the cube. The height of each pyramid is $h = \frac{1}{2}s$. The area of each base is $B = s^2$.

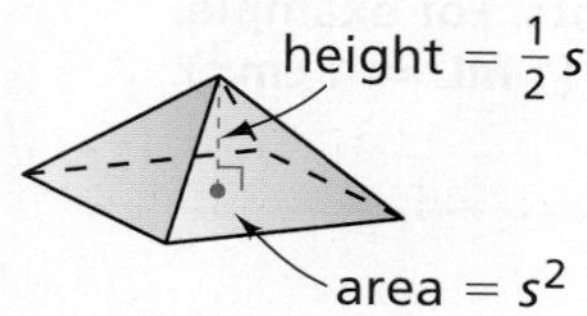

The volume of the cube must be s^3, so the volume of each pyramid must be $\frac{1}{6}s^3$.

$$\begin{aligned} V &= \tfrac{1}{6}s^3 \\ &= \tfrac{1}{3} \cdot \tfrac{1}{2} \cdot s \cdot s^2 \\ &= \tfrac{1}{3} \cdot s^2 \cdot \tfrac{1}{2}s \\ &= \tfrac{1}{3}Bh \end{aligned}$$

You can generalize this volume formula by visualizing a cone as a pyramid with a base of many, many sides.

Facts and Notation

In the following formulas, *B* is base area, and *h* is height of the solid.

Volume of prism or cylinder	**Volume of pyramid or cone**
$V = Bh$	$V = \frac{1}{3}Bh$

By substituting the area formulas for the bases, you have these common volume formulas:

Cube	$V = s^3$
Rectangular prism (box)	$V = \ell wh$
Cylinder	$V = \pi r^2 h$
Square pyramid	$V = \frac{1}{3}s^2 h$
Cone	$V = \frac{1}{3}\pi r^2 h$

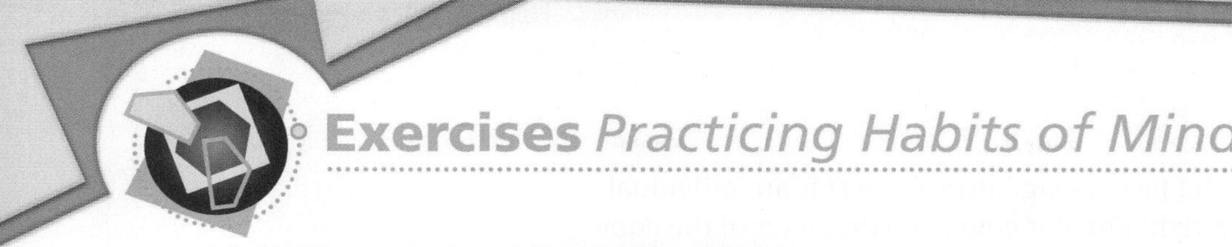

Exercises Practicing Habits of Mind

Check Your Understanding

1. Find the volume of each solid.
   a. a right triangular prism with a base that is an equilateral triangle of side length 4 inches, and with a height that is 10 inches
   b. a square pyramid with height 3 ft and base side length 2 ft
   c. a cylinder with radius 12 cm and height 13 cm
   d. a cone with radius 12 cm and slant height 13 cm
2. A pyramid and a prism have the same regular hexagonal base and the same volume. The pyramid has a base with side length 4 in. and height 13 in. Find the dimensions of the prism.
3. A cylinder and a cone have the same height and the same volume. The radius of the cylinder is 9 cm. What is the radius of the cone?

On Your Own

4. You have some apple cider in a cylindrical pot that has a radius of 4 in. You pour cider from the pot into a cylindrical cup that has a radius of $1\frac{1}{2}$ in. until the cider in the cup is 4 in. deep. How much did the level of cider in the pot go down?
5. A square prism and a cylinder have the same volume. The side length of the base of the prism is the same as the radius of the cylinder. The height of the prism is 7 cm. What is the height of the cylinder?
6. A factory has three cylindrical chimneys to release waste gases. Each chimney is 150 feet tall. The base of a chimney has a diameter of 15 feet. A can of paint can cover 100 square feet of surface. How many cans of paint are needed to paint the outsides of all three chimneys?
7. The factory in Exercise 6 needs to install filters inside the chimneys. The filter completely fills the interior of each chimney. The thickness of each chimney wall is $1\frac{1}{2}$ feet. How many cubic feet of filter are needed?
8. Sean is making a replica of the Washington Monument for history class. He decides to simplify the structure so that the replica resembles a square prism on the bottom and a square pyramid on the top. Sean's measurements are listed below. What is the volume of Sean's replica?
   - The total height of the replica is 24 inches.
   - The height of the pyramid at the top is 4 inches.
   - The length of one side of the square base of the replica is 3 inches.

9. **Standardized Test Prep** Chef Jasper's signature dessert is an individual carrot cake in the form of a right circular cone. The diameter of the cone is 3 in. and the height is 4 in. What is the approximate volume of carrot cake in each dessert?

A. 9.425 in.^{3} **B.** 12 in.^{3} **C.** 28.27 in.^{3} **D.** 37.70 in.^{3}

10. **Take It Further** Margherite wants to make a more accurate replica of the Washington Monument. She determined the measurements as follows.
    - The height of her replica is 22 inches.
    - The length of one side of the square at the base of her replica is 2 inches.
    - The length of one side of the square at the base of the pyramid at the top is $1\frac{3}{8}$ inches.
    - The height of the pyramid is 2 inches.

    Margherite has one quart of plaster. Does she have enough to make the model? Explain.

Remember...

1 gal = 231 in.^{3}

1 gal = 128 fl oz

1 gal = 4 qt

11. Terry wants to find out how much liquid a paper cup will hold. He measures the cup to be 4 inches high. The diameter of the bottom of the cup is 2 inches. The diameter of the top is 3 inches. How many fluid ounces of liquid can the cup hold?

12. **Take It Further** A tall cone has radius 5 m and height 9 m. A short cone has radius 9 m and height 5 m.

    a. Find the volume of each cone. Which has a greater volume, the tall cone or the short cone?

    b. Cut another cone off of the tip of the cone that has the greater volume. Your goal is to leave a frustum that has the same volume as the smaller of the two original cones. What must be the height of the cone you cut off?

Maintain Your Skills

13. Find the volume and total surface area of a right rectangular prism that measures 1 cm by 2 cm by 4 cm.

14. Two other right rectangular prisms with whole number centimeter measurements have the same volume as the prism in Exercise 13. Find their dimensions and surface areas.

15. A right rectangular prism with whole-number centimeter dimensions has volume 7 cm^3. What are its dimensions and total surface area?

16. Is it true that solids with greater volume have greater total surface area? If so, explain why. If not, provide a counterexample.

In this investigation, you found lateral surface area and total surface area of solids by visualizing their nets. You also used formulas to calculate volumes. These questions will help you summarize what you have learned.

1. Draw a net for the regular tetrahedron shown at the right.

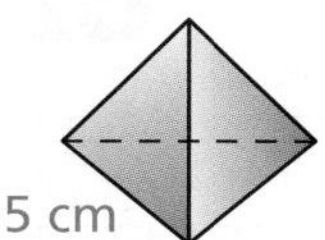

2. What is the total surface area of a cylinder with diameter 108 cm and height 18 cm?

3. Two cones have slant height 8 in. The first cone has a radius of 4 in. The second cone has a diameter of 12 in. What is the ratio of their lateral surface areas?

4. Stephanie has a goldfish who lives in a tank like the one shown at the right. The cone juts up into the tank to give the fish something to swim around. How much water does Stephanie need to fill the tank? (Disregard the volume of the fish.)

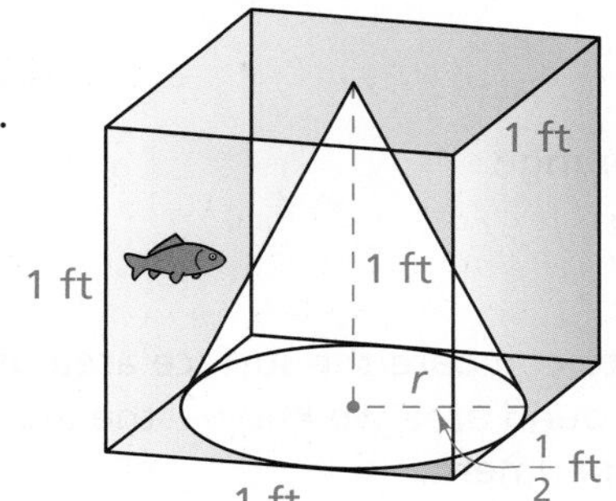

5. How can you use perimeter and area of two-dimensional shapes to find surface area and volume of three-dimensional solids?

6. What is the relationship between a prism and a cylinder? Between a pyramid and a cone?

7. A cylinder and a cone have the same base. The height of each is equal to the radius of its base. What is the ratio of their lateral surface areas?

Vocabulary

In this investigation, you learned these terms. Make sure you understand what each one means and how to use it.

- **apex**
- **base**
- **circumference**
- **cone**
- **cylinder**
- **face**
- **frustum**
- **lateral face**
- **lateral surface**
- **lateral surface area**
- **oblique prism**
- **oblique pyramid**
- **perimeter**
- **polyhedron**
- **pyramid**
- **right pyramid**
- **slant height**
- **surface area**
- **volume**

Project Using Mathematical Habits

Surface Area and Volume of a Sphere

The formulas for volume and surface area of a sphere are difficult to justify without quite a bit more mathematics. But you do not have to let that stop you from making sense of the formulas and using them.

Materials

paper, pencil, large orange

Surface Area

It might make sense to compare the surface area of a sphere to another round area we know—the area of a circle. Try this experiment:

- Cut in half an orange that is nearly spherical. Estimate your cut so that it passes through the center of the orange.
- Place a half of the orange cut-side side down on a piece of paper. Trace around it, making several copies of a great circle for your sphere.
- Peel the orange halves. Fit the pieces of peel into the circles you traced. How many circles can you fill?

1. Use the results of your experiment with the orange. Estimate the surface area of a sphere by comparing it to the area of a circle with the same radius. What formula for the surface area of a sphere would you write from your estimate?

Volume

To make sense of the formula for the volume of a sphere, you can compare it to formulas for the volumes of some other solids you know how to measure. If you find a solid that can contain the sphere, you will know that the sphere's volume is less than the solid. Then, if you find another solid that can fit inside the sphere, the sphere's volume must be greater.

2. Find the dimensions of the largest bicone—two cones joined at the base—that can be contained by a sphere of radius *r*. Then find the volume of the double cone. What can you conclude about the volume of the sphere?

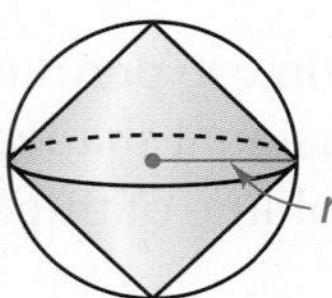

3. Find the dimensions of the smallest cylinder that could contain a sphere of radius *r*. Then find the volume of that cylinder. What can you conclude about the volume of the sphere?

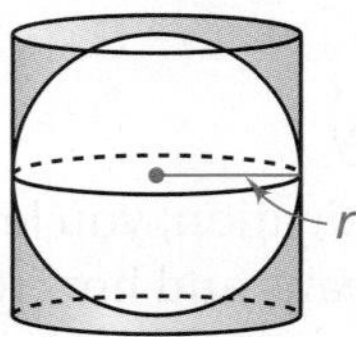

Although you have not derived the formula for the volume of a sphere, you can see that formula (given below) is at least within the limits you found in Problems 2 and 3.

Here are the formulas for a sphere.

The volume of a sphere is $V = \frac{4}{3}\pi r^3$.

The surface area of a sphere is $SA = 4\pi r^2$.

4. Find the surface area of a sphere with volume 10 cm^3.

5. Find the volume of a sphere with surface area 10 cm^2.

6. A cylindrical steel pipe is 12 feet long. It has an outer diameter of 4 inches and an inner diameter of $3\frac{3}{4}$ inches.

   a. What is the volume of the steel that makes up the pipe in cubic inches?

   b. What is the volume of the largest sphere that could fit inside the pipe?

   c. What is the surface area of that largest sphere?

7. a. Find the volume and surface area of a sphere with radius 8 in.

   b. A cylinder has the same volume and radius as the sphere in part (a). Find its height and surface area.

   c. A cone has the same volume and radius as the sphere in part (a). Find its height and surface area.

   d. Which of the solids of equal radius has the most surface area for the same amount of volume?

8. a. Suppose you double the radius of a cone but leave the height unchanged. How will the volume of the new cone compare to that of the original?

   b. Suppose you double the radius of a cylinder but leave the height unchanged. How will the volume of the new cylinder compare to that of the original?

   c. Suppose you double the radius of a sphere. How will the volume of the new sphere compare to that of the original?

9. A cone for ice cream has diameter 3 in. and height 5 in. The cone is completely filled with ice cream. There is a hemisphere of ice cream balanced on the base of the cone. Its diameter is also 3 in. What is the approximate volume of the ice cream?

10. A certain cold medicine comes in a capsule that is 20 mm long. The capsule shape is a cylinder of diameter 6 mm, with a hemisphere on each end. Each hemisphere also has diameter 6 mm. What is the volume available for the medicine inside the capsule?

Sections of a sphere were the basis for the roof design of the Opera House in Sydney, Australia.

Chapter 3

Review

Go Online
Pearsonsuccessnet.com

In **Investigation 3A** you learned how to

- change one shape into another by making cuts and rearranging the parts
- tell when two shapes are scissors-congruent
- prove the Midline Theorem using cuts and rearrangement

The following questions will help you check your understanding.

1. Describe an algorithm for dissecting this trapezoid into a rectangle.

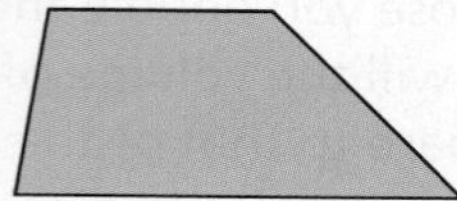

2. In the figure below, M is the midpoint of $\overline{AC}$, $\ell \parallel \overline{BC}$, and $EM = MF$. Prove each statement.

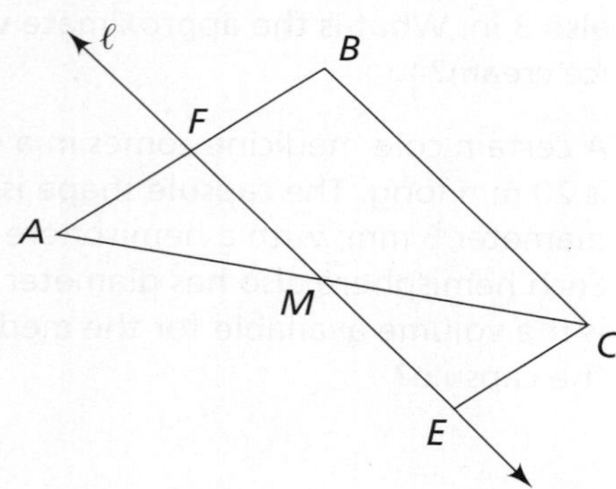

a. $\overline{EC} \parallel \overline{AB}$

b. $BCEF$ is a parallelogram.

c. $FM = \frac{1}{2}BC$

In **Investigation 3B** you learned how to

- calculate the area of a parallelogram, of a triangle, and of a trapezoid
- prove the formulas for calculating the areas above
- tell the difference between two figures being scissors-congruent and having the same area

The following questions will help you check your understanding.

3. In trapezoid $ABCD$, $\overline{AB} \parallel \overline{CD}$. What is the area of trapezoid $ABCD$?

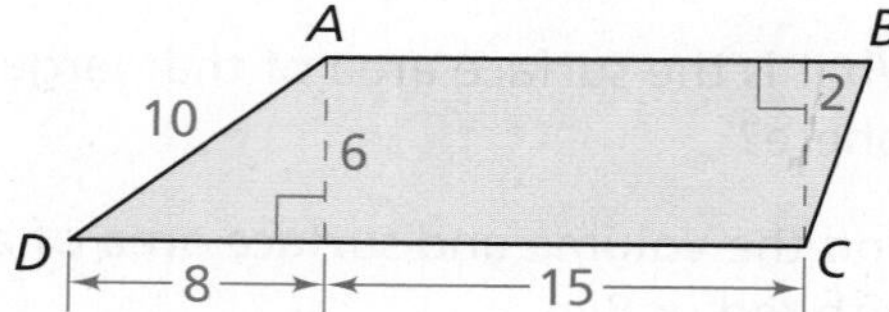

4. What is the area of this pentagon?

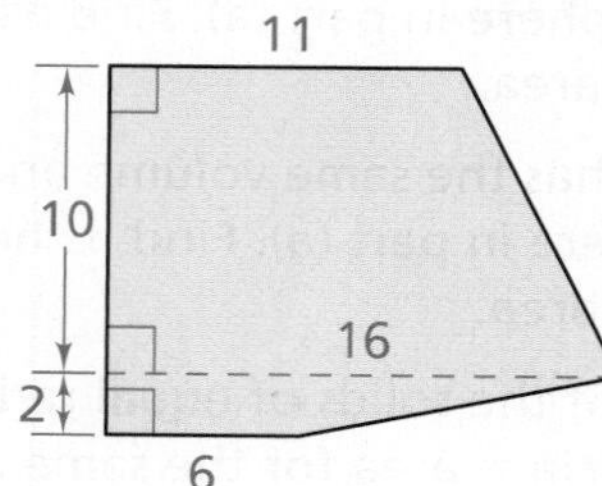

5. If two rectangles have the same area, are they scissors-congruent? Explain.

In **Investigation 3C** you learned how to

- follow the logical reasoning and fill in missing steps in proofs of the Pythagorean Theorem
- identify the critical features in a proof without words
- see where and how to use the Pythagorean Theorem to find missing lengths in figures

The following questions will help you check your understanding.

6. Write your favorite proof of the Pythagorean Theorem.

7. How far is the cat from the bird?

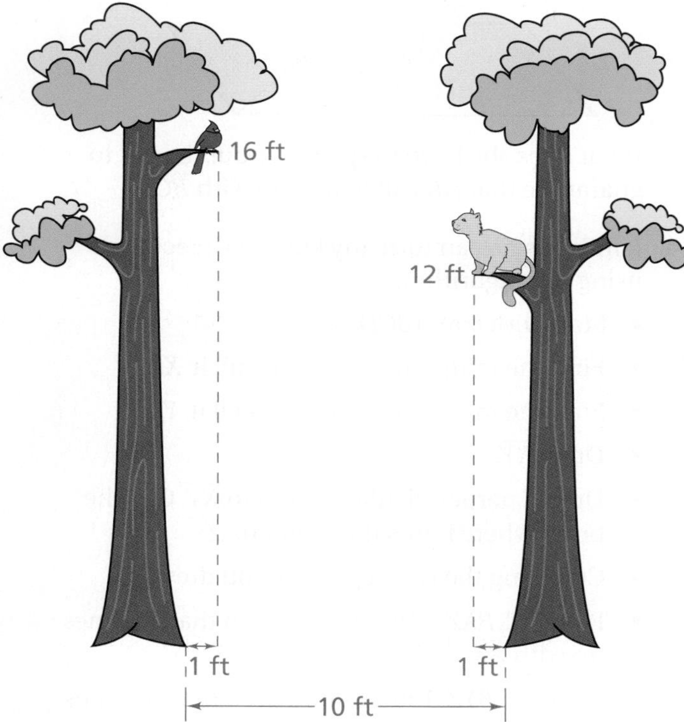

8. Draw two parallel lines ℓ and m that are 3 in. apart. Choose point A on line ℓ and point B on line m such that $AB = 5$ in. Draw line n through point B and perpendicular to line m. Let C be the intersection of lines ℓ and n. How far is C from A?

In **Investigation 3D** you learned how to

- find the surface area of solids by visualizing their nets
- estimate the volumes of solids
- use formulas for the volumes of certain solids

The following questions will help you check your understanding.

9. A friend of yours has made a replica of a traditional Sioux tepee, and she needs to know its volume. Suppose the inside of her tepee is a cone of radius 4 m, with slant height 8 m. What is the approximate volume of the tepee?

10. What is the total surface area of the cone shown below?

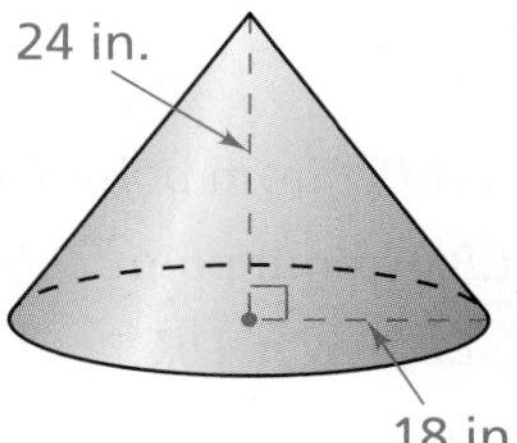

11. What is the volume of the solid below?

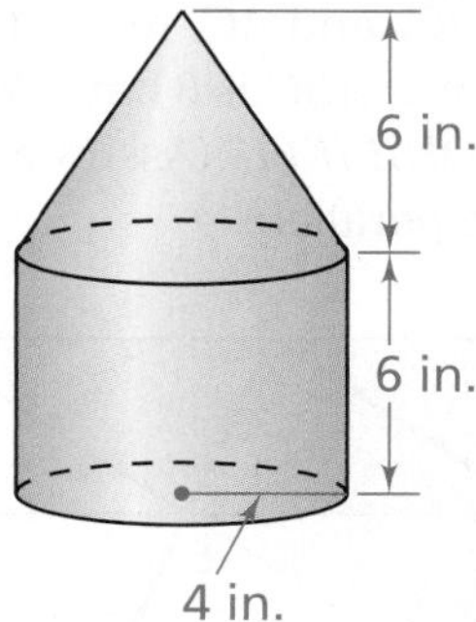

Test

Multiple Choice

1. Kendra started with $\triangle ABC$. Then she constructed the midpoint of $\overline{AB}$ and labeled it E. She used point E and $\triangle EBD$ to construct trapezoid $AFDC$. How did Kendra construct the trapezoid?

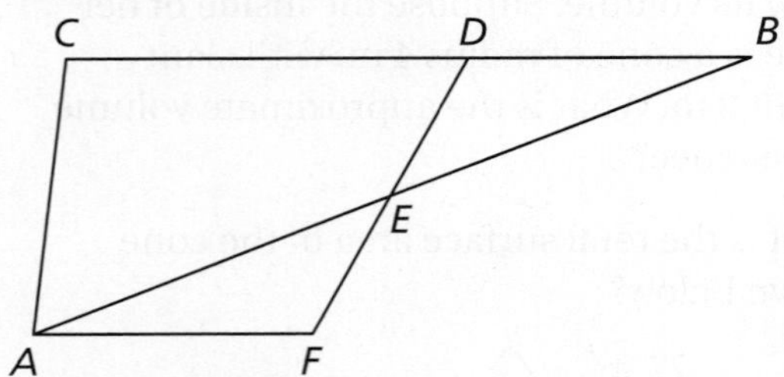

   A. She translated $\triangle EBD$ from point E to point A.

   B. She rotated $\triangle EBD$ about point D.

   C. She reflected $\triangle EBD$ over $\overline{DF}$.

   D. none of the above

2. In the diagram, points D, E, and F are the midpoints of $\overline{AB}$, $\overline{BC}$, and $\overline{AC}$, respectively. Suppose the area of $\triangle ABC$ is 8 cm^2. What is the area of polygon $GDHIEJKFL$? (Assume lines that appear parallel are parallel.)

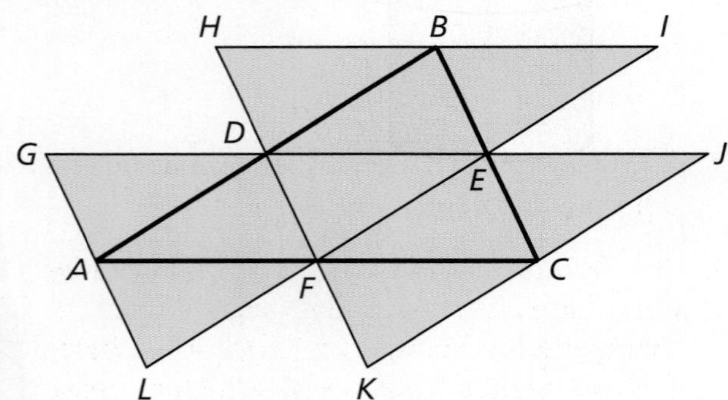

   A. 12 cm^2 **B.** 16 cm^2

   C. 18 cm^2 **D.** 20 cm^2

Open Response

3. Cori dissected the triangle into a parallelogram.

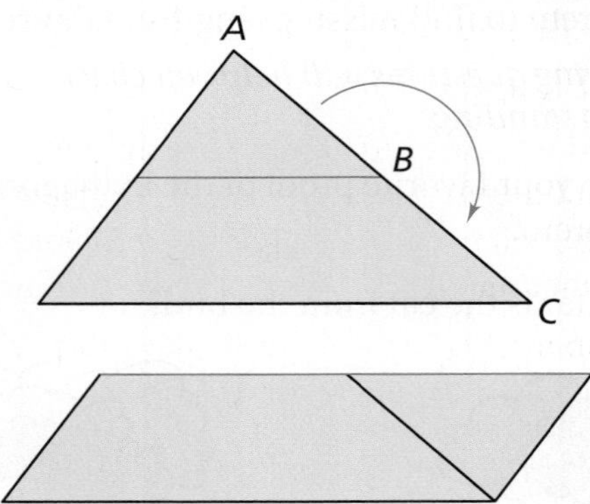

   What does she have to specify about the cut to guarantee that $\overline{AB}$ will match up with $\overline{BC}$?

4. Jamil says he can turn any kite into a rectangle using this algorithm.

   - Start with kite $ABCD$.
   - Find the midpoint of $\overline{AB}$ and call it X.
   - Find the midpoint of $\overline{BC}$ and call it Y.
   - Draw $\overline{XY}$.
   - Drop a perpendicular from B to $\overline{XY}$. Call the point where it hits the segment Z.
   - Cut along the two segments you drew.
   - Rotate $\triangle BXZ$ 180° around X, so that $\overline{BX}$ lines up with $\overline{AX}$.
   - Rotate $\triangle BYZ$ 180° around Y, so that $\overline{BY}$ lines up with $\overline{CY}$.
   - Now find the midpoint of $\overline{AD}$, and call it M.
   - Find the midpoint of $\overline{CD}$, and call it N.
   - Draw $\overline{MN}$.
   - Drop a perpendicular from D to $\overline{MN}$. Call the point where it hits the segment O.
   - Rotate $\triangle MOD$ 180° around M, so that $\overline{DM}$ lines up with $\overline{AM}$.
   - Rotate $\triangle DON$ 180° around N, so that $\overline{DN}$ lines up with $\overline{CN}$.
   - Now you have a rectangle!

a. Draw pictures to illustrate the steps of the algorithm.

b. Justify why the following pairs of segments are congruent.

- $\overline{BX}$ and $\overline{AX}$
- $\overline{BY}$ and $\overline{CY}$
- $\overline{DM}$ and $\overline{AM}$
- $\overline{DN}$ and $\overline{CN}$

c. Is the final figure really a rectangle? Justify your answer based on the cutting algorithm. (*Hint:* Is it really a quadrilateral? Does it have right angles?)

d. Explain how to use Jamil's algorithm to dissect the kite into a second rectangle.

5. Find the area and perimeter of each figure.

a.

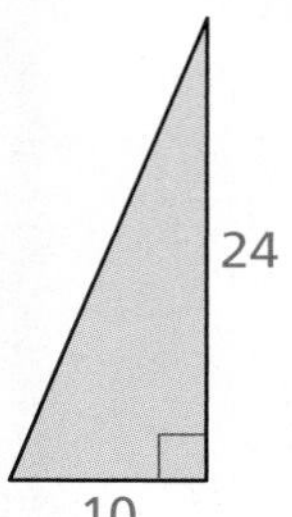

b.

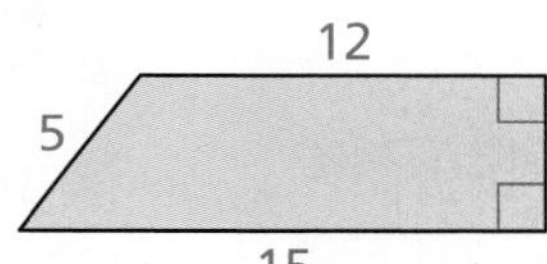

c.

12

6

7

6. Determine whether each triple is a Pythagorean triple. Explain.

a. (1, 2, 3)

b. (6, 8, 10)

c. (5, 13, 12)

d. (1, 3, 9)

e. (5, 3, 4)

f. (3, 4, 25)

7. A right square prism has volume 45 ft^3 and height 5 ft. Find each of the following.

a. the side length of a base

b. the total surface area of the prism

c. the volume of a pyramid with the same base and height

8. Find the slant height, total surface area, and volume of this cone.

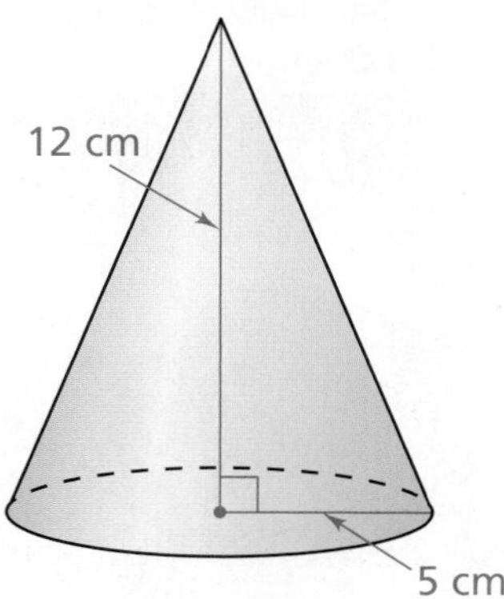

In Exercises 9 and 10, find the total surface area and volume of the indicated solid for the lengths given.

9. right rectangular prism

a. 4 cm by 5 cm by 6 cm

b. 3.5 cm by 3.5 cm by 3.5 cm

10. cylinder

a. radius 6 cm, height 18 cm

b. radius 18 cm, height 6 cm

11. Write About It Explain the difference between a right prism and an oblique prism.

12. Take It Further Cylinder A is a right cylinder. It has base radius 4 cm and height 6 cm. Cylinder B is an oblique cylinder. It has base radius 6 cm and height 4 cm. Which cylinder has greater volume?

Chapter
4
Investigations at a Glance
4A Scaled Copies
4B Curved or Straight? Just Dilate!
4C The Side-Splitter Theorems
4D Defining Similarity
Canon
FUNC. SET
DISP.

Similarity

Scaled images are an important application of mathematical similarity. A liquid crystal display (LCD) monitor on the back of a digital camera lets you see a scaled-down picture of what you are about to photograph.

A map is one kind of scale drawing. Its outline is the same as the region it represents, but it is obviously much smaller. By making a map to scale, you guarantee that distances you measure on the map are proportional to actual instances in the real world.

Architects also use scale drawings to plan buildings. The drawings ensure that the required features of a building fit together, illustrate traffic flow through the building, and allow the customer to visualize the design.

A microscope is a tool that changes the scale of what you view. It allows you to see objects on a large-enough scale to be able to distinguish critical features.

In art, the use of different scales for figures in a painting gives the illusion of depth. Smaller figures are perceived as being farther away from the viewer. Larger figures seem closer. In animation, a figure that becomes smaller appears to move away from the viewer.

Vocabulary and Notation

- center of dilation
- common ratio
- dilation
- nested triangles
- parallel method
- ratio
- ratio method
- scale a figure
- scaled figure
- scale factor
- similar figures
- splits two sides proportionally
- $\sim$ (is similar to)

Scaled Copies

In *Scaled Copies,* you will learn how you can model a very large or very small figure with a figure that is a manageable size. For example, you could sketch a rough map of your school on paper. You could show some important locations, such as drinking fountains and the cafeteria. You might, however, need the map for something more precise, such as a science project on air quality and ventilation. Then you would want to show more detail, such as the dimensions of rooms and hallways.

You could draw your map *to scale.* Then the dimensions of any room on your map would be proportional to the actual dimensions by the *scale factor* of your map.

By the end of this investigation, you will be able to answer questions like these.

1. Why is it important to know the scale factor when reading a map?
2. What is a well-scaled drawing?
3. How can you decide whether two rectangles are scaled copies of each other?

You will learn how to

- approximate the scale factor relating two pictures by measuring
- use a given scale factor to interpret a map or blueprint
- decide whether two figures are well-scaled copies of each other

You will develop these habits and skills:

- Identify scaled copies of figures.
- Use a scale factor to approximate distances on blueprints and maps.
- Apply a scale factor to make similar figures.

4.01 Getting Started

You can draw a whole city, a state, or an even larger region with a given scale so that it can fit on a piece of paper. In reading a map, it is important to keep the scale in mind.

For You to Explore

Here is a map of Sasha's neighborhood.

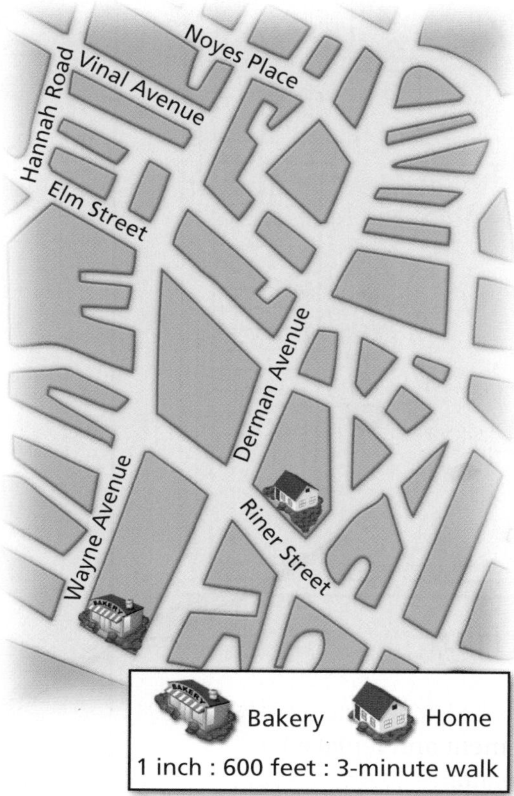

1. The scale shows that 1 inch on the map represents 600 feet of actual distance. It also says that an inch on the map represents about a three-minute walk. What distance does it suggest you can walk in one minute? Is this reasonable?

2. In Sasha's neighborhood, find the actual distance between the following locations. (Travel only on streets.)
   - a. the Bakery and the intersection of Wayne Avenue and Noyes Place
   - b. Sasha's house and the Bakery

3. Sasha is at the Bakery. She will walk to meet a friend at the intersection of Vinal Avenue and Hannah Road. About how much time will her walk take?

4. Recalculate your answers to Problem 2 using the scale 1 inch : 450 feet.

An architect's plans for an apartment building, a house, a school, an office, a park, or a sports complex can include many different sketches. Each sketch serves a different purpose. This blueprint drawing shows the floor plan of the second story of a house.

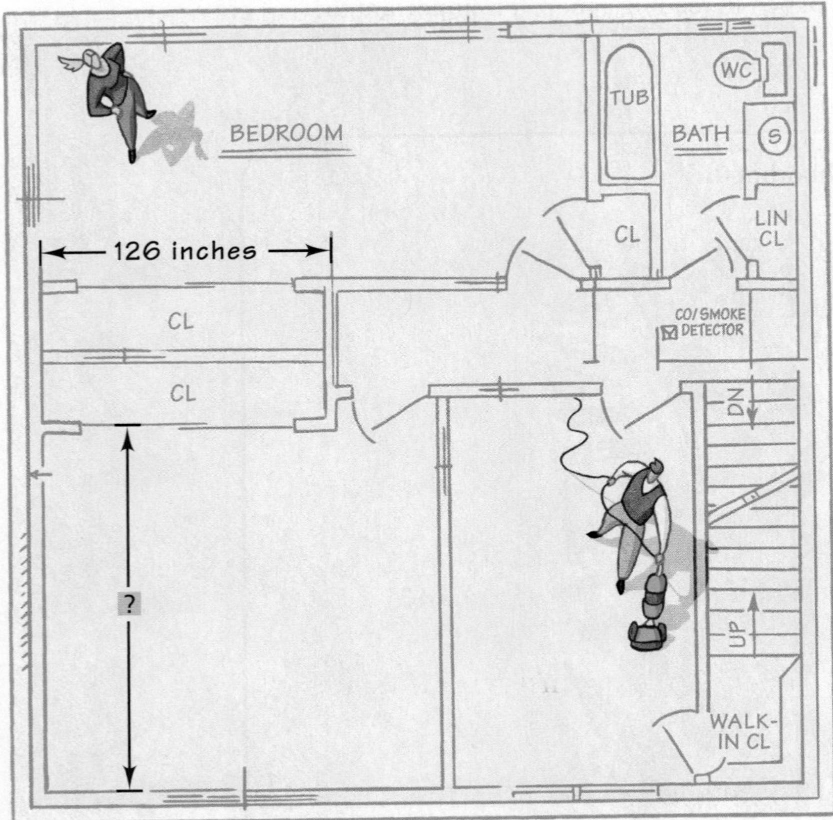

SECOND FLOOR PLAN

5. In this floor plan, someone erased a measurement and replaced it with a question mark. Calculate the missing value.

6. Find the actual dimensions of the entire second story.

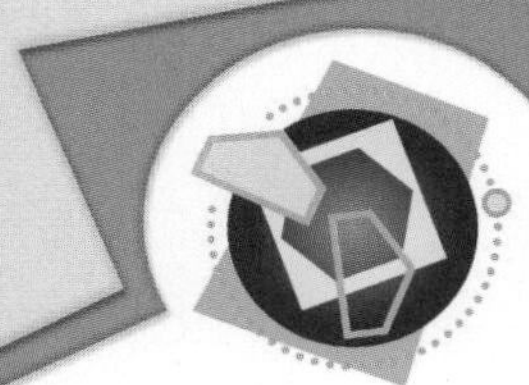

Exercises *Practicing Habits of Mind*

On Your Own

Go Online
Pearsonsuccessnet.com

7. Drivers sometimes estimate the driving time between two points based on their average driving speed and a map's scale. They are often surprised by how much longer the trip actually takes. What are some reasons that a trip can take longer than the length of the route suggests?

8. For traveling in Wisconsin, Sydney and Mark used a map that has a scale of 1 inch: 15 miles. Sydney's index finger is 3 inches long. On the trip from Madison to Greenlake, Sydney announced the following distances in "fingers." Convert Sydney's estimates to miles.
   a. At the beginning of the trip, Sydney said, "We're one finger away!"
   b. After a stop for ice cream, Sydney announced, "We've got only half a finger to go!"
   c. When they got back into the car after taking a picture of some cows, Sydney said, "Only one fingernail left in the trip!" (Her fingernail is about an eighth of her finger.)

9. The owners of the house with the floor plan shown in Problem 5 want to carpet the bedroom floor. They can use the floor plan to estimate how much carpet they need.
   a. What are the dimensions of the bedroom? (Do not include the closet.)
   b. How much carpet do the owners need to cover the bedroom floor? Give your answer in square inches.
   c. If carpet sells by the square yard, how many square yards of carpet do they need?

Maintain Your Skills

10. Find the perimeter and area of a rectangle with the given dimensions.
   a. 1 in. by 3 in.
   b. 2 in. by 6 in.
   c. 3 in. by 9 in.
   d. 4 in. by 12 in.
   e. n in. by $3n$ in.

4.02 Scale Factors

Maps and blueprints provide scales that allow you to calculate actual distances and lengths. Depending on the map, 1 inch might represent 1 mile, or 1 inch might represent 100 miles. The **scale factor** is a number that describes how much you reduce or enlarge a map, blueprint, or picture. In this lesson, you will develop a more precise definition of scale factor and learn how to calculate it.

For Discussion

Each side of this square has length 2 inches.

1. What do you think it means to "scale the square by the factor $\frac{1}{2}$"? Draw a figure to show what you think it means. Can you think of more than one way to interpret the statement? If so, draw a separate figure for each meaning.

Minds in Action — episode 9

Tony and Amy have different meanings for scaling the square by the factor $\frac{1}{2}$. See if you agree with either of their explanations.

Tony To scale by $\frac{1}{2}$, I drew a square that is half the size of the first one. You know, half the area. The area of the original square is 2×2 or 4 square inches. I made a square with an area of 2 square inches. A neat way to do this is to fold all four corners of the square to the center.

Habits of Mind

Visualize. Why does Tony's folding method work? How long are the sides of his new square?

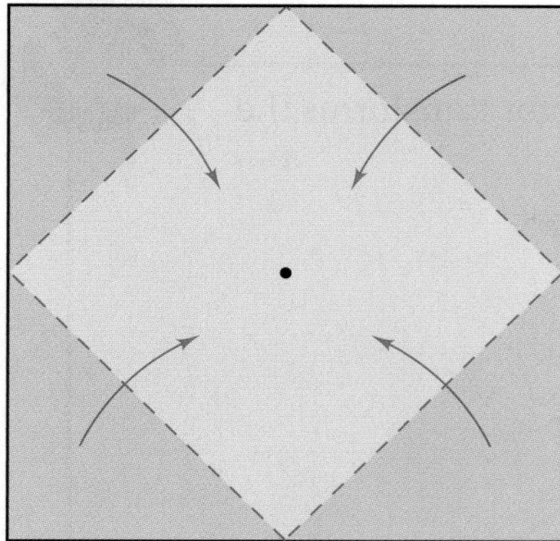

Amy I think that scaling by half means we are supposed to draw the sides half as long. The first square has sides that are 2 inches long, so the scaled square should have sides that are 1 inch long. I drew a horizontal line and a vertical line on the square to divide the length and width in half. This gives me four squares, each scaled by the factor $\frac{1}{2}$.

In fact, there is more than one correct way to interpret the phrase *scale by* $\frac{1}{2}$. Words can mean different things to different people. But Amy's meaning is the one that most people use.

Definition

When you scale a figure by the factor *r*, you draw a new figure, called a scaled figure, that is the same shape as the given figure. In the scaled figure, each length is *r* times the corresponding length of the original figure. The scale factor *r* can be any positive number, including a fraction.

Sometimes a scale factor is not given. You may, however, be able to compare parts of figures to calculate the scale factor.

Example

Problem For each pair of pictures below, what scale factor transforms the larger picture into the smaller scaled picture?

a.

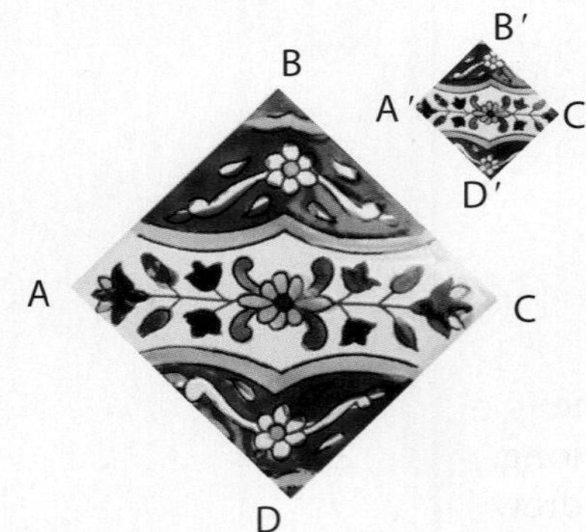

b.

Solutions

a. Measure each side of the first figure. Compare the lengths to the lengths of the sides in the second figure. You will find that each length in the second figure is $\frac{1}{3}$ the length in the first figure. The scale factor is $r = \frac{1}{3}$.

b. Rotate the kite on the right clockwise to match the orientation of the kite on the left. Once you have done this, measure the distances between corresponding points. For example, the distance from L to M is about 1.5 cm. The distance from L' to M' is about 1.2 cm. This gives a scale factor of $\frac{1.2}{1.5}$, or $\frac{4}{5}$.

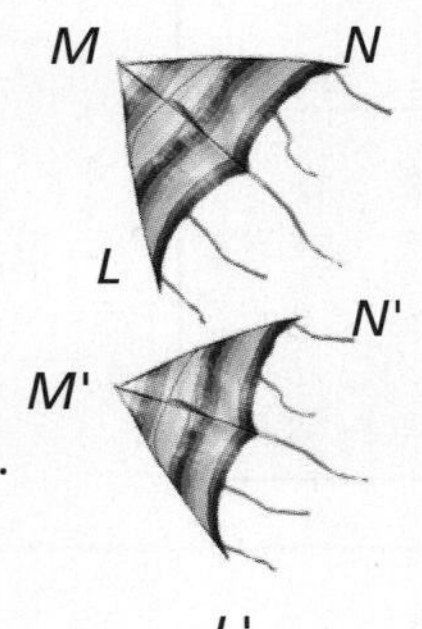

For You to Do

2. For each part of the Example, by what factor should you scale the smaller figure on the right to get the figure on the left?

In-Class Experiment

3. Draw a square with 1-inch sides. Scale the square by the factor 2. How many copies of the 1-inch square fit inside the scaled square?

4. Start with a 1-inch square again. Scale the square by the factor 3. How many copies of the 1-inch square fit inside the scaled square?

For Discussion

5. If you scale a 1-inch square by a positive integer r, how many copies of the 1-inch square fit inside the scaled square?

Minds in Action

episode 10

Derman and Tony have just finished the In-Class Experiment and are trying to apply what they learned to the following problem.

> A cube has edges of length 1 inch. You scale the cube by the factor 2. How long are the sides of the new cube? How many copies of the original cube fit inside the scaled cube?

Tony Well, if you scale the cube by the factor 2, then the new cube must be twice as big. Two cubes fit inside the scaled cube!

Derman That sounds right. The original cube has edges that are 1 inch long. The scaled cube must have edges that are 2 inches long.

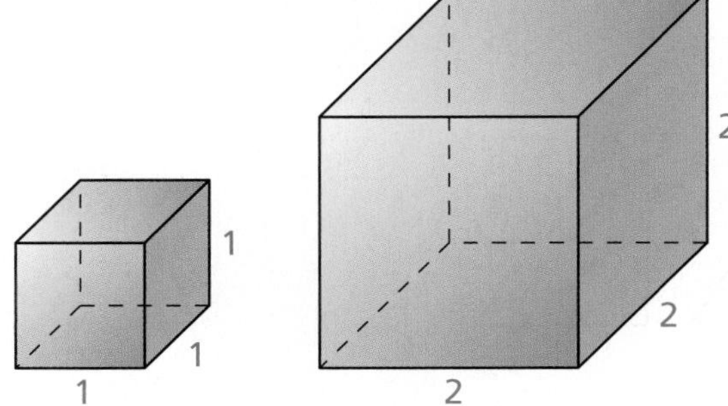

Derman Wait! Look at the picture, Tony. Your answer can't be right! More than two of the original cubes are going to fit into the big cube.

Tony Nothing is ever that easy. So, how many 1-inch cubes fit into the scaled cube?

Derman The volume of the original cube is $1 \times 1 \times 1$, or 1 cubic inch. The volume of the scaled cube is $2 \times 2 \times 2$, or 8 cubic inches. Think of the larger cube as a box. You pack in four small cubes to fill the bottom. Then pack in one more layer of four small cubes to fill the box.

For Discussion

6. If you scale the original cube by the factor 3, how long are the sides of the new cube? How many copies of the original cube fit inside the scaled cube?

7. If you scale the original cube by a positive integer r, how many copies of the original cube fit inside the scaled cube?

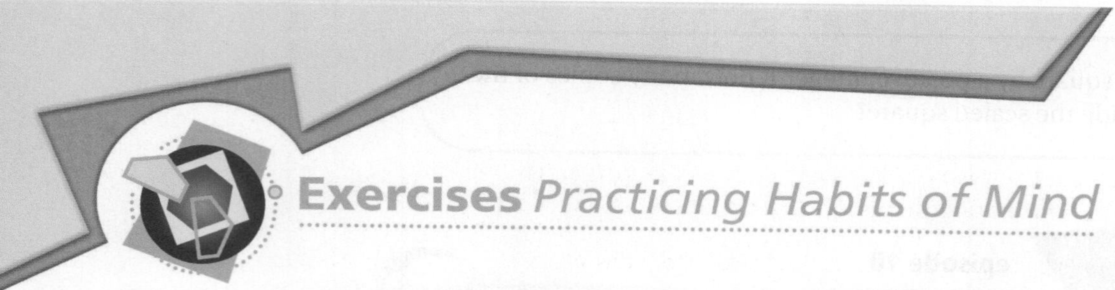

Exercises *Practicing Habits of Mind*

Check Your Understanding

1. What features of a square are invariant when you scale the square by the factor $\frac{1}{2}$?

2. You scale a figure by each given value of r. Will the new figure be smaller, larger, or the same size as the original figure?

   a. $r = \frac{3}{5}$

   b. $r = 1$

   c. $r = 3$

   d. $r = 0.77$

3. For each pair of figures, determine whether one figure was scaled by the factor $\frac{1}{2}$ to obtain the other figure. Explain.

   a.

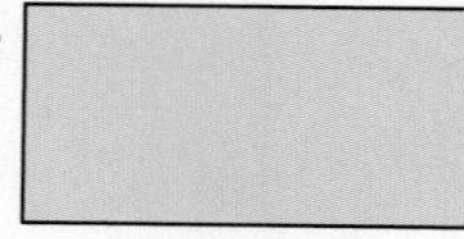

   b.

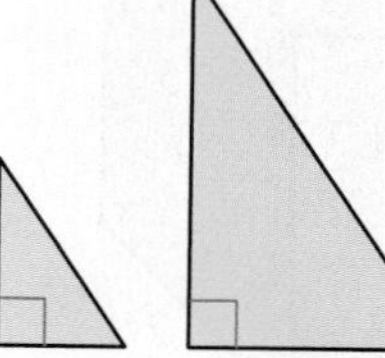

   c.

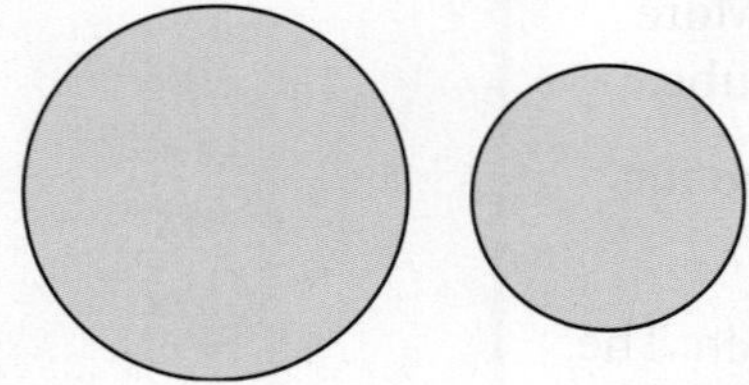

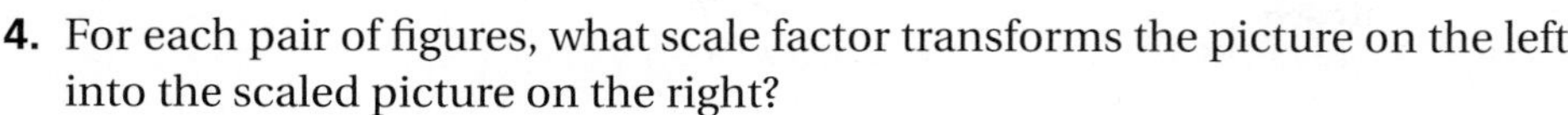

4. For each pair of figures, what scale factor transforms the picture on the left into the scaled picture on the right?

a.  

b.  

5. For each pair of figures in Exercise 4, what scale factor transforms the picture on the right into the scaled picture on the left?

6. Compare the scale factors you found for Exercises 4 and 5. How are they related?

7. This equilateral triangle has 2-inch sides.

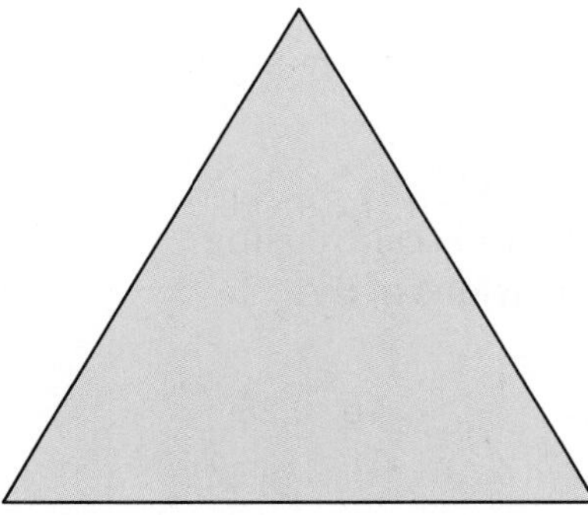

a. Draw a scaled version of the triangle. Use the factor $\frac{1}{2}$. How many of the scaled triangles fit inside the original triangle?

b. Draw a scaled version of the triangle using the factor $\frac{1}{3}$. How many of the scaled triangles fit inside the original triangle?

8. Suppose you scale a 6 in.-by-6 in. square by each factor. How many 1-in. squares will fit inside each scaled square?

a. $\frac{1}{3}$ b. 3 c. $\frac{2}{3}$

Scale the house at the far left by the factor $\frac{1}{42}$. You get a 4-ft-wide model.

On Your Own

9. Many photocopy machines allow you to scale (reduce or enlarge) a picture. You enter the desired percent and press Copy.

a. If you enter 80%, by what factor do you scale the picture?

b. To scale a picture by the factor $\frac{3}{4}$, what percent should you enter?

10. Label the two scalings as *same* or *different*.

a. scaling by 2 and scaling by $\frac{1}{2}$

b. scaling by $\frac{1}{3}$ and scaling by 30%

c. scaling by $\frac{3}{5}$ and scaling by 0.6

d. scaling by 1 and scaling by 100%

11. Give a scale factor that changes the quadrilateral *MEOW* as indicated.

a. shrinks it

b. enlarges it

c. shrinks it very slightly

d. keeps it the same size

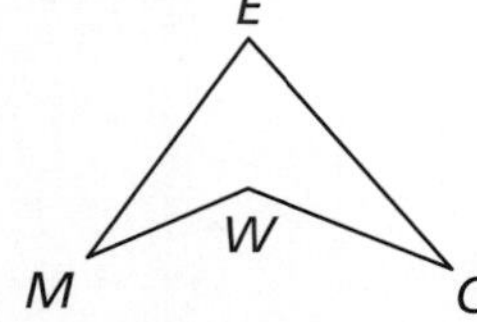

12. A rectangle has width 12 inches and length 24 inches. You scale it using the following factors. In each case, what are the dimensions of the scaled rectangle?

a. $\frac{1}{3}$ **b.** $\frac{1}{4}$ **c.** 0.3 **d.** 2.5 **e.** 0.25

13. Examine each pair of figures below.

- What scale factor can you apply to figure X to get figure Y?
- What scale factor can you apply to figure Y to get figure X?
- How are the two scale factors you found related?

a.

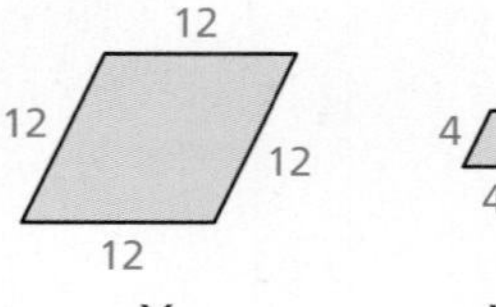

b.

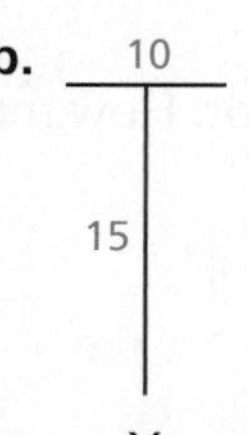

c.

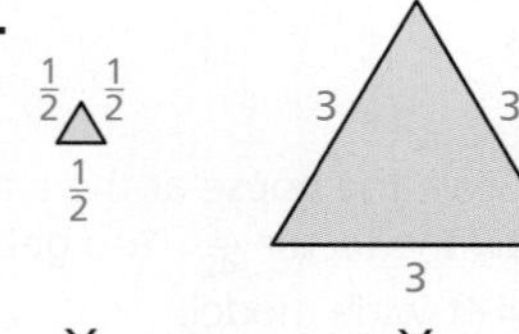

14. Standardized Test Prep Jamal scales a triangle by the factor 4. How many copies of the original triangle can he use to fill the scaled copy?

A. 4 **B.** 8 **C.** 12 **D.** 16

15. Take It Further Suppose you scale a picture by the factor $\frac{1}{2}$. Then you scale your scaled picture by the factor $\frac{1}{4}$. By what overall factor have you scaled the original picture?

Maintain Your Skills

16. Scale each figure below by the factor 4.

- What are the dimensions of the scaled figure?
- How many of the original figures fit into the scaled figure?

a.

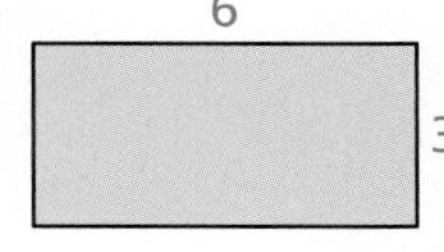

b.

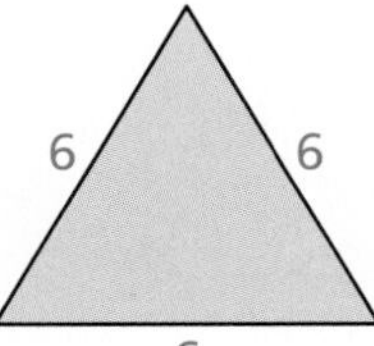

c.

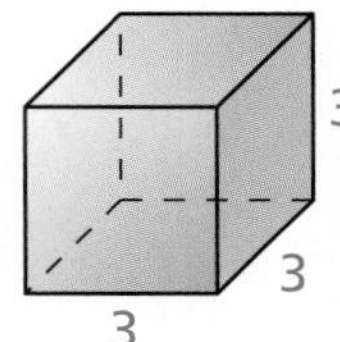

17. Apply the scale factor $\frac{1}{3}$ to each figure in Exercise 16.

- What are the dimensions of the scaled figure?
- How many of the original figure fit into the scaled figure?

18. Take It Further Apply a scale factor n to each figure in Exercise 16.

- What are the dimensions of the scaled figure?
- How many of the original figure fit into the scaled figure?

4.03 What Is a Well-Scaled Drawing?

The map and blueprint in Lesson 4.01 are both well-scaled drawings. Sometimes, though, a reduction or enlargement is not a good copy of the original. When you look at yourself in a funhouse mirror, you see that your body is scaled in a very unusual way indeed. The mirror might stretch your image so that you appear as skinny as a matchstick. It might shrink your image so that you appear one foot tall!

Here is a picture of a dog.

Here are four other images of the dog.

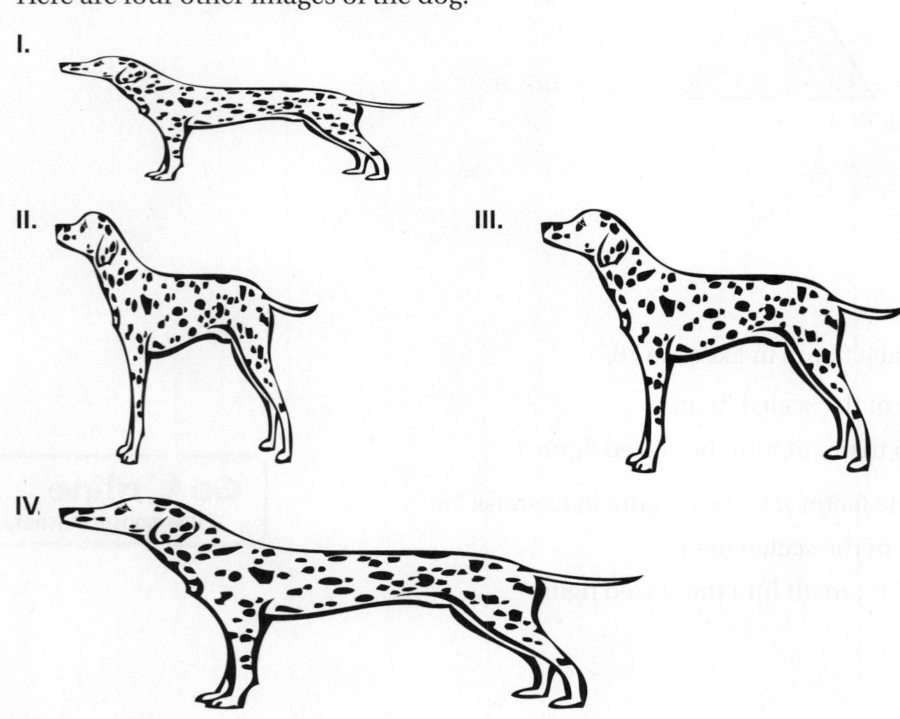

Minds in Action episode 11

Tony and Sasha try to decide which images could be accurate reductions or enlargements of the dog picture.

Tony If one of these pictures is an accurate copy of the original dog picture, it's got to look exactly like the original, right?

Sasha Well, we're not necessarily looking for an exact copy of the original. We're just looking for a picture that keeps the same shape, but not necessarily the same size. The original picture may have been enlarged or shrunk down—like on a copy machine.

Tony The first copy is shorter than the original, but it's not smaller all around. It just looks like someone stepped on it. If we're looking for an accurate smaller copy of the original picture, the copy needs to be smaller all around.

Sasha I know what you mean. The fourth copy is bigger than the original, but it's not bigger all around. It got bigger, but it's too long.

For Discussion

1. Decide which of the four images are accurate enlargements or reductions of the original dog picture.
2. What characteristics of the dog images helped you make your decisions?

Exercises *Practicing Habits of Mind*

Check Your Understanding

Exercises 1–3 on the next page will help you make decisions about whether you are looking at a good copy or a bad copy. You will use measurements rather than just judging by eye.

1. Here are drawings of two baby chicks with points labeled A through H.

Here are the distances between some of the points.

$AB = 4$ cm $\quad CD = 2$ cm $\quad EF = 2.5$ cm $\quad GH = 1.25$ cm

How can you use these measurements to help convince someone that the two chicks are well-scaled copies of each other? Are there other measurements that could be important to compare?

2. The labels A, B, C, and D name four points on this fish. The fish is not drawn to scale.

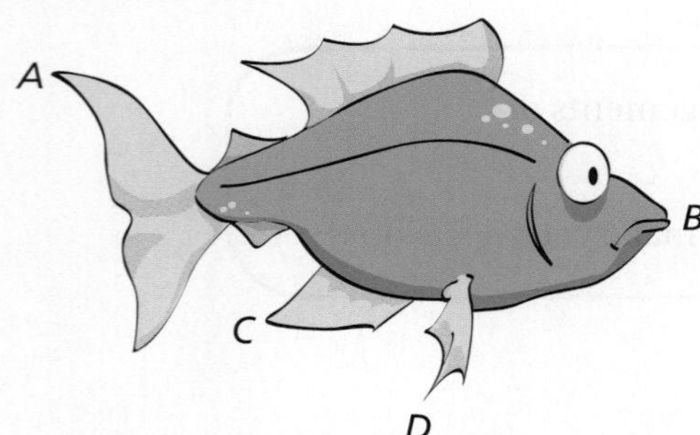

Jo measures the distance AB, as well as the distance CD. She calculates that $\frac{AB}{CD} = 2.6$. Michael sees her answer and asks, "But what's your unit? Is the answer 2.6 centimeters, 2.6 inches, 2.6 feet, or something else?"

How would you respond to Michael's question?

3. Name at least four different pairs of measurements you could take on these two figures to convince someone that the two figures are well-scaled copies of each other.

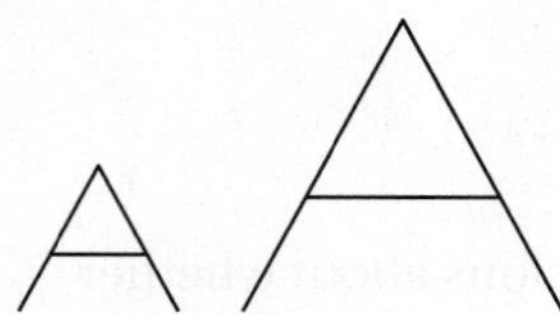

On Your Own

For Exercises 4–6, use graph paper to scale the pictures by the given scale factor.

4.

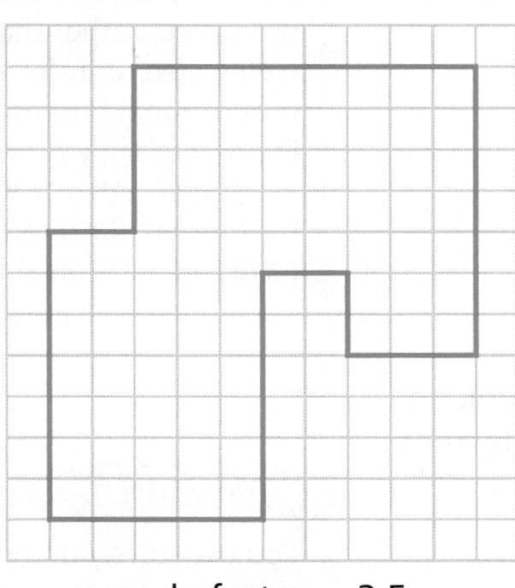

scale factor = 2.5

5.

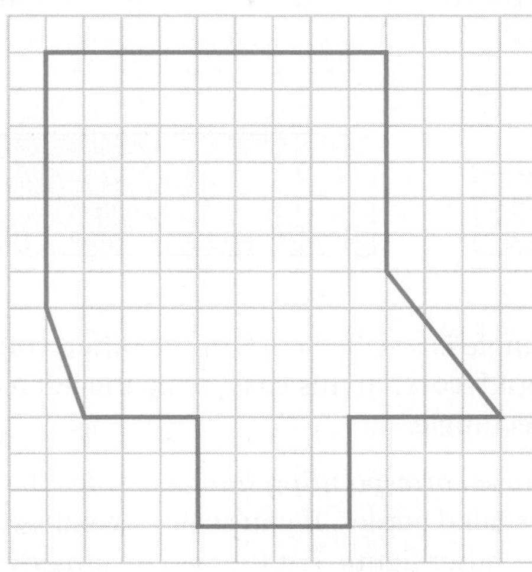

scale factor = 0.5

6.

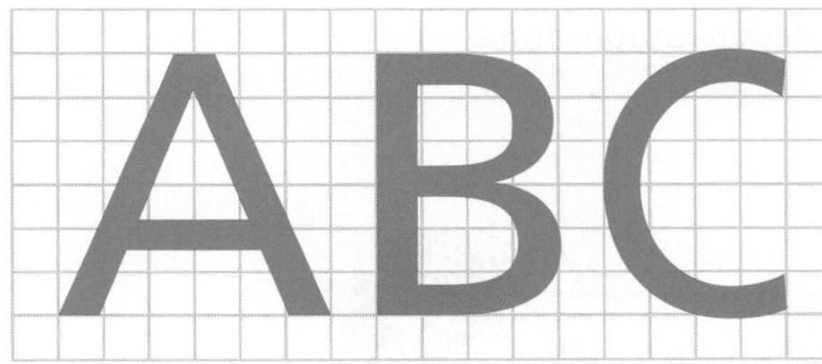

scale factor = 2

7. **Standardized Test Prep** A rectangle has dimensions 25 cm by 10 cm. It is scaled by the factor $\frac{3}{5}$. What is the perimeter of the scaled rectangle?

A. 35 cm **B.** 42 cm **C.** 70 cm **D.** 90 cm

Maintain Your Skills

8. A rectangle has dimensions 3 cm by 4 cm. You scale it using the following factors. Find the area of each scaled rectangle.

a. 2 **b.** 3 **c.** 0.5

d. $\frac{5}{12}$ **e.** n

4.04 Testing for Scale

In Lesson 4.03, you thought about the characteristics that did or did not make pictures of a dog well-scaled copies of each other. Now you will do the same for pairs of simple geometric figures such as rectangles, triangles, and other polygons.

Mathematicians usually use *scaled,* rather than *well-scaled,* to refer to proportional figures. From here on, you will use *scaled* rather than *well-scaled.* Both terms have the same meaning.

Here are two rectangles.

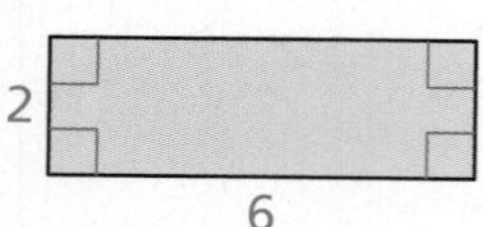

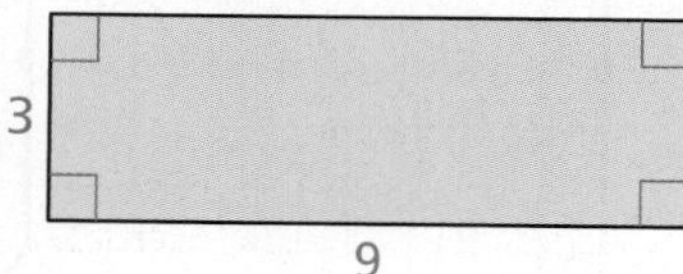

To tell whether one rectangle is a scaled copy of the other, you could look for a scale factor that would work. In this case, scale the left rectangle by the factor $\frac{3}{2}$ to get the right rectangle.

Some people use the phrase *corresponding sides,* or "sides that match up," when talking about scaled copies. If you scale one side, you get the corresponding side of the other figure. For the two rectangles above, the 2-unit side and the 3-unit side are corresponding. Also, the 6-unit side and the 9-unit side are corresponding. Corresponding sides of scaled figures are proportional. Corresponding sides in these rectangles are proportional because $\frac{2}{3} = \frac{6}{9}$.

Remember...

You use *corresponding sides* here the same way you used it for congruent figures.

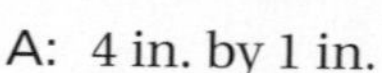

Example

Problem The lengths and widths of seven rectangles A–G are given. Match the rectangles that are scaled copies of each other.

A: 4 in. by 1 in.
B: 3 in. by 2 in.
C: 10 in. by 5 in.
D: 4 in. by 6 in.
E: 5 in. by 3 in.
F: 16 in. by 4 in.
G: 8 in. by 4 in.

Solutions There are three pairs of scaled copies. Rectangles C and G are scaled copies $\left(\text{since } \frac{10}{8} = \frac{5}{4}\right)$, as are A and F $\left(\text{since } \frac{4}{16} = \frac{1}{4}\right)$.

Rectangles B and D are also scaled copies. Notice, however, that $\frac{3}{4} \neq \frac{2}{6}$. To see that the rectangles have equal side-length ratios, you need to make your ratios in a consistent way. If one ratio is in the form of $\frac{\text{shorter side}}{\text{shorter side}}$, then the other must be $\frac{\text{longer side}}{\text{longer side}}$. Thus, you have $\frac{2}{4} = \frac{3}{6}$.

Exercises *Practicing Habits of Mind*

Check Your Understanding

1. The ratio of length to width for a particular rectangle is 1.5. A scaled copy has width 6. What is the length of the scaled copy?

A **ratio** is the quotient of two numbers. If only one number is given, the second number is understood to be 1. *A ratio of 1.5* really means "1.5 to 1."

2. Two rectangles are scaled copies of each other. The ratio of their lengths is 0.6. The smaller rectangle has width 3. What is the width of the larger rectangle?

3. Are the two triangles below scaled copies of each other? Take measurements and do calculations as necessary. Explain what you find.

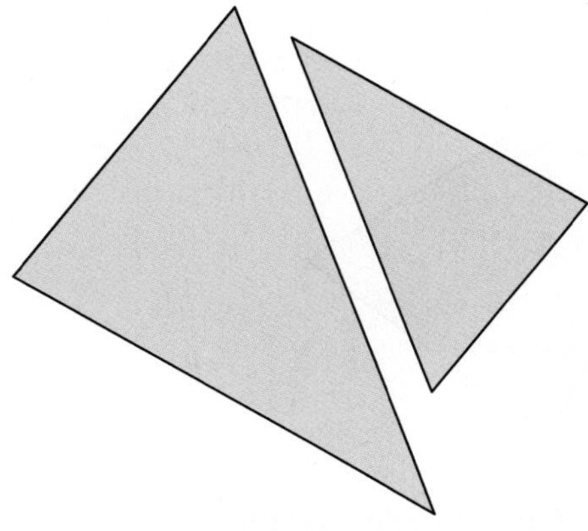

4. Kaori has two triangles that have all corresponding angles congruent. The sides of one triangle are 4, 6, and 8. The sides of the other are 9, 6, and 12. She says that because

$$\frac{4}{9} = 0.44\ldots,$$

$$\frac{6}{6} = 1,$$

and

$$\frac{8}{12} = 0.66\ldots,$$

the triangles are not scaled copies. Do you agree?

On Your Own

5. Can a 3 foot-by-9 foot rectangle be a scaled copy of a 3 foot-by-1 foot rectangle? Explain.
6. You scale a square by the factor 2.5. The resulting square has a side length of 8 inches. What is the length of a side of the original square?
7. One triangle has side lengths of 21, 15, and 18. Another triangle has side lengths of 12, 14, and 16. Are these triangles scaled copies? How can you tell?
8. Carefully trace the triangles below. Cut out the traced triangles. Decide whether any two of the triangles are scaled copies of each other. Use any of the methods discussed in class.

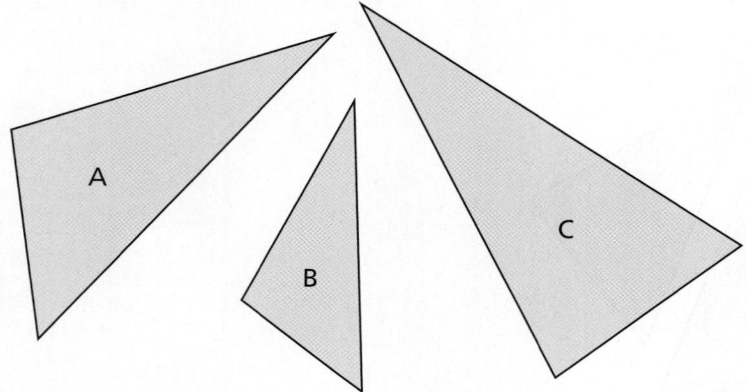

9. **Standardized Test Prep** Elisha has two triangles. One triangle has side lengths of 3 cm, 5 cm, and 7 cm. The other triangle has side lengths of 40 cm, 24 cm, and 56 cm. Are the two triangles scaled copies of each other? If so, what scale factor transforms the first triangle into the second triangle?

   A. No, the two triangles are not scaled copies of each other.

   B. yes; 8 **C.** yes; $\frac{40}{3}$ **D.** yes; $\frac{24}{5}$

Maintain Your Skills

10. Suppose $f(x, y) = xy$. Evaluate each of the following.

    a. $f(2, 3)$ **b.** $f(4, 6)$ **c.** $f(6, 9)$

    d. $f(a, b)$ **e.** $f(2a, 2b)$ **f.** $f(ka, kb)$

11. Write an algebraic equation to define a function that has a rectangle's length and width as input and the area of the rectangle as output.

4.05 Checking for Scaled Copies

Think for a moment about congruent triangles. Recall how you determine whether two triangles are congruent without taking measurements or performing calculations.

One way is to cut out the triangles and lay one on top of the other. If you can arrange the triangles so that they perfectly coincide, then they are congruent.

Perhaps there is also a visual way to test whether two shapes are scaled copies of each other without having to take measurements.

Minds in Action — episode 12

Hannah and Derman are trying to determine whether the pairs of rectangles in each figure below are scaled copies.

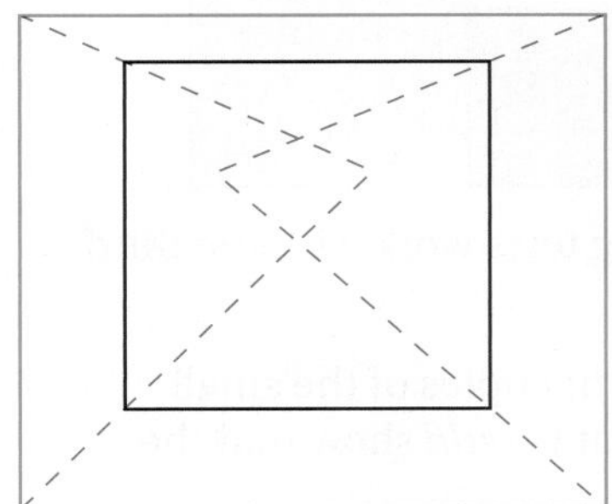

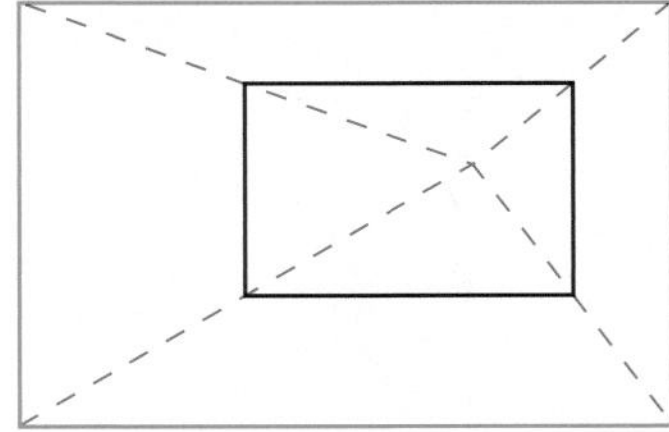

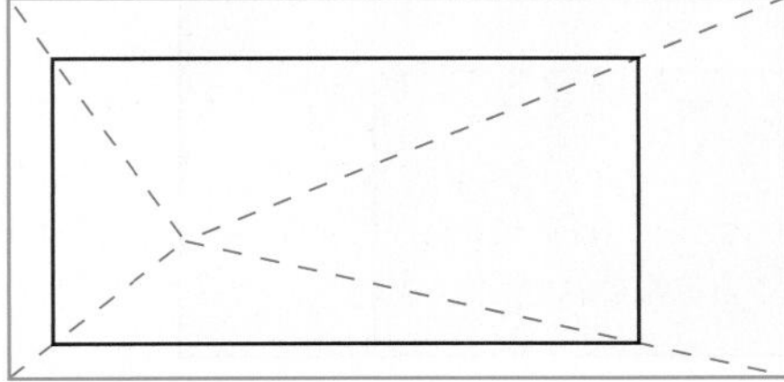

Hannah Why are there dashed lines in these figures? They're just confusing me!

Derman I don't know—let's just try to ignore them for now. How are we going to decide whether the rectangles are scaled copies?

Hannah Well, we've been taking measurements and comparing corresponding sides. Let's do that here.

Derman Do that with the first pair of rectangles. I'm going to try to decide this without measuring.

Moments later . . .

Hannah I measured the sides of the first pair of rectangles in centimeters. I made ratios of the sides for each rectangle. I got $\frac{2.8}{4.5}$ and $\frac{2.8}{4.0}$. The ratios aren't equal, so they're not scaled copies of each other.

Derman I thought the second pair might be scaled copies. I wanted to be sure, so I measured them, too. They are. So I decided to trace them, cut them out, and fool around with them. I wanted to see whether there is another way to show they're scaled copies.

I noticed a couple of things with the second pair of rectangles.

First, I can fit four copies of the small rectangle perfectly inside the big rectangle.

And, I can draw one diagonal in both rectangles. Then, when I slide the small rectangle down to one corner, the diagonals match up perfectly.

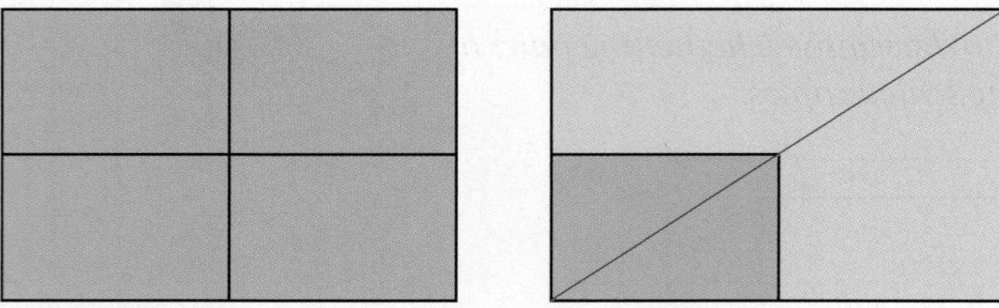

Hannah That's cool. Did your cutting and moving tests work with the third pair of rectangles?

Derman Well, the first test didn't work. I couldn't fit copies of the small rectangle perfectly inside the big one. But I *could* show that the diagonals match up.

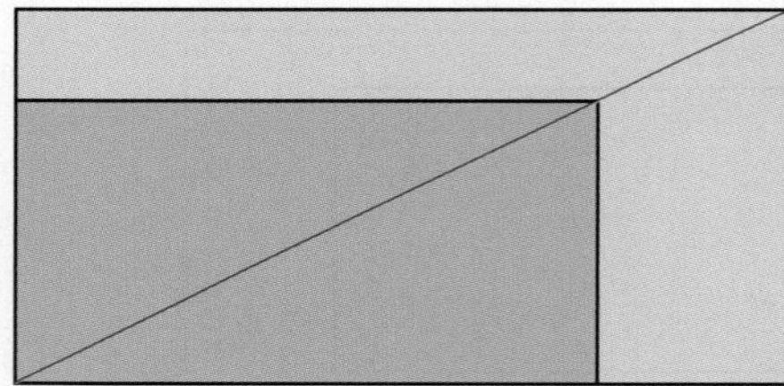

Hannah So, does that mean that the two rectangles in the third pair are scaled copies of each other?

For Discussion

1. What do you think? Are the rectangles in the second pair scaled copies? Are the rectangles in the third pair scaled copies? Can you figure out what the dashed lines in the original figures might be for? Explain.

In-Class Experiment

The triangles in each pair below are scaled copies of each other. Trace and cut out the triangles in each pair. Then move the triangles around. Look for some visual clues that suggest good tests for recognizing scaled triangles. For instance, if you place one angle on top of another and find they match, what do you notice about the triangles' corresponding sides?

2.

3.

For Discussion

4. Share your findings with your class. Did placing one angle on top of a matching angle help you decide whether the triangles are scaled copies? What other tests did you use?

In the figure below, $\overline{DE} \parallel \overline{BC}$. Prove that all pairs of corresponding angles for $\triangle ADE$ and $\triangle ABC$ are congruent.

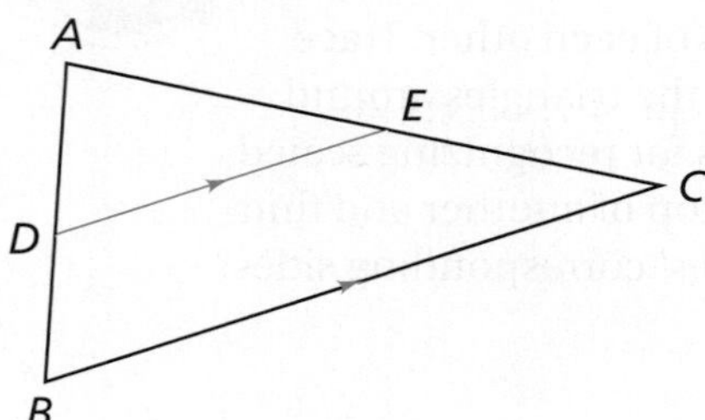

Habits of Mind

Understand context. *Corresponding angles* can have two different meanings in this discussion. Think about the context to understand the meaning.

Proof

Because $\overline{DE}$ is parallel to $\overline{BC}$, it follows that $\angle ADE \cong \angle ABC$ and $\angle AED \cong \angle ACB$. Since $\angle A \cong \angle A$, you know that $\triangle ADE$ and $\triangle ABC$ have congruent corresponding angles.

Remember...

When parallel lines are cut by a transversal, the corresponding angles formed are congruent.

If two triangles have congruent corresponding angles, does that mean that the triangles are scaled copies of each other? It seems like a reasonable conjecture, and it is, in fact, true. You will prove it in Investigation 4D.

Exercises *Practicing Habits of Mind*

Check Your Understanding

1. Martin thinks that the angle test for triangles might also be a good way to check whether other polygons (such as rectangles) are scaled copies. If the angles of quadrilateral $ABCD$ are congruent to the corresponding angles of quadrilateral $A'B'C'D'$, are the quadrilaterals scaled copies? Explain.

2. Sheena has an idea for making a scaled copy of a triangle.

   Measure the sides of the triangle. Then add the same constant value (such as 1, 2, or 3) to each side length. Draw a triangle with these new side lengths.

   Will this new triangle be a scaled copy of the original? Try it.

You now have tests for scaled rectangles and triangles. How can you test other polygons?

3. For each figure, decide whether the two polygons are scaled copies. Explain your decision.

a.

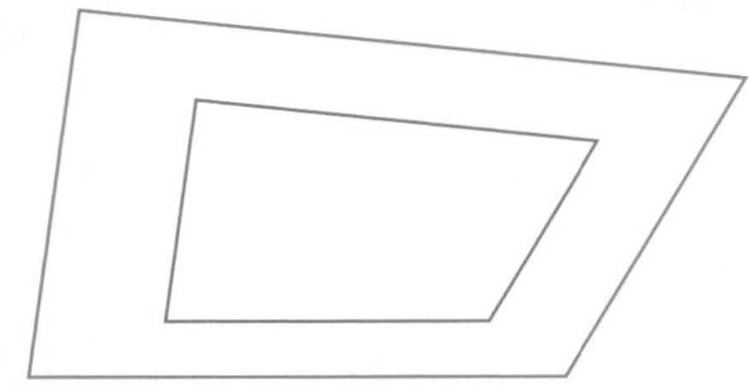

b.

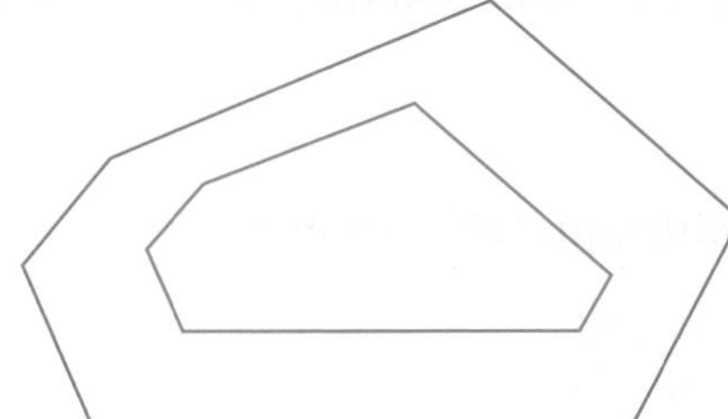

4. Trace trapezoid *ABCD*. Inside the traced trapezoid, draw another trapezoid that is a scaled copy. (You choose the scale factor.) Explain how you made the scaled copy.

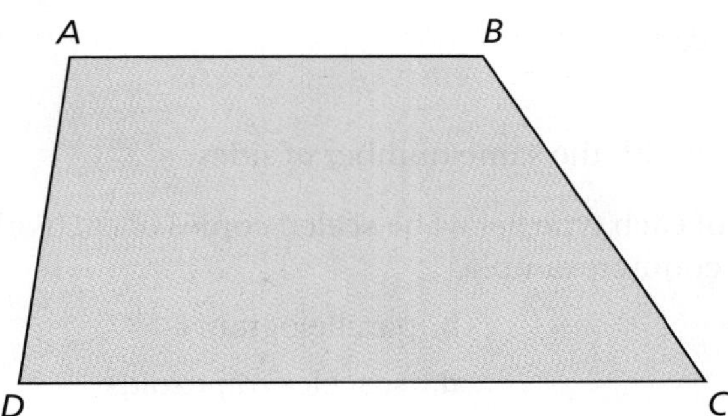

5. You scale a polygon by the factor $\frac{3}{4}$. You then compare the original polygon to the scaled one. Find each ratio.
   a. the lengths of any two corresponding sides
   b. the measures of any two corresponding angles

6. Is either statement below a valid test for whether two polygons are scaled copies? Explain. If the test is not valid, what additional requirement(s) would make each test work?
   - Two polygons are scaled copies if you can show that their corresponding angles all have equal measures.
   - Two polygons are scaled copies if you can show that the lengths of their corresponding sides are all in the same ratio.

On Your Own

7. Two angles of one triangle measure 28° and 31°. Another triangle has two angles that measure 117° and 31°. Are the triangles scaled copies? How can you tell?

8. How can you tell whether two squares are scaled copies of each other?

9. Draw two quadrilaterals that are not scaled copies but in which the sides of one quadrilateral are twice as long as the corresponding sides of the other quadrilateral.

Go Online
Pearsonsuccessnet.com

10. Explain why the figures in each pair below are scaled copies of each other, or give a counterexample to show that they need not be scaled copies.

    a. two quadrilaterals
    b. two squares
    c. two quadrilaterals with equal corresponding angle measures
    d. two triangles
    e. two isosceles triangles
    f. two isosceles right triangles
    g. two equilateral triangles
    h. two rhombuses
    i. two regular polygons with the same number of sides

11. Must any two figures of each type below be scaled copies of each other? Explain why or give a counterexample.

    a. rectangles
    b. parallelograms
    c. trapezoids
    d. isosceles trapezoids
    e. regular hexagons
    f. octagons
    g. circles
    h. cubes
    i. spheres
    j. cylinders
    k. boxes
    l. cones

12. **Standardized Test Prep** Which two figures are not necessarily scaled copies of each other?

    A. two rhombuses
    B. two squares
    C. two circles
    D. two isosceles right triangles

Maintain Your Skills

13. Scale this circle by the given scale factors.

    a. 2
    b. 2.5
    c. 0.5
    d. 1

Habits of Mind

Simplify. When you must show an example, keep it simple. For Exercise 13a, which length related to a circle is easy to double?

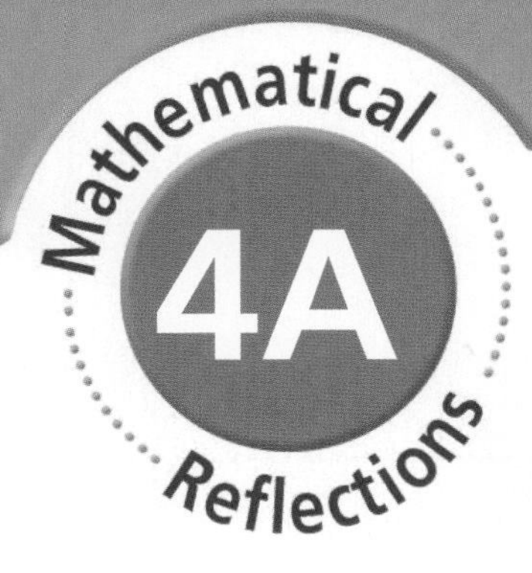

In this investigation, you studied scaled copies—accurate reductions or enlargements of given figures. You used scale factors to draw similar figures and to approximate distances on blueprints and maps. You also studied ways to decide whether two shapes were well-scaled copies of each other. These questions will help you summarize what you have learned.

1. Give an approximate scale factor for the following pairs of figures. If you think that the figures are not scaled copies of each other, explain why.

   a.

   b.

   c.

2. Scale the triangle at the right by the factor $\frac{1}{4}$.

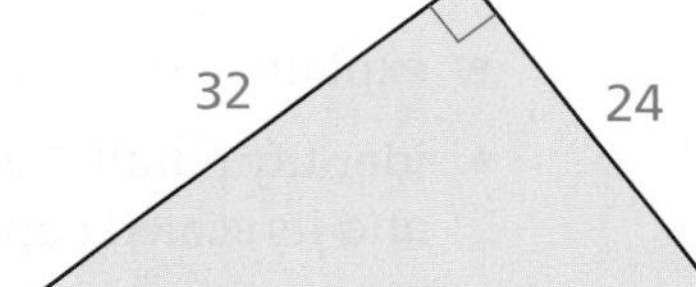

3. Check, without measuring, whether the two rectangles below are scaled copies of each other. Explain.

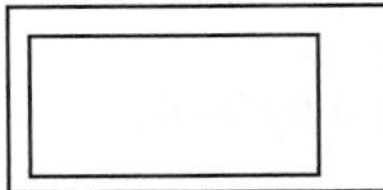

4. Why is it important to know the scale factor when reading a map?
5. What is a well-scaled drawing?
6. How can you decide whether two rectangles are scaled copies of each other?

Vocabulary

In this investigation, you learned these terms. Make sure you understand what each one means and how to use it.

- **ratio**
- **scale a figure**
- **scaled figure**
- **scale factor**

Curved or Straight? Just Dilate!

In *Curved or Straight? Just Dilate!*, you will learn two techniques for making scaled copies. The process of making a scaled copy is called *dilation*. The copy you make may sometimes be larger or smaller than the original figure, depending on the scale factor of the dilation.

By the end of this investigation, you will be able to answer questions like these.

1. What is the mathematical meaning of *dilation*?
2. How do you use the parallel method to scale a polygon?
3. What is the result of applying scale factor 3 to a polygon? The result of applying scale factor $\frac{1}{3}$?

You will learn how to

- describe and use methods for constructing enlargements or reductions of shapes
- explain and contrast the ratio method and parallel method for dilation
- identify parallel segments and corresponding segments in a drawing and its scaled copy

You will develop these habits and skills:

- Identify a dilation as an enlargement or reduction by looking at the scale factor.
- Dilate figures using the ratio method and the parallel method.
- Describe the effects of the choice for center of dilation on the resulting dilation.

Why is it important that Russian nesting dolls be scaled copies of one another?

4.06 Getting Started

You have thought about what a scaled copy is. You have learned to recognize a well-scaled copy. Now you may be wondering how to make scaled copies.

For You to Explore

1. Use only a ruler and pencil. Try to scale figures like these by the factor 2.

   a. 

   b. 

   c. 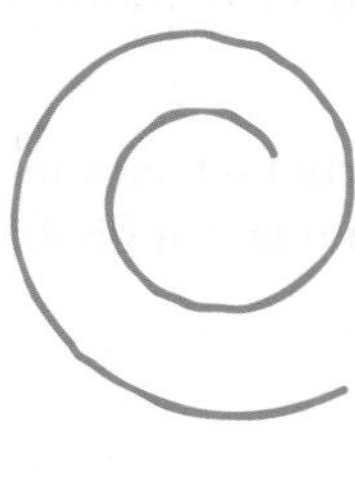

2. Share your drawings with classmates. Decide which drawings are well scaled. Discuss why.
3. Of the scaling processes that seem to work, describe the two that you think work best.

Exercises *Practicing Habits of Mind*

On Your Own

4. Find several meanings of the word *dilation*.
5. Trace this hexagon onto a sheet of paper. Then use a ruler to scale the traced figure by the given scale factors.

   a. 0.5 **b.** 1

   c. $\frac{3}{2}$ **d.** $\frac{3}{4}$

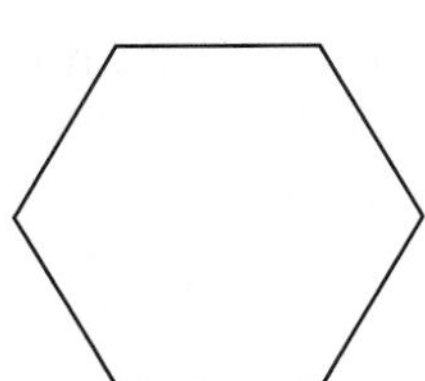

6. Describe the effect of each scale factor in Exercise 5.

7. Use geometry software. Construct a rectangle. Find its area and perimeter. Then scale your rectangle by each scale factor given below. Record the area and perimeter of the scaled copy.

a. 2 **b.** 3 **c.** $\frac{1}{2}$ **d.** $\frac{1}{3}$

See the TI-Nspire™ Handbook, p. 712, for help with finding the area of a polygon and scaling a figure.

8. For a given rectangle, describe the effects of a scale factor on the area and perimeter. Can you predict the area and perimeter of a scaled copy without first scaling the original rectangle? Without finding the dimensions of the scaled copy?

9. Use geometry software. Construct a triangle. Find its area and perimeter. Scale your triangle by each scale factor given below. Record the area and perimeter of each scaled copy.

a. 4 **b.** 0.1 **c.** $\frac{3}{5}$ **d.** $\frac{1}{7}$

10. For a given triangle, describe the effects of a scale factor on the area and perimeter. Can you predict the area and perimeter of a scaled copy without first scaling the original triangle? Without finding the dimensions of the scaled copy?

Maintain Your Skills

11. Use the figure below to find each length.

a. AZ

b. BY

c. CX

d. DW

e. EV

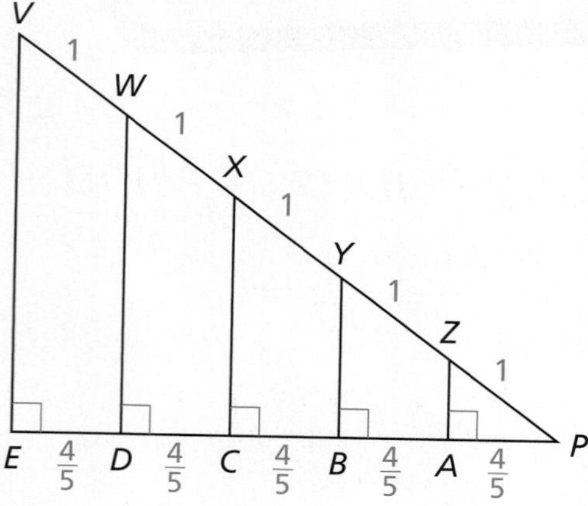

12. $\overline{AZ}$, $\overline{BY}$, $\overline{CX}$, $\overline{DW}$, and $\overline{EV}$ are corresponding sides in triangles AZP, BYP, CXP, DWP, and EVP, respectively. Use your results from Exercise 11. Find each ratio.

a. $\frac{AZ}{AZ}$ **b.** $\frac{BY}{AZ}$ **c.** $\frac{CX}{AZ}$ **d.** $\frac{DW}{AZ}$ **e.** $\frac{EV}{AZ}$

13. How do the ratios you found in Exercise 12 compare to the ratios of other pairs of corresponding sides in triangles AZP, BYP, CXP, DWP, and EVP?

4.07 Making Scaled Copies

To scale an image on film, a light source sends beams of light through the film. A screen that is parallel to the film catches the beams. This is a "point-by-point" process.

Here the enlargement is by the factor 2. Point A' is twice as far from the center of dilation as point A. Concisely put, $LA' = 2LA$. Likewise, $LB' = 2LB$.

In mathematics, the procedure of scaling a figure is called **dilation.** In the figure above, the point that corresponds to the light source is the **center of dilation.** The rays coming from it represent the beams of light. The points farther out along the rays (like A' and B') represent the screen images of points on the film (A and B, respectively). To get more image points, draw more rays.

You can think of dilation as a particular way of scaling a figure. If you are asked to "dilate a figure by 2," this means to use dilation to scale it by 2.

Habits of Mind

Communicate context. You can use *dilation* to refer to the dilation copy when this meaning is clear in context.

Developing Habits of Mind

Make strategic choices. Representing a scaled figure on paper is sometimes easy but can also be challenging. To dilate a line segment, you need to dilate only two points. Which two are they?

To dilate the film image above and get a reasonably good copy, you must dilate many points. The more points you choose to dilate and the more strategically you choose them, the more accurate your dilation.

How many points would you have to dilate to make a good sketch of each of the following?

- a triangle
- a square
- a circle with a given center
- a circle with its center not given

The number needed is not necessarily obvious. For a square, three points are enough. On the other hand, even four points (as suggested in the diagram) might not be enough if the points are not well chosen.

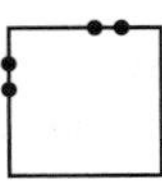

Exercises *Practicing Habits of Mind*

Check Your Understanding

1. Draw a circle on a piece of paper.

a. Use dilation to scale the circle by the factor 2. Choose enough points on the circle that you can judge whether your dilation really does produce a scaled copy.

Pick any center of dilation that you want.

b. Compare your results with your classmates' work. How does the choice of center of dilation affect the result?

2. a. Draw a tilted square on a piece of paper. Dilate it by the factor 2. Dilate at least eight points before drawing the entire dilation image.

b. How does the orientation of the dilated square compare with that of the original tilted square?

c. Is orientation affected by your choice for the center of dilation?

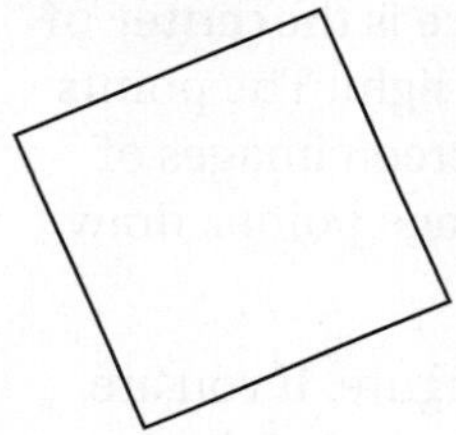

a tilted square

3. Explain how to dilate a circle or square by the factor $\frac{1}{2}$. Explain how to dilate it by the factor 3.

4. The ornamental pattern on the left below was dilated by the factor 2. The dilation copy is on the right. Trace the figures and locate the center of dilation.

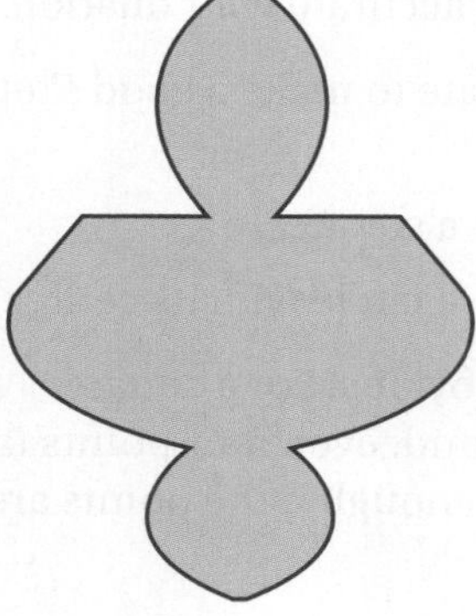

On Your Own

5. Choose a favorite picture. It might be like Trig, the horse shown here. Dilate the picture by the factor 2 to make a scaled sketch. You do not need to scale all the details from your picture. A rough outline is fine, but be sure to include at least the important ones.

In Exercises 6–9, you can investigate a dilation that has surprising results. Stand in front of a mirror (perhaps a bathroom mirror at home). Trace your image with a bar of soap. Include important features like your eyes, nose, mouth, and chin.

6. Use a ruler. Measure a few of the distances on your mirror picture. How far apart are your eyes? How wide is your mouth? How far is it from your chin to the top of your head?

7. Compare the distances you've measured on the mirror to the actual measurements of your face. Are they the same?

8. How can the concept of dilation help explain your results?

9. Stand in front of the mirror again. Have a friend trace the image of your face. Is the picture the same as the one you traced? Explain.

10. **Standardized Test Prep** Suppose you dilate a square by the factor 2. How does the area of the dilated square compare to the area of the original square?

A. It is the same. **B.** It is 2 times greater.

C. It is 4 times greater. **D.** It is 8 times greater.

11. **Take It Further** Dilating a figure with a pencil and ruler takes plenty of patience. You need to dilate many points to get a good outline of the scaled copy. Geometry software lets you speed up the process.

With geometry software, draw $\overline{AB}$. Construct its midpoint, M. Select points B and M. Use the Trace feature to indicate that you want the software to keep track of the paths of B and M.

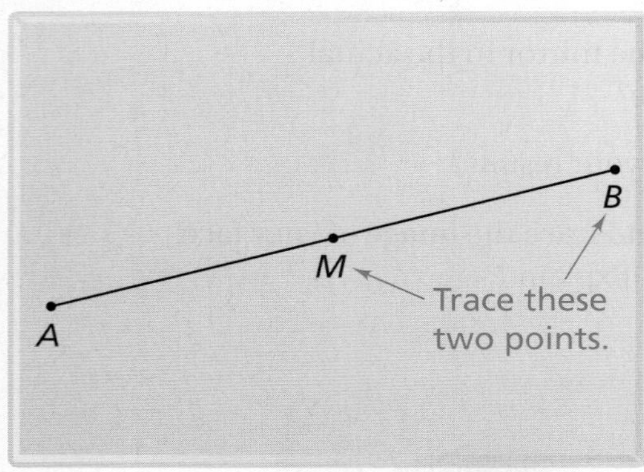

a. Move point B around the screen to draw a picture or perhaps sign your name. Compare point B's path to the path traced by point M. Are they the same? How are they related?

Point A should stay fixed as you move point B.

b. Use the software's segment tool. Draw a polygon on your screen. Move point B along the sides of the polygon. Describe the path traced by point M.

c. As you move point B, trace $\overline{AB}$ as well as points B and M. How does your final picture illustrate the concept of dilation?

Move point B fairly quickly. If you move it slowly, the screen fills up with traced segments and the picture is hard to see.

Maintain Your Skills

12. Trace this figure. Scale it using the given scale factors. You can choose your own center of dilation.

a. 2 **b.** 0.5

c. 1 **d.** 0.1

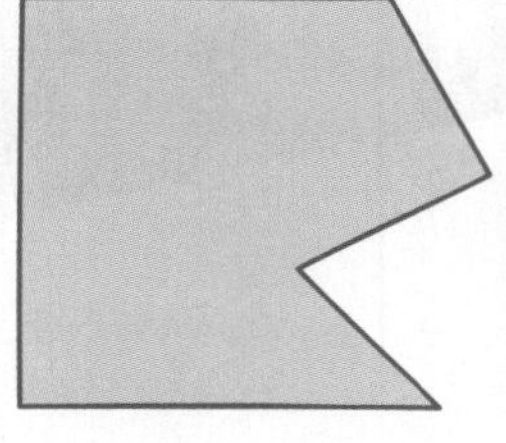

4.08 Ratio and Parallel Methods

When you use dilation to scale a figure such as a horse's head, you need to dilate a fair number of points before the scaled copy is recognizable. For figures made of line segments, such as polygons, you need to keep track of only a few critical points.

In this lesson, you will learn two shortcuts, the **ratio method** and the **parallel method**. You can use each method with those critical points to make the dilation process much faster.

Habits of Mind

Make strategic choices. For dilating a segment, you choose the endpoints of the segment. Are they strategically good choices? Explain.

Example 1

The Ratio Method

Problem Use point L as the center of dilation. Dilate polygon $ABCDE$ by $\frac{1}{2}$.

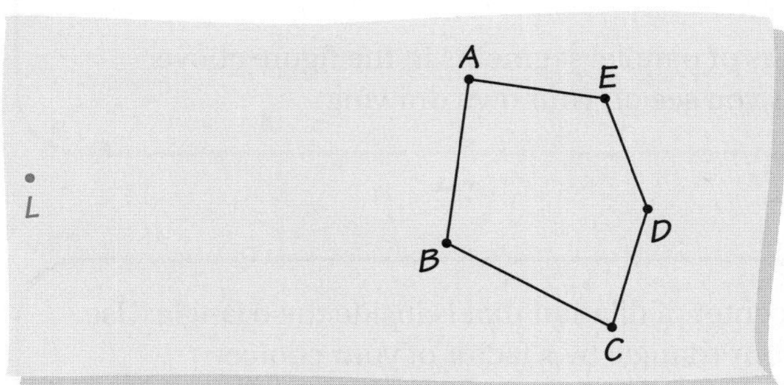

See the TI-Nspire Handbook, p. 712, to learn how to use the ratio method with geometry software.

Solution

Step 1 Draw a ray from point L through each vertex of the polygon.

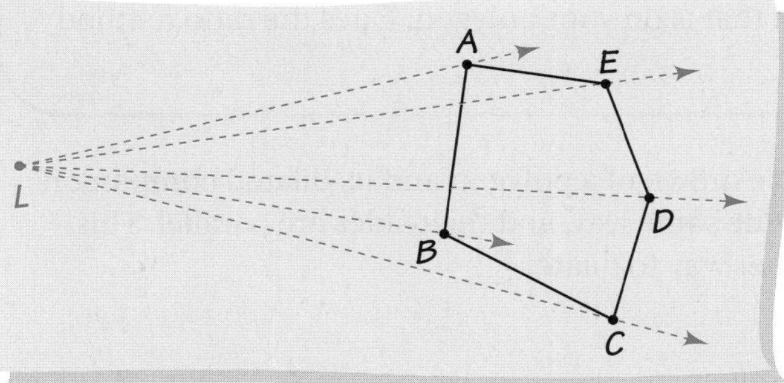

Step 2 Find the midpoint of each of the segments $\overline{LA}$ through $\overline{LE}$.

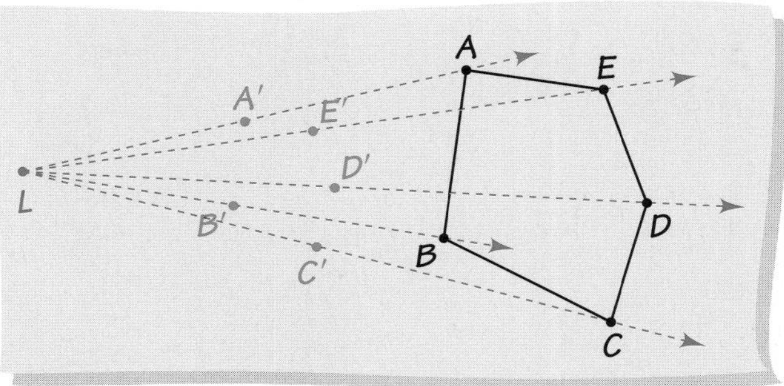

Step 3 Connect the midpoints to form a new polygon, $A'B'C'D'E'$.

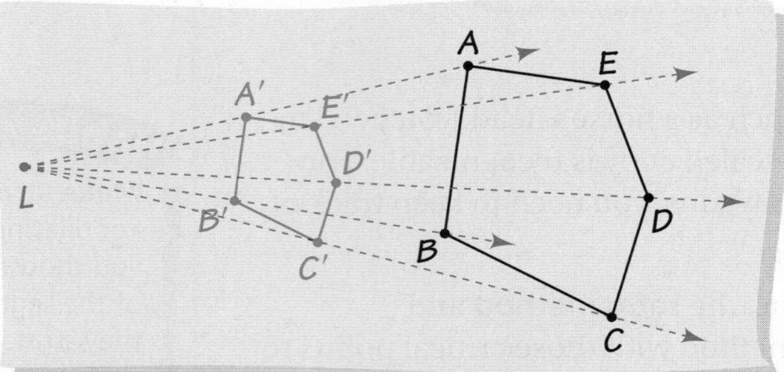

For Discussion

1. Is your new polygon a scaled $\left(\text{by } \frac{1}{2}\right)$ copy of the original? How can you tell?

2. There seem to be many pairs of parallel segments in the figure above. Label the parallel segments you see on your own drawing.

Habits of Mind

Check your results. You can take measurements to check your work. How many measurements would you take to convince yourself that the polygon is a scaled copy of the original? Explain.

For You to Do

3. Draw a triangle. Choose a center of dilation that is inside the triangle. Use the ratio method to scale your triangle by a factor of your choice.

   Does the ratio method work if the center of dilation is inside the polygon?

4. Choose a center of dilation that is on your polygon. Does the ratio method still work?

Look at each figure you have drawn of a polygon and its dilated companion. The polygons are oriented the same way, and their sides are parallel. This observation suggests another way to dilate.

Example 2

The Parallel Method

Problem Use point E as the center of dilation. Dilate polygon $ABCD$ by 2.

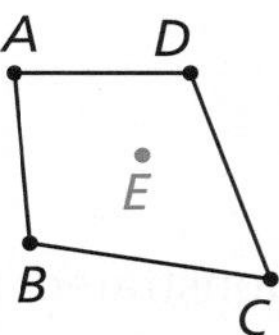

Solution

Step 1 Draw a ray from E through each vertex.

Step 2 Along one ray ($\overrightarrow{EA}$ below), find a point that is twice as far from E as the vertex A. Mark this location A'.

Step 3 Start at point A'. Draw segments parallel to $\overline{AB}$, $\overline{BC}$, $\overline{CD}$, and finally $\overline{DA}$.

Estimate the slope of the parallel segments as best you can.

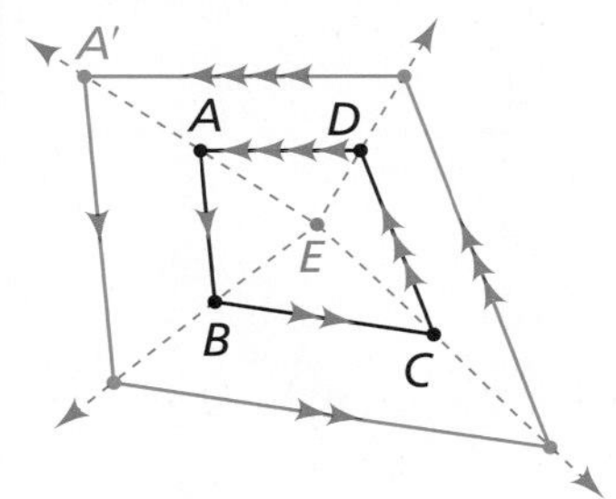

For Discussion

Draw a polygon. Follow the steps in Example 2 to dilate your polygon by 2.

5. Is your new polygon a scaled (by the factor 2) copy of the original? How can you tell?
6. Label the pairs of parallel segments on your drawing.

For You to Do

7. Draw a triangle. Choose a center of dilation that is on the triangle. Use the parallel method to scale your triangle by a factor of your choice. Does the parallel method work if the center of dilation is on the polygon?
8. Try the parallel method again. This time choose a center of dilation that is outside your polygon. Does the parallel method still work?

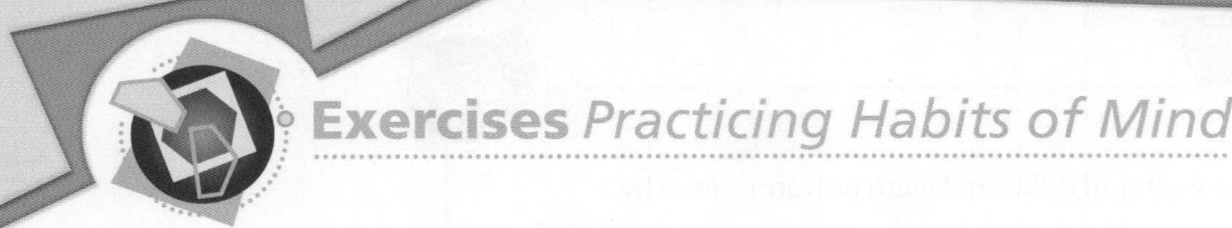

Exercises Practicing Habits of Mind

Check Your Understanding

As well as making half-size reductions, the ratio method demonstrated in this lesson can dilate a figure by any scale factor you choose.

1. Start with a polygon. Use the ratio method to dilate it by the factor $\frac{1}{3}$.

2. Use the ratio method to enlarge a polygon by the factor 2.

3. Rosie wants to make two scale drawings of $\triangle ABC$. One is to be dilated by the factor 2. The other is to be dilated by the factor 3. She decides to make the triangle vertex A her center of dilation. Draw a picture like the one below. Then finish her construction.

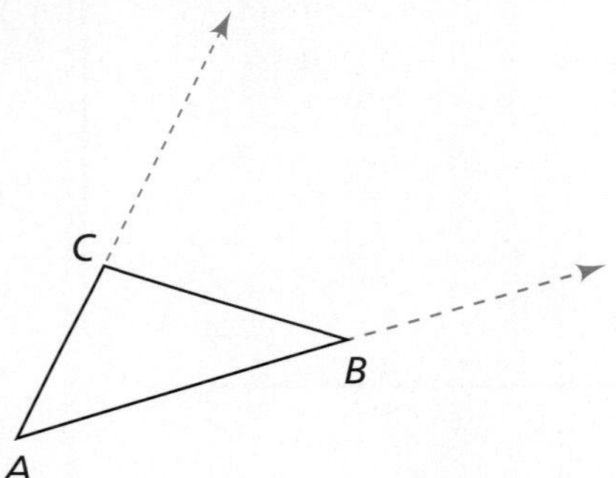

Habits of Mind

Visualize. When you have to draw a picture carefully, such as in a construction, it can be very helpful to first sketch what the final picture should look like.

4. **What's Wrong Here?** Steve uses the ratio method to enlarge $\triangle ABC$ below by the factor 2.

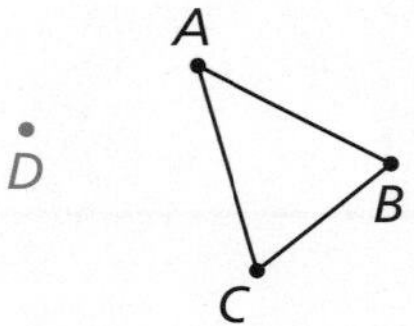

He follows this procedure. (See diagram at the top of the next page.)

- He measures the distance DA to be 1. He moves out along $\overrightarrow{DA}$ until he finds a point A' such that $AA' = 2$ (twice as much as DA).
- He measures the distance DB to be 2. He moves out along $\overrightarrow{DB}$ until he finds a point B' such that $BB' = 4$ (twice as much as DB).
- He measures the distance DC to be 1.5. He moves out along $\overrightarrow{DC}$ until he finds a point C' such that $CC' = 3$ (twice as much as DC).
- He draws $\triangle A'B'C'$.

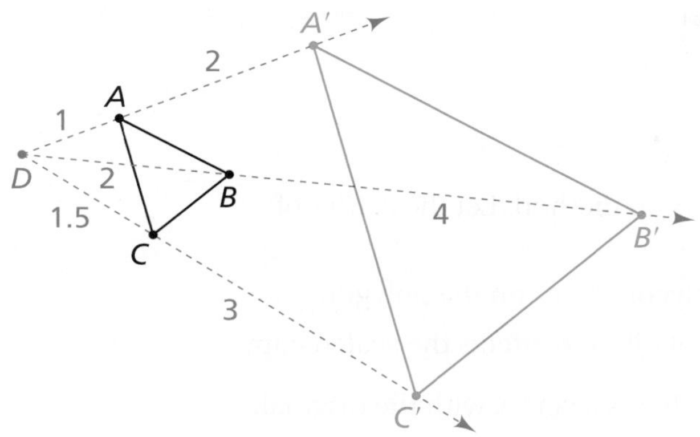

To Steve's surprise, $\triangle A'B'C'$ has sides that are proportional to the sides of $\triangle ABC$, but they are not twice as long. How many times as long are they? What is the matter here?

5. Oh no! There is a problem at the print shop. The picture below was supposed to show $\triangle ABC$ and its dilated companion, $\triangle A'B'C'$, but an ink spill spoiled the page. Can you salvage something from this disaster by calculating how much $\triangle ABC$ has been scaled?

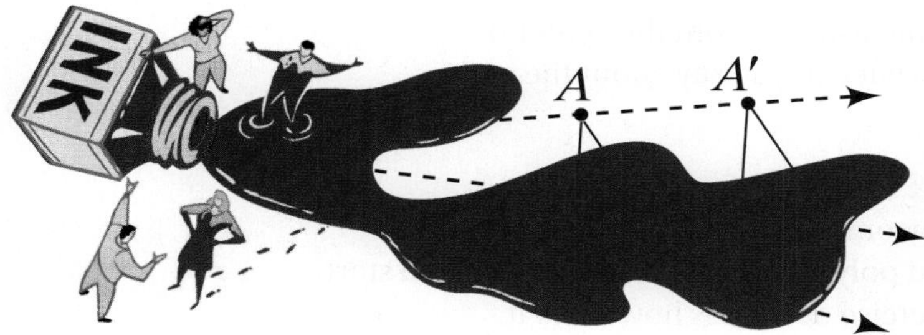

6. Trace the figure below onto a sheet of paper, including the center of dilation, D. Use the ratio method to scale the figure by the given factor.

a. $\frac{3}{4}$ **b.** 1.5

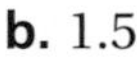

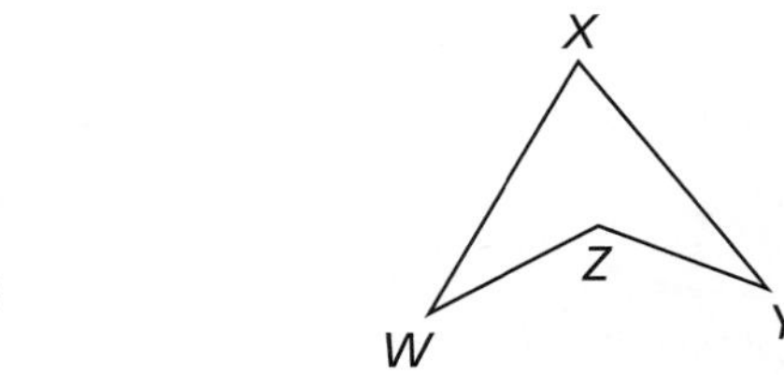

7. Draw a polygon. Use the parallel method to reduce the polygon by the factor $\frac{1}{2}$.

8. Draw a polygon. Use the parallel method to enlarge the polygon by the factor 3. Make three enlargements. Locate the centers of dilation inside the polygon, on the polygon, and outside the polygon.

On Your Own

9. Draw any polygon. Scale it by 2 using the ratio method. Let the center of dilation be as given.

   a. outside the polygon b. inside the polygon c. on the polygon

   d. Explain how the location of the center of dilation affects the scaled copy.

10. Draw a polygon. Make a scaled copy that shares a vertex with the original. Use any scale factor you like (other than 1).

11. Draw a polygon. Make a scaled copy that has one side containing the corresponding side of the original.

One side of the copy contains the corresponding side of the original. From this, what can you conclude about the dilation?

12. Julia scaled a polygon three times.

    a. The first scaled copy was closer to the center of dilation than the original polygon. What can you say about the scale factor?

    b. The second scaled copy was farther from the center of dilation than the original polygon. What can you say about the scale factor?

    c. The third scaled copy was the same distance from the center of dilation as the original polygon. What can you say about the scale factor? Be careful!

If you use the parallel method with geometry software, you can make a whole series of different-sized scaled polygons. And you do not have to start from scratch each time. The next exercise describes how to do it.

13. Use geometry software. Construct a polygon and a center of dilation. Construct rays from this center through the polygon's vertices. Then place a point anywhere along one of the rays. This will be a "slider point." It will control the amount of dilation.

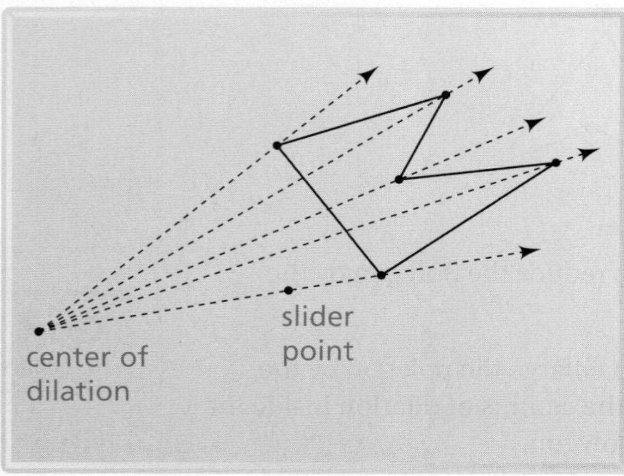

Use the slider point as the starting point for the dilated image. With the parallel method, complete a dilated copy of the polygon. When your dilated copy is complete, move the slider point back and forth along its ray. Describe what happens.

14. Take It Further With your polygon and its scaled copy from Exercise 13, use the software to calculate the scale factor. This scale factor should update itself automatically as you move the slider point. For what location(s) of the slider point is the scale factor as follows?

a. less than one **b.** greater than one **c.** equal to one

15. Standardized Test Prep One figure is made of segments. A second figure is made of segments *and* curved parts. Why is the first figure easier to dilate?

A. You can easily move the center of dilation of the first figure.

B. You only have to dilate the endpoints of the first figure's segments and then connect those points.

C. It is easier to place the center of the dilation inside the first figure.

D. You cannot dilate the curved parts.

16. Take It Further Draw $\triangle ABC$ with pencil and paper or geometry software. Your challenge is to construct a square with one side lying on $\overline{BC}$ and the other two vertices on sides $\overline{AB}$ and $\overline{AC}$.

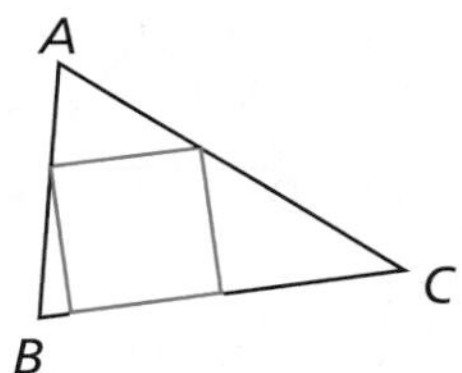

Habits of Mind

Visualize. You can shrink the square, keeping three vertices on the triangle. This should suggest an enlargement dilation that will reveal the construction steps.

Maintain Your Skills

17. Use both the ratio method and the parallel method to scale the figure below by the given scale factors.

a. 2.5

b. $\frac{1}{2}$

c. $\frac{5}{2}$

d. $\frac{1}{4}$

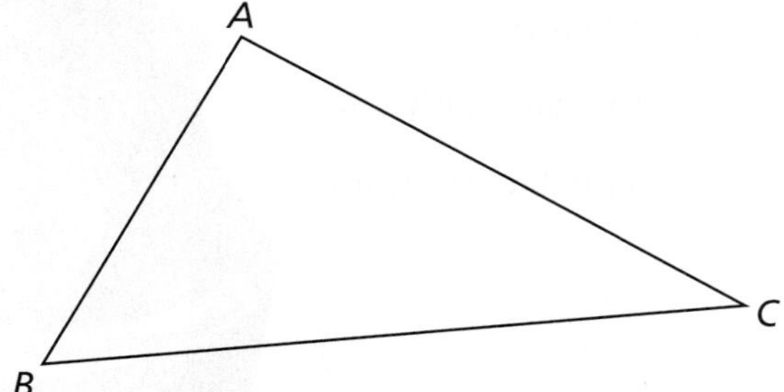

In this investigation, you explored dilations. You applied scale factors to construct enlargements and reductions. You explored choices for the center of dilation. Also, you learned the ratio and parallel methods. These questions will help you summarize what you have learned.

1. You scale a figure by the factor $\frac{3}{5}$. How do the areas of the original figure and the scaled copy compare?
2. Draw $\triangle ABC$ and a point X outside of $\triangle ABC$. Use the ratio method or parallel method. Scale $\triangle ABC$ by $\frac{3}{2}$. Use X as the center of dilation.
3. Trace polygon $ABCD$ and point X. Use the parallel method. Dilate $ABCD$ by the factor $\frac{1}{5}$. Use X as the center of dilation.
4. Explain how to find the center of dilation that maps $\triangle ABC$ to $\triangle DEF$.

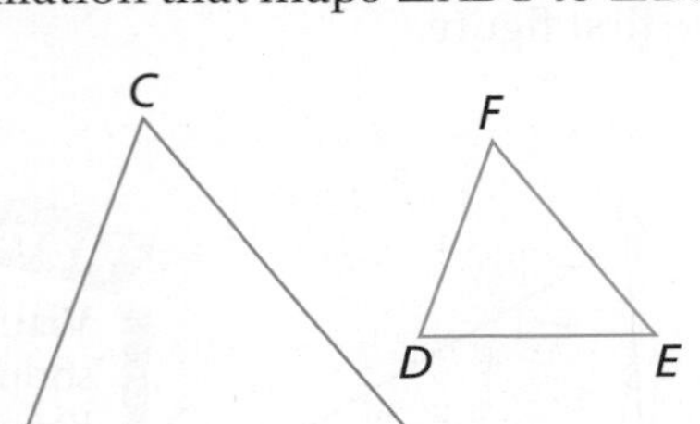

5. If you scale the regular tetrahedron at the right by the factor 2, how do the surface areas of the original figure and the scaled copy compare?

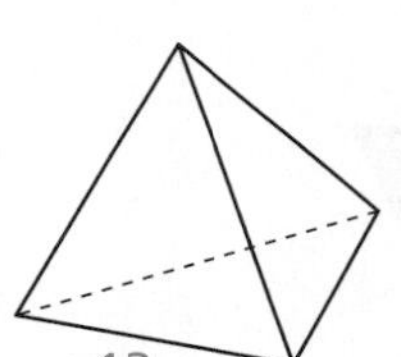

6. What is the mathematical meaning of *dilation*?
7. How do you use the parallel method to scale a polygon?
8. What is the result of applying scale factor 3 to a polygon? The result of applying scale factor $\frac{1}{3}$?

If nesting dolls are dilation images of one another, where is the center of dilation?

Vocabulary

In this investigation, you learned these terms. Make sure you understand what each one means and how to use it.

- **center of dilation**
- **dilation**
- **parallel method**
- **ratio method**

Mid-Chapter Test

Multiple Choice

1. You scale a triangle by the factor 3. Then you scale the resulting triangle by the factor 4. What is the ratio of a side length of the original triangle to the corresponding side length of the final triangle?

A. 1 : 12 **B.** 3 : 4 **C.** 4 : 3 **D.** 12 : 1

2. Cube A has a volume of 27 cm^3. Cube B is a scaled copy of cube A. You can fit exactly 27 copies of cube A inside cube B. What is the scale factor you can use to transform cube B into cube A?

A. $\frac{1}{9}$ **B.** $\frac{1}{3}$ **C.** 3 **D.** 9

3. You dilate the inner square by the factor 2. The image of the dilation is the outer square. Which point is the center of the dilation?

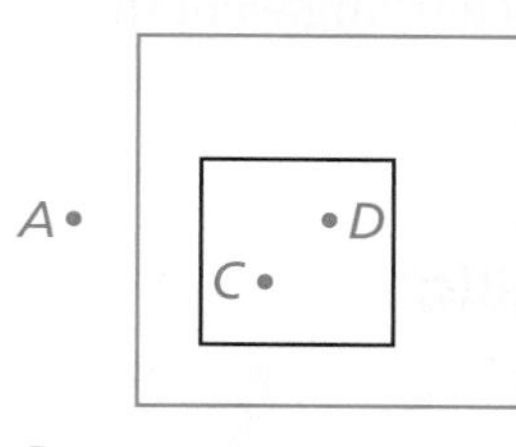

A. *A* **B.** *B* **C.** *C* **D.** *D*

Open Response

4. A map gives a scale factor of 1 inch : 5 miles : 10 minutes average driving time.

a. How far will you travel if your route measures 3.5 inches on the map?

b. About how long will a "3.5-inch trip" take?

c. What map length represents a 28-mile trip?

5. A square has an area of 80 square inches. Another square has an area of 5 square inches. Can these squares be scaled copies of each other? If so, give a scale factor. If not, explain why not.

6. Copy polygon *WORD* and point *A*. Use any method to dilate *WORD*. Use *A* as the center of dilation and scale factor $\frac{3}{4}$.

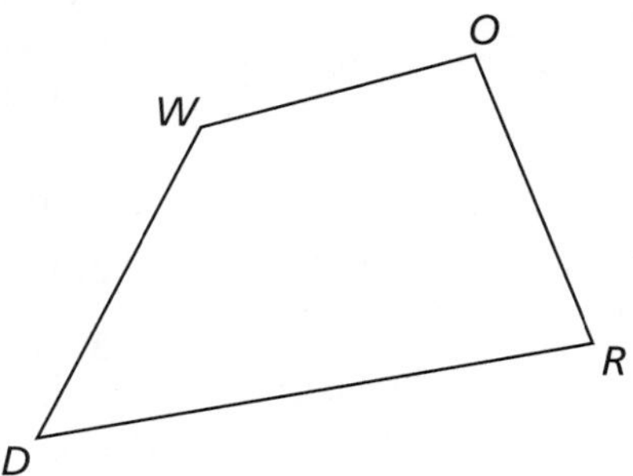

7. You want to scale a polygon by $\frac{1}{3}$. Where would you have to place the center of dilation to have the scaled copy located as follows?

a. to the left of (possibly overlapping) the original polygon

b. inside the original polygon

c. sharing a vertex with the original polygon

8. In the book *Gulliver's Travels,* a grown man from our world visits the land of Lilliput. In Lilliput, the people and things are scaled copies of the people and things in our world. Every length in Lilliput is $\frac{1}{12}$ the corresponding length in our world.

Trace your hand on a piece of paper. Pick a center of dilation. Dilate your tracing to find the size of a Lilliputian student's hand.

9. You scale a cube with 5-inch sides by the factor $\frac{1}{3}$. What is the volume of the scaled cube? How does the volume of the original cube compare to the volume of the scaled tube?

The Side-Splitter Theorems

In *The Side-Splitter Theorems,* you will dilate a triangle using one of its vertices as the center of dilation. You will examine the result in detail and develop some very useful theorems.

By the end of this investigation, you will be able to answer questions like these.

1. If a point D is on side $\overline{AB}$ of $\triangle ABC$, E is on $\overline{AC}$, and $\overline{DE}$ is parallel to $\overline{BC}$, then what can you say about the relationship between $\triangle ABC$ and $\triangle ADE$?
2. What are the side-splitter theorems?
3. If two triangles have the same height, and you know the ratio of their areas, what is the ratio of the lengths of their bases?

You will learn how to

- investigate proportional relationships in nested triangles
- investigate how lines parallel to a side of a triangle cut the other two sides
- prove the side-splitter theorems

You will develop these habits and skills:

- Use ratios and proportions.
- Prove conjectures using scaled figures.
- Identify invariants.

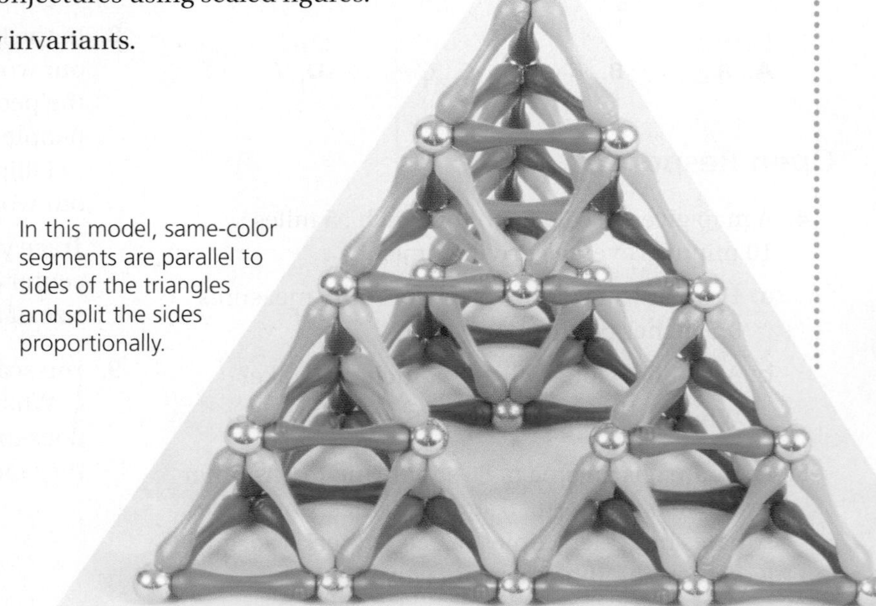

In this model, same-color segments are parallel to sides of the triangles and split the sides proportionally.

4.09 Getting Started

In this investigation, you will construct proofs for most parts of the side-splitter theorems. At the core of these proofs is an ingenious area argument devised by Euclid. To prepare for the proofs, you have several questions about area to work on first.

For You to Explore

1. Points A and B of $\triangle ABC$ are fixed on line ℓ. Line m is parallel to line ℓ. Point C, which is not shown, is free to wander anywhere along line m. For what location of point C is the area of $\triangle ABC$ the greatest? Explain.

Geometry software makes it easy for you to experiment with different locations of point C.

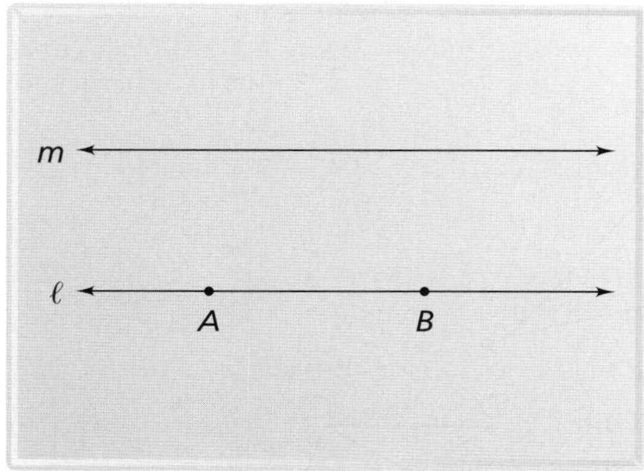

In Exercises 2 and 3, you prove that if two triangles have the same height, the ratio of their areas is the same as the ratio of their bases.

2. Both $\triangle ABC$ and $\triangle DEF$ have height h. Write an expression for the area of each triangle. Then show that the ratio of their areas is $\frac{AC}{DF}$.

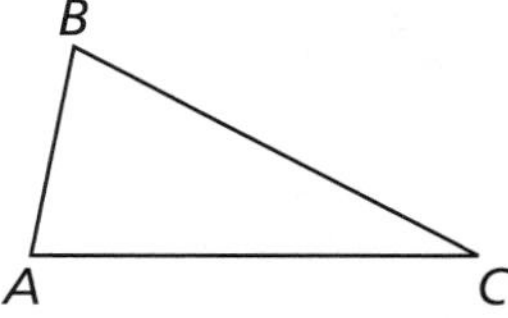

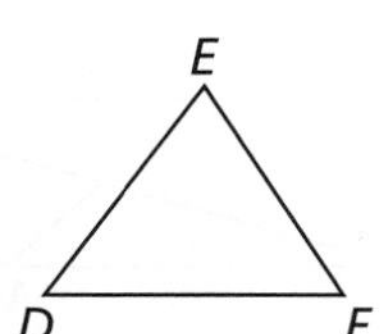

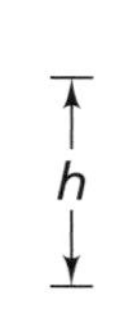

3. The area of $\triangle GEM$ is 3 square inches. The area of $\triangle MEO$ is 2 square inches. What is the value of $\frac{GE}{EO}$? Explain. What is value of $\frac{GE}{GO}$?

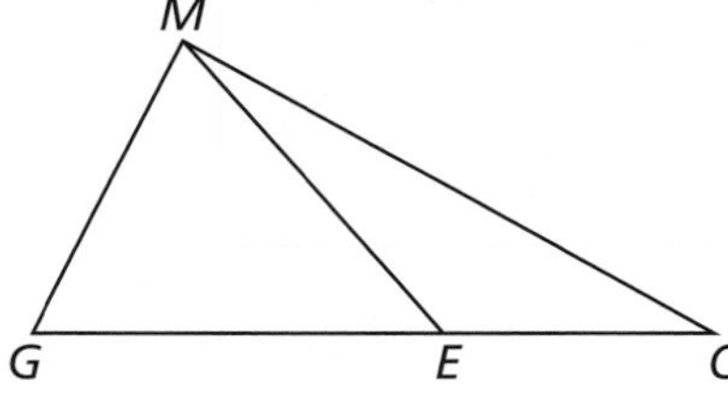

Exercises *Practicing Habits of Mind*

On Your Own

4. In this figure, $\frac{\text{area of } \triangle PQS}{\text{area of } \triangle RPS} = \frac{1}{2}$. If $SQ = 4$ and $PS = 6$, find the lengths PQ, SR, QR, and PR.

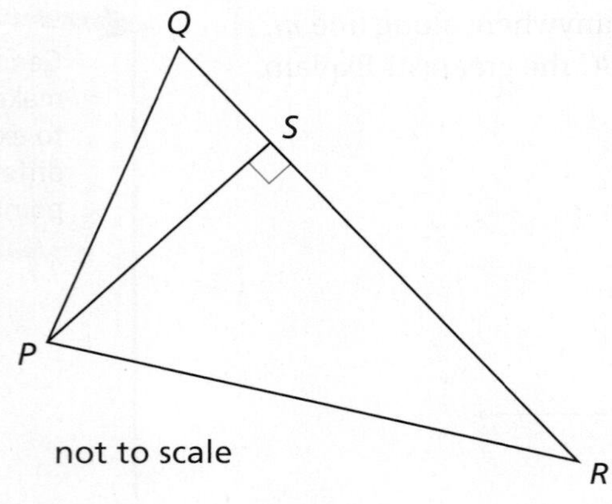

5. $ABCD$ is a trapezoid with $\overline{AB} \parallel \overline{DC}$.

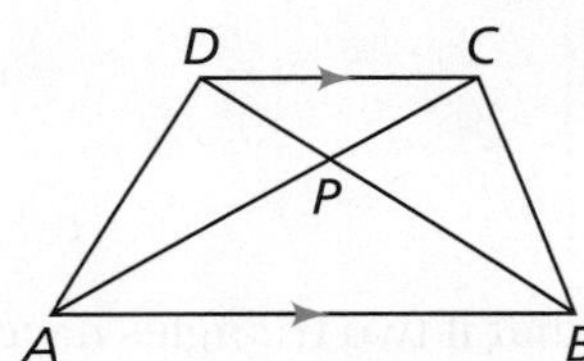

a. Explain why the area of $\triangle ACB$ is equal to the area of $\triangle ADB$.

b. Name two other pairs of triangles in the figure that have equal areas. Explain how you know.

6. $GRAM$ is a parallelogram. Which of $\triangle GAM$, $\triangle ARM$, $\triangle MRG$, and $\triangle RAG$ has the greatest area? Explain.

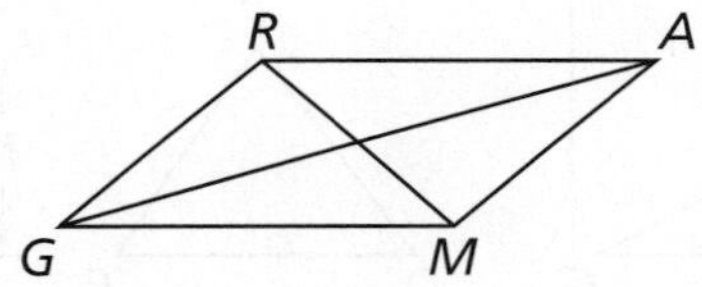

Maintain Your Skills

7. This figure is a scaled copy. Draw an original figure that would result in this copy for each of the following scale factors.

a. 2 **b.** 3

c. 0.5 **d.** 0.1

4.10 Nested Triangles

Here are a polygon (black) and a scaled copy (blue). The copy was made using the parallel method.

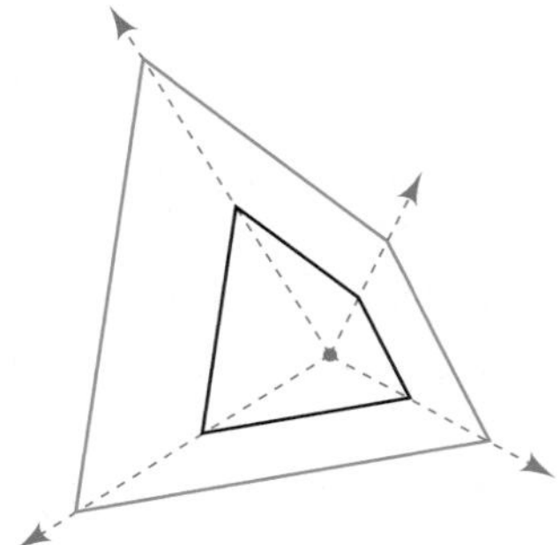

a polygon and a scaled copy

The four pictures below show the same polygons. Each picture highlights a pair of **nested triangles**—one triangle inside another. Notice that each pair of nested triangles contains a side from the original polygon and a parallel side from the scaled polygon.

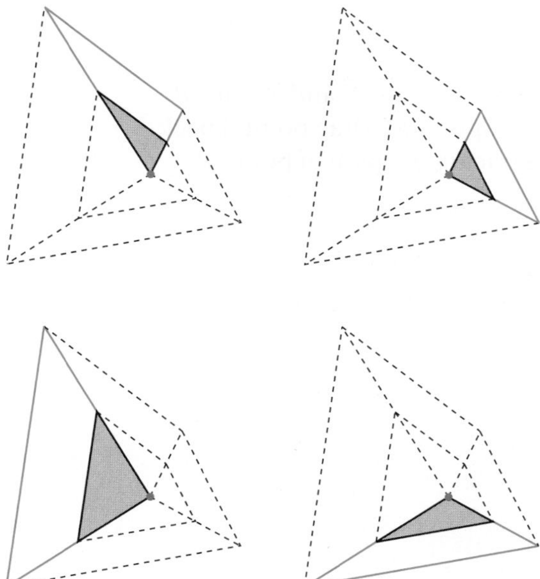

four pairs of nested triangles

In the In-Class Experiment that follows, you should discover some important relationships between parallel lines and the sides of the triangles that they intersect.

In-Class Experiment

Part 1A Parallel Lines and Midpoints

Draw a picture like the one below. Show two parallel lines and a point. Make the distance between the point and the closer line equal to the distance between the two lines.

1. Use your picture. Find a quick way to draw ten segments so that each will have its midpoint automatically marked.
2. Find a way to position two parallel lines and a point that gives a quick way to draw ten segments with each segment divided into two smaller segments with lengths in the ratio 1 to 3.

Part 1B Midpoints and Parallel Lines

Use geometry software. Draw $\overline{XY}$. Construct a point A on $\overline{XY}$ and a point B that is not on $\overline{XY}$. Draw $\overline{AB}$ and construct its midpoint M. Drag point A back and forth along the entire length of $\overline{XY}$ while tracing the path of point M.

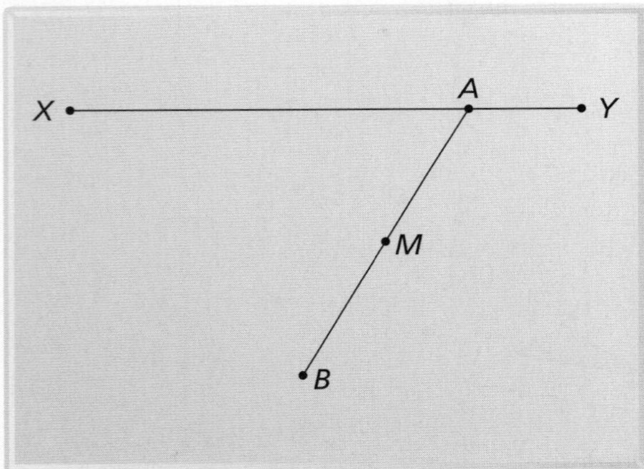

Drag point A along $\overline{XY}$.

3. a. Describe the path traced by M.
   b. How does the path traced by point M compare to $\overline{XY}$?
4. Repeat the construction above. This time, instead of constructing the midpoint of $\overline{AB}$, place the point M somewhere else on $\overline{AB}$. How does the position of M affect the path traced by M?

5. Use geometry software. Draw $\overline{XY}$. Locate a point A on $\overline{XY}$. Then construct three segments, each with A as an endpoint. Construct the midpoints M_1, M_2, and M_3 of the three segments. Move point A back and forth along $\overline{XY}$ while tracing the paths of these midpoints. Describe the paths of the midpoints, including what you know about their locations and lengths.

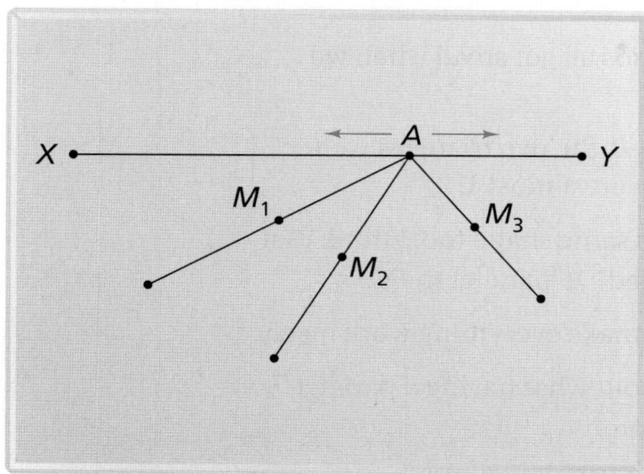

Part 2 Splitting Two Sides of a Triangle

Use geometry software. Draw $\triangle ABC$. Place a point D anywhere on side $\overline{AB}$. Then construct a segment $\overline{DE}$ that is parallel to $\overline{BC}$.

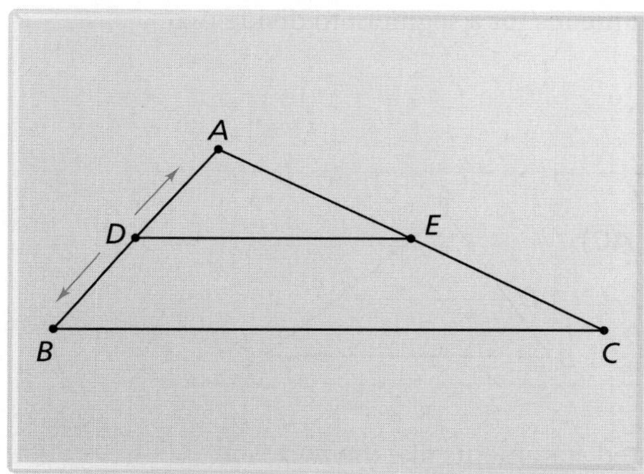

Drag point D along $\overline{AB}$.

$\triangle ADE$ and $\triangle ABC$ are a pair of nested triangles.

6. Use the software to find the ratio $\frac{AD}{AB}$.

7. Find two other length ratios with the same value. Do all three ratios remain equal to each other when you drag point D along $\overline{AB}$?

8. As you drag D along $\overline{AB}$, describe what happens to the figure. Make a conjecture about the effect of $\overline{DE}$ being parallel to $\overline{BC}$.

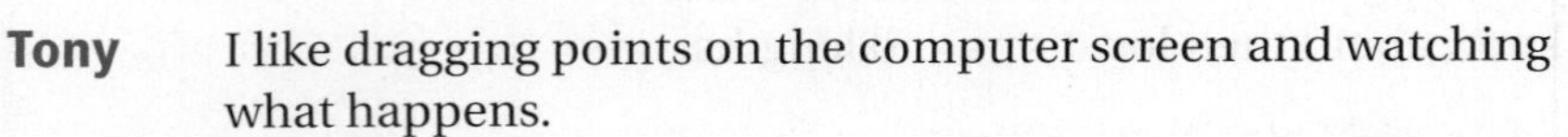

Tony and Sasha are finishing the In-Class Experiment.

Tony I like dragging points on the computer screen and watching what happens.

Sasha Me too. Triangle ADE and the ratios all got small when we dragged D close to A.

Tony And when we dragged D close to B, the two triangles were almost the same, and the ratios were almost 1!

Sasha The two triangles always had the same shape too. I think that happened because we constructed $\overline{DE}$ parallel to $\overline{BC}$.

Tony The parallel segment seemed to make everything work nicely.

Sasha So, can we make a conjecture about what having a parallel segment like $\overline{DE}$ does for the figure?

Tony Can we say something like "A parallel-to-one-side segment inside a triangle makes two proportional triangles"?

Sasha Hmm. I get the idea. I think we have to work on the wording.

Sasha and Tony need a definition of what it means for a segment to divide two sides of a triangle proportionally.

Definitions

In $\triangle ABC$ with D on $\overline{AB}$ and E on $\overline{AC}$, $\overline{DE}$ splits two sides proportionally ($\overline{AB}$ and $\overline{AC}$) if and only if $\frac{AB}{AD} = \frac{AC}{AE}$.

You call the ratio $\frac{AB}{AD}$ the common ratio.

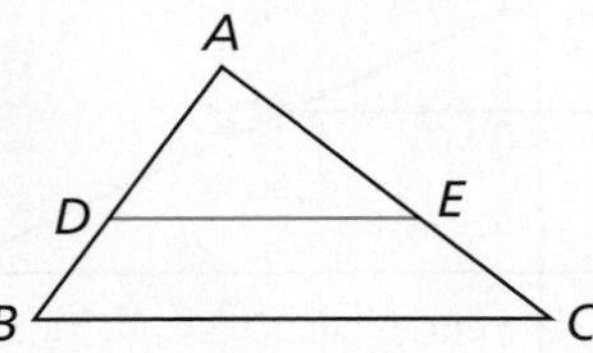

The In-Class Experiment may have suggested statements like the two theorems that follow. You will prove these theorems in the next two lessons.

Theorem 4.1 The Parallel Side-Splitter Theorem

If a segment with endpoints on two sides of a triangle is parallel to the third side of the triangle, then

- **the segment splits the sides it intersects proportionally**
- **the ratio of the length of the third side of the triangle to the length of the parallel segment is the common ratio**

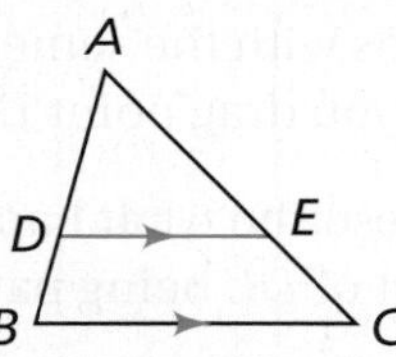

Theorem 4.2 *The Proportional Side-Splitter Theorem*

If a segment with endpoints on two sides of a triangle splits those sides proportionally, then the segment is parallel to the third side.

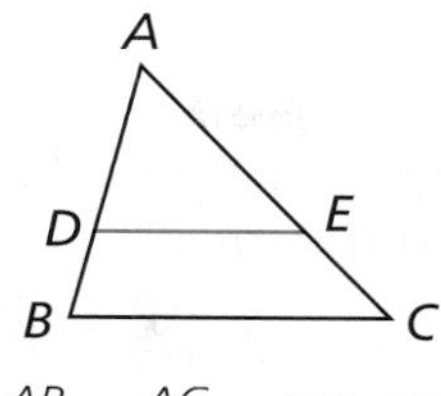

$\frac{AB}{AD} = \frac{AC}{AE} \Rightarrow \overline{DE} \parallel \overline{BC}$

Exercises *Practicing Habits of Mind*

Check Your Understanding

In Exercises 1–5, $\overline{DE} \parallel \overline{BC}$.

1. If $AD = 1$, $AB = 3$, and $AE = 2$, what is AC?

2. If $AE = 4$, $AC = 5$, and $AB = 20$, what is AD?

3. If $AD = 3$, $DB = 2$, and $AE = 12$, what is EC?

4. If $AE = 1$, $AC = 4$, and $DE = 3$, what is BC?

5. If $AD = 2$ and $DB = 6$, what is the value of $\frac{DE}{BC}$?

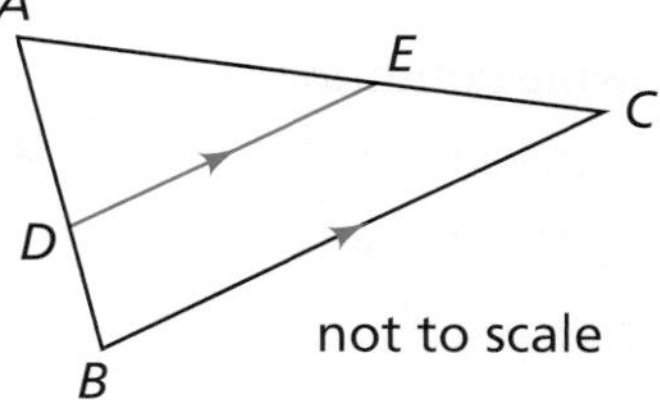

On Your Own

6. Understanding Theorems 4.1 and 4.2 by reading through their words can be difficult. It may help to replace some of the words with actual segment names. Rewrite each theorem using the nested triangles shown here as a reference. Make each theorem as specific as possible. If a theorem mentions a segment length or a proportion, substitute the name of that segment or proportion in place of the words.

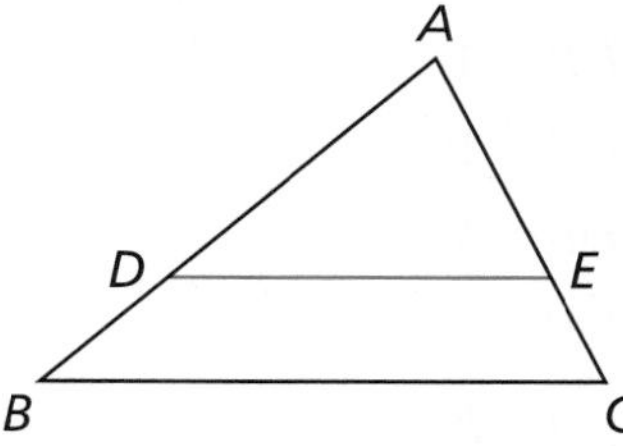

7. **Standardized Test Prep** In $\triangle ABC$, D lies on $\overline{AB}$ and E lies on $\overline{AC}$. Suppose $\overleftrightarrow{DE} \parallel \overleftrightarrow{BC}$. Which proportion is NOT correct?

A. $\frac{AD}{AB} = \frac{AE}{AC}$ **B.** $\frac{AD}{DB} = \frac{AE}{EC}$

C. $\frac{AD}{DB} = \frac{DE}{BC}$ **D.** $\frac{AD}{AB} = \frac{DE}{BC}$

8. **Write About It** The Parallel Side-Splitter Theorem says that a segment parallel to a side of a triangle with endpoints on the other two sides "splits the other two sides proportionally."

Tammy Jo has three sayings that help her remember this:

Whole is to part as whole is to part.

Part is to part as part is to part.

Part is to whole as part is to whole.

What do these sayings mean?

Maintain Your Skills

For Exercises 9 and 10, use the figure at the right. $\overline{DE} \parallel \overline{BC}$.

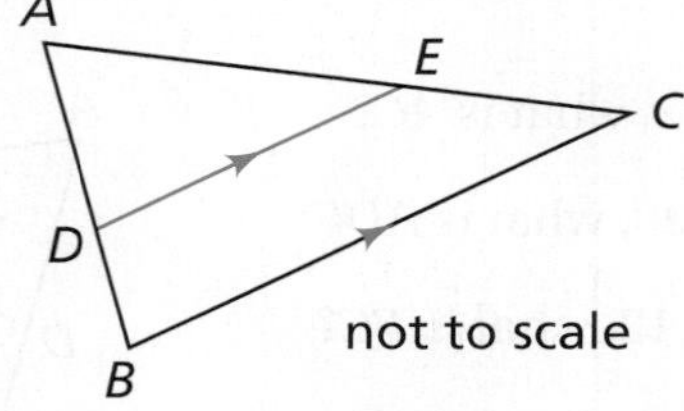

9. Find EC given the following conditions.
   a. $AD = 1$, $DB = 4$, and $AE = 3$
   b. $AD = 1$, $DB = 4$, and $AE = 7$
   c. $AD = 1$, $DB = 7$, and $AE = 4$
   d. $AD = 1$, $DB = 10$, and $AE = 10$
   e. $AD = 1$, $DB = \frac{1}{2}$, and $AE = 3$
   f. $AD = 1$, $DB = x$, and $AE = y$

10. Find EC given the following conditions.
   a. $AE = 1$, $AD = 4$, and $DB = 8$
   b. $AE = 1$, $AD = 8$, and $DB = 4$
   c. $AE = 1$, $AD = 2$, and $DB = 10$
   d. $AE = 1$, $AD = 2$, and $DB = \frac{1}{2}$
   e. $AE = 1$, $AD = \frac{1}{2}$, and $DB = 2$
   f. $AE = 1$, $AD = x$, and $DB = y$

Go Online
Pearsonsuccessnet.com

4.11 Proving the Side-Splitter Theorems

Recall what the first part of the Parallel Side-Splitter Theorem says:

> If a segment with endpoints on two sides of a triangle is parallel to the third side of the triangle, then it splits the sides it intersects proportionally.

To begin the proof of this theorem, you can show that, in the figure below, if $\overline{VW} \parallel \overline{RT}$, then $\frac{SV}{VR} = \frac{SW}{WT}$.

In the figures below, triangles *SVW* and *RVW* have the same height. This means that the ratio of their areas is equal to the ratio of their base lengths, *SV* and *VR*.

This fact comes from Lesson 4.09.

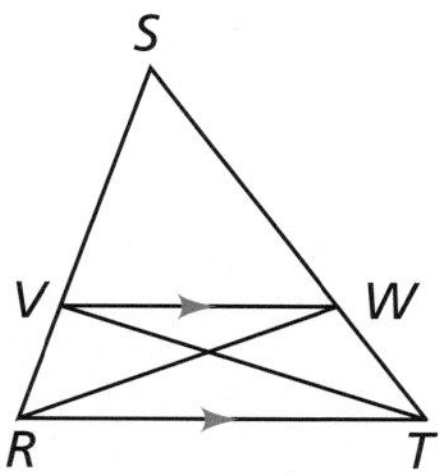

$$\frac{\text{area}(\triangle SVW)}{\text{area}(\triangle RVW)} = \frac{SV}{VR}$$

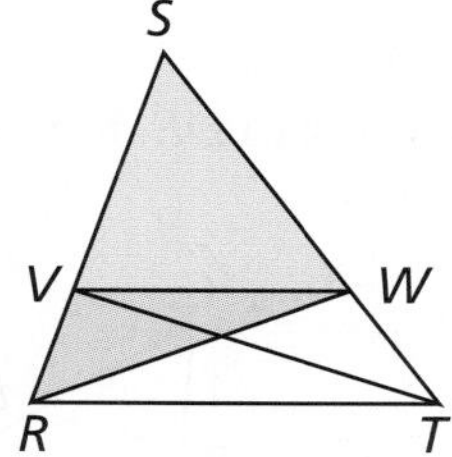

In the figures below, triangles *SVW* and *TVW* have the same height. Thus, the ratio of their areas is equal to the ratio of their base lengths, *SW* and *WT*.

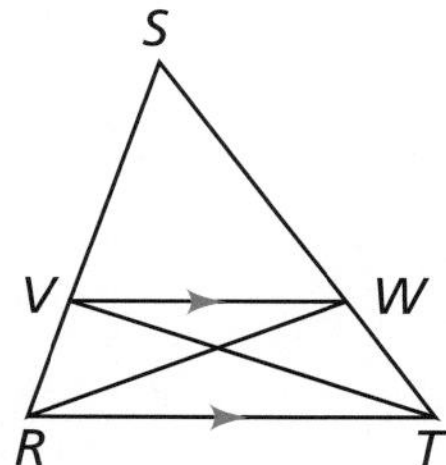

$$\frac{\text{area}(\triangle SVW)}{\text{area}(\triangle TVW)} = \frac{SW}{WT}$$

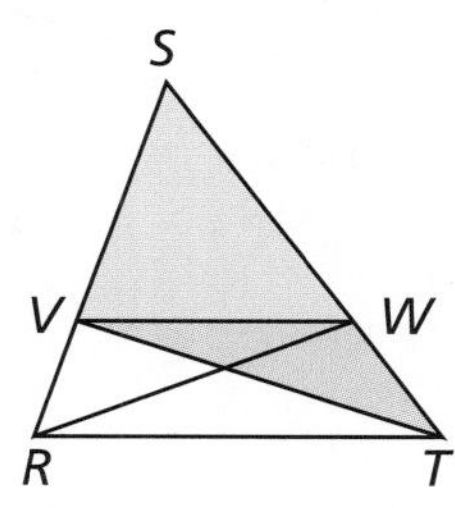

Habits of Mind

Understand the process. A "tidy" proof like this may not necessarily be easy to write. You build it from many notes, sketches, erasures, more sketches, more notes, and plenty of talking to yourself!

You have two fractions with the same numerator,

$$\frac{\text{area}(\triangle SVW)}{\text{area}(\triangle RVW)} \text{ and } \frac{\text{area}(\triangle SVW)}{\text{area}(\triangle TVW)}.$$

The denominators are not the same, but are they equal? Recall Problem 1 from Lesson 4.09. Triangles *RVW* and *TVW* share the same base $\overline{VW}$. They have the same height, since $\overline{VW}$ is parallel to $\overline{RT}$. So they have the same area.

You can combine all of these results to draw a conclusion about *SV*, *VR*, *SW*, and *WT*.

$$\frac{SV}{VR} = \frac{\text{area}(\triangle SVW)}{\text{area}(\triangle RVW)} = \frac{\text{area}(\triangle SVW)}{\text{area}(\triangle TVW)} = \frac{SW}{WT}$$

For You to Do

1. Using what has been outlined in this lesson, write a complete proof of the first part of the Parallel Side-Splitter Theorem.

Exercises *Practicing Habits of Mind*

Check Your Understanding

1. Recall the Proportional Side-Splitter Theorem:

If a segment with endpoints on two sides of a triangle splits those sides proportionally, then the segment is parallel to the third side.

This time, the proof is up to you. Use the same setup that you used to prove the Parallel Side-Splitter Theorem. Write your proof so that someone else can follow it.

2. In the diagrams below, $\overline{AB}$ is parallel to $\overline{DE}$. Find as many lengths as you can.

a.

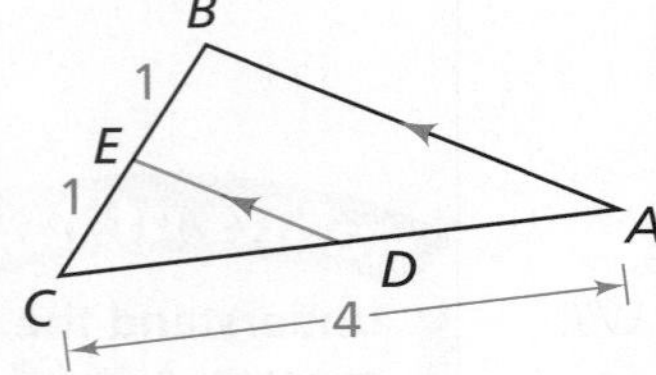

b.

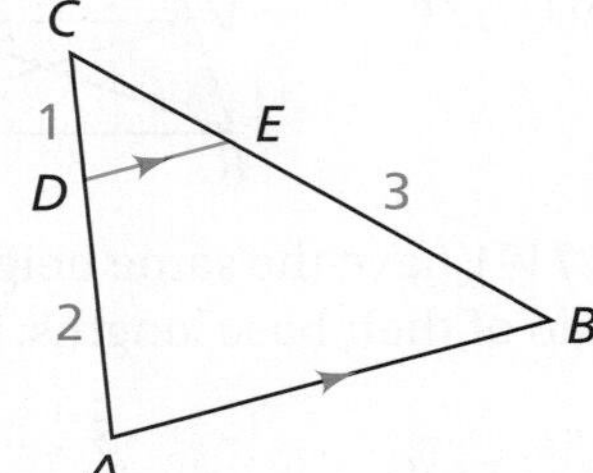

c.

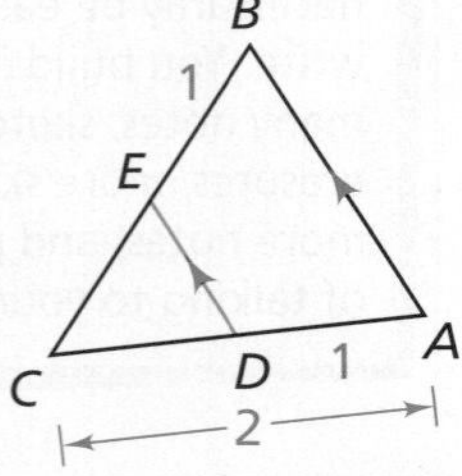

The main entrance to the Rock and Roll Hall of Fame is at the base of this glass-and-steel triangle. Can you find horizontal steel ribbing in the triangle that is half the length of the base? Three fourths the length of the base?

3. Use the lengths given in each figure below to decide whether $\overline{AB}$ is parallel to $\overline{DE}$. Explain.

a.

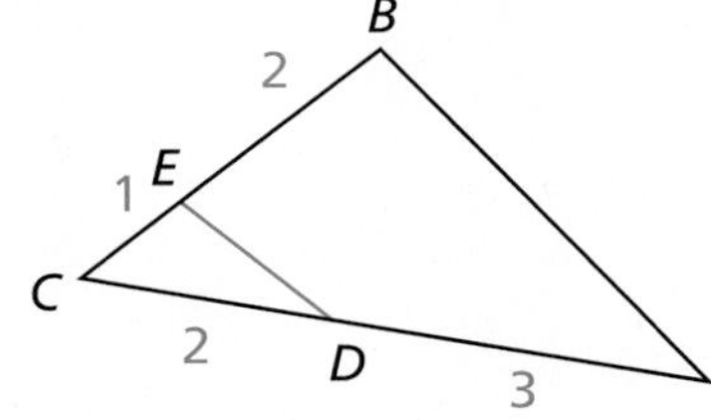

b.

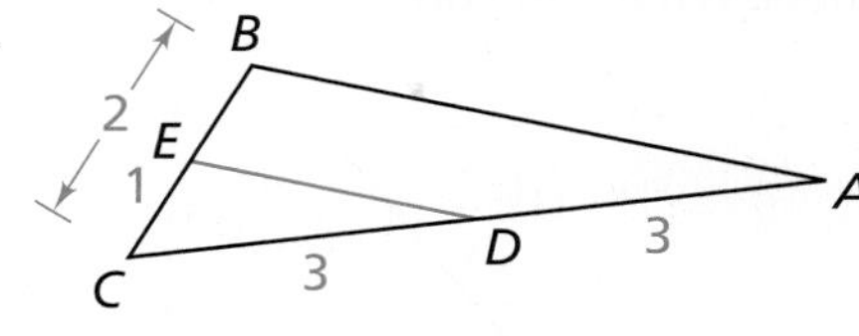

c.

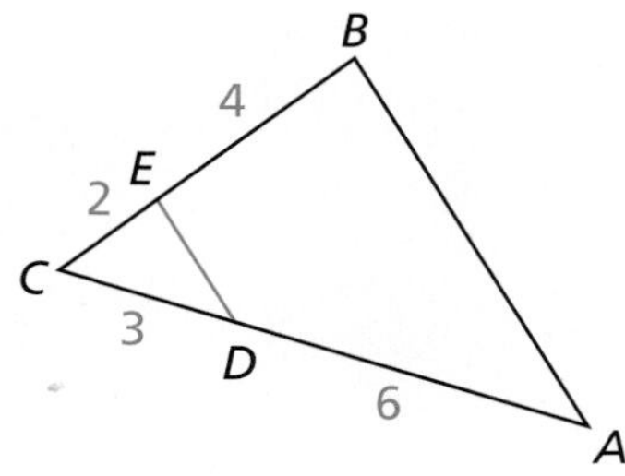

On Your Own

4. **Standardized Test Prep** In $\triangle STR$, U lies on $\overline{SR}$, V lies on $\overline{RT}$, and $\overline{VU} \parallel \overline{TS}$. Suppose that $TS = 540$, $VU = 180$, $US = 667$, and $RT = 600$. What is RV?

A. 200 **B.** 240 **C.** 270 **D.** 333

5. The dashed lines in the figure are all parallel to $\overline{AC}$ and equally spaced. What can you conclude about how they intersect $\overline{AB}$ and $\overline{BC}$?

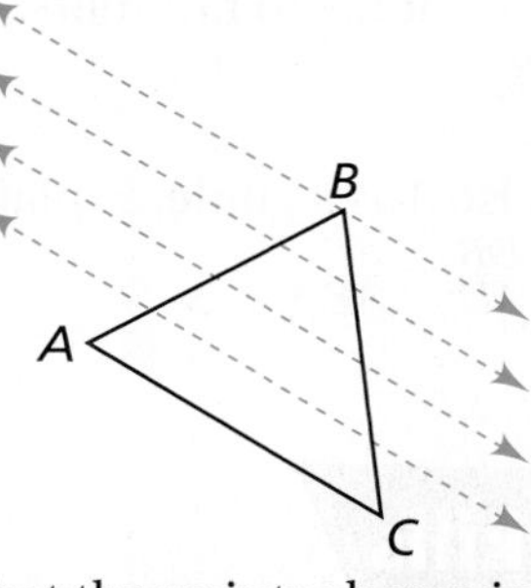

6. Make two copies of the diagram below. Use the fact that the points shown in red trisect $\overline{BC}$ to do the following.

a. Trisect $\overline{AB}$.

b. Trisect $\overline{AC}$.

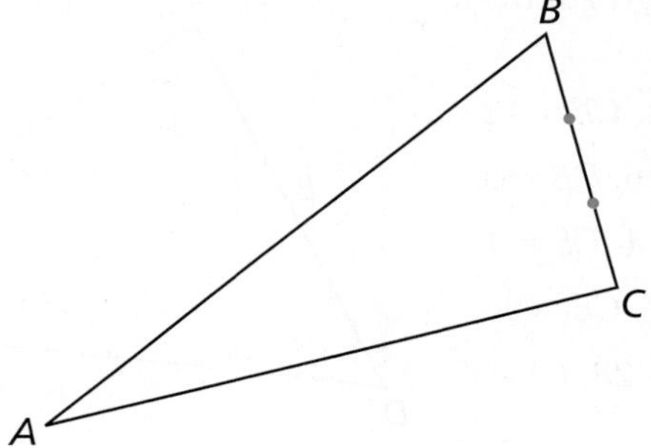

Habits of Mind

Make connections. How does the definition of *bisect* help you define *trisect*?

7. Both $\overline{AB}$ and $\overline{BC}$ are cut into five equal-length segments by the dashed lines. What can you conclude?

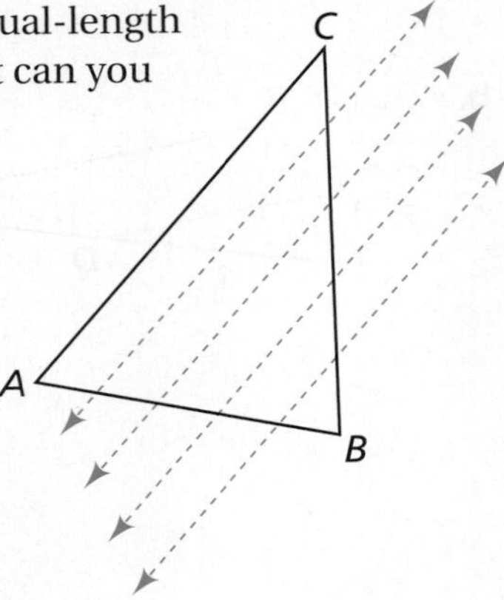

The first part of the Parallel Side-Splitter Theorem tells you that two sides of a triangle are split proportionally. By now, you should suspect that there are several proportions possible, such as $\frac{AB}{AD} = \frac{AC}{AE}$ and $\frac{DB}{AD} = \frac{EC}{AE}$ in the triangle at the right.

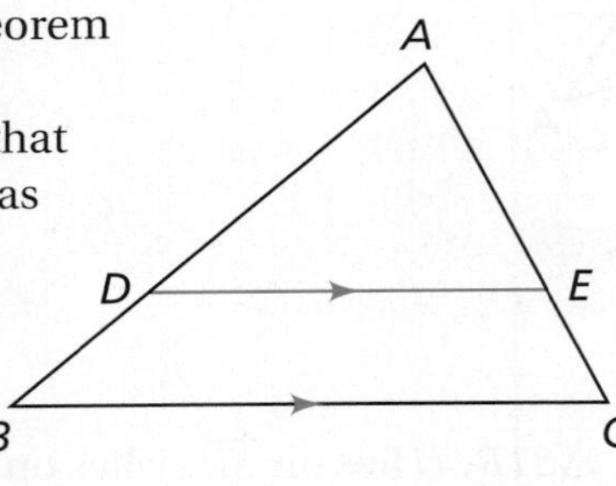

Exercises 8 and 9 show how to prove that these proportions are two different ways of writing the same information.

8. **Take It Further** First, you can prove a related fact using algebra. Suppose that r, s, t, and u are any four nonzero numbers. If $\frac{r}{s} = \frac{t}{u}$, explain why it is also true that $\frac{r - s}{s} = \frac{t - u}{u}$.

Hint: $\frac{r - s}{s} = \frac{r}{s} - \frac{s}{s}$

9. **Take It Further** Use Exercise 8 as a guide. Explain how the proportion $\frac{AB}{AD} = \frac{AC}{AE}$ leads directly to $\frac{DB}{AD} = \frac{EC}{AE}$.

Maintain Your Skills

10. Does the given information guarantee that $\overline{BC} \parallel \overline{DE}$?

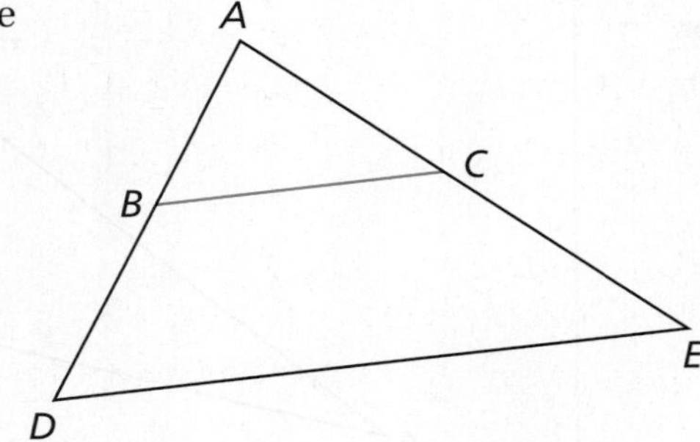

a. $AB = 1$, $BD = 4$, $AC = 3$, $CE = 12$

b. $AB = 8$, $BD = 4$, $AC = 16$, $CE = 8$

c. $AB = 3$, $BD = 12$, $AC = 4$, $CE = 1$

d. $AB = 7$, $BD = 3$, $AC = 7$, $CE = 8$

e. $AB = 0.5$, $BD = 7$, $AC = 28$, $CE = 2$

Go Online
Pearsonsuccessnet.com

4.12 The Side-Splitter Theorems (continued)

Now you will finish proving the Parallel Side-Splitter Theorem. Recall that the theorem says

If $\overline{VW}$ is parallel to $\overline{RT}$, then $\frac{SR}{SV} = \frac{ST}{SW} = \frac{RT}{VW}$.

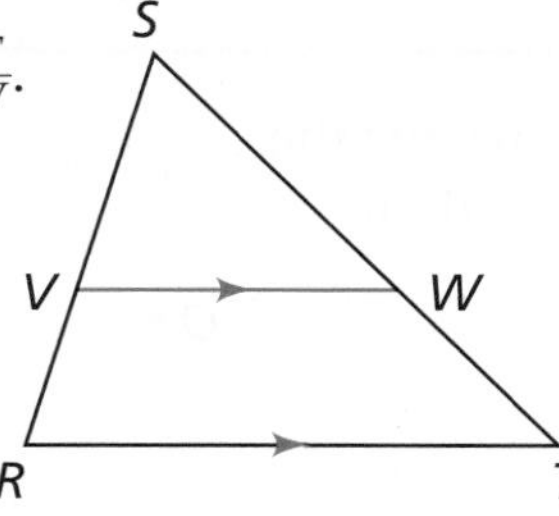

In Lesson 4.11, you proved that $\frac{SV}{VR} = \frac{SW}{WT}$. You can use this to show that $\frac{SR}{SV} = \frac{ST}{SW}$.

$$\frac{SV}{VR} = \frac{SW}{WT}$$

$$\frac{VR}{SV} = \frac{WT}{SW}$$

$$1 + \frac{VR}{SV} = 1 + \frac{WT}{SW}$$

$$\frac{SV}{SV} + \frac{VR}{SV} = \frac{SW}{SW} + \frac{WT}{SW}$$

$$\frac{SV + VR}{SV} = \frac{SW + WT}{SW}$$

$$\frac{SR}{SV} = \frac{ST}{SW}$$

In-Class Experiment

Trace and make paper cutouts of $\triangle SVW$ and $\triangle SRT$. Place them on top of each other. Slide $\triangle SVW$ along $\overline{SR}$ until vertices V and R coincide.

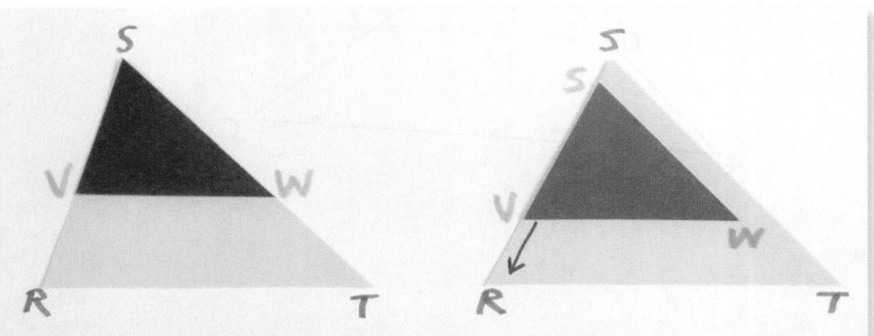

1. Why does $\angle SVW$ fall precisely on top of $\angle SRT$?
2. Draw a picture of how the triangles look after you slide $\triangle SVW$ to $\overline{RT}$.
3. Which two segments are now parallel? Explain.

For You to Do

4. Use the setup from the In-Class Experiment to prove the last part of the Parallel Side-Splitter Theorem—namely, that $\frac{RT}{VW}$ equals both $\frac{SR}{SV}$ and $\frac{ST}{SW}$.

For Discussion

5. Show that if $\overline{AB}$ is dilated from O using first the ratio method and then the parallel method, you get the same result.

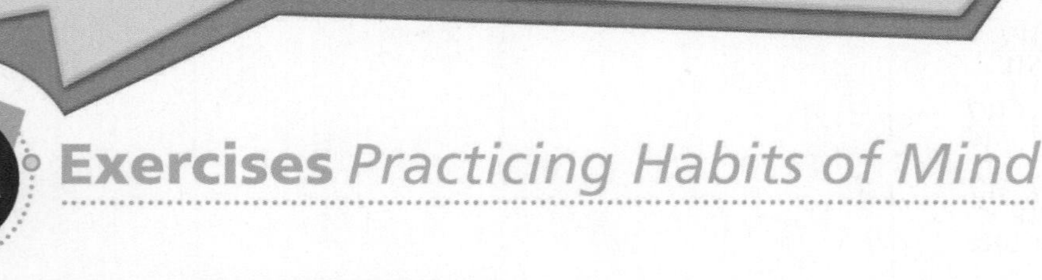

Check Your Understanding

In Exercises 1–3, $\overline{AC} \parallel \overline{DE}$. Copy the diagrams. Find as many lengths as you can.

1.

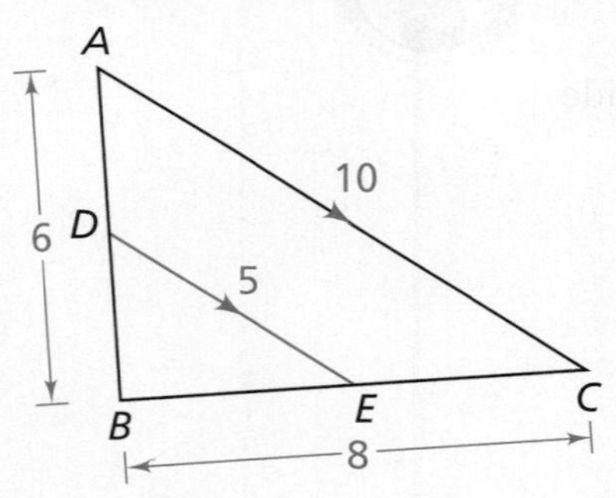

2.

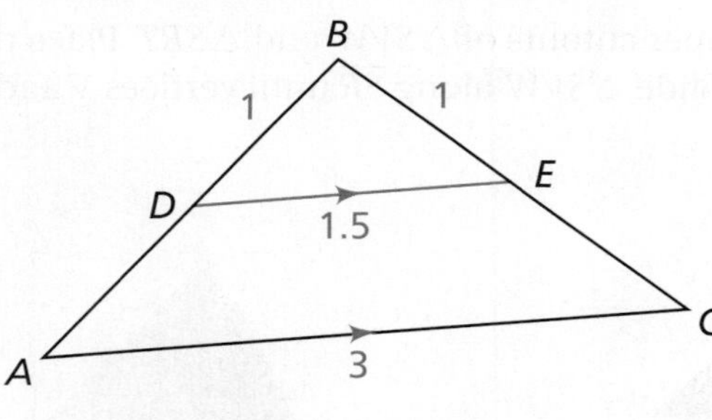

3.

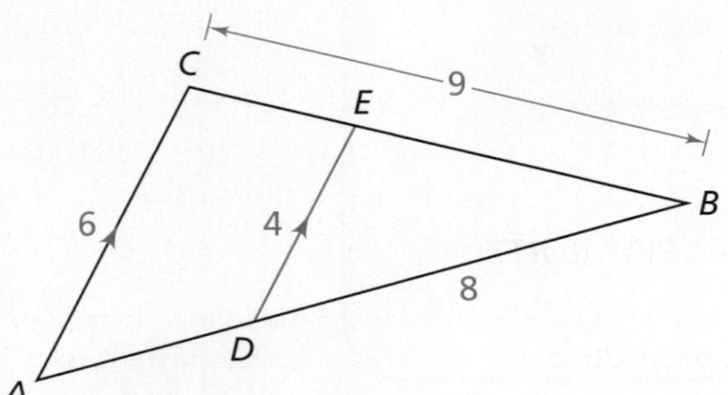

On Your Own

4. Use the side-splitter theorems. Explain why the two rectangles in each figure below are scaled copies of each other.

a.

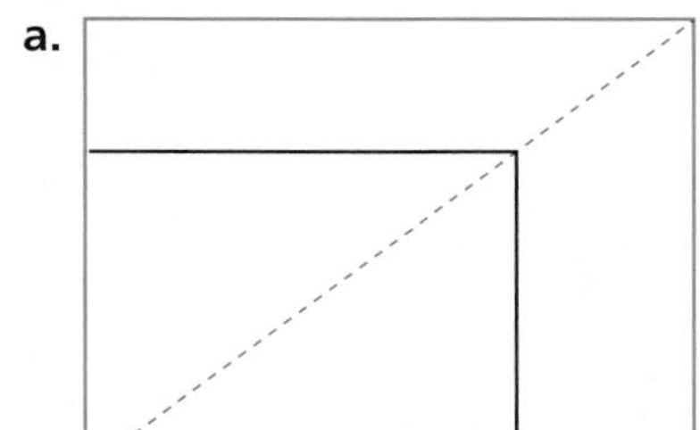

b.

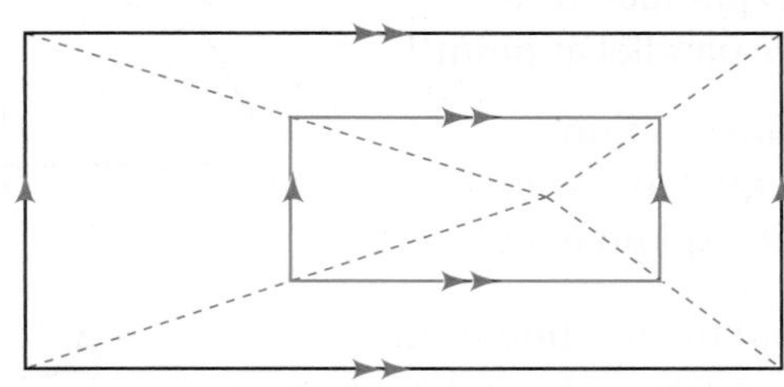

5. In the triangle shown here, $\overline{DE} \parallel \overline{BC}$. Explain why $\triangle ABC$ is a scaled copy of $\triangle ADE$.

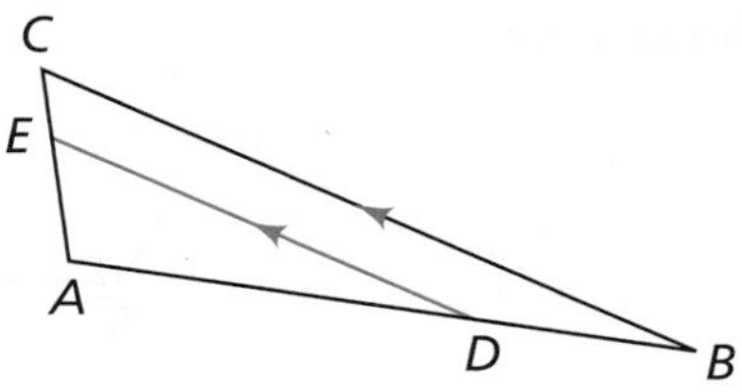

6. You draw the sides of the outer polygon parallel to the sides of the inner polygon as shown at the right. Explain why the polygons are scaled copies.

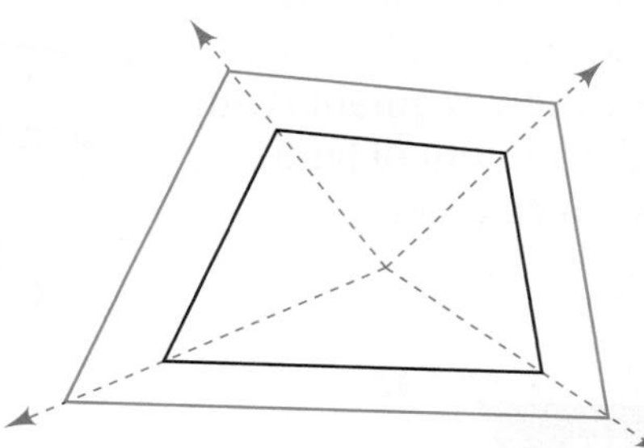

7. **Standardized Test Prep** Suppose $\triangle ABC$ is a scaled copy of $\triangle BED$. Which of the following lists the congruent corresponding angles of these two triangles?

A. $\angle A \cong \angle DBE$, $\angle ABC \cong \angle BDE$, $\angle C \cong \angle DEB$

B. $\angle A \cong \angle DBE$, $\angle ABC \cong \angle BED$, $\angle C \cong \angle BDE$

C. $\angle A \cong \angle DBE$, $\angle ABC \cong \angle BED$, $\angle B \cong \angle BDE$

D. $\angle A \cong \angle DBE$, $\angle ABC \cong \angle BDE$, $\angle C \cong \angle DEB$

How might you extend the idea of nested triangles to nested circles? What proportional relationships do nested circles suggest? Find out in Lesson 5.09.

8. Take It Further Here is a way to construct $\triangle ABE$ to have the same area as quadrilateral *ABCD*, without taking any measurements.

First, draw diagonal $\overline{AC}$. Then draw a line through point *D* parallel to $\overline{AC}$. Extend $\overline{BC}$ to meet the parallel at point *E*.

This completes the construction. The area of $\triangle ABE$ is equal to the area of quadrilateral *ABCD*. Explain why.

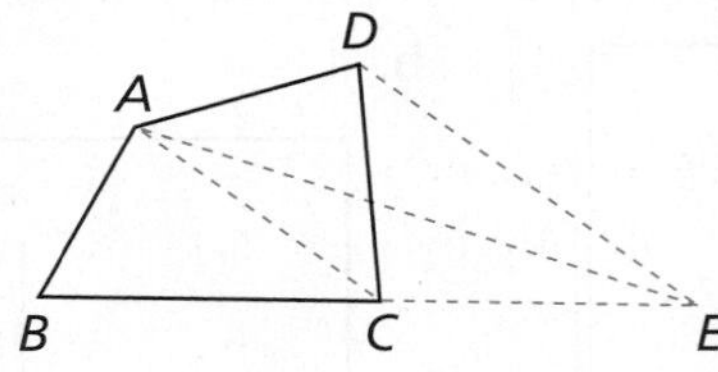

9. Take It Further Extend the method used in Exercise 8. Construct a triangle with area equal to that of pentagon *ABCDE* shown here.

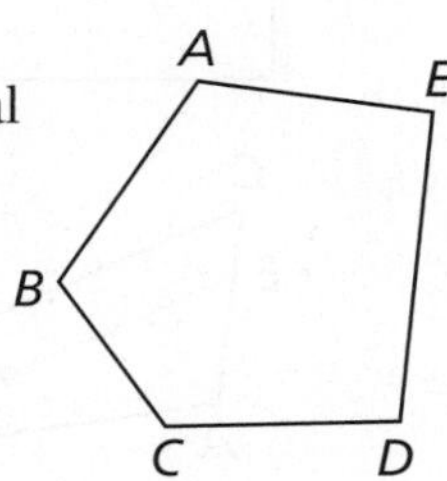

10. Take It Further $\overline{AB}$ and $\overline{BC}$ represent the border between land owned by Wendy and land owned by Juan. How can you replace these segments with a single segment such that the amount of land owned by each person does not change? Justify your answer.

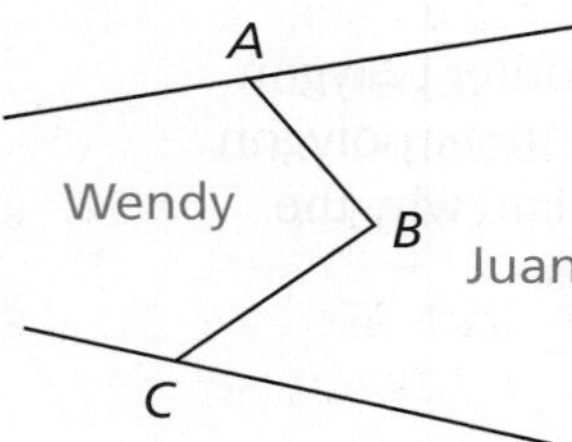

Maintain Your Skills

11. Decide whether $\overline{AB}$ is parallel to $\overline{DE}$. In each case, give a reason for your decision. The triangles are not necessarily drawn to scale.

a.

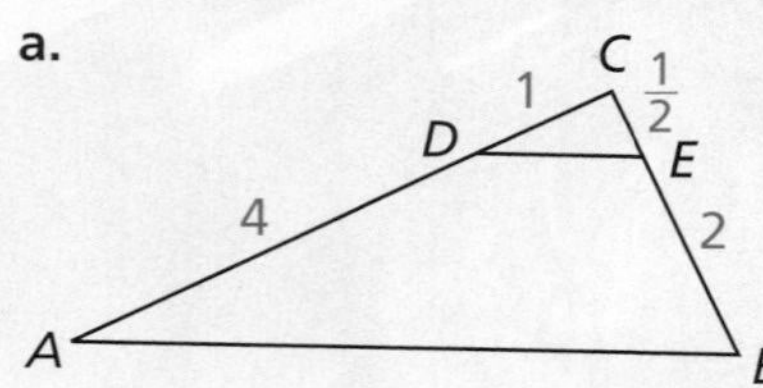

b.

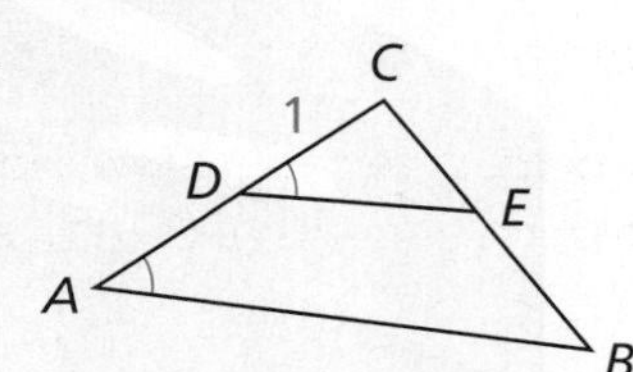

c.

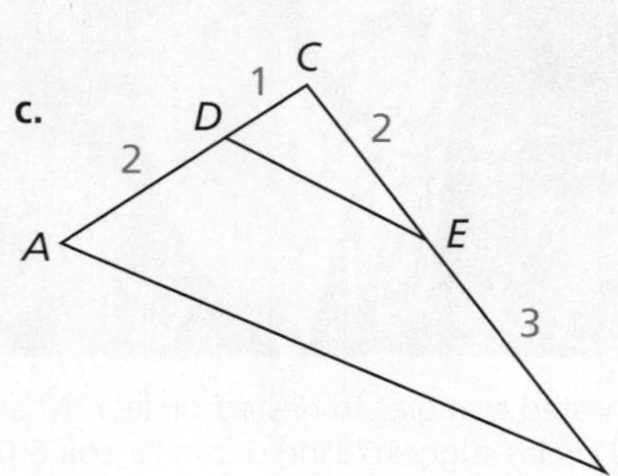

d.

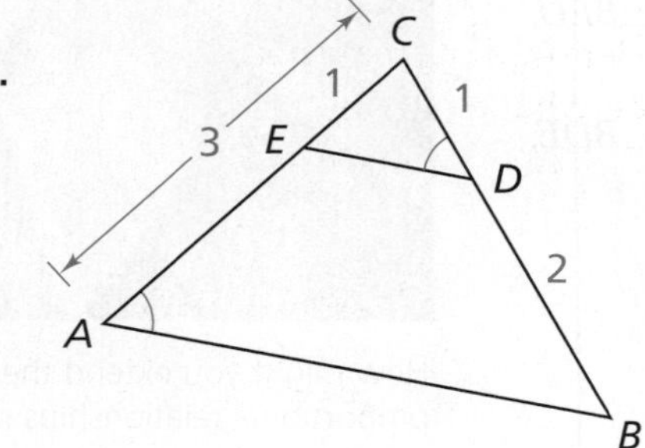

In this investigation, you explored parallels and proportions in nested triangles. You proved the side-splitter theorems. These questions will help you summarize what you have learned.

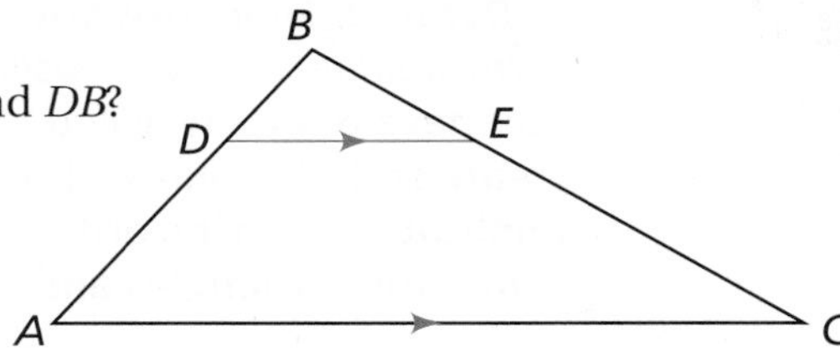

1. In $\triangle ABC$, $\overline{DE} \parallel \overline{AC}$, $DB = \frac{1}{3}AB$, $AB = 6$, $BE = 3$, and $AC = 12$. What are BC, DE, and DB?

2. $EFGH$ is a quadrilateral. $CH = \frac{1}{3}HE$, $HD = \frac{1}{3}HG$, $AF = \frac{1}{4}EF$, and $BF = \frac{1}{4}FG$. Prove that $\overline{AB} \parallel \overline{CD}$.

3. Use the side-splitter theorems to prove the Midline Theorem.

4. Suppose you want to scale a segment, $\overline{AB}$, by the factor $\frac{1}{3}$ and use a point O not on $\overline{AB}$ as the center of dilation. Describe each step you would use. Give a reason for each step.

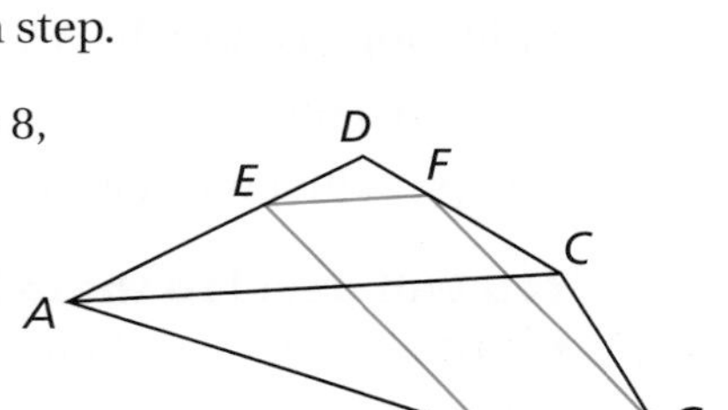

5. In the diagram at the right, $AD = 24$, $ED = 8$, $DC = 21$, and $DF = 7$. $\triangle HBG$ is a scaled copy of $\triangle ABC$ such that its area is $\frac{1}{9}$ the area of $\triangle ABC$. Prove that $EFGH$ is a parallelogram.

6. If a point D is on side $\overline{AB}$ of $\triangle ABC$, E is on $\overline{AC}$, and $\overline{DE}$ is parallel to $\overline{BC}$, then what can you say about the relationship between $\triangle ABC$ and $\triangle ADE$?

7. What are the side-splitter theorems?

8. If two triangles have the same height, and you know the ratio of their areas, what is the ratio of the lengths of their bases?

Vocabulary

In this investigation, you learned these terms. Make sure you understand what each one means and how to use it.

- **common ratio**
- **nested triangles**
- **splits two sides proportionally**

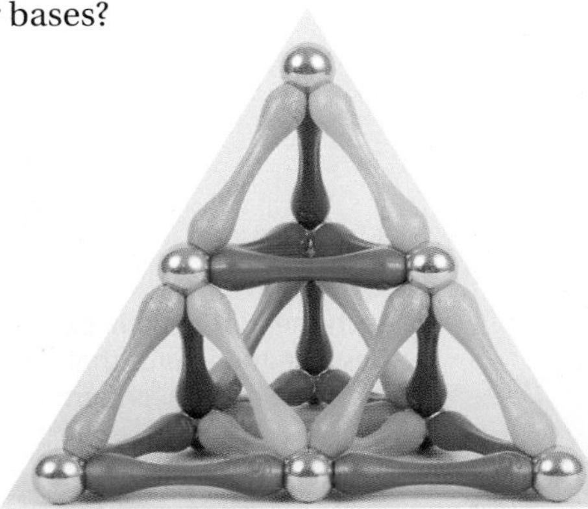

The Midline Theorem is a special case of the side-splitter theorems.

Defining Similarity

In *Defining Similarity,* you formally define the mathematical term *similar.* You will closely tie its definition to all the work you have done on scaled copies. Your ability to recognize and create scaled copies will be very useful. You will learn the implications of similarity. You will also learn how to test for similarity in triangles and other figures.

By the end of this investigation, you will be able to answer questions like these.

1. What does it mean for two figures to be similar?

2. What are some tests for triangle similarity?

3. If the common ratio of two similar figures is r, what is the ratio of their areas?

You will learn how to

- identify corresponding parts of similar triangles
- develop and use the AA, SAS, and SSS tests for similarity in triangles
- understand that the ratio between the area of a polygon and the area of a copy of that polygon scaled by the factor r will be r^2

You will develop these habits and skills:

- Visualize similar triangles.
- Look for invariant ratios.
- Make logical inferences to prove similarity.

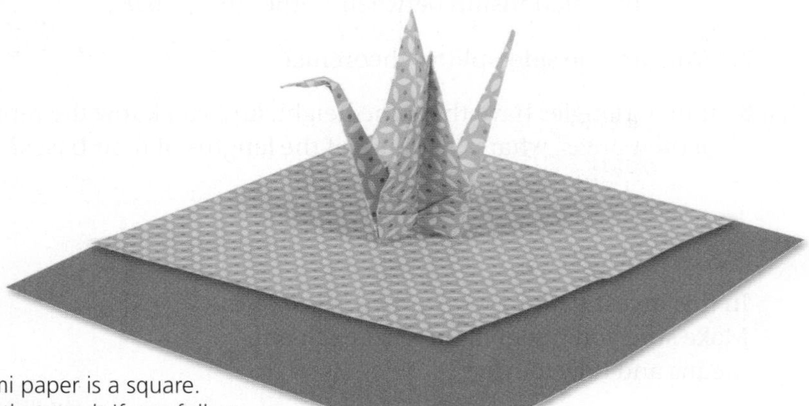

Each sheet of origami paper is a square. Describe the figures that result if you follow the same origami pattern to fold each sheet.

4.13 Getting Started

Words such as *enlargements, reductions, scale factors,* and *dilations* are some of the terms you have met again and again in this chapter.

The common theme uniting them is called *similarity.* By enlarging or reducing a picture, you make another picture that is similar to the first. One way to define *similar figures* in geometry is as follows.

- Two figures are similar if one is a scaled copy of the other.

The ratio method suggests another possible definition.

- Two figures are similar if one is a dilation of the other.

You can use dilation to refer to the dilation image when this meaning is clear in context.

To test this definition, look at the picture of the head of Trig the horse. Trig is accompanied here by his little sister, Girt. Girt is smaller than Trig but her head shares all of his features.

For You to Explore

1. Is Girt a dilated copy of Trig? If so, find the center of dilation.
2. Is the picture of Girt similar to the picture of Trig?

Here is another family portrait of Trig and Girt, this time in a different pose.

3. Is the picture of Girt still similar to the picture of Trig?
4. Can you still dilate one picture onto the other? Explain.
5. Expand the dilation definition of similar so you can say that even these two pictures are similar.

Exercises *Practicing Habits of Mind*

On Your Own

6. Look at your notes for Investigation 4A. Write your test for telling whether two figures are scaled copies of each other.

7. These two triangles are scaled copies of each other. List the angle measurements that are equal and the side lengths that are proportional.

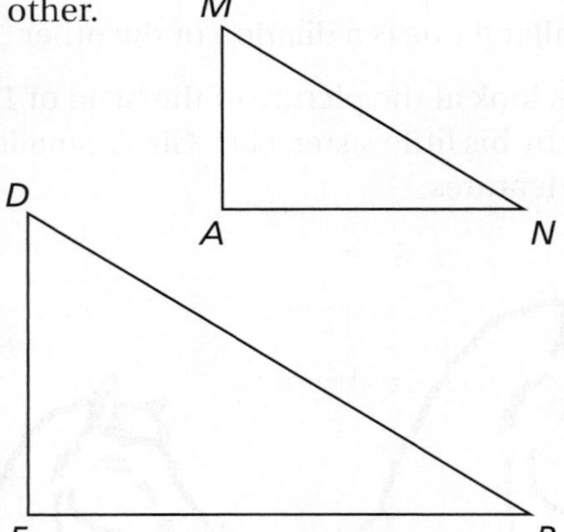

8. If two polygons are dilations of each other, describe how to find the center of dilation. Is that center unique?

9. Will you always be able to find a center of dilation for two similar polygons? If so, describe how to do it. If not, sketch a counterexample.

Maintain Your Skills

10. Use a standard rectangular sheet of paper that measures $8\frac{1}{2}$ in. by 11 in. For parts (a)–(d) below, fold the paper in half the given number of times by matching the two shorter sides. When done folding, do the following.

- Unfold the paper.
- Count the number of rectangles that are formed.
- Find the dimensions of each rectangle.
- Decide whether each rectangle is similar to the shape of the original sheet of paper.

a. Make one fold.

b. Make two folds.

c. Make three folds.

d. Make four folds.

e. Some numbers of folds produce rectangles that are similar to the shape of the original sheet of paper. What do these numbers have in common?

4.14 Similar Figures

Here are some suggestions for ways to define similar figures using dilation terminology.

Definitions

- **Two figures are similar if you can rotate and/or flip one of them so that you can dilate it onto the other.**
- **Two figures are similar if one is congruent to a dilation of the other.**

For Discussion

In Lesson 4.13, you tried to extend a dilation definition of similarity so that it would work with the second family portrait of Trig and Girt.

1. Do the two definitions above solve any problems you may have had?
2. Are the two definitions above equivalent?

Developing Habits of Mind

Consider the converse. If two figures are congruent, are they similar? If two figures are similar, are they congruent?

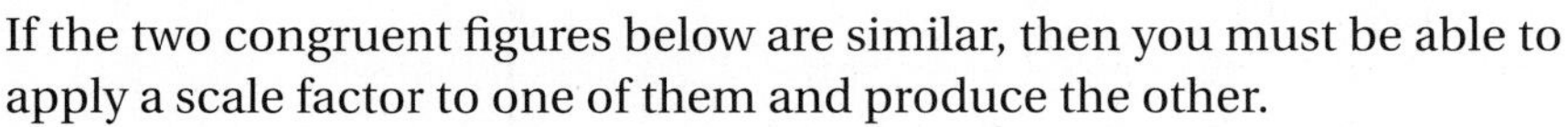

If the two congruent figures below are similar, then you must be able to apply a scale factor to one of them and produce the other.

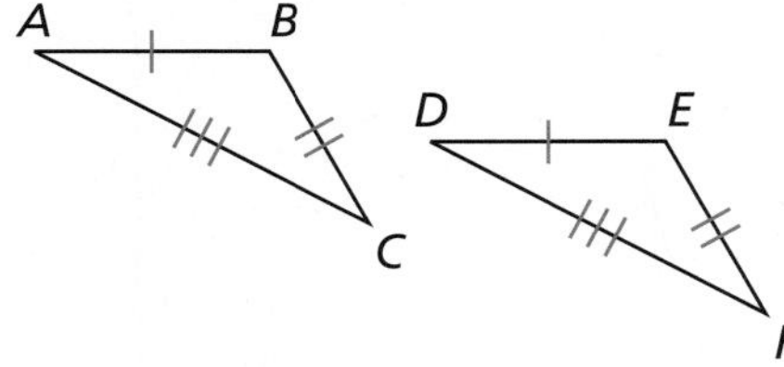

In this case, a scale factor of 1 applied to $\triangle ABC$ will produce $\triangle DEF$. But here are two similar figures that are obviously not congruent.

The symbol for similarity, ~, is the upper part of the symbol ≅ for congruence. Thus, you read the statement $ABCD \sim EFGH$ as "$ABCD$ is similar to $EFGH$." It means that the two polygons are scaled copies of each other.

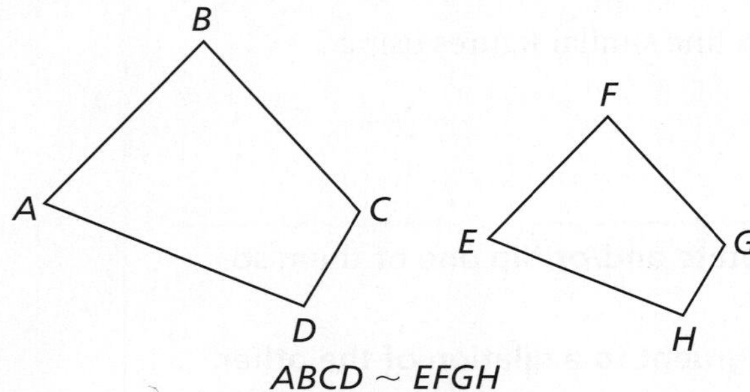

$ABCD \sim EFGH$

The similarity symbol, ~, means "has the same shape as," and the congruence symbol, ≅, means "has the same shape *and* the same size as."

For congruent triangles, the statement $\triangle ABC \cong \triangle XYZ$ conveys specific information about their corresponding parts. For figures that are similar, the order of their vertex letters also specifies which parts correspond, but the conclusions you draw will be different.

Remember...

When you say $\triangle ABC \cong \triangle XYZ$, you can draw many conclusions about congruence. Which segments are congruent to each other? Which angles are congruent?

For You to Do

$\triangle ABC \sim \triangle XYZ$ and $ABCDE \sim PQRST$. Copy the figures. Label the vertices of $\triangle XYZ$ and $PQRST$ correctly.

3.

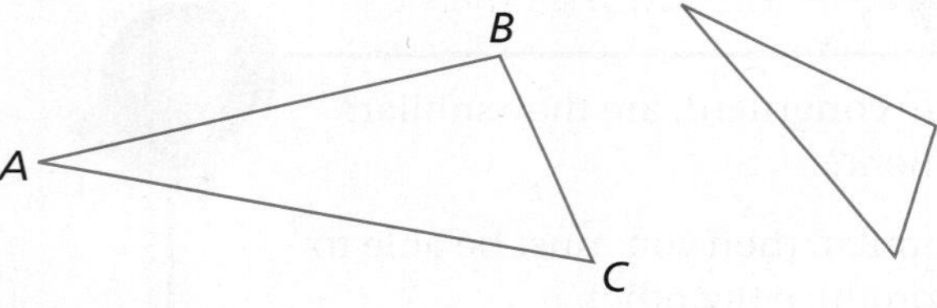

4.

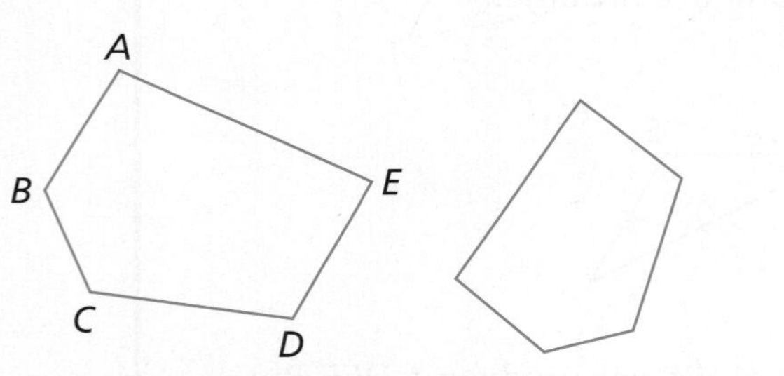

In Investigation 4A, you devised several ways to test whether two triangles are similar. (Only then, you used the phrase *scaled copies.*) One test was probably the following.

> Two triangles are similar (scaled copies) if their corresponding angles are congruent and their corresponding sides are proportional.

For future reference, you can call this the Congruent Angles, Proportional Sides test.

Using the word *dilation,* here is another test for similar triangles.

Two triangles are similar if one is congruent to a dilation of the other.

You can refer to this as the Congruent to a Dilation test.

For You to Do

5. Suppose that $\triangle NEW \sim \triangle OLD$. If $m\angle N = 19^\circ$ and $m\angle L = 67^\circ$, find the measures of the other angles.

Exercises *Practicing Habits of Mind*

Check Your Understanding

1. Is each given similarity statement true or false? Take measurements to decide. Explain your answer.

a. $ABCD \sim EFGH$

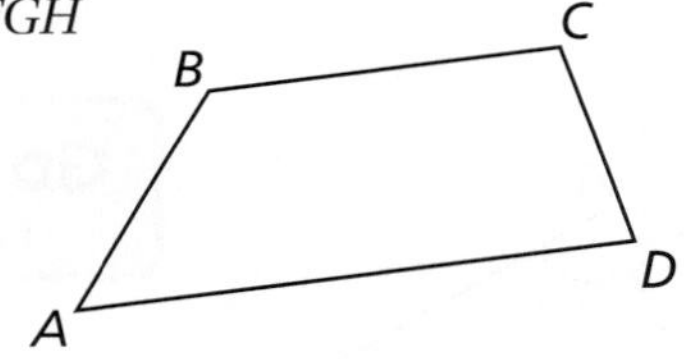

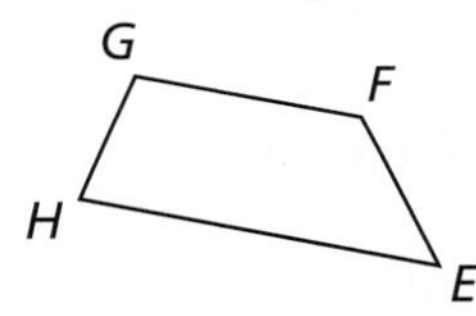

b. $ABCD \sim EFGH$

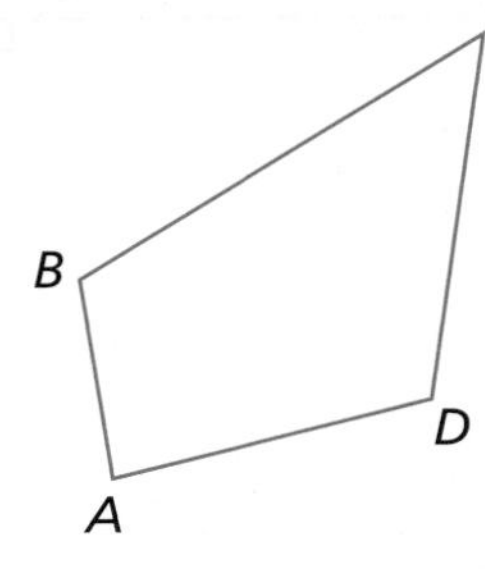

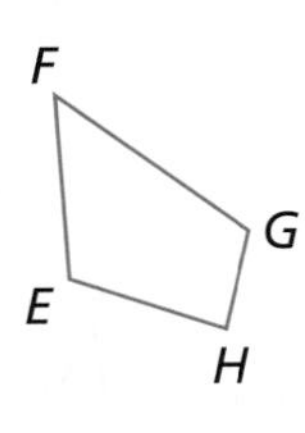

c. $\triangle ABC \sim \triangle DEF$

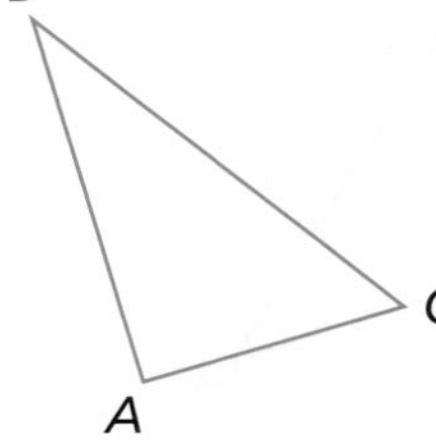

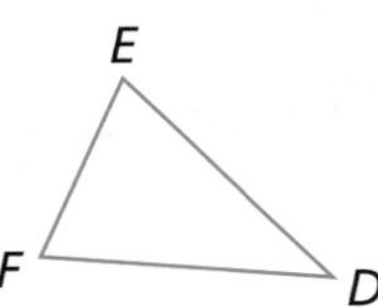

2. Suppose $\triangle ABC \sim \triangle DEF$. Must each statement be true?

a. $\frac{AB}{DE} = \frac{BC}{EF}$

b. $\frac{AC}{BC} = \frac{DF}{EF}$

c. $\frac{BC}{AB} = \frac{DF}{DE}$

d. $AC \cdot DE = AB \cdot DF$

3. In the figure below, $\triangle ABC \sim \triangle BDA$. Explain why $\triangle ABC$ is isosceles.

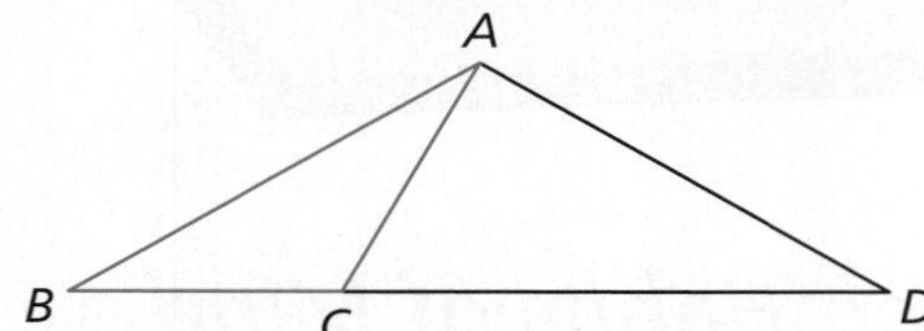

Habits of Mind

Think it through. Recall some conditions for a triangle to be isosceles.

4. In the figure at the right, F, G, and H are midpoints of the sides of $\triangle ABC$. Show that $\triangle ABC \sim \triangle GHF$.

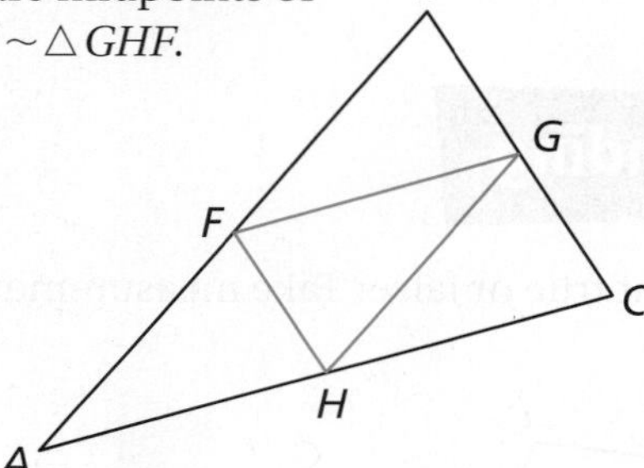

5. Make a large copy of the figure from Exercise 3. On your copy, mark the measurements shown at the right. Then fill in the rest of the angle measures and side lengths.

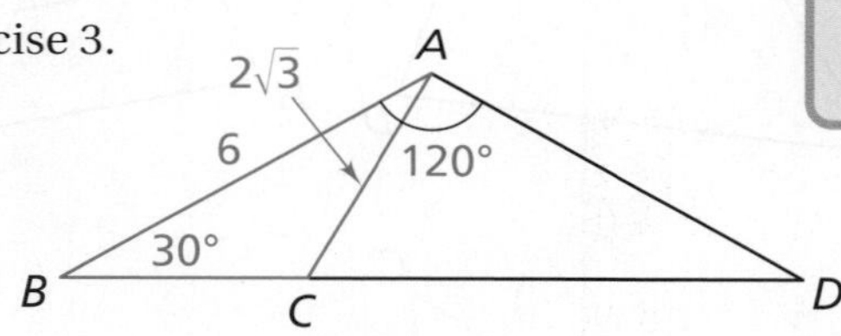

Go Online
Pearsonsuccessnet.com

On Your Own

6. In the figure, $\triangle ABC \sim \triangle CDE$.

Decide whether each statement is correct or incorrect.

a. $\triangle ABC \sim \triangle DEC$

b. $\triangle BCA \sim \triangle DEC$

c. $\triangle BAC \sim \triangle DEC$

d. $\triangle CAB \sim \triangle ECD$

e. $\triangle CBA \sim \triangle ECD$

f. $\triangle CBA \sim \triangle CDE$

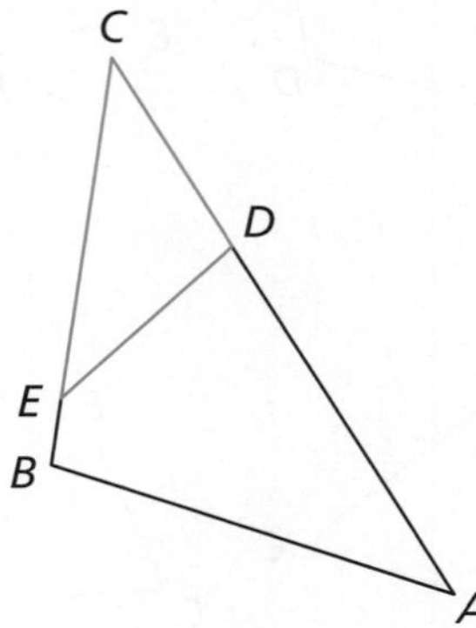

7. $\triangle QRS \sim \triangle VUT$.

Decide whether each statement is correct or incorrect.

a. $\frac{QR}{TU} = \frac{SR}{TV}$ b. $\frac{QR}{SR} = \frac{TU}{TV}$

c. $\frac{QR}{QS} = \frac{UV}{TV}$ d. $\frac{QT}{QV} = \frac{RT}{TU}$

e. $\frac{QR}{TV} = \frac{SR}{TU}$ f. $\frac{QS}{VT} = \frac{RS}{UT}$

8. $\triangle CAT \sim \triangle DOT$.

Complete each statement.

a. $\angle C \cong$ __?__ b. $\angle CTA \cong$ __?__

c. $\angle DTO \cong$ __?__ d. $\angle A \cong$ __?__

e. $\angle D \cong$ __?__ f. $\angle O \cong$ __?__

9. **Standardized Test Prep** In the figure at the right, $\triangle ABC \sim \triangle BED$. Which length correctly completes the following proportion?

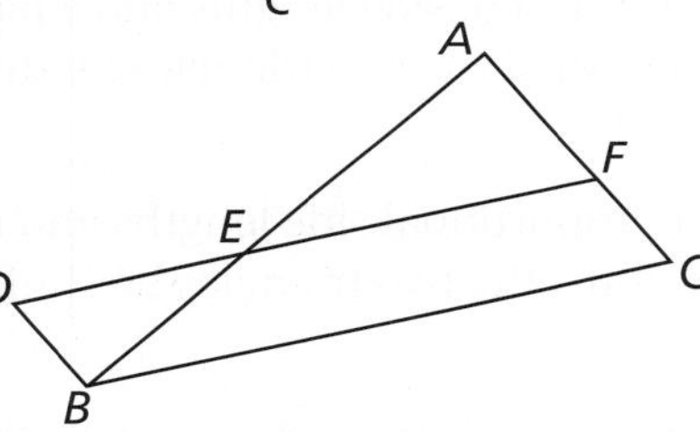

$$\frac{AB}{BE} = \frac{AC}{\blacksquare}$$

A. BD **B.** ED **C.** BC **D.** EB

Maintain Your Skills

10. $\triangle PLU \sim \triangle ABC$. Find AC and BC for each of the given lengths of AB.

a. $AB = 1$ b. $AB = 2$

c. $AB = 3$ d. $AB = 4$

e. $AB = x$

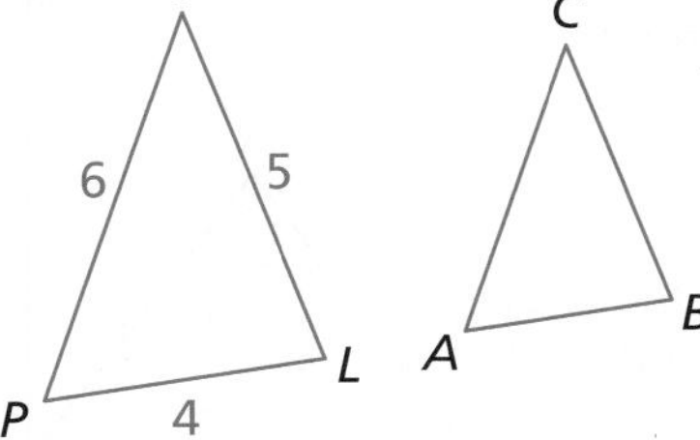

4.15 Tests for Similar Triangles

You know several tests to decide whether triangles are congruent, for example SSS. It would be useful to have comparable tests for similar triangles.

In-Class Experiment

The main tests for congruent triangles are SAS, ASA, AAS, and SSS. Are there similar tests for similar triangles? Below are some possibilities. For each proposed test, draw a pair of triangles that share the attributes listed. Then check to see whether they must be similar. See if you can find a counterexample.

1. Three angles of one triangle are congruent to three angles of the other. Must the two triangles be similar? (AAA similarity)
2. Two triangles have a pair of proportional side lengths and a pair of congruent corresponding angles. Must the two triangles be similar? (SA similarity)
3. Two triangles have two pairs of proportional side lengths and the included angles are congruent. Must the two triangles be similar? (SAS similarity)
4. Two triangles have three pairs of proportional side lengths. Must the two triangles be similar? (SSS similarity)

AAA Similarity

Suppose $\triangle ABC$ and $\triangle PQR$ have congruent corresponding angles. Can you prove that the triangles are similar?

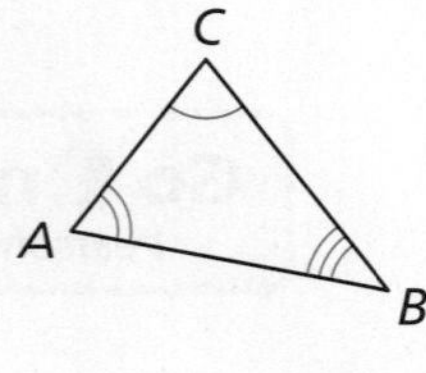

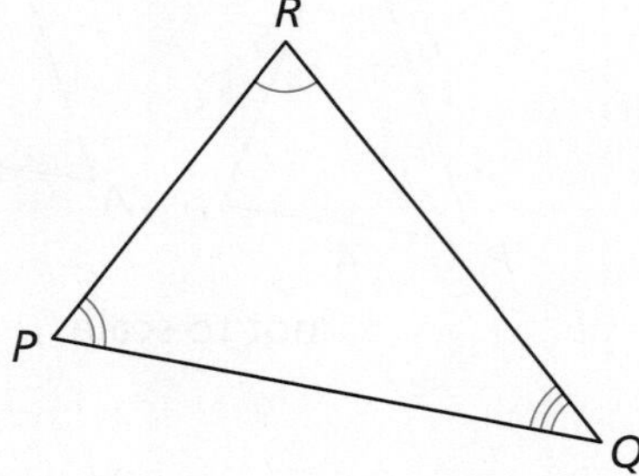

In previous lessons, you checked whether triangles were scaled copies (similar to each other) by placing one triangle inside the other triangle to form a pair of nested triangles.

So try placing $\triangle ABC$ inside $\triangle PQR$ so that congruent angles C and R coincide. The triangles line up because $\angle C$ and $\angle R$ are congruent. The rays that form the angles lie on top of each other.

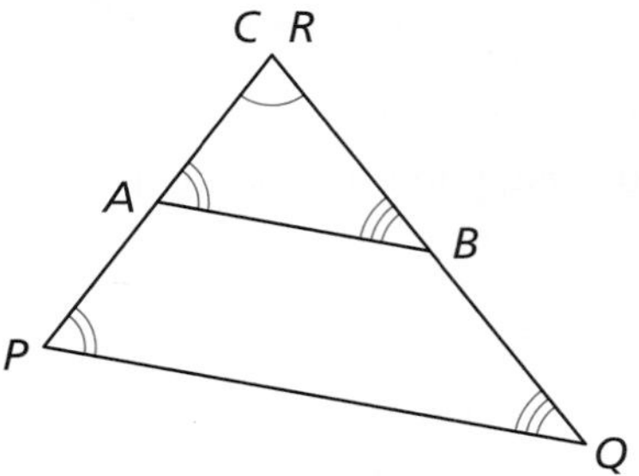

For You to Do

5. Use the figure above to prove that $\overline{AB}$ is parallel to $\overline{PQ}$. Then apply the Parallel Side-Splitter Theorem to write several proportions using the side lengths of the two triangles. Which definition of similarity allows you to conclude that $\triangle ABC \sim \triangle PQR$?

Theorem 4.3 AAA Similarity Theorem

If three angles of one triangle are congruent to three angles of another triangle, the triangles are similar.

$\triangle ABC \sim \triangle DEF$

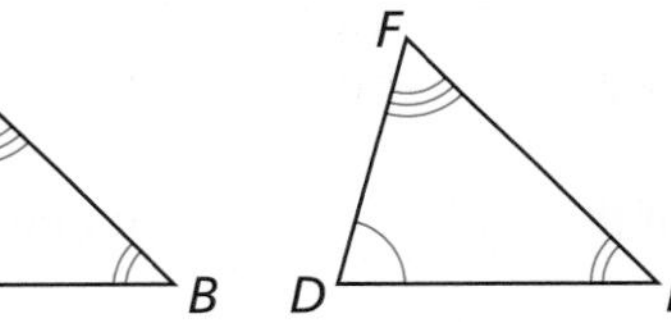

For Discussion

6. Use the information from Problem 5 to prove the AAA Similarity Theorem.

Developing Habits of Mind

Simplify. In a sense, the requirement that the three angles of one triangle be congruent to the three angles of the other triangle is too much.

The AAA test can actually be replaced by an AA test. Once you know the measures of two angles of a triangle, the measure of the third angle is completely determined, since the sum of the measures of the three angles of a triangle is $180°$. Thus, you can rewrite the theorem as follows.

If two angles of one triangle are congruent to two angles of another triangle, then the triangles are similar.

When you write proofs, you may use the AA Similarity Theorem, instead of the AAA Similarity Theorem.

For Discussion

7. Does it make sense to have an ASA test for triangle similarity? Explain.

SAS Similarity

Is there an SAS similarity test? If such a theorem did exist, you might state it as follows.

Theorem 4.4 SAS Similarity Theorem

If two triangles have two pairs of proportional side lengths and the included angles are congruent, the triangles are similar.

$\frac{AC}{DF} = \frac{AB}{DE}$; $\angle A \cong \angle D \Rightarrow \triangle ABC \sim \triangle DEF$

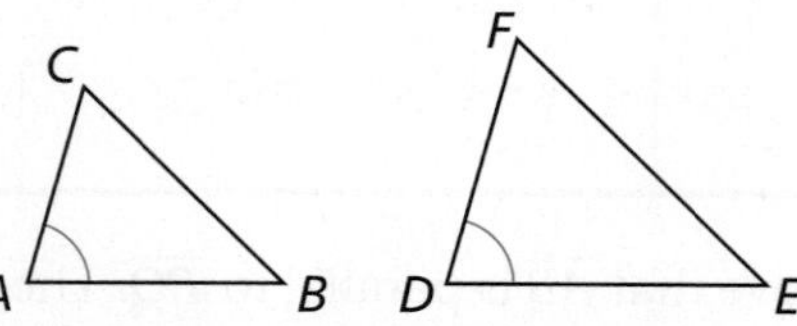

Developing Habits of Mind

Think it through. Suppose you have two triangles, $\triangle ABC$ and $\triangle DEF$, such that the following statements are true:

$$\frac{AC}{DF} = \frac{AB}{DE} \text{ and } \angle A \cong \angle D$$

These are the hypotheses of the SAS test. Now you need to show that the triangles are similar.

The key is to arrange the triangles, one inside the other, so that the congruent angles at A and D line up:

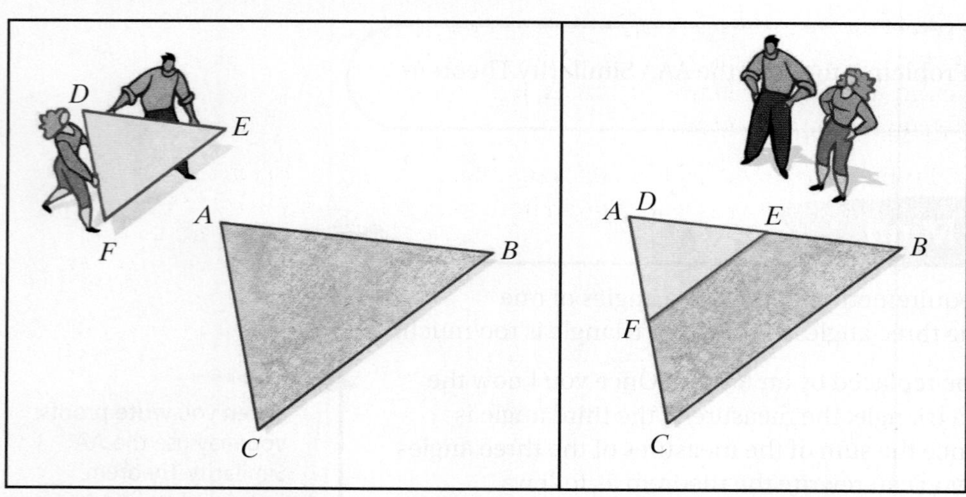

Because of the equal ratios given above, the Proportional Side-Splitter Theorem implies that $\overline{FE}$ is parallel to $\overline{CB}$. So you know that $\angle DFE \cong \angle ACB$ and $\angle DEF \cong \angle ABC$.

Moreover, the Parallel Side-Splitter Theorem tells you that

$$\frac{AC}{DF} = \frac{AB}{DE} = \frac{CB}{FE}$$

Thus, the angles of the two triangles are congruent and corresponding sides are proportional, so

$$\triangle ABC \sim \triangle DEF$$

This proves the SAS similarity theorem.

For Discussion

8. The AAA condition was too strong. Is SAS too strong as well?

SSS Similarity

Is there an SSS similarity test? If such a theorem did exist, you might state it as follows.

Theorem 4.5 SSS Similarity Theorem

If two triangles have all three pairs of side lengths proportional, the triangles are similar.

$$\frac{AC}{DF} = \frac{AB}{DE} = \frac{CB}{FE} \Rightarrow \triangle ABC \sim \triangle DEF$$

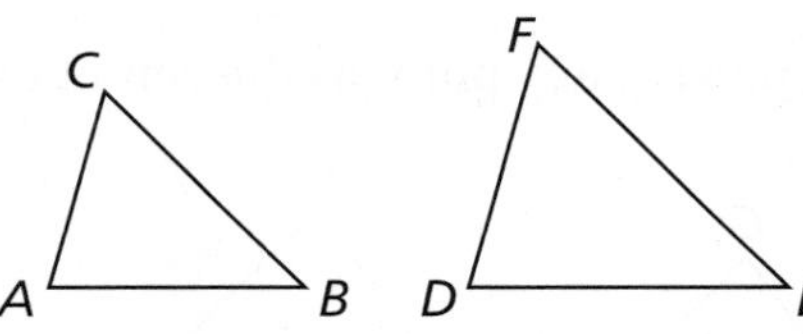

If you try to prove this theorem with the method used in the AAA and SAS proofs, something does not work.

In the AAA and SAS proofs, you had at least one pair of corresponding angles that you knew were congruent. This meant you could fit one triangle inside the other so that the congruent angles aligned perfectly. In the case of SSS, however, you have no congruent angles to use.

Since the Congruent Angles, Proportional Sides method does not seem well suited to prove SSS, try using the Congruent to a Dilation definition of similar triangles instead.

Habits of Mind

Make a choice. When you know equivalent definitions, use the one that best suits your needs.

For You to Do

9. Suppose the corresponding side lengths of $\triangle ABC$ and $\triangle PQR$ are proportional.

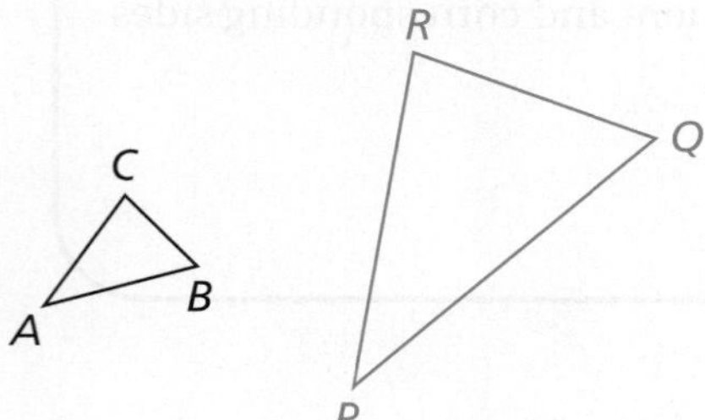

a. Write the proportionality statement for the side lengths of these two triangles.

b. If $\frac{PQ}{AB} = k$, where k is some positive number, complete each of the following statements.

- $\blacksquare = k(AB)$
- $\blacksquare = k(BC)$
- $\blacksquare = k(CA)$

Next, dilate $\triangle ABC$ by k, picking any point as the center of dilation.

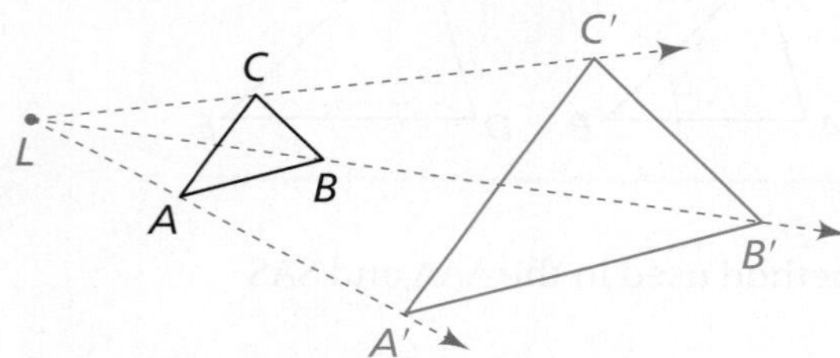

c. How do the sides of the dilated triangle $\triangle A'B'C'$ compare with the sides of $\triangle PQR$? Justify your answer.

d. Is it true that $\triangle A'B'C' \cong \triangle PQR$? Which congruence postulate can you use?

e. Is $\triangle PQR$ congruent to a dilation of $\triangle ABC$? Explain your answer.

For Discussion

10. Using your results from Problem 9, prove the SSS Similarity Theorem.

Exercises *Practicing Habits of Mind*

Check Your Understanding

1. $\triangle JKL$ has $JK = 8$, $KL = 12$, and $LJ = 16$. Points M and N are on $\overline{JK}$ and $\overline{KL}$ respectively, with $JM = 6$ and $LN = 9$.

a. Explain why $\overline{MN} \parallel \overline{JL}$.

b. Prove $\triangle MKN \sim \triangle JKL$ in three ways. Use each of the following similarity theorems.

- AA
- SAS
- SSS

2. $\triangle DEF$ is similar to $\triangle ABC$ and has sides that are three times as long. Find the ratios of the lengths of the segments listed below. Name the triangle similarity theorem that allows you to draw your conclusion.

a. two corresponding altitudes

b. two corresponding angle bisectors that terminate on the opposite side

c. two corresponding medians

For Exercises 3 and 4, decide whether quadrilaterals $ABCD$ and $EFGH$ are similar for the given conditions. Prove what you decide either as a theorem or by finding a counterexample.

3. The angles of one are congruent to the corresponding angles of the other.

4. Three corresponding sides are proportional and two corresponding included angles are congruent.

5. In the figure below, $\overline{DG} \parallel \overline{BC}$ and $\overline{EF} \parallel \overline{BA}$. Prove that $\triangle ABC \sim \triangle FHG$.

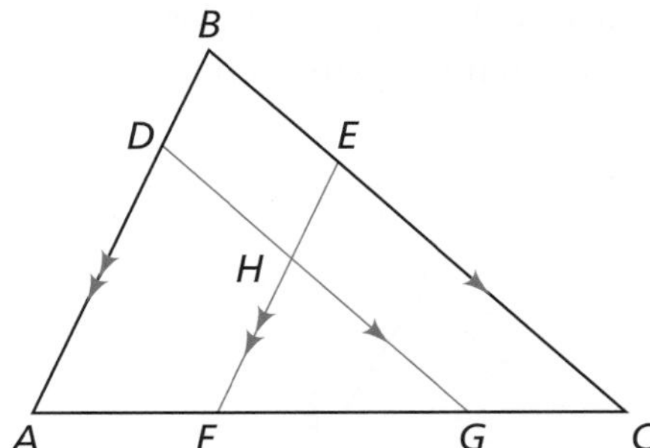

6. **Standardized Test Prep** Suppose $\triangle ABC \sim \triangle FHG$, $AB = 10$ ft, $AC = 20$ ft, $BC = 25$ ft, and $\frac{AB}{FH} = 2.5$. What is FG?

A. 4 ft **B.** 8 ft **C.** 10 ft **D.** 50 ft

On Your Own

7. The sides of a triangle have lengths 4, 5, and 8. Another triangle similar to it has one side of length 3. What are the lengths of its other two sides? Is more than one answer possible?

8. A triangle has sides of lengths 2, 3, and 4 inches. Another triangle similar to it has a perimeter of 6 inches. What are the side lengths of this triangle?

9. In the figure at the right, $\angle ADE \cong \angle ACB$. Explain why $\triangle ADE \sim \triangle ACB$.

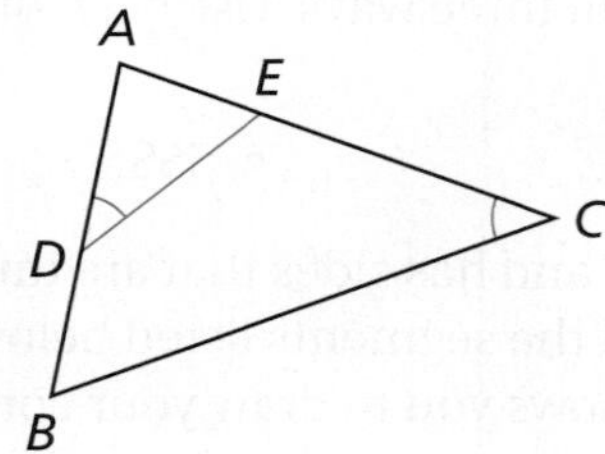

10. In the figure at the right, $AB = 2$ and $BC = 1$. Without making any measurements, find the values of $\frac{AD}{DE}$ and $\frac{AF}{FG}$. Explain how you got your answers.

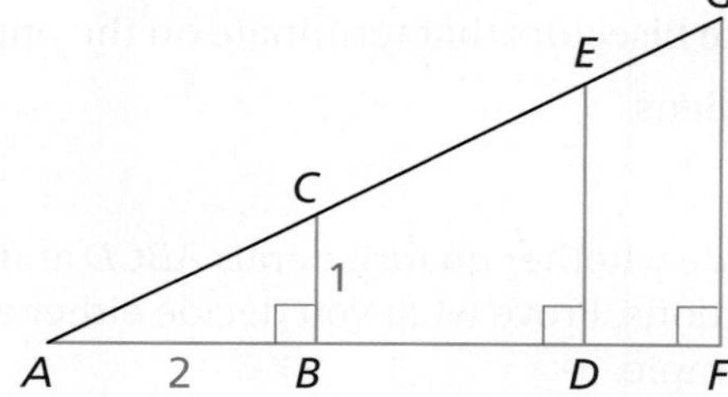

11. Draw a nonisosceles right triangle ABC. Draw the altitude from the right angle to the hypotenuse. The altitude divides $\triangle ABC$ into two smaller right triangles.
   a. There are two pairs of congruent angles (other than the right angles) in your picture. Find and label them.
   b. Make a copy of your triangle. Then cut out the two smaller right triangles. Position them in such a way as to convince yourself that they are similar to each other and to $\triangle ABC$.
   c. Explain why all three of these triangles are similar.

12. In the figure at the right, $AB = 4$, $BC = 5$, $AC = 6$, $DC = 2.5$, and $EC = 3$. Prove that $\triangle ABC \sim \triangle EDC$. Find the length of $\overline{DE}$.

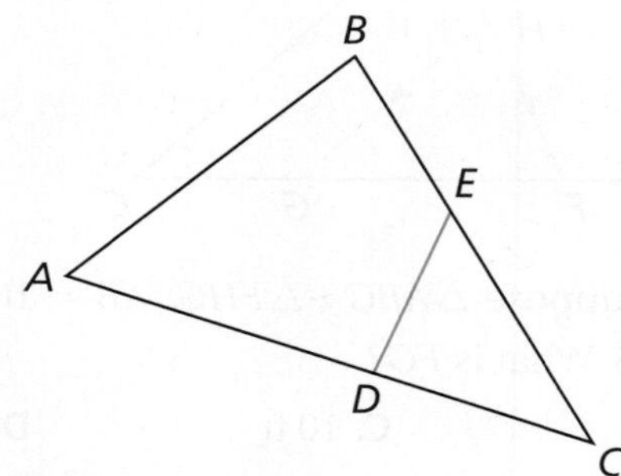

13. Quadrilateral $RATS$ is a trapezoid with $\overline{RA} \parallel \overline{ST}$. Diagonals $\overline{RT}$ and $\overline{AS}$ meet at O.

   a. Explain why $\triangle ROA \sim \triangle TOS$.

   b. From part (a) you can say that $\frac{RO}{TO} = \frac{OA}{OS}$. Explain.

   c. Mary Elizabeth knows that $\frac{RO}{TO} = \frac{OA}{OS}$ and $\angle ROS \cong \angle TOA$. She claims that $\triangle ROS \sim \triangle TOA$ by the SAS similarity test. Is this true? Explain.

14. **Take It Further** Take a square sheet of paper. Fold back one fourth of it. You are left with a rectangle. The challenge is to fold the sheet of paper to form a rectangle that is similar to this one, but has half its area. You may not use a ruler.

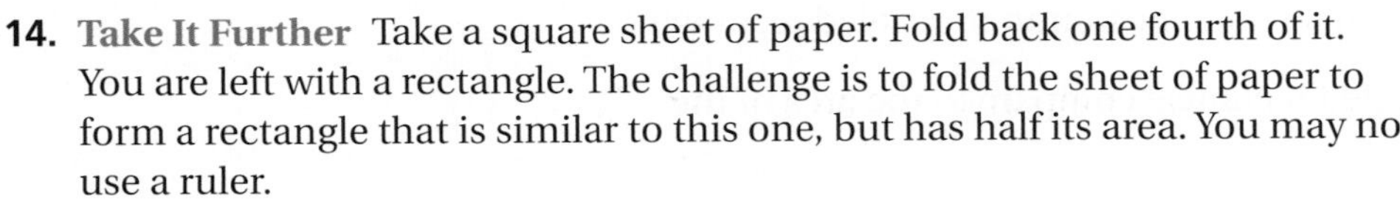

Even though you have folded part of the square, you can still unfold it and work with the entire square.

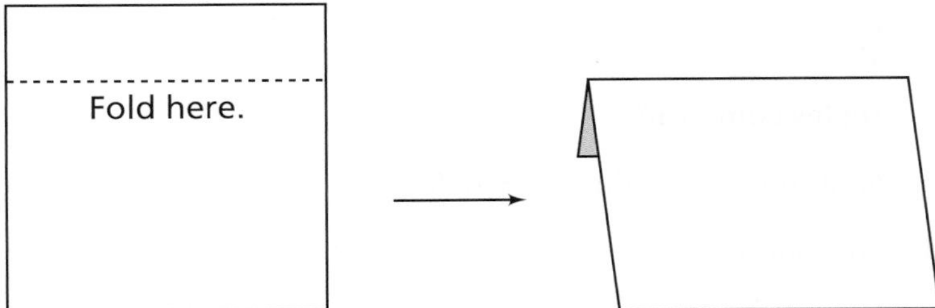

Maintain Your Skills

15. Although similarity for three-dimensional shapes has not been defined here, you can think about what it means to scale a three-dimensional figure. You would make a new figure with sides proportional to the sides of the original figure. For example, scale a rectangular prism 1 cm by 2 cm by 3 cm by the factor 2. You get a new rectangular prism measuring 2 cm by 4 cm by 6 cm.

   a. What are the surface area and volume of the original 1 cm-by-2 cm-by-3 cm rectangular prism?

   b. What are the surface area and volume of the scaled copy?

   In Exercises 16–18, scale a 1 cm-by-2 cm-by-3 cm rectangular prism by the given factor. What are the dimensions, the surface area, and the volume of the scaled copy?

16. scale factor 3

17. scale factor 4

18. scale factor k

4.16 Areas of Similar Polygons

How do the areas of similar polygons compare? Checking simple polygons, such as rectangles, is a good place to start.

In-Class Experiment

Draw a rectangle. Scale it by the factor 2.

1. How do the dimensions of the original rectangle compare with the dimensions of the scaled rectangle?
2. How many copies of the original rectangle fit into the scaled rectangle?
3. How does the area of the scaled rectangle compare to the area of the original rectangle?

Draw a rectangle. Scale it by the factor $\frac{1}{3}$.

4. How do the dimensions of the two rectangles compare?
5. How many copies of the scaled rectangle fit into the original rectangle?
6. How do the areas of the two rectangles compare?

If two triangles are similar and the scale factor is r, you know that the ratio of the lengths of two corresponding sides is r. Show that the following statements are true.

7. The ratio of their perimeters is r.
8. The ratio of the lengths of two corresponding altitudes is also r.
9. The ratio of their areas is r^2.

Minds in Action **episode 14**

Hannah and Derman complete the In-Class Experiment.

Hannah According to the In-Class Experiment, if you scale a triangle by 4, then 16 copies of the original triangle should fit inside the scaled copy.

Derman That sounds like a lot of triangles. Let's try to draw it out.

Hannah It's easy! Look, here's a small triangle. And here's a picture showing 16 copies of the small triangle inside the triangle that has been scaled by 4.

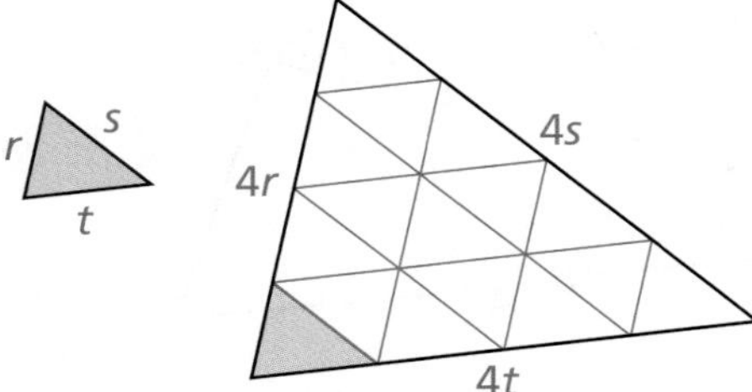

Derman Okay, that works. But what if you scale a triangle by $2\frac{1}{2}$? Then there should by $6\frac{1}{4}$ copies of the original triangle inside the scaled one. What would that look like?

For Discussion

10. Draw a figure that answers Derman's question. Show that if you scale a triangle by the factor $2\frac{1}{2}$, then the scaled triangle has $6\frac{1}{4}$ times the area of the original triangle.

Now that you have calculated the areas of similar rectangles and triangles, take a look at similar polygons with any number of sides.

For You to Do

In the figures below, you scale polygon 1 by the factor r to obtain polygon 2. You divide polygon 1 into four triangles with areas a, b, c, and d.

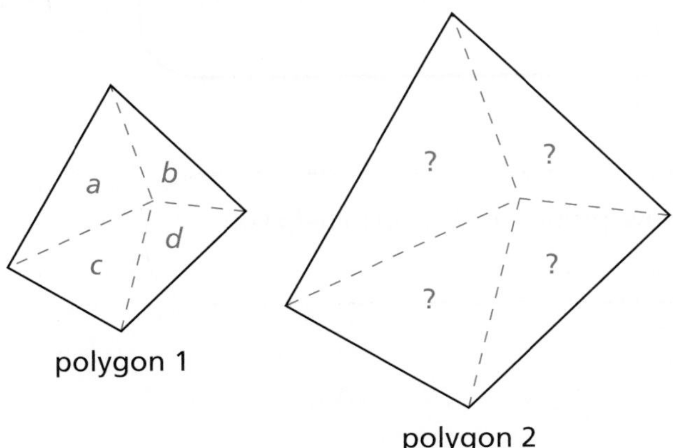

11. What are the areas of the corresponding triangles in polygon 2?

12. What is the total area of polygon 2?

13. What is the total area of polygon 1?

The results of your work lead to the following theorem.

Theorem 4.6

If you scale a polygon by some positive number *r*, then the ratio of the area of the scaled copy to the area of the original polygon is r^2.

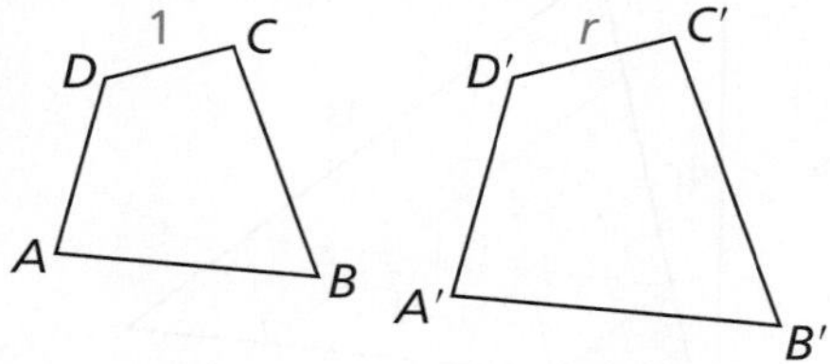

Developing Habits of Mind

Prove a special case. An argument for a special case can suggest how an argument could be made in general. Here's a proof of Theorem 4.6 for a quadrilateral. It suggests how a proof might proceed for any polygon.

Suppose you scale $ABCD$ by r to get $A'B'C'D'$. Pick a point O inside $ABCD$. Connect it to each of the vertices, dividing $ABCD$ into triangles. (There would be four in this case, but in general there would be as many as there are sides.) Let the areas of these triangles be a, b, c, and d. Then

$$\text{area}(ABCD) = a + b + c + d$$

If the image of O is O', then the triangle AOB gets scaled by a factor of r to triangle $A'O'B'$, and so on. So, by the results of Problem 9 of the In-Class Experiment, the area of the triangles in $A'B'C'D'$ are r^2a, r^2b, r^2c, and r^2d. Then

$$\begin{aligned}\text{area}(A'B'C'D') &= r^2a + r^2b + r^2c + r^2d \\ &= r^2(a + b + c + d) \\ &= r^2 \cdot \text{area}(ABCD)\end{aligned}$$

There are some quadrilaterals for which picking an inside point would not necessarily work. For example:

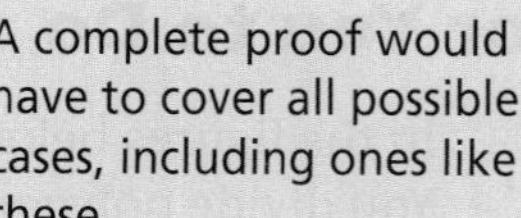

A complete proof would have to cover all possible cases, including ones like these.

For You to Do

14. Draw diagrams to go along with the above proof. Label them to help you understand this proof.

Exercises *Practicing Habits of Mind*

Check Your Understanding

1. One side of a triangle has length 10. The altitude to that side has length 12. If you make a new triangle for which all the sides of the original triangle are tripled, what is the area of the new triangle?

2. Jerry wants to plant two cornfields. One measures 400 ft by 600 ft. The other measures 200 ft by 300 ft. Becky, the owner of the seed-and-grain store, says, "The big field will take eight bags of seed. The small field has sides half as big, so you'll need four more bags for that. Will that be cash or charge?" A few days later, Jerry returns to the store very upset. Explain.

3. **a.** Trace this polygon onto a sheet of paper. Estimate its area in square centimeters.

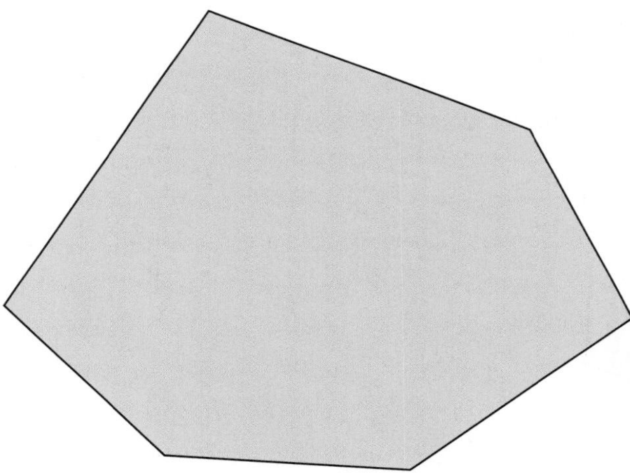

b. If you scale the polygon by the factor 1.5, what will be the area of the scaled copy?

Habits of Mind

Recall what you know. Think about figures for which a ruler can help you find area. Can you see such figures in this polygon?

On Your Own

4. The area of one square is 12 times the area of another square. Find the ratio of the lengths of the following.

a. their sides

b. their diagonals

5. You scale a rectangle by the factor $\frac{1}{4}$. Compare the area of the scaled rectangle to the area of the original rectangle.

6. You scale a triangle by the factor 5. Compare the area of the scaled triangle to the area of the original triangle.

7. The area of a polygon is 17 square inches. You scale the polygon by the factor 2. What is the area of the new polygon?

8. **Standardized Test Prep** The area of a regular hexagon with 10-cm sides is about 259.8 cm^2. To the nearest square centimeter, what is the area of a regular hexagon with 5-cm sides?

A. 130 cm^2 **B.** 100 cm^2 **C.** 65 cm^2 **D.** 52 cm^2

Maintain Your Skills

In Exercises 9–12, find the volume of each figure. Then apply the given scale factor and find the volume of the new figure.

9. scale factor = 3

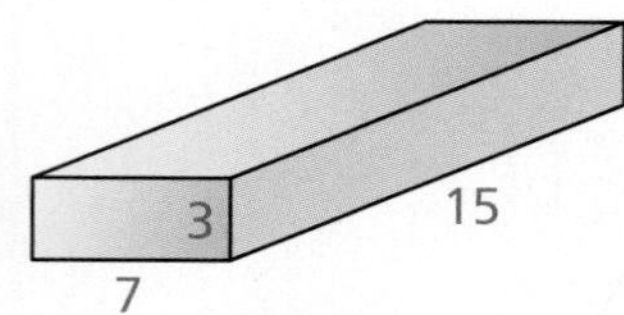

rectangular prism

10. scale factor = 2

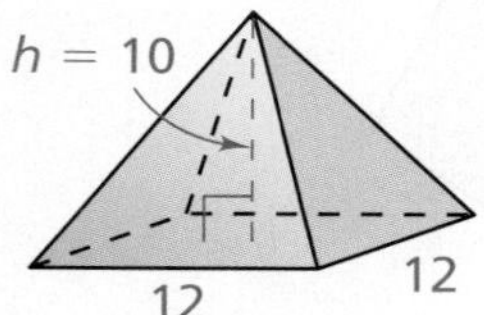

square pyramid

11. scale factor = 5

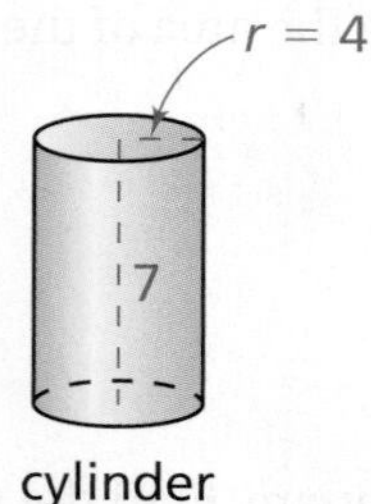

cylinder

12. scale factor = r

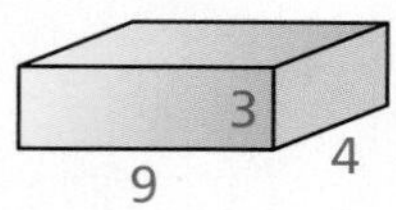

rectangular prism

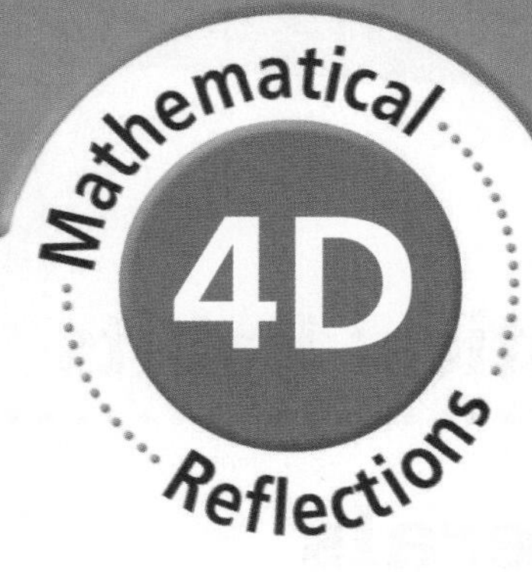

In this investigation, you studied similar figures—figures with congruent corresponding angles and proportional corresponding sides. You used the AA, SAS, and SSS tests to determine whether two triangles are similar. You also used scale factors to find the areas of two similar figures. These questions will help you summarize what you have learned.

1. In the figure at the right, suppose $\overline{CD} \perp \overline{AB}$. How many similar triangles can you find? Prove that all the ones you find are similar. Use the triangle similarity tests.

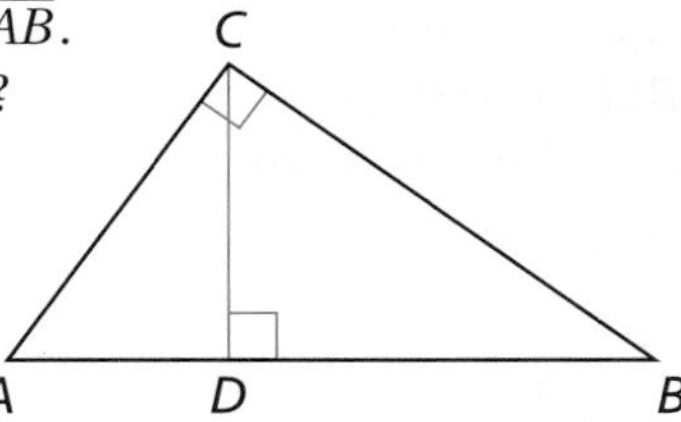

2. In the figure at the right, $\triangle ABC \sim \triangle EDC$. Prove that $\triangle FDA \sim \triangle FBE$.

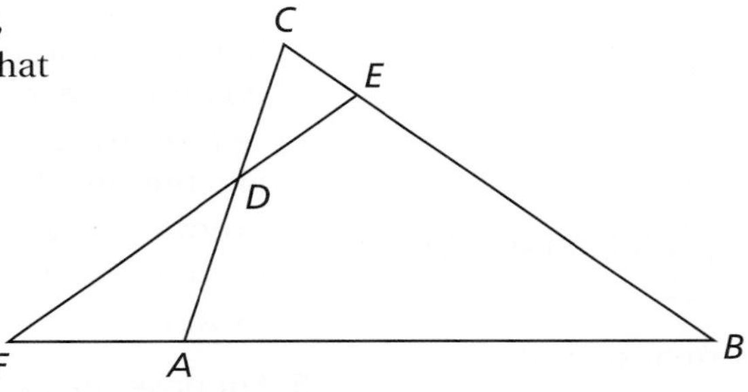

3. In quadrilateral $EFGH$, $\overline{EF} \parallel \overline{HG}$, $\overline{EH} \perp \overline{EF}$, $EF = 6$, $FG = 5$, $GH = 10$, and $EH = 3$.
   a. Find the area of $EFGH$.
   b. Scale $EFGH$ by 3. Call the scaled copy $IJKL$, so that $EFGH \sim IJKL$. Find the area of $IJKL$.
   c. What is the ratio of the areas of $EFGH$ and $IJKL$?
4. What does it mean for two figures to be similar?
5. What are some tests for triangle similarity?
6. If the common ratio of two similar figures is r, what is the ratio of their areas?

The two different-sized squares have similar fold patterns. Fold them and you get two origami figures that are similar.

Vocabulary and Notation

In this investigation, you learned this term and this symbol. Make sure you understand what each one means and how to use it.

- **similar figures**
- **$\sim$ (is similar to)**

Project Using Mathematical Habits

Midpoint Quadrilaterals

Use either pencil and straightedge or geometry software. Draw quadrilateral *ABCD*. Construct the midpoint of each side. Label the midpoints of $\overline{AB}$, $\overline{BC}$, $\overline{CD}$, and $\overline{DA}$ as *E*, *F*, *G*, and *H*, respectively.

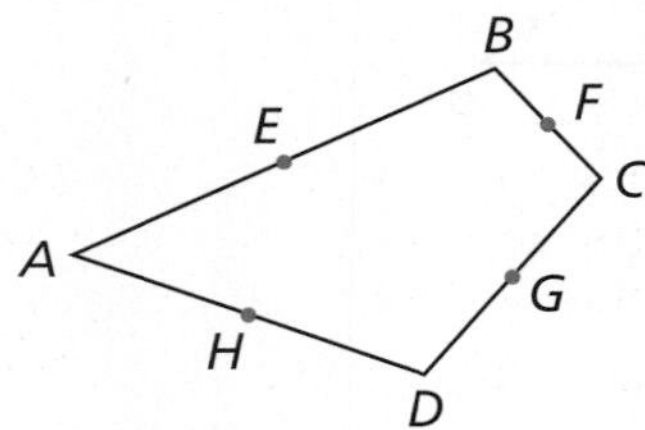

Connect the midpoints to form quadrilateral *EFGH*. Call this the midpoint quadrilateral.

1. Describe the features of your midpoint quadrilateral *EFGH*.
2. Try to classify it as a particular kind of quadrilateral.
   - If you are using geometry software, experiment by moving the vertices and sides of *ABCD*.
   - If you are working on paper, repeat the experiment with a significantly different starting quadrilateral.

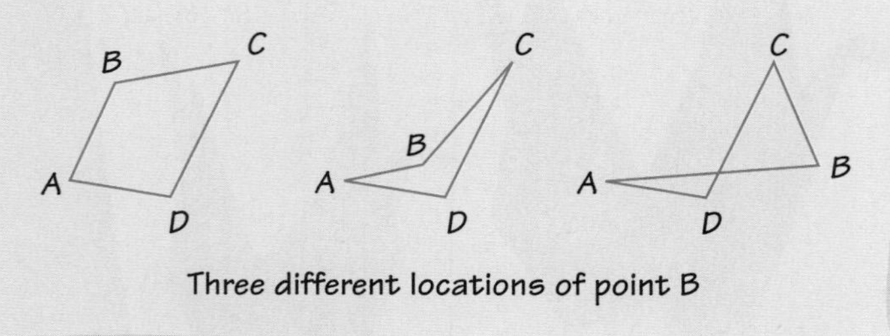

Three different locations of point B

3. Does the midpoint quadrilateral retain its special features?
4. Use the Proportional Side-Splitter Theorem. Prove that each conjecture you have made about a midpoint quadrilateral is correct. Make sure that your proof is valid for each of the three locations of *B* shown in the preceding diagram. It may help to draw the diagonals of each quadrilateral.

   Remember, in this book, the term *quadrilateral* does not include self-intersecting quadrilaterals like this one. However, your proof could work for self-intersecting quadrilaterals, as well.

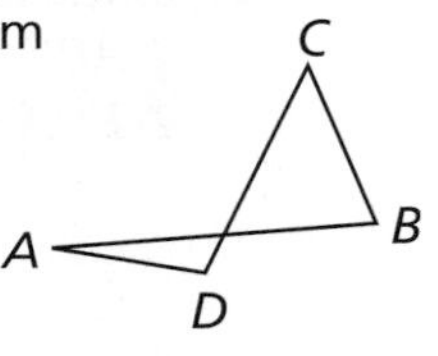

5. Suppose the diagonals of quadrilateral *ABCD* measure 8 inches and 12 inches. What is the perimeter of the midpoint quadrilateral?

Using the Midline Theorem

Juan said that he did not use a side-splitter theorem in his proof for his conjecture about midpoint quadrilaterals. Here is an outline of his proof.

- In quadrilateral *ABCD*, find the midpoints and connect them in order to make the midpoint quadrilateral.
- Draw the diagonal $\overline{AC}$. Two opposite sides of the midpoint quadrilateral are parallel to and half as long as $\overline{AC}$ because of the Midline Theorem. To see this, you just have to look at *ABCD* as two triangles that share a base $\overline{AC}$.

6. Write out Juan's proof. Include a statement of his conjecture, any helpful diagram(s), and a conclusion about the midpoint quadrilateral.

Special Quadrilaterals

Special types of quadrilaterals include

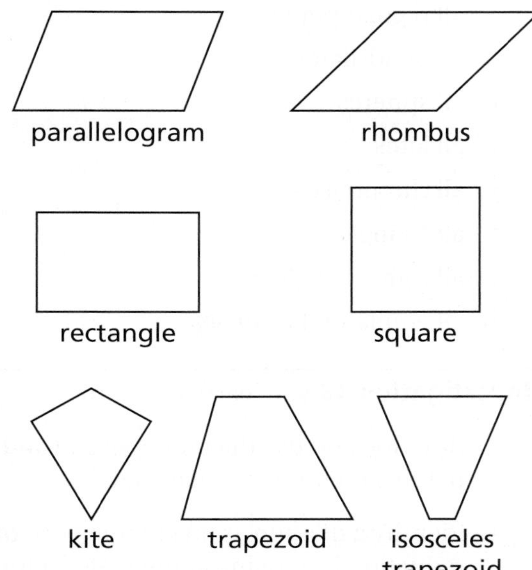

7. Does any special type of quadrilateral have a special midpoint quadrilateral (different from what you found in the preceding exercises)? Prove each conjecture you make.

8. If quadrilateral *ABCD* has a square (or rhombus or rectangle) as a midpoint quadrilateral, make a conjecture about *ABCD*. Prove your conjecture. How can you support your conjecture using software?

Extending the Idea

9. Describe a connection between midpoint quadrilaterals and dilations. (*Hint:* A midpoint quadrilateral has, of course, its own midpoint quadrilateral. Think about the sequence of midpoint quadrilaterals for a given figure. One such sequence is shown on the diagram that follows.)

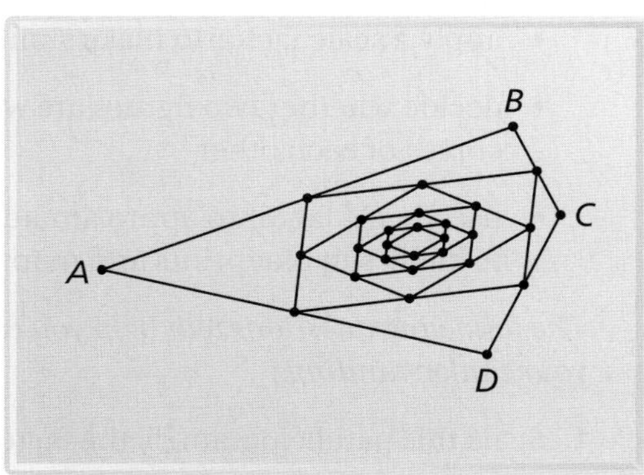

Jessica extended her investigation. She used a diagram like the one below to make a conjecture. She claimed that she could prove her conjecture using the Proportional Side-Splitter Theorem.

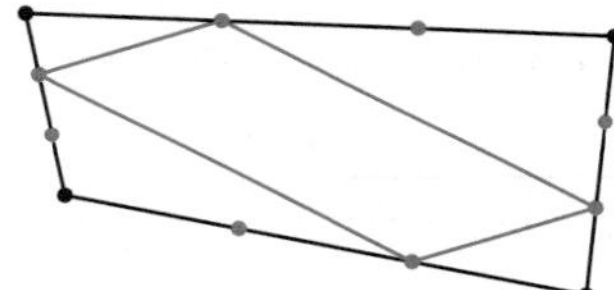

10. a. Describe the points that Jessica connected in her diagram. It may help to redraw the diagram and label some points.

    b. Use the Proportional Side-Splitter Theorem to prove that the inner quadrilateral is a parallelogram.

11. Here is another "inside quadrilateral" that Jessica's diagram suggests. Make a thoughtful conjecture about this quadrilateral. Prove, or at least give some support for, your conjecture.

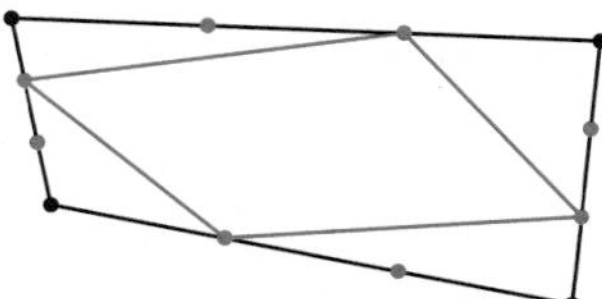

Review

Go Online
Pearsonsuccessnet.com

In **Investigation 4A** you learned how to

- apply a scale factor to make similar figures
- decide whether two figures are well-scaled copies of each other
- use a scale factor to approximate distances in blueprints and maps

The following questions will help you check your understanding.

1. Scale this parallelogram by the factor $\frac{1}{3}$.

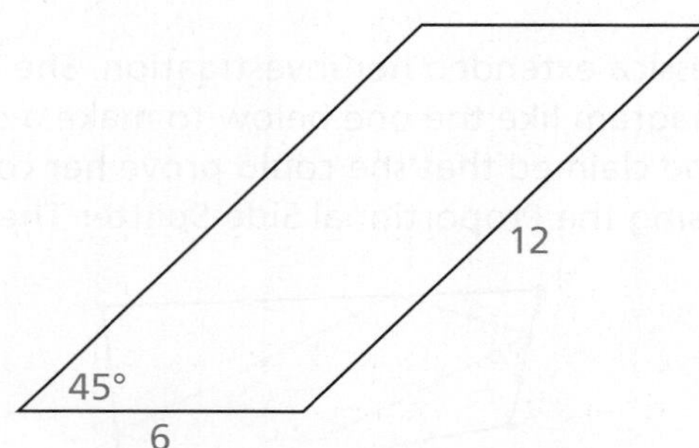

2. Without measuring, check whether the figures below are scaled copies of each other.

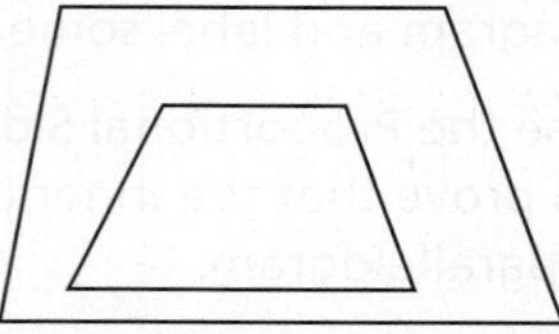

3. Decide whether all members of each collection below must be scaled copies of each other. Explain why they are, or find a counterexample.

a. all regular pentagons

b. all quadrilaterals

c. all spheres

d. all kites

e. all rhombuses

f. all triangles

g. all right triangles

h. all equilateral triangles

In **Investigation 4B** you learned how to

- describe and use the ratio method and the parallel method to make dilations
- identify a dilation as an enlargement or reduction by looking at the scale factor
- describe the effect of the choice for center of dilation on the resulting dilation

The following questions will help you check your understanding.

4. Trace the pentagon and point T onto a sheet of paper. Use the ratio method to scale the pentagon by the factor 1.5. Use T as the center of dilation.

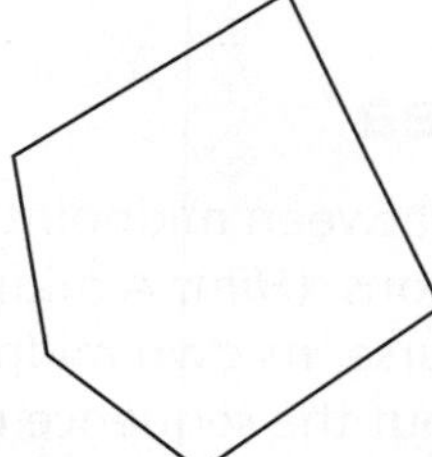

5. Trace *ABCDEF* and point *O* onto a sheet of paper. Use the parallel method to scale the hexagon by the factor $\frac{1}{3}$. Use *O* as the center of dilation.

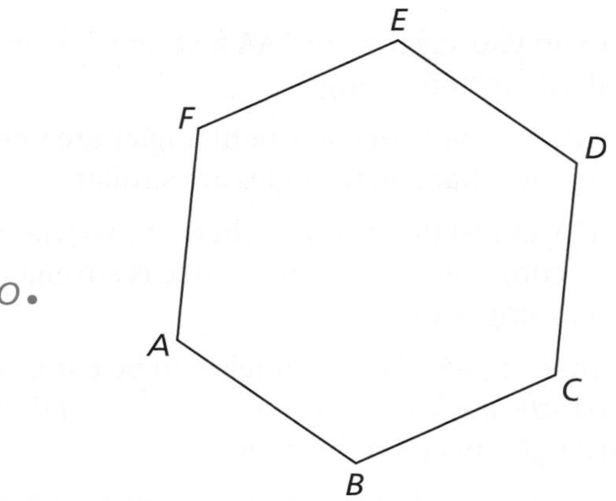

In **Investigation 4C** you learned how to

- decide how lines parallel to a side of a triangle split the other two sides
- understand and prove the side-splitter theorems
- use ratios and proportions.

The following questions will help you check your understanding.

6. In the diagram below, $EB = \frac{1}{3}AB$, $BC = 3BF$, $DA = 2AH$, and $DG = \frac{1}{2}DC$. Prove that *EFGH* is a trapezoid.

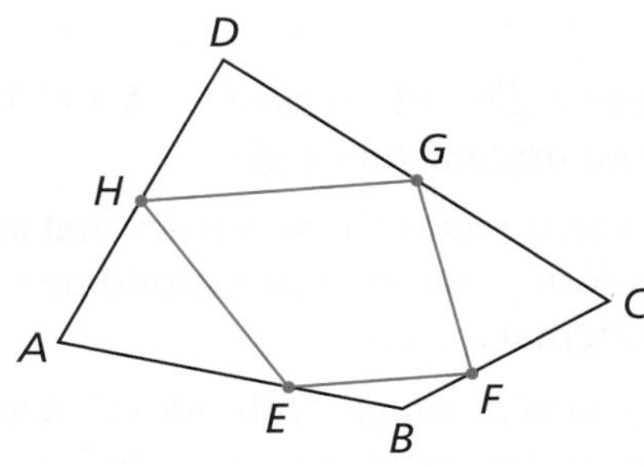

7. $\triangle ABC$ is a right triangle. $AC = 10$, $AD = 4$, $CB = 15$, and $EB = 6$. Prove that $\triangle DEC$ is a scaled copy of $\triangle ABC$.

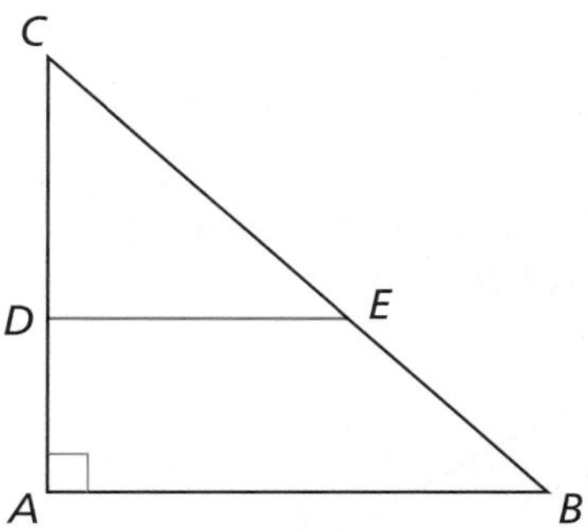

8. Draw a triangle. Label its vertices *A*, *B*, and *C*. Choose point *P* on $\overline{AC}$ such that $\frac{PA}{AC} = \frac{2}{9}$. Then choose point *Q* on $\overline{BC}$ such that $\frac{BQ}{CB} = \frac{6}{27}$. If $AB = 27$, what is *PQ*?

In **Investigation 4D** you learned how to

- identify corresponding parts of similar triangles
- use the AA, SAS, and SSS tests for similarity in triangles
- understand that the ratio between the area of a polygon and the area of a copy of that polygon scaled by the factor *r* must be r^2

The following questions will help you check your understanding.

9. Draw a square and its diagonals. How many similar triangles can you find? Prove that they are similar. Use the triangle similarity tests.

10. You scale an *n*-gon by the factor 7. What is the ratio of the areas of the scaled *n*-gon and the original *n*-gon?

Test

Go Online
Pearsonsuccessnet.com

Multiple Choice

1. In this triangle, $\overline{BC} \parallel \overline{DE}$. Also, $AB = DE = 5$, and $BC = 7$. What is DB?

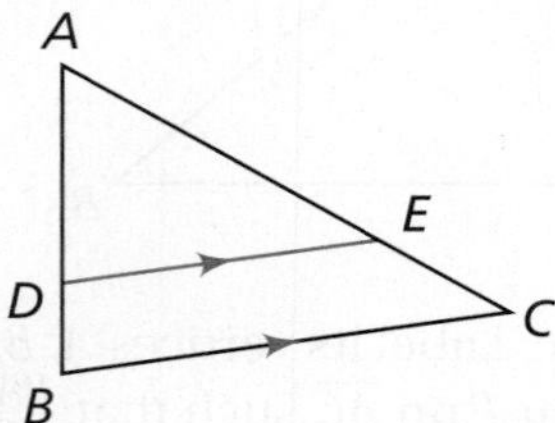

A. $\frac{7}{25}$ **B.** $\frac{25}{7}$ **C.** $\frac{10}{7}$ **D.** 7

2. In the triangle below, $\overline{DE} \parallel \overline{AB}$. Which of the following is true?

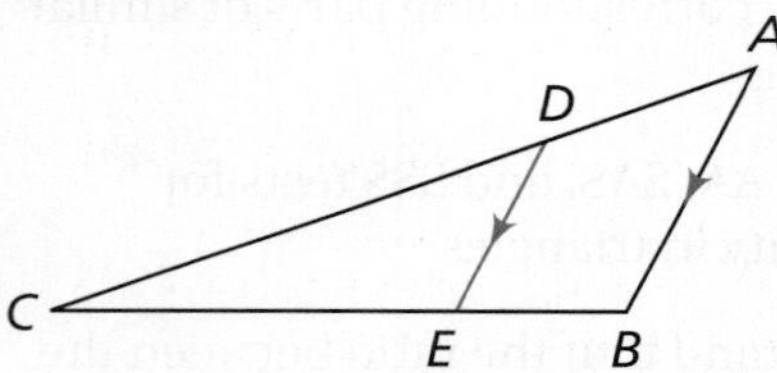

A. $\frac{AD}{BE} = \frac{CE}{AD}$ **B.** $\frac{AB}{DE} = \frac{BC}{BE}$

C. $\frac{DE}{AB} = \frac{CE}{BC}$ **D.** $\frac{DE}{CE} = \frac{AC}{BC}$

3. In the figure below, $\angle B \cong \angle E$. Which of the following does NOT allow you to conclude that $\triangle ABC \sim \triangle DEF$?

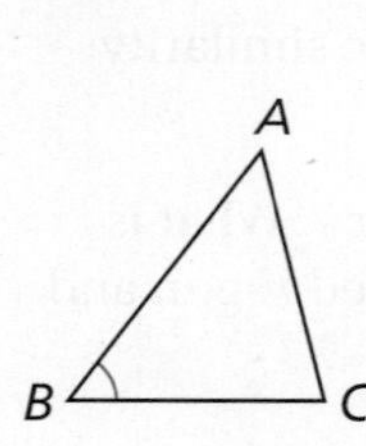

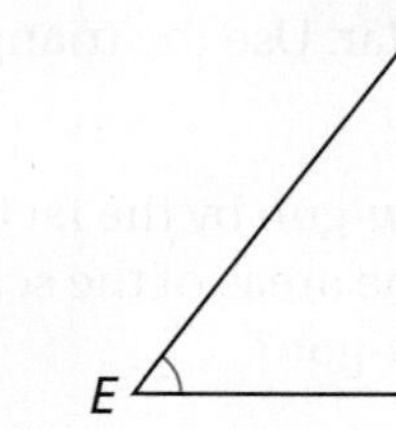

A. $\frac{AB}{DE} = \frac{BC}{EF}$ **B.** $\angle C \cong \angle F$

C. $\frac{AB}{DE} = \frac{AC}{DF}$ **D.** $\angle A \cong \angle D$

4. Why can you say that an AAA test for triangle similarity is "too strong?"

A. Only two pairs of congruent angles are needed to prove that two triangles are similar.

B. An AAA test determines whether two triangles are congruent, and congruence is stronger than similarity.

C. Three angles of one triangle can be congruent to three angles of another triangle, but the triangles need not be congruent.

D. You only need one pair of congruent angles to prove that two triangles are similar.

Open Response

5. Copy the figure below onto a sheet of paper. Use the ratio method or the parallel method to scale $\triangle ABC$ by $\frac{1}{4}$.

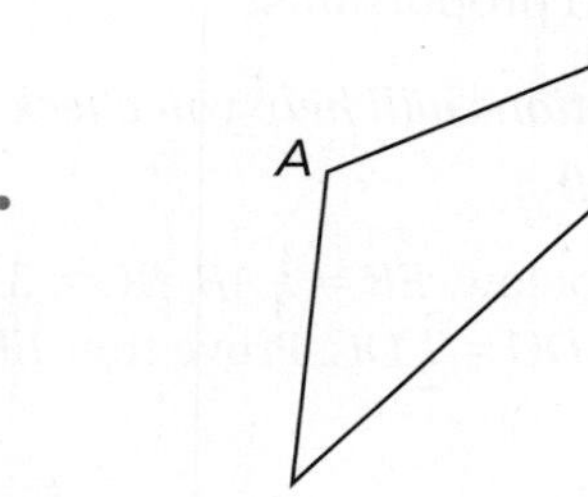

6. Draw a rectangle with sides of 6 cm and 4 cm. This is your original rectangle.

a. Draw a new rectangle with sides that are 2 cm shorter than the corresponding sides of your original rectangle.

b. Draw a new rectangle with sides that are $\frac{1}{2}$ as long as the corresponding sides of your original rectangle.

c. Is either of the rectangles you drew in parts (a) or (b) a scaled copy of the original rectangle? Are they both scaled copies? Explain.

d. What kind of rectangle must you start with to have the directions in both parts (a) and (b) produce scaled copies of the original rectangle?

7. Given: $SUZI \sim CUHE$. Determine whether each of the following statements is *true* or *not necessarily true.*

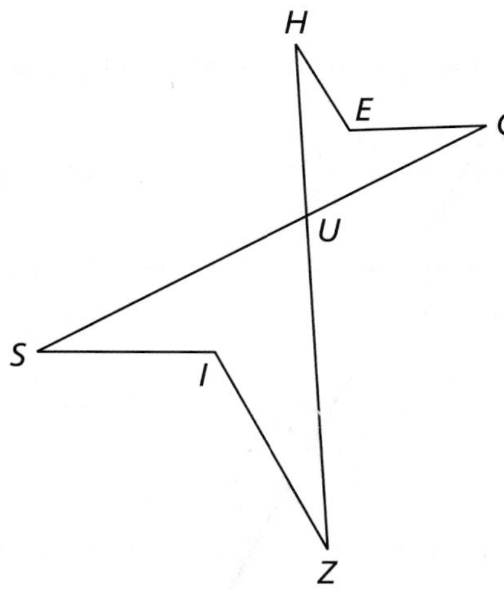

a. $\angle S \cong \angle C$

b. $\frac{CU}{SU} = \frac{ZU}{HU}$

c. $\angle E \cong \angle C$

d. $\angle CUH \cong \angle SUZ$

e. $\frac{HU}{ZU} = \frac{CU}{SU}$

f. $\frac{CH}{SZ} = \frac{CE}{IZ}$

8. Are the triangles in each pair scaled copies of each other? Explain.

a.

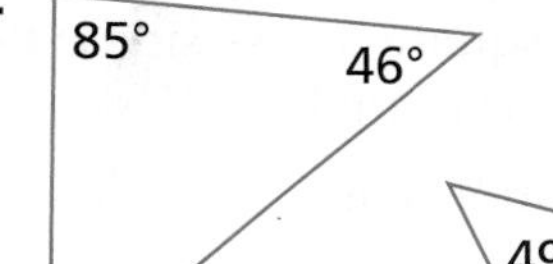

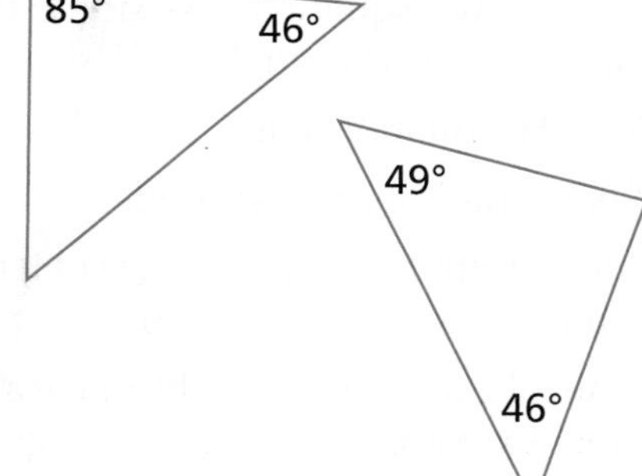

b.

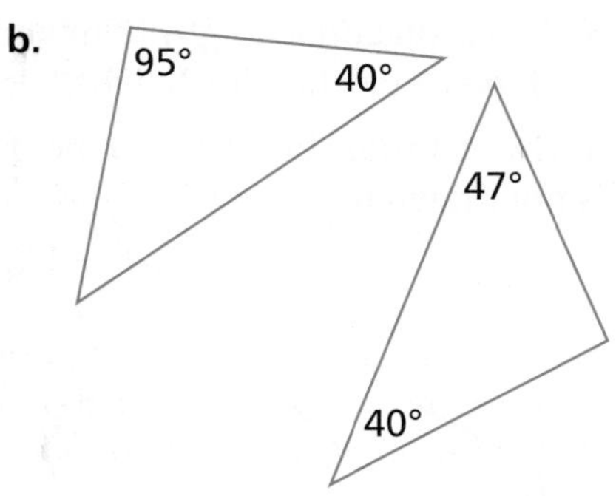

9. Explain how you know that any two squares are similar.

10. Consider the following figure.

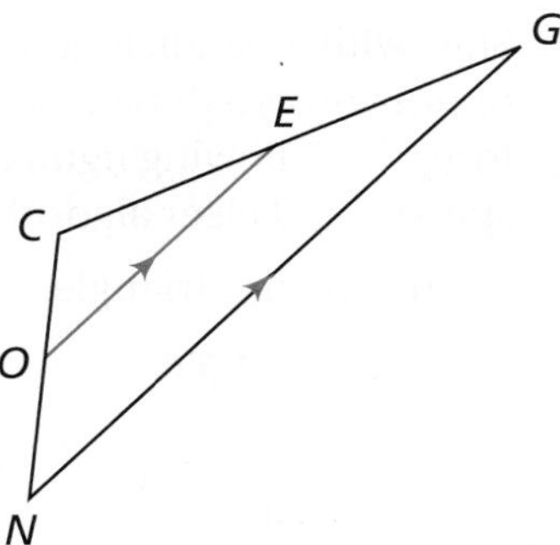

$\overline{OE}$ is parallel to $\overline{NG}$.

a. If $CN = 5$, $CO = 1$, and $CE = 2$, what is CG?

b. If $CG = 7.5$, $CO = 3$, and $CN = 6$, what is CE?

c. If $CE = 3$, and $CG = 12$, what is the value of $\frac{CO}{CN}$?

d. If $CO = 1$, and $ON = 4$, what is the value of $\frac{OE}{NG}$?

11. Given: $BC = 3 \cdot EC$, and $AC = 3 \cdot CD$

Prove: $\triangle BAC \sim \triangle EDC$

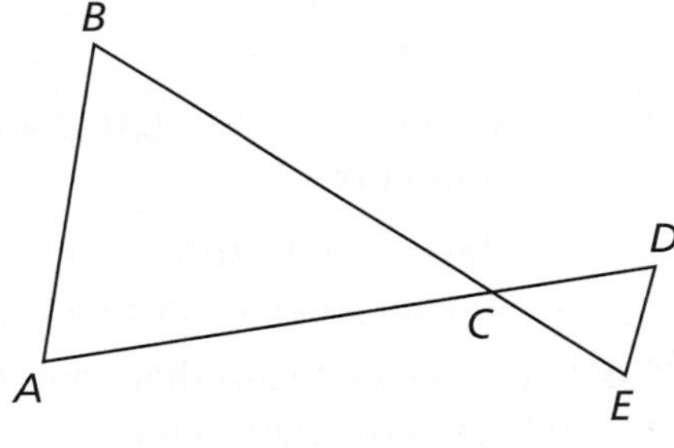

Cumulative Review

1. Start with a parallelogram. Decide whether or not you can dissect it into pieces that can form the following figures. If you can, write a specific and clear algorithm.

   a. an isosceles triangle

   b. a right triangle

   c. a trapezoid

   d. a rectangle

2. The base of a triangle has a length of 16 inches. How long is the segment that joins the midpoints of the other two sides?

3. Use $\triangle ACE$, below, with midline $\overline{BD}$.

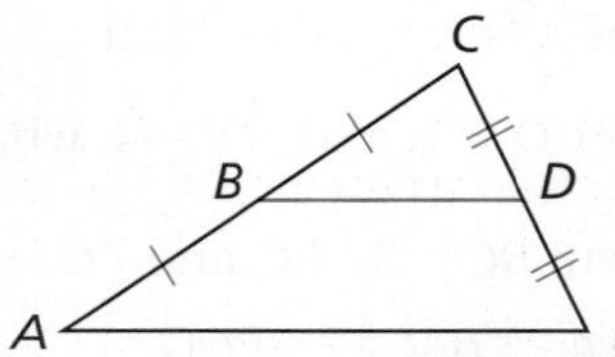

   a. In what ways are $\triangle ACE$ and $\triangle BCD$ the same?

   b. In what ways are $\triangle ACE$ and $\triangle BCD$ different?

   c. Make a conjecture about a triangle and a smaller triangle formed by a midline.

4. Suppose a kite has diagonals of 12 and 20. Find the perimeter and area of the quadrilateral formed by joining the midpoints of the kite's sides.

5. Which of the following quadrilaterals have the same area? Are any congruent?

i.

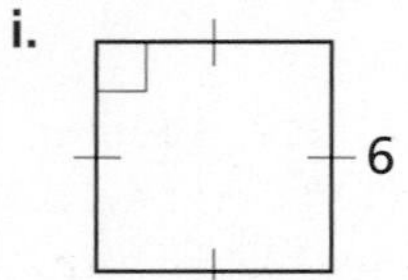

ii.

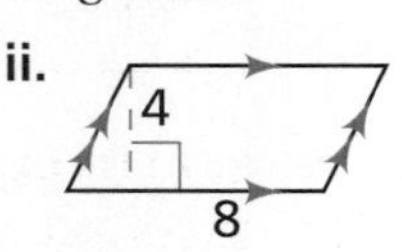

iii.

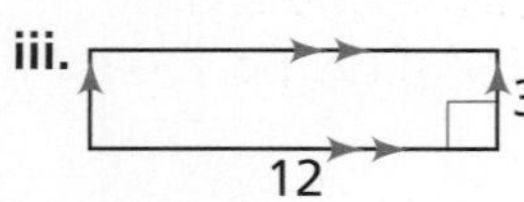

iv.

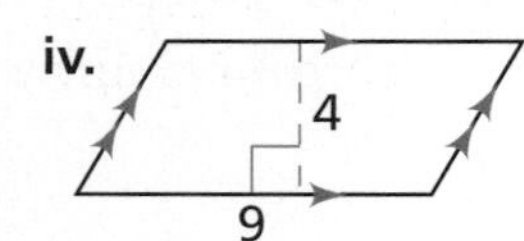

In Exercises 6–8, find the area of the figure.

6.

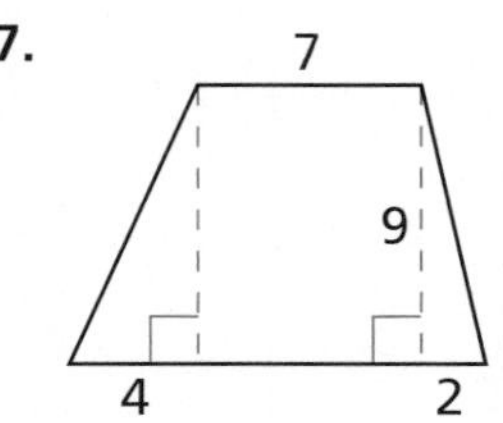

7.

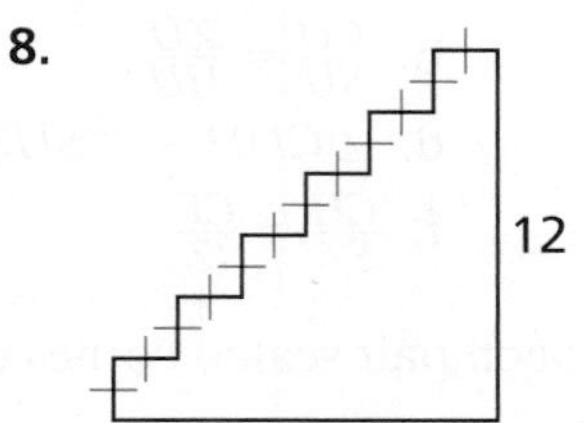

8.

9. Draw a right triangle with legs of lengths 6 and 8. Draw a square whose side is the hypotenuse of this triangle.

   a. Find the square's area.

   b. What is the square's perimeter?

   c. Draw a right triangle with legs of lengths 15 and 36. Repeat (a) and (b).

10. Can the following side lengths make a right triangle? Explain.

    a. 5, 9,12 b. 9, 40, 41 c. 10, 11, 21

11. A rectangle has diagonal length 17 m and a base 8 m. Find the rectangle's height.

12. Explain why $\angle A$ must be a right angle. The figure is not drawn to scale.

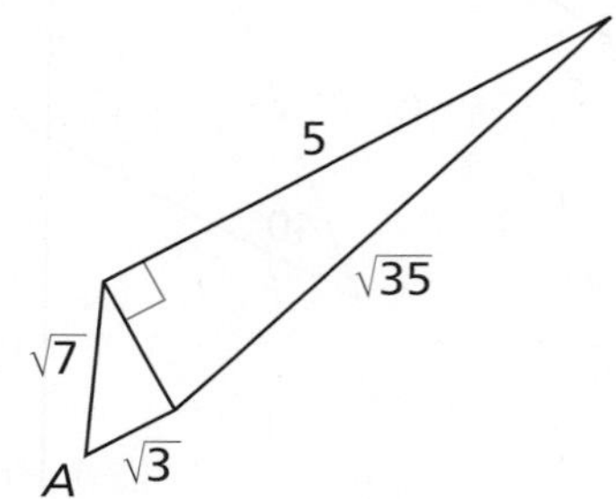

13. Find the area of a regular hexagon with side lengths of 12 m.

14. Find the lateral and total surface areas for each labeled figure.

a.

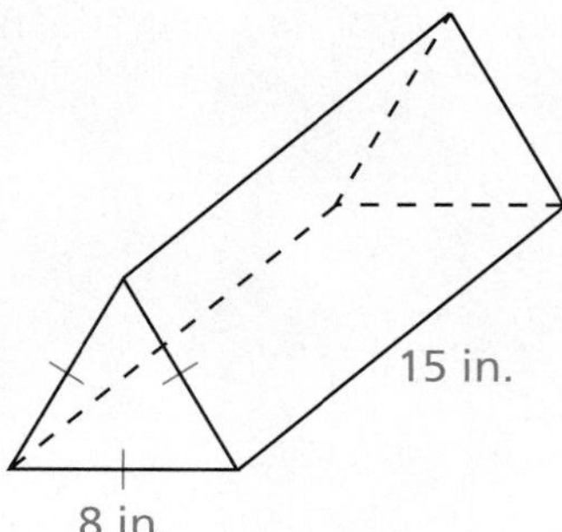

b.

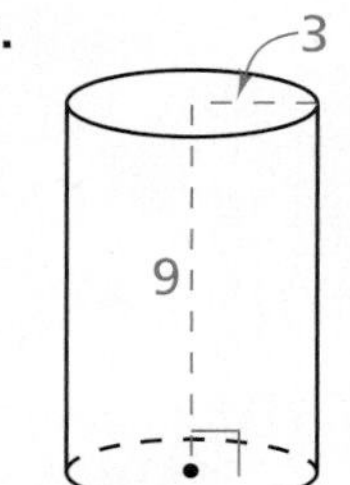

c.

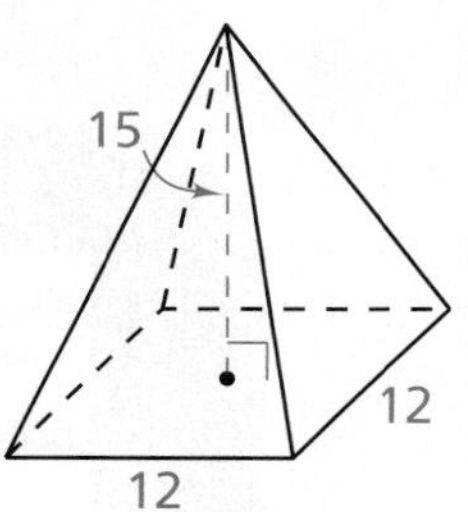

d.

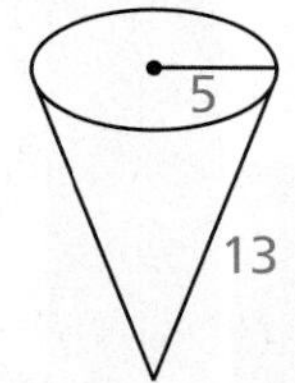

15. A parallelogram that has a length of 18 inches and a height of 9 inches is scaled using the following scale factors r. What are the parallelogram's new dimensions after being scaled?

a. $r = \frac{5}{3}$ **b.** $r = 3.5$ **c.** $r = \frac{4}{9}$

16. Name at least four different measurements you could take on the following pair of figures to convince someone that the two figures are well-scaled copies of each other.

17. Use graph paper to scale the figure by the factor 3.

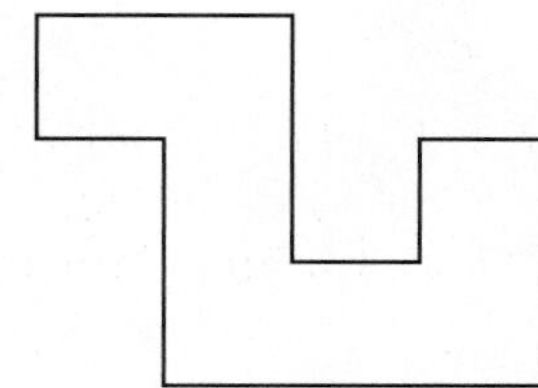

18. Determine whether or not the following can be scaled copies and explain your answer.

a. One triangle has side lengths of 3, 4, and 5. Another triangle has side lengths of 7.5, 10, and 12.

b. One rectangle has dimensions of 4 feet and 11 feet. Another has dimensions of 11 feet and 30 feet.

19. A scaled rhombus now has sides of length 12 cm. If the scale factor was $\frac{2}{3}$, what was the length of a side of the original rhombus?

20. Decide if the pair of polygons are scaled copies. Explain how you made your decision.

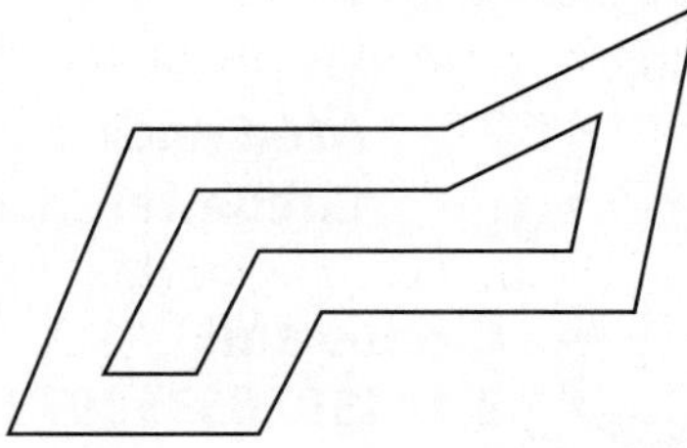

21. A polygon is scaled by a factor of 150%. The original polygon is then compared to the scaled one. Find the ratio of any two corresponding sides and any two corresponding angles of the polygons.

Chapter 5

Investigations at a Glance

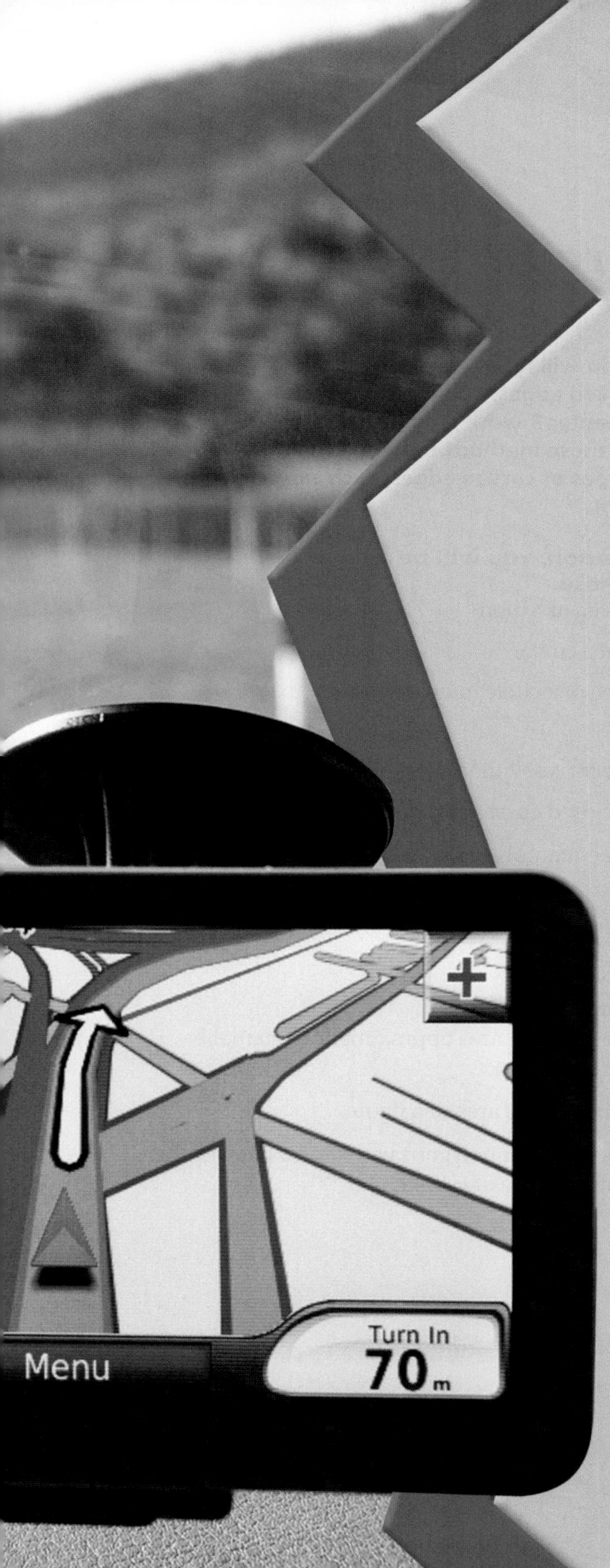

Circles

Trilateration is one way to determine a location relative to fixed reference points. If you have the equipment, you can measure your distance from a radio beacon. Draw a circle on a map, centered at the beacon, with your distance from the beacon as its radius. Next, measure your distance from a second radio beacon. That gives you a second circle to draw on your map. The distance from a third beacon pinpoints your location exactly.

A global positioning system or GPS works on a similar principle, but in three dimensions. The GPS receiver determines the distance from at least three GPS satellites. This information determines three spheres, each centered at a satellite, with radius equal to the corresponding distance to the receiver. The intersection of the spheres gives your location. GPS uses the signal from a fourth satellite to confirm your location.

Vocabulary and Notation

- apothem
- arc, $\widehat{AB}$
- central angle
- chord
- circumscribe
- concentric circles
- diameter
- inscribe
- inscribed angle
- limit
- linear approximation
- locus
- Monte Carlo Method
- pi, π
- power of a point, $\Pi(P)$
- probability
- secant
- secant angle
- sector
- tangent
- $a_n \rightarrow r$ (a_n approaches r)

Area and Circumference

In *Area and Circumference*, you will learn ways to find the areas of figures that have curved edges. The methods you learned for finding area in Chapter 3 work only for polygons and circles. Now you will use those methods to help you find areas of figures with other types of curved edges, such as figures formed by spilled paint.

By the end of this investigation, you will be able to answer questions like these.

1. How can you calculate the area of a blob?
2. What is the circumference of a circle?
3. What formula relates the area of a circle to its circumference?

You will learn how to

- approximate areas of closed curves with inner and outer sums
- approximate perimeters of closed curves with linear approximation
- establish that the area of a regular polygon is $\frac{1}{2}$ the perimeter times the apothem
- approximate areas and perimeters of circles with inscribed and circumscribed regular polygons

You will develop these habits and skills:

- Visualize the effect of a finer mesh on area approximation or smaller segments on perimeter approximation.
- Determine the effect of scaling on the area of a figure.
- Relate areas and perimeters of regular polygons with increasing numbers of sides to the area and circumference of a circle.

How would you measure the size of an oil spill?

5.01 Getting Started

Triangles and other polygons are convenient geometric shapes to study, but many objects in our world are not composed of line segments. Circles, egg shapes, and curves of all types are as common as polygons. How can you find the area of a shape that has curves?

For You to Explore

One way to find the area of a polygon is to divide it into triangles and then find the area of each triangle. What can you do for a figure that is not a polygon? For example, how can you estimate the area of this blob? Can you find it exactly?

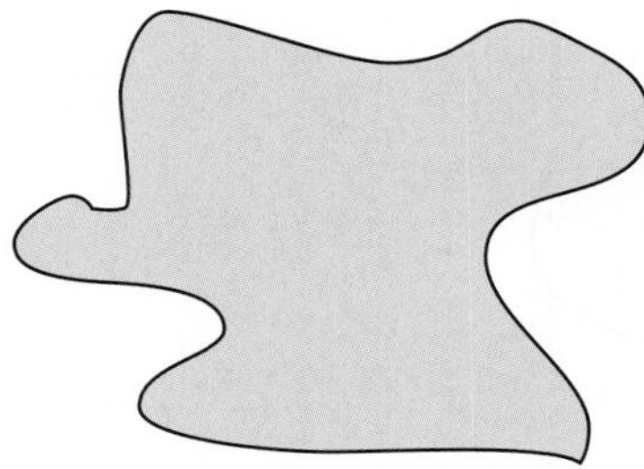

For shapes such as this, the best you can do is estimate the area.

1. List several ways that you can estimate the area of an irregular shape such as the blob above.
2. List several ways that you can estimate the perimeter of an irregular shape such as the blob above.
3. Try each of your methods with the blob or some other shape.

Exercises *Practicing Habits of Mind*

On Your Own

One mathematical habit for estimating a value is to find upper and lower bounds for the value. Then you squeeze those bounds together. Follow the steps in Exercises 4 and 5 to find bounds for the area of the blob.

4. Begin by placing the blob on a piece of graph paper that has $\frac{1}{2}$ in.-by-$\frac{1}{2}$ in. squares.

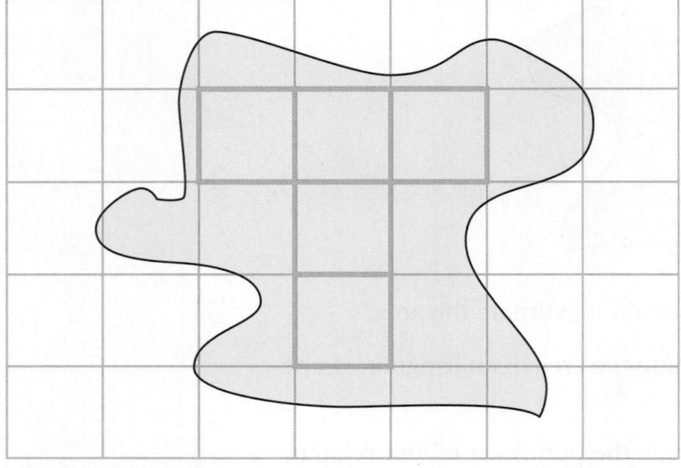

a. Count the number of squares that are completely inside the figure.

b. Add the areas of those inner squares to find an area that is definitely less than the area of the blob.

5. Now count all the squares that are either inside the blob or touching it.

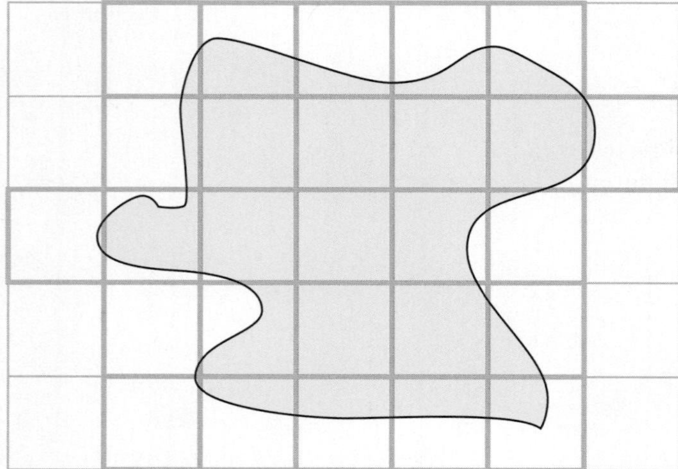

a. How many of these squares are there?

b. Add the areas of these squares to find an area that is definitely greater than the area of the blob.

Maintain Your Skills

6. Trace this square and scale it by a factor of $\frac{1}{2}$.

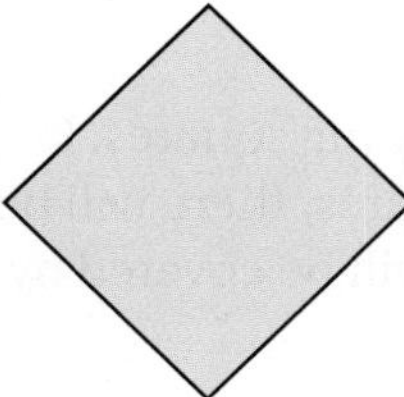

What is the area of the initial square? What is the area of the scaled square?

In order to scale these polygons, you should measure their sides. To calculate their areas, either use a formula or think of a way to estimate each area.

7. Trace this octagon and scale it by a factor of 2.

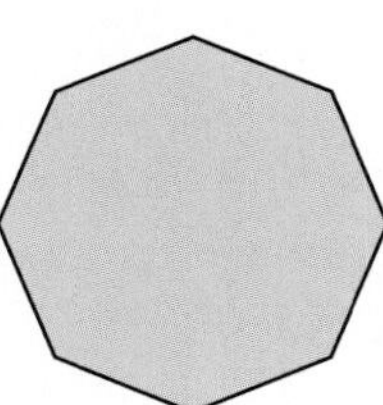

What is the approximate area of the initial octagon? What is the approximate area of the scaled octagon?

8. Trace this parallelogram and scale it by a factor of $\frac{1}{3}$.

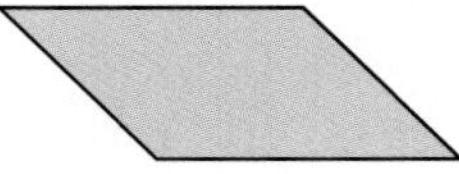

What is the approximate area of the initial parallelogram? What is the approximate area of the scaled parallelogram?

5.02 Area and Perimeter

Now you can refine your approach to find the area of an irregular shape, such as the area of the blob in Lesson 5.01.

Minds in Action

episode 15

Tony and Sasha are discussing the method for finding the area of the blob in Exercises 4 and 5.

Tony There's a pretty wide range between the inner and outer areas we found for the blob in these two exercises.

Sasha Well, the grid that the blob is on is made of really big squares. I bet if we put the blob on a grid with smaller squares, there will be less of a range. By doing that, more of the blob will be covered by whole squares.

Mathematicians say that you are making a "finer mesh."

Tony Let's try this grid. Each square is $\frac{1}{4}$ in. by $\frac{1}{4}$ in. So each square has an area of $\frac{1}{16}$ square inch.

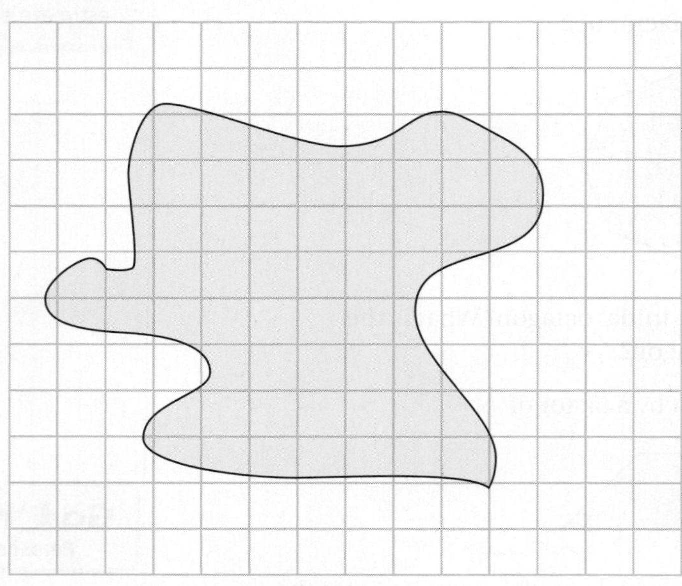

Sasha I'll take it from here. There are 32 squares completely inside the blob. So that's $32 \times \frac{1}{16}$ square inch, or $\frac{32}{16}$ square inches. There are 47 border squares. So that's $(32 + 47) \times \frac{1}{16}$ square inch, or $\frac{79}{16}$ square inches.

Tony Hmm, the area of the blob must be somewhere in between those two numbers.

Sasha That's still not very accurate. We'd better use smaller squares!

For You to Do

In this picture, the squares on the graph paper are $\frac{1}{8}$ in. by $\frac{1}{8}$ in.

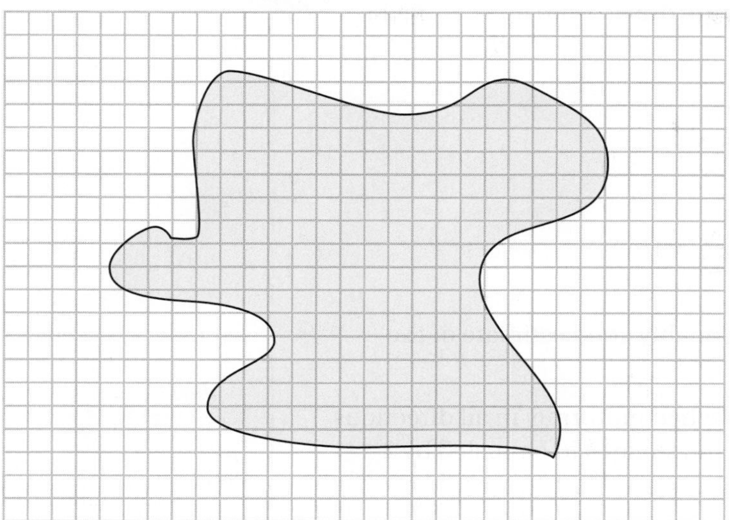

1. a. What is the area of each small square?
   b. Calculate the inner sum and the outer sum to place the area of the blob between two numbers.
   c. Are these numbers closer to each other than the numbers Sasha found?
2. Give an argument to support the claim that as the number of squares per inch increases (that is, as the mesh of the graph paper gets finer), the difference between the outer sum and the inner sum decreases.

You now have the basic idea behind how the area of a closed curve (like the blob) is defined. In summary:

- You cover the region with graph paper and compute the inner and outer sums. You make the mesh finer and repeat the process.
- This produces a sequence of inner and outer sums. The difference between these inner and outer sums can be made as small as you want by making the mesh even finer.
- This means the inner and outer sums get closer and closer to a single number. This is the **limit** of the whole process.
- This single number is the area of the region.

You already know a way to compare the areas of two polygons when one is a scaled copy of the other. If a polygon is scaled by some positive number r, then the ratio of the area of the scaled copy to the original is r^2. Is this true for blobs, too?

In-Class Experiment

Imagine that a blob and a grid of squares are drawn onto a big rubber sheet.

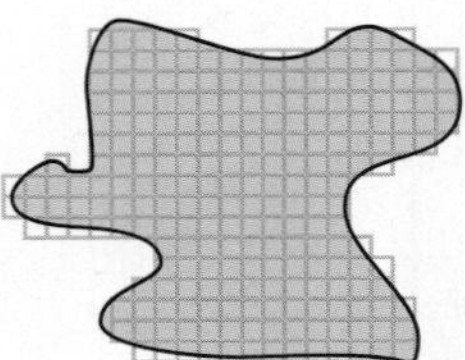

The area of these 228 squares gives a reasonably good estimate of the blob's area.

Now imagine that the rubber sheet is stretched uniformly in all directions by a factor of 2. This causes the blob and the squares to be scaled by 2 as well.

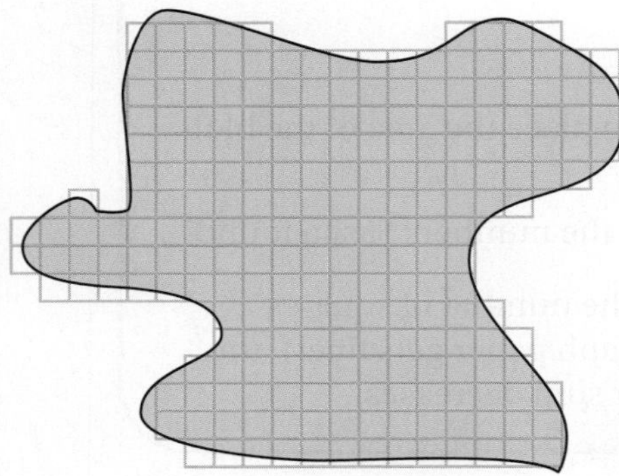

Estimate the area of the blob, now that the squares have been stretched by a factor of 2.

3. By what factor did the area of each square increase?
4. What is a good estimate for the blob's area in terms of the number of squares?
5. If the area of one square before was S, what is it now? What is the area of the 228 stretched squares?

For You to Do

6. What would have happened if you had stretched the rubber sheet uniformly in all directions by a factor of r? Answer the questions from the In-Class Experiment for a rubber sheet stretched by a factor of r.

Archimedes used a **linear approximation** method for estimating the length of a curved path that is easy to apply. Just approximate the curve with line segments and add the lengths of the segments.

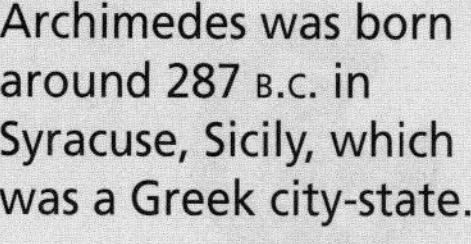

Archimedes was born around 287 B.C. in Syracuse, Sicily, which was a Greek city-state.

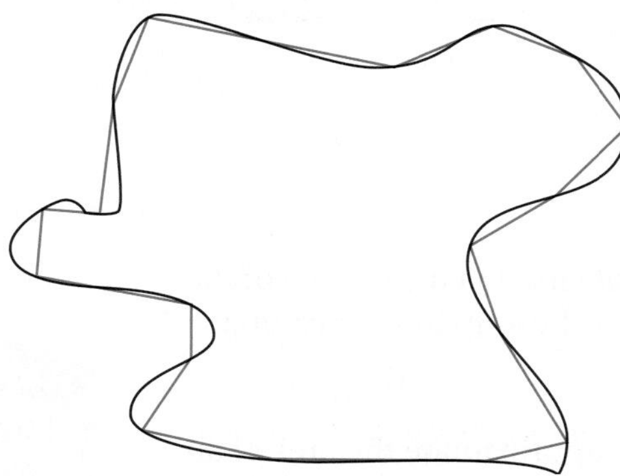

For You to Do

7. Approximate the perimeter of the blob above using this linear approximation technique.

For Discussion

8. How can you improve your estimate?

Perimeters of Circles

Of all curves, perhaps the most recognizable is the circle. The name given to the perimeter of a circle is one you already know—the circumference. Circumference is reserved for circles and the round cross sections of three-dimensional shapes such as spheres and cylinders.

The perimeter of a circle can be found through the following process.

- Inscribe a regular polygon in the circle. Circumscribe a regular polygon with the same number of sides around the circle.
- Calculate the perimeter of each polygon.
- Make another pair of inscribed and circumscribed polygons with double the number of sides. Then calculate the perimeters of the new polygons.
- Continue this process. The inner and outer perimeters will approach a common value. That number is the circle's circumference.

To **inscribe** a polygon in a circle means to draw it so that all of its vertices are on the circle. To **circumscribe** a polygon around a circle means to draw it so that all of its sides are touching the circle.

Exercises Practicing Habits of Mind

Check Your Understanding

1. Draw a circle of radius one inch and approximate its area using each of the following mesh sizes. Describe any patterns that show up in your estimates.
   a. $\frac{1}{2}$ in. **b.** $\frac{1}{4}$ in. **c.** $\frac{1}{8}$ in. **d.** $\frac{1}{16}$ in.

2. **a.** Explain in words a method you have used to approximate the area of an irregular shape.
   b. Using what you learned in Chapter 3, find the area of a right triangle with sides 3 in., 4 in., and 5 in.
   c. Suppose you did not know the area formula for a triangle. Go through the inner and outer sums process for a 3-4-5 triangle to approximate its area. See how close you can get to the actual area.

Habits of Mind

Strategize. Sometimes a shape has symmetry that allows you to make counting easier with shortcuts. Use shortcuts wherever possible.

3. The two crescent moons are scaled copies of each other. What is the ratio of their areas?

4. How do the areas of the two circles compare?
   a. A circle of radius 2 is scaled to a circle of radius 6.
   b. A circle of radius 2 is scaled to a circle of radius 1.

In Exercises 5–10, you will practice the process of drawing inscribed and circumscribed polygons for a circle. If you are not able to make the drawings yourself, just copy and complete the table in Exercise 8 by taking measurements directly from the drawings provided.

5. Draw a circle. Inscribe a square in the circle and circumscribe a square around the circle. Calculate the perimeters of the two squares and thus place the circumference of the circle between two numbers.

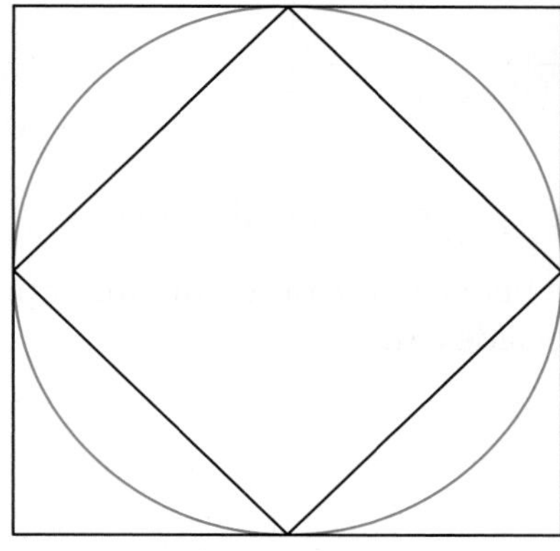

Remember...

Draw means to use either pencil-and-paper drawing tools or geometry software.

6. Using a circle of the same size, inscribe a regular octagon in the circle and circumscribe a regular octagon around the circle. Calculate the perimeter of the two octagons and thus place the circumference of the circle between two numbers.

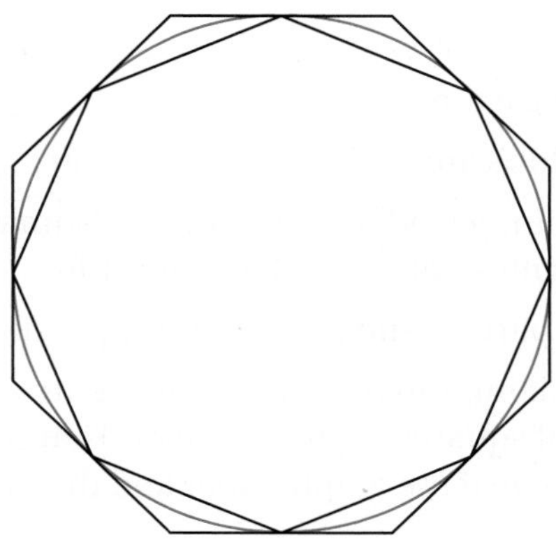

Go Online
Pearsonsuccessnet.com

7. Carry this process one step further with inscribed and circumscribed 16-gons.

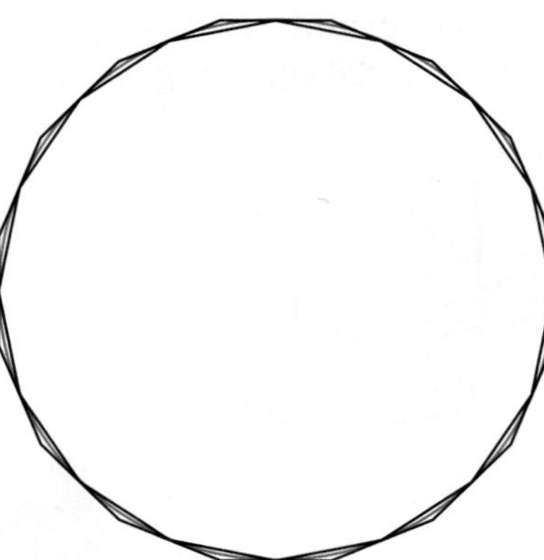

8. Copy the table. Use the data from Exercises 5–7 to complete it.

Number of Sides	Outer Perimeter	Inner Perimeter	Difference
4	■	■	■
8	■	■	■
16	■	■	■

9. Give an approximation for the perimeter of the circle.

10. Explain why the difference between the outer and inner perimeters decreases as the number of sides increases.

On Your Own

11. a. Draw a blob.
   - Estimate its area using a mesh of $\frac{1}{2}$ in.
   - Estimate the same blob's area using a mesh of $\frac{1}{4}$ in.

   b. Now draw the blob again, scaled by a factor of 2. Estimate the new blob's area three times. Use a mesh of $\frac{1}{2}$ in., $\frac{1}{4}$ in., and 1 in.

   c. Which estimates from part (a) and part (b) are approximately the same?

   d. Explain the following claim. You have a good estimate for a blob's area in terms of a number of squares on graph paper. That same number of squares is a good estimate if the graph paper and the blob get stretched by a factor of *r*.

12. **Take It Further** Imagine that a blob and a grid of squares are drawn onto a big rubber sheet. The area of these 228 squares gives a good estimate of the blob's area.

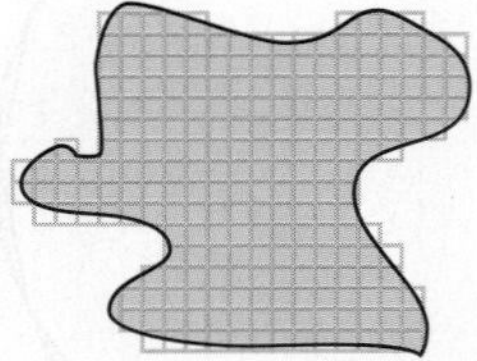

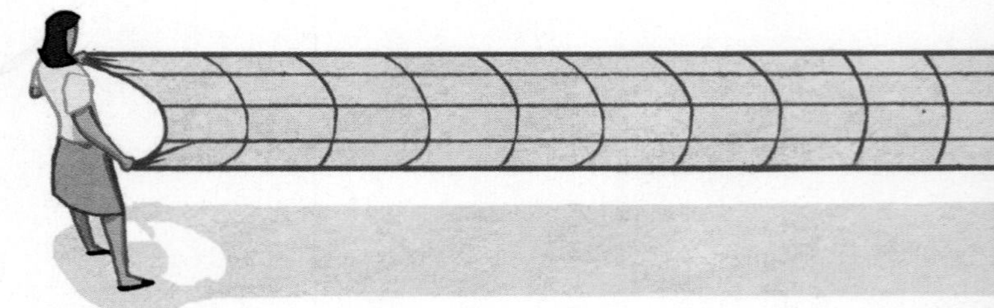

Imagine that the rubber sheet is stretched in just one direction. Now all of the squares have one side length doubled and one unchanged.

a. What shape do the squares become?

b. What is the area of the new shapes compared to the area of the squares?

c. What happens to the area of the blob?

d. Is the blob a scaled copy of the original? If your answer is yes, what is the scale factor? If your answer is no, explain why not.

Sasha has a way to make the linear approximation technique easier. She uses what she calls a regular approximation for a curve. She picks some length, say $\frac{1}{4}$ in., and marks it off around the curve until she gets too close to the starting point to mark another segment. Then she just multiplies the number of segments by $\frac{1}{4}$ and adds on the last little gap.

13. Use Sasha's regular approximation method to estimate the length of the curve below.

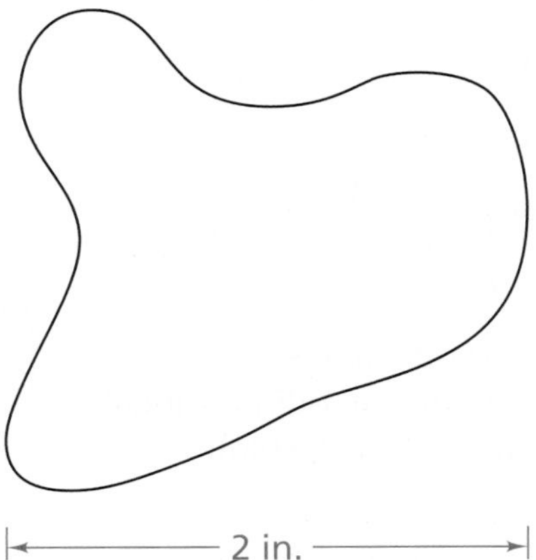

14. Many people use Sasha's regular approximation to estimate distance on road maps.

a. Explain how this works.

b. Use a road map and regular approximation to estimate the distance between your hometown and a city many states away.

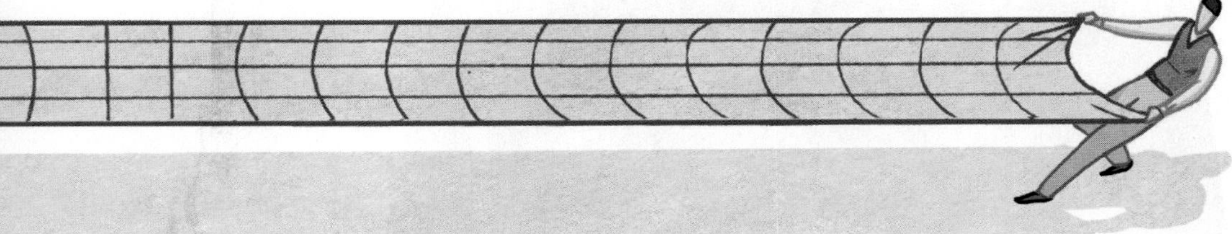

15. **Standardized Test Prep** The circle has a square circumscribed around it. It has another square inscribed inside it. What is the ratio of the perimeter of the circumscribed square to the perimeter of the inscribed square?

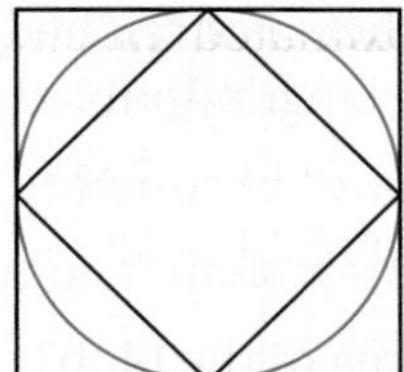

A. $\sqrt{2}$ **B.** 2

C. $2\sqrt{2}$ **D.** 4

Maintain Your Skills

For Exercises 16–19, answer parts (a), (b), and (c).

a. What is the new side length of the cube?

b. What was the area of a face on the original cube? What is the new area of a face?

c. What was the volume of the original cube? What is the new volume?

16. A cube with side length 1 cm is scaled by a factor of 2.
17. A cube with side length 1 cm is scaled by a factor of 3.
18. A cube with side length 1 cm is scaled by a factor of $\frac{1}{2}$.
19. A cube with side length 1 cm is scaled by a factor of r.
20. You learned how to approximate the area of 2-dimensional blobs with squares. In a similar way, you can approximate the volume of 3-dimensional blobs with cubes. Write a rule that tells how the volume of such a blob changes when it is scaled by a factor of r.

How can volume help you guess the number of pennies that would fill the jar?

5.03 Connecting Area, Circumference

In Lesson 5.02, you approximated the circumference of a circle with inscribed and circumscribed polygons. Now the idea is to find a formula that connects the area of a circle to its circumference. First you must learn about the *apothem* of a regular polygon.

Definition

The apothem *a* of a regular polygon is the length of the perpendicular segment from the center point of the polygon to one of its sides.

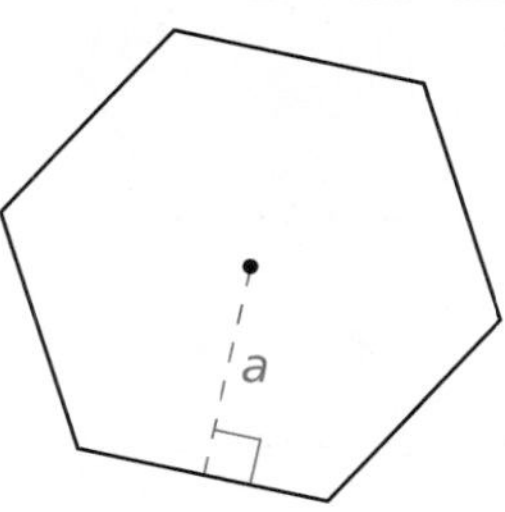

For Discussion

1. Find the area of a regular hexagon of side 12 in.

A regular hexagon's side is the same length as the radius of its circumscribed circle. Can you explain why?

In-Class Experiment

In this experiment, you will find a formula for the areas of regular polygons.

2. Look at the regular pentagon and divide it into five congruent triangles meeting at the center. What role does the apothem a of the pentagon play for each of these triangles?

3. If s is the length of each side of the pentagon, what is the area of each congruent triangle? What is the area of the whole pentagon?

4. What would change if the regular polygon had four sides, six sides, or n sides? Can you find the polygon's perimeter somewhere in the formula for its area?

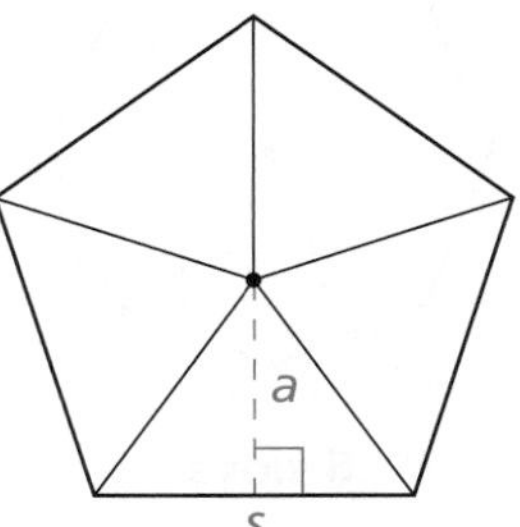

The result of the In-Class Experiment is important enough to record as a theorem.

Theorem 5.1

The area *A* of a regular polygon is equal to half of the product of its perimeter *P* and its apothem *a*.

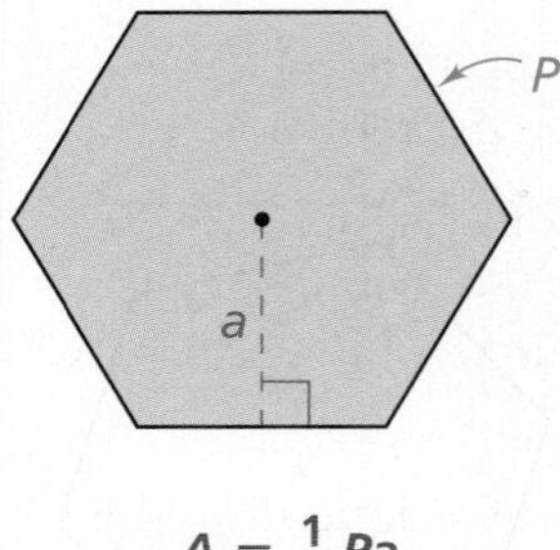

$$A = \frac{1}{2}Pa$$

For You to Do

5. What is the area of a regular hexagon with side length 8?

6. Use the area formula $A = \frac{1}{2}Pa$ to calculate the area of a square with side length 12. Check your result by calculating the area of the square another way.

For Discussion

7. Below are three regular polygons, each inscribed in a circle with radius r. The number of sides in each polygon increases from 4 to 8 to 16. Imagine that these pictures continue for a sequence of regular polygons with more and more sides inscribed in this same circle.

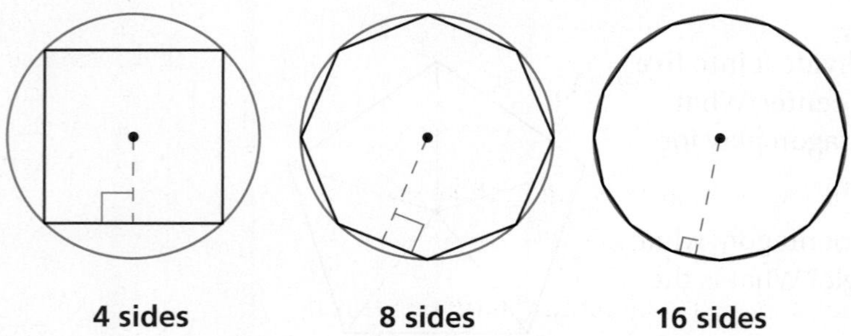

Think about how the length of each polygon's apothem changes as you draw polygons with more and more sides. Compare each polygon's perimeter and area with the circumference and area of the circle each is inscribed in.

Habits of Mind

Detect the key characteristics. As the number of sides in each polygon increases, it becomes very difficult to distinguish the polygon from the circle and an apothem from a radius.

Minds in Action episode 16

Tony and Sasha look at Theorem 5.1.

Sasha Tony, do you think we could find a similar formula relating the area of a circle to its perimeter?

Tony Well, I know that circumference is a circle's perimeter. How does the apothem a for different shapes compare to the radius r?

Sasha The apothem is the distance from the center of a regular polygon to any of its sides. And as the number of sides increases, a regular polygon starts to look like a circle. The equivalent of the apothem in a circle has to be the radius.

Tony Ah . . . now I get it! So the formula for the area of a circle should be something like one half the circumference times the radius.

Sasha I think we can basically prove that by approximating circles with polygons. We could inscribe a sequence of regular polygons in a circle and study their areas. Let's try . . .

Facts and Notation

To make this more precise, use the following notation.

- **Let A, C, and r be the area, circumference, and radius of the circle.**
- **Number the polygons in the sequence 1, 2, 3, ...**
- **Let the areas of the polygons be $A_1, A_2, A_3, \ldots$; let their perimeters be $P_1, P_2, P_3, \ldots$; and let their apothems be $a_1, a_2, a_3, \ldots$.**

Instead of saying that the length of the apothem approaches the radius as n gets larger and larger, write $a_n \to r$. Using this shorthand notation, rewrite the assumptions as follows.

1. $a_n \to r$ **2.** $P_n \to C$ **3.** $A_n \to A$

This arrow notation means something quite precise in calculus. It means that you can make the difference between the length of the apothem and the radius as small as you want by increasing the number of polygon sides enough.

Here is the formula for the area of the nth regular polygon in the sequence.

$$A_n = \frac{1}{2}P_n a_n$$

Now, because of the three assumptions, as n gets larger and larger, you can rewrite the formula.

$$\frac{1}{2}P_n a_n \to \frac{1}{2}Cr$$

You can conclude the following.

$$A_n \to A$$

You can think of it this way.

$$\begin{array}{ccc} A_n & = & \frac{1}{2} P_n \, a_n \\ \downarrow & & \downarrow \;\; \downarrow \\ A & = & \frac{1}{2} C \;\;\; r \end{array}$$

This argument leads to the following theorem.

Theorem 5.2

The area of a circle is one half its circumference times its radius.

$$A = \frac{1}{2}Cr$$

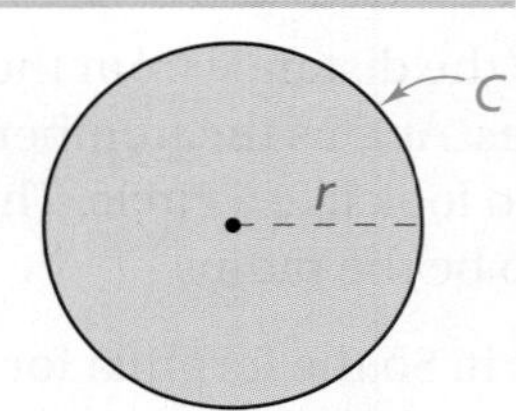

To make this proof completely rigorous, you would need to fill in several gaps about limits and be more precise about the definitions of area and circumference. For now, an intuitive understanding is sufficient.

For a precise proof of this theorem, you will have to wait until you study calculus.

For You to Do

8. A flying disc has an approximate area of 154 in.^{2} and a diameter of 14 in. Find its circumference to the nearest inch.

Exercises *Practicing Habits of Mind*

Check Your Understanding

1. A circular garden has a radius of 1 meter and a circumference of about 6.25 meters. What is the area of the garden?

2. A square with side 2 cm is inscribed in a circle.

a. Find the radius of this circle.

b. The circumference of the circle is about 8.9 cm. What is its area?

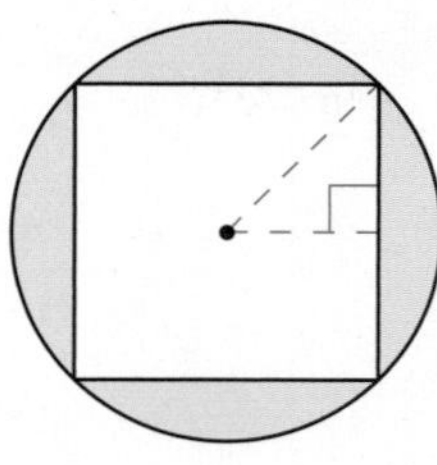

3. Why is a regular hexagon's side the same length as the radius of its circumscribed circle? Explain your answer with a proof.

4. A regular hexagon is inscribed in a circle of radius 1 in.

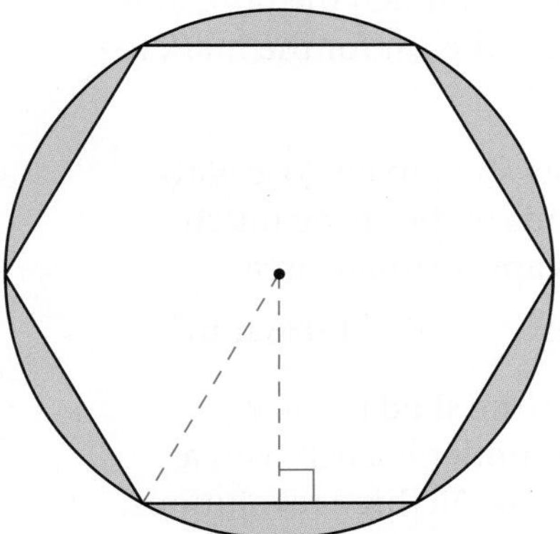

If the area of the shaded region is about 0.54 square inch, what is the circumference of the circle?

On Your Own

5. Find the area of each figure.

   a. A stop sign has sides that are 6 inches long and an apothem that is 7.2 inches.

   b. In the figure, an equilateral triangle is inscribed in a circle of radius 2 cm. The center of the circle that circumscribes a triangle is the triangle's circumcenter. The circumcenter of an equilateral triangle divides each of the triangle's medians into two segments. One is twice as long as the other. This should give you enough information to find the side length of the equilateral triangle using the shaded triangle in the figure.

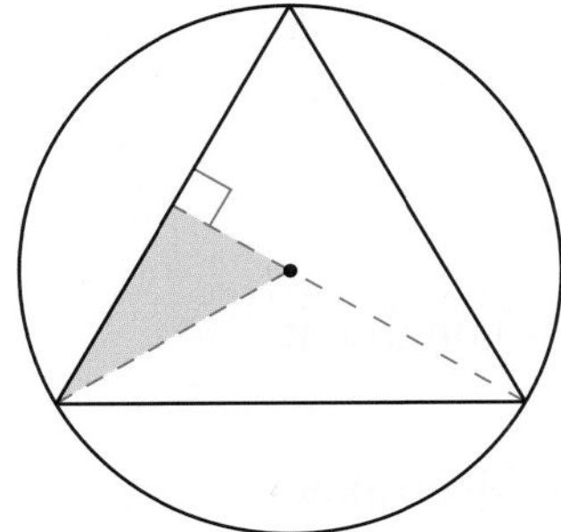

6. Can you use the formula $A = \frac{1}{2}Pa$ for irregular polygons? Explain.

7. A wheel of a toy car has an area of 5 cm^2 and a radius of about 1.26 cm. There is a mark on the point of the wheel that touches the floor. You start pushing the car forward and the marked point does not touch the floor any more. What is the shortest distance you have to push the car for the mark to touch the floor again?

8. **Standardized Test Prep** Beth wants to find the area she can enclose with 264 mm of string. She makes a circle so that the ends of the string touch. The circle has a radius of about 42 mm. What is its approximate area?

   A. 1764 mm^2 **B.** 3353 mm^2 **C.** 5544 mm^2 **D.** 11,088 mm^2

9. **Take It Further** The Moriarity sisters have to move the shed in their backyard. They jack up the shed and slip two pipes under it, each with a circumference of 8 inches. The sisters get the pipes to roll three revolutions. How far do the sisters move the shed?

10. **Take It Further** A regular polygon with n sides and side length s is inscribed in a circle of radius 1. Show that a regular polygon with $2n$ sides inscribed in the same circle has side length $\sqrt{2 - \sqrt{4 - s^2}}$.

Maintain Your Skills

11. J is the midpoint of side $\overline{NM}$ of an equilateral triangle inscribed in a circle. A regular hexagon is also inscribed in the circle. $\overline{OH}$ is an apothem of the triangle, and $\overline{OK}$ is an apothem of the hexagon.

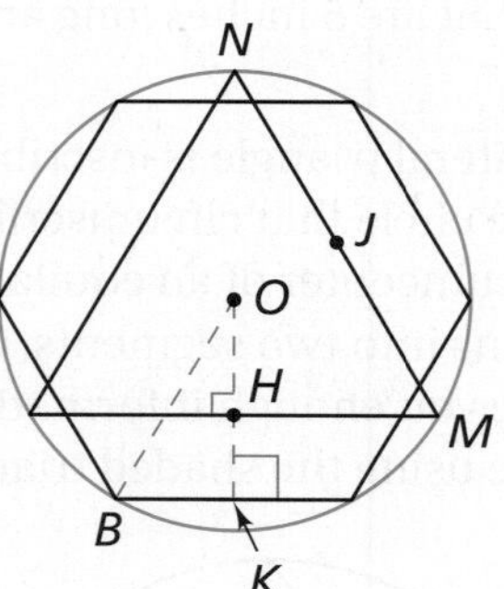

   a. Trace the figure onto a sheet of paper. Draw the radius $\overline{NO}$ and the segment $\overline{OJ}$.

   b. Find the degree measure for each of the following angles.

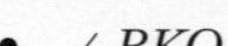

   - $\angle BKO$
   - $\angle KOB$
   - $\angle OBK$
   - $\angle JON$
   - $\angle ONJ$
   - $\angle NJO$

   c. Now consider $\triangle BKO$ and $\triangle OJN$. Prove that they are congruent.

   d. Now show that $\overline{OK}$ and $\overline{NJ}$ are congruent.

   e. Compare the hexagon's apothem with the triangle's side. Explain your conclusion.

In this investigation, you explored ways to find the perimeters and areas of shapes with curved edges. These questions will help you summarize what you have learned.

1. Describe a technique you learned in this investigation for approximating the perimeter of a curve. Use the method you described to approximate the perimeter of the curve at the right.

2. Bill spilled paint and left the blob at the right. Describe how you would use the grid method to estimate the area of Bill's mess.
3. What is the area of a regular octagon with apothem 15 in. and side length 12.4 in.?
4. What is the area of a regular hexagon with side length 3 cm?
5. What is the approximate area of a circular pool with an approximate circumference of 12.6 ft and radius 2 ft?
6. How can you calculate the area of a blob?
7. What is the circumference of a circle?
8. What formula relates the area of a circle to its circumference?

Is there a relationship between the length of the boom surrounding the oil and the area of the oil spill?

Vocabulary and Notation

In this investigation, you learned these terms and this symbol. Make sure you understand what each one means and how to use it.

- **apothem**
- **circumscribe**
- **inscribe**
- **limit**
- **linear approximation**
- $a_n \rightarrow r$ (**a_n approaches r**)

Circles and 3.14159265358979 . . .

In *Circles and 3.14159265358979 . . .*, you will examine the circle formulas that you have known for years. In Investigation 5A, you connected perimeter and area for inscribed and circumscribed polygons to circumference and area for circles. Now you can expand these concepts and develop a deeper understanding of circles and the role of π.

By the end of this investigation, you will be able to answer questions like these.

1. What is π?
2. How can you express the area and the circumference of a circle in terms of π?
3. What is the exact area of the shaded portion of the circle with center O?

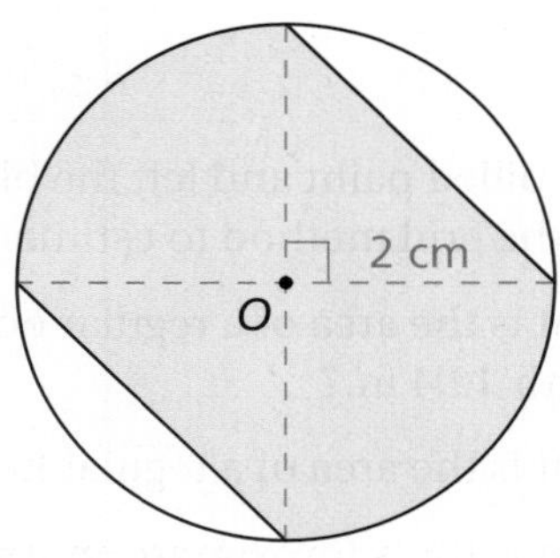

You will learn how to

- use the definition of π as the area of the unit circle
- develop and use the formula $A = \pi r^2$
- develop and use the formula $C = 2\pi r$

You will develop these habits and skills:

- Realize that any decimal or fractional representation of π is only an approximation.
- Apply the area formula for circles to find areas of composite shapes.
- Relate and use different definitions of π.

What questions could you ask about these crop circles?

5.04 Getting Started

You have already learned quite a bit about circles in this chapter. It is time to pull together some ideas.

For You to Explore

All circles are similar. This means that all circles have the same shape, but not necessarily the same size.

1. Two circles have radii 12 cm and 30 cm. Can one of them be scaled to give a congruent copy of the other? Explain.

2. Two circles have radii r and R. Can one of them be scaled to give a congruent copy of the other? Explain.

3. a. Use a ruler and compass or geometry software to copy and complete this table. All the polygons are regular.

Number of Sides	$\frac{\text{Perimeter}}{\text{Apothem}}$
4	■
6	■
8	■
16	■

b. Continue the table for larger numbers of sides.

c. Do the ratios seem to approach any particular number?

Habits of Mind

Visualize. Why do you think all circles are similar?

Exercises *Practicing Habits of Mind*

On Your Own

4. This figure is made up of a quarter circle with radius 1 cm and two equilateral triangles. If the circumference of the whole circle is 6.28 cm, what is the perimeter of the whole shape?

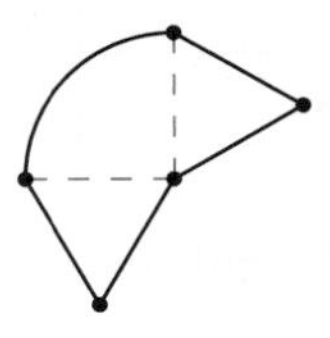

5. A circle's area is about 25.1 square centimeters. A square is inscribed in the circle. Its apothem is 2 cm. What is the total area of the shaded region shown in the figure?

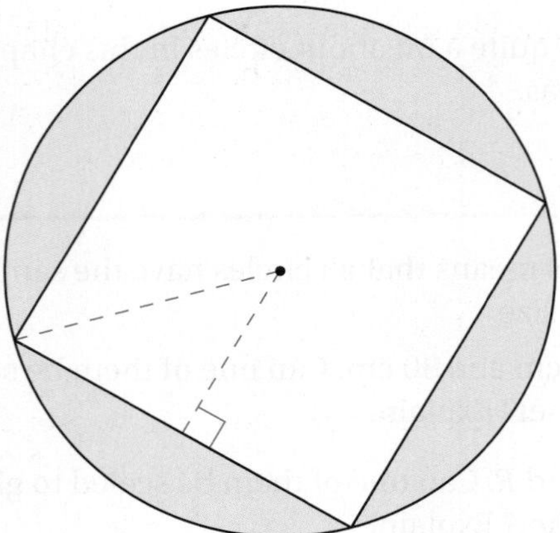

Maintain Your Skills

6. Look at the circles below.

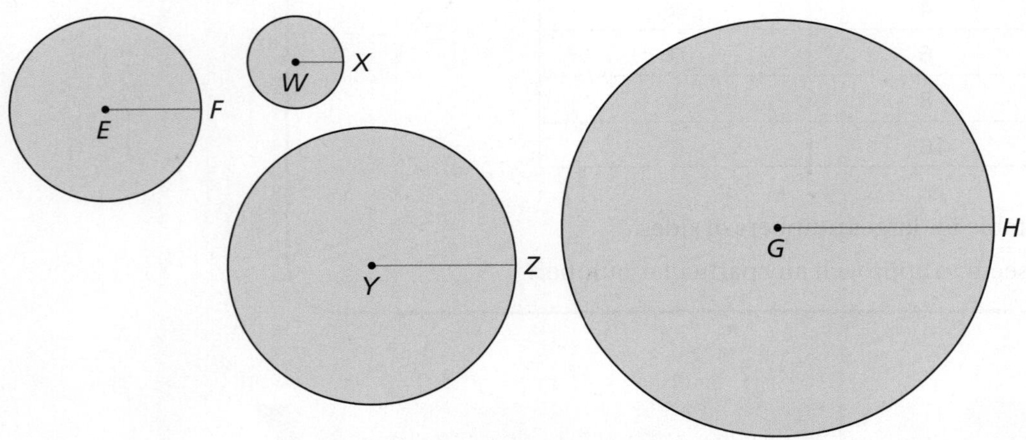

a. Estimate the area A of each circle using any method.

b. Use a ruler to measure each circle's radius r. Then copy and complete the following table.

Circle With Radius	A	$\frac{A}{r^2}$	C	$2r$	$\frac{C}{2r}$
$\overline{EF}$	■	■	■	■	■
$\overline{WX}$	■	■	■	■	■
$\overline{YZ}$	■	■	■	■	■
$\overline{GH}$	■	■	■	■	■

c. Compare the data in the columns of the table and look for invariants.

Habits of Mind

Look for relationships. You might want to look at your answer to Problem 3 in this lesson and see if there are any similarities.

5.05 An Area Formula for Circles

How does the area of a circle change when the circle is scaled? Since you know you can approximate a circle's area with a sequence of regular n-gons, you can scale all of the polygons by s to approximate the area of the scaled circle. The polygons' areas would all change by a factor of s^2, so it seems plausible that the circle's area would, too.

Below is a theorem that summarizes this.

Theorem 5.3

If a circle is scaled by a positive number s, then its area is scaled by s^2.

For You to Do

In Exercise 1 in Lesson 5.02, you approximated the area of a circle with radius one inch to be a bit more than three square inches. Use that result and the theorem above to find a good approximation for the area of a circle with each radius.

1. 2 inches

2. 5 inches

3. 6 inches

4. $\sqrt{3}$ inches

5. $7\frac{1}{2}$ inches

Theorem 5.4

If the area of a circle with radius 1 is k, then the area of a circle with radius r is kr^2.

This theorem says that you can find the area of any circle once you know the area of a circle with radius 1. As you have calculated, the value of that area is a bit more than 3. Rather than call it k, most people call it *pi* and represent it with the Greek letter π.

Definition

Pi (π) is the numerical value of the area of a circle with radius 1.

Therefore, thanks to Theorem 5.4, there is a formula you can use for calculating the area of a circle when you know only its radius.

Theorem 5.5

The area of a circle of radius r is π times the radius squared.

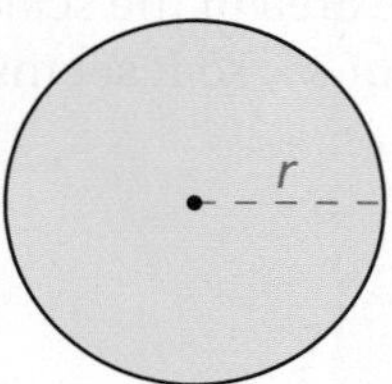

$$A = \pi r^2$$

If you ask a person to tell you the value of π, you might hear 3.14 or $\frac{22}{7}$. While these are indeed approximations of π, neither is equal to π. In fact, π cannot be represented as a ratio of two whole numbers because π is not a rational number. Since π is irrational, its decimal representation is infinite and nonrepeating.

π is usually defined as the ratio of the circumference of a circle to its diameter.

Often, people leave the result of calculations about circles in terms of π. That way, if you want a numerical approximation of the result, you can use whatever approximation for π you prefer.

For Discussion

6. Tony is puzzled. He asks himself, "What do they mean π is the area of a circle of radius 1? One what? If you have a circle of radius 1 foot, it can't have the same area as a circle whose radius is 1 inch. This is all nonsense." Suggest an answer to Tony's question.

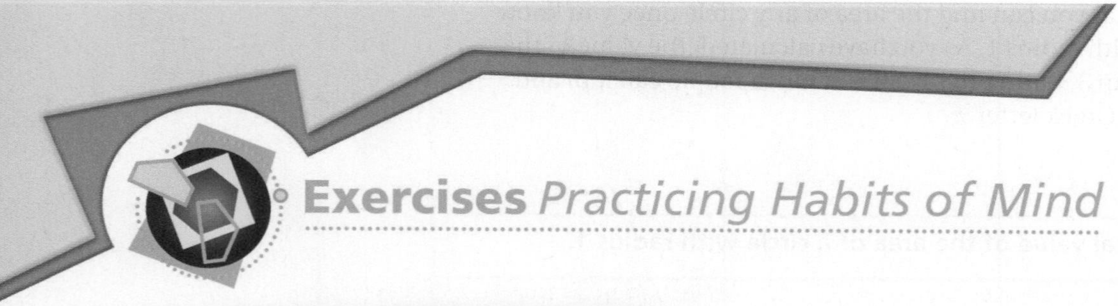

Exercises *Practicing Habits of Mind*

Check Your Understanding

1. Find the area of a circle with the given dimension.

a. a radius of 10 in. **b.** a radius of 5 cm **c.** a diameter of 3 ft

d. the circle obtained by scaling a circle of radius 2 in. by a factor of 5

2. The angle of the wedge in the circle is 45°. The radius of the circle is 1.

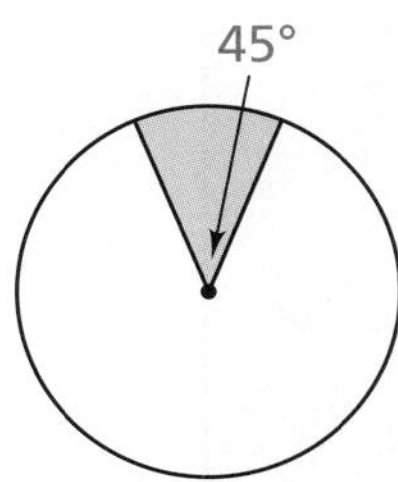

This wedge is really called a **sector** of the circle, which is a region bound by two radii and the circle.

a. What fraction of the circle's area is the wedge?

b. What is the exact area of the circle?

c. What is the exact area of the wedge?

d. Use two common approximations for π to find the area of the wedge.

3. Find the area of each shaded region.

a.
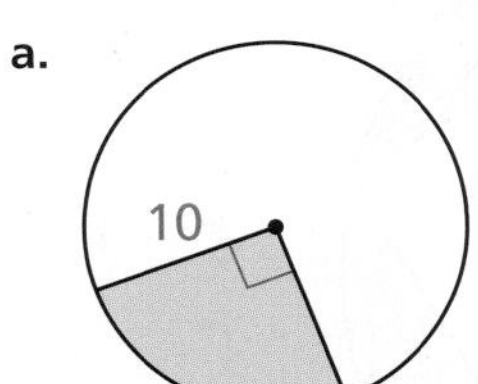

b.
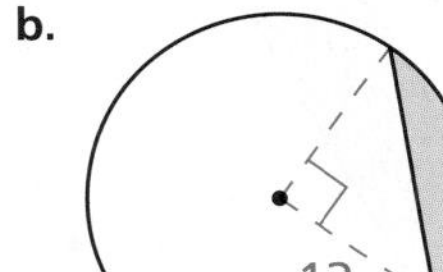

On Your Own

4. Find the area of each shaded region.

a.
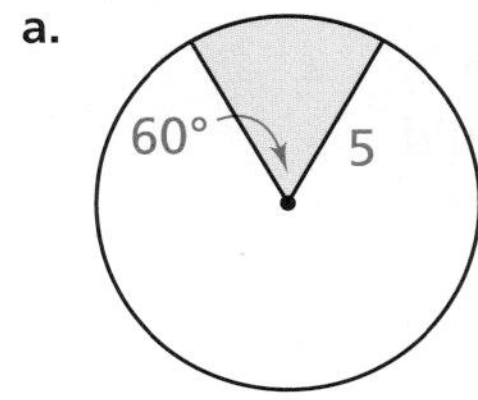

b.
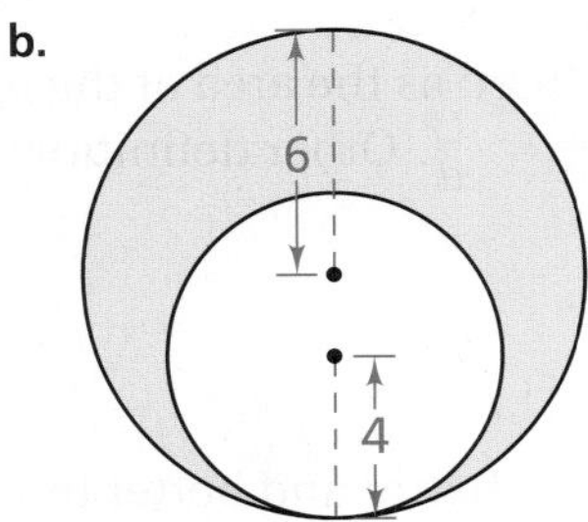

5. An equilateral triangle with sides of length 6.9 cm is inscribed in a circle.

a. Find the length of the apothem and draw a sketch.

b. Find the area of the circle.

c. Shade the part of the circle that is outside the triangle. Find that area.

6. Suppose the side length of each square is 6 cm. Find the area of each shaded region and each white region.

a.

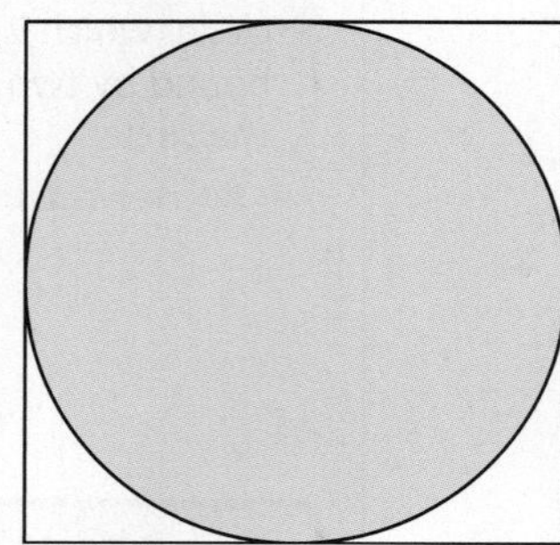

b.

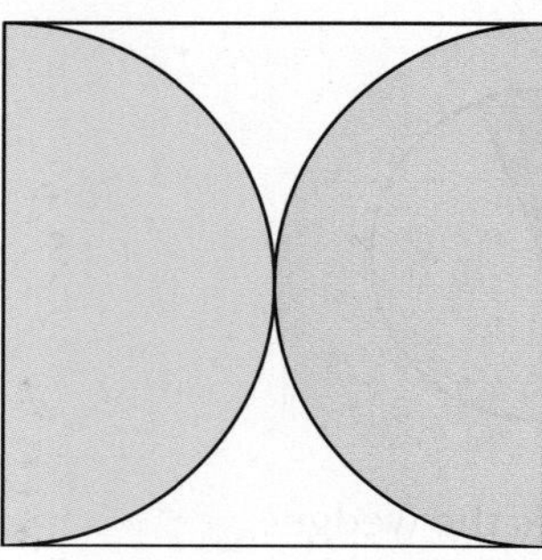

c. Compare your answers for parts (a) and (b) above. What do you notice? Explain.

7. The square at the right is inscribed in a circle. The square's apothem is 2 cm. What is the total area of the shaded region?

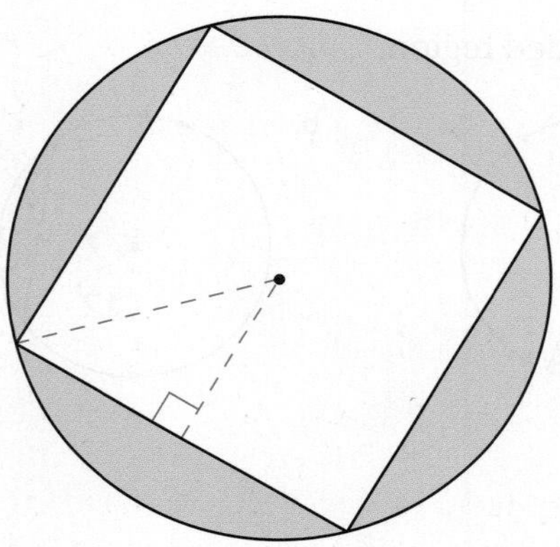

8. **Standardized Test Prep** For Zach's birthday, his grandmother makes an extra large cheesecake. She usually uses a pan that has a 7-inch diameter. This time she uses a pan with a 14-inch diameter. She usually serves wedges that are $\frac{1}{12}$ of the cake. This time Zach asks for a wedge with an angle twice the usual size. How many times greater than normal is the area of Zach's birthday serving?

A. 2 times B. 4 times C. 6 times D. 8 times

9. **Take It Further** In this lesson, π is defined as the area of the unit circle. In a note, another definition given is $\pi = \frac{C}{d}$. Other definitions of π could be as follows.

a. $\pi = \frac{A}{r^2}$

b. $\pi = \frac{C}{2r}$

c. π is the number you can approximate better and better by calculating the ratio $\frac{P}{2a}$ for regular polygons with perimeter P and apothem a that have more and more sides.

d. π is half the circumference of the unit circle.

e. π is the circumference of the circle with a unit diameter.

Choose at least two of these definitions of π and prove that they are equivalent to one of the two definitions given in this lesson.

Maintain Your Skills

10. The following figures are unit circles with a shaded sector. Find the area of each sector.

a.

b.

c.
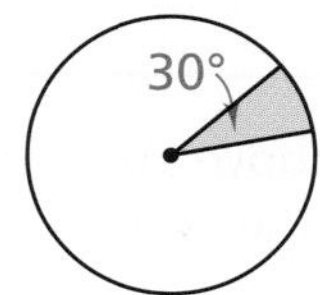

d.
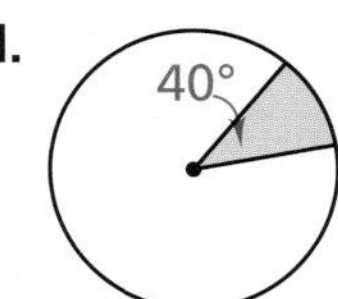

e.

f.
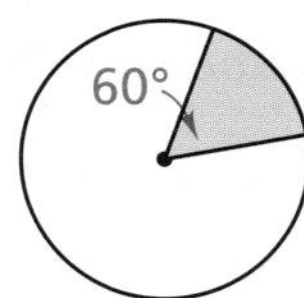

g. When the angle grows by 10°, how does the area of the sector change?

Historical Perspective

Representations of π

The number π has intrigued people for centuries. The number π is not the ratio of two integers, but there are many ways to represent it. Here are a few. The numbers given in parentheses represent the years in which the equations were discovered.

(1655, Wallis) $\frac{\pi}{2} = \frac{2 \cdot 2}{1 \cdot 3} \cdot \frac{4 \cdot 4}{3 \cdot 5} \cdot \frac{6 \cdot 6}{5 \cdot 7} \cdots$

(1593, Viète) $\frac{2}{\pi} = \sqrt{\frac{1}{2}} \cdot \sqrt{\frac{1}{2} + \frac{1}{2}\sqrt{\frac{1}{2}}} \cdot \sqrt{\frac{1}{2} + \frac{1}{2}\sqrt{\frac{1}{2} + \frac{1}{2}\sqrt{\frac{1}{2}}}} \cdots$

(1748, Euler) $\frac{\pi^2}{6} = 1 + \frac{1}{4} + \frac{1}{9} + \frac{1}{16} + \frac{1}{25} + \cdots$

(1914, Ramanujan)

$$\frac{1}{\pi} = \frac{5}{2^4} + \frac{47}{2^{13}} + \frac{3^3 \cdot 89}{2^{25}} + \frac{5^3 \cdot 131}{2^{34}} + \cdots + \binom{2n}{n}^3 \frac{42n + 5}{2^{12n+4}} + \cdots$$

The notation $\binom{n}{k}$ stands for the kth entry in the nth row of Pascal's Triangle. For example, $\binom{4}{3} = \frac{4!}{(4-3)! \cdot 3!} = \frac{4 \cdot 3 \cdot 2 \cdot 1}{1 \cdot 3 \cdot 2 \cdot 1} = 4$.

5.06 Circumference

You can use Theorem 5.2 to express the circumference of a circle in terms of its radius. Suppose a circle has radius r, circumference C, and area A. You know the following two formulas, so you just need to do some algebra.

$$A = \frac{1}{2}Cr \qquad A = \pi r^2$$

For Discussion

1. Combine the two equations above and write a formula for C (the circumference) in terms of r (the radius).

Your answer is very important and you should remember it as a theorem.

Theorem 5.6

The circumference of a circle of radius r is 2π times the radius.

$$C = 2\pi r$$

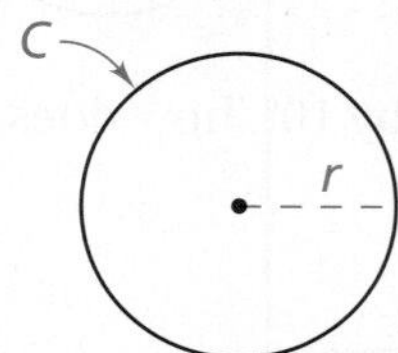

For You to Do

2. The circumference of a circle is approximately how many times its radius?

   A. five **B.** six **C.** seven

3. The circumference of a circle is approximately how many times its diameter?

   A. three **B.** four **C.** five

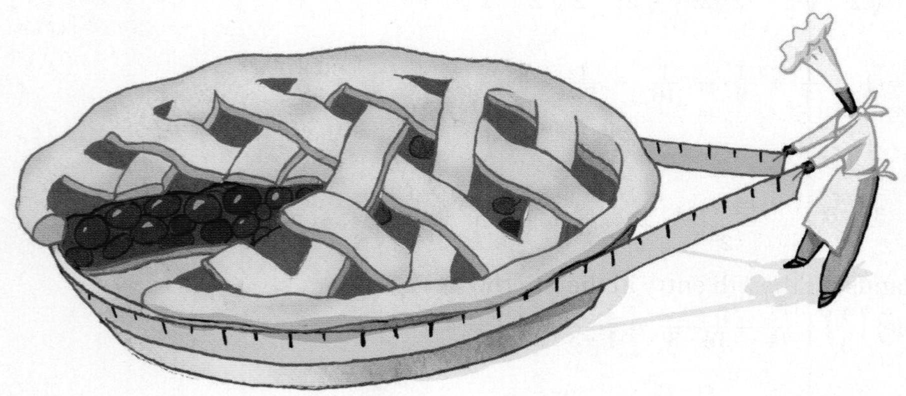

Exercises *Practicing Habits of Mind*

Check Your Understanding

For Exercises 1–3, you are given a circle of radius 2 cm. Draw a sector of the given size. The sector determines two arcs on the circle. How long is each arc in centimeters?

An *arc* is the set of points on a circle that lie on the round edge of a sector.

1. 60°

2. 30°

3. 45°

4. True or false: The ratio of a circle's circumference to its diameter is the same for all circles. Explain your answer.

On Your Own

5. The table gives one piece of information about four different circles. Copy the table and find the missing parts for each circle.

Radius	Diameter	Area	Circumference
3	■	■	■
■	3	■	■
■	■	3	■
■	■	■	3

6. A canister contains three tennis balls each with a diameter of 2.5 in. Which distance do you think is greater, the height of the canister or the circumference of the canister? Guess the answer and then do the calculations to see if your guess is correct.

Habits of Mind

Experiment. Find a tennis ball canister and check this out!

7. Good'n Yummy Spaghetti Company makes canned spaghetti. The cans measure 5 in. high and 3 in. in diameter. What size piece of paper does the company need to make a label for the outside of its can?

8. **Standardized Test Prep** The rotating globe Eartha in Yarmouth, Maine, is 12.535 meters in diameter. Imagine there is a satellite orbiting one meter above Eartha's equator. How much longer than Eartha's circumference would the path of this satellite be?

A. 1 meter　　**B.** 3.142 meters

C. 6.283 meters　　**D.** 12.535 meters

9. **Take It Further** A speedometer company makes electronic speedometers for bicycles. The device consists of a small magnet on a spoke and a sensor on the fork of the same wheel. The magnet sends a signal every time the wheel makes one revolution. When you install one on your bike, you need to know how far the wheel travels in one revolution. The instructions say to use the rollout method: Put a chalk mark on the tire where it touches the ground (and mark the ground, too). Then roll the bike until the mark comes back to the ground and measure the distance between the chalk marks. What is an easier way to find the distance for one revolution? Try both methods with a bike.

Maintain Your Skills

10. The Bernoulli sisters claim to have a way to calculate π. They calculate two sequences of numbers, n and s_n, and then find $\frac{ns_n}{2}$.

n	s_n	$\frac{ns_n}{2}$
6	1	3
12	0.51763809	3.105828541
24	■	■
48	■	■

Each n is twice the one above it. Each s_n is computed from the previous one with the following steps.

a. Square the previous s_n.

b. Subtract the result from 4.

c. Take the square root of the result from part (b).

d. Subtract the result from part (c) from 2.

e. Take the square root of the result from part (d).

You can represent steps (a)–(e) with this formula.

$$s_n = \sqrt{2 - \sqrt{4 - \left(s_{\frac{n}{2}}\right)^2}}$$

Copy the Bernoulli table. Use a calculator to complete it. See whether $\frac{ns_n}{2}$ gets close to π as n increases. The formula below is from Exercise 10 in Lesson 5.03. How is it related to the formula for s_n above?

$$\sqrt{2 - \sqrt{4 - s^2}}$$

11. **Take It Further** Explain why the steps described in the previous exercise work. Why does $\frac{ns_n}{2}$ get closer to π as n increases?

Marc Umile set an American record in 2007 by listing 12,887 digits of pi from memory.

Historical Perspective
Pieces of π

The number π has intrigued people for centuries. Below are a few interesting facts and an experiment you can try.

- Around 2000 B.C., the Egyptians knew π to nearly 2 decimal places and used the number $3\frac{13}{81}$.
- Around 200 B.C., Archimedes found π to be between $3\frac{10}{71}$ and $3\frac{1}{7}$ (about 3.14). To obtain these values, Archimedes calculated the perimeters of polygons with $6 \cdot 2^n$ sides inscribed and circumscribed about a circle of diameter 1. This is known as the method of exhaustion.
- In the 1500s, Ludolph van Ceulen calculated π to 35 decimal places and had the result carved on his tombstone. To this day, Germans still refer to π as *die Ludolphsche Zahl* (the Ludolphine number).
- In 1991, David and Gregory Chudnovsky calculated π to more than 2,260,821,336 decimal places. To perform the calculation, the brothers built a supercomputer assembled from mail-order parts and placed it in what used to be the living room of Gregory's apartment.
- Ten decimal places of π would be enough to calculate the circumference of Earth to within a fraction of an inch if Earth were a smooth sphere.
- Do an experiment, either with a computer or by polling people in the halls of your school or at lunch. Get many pairs of whole numbers, chosen at random. If you can, get 1000 such pairs. Count the number of pairs that have no common factor (such as (5, 8) or (9, 16)). Then take this number and divide it by the total number of pairs. Your answer should be close to $\frac{6}{\pi^2} \approx 0.6079$.

5.07 Arc Length

Earlier in this investigation, you learned that all circles are similar. Here is a quick proof. If a circle is dilated with center of dilation at the center of the circle, the new shape is still a circle. Two figures are similar if one is congruent to a dilation of the other. So, any two circles are similar because you can dilate the first circle so the radius of the image equals the radius of the second circle.

When two shapes are similar, any lengths in one shape have the same ratio as corresponding lengths in the other shape. In this lesson, you will focus on the lengths of *arcs* in circles and the relationship to their circles' radii. This relationship also leads to a new way to measure angles called *radian measure*.

For You to Do

For each circle O, do the following:

- Find L, the length of $\widehat{AB}$.
- Calculate the exact value of $\frac{L}{r}$, where r is the radius of the circle.

Unless otherwise stated, *arc AB* refers to the shorter of the two possible arcs from *A* to *B*. The two arcs are called the *minor arc* and *major arc*, and the shorter arc is the minor arc. Arc *AB* can also be written as $\widehat{AB}$.

1.

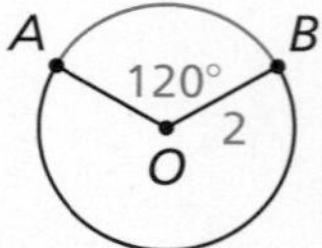

2.

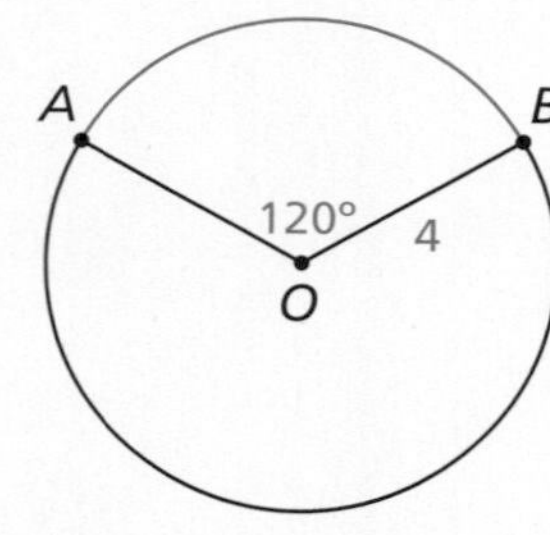

3.

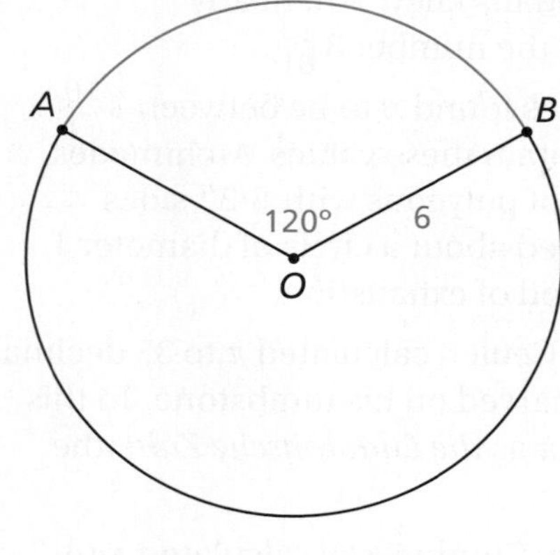

For Discussion

4. What do you notice about the value of $\frac{L}{r}$?
5. What is the value of $\frac{L}{r}$ when the arc is the entire 360° of the circle?

Developing Habits of Mind

Look for invariants. The ratio $\frac{L}{r}$ seems to be invariant for circles of any radius, as long as the central angle is 120°. This makes sense using what you learned about similarity in Chapter 4, that any lengths in one shape have the same ratio as the same lengths in another similar shape.

A *central angle* is an angle whose vertex is the center of the circle.

You can show that the ratio $\frac{L}{r}$ depends only on the central angle θ. First write an expression for the arc length L. Notice that L is some fraction of the circle's circumference C. That fraction is equal to the fraction of the entire circle's angle measure, 360°, that is taken up by the central angle θ. You can express this relationship using the equation below.

$$L = C \cdot \frac{\theta}{360}$$

Because $C = 2\pi r$, this equation can be rewritten as follows.

$$L = 2\pi r \cdot \frac{\theta}{360}$$

If you divide each side of the equation above by r, you obtain an equation for $\frac{L}{r}$.

$$\frac{L}{r} = 2\pi \cdot \frac{\theta}{360}$$

The only variable on the right side of the last equation is θ. This shows that the ratio $\frac{L}{r}$ depends only on the central angle, and not on the circle's radius or circumference. For example, when $\theta = 120°$ (as in the *For You to Do* on page 1), you get the following value for $\frac{L}{r}$.

$$\frac{L}{r} = 2\pi \cdot \frac{120}{360} = 2\pi \cdot \frac{1}{3} = \frac{2\pi}{3}$$

Example 1

Problem For each circle M, the radius and arc length are given. Find the measure of each central angle in degrees.

a.

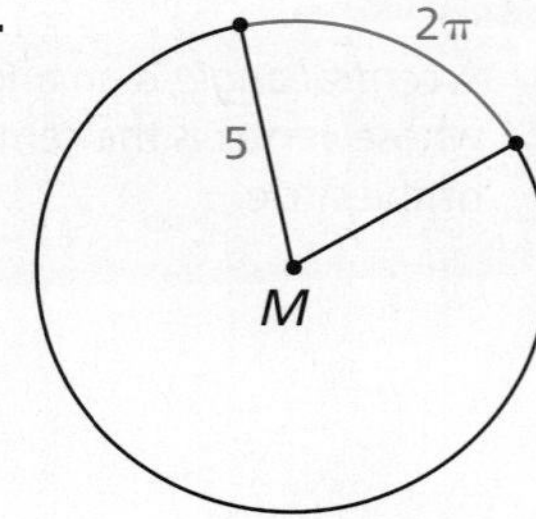

b.

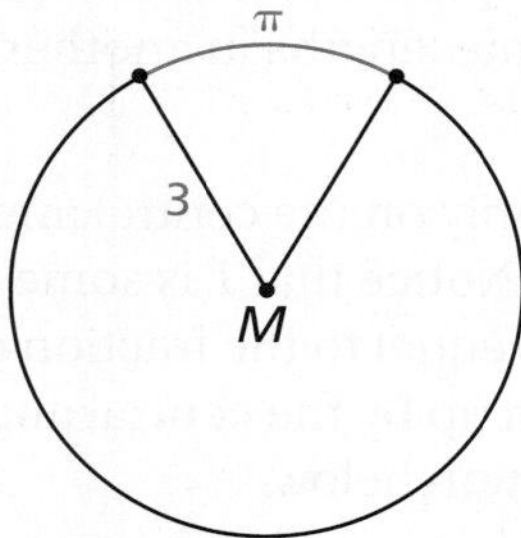

Solution Here are two different ways to solve these types of problems.

a. A circle of radius 5 has circumference 10π. The given arc length is 2π, which is one fifth of the circumference. The measure on the central angle is one fifth of 360°, which is **72°**.

b. Use the relationship $\frac{L}{r} = 2\pi \cdot \frac{\theta}{360}$. The values of L and r are known.

$$\frac{\pi}{3} = 2\pi \cdot \frac{\theta}{360}$$

$$\frac{1}{3} = 2 \cdot \frac{\theta}{360}$$

$$\frac{1}{6} = \frac{\theta}{360}$$

By solving the proportion, the measure of the central angle is **60°**.

What number is one sixth of 360?

It is possible to determine any central angle using the ratio of arc length to radius. For example, when the ratio is $\frac{2\pi}{3}$, the measure of the central angle is one third of the circle, and when the ratio is $\frac{2\pi}{5}$, the measure of the central angle is one fifth of the circle.

Angles are usually measured in degrees, where 360° is the measure of a full circle. There are other ways to measure angles. The ratio of arc length to radius defines a measure of angle called the **radian**.

Why are there 360 degrees in a circle? The degree is defined this way. No one knows the exact origin, but the Babylonians used a base-60 number system that could have led to 60 degrees in each angle of an equilateral triangle.

Definition (radian)

The measure in *radians* of a central angle of a circle is the ratio $\frac{L}{r}$ of the intercepted arc length L to the circle's radius r.

Alternately, the angle in radians is the arc length in a circle of radius 1, using the special case $r = 1$.

Example 2

Problem The circles and central angles from Example 1 are shown below. Find the measure of each central angle in radians.

a.

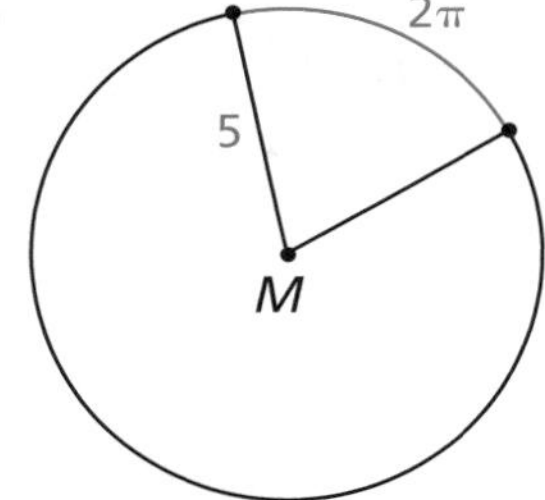

b.

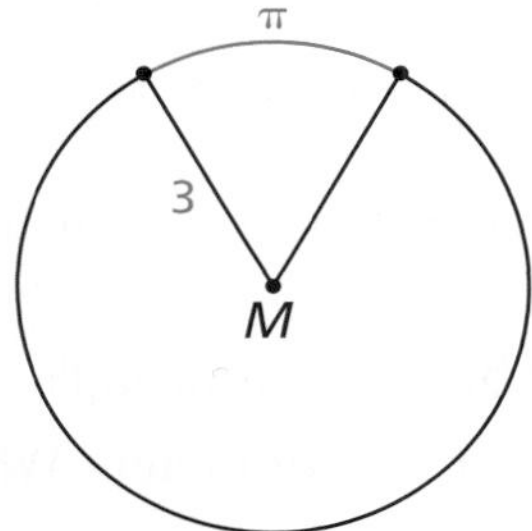

Solution

a. The angle measure in radians is given by the ratio $\frac{L}{r}$. Here, $L = 2\pi$ and $r = 5$, so the angle measure in radians is $\frac{2\pi}{5}$. The angle has not changed: it still measures one fifth of the entire circle.

b. The formula for the angle changes to the much simpler $\frac{L}{r} = \theta$.

Since $L = \pi$ and $r = 3$, the angle in radians is $\frac{\pi}{3}$. This angle is still one sixth of the circle.

As you can tell from the example, radian measure can make some calculations much easier. An angle's radian measure will not increase or decrease when the circle's radius changes, since arc length and radius both change in such a way that their ratio remains constant.

For Discussion

6. About how big is one radian? How many degrees are in one radian?

Exercises *Practicing Habits of Mind*

Check Your Understanding

1. How many radians are in a full circle? How many degrees?

2. Calculate, in radians and degrees, the measure of each central angle shown.

a.

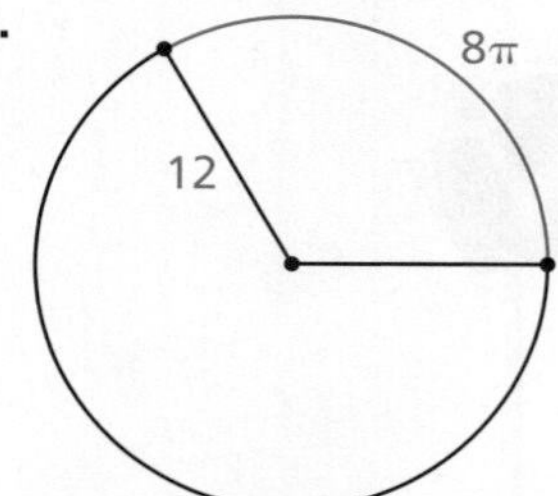

b.

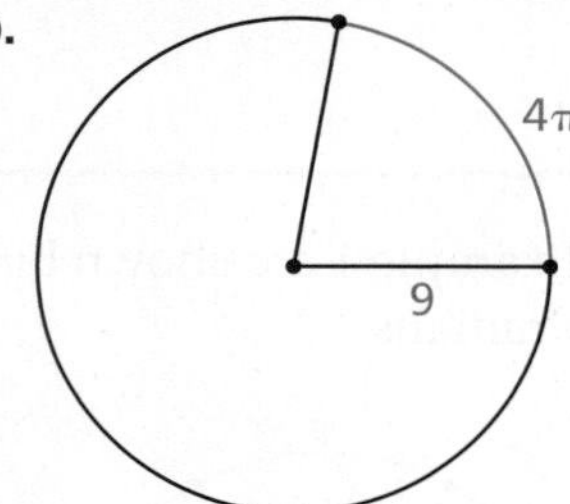

c.

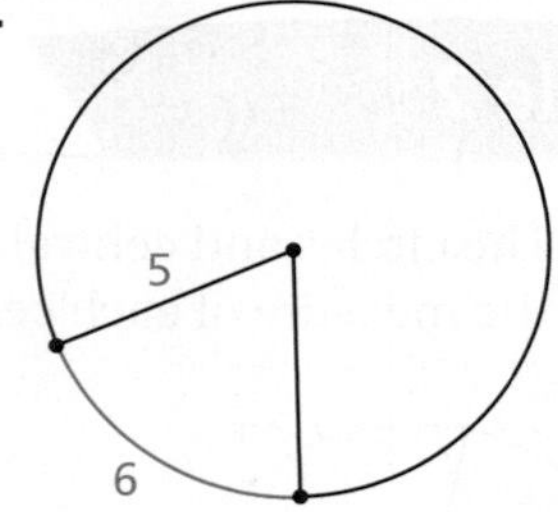

3. **a.** Draw a circle with a radius of 5 centimeters and a central angle of 2 radians.
   b. Find the length of the arc intercepted by this central angle.
   c. A similar figure is drawn with a radius of 10 centimeters. What happens to the radian measure of the central angle?

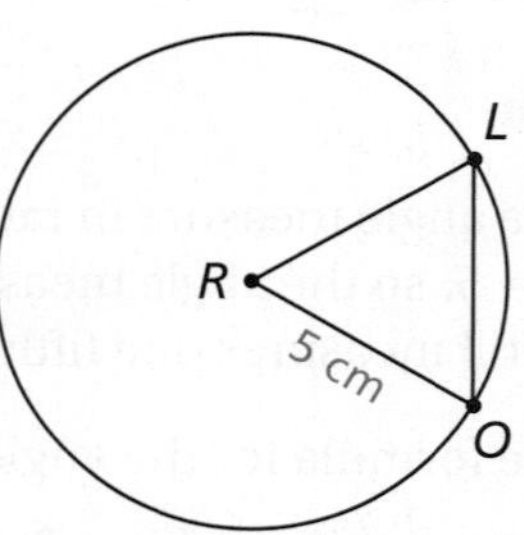

4. Triangle *RLO* is equilateral, and *R* is the center of the circle.
   a. Explain why the length of minor arc $\overset{\frown}{OL}$ *must* be more than 5 cm.
   b. Find the exact length of minor arc $\overset{\frown}{OL}$ and compare it to the length of chord $\overline{OL}$.
   c. Find the measure of angle *R* in radians.

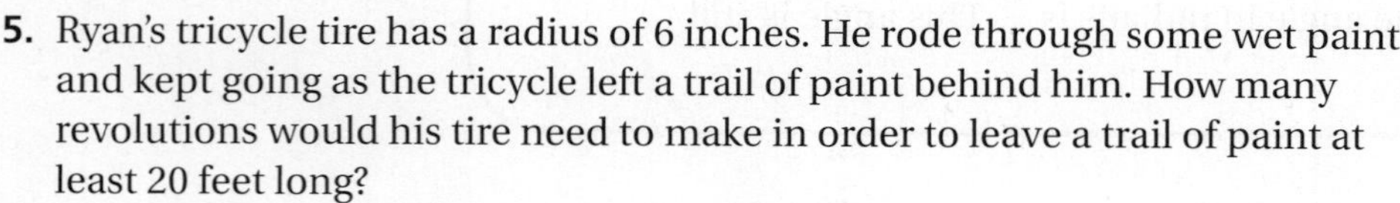

5. Ryan's tricycle tire has a radius of 6 inches. He rode through some wet paint and kept going as the tricycle left a trail of paint behind him. How many revolutions would his tire need to make in order to leave a trail of paint at least 20 feet long?

6. **Take It Further** Determine a formula relating the area of a sector to the radius and arc length of the sector.

On Your Own

7. What is the radian measure of a central angle that is a straight angle? What is the degree measure?

8. Determine the measure of the central angle, in radians and degrees, for each portion of a circle.

   a. $\frac{1}{3}$ of a circle
   b. $\frac{1}{5}$ of a circle
   c. $\frac{1}{9}$ of a circle
   d. $\frac{1}{4}$ of a circle
   e. $\frac{1}{360}$ of a circle

9. A circle has a circumference of 360 centimeters. Find the length of an arc with the given central angle measure.

   a. 120° b. 72° c. 40° d. 90° e. 1°

10. A circle has a radius of 1 centimeter. Find the length of an arc whose central angle is:

    a. 120° b. 72° c. 40° d. 90° e. 1°

11. Matt, Liz, and Benny were asked to find the measure of central angle P given the information at the right. Who is right? Explain.

    Matt: I divide the radius by the arc length. The angle in radians is $\frac{7}{21}$, or $\frac{1}{3}$.

    Liz: I divide the arc length by the radius. The angle in radians is $\frac{21}{7}$, which equals 3.

    Benny: You're both wrong. The whole circumference is 14π because the radius is 7. Then the angle is the solution to the proportion $\frac{21}{14\pi} = \frac{x}{360}$, which is $x \approx 172$.

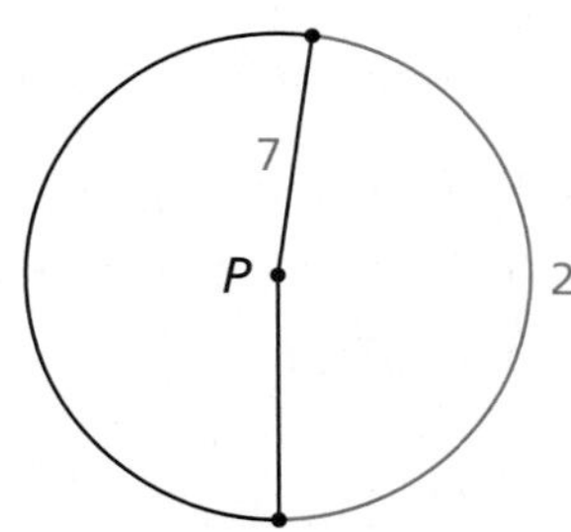

12. Given that major arc $\widehat{AB}$ has length 24, and central angle AOB measures 120°, find the length of minor arc $\widehat{AB}$.

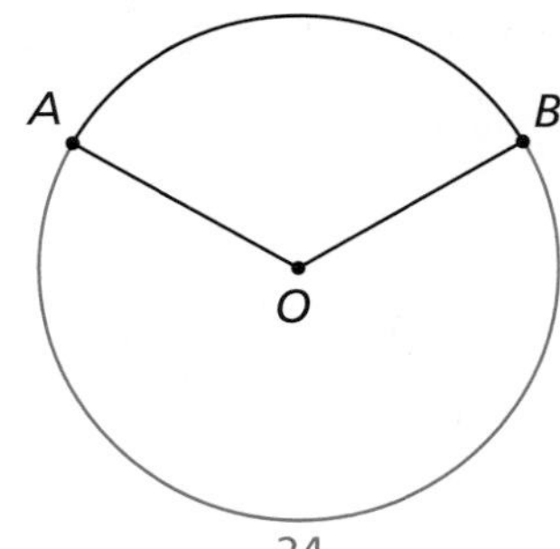

Maintain Your Skills

13. Two circles are centered at X.

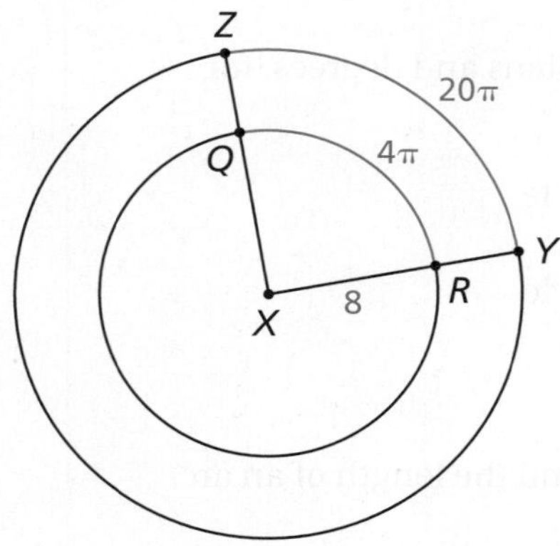

Is this figure drawn to scale?

a. Find the measure of central angle X in radians and in degrees.

b. Find the length of $\overline{QZ}$.

14. Find the area of a sector of a circle with radius 10 for each given arc length.

a. 5π **b.** 4π **c.** π **d.** 10

In this investigation, you explored relationships between π and measurements of circles. These questions will help you summarize what you have learned.

1. Why is it possible to calculate the circumference of a circle when you know only the length of its radius? Explain in detail.
2. What is the perimeter of a circle with diameter 2.5 in.?
3. What is the area of the shape at the right, composed of a square and a semicircle of radius 4 cm?

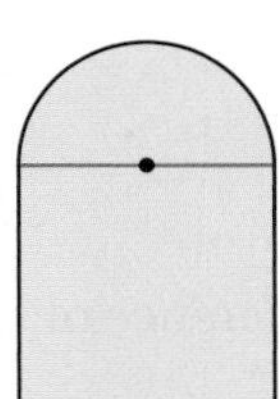

4. Find the radius of a circle with area 8π.
5. What is the area of the blue sector?

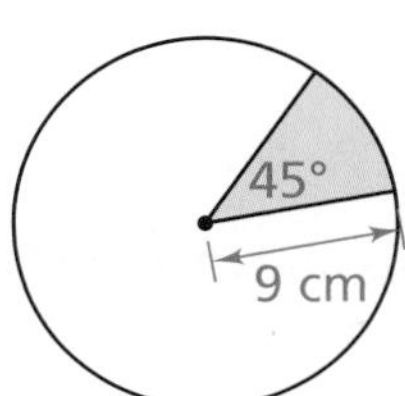

6. What is π?

7. How can you express the area and the circumference of a circle in terms of π?

8. What is the exact area of the shaded portion of the circle with center O?

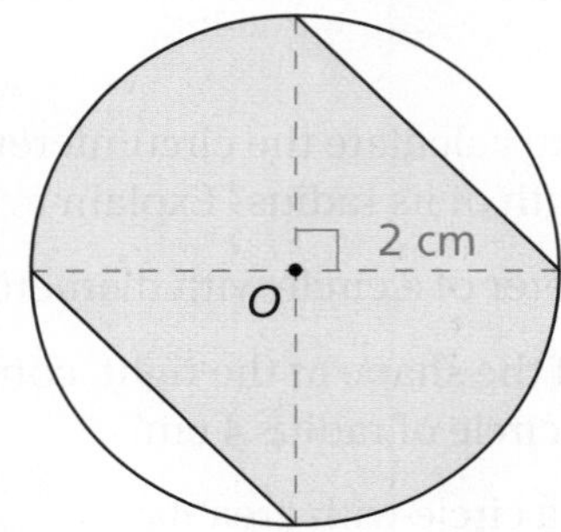

9. The circumference of a circle is 144π. Find the arc length of a 60° sector.

Vocabulary and Notation

In this investigation, you learned these terms and this symbol. Make sure you understand what each one means and how to use it.

- **pi,**
- **radian**
- **sector**

The technology behind crop circles is the compass.

Mid-Chapter Test

1. The area of a blob drawn on a sheet of rubber is 34 in.^{2} What is the area of the blob when the sheet is stretched or shrunk uniformly by the following factors?

   a. 2 **b.** 6 **c.** $\frac{1}{3}$ **d.** $\frac{1}{4}$

2. What is the formula for the area of a regular polygon in terms of its perimeter and apothem? What is the formula for the area of a circle in terms of its circumference and radius? Explain the analogies between the two formulas.

3. Find the area of each figure described below.

   a. a regular pentagon with side 4.52 in. and apothem 3.11 in.

   b. an equilateral triangle with apothem 2 cm

   c. a regular hexagon with apothem $\sqrt{5}$ in.

4. Calculate the areas of the following figures. The figures are made of polygons and circle sectors.

   a.

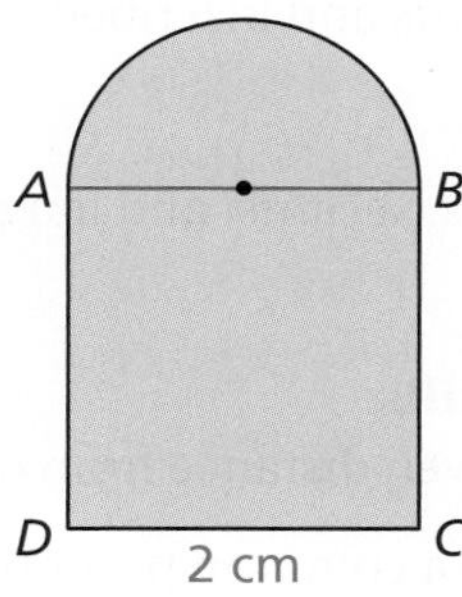

ABCD is a square and $\overset{\frown}{AB}$ is a semicircle.

   b.

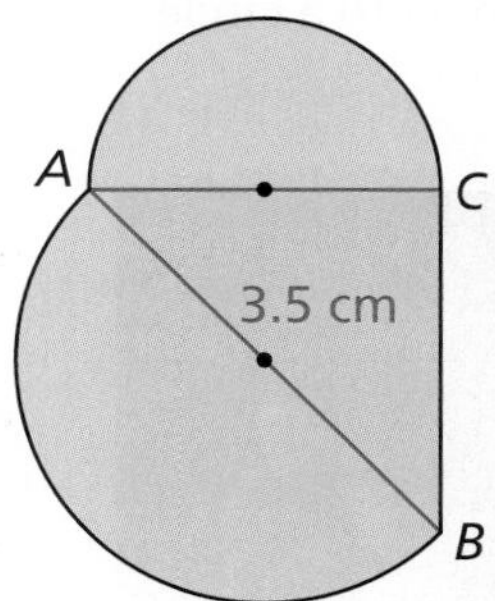

Triangle *ABC* has angles of 45°, 45°, and 90°. $\overset{\frown}{AC}$ and $\overset{\frown}{AB}$ are semicircles.

5. The wheel of a bicycle has a diameter of 2 ft. If you mark with chalk the point of the wheel that touches the ground, how many times does the mark touch the ground while the bicycle travels 27 ft?

6. Find the area and the perimeter of a regular hexagon with apothem 1 in.

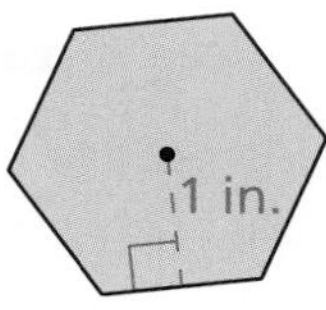

7. Find the area of a regular hexagon with apothem 4 cm.

8. Tony rolled his bicycle along a straight line that was 7 feet long. How long would the radius of his wheels have to be for each point on the wheel to touch the ground exactly once in that distance?

9. Suppose the area of the regular hexagon below is $6\sqrt{3}$. Find the area of the shaded region.

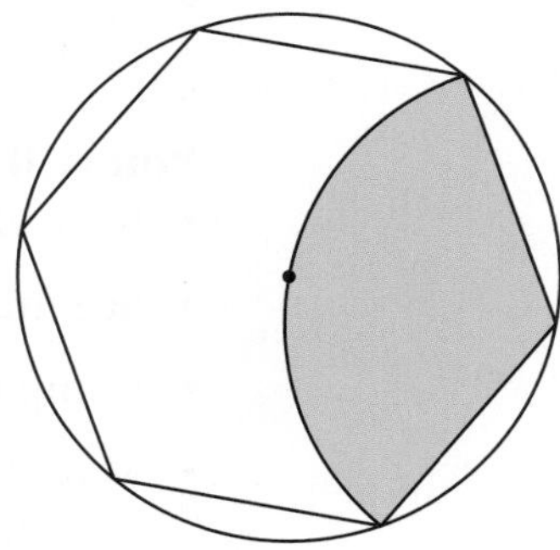

Classical Results About Circles

In *Classical Results About Circles*, you will study lines passing through circles and the angles formed by these lines. Studying their many relationships will improve your inductive reasoning, proof-writing skills, and understanding of circles.

By the end of this investigation, you will be able to answer questions like these.

1. What are arcs and chords in circles?
2. How much smaller is the measure of an inscribed angle than the measure of its corresponding central angle?
3. What is the power of a point? What are the maximum and minimum values of the power of a point in a circle with radius r?

You will learn how to

- recognize the relationship between inscribed angles and their corresponding central angles
- prove and use general theorems on chords and inscribed angles
- identify properties of tangents
- apply the theory of proportion to chords, secants, and tangents of circles

You will develop these habits and skills:

- See a circle as the set of points with a given distance from one point.
- See "traced paths" as sets of points with a common property.
- Compare chords and arcs of a circle.
- Make logical inferences to prove results about similar triangles with sides that are secants or tangents with respect to a circle.

In a windmill pitch, the hand sweeps out a circle centered on the pitcher's shoulder.

5.08 Getting Started

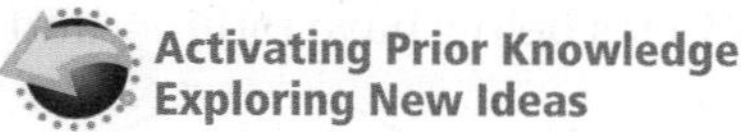

To understand relationships between circles and lines, it is helpful to see figures in motion. It is good practice to try visualizing such motion in your mind's eye. It is also helpful to see the motion on a computer screen.

For You to Explore

1. Draw a circle and a line. Depending on where you draw your line, you will notice a different number of intersection points. List all the possibilities.
2. Draw two circles. How many intersections can two circles have? List all the possibilities.
3. Use the figure to answer the following questions.

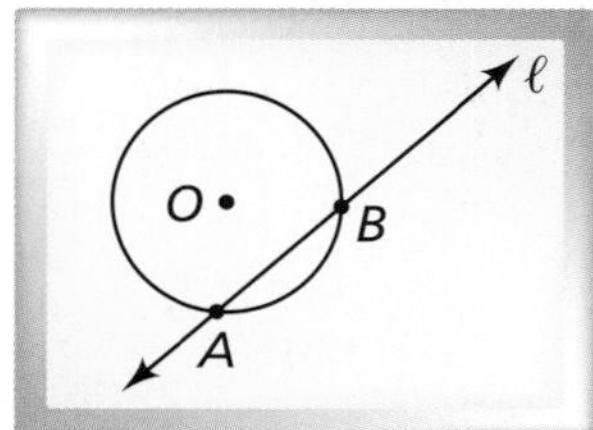

For help finding intersection points, see the TI-Nspire™ Handbook, p. 712.

   a. If you move ℓ around and leave A fixed, what happens to $\overline{AB}$? Under which conditions does $\overline{AB}$ disappear?
   b. In what position does $\overline{AB}$ have the greatest possible length? What does this length represent?
   c. Draw a segment that you could measure to find the distance of $\overline{AB}$ from the center of the circle. When is this distance at a maximum? When is it at a minimum?

4. The circles with centers A and B are congruent. For which points P on either of the two circles does $PA = PB$? Explain.

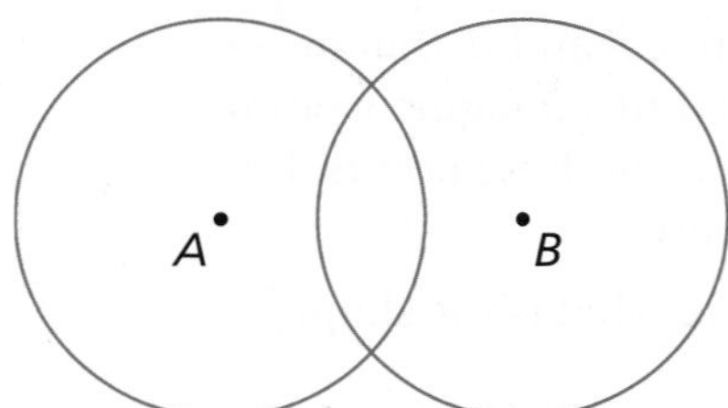

5. The two circles below have radii r_A and r_B respectively.

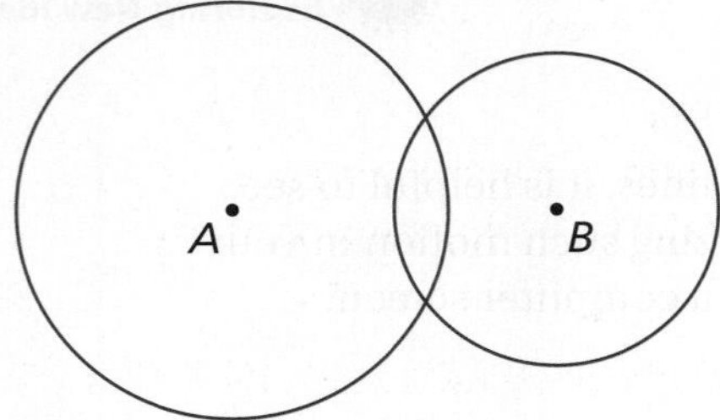

a. For which points P on either of the two circles is the sum of the distances from the two centers equal to the sum of the lengths of the two radii $(PA + PB = r_A + r_B)$?

b. Are there any other points P (not on either circle) for which $PA + PB = r_A + r_B$? Describe the locus of points.

A **locus** is a set of points that all have a given property. For example, the locus of points in a plane r units from a given point P is the circle with center P and radius r.

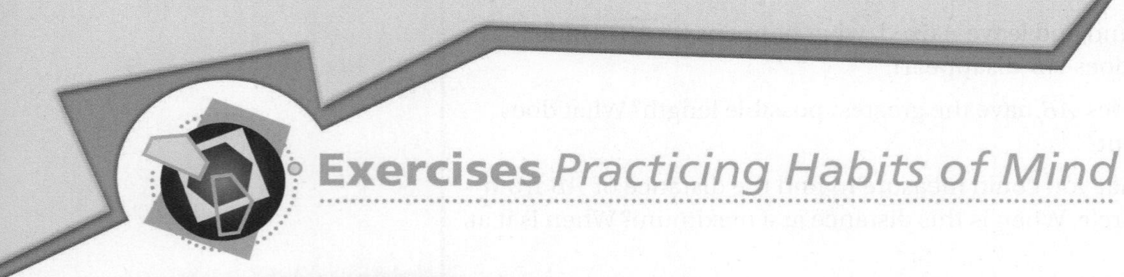

Exercises *Practicing Habits of Mind*

On Your Own

6. On paper or with geometry software, draw two points, A and B, that never move. Make the distance between them less than 6 units. Imagine a point P that can move along various paths described in terms of these points. Draw and describe what the path of P looks like in each case.

a. P moves along a path so that PA always equals PB. What is the shape of the path?

b. This time the path of P keeps $PA = 5$.

c. P moves along a path where $PA + PB = 6$.

d. $m\angle APB = 90°$, no matter where P is along this path.

e. $m\angle APB = 60°$, no matter where P is along this path.

f. $m\angle APB = 30°$, no matter where P is along this path.

7. Draw a circle with a diameter having endpoints A and B. Now choose a point P on the circle that is not A or B and answer the following questions.

   a. What kind of triangle is $\triangle APB$?

   b. On which side of $\triangle APB$ does the center of the circle lie, and what is its position on that side?

   c. Where would a point Q be if $m\angle AQB < 90°$? Where would Q be if $m\angle AQB > 90°$?

8. How could you draw a circle if you were given tacks, a length of string, and a pencil? Explain why your method works.

Maintain Your Skills

Use this construction for Exercises 9 and 10. A triangle inscribed in a semicircle has one side that is a diameter of the semicircle. All three of its vertices lie on the circle. Assume that the following statement is true: Any triangle inscribed in a semicircle is a right triangle. Draw a semicircle and inscribe a triangle in it. Then reflect your drawing about the diameter of the semicircle. Now you have a circle with a quadrilateral inscribed in it, as shown in this figure.

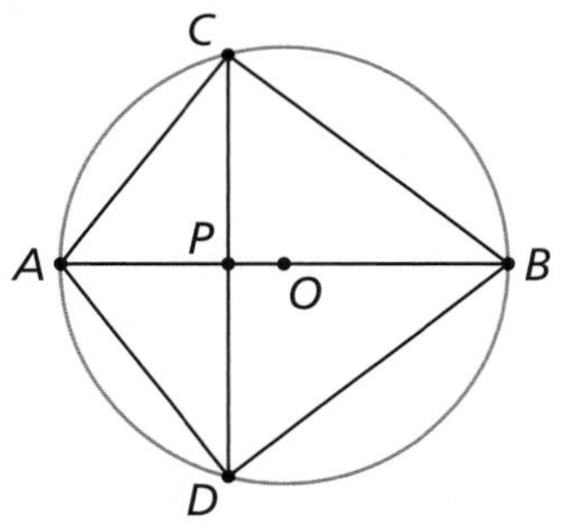

Habits of Mind

Look for relationships. Look for similar triangles in the semicircle that contains $\triangle ABC$. How many can you find? How can you compare the lengths of their sides?

9. Suppose $AP = 3\,\text{cm}$ and $PB = 5\,\text{cm}$. Find CD.

10. Use the construction above. Suppose $AP = a$ and $PB = b$. Find $CP = c$ as a function of a and b.

Circles are a compulsory element in the ribbon component of rhythmic gymnastics. What length ribbon would you use?

5.09 Arcs and Central Angles

Here are some definitions you need for this lesson.

Definitions

A central angle for a circle is an angle that has its vertex at the center of the circle.

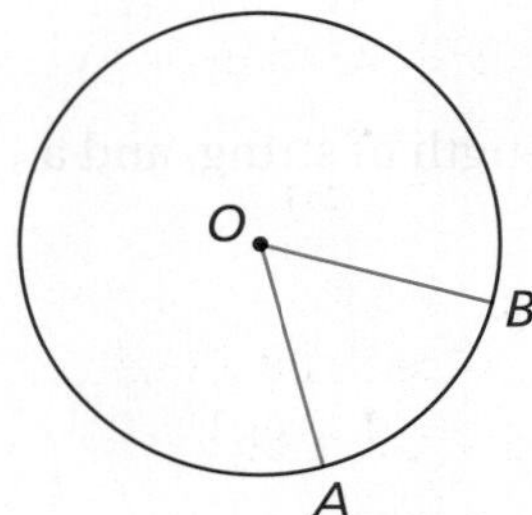

The set of points on a circle that lie on or in the interior of a particular central angle is called the arc intercepted by the angle. If the central angle is $\angle AOB$, then you refer to the arc as "the arc *AB* intercepted by angle *AOB*." You can write the arc *AB* as $\overset{\frown}{AB}$.

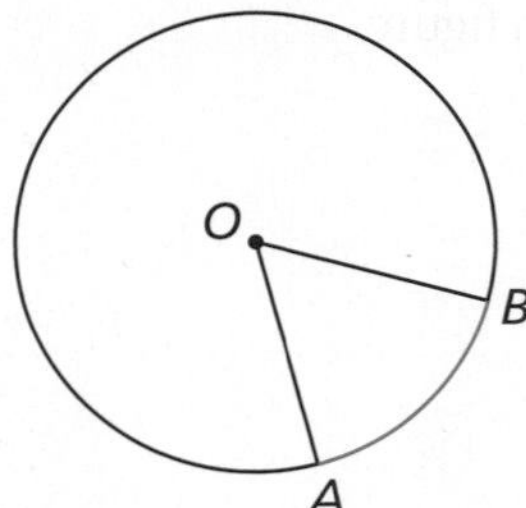

A chord is a segment that connects two points on a circle. Any chord through the center of the circle is a diameter.

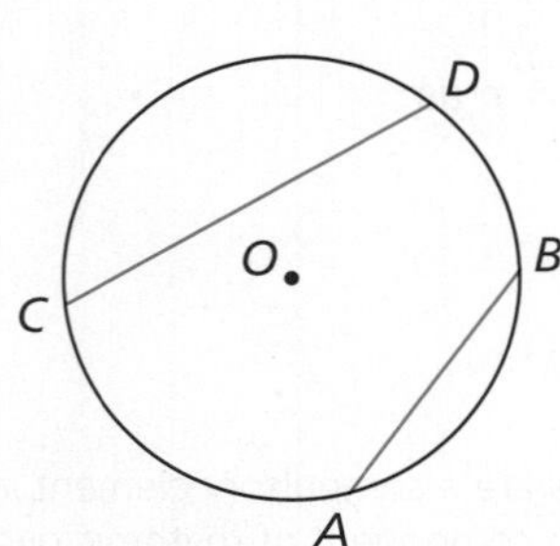

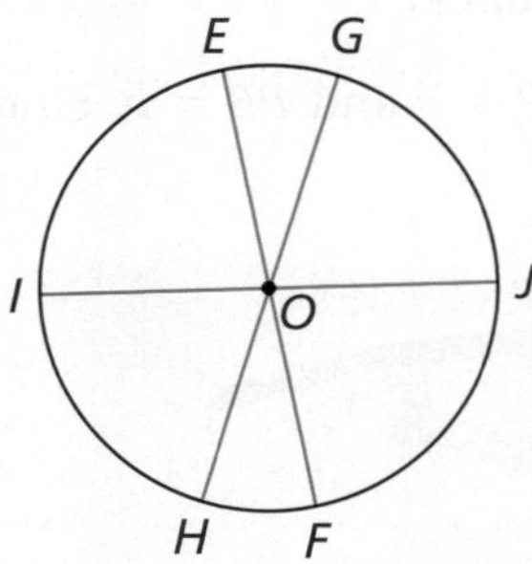

Minds in Action episode 17

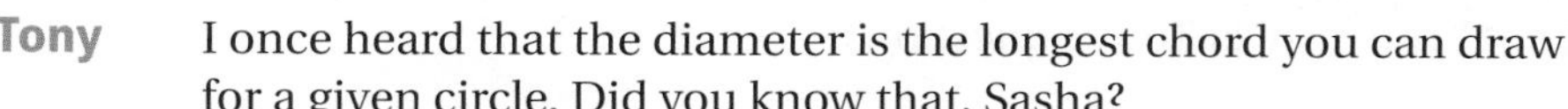

Looking at the definition of diameter, *Tony wonders about chords.*

Tony I once heard that the diameter is the longest chord you can draw for a given circle. Did you know that, Sasha?

Sasha As a matter of fact, I did! I think I can prove it. Let's see.

Tony Well, make life simple and start with the first circle at the bottom of the last page. You already have a chord, $\overline{CD}$.

Sasha Right! All we have to do is look for triangles, and I love triangles! Connect *C*, *D*, and *O*. Now I remember that in a triangle the sum of two sides is always greater than the third one. So $CD < CO + OD$.

Tony You're brilliant! I know what to do now. I just noticed that $\overline{CO}$ and $\overline{OD}$ are two radii, so their sum is equal to the diameter. So we've proven that any chord $\overline{CD}$ is shorter than a diameter.

For Discussion

1. How does Sasha and Tony's discussion prove that the diameter is the longest chord of a circle?

In-Class Experiment

2. Use tracing paper.
   a. Draw a black circle with center *O*. Choose points *A* and *B* on the circle.
   b. Choose two more points *C* and *D* such that $\widehat{AB} \cong \widehat{CD}$. You can do this by tracing your circle in blue on tracing paper and marking *A* and *B* on it. Then choose *C* on the black circle and pin the centers together with the blue circle on top. Rotate the blue circle until *A* is on top of *C*. Now mark the point on the black circle that corresponds to the position of *B*. This is point *D*.

   You have two arcs $\widehat{AB}$ and $\widehat{CD}$. Compare $\angle AOB$ and $\angle COD$.

For You to Do

3. Use a technique similar to the one above to prove the following statement.

   If two central angles are congruent, then their intercepted arcs are congruent.

Remember...

This is the converse of what you proved in the In-Class Experiment above.

For Discussion

4. Tony is a bit confused by the definition of arc. He thinks, "How can a single arc be intercepted by a central angle? I see two arcs intercepted by $\angle AOB$ because the circle is divided into a big part and a little part. Which part is the intercepted arc?" How could you answer Tony's questions?

The confusion arises from the uncertainty about the central angle. If it is not specified, the interior of $\angle AOB$ refers to the convex region enclosed by the angle. A good way to avoid confusion is to define a **major arc** and a **minor arc** for each central angle. The major arc is the larger part of the circle, and the minor arc is the smaller part of the circle. In this book, you may assume that an arc is a minor arc unless stated otherwise.

Arcs, as well as angles, can be measured in degrees. The **measure of an arc** is the measure of the central angle that intercepts it. If the measure of a minor arc is $x°$, then the measure of the corresponding major arc is $360° - x°$. You write the measure of an arc $\widehat{AB}$ as $m\widehat{AB}$.

The degree measure of an arc divided by 360 tells you how much of the circle is contained by the arc.

The chord of a minor arc is the segment with ends that are the intersections of the central angle with the circle. Now you can prove a theorem on minor arcs and chords.

Theorem 5.7

Two chords are congruent if and only if their corresponding arcs are congruent.

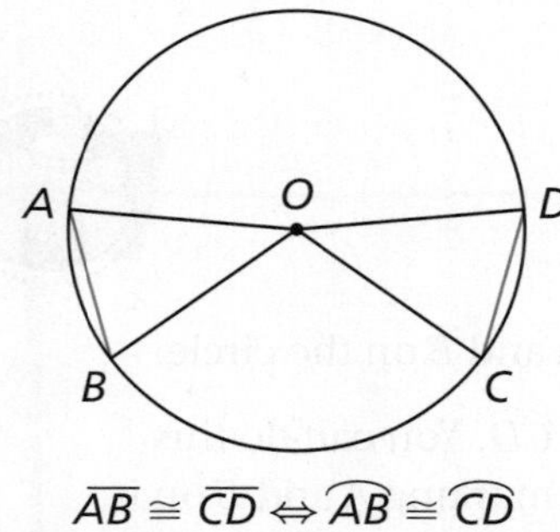

$\overline{AB} \cong \overline{CD} \Leftrightarrow \widehat{AB} \cong \widehat{CD}$

Proof If you start with two congruent chords, then $\triangle COD$ and $\triangle AOB$ are congruent by SSS. Therefore, all of their corresponding elements are congruent. In particular $\angle AOB \cong \angle COD$. So the corresponding arcs are congruent.

If you start with two congruent arcs $\widehat{AB}$ and $\widehat{CD}$, the two central angles that intercept them on the circle are congruent (as you saw in the In-Class Experiment on the previous page). Therefore, $\triangle AOB$ and $\triangle COD$ are congruent by SAS, because $\overline{OA}$, $\overline{OD}$, $\overline{OB}$, and $\overline{OC}$ are all radii of the same circle. All their corresponding elements are congruent, so sides $\overline{AB}$ and $\overline{CD}$ are congruent.

Exercises *Practicing Habits of Mind*

Check Your Understanding

1. What parts of the circle are the following elements?

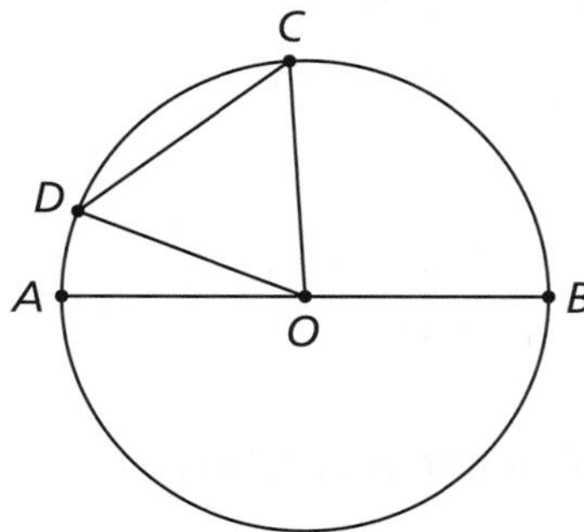

a. $\overline{AB}$ **b.** $\overline{OB}$ **c.** $\overline{OD}$

d. $\overline{CD}$ **e.** $\angle COD$ **f.** $\angle AOC$

g. $\widehat{CD}$ **h.** $\widehat{AB}$

2. In a circle with center O and radius 1 inch, $\widehat{MN}$ is an arc that measures 60°. What are $m\angle MON$, MN, and OH, where H is the base of the height through O of $\triangle MON$?

3. Look at this picture, where $m\widehat{AB} = 60°$, $m\widehat{CD} = 30°$, and $m\angle AOC = 45°$.

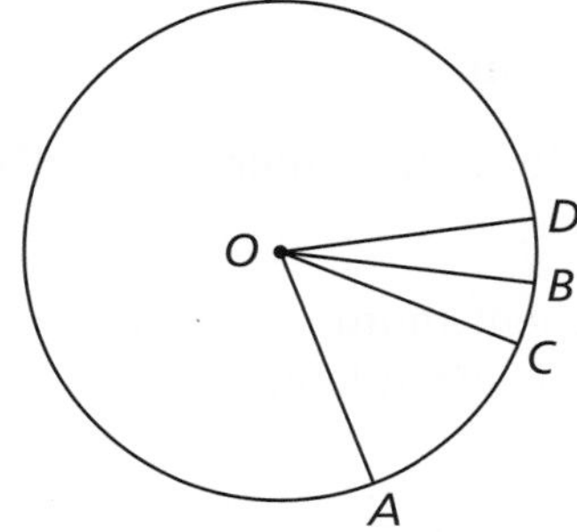

Find the measures of the following elements. (The arcs are all minor arcs.)

a. $\angle AOB$ **b.** $\angle COD$ **c.** $\widehat{AC}$

d. $\widehat{CB}$ **e.** $\angle COB$ **f.** $\angle BOD$

g. $\widehat{AD}$

4. Is it true that if point C is on minor arc $\widehat{AB}$ of a circle with center O, then $m\widehat{AC} + m\widehat{CB} = m\widehat{AB}$? Explain.

This is known as the Arc Addition Postulate.

On Your Own

5. $\overline{OZ}$ is the bisector of $\angle QOR$. Prove that $\overline{QP}$ is congruent to $\overline{PR}$.

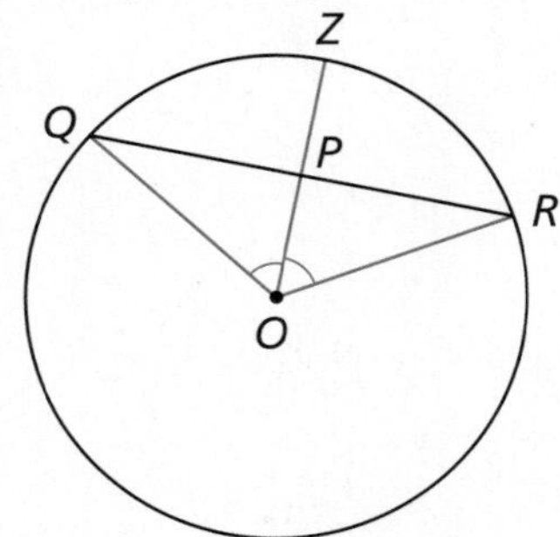

6. Draw a circle and two congruent chords $\overline{FH}$ and $\overline{JI}$ that intersect at point E (not the center O). Draw radii $\overline{OF}$, $\overline{OH}$, $\overline{OI}$, and $\overline{OJ}$.

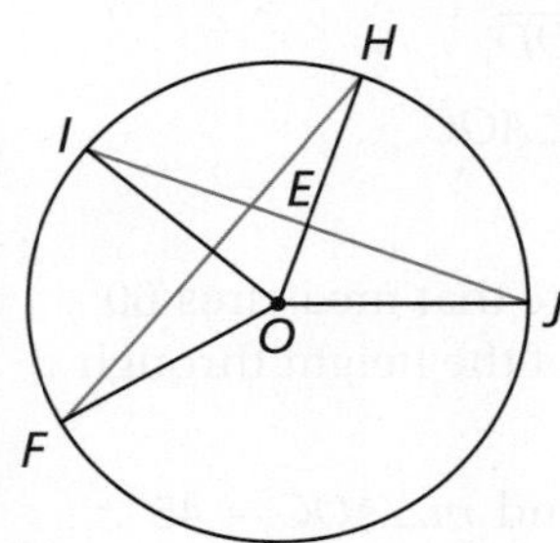

Prove that $\angle OFH$, $\angle FHO$, $\angle OJI$, and $\angle JIO$ are congruent.

7. Prove that chords of equal lengths are equally distant from the center of the circle.

How do you measure the distance from a chord to the center?

8. Construct two congruent circles. Draw two noncongruent chords—one in each circle. Which chord is closer to the center of its circle? Explain.

9. **Standardized Test Prep** In the diagram, O is the center of the circle and $\overline{AB} \cong \overline{CD}$. Which statement is NOT necessarily true?

A. $\triangle ABO \cong \triangle DCO$

B. $\triangle ABO$ is isosceles.

C. $\overset{\frown}{AC} \cong \overset{\frown}{DB}$

D. $\triangle DCO$ is equilateral.

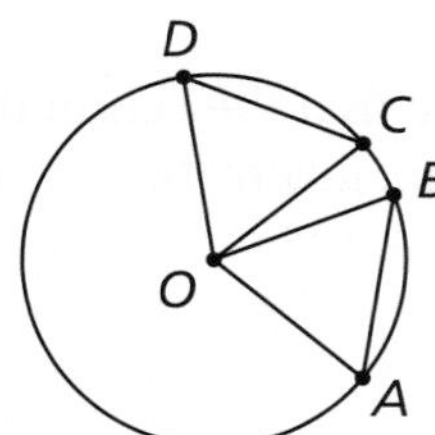

10. **Take It Further** Two lines r and r' cut a circle in four points as shown. If $\overset{\frown}{AB} \cong \overset{\frown}{CD}$, prove that $\angle APO$ and $\angle OPD$ are congruent.

Lines that cut a circle in two points are called *secants*.

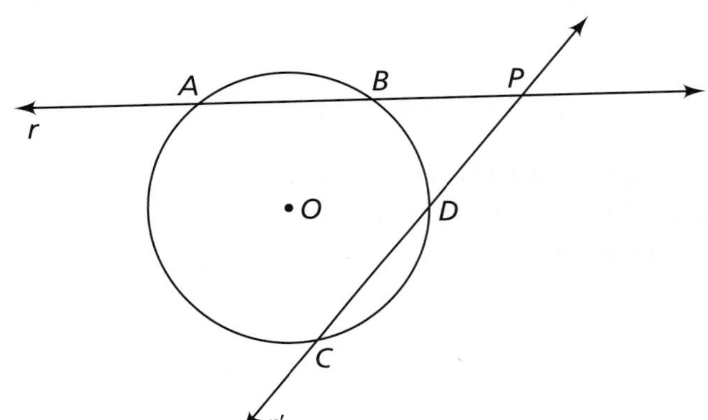

11. Look at the following figure.

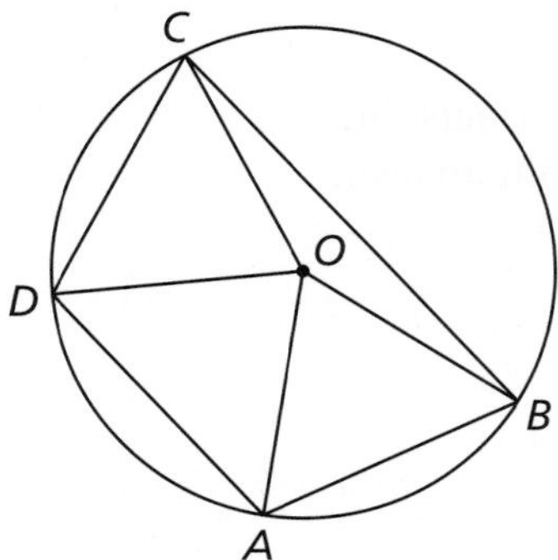

a. Knowing only that $\overset{\frown}{AB} \cong \overset{\frown}{CD}$, give a reason for each of the following statements.

- $\angle AOB \cong \angle COD$
- $\triangle AOB \cong \triangle COD$
- $\overline{AB} \cong \overline{CD}$

b. Copy the figure and draw the heights through O for the two triangles, $\triangle AOD$ and $\triangle BOC$. Prove that these heights lie on the same line and therefore $\overline{AD} \parallel \overline{BC}$.

Maintain Your Skills

12. $\overline{BA}$ is the perpendicular bisector of $\overline{DC}$. Assume that the center of the circle O is on $\overline{BA}$, as it appears to be in the figure. Then, given $BA = 5$ in. and $BE = 2$ in., find DC. Justify your answer.

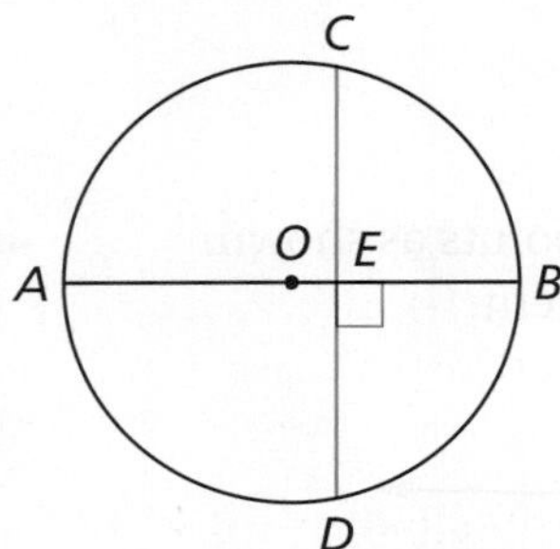

13. $\overline{CD}$ is the perpendicular bisector of $\overline{AB}$. Assume that $\overline{CD}$ is also a diameter of the circle, as it appears to be in the figure. Then, given $CK = 1.5$ cm and $OK = 2$ cm, find DC, AO, and AK. Justify your answers.

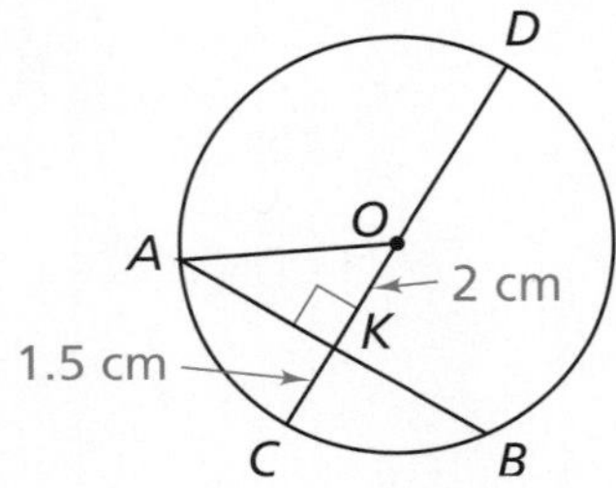

14. $\overline{AB}$ is the diameter perpendicular to $\overline{DC}$. Assume that $\overline{BA}$ bisects $\overline{DC}$. Then, given $BA = 12$ in. and $BE = 3$ in., find DC. Justify your answer.

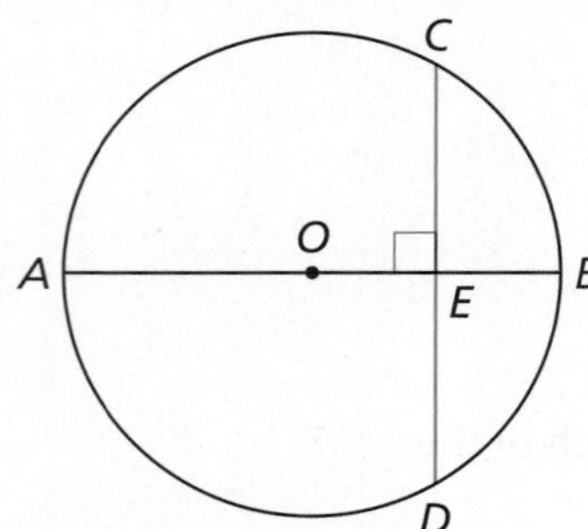

15. $\overline{DC}$ is the diameter perpendicular to $\overline{AB}$. Assume $\overline{DC}$ bisects $\overline{AB}$. Suppose $AK = 1.2$ cm and $KO = 3$ cm. Find DC and AB. Justify your answer.

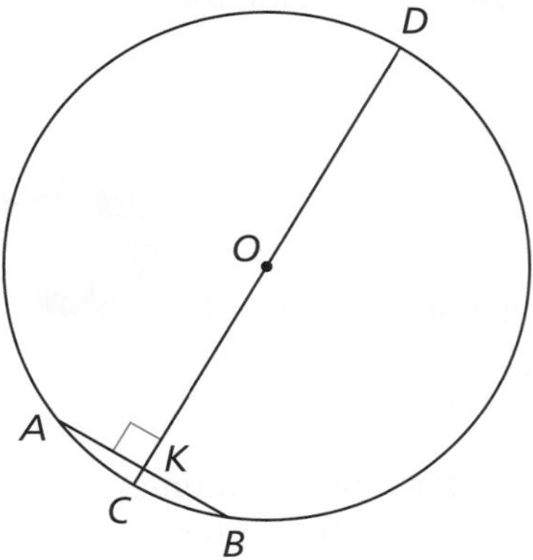

16. Diameter $\overline{JL}$ bisects $\overline{NK}$. Assume that $\overline{JL}$ is also perpendicular to $\overline{NK}$. Suppose $NA = 14$ cm and $OJ = 16$ cm. Find OA. Justify your answer.

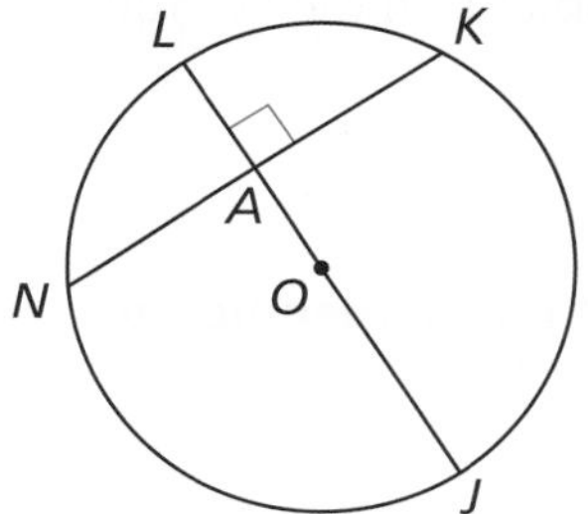

As the moon rises, the horizon forms a chord that gets longer and then shorter. When is the chord the longest?

5.10 Chords and Inscribed Angles

In Lesson 5.09, you studied angles that have a vertex at the center of a circle. In this lesson, angles of interest have their vertices elsewhere inside the circle, or on the circle itself.

In-Class Experiment

1. Draw a circle and a chord, $\overline{AB}$, that is not a diameter. Use a straightedge to draw various lines that are perpendicular to $\overline{AB}$. How many of these perpendicular lines can you draw through the center of the circle?
2. Using the figure from Problem 1, find a proof for the following statement. There is one and only one line perpendicular to $\overline{AB}$ through the center of the circle.

Now you can prove a theorem about chords and lines through the center of a circle. Learn the technique and use it to solve the problems in the For You to Do that follows.

Theorem 5.8

A line through the center of a circle bisects a chord if it is perpendicular to the chord.

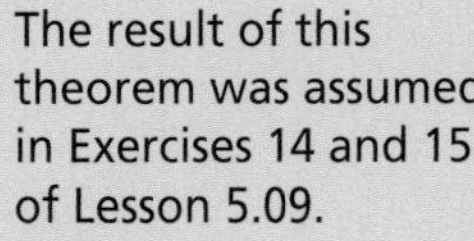

The result of this theorem was assumed in Exercises 14 and 15 of Lesson 5.09.

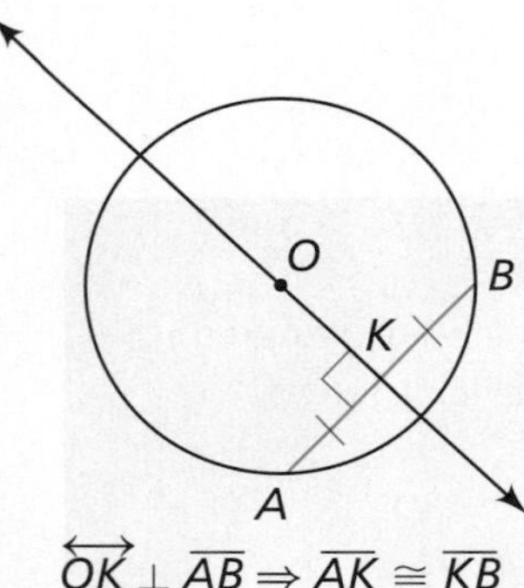

$\overleftrightarrow{OK} \perp \overline{AB} \Rightarrow \overline{AK} \cong \overline{KB}$

Proof Consider the line that contains $\overline{OK}$ through the center O of the circle above. Suppose it is perpendicular to $\overline{AB}$. You have to prove that it also bisects $\overline{AB}$. $\triangle AOB$ is isosceles because $AO = r = OB$, where r is the length of the radius of the circle. In any isosceles triangle, the height with respect to the base is also the bisector of the angle and the perpendicular bisector of the side it cuts. Therefore $\overline{AK}$ and $\overline{KB}$ are congruent, which is what you wanted to prove.

For Discussion

3. Prove the following theorems. Refer to the figure from Theorem 5.8.

Theorem 5.9

If a line through the center of a circle bisects a chord, then it is perpendicular to the chord.

The result of this theorem was assumed in Exercise 16 of Lesson 5.09.

Theorem 5.10

The center of a circle lies on the line perpendicular to a chord if and only if the line bisects the chord.

The result of this theorem was assumed in Exercises 12 and 13 of Lesson 5.09.

Definition

An inscribed angle is an angle that has its vertex on the circle and has sides that are chords of the circle. You say that $\angle ABC$ intercepts $\overset{\frown}{AC}$ and that it is inscribed in $\overset{\frown}{ABC}$.

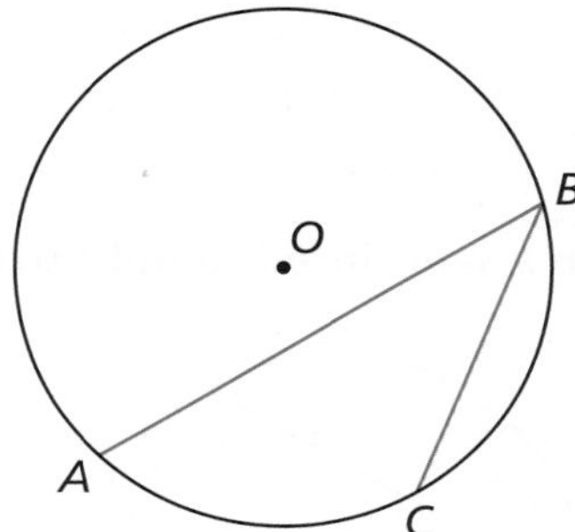

In-Class Experiment

4. Draw a circle and a central angle, $\angle AOC$. How many inscribed angles can you draw that intercept $\overset{\frown}{AC}$? Draw a few of these inscribed angles.

5. Measure $\angle AOC$ and then measure all the inscribed angles you drew. Can you find a relationship between them?

Theorem 5.11

The measure of an inscribed angle is equal to half the measure of its intercepted arc.

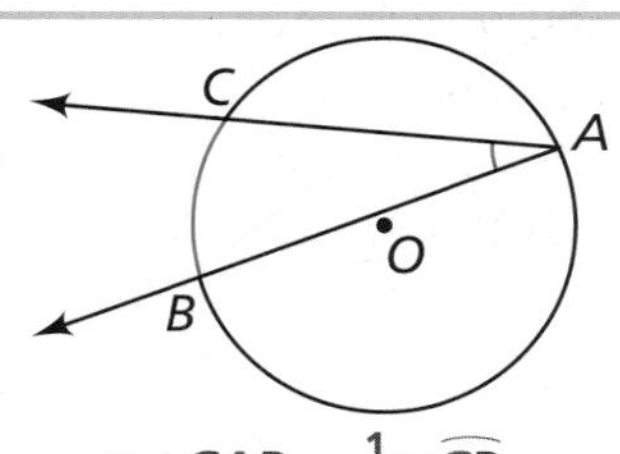

$m\angle CAB = \frac{1}{2} m\overset{\frown}{CB}$

For Discussion

6. Prove Theorem 5.11 for $\angle ACB$.

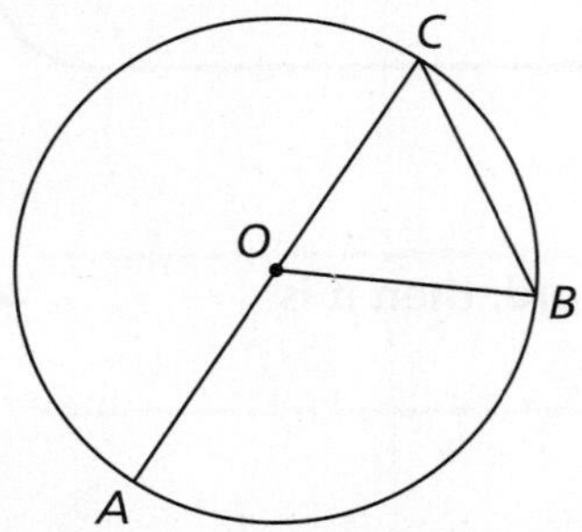

Habits of Mind

Prove. Can you use the Arc Addition Postulate to prove Theorem 5.11 in general? See Exercise 4 in Lesson 5.08 for a reminder.

Theorem 5.11 has two important corollaries.

Corollary 5.11.1

Inscribed angles are congruent if and only if they intercept the same arc or congruent arcs.

Corollary 5.11.2

Any triangle inscribed in a semicircle is a right triangle.

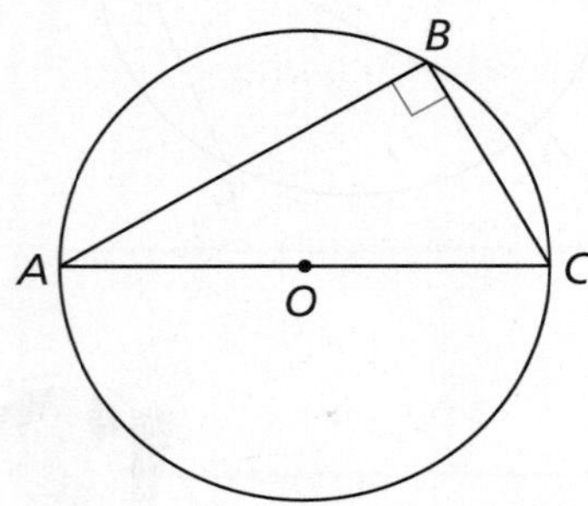

Remember...

One side of a triangle inscribed in a semicircle is a diameter of the circle. So $\angle ABC$ intercepts an arc of 180° and therefore measures 90°.

For You to Do

7. In a circle, two parallel chords contain opposite endpoints of a diameter. Prove that the chords are congruent.

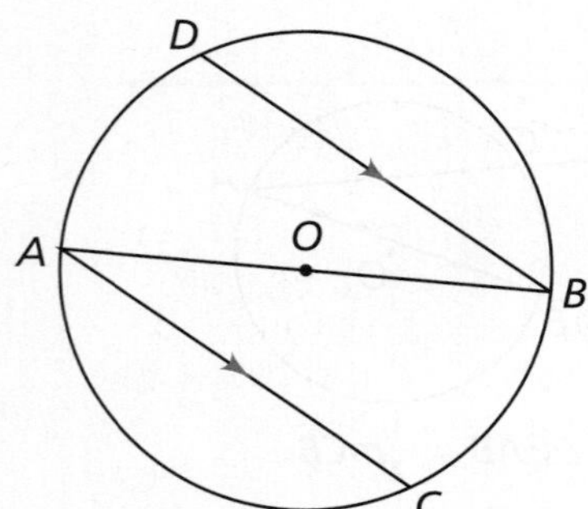

Exercises *Practicing Habits of Mind*

Check Your Understanding

1. What is the measure of any angle inscribed in a semicircle?
2. Choose a point A inside a circle. Describe the shortest chord that you can draw through A. Justify your answer.
3. Draw a circle and two congruent chords and letter the endpoints A, B, C, and D as you go counterclockwise around the circle. Connect A with C and B with D. Prove that $\overline{AC}$ and $\overline{BD}$ are congruent.

4. Prove that in a circle two adjacent chords that form equal angles with a radius are congruent.

Adjacent chords share an endpoint.

5. In the figure, $m\widehat{ABC} = 46^\circ$ and $\widehat{AB} \cong \widehat{BC}$. Find the measures of the inscribed angles.

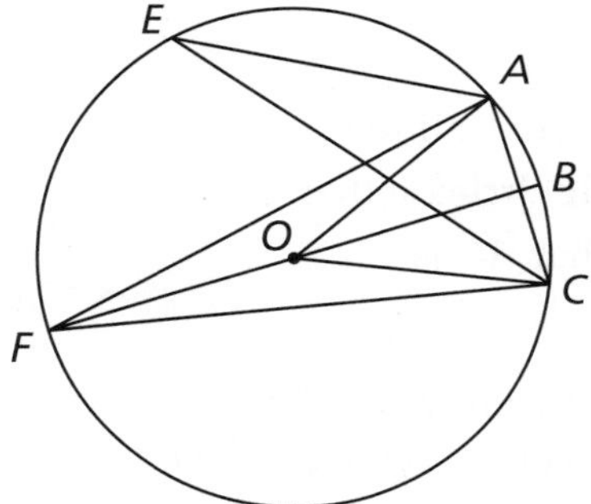

   a. $\angle CFB$
   b. $\angle CFA$
   c. $\angle CEA$
   d. $\angle FAC$
   e. $\angle FCA$

On Your Own

6. The midpoints of two chords of a circle are the same distance from the center O. Prove that these chords are congruent.
7. Draw a circle with a 3-cm radius. Consider a chord that is 2 cm long and draw at least ten other chords 2 cm long on the circle. What is the locus of the midpoints of these chords?

Remember...

A locus is a set of points with a given property. In this case, the points are all midpoints of equal-length segments.

8. $\overline{AB}$ is a diameter of a circle. $AB = 2$ in. Draw this circle and diameter and then select a point C on the circle such that $m\angle BAC = 30°$. In how many ways can you choose C? Shade the part of the circle that lies in the interior of $\angle BAC$. What is its area?

9. The line through the center of the circle below is the bisector of $\angle AOB$. Prove that $\overline{AE}$ is congruent to $\overline{BF}$.

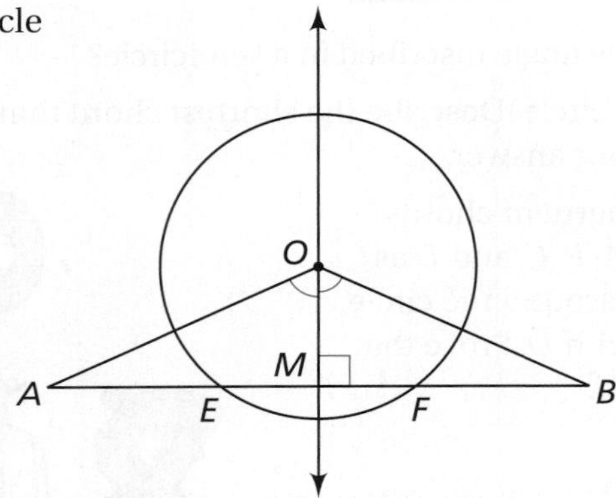

10. In the figure at the right, $m\angle CAD = 20°$ and $DP = PB$. What is the measure of each angle?

a. $\angle DPA$, $\angle DPC$, $\angle CPB$, $\angle BPA$

b. $\angle ADB$

c. $\angle AOB$

d. $\angle ACB$

e. $\angle COB$

11. Two concentric circles are cut by line ℓ. (Two circles are **concentric circles** if their centers coincide.) Prove that $\overline{AC}$ is congruent to $\overline{DB}$.

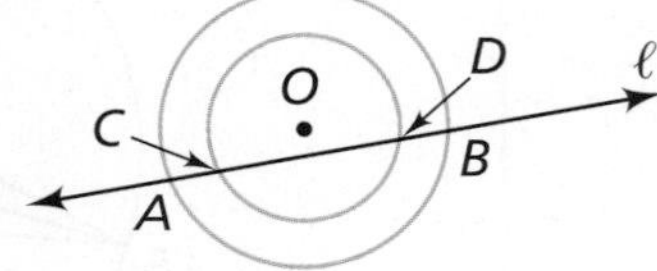

12. In the figure below, $FZ = 10$ cm, $PQ = 5$ cm, and the distance from the center of the circle O to $\overline{MN}$ is 2.5 cm. $\overline{FZ}$ is perpendicular to $\overline{MN}$, which is parallel to $\overline{PQ}$. Answer the following questions.

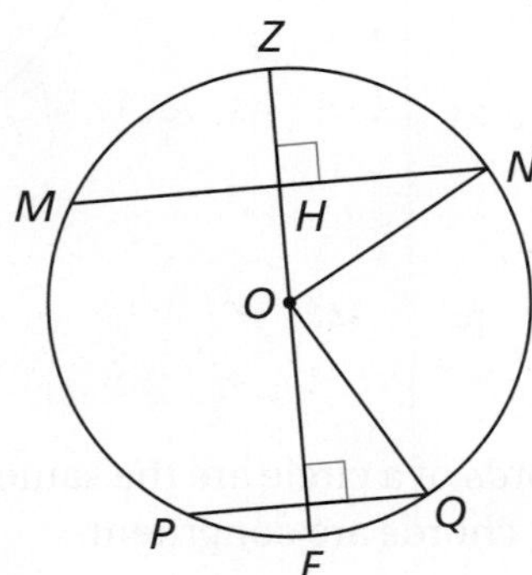

a. Why is $\overline{FZ}$ the perpendicular bisector of $\overline{PQ}$ and $\overline{MN}$?

b. What is the radius of the circle?

c. How long is $\overline{MN}$?

d. How far is $\overline{PQ}$ from O?

e. What is $m\angle NOQ$?

13. Given $m\widehat{AB} = 30°$ and $m\widehat{CD} = 60°$, find $m\angle APB$.

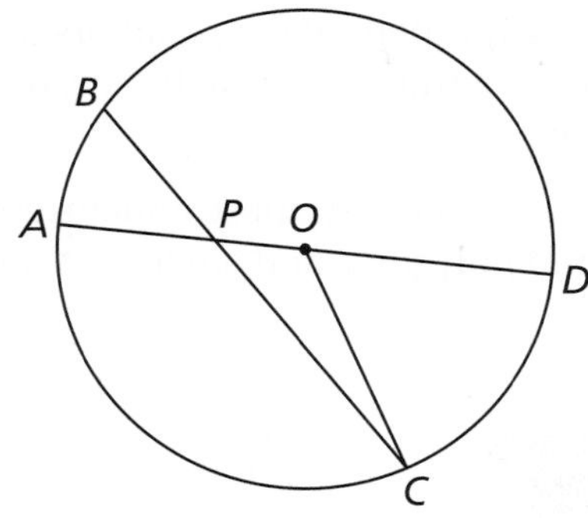

14. The diagram shows a pair of nested circles. One circle is inside the other, and the two circles have point A in common.

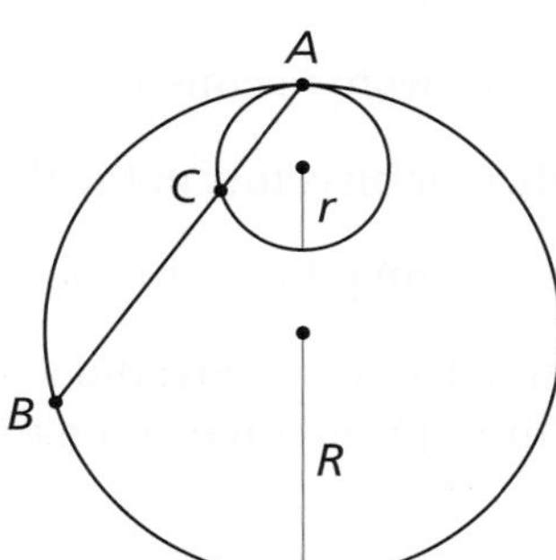

a. Why are the circles similar?

b. Let the ratio of corresponding lengths be the common ratio for the two circles. In terms of the radii r and R, what is the common ratio?

c. Any chord $\overline{AB}$ of the larger circle determines a chord $\overline{AC}$ of the smaller circle. Explain why the ratio of AB to AC equals the common ratio.

15. **Standardized Test Prep** What is $m\angle EFH$ if $m\angle EOF = 30°$ and $m\angle FGH = 40°$?

A. 80° B. 110° C. 125°

D. not enough information to answer

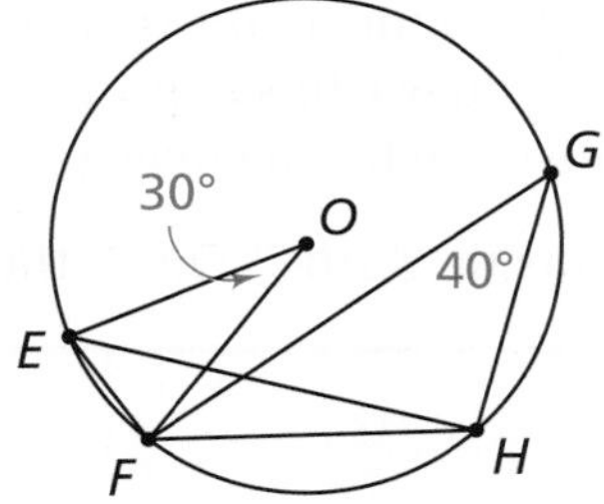

Maintain Your Skills

16. Draw a unit circle with center O and a radius $\overline{OA}$. Label the midpoint of the radius M_1.

a. Draw a chord with midpoint M_1. How many can you draw? Explain.

b. Label one of the chords you drew $\overline{C_1D_1}$. How long is it?

c. Label the midpoint of $\overline{M_1A}$ M_2. Draw a chord $\overline{C_2D_2}$ with midpoint M_2. How long is $\overline{C_2D_2}$?

d. Label the midpoint of $\overline{M_2A}$ M_3. Draw a chord $\overline{C_3D_3}$ with midpoint M_3. How long is $\overline{C_3D_3}$?

e. As you continue this process, what happens to $\overline{OM_n}$? To $\overline{C_nD_n}$?

f. Draw a series of lines ℓ_n through C_n and D_n. What happens to the lines ℓ_n as the value of n increases?

5.11 Circumscribed and Inscribed Circles

In Lesson 1.12, you constructed the perpendicular bisectors of the sides of a triangle and the angle bisectors of a triangle. In each case, the three lines you constructed were concurrent.

This lesson explores the connections between these concurrencies and ways to draw circles that surround polygons, and circles that are contained within polygons.

In-Class Experiment

1. Use dynamic geometry software to construct $\triangle ABC$.
2. Construct the perpendicular bisectors of the three sides of the triangle.
3. Label point X, the intersection point of the perpendicular bisectors.
4. Construct a circle centered at X with an adjustable radius. Adjust the radius until the circle passes through all three of the triangle's vertices.

Remember...

The name *perpendicular bisector* should remind you of its properties.

For Discussion

5. Use properties of perpendicular bisectors to prove that $\overline{AX}$, $\overline{BX}$, and $\overline{CX}$ are all the same length. How can you use this to prove that if point A is on circle X, then points B and C must also be on circle X?
6. Is it possible for point X to lie outside $\triangle ABC$? On $\triangle ABC$? If so, how?

Definitions

A circumscribed circle of a polygon is a circle that passes through all of the polygon's vertices. The center of a circumscribed circle is the *circumcenter*, equidistant from the polygon's vertices.

An inscribed circle of a polygon is a circle that is tangent to all of the polygon's sides. The center of an inscribed circle is the *incenter*, equidistant from the polygon's sides.

Habits of Mind

Use precise language. The word *circumscribed* means *drawn around,* and is closely related to *circumference.*

The In-Class Experiment shows how to construct a circumscribed circle for any triangle. If point X is the intersection of any two perpendicular bisectors of the sides of a triangle, then the circle with center X that passes through any vertex must pass through them all.

Every triangle has a circumscribed circle. In Exercises 3 and 4, you'll learn how to construct the inscribed circle for any triangle.

For You to Do

7. In the following diagram, quadrilateral $ABCD$ has a circumscribed circle. Angle D measures 50°. Determine any other angle measures, arc measures, or lengths that are possible to find.

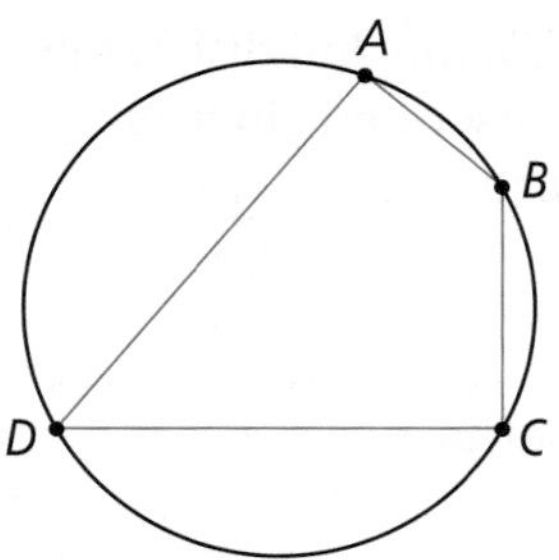

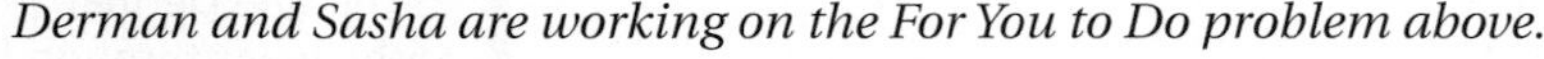

Minds in Action

Derman and Sasha are working on the For You to Do problem above.

Derman I don't think we can measure anything else. We don't even know how big the circle is.

Sasha Good point. We definitely can't measure any *lengths* without knowing the size of the circle. But angles, maybe.

Derman Could we use the fact that there are 360 degrees in a quadrilateral?

Sasha We only know that angles A, B, and C add up to 310 degrees, but we don't know the exact measure of any of them.

Derman Fine! No lengths, no angles. That leaves arcs. Isn't angle D a circumscribed angle or something?

Sasha It's an *inscribed* angle. Oh cool, we can measure something. It's arc AC.

Derman Huh? Which one?

Sasha Arc AC. It measures 100 degrees. Angle D has half the measure of arc AC, because of the inscribed angle theorem.

Derman But which one? There are two arcs we could call AC. What about the big AC?

Sasha Oh, the major arc. Could we figure that out? Oh wow, we can. And we can use that to find the measure of angle B! That's really clever, Derman.

Derman Ummm… sure, thanks!

Habits of Mind

Use precise language. The angle is *inscribed* in the circle, and the circle is *circumscribed* around the quadrilateral.

To clarify this confusion about arcs, a third point is sometimes used. Saying *arc ABC* or *arc ADC* would also answer Derman's question.

For You to Do

8. Find the measure of major arc $\widehat{AC}$ and the measure of $\angle B$. Explain your reasoning.

The argument used above is general in nature; it works for any quadrilateral with a circumscribed circle. A quadrilateral with a circumscribed circle is called a *cyclic quadrilateral* and has the following property.

Theorem 5.12

In a cyclic quadrilateral, opposite angles are supplementary.

Proof Suppose $\angle D$ measures x degrees. It is an inscribed angle, so its intercepted arc $\widehat{ABC}$ measures $2x$ degrees.

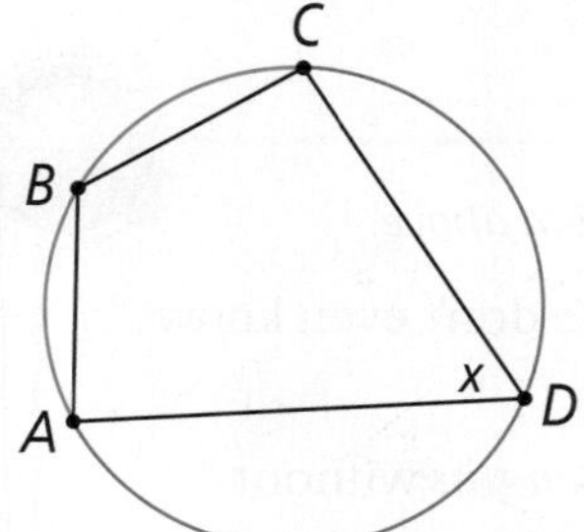

Habits of Mind

Generalize from calculation. This proof follows the same process as the one Derman and Sasha went through but uses a variable for the measure of angle D to represent any number.

$\widehat{ADC}$ is the rest of the circle, so it measures $(360 - 2x)$ degrees.

Inscribed angle B intercepts $\widehat{ADC}$, so it measures half of $(360 - 2x)$ degrees, or $(180 - x)$ degrees. It is supplementary to angle D, which measures x degrees.

The measures of the four angles in a quadrilateral add up to 360 degrees. If angles B and D measure 180 degrees together, the remaining 180 degrees must come from angles A and C. They also must be supplementary.

For Discussion

9. Do *all* quadrilaterals have circumscribed circles? Explain.
10. Do *some* quadrilaterals have inscribed circles?
11. Do *all* quadrilaterals have inscribed circles?

Exercises *Practicing Habits of Mind*

Check Your Understanding

1. If possible, determine the values of x and y. If it is not possible to determine the values of x and y, explain why.

a.

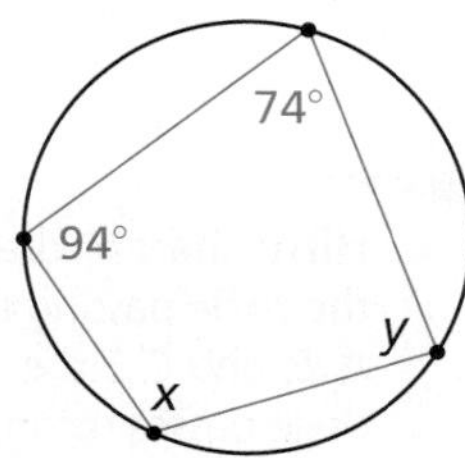

b.

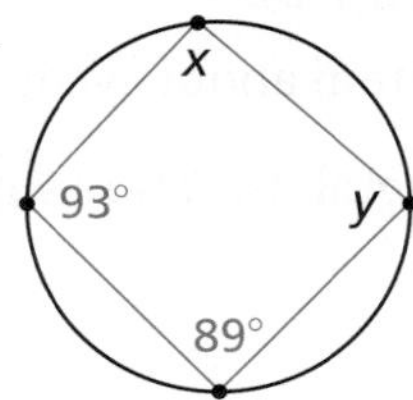

c.

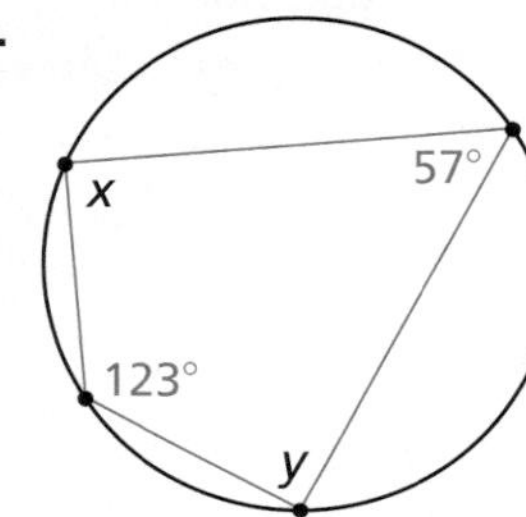

d.

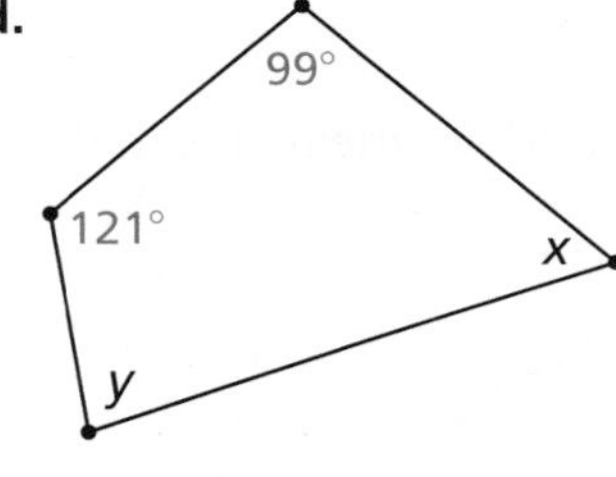

2. In the diagram below, O is the center of the circle, and $AB = BC = 10$.

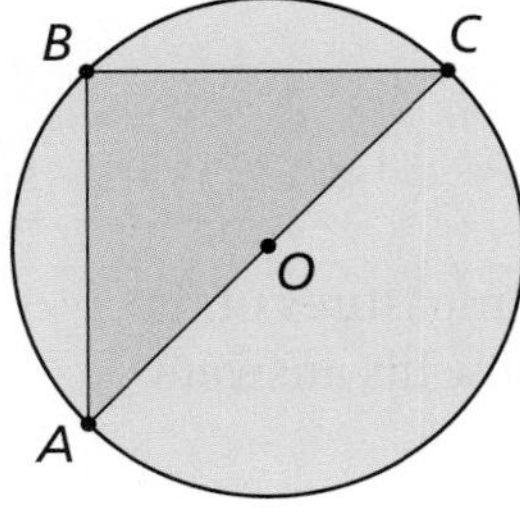

Is $\triangle ABC$ acute, right, or obtuse? How do you know?

a. Find the area of the triangle.

b. Find the area of the circle.

3. Complete this experiment to construct the *inscribed circle* for any triangle.

a. Use dynamic geometry software to construct $\triangle ABC$.

b. Construct the angle bisector of two angles of the triangle.

c. Label point X, the intersection point of the two angle bisectors.

d. Construct the angle bisector of the third angle.

e. Construct a circle centered at X with a movable radius. Adjust the radius until the circle just touches all three sides of the triangle.

Remember...

The points on an angle bisector are equidistant from the two rays that form the angle.

4. **a.** Explain why point X in the construction from Exercise 3 must be equidistant from all three sides of the triangle.

   b. How could you *construct* the inscribed circle, instead of adjusting the radius of the circle centered at X?

5. Trapezoid $TRAP$ is cyclic and has a 50° angle.

   a. Draw a sketch of what $TRAP$ might look like.

   b. Find the other angle measures of trapezoid $TRAP$.

   c. Use this example to find and prove a theorem about cyclic trapezoids.

6. Prove that if the opposite angles of quadrilateral $ABCD$ are supplementary, then the quadrilateral is cyclic.

Hint: Start by drawing the circle passing through *A, B,* and *C.* Either this circle passes through *D*, or it does not.

On Your Own

7. Calculate all missing angle measures and arc measures in the diagram below.

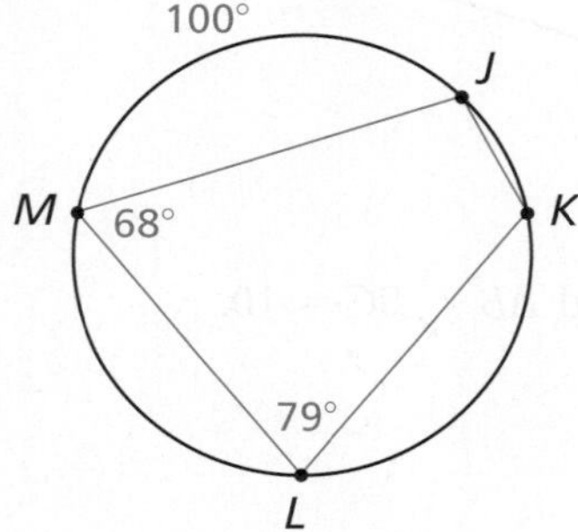

8. **What's Wrong Here?** James was asked to determine the measures of the angles in cyclic quadrilateral $ABCD$. Explain how you know his answers cannot be correct, and find the correct measures.

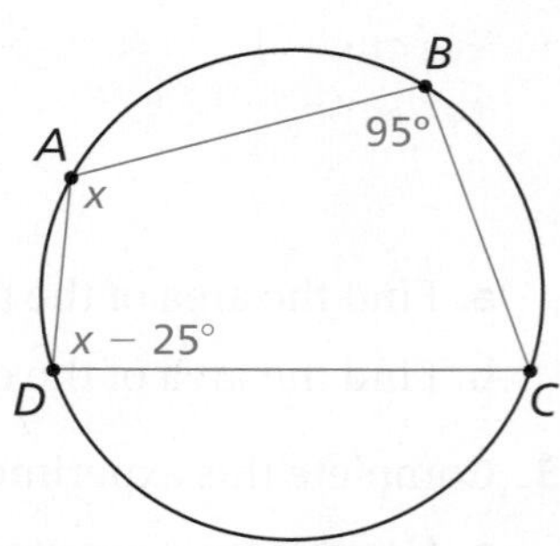

   James: It's a cyclic quadrilateral, so that means $x + 95 = 180$. Then x is 85 degrees. Angle D is $x - 25$, so it's 60 degrees. I can use the fact that there are 360 degrees in a quadrilateral to find the measure of angle C. It's 120 degrees.

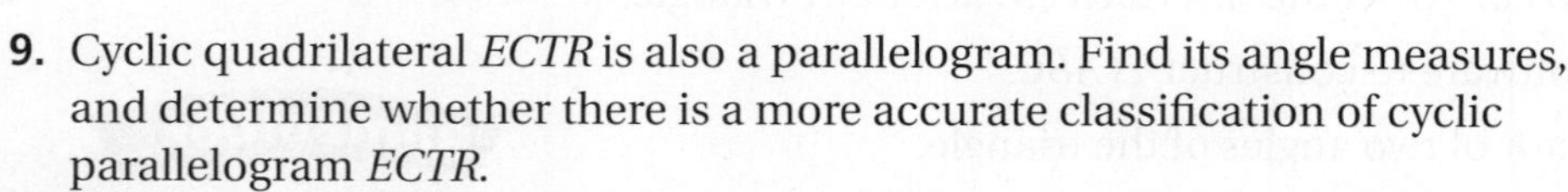

9. Cyclic quadrilateral $ECTR$ is also a parallelogram. Find its angle measures, and determine whether there is a more accurate classification of cyclic parallelogram $ECTR$.

10. Find the area of a cyclic quadrilateral with side lengths 1, 8, 4, and 7. The angle between the sides of length 1 and 8 is 90 degrees.

11. Draw or construct $\triangle ABC$ and its inscribed circle with center X.

a. Find the area of $\triangle AXC$ in terms of other measurements in your diagram.

b. Similarly, find the area of $\triangle AXB$ and $\triangle BXC$ in terms of other measurements in your diagram.

c. Show that the area of $\triangle ABC$ is given by $A = \frac{1}{2}Pr$, where P is the perimeter of the triangle and r is the radius of its inscribed circle.

12. Do all regular polygons have inscribed circles? For regular polygons that do have inscribed circles, what is the radius of the inscribed circle?

13. **Take It Further** Some, but not all, quadrilaterals can have an *inscribed circle,* a circle tangent to all four sides. Find a property for a quadrilateral that determines whether or not it can have an inscribed circle.

Maintain Your Skills

14. Given circle A and cyclic quadrilateral $BDCE$, find the values of x and y.

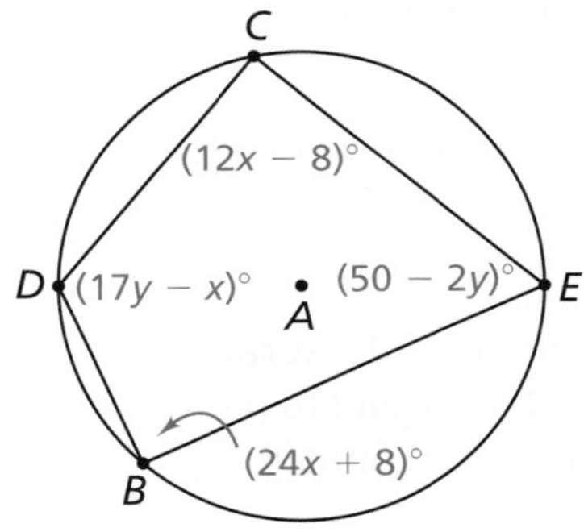

15. Use circle A below to determine all missing angle measures and arc measures.

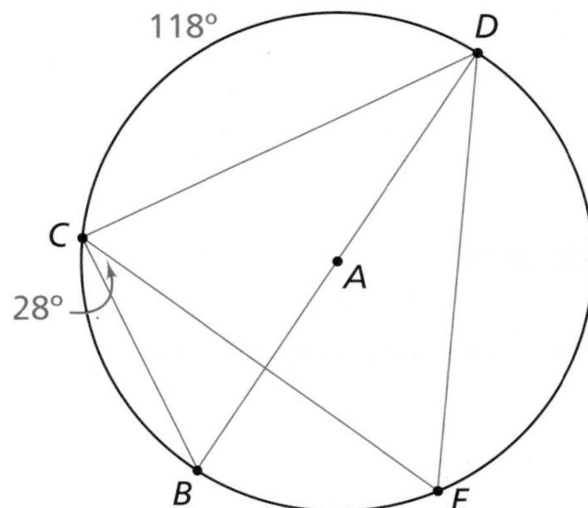

5.12 Secants and Tangents

Just as chords have special relationships with circles, so do lines that contain the chords.

In-Class Experiment

Use geometry software or a compass and straightedge for the following experiment.

1. Draw a circle of radius 1 and a diameter $\overline{AB}$.
2. Select a point C on the circle and draw $\triangle ABC$. What kind of triangle is it?
3. Move C along the circle. What kind of triangle do you have when C is on the diameter perpendicular to $\overline{AB}$?
4. Is it always true that $m\angle ACB = 90°$? Explain. What is the measure of $\angle ACB$ if C is very close to A or B?
5. If ℓ is the line that coincides with $\overline{CA}$, what happens to ℓ as you move C around? How many intersections does ℓ have with the circle in every position, including when C and A coincide?
6. What is the maximum distance you can find from ℓ to the center of the circle?

In general, if a line has two intersections with a circle it is called a **secant.** When a line has only one intersection point with a circle, it is said to be a **tangent** of the circle or tangent to the circle at the point of contact.

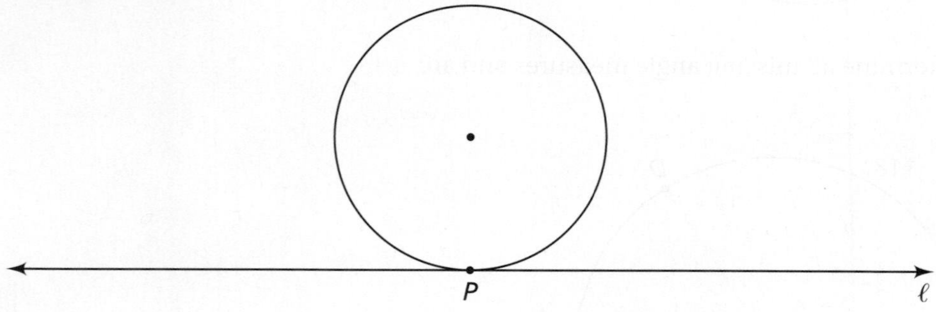

Line ℓ is tangent to the circle at P.

Now you can prove a theorem about your answers to questions 4, 5, and 6 of the In-Class Experiment.

Theorem 5.13

If a line intersects a circle in one point (that is, the line is tangent to the circle), it is perpendicular to the radius drawn to the point of contact.

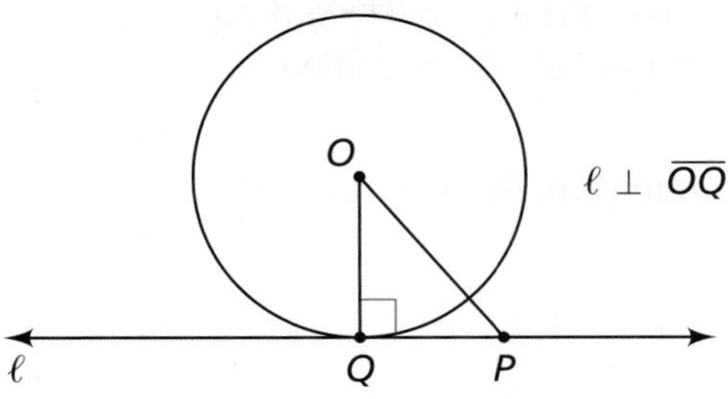

Proof Suppose ℓ is tangent to the circle with center O at point Q. Then $\overline{OQ}$ is a radius and $OQ = r$. If you choose a point P on ℓ, other than Q, $OP > r$, because P is outside the circle. So the shortest way to get from O to ℓ is along $\overline{OQ}$. The shortest way to get from O to ℓ is measured along the perpendicular to ℓ, so $\overline{OQ}$ is perpendicular to ℓ.

For You to Do

7. Draw a circle and a point outside of it. Think of all the tangent lines to the circle through that point. How many are there?
8. Draw two circles that intersect. How many lines are tangent to both circles?
9. Draw two circles that do not intersect and neither of which contains the other. How many lines are tangent to both circles?

Definition

A secant angle is an angle with sides that are two secants of a circle. A secant angle's vertex can be inside or outside the circle.

Remember...

What do you call a secant angle with its vertex on the circle?

Minds in Action

episode 18

Tony and Sasha were told to find $m\angle APD$ (and therefore $m\angle APC$). They know that $m\widehat{AD} = 122°$ and $m\widehat{BC} = 140°$.

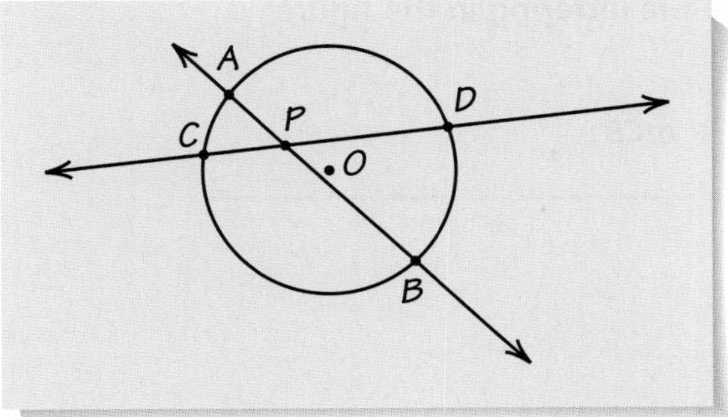

Tony I don't know how to relate the measures of the minor arcs to the angle we are looking for. What can we do?

Sasha Well, we have to work from the information we have. The measures of the arcs give us the measures of their corresponding central angles and therefore the measures of all the inscribed angles that intercept them.

Tony Let's try to use triangles. I know how much you like to work with them. You find triangles everywhere!

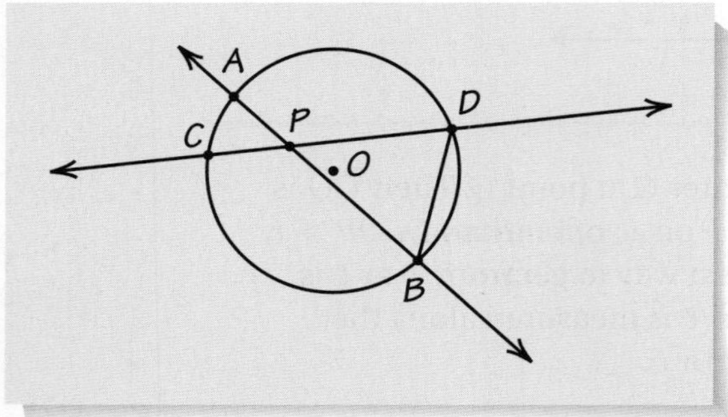

Sasha Good idea! I see $\triangle PBD$, for example. From the theorem on the exterior angles of a triangle, we know that $m\angle APD = m\angle PDB + m\angle PBD$.

Tony I know that

$$m\widehat{AD} = m\angle AOD = 2m\angle ABD = 2m\angle PBD$$

Sasha Right! And the same is true for $\angle CDB$, so

$$m\widehat{CB} = m\angle COB = 2m\angle CDB = 2m\angle PDB$$

Tony So $m\widehat{AD} + m\widehat{CB} = 2m\angle PBD + 2m\angle PDB = 2m\angle APD$.

Sasha Therefore, $m\angle APD = \frac{1}{2}(m\widehat{AD} + m\widehat{CB})$.

That's pretty neat, isn't it?

You can express the theorem Tony and Sasha found this way.

Theorem 5.14

A secant angle with vertex inside a circle is equal in measure to half of the sum of the arcs it intercepts. If you use the lettering in the figure from Minds in Action, the result is below.

$$m\angle APD = \frac{1}{2}(m\widehat{AD} + m\widehat{CB})$$

For You to Do

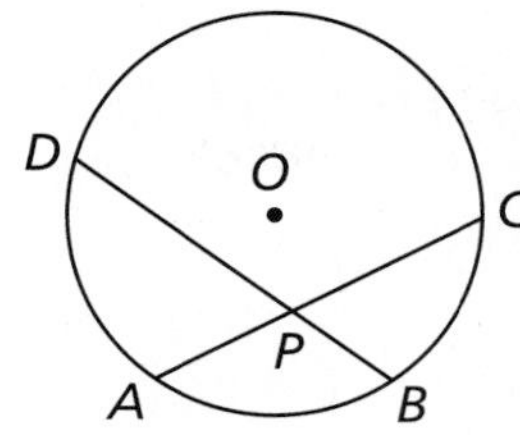

10. If $m\widehat{AB} = 69^\circ$ and $m\widehat{DC} = 163^\circ$, what is $m\angle APB$?

Theorem 5.15

A secant angle with vertex outside a circle is equal in measure to half of the difference of the measures of the arcs it intercepts. If you use the lettering in the figure below, the result is as follows.

$$m\angle APD = \frac{1}{2}(m\widehat{AD} - m\widehat{CB})$$

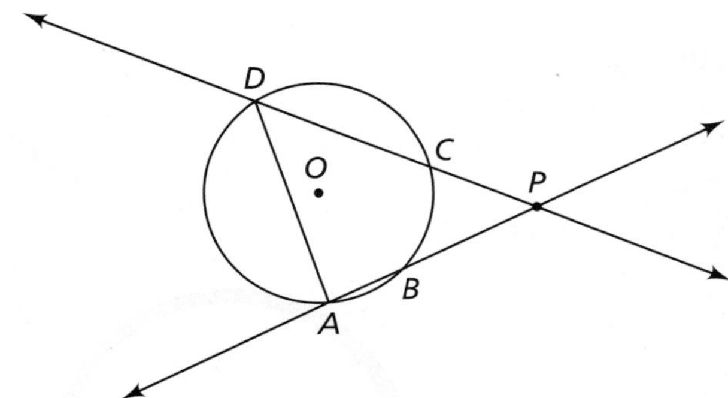

Habits of Mind

Develop your understanding. The difference has to be positive because it is a measure. So it is the measure of the greater of the two intercepted arcs minus the measure of the smaller of the two. You can also say it is the absolute value of the difference of the measures of the arcs.

For Discussion

11. Use the figure above to prove Theorem 5.14.

For You to Do

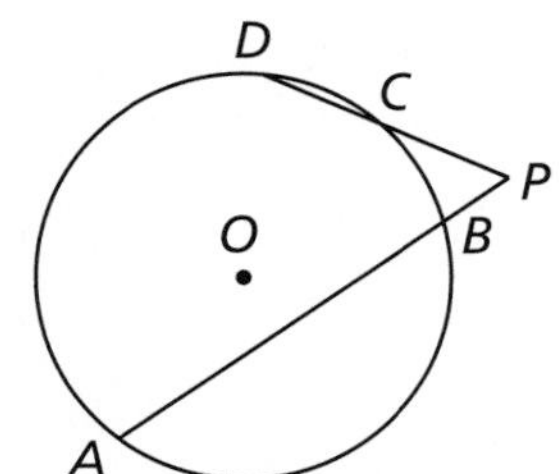

12. If $m\widehat{AD} = 133^\circ$ and $m\widehat{BC} = 48^\circ$, what is $m\angle APD$?

Exercises *Practicing Habits of Mind*

Check Your Understanding

1. $\overline{PA}$ and $\overline{PB}$ are the tangents to a circle through P. Prove that $\overline{PA} \cong \overline{PB}$.

$\overline{PA}$ and $\overline{PB}$ are called *tangent segments.*

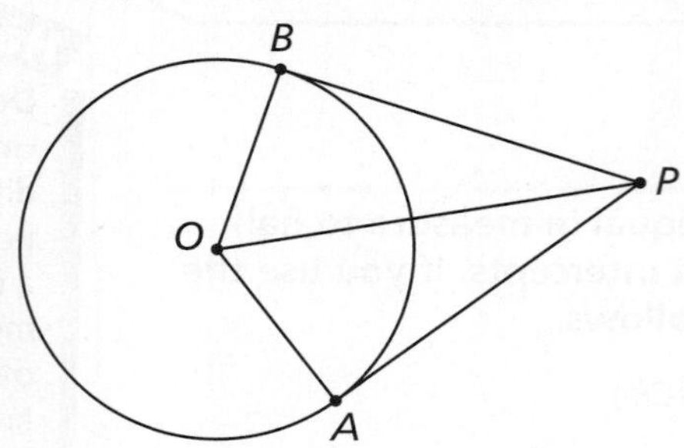

2. $\overline{PA}$ and $\overline{PB}$ are the tangents to a circle through P.

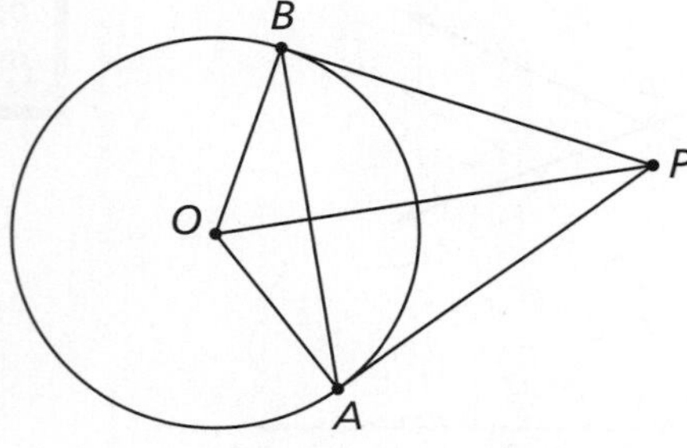

Prove that $\overline{PO}$ is the perpendicular bisector of $\overline{AB}$.

3. Construct a circle, an external point, and the tangents from the external point to the circle. Describe the steps you take and why your construction works.

4. In the figure, $m\widehat{CB} = 45°$, $m\widehat{AD} = 69°$, $m\angle DCE = 13°$, and $m\angle CPF = 68°$. Find the measures of the following angle and arcs.

a. $\angle CQB$ **b.** $\widehat{ED}$ **c.** $\widehat{FB}$

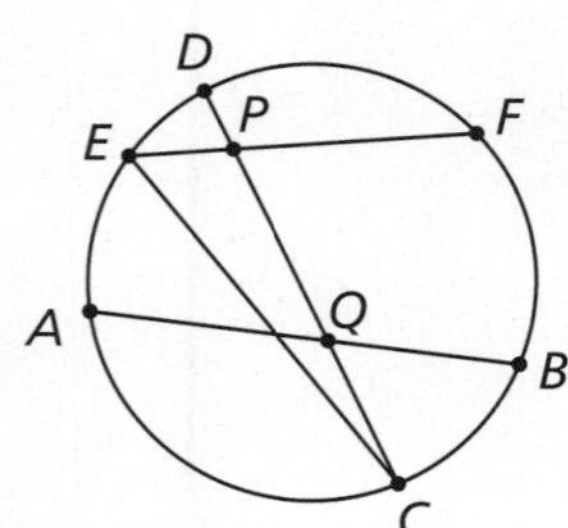

5. In this figure, $m\widehat{CE} = 69°$ and $m\widehat{EF} = 97°$

   a. What is $m\widehat{FB}$?

   b. What is $m\angle CAD$?

   c. Suppose you do not know that a tangent is perpendicular to the radius through its point of tangency. Use the formula from Theorem 5.13 or Theorem 5.14 to prove that $\overline{DC}$ is perpendicular to $\overline{AC}$.

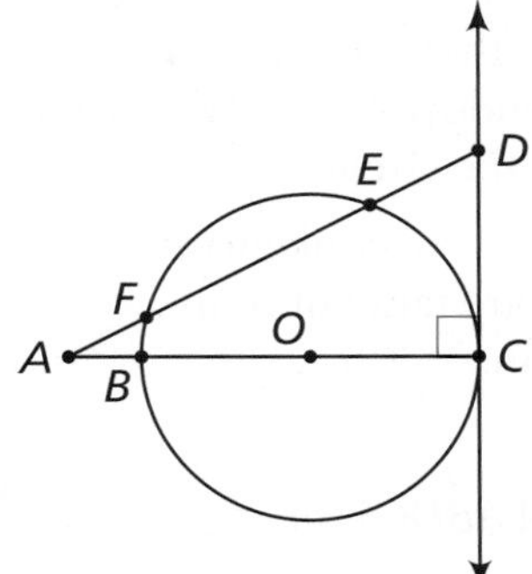

On Your Own

6. In the circle with center O, $OP = 1$ in., $m\angle POQ = 30°$, and $\overline{PQ}$ is tangent to the circle. Find OQ and PQ. Then calculate OQ and PQ for $m\angle POQ = 45°$ and for $m\angle POQ = 60°$.

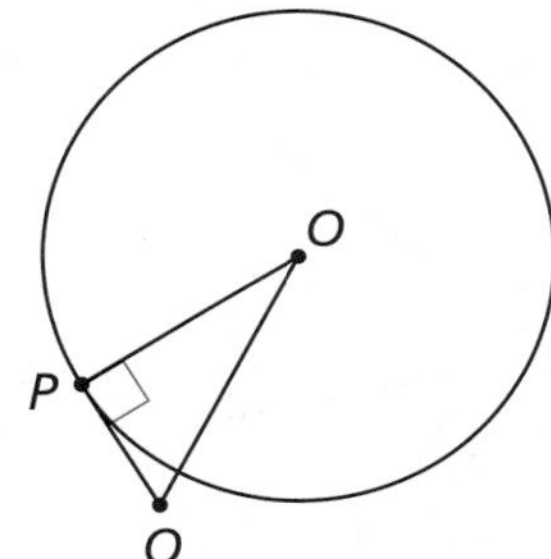

7. Draw two parallel lines and inscribe a circle between them. What can you say about the segment that connects the intersections of the circle with the parallel lines? Explain.

8. **Standardized Test Prep** Given $m\angle AQF = 22°$ and $m\widehat{QHP} = 110°$, what is $m\angle QRP$?

   A. 67°

   B. 77°

   C. 82°

   D. 88°

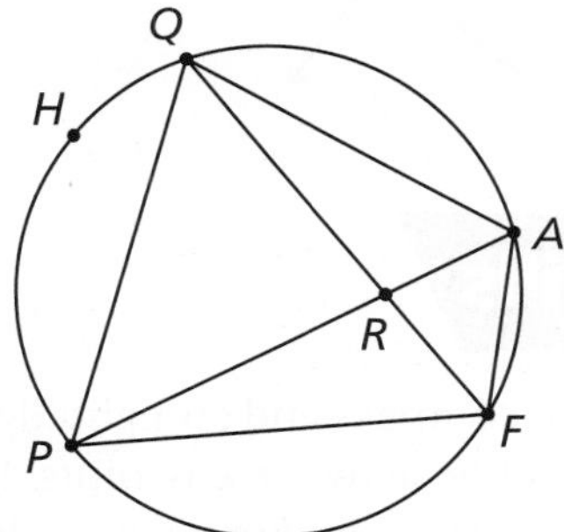

9. Draw a circle and two different-length adjacent chords $\overline{AB}$ and $\overline{AC}$. Mark the midpoints P and Q of the minor arcs $\widehat{AB}$ and $\widehat{AC}$ and connect them. M and N are the points in which this segment intersects $\overline{AB}$ and $\overline{AC}$. Prove that $\overline{AM} \cong \overline{AN}$.

10. **Take It Further** Draw a circle and inscribe a right triangle so that $m\angle ABC = 90°$. Through the center of the circle O, draw a line ℓ parallel to $\overline{AB}$. Draw a line through C that intersects ℓ at P so that $\angle CPO \cong \angle ACB$. In how many ways can you choose P on ℓ? In how many points does the line through C and P intersect the circle?

11. In this figure, the two circles are concentric and $\overline{PA}$, $\overline{PB}$, $\overline{PC}$, and $\overline{PD}$ are tangent to the circle their endpoints lie on.

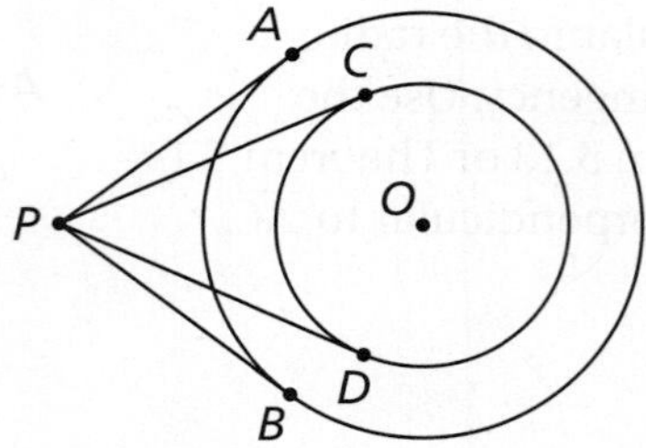

   a. Prove $\angle APC \cong \angle DPB$.

   b. Prove that quadrilateral $ABDC$ is an isosceles trapezoid.

12. **Take It Further** In the figure below, O is the center of the circle and ℓ is tangent to the circle at point C. Prove that M is the midpoint of $\overline{EF}$.

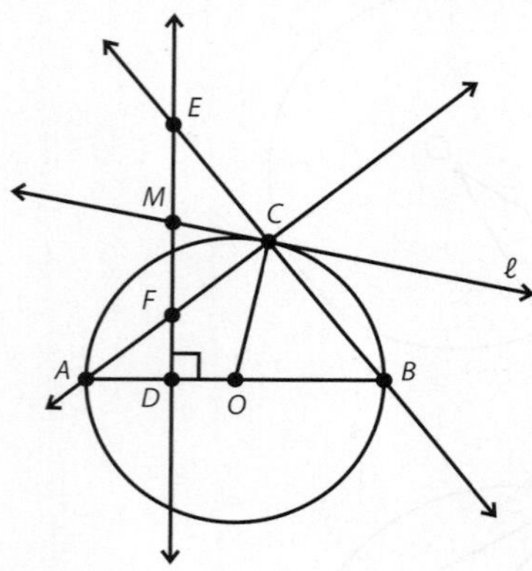

Maintain Your Skills

13. Use geometry software or a compass and straightedge for the following exercise. Draw a circle and choose two fixed points A and C on it. Now choose a third point B on the circle and move it gradually toward A.

   a. What is the measure of $\angle ABC$ as you move B along the circle?

   b. Draw the line ℓ that contains $\overline{BA}$ and move B until it coincides with A. What does ℓ become? Explain.

   c. When B coincides with A, what arc does the angle that ℓ forms with $\overline{AC}$ intercept?

   d. Think about the angle that ℓ forms with $\overline{AC}$ when B coincides with A. Can you prove that its measure is the same as the measure of $\angle ABC$ that is formed when B does not coincide with A? Explain.

14. Can Theorem 5.11 be considered a special case of Theorem 5.13 or of Theorem 5.14?

5.13 Power of a Point

Every point in the plane of a circle has a number associated with it. That number is called the power of the point.

In-Class Experiment

The Power of a Point

1. Draw a circle and pick a point P anywhere inside it. Then draw a chord of the circle that passes through P. Point P divides the chord into two segments $\overline{PA}$ and $\overline{PB}$.

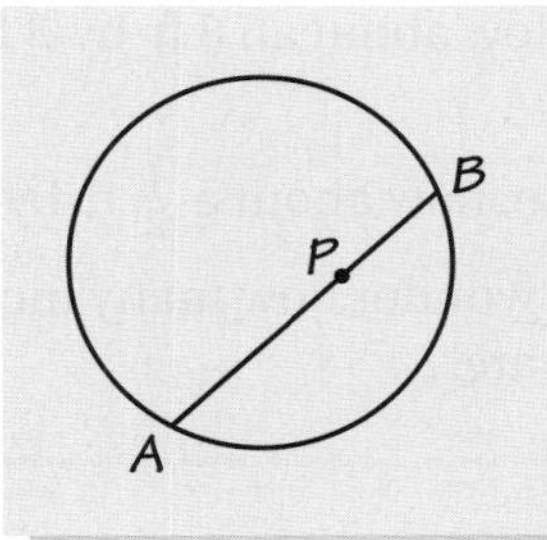

   a. Measure the lengths of these segments and calculate the product $(PA) \cdot (PB)$.

   b. Draw another chord through P and calculate the same product of the lengths of its two segments. Record your observations and repeat the process for several more chords.

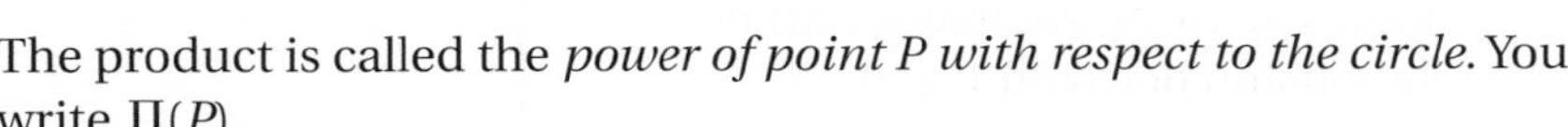

The product is called the *power of point P with respect to the circle.* You write $\Pi(P)$.

If you see $\Pi(P) = \ldots$ in reference to a circle and a point P, you say "the power of P with respect to the circle is . . . ."

2. The circle at the right has two chords $\overline{AB}$ and $\overline{CD}$ that intersect at point P.

   a. What can you predict about the lengths PA, PB, PC, and PD?

   b. Copy the figure and add segments $\overline{AC}$ and $\overline{BD}$ to the illustration. The first step in proving your conjecture from part (a) is to show that $\triangle APC \sim \triangle DPB$. Explain why these two triangles must be similar.

   c. Use the fact that $\triangle APC \sim \triangle DPB$ to write a proportion that includes PA, PB, PC, and PD. Rearrange the proportion to prove your conjecture from part (a).

   d. How does this result prove that the product of the chord lengths is the same for any chord through P?

Hint: $\angle ACD$ and $\angle ABD$ intercept the same arc.

One of the pleasures of mathematics comes from finding an unexpected connection between two topics that seem to have nothing in common. For example, you can use your findings about the power of a point to answer the following question.

Is there a way to construct a rectangle with geometry software so that when you drag a vertex the perimeter changes but the area remains the same?

If you could build such a rectangle, you could call it a *constant-area rectangle.*

Minds in Action episode 19

Derman and Tony are discussing the possible dimensions of different rectangles with an area of 24 square feet.

Derman Tony, I found two rectangles that have an area of 24 square feet—a 24 ft-by-1 ft and a 12 ft-by-2 ft.

Tony I think there are more than two rectangles that have an area of 24 square feet! How about an 8 ft-by-3 ft rectangle, or a 6 ft-by-4 ft rectangle?

Derman Okay, in that case, how about a $\frac{1}{2}$ ft-by-48 ft rectangle?

Tony Wow, Derman, I wonder how many more 24-square-foot rectangles there are.

For Discussion

3. If ℓ represents the lengths of the rectangles in the above dialog and w represents their widths, what is the relationship between ℓ and w?

4. How many rectangles are there with an area of 24 square feet?

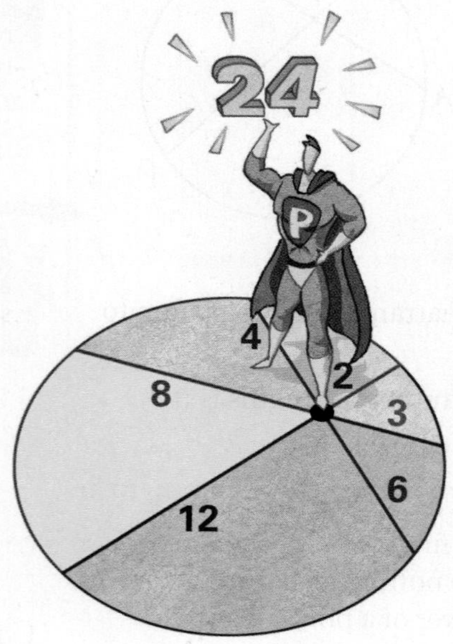

Using what you found out about the power of a point, you can construct constant-area rectangles. To begin, the computer screen shows a rectangle on one side and the power-of-a-point construction on the other. The length *PA* and the width *PB* of the rectangle are linked to the corresponding chord segments and are equal to them. So when the chord segment lengths change, the rectangle's dimensions will, too.

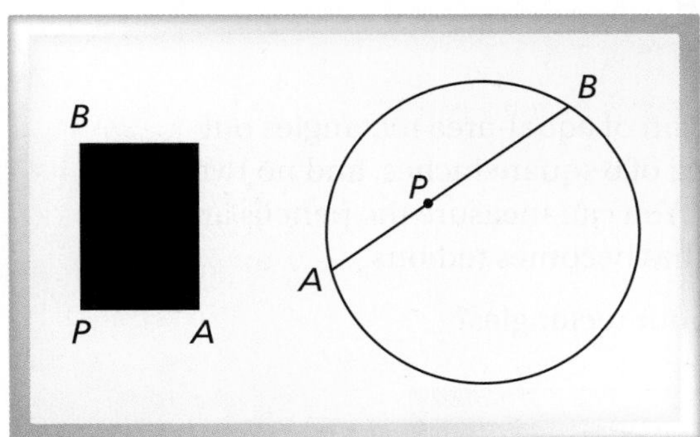

As you move point *A* around the circle, the chord $\overline{AB}$ spins, always passing through the stationary point *P*.

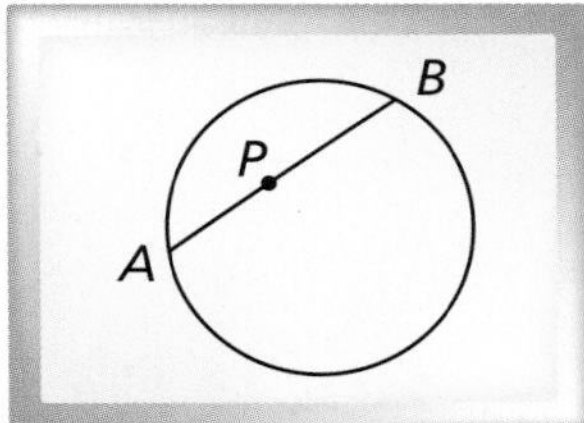

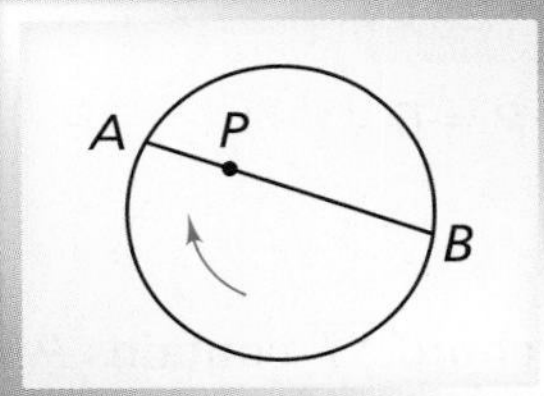

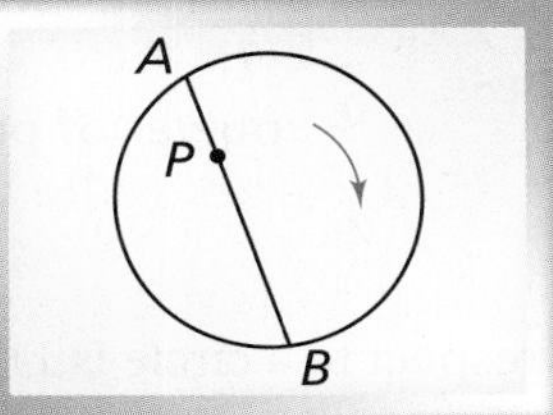

For You to Do

Use geometry software to build a construction like the one described above. Your construction might include an animation button that allows point *A* to travel automatically around the circle.

5. As chord $\overline{AB}$ spins, describe what happens to the rectangle.

6. The purpose of this geometry construction is to create a rectangle of constant area. Explain why you think this construction does or does not satisfy this goal.

7. Does your construction show all possible rectangles that share the same area? Explain.

Exercises *Practicing Habits of Mind*

Check Your Understanding

1. Suppose that you decide to build a collection of equal-area rectangles out of pencils. Each rectangle is to have an area of 6 square inches, and no two rectangles can have the same dimensions. You can measure the pencils and then cut them at appropriate places, but that becomes tedious.

   How can the setup below help you make your rectangles?

a few pencils

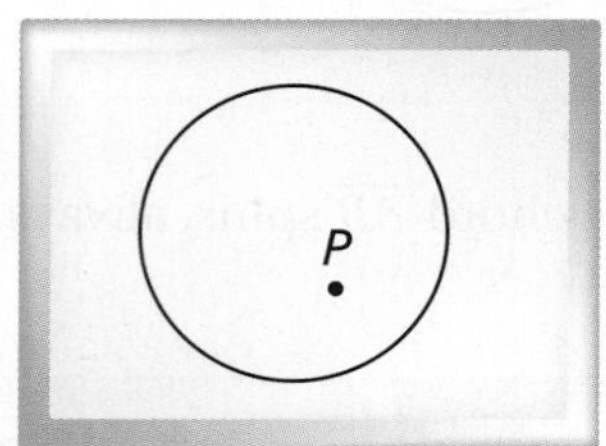

power of point $P = 6$

The actual circle and pencils would be larger.

2. The power of point P with respect to a circle is 112. A chord $\overline{ST}$ contains P. If $PT = 32$ in., how long is $\overline{ST}$?

3. Draw a circle with center O, radius r, and a diameter $\overline{AE}$. Find and label the midpoint of $\overline{OE}$ B, the midpoint of $\overline{BE}$ C, and the midpoint of $\overline{CE}$ D. Find $\Pi(B)$, $\Pi(C)$, $\Pi(D)$, and $\Pi(O)$. How would you define $\Pi(E)$?

On Your Own

4. **Write About It** Suppose you want to make a constant-area triangle instead of a rectangle. Describe at least one way to alter the methods in this lesson to make a triangle instead. Include pictures.

5. Parts (a)–(d) give an outline for a proof that the power of a point is invariant. Justify each step and then write the proof.

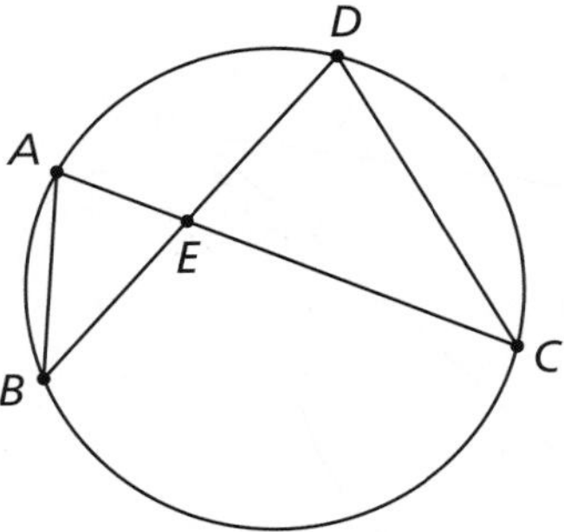

a. $\angle ABE \cong \angle DCE$

b. $\angle AEB \cong \angle DEC$

c. $\triangle ABE \sim \triangle DCE$

d. $\frac{AE}{DE} = \frac{BE}{CE}$

e. Write the complete proof showing that $(AE)(CE) = (BE)(DE)$.

Hint: Look for inscribed angles.

6. The power of a point P with respect to a circle is 126. Draw two chords $\overline{AB}$ and $\overline{CD}$ through P, such that $AP = 21$ cm and $CD = 25$ cm. Find PB, CP, and DP.

7. Two chords $\overline{AB}$ and $\overline{CD}$ through a point P inside a circle measure 7 cm and 13 cm respectively. If $AP = 3$ cm, find PB, CP, and PD.

8. **Standardized Test Prep** In the figure, $CD = 7$ cm, $CP = 3$ cm, and $PG = 5$ cm. What is FP?

A. 2.0 cm

B. 2.4 cm

C. 2.5 cm

D. 4.2 cm

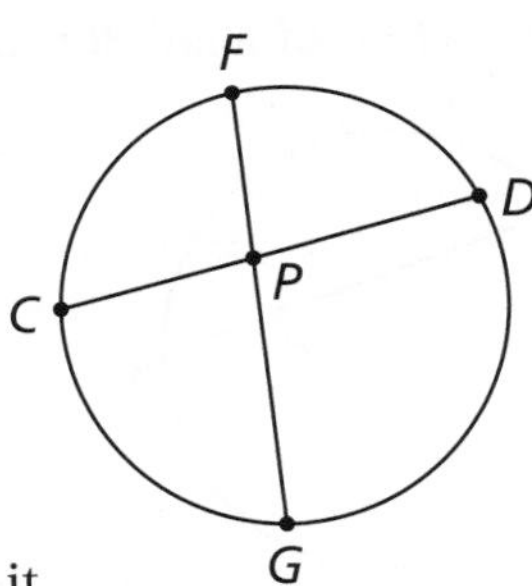

9. **Take It Further** Draw a circle and a point P within it. Measure to calculate the power of P.

a. Are there other locations for P within the same circle that have the same power? Find a few and explain your reasoning.

b. Find the locations of all points within your circle that have the same power as P. What does this collection of points look like?

10. **Take It Further** If P is a point outside the circle, as in the figure below left, you can still prove that the product $(PA)(PB)$ is invariant. Copy the figure below right and connect B to C and A to D.

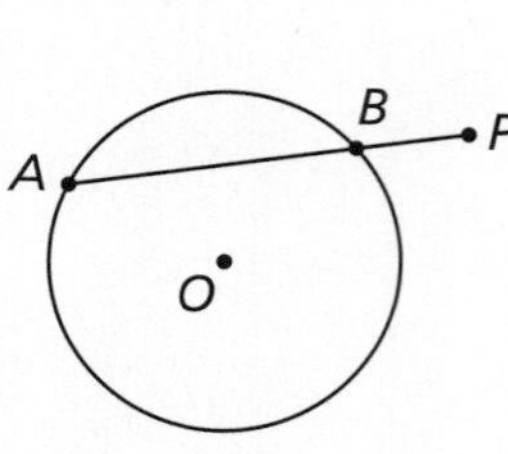

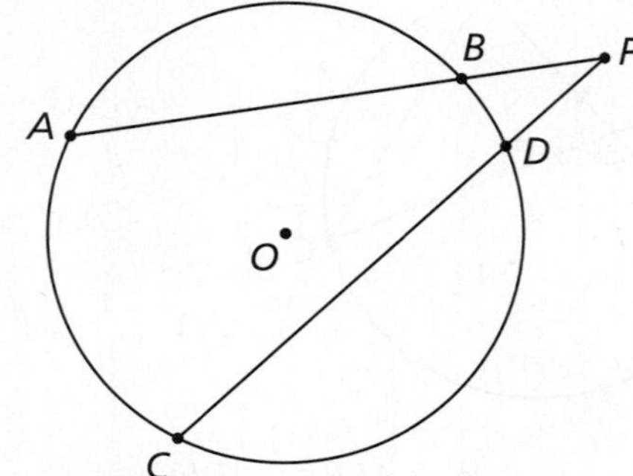

a. Prove that $\triangle PAD \sim \triangle PCB$.

b. Write proportions for the sides of the triangles and deduce that $(PA)(PB)$ is invariant.

You can, therefore, generalize the definition of $\Pi(P)$ this way.

Definition

The power of a point P with respect to a circle is the product $(PA)(PB)$, where A and B are the points of intersection of a line through P and the circle.

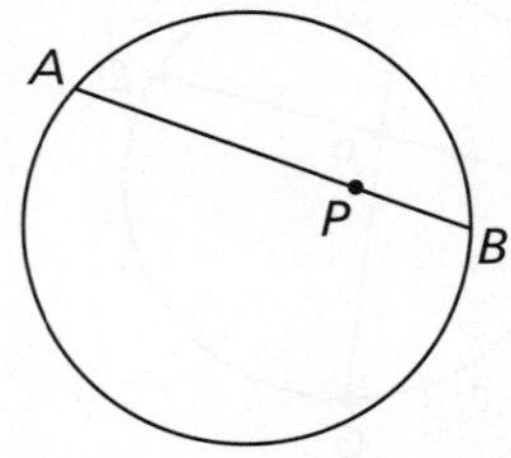

Habits of Mind

Explore. What is the power of P if P lies *on* the circle?

Maintain Your Skills

For Exercises 11–14, draw a circle and a chord $\overline{AB}$ through a point P inside the circle.

11. For $\Pi(P) = 6$ and $PA = 3$ cm, find PB and AB.

12. For $\Pi(P) = 9$ and $AB = 10$ in., find PA and PB.

13. For $\Pi(P) = 28$ and $AB = 16$ cm, find PA and PB.

14. For $\Pi(P) = k$ and $AB = a$ cm, find PA and PB as functions of k and a.

In this investigation, you examined chords, secants, and tangents of circles and proved many relationships involving these figures. These questions will help you summarize what you have learned.

1. In the circle at the right with center O, M is the midpoint of $\overline{AB}$. Prove that $\triangle AOM$ is a right triangle.
2. Draw any right triangle ABC and let $m\angle ABC = 90°$. Why is the median from B to the midpoint of $\overline{AC}$ always half as long as $\overline{AC}$?
3. In the figure at the right below, $m\angle ABC = 31°$ and O is the center of the circle. What is the measure of each angle?
   a. $\angle AOC$
   b. $\angle AEC$
   c. $\angle CDA$
4. Draw a circle with center O and radius 35 mm, choose a point P on the circle, and draw the line ℓ through P tangent to the circle. What is the distance from O to ℓ?
5. What are arcs and chords in circles?
6. How much smaller is the measure of an inscribed angle than the measure of its corresponding central angle?
7. What is the power of a point? What are the maximum and minimum values of the power of a point in a circle with radius r?

Vocabulary and Notation

In this investigation, you learned these terms and symbols. Make sure you understand what each one means and how to use it.

- **arc, $\widehat{AB}$**
- **central angle**
- **chord**
- **circumscribed circle**
- **concentric circles**
- **diameter**
- **inscribed angle**
- **inscribed circle**
- **locus**
- **major arc**
- **measure of an arc, $m\widehat{AB}$**
- **minor arc**
- **power of a point, $\Pi(P)$**
- **secant**
- **secant angle**
- **tangent**

The ball flies off on a tangent.

Geometric Probability

In *Geometric Probability*, you may be surprised to see concepts from probability applied to geometric situations. Most people have thought about probability in contexts such as rolling number cubes, flipping coins, drawing playing cards, or other random events. How does probability relate to geometry? As you will see, you can use certain types of random events to approximate areas of figures. Through these experiments, you will experience a new way to think about measurement.

By the end of this investigation, you will be able to answer questions like these.

1. What is the probability that a tiny rain drop will hit a certain region on a board?
2. How can you estimate areas with the Monte Carlo Method?
3. What is the probability of a spinner landing on a line?

You will learnw how to

- compute the probability that a tiny rain drop will hit a certain area of a board
- use the Monte Carlo Method to approximate areas
- recognize sets of measure zero

You will develop these habits and skills:

- Relate ratios of areas to probability.
- Use probability experiments to approximate π.
- Work to understand an abstract definition of a mathematical object.

The larger the web, the smaller is the probability that a bug can fly by without getting caught.

5.14 Getting Started

In some games you spin a pointer. You proceed with the game based on the outcome of the spin.

In-Class Experiment

For this experiment, you will need a spinner provided by your teacher.

1. Label the sections on your spinner A, B, C, D, E, and F. Spin the spinner 50 times and keep track of which letter the pointer lands on each time. Compare your results with other students' results.

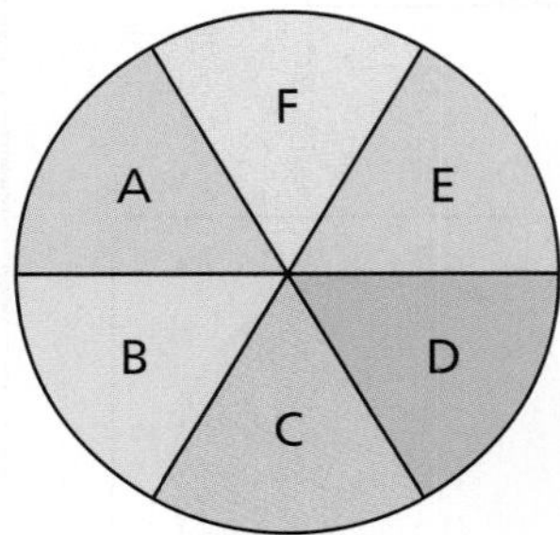

2. Change the names of the slices so that your spinner looks like this:

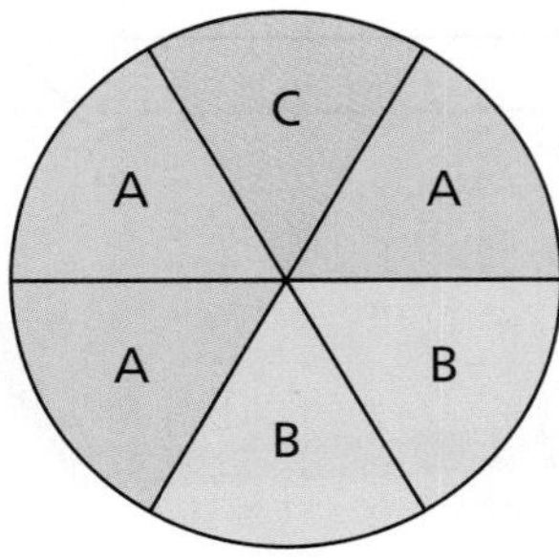

Spin the spinner 50 times. Keep track of which letter the pointer lands on each time. Compare your results with other students' results. Do you get the same results as in Problem 1? Explain.

3. Draw another circle with the same radius as your spinner. Cut it out and tape it to the spinner. Now divide your spinner so that $\frac{1}{4}$ of it is the A region, $\frac{5}{8}$ of it is the B region, and $\frac{1}{8}$ of it is the C region. Did all of your classmates divide the spinner in the same way? Does it matter? Spin the spinner 50 times and mark what letter the pointer lands on. What is the greatest number of times the pointer lands on a zone? Why do you think this region has the greatest number?

For You to Explore

For the following problems, imagine poppy seeds falling on the figures. For each figure, predict whether the seeds will land more frequently on the blue part or on the white part. Explain your reasoning. You may wish to measure the figures with a ruler.

Imagine that the seeds fall with equal probability anywhere on the figure.

4.

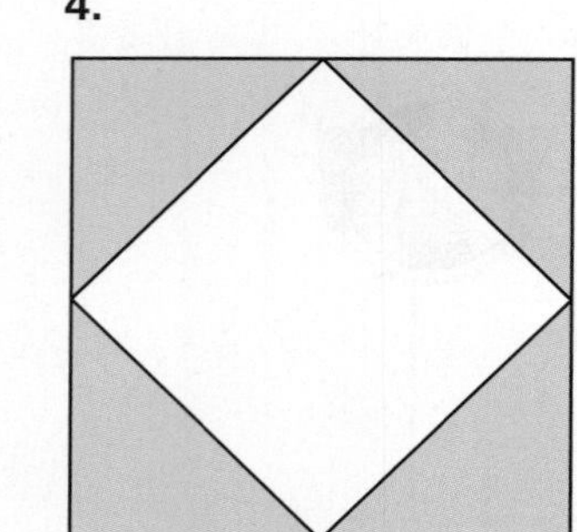

5.

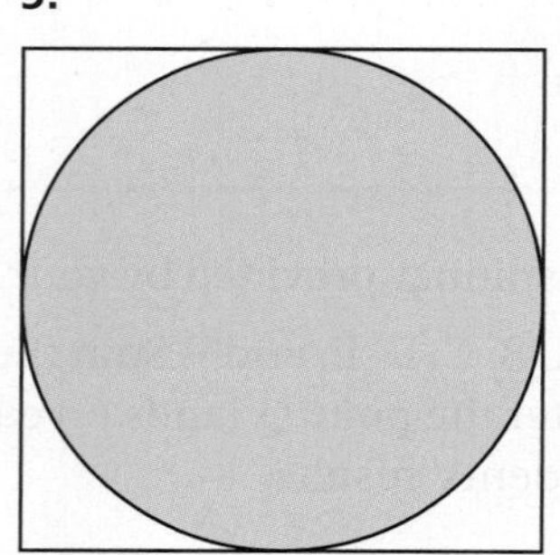

6.

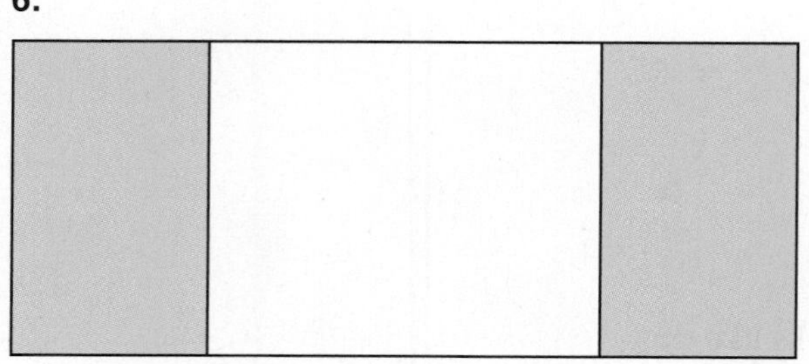

7.

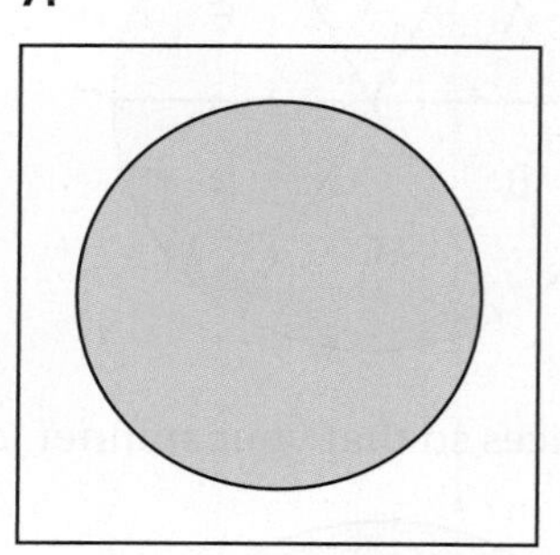

Exercises *Practicing Habits of Mind*

On Your Own

For the following exercises, imagine poppy seeds falling anywhere on a board with equal probability.

8. Shade the board with two different colors so that there is a 50% probability that a poppy seed will fall on each color.

9. Shade the board with two different colors so that there is a 25% probability that a poppy seed will fall on one of the colors.

10. Shade the board with two different colors so that there is a 75% probability that a poppy seed will fall on one of the colors.

11. Shade the board with two different colors so that there is a $33\frac{1}{3}\%$ probability that a poppy seed will fall on one of the colors.

Maintain Your Skills

12.

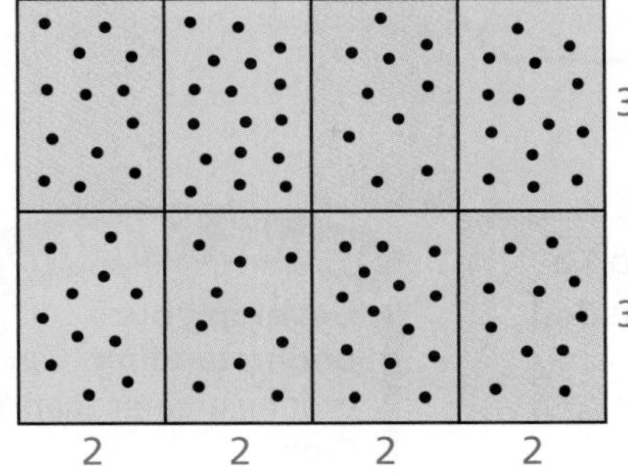

Ms. Belanger's class made a board that measures 8 feet by 6 feet and divided it into eight color regions. The class threw a table-tennis ball dipped in yellow paint 100 times. The ball had equal probabilities of hitting any of the eight regions. The center of each hit was marked with a black dot. The figure shows the black dots as they appeared on the full-sized board. Count the black dots in each region. Copy and complete the table.

Color	h = number of hits (out of 100)	A = area of the region	$\frac{h}{100}$	$\frac{A}{48}$
R	■	■	■	■
G	■	■	■	■
B	■	■	■	■

Are the last two columns similar? What do you think would have happened if the class had thrown the table-tennis ball 200 times or 1000 times?

5.15 Probability as a Ratio of Areas

The sizes of shapes affect geometric probability.

For Discussion

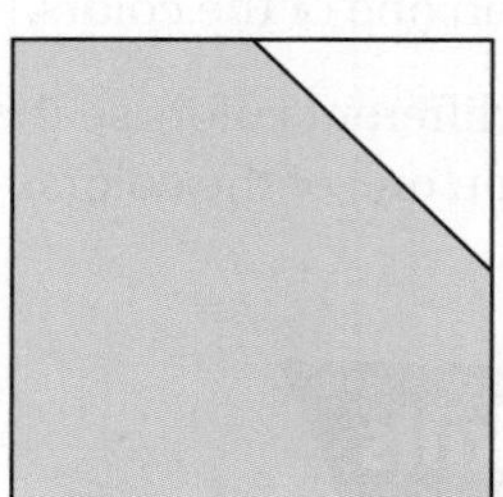

1. If a tiny drop of ink randomly hit the figure, would the drop be more likely to land on the blue region or the white region?
2. If the probability of the drop landing on the blue region is P, would you reduce or enlarge the blue region to make the probability $\frac{P}{2}$? To make the probability $\frac{P}{4}$?
3. What is the relationship between P and the blue region?

Facts and Notation

The probability P that a tiny drop will land on a region of area s on a board of area b ($b \neq 0$) is equal to the ratio of the areas of the shaded region and of the whole board.

$$P = \frac{s}{b}$$

Habits of Mind

Develop your understanding. Can P ever be greater than 1? Explain.

For You to Do

A circular board has radius r. There is a shaded concentric circle on the board. What would the radius of this shaded circle have to be in order for the probability of a tiny drop landing on it to be the following?

4. $\frac{1}{4}$
5. $\frac{1}{3}$
6. $\frac{1}{2}$

Minds in Action episode 20

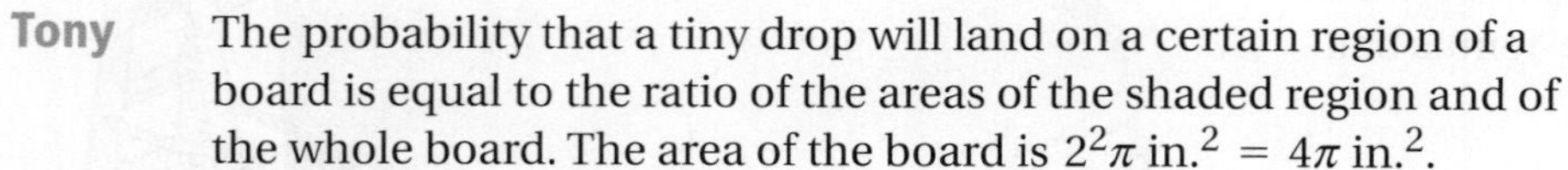

Sasha and Tony were asked to estimate the area of a blob inside a circular board with a radius of 2 in., without using the grid method.

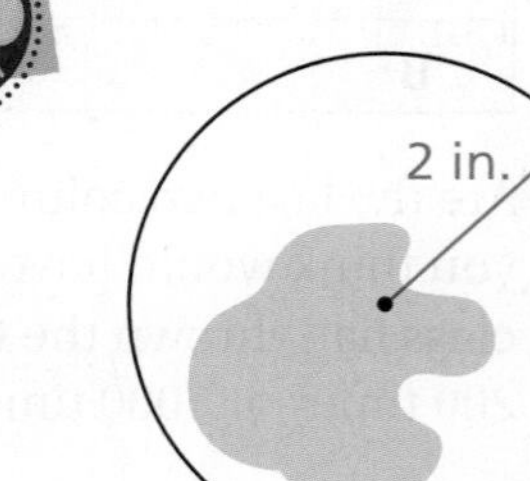

Tony The probability that a tiny drop will land on a certain region of a board is equal to the ratio of the areas of the shaded region and of the whole board. The area of the board is $2^2\pi$ in.^{2} $= 4\pi$ in.^{2}.

Sasha I think you're going in the right direction, but if we want to use the formula $P = \frac{s}{b}$, we need to know the probability a tiny drop will land in the blob. How can we get that?

Tony Well, I remember the In-Class Experiment at the beginning of this investigation. We related the number of times the pointer landed on a certain slice of the spinner to the area of that region of the spinner. Do you think we could do something like that?

Sasha That's a good idea, Tony! Let's think. We could find the ratio between the number of times a drop lands on the blob and the number of times a drop hits the board anywhere. How could we relate this to the probability P, which is the likelihood a drop will hit the blob rather than some other point on the board?

Tony We may not know P exactly, but the more drops we use, the more accurate our guess will be.

Sasha Then we can use our guess at P to make a good guess for the area of the blob! Good thinking, Tony.

It is hard to randomly generate tiny ink drops, so Sasha and Tony simulate this using the following method.

Step 1 Cut out the board with the blob.

Step 2 Sprinkle 200 poppy seeds randomly on the board.

Step 3 Count the poppy seeds that landed on the blob.

Step 4 Calculate the ratio of poppy seeds on the blob to the total number of poppy seeds you sprinkled (200).

This ratio R will be close to the actual probability P, as long as the number of poppy seeds is relatively large. You can use the ratio R in place of P to estimate the area A of the blob by calculating the following.

$$A \approx R(4\pi)$$

In the case of the poppy-seed experiment, the definition of probability is the number of seeds on the blob divided by the total number of seeds on the board.

Monte Carlo Method

The method Tony and Sasha just used is called the **Monte Carlo Method.** In general, the Monte Carlo Method is a statistical simulation method that utilizes sequences of random numbers to perform a simulation. It is used in many fields, from the simulation of physical phenomena such as radiation transport in Earth's atmosphere to the simulation of a game.

Because the method can simulate games of chance, it is named after a small European city that is a center for gambling.

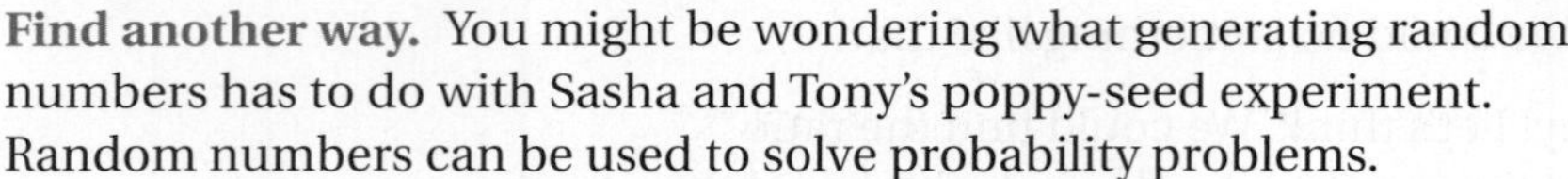

Developing Habits of Mind

Find another way. You might be wondering what generating random numbers has to do with Sasha and Tony's poppy-seed experiment. Random numbers can be used to solve probability problems.

Here is a way that a random number generator could simulate the poppy-seed experiment. Think of a board divided into thousands of regions, each the size of a poppy seed. A computer could randomly generate a sequence of numbers from 0 to the total number of regions. Each number would correspond to a tiny region on the board. The generated numbers would correspond to the event of a poppy seed landing inside or outside the shaded region.

To get a better estimate for P, you must make sure the number of times you repeat the event is relatively high.

For You to Do

7. Tony and Sasha repeat the poppy-seed experiment three times on a second blob drawn on a circular board with 2-in. radius. The first time they use 100 poppy seeds, the second time 200 poppy seeds, and the third time 400 poppy seeds. They calculate the ratios $R_1 = 0.720$, $R_2 = 0.765$, and $R_3 = 0.755$. What is the best estimate for the blob's area? Explain.

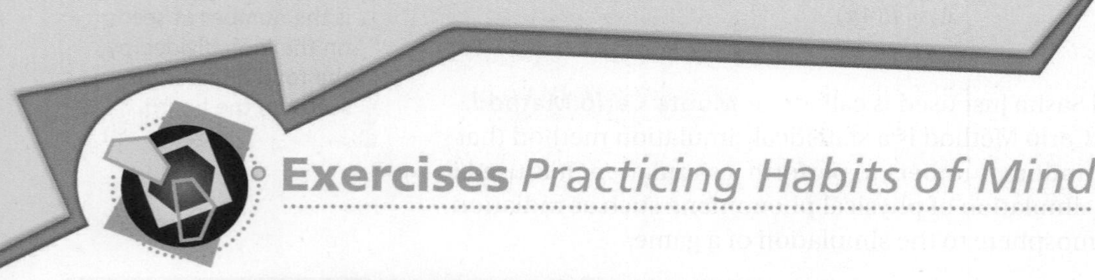

Exercises *Practicing Habits of Mind*

Check Your Understanding

What is the probability a tiny drop of ink will land on the blue regions of the following square boards? The side length of the square is 3 inches.

1.

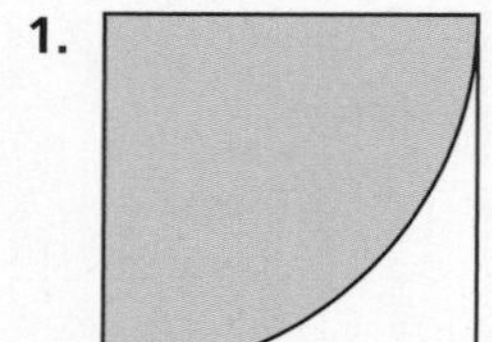

2.

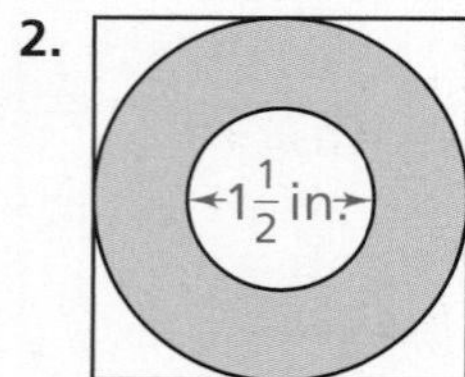

3.

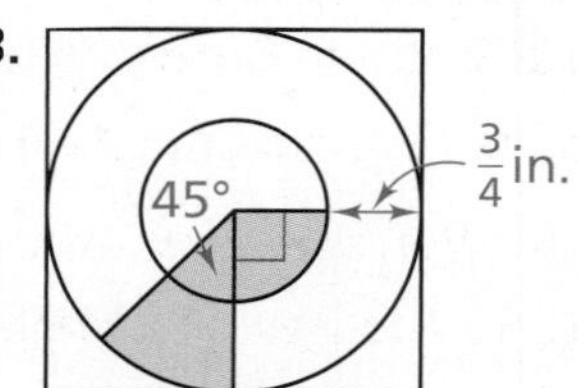

On Your Own

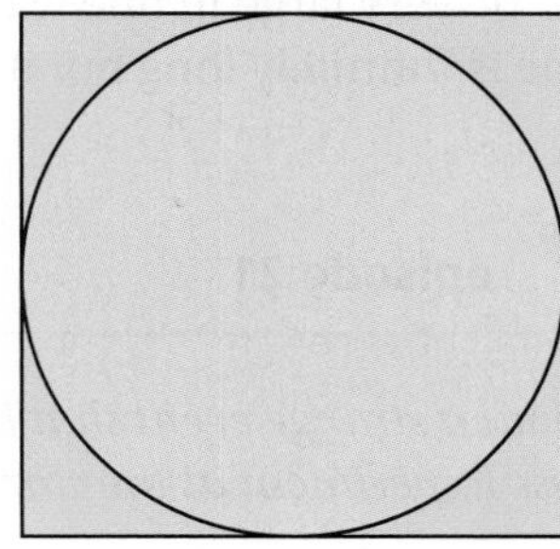

4. A circle is inscribed in a square.

Use the Monte Carlo Method to estimate the value of π.

5. Think of a checkerboard made of squares of alternating colors, each with an area of 4 square inches. Assume the board extends infinitely in all directs like a plane. If you drop a penny (its diameter is $\frac{3}{4}$ in.) on the board, what is the probability it will touch two colors?

6. How could you change the side length of the squares on the checkerboard from Exercise 5 in order for the probability of the penny landing on two colors to be $\frac{1}{2}$, $\frac{1}{3}$, or $\frac{1}{4}$?

7. Two circles are painted on a board. The probability of a drop landing inside exactly one of the two circles is 0.4. The probability of it landing outside both circles is 0.5. How can this be? What is the probability of the drop landing in the intersection of the two circles? How big is this area if the board's area is 5 square feet?

8. **Standardized Test Prep** Ms. Pryce challenged her students to divide a square into three regions with equal areas. Linette did it by drawing a circle of radius 2 cm inside the square and a smaller concentric circle inside the first circle. What is the radius of the smaller circle?

A. 1 cm **B.** $\sqrt{2}$ cm **C.** 1.5 cm **D.** $\sqrt{3}$ cm

9. **Take It Further** A circle and a square are painted on a board. The probability of a drop landing on the circle is 0.4. The probability of a drop landing on the square is 0.7. Suppose the area of the whole board is 5 square feet and the probability of a drop landing on neither the square nor the circle is 0.3. What is the area of the intersection of the square and the circle? What are the areas of the square and the circle?

Maintain Your Skills

10. Find a toothpick and measure it. Call its length ℓ. On a sheet of paper, draw many parallel lines with a distance of ℓ between them. Drop the toothpick on the sheet of paper many times and mark how many times it landed touching a line. This is known as Buffon's Experiment.

a. Give an estimate for the probability P that the toothpick falls on a line.

b. The exact theoretical value for P is $\frac{2}{\pi}$. Is your estimate close?

c. Design an experiment using the Monte Carlo Method and Buffon's Experiment for estimating π.

You will be able to exactly calculate the value of P after you learn some calculus.

5.16 Sets of Measure 0

It is possible for a region to be very large in one way and very small in another. For example, a line is infinitely long but it has area 0.

Minds in Action episode 21

Tony has been thinking about a strange event that happened while he was working on the In-Class Experiment at the start of the investigation.

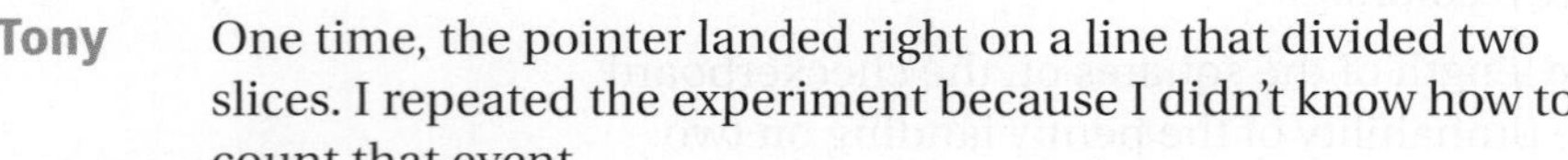

Tony One time, the pointer landed right on a line that divided two slices. I repeated the experiment because I didn't know how to count that event.

Sasha Maybe if you had looked harder you would have seen that the pointer was a tiny bit more on one side of the line. I don't think it could really land exactly on a line, because the width of a line is zero. So the probability of the pointer landing on it is zero.

Tony No, I'm sure it landed right on the line! That event can happen!

For Discussion

1. Who is right? Do you agree with Tony or Sasha? Choose a point of view and argue why it is correct.

In real life, no line or point really has a zero area. Any line you draw is actually a very thin rectangle, and any point is a circle with a very small radius. So in real life, the probability of a pointer landing on a line or a tiny drop of ink landing on a point is very small but not zero.

How thin the rectangle is and how small the circle's radius is depend on how fine a pen you use for drawing lines and points.

Developing Habits of Mind

Explore real-world constraints. A segment with zero area exists only in an idealized mathematical world. It is often helpful to picture this world when you are conducting an experiment in the real world.

If you imagine a spinner divided into a number of regions, you are pretending that the border between two regions has no width, and therefore no area. You are also pretending that the pointer has no width. The calculated theoretical probability P of the pointer landing on the border is 0. It is important to note that it is not impossible for a pointer with no width to land on a border with no width. However, it is so unlikely in this idealized world that the probability it will occur is zero.

In the real world, you can repeat the experiment many times with an actual spinner. The pointer will land on the border with a probability greater than 0 because of real-life constraints. The pointer and border have real width even if it is quite small.

The probability that a dart lands on a border in this game is nearly 0.

For You to Do

2. If you throw a ball at a circular board, can you hit the center? Think of a way to tell exactly where the ball hits the board. What is the probability of hitting the center? What are the real-life limitations?

Measure

You could try to calculate the probability of hitting the exact center of the board in the For You to Do above. Suppose you draw a small circle around the center of the board and calculate the probability of hitting it. If this little circle has a radius of $r_1 = 1$ in. and the board has a radius of 2 feet, the probability is $\frac{1}{576}$, which is small. If the little circle has a radius of $r_2 = \frac{1}{2}$ in., the probability of hitting it is $\frac{1}{2304}$, which is even smaller. Continue this process for r_3, r_4, and r_5, where each radius is half the previous radius. What does the probability of hitting the little circle approach? What happens when that circle becomes a point (a circle of radius zero)?

You are used to measuring a segment by finding its length or measuring a figure on a plane by calculating its area. Probability is another kind of measure. Here is a list of properties of measures you have been working with.

- The measure of something is always greater than or equal to zero.
- The measure of a set of separate elements is the sum of the measures of the individual elements.
- The measure of a set of nonseparate elements is less than or equal to the sum of the measures of the single elements.
- The measure of the intersection of many elements, each contained in the previous one, is the measure of the smallest one.
- When probability is the measure, the probability of an event can never be greater than 1.

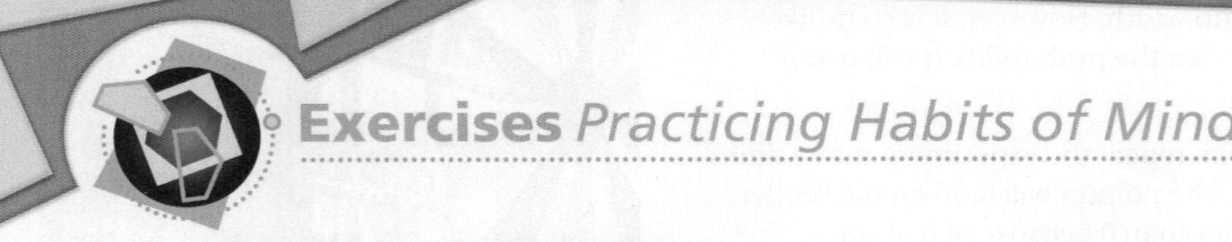

Exercises *Practicing Habits of Mind*

Check Your Understanding

1. If each of the squiggly lines shown on the board is an idealized line with no width, what is the probability of a tiny drop (so small that it has no area) landing on a line? Explain.

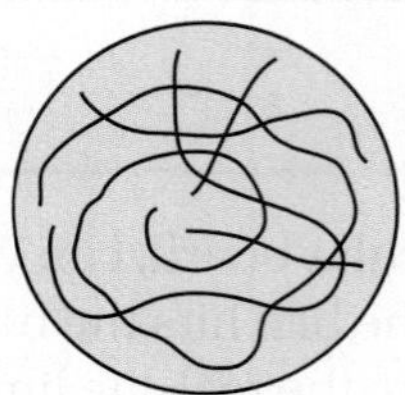

2. The side of this square is 6 units and the radius of each circle is 2 units. Choose a circle and find the probability of a tiny drop landing inside that circle. Is the probability of the drop landing inside either of the two circles twice the number you just found? If the probability that the drop does not land inside any circle is $\frac{1}{2}$, what is the probability of the drop landing inside both circles? What properties of a measure did you use to solve this exercise?

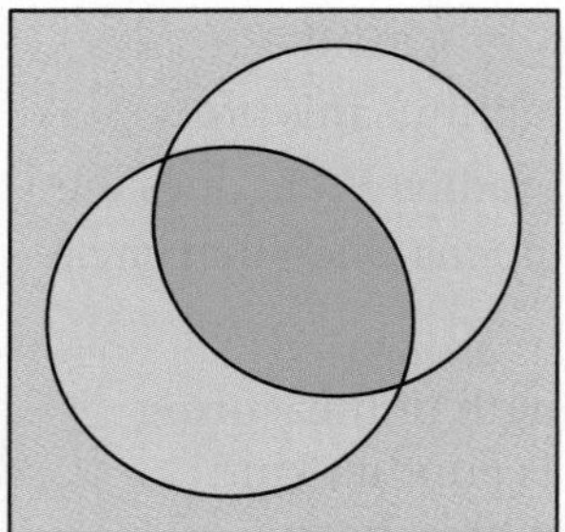

3. The board below is a square with side length 5 cm, and each region is also a square with a side length half the length of the previous one. What is the probability of a tiny drop landing in each of the regions R_1, R_2, R_3, and R_4? Find the probability of a tiny drop landing in each of the regions R_5, R_6, R_7, ... R_n. The last region is a point. What is the probability of a tiny drop landing on it? Of which property of measure is this exercise an example? Explain.

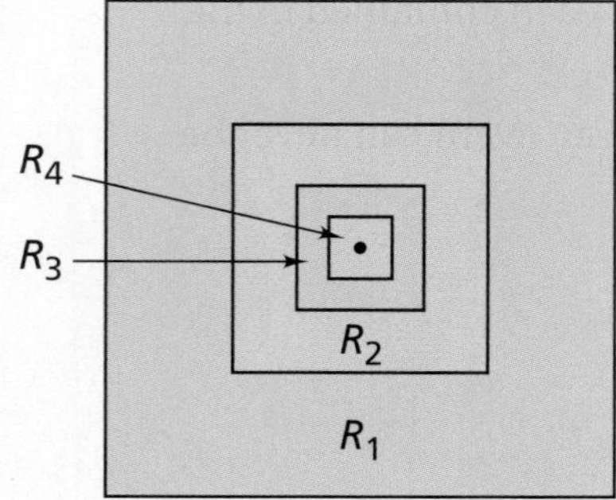

On Your Own

4. Look at the figure below. The board's side length is 4 inches.

   a. What is the probability of a tiny drop landing on a white square?

   b. What is the probability of a tiny drop landing on a black square?

   c. Of which property of measure is this exercise an example? Explain.

5. An isosceles trapezoid's dimensions are as labeled.

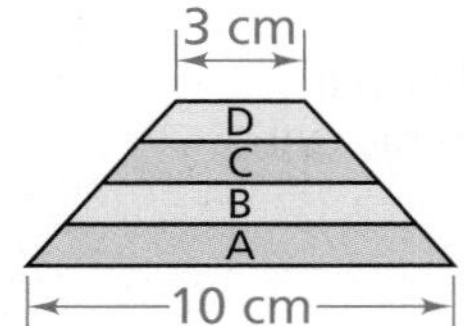

   It is cut by three parallel lines separated from each other and from the bases of the trapezoid by a distance of 1 cm. What is the probability of a tiny drop landing in each of the regions A, B, C, and D of the trapezoid? Choose two regions. What is the probability of the drop landing in one of the two regions you chose? Are there other ways of getting the same answer?

6. All four of the regions of this board are squares of side length ℓ. What is the probability that a randomly dropped coin with radius r would touch all four? What is the probability a tiny drop would land touching all four regions? Explain.

7. **Standardized Test Prep** Mario wants to estimate how often a quarter would land completely inside a square on his chessboard (without touching any other square). Mario makes 1000 trials. Assume that in each trial the coin lands randomly on the chessboard. A side of a square on the chessboard is 38.1 mm. The diameter of a quarter is 24.26 mm. Which of the following is the best estimate for the expected number of times that the quarter will land completely inside a square?

   A. 104 **B.** 111 **C.** 132 **D.** 405

8. **Take It Further** An interesting problem consists of randomly placing a rectangle on a chessboard with its sides parallel to the sides of the chessboard. The rectangle is large enough that it cannot fit in a single square, so it must touch more than one color. The area of the rectangle can be expressed as the sum of the areas of each of the colors it covers. Draw various rectangles, cut them out, and place them on a chessboard. What conditions have to be present for the rectangle to cover an equal area of each color? What is the probability that the rectangle will cover equal amounts of each color?

   If you do not have a chess board, you can divide a square piece of paper into an 8-by-8 grid.

   (Adapted from Alexander Bogomolny's problem Rectangle on a Chessboard on his Web site "Cut the Knot." Copyright © 1996–2007 Alexander Bogomolny.)

Maintain Your Skills

9. Imagine dropping a coin of radius r on a checkerboard with squares of side length ℓ. Assume the board extends infinitely in all directions, like a plane. What is the probability of the coin landing in each of the following ways?

   a. on only one color
   b. on two different squares
   c. on three different squares
   d. on four different squares
   e. on two different colors

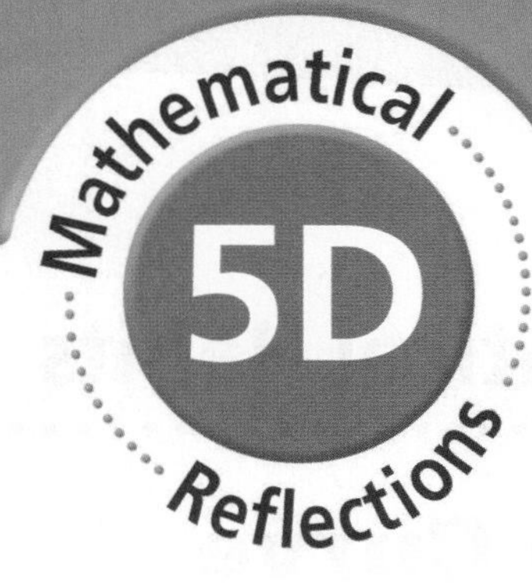

In this investigation, you used areas of regions to find geometric probabilities. You also used geometric probabilities to estimate areas of geometric figures. These questions will help you summarize what you have learned.

1. Find the probability of a tiny drop landing on the blue region of the regular hexagon.

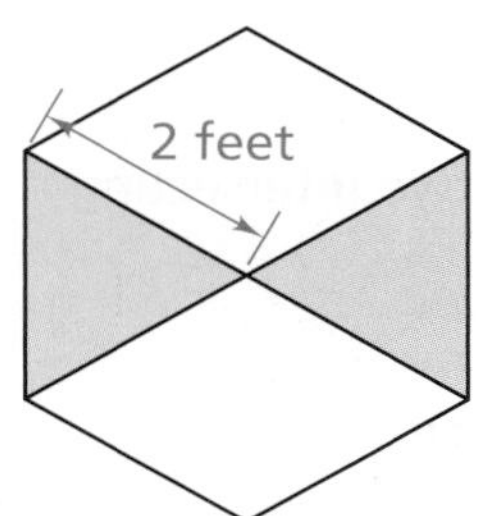

2. When you sprinkled 500 poppy seeds randomly on a black and white tablecloth, 310 landed on white regions. Approximately what fraction of the tablecloth is black?
3. What is the probability of a tiny drop landing on the blue region of the board?

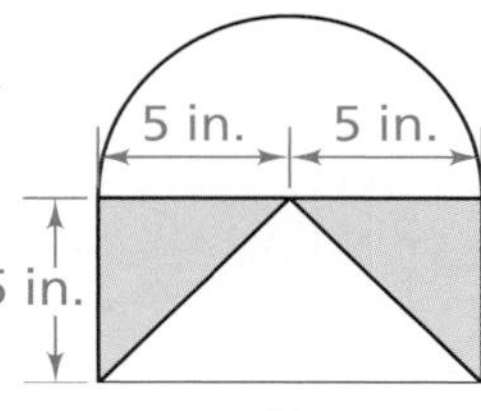

4. What is the probability of a tiny drop landing on the blue region on the board?

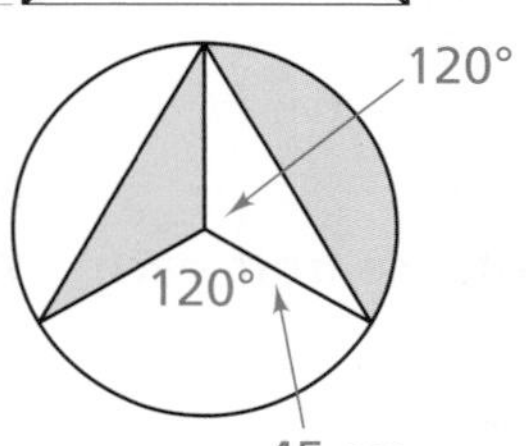

5. Describe a set of measure zero and give an example.
6. What is the probability that a tiny rain drop will hit a certain region on a board?
7. How can you estimate areas with the Monte Carlo Method?
8. What is the probability of a spinner landing on a line?

Vocabulary

In this investigation, you learned these terms. Make sure you understand what each one means and how to use it.

- **Monte Carlo Method**
- **probability**

The larger the bug, the smaller the probability that it can fly through the web without getting caught.

Project: Using Mathematical Habits

Another Interesting Curve

Use geometry software to construct two intersecting circles in the following way.

- Construct $\overline{AB}$.
- Place point C on $\overline{AB}$ near its midpoint.
- Construct $\overline{AC}$ and $\overline{CB}$.

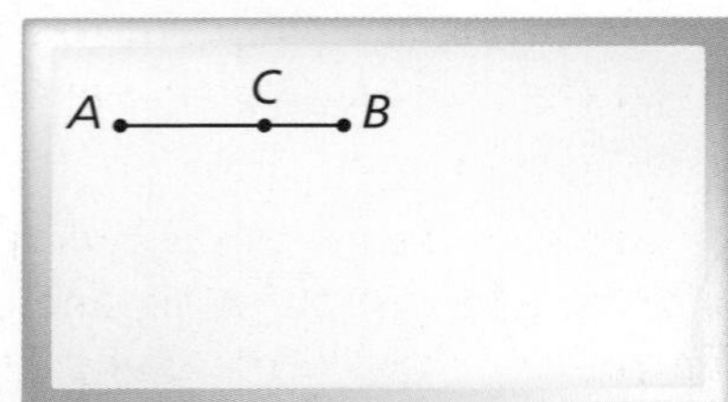

Both $\overline{AC}$ and $\overline{CB}$ have been constructed as segments on top of $\overline{AB}$.

Place points D and E so that their distance from each other is less than AB.

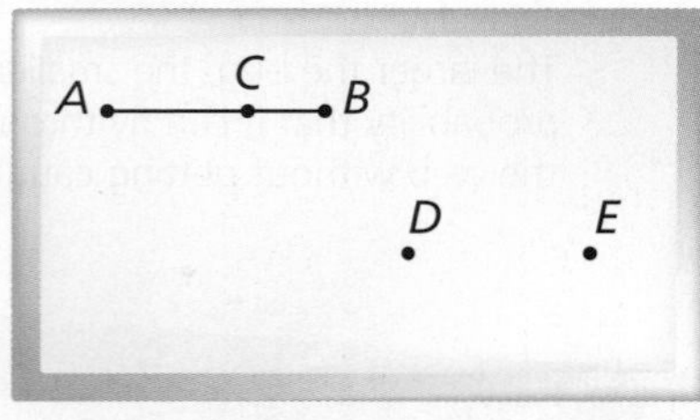

$DE < AB$

- With D as center and AC as radius, construct a circle.
- With E as center and BC as radius, construct a second circle.
- Find the intersections of these two circles.
- Label your entire construction as illustrated below.

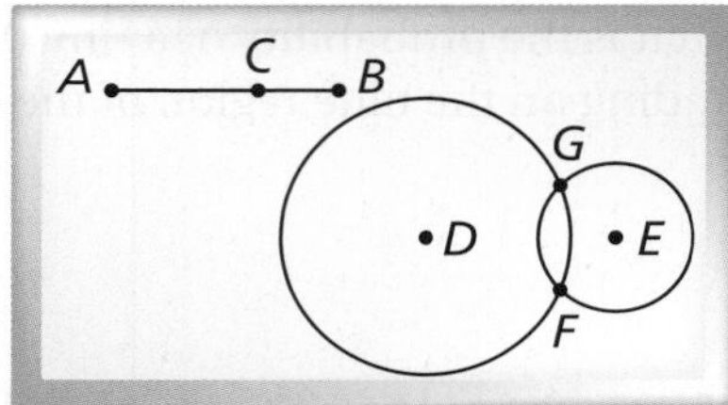

Now work through these exercises to understand what is happening.

1. As you move C back and forth on $\overline{AB}$, notice that the circles do not always intersect. Use the triangle inequality theorem to explain why the circles sometimes intersect and sometimes do not intersect.
2. **Trace** the intersections of these two circles and then experiment with the diagram by dragging A, B, C, D, and E. Patterns that you see as you move these points are kinds of invariants.
3. **Trace** the intersection points (F and G in the picture above). Describe what you see when you move A.

4. What shapes do the points trace out as A moves?

5. Does the pattern you see as you drag A depend on where C was initially along $\overline{AB}$? (For example, does it matter if C starts out near A, far from A, or close to the middle of $\overline{AB}$?) What is the invariant?

6. Make a reasoned argument for or against this statement. "Whatever pattern (invariant) I see when I move A, I should see exactly the same one when I move B."

7. Leave A and B fixed and move C along $\overline{AB}$. What pattern do you find in the intersection points of the circles?

8. Now move D or E around while leaving everything else fixed. Describe what happens.

9. An ellipse is a set of points such that the sum of the distances from each point to two given points is constant. When you move C, you get an ellipse. Explain.

10. Handy objects to have when drawing a circle include tacks, a length of string, and a pencil. How can you use these same objects to build an ellipse maker? Build one and draw several ellipses of various sizes.

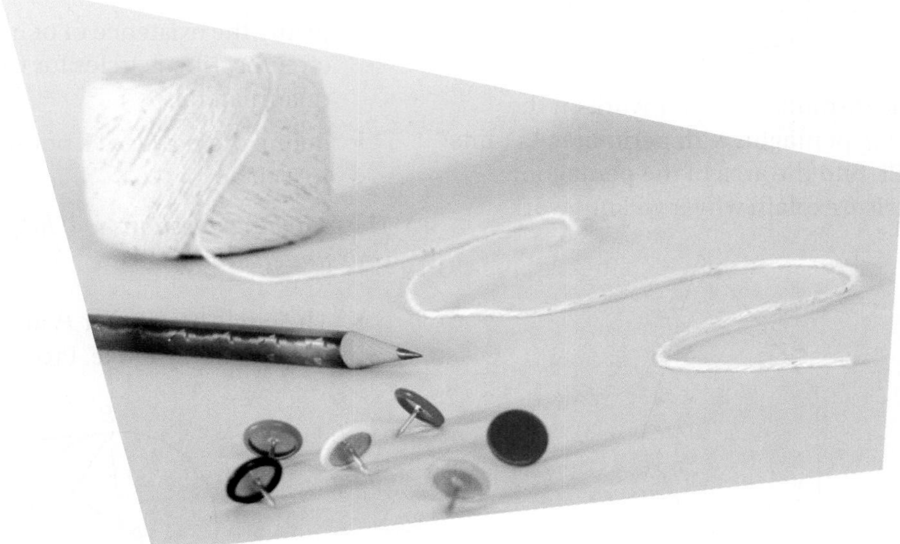

Review

Go Online
Pearsonsuccessnet.com

In **Investigation 5A** you learned how to

- approximate the area and perimeter of blobs
- find the area of regular polygons
- solve problems using the relationship between a regular hexagon's side and the radius of the circle it is inscribed in
- find the area of a circle given its circumference
- use proportional reasoning to determine the lengths of arcs of circles

The following questions will help you check your understanding.

1. Estimate the perimeter of the blob and describe your technique.

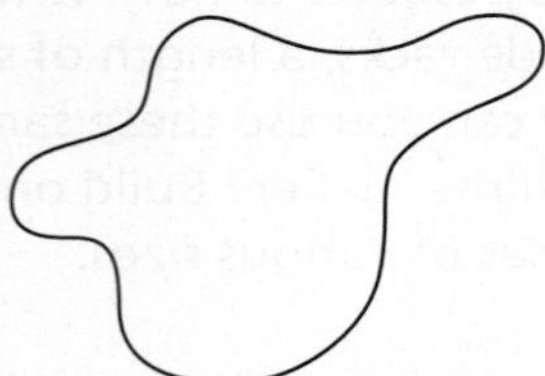

2. Will the formula $A = \frac{1}{2}Pa$ work on the following pentagon with perimeter 45 units? If it will, find the area of the pentagon; otherwise, explain why it will not work.

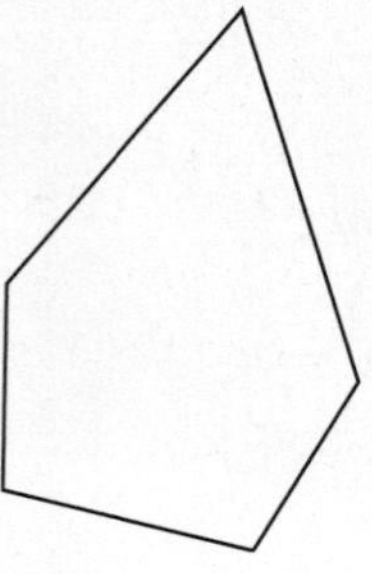

In **Investigation 5B** you learned how to

- calculate the area of a circle, given its radius
- find the perimeter of a circle, given its radius

The following questions will help you check your understanding.

3. If you scale a circle by 6, how does the radius of the scaled circle compare to the radius of the original circle? How does the area of the scaled circle compare to the area of the original circle?

4. What is the perimeter of a circle of radius 216 cm? What is its area?

In **Investigation 5C** you learned how to

- prove and apply theorems about arcs, chords, and inscribed angles of a circle
- prove and apply theorems about secants and tangents of a circle
- look for invariants in circles
- justify the existence of of inscribed and circumscribed circles for triangles and quadrilaterals
- define the power of a point with respect to a circle

The following questions will help you check your understanding.

5. The circle has center P, and $\overline{CB}$ and $\overline{CA}$ are tangent to the circle. Prove that $\overline{PC} \perp \overline{AB}$.

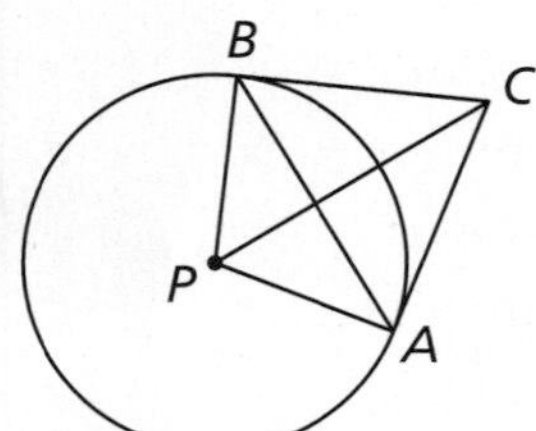

6. If $m\widehat{AB} = 62°$ and $m\widehat{DQC} = 170°$, what is $m\angle APB$?

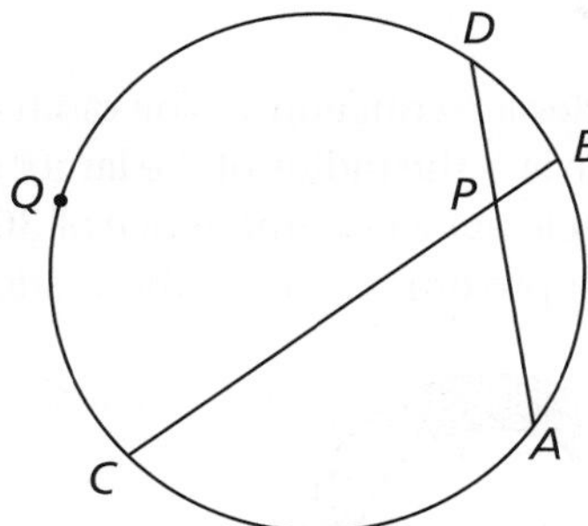

7. What is $\Pi(P)$ in the figure below?

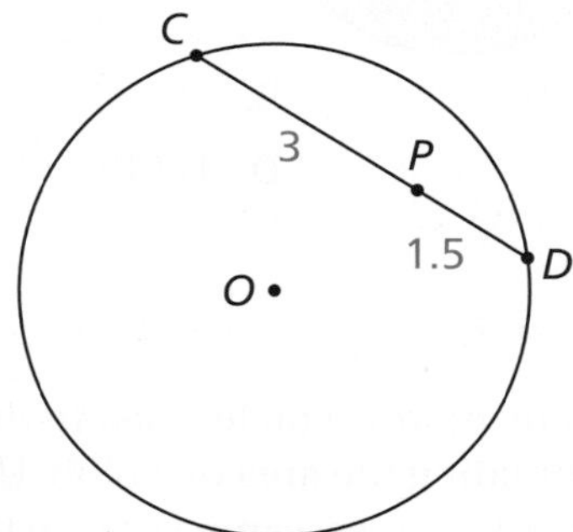

8. Without using a ruler, explain why the measures of the segments in this diagram must be incorrect.

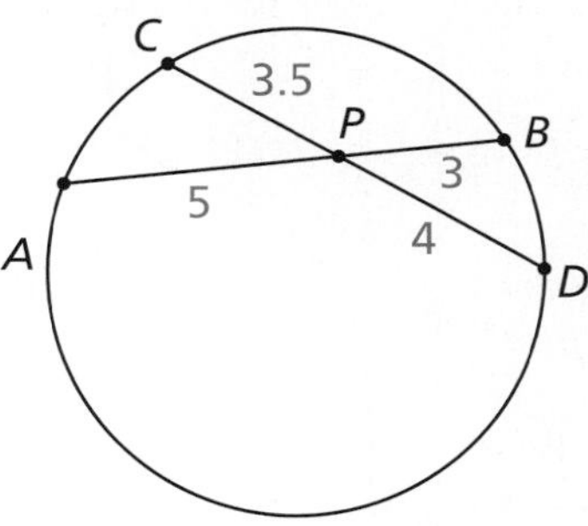

In **Investigation 5D** you learned how to

- calculate the probability of a tiny drop landing on a given area of a board
- find the probability of a spinner landing on a line
- use the Monte Carlo Method
- recognize sets of measure zero

The following questions will help you check your understanding.

9. At a fair, Sam wants to win the goldfish game. To play, you toss a table-tennis ball at a table covered with spherical goldfish bowls that have circular openings on top. The diagram below shows a top view. If your ball lands in the water, you win the fish in that bowl; otherwise you have wasted your money.

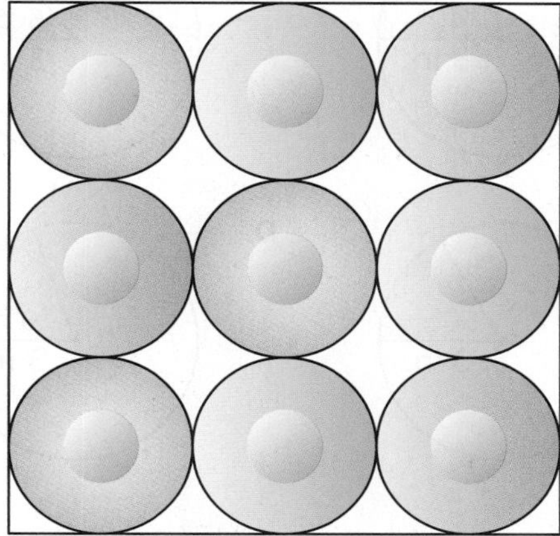

There are 9 adjacent bowls and the diameter of the tops are $\frac{1}{3}$ the diameter of the bowl. The table-tennis ball can fall anywhere on the square table on which the bowls are set. Assume the ball is a dimensionless point. What is the probability that Sam will take home a goldfish if he tosses the ball randomly (but on the table)?

10. Sarah's grandmother is turning 100, so Sarah baked her a birthday cake and covered it completely with red and purple frosting. She placed the 100 candles randomly and 65 of them are on the red frosting. Compare the amount of red frosting to the amount of purple frosting that Sarah used.

11. Can a spinner land on the line separating two of its regions? Explain.

Test

Go Online
Pearsonsuccessnet.com

Multiple Choice

1. Which pink region has an area of π square inches?

A.

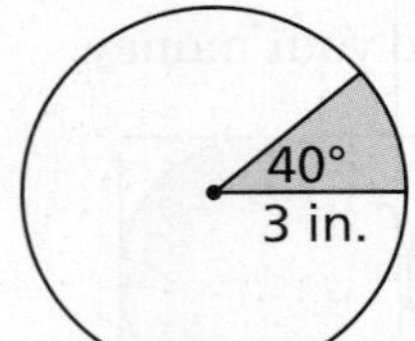

B.

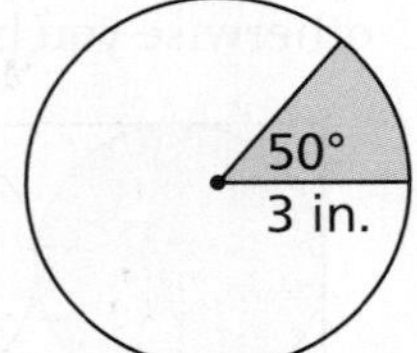

C.

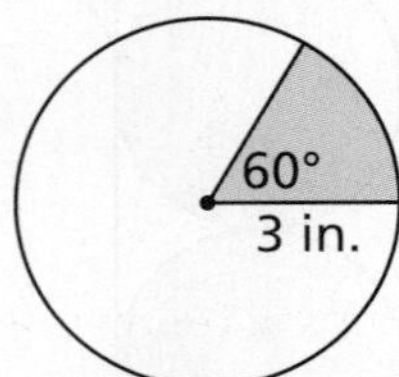

D.

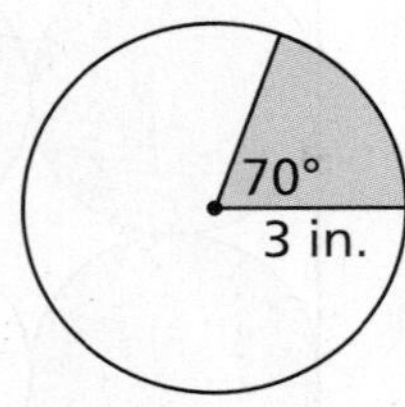

2. If $m\angle ZPY = 83°$ and $m\widehat{ZY} = 112°$, what is $m\widehat{WX}$?

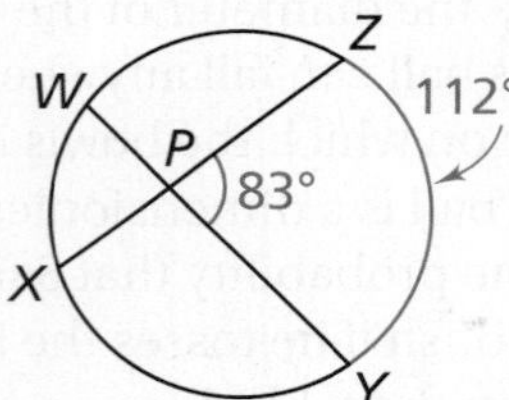

A. 29° **B.** 54° **C.** 56° **D.** 165°

3. The two circles are concentric. The radius of the smaller circle is $\frac{2}{3}$ the radius of the larger circle. If the larger circle has a circumference of 30π feet, what is the approximate area of the shaded region?

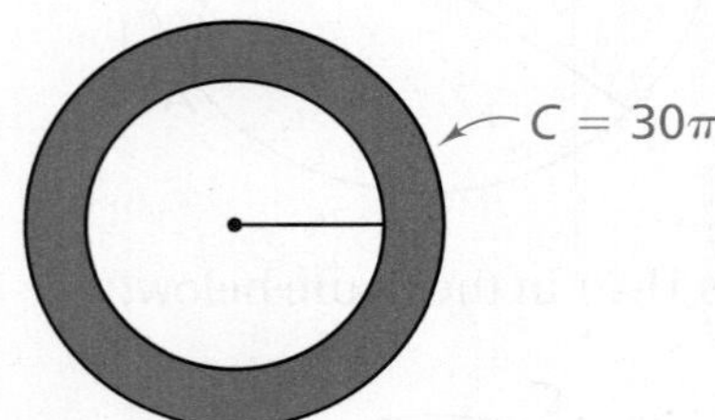

A. 63 ft^2 **B.** 314 ft^2

C. 393 ft^2 **D.** 471 ft^2

Open Response

4. Describe a technique you learned in this chapter for approximating the area of a blob. Use the method you describe to approximate the area of this blob.

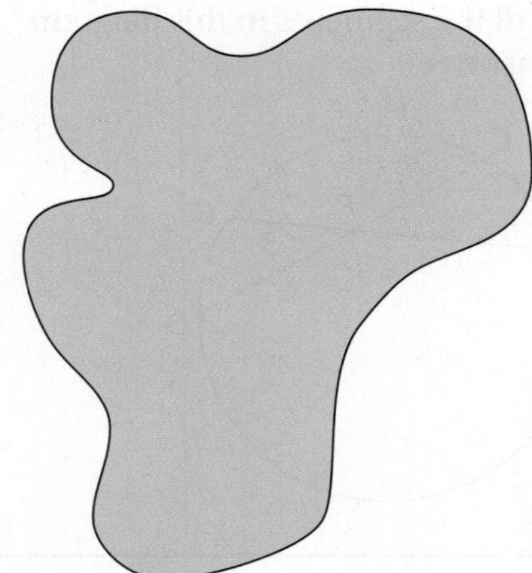

5. Find the areas of the following blue circle sectors.

a. b.

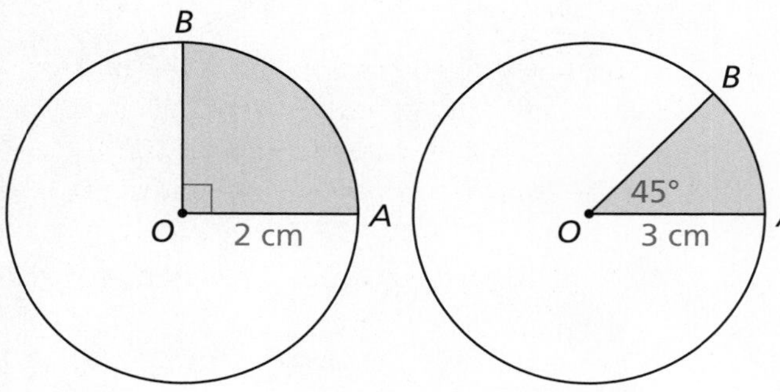

c. d.

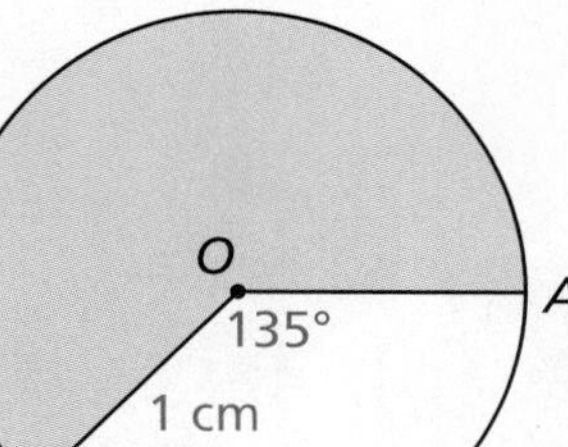

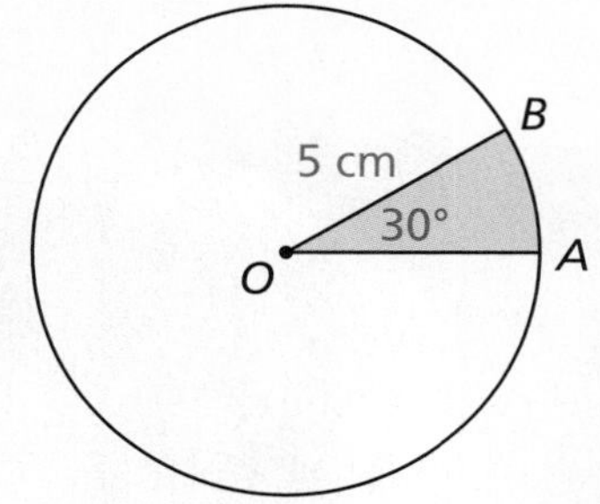

6. Give a definition for the diameter of a circle and prove that a diameter is the longest of all chords of a circle.

7. In the figure at the below, find the measures of $\angle OBC$, $\angle BCA$, and $\angle CAO$ in radians.

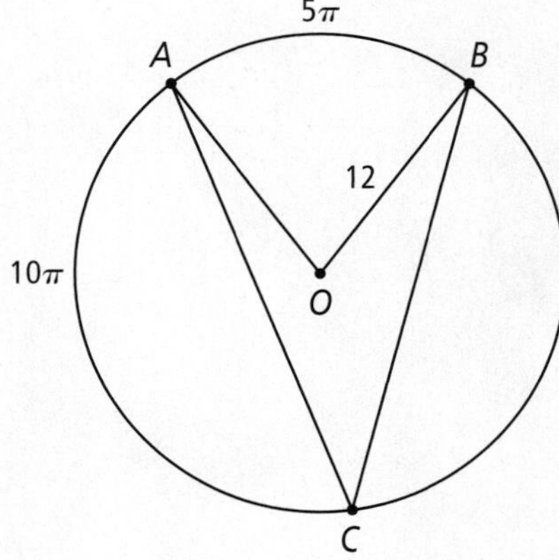

8. In the figure, $m\widehat{ABC} = 52°$. Find the measure of each angle.

a. $\angle ADC$ b. $\angle AOC$

c. $\angle CEA$ d. $\angle ACF$

e. $\angle AFC$ f. $\angle OCF$

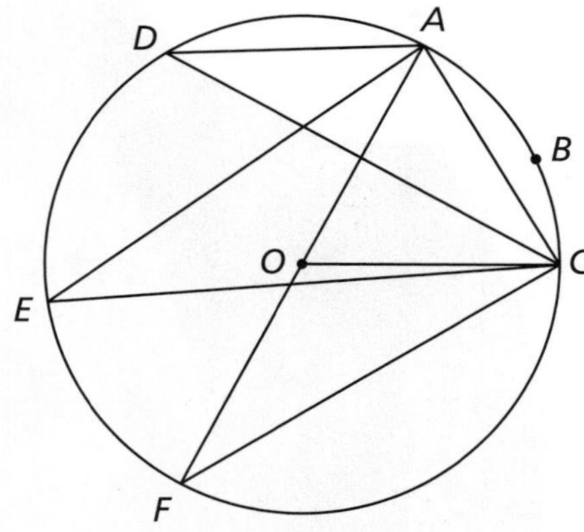

9. What is the power of P in the following figure?

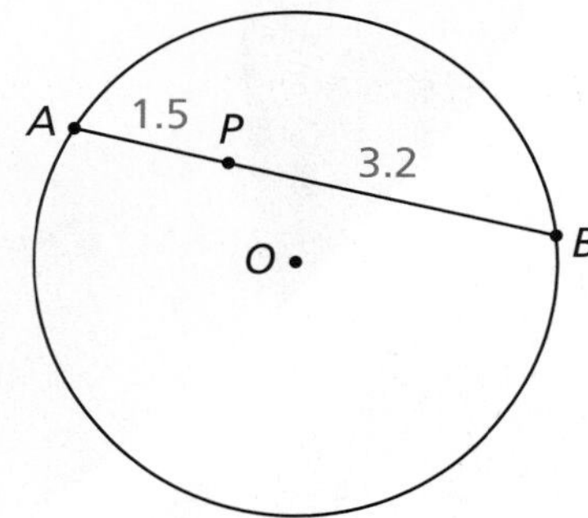

10. What is the probability of a tiny drop landing on the blue region of this board? $ABCD$ is a square inscribed in the circle with center O and radius 2.5 cm.

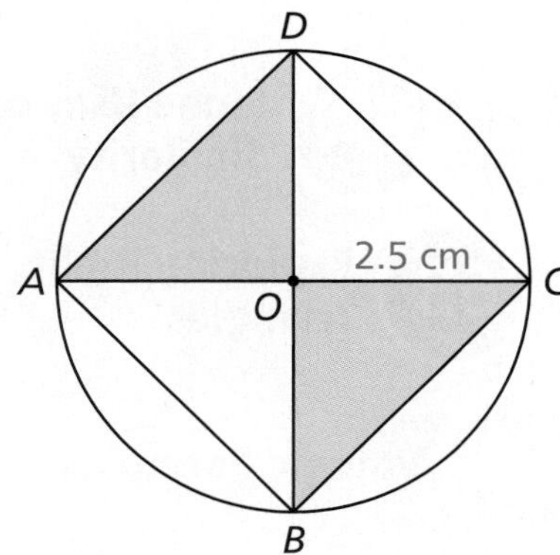

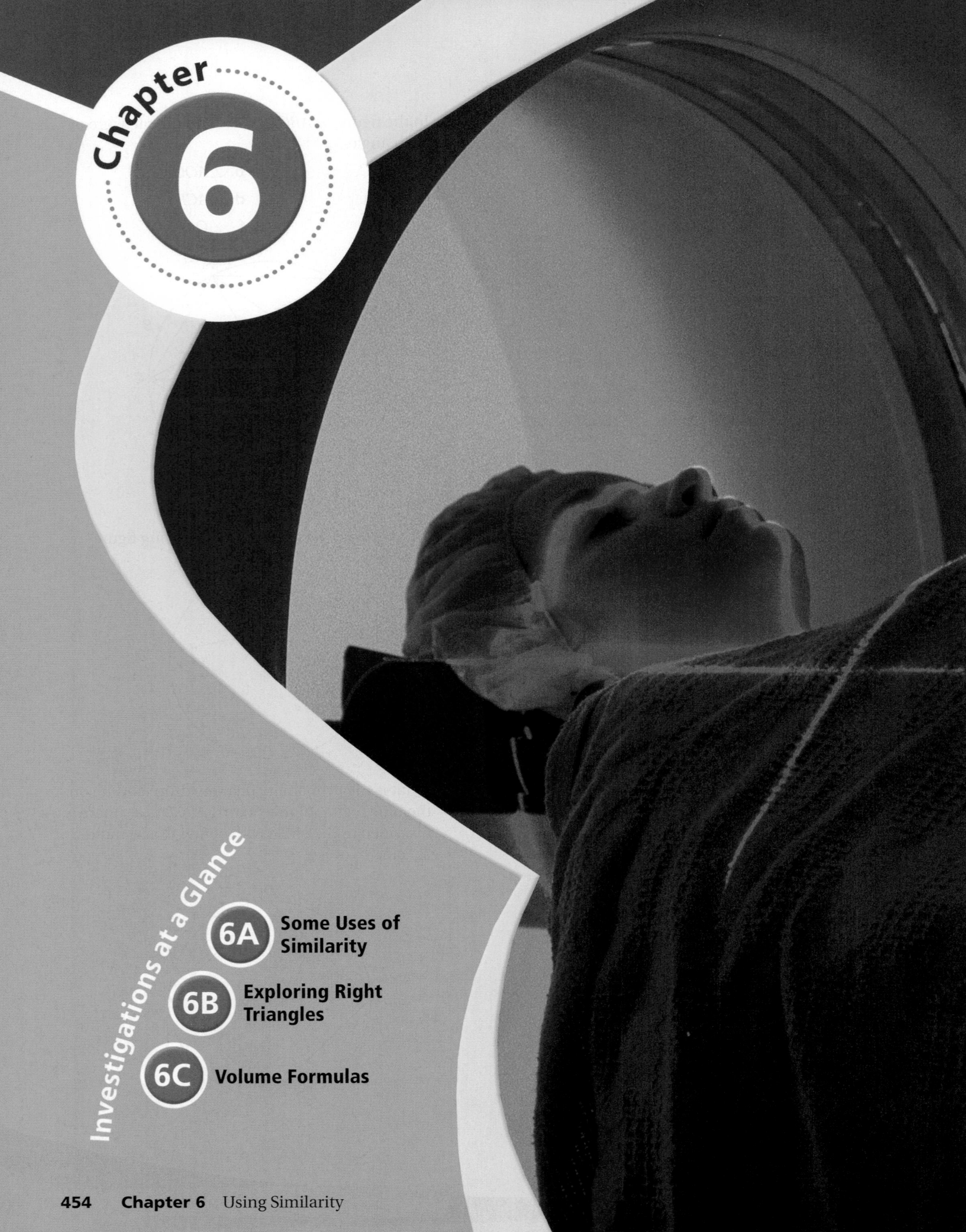
Chapter
6
Investigations at a Glance
6A Some Uses of Similarity
6B Exploring Right Triangles
6C Volume Formulas

Using Similarity

One application of *trigonometry* (a topic introduced in this chapter) is in *tomographic reconstruction*. This is the process by which three-dimensional images are created in diagnostic medical tests such as CT scans.

In a CT scan, an X-ray machine moves around above the patient as a sensor moves around below. The area to be scanned is between them. The X-ray emission is absorbed in differing amounts by materials of differing density within the patient's body. The intensity of the X-rays coming through the patient is recorded from moment to moment as the scanner moves around. The X-ray sensor data are converted into density readings through a complicated formula involving trigonometric functions and some operations of calculus.

These readings are used to create a two-dimensional scan of a horizontal "slice" of the patient. Many horizontal slices, or cross sections, are "stacked" to create a three-dimensional image. You can picture a three-dimensional object as a stack of two-dimensional cross sections. You can think of this as a CT scan of a geometric solid!

Vocabulary and Notation

- arithmetic mean
- geometric mean
- projection
- trigonometry
- sine, $\sin\theta$
- cosine, $\cos\theta$
- tangent, $\tan\theta$
- $\sin^{-1} x$
- $\cos^{-1} x$
- $\tan^{-1} x$

Some Uses of Similarity

In *Some Uses of Similarity,* you will explore applications of similarity, including its use in some classical Greek proofs. Similarity and proportionality are important ideas in mathematics. They allow you to calculate and prove many things.

By the end of this investigation, you will be able to answer questions like these.

1. What is the Arithmetic-Geometric Mean Inequality?
2. Why does the altitude to the hypotenuse of a right triangle form three similar triangles?
3. In $\triangle ABC$, suppose that $AH = 12$ cm and $BA = 15$ cm. What is HC?

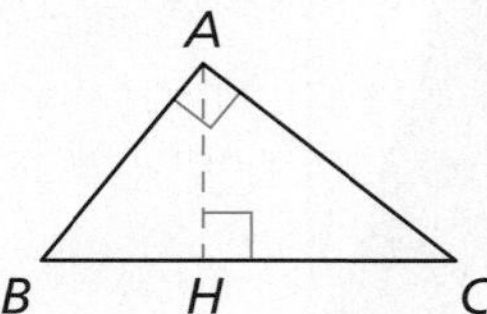

You will learn how to

- state and use the Arithmetic-Geometric Mean Inequality
- use similar triangles to find unknown lengths
- prove theorems using similarity

You will develop these habits and skills:

- Find invariants in triangles.
- Visualize similar triangles to solve problems.
- Choose and draw strategic circles, segments, and points to solve problems.

Drawing details square by square can help you capture a similar image.

6.01 Getting Started

You can use similar triangles to measure inaccessible distances by comparing them to distances between objects close at hand. You have likely seen (or even used) this technique before.

For You to Explore

1. Choose an object and measure the length of the shadow the object casts in sunlight. Also measure the shadow cast by a yardstick (or some other object of known height) standing straight up on the ground at the same time of day.

   Use the fact that the sun's rays are approximately parallel to set a proportion using similar triangles. Find the height of your object.

2. From their boat off the coast, two sailors can see the faraway top of Mount Pythagoras, towering 6600 feet above sea level. One of the two sailors holds her left arm straight out in front of her in a "thumbs up" gesture to get an idea of their distance from the base of the mountain.

   She positions herself so that she can see how much of her thumb covers the mountain. She covers the mountain completely—the whole 6600 feet behind her thumb!

   Her companion measures the distance from her eye to the place on her thumb that lines up with the edge of the shore. Then they measure the length of the thumb that covers Mount Pythagoras. Using similar triangles, they calculate their distance to the base of the mountain.

   Here is a rough sketch of the situation.

   a. What assumption is built into the sketch?

   b. Name a pair of similar triangles in the sketch.

   c. The length of your thumb covering the mountain is 1 inch. The distance from your eye to the bottom of your thumb is 14 inches. Calculate your distance from the mountain.

   d. Measure the length of your thumb. Also measure the distance from the base of your thumb to your eye when your arm is fully extended. If you know the height of an object that is covered by your thumb, you can then determine your distance from that object. Pick an object you know the height of. Use the sailors' technique to figure out how far away it is. Check your results by measuring the actual distance.

Remember...

You already know that the height of the mountain is 6600 feet.

Habits of Mind

Estimate. You can estimate what your thumb covers. If your thumb covers about one third of a 60-meter building, then about 20 meters are covered.

3. You look out a window and see a person standing far away. The person's image fills just part of the window. If you could trace the image on the window, you could measure the height of the image. You could also find the height of the image if you knew the following.

- the person's height
- your distance from the window
- your distance from the person

Here is a sketch of that situation. Carefully describe how you could use similar triangles to determine how tall the image on the window would be.

4. A tree's shadow is 20 feet long, and a yardstick's shadow is 17 inches long.

  a. Draw a diagram that shows the tree, the yardstick, the sun's rays, and the shadows.

  b. Find a pair of similar triangles and explain why they are similar.

  c. How tall is the tree?

Exercises *Practicing Habits of Mind*

On Your Own

5. On a sunny day, Melanie and Nancy noticed that their shadows were different lengths. Nancy measured Melanie's shadow and found that it was 96 inches long. Melanie found that Nancy's was 102 inches long.

  a. Who do you think is taller, Nancy or Melanie? Explain.

  b. If Melanie is 5 feet 4 inches tall, how tall is Nancy?

  c. If Nancy is 5 feet 4 inches tall, about how tall is Melanie?

Habits of Mind

Represent the situation. Drawing a picture might help you answer these questions.

6. Use the shadow method to find the height of some tall object for which you can obtain the actual height. Record the details of your measurements and prepare a presentation for your class. By how much did the result of your calculations differ from the actual height? What might cause these differences?

7. Apply your theory from Problem 3. You see a person 5 feet tall standing outside your window about 30 feet away from you. You are about 2 feet from the window. About how tall will the image be?

8. A light-year is a unit of distance—the distance that light travels in 1 year. The star nearest to us (other than our own sun) is about 4 light-years away. Light travels at 186,000 miles per second. How far does light travel in one year? How far away is the nearest star?

9. A planet is the same distance away as the star in Exercise 8 and has the same diameter as Earth. How large will the planet's image appear on a window that is 2 feet away from you?

Remember...

The diameter of Earth is approximately 7900 miles.

10. About how much must that image be magnified to be as big as the letter o on this page? Use $\frac{1}{20}$ inch for the width of the letter o.

11. A child $3\frac{1}{2}$ feet tall is standing next to a very tall basketball player. The child's sister notices that the player's shadow is about twice as long as the child's. She quickly estimates the player's height. What value does she get?

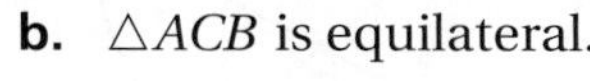
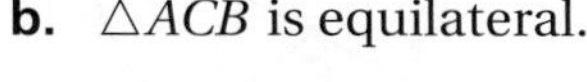

Maintain Your Skills

12. Find all the similar triangles in each diagram. Explain your answers.

a. $\triangle ABC$ is isosceles. D, E, and F are midpoints.

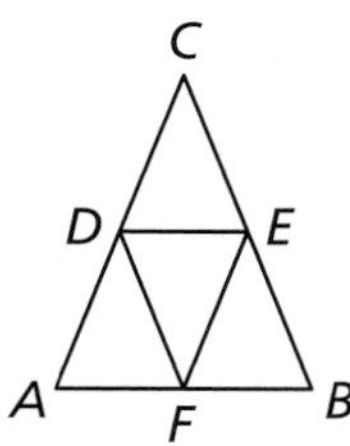
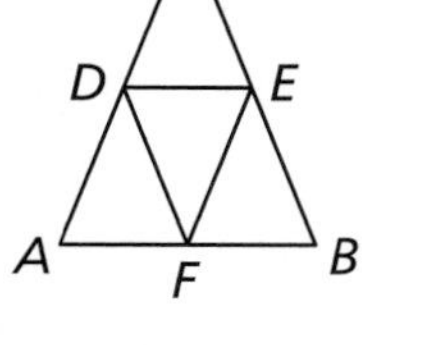

b. $\triangle ACB$ is equilateral.

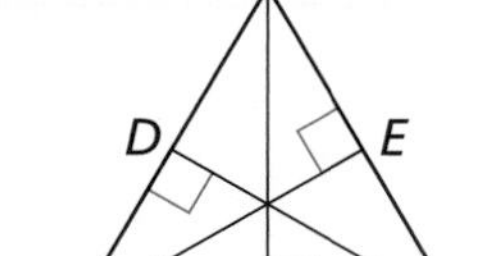

c. $\angle ACB$ is a right angle.

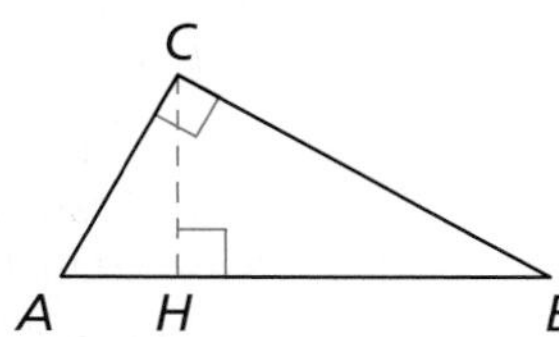

d.

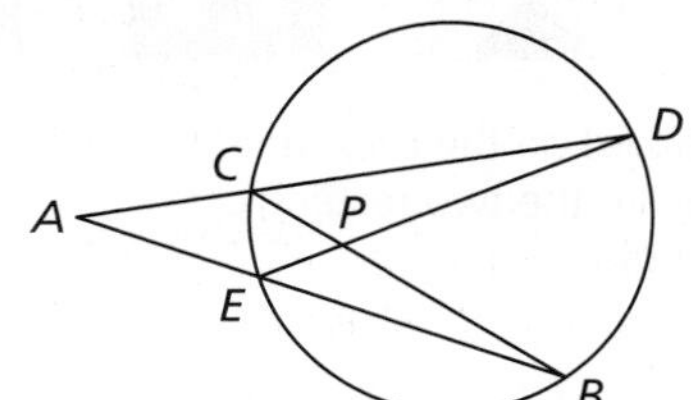

6.02 An Inequality of Means

The figure below shows a complete rectangle on the left and only the length of another rectangle on the right.

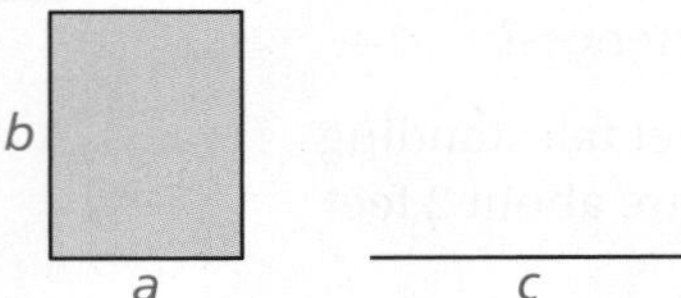

For Discussion

1. How can you construct the missing width of a rectangle with length c, so that both rectangles have the same area? Look at the following pictures and think about how they might be useful to solve your problem.

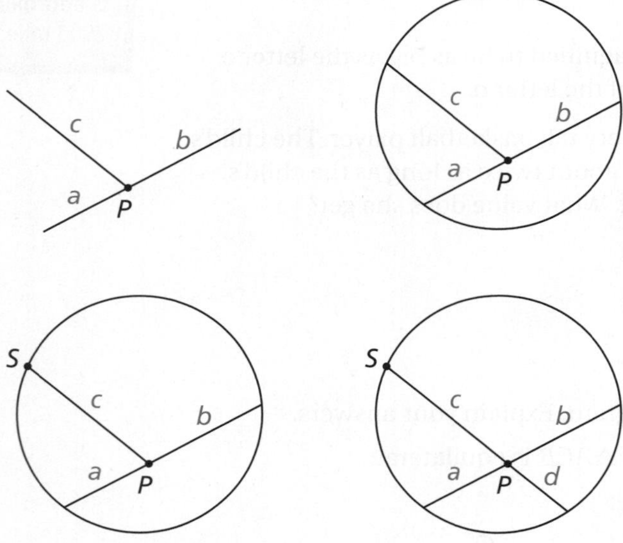

Remember...

The power of a point with respect to a circle is the product $PA \cdot PB$.

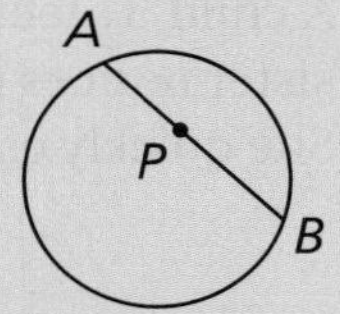

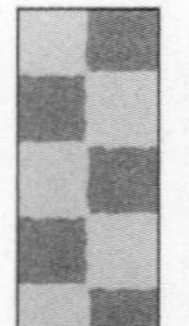 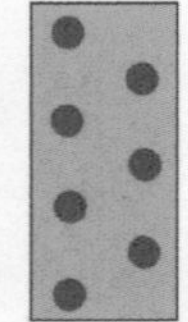 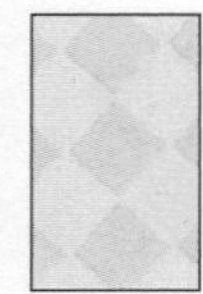 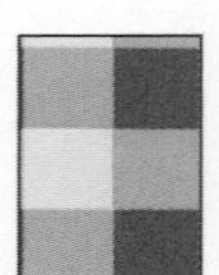   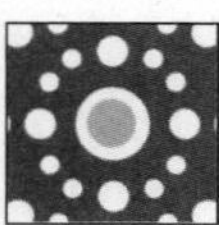

You can construct these equal-area rectangles based on the circle and point P given in the For Discussion section. How are the two rectangles at the ends related? (*Hint:* The rectangle at the right is square.)

Minds in Action episode 22

Tony wants to take the For Discussion idea further.

Tony It's cool how we can use the power-of-a-point construction to construct the missing width of the rectangle, so that both rectangles have the same area. But I was thinking that it would be even cooler to use the construction to find a square with the same area as this rectangle.

Tony points to a rectangle like the one below.

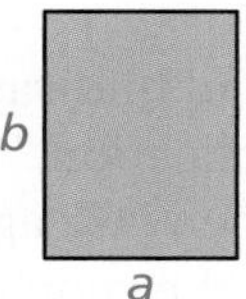

Tony But I'm stuck.

Sasha Well, it's an interesting idea. Let me think about it.

After a while Sasha draws the following diagrams, in which $\overline{AB}$ is a diameter.

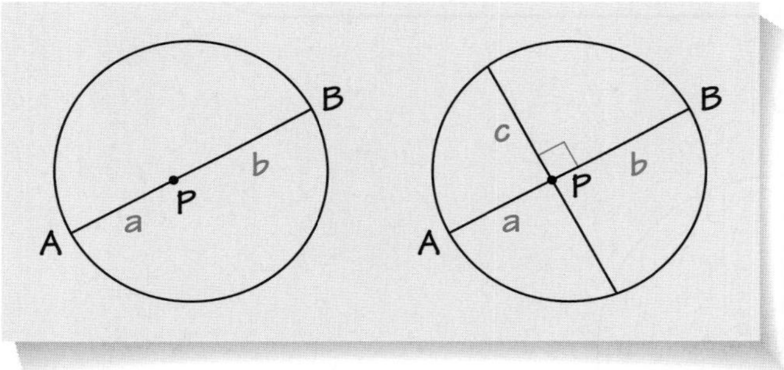

Tony So you're saying that c is the length of the side of the square we're looking for? How do you know?

For You to Do

2. Explain why Sasha's construction method works.

3. Write a formula that relates a, b, and c. What is the algebraic relationship between a, b, and c?

Definition

The geometric mean of a and b is c if $c > 0$ and $c^2 = ab$. Equivalently, $c = \sqrt{ab}$.

Developing Habits of Mind

Explore Relationships. The **arithmetic mean,** or average, of two numbers a and b is $\frac{a + b}{2}$.

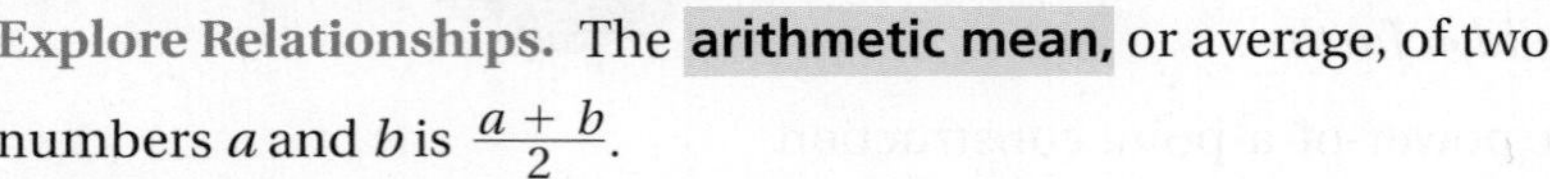

So the arithmetic mean of 10 and 40 is $\frac{10 + 40}{2} = 25$. The mean 25 is midway between 10 and 40. Examine the following pairs of equations to see how the arithmetic mean 25 relates to the two numbers 10 and 40.

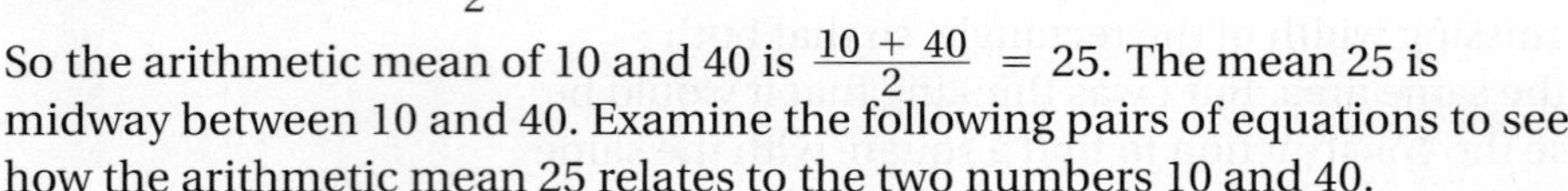

$25 - 10 = 15$ $10 + 15 = 25$

$40 - 25 = 15$ $25 + 15 = 40$

The geometric mean of two numbers defines a different kind of midway point. The geometric mean is "midway with respect to multiplication." To get from 10 to 40, you can multiply by 2 $(10 \times 2 = 20)$ and then by 2 again $(20 \times 2 = 40)$. Thus 20, the midway point in your journey, is the geometric mean of 10 and 40. Another way to say that 20 is midway with respect to multiplication between 10 and 40 is to write the proportion $\frac{10}{20} = \frac{20}{40}$.

$$10 \xrightarrow{+15} 25 \xrightarrow{+15} 40$$

arithmetic mean

$$10 \xrightarrow{\times 2} 20 \xrightarrow{\times 2} 40$$

geometric mean

The Arithmetic-Geometric Inequality

Look at the figure below.

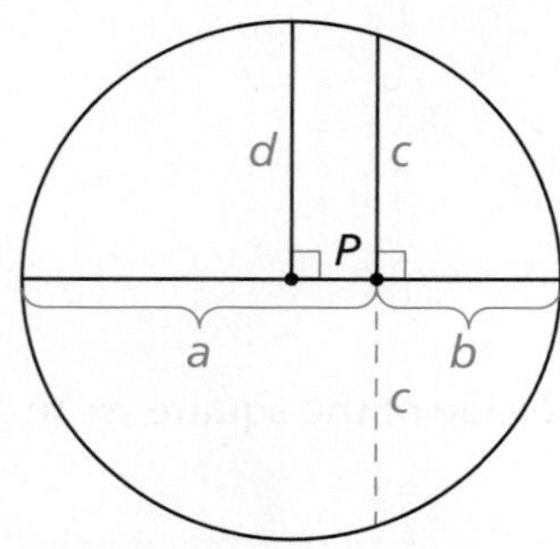

The following relationships hold. If you calculate the power of point P, you get

$$c^2 = a \cdot b$$

$$c = \sqrt{ab}$$

Since d is a radius of the circle, it is half the diameter $a + b$.

$$d = \frac{a + b}{2}$$

Can you explain why these relationships are true?

You can see from your work that $d \geq c$.

Therefore, you get the Arithmetic-Geometric Mean Inequality.

arithmetic mean $\geq$ geometric mean

$$\frac{a + b}{2} \geq \sqrt{ab}$$

Exercises *Practicing Habits of Mind*

Check Your Understanding

1. Compute the geometric mean and the arithmetic mean of the following pairs of numbers.

a. 2 and 8 **b.** 3 and 12

c. 4 and 6 **d.** 5 and 5

2. If you add two extra segments to the geometric mean, as shown below, three right triangles are formed in the semicircle. Explain.

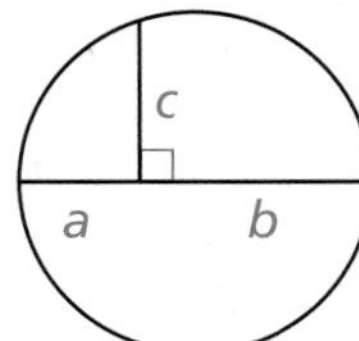

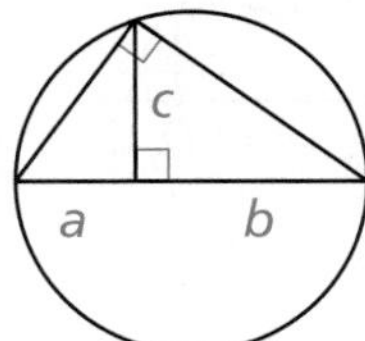

Usually, just the right triangles are shown and not the circle that is used to construct them. In the next exercise, the circles were erased after the right triangles were constructed.

3. Find all of the unknown segment lengths in these two figures.

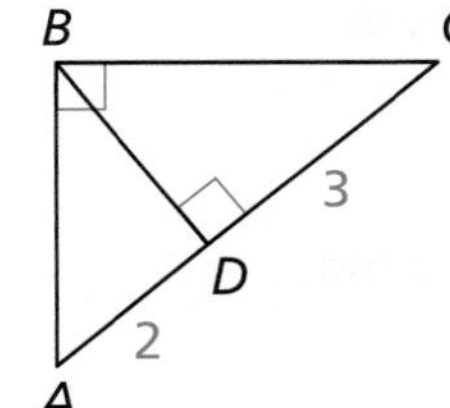

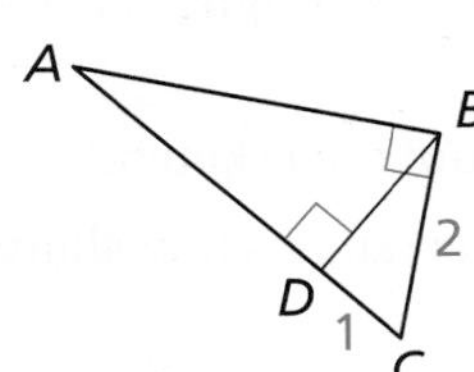

4. Construct a segment with length that is the geometric mean of a 1-inch segment and a 3-inch segment.

On Your Own

5. **Standardized Test Prep** Three of the following pairs of numbers have the same geometric mean. Which pair has a geometric mean that is different?

   A. 2 and 72 **B.** 3 and 48

   C. 4 and 36 **D.** 6 and 30

6. The illustration below shows four frames from a geometric mean construction as point D moves to the left and point A remains stationary.

   1

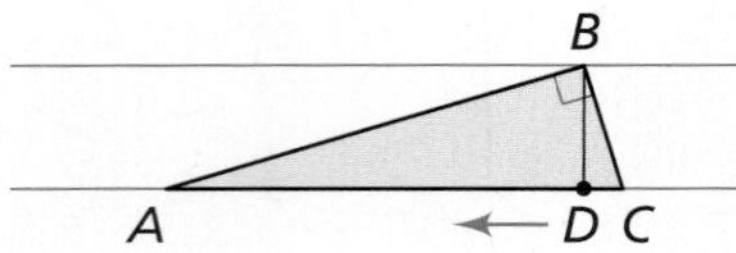

   2

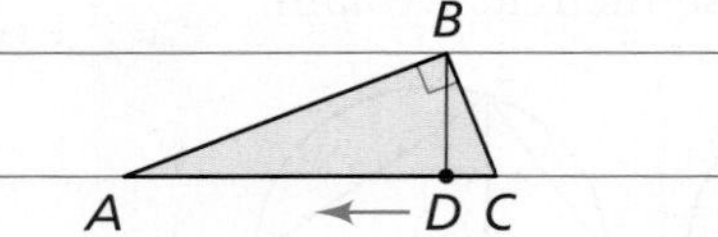

   3

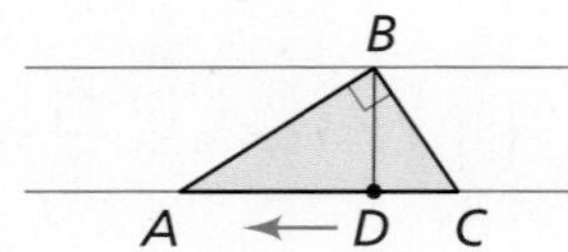

   4

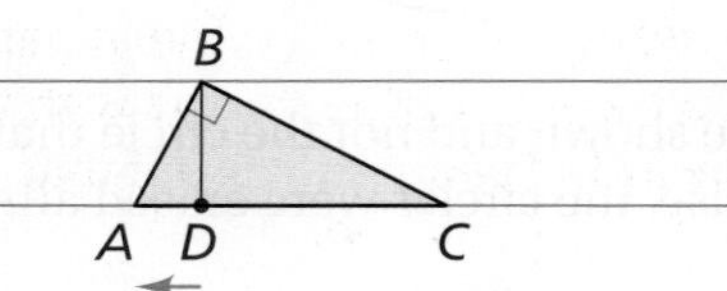

   Make a sketch like this using geometry software.

   a. The product of two lengths remains the same throughout each of these four frames. Which lengths are they?

   b. Use this setup to build a rectangle of constant area sketch.

   c. Does your construction show *all* possible rectangles that share the same area? Explain.

7. **Write About It** Your constant-area-rectangle sketches show rectangles that range from narrow and tall to wide and short. Which of the two constructions—the power of a point or the geometric mean—seems to generate a larger range of constant-area rectangles? Explain.

8. Here is a diagram of a square and a rectangle.

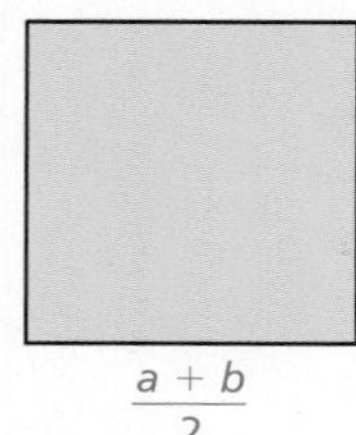

b

a

   a. Which has the greater perimeter? **b.** Which has the greater area?

Try it with numbers.

9. Begin with an $a \times b$ rectangle. Explain how to construct a rectangle with length c that has the same area as the $a \times b$ rectangle.

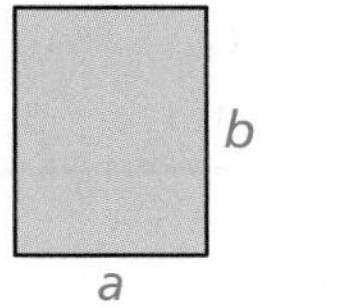

a. Can you use the same circle as in the Minds in Action dialog to complete this construction? Explain.

b. What difficulties do you encounter?

c. Explain how to redraw the circle so that the construction works.

Maintain Your Skills

10. The segments below have lengths a and b. For each value in parts (a)—(d), construct either a segment with that length or a rectangle with that area. Your constructions should lead towards a geometric proof that

$$\left(\frac{a+b}{2}\right)^2 - \left(\frac{a-b}{2}\right)^2 = ab$$

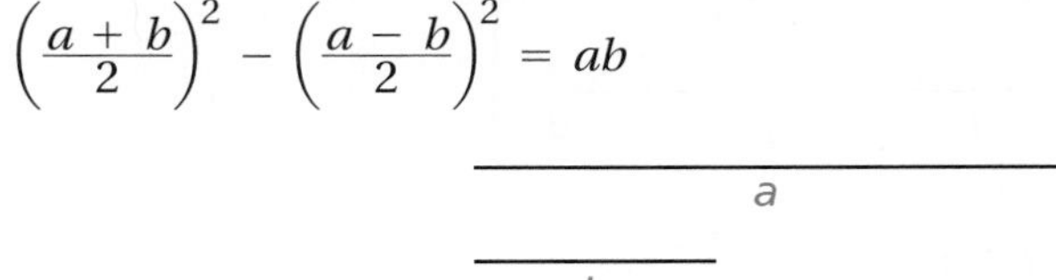

All of the constructions can be done with just an unmarked straightedge, a compass, and some lined notebook paper. Resist the urge to measure with a ruler—you will not need to!

In which cases will you construct a segment? In which cases will you construct a rectangle?

a. $a + b$ and $\left(\frac{a+b}{2}\right)^2$

b. $a - b$ and $\left(\frac{a-b}{2}\right)^2$

c. $\left(\frac{a+b}{2}\right)^2 - \left(\frac{a-b}{2}\right)^2$

d. ab

e. Use algebra to prove $\left(\frac{a+b}{2}\right)^2 - \left(\frac{a-b}{2}\right)^2 = ab$. Use the equation to prove the Arithmetic-Geometric Mean Inequality.

6.03 Similarity in Ancient Greece

As you have seen in these lessons and in Chapter 4, similarity is very useful and has a wide variety of applications. In this lesson you will use similarity to prove the Pythagorean Theorem and other theorems of ancient Greece.

For You to Do

In $\triangle ABC$, $\angle ACB$ is a right angle.

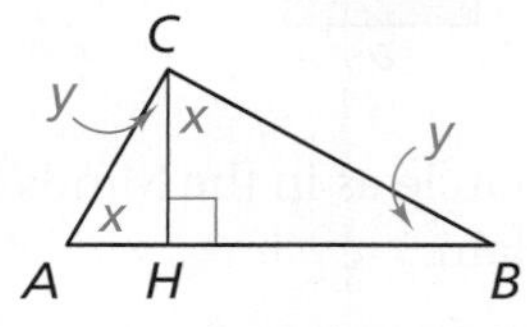

1. Why are $\triangle CAH$, $\triangle ABC$, and $\triangle CHB$ right triangles?

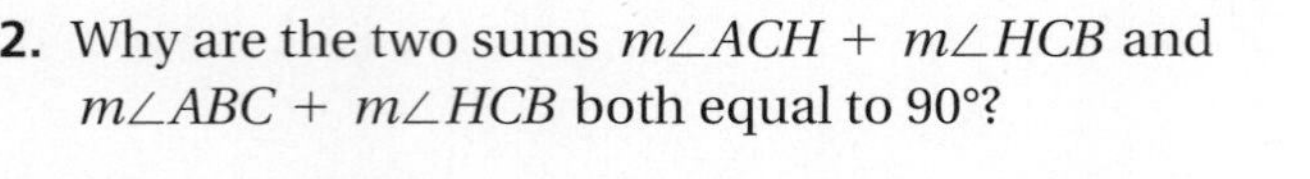

2. Why are the two sums $m\angle ACH + m\angle HCB$ and $m\angle ABC + m\angle HCB$ both equal to 90°?
3. Why are the three triangles, $\triangle CAH$, $\triangle ABC$, and $\triangle CHB$, similar?

Example

Problem $\triangle ABC$ is a right triangle with $m\angle ACB = 90°$. Prove the Pythagorean Theorem using similar triangles.

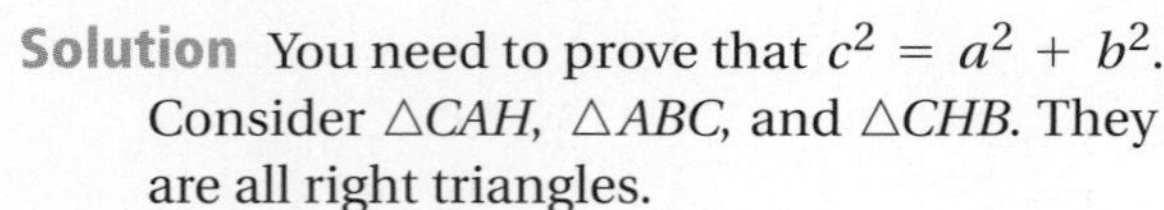

Solution You need to prove that $c^2 = a^2 + b^2$. Consider $\triangle CAH$, $\triangle ABC$, and $\triangle CHB$. They are all right triangles.

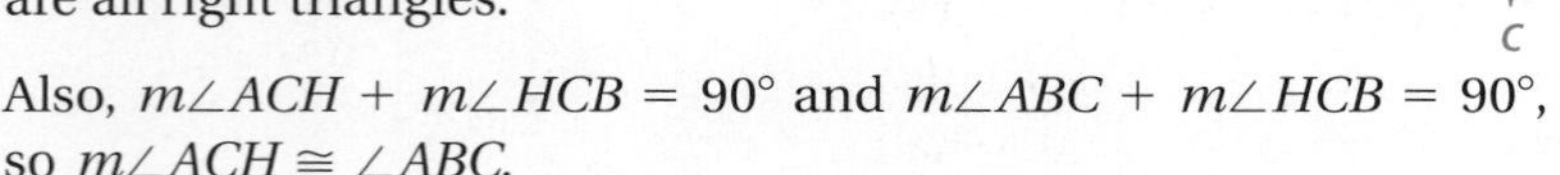

Also, $m\angle ACH + m\angle HCB = 90°$ and $m\angle ABC + m\angle HCB = 90°$, so $m\angle ACH \cong \angle ABC$.

By the AA Similarity Theorem, the three triangles are similar. Therefore, the ratios of corresponding sides are the same.

$$\frac{b}{c} = \frac{x}{b} \text{ and } \frac{a}{c} = \frac{y}{a}$$

So $b^2 = cx$ and $a^2 = cy$. Add these two equations and remember that $x + y = c$.

$$\begin{aligned} b^2 + a^2 &= cx + cy \\ &= c(x + y) \\ &= c^2 \end{aligned}$$

There are many other proofs of the Pythagorean Theorem. You saw some of the proofs by dissection in Chapter 2. The following is another proof that goes back to Euclid.

In this figure, *ACRS*, *BCPQ*, and *ABNM* are squares constructed on the sides of right triangle *ABC*.

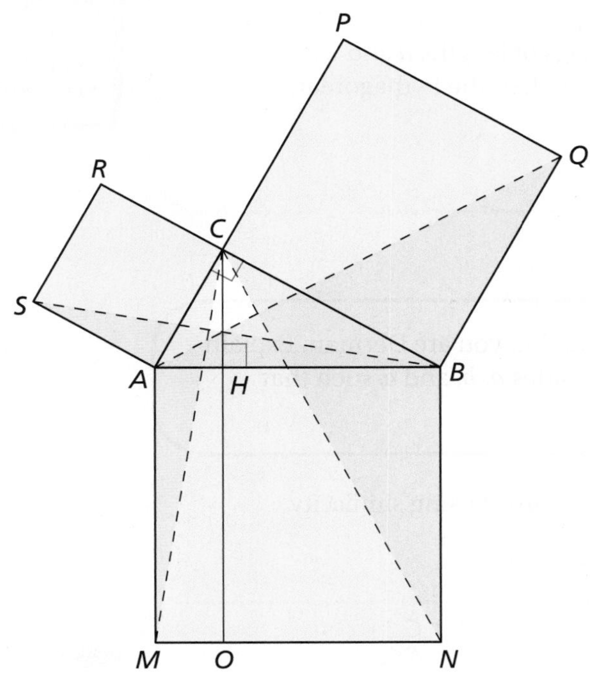

$\triangle ACM$ and $\triangle ASB$ are congruent and $\triangle ABQ$ and $\triangle CBN$ are congruent. Also, remember that the area of a triangle is equal to half the area of a parallelogram with a congruent base and height. So, the area of $\triangle ACM$ is equal to half the area of *AMOH*. The area of $\triangle ASB$ is equal to half the area of *ACRS*.

Why are these two pairs of triangles congruent?

$$A_{ACRS} = 2A_{ASB} = 2A_{CAM} = A_{AMOH}$$

What are the common bases and heights of *ACRS* and *ASB*? Of *AMOH* and *CAM*?

For You to Do

4. Finish proving the Pythagorean Theorem using the method above. Prove that $A_{CBQP} = A_{HONB}$ and that therefore $A_{ABNM} = A_{ACRS} + A_{CBQP}$.

Minds in Action episode 23

Derman and Sasha are thinking about the following question.

If a triangle has side lengths *a*, *b*, and *c*, such that $c^2 = a^2 + b^2$, is the triangle a right triangle?

Derman It has to be a right triangle with legs of lengths *a* and *b* and hypotenuse *c*, because if it weren't, then the Pythagorean Theorem wouldn't be true.

Sasha What do you mean?

Habits of Mind

Explore. *a*, *b*, *c* are not zero . . . what would happen if one of them was zero?

For Discussion

5. What do you think Derman means? Pretend that you are Derman. Explain to Sasha why you think that a triangle with sides *a*, *b*, and *c*, such that $c^2 = a^2 + b^2$, must be a right triangle.

There are many more theorems that you can prove using similarity.

Theorem 6.1

In a right triangle, the length of either leg is the geometric mean of the length of its projection on the hypotenuse and the length of the whole hypotenuse.

$$CA^2 = AH \cdot AB$$

$$CB^2 = HB \cdot AB$$

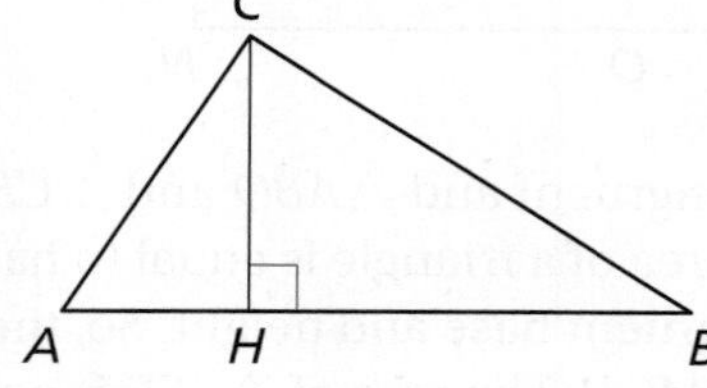

The **projection** of $\overline{AB}$ onto $\overline{CD}$ is $\overline{EF}$.

Theorem 6.2

In a right triangle, the length of the altitude relative to the hypotenuse is the geometric mean of the lengths of the two segments of the hypotenuse.

$$CH^2 = AH \cdot HB$$

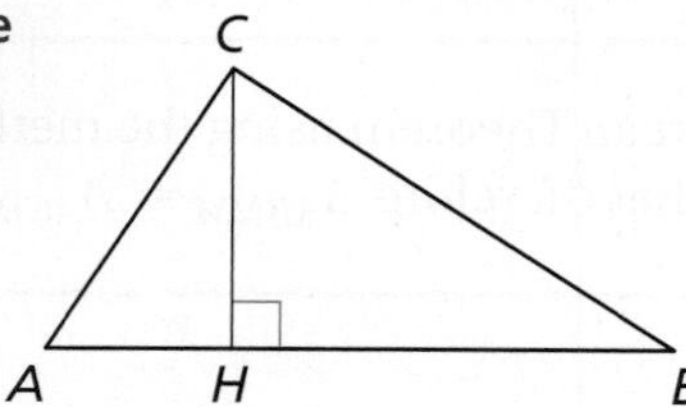

Exercises Practicing Habits of Mind

Check Your Understanding

1. Prove Theorem 6.2.

2. In $\triangle ABC$, $\frac{AH}{CH} = \frac{CH}{HB}$. Prove that $\triangle ABC$ is a right triangle.

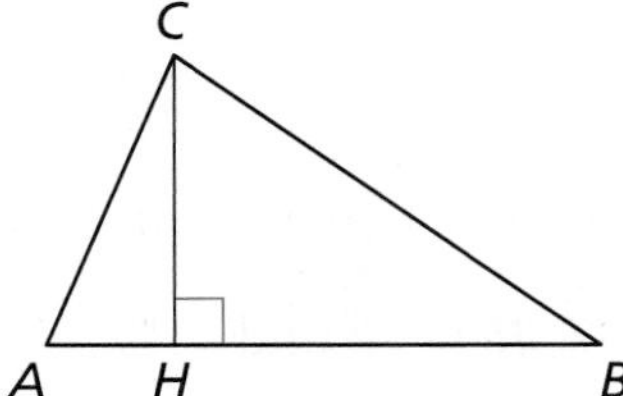

3. Copy the figure onto a separate sheet of paper. Then draw a diameter of the circle below, so that A or B lies on the diameter.

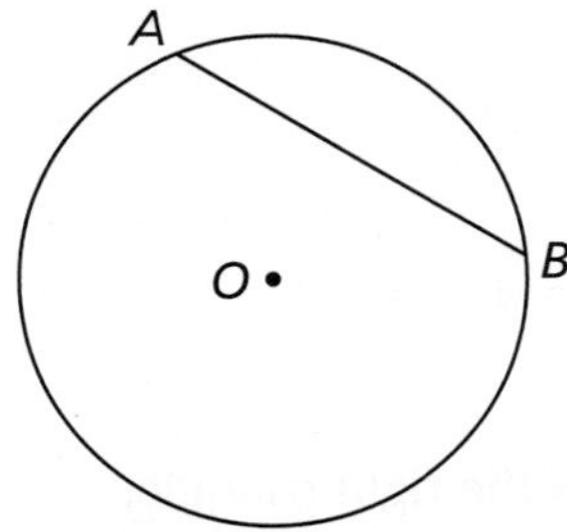

Prove that AB^2 is equal to the product of the diameter and the chord's projection on the diameter.

4. If $AH = r$ and $HB = s$ in the right triangle below, what is CH?

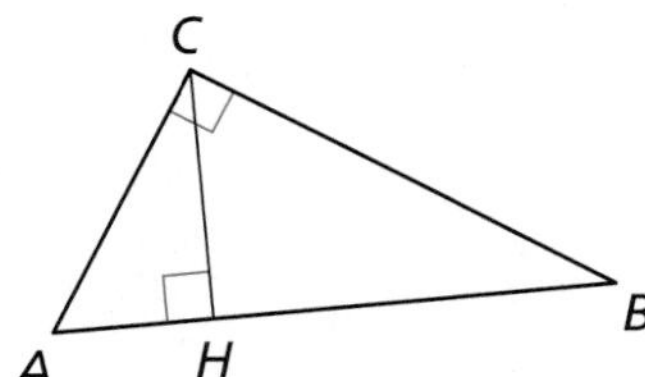

On Your Own

5. In the right triangle below, $AH = r$ and $AB = c$. Using similarity, find AC and CB.

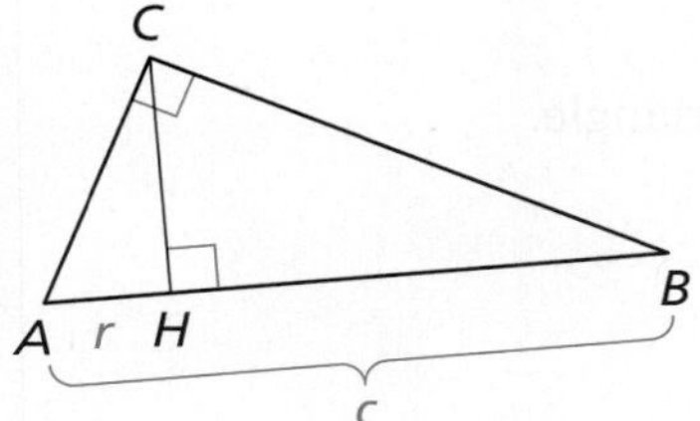

6. **Standardized Test Prep** $\overline{RT}$ is the hypotenuse of $\triangle RST$. $RU = 2$ and $UT = 6$. What are the values of x and y?

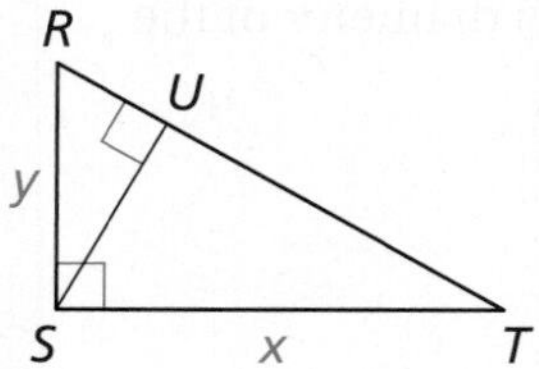

A. $x = 2\sqrt{3},\ y = 3$
B. $x = 4\sqrt{3},\ y = 4$
C. $x = 4,\ y = 2\sqrt{3}$
D. $x = 8,\ y = 6$

7. Draw a right triangle. Draw a semicircle on each side of the right triangle, such that each side of the right triangle is a diameter of a semicircle. Prove that the area of the semicircle on the hypotenuse is equal to the sum of the areas of the semicircles on the legs of the triangle.

8. In $\triangle ABC$, $AC = BC$. Prove that $\frac{AC}{AB} = \frac{AB}{2HB}$.

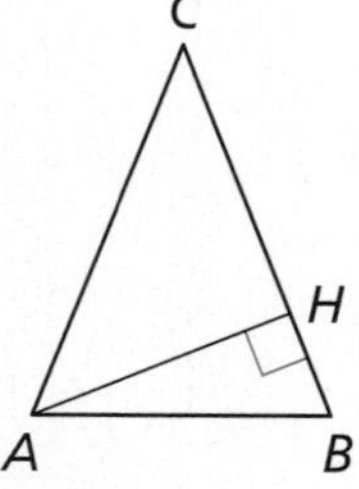

Use $\triangle POD$ for Exercises 9 and 10.

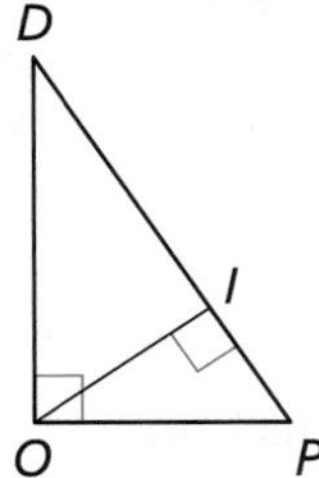

9. $PI = 4$ and $DI = 9$. What is OI?

10. $PI = 7.2$ and $DI = 12.8$. What is PO?

11. In a right triangle ABC with hypotenuse $\overline{BC}$, the altitude from vertex A reaches side $\overline{BC}$ at H. $BH = 3.6$ and the length of the hypotenuse is 10. What are the lengths of the legs of $\triangle ABC$?

H is also called the projection of vertex *A* onto the hypotenuse $\overline{BC}$.

12. **Take It Further** The mathematicians of ancient Greece proved Theorem 6.1 using a technique like the one in Euclid's proof of the Pythagorean Theorem. At the right is a diagram of the proof. Think about the diagram and write a proof.

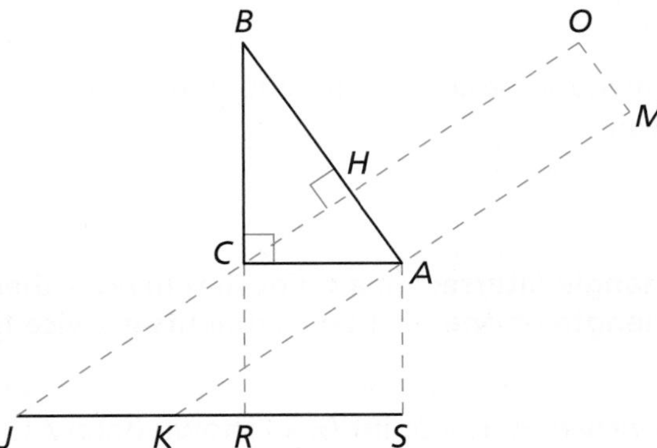

Maintain Your Skills

13. a. The height from the hypotenuse of a right triangle is 6 cm. A projection of a leg onto the hypotenuse is 4 cm. What is the length of the hypotenuse of the triangle?

b. The two projections of the legs of a right triangle onto its hypotenuse are 5 in. and 45 in. What is the area of the right triangle?

c. In a right triangle the hypotenuse measures 24 cm. The projection of a leg onto the hypotenuse measures 6 cm. What is the triangle's perimeter?

6.04 Concurrence of Medians

A median of a triangle is a segment with endpoints that are a vertex of the triangle and the midpoint of the opposite side. Every triangle has three medians.

In-Class Experiment

1. Using geometry software, draw $\triangle ABC$. Construct the medians from A and B.
2. Drag the vertices of your triangle and describe all the invariants that you can find.
3. Construct the median from C.
4. Drag the vertices of your triangle again. Do the invariants you found in Problem 2 still hold for the new median?

During the experiment, you made some conjectures about invariants that may have included the following.

Conjecture 6.1

1. **Any two medians of a triangle intersect in a point that divides them into two segments. The length of one of these segments is twice the length of the other.**
2. **The three medians are concurrent at a point *G*, as shown below.**

G is the *centroid* of the triangle.

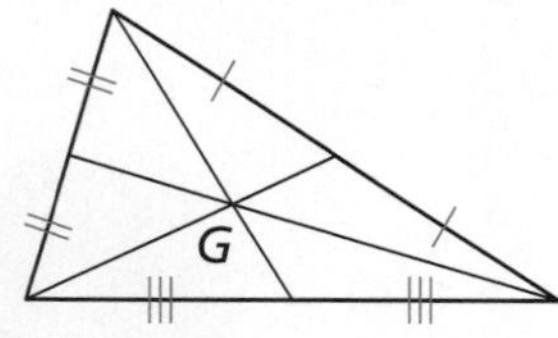

Minds in Action

episode 24

Tony and Sasha are trying to prove both parts of Conjecture 6.1.

Sasha I have an idea. In $\triangle ABC$, M and N are the midpoints of the sides $\overline{AC}$ and $\overline{CB}$. The medians $\overline{AN}$ and $\overline{BM}$ intersect at G. P and Q are the midpoints of $\overline{AG}$ and $\overline{GB}$.

Look at triangles PQG and NMG.

Tony I wouldn't be surprised if those were congruent triangles.

Sasha They are, and here's why. Apply the Midline Theorem to $\triangle ABC$. You get $\overline{MN} \parallel \overline{AB}$ and $MN = \frac{1}{2}AB$. Apply the Midline Theorem to $\triangle ABG$. You get $\overline{PQ} \parallel \overline{AB}$ and $PQ = \frac{1}{2}AB$. So $\overline{MN} \parallel \overline{PQ}$ and $MN = PQ$. This means that $\angle QPN \cong \angle PNM$ and $\angle PQG \cong \angle QMN$. Finally, $\triangle PQG \cong \triangle NMG$ by ASA. Neat, huh?

Tony That means we've proven the first conjecture. After all, $\overline{GM} \cong \overline{GQ} \cong \overline{QB}$. That tells us that G divides $\overline{BM}$ into two pieces, one of which is twice as long as the other.

Sasha Right, and $\overline{GN} \cong \overline{GP} \cong \overline{PA}$, so G also divides $\overline{AN}$ the same way.

Tony Wait! There wasn't anything special about G. The result must be the same for any two medians. The point of intersection must divide the medians into two segments with one segment twice the length of the other. That means if the third median $\overline{CK}$ intersects $\overline{BM}$ in point G', G' has to have the same property. So $CG' = 2G'K$ and $BG' = 2G'M$.

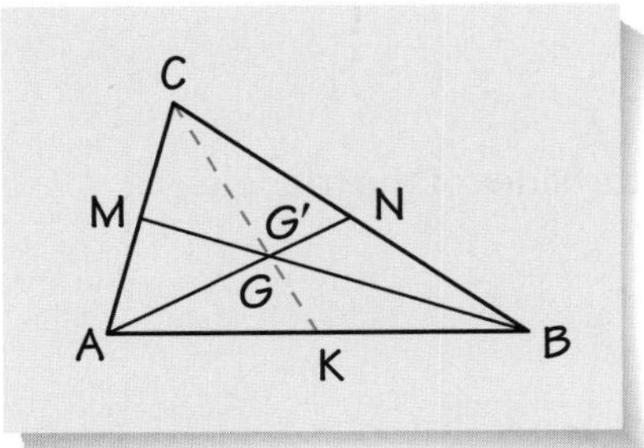

Sasha But you already know that G is the point that divides $\overline{BM}$ into two segments and that one segment is twice the length of the other.

Tony Right! So $G = G'$ and therefore, G lies on $\overline{CK}$, too.

Habits of Mind

Explore. Think about why this lesson is in an investigation on similarity.

Remember...

You proved the Midline Theorem in Chapter 3.

For You to Do

5. Explain why knowing that $\triangle PQG \cong \triangle NMG$ is enough to conclude that $AG = 2GN$ and $BG = 2GM$.

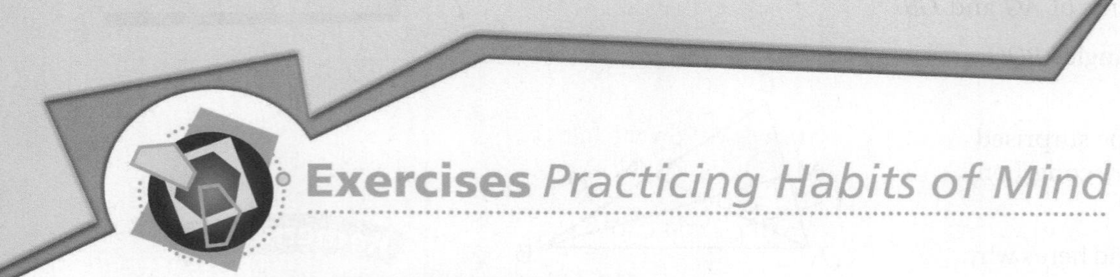

Exercises *Practicing Habits of Mind*

Check Your Understanding

1. **Write About It** Use Sasha's triangle. In your own words, prove Conjecture 6.1, namely that $AG = 2GN$ and $BG = 2GM$.

2. Think about how Sasha proved that $AG = 2GN$ and $BG = 2GM$ in her figure. Can you think of another way of proving the same thing that does not use the congruence of $\triangle PQG$ and $\triangle NMG$? Explain.

Hint: Think about parallelograms.

3. Do you know other special three-segment sets that are concurrent in triangles? List each set of three segments you know. Draw a diagram for each set.

On Your Own

4. **Standardized Test Prep** Which of the following statements does the diagram below illustrate?

A. The altitudes of a triangle are concurrent.

B. The medians of a triangle are perpendicular to the sides of the triangle.

C. The medians of a triangle are concurrent.

D. The altitudes of a triangle are parallel.

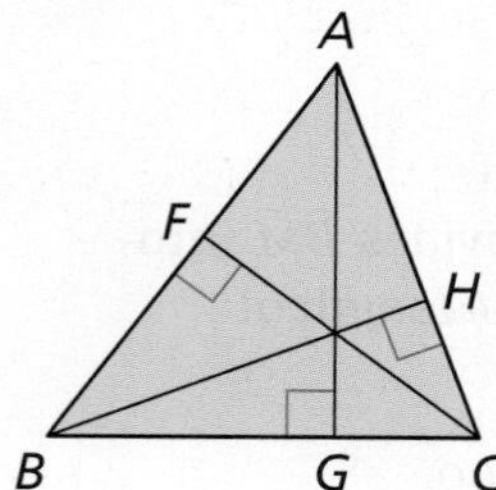

5. For this exercise, you need a piece of cardboard or thick paper and a piece of string knotted at one end.
   - Cut a triangle from the cardboard or paper.
   - Construct the medians of the triangle. Mark the point of concurrence.
   - Poke a tiny hole through the centroid you found. Thread the string through the hole.
   - Hold the end of the string. Let the triangle hang down on the knot.
   - Describe the triangle's position when it stabilizes.

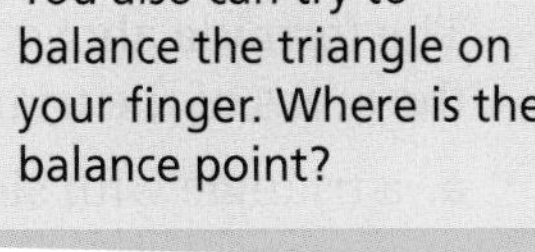

You also can try to balance the triangle on your finger. Where is the balance point?

6. Copy the figure below onto a separate sheet of paper. Then choose a point P on the median $\overline{CM}$ of $\triangle ABC$.

   a. Draw the altitudes from P for $\triangle APM$ and $\triangle BPM$.

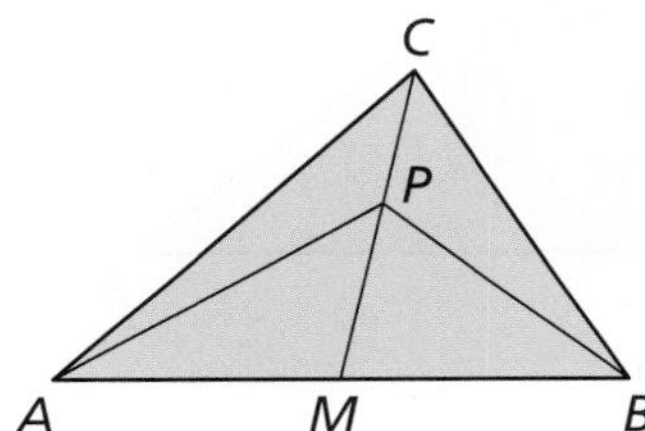

   b. Complete the following statements and justify your answers.

$$A_{\triangle APC} = A_{\triangle ACM} - A_{\triangle \underline{\ ?\ }}$$

$$A_{\triangle BPC} = A_{\triangle \underline{\ ?\ }} - A_{\triangle \underline{\ ?\ }}$$

   c. Prove that if P is not on the median $\overline{CM}$, then $A_{\triangle APC} \neq A_{\triangle BPC}$.

   d. Now describe the median $\overline{CM}$ as the set of points with a given property.

Remember...

A *locus* is a set of points with a given property.

7. Use $\triangle ABC$ from Exercise 6. Consider the medians of a triangle as the set of points P with the following property: $A_{\triangle APC} = A_{\triangle BPC}$, (in the case of median $\overline{CM}$). Use an argument similar to Tony's to prove that the three medians of a triangle are concurrent.

8. In this exercise, you will prove that the three altitudes of a triangle are concurrent.

   a. Draw $\triangle ABC$ and its three altitudes.

   b. Through vertex A draw the perpendicular to the altitude through A. Repeat this for the other two vertices.

   c. Mark the three points of intersection of the lines you drew in part (b) and label them D, E, and F.

   d. What are the altitudes of $\triangle ABC$ with respect to $\triangle DEF$?

   e. Explain why the three altitudes of $\triangle ABC$ are concurrent.

Maintain Your Skills

9. You can use the following formula to find the area A of a triangle if you know the lengths, a, b, and c, of its sides.

$$A = \sqrt{\left(\frac{a+b+c}{2}\right)\left(\frac{b+c-a}{2}\right)\left(\frac{a-b+c}{2}\right)\left(\frac{a+b-c}{2}\right)}$$

The formula above is called *Heron's formula.* Use Heron's formula to find the areas of the triangles below.

a. a triangle with sides 6 in., 12 in., and 13 in.

b. $\triangle ABC$

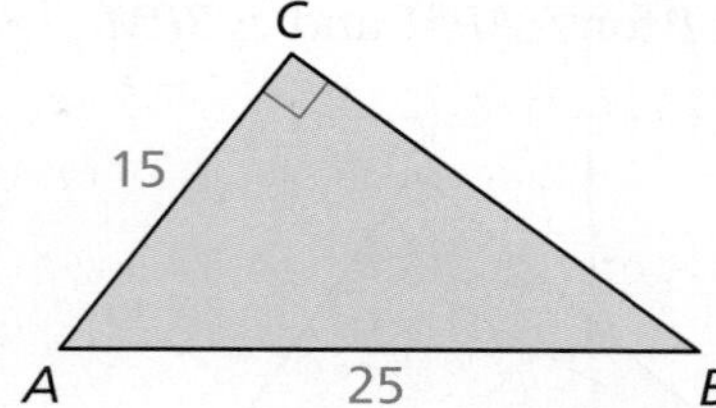

c. an equilateral triangle with sides 3 cm

d. an isosceles triangle with base 43 cm and perimeter 89 cm

e. a triangle with sides 6 cm, 8 cm, and 10 cm

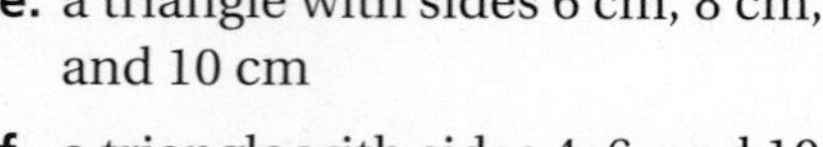

f. a triangle with sides 4, 6, and 10

Does Heron's formula make sense? Find the areas of the triangles above in a different way and check the answers you found with Heron's formula.

10. **Take It Further** Brahmagupta's formula is similar to Heron's formula from Exercise 9. Suppose a quadrilateral with side lengths a, b, c, and d is inscribed in a circle. Brahmagupta's formula finds the area A of the quadrilateral.

$$A = \sqrt{\left(\frac{a+b+c-d}{2}\right)\left(\frac{a+b-c+d}{2}\right)\left(\frac{a-b+c+d}{2}\right)\left(\frac{-a+b+c+d}{2}\right)}$$

a. Use Brahmagupta's formula to find the area of the cyclic quadrilateral at the right.

b. **Write About It** Compare Heron's formula with Brahmagupta's formula. If $d = 0$, what does Brahmagupta's formula become?

c. Is Brahmagupta's formula a generalization of Heron's formula? Explain.

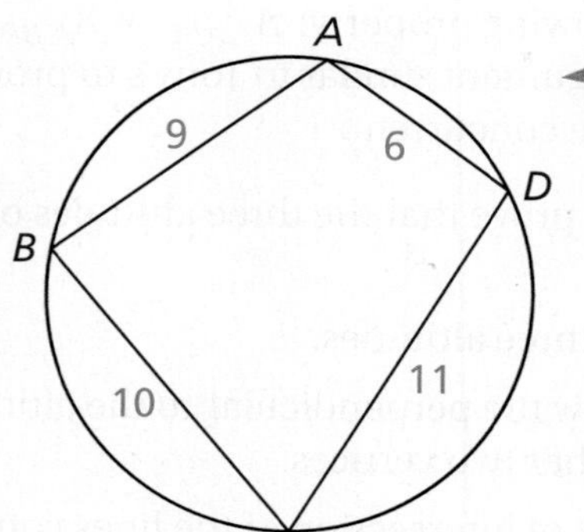

Cyclic quadrilaterals are quadrilaterals inscribed in a circle.

Go Online
Pearsonsuccessnet.com

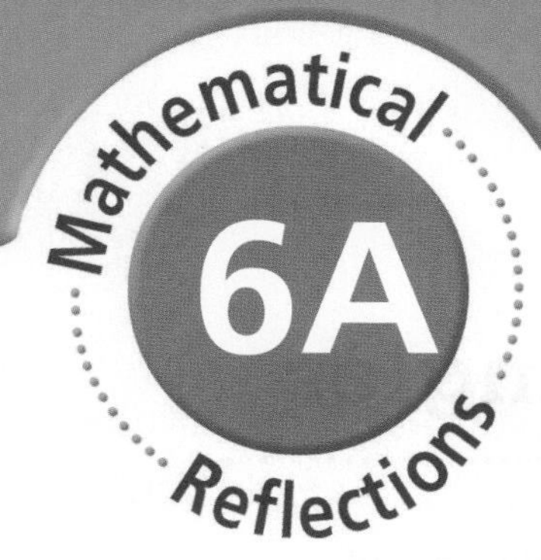

In this investigation, you learned how to apply properties of similarity, prove theorems using similarity, and draw strategic circles, segments, and points to solve problems. These questions will help you summarize what you have learned.

1. Sophie and Erin are measuring things for a school project. They accidentally drop their yardstick down a hole, where it lies flat along the bottom.

   Erin holds a 12-in. ruler out over the hole at ground level. Sophie looks straight down into the hole and notices that, from her perspective, the ruler *exactly* covers the yardstick.

   If Sophie's eyes are 5 feet above the ruler, how deep is the hole?

2. Find the arithmetic and geometric mean for the numbers 6 and 24. Explain how each of the means is halfway between the two numbers.

3. If the altitude to the hypotenuse of a right triangle is also a median, what can you conclude about the original right triangle? Explain.

4. Prove that if $\triangle ABC \sim \triangle AHB$, then $\triangle AHB \sim \triangle BHC$.

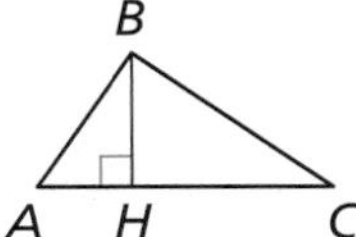

5. Describe how to locate the centroid of a triangle without constructing more than one of its medians.

6. What is the Arithmetic-Geometric Mean Inequality?

7. Why does the altitude to the hypotenuse of a right triangle form three similar triangles?

8. In $\triangle ABC$, suppose that $AH = 12$ cm and $BA = 15$ cm. What is HC?

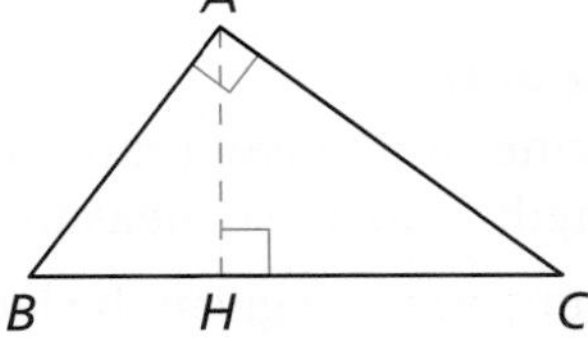

Vocabulary

In this investigation, you learned these terms. Make sure you understand what each one means and how to use it.

- **arithmetic mean**
- **geometric mean**
- **projection**

Use 1-inch grid paper to capture an image similar to this prince.

Exploring Right Triangles

In *Exploring Right Triangles,* you will learn a great deal about all triangles, and even all polygons. Every *n*-sided polygon can be subdivided into $n - 2$ triangles by connecting one vertex of the polygon to each nonadjacent vertex.

In this investigation, you will see how to use ratios of side lengths in right triangles to determine side lengths and angle measures in triangles and in other figures.

By the end of this investigation, you will be able to answer questions like these.

1. How can you use half of a square or half of an equilateral triangle to evaluate trigonometric functions for angles measuring 30°, 45°, and 60°?
2. Find the sine, cosine, and tangent of α and β in terms of the side lengths of $\triangle ABC$.

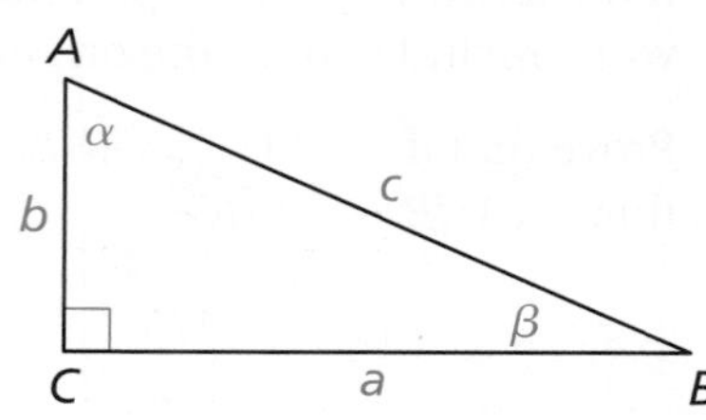

3. What is the area of $\triangle LMN$? What is the approximate length of $\overline{MN}$?

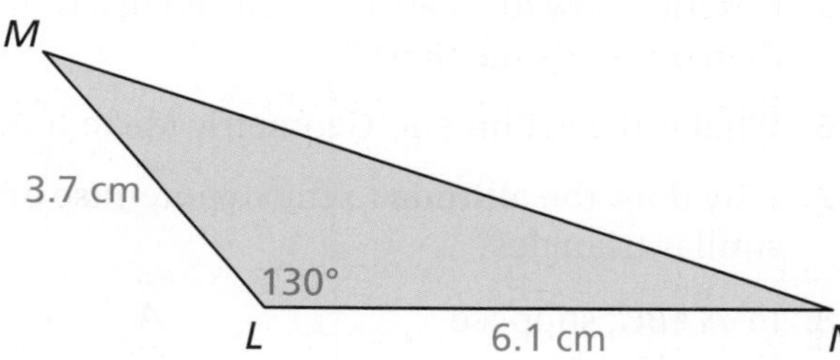

You will learn how to

- use the sine, cosine, and tangent ratios and their inverses to find missing side lengths and angle measures in triangles
- find the area of any triangle given the lengths of two sides and the measure of their included angle
- find the length of the third side of a triangle given the lengths of two sides and the measure of their included angle

You will develop these habits and skills:

- Find invariants in classes of right triangles.
- Visualize right triangles in different problem situations.
- Choose appropriate strategies to find missing angle measures and side lengths.

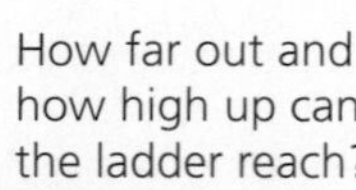
How far out and how high up can the ladder reach?

6.05 Getting Started

You have already investigated the Pythagorean Theorem, which explains how the lengths of the sides of right triangles are related to each other. But how can you use information about the lengths of the sides of a right triangle to tell you about the measures of its angles?

In the following In-Class Experiment, you will study a right triangle that is the side view of a ramp. You will vary the lengths of the sides of the triangle. You will develop some conjectures about how different side lengths relate to the ramp's angle of inclination.

In-Class Experiment

You can specify a ramp by giving any two of the measurements indicated in the figure below.

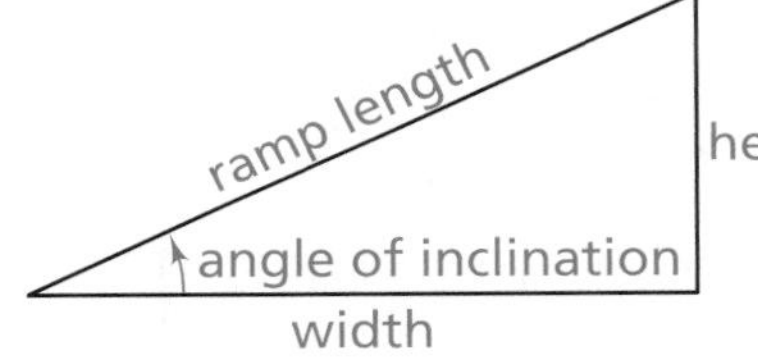

Habits of Mind

Visualize. Why are only two of these measurements enough? What else do you know about the ramp?

1. Decide which ramp is the steepest.

   Use any method you like, such as constructing physical scale models, making graphical models, or using calculations. Be prepared to explain why your method is valid as well as why your choice is the steepest ramp.

   Ramp A: width 9.2 feet, height 3.3 feet

   Ramp B: ramp length 10.2 m, height 3.8 m

   Ramp C: height 3.1 feet, width 8.5 feet

   Ramp D: width 9 m, ramp length 10.8 m

   Ramp E: ramp length 3 yards, angle of inclination 30°

   Ramp F: height 3 feet, width 7 feet

For You to Explore

2. Two ladders are leaned against a wall so that they make the same angle with the ground.

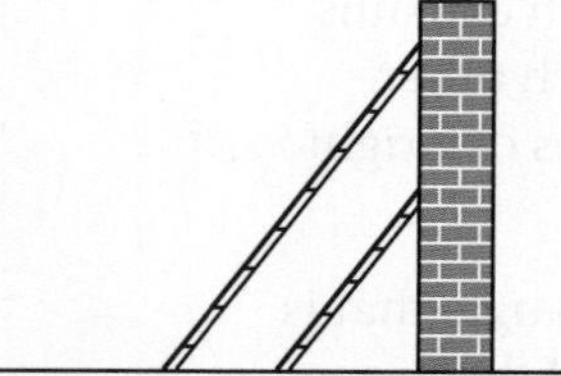

The 10-foot ladder reaches 8 feet up the wall. How much farther up the wall does the 18-foot ladder reach?

3. Workers accidentally drop a metal pipe that is 10 feet long. It falls into a cylindrical hole with a radius of 4 feet and a grate across the top. The pipe comes to rest leaning across the bottom of the hole. The workers are able to just reach the upper end of the pipe through the grate with a magnet at the end of a rope that is 7 feet long. About how deep is the hole?

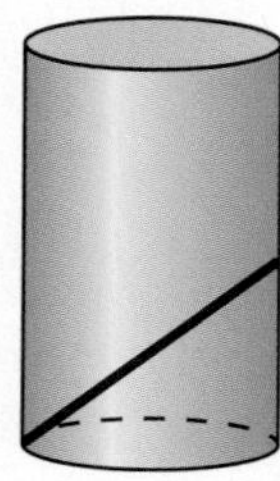

4. **Write About It** Describe how to compare the steepness of two ramps given the following measurements for each ramp.
   - ramp length and width
   - ramp length and height
   - width and height

As you raise the truck bed, which measures change?

Exercises *Practicing Habits of Mind*

On Your Own

5. The width and height of four ramps are given. Which ramp is the steepest? Explain.

Ramp A: width 10 feet, height 6 feet

Ramp B: width 5 miles, height 3 miles

Ramp C: width 15 inches, height 9 inches

Ramp D: width 50 cm, height 30 cm

6. **What's Wrong Here?** Derman says that Exercise 5 proves that units are completely irrelevant when you compare the steepness of ramps. Explain how units *can* have an effect when you compare the steepness of two ramps.

7. Hannah's method for comparing the steepness of ramps is to construct a triangle that is similar to the triangle formed by the ramp, but with a width of 1. Then she compares the heights of the similar triangles in order to choose the steepest ramp. Try Hannah's method to determine which of the following ramps is the steepest.

Ramp A: ramp length 18 cm, height 6 cm

Ramp B: ramp length 43 inches, width 41 inches

Ramp C: width 50.9 mm, height 18.5 mm

8. Ramp A has an angle of inclination of 30°. Ramp B has width 8.9 feet and height 5.3 feet. Which ramp is steeper? How did you decide?

9. When you are standing at point *A*, you have to tilt your head up 27° to see the very top of a tree. You are 40 feet from the tree. Approximately how tall is the tree?

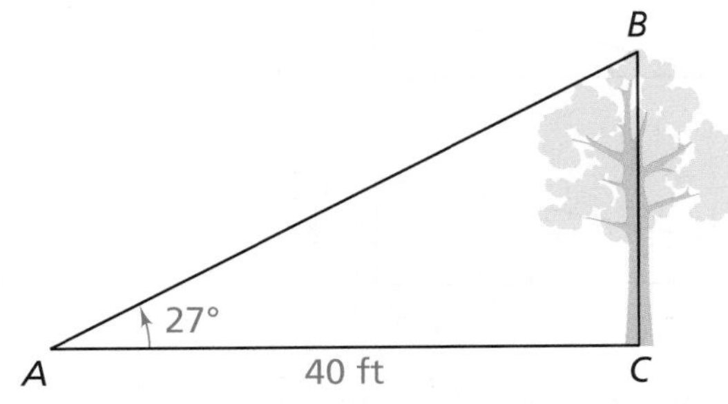

This picture is not exactly right. To simplify the problem, something was ignored. What is it?

10. When you are in a boat at point A, you have to tilt your head up 27° to see the very top of the Statue of Liberty. The statue (including its base) is about 300 feet tall. Approximately how far are you from the bottom of the base?

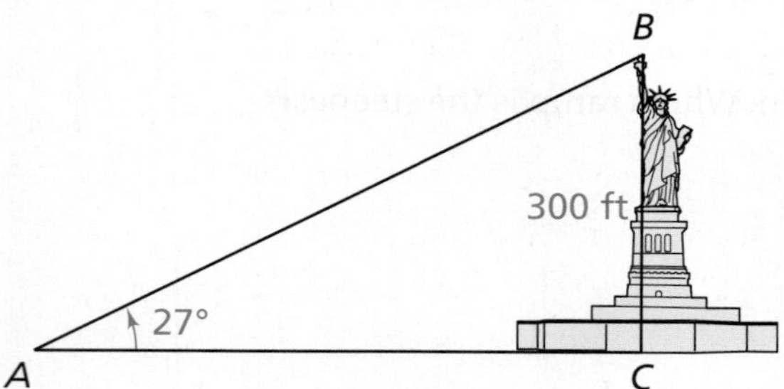

11. Refer to Exercises 9 and 10 to answer the following questions.

a. List some things that these two exercises have in common.

b. Explain why the value of $\frac{BC}{AC}$ is the same for both triangles.

c. Measure one of the triangles and calculate this constant value. Did you use this relationship in your solutions to Exercises 9 and 10?

12. You have likely conjectured that there is a relationship between the height-to-width ratio of a ramp and its angle of inclination. The larger the height-to-width ratio, the larger the angle. Estimate the height-to-width ratio for each angle of inclination.

a. 30° **b.** 37° **c.** 45° **d.** 60°

Maintain Your Skills

13. In the following series of ramps, the height is always 1 foot, but the width of the ramp gets progressively wider.

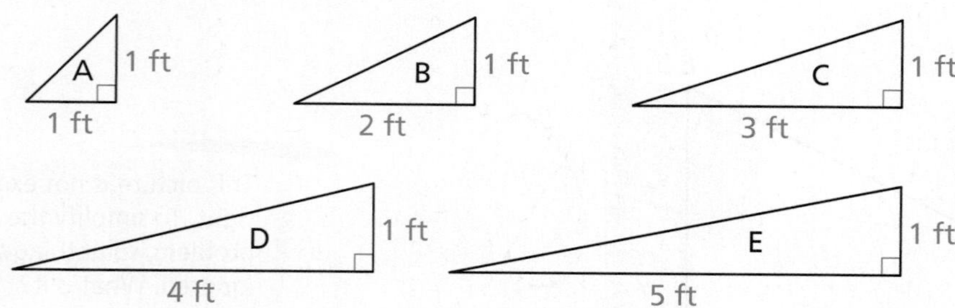

Compute or measure the following quantities for each ramp. Describe how the quantity changes from Ramp A to Ramp E.

a. ramp length

b. angle of inclination

c. ratio of height to width

d. ratio of height to ramp length

6.06 Some Special Triangles

Every triangle has three side lengths and three angle measures. In Chapter 2, you saw that you do not have to know all six measurements to prove that two triangles are congruent. In fact, you only need to know three of the measurements—all three side lengths (SSS), two sides and the included angle (SAS), or two angles and one side length (ASA and AAS). There must be some way to figure out what the other three measurements are from the ones you know.

Minds in Action episode 25

Tony and Sasha are talking about situations in which they could use three triangle facts to determine the others.

Tony If you just know three sides of a triangle, how could you ever figure out what the angles are without constructing it?

Sasha Well, I don't know how to do it for *every* triangle. I bet I can give you three facts that you could use to solve for the other three.

Here's one I *know* you know. What if $\triangle ABC$ has three sides that all measure 6.17 cm? What are its angle measures?

Tony Okay. That one I get. So I agree that there are some special cases that are possible to do. How about a side-angle-side set?

Sasha How about $\triangle DEF$ with $DE = 4$ in., $EF = 4$ in., and $m\angle E = 90°$?

Tony With two sides of a right triangle, I can always figure out the length of the third side, but how can I figure out the other two angle measures? Oh, it's an isosceles right triangle.

Now I've got an angle-side-angle set for you, Sasha: $\triangle GHI$ where $m\angle G = 30°$, $m\angle H = 60°$, and $GH = 6$ mm.

Sasha That one's tricky, but at least it must be a right triangle. I'll draw a sketch.

Hey! This is just half of an equilateral triangle!

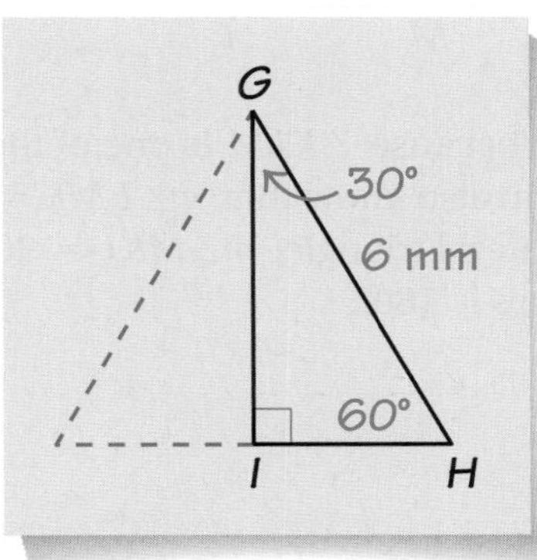

For You to Do

Answer these questions about the several triangles that were mentioned in the Minds in Action.

1. What are the measures of the angles of $\triangle ABC$? Explain.
2. What are the missing measures of $\triangle DEF$? Explain.
3. What are the missing measures of $\triangle GHI$? Explain.
4. Create a new problem in which you specify only three measurements for a triangle. Make sure the other three measurements can be determined from the given information. Exchange problems with a classmate.

In the Minds in Action, Tony and Sasha discussed an isosceles right triangle and a triangle that is half of an equilateral triangle. You already know many properties of these two triangles. Now it is time to learn how the angle measures and the three side lengths in each are related.

A 30-60-90 triangle is a right triangle that is half of an equilateral triangle.

Example

Problem An altitude of an equilateral triangle cuts it into two right triangles. If the side length of the original triangle is *a*, find all the side lengths and angle measures for one such right triangle.

Solution Here is a diagram of the situation.

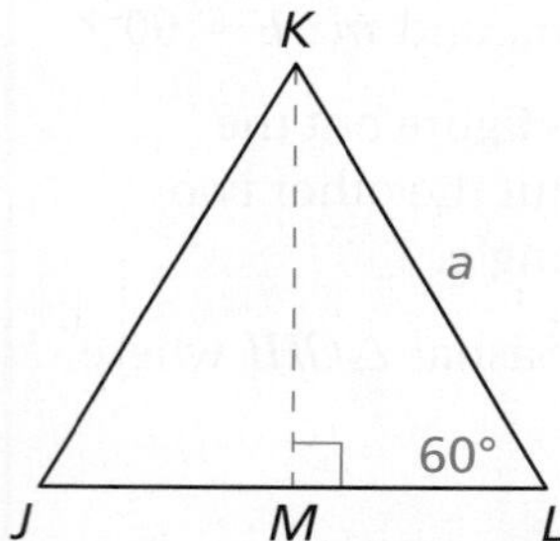

The measure of $\angle KLM = 60°$, because $\angle KLM$ is one of the angles of the original equilateral triangle. You also know that $m\angle LMK = 90°$, because $\overline{KM}$ is an altitude of the equilateral triangle. $m\angle MKL = 30°$, because the sum of the three angle measures is 180°.

$KL = a$, because $\overline{KL}$ is one of the sides of the original equilateral triangle. $LM = \frac{a}{2}$, because the altitude of an isosceles triangle bisects the base. You can find KM by using the Pythagorean Theorem.

$$KM^2 + LM^2 = KL^2$$

$$KM^2 + \left(\frac{a}{2}\right)^2 = a^2$$

$$KM^2 = \frac{3a^2}{4}$$

$$KM = \frac{\sqrt{3}a}{2}$$

Here is the triangle with all of its angle measures and side lengths marked. Learn to look for and recognize triangles with these angles, or with side lengths that are proportional to those in this triangle.

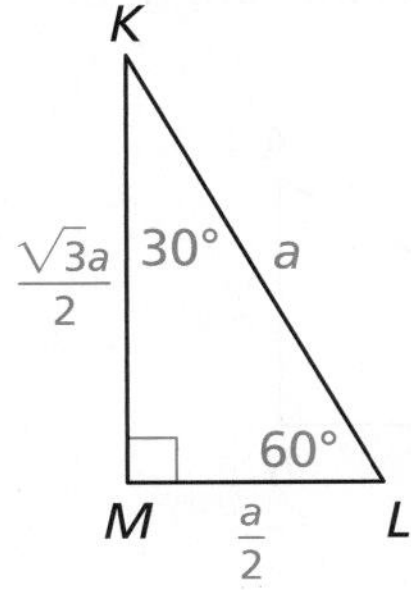

You can also call this triangle a 30-60-90 triangle. The ratio of side lengths in a 30-60-90 triangle is $1 : \sqrt{3} : 2$.

> **Habits of Mind**
>
> **Prove.** If you did not remember that the altitude of an isosceles triangle must bisect its base, you could quickly prove it using AAS congruence of the two right triangles.

For You to Do

A diagonal of a square cuts it into two congruent right triangles.

5. If the side length of the square is a, find all the side lengths and angle measures for one such right triangle.

A right triangle that is half of a square is an isosceles right triangle. You can also call it a 45-45-90 triangle. Learn to look for and recognize triangles with these angles, or with side lengths that are proportional to those of an isosceles right triangle. The ratio of side lengths in a 45-45-90 triangle is $1 : 1 : \sqrt{2}$.

Exercises *Practicing Habits of Mind*

Check Your Understanding

1. When you are trying to recognize the special right triangles discussed in this lesson, it will be useful to remember the converse of the Pythagorean Theorem. If the three side lengths a, b, and c are such that $a^2 + b^2 = c^2$, then the triangle they form must be a right triangle. Prove this.

For Exercises 2 and 3, find the missing angle measures and side length of each triangle. Explain your answers.

2.

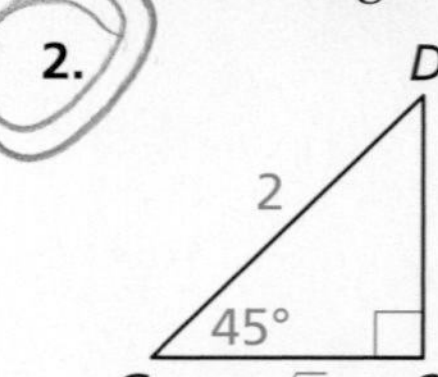

3.

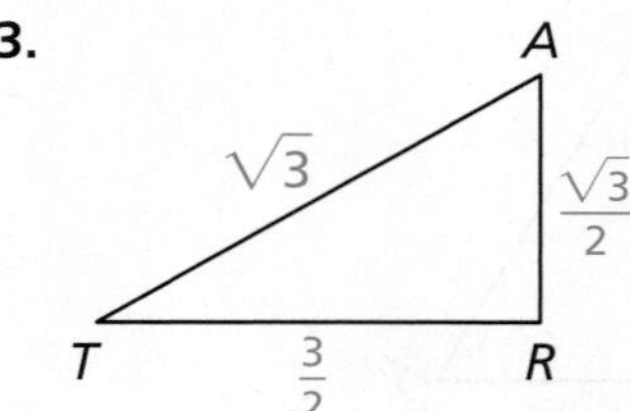

4. Suppose you know that two sides of a triangle measure 1 in. and 2 in. One of the angles of this triangle measures 60°. Is this triangle a 30-60-90 triangle? Sketch any possible triangles that meet these requirements.

On Your Own

For Exercises 5–8, find any missing angle measures or side lengths. Explain your answers.

5.

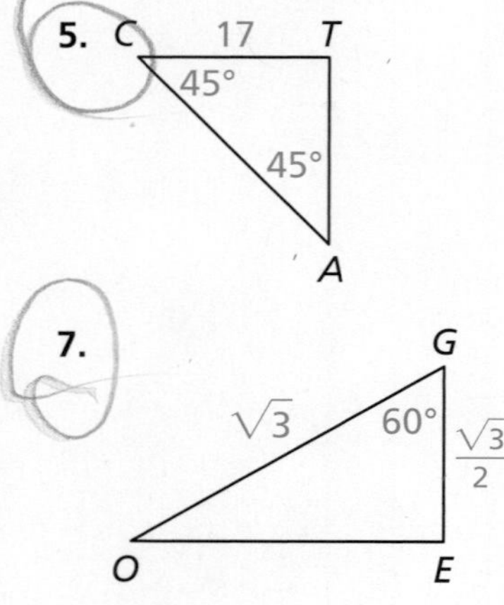

6.

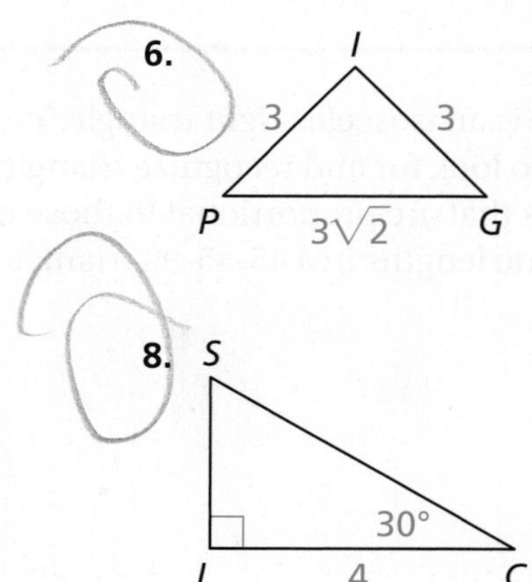

7.

8.

9. **Standardized Test Prep** The Garden Club is building a flower garden for Lincoln High School. The design is a square with diagonal walkways. The length of each walkway is 49.5 ft. Find the approximate area of the garden.

A. 1225 ft^2 **B.** 1980 ft^2 **C.** 2450 ft^2 **D.** 4900 ft^2

10. **What's Wrong Here?** Derman and Sasha made up triangle problems so they could practice with the special right triangles from this lesson.

Derman wrote this problem:

In $\triangle DER$, $DE = 2$ cm, $DR = 1$ cm, and $m\angle EDR = 30°$. Find the missing side lengths and angle measures.

Sasha said, "I don't think we can solve that one yet." Derman said, "Oh come on, it's easy. Here's a picture."

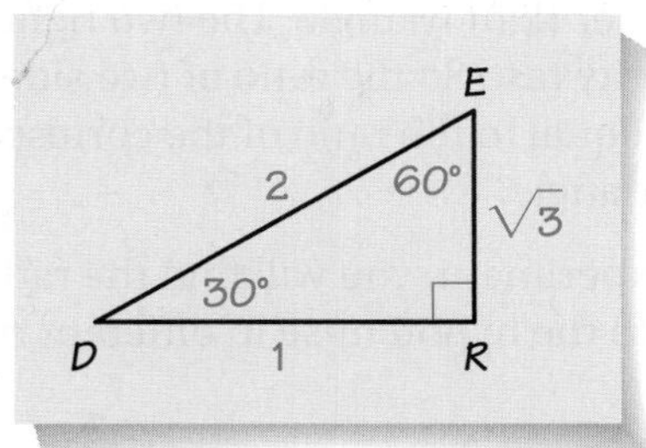

Explain what is wrong with Derman's solution. Use paper and pencil or geometry software to construct the triangle with Derman's given information.

11. A right triangle with a 30° angle has one side that is 1 inch long. Show all possible triangles. Find and label the lengths of the other two sides in each case.

12. A right triangle with a 45° angle has one side that is 1 inch long. Show all possible triangles. Find and label the lengths of the other two sides in each case.

13. Given $AB = 4\sqrt{3}$ cm, find AE.

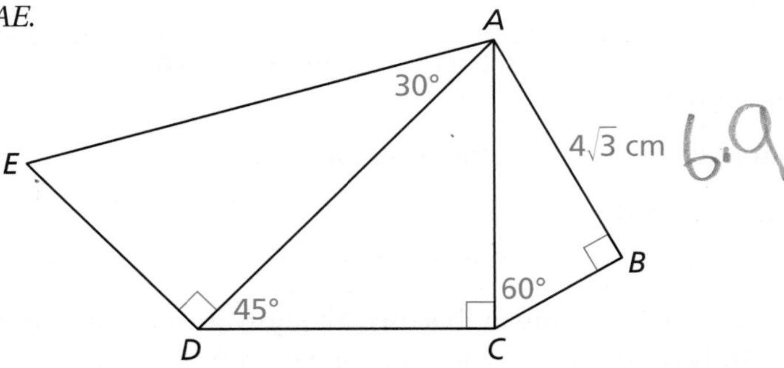

Maintain Your Skills

Go Online
Pearsonsuccessnet.com

14. $\triangle ABC$ is a right triangle with $m\angle B = 90°$. Find $\frac{AB}{AC}$, $\frac{BC}{AC}$, and $\frac{AB}{BC}$ for each measure of $\angle C$ below.

a. $m\angle C = 30°$ **b.** $m\angle C = 45°$ **c.** $m\angle C = 60°$

6.07 Some Special Ratios

If you have enough information to determine a triangle completely, then there ought to be a way to figure out all of the missing measurements. Right now, you can figure out the missing measurements for two special triangles: a 30-60-90 triangle and a 45-45-90 triangle.

> *To determine a triangle completely* means that you know enough measurements to guarantee that any other triangle with those measurements must be congruent to your triangle.

For example, suppose you know that the hypotenuse of a 30-60-90 triangle is 4 feet long. From this information, you can conclude that the side opposite the 30° angle is 2 feet long. This is because you know that the ratio of the side opposite the 30° angle to the hypotenuse of a 30-60-90 triangle is always $\frac{1}{2}$.

The ratios of the side lengths of other right triangles are also constant ratios. For instance, suppose a nonright angle in one right triangle is congruent to a nonright angle in another right triangle. The two right triangles must be similar by the AA similarity test. So the ratio of two side lengths of the first right triangle must be equal to the ratio of the corresponding two side lengths of the other right triangle.

In the following In-Class Experiment, you will find the ratio of the side opposite a nonright angle to the hypotenuse in different right triangles.

In-Class Experiment

Use geometry software to construct $\triangle ABC$ with $m\angle ABC = 90°$. Start with a small value for $m\angle C$ and gradually increase it. Make a table showing $m\angle C$ and the ratio $\frac{AB}{AC}$.

> If you do not have access to geometry software, you can still make this table, but your measurements will be less accurate.

1. As $m\angle C$ increases, what happens to the value of $\frac{AB}{AC}$?
2. What is the value of $\frac{AB}{AC}$ when $m\angle C = 30°$? When $m\angle C = 45°$? When $m\angle C = 60°$?
3. What value does the ratio $\frac{AB}{AC}$ approach as $m\angle C$ approaches 0°? As $m\angle C$ approaches 90°?
4. If $\frac{AB}{AC} \approx 0.34$, what is an approximate measure for $\angle C$?

Discuss your results with your classmates.

The problems you have been solving in this investigation are all examples of **trigonometry,** the study of triangles, in action. For easy reference, names are given to some of the constant ratios found in right triangles. In right triangle *ABC*, the names of these ratios are given and defined on the following page.

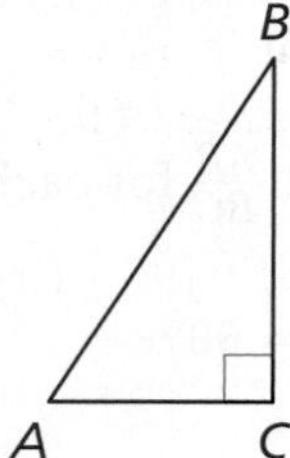

Trigonometric Ratios

The **sine** of $\angle A$ is defined as $\frac{BC}{AB}$, the ratio of the length of the side opposite $\angle A$ to the length of the hypotenuse.

Sine is often abbreviated as sin, so sin A is the same as sine A.

The **cosine** of $\angle A$ is defined as $\frac{AC}{AB}$, the ratio of the length of the side adjacent to $\angle A$ to the length of the hypotenuse.

Cosine is often abbreviated as cos, so cos A is the same as cosine A.

The **tangent** of $\angle A$ is defined as $\frac{BC}{AC}$, the ratio of the length of the side opposite $\angle A$ to the length of the side adjacent to $\angle A$.

Tangent is often abbreviated as tan, so tan A is the same as tangent A.

In this course, you define the sine, cosine, and tangent ratios of an acute angle of a right triangle as the ratios of the side lengths of the right triangle. So, you define the trigonometric ratios for angles with measures that are greater than 0° and less than 90°.

In later courses, you will extend the domain of the trigonometric ratios and be able to evaluate them for angles that cannot occur in right triangles.

Facts and Notation

When you find the trigonometric ratio of an acute angle of a right triangle, you can identify the acute angle in three ways.

- by degree measure: sin 27°
- by vertex: sin A
- by Greek letter: sin θ

The notation you choose will depend on the figure you are considering. If more than one angle has the same vertex, you have to use a three-letter angle name, such as sin $\angle BAC$. The alternative is to name the interior of each angle with a Greek letter, such as θ.

You can find the values of sine, cosine, and tangent for any angle using the trigonometric functions on your calculator. For example, if you enter "tan 27°" into a calculator, it gives the value 0.51, to the nearest hundredth. Different calculators may evaluate trigonometric functions differently. Determine the keystrokes needed on your calculator to evaluate tan 27°.

Note that your calculator can give you the values of these ratios to many decimal places of accuracy. However, even when your calculator shows a full display of digits, it may still be expressing an approximation of the actual value.

Example

Problem In $\triangle ABC$, $m\angle B = 90°$ and $BC = 8$. The area of $\triangle ABC$ is 24 cm^2. Find the rest of the side lengths and angle measures of the triangle. Indicate whether your measurements are *exact* or *approximate* in each case.

Solution The height of the triangle relative to $\overline{BC}$ is AB.

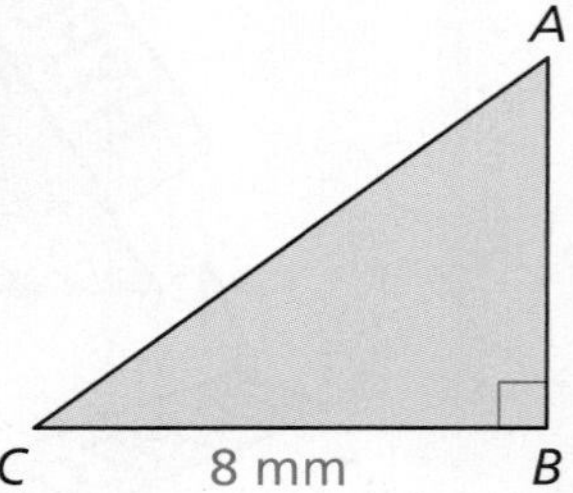

To find AB, use the area formula for a triangle.

$$A_{\triangle ABC} = \frac{1}{2}(BC)(AB)$$
$$24 = \frac{1}{2}(8)(AB)$$
$$AB = 6$$

$\overline{AB}$ is exactly 6 cm long.

Since $\triangle ABC$ is a right triangle, use the Pythagorean Theorem to find AC.

$$8^2 + 6^2 = (AC)^2$$

This gives $AC = 10\,\text{cm}$, so $\overline{AC}$ is exactly 10 cm long.

To find the angle measures, use the inverse of a trigonometric function on your calculator. The notation $\sin^{-1} 0.6$ is used for the *inverse* of the sine function. It means, "Find the angle with a sine of 0.6."

$$\sin C = \frac{6}{10}, \text{ so } m\angle C = \sin^{-1} 0.6$$
$$m\angle C \approx 36.87°$$

Similarly,

$$\cos A = \frac{6}{10}, \text{ so } m\angle A = \cos^{-1} 0.6$$
$$m\angle A \approx 53.13°$$

These angle measures are approximate.

For You to Do

5. In $\triangle MIN$, $m\angle M = 25°$, $m\angle N = 90°$, and $MI = 5$ inches. Find the rest of the side lengths and angle measures of the triangle. Indicate whether your measurements are *exact* or *approximate* in each case.

Exercises *Practicing Habits of Mind*

In the exercises for this lesson, be sure to indicate whether your solutions are *exact* or *approximate*. Find exact answers when possible.

Check Your Understanding

1. Rewrite these statements using the language of trigonometry:

a. In right triangle ABC with $m\angle A = 40°$, the ratio of the length of the side opposite $\angle A$ to the length of the hypotenuse is 0.64.

b. In right triangle DEF with $m\angle E = 70°$, the ratio of the length of the side adjacent to $\angle E$ to the length of the hypotenuse is 0.34.

c. In right triangle GHI with $m\angle H = 55°$, the ratio of the length of the side opposite $\angle H$ to the length of the side adjacent to $\angle H$ is 1.43.

The ratios in parts (a)–(c) are accurate to two decimal places.

In Exercises 2 and 3,

a. Find $\sin A$, $\cos A$, and $\tan A$ for each triangle.

b. Find $\sin B$, $\cos B$, and $\tan B$ for each triangle.

c. Which of your answers from parts (a) and (b) are the same? Explain.

2.

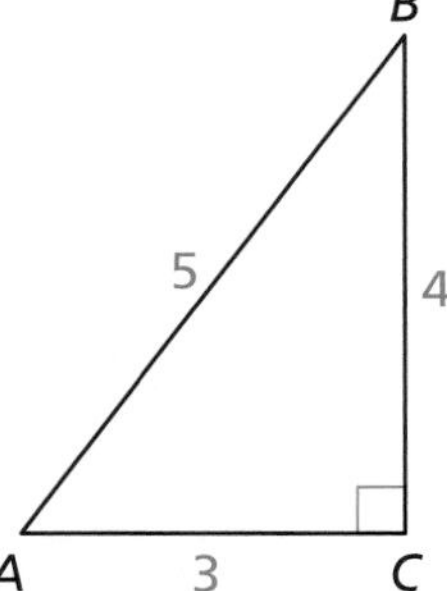

3.

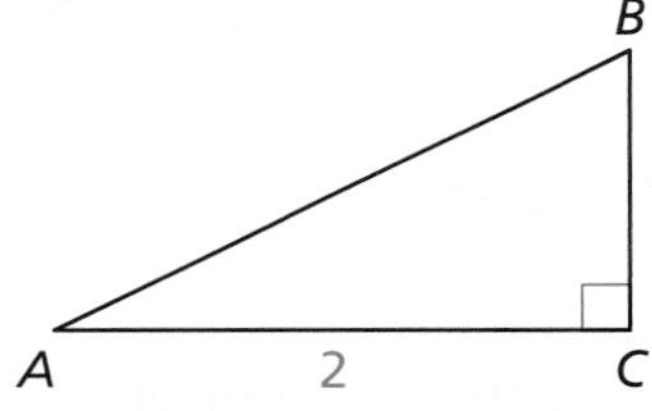

4. Find $\sin B$ and $\cos B$ for isosceles triangle ABC at the right.

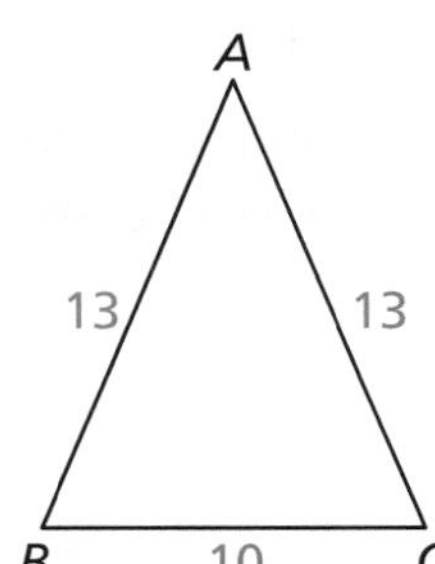

5. An airplane takes off and flies 10,000 feet in a straight line, making a 25° angle with the ground. How high above the ground does the airplane rise?

On Your Own

6. In $\triangle TUB$, $m\angle T = 90°$, $m\angle U = 70°$, and $TU = 8$ cm. Find the rest of the side lengths and angle measures.

7. **Standardized Test Prep** Find $\sin\theta$, $\cos\theta$, and $\tan\theta$ for the triangle below.

A. $\sin\theta = \frac{1}{4}$, $\cos\theta = \frac{3}{4}$, $\tan\theta = 3$

B. $\sin\theta = \frac{3}{\sqrt{10}}$, $\cos\theta = \frac{1}{\sqrt{10}}$, $\tan\theta = 3$

C. $\sin\theta = 1$, $\cos\theta = 3$, $\tan\theta = \sqrt{10}$

D. $\sin\theta = \frac{1}{\sqrt{10}}$, $\cos\theta = \frac{3}{\sqrt{10}}$, $\tan\theta = \frac{1}{3}$

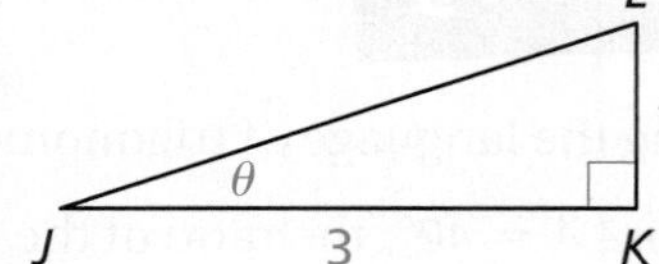

8. Triangle RST is a right triangle with right angle at S. If $\tan R = \frac{2}{3}$, find $\sin R$ and $\cos R$.

Drawing a sketch will help.

9. Triangle JKL is a right triangle with right angle at K. $\overline{JK}$ is three times the length of $\overline{KL}$. Find the sine, cosine, and tangent of $\angle J$ and of $\angle L$.

10. For each right triangle below, find the exact values for the sine, cosine, and tangent of $\angle A$ and $\angle B$.

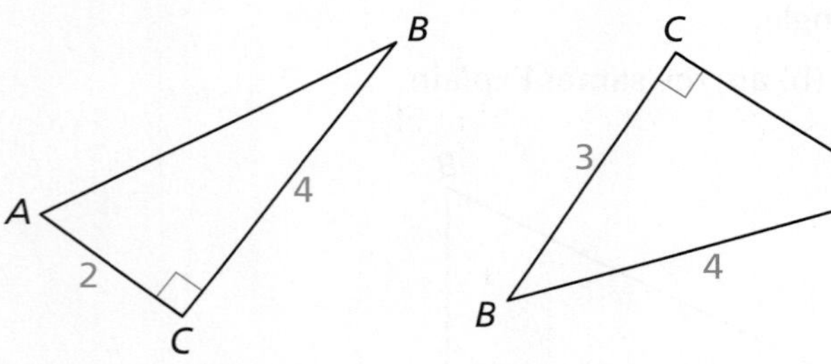

11. Use your calculator to evaluate the following expressions. Round your answers to the nearest hundredth.

a. $\sin 33°$ **b.** $\cos 33°$ **c.** $\tan 33°$ **d.** $\frac{\sin 33°}{\cos 33°}$

e. $\sin 57°$ **f.** $\cos 57°$ **g.** $\tan 57°$ **h.** $\frac{\sin 57°}{\cos 57°}$

12. In Exercise 11, there are several expressions that have the same value. Identify those expressions. In each case, explain why the two expressions are equal.

Refer to $\triangle ABC$ for Exercises 13–16.

13. Find $\sin\theta$, $\cos\theta$, and $\tan\theta$.

14. How is $\tan\theta$ related to $\sin\theta$ and $\cos\theta$? Write an equation that represents this relationship.

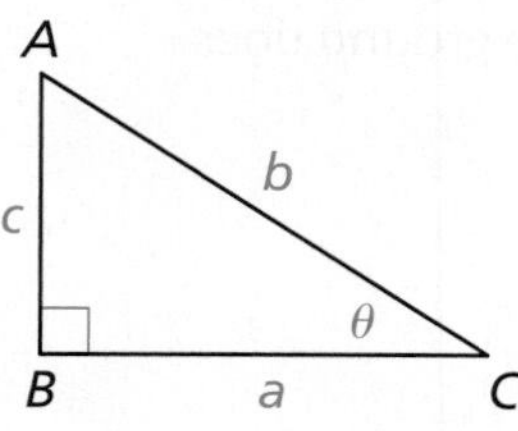

15. Sophia says the following equations are true for all values of θ.

$$\sin \theta = \cos (90^\circ - \theta) \qquad \cos \theta = \sin (90^\circ - \theta)$$

Is she right? Explain.

16. Joe says the following equation is true for all values of θ.

$$(\sin \theta)^2 + (\cos \theta)^2 = 1$$

Is he right? Try it out for a few numerical values of θ and then in a general triangle with sides a, b, and c.

You will often see $(\sin \theta)^2$ written as $\sin^2 \theta$. This is a common notation used to show a trigonometric ratio raised to a power.

17. To the nearest tenth, the value of $\tan 57^\circ$ is 1.5. To the nearest thousandth, it is 1.540. Solve for the length of $\overline{BC}$ in $\triangle ABC$ using each of these values. By how much do your two answers differ?

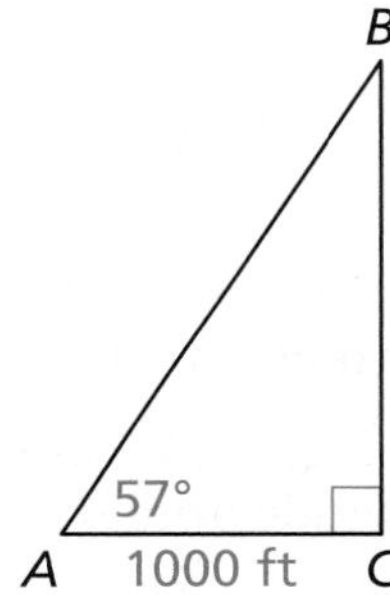

18. The piece of paper below originally showed a complete right triangle, $\triangle ABC$, with right angle at C. The paper was ripped, though, so that all you can see now is $\angle A$.

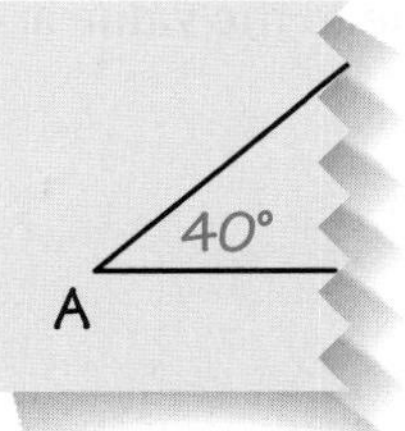

Find as many of these values as you can using a calculator. Some values might not be possible to find.

a. $\frac{BC}{AC}$ **b.** $AC + BC$ **c.** $\frac{BC}{AB}$ **d.** $AB \cdot AC$

e. $\frac{AC}{AB}$ **f.** $AB - BC$ **g.** $\frac{AC}{BC}$

19. **Take It Further** Follow the steps in parts (a)–(f) below to find the exact value of $\cos 72^\circ$. The isosceles triangle ABC at the left has base angles measuring 72°. $AB = 1$ and $AC = 1$. The same triangle is at the right with $\overline{BD}$ bisecting $\angle B$. $BD = x$.

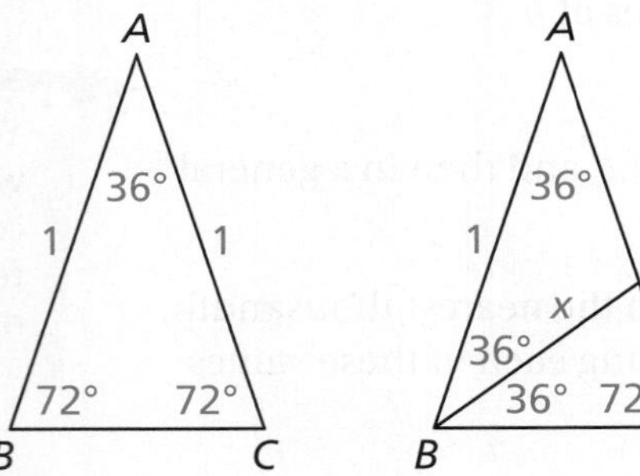

a. Find the lengths of $\overline{BC}$, $\overline{AD}$, and $\overline{DC}$ in terms of x.

b. Explain why $\triangle ABC \sim \triangle BCD$.

c. Write a proportion involving AB, BC, and CD.

d. Use your proportion from part (c) and the Quadratic Formula to solve for x.

e. Divide $\triangle ABC$ into two right triangles by drawing its altitude from A.

f. Use either of these right triangles and the value of x to find $\cos 72^\circ$.

Now find $\cos 72^\circ$ on a calculator. Compare the value the calculator gives to the exact value you found.

20. **Take It Further** Find $\cos 36^\circ$ by dividing $\triangle ABD$ in Exercise 19 into two right triangles. As in Exercise 19, compare this exact value to the value a calculator gives for $\cos 36^\circ$.

Maintain Your Skills

For each triangle, find the missing side lengths and angle measures.

21.

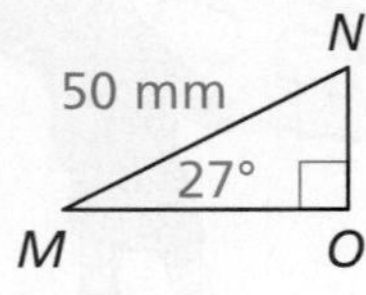

22.

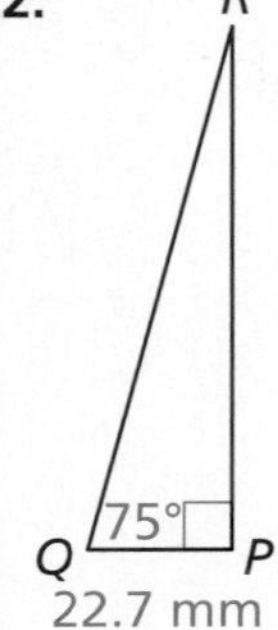

23.

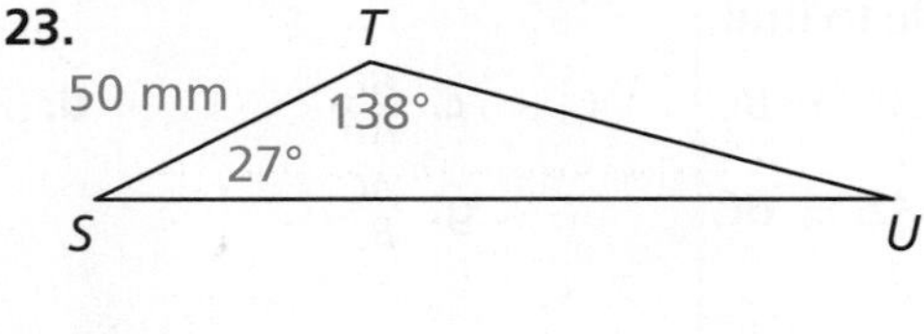

6.08 Finding Triangle Areas

The trigonometric functions sine, cosine, and tangent have proven very valuable in determining missing side lengths and angle measures in right triangles. In this lesson, you will use trigonometric functions to determine areas and other measurements in nonright triangles.

Minds in Action episode 26

Derman has made a discovery!

Derman I can find the area of any triangle if you tell me two sides and the included angle!

Tony Any triangle? Really? Okay, in $\triangle ABC$, $AB = 6$ cm, $AC = 8$ cm, and $m\angle B = 20°$.

Derman Here's my sketch.

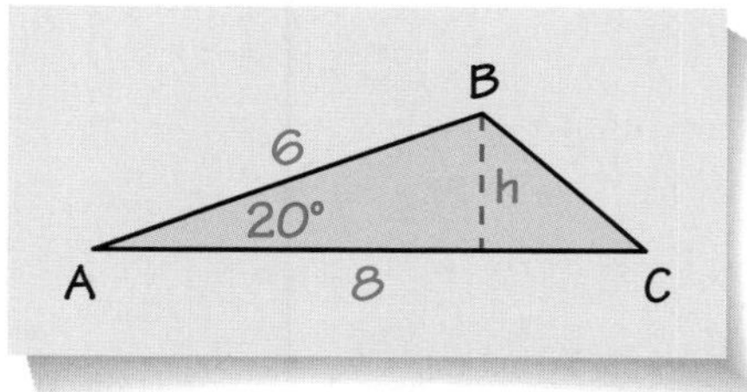

So $\frac{h}{6} = \sin 20°$ and $h = 6 \sin 20°$, which is about 2 cm. That means the area of $\triangle ABC$ is about $\frac{1}{2}(2)(8)$, or about 8 cm^2.

Tony Nice! Does it work if the angle is obtuse? After all, we've only defined the sine function for acute angles.

Derman I'm not sure. Let's try one.

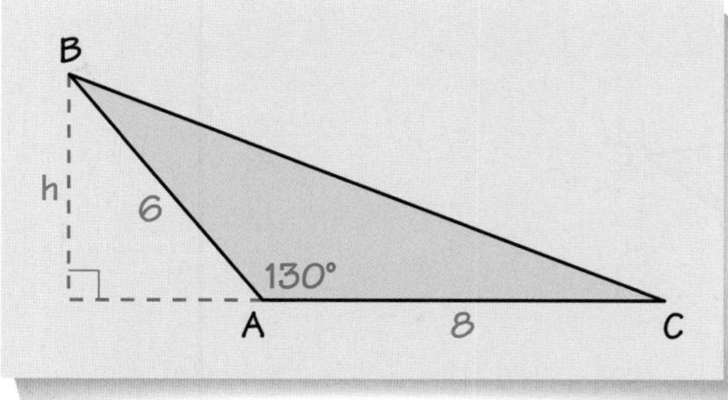

Tony I see how to do it. You just use the little right triangle that has the height as one of its legs.

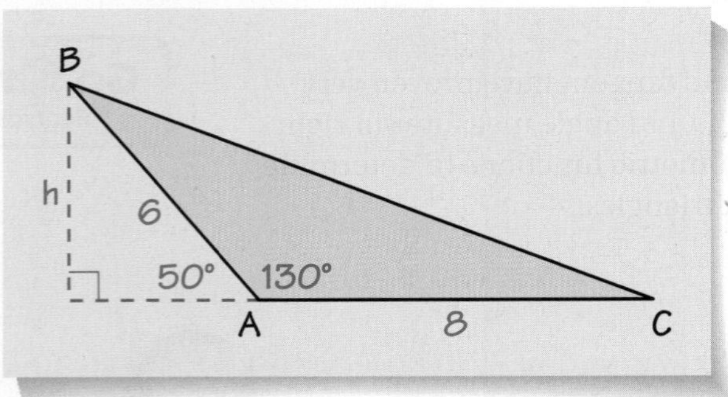

And we've got it. The area is approximately 18.4 cm^2.

Check Tony's calculations.

For You to Do

Find the area of each triangle.

1.

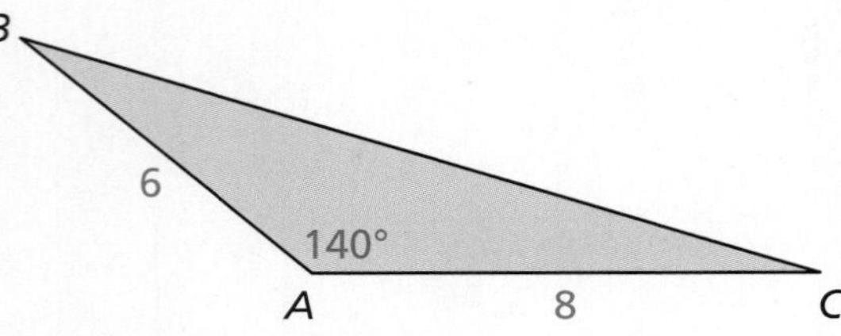

2.

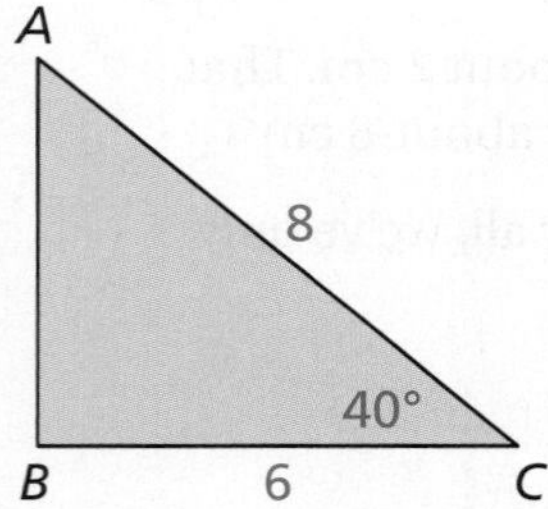

3.

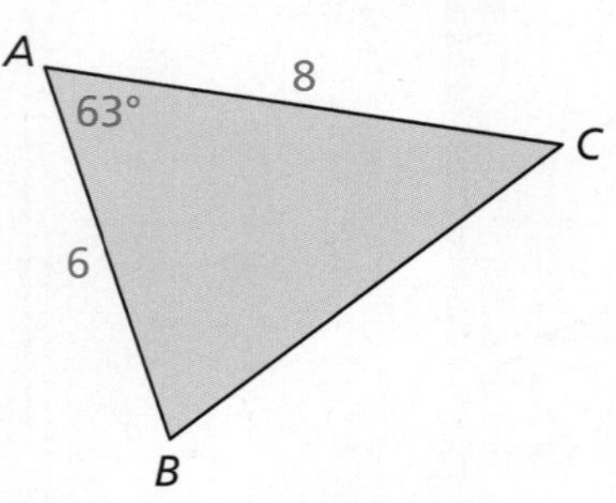

In this lesson, you have already seen that you can determine the area of any triangle given two sides and their included angle. There should be a way to find approximations for the other two angle measures, and the missing side length, as well. The following example shows one way to do this.

Example

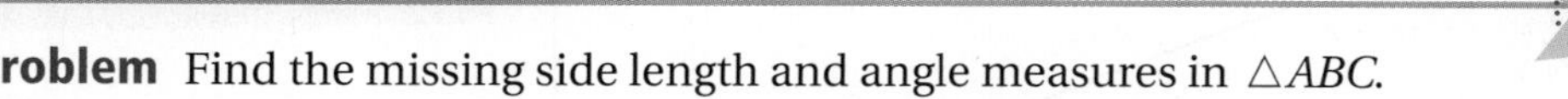

Problem Find the missing side length and angle measures in $\triangle ABC$.

B, 6, h, 20°, A, 8, C

Solution Derman has already found that the height of this triangle is approximately 2 cm. You can use the same technique to find the length marked x, and then y.

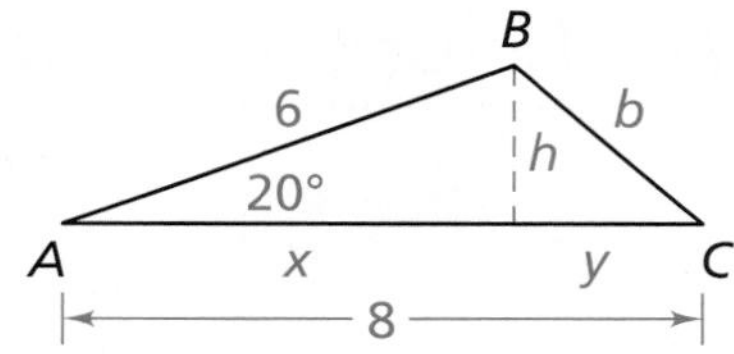

$$\frac{x}{6} = \cos 20^\circ \qquad y = 8 - x$$

$$x = 6\cos 20^\circ \qquad y \approx 8 - 5.6$$

$$\approx 5.6 \text{ cm} \qquad \approx 2.4 \text{ cm}$$

Since $\tan C = \frac{h}{y}$, you can find $m\angle C$ and $m\angle B$.

$$\tan C = \frac{h}{y} \qquad m\angle B = 180^\circ - m\angle A - m\angle C$$

$$m\angle C = \tan^{-1}\left(\frac{2}{2.4}\right) \qquad \approx 180^\circ - 20^\circ - 39.8^\circ$$

$$\approx 39.8^\circ \qquad \approx 120.2^\circ$$

All that is left to find is b. One way to find it is to see that $\frac{h}{b} = \sin C$.

$$b = \frac{h}{\sin C}$$

$$\approx \frac{2}{0.64}$$

$$\approx 3.1 \text{ cm}$$

For You to Do

4. Find the missing side length and angle measures.

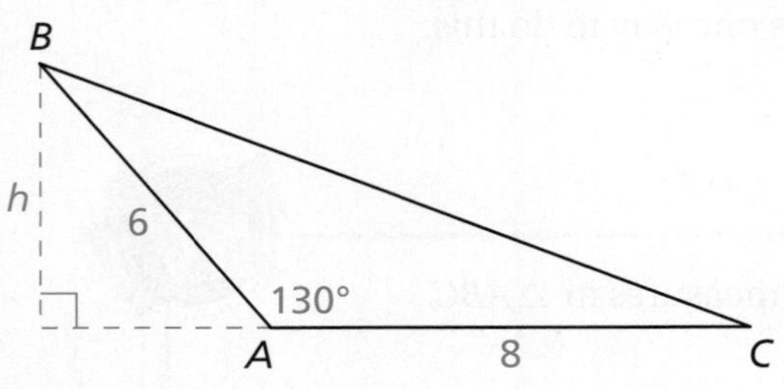

Remember...

Since you can find the sine ratio of an acute angle only, look in the diagram for an acute angle that will help you.

Exercises *Practicing Habits of Mind*

Check Your Understanding

In Exercises 1–3, find all the missing side lengths and angle measures of each triangle.

1.

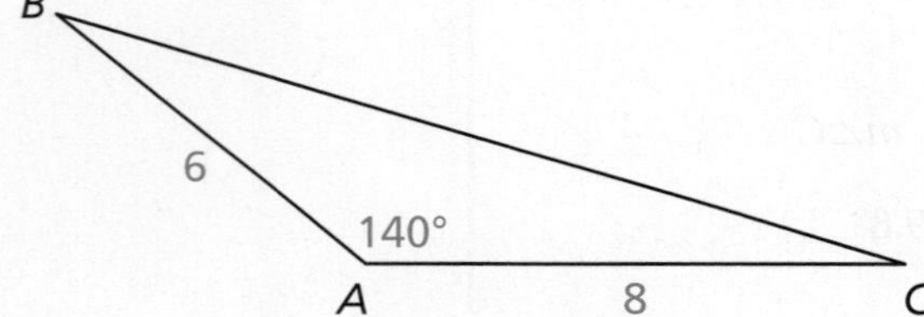

2.

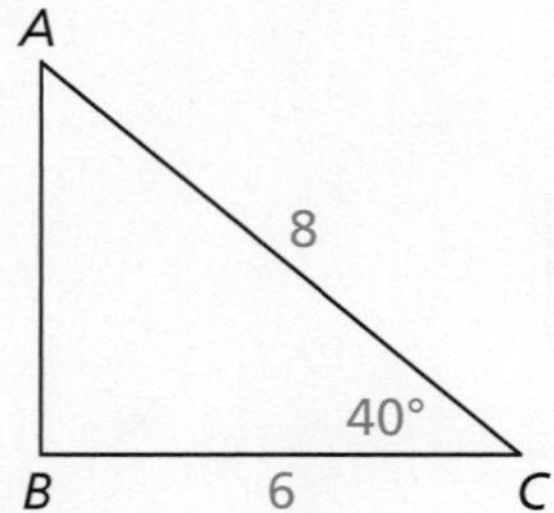

3.

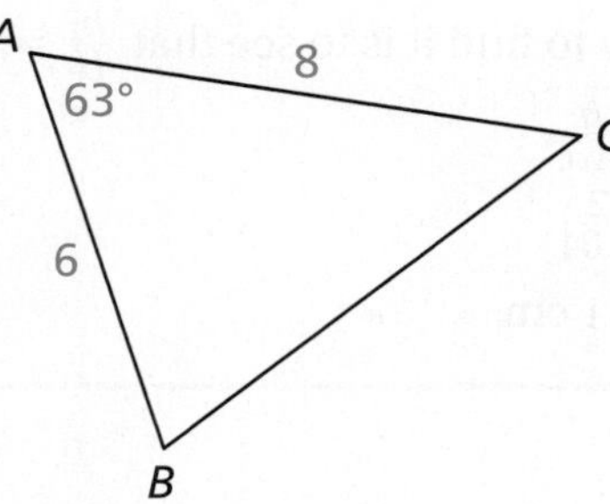

4. **a.** Find the area of the triangle in terms of a, b, and θ.

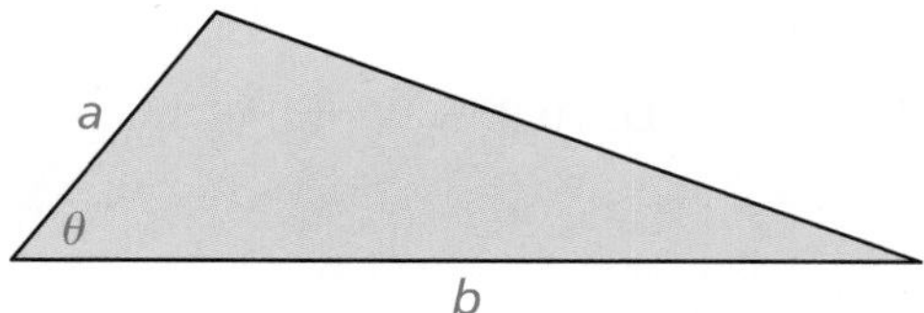

Remember...

θ (the Greek letter *theta*) is a variable that is often used to represent angle measures.

b. Use the area formula from part (a) to show that if you scale the triangle by the factor r, then you scale its area by r^2.

5. Find the area of parallelogram $ABCD$.

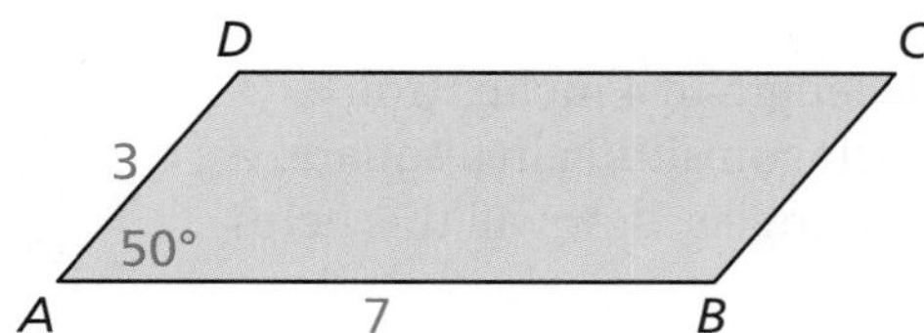

On Your Own

6. The altitude of $\triangle ABC$ from B intersects $\overline{AC}$ at D.

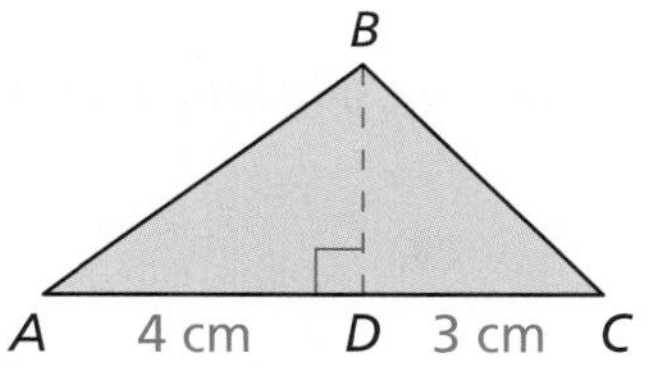

The area of $\triangle ABC$ is exactly 10.5 cm^2. $AD = 4$ cm and $DC = 3$ cm. Find the missing side lengths and angle measures.

Hint: Find the right triangles.

7. $\triangle DEW$ is isosceles. $DE = 65.3$ mm, $EW = 65.3$ mm, and $DW = 100$ mm. Find the angle measures and area of $\triangle DEW$.

8. In $\triangle RAT$, $m\angle A = 80°$, $RA = 1.74$ in., and $AT = 5$ in. Find TR, the other angle measures, and the area of the triangle.

9. The area of $\triangle ABC$ is 30 in.^{2}, $AC = 10$ in., and $m\angle A = 45°$. Find the rest of the side lengths and angle measures.

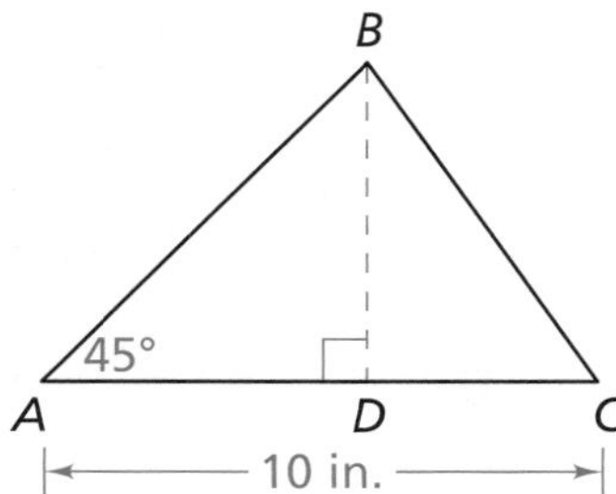

10. **Standardized Test Prep** You are given that $AB = 4$, $BC = 5$, $AC = 7$, and the area of $\triangle ABC$ is 9.798. Which value is closest to $m\angle A$?

A. 39.68° **B.** 44.48° **C.** 68.48° **D.** 70.8°

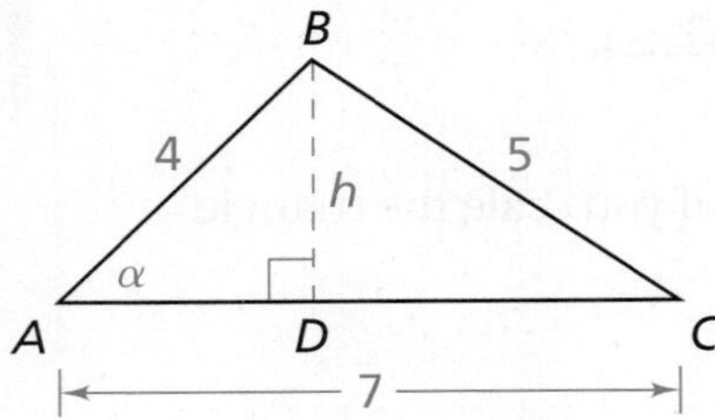

11. Find the area of a regular octagon that has a side length of 4 inches. You might also consider this picture that shows the octagon sitting in a square. If you can find the area of the square and the four triangles, how will this help?

Hint: Divide the octagon into triangles and find the area of each one.

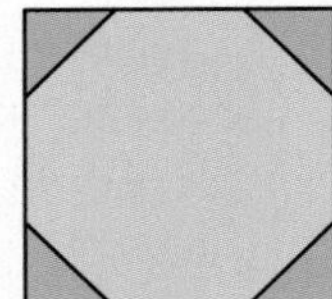

In Exercises 12–15, find the missing side length and angle measures of each triangle.

12.

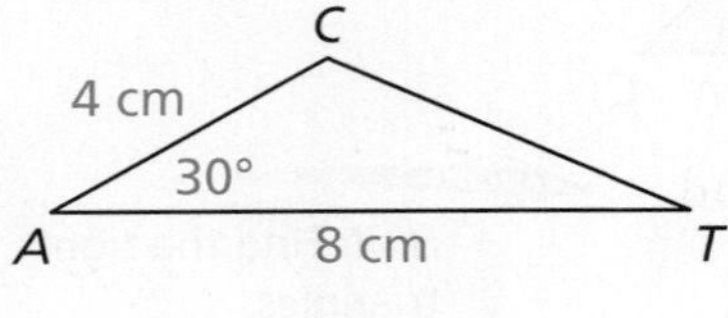

13.

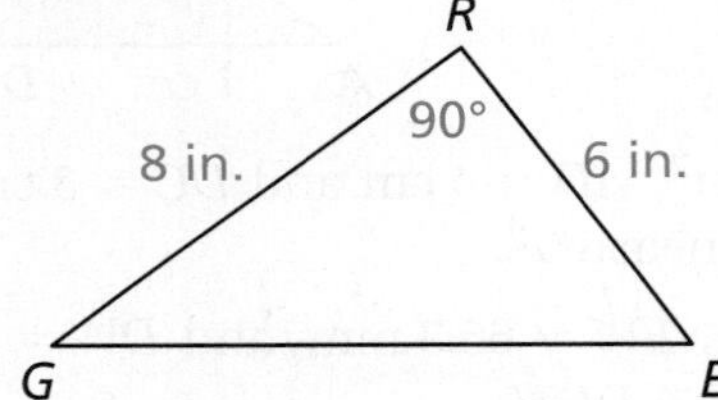

14.

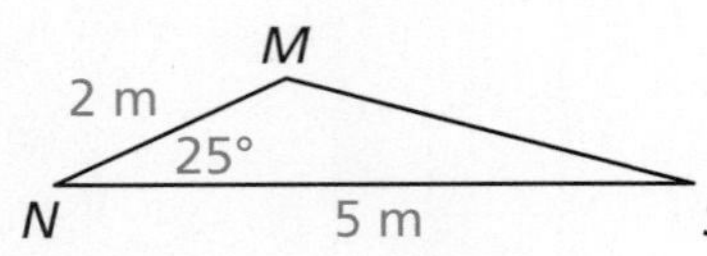

15.

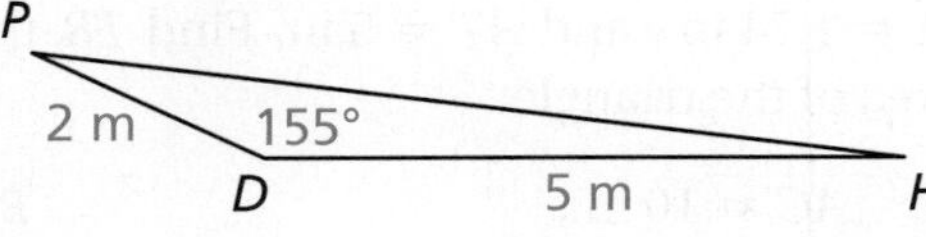

The Example earlier in this lesson demonstrated a technique you could use to find all the missing measurements for a triangle given the lengths of two sides and the measure of their included angle.

In Exercises 16–18, you will work through a technique that allows you to find all the missing measurements of a triangle given the measures of two angles and the length of their included side.

16. Explain why each equation is valid for $\triangle ABC$.

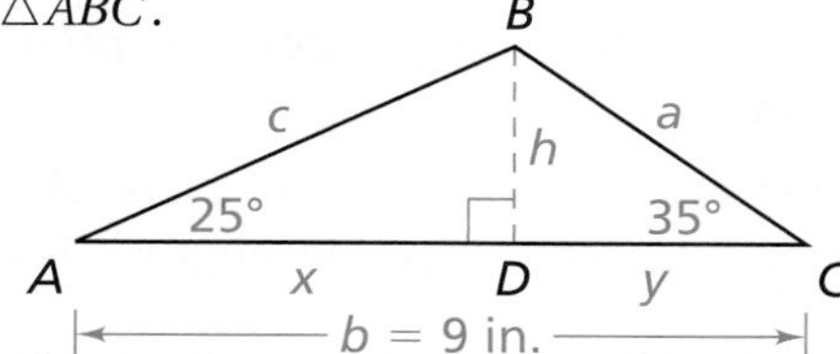

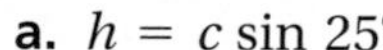

a. $h = c \sin 25°$

b. $h = a \sin 35°$

c. $c = \dfrac{a \sin 35°}{\sin 25°}$

d. $x = c \cos 25°$

e. $y = a \cos 35°$

f. $a \cos 35° + c \cos 25° = 9$

17. Find approximations for a and c in $\triangle ABC$ from Exercise 16.

18. Use the value you found for a and the given values for AC and $m\angle C$ to find c using the method from the Example. Did you get the same value for c as you did in Exercise 17?

19. Find the missing side lengths and angle measure of $\triangle REX$.

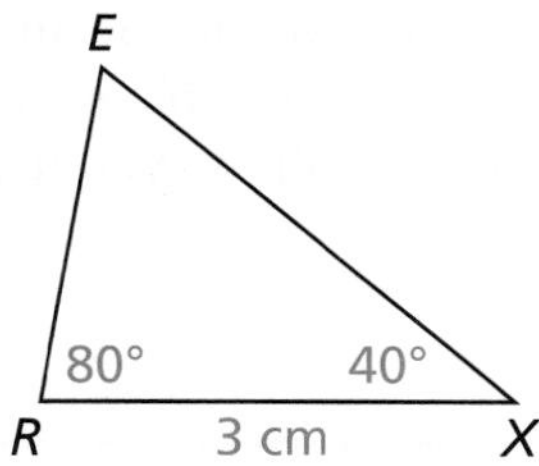

20. **Take It Further** Find the value of α in the triangle at the right.

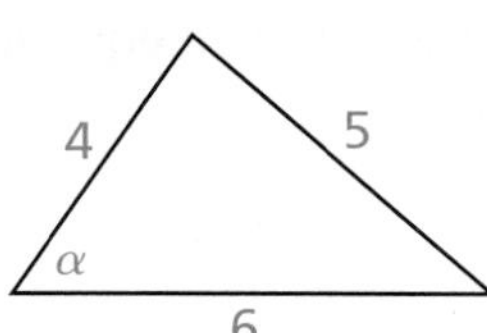

Maintain Your Skills

21. There are many triangles with two sides measuring 4 in. and 6 in. Among those triangles, which one has the maximum area? To investigate this question, use $\triangle ABC$ with $AB = 4$ in. and $BC = 6$ in. Using the different values for $m\angle B$ below, calculate the area. Which value of $m\angle B$ gives the greatest area for the triangle?

a. $m\angle B = 10°$ **b.** $m\angle B = 30°$ **c.** $m\angle B = 50°$ **d.** $m\angle B = 70°$

e. $m\angle B = 90°$ **f.** $m\angle B = 110°$ **g.** $m\angle B = 130°$

6.09 Extend the Pythagorean Theorem

You have determined missing side lengths and angle measures in triangles for which you have enough information to determine the triangle completely. Use the For Discussion questions below to reflect on what you have learned.

For Discussion

In your group, discuss one of the following questions. Be prepared to present your results to the class.

1. You have two angle measures and one side length of a triangle. Can you find the missing angle measure and the other two side lengths? If so, explain how.
2. You have two side lengths of a triangle and the measure of their included angle. Can you find the missing angle measures and the other side length? If so, explain how.
3. You have three side lengths of a triangle. Can you find its angle measures? If so, explain how.

If your group discussed Problem 3, you may have felt that it must be possible to use inverse trigonometric functions to find the angle measures of a triangle if you know its side lengths. But you may have had trouble describing a technique. Here is an example that shows you how to do it.

Example

Problem Given $\triangle ABC$ with side lengths a, b, and c, find an equation that relates these side lengths to the measure of $\angle C$.

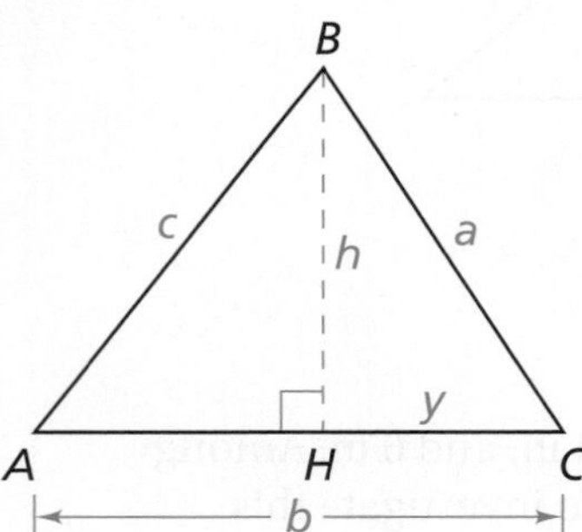

Solution $\triangle BCH$ is a right triangle, so you can use the Pythagorean Theorem.

$$a^2 = y^2 + h^2$$

Similarly, $\triangle ABH$ is a right triangle.

$$c^2 = (b - y)^2 + h^2$$

This leads to the following equation.

$$c^2 = b^2 - 2by + y^2 + h^2$$

Remember that $a^2 = y^2 + h^2$. This means that you can write the following.

$$c^2 = b^2 - 2by + a^2$$

You know that $y = a \cos C$, so with a little rearrangement you get the following.

$$c^2 = a^2 + b^2 - 2ab \cos C$$

You can use a similar process to relate the same three side lengths of $\triangle ABC$ to either of its other angles. Here are the resulting equations.

$$a^2 = b^2 + c^2 - 2bc \cos A$$

$$b^2 = a^2 + c^2 - 2ac \cos B$$

The equations above, called the Law of Cosines, relate the side lengths of a triangle to the measure of one angle of the triangle. You can use the Law of Cosines to find

- the third side length of a triangle when you know two side lengths and the measure of the included angle
- the measure of an angle of a triangle when you know the three side lengths

In the second application, you solve for the cosine of the angle. Then you use the inverse of the cosine function to find the angle measure.

In a later course, you will learn the meaning of cosine for *any* angle. For now, when you use the Law of Cosines with a triangle, you must use the Law of Cosines equation that refers to an angle that you know is acute.

For You to Do

4. Find AC for $\triangle ABC$.

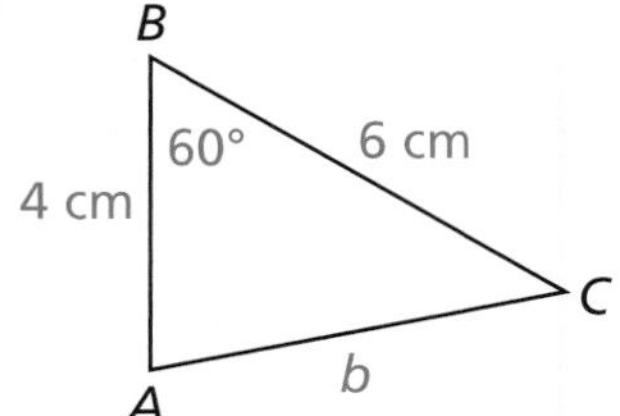

5. Find $m\angle A$ for $\triangle ABC$.

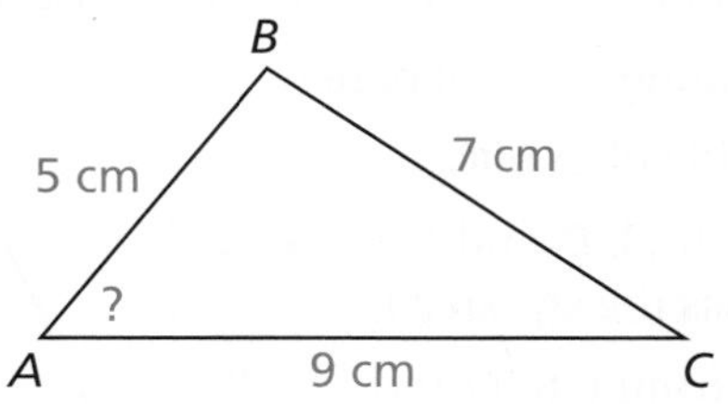

Developing Habits of Mind

Understand the Process. An efficient way to present an argument is to give its major steps. If the major steps convince others, then you can move on. If not, you can fill in selected details. This saves you from having to provide the details that are already common knowledge.

Watch how this works in the following colorful proof of the Law of Cosines.

Proof of the Law of Cosines, $c^2 = a^2 + b^2 - 2ab\cos C$

The diagram shows $\triangle ABC$ with squares on each side of the triangle. You divide each square into two rectangles by drawing perpendiculars from A, B, and C. You also need dashed $\overline{CQ}$ and $\overline{BV}$.

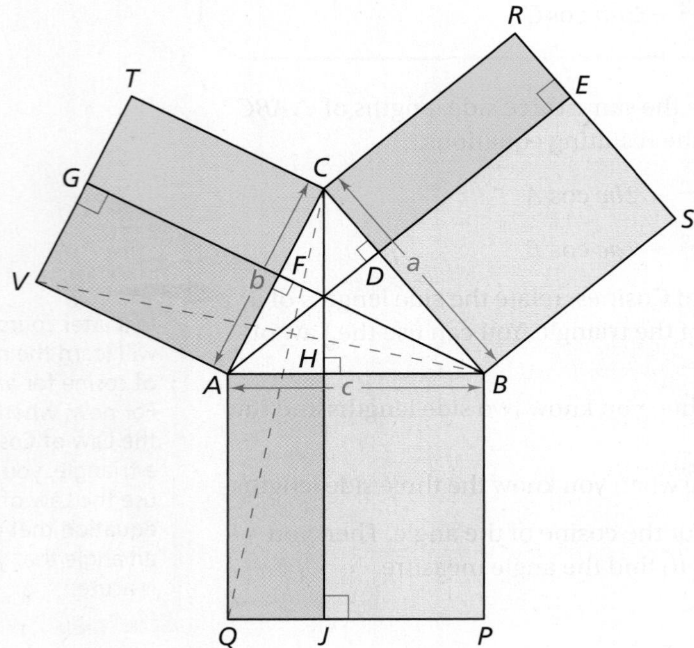

Complete the steps below to draw the diagram used in this proof. This will help you understand the proof. Use labels to match those shown below.

- Copy $\triangle ABC$ onto a separate sheet of paper.
- Draw squares on each side of $\triangle ABC$.
- Draw perpendiculars from A, B, and C. (Extend the perpendiculars across the squares.)
- Draw dashed segments from C to Q and V to B.

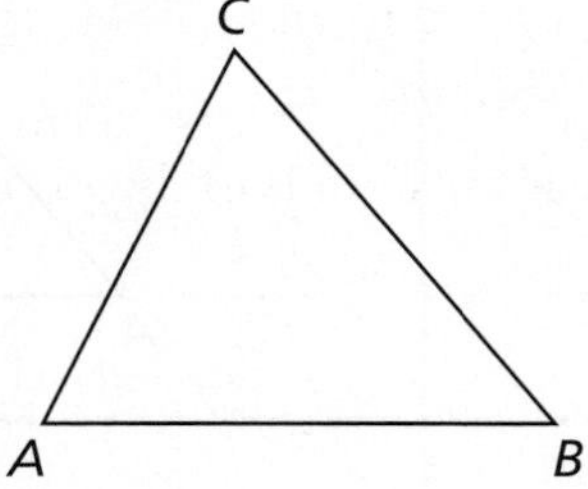

Habits of Mind

Explore the possibilities. If you have access to geometry software, construct the figure. Drag a vertex of $\triangle ABC$ and see what happens to the colored rectangles. When do the blue and green ones disappear?

Convince yourself that if each step below is true, then the Law of Cosines is true.

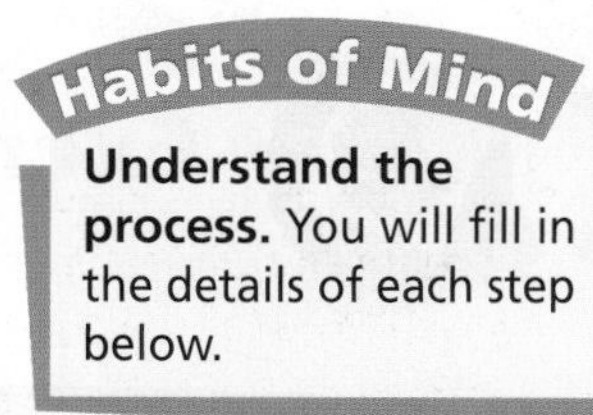

Understand the process. You will fill in the details of each step below.

Step 1 The purple rectangles have equal areas.

Step 2 The yellow rectangles have equal areas.

Step 3 The green rectangles have equal areas. The area of each rectangle is $ab \cos C$.

Step 4 This equation refers to the area of each figure:

$\square ABPQ = \square ACTV + \square BCRS - 2$ green rectangles

Step 5 $c^2 = a^2 + b^2 - 2ab \cos C$

The details below may help you convince yourself that each step above is correct.

Step 1 area $\square AHJQ = 2 \cdot$ area $\triangle AQC$

area $\square AFGV = 2 \cdot$ area $\triangle ABV$

area $\triangle AQC$ = area $\triangle ABV$

area $\square AHJQ$ = area $\square AFGV$

Step 2 You will provide the details for Step 2 in the For You to Do section below.

Step 3 area $\square FCTG = b \cdot CF$

$\cos C = \frac{CF}{a}$ (in $\triangle CFB$)

$CF = a \cos C$

So, area $\square FCTG = ab \cos C$.

area $\square DCRE = a \cdot CD$

$\cos C = \frac{CD}{b}$ (in $\triangle CDA$)

$CD = b \cos C$

So, area $\square DCRE = ab \cos C$.

Step 4 In terms of colors, Step 4 says the following.
(purple + yellow) = (purple + green) + (yellow + green) − 2 greens

Step 5 This step follows from the original Step 4 by substituting the equivalent expressions for areas into Step 4.

You may want to fill in even more details.

Step 1 $\square AHJQ$ and $\triangle AQC$ have the same base and height,
so area $\square AHJQ = 2 \cdot$ area $\triangle AQC$.
Area $\triangle AQC = \triangle ABV$ because $\triangle AQC \cong \triangle ABV$ by SAS.
$\square AFGV$ and $\triangle ABV$ have the same base and height,
so area $\square AFGV = 2 \cdot$ area $\triangle ABV$.

If you need to clarify even more details of the proof, work with a classmate.

For You to Do

6. Fill in the details for Step 2.

Exercises Practicing Habits of Mind

Check Your Understanding

1. Find AC.

2. Find BC.

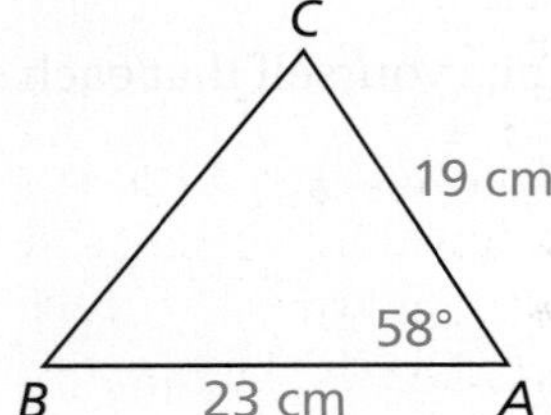

3. Find $m\angle B$.

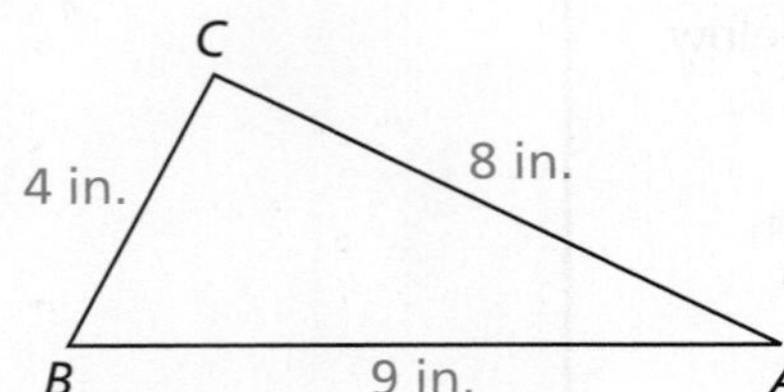

4. Find $m\angle A$.

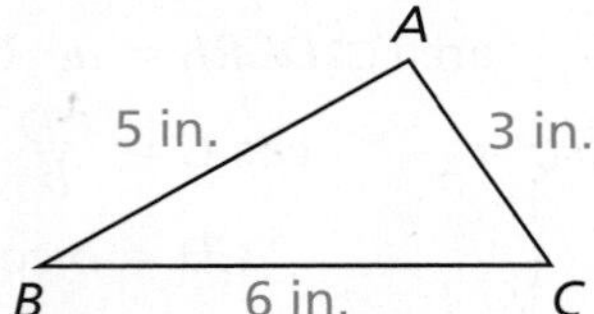

On Your Own

5. Find the missing side length, angle measures, and area of $\triangle CAT$.

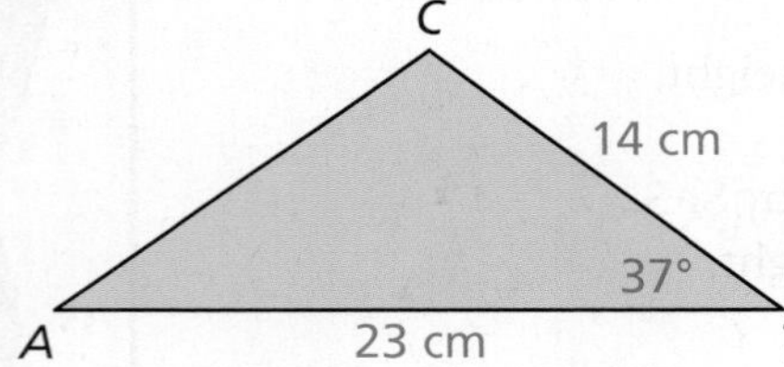

6. Find the missing angle measures and area of $\triangle DOG$.

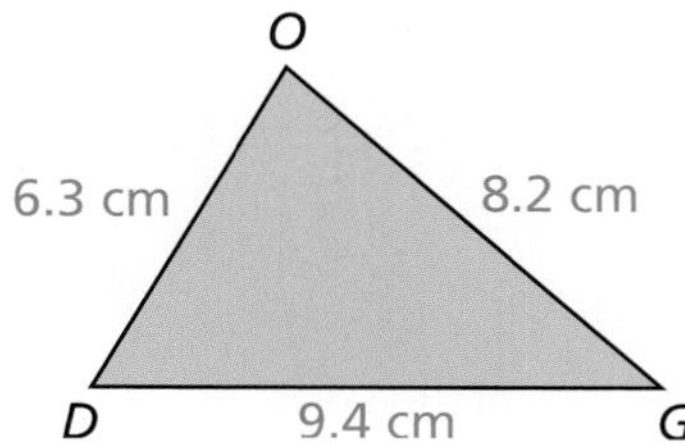

7. **Standardized Test Prep** A community group is building a fenced-in triangular space for a dog park. They know that two sides of the park will be 35 m and 25 m. Because of a nearby pond, the angle between these two sides will have to measure 40°. What will be the perimeter of the dog park?

   A. 65 m B. 78 m
   C. 83 m D. 110 m

8. A regular pentagon is inscribed in a circle of radius 1. What is the length of one of its sides?

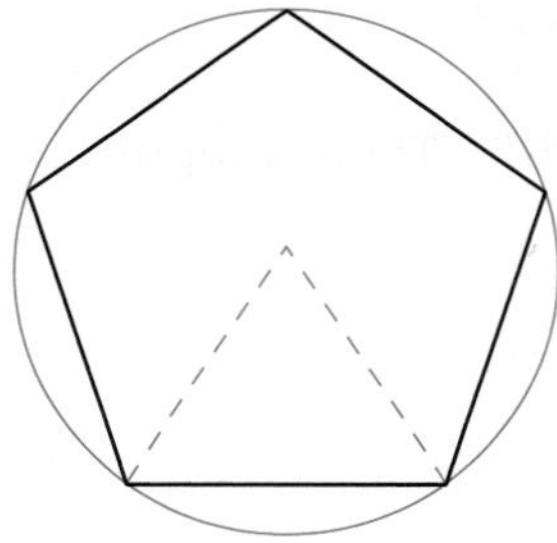

9. **Write About It** Explain how the Law of Cosines is an extension of the Pythagorean Theorem.

10. **Write About It** Explain how you would approach the problem of finding all of the missing angle measures and the area of a triangle for which you know the three side lengths.

11. **Write About It** You know the lengths of two sides of a triangle and the measure of their included acute angle. Explain how you would find the length of the third side, the measures of the other two angles, and the area of the triangle. How would your work be different if the angle measure you knew was obtuse?

12. Find the missing angle measures of $\triangle ABC$. Then compute the ratios below.

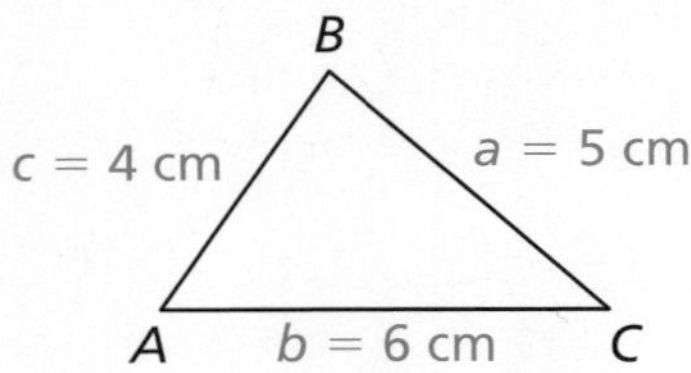

a. $\frac{\sin A}{a}$ **b.** $\frac{\sin B}{b}$ **c.** $\frac{\sin C}{c}$

13. Find the missing side lengths and angle measure of $\triangle ABC$. Then compute the ratios below.

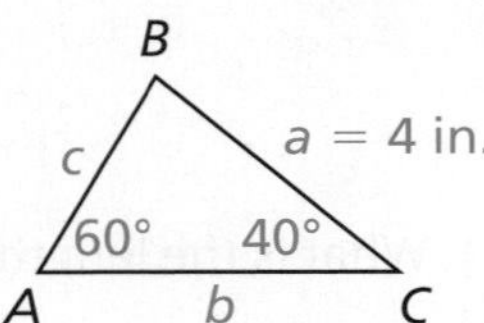

a. $\frac{\sin A}{a}$ **b.** $\frac{\sin B}{b}$ **c.** $\frac{\sin C}{c}$

14. Find the missing side length and angle measures of $\triangle ABC$. Then compute the ratios below.

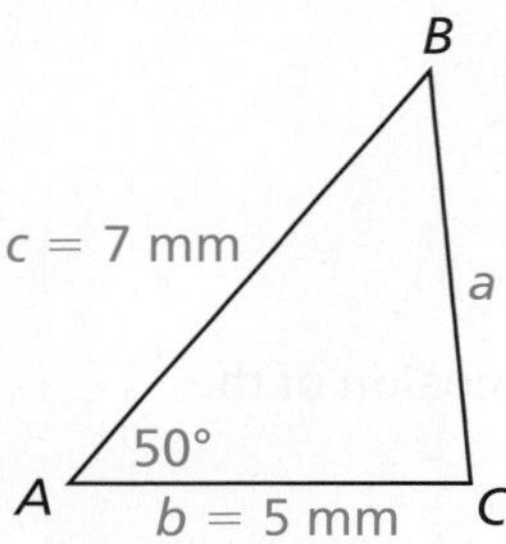

a. $\frac{\sin A}{a}$ **b.** $\frac{\sin B}{b}$ **c.** $\frac{\sin C}{c}$

Maintain Your Skills

For Exercises 15–18, prove that the area of the figure on the hypotenuse is equal to the sum of the areas of the figures on the legs of the right triangle.

15.

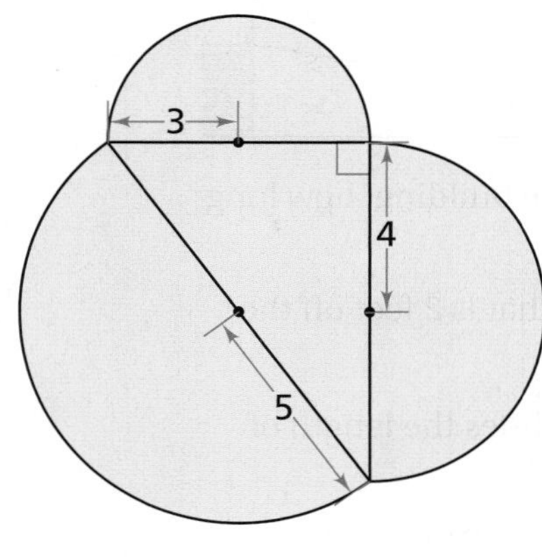

16.

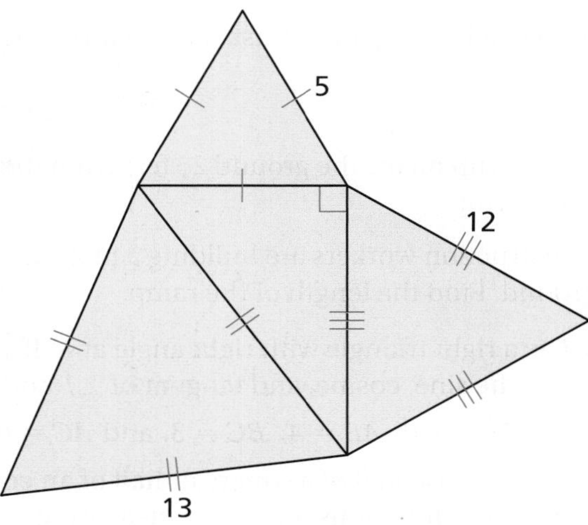

17.

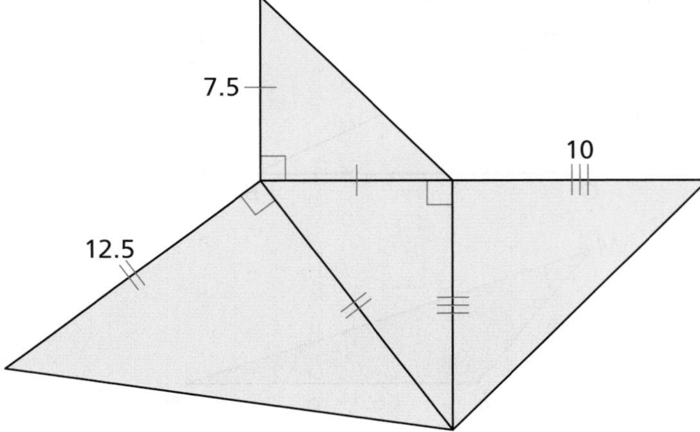

18.

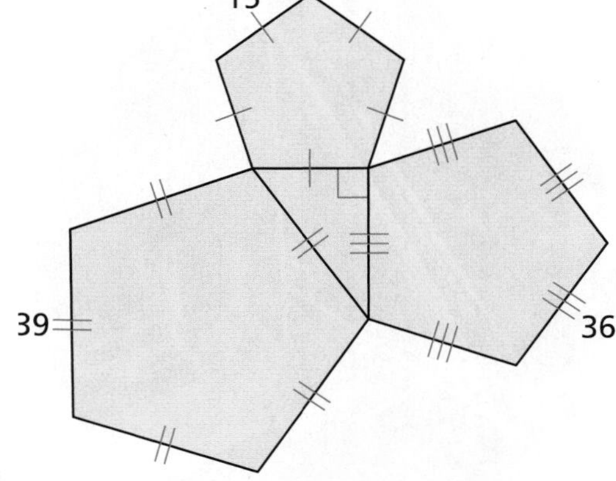

In this investigation, you learned how to use trigonometric functions. You found areas, angle measures, and side lengths of triangles. You used right triangles to solve problems. These questions will help you summarize what you have learned.

1. A ramp to a loading dock must slope at a 10° angle.

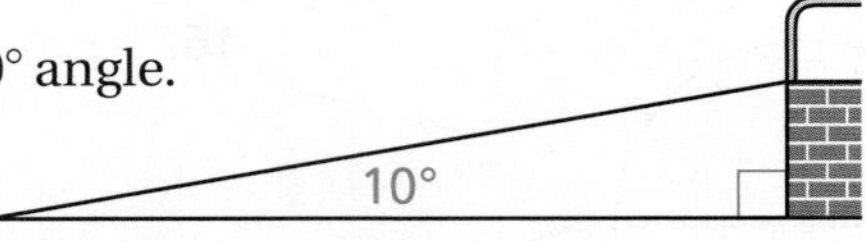

   a. If the ramp meets the ground 25 feet from the base of the building, how long is the ramp?

   b. Construction workers are building a ramp up to a door that is 2 feet off the ground. Find the length of the ramp.

2. $\triangle JKL$ is a right triangle with right angle at K. If $\overline{JK}$ is four times the length of $\overline{KL}$, find the sine, cosine, and tangent of $\angle J$ and $\angle L$.

3. Given $\triangle ABC$ with $AB = 4$, $BC = 3$, and $AC = 6$, find the measure of angle C.

4. How can you use half of a square or half of an equilateral triangle to evaluate trigonometric functions for angles measuring 30°, 45°, and 60°?

5. Find the sine, cosine, and tangent of α and β in terms of the side lengths of $\triangle ABC$.

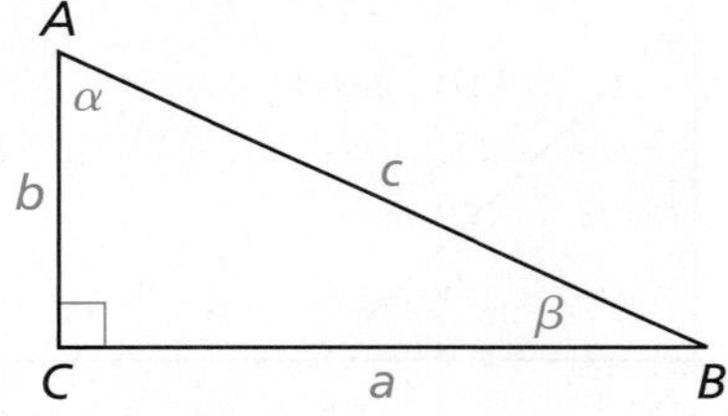

6. What is the area of $\triangle LMN$? What is the approximate length of $\overline{MN}$?

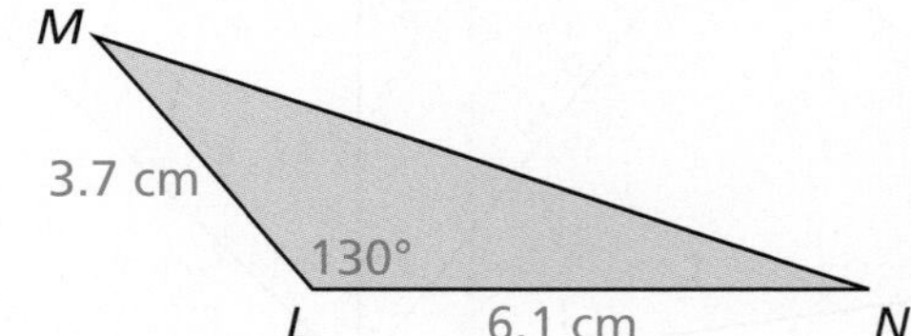

Vocabulary and Notation

In this investigation, you learned these terms and symbols. Make sure you understand what each one means and how to use it.

- **trigonometry**
- **sine, sin θ**
- **cosine, cos θ**
- **tangent, tan θ**
- **$\sin^{-1} x$**
- **$\cos^{-1} x$**
- **$\tan^{-1} x$**

The ladder can reach out $\ell \cos \theta$ and up a height of $t + \ell \sin \theta$. ℓ can extend as θ increases.

Chapter 6

Mid-Chapter Test

Go Online
Pearsonsuccessnet.com

Multiple Choice

1. In $\triangle ABC$, $AH = 12$ cm and $HB = 3$ cm. Find CB.

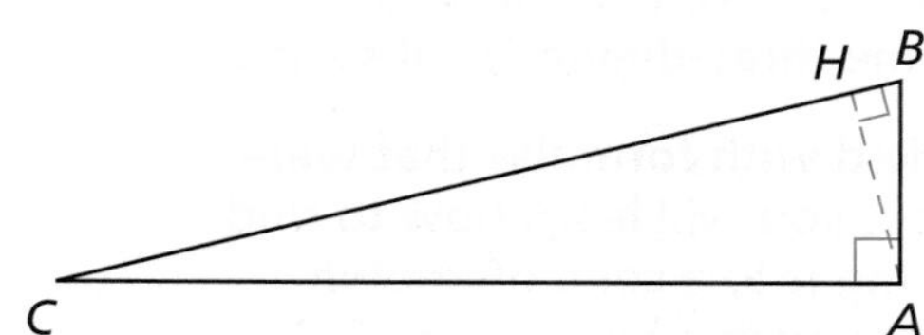

A. 12.4 **B.** 36 **C.** 51 **D.** 153

2. A right triangle with a 45° angle has a hypotenuse of 16. Find the measure of the third angle and the lengths of its legs.

A. 90°, $8\sqrt{2}$, 16 **B.** 45°, $8\sqrt{2}$, $8\sqrt{2}$

C. 45°, 16, 22.6 **D.** 135°, $8\sqrt{2}$, $8\sqrt{2}$

Open Response

3. Find the arithmetic mean and the geometric mean of 4 and 16. Use a numerical computation and then a geometric construction.

4. Construct a rectangle with the same area as $ABCD$ that has $\overline{EF}$ as a side.

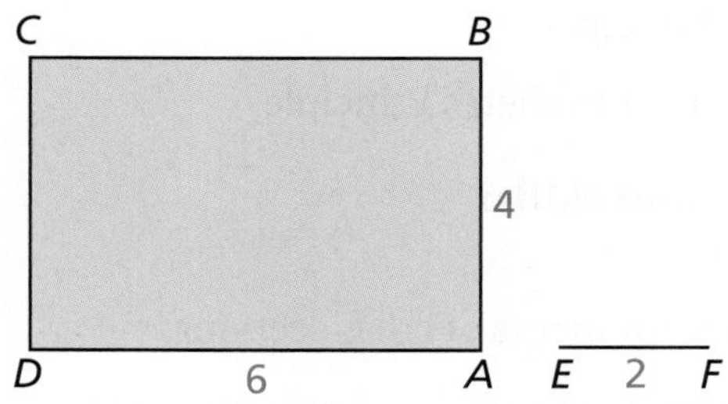

5. Determine whether each statement must be true. Explain your reasoning.

a. A triangle has three altitudes.

b. The altitudes of a triangle are concurrent.

c. The point in which two altitudes of a triangle intersect divides each altitude into segments with ratio 1 : 2.

d. In an equilateral triangle, the altitudes are concurrent.

e. In an equilateral triangle, the point in which two altitudes intersect divides each altitude into segments with ratio 1 : 2.

6. Find the missing side lengths and angle measures of $\triangle ABC$.

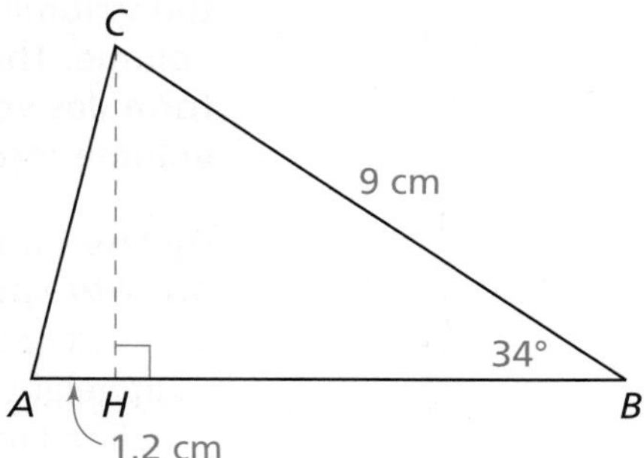

7. The area of the triangle below is 78 cm^2. $AD = 8$ cm and $m\angle BAD = 60°$. Find the rest of the side lengths and angle measures.

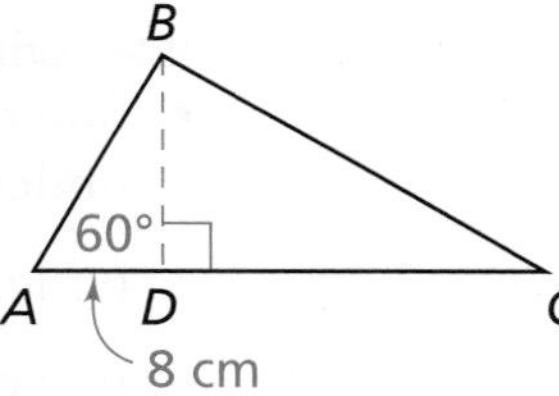

8. For each right triangle below, find the exact values for sine, cosine, and tangent of $\angle A$ and $\angle B$.

a.

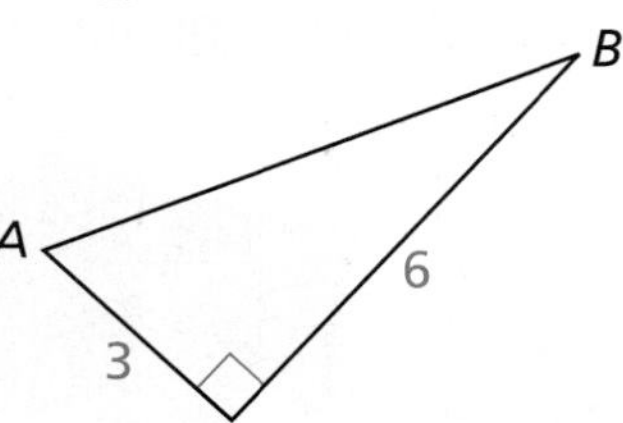

b.

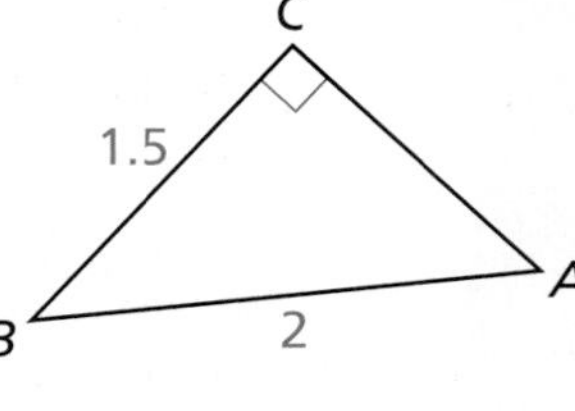

Volume Formulas

In *Volume Formulas,* you will learn a new technique for finding the volume of a solid. In Investigation 3D, you found the volumes and surface areas of some three-dimensional solids.

For many of the solids, you worked with formulas that were given to you. In this investigation, you will learn how to find the volume of a solid by comparing it to a solid of known volume. This technique will allow you to prove some of the formulas you were told about in Chapter 3, including the volume formula for spheres.

By the end of this investigation, you will be able to answer questions like these.

1. A hexagonal pyramid of height h is cut by a plane parallel to its base at height r above the base. How is the shape of the resulting cross section related to the shape of the base of the pyramid? How are their areas related?
2. Explain Cavalieri's Principle.
3. A spherical melon has radius 3 inches. You cut a slice 2 inches from its center. What is the volume of the piece you cut from the melon?

You will learn how to

- find the areas of cross sections formed when planes intersect with solids under certain conditions
- understand and use Cavalieri's Principle
- prove basic volume formulas using Cavalieri's Principle

You will develop these habits and skills:

- Visualize cross sections of solids.
- Use similar triangles to find measurements of cross sections.
- Choose appropriate solids to compare using Cavalieri's Principle.

The two stacks have identical bases and the same height. How do the numbers of napkins in the stacks compare?

6.10 Getting Started

In Chapter 1, you did some preliminary work in visualizing the cross sections of different three-dimensional objects cut by planes. Now you can describe these cross sections more thoroughly. The Ratio and Parallel methods for dilation that you learned in Chapter 4 also work in three dimensions. Work in groups of at least three to complete the following experiment.

In-Class Experiment

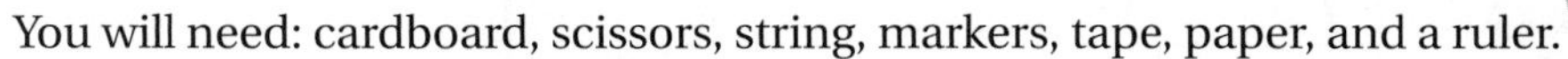

You will need: cardboard, scissors, string, markers, tape, paper, and a ruler.

Step 1 Cut a triangle out of a piece of cardboard.

Step 2 Now punch three small holes near the vertices of your cardboard triangle.

Step 3 Pass the end of a piece of string through each hole.

Step 4 Have one student hold the cardboard triangle so that it is in a plane parallel to the plane of the desk.

This is a very important job. You must hold the triangle in a plane parallel to the plane of the desk at all times.

Step 5 Have another student gather the three pieces of string together above the triangle.

Step 6 Have the third student stretch the other ends of the strings out and tape them to a piece of paper on the desk. Mark the three points where the strings touch the desk, and connect them to form a new triangle.

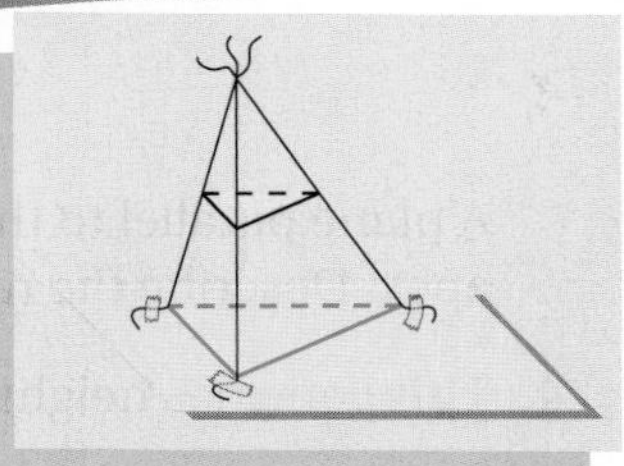

Step 7 Mark the strings where they touch the apex A, the cardboard triangle B, and the paper triangle C. Find the ratios $\frac{AB}{AC}$ for each string. How do they compare?

Step 8 Now compare the cardboard triangle to the triangle drawn on the paper.

As you discuss your results with the whole class, relate the experience to dilation by the Ratio Method.

- Where is the center of dilation in this experiment?
- Why were the strings cut proportionally by the cardboard triangle?
- What is the relationship between the cardboard triangle and the paper triangle?

In the In-Class Experiment, you showed that the Ratio Method works in three dimensions. So when you cut a pyramid with a plane parallel to the base of the pyramid, the resulting cross section will be a polygon similar to the base of the pyramid.

For You to Explore

1. A right square pyramid has a base with side length 6 in. and height 9 in. A plane cuts the pyramid 3 inches above and parallel to the base.

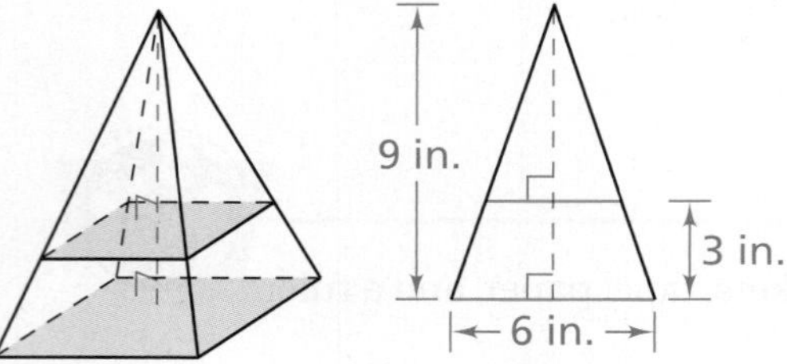

Describe the shape of the intersection of the pyramid with the cross-sectional plane. Calculate the area of the cross section.

2. The pyramid from Exercise 1 is cut by a plane that is parallel to its base and h inches above its base. Describe the resulting cross section. Calculate the area of the cross section in terms of h.

3. The square pyramid below has a base with side length 8 cm and height 5 cm.

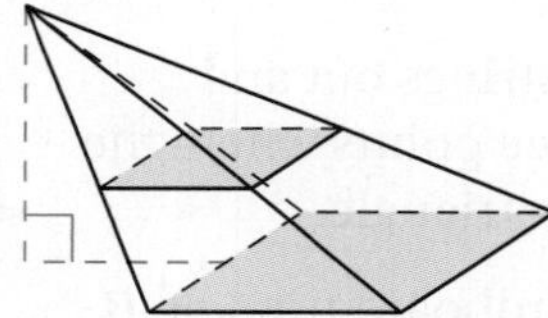

A plane parallel to the plane of its base cuts the pyramid 3 cm below its apex. Describe the resulting cross section. Calculate its area.

4. This cone has height 6 inches and a base with radius 2 inches.

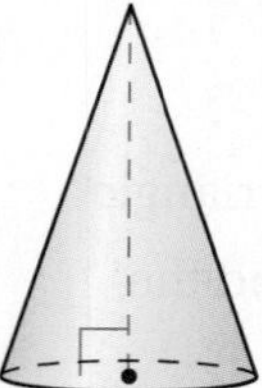

You plan to cut the cone parallel to its base so that the area of the resulting cross section will be 2 square inches. At what height from the base should you cut the cone?

Exercises *Practicing Habits of Mind*

On Your Own

5. A line parallel to $\overline{BC}$ intersects $\triangle ABC$ in $\overline{DE}$ as shown.

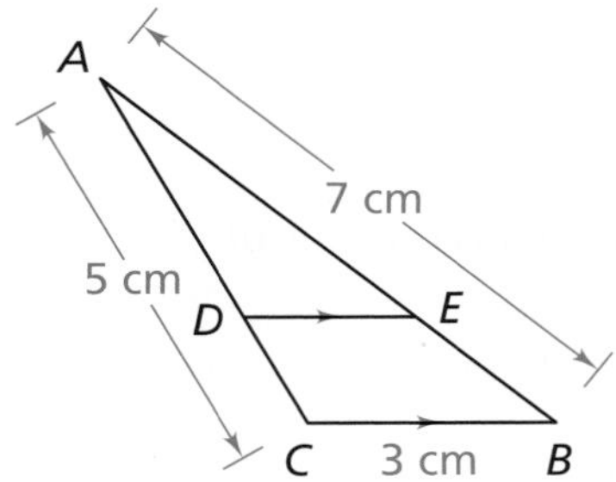

a. Find DE if the distance from D to $\overleftrightarrow{BC}$ is 1 cm.

b. What is the distance from D to $\overleftrightarrow{BC}$ when DE is 2 cm?

6. This triangular pyramid has a base with area 4 cm^2 and height 2 cm.

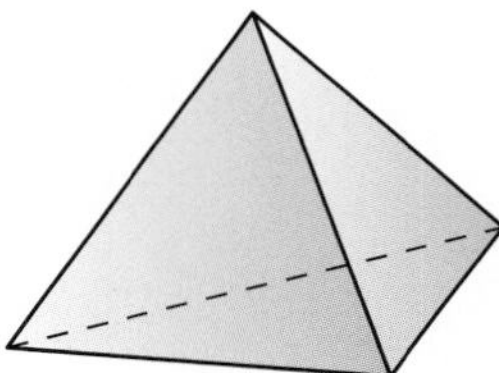

a. The pyramid is cut by a plane parallel to its base and 1 cm above it. Find the area of the cross section.

b. You want to make a parallel cross section of the pyramid with area 3 cm^2. How high above the base of the pyramid must you cut?

Go Online
Pearsonsuccessnet.com

7. A line intersects a circle of radius 6 cm.

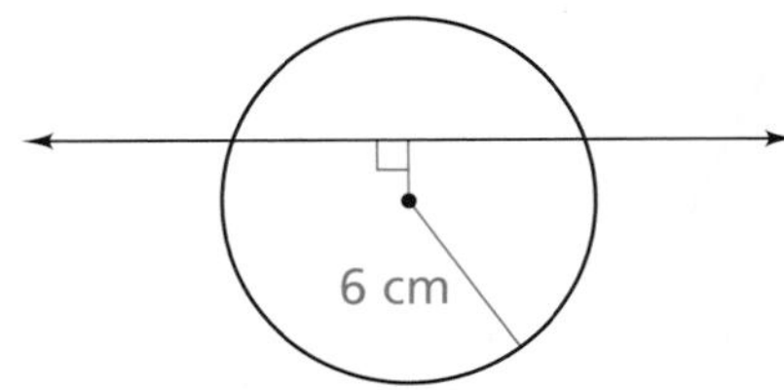

a. If the line is 2 cm from the center of the circle, what is the length of the chord?

b. If the chord has length 10.4 cm, how far is the line from the center?

8. A plane intersects a sphere of radius 12 cm.

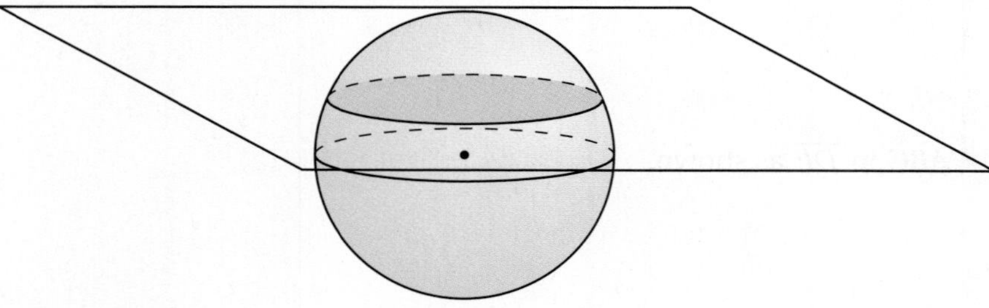

a. If the plane is 3 cm from the center of the sphere, what is the area of the cross section?

b. If the cross section has area 4π cm^2, how far is the plane from the center?

9. In the figure below, $\overline{VH}$ is the altitude of the pyramid *VABC*. $\overline{VH'}$ is an altitude of the smaller pyramid $VA'B'C'$. Determine the scale factor of $\triangle ABC$ and $\triangle A'B'C'$ in terms of *VH* and *VH'*.

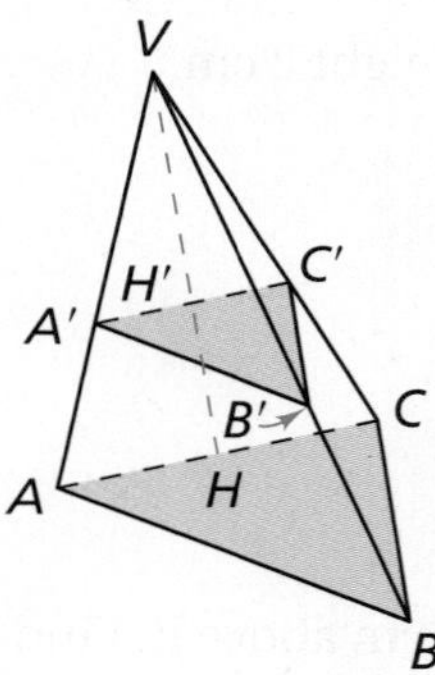

10. The rectangular prism and cone below both have height 8 in.

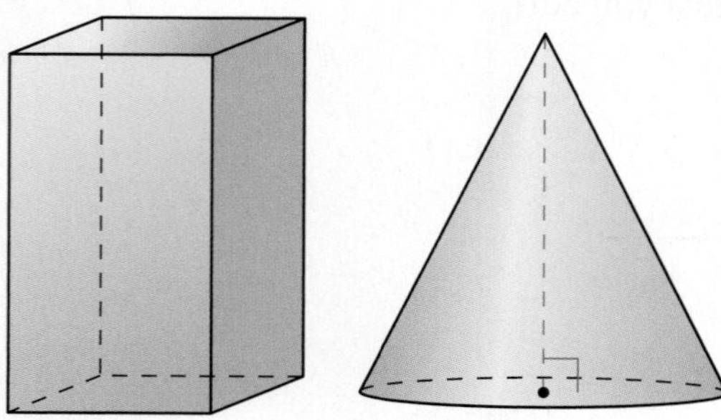

The prism has a square base. The radius of the base of the cone is 4 in. The cross section of the prism has the same area as the cross section of the cone at a height of 3 in. from their bases. What is the side length of the square base of the prism?

11. You drop a bowling ball with diameter 9.4 inches into a square hole with side length 6 inches. How far into the hole does the bowling ball get stuck?

Maintain Your Skills

For each pair of solids in Exercises 12–14, find the height from the bottom at which both solids have the same cross-sectional area.

12. The cylinder has radius 2 in. The cone has radius 4 in. They both have height 5 in.

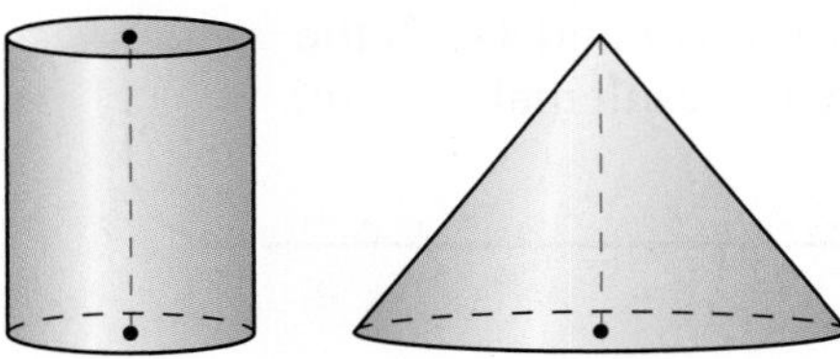

13. The cylinder has radius 3 in. and height 8 in. The sphere has radius 4 in.

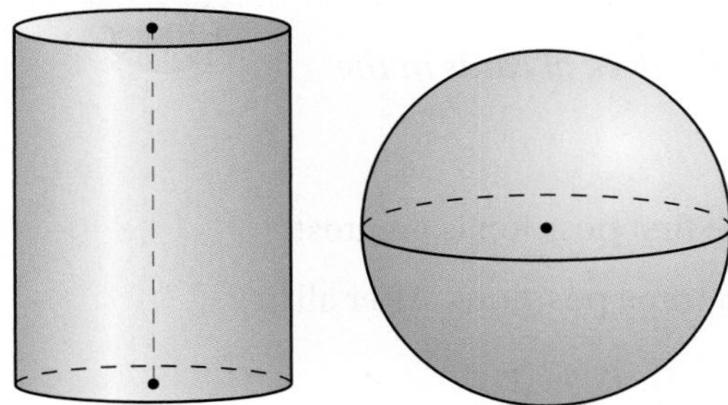

14. The cone has radius 5 in. and height 6 in. The sphere has radius 3 in.

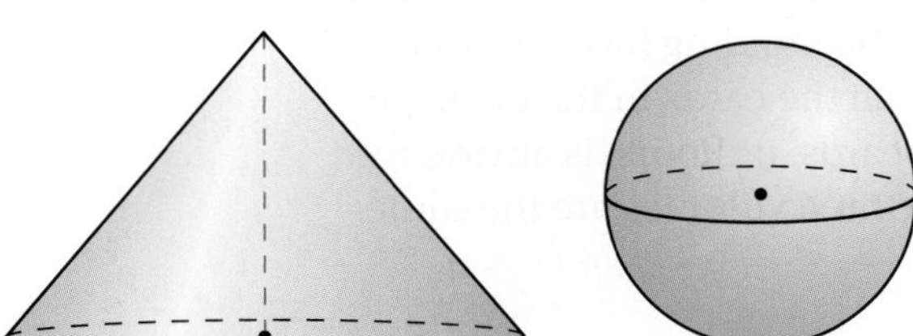

6.11 Cavalieri's Principle

Below are three diagrams of the same deck of cards in three different positions.

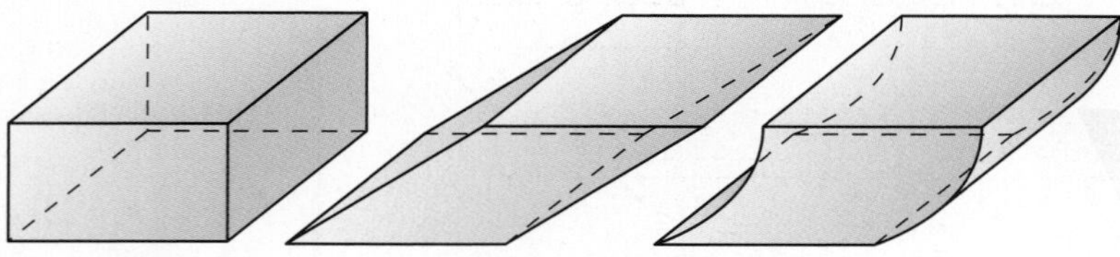

For Discussion

1. Compare the volumes of the deck of cards in positions 2 and 3 with the volume of the deck of cards in position 1. Does your result make sense? Explain and discuss your ideas with the class.

Minds in Action episode 27

Sasha, Tony, and Derman are thinking about the deck of cards in the pictures above.

Tony I think the volume of the deck in the first position is greatest.

Derman I think the volume is the same in all three positions. After all, it's the *same* deck of cards!

Tony But the deck in position 1 *looks* bigger.

Sasha Well, you know that looks can be deceiving. Think of the deck of cards as a building. Every "floor" of the building has the same area. Each floor is a single card and all the cards in the deck are the same size. Since the number of cards, or floors, is always the same, it would make sense that the three volumes are the same.

In the 1600s, an Italian mathematician named Bonaventura Cavalieri formalized Sasha's idea.

This is why his name is the one attached to the principle.

Postulate 6.1 Cavalieri's Principle

Two solids of the same height are cut by a plane so that the resulting cross sections have the same area. If the solids also have cross-sectional areas equal to each other when cut by any plane parallel to the first, then they have the same volume.

Picture how Cavalieri's Principle can be used to find the volume of the deck of cards in positions 2 and 3. The bottom card of the deck, in each position, lies in the same plane—the plane of the table. The plane in the figure below is parallel to this bottom plane.

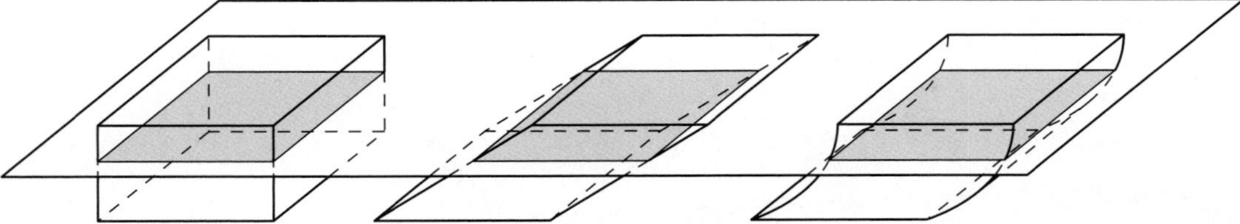

You can see that the intersection of this plane with each solid is a rectangle of equal area—the area of a single card. This means that each cross section has equal area. This is also true for *every* plane parallel to the bottom plane, all the way up to the plane that passes through the top card of each deck.

Cavalieri's Principle states that all three decks must have the same volume.

Example

Problem Show that all pyramids that have the same height and the same base area must have the same volume.

Solution Start with two pyramids with height h and bases with area A. The two bases can be any polygonal shape. Position the pyramids so that their bases both lie in the same plane. Then find any other plane parallel to the plane of the bases that intersects the two pyramids.

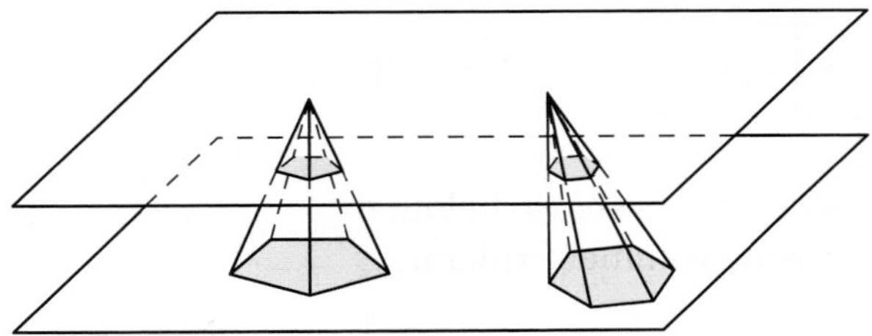

Call the distance of this cutting plane from the apexes of the pyramids b. Think of the apex of each pyramid as a center of dilation in the ratio method. You can conclude that the cross sections created by the cutting plane are similar to the bases of their corresponding pyramids.

You also know the scale factor of the dilation must be $\frac{b}{h}$. Since the area of each base is A, the areas of these cross sections must both be $A\left(\frac{b}{h}\right)^2$.

Both cross sections must have the same area for any height b. So you can conclude that these two pyramids must have the same volume.

Remember...

The area of a dilation is equal to the square of the scale factor multiplied by the area of the original figure.

For You to Do

2. A triangular pyramid and a square pyramid have equal volume and the same height, 3 in. The base of the triangular pyramid has side lengths 3 in., 4 in., and 5 in. Find the side length of the base of the square pyramid.

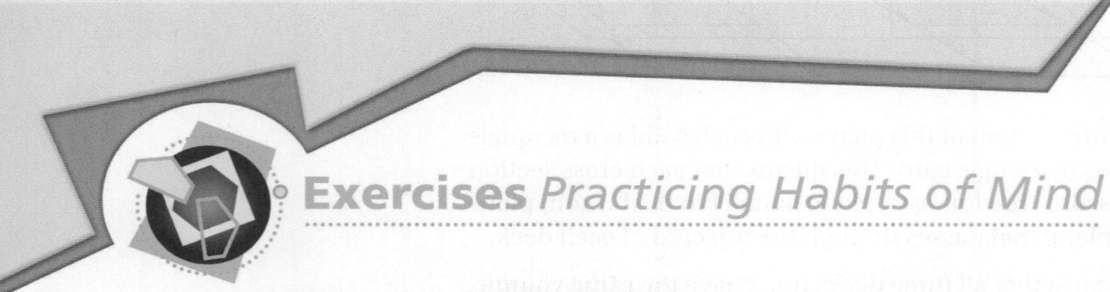

Exercises *Practicing Habits of Mind*

Check Your Understanding

1. The two shaded circles in the figure below have the same area. Must the two solids have the same volume? Explain.

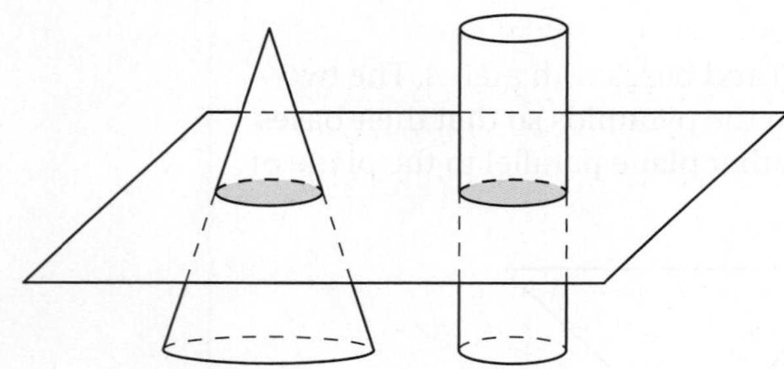

2. You can deform a right prism by pushing it sideways as shown below, to form a new solid. Do the two solids have the same volume? Explain.

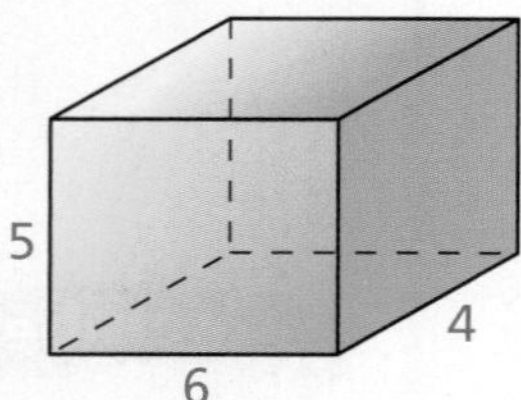

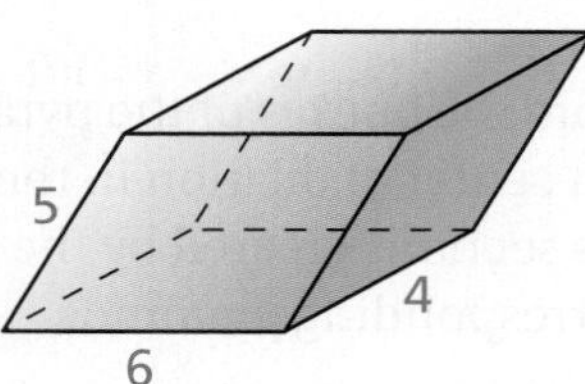

3. Here are two rectangular prisms.

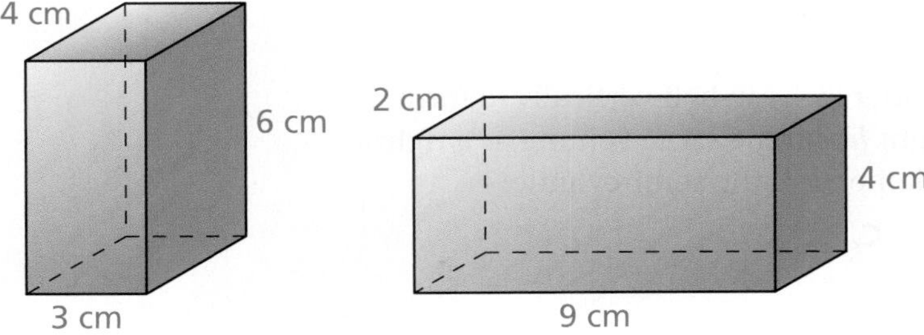

a. Calculate the volume of each prism.

b. Can you use Cavalieri's Principle to conclude that the two prisms have the same volume? Explain.

On Your Own

4. The converse of Cavalieri's Principle is not necessarily true.

You have two solids that have equal volumes. Suppose there is a plane that intersects those two solids in equal-area cross sections. This does *not* guarantee that every plane parallel to the first plane will also intersect the solids in equal-area cross sections.

Show an example that demonstrates this. Give enough measurements to define each of the solids. Locate a plane that produces equal-area cross sections and a parallel plane that produces unequal-area cross sections.

5. **Write About It** What happens to the assertion in Exercise 4 if you are comparing two prisms of equal height? Are there any other shapes that could be included in this exception? Explain.

6. A cylinder has height 6 inches and radius 3 inches. A prism with a square base has the same volume and height. What is the side length of the base of the prism?

7. A cylinder and a prism with a square base have the same volume V and height h. The cylinder has radius r. What is the side length of the square base of the prism?

8. **Standardized Test Prep** A right cylinder is cut in half vertically to form a semi-cylinder. It has the same height h and the same volume as a right cylinder with radius r. What is the diameter of the semi-cylinder?

   A. $2r$ **B.** $r\sqrt{2}$ **C.** $2r\sqrt{2}$ **D.** $4r$

Exercises 9 and 10 ask you to think about Cavalieri's Principle in two dimensions.

You can divide the two quadrilaterals in the figure into an equal number of congruent rectangles with height that can be as small as you want. Because the corresponding rectangles in each quadrilateral are always congruent no matter how small they get, the two quadrilaterals must have the same area.

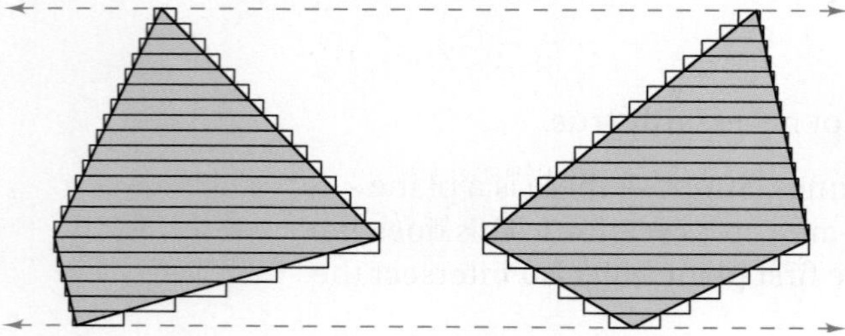

Habits of Mind

Reason. Reason by continuity, making the heights smaller and smaller. What happens as the height of the rectangles approaches zero?

In two dimensions, Cavalieri's Principle can be stated as follows.

Suppose you have two 2-dimensional figures. Draw a line that intersects both figures. In each figure, that intersection will be a segment. If both segments have equal length, and if every line parallel to your original line also intersects both figures in segments of equal length, then the two figures must have equal area.

9. Use Cavalieri's Principle to show that any two triangles that have the same base and height must also have the same area.

10. Two polygons have the same area. Line ℓ intersects them both in segments of equal length. Does this guarantee that every line parallel to ℓ intersects both polygons in segments of equal length? If so, explain your reasoning. If not, give a counterexample.

11. A hollow square prism with height 1 foot, as pictured below, has the same volume as a solid square prism with the same height and a base with a 2-inch side length.

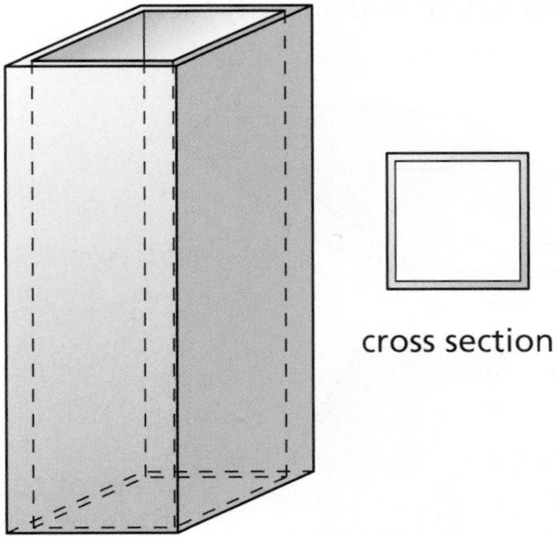

The thickness of the sides of the hollow square prism is $\frac{1}{4}$ inch. What is the side length of the outside square?

12. A hollow cylindrical pipe with height 1 foot has the same volume as a solid square prism with the same height and a base with a 2-inch side length.

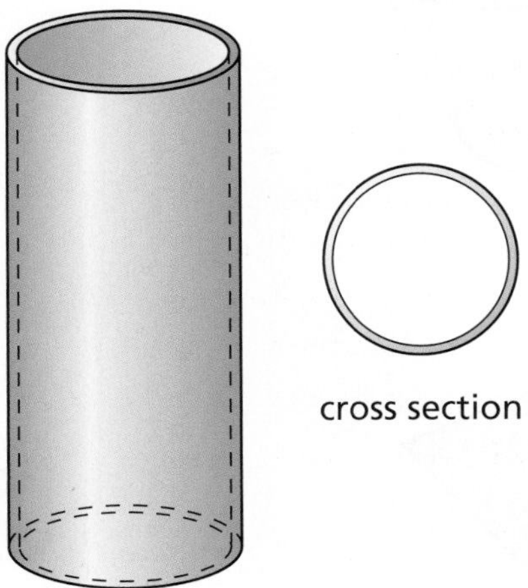

The thickness of the wall of the cylindrical pipe is $\frac{1}{4}$ inch. What is the radius of the outside circle?

Maintain Your Skills

13. Compare the volumes of each pair of solids. In each case, explain why their volumes are the same or different.

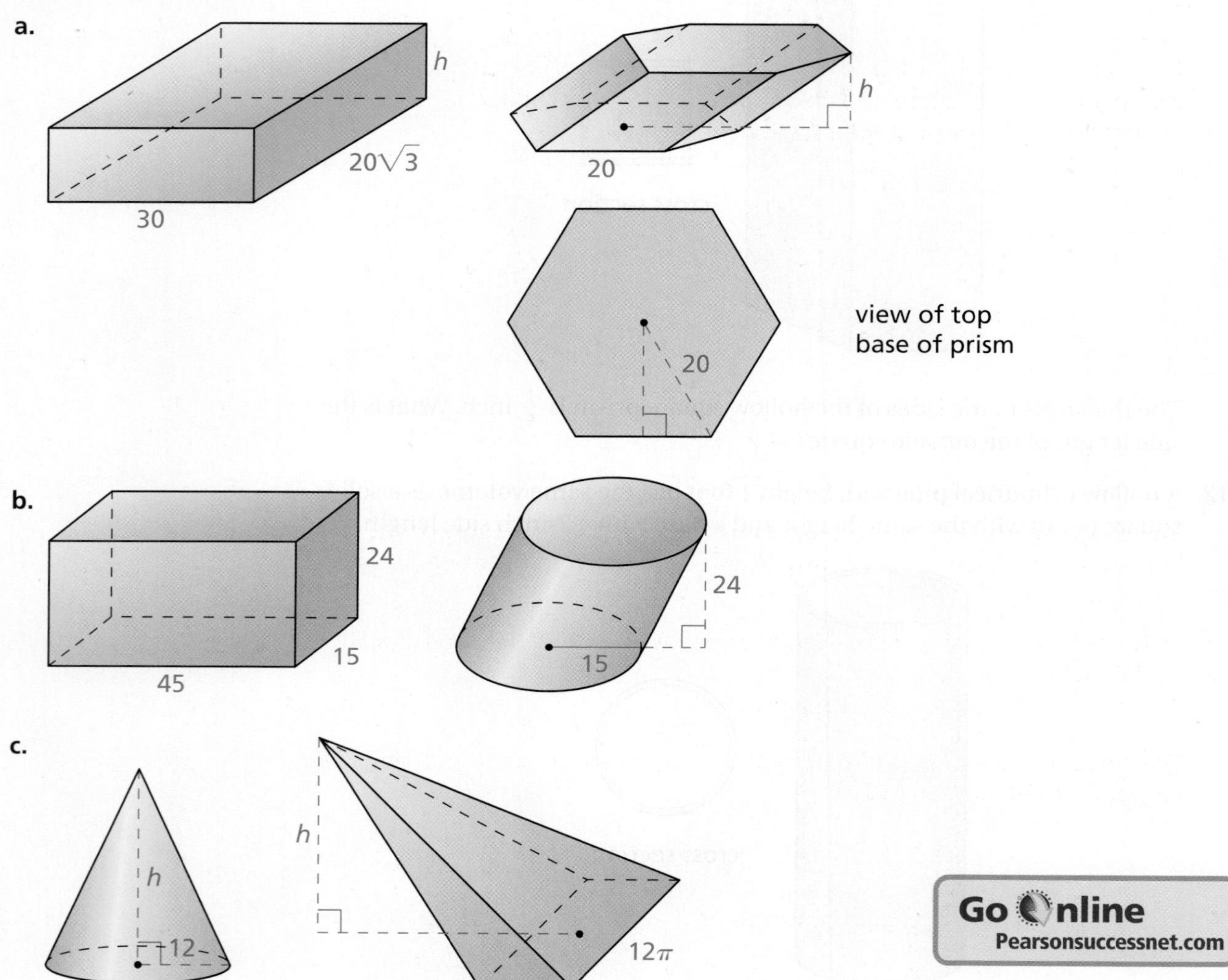

Go Online
Pearsonsuccessnet.com

6.12 Proving Volume Formulas

Cavalieri's Principle is very useful when it comes to proving volume formulas. In this lesson, you will prove formulas for a general prism, a cylinder, a pyramid, and a cone. You will start with the formula for the volume of a right rectangular prism and use Cavalieri's Principle.

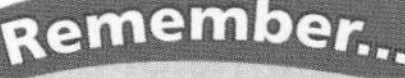

Do you remember how to find the volume of a right rectangular prism with dimensions *a*, *b*, and *c*?

For You to Do

The picture below represents two prisms: the prism on the left is a right rectangular prism, and the prism on the right has a triangular base and is not right. Both prisms have the same height.

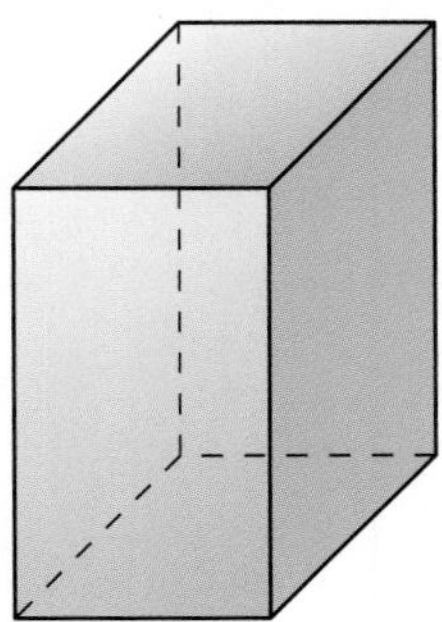

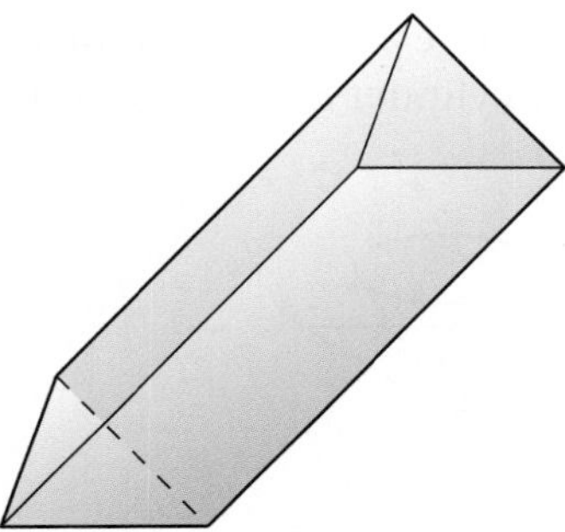

The area of the base of the rectangular prism is 24 cm^2. The area of the base of the triangular prism is also 24 cm^2. The heights of the two prisms are both 7 cm.

1. Determine the volume of the triangular prism, if possible. If you cannot, explain why.

You can generalize your solution for the problem above in the For You to Do with the following theorem.

Theorem 6.3

The volume of a prism is equal to the product of the area of its base and its height.

h

A_{base}

$$V_{prism} = A_{base} \cdot h$$

Suppose the base of the triangular prism in the For You to Do is a circle. You can generalize Theorem 6.3 as follows.

Theorem 6.4

The volume of a cylinder is equal to the product of the area of its base (a circle) and its height.

$V_{\text{cylinder}} = A_{\text{base}} \cdot h$

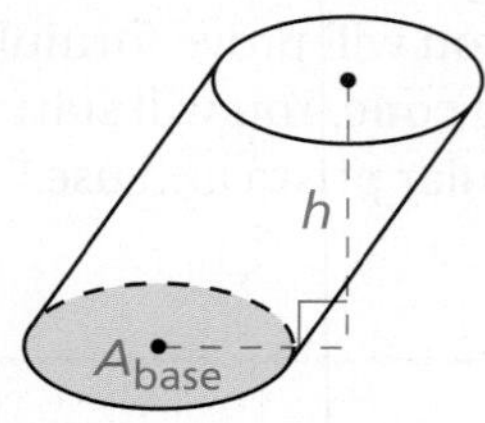

For Discussion

The area of the base of the cylinder is the same as the area of the base of the rectangular right prism. The height of the cylinder is the same as the height of the rectangular prism.

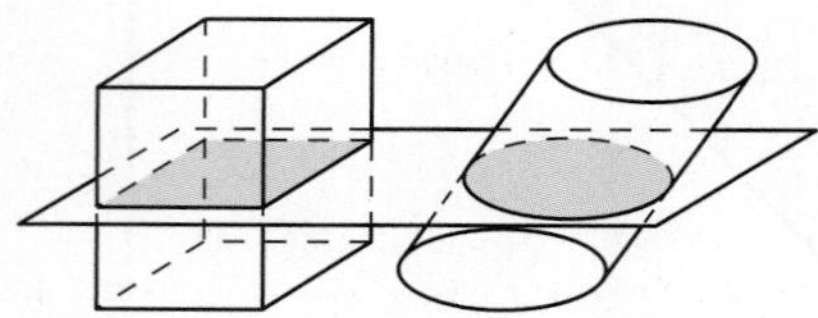

2. Explain how to apply Cavalieri's Principle to the two solids.

3. What can you prove about their volumes?

Minds in Action episode 28

Tony, Sasha, and Derman are trying to use Cavalieri's Principle to find the formula for the volume of the pyramid below.

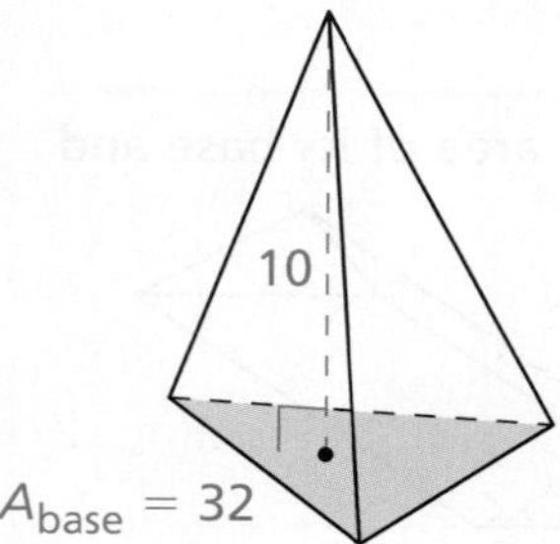

Sasha Let's think of some kind of pyramid we already know how to find the volume of.

Tony I know! Look at this. A cube contains exactly three congruent square pyramids.

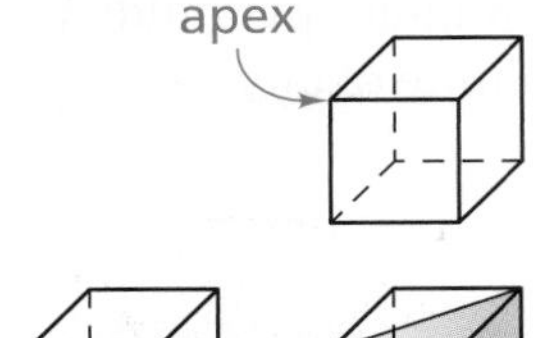

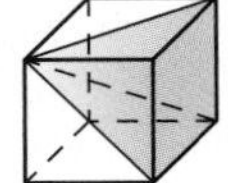

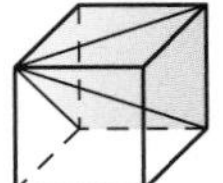

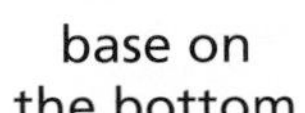

base on the bottom   base on the right   base at the back

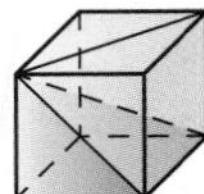

Sasha Great, that's really cool! So we know that the volume of a square pyramid with height equal to the side length of its base is $\frac{1}{3}$ the volume of the cube it's contained in.

Now what if we had a square pyramid with height different from its base?

Derman Oh, that's easy. If the cube's height is scaled by some factor, say, 3, then its volume is three times larger. So the volume of the pyramid must also be three times larger, too, because it was scaled in the same way.

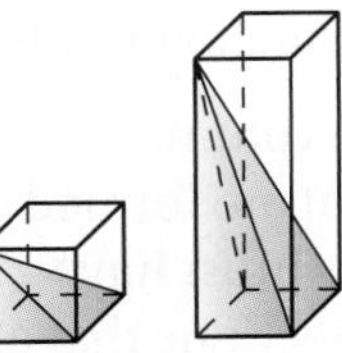

Tony OK, so now if we construct a square pyramid with the same height as our pyramid with base area 32, we can use Cavalieri's Principle.

Each pair of cross sections is similar to the base. For any cutting plane, the scale factor for both cross sections is the same. That means each pair of cross sections will have the same area.

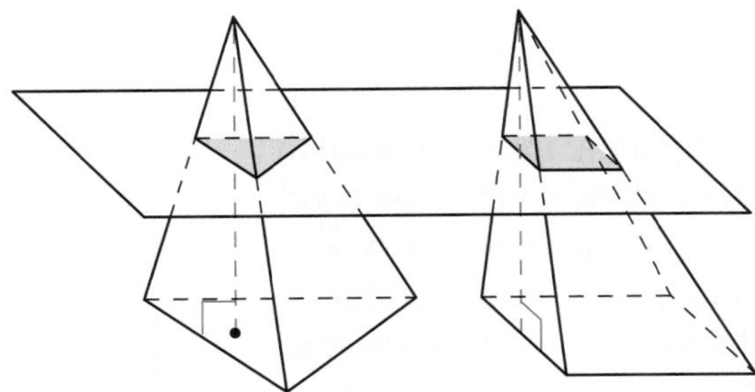

Sasha Right! So the volume of our pyramid is $\frac{32 \cdot 10}{3}$. That's one third of the corresponding prism's volume.

Remember...

Remember the In-Class Experiment in Lesson 6.10? The intersection of a plane parallel to the base of a pyramid with the pyramid is a polygon similar to the base of the pyramid.

For You to Do

4. Use Cavalieri's Principle to help you find the volume of a triangular pyramid by comparing it to a square pyramid. Could you find the volume of any pyramid in this way?

Theorem 6.5 summarizes your work.

Theorem 6.5

The volume of a pyramid is equal to one third of the product of the area of its base and its height.

$$V_{\text{pyramid}} = \frac{A_{\text{base}} \cdot h}{3}$$

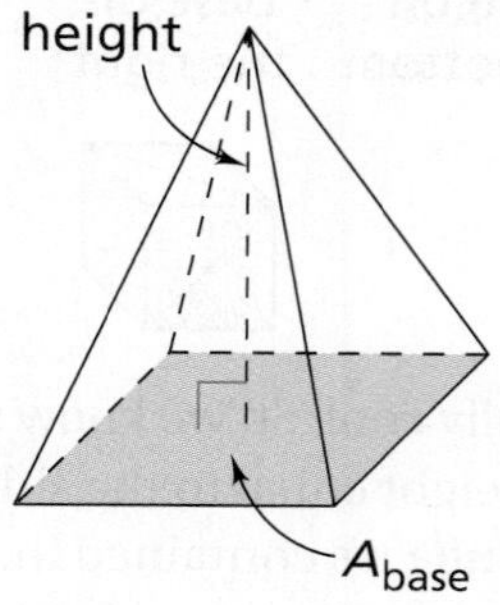

Example

Problem Find a square pyramid that has the same height and volume as a cone of radius r and height h. What is the volume of the square pyramid?

Solution To show that the pyramid and the cone have the same volume, consider the cross sections of the pyramid and the cone that are formed by a set of parallel planes. The corresponding cross sections must have equal areas. It makes the most sense to consider the cross sections that are formed by planes that are parallel to the base of each figure.

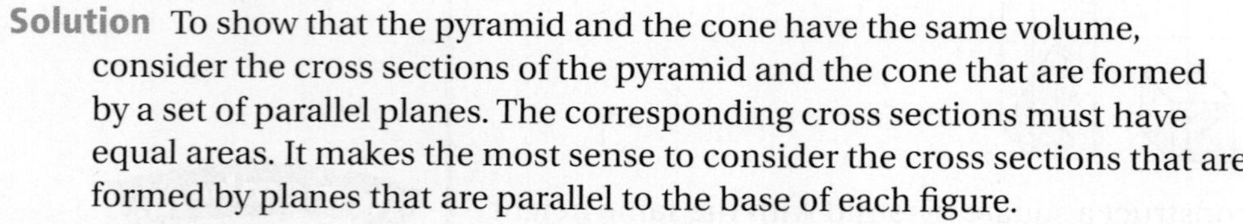

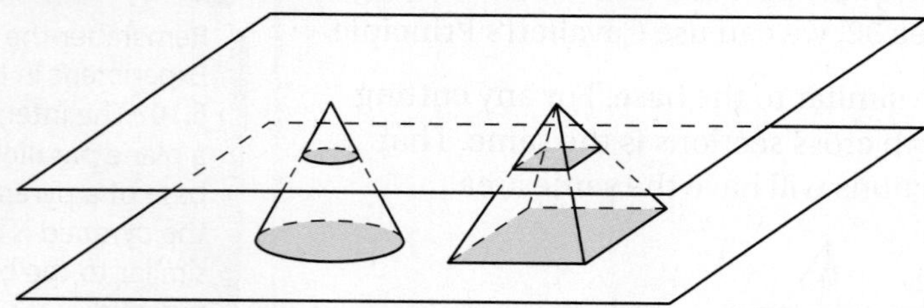

In particular, the area of the square base of the pyramid must be equal to the area of the circular base of the cone. The area of the cone's base is πr^2. For the square to have this area, its side length must be $\sqrt{\pi r^2}$, or $r\sqrt{\pi}$. To be certain that the areas of the corresponding cross sections of the pyramid and cone are the same, remember the ratio method. Suppose a plane intersects the pyramid and the cone at some distance d from the plane that contains the apexes of the pyramid and cone. This plane forms two corresponding cross sections. You can think of these cross sections as the bases of a dilated pyramid and cone. The scale factor is $\frac{d}{h}$. The areas of the dilated bases, or cross sections, will both be equal to $\left(\frac{d}{h}\right)^2$ times the areas of the bases of the original pyramid and cone.

Since the pyramid and the cone have the same height and the same cross-sectional area for any plane that is parallel to their bases, the pyramid and the cone have the same volume. The volume of the square pyramid is $\frac{1}{3}(r\sqrt{\pi})^2 \cdot h$, or $\frac{1}{3}(\pi r^2)(h)$.

Theorem 6.6 is a result of the example above.

Theorem 6.6

The volume of a cone is equal to one third of the product of the area of its base (a circle) and its height.

$$V_{\text{cone}} = \frac{A_{\text{base}} \cdot h}{3}$$

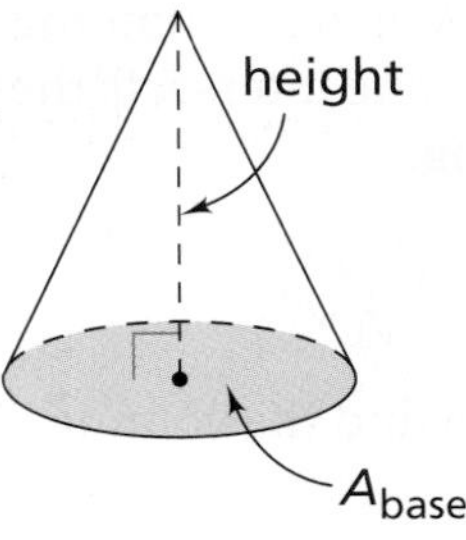

For Discussion

5. Explain why you cannot use the techniques from this lesson to find a volume formula for a figure like the one below.

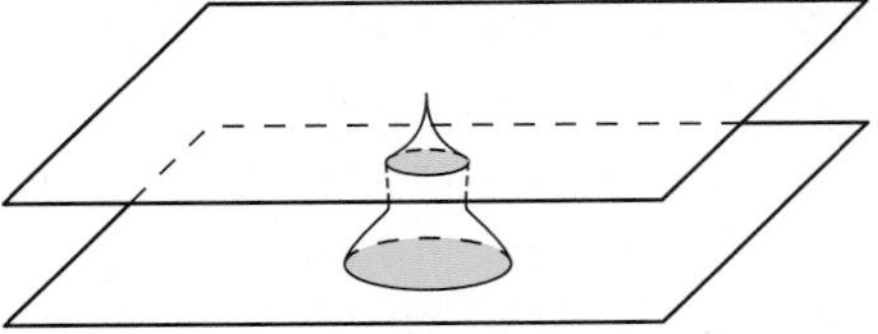

What angle cut at the center of a circle will give you a cone with the greatest volume?

Exercises *Practicing Habits of Mind*

Check Your Understanding

1. Use the cone at the right. A plane containing O' and parallel to the base of the cone intersects the cone in a circle. Prove the following.

$$\frac{A_{circle}}{A_{base}} = \frac{(VO')^2}{VO^2}$$

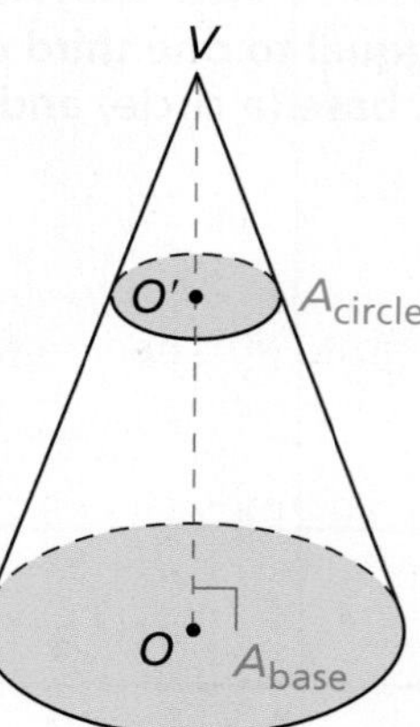

2. Use Cavalieri's Principle to find the volume of the pyramid below.

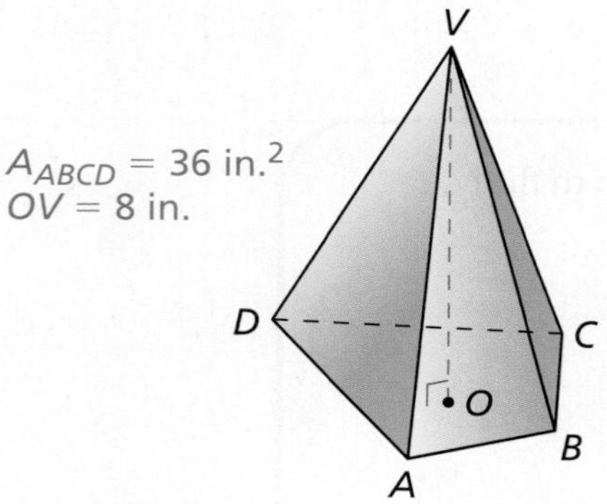

3. a. Find the volume of a triangular pyramid of height 5 cm that has a right triangle base with legs that measure 4 cm and 6 cm.

b. Find the radius of the cone that has the same volume and height as the triangular pyramid.

4. A triangular pyramid and a cone are standing on the same plane. They have equal base areas and the same height h. The cone has base radius r.

a. Give a possible set of dimensions for the base of the pyramid.

b. A plane parallel to the bases intersects the two solids. What can you say about the resulting cross sections?

5. Use Cavalieri's Principle to conclude that the volume of the cone and the volume of the pyramid from Exercise 4 are the same.

On Your Own

6. The base of a cone has radius 2 ft. The height of the cone is 6 ft. What is the volume of the cone?

7. A prism has a square base of side 4 cm. Its lateral faces are two rectangles and two parallelograms like the ones below. Determine the volume of the prism.

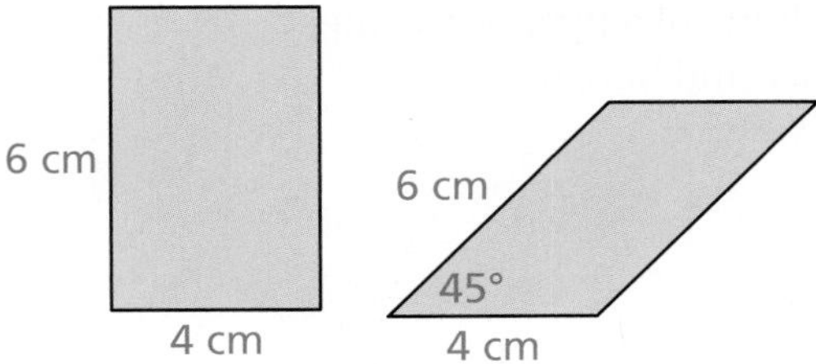

Remember...

A tetrahedron is a pyramid that has congruent equilateral triangles for all faces.

8. The area of one face of a regular tetrahedron is $16\sqrt{3}\text{ cm}^2$. What is its volume?

9. Another way to see that the volume of a pyramid is one third the volume of the prism with the same base and height is to look at a triangular prism.

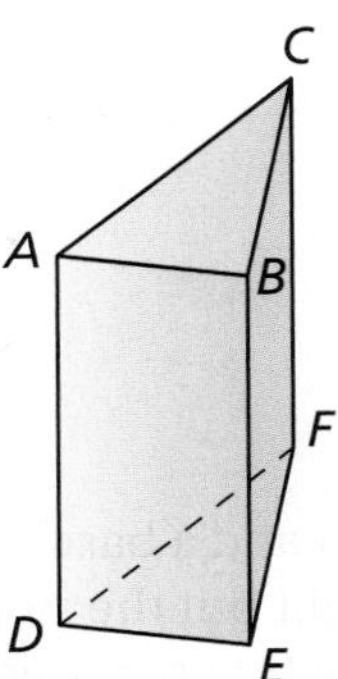

You can cut a triangular prism into three triangular pyramids. In the dissection of the cube in the lesson, the three pyramids were congruent. Here they are not, but you can show that they do have the same volume.

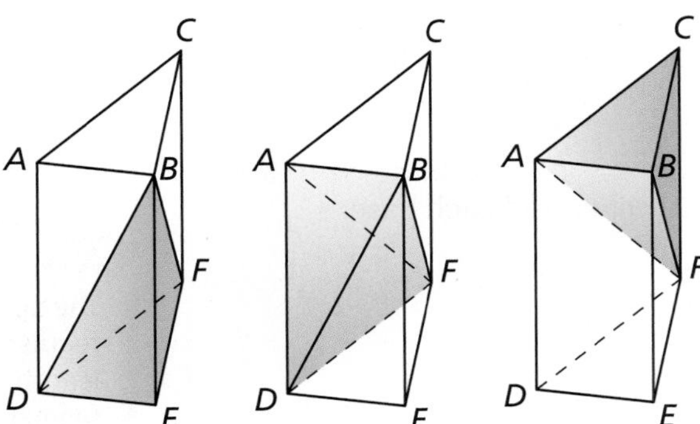

a. Consider the green and blue pyramids. The height of each pyramid is the length of a perpendicular from C to plane $ABED$. If the bases are congruent, then they have the same volume. Show that $\triangle BDE \cong \triangle DBA$.

b. Consider the green and purple pyramids. The green pyramid has base $\triangle DEF$ and height BE. What base and height for the purple pyramid would show that these two pyramids must have the same volume?

c. Complete the argument to show that the volume of a pyramid is one-third the area of the prism with the same base and height.

10. What is the volume of the solid below?

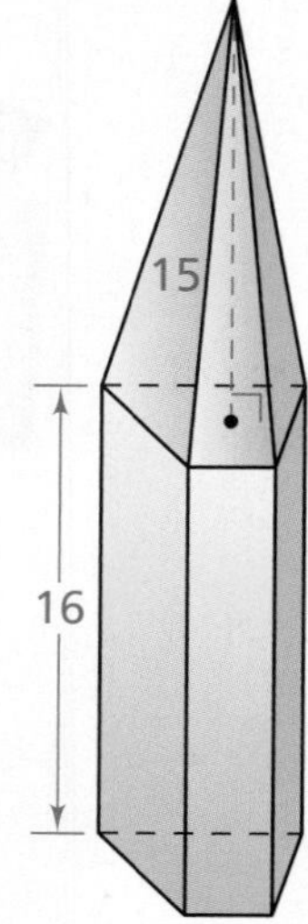

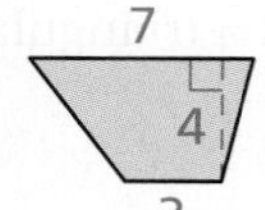

The base is a trapezoid.

11. **Standardized Test Prep** A square pyramid has height 10 cm and a base area of 36 cm^2. A second square pyramid has the same height but the side lengths of its base are double those of the side lengths of the first pyramid. What is the ratio of the volume of the second pyramid to the volume of the first pyramid?

A. 2 : 1 **B.** 4 : 1 **C.** 6 : 1 **D.** 8 : 1

Maintain Your Skills

12. Find the volume of a pyramid with height 12 inches and each base described below. Approximate if necessary.

a. an equilateral triangle with apothem 1 in.

b. a square with apothem 1 in.

c. a regular pentagon with apothem 1 in.

d. a regular hexagon with apothem 1 in.

e. a regular octagon with apothem 1 in.

13. Find the volume of a cone with height 12 in. and radius 1 in.

Remember...

The apothem *a* of a regular polygon is the length of a perpendicular segment from the center point of the polygon to one of its sides.

6.13 Volume of a Sphere

You can use Cavalieri's Principle to show that two different solids have the same volume. If you know how to find the volume of one of the solids, you can use that result as the volume of the other. You can even develop new volume formulas for new classes of solids. However, the tricky part of using Cavalieri's Principle is that you have to know which two solids to compare.

For Discussion

To find a solid to compare to a sphere of radius r using Cavalieri's Principle, it might be a good idea to use one of the round solids with a volume formula that you already know. The cross sections of a sphere are small circles at first. Then the circles get larger and larger as you approach the center of the sphere. The circles then gradually decrease in size as you move away from the center of the sphere.

1. Would a bicone work?

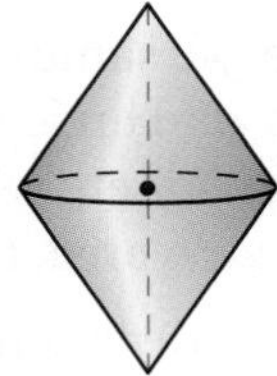

If so, describe the dimensions of the bicone as completely as possible. If not, describe the problems you encounter.

In fact, this is not a simple problem to solve. The Greek mathematician Archimedes was finally able to prove the volume formula for a sphere. It is said that he was so thrilled that he wanted his solution to the problem to be engraved on his tombstone.

You and your classmates may not have been able to think of a choice of what solid to compare to the sphere. But you can still demonstrate the comparison.

Minds in Action

episode 29

Sasha and Tony are comparing the cross sections of a sphere and a cylinder with a double cone removed from it. The sphere has radius r, and the cross section of the sphere is at a distance h from the center of the sphere. The cylinder with the double cone removed from it has radius r and height 2r.

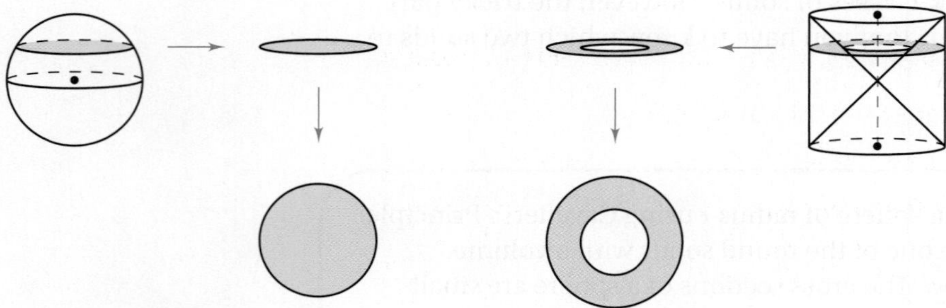

Sasha The cross sections of the cylinder-minus-cones solid will be rings. The outside radius of the ring will always be the same, but the inside radius will get smaller and then larger as you move downward from the top.

Tony We can say that the areas of three cross sections are the same right away. At the very top and bottom, the ring has zero area. At those same two heights, the plane that intersects the sphere will intersect it in a point, so that intersection will have zero area, too.

Sasha Yes, and halfway up the cylinder, the radius of each cone is zero. The intersection with the plane is just a circle of radius r. That's exactly the same area and shape as the intersection of that plane with the sphere.

Tony But now we have to prove it works for all the planes parallel to the base of the cylinder-minus-cones solid.

Sasha I'm guessing similar triangles are going to help us.

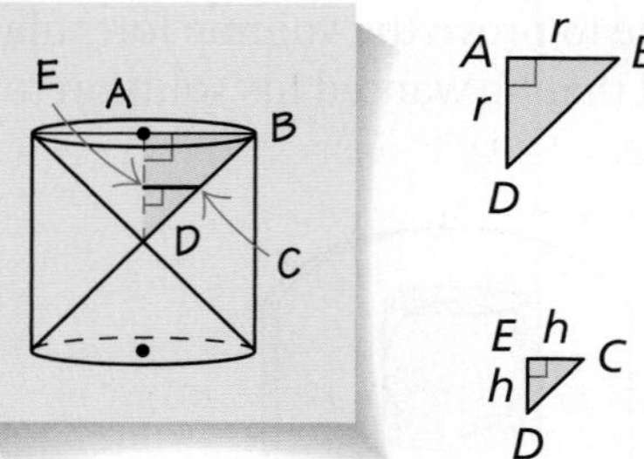

We know $\triangle ABD$ is an isosceles right triangle, because the cones both have base radius r and height r. Since $\triangle ECD \sim \triangle ABD$, then it's an isosceles right triangle, too! So we know the inner radius and the outer radius. So we can find the area of the ring.

How does Sasha know that the two triangles are similar?

Tony So now we have to find the area of the intersection of the plane at height h with the sphere. I'm going to label the sphere with everything I know.

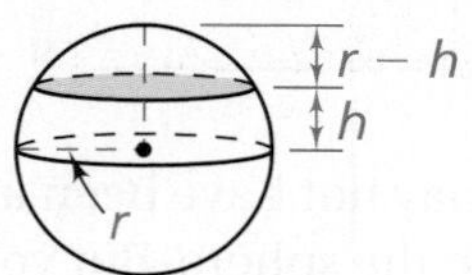

If the area of the cross section of the sphere is the same as the ring, we've done it!

For You to Do

Use the figures and dimensions from the Minds in Action. Finish Tony and Sasha's work.

You may want to use the ratio method.

2. Find the area of the intersection of the plane and the cylinder-minus-cones solid using Sasha's similar triangles.
3. Find the area of the cross section of the sphere using Tony's sketch.
4. How can you be sure that these two solids have the same volume? Explain.
5. What is the volume of the cylinder-minus-cones solid?

Your work so far is proof of the following formula.

Theorem 6.7

The volume of a sphere with radius r is $\frac{4}{3}\pi r^3$.

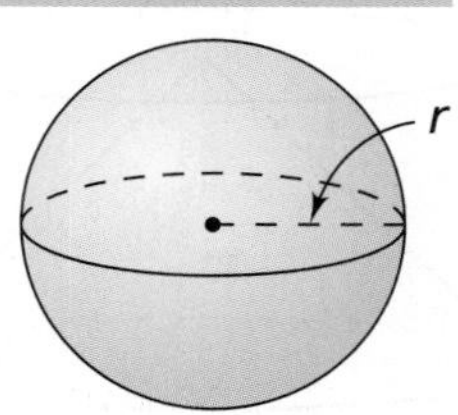

You also can confirm the formula for the surface area of a sphere now that you are sure about its volume. Think of the sphere as being made of some large number n of tiny congruent square pyramids that are all joined so that the apex of each pyramid is at the center of the sphere.

Each pyramid has height r and a square base that is on the sphere. Call the area of each square base b. The areas of all n bases, or nb, is the surface area of the sphere.

Each pyramid has volume $\frac{1}{3}br$. If you add the volumes of the n pyramids, you get the total volume of the sphere, so

$$V_{\text{sphere}} = n\left(\frac{1}{3}br\right)$$

Set the two volume formulas equal to each other.

$$n\left(\frac{1}{3}br\right) = \frac{4}{3}\pi r^3$$

If you solve this equation for nb, you get the formula for the surface area of the sphere.

Habits of Mind

Look for connections. The argument here is very similar to the argument in Chapter 5 relating the area and circumference of a circle.

Theorem 6.8

The surface area of a sphere with radius r is $4\pi r^2$.

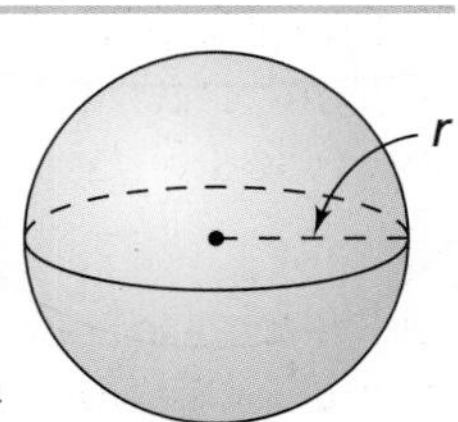

Exercises *Practicing Habits of Mind*

Check Your Understanding

1. Can two parallel planes intersect a sphere and result in cross sections with equal areas? If so, in how many ways can this happen?

Can two nonparallel planes intersect a sphere and create cross sections with equal areas? If so, in how many ways can this happen? Explain.

2. The figure shows a cylinder with a cone cut out of it.

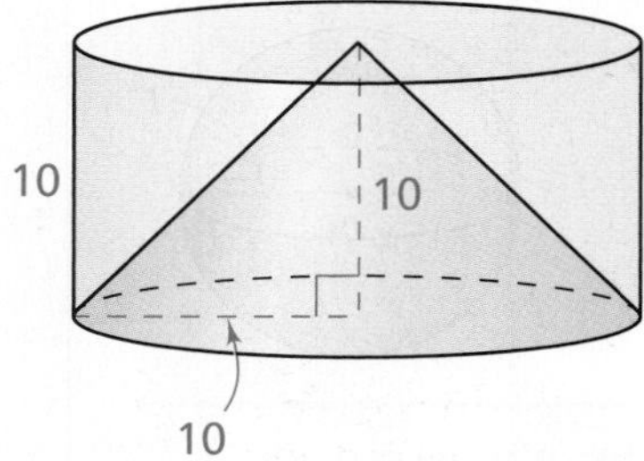

Find the volume of the cylinder-minus-cone solid. Now, use Cavalieri's Principle to compare that solid to a part of a sphere. What is the radius of the sphere the piece comes from? What is the volume of the piece of the sphere?

> What fraction of a sphere should you use?

3. You have a piece of cloth with area 45 cm^2. You can cut the cloth and arrange the pieces any way you like. What is the volume of the greatest sphere you can cover with it?

On Your Own

4. A sphere has radius 15 cm. If the shaded circle has area 25π cm^2, what is h?

> Try using Cavalieri's Principle for this.

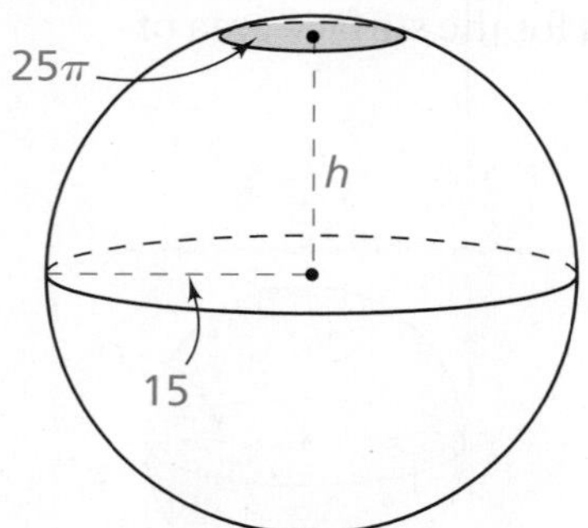

5. Standardized Test Prep Sasha peels an orange. The peel is 0.5 cm thick and each slice of orange is 5 cm long. What was the volume of the unpeeled orange?

A. 65.4 cm^3 **B.** 113.1 cm^3 **C.** 523.5 cm^3 **D.** 904.8 cm^3

In Exercises 6–9, you will investigate the problem of drilling a cylindrical hole through the center of a sphere. You begin with a wooden sphere with a radius of 5 mm. You plan to drill a cylindrical hole of radius 3 mm through its center to make it into a bead.

The original sphere and the finished bead are shown below.

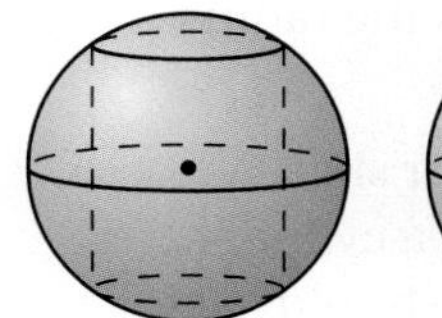

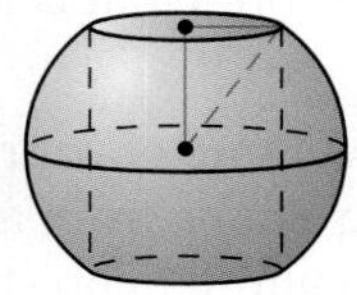

Notice that the bead is shorter than the original sphere. By drilling the cylinder, you have not precisely cut out a cylinder of wood. Instead you have cut out a sort of cylinder with a rounded top and bottom. In effect, a cap has been cut off of both the top and bottom of the sphere in addition to the cylindrical hole.

6. What is the height of the finished bead?

7. Find the volume of the finished bead. You will want to use the volume of the original wooden sphere, the volume of the cylindrical hole, and the volumes of the rounded caps that were cut off.

8. **a.** What is the radius of the sphere that has the same volume as the finished bead?

b. Show that the bead and this same-volume sphere actually have the same area at every cross section for planes perpendicular to the bead's cylindrical hole.

9. Find the volume of a bead formed by drilling a cylindrical hole of radius 2 mm through a sphere of radius 6 mm.

10. You have a perfectly spherical onion with a diameter of 13 cm. You cut off a slice $\frac{1}{2}$ cm thick as shown below.

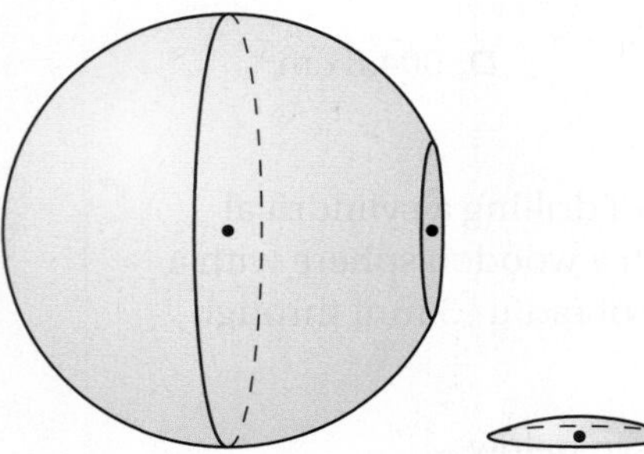

a. The slice created a circular cross section of the onion. What is the radius of that cross section?

b. You want to use Cavalieri's Principle to find the volume of your slice. As in the lesson, you will use the idea of subtracting a cone from a cylinder. What are the dimensions and the volume of the cylinder you should use?

c. You will need to subtract the volume of the frustum of a cone from that of your cylinder because you're not finding the volume of an entire sphere—just a piece. The frustum has two radii—a large radius on top and a smaller radius on the bottom. What are its radii and height?

d. What is the volume of the frustum?

e. What is the volume of your onion slice?

Remember...

Just think of a frustum as the difference of two cones. You start with a large cone and remove its tip by making a cut parallel to the base of the cone.

11. The volume of the hemisphere is 9216 in.^{3}.

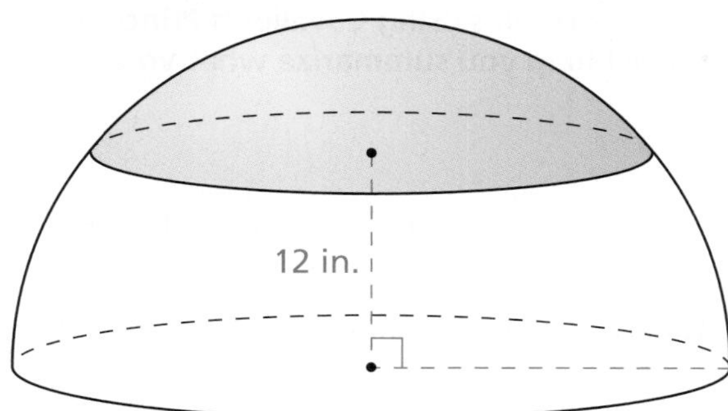

The vertical segment is 12 inches long. What is the volume of the shaded region?

Remember...

A *hemisphere* is half of a sphere.

Maintain Your Skills

12. Each figure below is rotated around line ℓ to make a solid. Find the surface area and volume of each solid.

a.

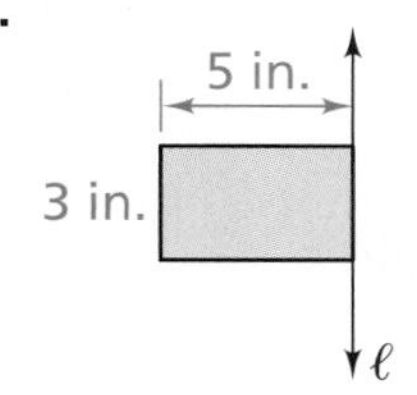

b.

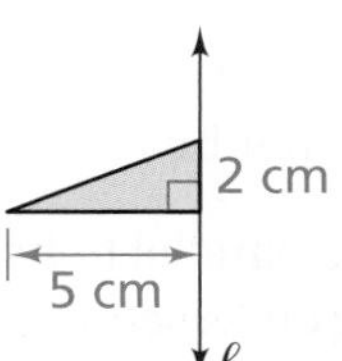

c.

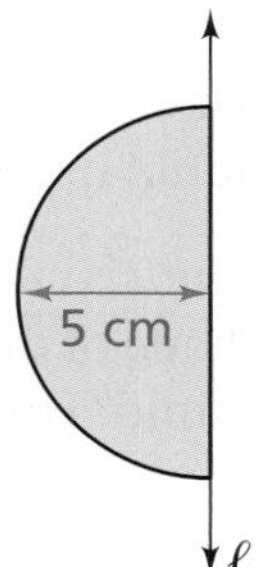

d.

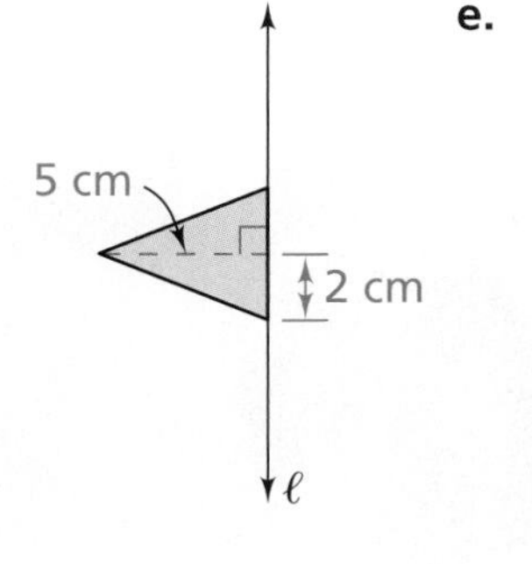

e.

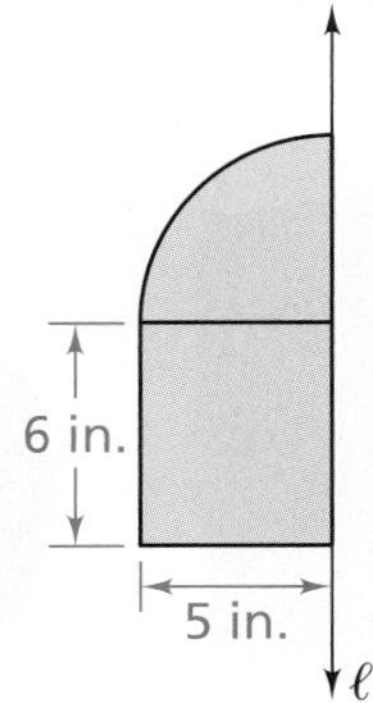

Habits of Mind

Visualize. If you have trouble visualizing this, tape a cutout of the shape to a pencil, and spin the pencil between your hands. This should help you see what the solid will look like.

Go Online
Pearsonsuccessnet.com

In this investigation, you learned how to find areas of cross sections of solids, apply Cavalieri's Principle, and prove basic volume formulas using Cavalieri's Principle. These questions will help you summarize what you have learned.

1. A sphere with radius 5 cm is cut by a plane 3 cm from the top. Find the area of the resulting cross section.

2. An architect created a plan for a four-story building with a central courtyard.

   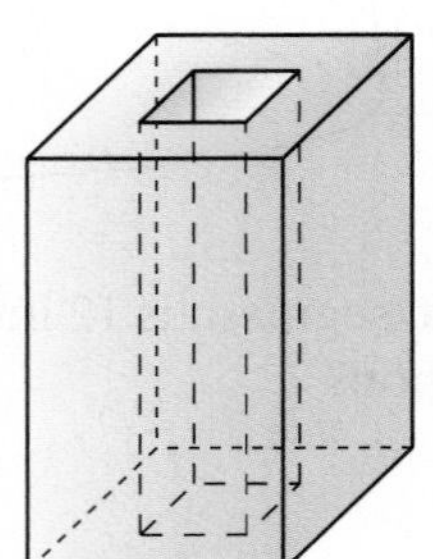

   The building measures 96 feet on each side. The courtyard measures 40 feet on a side. His clients asked him to work out an alternative design with the same volume but without the courtyard. Find the side length of such a building if it is designed as a four-story square prism.

3. **a.** Kirima lives in a hemispherical dome with radius 12 feet. How many square feet should her air conditioner be rated for?

   Kirima discovers that the air conditioner ratings are really based on the cubic footage of air to be cooled, and that the square footage listed is assumed to be in a rectangular room with an 8 foot ceiling.

   b. If she decides to buy an air conditioner based on this discovery, how many square feet should her air conditioner be rated for?

4. A hexagonal pyramid of height h is cut by a plane parallel to its base at height r above the base. How is the shape of the resulting cross section related to the shape of the base of the pyramid? How are their areas related?

5. Explain Cavalieri's Principle.

6. A spherical melon has radius 3 inches. You cut a slice 2 inches from its center. What is the volume of the piece you cut from the melon?

Horizontal cross sections are congruent at every level. The two stacks have equal volumes.

Project Using Mathematical Habits

Demonstrating a Volume Relationship

In Investigation 6C, you saw two different ways to explain why the volume of a pyramid is always one third the volume of the prism with the same base and height. One way, shown in episode 28 of Minds in Action, was to decompose a cube into three congruent square pyramids.

The other method, described in Lesson 6.12, showed how to decompose a triangular prism into three triangular pyramids. These pyramids were not necessarily congruent, but they all had equal volumes.

1. Make models of a cube and its corresponding congruent square pyramids to demonstrate the 3 to 1 volume ratio concretely. You should make two sets of nets. You can use your new experience in trigonometry to help you make the nets for the cube and the pyramids.
2. Keep one set of nets flat and unfolded. You can use that set to verify congruence of faces. Cut out, fold, and tape the other set of nets. You can use the three-dimensional models to verify congruence of heights. Confirm that you can fit the three pyramids together to make the cube.
3. Decide on the measurements of the triangular prism that you will decompose into three triangular pyramids of equal volume. Make its net. Again, trigonometry will help you construct this net.
4. Make nets for the three pyramids that the triangular prism can be decomposed into. Use the nets and the three-dimensional models of the solids as before to confirm that the pyramids have equal volumes and that they can fit together to make a copy of the prism.
5. If you are looking for a challenge, repeat Exercises 3 and 4 with a nonright triangular prism like this.

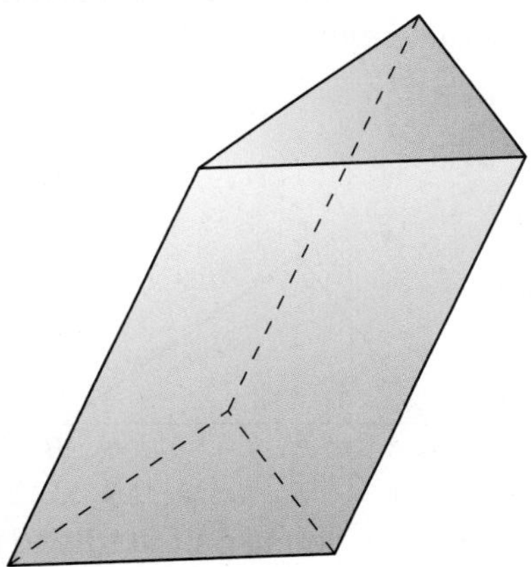

Chapter 6

Review

Go Online
Pearsonsuccessnet.com

In **Investigation 6A** you learned how to

- state and use the Arithmetic-Geometric Mean Inequality
- use similar triangles to find unknown lengths
- use similarity to prove theorems

The following questions will help you check your understanding.

1. Find the arithmetic mean and geometric mean of 4 and 7 in two ways.

a. Use a numerical calculation.

b. Use a geometric construction.

2. In the triangle below, $m\angle ACB = 90^\circ$, $AC = 15$, and $AH = 9$. Find the following side lengths.

a. AB

b. BC

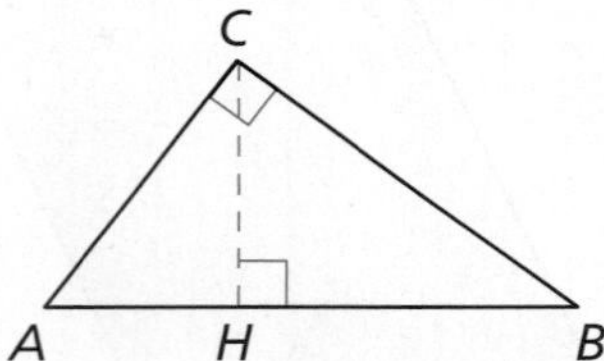

3. How can you use similarity to prove that the medians of a triangle are concurrent?

In **Investigation 6B** you learned how to

- use the sine, cosine, and tangent functions and their inverses to find missing sides and angles in triangles
- find the area of any triangle given two sides and the included angle
- find the length of the third side of a triangle given two sides and the included angle

The following questions will help you check your understanding.

4. A triangle has sides of length 52 meters and 16 meters. If the angle between these two sides is 38°, what is the triangle's area?

5. Find the missing side lengths and angles of the triangle below.

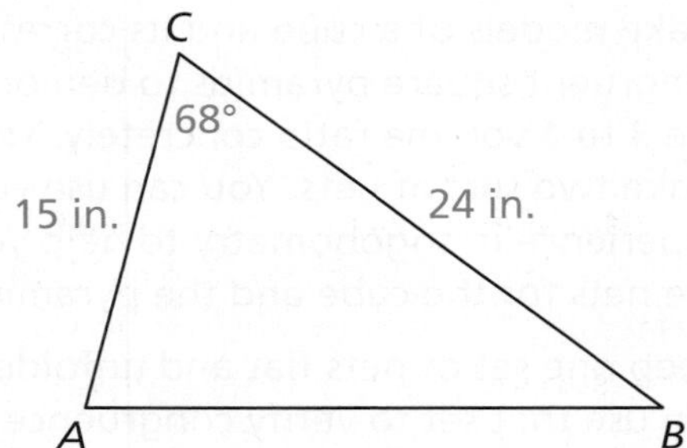

6. Find the perimeter of the triangle below.

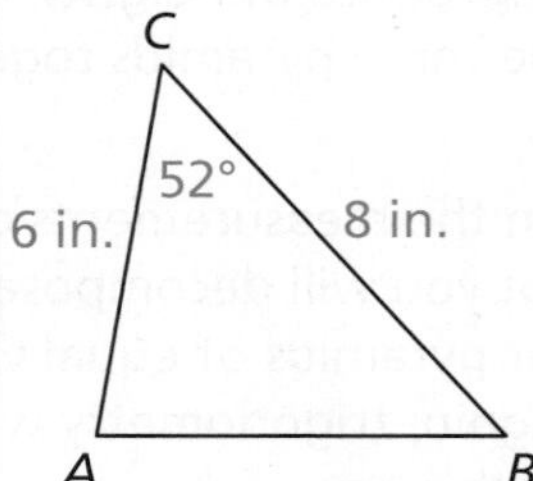

7. The lengths of two sides of a triangle are 11 m and 6 m. The measure of their included angle is 57°. What is the area of the triangle?

In **Investigation 6C** you learned how to

- find the areas of cross sections created when planes intersect solids
- understand and use Cavalieri's Principle
- prove basic volume formulas using Cavalieri's Principle

The following questions will help you check your understanding.

8. Can you use Cavalieri's Principle to determine the volume of the solid below? The solid is made from a deck of cards with volume 90 cm^3.

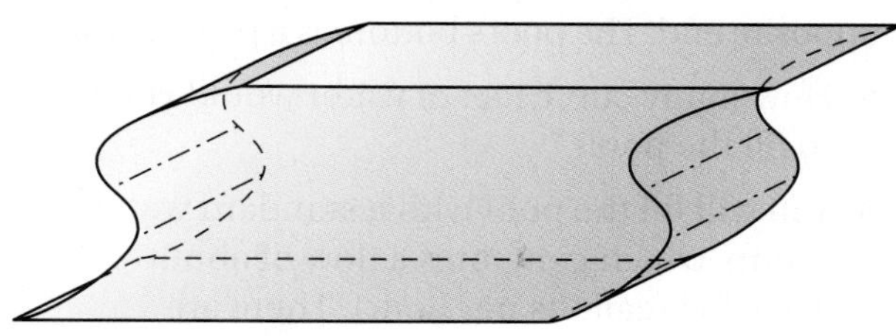

9. You have a piece of cloth with area 64 cm^2. You can cut and rearrange the cloth however you would like. What is the volume of the greatest cube that you can cover with the cloth?

10. Find the combined volume of the two right pyramids below.

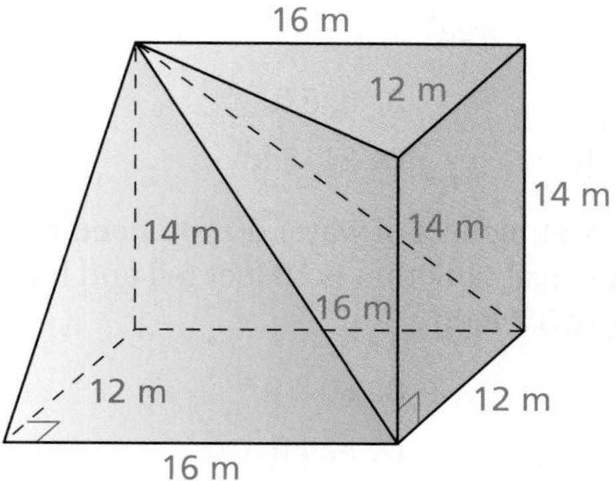

11. Explain how you can use Cavalieri's Principle to prove the volume formula for a sphere of radius *r*.

Chapter 6

Test

Go Online
Pearsonsuccessnet.com

Multiple Choice

1. A triangle has sides of length 45 feet and 57 feet. If the angle between these two sides is 47°, what is the triangle's area?

A. 682 ft^2 **B.** 938 ft^2
C. 1876.5 ft^2 **D.** 2115 ft^2

2. How many cubic feet of water do you need to fill a cylindrical tank that is 10 feet tall and has a diameter of 3.2 feet?

A. 32 ft^3 **B.** 80.4 ft^3
C. 100.5 ft^3 **D.** 320 ft^3

3. The cone has radius 8 inches and height 12 inches. You place the cone in a cylindrical hole of radius 3 inches. How deep into the hole is the apex of the pyramid?

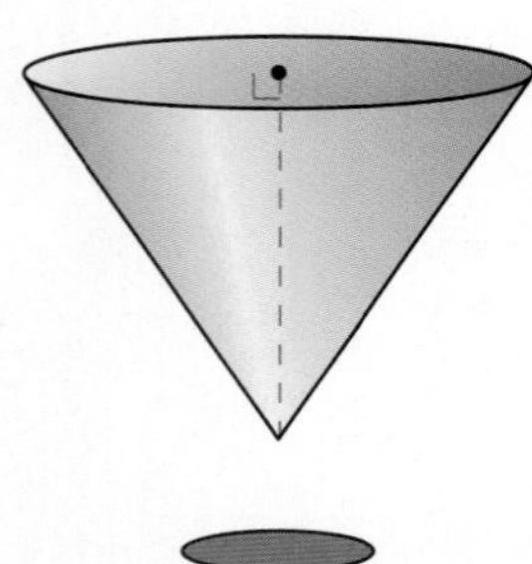

A. 1 in. **B.** 3 in.
C. 4.5 in. **D.** 5.5 in.

Open Response

4. State Cavalieri's Principle and show an example of when you can use it.

5. Calculate the arithmetic and geometric mean of the following pairs of numbers.

a. 3, 16 **b.** 45, 56 **c.** 21, 7

6. Find the volume of the prism below.

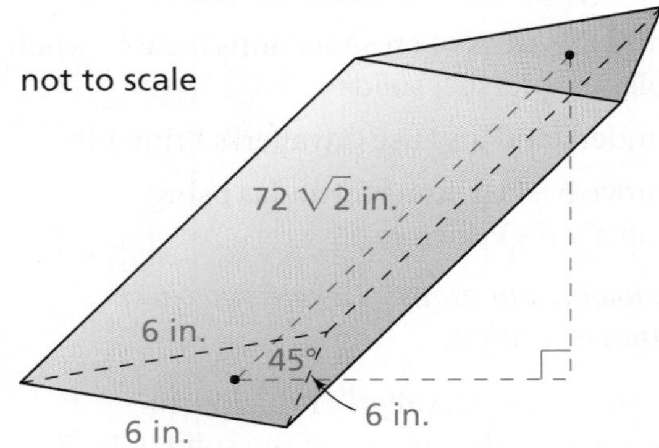

7. A swimming pool is 50 feet long and 23 feet wide. The pool is 2 feet deep at one end and 12 feet at the opposite end. The pool's bottom is a plane surface.

a. How many cubic feet of water would you need to fill the pool?

b. You will fill the pool with a standard water pump, which generates a flow of about 300 GPH (gallons per hour). There are approximately 0.134 cubic feet in a gallon. How long will it take you to fill the pool?

8. The area of the base of the cone below is 40 cm^2 and its height is 15 cm. The heights of the two solids are the same and the areas of the shaded regions are the same.

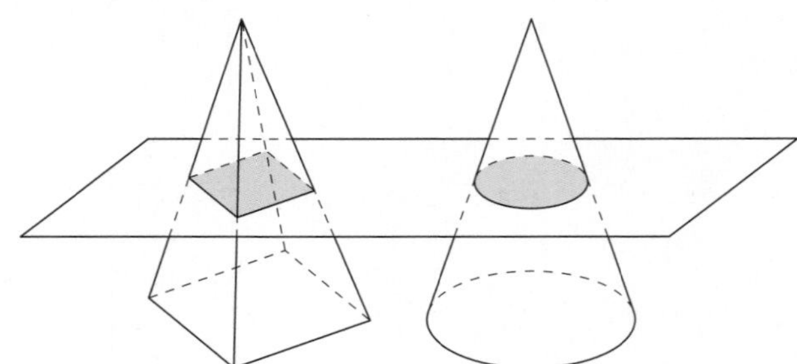

Can you use Cavalieri's Principle to determine the volume of the pyramid? Explain.

9. For each of the right triangles below, find the exact values for sine, cosine, and tangent of $\angle A$ and $\angle B$.

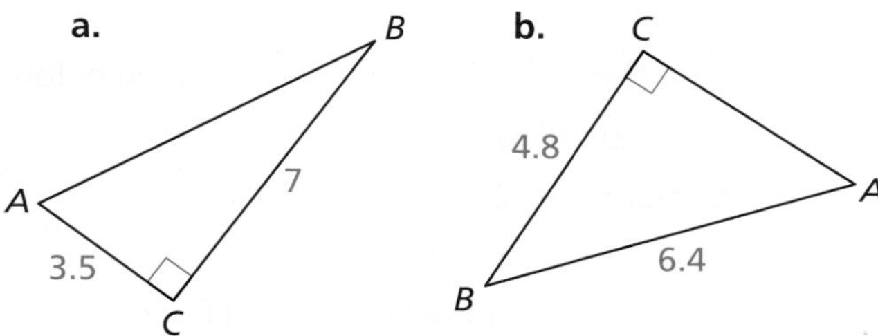

10. Find the missing angle and side lengths for $\triangle MNO$.

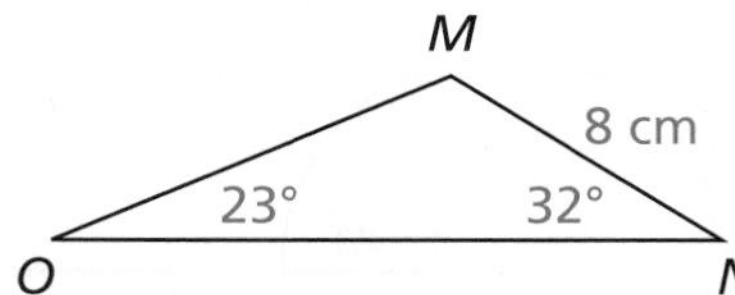

11. You are given a rectangle with the dimensions shown, as well as the length of another rectangle.

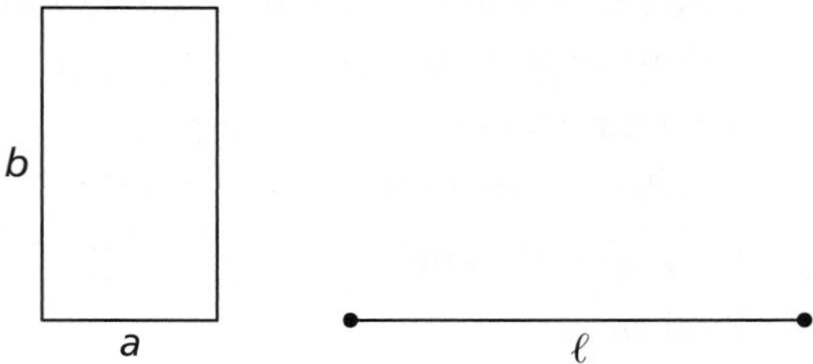

Explain how to construct the width of the second rectangle so that both rectangles have the same area.

12. Find the following measures for the cone.

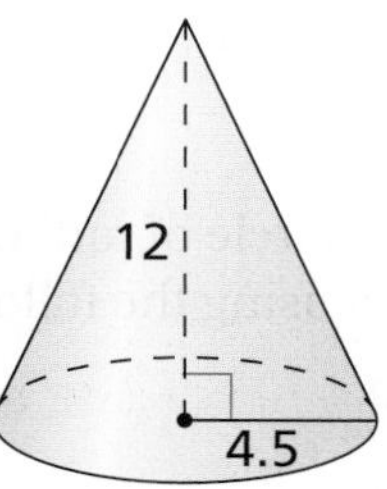

a. volume

b. lateral surface area

c. total surface area

13. What is the volume of the shaded region of the hemisphere?

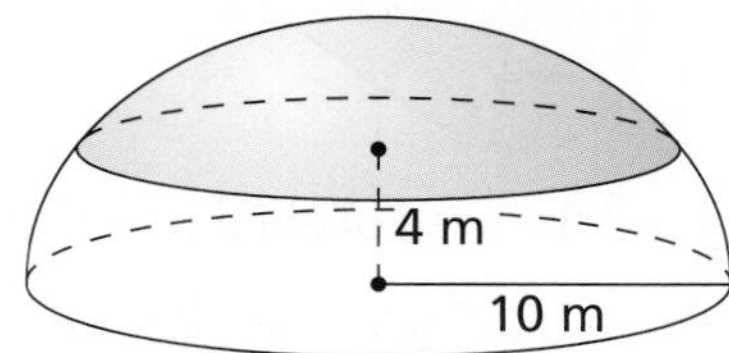

14. You have two beads, one shaped like a rectangular prism and one shaped like a cylinder.

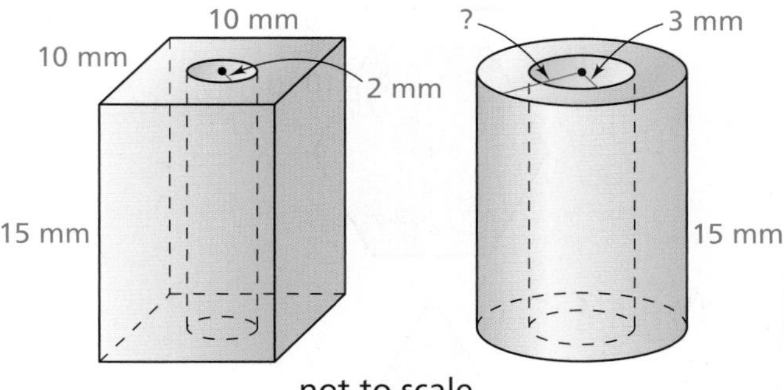

The rectangular prism has height 15 mm and a square base with 10-mm side lengths. The hole drilled through the rectangular prism has radius 2 mm. The cylindrical bead has the same height as the rectangular bead, but the hole drilled through it has radius 3 mm. Find the outer radius of the cylindrical bead such that the two beads have equal volume.

Chapter 6

Cumulative Review

1. Draw a circle of radius 2 inches. Approximate its area using the following mesh sizes.

   a. $\frac{1}{2}$ in. b. $\frac{1}{4}$ in.

   c. $\frac{1}{8}$ in. d. $\frac{1}{16}$ in.

2. Use the linear approximation technique to find the perimeter of the lake below.

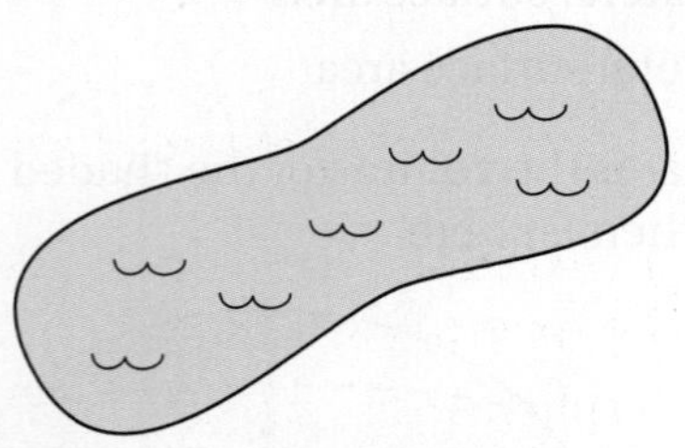
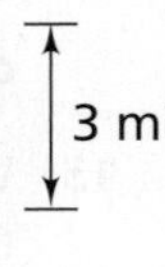

3. Find the area of each regular polygon.

   a.

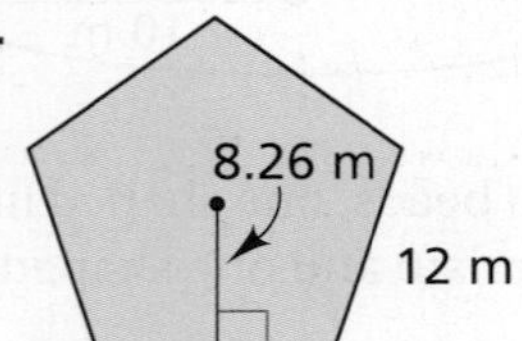

   b.

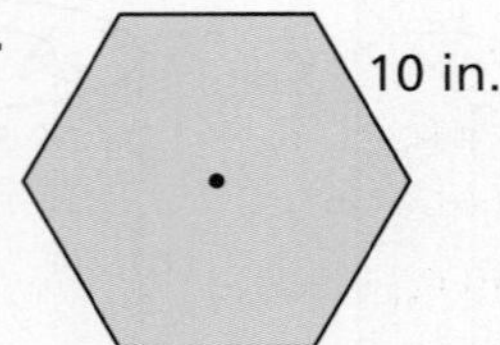

   c.

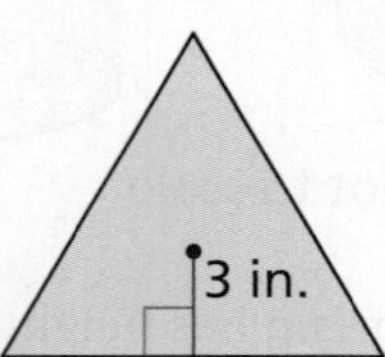

4. Find the total area of the shaded region in each figure below.

   a.

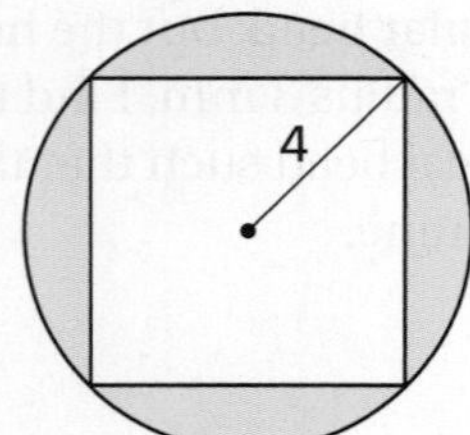

   b.

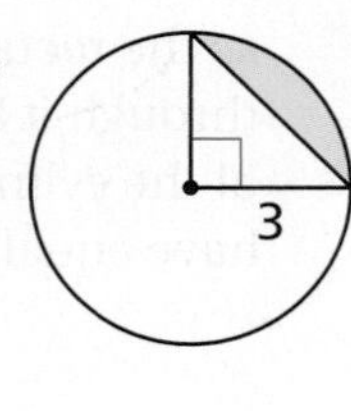

5. Find the area of each circle described below.

   a. radius 18 m

   b. diameter 13 in.

   c. circumference is 19π cm

   d. a circle of radius 9 in. scaled by the factor $\frac{2}{3}$

6. Find the exact length of each arc shown in red.

   a. b.

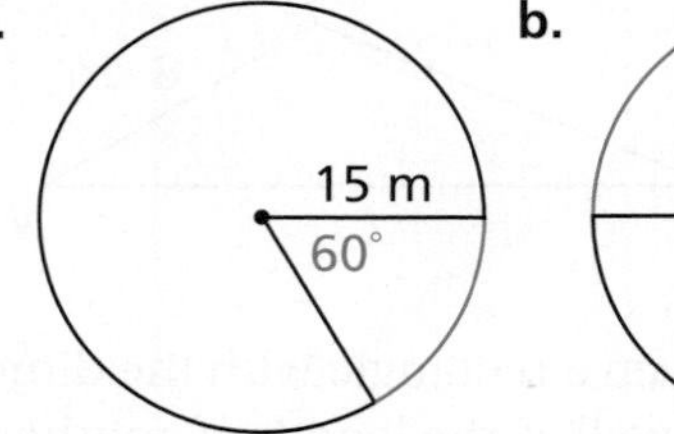

7. Find the circumference of the circle with the following dimensions.

   a. radius of 8 m

   b. diameter of 22 in.

   c. area of 81π cm^2

8. Find $m\angle 1$.

   a.

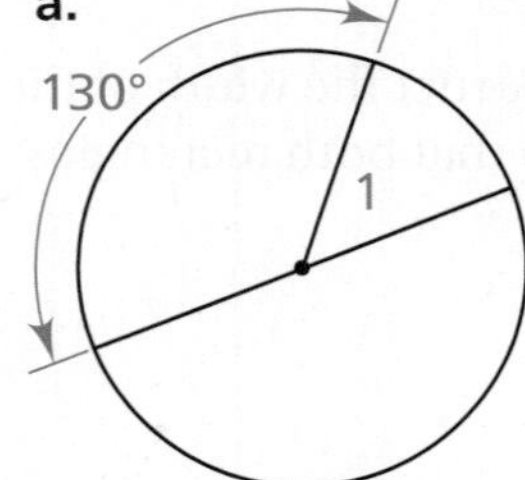

   b.

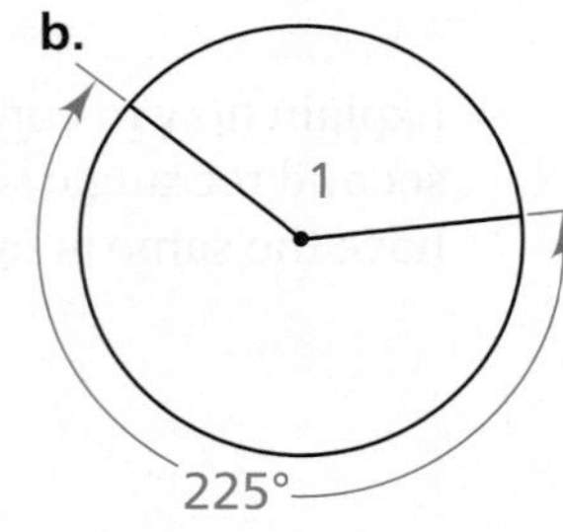

9. Find the values of x and y.

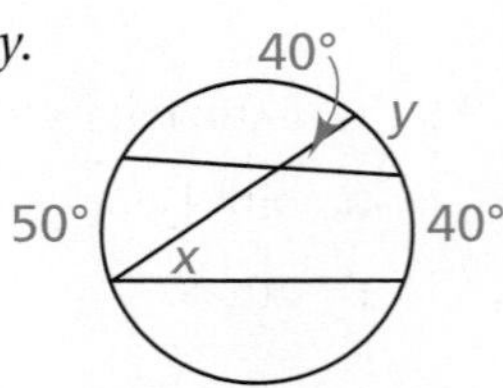

10. The power of point P with respect to a circle is 64. Chord $\overline{JK}$ goes through P such that $PK = 16$ in. What is JK?

11. A dart is thrown randomly at the dartboard. What is the probability that it lands in the gold region?

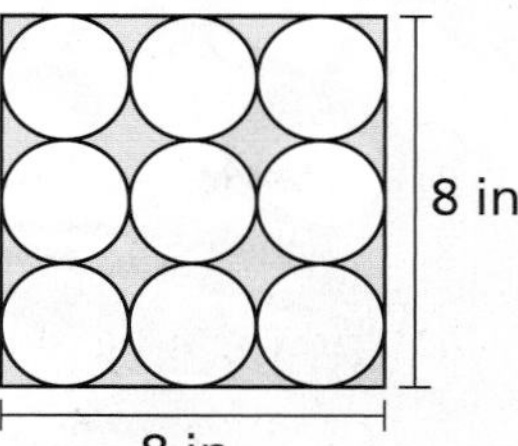

12. Find the value of each variable.

a.

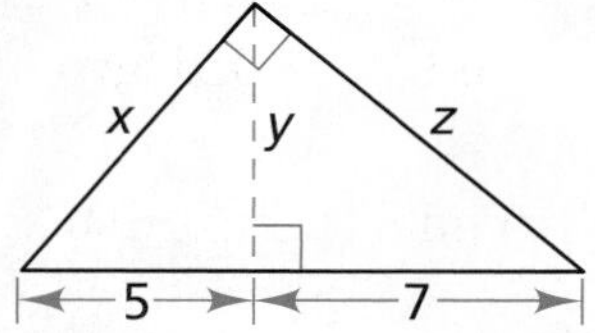

b.

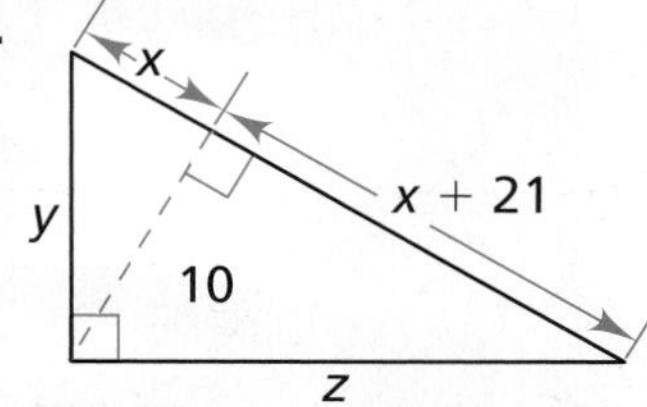

13. Draw each of the following.

a. a right triangle and its three perpendicular bisectors

b. an obtuse triangle and its three altitudes

c. an acute triangle and its three angle bisectors

14. Given: In $\triangle ABC$, $\overline{DE}$ is the perpendicular bisector of $\overline{AB}$.

Prove: $\overline{BE}$ is a median.

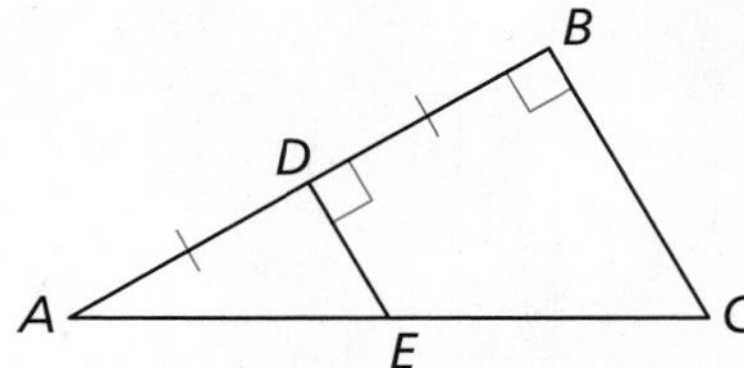

15. Use the triangle to find the following.

a. $\sin A$ **b.** $\cos A$ **c.** $\tan A$

d. $\sin B$ **e.** $\cos B$ **f.** $\tan B$

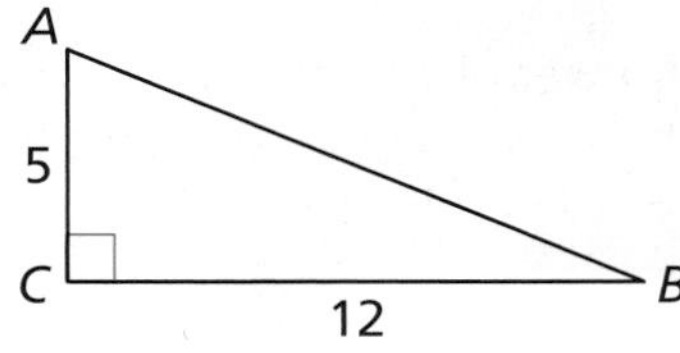

16. A redwood that is 100 feet tall casts a shadow that is 179 feet long. What is the angle of elevation from the tip of the shadow to the top of the tree?

17. a. Find all missing angle measures and side lengths of the triangle below.

b. Find the area of the triangle.

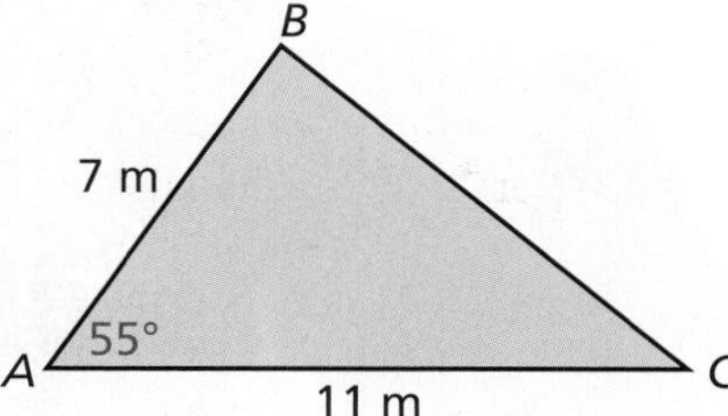

18. A plane intersects a sphere h inches from its center. The sphere has radius r.

a. Draw a sphere that represents the situation.

b. Find the exact area of the circle formed by this cross section if $h = 6$ and $r = 10$.

19. A triangle with side lengths of 5, 9, and 11 inches is scaled by the factor 3.5.

a. Find the side lengths of the scaled triangle.

b. By what scale factor has the area of the original triangle been changed?

20. Construct an equilateral triangle and a square that have equal areas.

21. Given: Circle A and Circle B with common tangent $\overline{CD}$

Prove: $\triangle ACE \sim \triangle BDE$

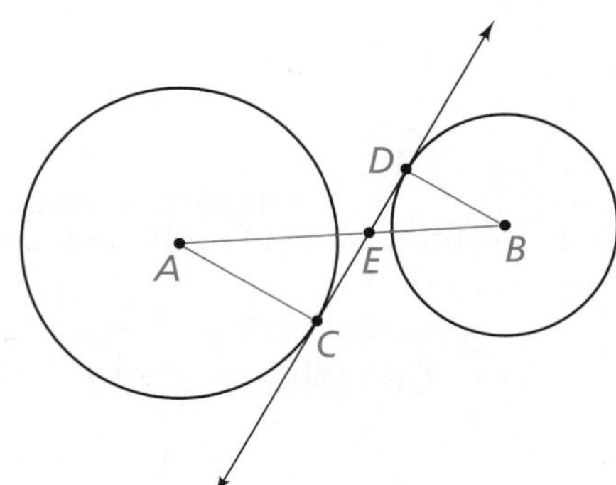

Chapter
7
Investigations at a Glance
7A Transformations
7B Geometry in the Coordinate Plane
7C Connections to Algebra

Coordinates and Vectors

Mathematics is at the core of computer graphics technology. Any drawing on a computer depends on analytic geometry, which assigns coordinates to every location in the plane (or in three-dimensional space). Analytic geometry also allows mathematical operations on those coordinates. Computers store drawings as a series of coordinates, along with functions that define relationships and connections between them.

You can draw curves on a computer with a vector pen. This tool allows you to select points and assign a vector to each point. The direction of the vector indicates the slope that the curve will have at that point. The size (or magnitude) of the vector indicates the degree to which that slope will affect surrounding points on the curve.

Computer animation depends heavily on the use of transformations. Transformations are functions on geometric objects. They produce images that are in new locations or orientations—reflections, rotations, and translations. You animate a figure by making a sequence of images under a set of transformations and dilations.

Vocabulary and Notation

- composition
- congruent
- equivalent vectors
- fixed point
- image
- isonetry
- line of reflection
- ordered triple
- preimage
- reflection
- rigid motion
- rotation
- transformation
- translation
- vector, $\overrightarrow{AB}$
- z-axis
- $x \mapsto y$ (x maps to y)

Transformations

In *Transformations,* you will explore reflections using paper folding or mirrors as well as the coordinate plane. You will also perform multiple reflections to make transformations called translations and rotations.

By the end of this investigation, you will be able to answer questions like these.

1. When you reflect an object over a line, what properties of the object are present in its image?
2. What happens when you compose two reflections? Three reflections? Four reflections?
3. $\triangle ABC$ has vertices $A(2, -1)$, $B(-2, -3)$, and $C(2, -3)$. When you reflect $\triangle ABC$ over the x-axis, what are the coordinates of its image $\triangle A'B'C'$?

You will learn how to

- model reflections using paper-folding techniques
- model compositions of reflections and classify the resulting transformation as a reflection, rotation, translation, or combination of transformations
- model rotations and translations in the plane, with and without coordinates
- understand properties of reflection, translation, and rotation in the plane
- identify fixed points for a given transformation or composition of transformations

You will develop these habits and skills:

- Use geometric properties of transformations in the coordinate plane.
- Recognize rules that map points onto other points and classify rules as particular transformations.
- Apply transformations to figures and to graphs of functions in the coordinate plane.

If a figure reflects onto itself o a line, then the line is a line o symmetry.

7.01 Getting Started

There are different types of **transformations** in a plane. A reflection suggests a mirror. But you can also experiment with reflections by folding paper.

In-Class Experiment

On a piece of plain paper, draw a capital letter F an inch or two high. Here is how to find the **image** of your letter F (the **preimage**) after reflection over a fold line.

- Fold the paper to cover the letter. The crease, or fold line, can be anywhere you like, but it should not intersect the letter.
- Trace the letter onto the back of the paper.
- Unfold the paper. Trace your tracing onto the front of the paper. Also, draw along the crease to show the fold line better.

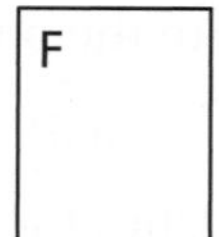

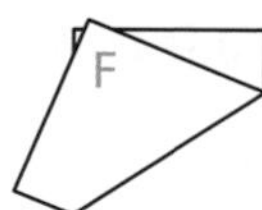

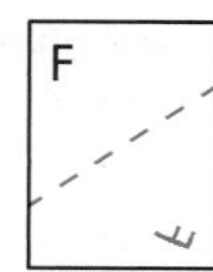

This new picture is the image of your original picture after reflection over your fold line. Place a mirror along the fold line and look into the mirror from the side with the preimage. You will see this image in the mirror.

- Label the image with an uppercase letter different from F. Label the fold line with the corresponding lowercase letter.
- Choose some other lines of reflection and repeat this process using your original preimage F. You can have one or two fold lines intersect F.
- Visualize the process to avoid lines that will reflect the preimage off your paper and predict where the image will be on the paper. Check each prediction.

For You to Explore

1. On a plain piece of paper, use a ruler to draw a line segment $\overline{AB}$. Fold the paper by matching point A to point B. Call the fold line ℓ. Call the point where ℓ and $\overline{AB}$ intersect point X.

a. Which segment has greater length, $\overline{AX}$ or $\overline{BX}$? Explain.

b. Choose a point C on ℓ but not on $\overline{AB}$. What is the measure of $\angle AXC$?

c. Describe $\triangle ABC$. Does it have any special characteristics?

d. Describe the relationship between ℓ and $\overline{AB}$.

2. Look at a reflection you did in the In-Class Experiment. Mark several points on the preimage F. From each point, draw a segment to the corresponding point on the image. How do all these segments seem to relate to one another? How do they relate to the fold line?

3. Mark coordinate axes on a sheet of graph paper. Graph the rectangle $ABCD$ with vertices $A(-3, 4)$, $B(-1, 4)$, $C(-1, 1)$, and $D(-3, 1)$.

   Use rectangle $ABCD$ as a preimage. Find the coordinates of its image after reflection over each of the following lines.

   a. the x-axis (Label the image $EFGH$.)

   b. the y-axis (Label the image $IJKL$.)

   c. the line with equation $x = -1$ (Label the image $MNOP$.)

   You can fold your paper to find image points or to check the correspondence. Also, redraw rectangle $ABCD$ on new sections of graph paper as needed.

4. Look at rectangle $ABCD$ and its images from Exercise 3. For each rectangle listed below, describe the path from vertex to vertex, in alphabetical order, as either clockwise or counterclockwise looking at the front of the paper.

   a. $ABCD$ b. $EFGH$ c. $IJKL$ d. $MNOP$

   e. Do all the paths for the images go in the same direction? Does the path for the preimage go in the same direction?

5. Graph the points $U(-3, -4)$, $V(5, 0)$, and $W(2, 5)$. Find and graph their respective images U', V', and W' from reflection over the line $y = 2$. Then find the following distances.

   a. U to U' b. U to the line $y = 2$ c. V to V'

   d. V to the line $y = 2$ e. W to W' f. W to the line $y = 2$

In this reflection, dotted lines are drawn between pairs of corresponding points.

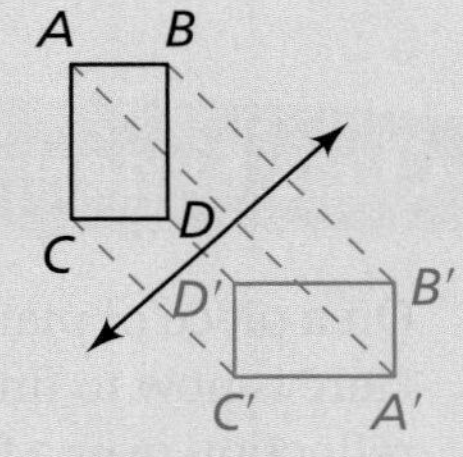

Habits of Mind

Be systematic. In your answers to Exercise 3, list the points in order as they correspond to the points *A*, *B*, *C*, and *D* in the preimage.

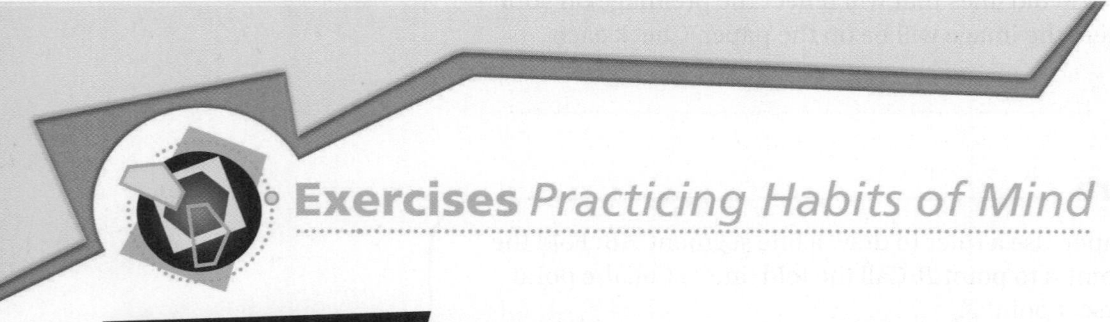

Exercises *Practicing Habits of Mind*

On Your Own

6. When you reflect a figure using the paper-folding method of the In-Class Experiment, is the image congruent to the original figure (the preimage)? Explain.

7. **a.** Graph quadrilateral $PQRS$ with $P(1, 0)$, $Q(5, 4)$, $R(9, 2)$, and $S(5, -2)$. Find the slope of each side of $PQRS$. Show that $PQRS$ is a parallelogram.
   b. Graph the image $P'Q'R'S'$ of $PQRS$ after reflection over the line $y = -2$.
   c. Is $P'Q'R'S'$ also a parallelogram? Explain.
   d. Are the sides of the image $P'Q'R'S'$ parallel to the corresponding sides in the preimage $PQRS$? Explain.

Remember...

Slope is the ratio of the change in the y-coordinates to the change in the x-coordinates. If two lines have the same slope, then they are parallel.

8. **a.** Graph any quadrilateral and label it $ABCD$.
   b. Suppose you walk around your quadrilateral from A to B to C to D and then back to A. Will a person watching from above see your path as clockwise or counterclockwise?
   c. Reflect your quadrilateral over the line $x = -2$. Label the image $EFGH$ so that $EFGH \cong ABCD$.
   d. Suppose you walk around this new quadrilateral from E to F to G to H and then back to E. Will a person watching from above see your path as clockwise or counterclockwise?
   e. Was the direction (clockwise or counterclockwise) the same for your preimage and for its image after reflection?

9. Plot $\overline{AB}$ on a coordinate plane, with endpoints $A(2, 5)$ and $B(4, 2)$. Reflect $\overline{AB}$ over the x-axis. Write the coordinates of A' and B', the images of A and B.

10. Graph the line with equation $2x + y = 6$. Write an equation for its image after a reflection over the y-axis.

For help graphing an equation, see the TI-Nspire™ Handbook, p. 712.

Maintain Your Skills

11. On a plain piece of paper, use a ruler to draw scalene $\triangle ABC$. Use the paper-folding method of the In-Class Experiment. Reflect $\triangle ABC$ over different lines of reflection. Describe where you fold the paper so that $\triangle ABC$ and its image have the following in common.
    a. no points
    b. one point
    c. two points
    d. one side

12. On a plain piece of paper, draw isosceles $\triangle DEF$ with $\overline{DE} \cong \overline{DF}$. Fold the paper to find the **line of reflection** for which $\triangle DEF$ and its image have all their points in common. Describe the position of this line of reflection.

7.02 Reflections

In Lesson 7.01, you worked with reflections in the plane. You saw how you can map all the points of the plane to the points of the plane by reflecting over a line. You learned to find the images of points by folding paper, or by using the "mirror-image" technique.

In other words, every point is mapped somewhere by the reflection.

Does every point map onto a point different from itself? For some reflections the points do, but for some they do not. Look at the following figure.

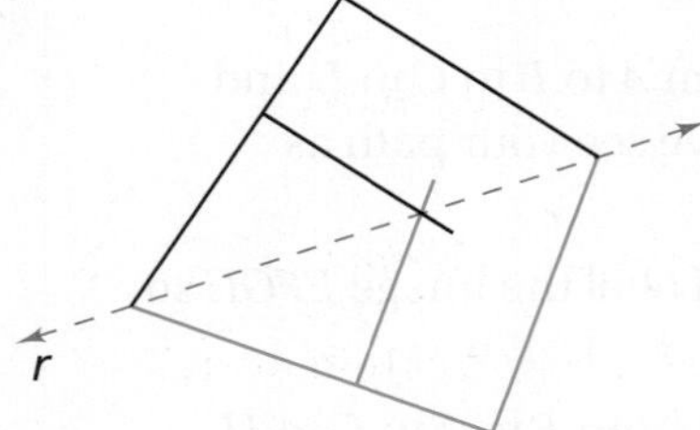

Definition

A point that is its own image after a transformation is a **fixed point.**

For Discussion

1. In the figure above, can you see points that are mapped onto themselves by reflection over r?
2. Draw a geometric object (such as a line, a triangle, or a circle) so that its image after the reflection over r is itself. Are all of its points fixed?
3. Describe all the fixed points for the reflection over line r.

You have seen what happens when you reflect a point over one line. What happens when you reflect a point over one line and then reflect the image of that point over a second line?

A figure that reflects onto itself over a line has line symmetry.

In-Class Experiment

Use geometry software or paper and pencil.

4. Draw two parallel lines *r* and *s*. Also, draw a letter F like the one on the right.

5. Reflect F over *r*. Refer to this image of F as F′.

6. Reflect F′ over *s*. Refer to this image of F′ as F″.

7. Are there any points in the plane that remained fixed through both reflections?

8. Compare F and F″. Is there a single transformation (not necessarily a reflection) that maps F onto F″? Explain.

9. Draw a different line for *s*. Make *s* intersect *r*. Construct F″ as before.

10. Are there any points in the plane that remained fixed after reflection over *r* and *s* for your new choice for *s*?

11. Compare F and F″. Is there a single transformation that maps F onto F″? Explain.

For help reflecting an object over a line, see the TI-Nspire Handbook, p. 712.

Read F″ as "F double prime."

For Discussion

Compare your results for the In-Class Experiment with the results of other students in your class. Discuss possible reasons for the differences and similarities you see.

12. What single transformation mapped F onto F″? Did this transformation map F onto F″ in both cases?

13. Did anyone have a different kind of single transformation?

14. When *r* and *s* intersected, what were the fixed points after reflection over *r* and then *s*? What were the fixed points when they were parallel?

15. What happens if *r* and *s* are the same line?

In Lesson 7.1, you folded paper and traced to produce a reflected image. You found that the fold line (which is the line of reflection) has a special property. It is the perpendicular bisector of every segment joining a point in the preimage to the corresponding point in the image.

You can use this special property to define *reflection.*

Definition

Suppose *P* is a point and ℓ is a line not containing *P*. A reflection over ℓ maps the point to *P*′ such that ℓ is the perpendicular bisector of $\overline{PP'}$. If ℓ contains *P*, *P* is its own reflection image.

Exercises *Practicing Habits of Mind*

Check Your Understanding

1. Decide whether each statement is *always*, *sometimes*, or *never* true for reflection over a line. If a statement is always true or never true, prove it. If a statement is sometimes true and sometimes false, give an example of each case.

a. A segment in a preimage must be the same length as the corresponding segment in the image.

b. An angle in a preimage must have the same measure as the corresponding angle in the image.

c. Collinear points in a preimage must have collinear image points.

d. The slope of a segment in an image must be the same as the slope of the corresponding segment in the preimage.

e. Segments in an image that correspond to segments that are parallel in the preimage must be parallel to each other.

f. Segments in an image that correspond to segments that are perpendicular in the preimage must also be perpendicular.

2. a. Reflect $\overline{AB}$ with endpoints $A(2, 5)$ and $B(4, 2)$ over the line with equation $x = 4$. Write the coordinates of the endpoints of the image.

b. Now reflect the image of $\overline{AB}$ over the line with equation $x = 8$. Write the coordinates of the endpoints of this new image.

c. Describe a single transformation that maps $\overline{AB}$ onto the final image.

3. In the diagram below, P' is the image of P over ℓ. The points O and R are on ℓ. Prove $\angle POR \cong \angle P'OR$.

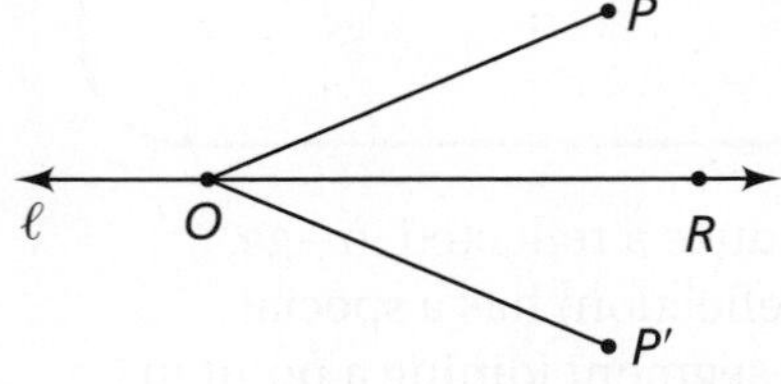

4. Prove that if a segment is parallel to a line of reflection, the image of the segment after reflection is also parallel to the line of reflection.

On Your Own

5. Complete parts (a) and (b) to show that the definition of reflection in the lesson describes a unique reflection image.

a. Given a line ℓ and a point P not on ℓ, how many lines are there through P that are perpendicular to ℓ? Explain how you know.

b. Given a line ℓ, a point P, and another line m through P and perpendicular to ℓ, explain how you can find a point P' on m such that ℓ is the perpendicular bisector of $\overline{PP'}$. Is there only one such point?

6. Use the definition of reflection to prove that a segment and its reflection image are congruent. In other words,

Show that if ℓ is the perpendicular bisector of both $\overline{AA'}$ and $\overline{BB'}$, then $\overline{AB} \cong \overline{A'B'}$.

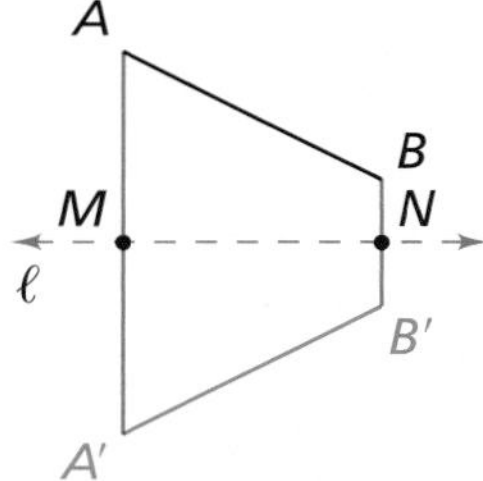

7. a. Reflect $\overline{AB}$ with endpoints $A(1, 2)$ and $B(3, 3)$ over the line $y = \frac{1}{2}$. Write the coordinates of the endpoints of the image.

b. Now reflect the image of $\overline{AB}$ over the line $y = -1$. Write the coordinates of the endpoints of this new image.

c. Describe a single transformation that maps $\overline{AB}$ onto the final image.

8. Reflect $\overline{AB}$ with endpoints $A(1, 2)$ and $B(3, 3)$ over the line $x = 4$. Now reflect the image over the line $y = -1$. Write the coordinates of the endpoints of the image of $\overline{AB}$ after these two reflections. Describe a single transformation that maps $\overline{AB}$ onto the final image.

9. Graph the line $x + 3y = 6$. Write an equation for its image after a reflection over the x-axis.

10. **Standardized Test Prep** Reflect point $R(2, -3)$ over the line $y = x$. What are the coordinates of the reflection image of point R?

A. $(-2, -3)$ **B.** $(-2, 3)$ **C.** $(-3, 2)$ **D.** $(2, 3)$

In Exercises 11–14, you are given an equation and its graph. Decide whether each graph has any lines of symmetry. Prove your conjecture.

Remember...

If a figure maps onto itself after reflection over a line, then that line is a line of symmetry for the figure.

11. $y = |x|$

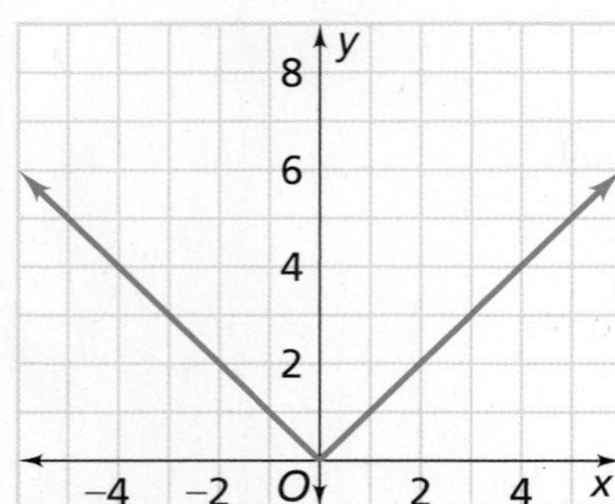

12. $y = x^2$

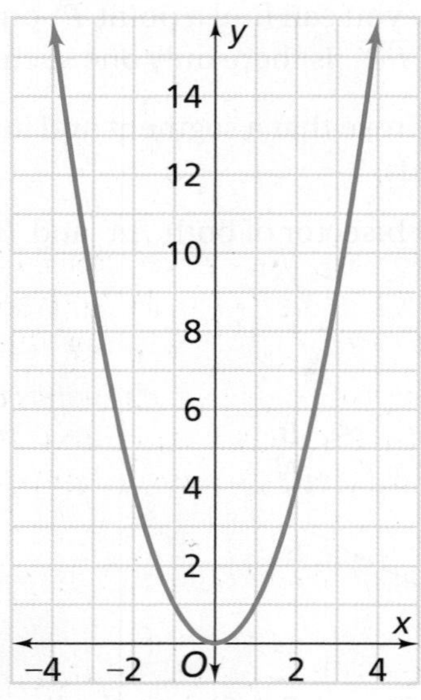

13. $y = x^2 + 2$

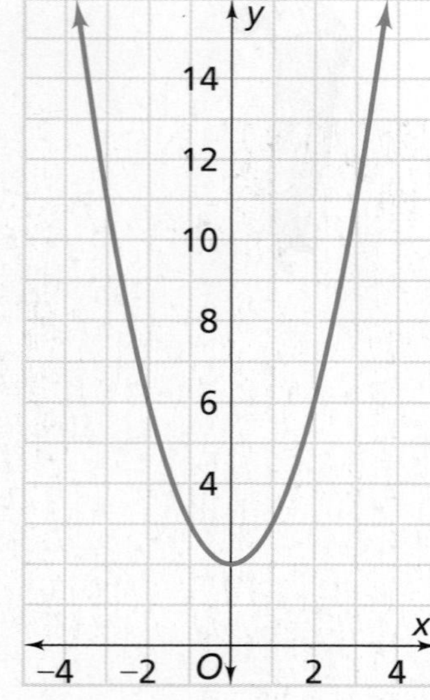

14. $y = x^2 + 2x + 1$

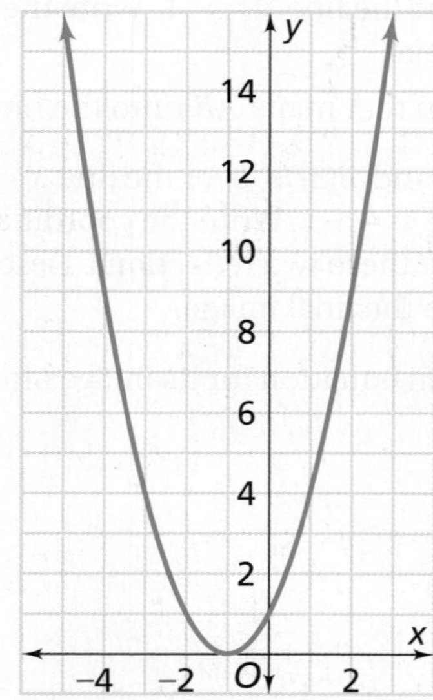

15. Trace the diagram below onto a sheet of plain paper. Use the letter F in this picture as a preimage.

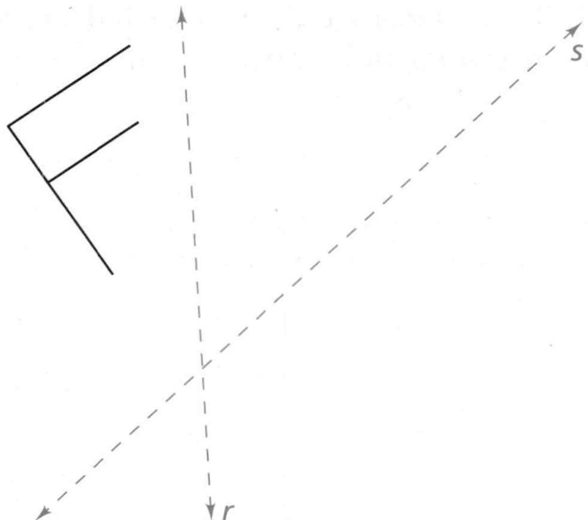

a. Reflect F over line r. Label this image $r(\text{F})$. Then reflect $r(\text{F})$ over line s. Label this image $s(r(\text{F}))$. Compare F and $s(r(\text{F}))$. Is there a single transformation that maps F onto $s(r(\text{F}))$ without using reflection?

b. Using the same diagram, draw two more lines. Call them t and w. Reflect $s(r(\text{F}))$ over t to obtain $t(s(r(\text{F})))$. Compare F and $t(s(r(\text{F})))$. Is there a single transformation that maps F onto $t(s(r(\text{F})))$ without using reflection?

c. Is there a single transformation that would map $r(\text{F})$ onto $t(s(r(\text{F})))$ without using reflection?

d. Compare F and $w(t(s(r(\text{F}))))$. Is there a single transformation that maps F onto $w(t(s(r(\text{F}))))$ without using reflection?

e. Find a pattern for your answers to parts (a)–(d).

Is this photograph upside down?

16. Think of the circle O and its chord AB as a single figure. Find all lines of symmetry for the figure. Write the equation of each line of symmetry.

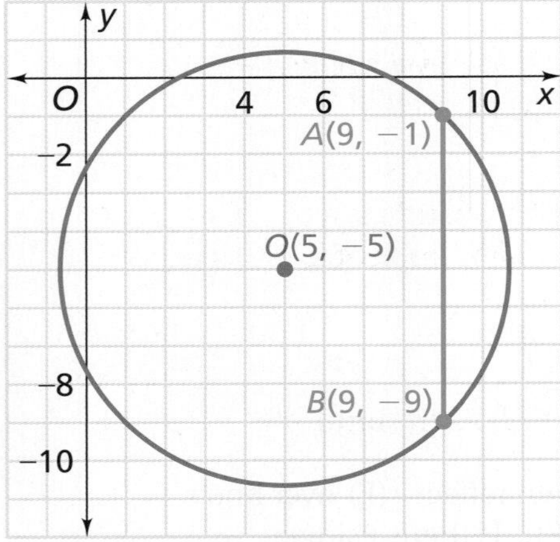

Maintain Your Skills

17. For the letters of the alphabet below, list those that appear to have each of the following.

ABCDEFGHI
JKLMNOPQR
STUVWXYZ

a. a vertical line of symmetry

b. a horizontal line of symmetry

c. both vertical and horizontal lines of symmetry

d. lines of symmetry that are neither horizontal nor vertical

e. rotational symmetry (other than full-turn rotational symmetry)

Having rotational symmetry means that, when you turn the paper, at some angle or angles the letter looks exactly as it did at the start.

7.03 Translations

In the In-Class Experiment of Lesson 7.02, you reflected the letter F over two parallel lines. Here are some conclusions you may have reached.

- The final image was congruent to the original F.
- You could obtain the final image from the original F by a single transformation—a "slide" with no spins or turns.
- No points on the plane were fixed.

This type of transformation is a **translation**. Any translation is a **composition** of two reflections, but you usually do not think of it that way.

In Exercise 6, you will prove that the composition of two reflections over parallel lines produces a translation.

For Discussion

1. How can you describe the transformation that maps $ABCD$ onto $A'B'C'D'$?

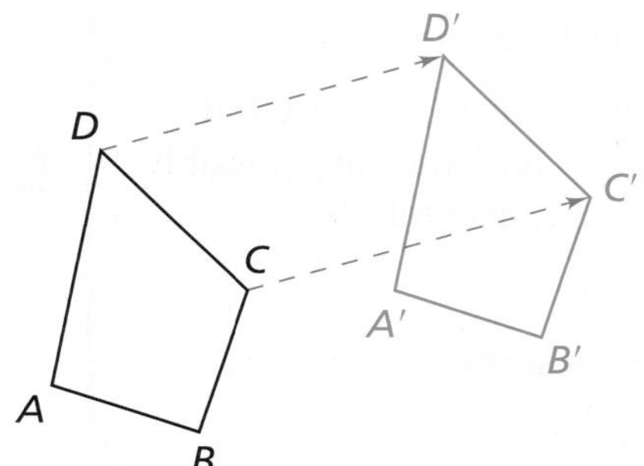

Try drawing more arrows to corresponding points. Some people call these arrows *vectors*.

How are the arrows related? Explain.

Digital artists use translations to make new arrangements of images.

Developing Habits of Mind

Write a description. The coordinate plane gives you an algebraic way to describe a translation. The diagram shows a translation of a quadrilateral.

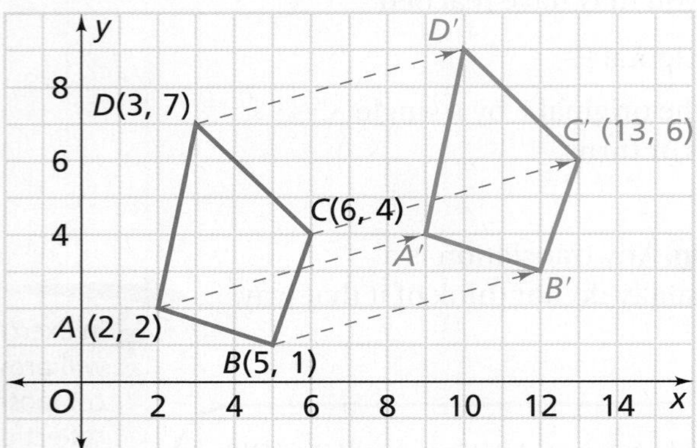

What are the coordinates of A', B', and D'?

Here, you "add" (7, 2) to each point of the preimage to get the image.

In general, a translation on the coordinate plane is a transformation that adds one value to every *x*-coordinate of the preimage and another (possibly the same) value to every *y*-coordinate of the preimage. In symbols,

$$(x, y) \mapsto (x + a, y + b)$$

where *a* and *b* are any real numbers. This notation describes a mapping. You say, "The translation (a, b) maps (x, y) to $(x + a, y + b)$."

Habits of Mind

Check your work. Verify your conjectures from Problem 1. Use numbers and the coordinate plane.

The relationships you described in Problem 1 are still true, but now you give such descriptions using numbers.

For You to Do

Graph a scalene right triangle. Find its image after applying each rule.

2. $(x, y) \mapsto (x + 8, y + 5)$

3. $(a, b) \mapsto (a - 8, b + 5)$

4. $(a, b) \mapsto (-a, b)$

5. $(x, y) \mapsto (x + 1, y + 2)$

6. $(x, y) \mapsto (x, -y)$

Which rules are translations? What are the other rules?

Minds in Action — episode 30

Tony and Sasha want to translate the parabola $y = \frac{1}{2}x^2 + 1$ *by* $(2, -1)$. *They also want to write an equation for the image of the parabola after the translation.*

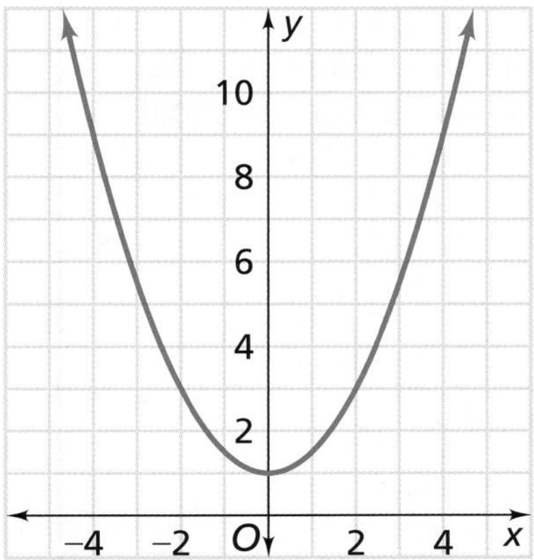

Tony This should be easy. I mean, we know that every point (x, y) maps to $(x + 2, y - 1)$. We can just plug those new expressions in for x and y. That should move everything 2 units to the right and 1 unit down.

Sasha That sounds reasonable enough.

Tony and Sasha graph $(y - 1) = \frac{1}{2}(x + 2)^2 + 1$.

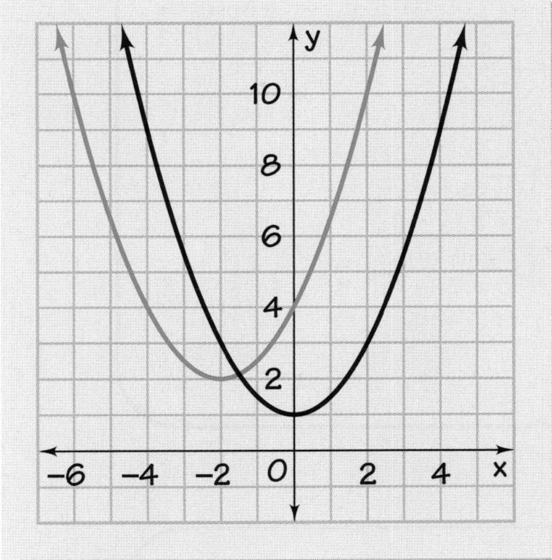

Tony Hey, that's out of order! The image parabola was translated in exactly the wrong direction! Where did we mess up?

Sasha Hmmm . . . wait a minute. The old equation was $y = \frac{1}{2}x^2 + 1$, right?

Tony Yes, so what?

Sasha That was written with the old x and the old y. We know that

$$y_{old} = \frac{1}{2}(x_{old})^2 + 1$$

But now we're talking about a different x and y.

$$x_{new} = x_{old} + 2$$

$$y_{new} = y_{old} - 1$$

Look, the only equation we have is in terms of x_{old} and y_{old}. We have to substitute something with x_{new} and y_{new} that are equal to x_{old} and y_{old}.

Tony Oh, I get it! Since

$$x_{old} = x_{new} - 2$$

$$y_{old} = y_{new} + 1$$

we have to plug in $x - 2$ for x and $y + 1$ for y.

Sasha Cross your fingers. Let's try it.

Tony and Sasha graph $(y + 1) = \frac{1}{2}(x - 2)^2 + 1$.

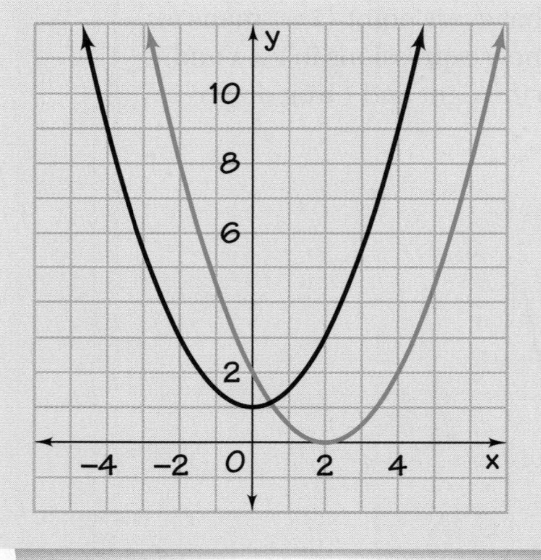

Tony Go, Sasha!

For You to Do

Translate the parabola with equation $y = \frac{1}{2}x^2 + 1$ by each translation below. Write an equation for the parabola's image after each translation.

7. (0, −2)

8. (3, 0)

9. (1, 5)

For help translating an object by a given vector, see the TI-Nspire Handbook, p. 712.

Exercises Practicing Habits of Mind

Check Your Understanding

1. The diagram shows the transformation $AKLJ \rightarrow A'K'L'J'$.

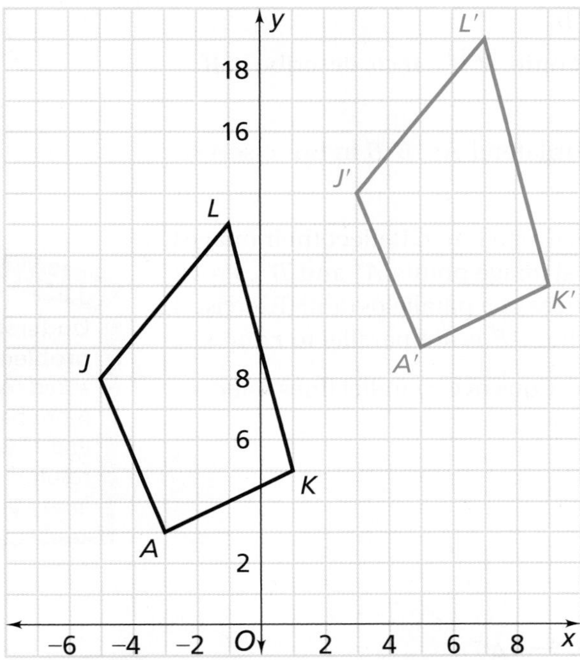

a. How do you know that the transformation is a translation?

b. Describe the translation.

c. Describe what you have to do to the coordinates of the vertices of $AKLJ$ to get the coordinates of the vertices of $A'K'L'J'$.

2. Apply the rule $(x, y) \mapsto (x + 10, y + 6)$ to the vertices of a triangle. Then connect the three image points. What figure do you get? How is it related to your original triangle?

3. Find an equation of the image of line s with equation $2x + y = 3$ after the translation $(6, 7)$.

On Your Own

4. Graph $\overline{AB}$ with endpoints $A(1, 2)$ and $B(2, 5)$.
   a. Reflect $\overline{AB}$ over the line $x = 3$. Call its image $\overline{A'B'}$.
   b. Reflect $\overline{A'B'}$ over the line $x = 6$. Call its image $\overline{A''B''}$.
   c. Find the coordinates of A', B', A'', and B''.
   d. Is there a single mapping that sends $\overline{AB}$ onto $\overline{A''B''}$? If so, describe it. If not, explain why not.

5. Use coordinate methods to show that quadrilateral $AA''B''B$ in Exercise 4 is a parallelogram.

6. **Take It Further** Reflect two points A and B over a line r. Reflect their images over a line s parallel to r, producing the final image points A'' and B''. Prove that the points A, B, B'', and A'' are the vertices of a parallelogram. (Exercise 4 is a specific case of this process.) Assume that $\overline{AB}$ is not parallel to r and s.

   Show also that the composition of the reflections over parallel lines r and s is a translation.

Habits of Mind

Understand the problem. Why are you asked to assume that $\overline{AB}$ is not parallel to lines r and s? Can you prove the result if $\overline{AB}$ is parallel to lines r and s? Try it.

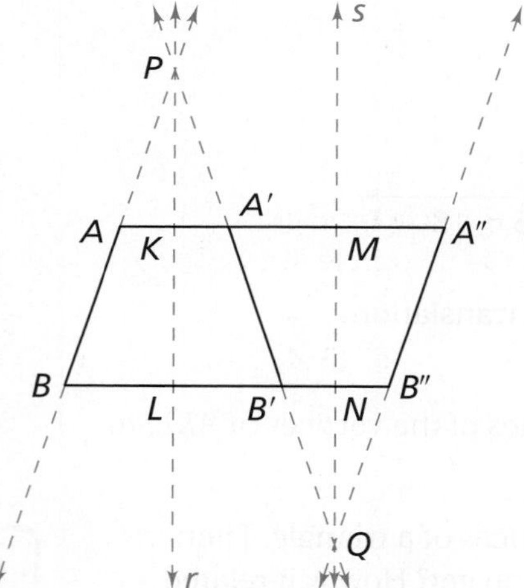

The points P and Q in the diagram might be useful.

7. Here is a graph of the parabola with equation $y = -x^2 + 2x$.

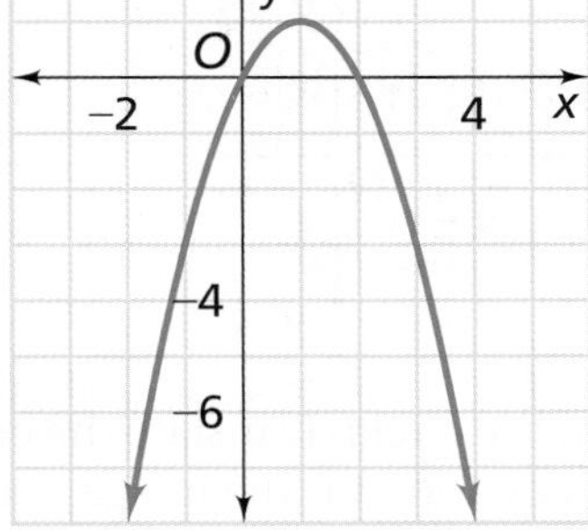

a. Substitute $x + 3$ for x in the equation of the parabola. Graph the result. Describe this result as a translation of the original parabola.

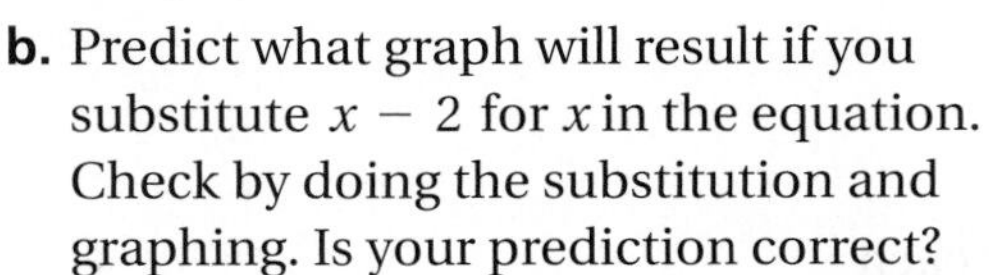

b. Predict what graph will result if you substitute $x - 2$ for x in the equation. Check by doing the substitution and graphing. Is your prediction correct?

c. Substitute $y - 2$ for y in the equation of the parabola. Graph the result. Describe this result as a translation of the original parabola.

d. Predict what graph will result if you substitute $y + 3$ for y in the equation. Check by doing the substitution and graphing the new equation. Is your prediction correct?

8. Use this graph of the circle with equation $x^2 + y^2 = 4$.

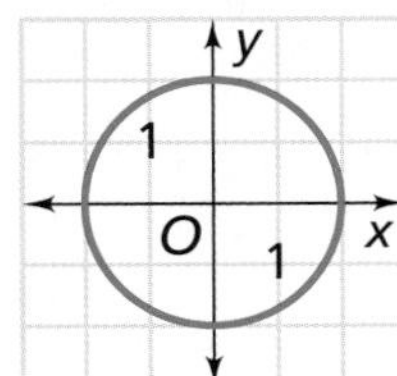

Find at least three points on the circle. Translate the circle by each translation below. Write an equation for the image of the circle after each translation.

a. $(0, -1)$ **b.** $(0, 1)$ **c.** $(6, 0)$ **d.** $(3, 4)$

For help finding the coordinates of a point, see the TI-Nspire Handbook, p. 712.

9. Look at the circle with equation $x^2 + y^2 + 2x = 3$.

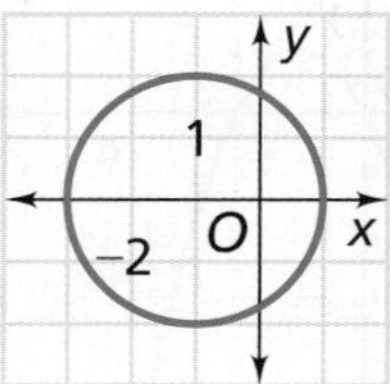

Find at least three points on the circle. Translate the circle by each translation below. Write an equation for the image of the circle after each translation.

a. (0, −2) **b.** (0, 2) **c.** (3, 0) **d.** (1, 4)

10. **Standardized Test Prep** The transformation $(x, y) \rightarrow (x, 2a - y)$ defines a reflection over the line with equation $y = a$. Suppose you reflect the point $F(5, 3)$ over the line with equation $y = c$ to get the image F'. Then you reflect F' over the line with equation $y = d$ to get the image F''. What are the coordinates of F''?

A. $(5, 2(c + d) - 3)$

B. $(5, 2(d - c) - 3)$

C. $(5, 2(c + d) + 3)$

D. $(5, 2(d - c) + 3)$

Maintain Your Skills

11. This is an equation of the circle with radius 5 centered at the origin.

$$x^2 + y^2 = 25$$

Find an equation for the circle with radius 5 centered at each point.

a. (4, 3)

b. (−2, 6)

c. (5, −1)

12. What translation maps the graph of the equation you found in each part of Exercise 11 to an image centered at the origin? How does each translation transform the coordinates of a point (x, y)?

13. Show that the translations you described in Exercise 12 transform the respective equations you found in Exercise 11 into the equation $x^2 + y^2 = 25$.

7.04 Rotations

In the In-Class Experiment in Lesson 7.2, you saw what happened when you reflected the letter F over two lines that are not parallel.

Recently, a large study of cell phone use among people with brain tumors was conducted. Overall, 54% of the patients interviewed had a cancerous tumor. Of those with a cancerous tumor, 61% were men. Of those with a benign tumor, only 23% were men.

Data like these need to be organized. There are two categorical variables here, gender and tumor type. A two-way table is useful as an organizational tool for this data.

Minds in Action

Derman is looking at his work from a recent In-Class Experiment.

Derman Hey Sasha, I've been thinking about the experiment we did in class for Lesson 7.2. I understand how you get a translation when you compose two reflections over parallel lines. But I have trouble understanding what happens when the lines aren't parallel.

Sasha Well, try to think how the final image was different from the original letter F you drew.

Derman Hmmm . . .

The original F and its final image were congruent.

I could have moved the final image and made it match up with the original F without flipping it.

But I couldn't have just translated it, because the transformation was different.

Sasha Right! The transformation involved some kind of a turn.

Derman Yes, and I also thought of another mysterious thing. You know how in a reflection, the line of reflection is fixed? Well, the first line is fixed for the first reflection. The second line is fixed for the second reflection. But the point of intersection is the only point fixed for both reflections! Doesn't that make it special?

Sasha I think there *is* something special about that point, but I don't think it's mysterious!

You can investigate this intersection point in the In-Class Experiment on the next page.

In-Class Experiment

You will need geometry software, or paper, a ruler, a pencil, and a protractor.

Draw two lines, r and s, that intersect at P so that you can choose two points R and S on r and s, respectively, such that $m\angle RPS = 35°$. Choose at least 5 points $A, B, C, D, E\ldots$ in the plane.

You may choose some points on r or s, but make sure you choose some that are not on the lines, too.

1. Reflect your points once over r and then reflect their images over s. Use the following notation. Call A' the image of point A after the reflection over r. Call A'' the image of A' after the reflection over s. Use the same notation for the other points B, B', B'', and so on.
2. Compare $\angle APA''$, $\angle BPB''$, $\angle CPC''$, and so on. If you are using a protractor, your measurements may be inaccurate.
3. Compare $\angle RPS$ with the angles above.
4. What happens if you perform the reflections in the opposite order, that is, first over s and then over r?

The In-Class Experiment suggests another way to obtain the image of a point after reflections over two intersecting lines. This other transformation is a **rotation.**

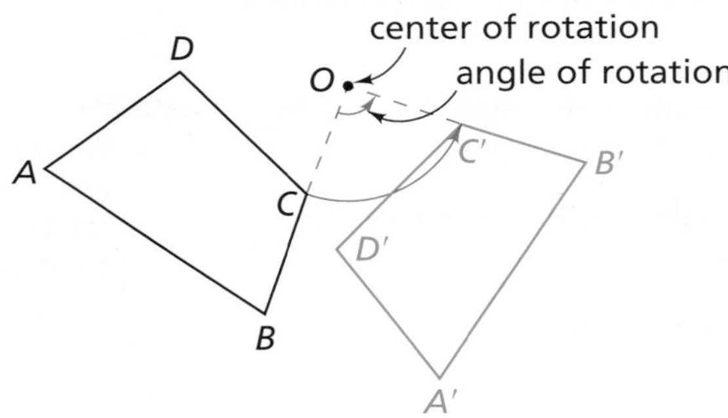

In the figure above, O is the center of rotation. Arcs connecting corresponding points in the preimage and the image lie on concentric circles. If P is a point in the preimage and P' is the image of P, all angles of the form $\angle POP'$ are congruent. For example, in the figure above, $\angle DOD' \cong \angle AOA'$.

Remember...

Concentric circles have the same center. In this case, the center is O.

For Discussion

5. In the figure, $A'B'C'D'$ is the image of $ABCD$ after a rotation.

How can you find the center of rotation and the angle of rotation? Form a conjecture and prove it.

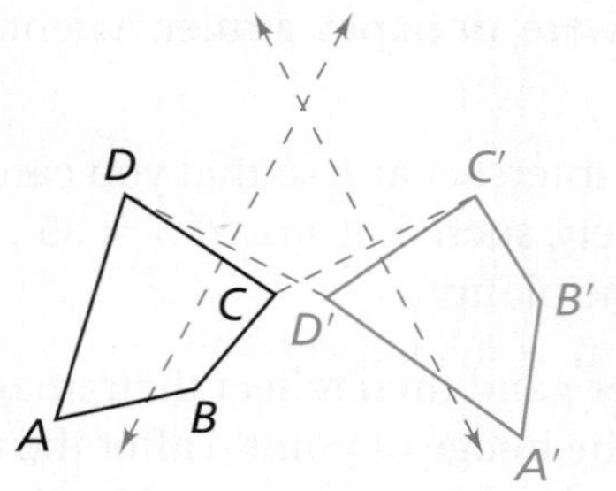

What lines have been drawn in to help you?

Theorem 7.1

The composition of two reflections over intersecting lines produces a rotation. Its center is the intersection of the lines. The measure of the angle of rotation is equal to twice the measure of the smaller angle formed by the two lines.

Proof Begin with two lines ℓ and m, intersecting at O. Reflect a point P over line ℓ and call the image P'. Then reflect P' over m and call its image P''. Mark Q at the intersection of ℓ and $\overline{PP'}$ and R at the intersection of m and $\overline{P'P''}$. You want to show that a rotation about O through an angle twice the measure of the angle formed by ℓ and m will map P onto P''. You can break this proof down into two parts.

Part 1 Show that $m\angle POP''$ is twice the measure of the angle formed by lines ℓ and m. In other words, $m\angle POP'' = 2m\angle QOR$.

Part 2 Show that the rotation about O through $\angle POP''$ maps P to P''. In other words, show that $OP'' = OP$.

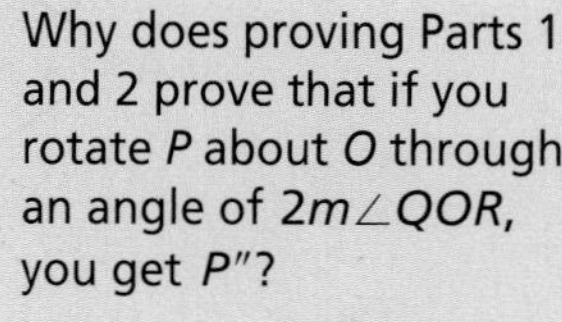

For a proof of Part 1, you can use triangle congruencies you have already shown.

Since $\triangle PQO \cong \triangle P'QO$, the two angles labled α in the diagram are congruent. Since $\triangle P'RO \cong \triangle P''RO$, the two angles labled β are congruent. The angle of rotation, $\angle POP''$, has measure $2\alpha + 2\beta$ or $2(\alpha + \beta)$. The angle formed by lines ℓ and m, $\angle QOR$, has measure $\alpha + \beta$. So the angle of rotation is twice the measure of the angle formed by the intersecting lines of reflection.

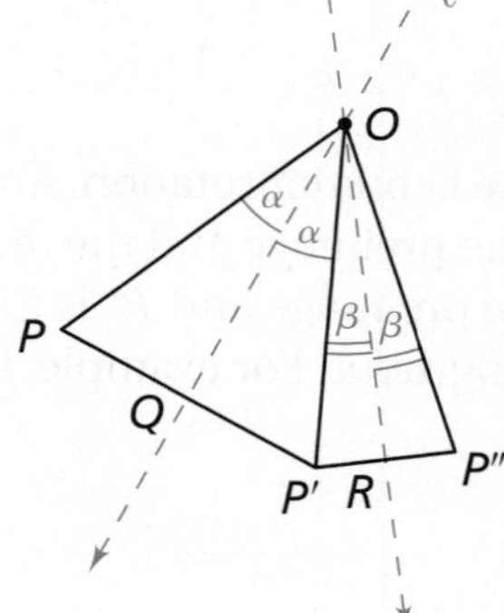

Does the position of point P change the proof? What if lines m and ℓ are perpendicular?

For You to Do

6. Prove Part 2 in the proof of Theorem 7.1.

As you learned in Lesson 7.2, some geometric figures have a *line of symmetry,* a line where a figure maps to itself under reflection. The same can happen under rotation, with a specific center of rotation and angle of rotation. It is possible for a figure to be mapped onto itself in multiple ways.

Example

Problem Find all of the rotations and reflections that map rectangle *RECT* onto itself.

Solution Picture another copy of the rectangle placed on top of *RECT*. How could *RECT* be rotated to land exactly on itself? The center of rotation would have to be at the center of the rectangle, the intersection of its diagonals. Two rotations work. The first rotation is 180°, taking *R* onto *C* and *E* onto *T*:

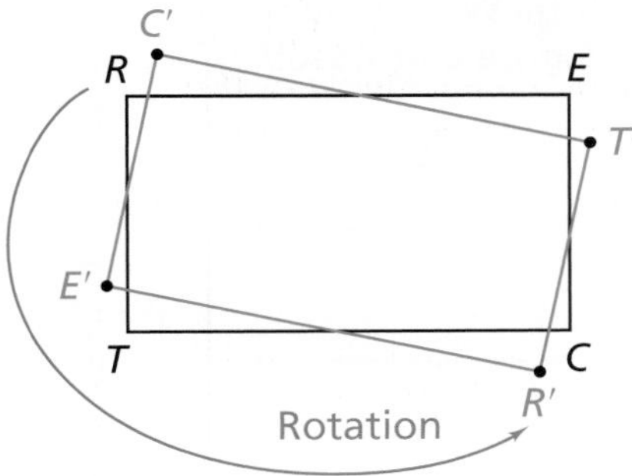

The second rotation is 360° (or 0°), leaving *RECT* in its starting orientation.

Rotations larger than 360° are equivalent to a rotation less than 360°. If these are allowed, any figure has an infinite number of rotations that map the figure onto itself!

What about reflections? Look for lines of symmetry. A rectangle has two lines of symmetry, through the midpoints of opposite sides:

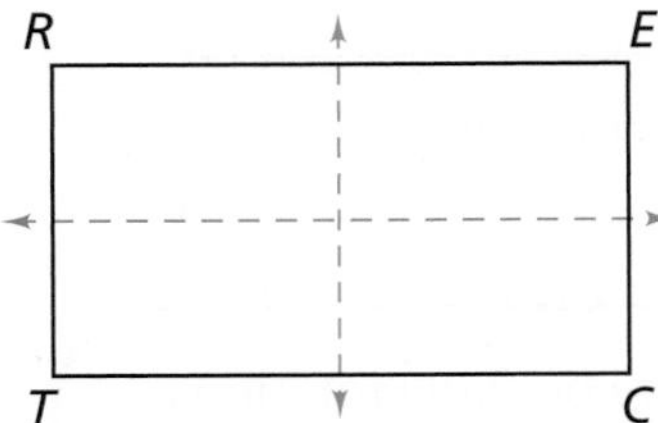

Through each of these lines of symmetry, the rectangle can be mapped onto itself. In total, there are 2 rotations and 2 reflections that map *RECT* onto itself.

For You to Do

7. Draw what *RECT* would look like after each of its two possible reflections. Label the vertices of your images.

8. Draw what *RECT* would look like after performing *both* reflections, back-to-back. Label the vertices of your image.

Habits of Mind

Look for connections. Reflect *RECT* over one line, then reflect it over another line. What kind of transformation is that?

In-Class Experiment

For each figure in the table, answer the following questions.

9. How many lines of symmetry does the shape have?

10. If there is a line that the shape can be reflected over to map the shape onto itself, draw the line.

11. If a shape can be rotated so that it is mapped onto itself, describe the rotation.

12. Fill in the table with the information you found.

Shape	Number of Rotations	Number of Reflections	Total Ways to Map Figure Onto Itself
Non-Square Rectangle	2	2	4
Equilateral Triangle	■	■	■
Isosceles Triangle	■	■	■
Scalene Triangle	■	■	■
Parallelogram	■	■	■
Trapezoid	■	■	■

For Discussion

13. Do any special parallelograms or trapezoids have more possible rotations or reflections than others? Look for special cases.

Exercises *Practicing Habits of Mind*

Check Your Understanding

1. In the diagram, reflect quadrilateral $ABCD$ over the y-axis to obtain $A'B'C'D'$. Reflect $A'B'C'D'$ over the x-axis to obtain $A''B''C''D''$.

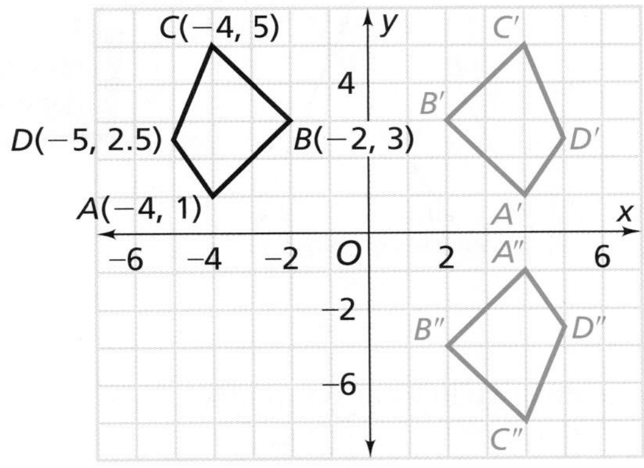

a. Find the coordinates of the vertices of $A'B'C'D'$.

b. Find the coordinates of the vertices of $A''B''C''D''$.

c. You can find a single rotation that maps $ABCD$ onto $A''B''C''D''$. What tells you that such a rotation is possible?

d. Describe the rotation.

e. Compare the coordinates of the vertices of $ABCD$ and of $A''B''C''D''$. What do you find?

2. a. For each regular polygon, draw all lines of symmetry and find all ways to rotate the regular polygon onto itself. Complete the table.

Shape	Number of Rotations	Number of Reflections	Total Ways to Map Figure Onto Itself
Equilateral Triangle	■	■	■
Square	■	■	■
Regular Pentagon	■	■	■
Regular Hexagon	■	■	■

b. Find a rule for the total number of ways to map a regular polygon onto itself.

c. Describe all the lines of symmetry for a regular polygon. Does the description change depending on the number of sides?

3. Use geometry software or a pencil and paper. Draw $\overline{AB}$ and a point O not on $\overline{AB}$. Find the image of $\overline{AB}$ after a counterclockwise rotation of 30° about O.

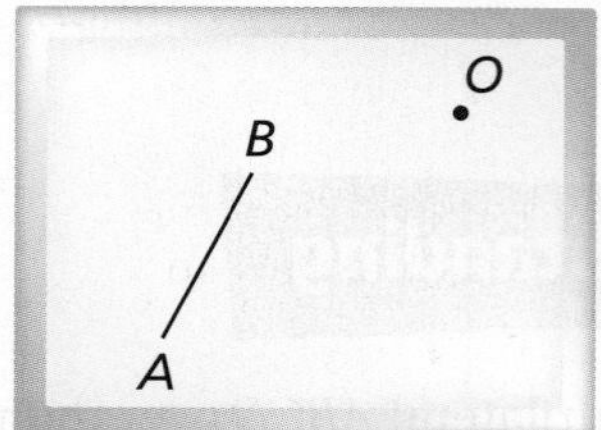

Habits of Mind

Experiment. What can you conclude if O is on $\overline{AB}$?

4. Think about the rotation that is the composition of reflections over r and then s.

Find the rotation image of $\overline{AB}$. Which point is the center of rotation? What is the angle of rotation? Could you have known either without finding the image of $\overline{AB}$?

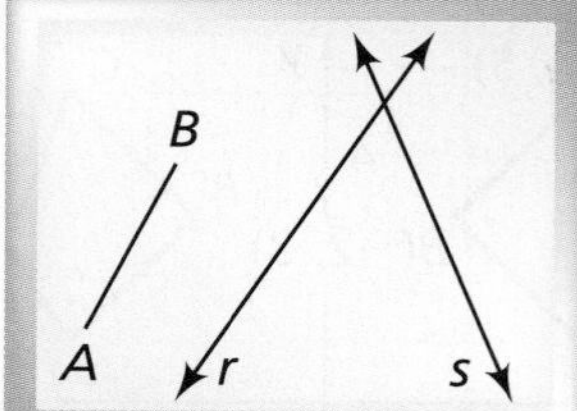

For help rotating an object, see the TI-Nspire Handbook, p. 712.

5. **a.** Draw a pentagon that has exactly one line of symmetry, or explain why it cannot be done.

   b. Take It Further Draw a pentagon that has exactly two lines of symmetry, or explain why it can't be done.

6. Square $SQRE$ has four lines of symmetry.

   a. Reflect $SQRE$ over any line of symmetry, and draw its new orientation. Label the vertices of your image.

   b. Reflect the new square over a *different* line of symmetry, and draw its new orientation. Label the vertices of your image.

   c. Describe a way to go directly from $SQRE$ to the orientation found after the two reflections.

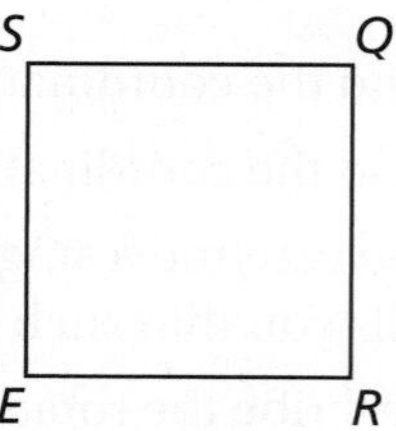

On Your Own

7. Draw $\triangle ABC$ and a point O. Find the image of $\triangle ABC$ after a counterclockwise rotation of 65° about O.

Try using your compass and protractor for this exercise.

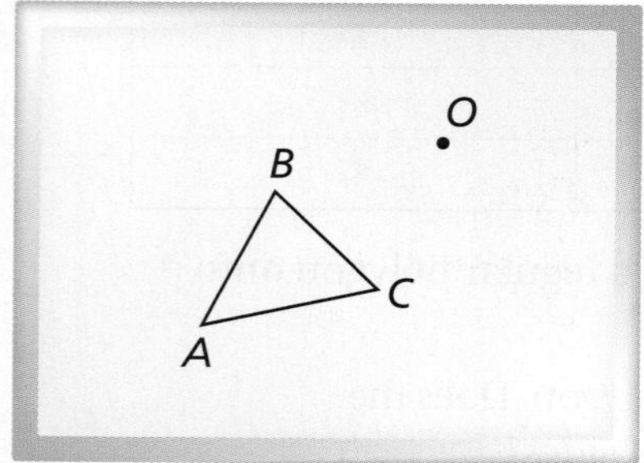

8. Draw a quadrilateral and a point P. Find the image of the quadrilateral after a counterclockwise rotation of 90° with center P.

9. Explain why the vertex C of an isosceles triangle with $\overline{AB}$ as its base is a possible center of a rotation that maps A onto B. What is the angle of rotation?

10. Draw all of the lines of reflection that map a regular octagon onto itself.

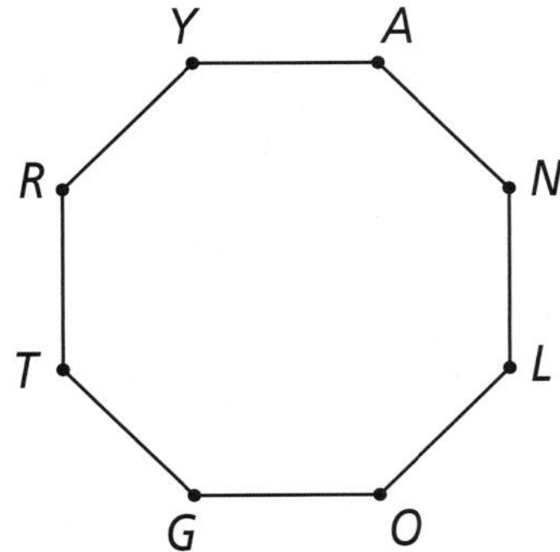

11. **Take It Further** Here $\triangle A'B'C'$ is the image of $\triangle ABC$ after a rotation about center O. (The label for B' is off of the screen.)

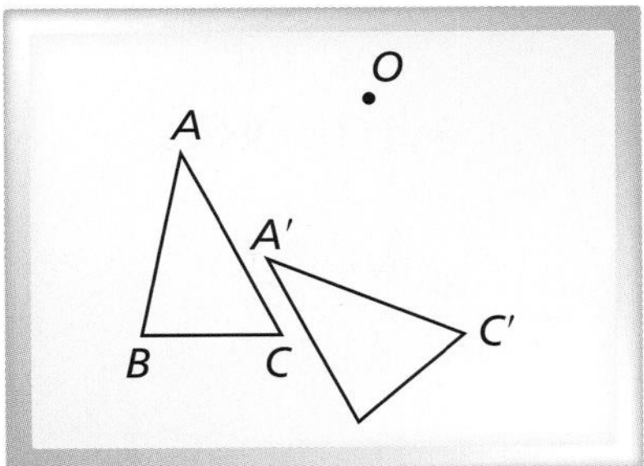

Find two lines over which a composition of reflections maps $\triangle ABC$ onto $\triangle A'B'C'$.

What angle will these two lines form?

12. **Standardized Test Prep** Rotate the letter W about a point P. Which of the following statements may NOT be true?

A. The image letter is congruent to the original letter.

B. The upper left point of the original W and the corresponding point of the image are the same distance from the point of rotation.

C. The two angles at the bottom of the original W are congruent to the corresponding angles of the image.

D. The original W and its image do not intersect.

Maintain Your Skills

13. You can obtain this figure by beginning with one of the F figures and repeatedly reflecting it over one and then over the other of the two lines.

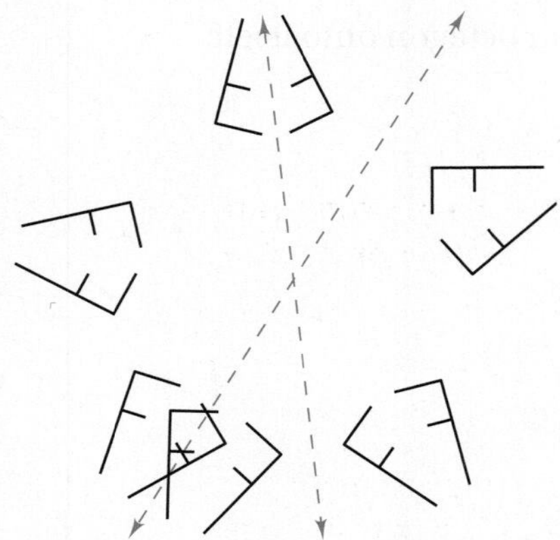

a. Which F might have been the first? How many could have been the first?

b. How might this figure continue?

c. Do you see any other repeated transformations?

d. Describe the patterns you see.

7.05 Congruence and Isometry

In this chapter, you have studied reflections, translations, and rotations. Each of these transformations map segments to segments of the same length, and angles to angles of the same measure. An **isometry** is any composition of reflections, translations, and rotations.

The name *isometry* comes from the Greek words *isos* (same) *métron* (measure).

Another name for isometry is **rigid motion,** a name that implies movement without a change in shape or size.

For Discussion

1. Draw two segments $\overline{AB}$ and $\overline{DE}$ on paper with $AB = DE$. Describe an isometry that maps point A onto point D and point B onto point E.

Remember...

The isometry may involve more than one step, such as a translation followed by a rotation.

For You to Do

For each pair of triangles, describe an isometry that maps triangle ABC onto triangle DEF, or explain why no isometry exists. In each case, $\triangle ABC \cong \triangle DEF$.

2. 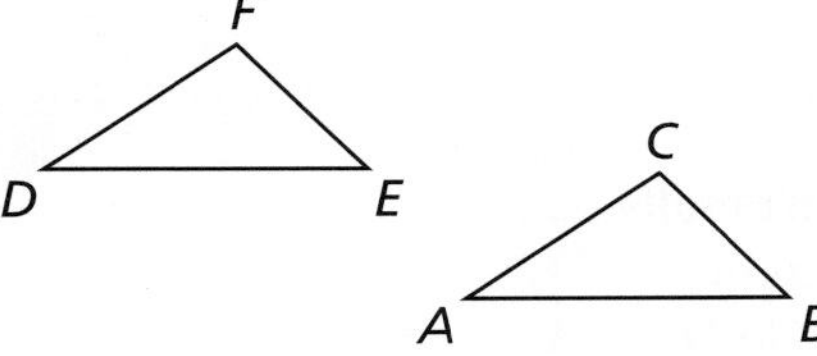

3. 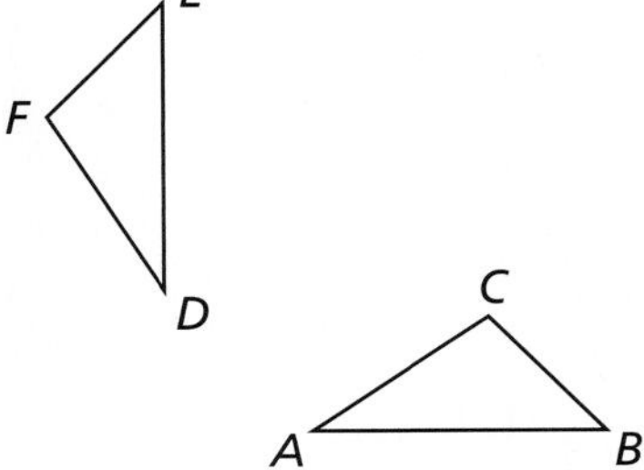

4. 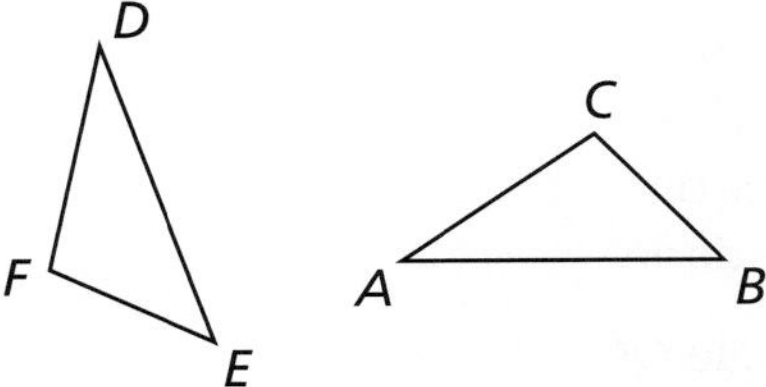

Given two congruent triangles, there is always an isometry that maps one onto the other. In fact, this is not restricted to triangles. In Chapter 2, you learned an alternate definition for congruence: "Given two shapes drawn on paper, if you can cut one out and fit it exactly on top of the other, then the two shapes are congruent." This can be stated as a definition using the language of isometry:

Remember...

You first explored definitions of congruence in Lesson 2.1.

Definition (congruence)

Two shapes are congruent if there is an isometry that maps one shape onto the other.

Minds in Action

Tony looks back at Lesson 2.4 about triangle congruence.

Tony Back in Chapter 2 we learned some ways to prove triangles are congruent, like side-angle-side. Does that work here?

Sasha Sure! Whenever you use side-angle-side, the triangles are congruent.

Tony That's not what I meant. I meant that if you only knew side-angle-side, could you make everything else line up right, and force the triangles to be congruent?

Sasha Wow, that would be like *proving* SAS. Go on.

Tony Imagine you start with two triangles ABC and DEF. You don't really know where they are. But you know $\overline{AB}$ and $\overline{DE}$ are congruent, $\overline{AC}$ and $\overline{DF}$ are congruent, and angle A is congruent to angle D.

Sasha Wait, let me draw that.

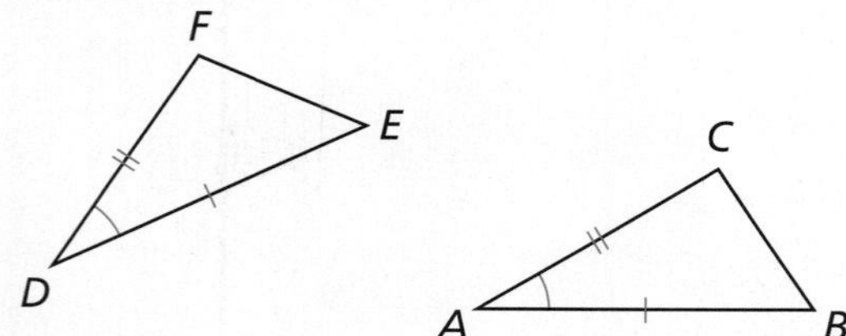

Tony There's definitely a way to move $\overline{AB}$ without changing its size or shape so it lines up exactly with $\overline{DE}$. Put A on top of D. Then I can rotate triangle ABC to put B on top of E, since I know $\overline{AB}$ and $\overline{DE}$ have the same length. Now, if I can convince you that C has to be on top of F, then both triangles are in the same position, and we're done.

Sasha Maybe. So you lined up one side. What about angle A and angle D?

Tony It's beautiful! Since I put A on top of D, angle A and angle D have to be in the same place. They are on top of each other, so $\overline{AC}$ and $\overline{DF}$ line up.

Sasha Wait, wait! That's not right. It could look like this:

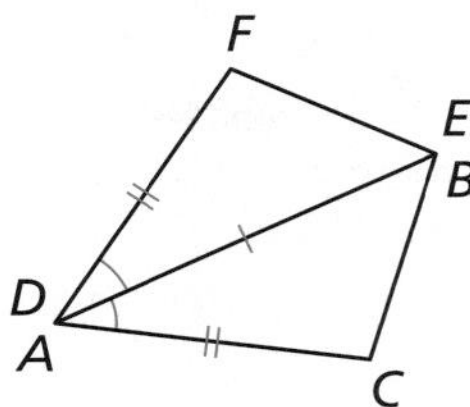

Tony Oh, whoops. I need to say that triangle *ABC* is set up with *C* on the same side that *F* is. You can do that, since it's just a reflection.

Sasha Really? That's okay? In that case, angle *A* and angle *D* do line up. I still don't see where you're going. You haven't proven point *C* is on top of point *F*.

Tony Use the second side! $\overline{AC}$ and $\overline{DF}$ are congruent, so they have the same length. That means points *C* and *F* now have to share the same location, too! And we're done: if we can get all the points in the same spots, all the corresponding sides and angles are congruent.

Sasha It's the same triangle now. I'm convinced.

For Discussion

5. In Chapter 2, SAS was a postulate, a statement assumed to be true without proof. What, if any, new postulates allow Tony to prove SAS here?

There were three postulated triangle congruencies in Chapter 2: SAS, ASA, and SSS. It is possible to prove all three using the properties of isometries.

Example 1

Problem Use isometries to show that two triangles with an ASA (Angle-Side-Angle) correspondence are congruent.

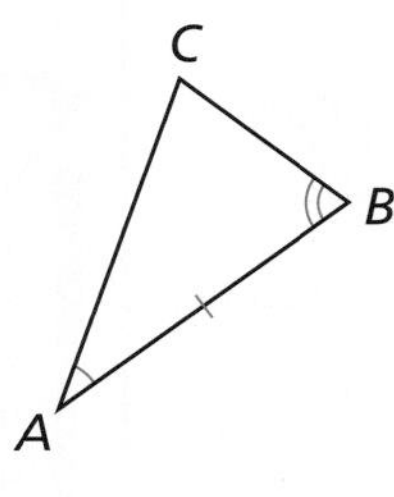

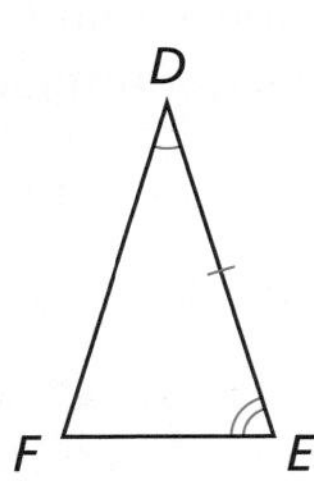

Solution Start with two triangles ABC and DEF with $\overline{AB} \cong \overline{DE}$, $\angle A \cong \angle D$, and $\angle B \cong \angle E$. As with Tony's description for SAS, begin by aligning the matching sides: map A onto D and B onto E.

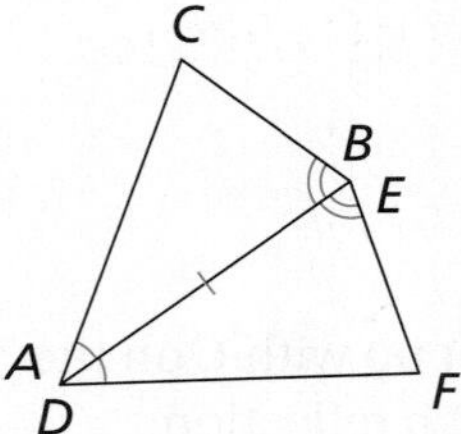

If necessary, reflect so that points C and F are on the same side of $\overline{DE}$. Now we must show that points C and F coincide.

We must show that points C and F will be in the same place.

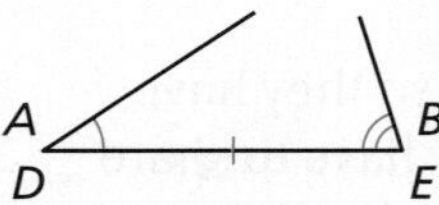

Angle A is in the same orientation and has the same measure as angle D. Therefore $\overline{AC}$ and $\overline{DF}$ must be in the same direction. Specifically, C must lie somewhere along $\overline{DF}$ or its extension. Angle B has the same relationship with angle E. Therefore C must also lie somewhere on $\overline{EF}$ or its extension. Since point C is on both of these lines, it must lie at the intersection of $\overline{DF}$ and $\overline{EF}$. The intersection is point F, so C and F coincide.

Once the correspondence of all three pairs of vertices is established, all sides and angles must be congruent. Because there is an isometry from one triangle to the other, any two triangles with an ASA correspondence must be congruent.

Example 2

Problem Use isometries to show that two triangles with a SSS (Side-Side-Side) correspondence are congruent.

Solution Start with two triangles ABC and DEF with $\overline{AB} \cong \overline{DE}$, $\overline{AC} \cong \overline{DF}$, and $\overline{BC} \cong \overline{EF}$. As before, begin by aligning A onto D and B onto E. If necessary, reflect so that points C and F are on the same side of $\overline{DE}$.

Now we must show that points C and F coincide. Suppose that C and F are *not* the same point. Then segment $\overline{CF}$ exists and does not intersect $\overleftrightarrow{DE}$, since C and F are on the same side of it.

Habits of Mind

Construct arguments. The method used here is a *proof by contradiction*. The goal is to find an impossible consequence, a contradiction. If one is found, then C and F must be the same point.

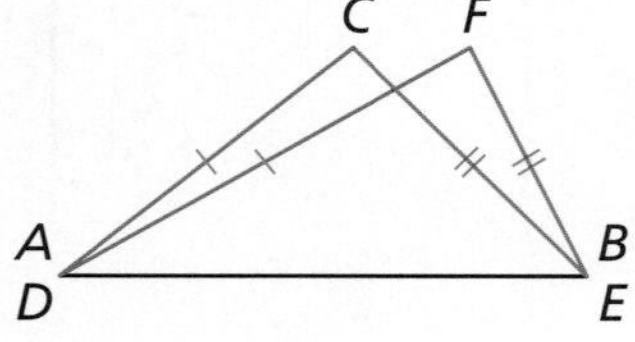

Because the two triangles' sides are congruent, $DC = DF$ and $EC = EF$. By the converse of the Perpendicular Bisector Theorem, $\overleftrightarrow{DE}$ is the perpendicular bisector of $\overline{CF}$! This doesn't make sense, since $\overleftrightarrow{DE}$ doesn't even intersect $\overline{CF}$. This is a contradiction! Therefore, points C and F must be identical. Since there is an isometry that maps triangle ABC onto DEF, the triangles are congruent.

For Discussion

6. Why is there no need for a proof of AAS congruence here?

Developing Habits of Mind

Understand logic. Throughout this book you have been developing *mathematical theory*. Starting from axioms and postulates (statements assumed to be true), you have constructed definitions, made conjectures, and proven theorems. Proven theorems are then used as building blocks to prove other theorems.

The current lesson can be confusing for two reasons:

- The lesson uses a new definition of *congruence*, given with respect to isometries.
- This lesson *proves* the SAS, ASA, and SSS criteria for triangle congruence, even though until now they had been assumed as postulates.

When Euclid first wrote his geometric theory, he used some ideas that were intuitive but that contained hidden assumptions. His notion of congruence involved the "method of superposition," similar to the use of isometry in this lesson. These assumptions can be considered additional postulates, though Euclid probably felt they were intuitive enough to be true without argument.

There are multiple possible starting points in Geometry, different lists of initial postulates and axioms. By adding properties of rigid motions (isometries) to the postulates, it becomes possible to prove the triangle congruencies as theorems.

Exercises *Practicing Habits of Mind*

Check Your Understanding

Habits of Mind

It is useful to learn to represent mathematical concepts in different ways. So try to interpret isometries as special kinds of functions.

1. Why can an isometry be considered a function? Explain.

2. If you know a certain transformation is an isometry, what other information do you need to know to determine where it maps a point? Explain.

3. Consider $\overline{AB}$ and a point P on the same plane, but not on $\overline{AB}$.

a. If an isometry maps A onto P, describe all possible points the isometry could map B onto.

b. What other information about the isometry would you need to know to determine exactly where point B is mapped?

4. Find some congruent figures from Chapter 2. For each pair of figures, describe an isometry that maps one figure onto the other figure.

5. The figures below show various transformations of the drawing at the right. Which figures represent isometries and which do not? Explain your answer.

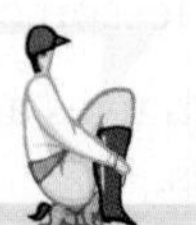

a.

b.

c.

d.

e.

f.

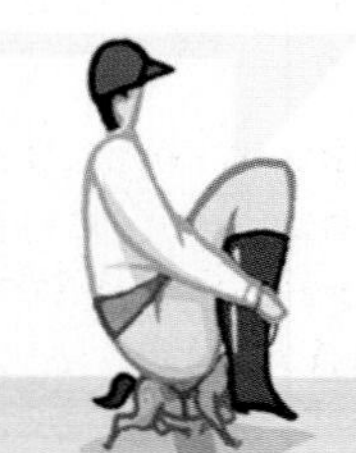

6. Draw a triangle and consider an isometry made up of a translation and a reflection. Draw the vector of the translation and the axis of symmetry of the reflection. Construct the image of your triangle under the isometry. Is the image a triangle that is congruent to your original triangle? How do you know?

Try using dynamic geometry software for this problem.

On Your Own

7. Does an isometry exist that maps the circle with center O to the circle with center O' shown below? Explain why or why not.

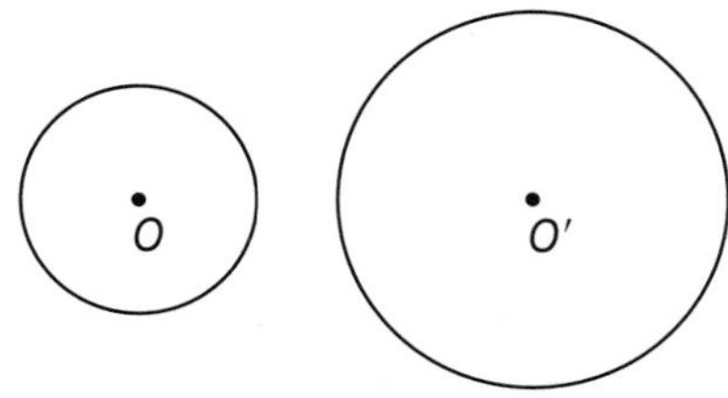

8. Consider the two triangles shown below with $\overline{AB} \cong \overline{A'B'}, \overline{BC} \cong \overline{B'C'}$, and $\overline{CA} \cong \overline{C'A'}$.

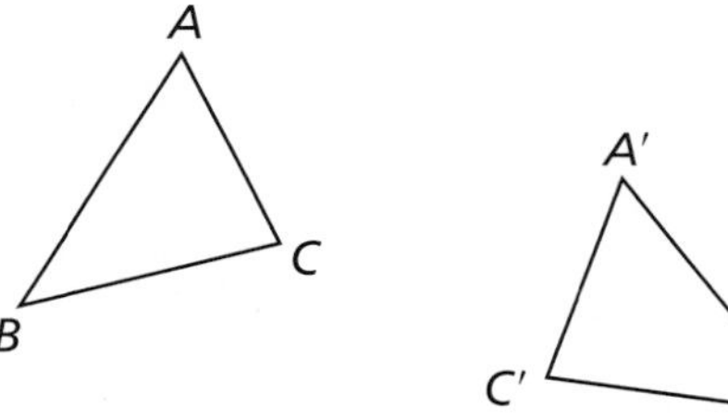

a. Describe an isometry that maps $\triangle ABC$ onto $\triangle A'B'C'$.

b. With dynamic geometry software, construct a third triangle A_1BC, as described in the SSS proof in Example 2. Triangle A_1BC is congruent to triangle $A'B'C'$, with $\overline{BC}$ congruent to $\overline{B'C'}$, and with A_1 lying on the same side of $\overline{BC}$ as A. Construct A_1 using the property that $\overline{BA_1}$ is congruent to $\overline{B'A'}$ and $\overline{CA_1}$ is congruent to $\overline{C'A'}$.

In this case $A'B'C'$ and A_1BC are congruent by SSS.

c. Explain why, even if you do not use point A, your point A_1 always coincides with point A.

d. Try using different properties to construct $\triangle A_1BC$ as a triangle congruent to $\triangle A'B'C'$ such that $\overline{BC}$ is congruent to $\overline{B'C'}$ and triangle A_1BC lies on the same side of $\overline{BC}$ as triangle ABC. For example, construct $\triangle A_1BC$ as congruent to $\triangle A'B'C'$ by SAS. Explain why, even if you do not use point A, your point A_1 always coincides with point A.

9. Once you have the SAS criterion, you can prove the SSS criterion in different ways. You completed one proof in Example 2. The following outline can help you prove the SSS criterion of congruence using isometries and the SAS criterion.

Given two triangles $\triangle ABC$ and $\triangle A'B'C'$ such that $\overline{AB} \cong \overline{A'B'}$, $\overline{BC} \cong \overline{B'C'}$, and $\overline{CA} \cong \overline{C'A'}$, construct a third triangle ABD such that $\angle BAD \cong \angle B'A'C'$, as shown below.

Remember that you know nothing about how $\triangle ABC$ and $\triangle A'B'C'$ are placed on the plane.

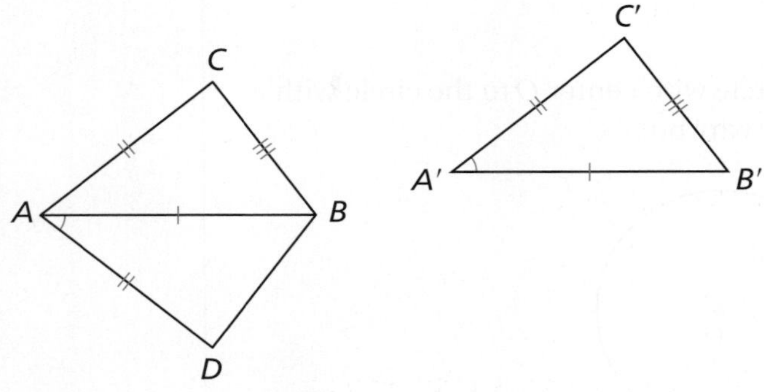

a. Prove that there exists a rigid motion mapping $\triangle A'B'C'$ to $\triangle ABD$.

b. Prove that triangle CBD is isosceles.

c. Prove that triangle CDA is isosceles.

d. Prove that $\angle ACB \cong \angle ADB$.

e. Prove that $\triangle ABC$ and $\triangle A'B'C'$ are congruent.

Maintain Your Skills

10. Use dynamic geometry software to construct two triangles with congruent sides. Do isometries exist that map one triangle onto the other? If so, describe one of these isometries.

11. Construct two triangles with congruent sides, given the first triangle and one of the sides of the second triangle, as shown below.

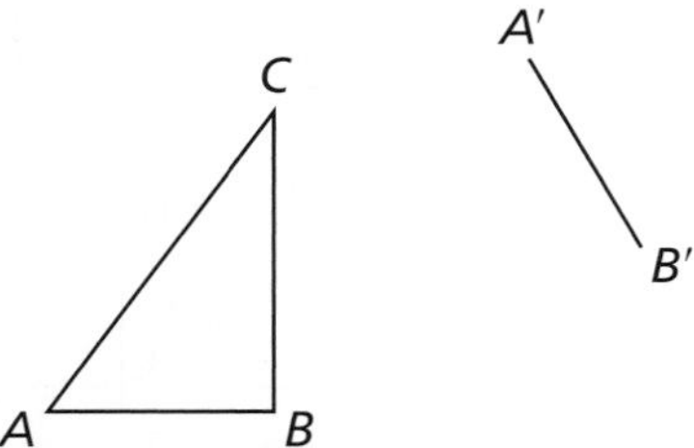

a. How many different triangles are possible to construct for the second triangle?

b. Describe an isometry that maps the first triangle onto the second one you constructed.

12. Construct two triangles with two respectively congruent sides and congruent included angles. You are given the first triangle and one congruent side and the congruent angle of the second triangle, as shown below.

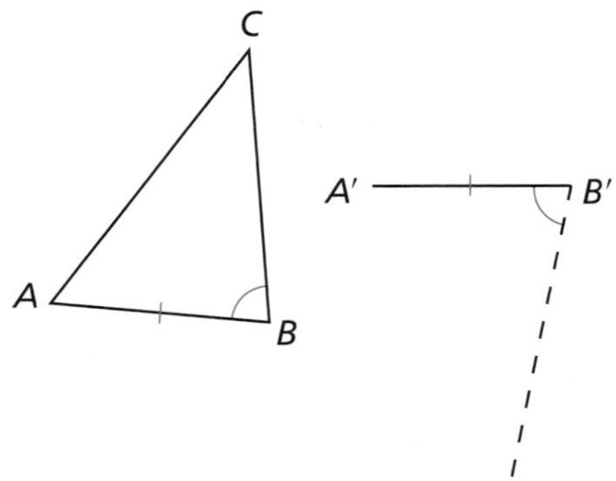

a. How many different triangles are possible to construct for the second triangle?

b. Describe an isometry that maps the first triangle onto the second one you constructed.

In this investigation, you learned how to reflect figures over a line, rotate figures in the plane, apply transformations to figures and graphs of functions in the coordinate plane, and define isometry. These questions will help you summarize what you have learned.

1. Reflect $\overline{AB}$, with endpoints $A(-6, -2)$ and $B(1, 5)$, over the line with equation $x = 3$. Write the coordinates of the endpoints of the image.

2. This parabola is a graph of the equation $y = 2x^2 + 3$.

   Translate the parabola by $(1, 2)$. Write an equation for the translated parabola.

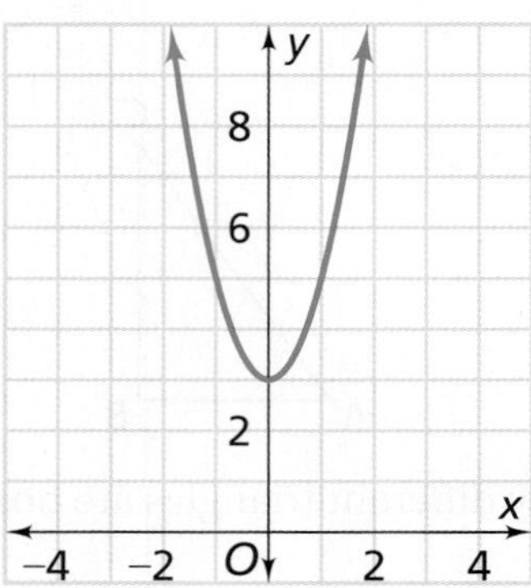

3. Find the coordinates of the endpoints $O(0, 0)$ and $P(3, 2)$ of $\overline{OP}$ after two reflections, the first over the line $y = 1$ and the second over the line $y = 5$. What transformation is the composition of these two reflections? Write a rule in the form $(x, y) \mapsto (\blacksquare, \blacksquare)$ to summarize this transformation.

4. Can you obtain a rotation by composing two other transformations? Explain with an example.

5. When you reflect an object over a line, what properties of the object are present in its image?

6. What happens when you compose two reflections? Three reflections? Four reflections?

7. $\triangle ABC$ has vertices $A(2, -1)$, $B(-2, -3)$, and $C(2, -3)$. When you reflect $\triangle ABC$ over the x-axis, what are the coordinates of its image $\triangle A'B'C'$?

Vocabulary and Notation

In this investigation, you learned these terms and symbols. Make sure you understand what each one means and how to use it.

- **angle of rotation**
- **center of rotation**
- **composition**
- **fixed point**
- **image**
- **line of reflection**
- **preimage**
- **reflection**
- **rotation**
- **transformation**
- **translation**
- **F' (F prime)**
- **F'' (F double prime)**
- **$x \mapsto y$ (x maps to y)**

Does the face have line symmetry?

Geometry in the Coordinate Plane

In *Geometry in the Coordinate Plane,* you will use coordinates in one, two, and three dimensions. You will learn the Midpoint Formula and the Distance Formula, and you will use these formulas in a variety of proofs.

By the end of this investigation, you will be able to answer questions like these.

1. How can you tell by examining the coordinates of two points whether they lie on a horizontal line? On a vertical line?
2. How do you calculate the distance between two points?
3. A box has dimensions 3 in. by 5 in. by 4 in. What is the length of a diagonal?

You will learn how to

- calculate the distance between two points with given coordinates
- calculate the coordinates of the midpoint of a segment
- prove algebraically that three points are or are not collinear
- recognize when two lines are parallel or perpendicular
- plot points in three dimensions and find the distance between them

You will develop these habits and skills:

- Plot points with given coordinates in two and three dimensions.
- Describe the location of a point on a coordinate plane.
- Write equations of lines with given characteristics.
- Use subscript notation.
- Write proofs combining geometric and algebraic ideas.

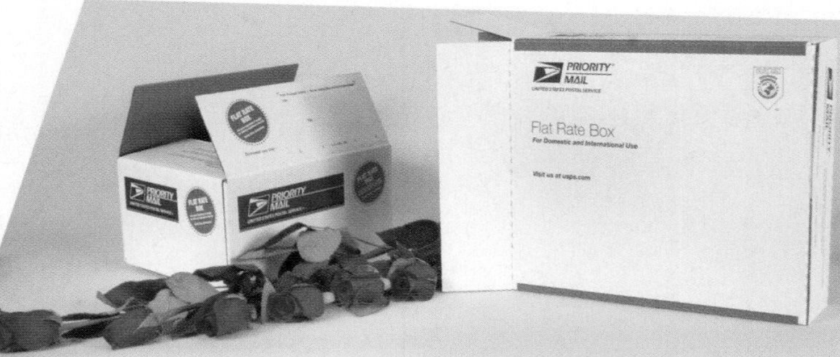

The boxes are 11 in. by $8\frac{1}{2}$ in. by $5\frac{1}{2}$ in. and $13\frac{5}{8}$ in. by $11\frac{7}{8}$ in. by $3\frac{3}{8}$ in. What is the longest rose you could ship in one of these boxes?

7.06 Getting Started

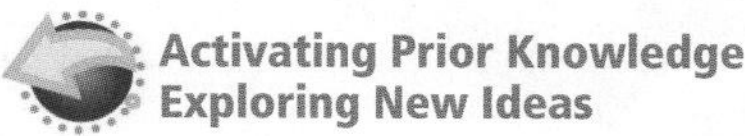

The coordinate plane allows you to make connections between geometry and algebra.

You have been working with polygons and circles geometrically, proving results through logic and reasoning. Now you can use your algebra skills to investigate some of these geometric ideas in the coordinate plane.

For example, coordinates locate points, so they are helpful for locating special parts, such as the midpoint of a line segment. Since coordinates involve numbers, you can use them to calculate lengths and distances exactly rather than relying on approximate measurements.

For You to Explore

1. The coordinates of three vertices of a rectangle are given. Find the coordinates of the points described below.

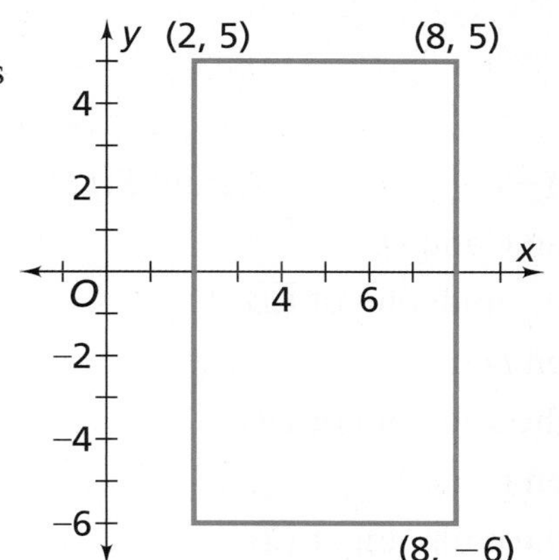

a. the fourth vertex

b. four points that are inside the rectangle

c. four points that are outside the rectangle

d. four more points that lie on the rectangle

e. How can you tell whether a point is inside the rectangle just by looking at its coordinates?

2. Suppose you have points $A(2, 5)$ and $B(2, 396)$.

a. What is the distance between A and B?

b. Find the coordinates of the midpoint of $\overline{AB}$.

3. a. How many vertical lines contain the point $(-1, 9)$?

b. Name the coordinates of the intersection I of a horizontal line through $T(3, -5)$ and a vertical line through $R(-1, 9)$.

c. Plot the points T, R, and I. Find the lengths of all three sides of $\triangle TRI$.

4. Suppose that $F(-1, 4)$ and $G(-3, -2)$.

a. Find the coordinates of the midpoint of $\overline{FG}$.

b. Find the length of $\overline{FG}$.

Exercises *Practicing Habits of Mind*

On Your Own

5. Find the coordinates of the midpoint of the segment below. Describe the method you used.

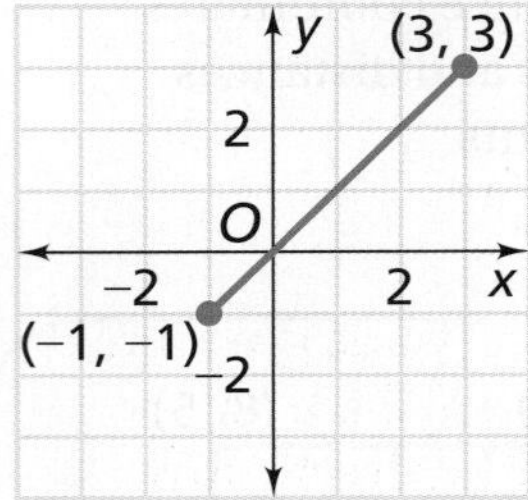

6. Suppose you have points $C(-5, -7)$, $D(12, -7)$, and $E(12, 3)$.

a. Find the distance between C and D.

b. Find the coordinates of the midpoint of $\overline{CD}$.

c. Find the distance between D and E.

d. Find the coordinates of the midpoint of $\overline{DE}$.

e. Find the distance between C and E.

f. Find the coordinates of the midpoint of $\overline{CE}$.

7. In the diagram, m is a vertical line. Find each of the following.

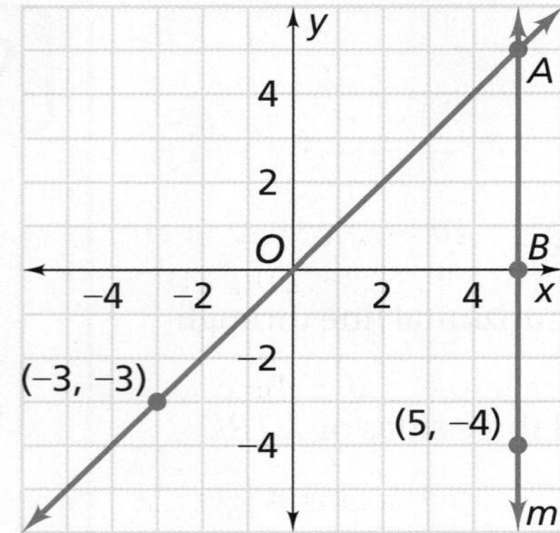

a. the coordinates of A and B

b. the length of $\overline{AB}$

c. the coordinates of the midpoint of $\overline{AB}$

d. the area of $\triangle AOB$

e. the length of $\overline{AO}$

f. the coordinates of the midpoint of $\overline{AO}$

8. List coordinates of points to make a connect-the-dots puzzle that draws your initials. Give it to a friend to try.

9. **Take It Further** How many quadrants in the coordinate plane does each line pass through?

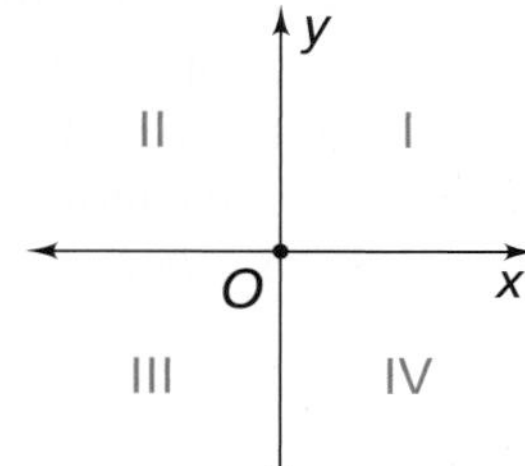

   a. a vertical line through the origin
   b. a vertical line not through the origin
   c. a nonvertical, nonhorizontal line through the origin
   d. a nonvertical, nonhorizontal line not through the origin

10. **Take It Further** Is it possible for a line to pass through only one quadrant? Is it possible for a line to pass through all four quadrants? Is there any slanting (nonvertical, nonhorizontal) line that passes through only two quadrants and does not contain the origin?

Maintain Your Skills

11. a. Copy and complete the table below.

A	B	C	D	E	F	G
(x, y)	$(x + 3, y)$	$(-x, y)$	$(x, -y)$	$(2x, 2y)$	$\left(\frac{x}{2}, \frac{y}{2}\right)$	$(-y, x)$
(2, 1)	■	■	■	■	$\left(1, \frac{1}{2}\right)$	■
(−4, 0)	(−1, 0)	■	■	■	■	■
(−5, 4)	■	(5, 4)	■	■	■	(−4, −5)

   b. On a piece of graph paper, plot the three points in Column A and connect them to form triangle A. Plot the three points in Column B and connect them to form a triangle B. Describe how the two triangles differ.

   c. On a new section of graph paper, draw triangles A and C. Describe how they differ.

   d. Use clean graph paper each time. Pair triangle A with each of triangles D, E, F, and G. Each time describe how the two triangles differ.

7.07 Midpoint and Distance Formulas

Here is some very convenient notation.

When only a few points need names, you can call them *A*, *B*, *C*, and so on, and name their coordinates (a, b), (c, d), (e, f), and so on. If you have too many points, however, you can run out of letters. Since you can never run out of numbers, the convention is to use numbers as subscripts. For example, you could name the vertices of a decagon $A_1, A_2, A_3, \ldots, A_{10}$. You could name the vertices of an *n*-gon $B_1, B_2, B_3, \ldots, B_n$.

In-Class Experiment

Copy and complete the table below. Then answer the questions that follow.

Assume that point V_1 has coordinates (x_1, y_1), point V_2 has coordinates (x_2, y_2), and so on.

i	Coordinates of V_i	x_i	y_i
1	(■, ■)	■	■
2	(■, ■)	−2	■
3	(−4, −2)	−4	−2
4	(■, ■)	2	■

1. Here is a claim about the coordinates of the vertices of square $V_1V_2V_3V_4$.

$$x_i = y_{i+1}$$

Is the claim true when $i = 1$? That is, is it true that $x_1 = y_2$? Is the claim true when $i = 2$? When $i = 3$? When $i = 4$?

For example, is it true that $x_1 = y_{1+1} = y_2$?

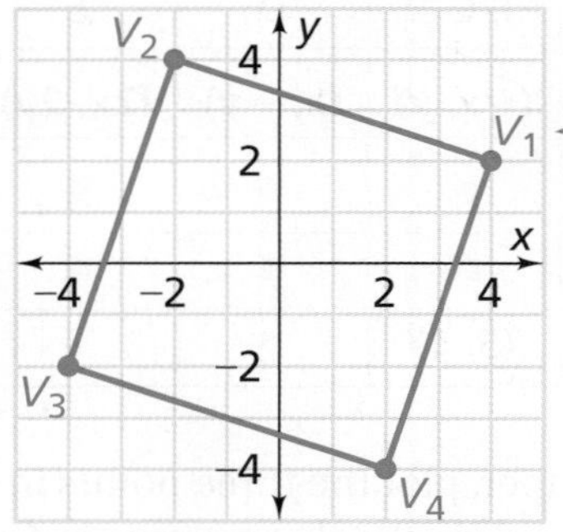

square $V_1V_2V_3V_4$

2. Here is another claim about the vertices of square $V_1V_2V_3V_4$.

If V_i has coordinates (x_i, y_i), then V_{i+1} has coordinates $(-y_i, x_i)$.

a. When $i = 2$, the claim says, "If V_2 has coordinates (x_2, y_2), then V_3 has coordinates $(-y_2, x_2)$." Look at the table and decide whether this is true.

b. Find a value of *i* for which the statement does not make sense.

3. Name the vertices of the square for which it is true that $y_i = \frac{1}{2}x_i$.

4. Here is a rule for deriving a new set of points Q_i from the points V_1, V_2, V_3, and V_4.

If $V_i = (x_i, y_i)$, then $Q_i = (x_i - 3, y_i + 4)$.

a. The rule is written in algebraic symbols. Explain the rule in words.

b. Find the new points Q_1, Q_2, Q_3, and Q_4 and plot them.

5. If $P_1 = (x_1, y_1)$, and you know that P_2 is a second point on the same horizontal line, how can you write its coordinates?

6. Let $P_i = (x_i, y_i)$, $x_i = i + 3$, and $y_i = x_i - 4$. Plot P_i as i goes from 1 to 8. Describe the result.

Minds in Action episode 32

Sasha and Derman are trying to write a formula for finding the distance between two points. They are given

$$G = (x_1, y_1),\ H = (x_2, y_2)$$

Sasha Well, the distance between two points on a vertical or horizontal line is easy to find. Just subtract the unlike coordinates. If G is $(3, 4)$ and H is $(3, 90)$, then the distance between G and H is $90 - 4 = 86$.

Derman But we don't know that G and H are on a horizontal or vertical line. They're just *any* two points.

We used the Pythagorean Theorem to help us find the distance between two points that weren't on the same horizontal or vertical line before. Let's try that here.

Sasha Don't we need three points to make a triangle so we can use the Pythagorean Theorem?

Derman Watch! I'll make a third point:

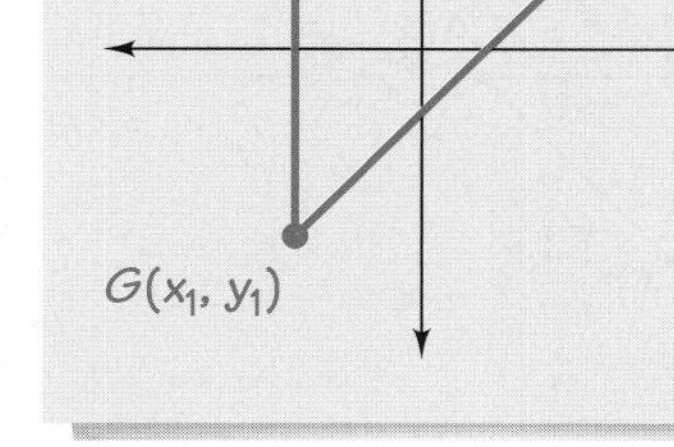

What are the lengths of the legs of this right triangle?

Before you ask, I know that the third point is (x_1, y_2). In my picture I had to go over as far as the (x_1, y_1) point—that's where I got the x_1—and up as far as the (x_2, y_2) point—that's where I got the y_2.

Sasha Great! Now let's use the Pythagorean Theorem to find the length of the hypotenuse of that triangle.

$$(x_2 - x_1)^2 + (y_2 - y_1)^2 = GH^2$$

So,

$$GH = \sqrt{(x_2 - x_1)^2 + (y_2 - y_1)^2}$$

Derman and Sasha's explanation is a proof of the following theorem.

Theorem 7.2 Distance Formula

The distance between two points (x_1, y_1) and (x_2, y_2) can be found using the Pythagorean Theorem. It is the square root of the sum of the square of the difference in the *x*-coordinates and the square of the difference in the *y*-coordinates.

Habits of Mind

Use facts you know. If you remember how you found it, you do not have to remember the Distance Formula. You can figure it out just by remembering the Pythagorean Theorem.

For You to Do

Find the distance between each pair of points.

7. (1, 1) and (−1, −1)

8. (1, 1) and (4, 5)

9. (2, 4) and (−4, −2)

When you found the midpoint of a segment in Lesson 7.5, you may have used a method like this:

The *x*-coordinate is equal to the average of the *x*-coordinates of the endpoints. The *y*-coordinate is equal to the average of the *y*-coordinates of the endpoints.

Or, you can write it algebraically.

$$\left(\frac{x_1 + x_2}{2}, \frac{y_1 + y_2}{2}\right)$$

You can use Derman's diagram from Minds in Action to help justify this method for finding the midpoint.

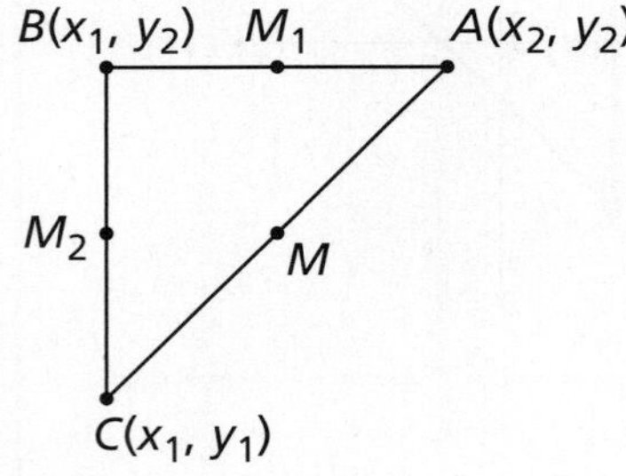

Theorem 7.3 Midpoint Formula

Each coordinate of the midpoint of a line segment is equal to the average of the corresponding coordinates of the endpoints of the line segment.

Proof First, find the midpoint M_1 of $\overline{AB}$. This segment is horizontal, so every point on it has the same y-coordinate. You also know that $\frac{x_1 + x_2}{2}$ is the number halfway between x_1 and x_2. This means that the coordinates of M_1 are $\left(\frac{x_1 + x_2}{2}, y_2\right)$.

You can show that the distance from M_1 to A is the same as the distance from B to M_1 by looking at the difference in the x-coordinates of these points, since they are all on the same horizontal line.

$$M_1 \text{ to } A\text{: } x_2 - \left(\frac{x_1 + x_2}{2}\right) = \frac{x_2 - x_1}{2}$$

$$B \text{ to } M_1\text{: } \frac{x_1 + x_2}{2} - x_1 = \frac{x_1 + x_2}{2} - \frac{2x_1}{2} = \frac{x_2 - x_1}{2}$$

The same reasoning shows that the midpoint M_2 of the segment with coordinates (x_1, y_1) and (x_1, y_2) has coordinates $\left(x_1, \frac{y_1 + y_2}{2}\right)$. In this case, the three points are on a vertical line, so they must all have the same x-coordinate.

Now you need to find the coordinates of M, the midpoint of $\overline{AC}$. The Midline Theorem (Theorem 2.10) says that the segment joining the midpoints of two sides of a triangle is parallel to the third side. Also, its measure is equal to half the measure of the third side.

About halfway between Penzance and Land's End is the hamlet of Crows-an-wra. About how far, and in what direction, is the hamlet from this marker?

This means that if you draw a line through M_1 and M (wherever it is), that line must be parallel to $\overline{BC}$. And that means that the line through M_1 and M is vertical. Because you know that on a vertical line all points have the same x-coordinate, you know that the x-coordinate of M is $\frac{x_1 + x_2}{2}$.

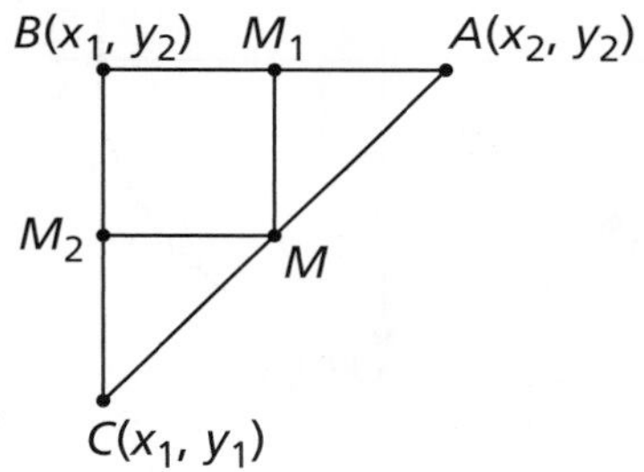

Similarly, if you draw a line through M_2 and M, that line will be parallel to $\overline{AB}$. It will be horizontal and will have the same y-coordinate as M_2, namely $\frac{y_1 + y_2}{2}$.

So the coordinates of M are $\left(\frac{x_1 + x_2}{2}, \frac{y_1 + y_2}{2}\right)$.

For You to Do

10. Find the midpoint of the segment with endpoints (1327, 94) and (−668, 17).

11. Find the midpoint of the segment with endpoints (1776, 13) and (2000, 50).

Exercises Practicing Habits of Mind

Check Your Understanding

1. Points A and B are endpoints of a diameter of a circle. Point C is the center of the circle. Find the coordinates of C given the following coordinates for A and B.

   a. $(-79, 687)$, $(13, 435)$

   b. $(x, 0)$, $(5x, y)$

2. Points A through G lie on a circle of radius 10, as shown in the figure. Find their missing coordinates.

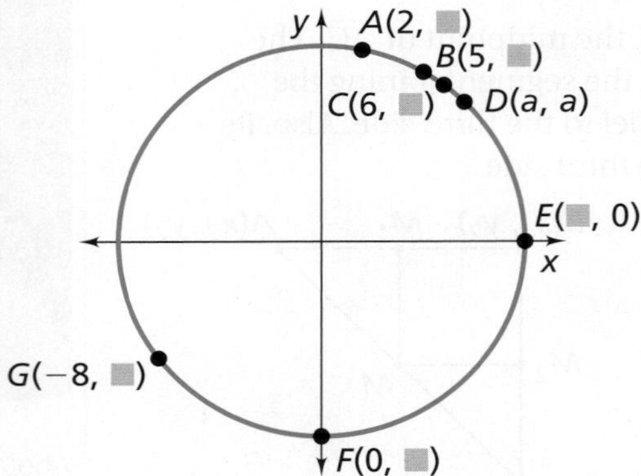

3. The vertices of $\triangle ABC$ are $A(2, 1)$, $B(4, 8)$, and $C(6, -2)$.

   a. Find the lengths of the three sides of the triangle.

   b. Find the lengths of the three medians of the triangle.

4. Consider the six points $A(5, 1)$, $B(10, -2)$, $C(8, 3)$, $A'(2, 3)$, $B'(7, 0)$, and $C'(5, 5)$. Show that $\triangle ABC \cong \triangle A'B'C'$.

5. Consider the six points $A(-800, -500)$, $B(160, 12)$, $C(-737, -484)$, $A'(0, 0)$, $B'(3840, 2048)$, and $C'(252, 64)$. Show that $\triangle ABC \sim \triangle A'B'C'$.

6. **Write About It** Explain how to tell whether two triangles are congruent by doing calculations on the coordinates of their vertices.

7. **Write About It** Explain how to tell whether two triangles are similar by doing calculations on the coordinates of their vertices.

8. Quadrilateral $STAR$ has vertices $S(-2, 8)$, $T(8, 2)$, $A(0, -4)$, and $R(-2, 0)$. Find the coordinates of the midpoints of the four sides of quadrilateral $STAR$. These points determine a new quadrilateral. Show that this new quadrilateral is a parallelogram.

One way to show that a quadrilateral is a parallelogram is to show that opposite sides are parallel. What is another way?

9. Pick any four points that form a quadrilateral in the coordinate plane. Find the midpoints of all four sides. Show that if you connect the midpoints in order, you get a parallelogram.

On Your Own

10. Three vertices of a square are $(-1, 5)$, $(5, 3)$, and $(3, -3)$.

a. Find the center of the square.

b. Find the fourth vertex.

11. Three vertices of a square are $(-114, 214)$, $(186, 114)$, and $(-214, -86)$.

a. Find the center of the square.

b. Find the fourth vertex.

12. $\overline{DE}$ has midpoint $F(4.5, 17)$ and one endpoint $D(2, 16)$. What are the coordinates of the other endpoint, E?

13. $\overline{AB}$ and $\overline{CD}$ bisect each other. Given the points $A(110, 15)$, $B(116, 23)$, and $C(110, 23)$, find E, the point of bisection. Also, find the coordinates of D.

Remember...

Two segments bisect each other if they intersect at each other's midpoint.

14. A segment has length 25. Give possible coordinates for the endpoints of this segment in each case below.

a. The segment is on a horizontal line.

b. The segment is on a vertical line.

c. The segment is neither horizontal nor vertical.

15. A segment has its midpoint at $(8, 10)$. List four possibilities for the coordinates of its endpoints.

16. A segment has one endpoint at $(-7, -2)$ and its midpoint at $(-2, 1.5)$. What are the coordinates of the other endpoint?

17. **Standardized Test Prep** Julio is planning to swim across the lake at his summer camp. On a map, the coordinates of his starting point are $(-2 \text{ cm}, 3.5 \text{ cm})$. The dock to which he will swim has coordinates $(14 \text{ cm}, -8.5 \text{ cm})$. The scale on the map is 1 cm : 100 m. What distance will Julio have to swim?

A. 1200 meters   **B.** 1300 meters

C. 1600 meters   **D.** 2000 meters

18. Suppose you have points $P(5, 0)$ and $Q(15, 0)$.

a. Find six points that are just as far from P as they are from Q.

b. Find six points that are closer to P than they are to Q.

c. How can you tell if a point is equidistant from P and Q just by looking at its coordinates?

19. The endpoints of a line segment are the midpoints of two sides of a triangle. Show that the length of this segment is one half the length of the third side of that triangle. Show that this is true for any triangle. (Use subscript notation.)

Habits of Mind

Use a symbol. You could use d_s for the length of a side of the triangle. You must show that d_m, the distance between the midpoints, is $\frac{1}{2}d_s$. But think ahead. Would it be helpful to use $2d_s$ for the length of a side?

Maintain Your Skills

Find the slope between each pair of points.

20. (3, 85) and (0, 124)

21. (0, 124) and (4, 72)

22. (4, 72) and (−111, 1567)

23. (−111, 1567) and (2, 98)

24. (2, 98) and (3, 85)

Remember...

You find slope by calculating the ratio between the change in *y*-coordinates and the change in *x*-coordinates.

Go Online
Pearsonsuccessnet.com

7.08 Parallel Lines and Collinear Points

This In-Class Experiment should help you remember what you learned in Algebra 1 about the equations of lines.

In-Class Experiment

1. Plot several points with y-coordinates that have each property.
   a. 1 more than the x-coordinate
   b. 2 more than the x-coordinate
   c. 1 less than the x-coordinate

   For each property, draw a picture that shows all the points with that property.

2. Plot several points with y-coordinates that have each property.
   a. twice the x-coordinate
   b. three times the x-coordinate
   c. four times the x-coordinate

   For each property, draw a picture that shows all the points with that property.

3. Some of the lines you drew have points with coordinates of the form $(x, x + \text{something})$.
   a. What do those lines have in common?
   b. Write the equations of those lines in the form $ax + by = c$.
   c. What do these equations have in common?

4. Some other lines you drew have points with coordinates of the form $(x, x \times \text{something})$.
   a. What do those lines have in common?
   b. Write the equations of those lines in the form $ax + by = c$.
   c. What do these equations have in common?

In Algebra 1, you proved the following theorem.

Theorem 7.4

Two nonvertical lines are parallel if and only if they have the same slope.

The proof of Theorem 7.4 depends on the following theorem.

Theorem 7.5

Let A, B, and C be three points, no two of which are in line vertically. Points A, B, and C are collinear if and only if the slope between A and B, $m(A, B)$, is the same as the slope between B and C, $m(B, C)$. In symbols:

$$A, B, \text{ and } C \text{ are collinear} \Leftrightarrow m(A, B) = m(B, C).$$

Remember...

Points that lie on a line are collinear.

Proof Without affecting the generality of the argument, you can choose to name the three points so that A is the point with the smallest x-coordinate, B is the point with the next-largest x-coordinate, and C is the point with the largest x-coordinate.

Step 1 Suppose that A, B, and C are collinear. Then you know $m\angle ABC = 180°$.

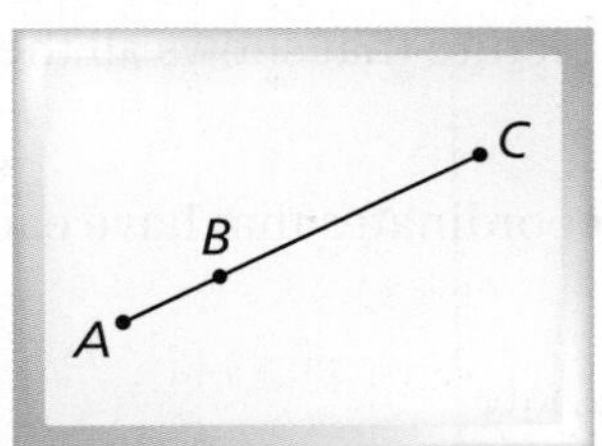

Step 2 Through points B and C, draw lines parallel to the y-axis. Through points A and B, draw lines parallel to the x-axis. By the Parallel Postulate, these lines are unique. You also know that any line parallel to the x-axis is perpendicular to any line parallel to the y-axis.

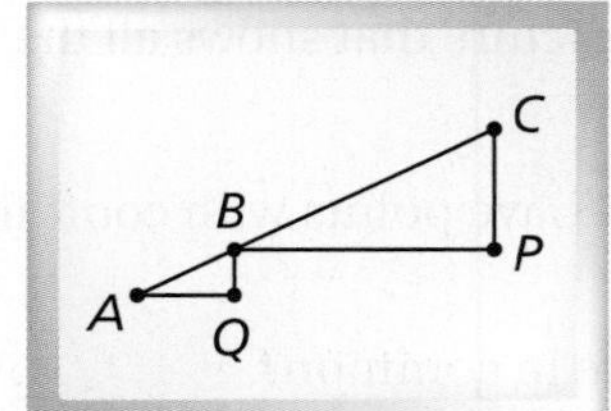

How do you treat the case in which the line containing A, B, and C is horizontal?

Let P be the intersection of the horizontal line from B and the vertical line from C. Let Q be the intersection of the horizontal line from A and the vertical line from B.

Step 3 Show that $m\angle AQB = m\angle QBP = m\angle BPC = 90°$.

Step 4 Show that $m\angle ABQ + m\angle BAQ = 90°$.

Step 5 Look at the three angles with vertex B ($\angle ABQ$, $\angle QBP$, and $\angle PBC$). From their relationship and from Step 4, you can conclude that $m\angle BAQ = m\angle CBP$.

Step 6 Use your previous results to show $\triangle AQB \sim \triangle BPC$. Then conclude that $\frac{BQ}{QA} = \frac{CP}{PB}$. This relationship tells you that $m(A, B)$ (the slope between points A and B) is equal to $m(B, C)$.

You have just proven half of Theorem 7.5!

Minds in Action episode 33

Tony seems a bit puzzled.

Tony Okay, so I understand how we proved that

$$A, B, \text{ and } C \text{ are collinear} \Rightarrow m(A, B) = m(B, C).$$

But how can we prove the other direction?

Sasha Well, it shouldn't be too hard. Somehow we have to reverse the steps. We want to start at the end of the proof we just did and work back to the beginning.

Tony That reminds me of the reverse-list strategy.

Sasha Yes, it sounds pretty easy, and if it works we will have proved the rest of the theorem.

For You to Do

5. Use Sasha's idea to prove the rest of Theorem 7.5.

$$A, B, \text{ and } C \text{ are collinear} \Leftarrow m(A, B) = m(B, C)$$

Developing Habits of Mind

Visualize. Here is another way to think about three collinear points, and this way has a bonus result! Think of points A, B, and C as vertices of a triangle. Also, think of B as moving continuously closer and closer to $\overline{AC}$.

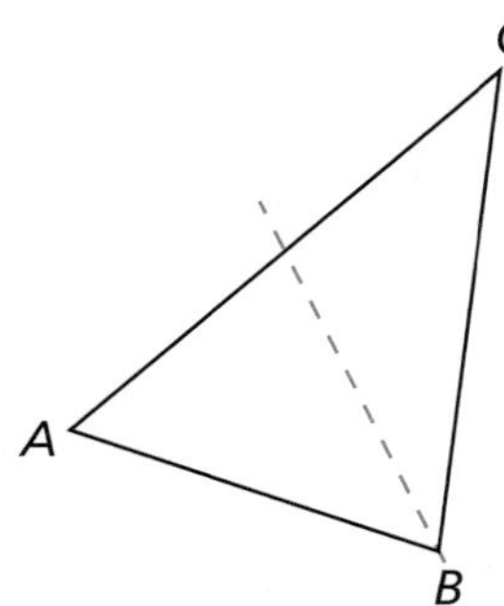

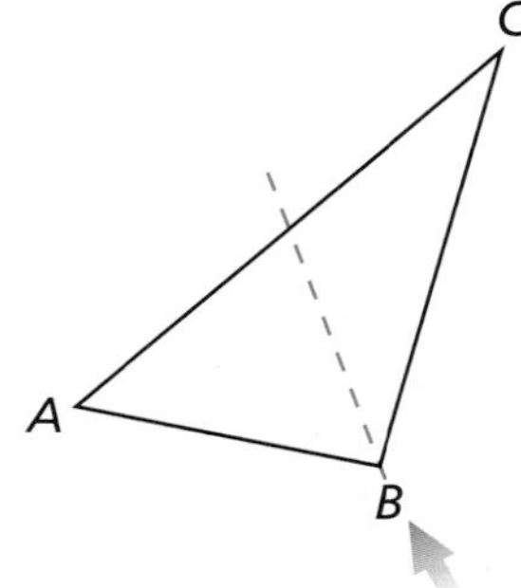

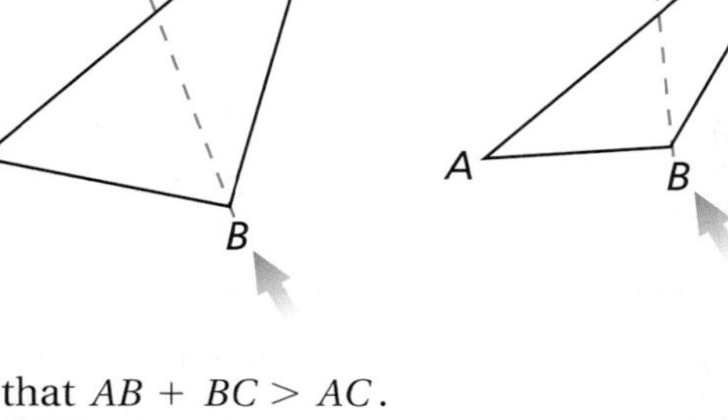

The Triangle Inequality says that $AB + BC > AC$. As B gets closer and closer to $\overline{AC}$, $AB + BC$ gets closer and closer to AC. When B is on $\overline{AC}$, $AB + BC$ is no longer greater than AC. In fact, $AB + BC = AC$.

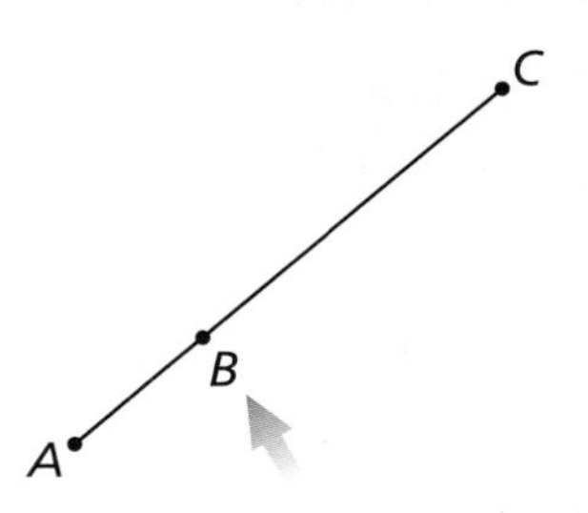

Now, suppose you are given three points, A, B, and C. Would knowing that $AC = AB + BC$ be enough to prove that the three points are collinear?

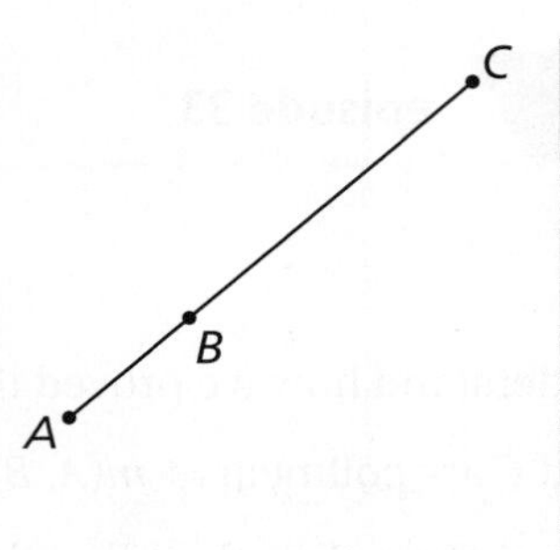

Yes, it would be enough, because if B were not in line with A and C, then A, B, and C would be the vertices of a triangle. The three segment lengths would satisfy the Triangle Inequality. But the segment lengths do not satisfy the Triangle Inequality, so the points cannot be the vertices of a triangle. The points have to be collinear.

Example

Problem Decide whether the following three points are collinear.

$A(1, 5)$ $B(0, 1)$ $C(3, 13)$

Solution Use the Triangle Inequality.

$$AB = \sqrt{(1-0)^2 + (5-1)^2} = \sqrt{1 + 16} = \sqrt{17}$$
$$BC = \sqrt{(3-0)^2 + (13-1)^2} = \sqrt{9 + 144} = 3\sqrt{17}$$
$$AC = \sqrt{(3-1)^2 + (13-5)^2} = \sqrt{4 + 64} = 2\sqrt{17}$$

For the three lengths, $AC + AB = 2\sqrt{17} + \sqrt{17} = 3\sqrt{17} = BC$. This means that A, B, and C are collinear, with A between B and C.

Habits of Mind

Check your work. You can use another method—namely Theorem 7.5—to check the result in the Example.

For You to Do

Use the Triangle Inequality or Theorem 7.5 to decide whether the three points are collinear. Use the other method to check your result.

6. $A\left(\frac{2}{7}, 0\right)$ $B(0, 2)$ $C(1, 9)$

7. $A\left(\frac{1}{25}, 2\right)$ $B(1, 26)$ $C(7, 0)$

8. $A(2, 2)$ $B(3, 3)$ $C(5, 9)$

9. $A(2, 4)$ $B(0, 0)$ $C(3, 6)$

10. $A(-1, 3)$ $B(-2, 2)$ $C(2, 6)$

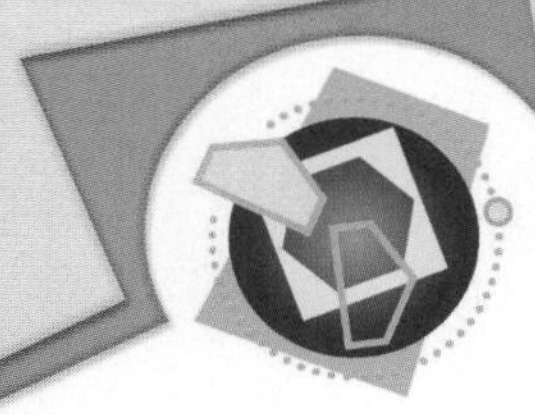

Exercises *Practicing Habits of Mind*

Check Your Understanding

1. Are the two lines with the given equations parallel? Explain.

a. $2x + 3y = 0$ $\quad 2x + 3y = 4$

b. $x + \frac{1}{3}y = 7$ $\quad 3x + y = 1$

c. $x + \frac{1}{3}y = 7$ $\quad 3x + y = 21$

d. $\sqrt{2}x + 4y = 0$ $\quad 2x + 4y = 0$

e. $2\sqrt{2}x + 4y = 1$ $\quad x + \sqrt{2}y = 3$

2. Find a point that is collinear with $A(5, 1)$ and $B(8, -3)$. Explain your method.

3. Give a set of instructions for finding points that are collinear with $A(5, 1)$ and $B(8, -3)$. Explain why your method works.

4. Is $P(-4, -14)$ collinear with $R(-40, -30)$ and $S(80, 20)$? Explain.

On Your Own

5. Suppose you have points $A(4, 1)$, $B(8, -2)$, $C(7, 1)$, and $D(3, 4)$.

a. Show that the diagonals of quadrilateral *ABCD* bisect each other.

b. What does this tell you about what kind of quadrilateral *ABCD* is? Explain.

6. Two vertices of an equilateral triangle are at $(1, 0)$ and $(9, 0)$. Find coordinates for the third vertex.

7. For each possible pairing of lines, tell whether the lines

- are parallel
- meet at the origin
- intersect elsewhere
- are the same line

How many possible pairs are there to consider?

ℓ: The y-coordinates are $\frac{1}{2}$ their x-coordinates.

m: The y-coordinates are 3 more than their x-coordinates.

n: The y-coordinates are 2 less than their x-coordinates.

p: The y-coordinates are -2 times their x-coordinates.

q: The y-coordinates are 5 times their x-coordinates.

r: The y-coordinates are $\frac{1}{3}$ their x-coordinates.

8. Is $(110, 9)$ collinear with $(60, 10)$ and $(10, 11)$? Explain.

9. **Standardized Test Prep** The coordinates of point A are $(3, 4)$. The coordinates of point B are $(5, -1)$. Which point is NOT collinear with A and B?

A. $(2, -5)$ **B.** $(1, 9)$ **C.** $(0, 11.5)$ **D.** $(4.6, 0)$

10. Draw two lines, a and b, with the following characteristics, on the coordinate plane.

- Line a passes through $(0, 1)$ and $(1, 0)$.
- Line b passes through the origin and makes a 45° angle with the axes as it enters Quadrant I.

Find the coordinates of the point where lines a and b intersect.

Maintain Your Skills

11. Use the Triangle Inequality to test whether points lie on $\overline{RS}$ with endpoints $R(-40, -30)$ and $S(80, 20)$. Test some points that are collinear with R and S and some that are not.

12. **Take It Further** Now generalize your method. Suppose $R(r_1, r_2)$ and $S(s_1, s_2)$ are two points. Write an equation that has to be true if and only if a third point $P(p_1, p_2)$ lies on $\overleftrightarrow{RS}$. Simplify your equation until you come to a form like this.

$$(a - b) \cdot (c - d) = (e - f) \cdot (g - h)$$

(*Hint:* If an equation contains a square root, isolate it on one side and then square each side. You can repeat this step if necessary.)

Habits of Mind

Establish a process. When you see that an expression becomes complex, take time to organize your work. This slows you down at first, but it will save you time in the end.

Besides having the same slope, parallel lines are everywhere the same distance apart.

7.09 Perpendicular Lines

The slopes of two perpendicular lines have a special relationship.

In-Class Experiment

Study the diagram.

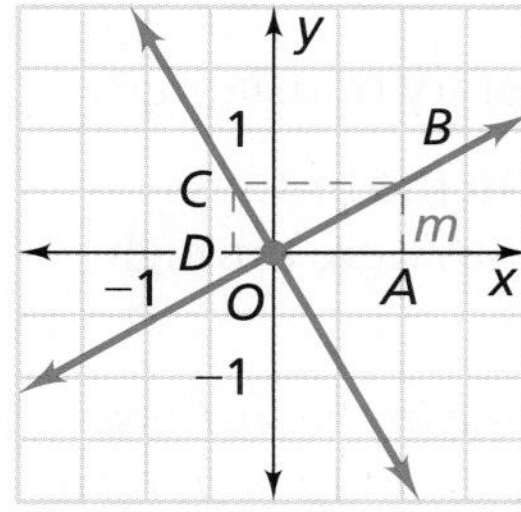

- $\overleftrightarrow{OB}$ and $\overleftrightarrow{OC}$ are perpendicular.
- Quadrilateral $ABCD$ has sides $\overline{AB}$ and $\overline{CD}$ parallel to the y-axis.
- Its other sides $\overline{BC}$ and $\overline{AD}$ are parallel to the x-axis.
- $AB = m$ and $OA = 1$.

1. Find CD and DO.

2. What is the slope of $\overleftrightarrow{OB}$?

3. What is the slope of $\overleftrightarrow{OC}$?

4. What is the product of the two slopes you found in Problems 2 and 3?

You just proved part of a very important theorem.

Theorem 7.6

Two nonvertical lines are perpendicular if and only if the product of their slopes is -1.

Also, any horizontal line is perpendicular to any vertical line.

Minds in Action episode 34

Tony wonders whether he has just seen a special case.

Tony Hey Sasha, suppose the lines don't intersect at the origin. Is Theorem 7.6 still true?

Sasha Well, Theorem 7.6 doesn't say anything about the lines having to intersect at the origin. But I agree that we have proved one direction of the theorem only for lines like that. Let's try to prove it for lines that could intersect anywhere.

Tony Let's try to avoid a lot of work. Why don't we just try translating?

Sasha That should work. The proof we came up with in the In-Class Experiment didn't really use the fact that the lines were through the origin. Look!

Sasha draws a diagram. She labels the rectangle like the one in the In-Class Experiment. She uses E instead of O for the intersection of the lines because it is no longer at the origin.

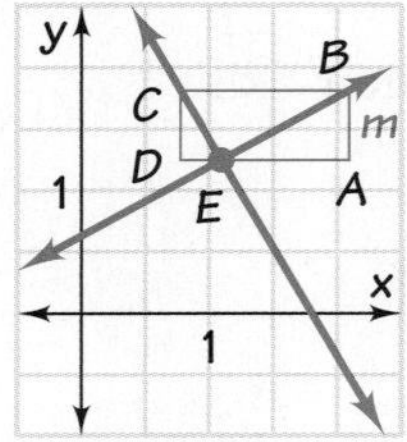

Tony Wow, that's true! Everything is the same as before:

$$AB = CD = m$$

$$EA = 1$$

and

$$CB = DA = 1 + DE$$

Knowing that $\overleftrightarrow{EB}$ and $\overleftrightarrow{EC}$ are perpendicular and that $\angle EAB$ and $\angle EDC$ are right angles, we know that $\triangle EAB$ and $\triangle CDE$ are similar. So

$$\frac{CD}{EA} = \frac{DE}{AB}$$

This means that $DE = \dfrac{AB \cdot CD}{EA} = \dfrac{m^2}{1} = m^2$.

Sasha Good, Tony! You really got it! So what are the slopes of $\overleftrightarrow{EB}$ and $\overleftrightarrow{EC}$?

Tony That's easy! The slope of $\overleftrightarrow{EB}$ is m, just as before. The slope of $\overleftrightarrow{EC}$ is

$$-\frac{CD}{DE} = -\frac{m}{m^2} = -\frac{1}{m}$$

So the product of the slopes is $m \cdot -\frac{1}{m} = -1$.

For Discussion

Now prove the second part of Theorem 7.6: *If the product of the slopes of two lines is* -1*, then the lines are perpendicular.*

Look at the figure below, where $m \geq 0$.

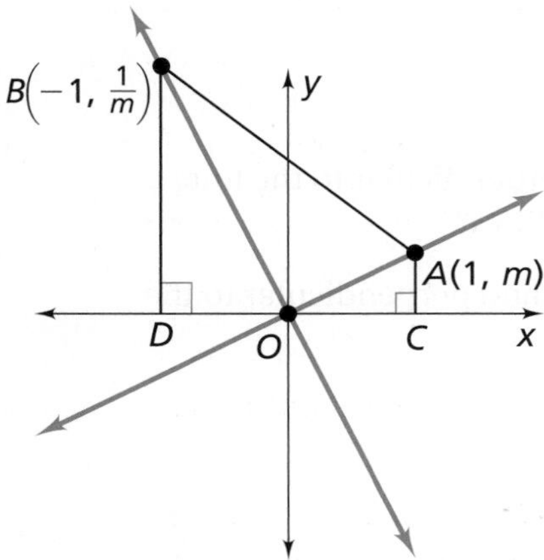

5. Find the slopes of $\overleftrightarrow{OA}$ and $\overleftrightarrow{OB}$. Show that the product of the slopes is -1.

6. Find *BD*, *DO*, *OC*, and *AC*.

7. Prove $\triangle BDO \sim \triangle OCA$.

8. Provide a justification for each step of the following proof.

Given $\triangle BDO \sim \triangle OCA$

Proof $m\angle DBO = m\angle COA$

$m\angle DBO + m\angle DOB = 90°$
$m\angle COA + m\angle DOB = 90°$
$m\angle BOA = 90°$

You can use Theorem 7.6 to find the distance between a point and a line.

For You to Do

9. Find an equation of the line through $P(3, 5)$ that is perpendicular to line ℓ with equation $2x + y = 9$.

10. Find the point of intersection *Q* of line ℓ and the perpendicular line you found.

11. What is the distance from *P* to ℓ?

Remember...

The distance from a point to a line is the length of the shortest segment from the point to the line. This segment is perpendicular to the line.

Exercises Practicing Habits of Mind

Check Your Understanding

1. Write equations for two different lines that are perpendicular to the line with equation $x + y = 3$. Are there other possibilities?

2. Write an equation of the line through point (1, 0) and perpendicular to the line with equation $x + 2y = 4$.

3. Find the distance from P to s in the figure below.

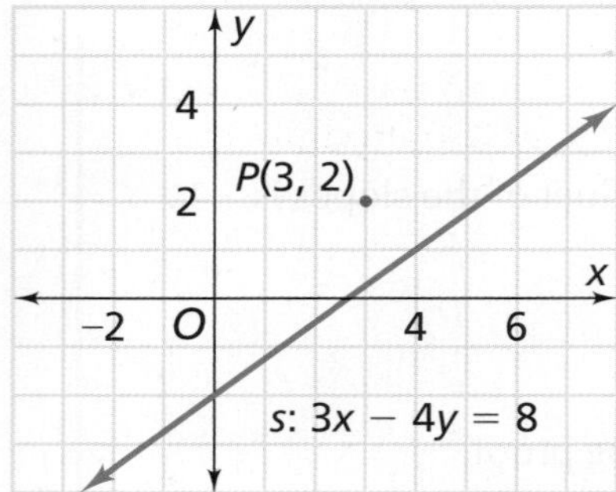

4. A circle has its center at the origin and radius 1. Find equations of two tangents to the circle through the point (3, 0).

Remember...

What is the distance from a tangent to the center of the circle?

On Your Own

5. Write an equation for at least one line perpendicular to the line with each equation.

   a. $x + y = 2$ **b.** $x - y + 2 = 0$ **c.** $19x + 3y = 17$ **d.** $y = 3 + 4x$

6. Write an equation of the line through the given point and perpendicular to the line with the given equation.

   a. (0, 0), $2x - 3y = 14$
   b. (0, −3), $y = -x + 2$
   c. (−4, −3), $2x + y + 6 = 0$
   d. (1, 2), $2x - 3y + 1 = 0$

7. Find the distance from the given point to the given line.

   a. (1, −2) to the line with equation $3x - y = -5$
   b. (−1, 0) to the line with equation $y = 5x - 1$
   c. (2, 2) to the line through points (3, 1) and (7, 4)
   d. (1, 2) to the line with equation $20x - 21y = 58$

8. Find the area of the triangle with the given vertices.

a. $A(1, 1)$, $B(4, 5)$, $C(13, -4)$ b. $A(1, 1)$, $B(4, 2)$, $C(2, 3)$

9. **Standardized Test Prep** What is the equation of the line that is perpendicular at the point $(4, 1)$ to the line with equation $y = -\frac{1}{2}x + 3$?

A. $y = \frac{1}{2}x - 1$ B. $y = 2x + 7$

C. $-x + y = -3$ D. $2x - y = 7$

10. Graph quadrilateral $ABCD$ with vertices $A(\sqrt{2}, 4)$, $B(3, 3)$, $C(-\sqrt{2}, -4)$, and $D(-3, -3)$. How many right angles does it have? Prove your answer.

11. a. Draw $\triangle ABC$ on the coordinate plane, with vertices $A(1, 1)$, $B(5, 1)$, and $C(3, 6)$.

b. Write an equation for the line containing the triangle's altitude relative to $\overline{AB}$.

c. Find the coordinates of H, the point of intersection of the altitude in part (b) and the base $\overline{AB}$.

d. Show algebraically that H is the midpoint of $\overline{AB}$.

12. a. Draw $\triangle ABC$ on the coordinate plane, with vertices $A(2, 3)$, $B(2, 7)$, and $C(8, 5)$.

b. Find the coordinates of the midpoint M of $\overline{AB}$.

c. Find an equation of the line through M and C.

d. Show algebraically that the line through M and C is perpendicular to $\overline{AB}$.

To do this, you should write an equation for $\overleftrightarrow{AB}$.

Maintain Your Skills

13. Line r has equation $2x + 3y = 4$. Line s has equation $ax + by = c$.

a. Find the distance of $(1, 2)$ from r.

b. Find the distance of (x_P, y_P) from r as a function of x_p and y_p.

c. Find the distance of $(1, 2)$ from s as a function of a, b, and c.

d. Find the distance of (x_P, y_P) from s as a function of x_p, y_p, a, b, and c.

A pier generally is built to be perpendicular to the shoreline. Why might this be so?

7.10 Coordinates in Three Dimensions

In the Cartesian coordinate plane, you describe the location of any point with an ordered pair (x, y). In three-dimensional space, you describe the location of a point with an **ordered triple** (x, y, z).

In mathematics, the conventional way to extend Cartesian coordinates to three dimensions is to show a third coordinate axis. It is perpendicular to the other two.

Conventional here means that most people do it or write it this way.

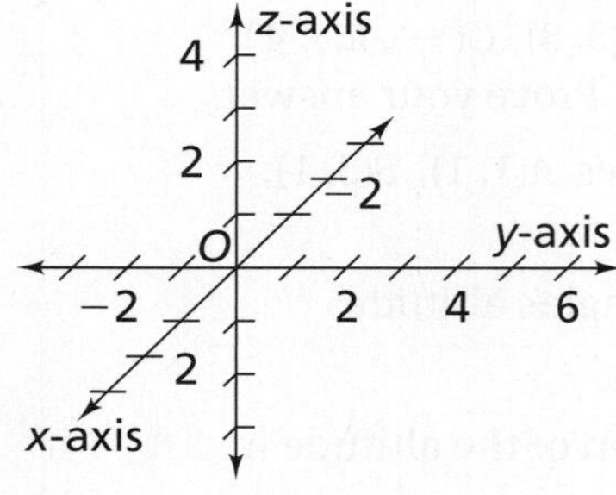

In this picture, the x-y coordinate plane lies flat, like the surface of your desk, and "face down." The new third axis—the ***z*-axis**—pierces the desk vertically and allows you to locate points above and below the x-y plane.

In this picture, B lies in the x-y plane and has coordinates (3, 4, 0). Point A lies above the x-y plane and has coordinates (3, 4, 2).

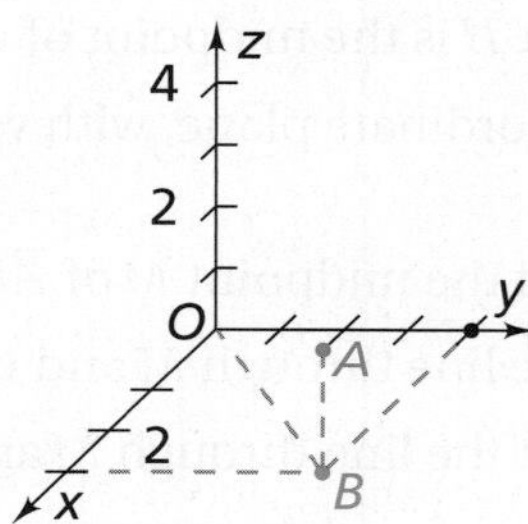

Example

Problem

a. Name and plot five ordered triples that have x-coordinate 3 and y-coordinate 4. What shape is the collection of all points with this property?

b. Name and plot five ordered triples that have z-coordinate 3. Describe where you find every point with z-coordinate 3.

Habits of Mind

Extend the description. You use an ordered pair for a point in two dimensions. You use an ordered triple for a point in three dimensions.

Solution

a. Here are five points that have the form $(3, 4, z)$.

$(3, 4, 0)$ $(3, 4, -2)$ $(3, 4, 2)$ $(3, 4, 4)$ $(3, 4, 6)$

All such points form a line that is parallel to the z-axis.

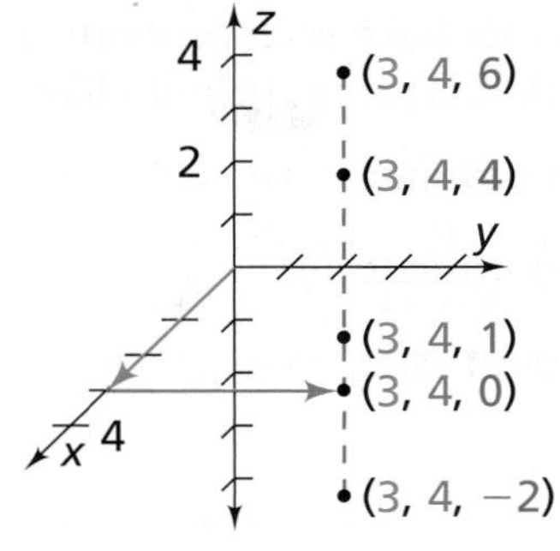

b. Here are five points that have the form $(x, y, 3)$.

$(0, 0, 3)$ $(0, 3, 3)$ $(-2, -3, 3)$ $(-2, 3, 3)$ $(4, 0, 3)$

It may not look like these points have anything in common, but every point with z-coordinate 3 lies on the plane that is three units above the x-y plane.

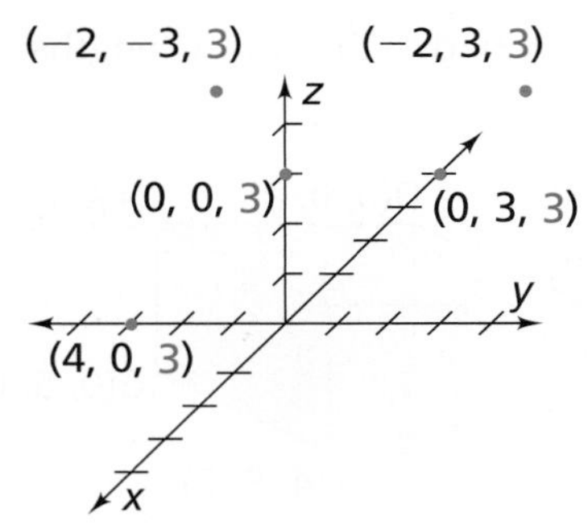

Developing Habits of Mind

Visualize. It is difficult to picture a three-dimensional figure, such as a plane, on a two-dimensional sheet of paper.

The diagram at the right might help you visualize three different planes in space. It looks like a corner of a room with no windows.

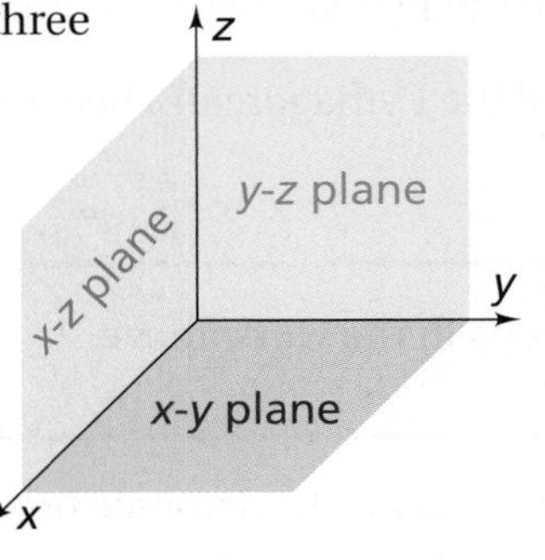

The x-y plane is the floor. All ordered triples that lie on this plane have a z-coordinate of 0: $(1, 2, 0)$, $(3, 5, 0)$, $(8, -2, 0)$, and so on.

The y-z plane is the wall at the back. All ordered triples that lie on this plane have an x-coordinate of 0: $(0, 1, 2)$, $(0, 3, 5)$, $(0, -2, 8)$, and so on.

The x-z plane is the wall at the left. All ordered triples that lie on this plane have a y-coordinate of 0: $(3, 0, 2)$, $(1, 0, 5)$, $(-12, 0, -2)$ and so on.

For You to Do

Name five ordered triples that have each property. Then describe what the collection of all points with this property looks like.

1. x-coordinate 2 and y-coordinate -3

2. x-coordinate 2 and z-coordinate -3

3. y-coordinate 2 and z-coordinate -3

4. x-coordinate 2

For the diagram below, Tony had to find these lengths: AE, EF, GF, EG, and AG.

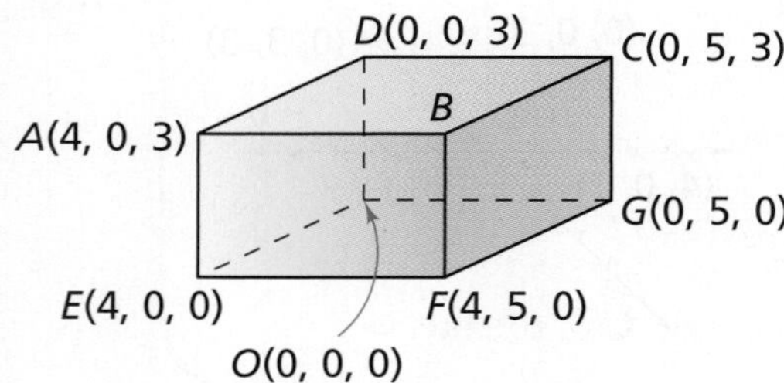

Here is Tony's work.

$AE = 3$ because $\overline{AE}$ is parallel to the z-axis.

$EF = 5$ because $\overline{EF}$ is parallel to the y-axis.

$GF = 4$ because $\overline{GF}$ is parallel to the x-axis.

$EG = \sqrt{41}$ because of the Pythagorean Theorem.

$AG = \sqrt{50}$ because of the Pythagorean Theorem.

For Discussion

5. Explain each of Tony's steps in the work above.

Tony's work leads to a formula for the distance between two points in three dimensions.

$$d = \sqrt{(x_2 - x_1)^2 + (y_2 - y_1)^2 + (z_2 - z_1)^2}$$

Proof This proof uses two successive applications of the Pythagorean Theorem. (See Tony's work above.)

Let $K = (x_1, y_1, z_1)$ and $M = (x_2, y_2, z_2)$.

You can form a right triangle by drawing $\overline{KN}$, a diagonal of the base of the box below.

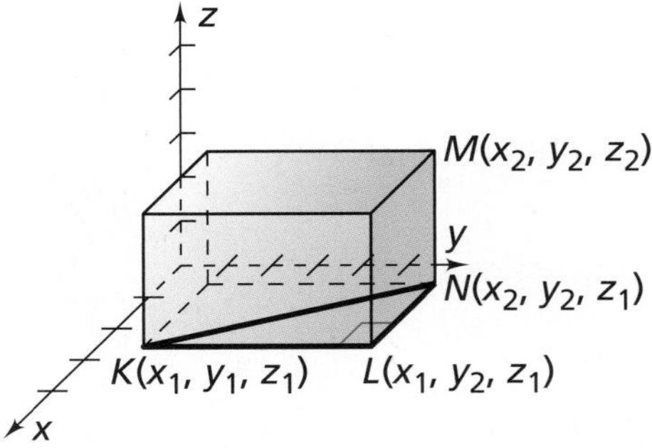

Apply the Pythagorean Theorem to get

$$KN^2 = LN^2 + KL^2$$

You can form right $\triangle KNM$ by drawing $\overline{KM}$, a diagonal of the box.

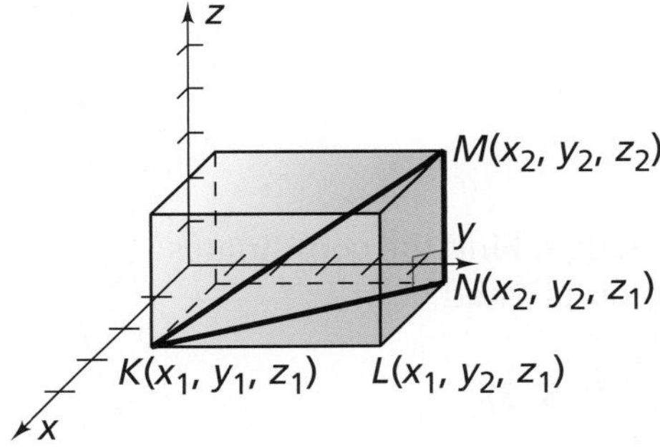

$$KM^2 = KN^2 + MN^2$$

Substituting $LN^2 + KL^2$ for KN^2 gives

$$KM^2 = LN^2 + KL^2 + MN^2$$

So $KM^2 = (x_2 - x_1)^2 + (y_2 - y_1)^2 + (z_2 - z_1)^2$.

A puffy dandelion suggests a sphere.

Exercises *Practicing Habits of Mind*

Check Your Understanding

1. Imagine that this room in your home is on a three-dimensional coordinate system.

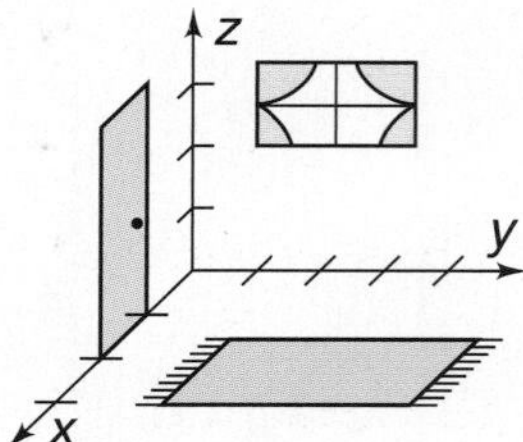

a. Describe where the origin is.

Estimate the ordered triples that describe each of the following.

b. the four corners of the door

c. the four corners of the window

d. the four corners of the rug

2. Here is the picture that Tony was working with earlier. Find the coordinates of the midpoint for each segment with the endpoints listed.

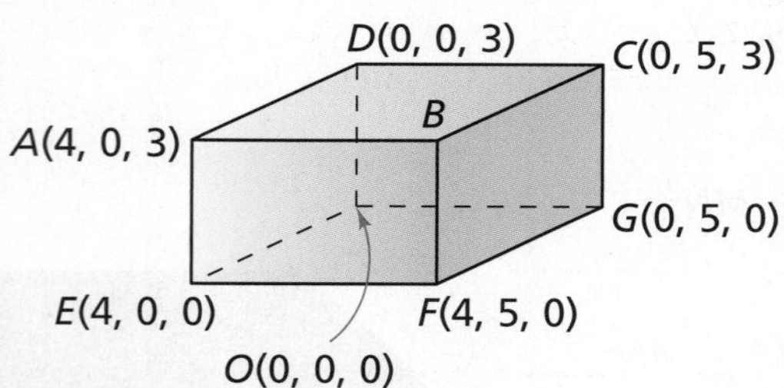

a. $A(4, 0, 3)$ and $C(0, 5, 3)$

b. $A(4, 0, 3)$ and $E(4, 0, 0)$

c. $O(0, 0, 0)$ and $A(4, 0, 3)$

d. $A(4, 0, 3)$ and $G(0, 5, 0)$

3. The diagonal $\overline{AH}$ of the box shown here is one side of $\triangle ABH$.

   a. What kind of triangle is $\triangle ABH$?

   b. What is BH?

   c. What is AH?

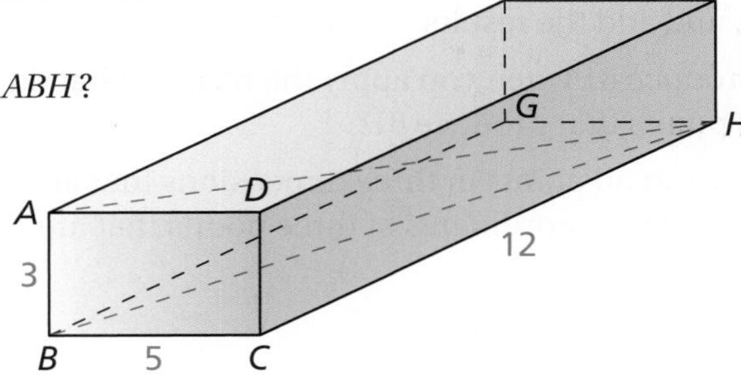

4. Here is a recipe to perform on points in the plane: square each coordinate and add the results.

   a. Find eight points that produce 5 when you apply the recipe to them.

   b. What figure do you see if you look at all the points that produce 5?

   Find eight points that produce each result.

   c. 13 d. 625 e. 100

   f. 169 g. 1

Developing Habits of Mind

Consider more than one strategy. One way to find a point that produces 5 in Exercise 4a is to use a calculator. Just decide, for example, that one coordinate of the point is 1.5. Then square 1.5, subtract the result from 5, and take the square root of what is left.

Another way is to think about sums of square integers. Can you express every integer as the sum of two squares? Can you express 5 as the sum of two squares?

5. a. If you draw a picture of all the points in the plane that are 13 units from the point (0, 0), what figure do you get?

   b. Find the coordinates of eight points that are 13 units from the point (0, 0). How can you tell if some new point (a, b) is on this figure by doing a quick calculation on its coordinates?

   c. If you draw a picture of all the points in the plane that are 13 units from the point $(4, -1)$, what figure do you get?

   d. Find the coordinates of eight points that are 13 units from the point $(4, -1)$. How can you tell if some new point (a, b) is on this figure by doing a quick calculation on its coordinates?

6. Suppose you apply the following recipe to points in three dimensions: take each coordinate, square it, and add the results.

   a. Find eight points that produce 81 when you apply the recipe. What do you get if you look at all points that produce 81?

   b. What do you get if you look at all points in three dimensions that are 7 units from the origin? Find the coordinates of three points that are 7 units from the origin.

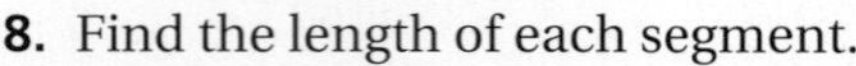

On Your Own

Use the diagram for Exercises 7–9.

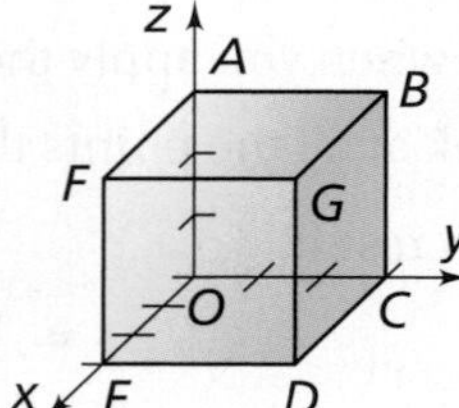

7. Find the coordinates of each vertex of the box.

8. Find the length of each segment.

   a. $\overline{OE}$ b. $\overline{OB}$

   c. $\overline{AE}$ d. $\overline{FC}$

9. Name another segment with the same length as the given segment.

   a. $\overline{OE}$ b. $\overline{OB}$

   c. $\overline{AE}$ d. $\overline{FC}$

10. A cube has a vertex at the origin and sides of length 1 along the axes.

   a. List one possible set of points that could be the other vertices of the cube.

   b. What is the length of a diagonal of the cube?

11. $\triangle LMN$ has vertices $L(1, 0, 0)$, $M(0, 1, 0)$, and $N(0, 0, 1)$.

   a. Sketch $\triangle LMN$.

   b. Find the perimeter of $\triangle LMN$.

   c. Find the midpoint of each side of $\triangle LMN$.

12. $\triangle ABC$ has vertices $A(2, -1, 7)$, $B(4, 0, 5)$, and $C(0, 0, 5)$.

   a. Find the perimeter of $\triangle ABC$.

   b. Find the midpoint of each side of $\triangle ABC$.

   c. Find the perimeter of the triangle formed by connecting the midpoints of the sides of $\triangle ABC$.

13. Standardized Test Prep A dowel is a long, straight rod with a small diameter. You want to ship a dowel in a rectangular box. The dimensions of four boxes are listed. Which dimensions allow for the longest dowel if the dowel extends from one corner to the opposite corner of the box?

A. 44 inches by 24 inches by 12 inches

B. 40 inches by 30 inches by 4 inches

C. 35 inches by 35 inches by 2 inches

D. 27 inches by 27 inches by 27 inches

14. Name six points in three dimensions that fit the rule: the sum of the coordinates is 30. What shape does this rule produce if you look at all of the points that fit it?

15. In a two-dimensional coordinate system, a square with a one-unit side length has one vertex at the origin. Two of its sides lie along the axes. Its vertices have no negative coordinates.

a. What are the coordinates of the vertex farthest from the origin?

b. How far is that vertex from the origin?

16. In a three-dimensional coordinate system, a cube with a one-unit side length sits with one vertex at the origin. Three of its edges lie along the axes. Its vertices have no negative coordinates.

a. What are the coordinates of the vertex farthest from the origin?

b. How far is that vertex from the origin?

17. Take It Further Two vertices of an equilateral triangle lie in the Cartesian plane at (1, 0) and (9, 0).

a. Find coordinates for the third vertex.

b. Embed the three points from part (a) in three dimensions. The coordinates become (1, 0, 0), (9, 0, 0), and $(a, b, 0)$, where (a, b) is your answer to part (a). Find the coordinates of the fourth vertex of a regular tetrahedron that has these three points as vertices.

Habits of Mind

Visualize. The four faces of a regular tetrahedron are equilateral triangles. The fourth vertex is the same distance from the other three vertices as they are from each other.

Maintain Your Skills

Points (0, 0, 2), (0, 1, 3), and (0, 1, 2) are the vertices of a triangle. Describe the triangle that results if you apply each rule to the coordinates.

18. Multiply each coordinate by 4.

19. Multiply each coordinate by $\frac{1}{3}$.

20. Add 3 to the x-coordinates.

21. Add 3 to the y-coordinates.

22. Subtract 3 from the z-coordinates.

In this investigation, you learned how to calculate the midpoint and length of a segment, write equations of lines with given characteristics, and prove whether three points are collinear. These questions will help you summarize what you have learned.

1. For $A\left(-3, \frac{1}{2}\right)$ and $B\left(\frac{2}{3}, \frac{1}{4}\right)$, find the distance of A from the origin O and the distance from A to B.
2. Calculate the coordinates of the midpoint of $\overline{JK}$ with endpoints $J(0, 3)$ and $K(-4, -6)$.
3. Are the following points collinear? Explain.
$$\left(0, \tfrac{1}{2}\right), \left(-1, -\tfrac{5}{2}\right), \left(\tfrac{1}{2}, 2\right)$$
4. Write an equation for the line through the origin and perpendicular to the line with equation $2x + 3y = 0$.
5. Here is a box in three dimensions.

   Find the length of its diagonal $\overline{EC}$.

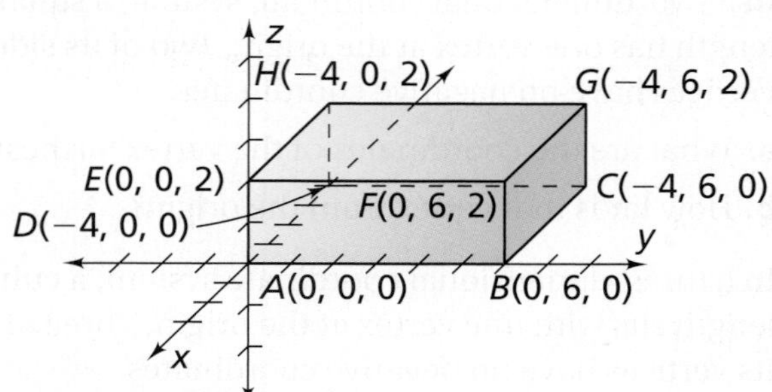

6. How can you tell by examining the coordinates of two points whether they lie on a horizontal line? On a vertical line?
7. How do you calculate the distance between two points?
8. A box has dimensions 3 in. by 5 in. by 4 in. What is the length of a diagonal?

Vocabulary and Notation

In this investigation, you learned these terms and this symbol. Make sure you understand what each one means and how to use it.

- **ordered triple**
- ***z*-axis**
- **V_1 (*V* sub 1)**

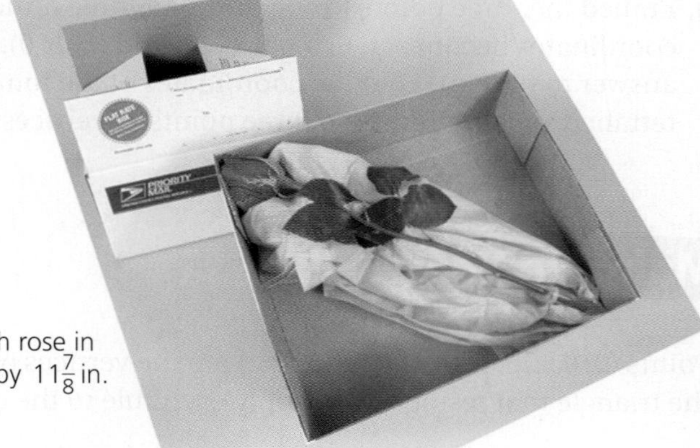

You can ship an 18-inch rose in the box that is $13\frac{5}{8}$ in. by $11\frac{7}{8}$ in. by $3\frac{3}{8}$ in.

Mid-Chapter Test

Go Online
Pearsonsuccessnet.com

Multiple Choice

1. Graph quadrilateral $ABCD$ with vertices $A(2, 4)$, $B(6, 4)$, $C(6, -4)$, and $D(2, -4)$. Graph its image $A'B'C'D'$ after a reflection over the x-axis. Which statement about $ABCD$ and $A'B'C'D'$ is true?

A. $ABCD$ and $A'B'C'D'$ are not congruent.

B. $ABCD$ and $A'B'C'D'$ are not identical.

C. $ABCD$ and $A'B'C'D'$ are not parallelograms.

D. $ABCD$ and $A'B'C'D'$ are not squares.

2. Three vertices of a square are $(-1, -3)$, $(-1, 5)$, and $(7, 5)$. What are the coordinates of the center of the square?

A. $(3, 1)$

B. $(\sqrt{3}, 1)$

C. $(3, \sqrt{3})$

D. $(1, 1)$

3. A right rectangular prism has three vertices $(0, 0, 0)$, $(3, 5, 0)$, and $(3, 5, 4)$ and three faces on the coordinate planes. Which must be the coordinates of a fourth vertex?

A. $(3, 0, 4)$

B. $(3, 0, 5)$

C. $(0, 5, 3)$

D. $(4, 5, 0)$

Open Response

4. Graph the line with equation $4x + 2y = 3$. Write an equation of its image after a reflection over the y-axis.

5. Copy $\overline{AB}$ and point O. Then rotate $\overline{AB}$ around O by 60° in the counterclockwise direction.

O

6. Find the coordinates of the midpoint of $\overline{AB}$ with endpoints $A(-3, 7)$ and $B(4, -9)$.

7. Pentagon $ABCDE$ has the following vertices.

- $A(1, 2)$
- $B(6, 1)$
- $C(5, -5)$
- $D(-8, -4)$
- $E(-6, 1)$

Graph the pentagon. Find its perimeter without using a ruler.

8. Point A has coordinates $(8, 6)$. Line ℓ has equation $3x - 5y = 2$. Write an equation for the line through A and parallel to ℓ.

9. Point B has coordinates $(-8, 3)$. Line m has equation $2x - 5y = 1$. Write an equation for the line through B and perpendicular to m.

10. The coordinates of two points in three-dimensional coordinate space are given.

- $A(1, -3, 12)$
- $B(-5, -9, 10)$

Calculate the length of $\overline{AB}$.

Connections to Algebra

In *Connections to Algebra,* you will use points on the coordinate plane as algebraic objects. In other words, you will think of points as things that you can add or that you can multiply by any real number. Since points are also geometric objects, you will see the corresponding geometric consequences of these operations.

By the end of this investigation, you will be able to answer questions like these.

1. What are vectors?

2. How can you tell whether two vectors are equivalent?

3. Find the vector equation for the line through $A(1, 2)$ and $B(3, -4)$.

You will learn how to

- add points and multiply points by any real number and write the results both algebraically and geometrically
- work with vectors
- write a vector equation for any line on the coordinate plane

You will develop these habits and skills:

- See mathematical objects from a different perspective.
- Operate on points and vectors as algebraic objects.
- Use vectors to write equations of lines.

Geese stay in the V formation by flying with equivalent velocity vectors.

7.11 Getting Started

To help prepare for the study of vectors, you need to know how to multiply a point by a number and how to add two points. To multiply a point by a number (scale a point), you simply multiply each of its coordinates by that number. To add two points, you simply add the corresponding coordinates.

For You to Explore

1. Use one coordinate grid for parts (a)–(g). For each exercise, graph A and cA on the coordinate plane. How is the location of cA related to the location of A?

   a. $A(5, 1),\ c = 2$

   b. $A(5, 1),\ c = \frac{1}{2}$

   c. $A(3, 4),\ c = 3$

   d. $A(3, 4),\ c = \frac{1}{2}$

   e. $A(3, 4),\ c = -1$

   f. $A(3, 4),\ c = -2$

   g. $A(3, 4),\ c = -\frac{1}{2}$

cA is the point you get when you *scale A* by *c*.

What happens if, instead of scaling one point by many different numbers, you take many collinear points and scale them by the same number? The next few exercises ask you to look at that question.

2. Draw a picture of what you get if you scale each of the collinear points below by 2. Describe in words what you get.

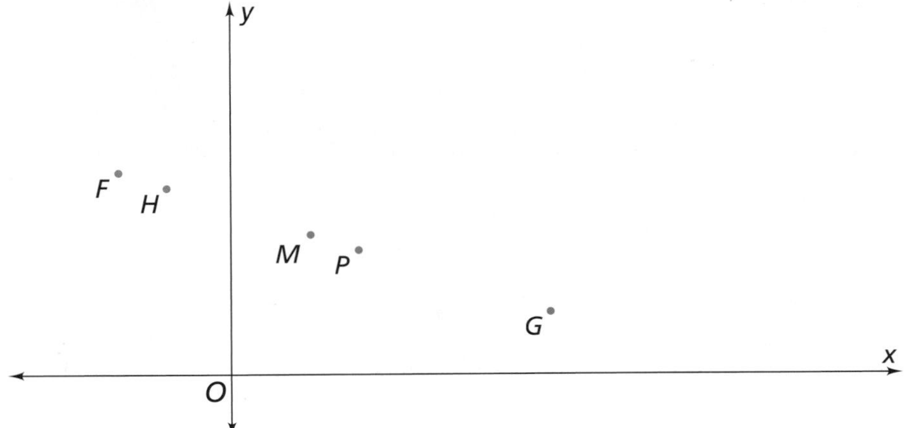

3. Think of a circle with radius 6 and center at the origin. What do you get if you scale all the points on the circle by 2? By $\frac{1}{2}$? By $-\frac{1}{2}$?

You may want to sketch a picture on graph paper.

4. Use a separate coordinate grid for each part. On each grid, show O (the origin), A, B, and $A + B$.

   a. $A(5, 1)$ $B(3, 6)$

   b. $A(4, -2)$ $B(0, 6)$

   c. $A(4, -2)$ $B(-3, -5)$

   d. $A(4, -2)$ $B(-4, 2)$

   e. $A(4, -2)$ $B(-1, 4)$

   f. $A(3, 1)$ $B(6, 2)$

Remember...

To add points, you add their corresponding coordinates. For example, $(-2, 7) + (4, 1) = (2, 8)$.

5. Suppose you have points $A(3, 5)$ and $B(6, -1)$.

   a. Plot B, $2B$, $0.5B$, $-1B$, $4B$, $-\frac{18}{5}B$, and three other multiples of B.

   b. What does the graph look like if you plot every possible multiple of B?

   c. Add A to each of the points you plotted in part (a). Plot the results on the same coordinate grid.

   d. What would your picture look like if you plotted the sum of A and each possible multiple of B?

6. Draw a polygon (like the one shown here if you like) on a coordinate grid. Apply each rule below to the vertices of the polygon. Draw the resulting polygon. Describe how each resulting polygon is related to the original.

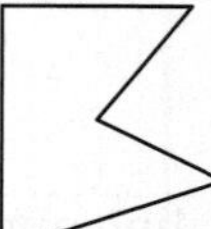

   a. $(x, y) \mapsto (x + 8, y + 5)$

   b. $(x, y) \mapsto (x - 8, y + 5)$

   c. $(x, y) \mapsto (3x, 3y)$

   d. $(x, y) \mapsto \left(\frac{x}{2}, \frac{y}{2}\right)$

   e. $(x, y) \mapsto \left(\frac{x}{2} + 7, \frac{y}{2} + 10\right)$

   f. $(x, y) \mapsto (-x, y + 2)$

   g. $(x, y) \mapsto (2x, y + 2)$

Habits of Mind

Look for patterns. Can you make connections between the rules in Problem 6 and adding and scaling points?

Exercises *Practicing Habits of Mind*

On Your Own

7. **Write About It** Suppose A is a point and c is some real number. Describe geometrically how cA is related to A. How can you tell someone how to locate $2A$ if that person knows where point A is, but you do not? How are the coordinates of cA related algebraically to the coordinates of A?

8. **Write About It** Why is *scaling* a better term than *multiplying* when you refer to the operation that gives you cA?

9. Draw a picture of what you get if you scale each point shown by $\frac{1}{2}$. Describe what you get in words.

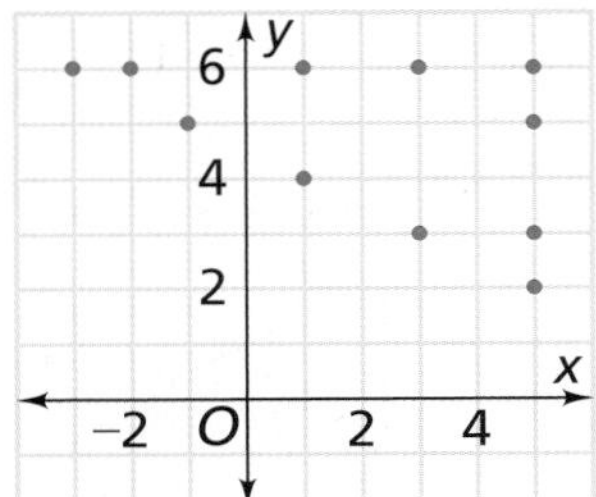

10. Draw what you get if you scale every point on the rectangle by -1. Then draw what you get if you scale each point by $\frac{5}{3}$.

11. Plot the sum of $P(1, 4)$ and each point on the rectangle below.

Habits of Mind

Visualize. Of course, you cannot add P to every point of the rectangle, but what would you get if you could?

12. For each of the diagrams, write a rule that transforms the vertices of polygon *JKLM* to the vertices of polygon *J′K′L′M′*. (Use the $\mapsto$ notation.)

a.

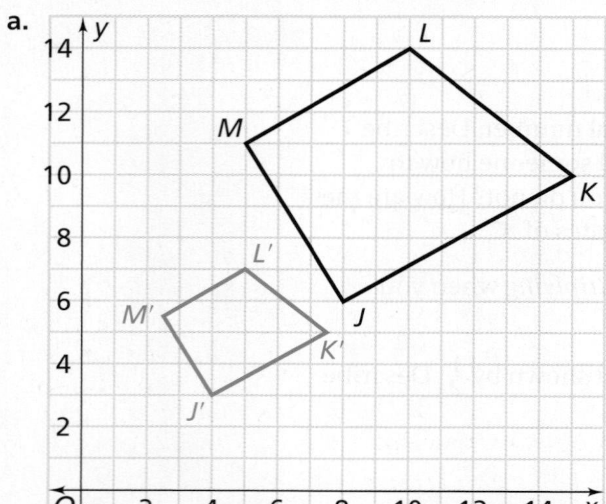

b.

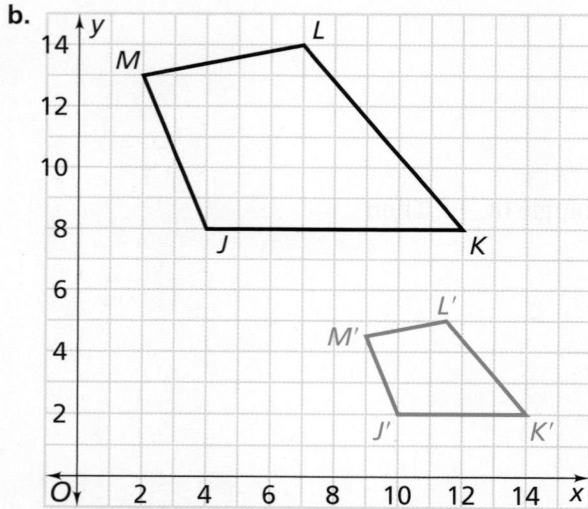

13. Jorge and Yutaka are both asked to transform $\triangle ABC$ with vertices $A(3, 6)$, $B(9, 6)$, and $C(9, 3)$. They are to scale it by $\frac{1}{4}$ and translate it 16 units to the right, but they are not told in which order to perform the transformations. Jorge chooses to scale the triangle first and then translate it. Yutaka translates first and then does the scaling.

a. Pick two vertices of $\triangle ABC$. Follow Jorge's and Yutaka's methods for each vertex. Write down where the images are.

b. Do both methods result in the same image triangle?

c. The two algebraic statements below describe Jorge's and Yutaka's methods. Which is Jorge's? Which is Yutaka's?

- $(x, y) \mapsto \frac{1}{4}(x, y) + (16, 0)$
- $(x, y) \mapsto \frac{1}{4}(x + 16, y)$

Maintain Your Skills

14. Here is a complicated rule.

$$(a, b) \mapsto \left(\tfrac{1}{2}(a - 3) + 5, \tfrac{1}{2}(b + 4) + 2\right)$$

a. Describe in words what this rule does.

b. Simplify the algebra of the rule. Describe in words what your new (but equivalent) rule does.

15. Here is another complicated rule.

$$(x, z) \mapsto \left(\tfrac{1}{2}(2(x - 4) + 6), \tfrac{1}{2}(2(z + 3) - 4)\right)$$

a. Describe in words what this rule does.

b. Simplify the algebra of the rule. Describe in words what your new (but equivalent) rule does.

Habits of Mind

Check your work. Apply your rule to some points on a specific picture to check that your description is right.

16. Compare $(x, y) \mapsto 2(x, y) + (2, 3)$ and $(x, y) \mapsto 2((x, y) + (1, 2))$. Do these rules give the same result?

17. Pick a point. Think about the following rule.

Add $(2, 3)$.

Scale by 3.

Subtract $(1, 2)$.

Now answer the following questions.

a. If you start with $(4, 5)$, where do you end?

b. If you start with $(-1, 3)$, where do you end?

c. If you end with $(7, 1)$, where did you start?

d. If you end with $(4, 6)$, where did you start?

e. What simple rule is equivalent to the one above?

7.12 Introduction to Vectors

In Lesson 7.10, you saw some geometric effects of adding and scaling points. There is a very convenient language for using these concepts. It involves the notion of a vector.

In physics, people distinguish speed (such as 30 mi/h) from velocity. Velocity has a **direction** as well as a size, so that 30 mi/h northeast is different from 30 mi/h due south. You can model this idea on a coordinate system by thinking about line segments that have a direction.

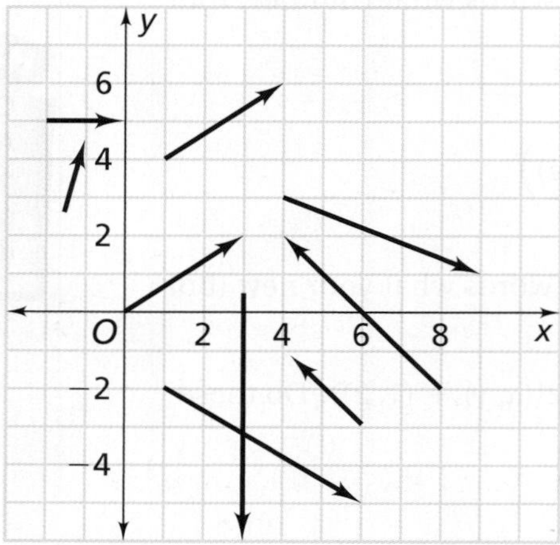

Each arrow in this figure can stand for a velocity. The length of the arrow is the speed. The direction of the arrow tells you which way the velocity is directed. The arrows are often called *vectors.* If A and B are points, the "vector from A to B" can be thought of as the arrow that starts at A and ends at B.

For navigators, vectors might stand for trips or currents or wind velocities.

Definition

Given two points A and B, the vector from A to B is the ordered pair of points (A, B). Point A is the tail of the vector and point B is the head.

You can write the vector from A to B as $\overrightarrow{AB}$.

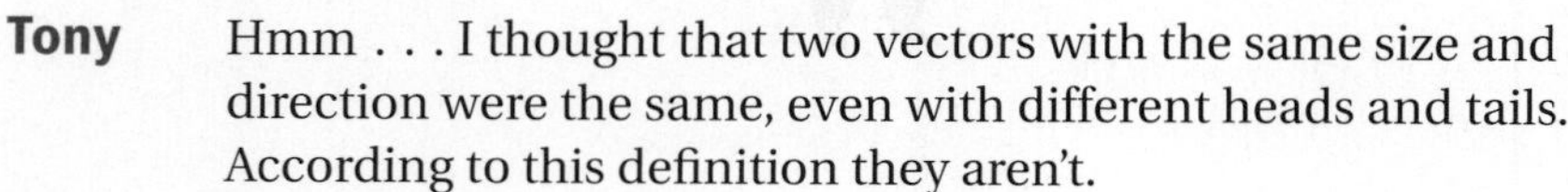

Tony has seen vectors before and is a bit confused by this definition.

Tony Hmm . . . I thought that two vectors with the same size and direction were the same, even with different heads and tails. According to this definition they aren't.

Sasha If two vectors have the same size and direction, but different heads and tails, they are **equivalent vectors.**

For You to Do

Use the points $A(5, 1)$, $B(-2, 5)$, $C(9, -2)$, and $D(16, -6)$. On a coordinate system, draw each vector.

- $\overrightarrow{AB}$
- $\overrightarrow{CD}$
- $\overrightarrow{AC}$
- $\overrightarrow{BA}$
- $\overrightarrow{OA}$
- $\overrightarrow{OB}$
- $\overrightarrow{B(A + B)}$
- $\overrightarrow{A(A + B)}$
- $\overrightarrow{O(B + A)}$

$\overrightarrow{B(A + B)}$ means the vector with tail B and head $A + B$.

1. Which vectors that you drew have the same direction?
2. Which have opposite directions?
3. Which have the same size?
4. Which have the same head?
5. Which have the same tail?

In-Class Experiment

Suppose you are working on the coordinate plane.

6. For $A(5, 3)$ and $B(8, 7)$, find a vector with tail at the origin and the same size and direction as $\overrightarrow{AB}$.
7. For $A(3, 5)$ and $B(8, 1)$, find two points C and D (neither at the origin) such that the vector from A to B is equivalent to the vector from C to D. Find another point E such that the vector from the origin to E is equivalent to $\overrightarrow{AB}$ and $\overrightarrow{CD}$.

Equivalent vectors have the same size and direction.

8. Two vectors are shown below. Find a way to tell whether the two vectors are equivalent just by looking at their coordinates (and doing some calculations with them).

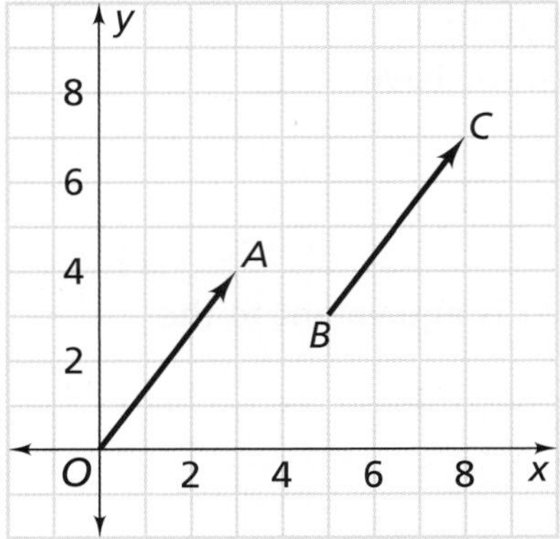

Here is a test you can use for deciding whether two vectors are equivalent.

Theorem 7.7 The Head-Minus-Tail Test

Two vectors are equivalent if and only if head minus tail for one vector gives the same result as head minus tail for the other. In symbols: $\overrightarrow{AB}$ is equivalent to $\overrightarrow{CD}$ if and only if $B - A = D - C$.

Proof In general, you can write the coordinates of A, B, C, and D this way.

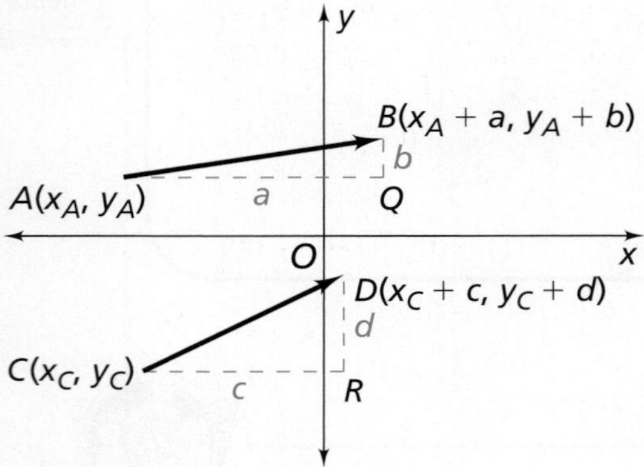

If $\overrightarrow{AB}$ and $\overrightarrow{CD}$ are equivalent, then $\overline{AB}$ is parallel to and congruent to $\overline{CD}$. Since the segments are parallel, the lines containing them have the same slope, so

$$\frac{b}{a} = \frac{d}{c}$$

This means that right $\triangle ABQ$ and right $\triangle CDR$ are similar. But the fact that $\overline{AB} \cong \overline{CD}$ implies that the two triangles are congruent. So, in particular, their corresponding legs are congruent.

$$(a, b) = (c, d), \text{ so } B - A = D - C$$

Conversely, if $B - A = D - C$, then $(a, b) = (c, d)$. So the legs of the two right triangles are congruent. This implies that $\overline{AB} \parallel \overline{CD}$ and that they have the same orientation. It also means that $AB = \sqrt{a^2 + b^2} = \sqrt{c^2 + d^2} = CD$. As a corollary, you have the following.

Corollary 7.7.1

If A and B are points, the vector from O to $(B - A)$ is equivalent to the vector from A to B.

Developing Habits of Mind

Look for relationships. To think about a class of equivalent objects, it is often enough to think of only one member of the class. Fractions provide a good example.

The fractions $\frac{1}{2}, \frac{2}{4}, \frac{3}{6}, \frac{4}{8}, \frac{5}{10}, \ldots$, all belong to the same class. It is usually enough to let the simplified fraction $\frac{1}{2}$ represent the class.

Vectors provide another example. Because of Corollary 7.7.1, any vector in the coordinate plane is equivalent to a vector with its tail at the origin. So, you can think of any vector with its tail at the origin as a representative of a whole class of equivalent vectors. If you think of it this way, the collection of all vectors with tails at the origin represents all the vectors in the coordinate plane!

Twenty-two vectors are shown here. How many classes of equivalent vectors are there?

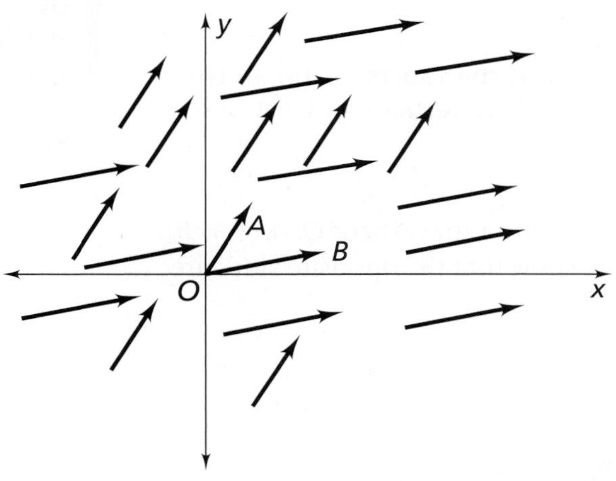

Corollary 7.7.1 lets you identify any vector with a point in the coordinate plane. Think of point A as $\overrightarrow{OA}$, for example. To add vectors, you add points as you did in the Getting Started lesson. Vectors, however, give this addition a geometric flavor. If A and B are points (and vectors), how can you locate $A + B$ using geometry?

Vectors must have the same direction and magnitude to be equivalent.

In-Class Experiment

- For each pair of points A and B given below, plot the following four points: the origin O, A, B, and the sum $A + B$.
- Describe how $A + B$ is located with respect to the other three points.
- Draw segments connecting O to A and B. Draw segments connecting A and B to $A + B$. What kind of figure do you get in each case?

9. $A(-3, 5)$, $B(5, 1)$

10. $A(2, 3)$, $B(5, 1)$

11. $A(-2, -2)$, $B(0, 6)$

12. $A(-3, 3)$, $B(5, -5)$

13. $A(-3, 5)$, $B(10, 2)$

14. $A(-3, 5)$, $B\left(\frac{5}{2}, \frac{1}{2}\right)$

The In-Class Experiment suggests a theorem.

Habits of Mind

Use your own words. State the theorem in a way that makes the most sense for you.

Theorem 7.8

If $A = (a_1, a_2)$ and $B = (b_1, b_2)$, then $A + B$ is the fourth vertex of the parallelogram that has A, O, and B as three of its vertices and $\overline{OA}$ and $\overline{OB}$ as two of its sides.

Basically, you want to show that the quadrilateral with vertices O, A, $A + B$, and B is a parallelogram. One strategy is to show that the opposite sides are parallel.

Let $A = (a_1, a_2)$ and $B = (b_1, b_2)$.

Let $P = A + B = (a_1 + b_1, a_2 + b_2)$.

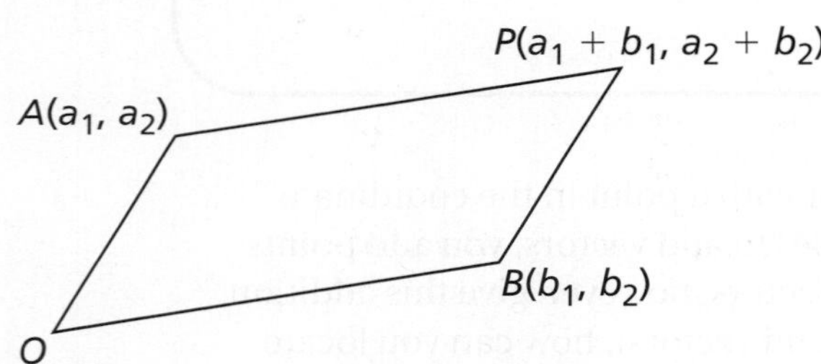

For You to Do

15. Prove that $\overline{OA}$ is parallel to $\overline{BP}$ and that $\overline{OB}$ is parallel to $\overline{AP}$.

16. Does Theorem 7.8 hold if O, A, and B are collinear? For example, where is the parallelogram if $A(9, -1)$ and $B(18, -2)$?

Identifying vectors with points in the coordinate plane also gives the scaling of points a geometric flavor.

Theorem 7.9

Suppose A is a point, c is a number greater than or equal to 1, and $B = cA$. Then,

- **B is collinear with A and the origin.**
- **B is c times as far from the origin as A.**

For $c > 1$, part 2 of the theorem implies that A is between O and B.

For You to Do

For each point A and value c given below, let $B = cA$. Then, show that the two statements in Theorem 7.9 are true. That is, show

a. $OA + AB = OB$ **b.** $OB = cOA$

17. $A(3, 4),\ c = 3$

18. $A(-5, 12),\ c = 2$

19. $A(6, 8),\ c = 1.5$

20. $A(3, 8),\ c = 4$

Exercises *Practicing Habits of Mind*

Check Your Understanding

1. Use the points $A(5, 3)$ and $B(8, 7)$. Find a vector that starts at the origin, has the same direction as $\overrightarrow{AB}$, and is twice as long as $\overrightarrow{AB}$.

2. Use the points $R(7, 2)$ and $S(15, 6)$. Find the head of a vector that starts at $(4, -3)$ and is equivalent to the vector from R to S.

3. True or false: If A and B are any points, the vector from O to B is equivalent to the vector from A to $A + B$. Explain.

4. Use the points $A(8, 15)$, $B(-4, 3)$, and $P = A + B$. Draw a picture of O, A, B, and P. Show that $OA = BP$ and $OB = AP$.

5. Use the points $A(8, 6)$, $B(3, 1)$, and $P = A + B$. Draw a picture of O, A, B, and P. Show that $OA = BP$ and $OB = AP$.

6. For $A(3, 2)$ and $P(4, 5)$, locate each of the following.

   a. $P + A$ **b.** $P + 2A$ **c.** $P + 3A$ **d.** $P + 4A$

   e. $P + \frac{1}{2}A$ **f.** $P + \frac{1}{3}A$ **g.** $P + \frac{1}{4}A$

On Your Own

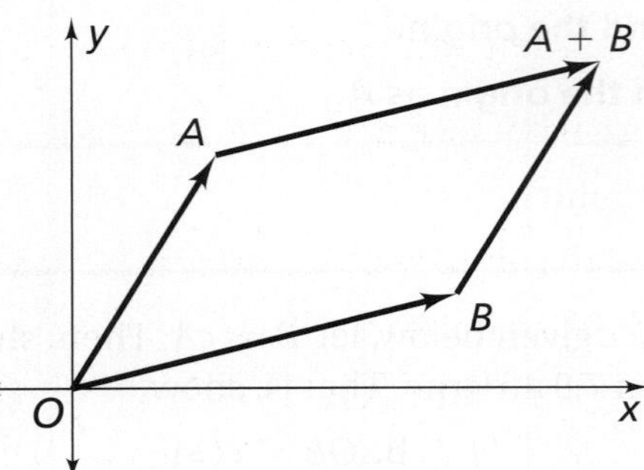

7. Here is a pair of fancy sentences: $\overrightarrow{A(A + B)}$ is equivalent to $\overrightarrow{OB}$, and $\overrightarrow{O(A + B)}$ is one diagonal of the parallelogram with vertices O, A, $A + B$, and B. Also, $\overrightarrow{OA}$ is equivalent to $\overrightarrow{B(A + B)}$.

Copy the figure shown here. Label the five vectors that are mentioned in the sentences above. Use $A(3, 5)$ and $B(8, 2)$ to show that $\overrightarrow{A(A + B)}$ is equivalent to $\overrightarrow{OB}$. Also, show that $\overrightarrow{OA}$ is equivalent to $\overrightarrow{B(A + B)}$. Use the head-minus-tail method.

8. Suppose T is the function that maps a point X to the point $X + (10, 5)$. Pick two points A and B. Draw the vectors from A to $T(A)$ and from B to $T(B)$. Show that these vectors are equivalent.

Remember...

This means that, for example, $T((4, 2)) = (4, 2) + (10, 5) = (14, 7)$.

9. For $A(3, 4)$, $B(5, -12)$, and $P = A + B$, draw a picture of O, A, B, and P. Show that $OA = BP$ and $OB = AP$.

10. Let A, B, and C be any three points. Show that the quadrilateral with vertices B, C, $C + A$, and $B + A$ is a parallelogram by showing that opposite sides are congruent. Draw a picture.

Corollary 7.7.1 says that $\overrightarrow{AB}$ is equivalent to the vector from O to $B - A$. Some people think of this as moving $\overrightarrow{AB}$ so its tail is at the origin. They say, "To move $\overrightarrow{AB}$ to the origin, just draw the vector from O to $B - A$."

Other people say it this way: "To move a vector to the origin, just subtract the tail from the head." The next exercises show you how you can apply this technique to the geometry of vectors.

11. Point A has coordinates $(1, 6)$. Point B has coordinates $(7, 8)$.

a. Calculate head minus tail for $\overrightarrow{AB}$. Draw a diagram that shows both $\overrightarrow{AB}$ and $\overrightarrow{O(B - A)}$. You have moved $\overrightarrow{AB}$ to the origin.

b. Now take the vector anchored at the origin. Move it to $P(3, -2)$ by adding P to the head and to the tail. Draw this new vector. What are the coordinates of its head and tail?

12. Prove the following theorem.

Theorem 7.10

Adding the same point to the tail and to the head of a vector produces an equivalent vector.

Habits of Mind

Check the theorem. Use specific values to test this generalization. Draw a picture in the coordinate plane.

13. Show that if A and B are points, the midpoint of $\overline{AB}$ is $\frac{1}{2}(A + B)$.

14. Mathematical convention usually assigns

- capital-letter names to points
- lowercase names early in the alphabet to constants (numbers you know)
- lowercase names late in the alphabet to variables or unknowns (numbers you do not know yet, or numbers that can vary)

In the expressions below, A, B, C, M, X, Y, and Z are names of points. O is the name of a special point, the origin. The letters c, k, and x are names for numbers. Classify each expression as a *point*, a *number*, or just plain *meaningless*.

a. cB	b. $c + A$	c. AB	d. $c(AB)$	e. $k(OA)$
f. $A + B + C$	g. xX	h. $(c + k)A$	i. $cA + B$	j. $A + B$
k. $c(A + B)$	l. $A(c + B)$	m. cZ	n. $c(XY)$	o. $c(X + Y)$
p. $A(X + Y)$	q. AX	r. $X + Y$	s. $M(C + X)$	

15. Given two points A and B, how can you find a point that is on $\overleftrightarrow{AB}$ and one third of the way from A to B? Explain.

16. **Standardized Test Prep** Equivalent vectors have the same magnitude and direction. Which vector is equivalent to $\overrightarrow{EF}$? (Point O is the origin.)

A. $\overrightarrow{FE}$ B. $\frac{1}{2}\overrightarrow{O(E + F)}$ C. $\overrightarrow{O(E - F)}$ D. $\overrightarrow{O(F - E)}$

17. Suppose A, B, C, and D are the vertices of a quadrilateral.

a. Express the midpoints of the sides of the quadrilateral in terms of A, B, C, and D.

b. Show that the quadrilateral formed by joining the midpoints from part (a) is a parallelogram.

Maintain Your Skills

18. Use $\overrightarrow{AB}$ from Exercise 11. Find (and draw) vectors equivalent to $\overrightarrow{AB}$ with the following properties.

a. tail at $C(8, 3)$ b. tail at $J(-8, 3)$

c. tail at $K(0, 3)$ d. head at O

e. head at $C(8, 3)$ f. tail at B

19. Suppose $A(3, 4)$, $B(9, 0)$, $C(-1, 2)$, and $D(5, -2)$. Show that $\overrightarrow{AB}$ is equivalent to $\overrightarrow{CD}$ by moving both vectors to the origin. Show also that $\overrightarrow{AC}$ is equivalent to $\overrightarrow{BD}$.

7.13 The Vector Equation of a Line

Theorem 7.9 in the previous lesson describes points that are on the line containing the vector from the origin to a point *A*. You can generalize this theorem to describe the line through the origin and *A*.

Theorem 7.11

If *A* is a point different from the origin, the set of all multiples of *A* is the line through the origin and *A*.

You might remember words such as *slope*, *y-intercept*, and *point-slope equation*. These terms had to do with equations of lines. In this lesson, you will revisit these terms and connect them with vectors.

Points $A(3, 1)$ and $B(8, -2)$ determine line $\overleftrightarrow{AB}$. How do you know if point $P(13, -5)$ or point $Q(13, -6)$ lies on $\overleftrightarrow{AB}$?

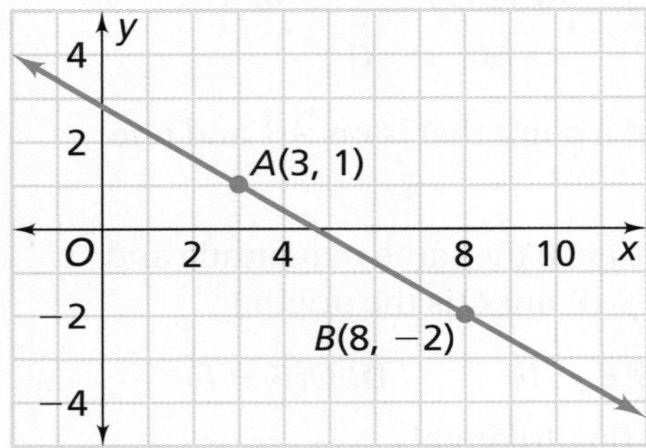

Minds in Action episode 36

Tony seems perplexed.

Tony I guess we are going to have to use Theorem 7.11, but I don't have the faintest idea how!

Sasha Well, what would happen if *P* were on $\overleftrightarrow{AB}$? If we moved everything to the origin *O* by subtracting *A*, then $P - A$ would be on the line through *O* and $B - A$.

Tony Stop! You're giving me a headache! Let me try to understand what you are saying with a picture. I calculated $B - A$ in my head, so . . .

Remember...

Sasha is using the technique from Exercise 11a in the previous lesson.

Tony draws a diagram showing his calculations.

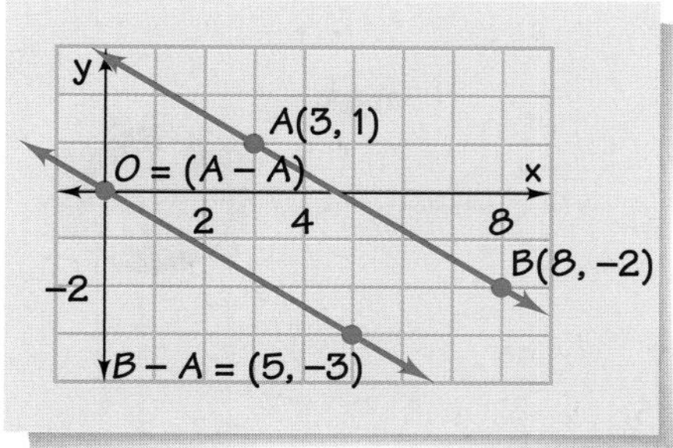

Sasha Good! Do you see it now? $P - A = (10, -6)$. Thanks to Theorem 7.11, we know that the point $P - A$ is on the line through $B - A$ and O only if $(10, -6)$ is a multiple of $(5, -3)$.

Tony And it is! So now we can move everything back and know that P lies on $\overleftrightarrow{AB}$. Hurray!

Sasha Okay, now it's your turn to see if Q is on $\overleftrightarrow{AB}$.

Tony $Q - A = (10, -7)$. I can't find any number k such that $(10, -7) = k(5, -3)$. It looks like Q isn't on $\overleftrightarrow{AB}$, because Theorem 7.11 says that otherwise there would be such a number k.

Sasha Good work, Tony!

So, in general, if a point X is on a line $\overleftrightarrow{AB}$, $X - A$ is a multiple of $B - A$. That is, there is a number k such that $X - A = k(B - A)$. So X lies on $\overleftrightarrow{AB}$ if

$$X = A + k(B - A)$$

This is a vector equation in X and k.

The converse is also true. If $X = A + k(B - A)$ for some number k, then X lies on $\overleftrightarrow{AB}$.

For You to Do

Find a vector equation of the line containing the two given points. Give three more points that satisfy each equation and three that do not.

1. $A(3, 5)$, $B(-1, -5)$
2. $P(8, -1)$, $Q(1, 7)$
3. $R(6, 7)$, $S(2, -3)$
4. $T(3, 5)$, $U(11, 11)$

You can describe parallel lines using vectors. This In-Class Experiment will help you gather ideas about parallel vectors.

In-Class Experiment

Here are some vectors.

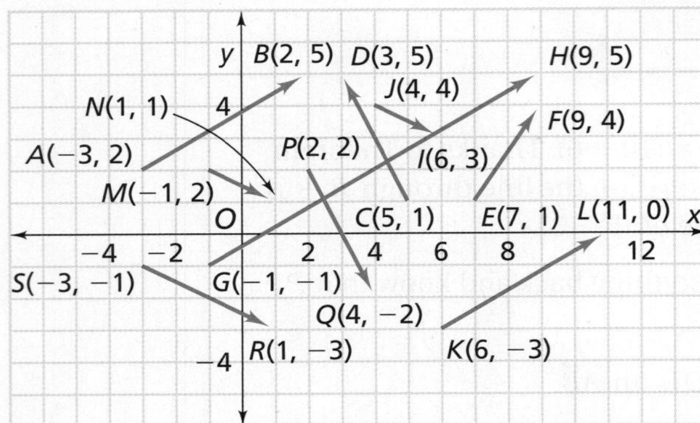

5. Which vectors are parallel?
6. Which are parallel in the same direction?
7. Which are parallel in opposite directions?
8. Which are equivalent?
9. Find a rule that uses head minus tail to tell you when two vectors are
   - parallel in the same direction
   - parallel in opposite directions

You can summarize the results of the In-Class Experiment in one general theorem.

Theorem 7.12

Two vectors $\overrightarrow{AB}$ and $\overrightarrow{CD}$ are parallel if and only if there is a number k such that

$$B - A = k(D - C)$$

If $k > 0$, the vectors have the same direction. If $k < 0$, the vectors have opposite directions. If $k = 1$, the vectors are equivalent.

For Discussion

10. Write a proof for Theorem 7.12.

For You to Do

11. Now prove the following theorem.

Theorem 7.13

If A and B are points, then the segment from O to $B - A$ is parallel and congruent to $\overline{AB}$.

$$\overline{O(B - A)} \parallel \overline{AB}$$

$$\overline{O(B - A)} \cong \overline{AB}$$

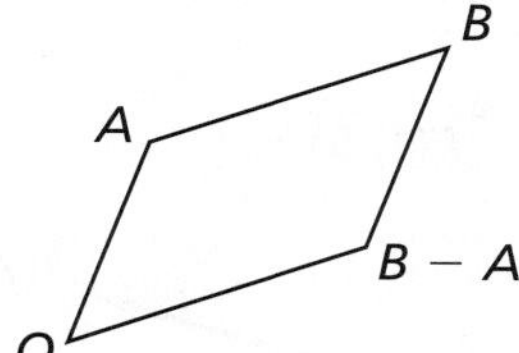

Exercises *Practicing Habits of Mind*

Check Your Understanding

1. Suppose you have points $A(4, 1)$, $B(9, 5)$, $C(3, -1)$, and $D(13, 7)$. Prove that $\overleftrightarrow{AB} \parallel \overleftrightarrow{CD}$.

2. Show that if P and A are points and t is a number, the segment from P to $P + tA$ is parallel to the segment from O to A.

For Exercise 2, refer to Exercise 6 from Lesson 7.11.

3. For $A(4, 4)$ and $B(8, -4)$, look at $\triangle OAB$. Let M be the midpoint of $\overline{OA}$ and N be the midpoint of $\overline{OB}$. Show that $\overline{MN} \parallel \overline{AB}$ and $MN = \frac{1}{2}AB$.

Exercise 3 shows a special case of the Midline Theorem.

4. Show that Theorem 7.13 holds for $A(3, 5)$ and $B(7, 9)$.

On Your Own

5. Use the points $A(-1, 3)$ and $B(2, 6)$. Find the head and tail of the vector that is equivalent to $\overrightarrow{AB}$, lies on $\overleftrightarrow{AB}$, and has its head on the line with each given equation.

a. $y = 2$

b. $x = -3$

6. For $A(3, 2)$, $B(-4, 5)$, and $C(7, 4)$, show that $\triangle ABC \cong \triangle O(B - A)(C - A)$. Draw a picture.

7. Show that if A, B, and C are any three points, $\triangle ABC \cong \triangle O(B - A)(C - A)$.

8. The coordinates of P and A are given in the figure. Find a vector equation of the line through P and parallel to $\overrightarrow{OA}$.

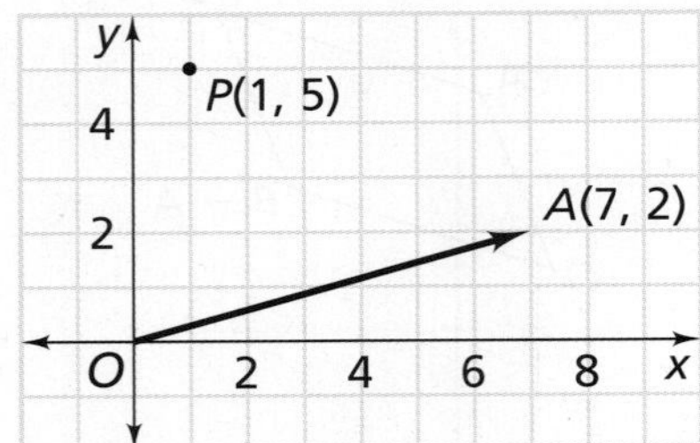

9. Show that the point $\frac{2}{3}A + \frac{1}{3}B$ is on $\overline{AB}$ $\frac{1}{3}$ of the way from A to B.

10. What point is on $\overline{AB}$ $\frac{1}{4}$ of the way from A to B?

11. For $A(3, 5)$ and $B(7, 1)$, find C if B is the midpoint of $\overline{AC}$.

12. **Standardized Test Prep** Points G and H have coordinates $(1, 3)$ and $(6, 5)$, respectively. Which point is NOT on $\overleftrightarrow{GH}$?

A. $J(-4, 1)$ **B.** $K(-9, -1)$

C. $L(0, 2.6)$ **D.** $M(-6, 0)$

13. Find vector equations of the three medians of $\triangle ABC$ with vertices $A(-1, 5)$, $B(5, -2)$, and $C(3, 5)$.

What points of $\triangle ABC$ lie on its medians?

14. In the coordinate plane, draw $\triangle AOB$ with vertices $A(3, 6)$, $B(8, 1)$, and O, the origin. Find the midpoint M of $\overline{OA}$ and the midpoint N of $\overline{OB}$. Prove that $\overrightarrow{MN}$ is parallel to $\overrightarrow{AB}$ and that the size of $\overrightarrow{MN}$ is half the size of $\overrightarrow{AB}$.

Maintain Your Skills

Go Online
Pearsonsuccessnet.com

15. Suppose A and B are points. Using vectors, explain how to locate each point.

a. $\frac{1}{3}A + \frac{2}{3}B$ **b.** $\frac{2}{3}A + \frac{1}{3}B$

c. $\frac{1}{4}A + \frac{3}{4}B$ **d.** $\frac{3}{4}A + \frac{1}{4}B$

e. $\frac{3}{5}A + \frac{2}{5}B$ **f.** $kA + (1 - k)B$ for $0 \le k \le 1$

16. The head of $\overrightarrow{OA}$ is $(1, 3)$. The head of $\overrightarrow{OB}$ is $(2, 0)$.

Find x and y such that $x\overrightarrow{OA} + y\overrightarrow{OB}$ has its head at each of the following points.

a. $(2, 1)$ **b.** $(4, 3)$ **c.** $(11, 1)$

d. $(5, 6)$ **e.** $(0, 8)$ **f.** $(1, -10)$

Habits of Mind

Visualize. Draw the two vectors on graph paper. For each point, sketch how you could get from the origin to that point if you could travel only in the directions allowed by the two vectors.

7.14 Using the Vector Equation of a Line

In this lesson, you use vector equations of lines to find the point of intersection of two lines, when it exists. You also learn how to tell whether a point of intersection exists just by looking at the equations of the lines. Then you will see how to prove that the medians of a triangle are concurrent by using vector equations of lines.

In-Class Experiment

Use point $A(1, 2)$, point $B(-2, 6)$, and the origin O.

1. Plot line ℓ with equation $P = A + p(-3, 4)$ and line s with equation $Q = B + q(1, 1)$.
2. Explain how you can find the point of intersection of ℓ and s. Then find it.
3. Now plot the line r with equation $T = O + m(1, 1)$. Can you find the point of intersection for ℓ and r? The point of intersection for s and r?
4. Plot line t with equation $H = (3, 5) + v(4, 4)$. Can you find the point of intersection for ℓ and t? For s and t? For r and t? Make conjectures about when it is possible to find the point of intersection and when it is not. Can you tell by simply looking at the vector equation?

For Discussion

5. Discuss with your class your results to the In-Class Experiment above. Write a summary of what you discovered.

For You to Do

6. **What's Wrong Here?** Tony tried to solve the following problem, but got an inconsistent answer. Help him find his mistake.

Problem Write a vector equation of the line through $A(-1, 4)$ and $B(2, 6)$. Also, write a vector equation of the line through $C\left(\frac{1}{2}, 3\right)$ and $D(5, -1)$. Do the two lines intersect? If they do, find the point of intersection.

Solution Since $\overrightarrow{AB} = (2 - (-1), 6 - 4) = (3, 2)$, $\overrightarrow{CD} = \left(5 - \frac{1}{2}, -1 - 3\right) = \left(\frac{9}{2}, -4\right)$, and for any k

$$(3, 2) \neq k\left(\frac{9}{2}, -4\right)$$

you know the two lines intersect.

A vector equation for $\overleftrightarrow{AB}$ is

$$P = A + t(B - A)$$
$$P = (-1, 4) + t(3, 2)$$

A vector equation for $\overleftrightarrow{CD}$ is

$$Q = C + t(D - C)$$
$$Q = \left(\frac{1}{2}, 3\right) + t\left(\frac{9}{2}, -4\right)$$

So the value of t that gives the point of intersection can be found by solving the following system of equations.

$$-1 + 3t = \frac{1}{2} + \frac{9}{2}t$$
$$4 + 2t = 3 - 4t$$

The first equation has solution $t = -1$. The second equation has solution $t = -\frac{1}{6}$. This means the system has no solution. But the lines do intersect. What is wrong here?

There is a variation of the point-tester rule from first-year algebra that works for vector equations of lines.

Example

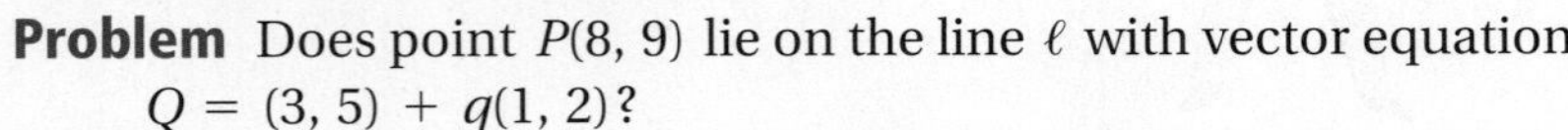

Problem Does point $P(8, 9)$ lie on the line ℓ with vector equation $Q = (3, 5) + q(1, 2)$?

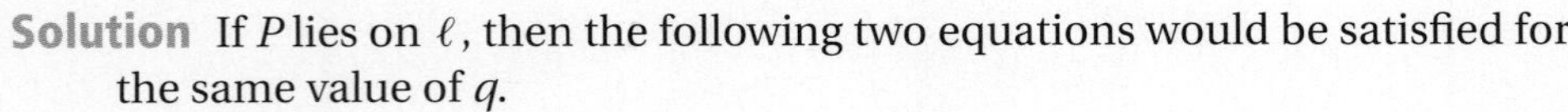

Solution If P lies on ℓ, then the following two equations would be satisfied for the same value of q.

$$8 = 3 + 1q$$
$$9 = 5 + 2q$$

Why is this the case?

The first equation has solution $q = 5$, but the second equation has solution $q = 2$. Therefore, P does not lie on ℓ.

Exercises *Practicing Habits of Mind*

Check Your Understanding

In Chapter 6, you proved that the three medians of a triangle are concurrent and that the point of intersection is $\frac{2}{3}$ of the way from a vertex to the midpoint of the opposite side. You can use vector equations to check it out.

1. Plot points $A(3, 1)$, $B(5, 2)$, and $C(7, 7)$ on the coordinate plane and connect them to form $\triangle ABC$. Translate the triangle to the origin by subtracting A from each vertex. Call the new vertices $A_0 = O$, B_0, and C_0. Find the midpoints M, N, and K of sides $\overline{A_0B_0}$, $\overline{B_0C_0}$, and $\overline{C_0A_0}$, respectively.

What does translating the triangle to the origin change in the results?

2. Use the figure you drew for Exercise 1 and write vector equations for $\overleftrightarrow{C_0M}$ and $\overleftrightarrow{B_0K}$. Do these lines intersect? Explain. If they do, find their point of intersection and label it G_0.

3. Refer to the figure you drew for Exercise 1 and write the vector equation of line $\overleftrightarrow{A_0N}$. Does G_0 lie on $\overleftrightarrow{A_0N}$?

4. Refer to Exercises 1–3. What are the values of the parameters in the vector equations of lines $\overleftrightarrow{A_0N}$, $\overleftrightarrow{B_0K}$, and $\overleftrightarrow{C_0M}$ that give point G_0? What does this result mean geometrically?

On Your Own

5. You are given point $A(-3, 4)$. How can you find the coordinates of a point B such that $\overrightarrow{OA}$ is perpendicular to $\overrightarrow{OB}$?

6. Find a vector equation of a line through $A(2, 4)$ and perpendicular to $\overrightarrow{OA}$.

7. Use vectors to show that the diagonals of a parallelogram bisect each other.

Habits of Mind

Simplify the problem. Assume that one vertex of the parallelogram is the origin O. If A, O, and B are consecutive vertices, the fourth vertex is $A + B$.

8. George has a way to find the population center for three cities of the same size. He puts the cities on a coordinate system, adds the coordinates of the three cities, and scales by $\frac{1}{3}$. In what sense is George's point the population center?

9. Martha extends George's method to allow for cities of different sizes. She first draws coordinates on the map and scales the coordinates of each city by its population. Next she adds the results, and then she divides the resulting point by the sum of the populations of all three cities. In what sense is Martha's point the population center?

10. **Standardized Test Prep** Which point is on the line with vector equation $F = (-2, 3) + r(1, -2)$?

A. $A(3, -7)$	**B.** $B(2, -3)$
C. $C(-3, 6)$	**D.** $D(1, 3)$

Maintain Your Skills

Exercises 11–13 will guide you through a proof of the fact that the three perpendicular bisectors of the sides of a triangle are concurrent. Use $\triangle OAB$, with $A(9, 2)$, $B(1, 8)$, and the origin O.

11. Write vector equations for the lines $\overleftrightarrow{OA}$, $\overleftrightarrow{OB}$, and $\overleftrightarrow{AB}$. Find three vectors, each perpendicular to one of these lines.

12. Write vector equations for the line that contains the midpoint of $\overline{OA}$ and is perpendicular to $\overleftrightarrow{OA}$, the line that contains the midpoint of $\overline{OB}$ and is perpendicular to $\overleftrightarrow{OB}$, and the line that contains the midpoint of $\overline{AB}$ and is perpendicular to $\overleftrightarrow{AB}$. These lines contain the three perpendicular bisectors of the sides of the triangle.

13. Find the intersection point of the perpendicular bisector of $\overline{OA}$ and the perpendicular bisector of $\overline{OB}$. Check to see whether this point lies on the perpendicular bisector of $\overline{AB}$.

14. **Write About It** Think about how you proved that both the medians and the perpendicular bisectors of the sides of a triangle are concurrent.

a. Write general steps you can use to prove that three lines are concurrent.

b. Prove that the three altitudes of a triangle are concurrent. You can use $\triangle OAB$.

In this investigation, you learned how to identify characteristics of vectors, add points and multiply them by any real number, and write a vector equation for any line on the coordinate plane. These questions will help you summarize what you have learned.

1. Use the points $A(-1, 5)$, $B(6, 2)$, and the origin O. What are the coordinates of M if $\overrightarrow{OM}$ is equivalent to $\overrightarrow{AB}$?
2. Use the points $A(-6, 8)$, $B(2, 7)$, $C(-3, 3.5)$, and $D(1, 3)$. Are $\overrightarrow{AB}$ and $\overrightarrow{CD}$ equivalent?
3. Use the points $A(-2, 1)$, $B(1, 6)$, $C(1, 1)$, and $D(7, 11)$. Compare $\overrightarrow{AB}$ and $\overrightarrow{CD}$.
4. Use the points $A(-1, -1)$ and $B(2, 3)$. Write coordinates for a point C such that $\overrightarrow{OC}$ is three times as long as $\overrightarrow{AB}$ and parallel to $\overrightarrow{AB}$.
5. Find a vector equation for the line through $A\left(\frac{2}{3}, 1\right)$ and $B(0, 4)$.
6. What are vectors?
7. How can you tell whether two vectors are equivalent?
8. Find a vector equation for the line through $A(1, 2)$ and $B(3, -4)$.

Vocabulary and Notation

In this investigation, you learned these terms and this symbol. Make sure you understand what each one means and how to use it.

- **direction**
- **equivalent vectors**
- **head**
- **tail**
- **vector, $\overrightarrow{AB}$**

By flying behind and slightly higher than another goose, a goose faces less wind resistance. In this way, it uses less energy to maintain its velocity vector.

Project: Using Mathematical Habits

Equations of Circles

A circle is the set of points that are a fixed distance from one particular point, called the circle's center. You can use equations to represent circles in a coordinate plane, such as the circles below.

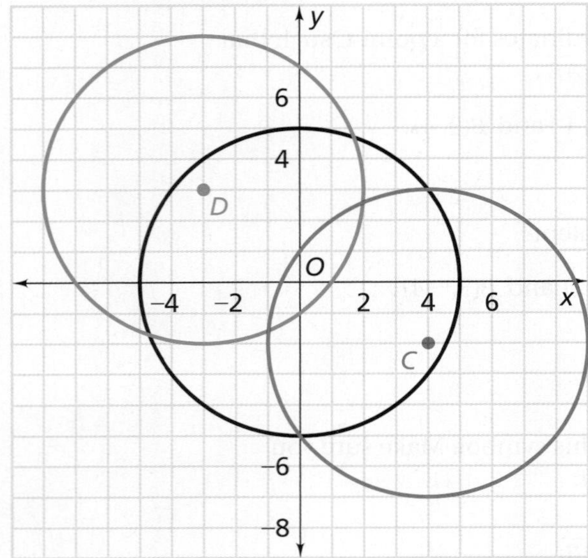

Let circle O be the circle with center (0, 0).

1. How can you tell if a point is on the circle O?
2. Find any points on circle O that are also on the vertical line through (4, −9).
3. Find the intersection(s) of circle O with the vertical line through (3, 2).
4. Find any points on circle O that are also on the horizontal line through (8, 0).
5. Find the intersection(s) of circle O with the horizontal line through (8, 3).
6. Find any points on circle O that are 13 units from the origin.
7. Find any points on circle O that are 11 units from (0, 16).

Circle O is the set of all points (x, y) that are 5 units from the center, the origin (0, 0). You can use the distance formula to write an equation for the circle.

Step 1 Use the distance formula.

$$\sqrt{(x-0)^2+(y-0)^2}=5$$

Step 2 Square both sides to get rid of the radical.

$$(x-0)^2+(y-0)^2=5^2$$

Remember that equations are point testers, so all the points on the circle should satisfy this equation.

Step 3 Simplify.

$$x^2+y^2=5^2\text{, or }25$$

Suppose, though, that you want to write an equation for a circle with center somewhere other than the origin. To do that, you have to go back to the distance formula. Let circle C be the circle with center C.

8. Find any points on circle C that are also on the vertical line through (4, –9).
9. Find the intersection(s) of circle C with the horizontal line through (8, 3).
10. **a.** What point is the center of circle C?

    b. What is the radius of the circle?

    c. Copy and complete the distance formula below to write an equation for circle C. Use the steps above to simplify your equation.

$$\sqrt{(x-\blacksquare)^2+(y-\blacksquare)^2}=\blacksquare$$

(x, y)
5
|y + 2|
C(4, −2)
(x, −2)
|x − 4|

Another way to write an equation for circle *C* is to use a translation.

You can translate circle *C* left 4 and up 2—a translation of $(-4, 2)$—to move its center to the origin.

Point $P(p_1, p_2)$ on circle *C* translates to point $P'(p_1 - 4, p_2 + 2)$. This point is a solution to the equation for circle *O*, $x^2 + y^2 = 25$.

$$x^2 + y^2 = 25, \text{ so}$$

$$(p_1 - 4)^2 + (p_2 + 2)^2 = 25$$

11. Expand and simplify the following equation.

$$(p_1 - 4)^2 + (p_2 + 2)^2 = 25$$

Compare this equation to the equation you wrote for circle *C* in Problem 10c above.

12. Write an equation for the circle with center *D* above.

13. Write an equation for a circle with center (0, 2) and radius 3 units.

14. **Take It Further** Consider the equation

$$\frac{x^2}{4} + \frac{y^2}{25} = 1$$

a. **Write About It** How is the equation similar to the equation of a circle? How is it different?

b. Graph the equation on a coordinate plane. What shape do you have?

If the center axle of this double Ferris wheel is at the origin, equations for the circles are $(x - a)^2 + (y - b)^2 = r^2$ and $(x + a)^2 + (y + b)^2 = r^2$.

Review

In **Investigation 7A** you learned how to

- use multiple methods for reflecting a figure over a line
- rotate a figure on the plane given a center and angle of rotation
- apply transformations to figures and the graphs of functions in the coordinate plane
- prove the SAS, ASA, and SSS triangle congruence criteria using isometry

The following questions will help you check your understanding.

1. Graph the line with equation $2x + y = 4$. Write an equation for its image after a reflection over the x-axis.

2. The point $Q'(-1, -3)$ is the reflection image of point $Q(3, 1)$. What is the reflection line? Explain how you know.

3. In the figure at the below, $\triangle ABC$ is congruent to $\triangle DEF$. For Exercises 1–4, describe the isometry that maps $\triangle ABC$ to $\triangle DEF$.

a. a translation

b. a reflection

c. a rotation followed by a reflection

d. a reflection followed by a rotation

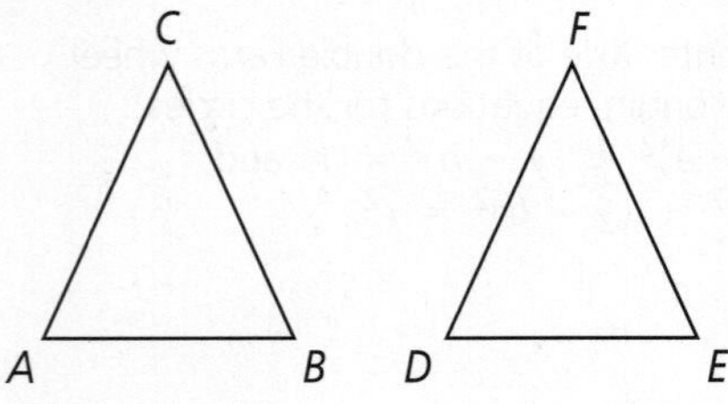

4. Copy the figure below. Draw the image of $\triangle ABC$ after a rotation of 70° around O in the counterclockwise direction.

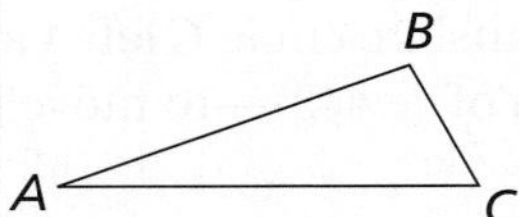

In **Investigation 7B** you learned how to

- plot points in two and three dimensions
- calculate the coordinates of the midpoint of a segment and find the length of a segment given the coordinates of its endpoints
- write equations of lines with given characteristics
- prove whether three points are collinear

The following questions will help you check your understanding.

5. $\overline{AB}$ has endpoints $A(-1, 1)$ and $B(3, 4)$. Find the length of $\overline{AB}$ and the coordinates of the midpoint of $\overline{AB}$.

6. Find the midpoint of the line segment with endpoints $(-2.5, 3.1)$ and $(6.7, -3.3)$.

7. Are the three points collinear?

a. $\left(2, \frac{1}{2}\right), \left(0, \frac{3}{2}\right), (1, 1)$

b. $(0, 5), (1, 12), (-1, 1)$

c. $(-7, 20), (7, 6), (3, 10)$

8. Quadrilateral $ABCD$ has coordinates $A(-3, -3)$, $B(4, -1)$, $C(3, 7)$, and $D(-1, 1)$. Find the coordinates of the midpoints of each side of the quadrilateral. Prove that these four points form a parallelogram.

9. Are the lines with equations $4x - 6y = 24$ and $4x + 6y = 24$ parallel? Explain.

10. Write an equation of the line through $P(5, 6)$ and perpendicular to the line through $A(-3, 4)$ and $B(4, -2)$.

11. What is the slope of all lines perpendicular to the line with equation $3x + 7y = 42$?

12. Plot points $A(3, 4, 5)$ and $B(0, 1, -6)$ on a three-dimensional coordinate system. Calculate the length of $\overline{AB}$.

In **Investigation 7C** you learned how to

- identify characteristics of vectors
- add points and multiply them by any real number, and write the results both algebraically and geometrically
- write a vector equation for any line on the coordinate plane

The following questions will help you check your understanding.

13. Use the points $A(4, 5)$ and $B(-3, 8)$. Point O is the origin. What are the coordinates of the head of $\overrightarrow{O(A + B)}$?

14. Answer the following questions for $\overrightarrow{AB}$ and $\overrightarrow{CD}$ in parts (a)–(c) below.

- Are $\overrightarrow{AB}$ and $\overrightarrow{CD}$ parallel?
- Are they oriented in the same direction?
- Are they oriented in opposite directions?
- Are they equivalent?

a. $A(1, 4)$, $B(4, 7)$, and $C(2, 3)$, $D(-1, 0)$

b. $A(-5, 3)$, $B(-2, 4)$, and $C(5, 7)$, $D(8, 6)$

c. $A(1, -6)$, $B(-2, 3)$, and $C(3, -9)$, $D(0, 0)$

15. Write a vector equation for the line through point A with coordinates $(2, 3)$ and parallel to $\overrightarrow{OB}$, where $B(6, 1)$.

16. Line m has vector equation

$$E = (-6, -1) + s(4, -1)$$

Line n has vector equation

$$H = (7, -1) + t(5, 2)$$

What are the coordinates of the intersection of lines m and n?

Chapter 7 Test

Go Online
Pearsonsuccessnet.com

Multiple Choice

1. Which line is the reflection of $2x + y = -4$ over the y-axis?
   A. $y = 2x - 4$
   B. $y = -2x - 4$
   C. $y = 2x + 4$
   D. $y = -2x + 4$

2. $\overline{FG}$ has endpoints $F(-1, 0)$ and $G(2, 3)$. It is reflected first over the y-axis (as $\overline{F'G'}$) and then over the x-axis (as $\overline{F''G''}$). What are the coordinates of F'' and G''?
   A. $F''(1, 0)$ and $G''(-2, 3)$
   B. $F''(1, 0)$ and $G''(-2, -3)$
   C. $F''(-1, 0)$ and $G''(2, -3)$
   D. $F''(-1, 0)$ and $G''(-2, -3)$

3. Which rule translates $A(-2, 4)$ to $A'(-7, -3)$?
   A. $(x, y) \mapsto (x - 5, y - 3)$
   B. $(x, y) \mapsto (x - 5, y - 7)$
   C. $(x, y) \mapsto (x + 5, y - 7)$
   D. $(x, y) \mapsto (x + 5, y - 1)$

4. $\overline{XY}$ has endpoints $X(-4, -2)$ and $Y(2, 3)$. What are the coordinates of the midpoint of $\overline{XY}$?
   A. $\left(-1, \frac{1}{2}\right)$
   B. $\left(-1, \frac{3}{2}\right)$
   C. $\left(3, -\frac{1}{2}\right)$
   D. $\left(3, \frac{5}{2}\right)$

5. What is the distance between $G(-3, 5)$ and $H(-1, -3)$?
   A. 8.2
   B. 4.4
   C. 2.8
   D. 2.4

6. Three vertices of a square are $(-2, 5)$, $(6, 5)$, and $(6, -3)$. What are the coordinates of the center of the square?
   A. $(-3, -3)$
   B. $(\sqrt{3}, \sqrt{3})$
   C. $(2, 1)$
   D. $\left(1\frac{1}{2}, 1\right)$

7. Which point is NOT collinear with (15, 5) and (60, 20)?
   A. $(-18, -6)$
   B. $(-3, -1)$
   C. $(0, 2)$
   D. $(24, 8)$

8. A cube has a vertex at the origin and sides of length 4 along the axes. What is the length of a diagonal of the cube?
   A. 2
   B. $4\sqrt{2}$
   C. 4
   D. $4\sqrt{3}$

9. For $A(-3, 2)$ and $B(-3, -5)$, what is $B - A$?
   A. $(-6, -3)$
   B. $(0, -7)$
   C. $(9, -10)$
   D. $(9, -7)$

10. For $G(-2, 10)$ and $K(3, -10)$, what is $G + 3K$?

A. $(9, -30)$

B. $(7, -20)$

C. $(7, 20)$

D. $(1, 0)$

11. For $X(-2, 4)$ and $Y(3, 2)$, what value of k puts the head of the vector $\overrightarrow{X(X + kY)}$ on the line with equation $y = -4$?

A. 3

B. 4

C. -3

D. -4

Open Response

12. Plot the points $A(1, 2)$ and $B(6, 8)$. Reflect $\overline{AB}$ over the x-axis. Write the coordinates of the images of its endpoints.

13. Here are equations of two lines.

$s: 3x + 4y = 3$ $\qquad$ $r: 16x - 12y = 28$

Prove that $s \perp r$.

14. Here are the coordinates of two points in three-dimensional coordinate space.

- $A(3, -13, 15)$
- $B(-15, 9, 26)$

Calculate the length of $\overline{AB}$.

15. Point A has coordinates $A(3, 8)$. Point B has coordinates $B(6, -3)$. O is the origin. Draw each vector on a coordinate plane.

a. $\overrightarrow{AB}$ $\qquad$ **b.** $\overrightarrow{OA}$

c. $\overrightarrow{OB}$ $\qquad$ **d.** $\overrightarrow{BA}$

16. Write the coordinates of the heads and tails of two vectors that are

a. are parallel

b. are parallel and oriented in the same direction

c. are parallel and oriented in opposite directions

Check your answers and explain why they are correct.

17. Quadrilateral $OACB$ is a parallelogram with vertices $A(4, 5)$, $C(3, 6)$, and O the origin. What are the coordinates of B?

18. For $P(1, 4)$ and $S(8, 12)$, find the coordinates of the tail of the vector that is equivalent to $\overrightarrow{PS}$ with its head at $(4, -3)$.

19. Line ℓ has a vector equation $T = t(3, 4)$, where T is a point on the line and t is any real number. Write a vector equation of the line through $A(-3, 5)$ and parallel to line ℓ.

20. Write a vector equation of the line through $A(0, -4)$ and $B(13, 20)$.

21. Find a vector equation of the line that passes through $A(5, 8)$ and is perpendicular to $\overrightarrow{OA}$.

22. For $A(6, 12)$ and $B(-2, 8)$, find C if B is the midpoint of $\overline{AC}$.

23. Find the intersection, if it exists, of the following pair of lines. If the point of intersection does not exist, explain why not.

$$S = (3, 4) + s(-3, 2)$$

$$R = (15, 3) - r(9, -6)$$

Investigations at a Glance

Optimization

Optimization is a process of evaluating alternatives to determine the best solution to a problem. It is a rich topic because the best solution often depends on many factors. People develop mathematical models to find the best solutions to both theoretical and practical problems. Many topics in math have been developed to answer the optimization questions that follow.

- What is the fastest way?
- What is the shortest way?
- What is the least?
- What is fairest?
- What is the cheapest way?
- What is the longest way?
- What is the largest?

Vocabulary and Notation

- angle of incidence
- angle of reflection
- contour line
- contour plot
- distance
- ellipse
- focus
- isoperimetric problem
- path
- topographic map

Making the *Least* of a Situation

In *Making the* Least *of a Situation,* you will minimize things. You minimize quantities in architecture, computer programming, economics, engineering, and medicine. This is because real-world optimization often involves making something as small as possible. You can minimize a rate, time, distance, area, volume, or angle measure.

By the end of this investigation, you will be able to answer questions like these.

1. What is the difference between the length of a path from one point to another and the distance between the points?
2. When and how can reflection help you find the shortest path for a situation?
3. In the following figure, $\overline{AS}$ and $\overline{BF}$ are perpendicular to $\overleftrightarrow{AB}$. $AS = 54$ ft, $BF = 27$ ft, and $AB = 84$ ft.

   Describe the location of P on $\overleftrightarrow{AB}$ such that the path from S to P to F is as short as possible.

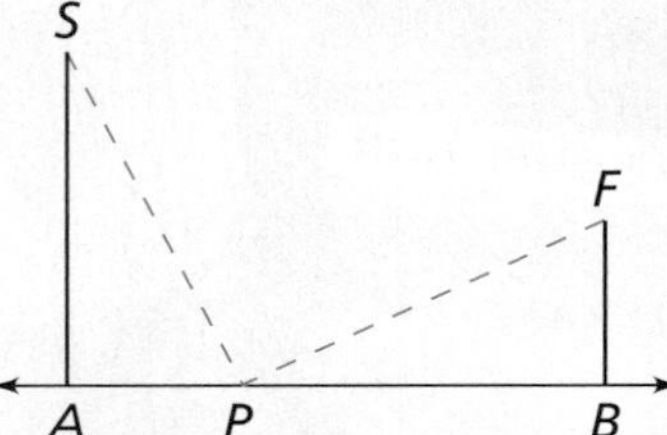

You will learn how to

- find the length of a path under given restrictions
- choose points that result in a minimum length for a path
- compute lengths and distances on the coordinate plane

You will develop these habits and skills:

- Distinguish between distance and the length of a path.
- Draw conclusions from trends in experimental data.
- Visualize reflections that will help minimize a path.
- Recognize key problem situations and choose techniques based on experience.

In this game, the least number of turns possible for moving one peg across the board is 1.

8.01 Getting Started

The **distance** between two fixed points is the length of the segment that contains them as endpoints. The distance is fixed. You cannot minimize or maximize it. A **path** between two points can be as long as you would like. A path between two points cannot be shorter than the distance between the points.

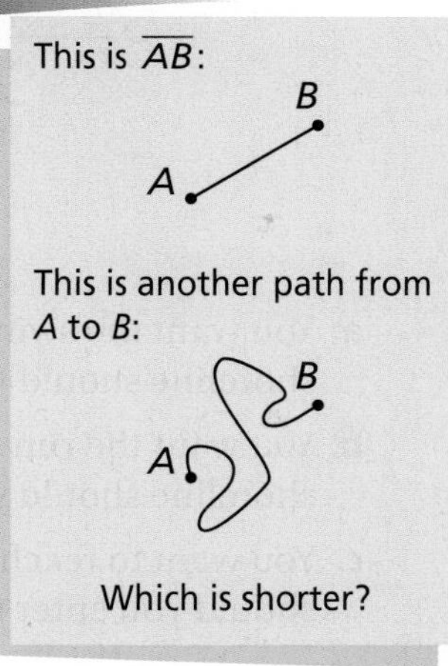

In the real world, the shortest possible path between two points may not be the segment containing them as endpoints. There may be obstacles in the way, or there may be an intermediate destination. In this investigation, you will find the shortest path from one point to another given a set of restrictions.

Habits of Mind

Visualize. Would it be possible to travel along the segment with endpoints at New York and Tokyo?

For You to Explore

1. Suppose you and a friend are at a corner of a parking lot and it is raining hard. All the spaces are taken and you want to get to your car by the shortest way possible. You can run around the cars or between them. What route minimizes the length of your path to the car? Is there more than one best route to the car?

2. This time, suppose you are standing in a courtyard with regularly spaced columns.

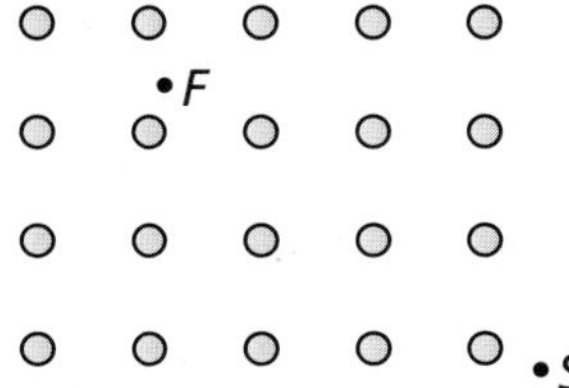

Find the shortest path you can from S to F. Did you use a different technique than you did in Problem 1? Explain.

3. You are lounging on the beach at L. You want to run to the shoreline and swim out to your friends at K.

This run-and-swim problem will be referenced later in the chapter.

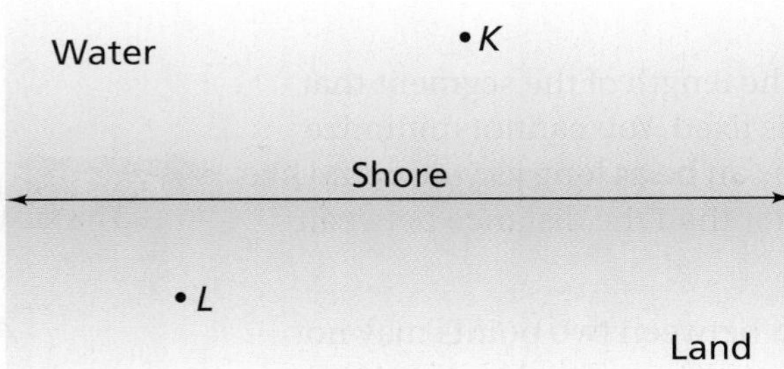

a. You want the swim to be as short as possible. To what point on the shoreline should you run to minimize the path you swim? Explain.

b. You want the run to be as short as possible. At what point on the shoreline should you enter the water now? Explain.

c. You want to reach K in the least possible total distance. Now where should you enter the water? Explain.

4. Use the following figure to answer parts (a) and (b).

a. Find the distance from $A(-2, 3)$ to $B(5, 7)$.

b. Add the restriction that no path from A to B may intersect $\overline{MN}$. Now find the length of the shortest path.

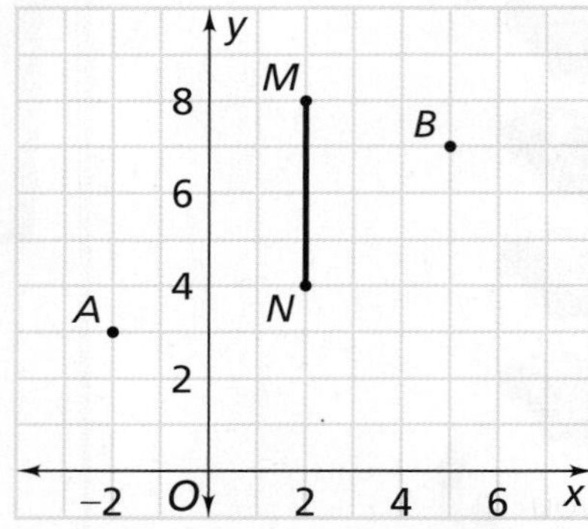

Exercises Practicing Habits of Mind

On Your Own

5. How do you measure the distance between two points when you are not in math class? How do you measure the distance between two points on the coordinate plane?

6. How do you measure the distance from a point to a line outside of math class? On the coordinate plane? Describe the process you would go through, rather than giving a formula.

For Exercises 7–10, use this new way to think about a coordinate grid. Imagine that the coordinate grid is actually a wire mesh set in a vertical plane, and an ant walks on it. There are wires at each whole-number value for x and y. The ant can walk only horizontally or vertically along the wires. The distance between two adjacent horizontal or vertical wires is 1 unit.

7. a. Describe the ant's path from A to B.

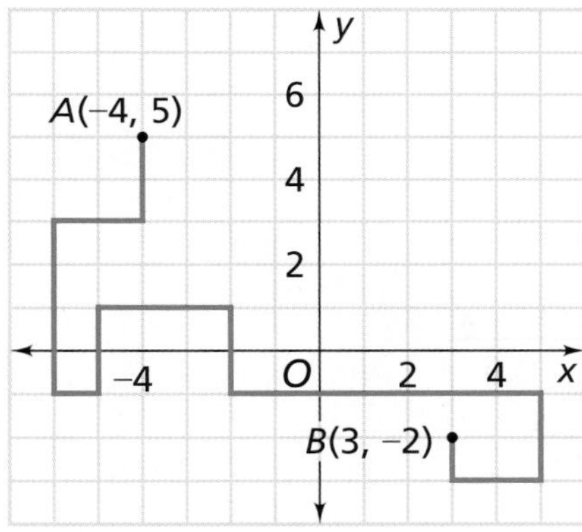

b. What is the length of this path?

c. Describe three different paths that an ant could take from A to B and give the length for each.

d. What is the length of the shortest possible path of an ant from A to B? Explain your answer.

e. Is the shortest path of an ant from A to B unique? If not, what do all the shortest paths from A to B have in common?

8. Find the distance between each pair of points on the coordinate plane. Then find the length of a shortest path of an ant between them.

a. $(-1, 3)$ and $(3, -1)$

b. $(2, 4)$ and $(-1, -5)$

c. $(4, 0)$ and $(-3, 8)$

9. **Take It Further** Name several pairs of points for which the distance between them is the same as the length of a shortest path of an ant. What relationship must the two points have for this to be true?

10. **Take It Further** Write a formula that gives the length of the shortest path of an ant from (x_1, y_1) to (x_2, y_2). Check that your formula works for points in any quadrant.

Maintain Your Skills

11. In the following graph, A, B, S, and F are fixed and P can be anywhere along $\overleftrightarrow{AB}$.

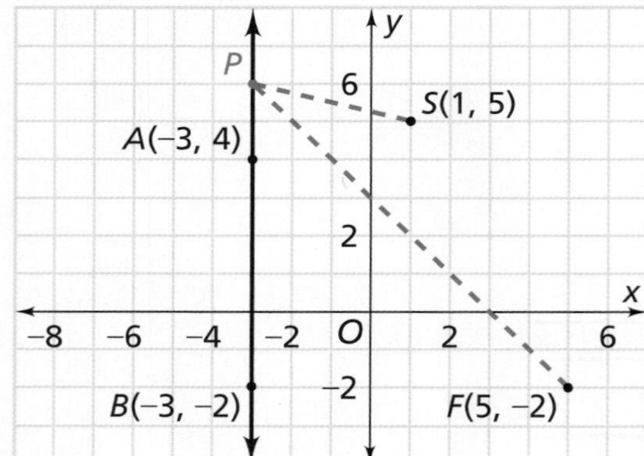

Find the length of the path from S to P to F for the following coordinates of P.

a. $P(-3, 6)$

b. $P(-3, 4)$

c. $P(-3, 2)$

d. $P(-3, 0)$

e. $P(-3, -2)$

f. $P(-3, -4)$

12. Refer to the information in Exercise 11.

a. What is the distance from S to F?

b. What location of P makes the length of the path from S to P to F the shortest possible? Explain.

c. What is the length of the shortest path from S to P to F?

8.02 Finding the Shortest Path

As you saw in Lesson 8.1, you cannot always take the shortest path between two points. There may be something in the way, or you may have an intermediate stop.

Remember...

In the parking lot problem, cars were in the way.

Imagine that you are motorboating on a river and you need fuel. First you must drop a passenger off on one river bank. Then you must refuel at a station on the other river bank.

Below are some pictures of the situation. The boat is at A. After you drop the passenger off at P, you will refuel at B. You can choose the location for P anywhere along the south bank. Because you are low on fuel, you want to minimize the length of the path you travel.

Should you land here?

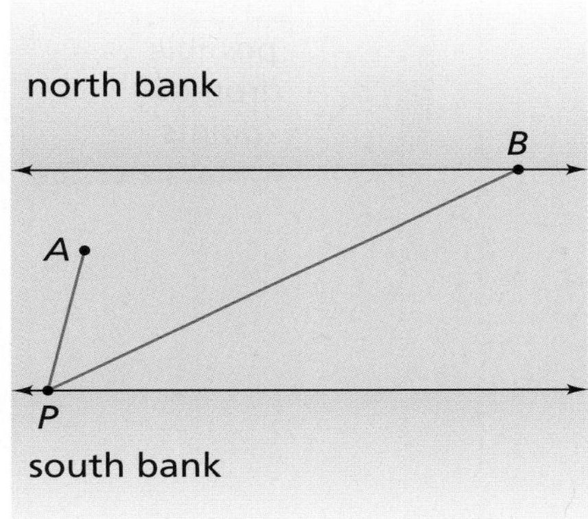

. . . or here?

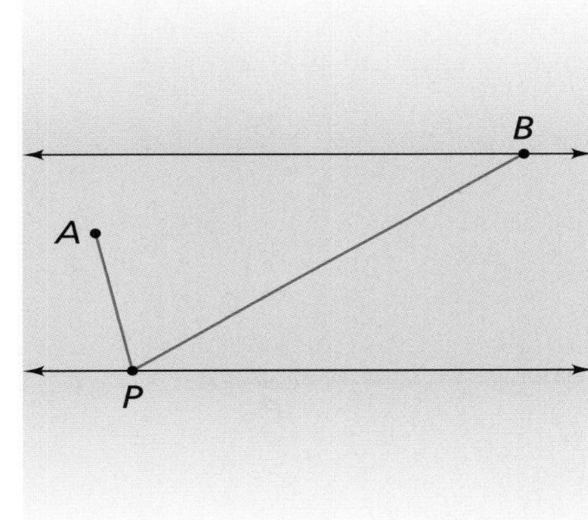

. . . or maybe here?

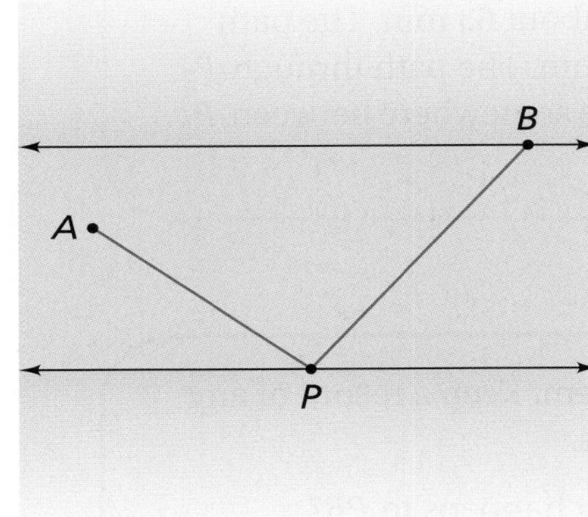

Minds in Action — episode 37

Tony and Sasha think about the refueling problem.

Sasha If you are traveling downstream, there's no way that you'd go back upstream from A to drop off the passenger before refueling.

Tony And you'd never go farther downstream than the fuel station at B.

Sasha So the best solution has to be somewhere downstream from A and upstream from B.

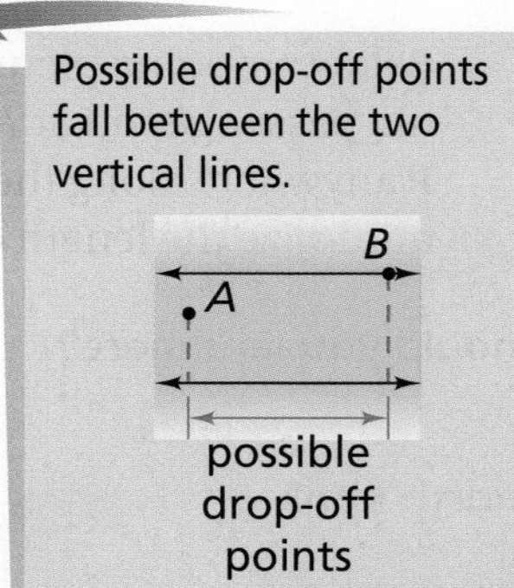

Possible drop-off points fall between the two vertical lines.

Tony Let's try some different places for P. We can measure to see what happens to the total distance traveled as we move P from left to right.

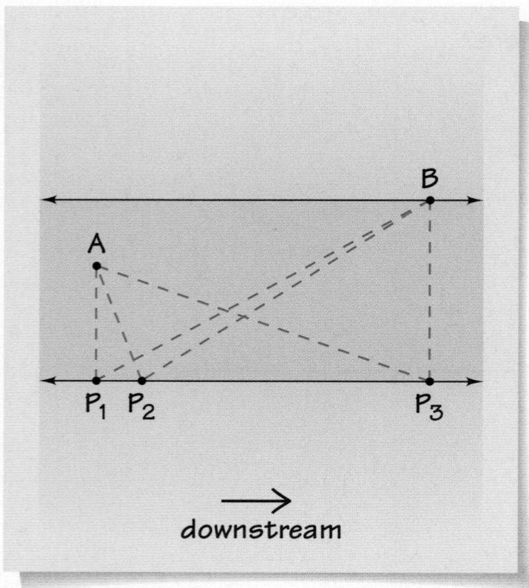

Sasha The path through P_1 directly below A is about 63 mm. The path through P_3 directly below B is about 68 mm. The path through P_2 measures 59 mm. The best path has to be somewhere between P_1 and P_3.

For You to Do

Here are some questions about the refueling problem. Keep a record of any conjectures you make, and justify your conclusions.

1. What happens to AP as P moves downstream? What happens to PB?
2. How does the sum $AP + PB$ change as P moves downstream?
3. Visualize, or draw, a sketch in which you hold A constant, but widen the river and move B farther away. Does the best location for P move to the left or right?

Developing Habits of Mind

Visualize. Here is another way to think about the refueling problem. When you look into a mirror, an object's reflection appears to be the same distance from the mirror as the real object. However, the reflection appears to be on the opposite side of the mirror from the real object. This makes the image and the real object symmetric with respect to the mirror.

Picture a mirror along the south bank of the river. You are standing on the north bank looking across the river.

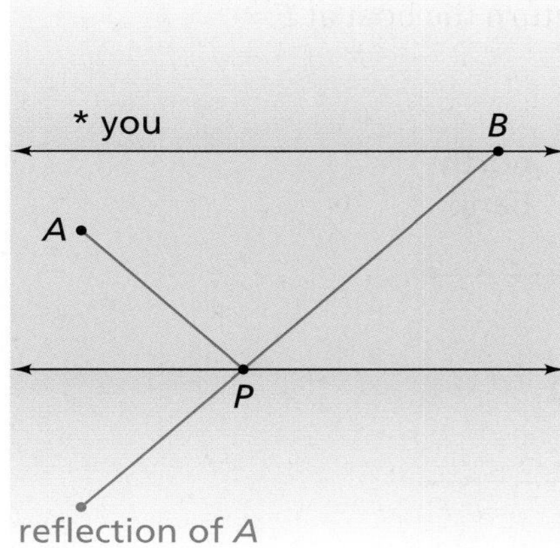

You can make the path from the *reflection of A* to B as short as possible by connecting the two points with a line segment. The point where this path crosses the south bank is also the point that minimizes the trip from A to P to B.

Remember...

In Chapter 7, you found that the mirror line is the perpendicular bisector of the segment joining a point and its reflected image.

For Discussion

4. The length of the path from the *reflection of A* to P to B is the same as the length of the path from A to P to B. Explain. Make a sketch using reflection to solve the refueling problem. Does it matter whether A or B is reflected? Explain.

Exercises *Practicing Habits of Mind*

Check Your Understanding

Use the figure below for Exercises 1–3.

You are in a rowboat, docked on the south bank of a river at D. You have to drop off a passenger on the north bank and then return the boat at F.

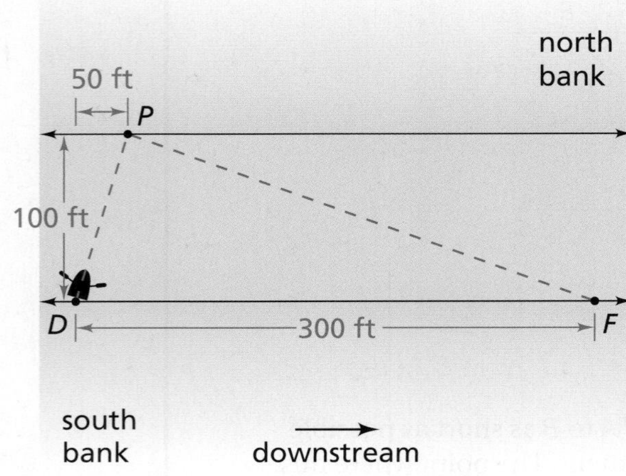

1. Find the total distance you have to row if the drop-off point P is 50 feet downstream from D. Assume that you can row in a straight line in spite of the river's current.

If P were x feet downstream, what would be the length of the path?

2. In the figure above, P is 50 feet downstream from D. Describe the location of Q on the north bank if the path from D to Q to F has the same length as the path from D to P to F. Explain how you know the length is the same without calculating it. Where would Q be if P were x feet downstream from D?

Habits of Mind

Visualize. As you move P to the right, what happens to Q?

3. Refer again to the figure above. Use reflection to find a location on the north bank for P that minimizes the length of the path from D to P to F. How far downstream is P? Is there another point on the north bank that has a path equal in length to the path from D to P to F?

On Your Own

4. **Write About It** Returning from picking berries near a campground, you find your tent on fire. Luckily, the river is nearby. You must quickly empty your berry bucket and figure out at which point P you should fill your bucket with water to minimize the distance you travel. Write about methods you could use to find the shortest path from where you are, to the river, and then to the tent.

This "burning-tent" problem will appear later in the text.

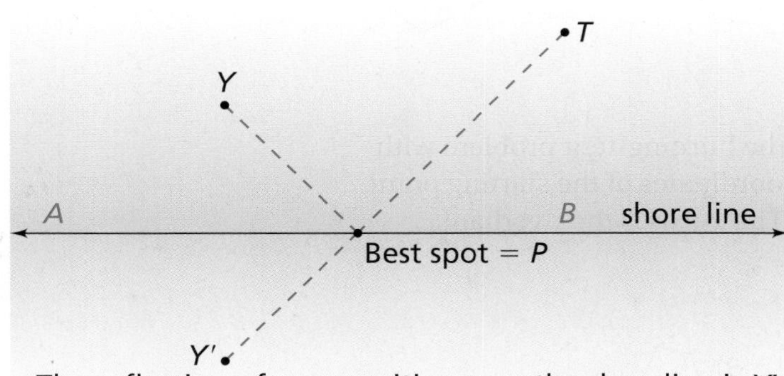

The reflection of your position over the shoreline is Y'.

5. Find the shortest path from $A(-4, 3)$ through any point P on the line $3x - 2y = 0$, to $B(4, -1)$.
   a. Sketch a graph of the situation.
   b. What point P on the line $3x - 2y = 0$ should the path go through? Explain.
   c. What is the length of the shortest path?
6. Find the shortest path from $A(-4, 3)$ to any point P on the line $y = 5$, to $B(4, -1)$.
   a. Sketch a graph of the situation.
   b. What point P on the line $y = 5$ should the path go through? Explain.
   c. What is the length of the shortest path?
7. Line ℓ has equation $2x - y = 0$. Because ℓ can also be written in the form $y = 2x$, points in ℓ are of the form $(x, 2x)$. Find a function that will give the distance between $(1, 2)$ and any other point on ℓ. For what value of x is this function at a minimum?
8. **Standardized Test Prep** Points $D(0, 1)$, $E(9, 13)$, and $F(25, 1)$ are the vertices of $\triangle DEF$, as shown at the right. Point $C(10, 6)$ is the intersection of the angle bisectors of $\triangle DEF$. $\overline{CH} \perp \overline{DE}$. What are the coordinates of point H? What is CH?

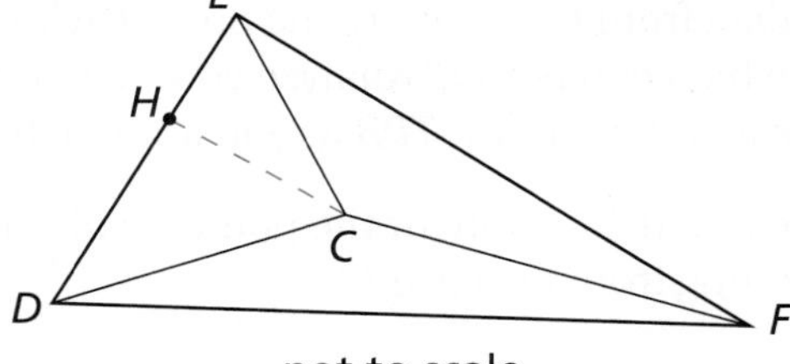

   A. $H(4.5, 7)$; $CH = \frac{5\sqrt{5}}{2}$
   B. $H\left(5, \frac{23}{3}\right)$; $CH = \frac{5\sqrt{10}}{3}$
   C. $H(5.25, 8)$; $CH = \frac{5\sqrt{17}}{4}$
   D. $H(6, 9)$; $CH = 5$

9. You are at an arbitrary point M in a swimming pool with many sides. Describe the shortest path out of the pool. Is the path to a corner or to a side?

10. Draw a new pool and a position for M such that the shortest path is to a corner.

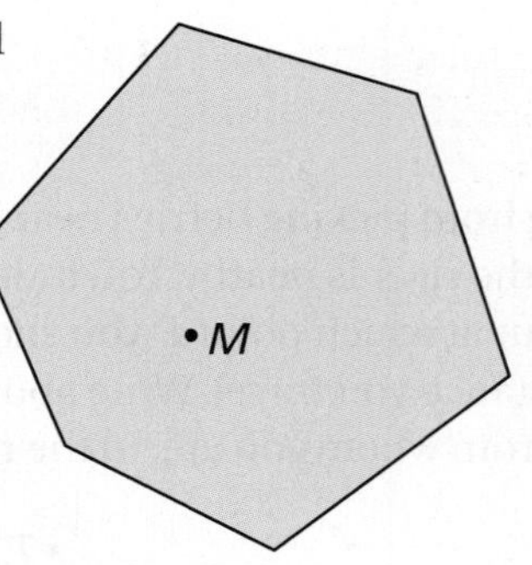

Habits of Mind

Expand your thinking. How would you describe all the points that are a given distance away from where you are in the pool?

Maintain Your Skills

In Exercises 11–14, you will examine the burning-tent problem with trigonometry. This figure shows the coordinates of the starting point and the location of the burning tent. The x-axis is the riverbank.

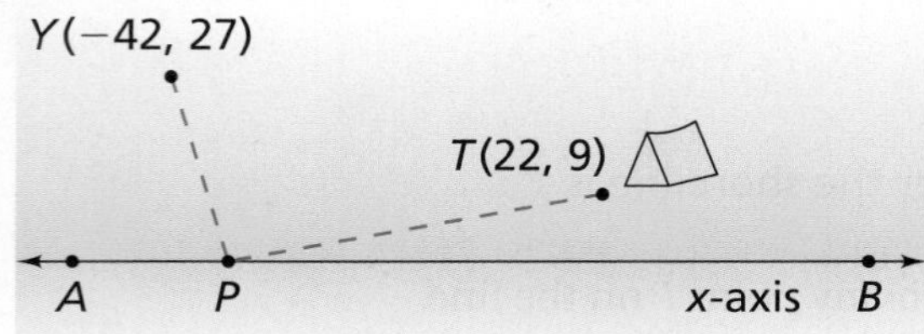

11. For each proposed location of P, the place you fill up your bucket, find the total length of the path.

a. $(-42, 0)$ **b.** $(-30, 0)$

c. $(-15, 0)$ **d.** $(-3, 0)$

e. $(10, 0)$ **f.** $(22, 0)$

12. For each proposed location of P, find and compare the approximate measures of $\angle YPA$ and $\angle TPB$.

a. $(-42, 0)$ **b.** $(-30, 0)$

c. $(-15, 0)$ **d.** $(-3, 0)$

e. $(10, 0)$ **f.** $(22, 0)$

13. Analyze your data from Exercise 11. The point P with the shortest path falls between which two points? Analyze your data from Exercise 12. What happens to $\angle YPA$ and $\angle TPB$ as you approach this location for P?

14. Find the approximate location for the point P with the shortest path. Use your reasoning from Exercise 13.

8.03 Reflecting to Find Shortest Paths

When you used reflection in the burning-tent and boating problems, you may have noticed similarities. Think about the angles at which the minimum-length paths intersect the riverbank. The situation is similar to the game of pool. The angle at which a ball hits the bumper is the same as the angle at which it ricochets off the bumper.

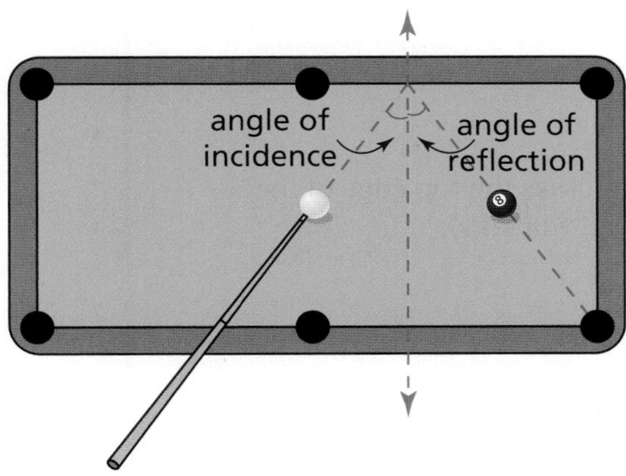

The **angle of incidence** is the angle between the incoming ball and the line perpendicular to the bumper at the collision point. The **angle of reflection** is the angle between the ball and the perpendicular line as the ball leaves the bumper.

For Discussion

1. Does this relationship hold for the minimum path length in the burning-tent problem? Is the angle at which you approach the river the same as the angle at which you leave the river? Does the reflection method guarantee this result? Explain.

In pool, friction affects the ball, and the ball's collision with the bumper is not perfectly elastic. This means that the measure of its angle of reflection is only approximately equal to the measure of its angle of incidence. In this lesson, imagine an ideal pool table, with no friction and perfectly elastic collisions.

Example

Problem Your goal is to hit the white ball in the figure off the top bumper, the right bumper, and then knock the black ball into the bottom center pocket.

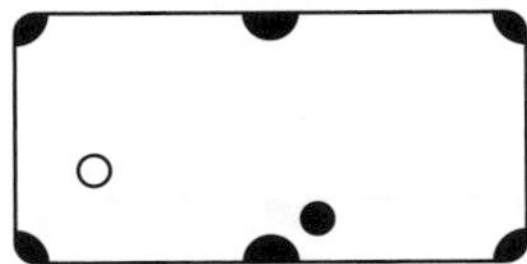

Find the point on the top bumper where the white ball should hit.

Solution You want to make a straight line through the top bumper of the table, the right bumper, and the target pocket. Reflect the pool table over its top edge. Reflect it again over its right edge. Now you can draw the straight line you want, as in the figure below. (The word *pool* is in the figure to help you visualize the reflections.)

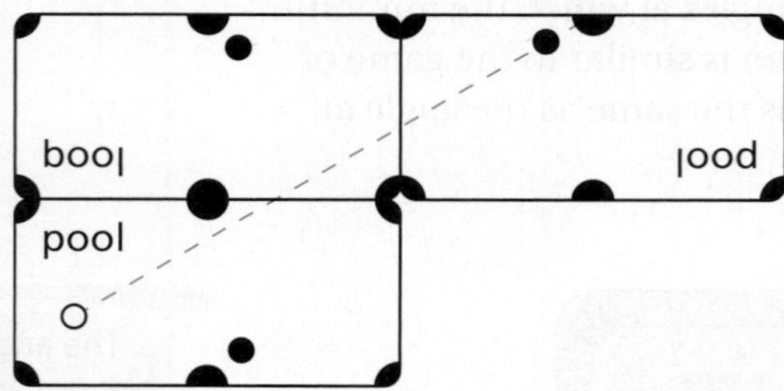

You should aim for the point where this line crosses the top edge of the table. Here is a sketch of the path the white ball will take.

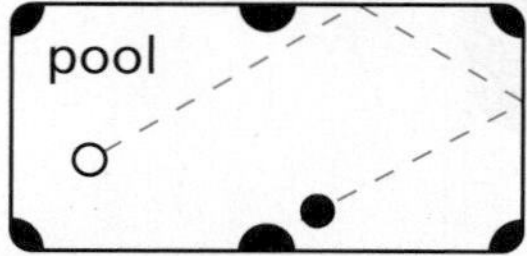

For You to Do

2. Use the figure from the Example for the starting point of the white ball. This time, you want the white ball to hit the right bumper, the left bumper, and then go into the bottom center pocket. Find the point you should aim for and sketch the path of the ball.

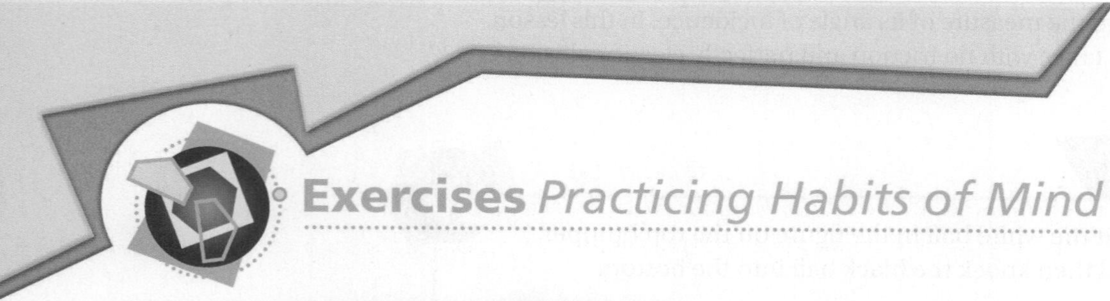

Exercises *Practicing Habits of Mind*

Check Your Understanding

1. Your goal is to hit the white ball off the top bumper, the bottom bumper, and then knock the black ball into the top left corner pocket.

   Locate the point you should aim for and sketch the path you expect the ball to take.

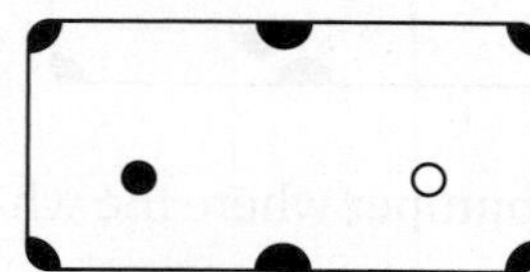

2. Design your own pool-shot problem involving at least two bumpers. Solve the problem yourself. Then give your problem to a classmate and compare your solutions.

3. A canoe is at R in the figure at the right. First, a passenger must be let off on the west bank. Then a passenger must be picked up on the east bank and dropped off at island S. Find the drop-off and pickup points that minimize the total distance traveled. Explain your reasoning. Check your answer with a ruler and string, or geometry software.

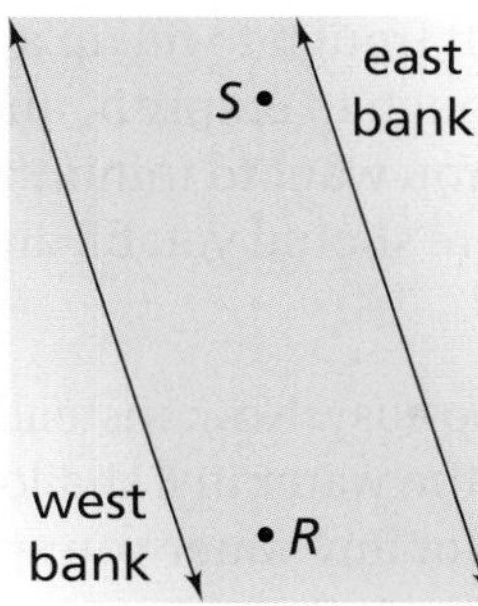

On Your Own

4. **Write About It** You are given line ℓ and two points S and F that are not on the line. Describe a strategy for finding P on ℓ that minimizes the length of the path from S to P to F.

5. You are in a rectangular swimming pool at K, out of reach of the sides of the pool. Before swimming to L, you want to swim to a side of the pool to put down your sunglasses.

   Explain how to find the place to put your sunglasses that minimizes the length of the path you swim.

6. A path on the coordinate plane must go from $P(3, -1)$ to point L on line ℓ with equation $x = -1$. Then the path goes to point M on line m with equation $x = 7$, and finally to $Q(3, 8)$. Graph the shortest path and find the coordinates of L and M.

7. In Exercise 6, P is exactly halfway between lines ℓ and m.

   a. If P moves closer to line ℓ than to line m, how does the path from P to ℓ, to m, and then to Q change?

   b. Check your prediction in part (a) by solving the problem again, but with $P(0, -1)$.

8. You are running a race at a July Fourth party. There are water troughs all along the left and right sides of the course.

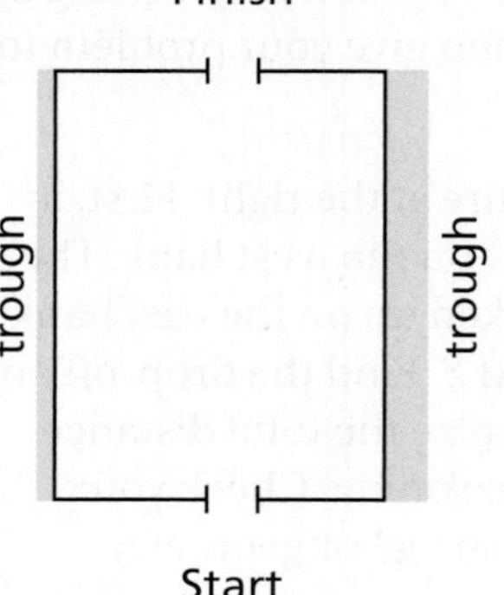

The goal is to run to the left trough to fill up a pitcher, run to the right trough to empty it, and then cross the finish line. You want to minimize the distance you run. Where should you fill and empty the pitcher?

9. The race in Exercise 8 is too easy. Now, instead of a pitcher, you have to carry the water in a shallow bowl and you will get penalties for any water you spill. Find a new route that minimizes the distance you have to carry the water-filled bowl.

10. **Standardized Test Prep** The measure of the angle at which a ray of light hits a mirror is 30°. What is the measure of the angle at which the ray of light reflects off the mirror?

A. 30° **B.** 60° **C.** 90° **D.** 150°

Maintain Your Skills

You have been minimizing lengths of paths that go through only two or three points. In this next series of problems, you will explore situations with more stopping points. In Exercises 11–13, you have $A(-3, -2)$, $B(1, 3)$, and $C(4, -1)$. A path is defined as follows.

- The path must start and end at *A*.
- It must pass through each of the other given points once and only once.
- For two paths to be considered different, one must contain at least one point that is not on the other path.

Answer the following questions for each of the given situations.

a. How many different paths meet the requirements?

b. Find the length of each path that fits the requirements. Which path is the shortest?

11. A path in this situation is made up of segments having *A*, *B*, and *C* as endpoints. (A path must pass through *B* and *C* once and only once.)

12. Include a fourth point $D(-2, 0)$ in the situation. Now the path consists of segments having *A*, *B*, *C*, and *D* as endpoints.

13. Include a fifth point $E(0, 5)$ in the situation. Now the path consists of segments having *A*, *B*, *C*, *D*, and *E* as endpoints.

Mathematical Reflections 8A

In this investigation, you learned to distinguish between path and distance, and find the length of a path under given restrictions. These questions will help you summarize what you have learned.

1. Describe this ant's path from A to B and find the path's length.

   Is this the shortest possible path between A and B? Explain your answer.

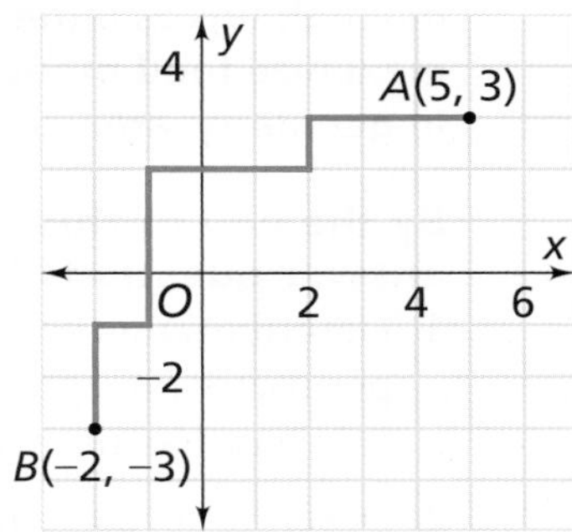

In Exercises 2 and 3, a path must lead from $(-3, 2)$, to the x-axis, and then to $(5, 2)$.

2. One path touches the x-axis at $(2, 0)$. Find the length of the path.
3. Find a different path that has the same length as the path in Exercise 2.
4. A path must lead from $(3, 5)$, to the line $2x + y = 4$, and then to $(1, 1)$. Where does the shortest path cross the line?
5. Find the path of minimum length that goes from $(-1, 4)$, to the line $y = 5$, to the line $y = -2$, and ends at $(2, 2)$. Your solution should include a graph and the coordinates of any significant points.
6. What is the difference between the length of a path from one point to another and the distance between the points?
7. When and how can reflection help you find the shortest path for a situation?

It's your turn. Can you move one peg across the board?

8. In the figure, $\overline{AS}$ and $\overline{BF}$ are perpendicular to $\overleftrightarrow{AB}$. $AS = 54$ ft, $BF = 27$ ft, and $AB = 84$ ft.

   Describe the location of P on $\overleftrightarrow{AB}$ such that the path from S to P to F is as short as possible.

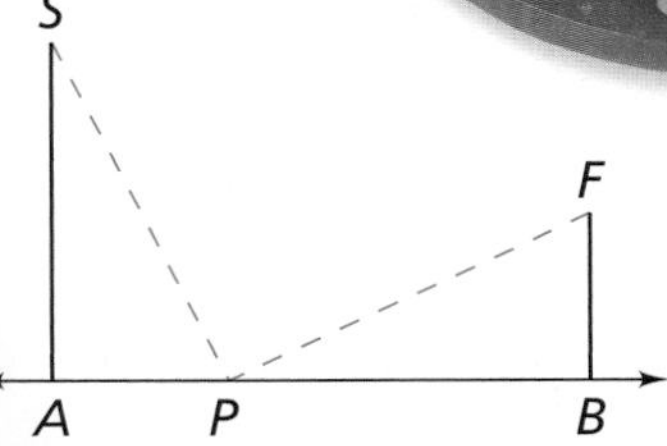

Vocabulary

In this investigation, you learned these terms. Make sure you understand what each one means and how to use it.

- **angle of incidence**
- **angle of reflection**
- **distance**
- **path**

Making the *Most* of a Situation

In *Making the* Most *of a Situation*, you will maximize things—make things as large as possible. In general, people want to maximize food production, profit, gas mileage, fun, or comfort. In geometry, area, angles, and height are often maximized.

By the end of this investigation, you will be able to answer questions like these.

1. Describe some characteristics of a rectangle that has maximum perimeter for a given area. Describe some characteristics of a rectangle that has maximum area for a given perimeter.
2. Describe several situations in which reflection can help you find the maximum area for a figure.
3. You want to build a rectangular garden against one wall of your house. You have 29 feet of border fencing. What are the area and dimensions of the largest possible garden you can build?

You will learn how to

- find grid polygons with a given area or perimeter
- maximize area for a triangle or rectangle under given conditions
- find the maximum area for a shape with a given perimeter

You will develop these habits and skills:

- Draw conclusions from trends in experimental data.
- Visualize reflections that will help maximize area.
- Reason by continuity to find maximums.

In-car monitors help you get the most miles per gallon.

8.04 Getting Started

Area and perimeter seem as though they should be related to each other. For example, if one fence encloses a greater area than another, it seems that the walk around the first fence should be longer. However, it does not always work that way. Here are two fields entirely enclosed by fences. You have to check the fences to see if they are in good repair.

Field A

Field B

Which field has more acreage? Which field has more fence for you to check?

An acre is a unit of area equal to 43,560 square feet.

For You to Explore

1. Use only the grid lines on a sheet of graph paper. Draw several polygons with area 8 square units. Find the perimeter of each one. What are the greatest and least possible perimeters for grid polygons of this area?
2. Use only the grid lines on a sheet of graph paper. Draw several polygons with perimeter 12 units. Find the area of each one. What are the greatest and least possible areas for grid polygons of this perimeter?
3. Use only $1 \times 1 \times 1$ unit cubes joined face to face. Build and sketch several three-dimensional shapes with volume 8 cubic units. Find the surface area of each structure. What are the greatest and least possible surface areas for cube structures of this volume?
4. Use only $1 \times 1 \times 1$ unit cubes joined face to face. Build and sketch several three-dimensional shapes with surface area 22 square units. Find the volume of each structure. What are the greatest and least possible volumes for cube structures that have this surface area?

Habits of Mind

Find another way. You do not need a formula to find the surface area of your structures. Just count the exposed cube faces on the top, bottom, and sides of your structure. What is the area of each cube face?

Exercises *Practicing Habits of Mind*

On Your Own

5. Describe several situations in which maximizing area would help in making food or money, saving time, or providing other benefits.

6. Each of the following grid polygons is changing. One square unit of area will be added to the polygon in the location shown. Find the perimeter and area for both the original and the new polygon.

In part (d), the original figure is not a polygon. The new figure is a polygon. The square with the missing center is included for the sake of completeness.

a.

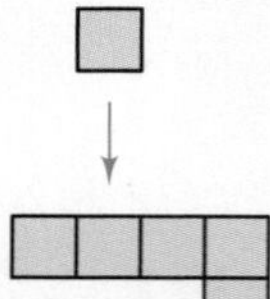

b.

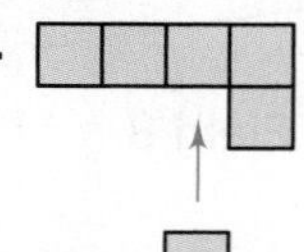

c.

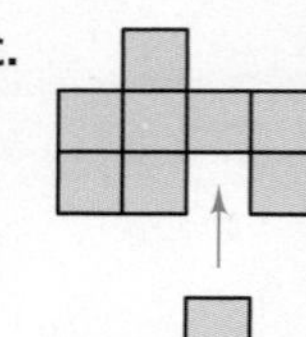

d.

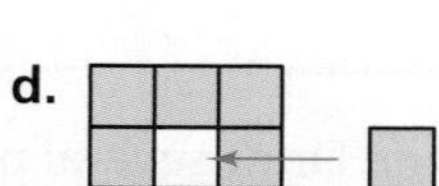

Habits of Mind

Look for patterns. Are there any cases not included in this exercise? Explain.

7. Change this grid polygon by adding as many square units to the polygon as you can without changing its perimeter. Show each step you take and check that the perimeter is unchanged. What is the greatest area you can get?

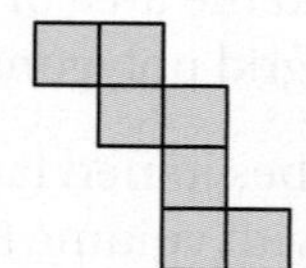

8. Each cube structure is changing. One cubic unit of volume will be added to the structure in the location shown. Find the surface area and volume of both the original and the new structures.

a.

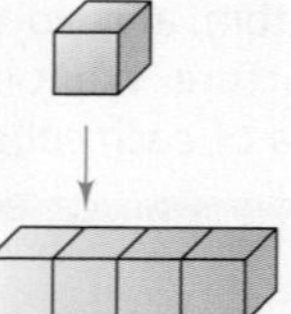

b.

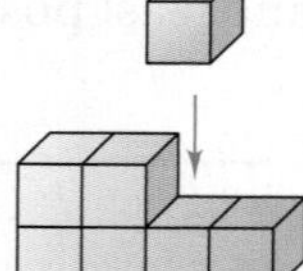

c.

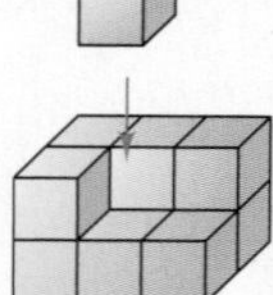

d.

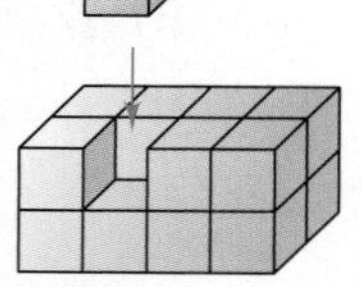

Parts (e) and (f) may be difficult to visualize. Each figure is shown with an exploded view that shows the floors of the structure separately.

Original Structure

e.

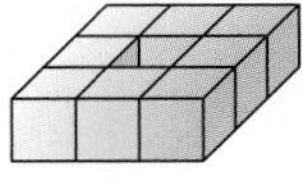

top floor: 8 cubes

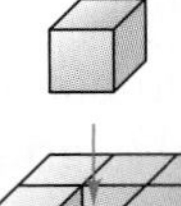

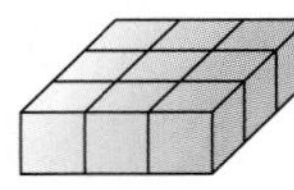

bottom floor: 9 cubes

f. Defining the surface area of the original structure is difficult because the structure has a hollow space in the middle. Count any square face that is touched by air as part of the surface area.

Original Structure

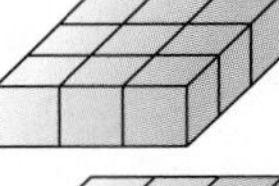

top floor: 9 cubes

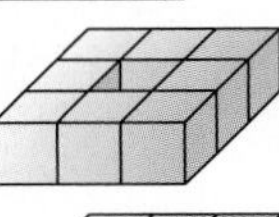

middle floor: 8 cubes

bottom floor: 9 cubes

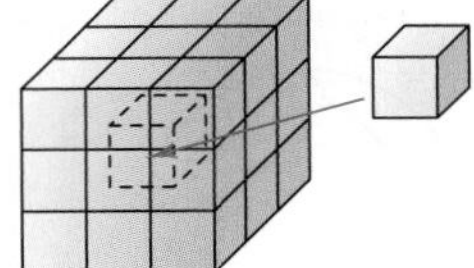

The added cube fills in the hollow space.

9. Change this cube structure by adding as many cubic units as you can without changing its surface area. Show each step you take and check that the surface area is unchanged. What is the greatest volume you can get?

10. **Write About It** Describe the characteristics of grid polygons that have maximum perimeter for a given area. What do they look like? What features *don't* they have?

11. **Write About It** Describe the characteristics of grid polygons that have minimum perimeter for a given area. What do they look like? What features *don't* they have?

12. Find four polygons with area 12 square units. Each must meet one of the following criteria.

- It is a grid polygon that has maximum perimeter.
- It is a grid polygon that has minimum perimeter.
- It is a polygon of any type that has a greater perimeter than the maximum for grid polygons. (This polygon is not restricted to grid lines on graph paper.)
- It is a polygon of any type that has a perimeter less than the minimum for grid polygons.

Maintain Your Skills

For Exercises 13–16, the regular polygon is inscribed in a circle of radius 1.

- Find the measure of the central angle θ, which intersects two adjacent vertices of the polygon.
- Find the length of one side of the polygon.
- Find the perimeter of the polygon.

13.

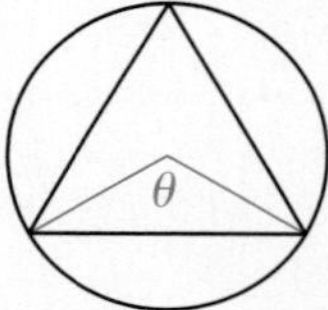

14.

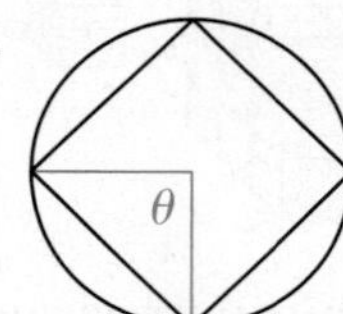

15.

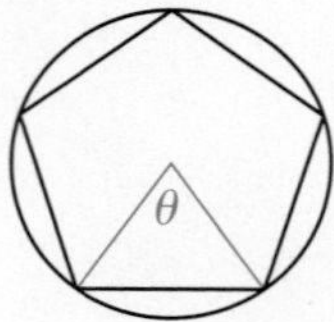

16.

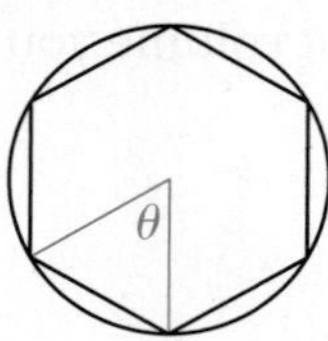

17. Look at your results for Exercises 13–16. Describe any patterns that allow you to predict results for inscribed polygons with more sides.

8.05 Maximizing Areas, Part 1

In Lesson 8.4, you were able to find maximums by trial and error. You were working in a restricted environment, so you could try each of the possible structures that met the given requirements. Now, you are going to prove some results about maximum area using familiar shapes.

Minds in Action episode 38

Sasha and Derman are working on the following problem.

Suppose you want to build a house with a rectangular base. The most expensive part of the house to frame is the exterior walls. You decide you can afford a house with a base (or floor) that has a total perimeter of 128 feet. What dimensions should you choose for the base if you want to maximize the floor area?

Derman After working with the grid polygons, we know it has to be a square. So it's a square with sides 32 feet long.

Sasha Well, we *think* it has to be a square. We haven't proven anything yet.

Derman Okay, I'll take a stab at it. The 32×32 square is better than a 40×24 rectangle. The area of the square is 1024 ft^2, while the area of the 40×24 rectangle is only 960 ft^2.

Is this a good example? (What is the perimeter of a 40×24 rectangle?)

Sasha True, but that's just one case. We have to show that the square has a greater area than any rectangle we could choose. Let's draw a picture.

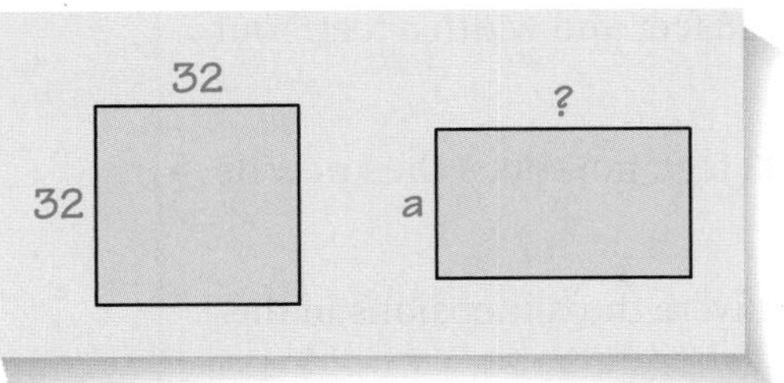

Derman Okay, the width of the rectangle is *a*, which is supposed to be less than 32 feet. How can we find the length of the rectangle?

Habits of Mind

Strategize. Use the perimeter.

Sasha We can try a cutting proof like the ones we used in Chapter 3. The length of the rectangle has to be greater than 32. Our rectangle has a width a and a length greater than 32 feet, so we can cut off a rectangle a feet by 32 feet.

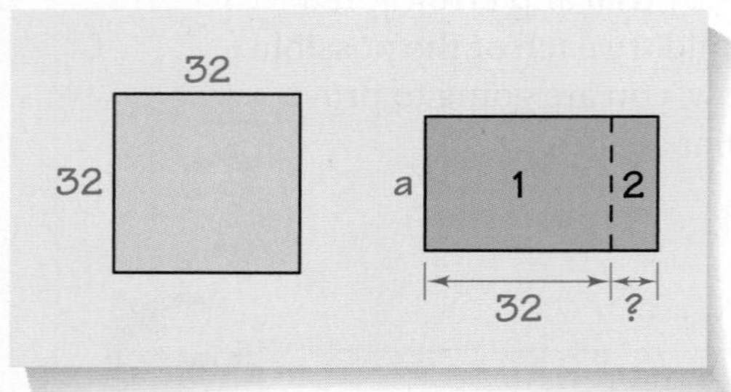

Derman Then we can fit both pieces inside the square like this!

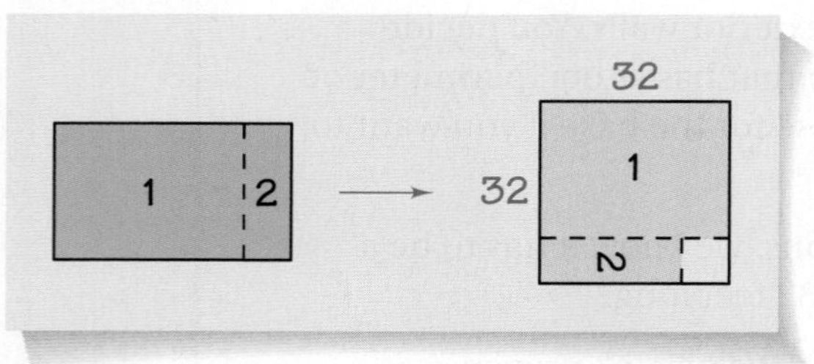

Sasha Great. Now you can see that the area of the rectangle is less than the area of the square.

Habits of Mind

Develop your understanding. What are the dimensions of the rectangle that is left after the cut?

For You to Do

There are some details missing in the dialog above.

1. Find the length of a rectangle with perimeter 128 feet and width a feet. Your answer should be in terms of a.
2. If the width a of Sasha's rectangle is less than 32 feet, how does she know its length is greater than 32 feet?
3. When Sasha cut off the $32 \times a$ rectangle, what were the dimensions of the little rectangle that was left?
4. Do both pieces of the rectangle really fit into the square as Derman said they would? Explain.
5. Write out a proof of Sasha's cutting argument in your own words. Prove that any nonsquare rectangle with a perimeter of 128 feet has less area than a square with the same perimeter.

Example

Problem You want to fence in a rectangular exercise run for your dog. You have 36 feet of fencing material. You decide that to enclose more area, you will use a wall of your house as the fourth side of the run. What are the dimensions of the greatest area you can enclose?

Solution This figure shows a run with width a and length b.

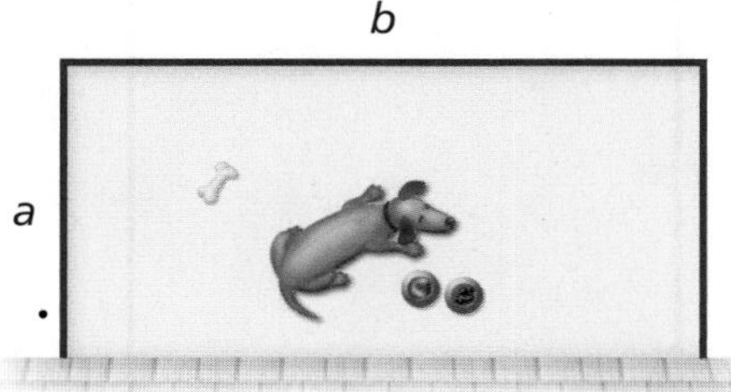

The total amount of fencing is 36 feet, so the perimeter equation is as follows.

$$2a + b = 36$$

You want to maximize A_{run}, which is the area of the run. The formula follows.

$$A_{\text{run}} = ab$$

Rewrite this formula in terms of one variable, say a, using the previous perimeter equation.

$$\begin{aligned} A_{\text{run}} &= a(36 - 2a) \\ &= 36a - 2a^2 \end{aligned}$$

Graph A_{run} as a function of a on a coordinate grid, either by hand or with a graphing calculator.

For help graphing a function, see the TI-Nspire™ Handbook, p. 712.

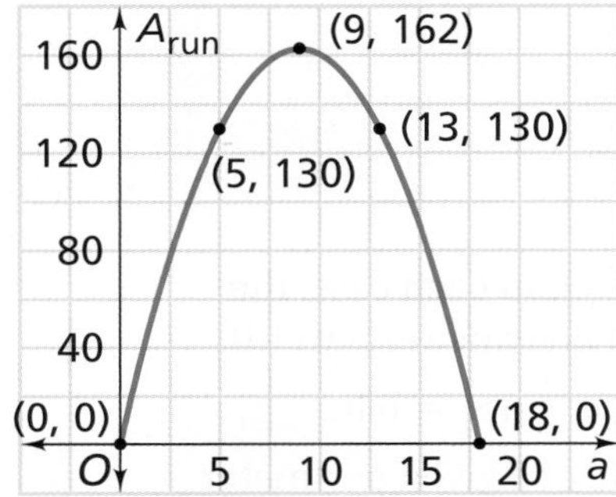

The graph is a parabola opening downward. The maximum value for A_{run} occurs at $a = 9$ feet. The dimensions of the run with the greatest area are 9 feet by 18 feet. Its area is 162 square feet.

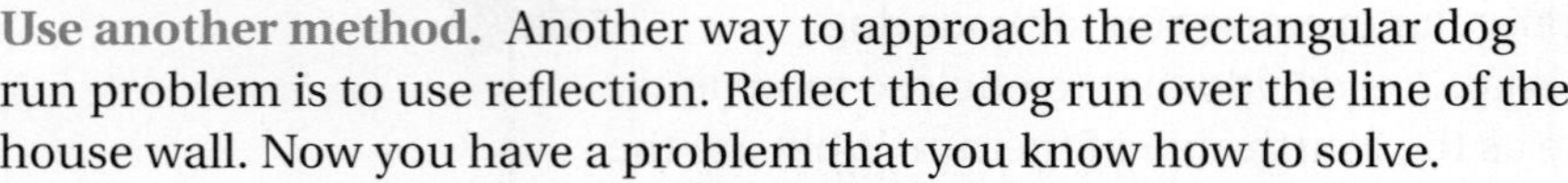

Developing Habits of Mind

Use another method. Another way to approach the rectangular dog run problem is to use reflection. Reflect the dog run over the line of the house wall. Now you have a problem that you know how to solve.

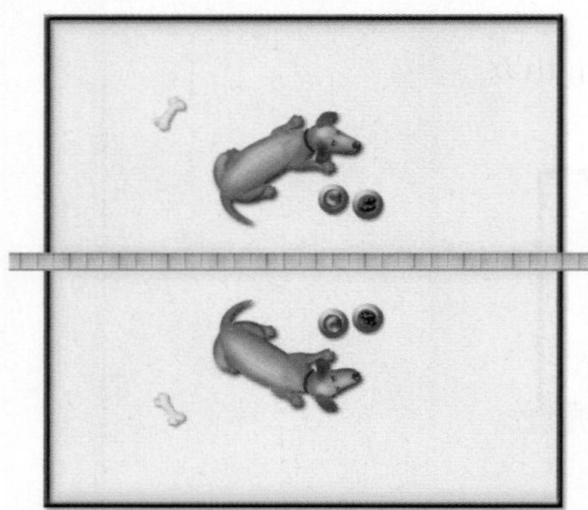

The new rectangle has a perimeter of 72 feet. You want to maximize the area. The maximum area will occur when the rectangle is a square with a side length of 18 feet. The real dog run is half of that square, so it measures 9 feet by 18 feet.

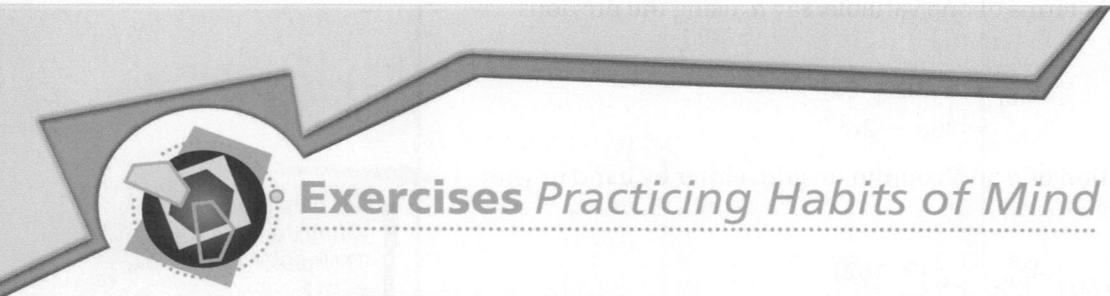

Exercises *Practicing Habits of Mind*

Check Your Understanding

1. Find the area of the triangle described in parts (a)–(c). In each case, the triangle is isosceles with a perimeter of 15 inches. Then answer part (d).

a. base = 4 in. **b.** base = 5 in. **c.** base = 6 in.

d. Make a conjecture about which isosceles triangle of a given perimeter will enclose the most area.

2. A triangle has a perimeter of 36 cm, and one side is 10 cm long. What should the lengths of the other two sides be to maximize the area of the triangle? Experiment and make a conjecture about the maximum area for this triangle.

You will prove your conjecture in Exercise 8.

3. Of all the rectangles with a given perimeter, which one has the greatest area? Explain.

On Your Own

4. Standardized Test Prep Ned draws a rectangle such that its length is twice its width, and its perimeter is half its area. What is the area of Ned's rectangle?

A. 8 units^2 **B.** 18 units^2 **C.** 32 units^2 **D.** 72 units^2

5. Refer back to the cutting method used in this lesson's Minds in Action. Show that an $a \times b$ nonsquare rectangle has less area than a square with the same perimeter. (This is not the same problem as in Minds in Action. Here the perimeter is fixed, but you do not know what it is.)

6. Suppose as in the Example you have 36 ft of fencing. You want to build a rectangular dog run against a barn wall that is 13 ft long. Again, you plan to use the barn as one side of the run. What size rectangle maximizes the area of the run now?

7. Triangles of many different shapes may have one side of length 5 in. and one of length 6 in. Which of these triangles encloses the most area? Explain.

Habits of Mind

Experiment. You might use geometry software.

8. In Exercise 2, you studied triangles with one side 10 cm and perimeter 36 cm. You may have conjectured that the triangle with maximum area is isosceles. It would have two 13-cm sides. The conjecture is true. In this exercise, you will prove it.

Suppose the height you conjectured is not the maximum. So there is another point that gives a greater height for the triangle. Therefore, the two unknown sides are not equal. One must be greater than 13 cm and one must be less by the same amount. Also, the perpendicular from the third vertex of the triangle does not intersect the 10-cm side at its midpoint. The point of intersection is closer to one side.

This scenario is shown in the figure.

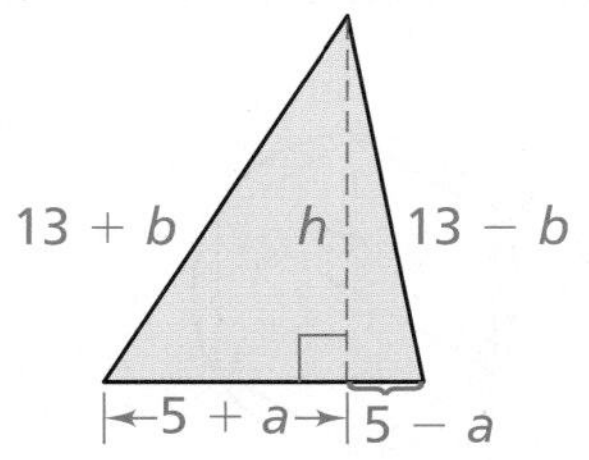

13 + b
h
13 − b
5 + a
5 − a

a. Write equations relating a, b, and h for each of the small right triangles in the figure. Use the Pythagorean Theorem.

b. Expand and simplify each side of the equation. Subtract one equation from the other. Find an expression for a in terms of b.

c. Using either of the two equations you wrote in part (a), write an equation for h in terms of b.

d. Show that the value of h is greatest when $b = 0$ and the triangle is isosceles.

9. A triangle has one side that measures s cm and a total perimeter of p cm. What lengths for the other two sides will maximize its area?

10. Out of all the triangles with perimeter 18 cm, which has the greatest area? Explain.

11. Find the maximum area for a triangle with perimeter 24 in. Now, find the maximum area for a rectangle with perimeter 24 in. Which is greater?

Maintain Your Skills

12. Find the area of a regular triangle (an equilateral triangle) with perimeter 60 cm.

13. Find the area of a regular quadrilateral (a square) with perimeter 60 cm.

14. Take It Further

a. This regular pentagon is inscribed in a circle and cut into 5 congruent isosceles triangles.

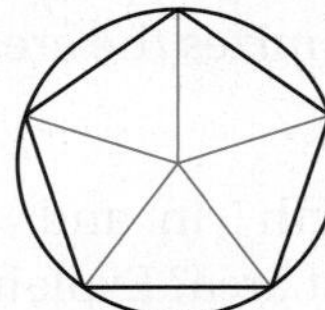

Find the measurements of all three angles in one of the triangles.

b. Here is one of the triangles by itself.

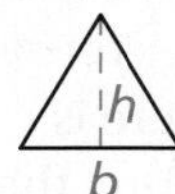

Use the tangent function to find an approximation for h in terms of b.

c. Find the area of a regular pentagon with perimeter 60 cm.

15. a. This regular hexagon is inscribed in a circle and cut into 6 congruent isosceles triangles.

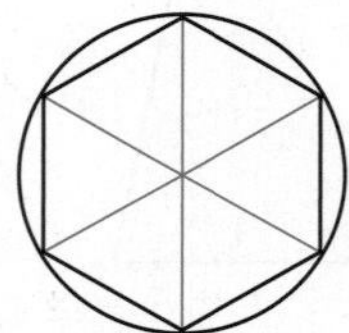

Find the measurements of all three angles in one of the triangles.

b. Here is one of the triangles by itself.

Use the tangent function to find an approximation for h in terms of base b.

c. Find the area of a regular hexagon with perimeter 60 cm.

16. Refer to Exercises 12–15. Make some conjectures about what kind of shape will have the maximum area for a given perimeter.

8.06 Maximizing Areas, Part 2

In Lesson 8.5, you explored problems in which the perimeter of a polygon is fixed. You discovered that the triangle with the greatest area is equilateral. The rectangle with the greatest area is a square. These two results may have led you to a conjecture similar to the following theorem.

Theorem 8.1 The Regular Polygon Theorem

Of all the polygons having a given perimeter and a given number of sides, the regular polygon has the greatest area.

You will work toward a proof of this theorem in the exercises for this lesson and in Investigation 8D.

In Exercise 11 of the previous lesson, an equilateral triangle and a square have the same perimeter. The area of the square is greater. Exercises 12–15 support the conjecture that for a fixed perimeter, the more sides a regular polygon has, the greater is its area.

For Discussion

Suppose for now that Theorem 8.1 is true, even though you have not seen it proven. Also suppose that for a given perimeter, a regular polygon with more sides encloses more area than a polygon with fewer sides. Propose an answer to the following area-maximization problem.

1. For all shapes with the same perimeter, which has the greatest area?

You will explore this question thoroughly in Investigation 8D.

Exercises *Practicing Habits of Mind*

Check Your Understanding

1. Which polygon has the greater area? Find a way to convince your teacher or someone else that your answer is correct.

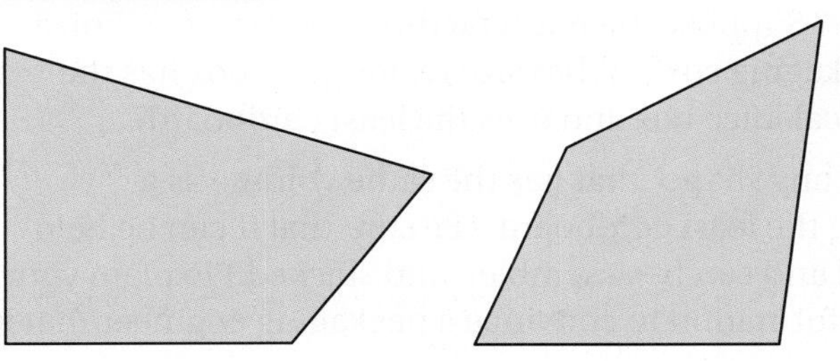

Habits of Mind

Consider more than one strategy. Could you trace and then cut up the polygons to compare the parts? What else might you do?

2. Consider the polygon at the right. Describe a way to make a polygon with the same side lengths, but with greater area.

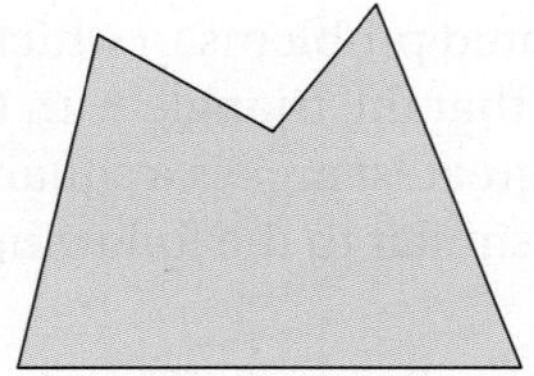

3. Consider all the parallelograms with side lengths 20, 30, 20, and 30. Which one encloses the most area? Explain.

On Your Own

4. **Standardized Test Prep** Suppose you have four regular polygons: a triangle, a quadrilateral, a pentagon, and a hexagon. The perimeters of the polygons are the same. Which polygon has the greatest area?

   A. triangle **B.** quadrilateral **C.** pentagon **D.** hexagon

5. Consider all the quadrilaterals of a given perimeter. Prove that the one that encloses the most area is a rhombus. You might draw a diagonal that cuts the quadrilateral into two triangles. How can you guarantee that the triangles both have maximum area? What do you find if you draw the other diagonal?

6. Show that the n-gon of a given perimeter that encloses the most area must be equilateral. Use your reasoning from Exercise 5.

7. Prove that the rhombus of a given perimeter that encloses the most area is a square.

8. Use Theorem 8.1 to solve the following problem, which is similar to the example in Lesson 8.5.

   Suppose you want to build a four-sided pen that is not necessarily a rectangle. You plan to use a stone wall as one side of the pen. The other three walls will be built with 840 feet of fencing. What shape and dimensions maximize the area of the pen?

9. Explain why the hypotenuse is always the longest side of a right triangle.

Remember...

The hypotenuse of a right triangle is the side opposite the right angle.

10. A typical juice box contains about 250 milliliters (mL) of juice. It measures 10.5 cm by 6.5 cm by 4 cm.

    a. What is the volume of this box in cubic centimeters?

    b. Is this the best box size? Suppose the manufacturer wants to maximize profit by reducing packaging costs. What size rectangular box has the same volume as a typical juice box and uses the least cardboard?

    c. Design a container (of any shape) that has the same volume as a typical juice box, using the least cardboard. (Be sure that it can be held comfortably by a child and can be assembled and stacked.) Explain your choice with enough information to convince a packaging engineer that it is the best shape.

11. Cut wood is often sold by the cord. A cord is a stack that measures 4 feet $\times$ 4 feet $\times$ 8 feet. This picture shows one way to stack a cord of 8-foot logs, all with the same diameter.

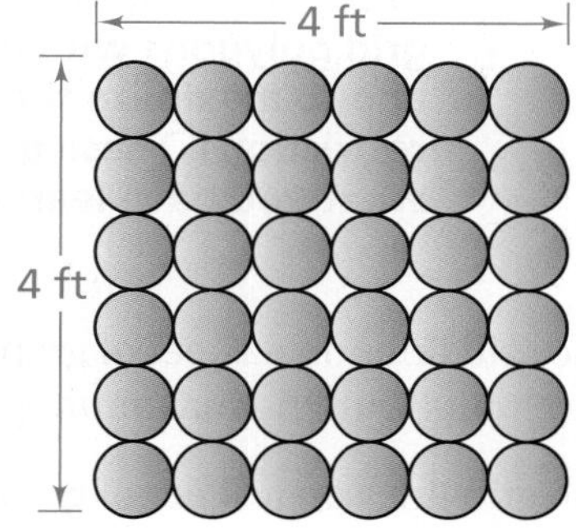

Jamal is ordering a cord of wood stacked this way. Suppose he can choose the diameter of the logs he buys. (In reality, there are many different diameters in a cord of wood.) What diameter should Jamal choose if he wants to maximize the amount of wood in the stack? (He wants to minimize the amount of air he buys.) Should Jamal buy one big log or many small logs?

Maintain Your Skills

Use the following description for Exercises 12–15.

Danae wants to build a rectangular dog run for her beagle, Bruiser. She has 48 feet of fencing to use. One wall of her house will serve as a side of the run. She wants Bruiser to have the maximum area possible.

12. What are the dimensions and area of the run she should build?

13. You tell Danae that the rectangular dog run is not the best possible 4-sided run. Instead, her run should be half of a regular hexagon. Give Danae directions (including lengths and angles) and the area of this dog run.

14. The wall of Danae's house is only 20 feet long. She cannot build the optimal rectangular run or the optimal half-hexagonal run. Find the new best rectangular run. Find the new best hexagonal run.

15. Danae has another problem. If she builds more than 9 feet from the house, she will run into the neighbor's property line. She has two possible solutions. Find the dimensions and the area of the best run of each type described below.

a. The run is a 9-foot wide rectangle. The 20-foot wall is part of one side.

b. The run is a 9-foot-wide isosceles trapezoid. The 20-foot wall is one complete base of the trapezoid.

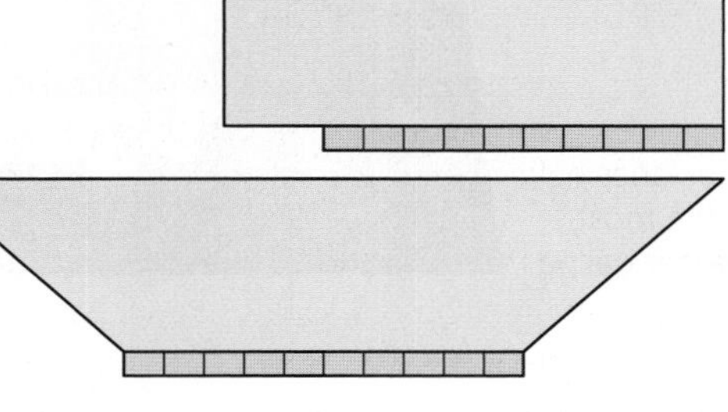

c. Which run should Danae choose?

In this investigation, you learned how to find grid polygons with a given area or perimeter, and to maximize the area for a shape with certain restrictions. These questions will help you summarize what you have learned.

1. Use only the grid lines on a sheet of graph paper. Find the polygon that has area 8 square units with the maximum perimeter possible.
2. Use only the grid lines on a sheet of graph paper. Find the polygon that has perimeter 12 units with the maximum area possible.
3. Several triangles have one side of length 7 cm and one side of length 5 cm. Which of these triangles encloses the most area? What is its perimeter?
4. Find the maximum possible area for a triangle with perimeter 24 in.
5. Find the maximum possible area for a quadrilateral with perimeter 24 in.
6. Describe some characteristics of a rectangle that has a large perimeter for a given area. Describe some characteristics of a rectangle that has maximum area for a given perimeter.
7. Describe several situations in which reflection can help you find the maximum area for a figure.
8. You want to build a rectangular garden against one wall of your house. You have 29 feet of border fencing. What are the area and dimensions of the largest possible garden you can build?

Carpool lanes help move the most people per gallon.

Mid-Chapter Test

Multiple Choice

1. Recall from Lesson 8.1 the ant that can travel only on the wire mesh of a coordinate grid. If an ant travels from $A(1, 4)$ to $B(-4, 0)$, what is the length of the shortest possible path?

   A. 6 units **B.** 9 units
   C. 12 units **D.** 15 units

2. Suppose a square is inscribed in a circle of radius 3 cm. Find the area of the square.

   A. 9 cm^2 **B.** 18 cm^2
   C. $6\sqrt{18}$ cm^2 **D.** 36 cm^2

Open Response

3. Trace these lines and draw the shortest path from A to B.

4. Trace these lines. Draw the shortest path from A to B through some point P on line m. Label P.

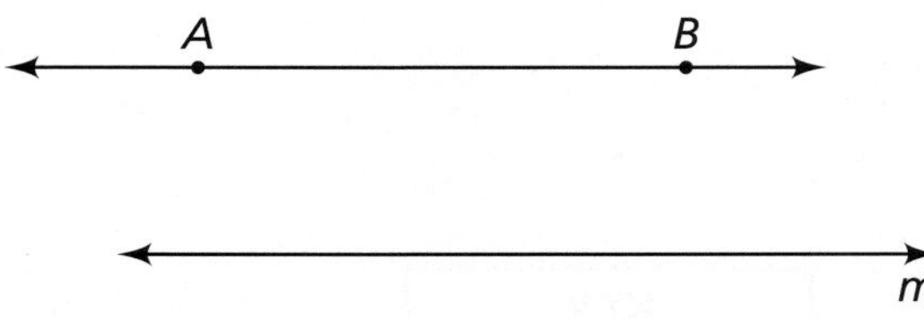

5. Describe and draw the shortest path from X to any point on polygon $ABCDEFG$.

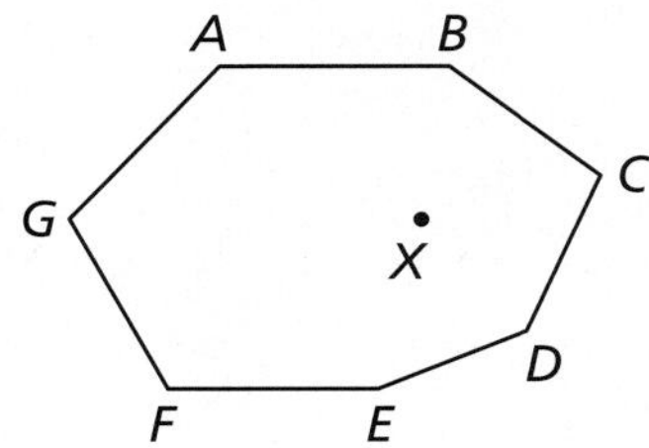

In Exercises 6 and 7, a path must lead from (4, 5), to the y-axis, and then to $(4, -4)$.

6. One path touches the y-axis at $(0, -3)$. Find the length of the path.

7. Find a different path that follows the rules and has the same length as the path in Exercise 6.

8. A town ordinance says you must have a fence around your swimming pool. You can afford 36 meters of fence to enclose a rectangle around your pool.

   a. What dimensions maximize the area of this rectangle if all four sides are made from your fencing?

   b. Suppose you want to enclose an even greater area. You decide to build against your neighbor's existing 20-meter fence. The 36 meters of fencing will be used for the other three sides. What dimensions maximize the area of this rectangle?

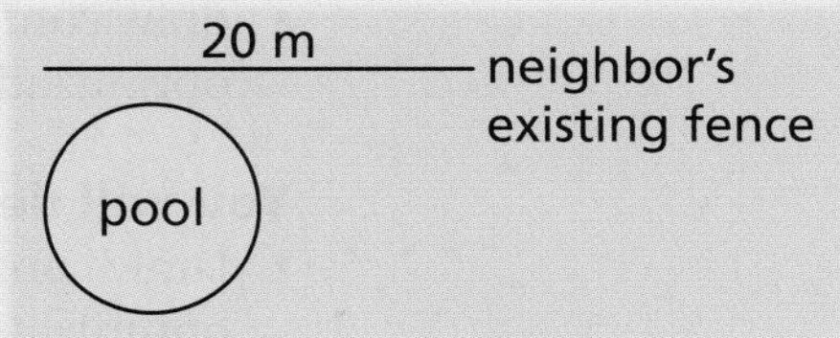

9. Suppose you have a group of 16 pictures, each 6 inches by 6 inches. You want to arrange them edge to edge and then frame the group. The frame store charges $2 per foot of frame.

   a. How should you arrange your 16 pictures to minimize the cost? What is the cost? Draw a picture and explain your answer.

   b. What is the most expensive arrangement? What is the cost? Draw a picture and explain your answer.

Contour Lines

In *Contour Lines*, you will explore functions on the plane. You will draw pictures that show where a function takes on specific values. You will use these drawings to find minimum values for functions under certain restrictions. Then you will use the new techniques to revisit the burning-tent problem.

By the end of this investigation, you will be able to answer questions like these.

1. Describe how a contour plot can help you solve the burning-tent problem.
2. Can two contour lines of a contour plot intersect? Explain.
3. Below is a contour plot showing depth in feet of a lake. You drop your keys into the deepest part of the lake. How far down will you have to swim to get them?

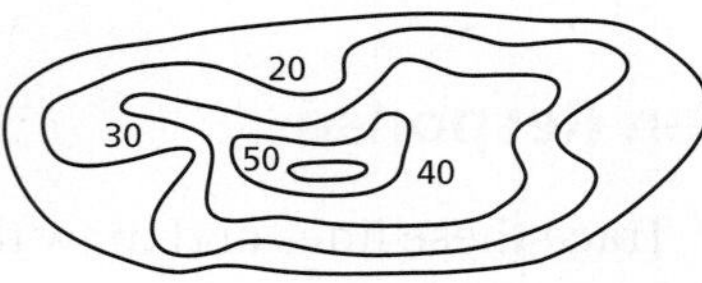

You will learn how to

- read and understand topographic maps and temperature maps
- interpret contour plots
- draw contour lines to make contour plots and solve optimization problems

You will develop these habits and skills:

- Draw contour lines to visualize a possible solution for an optimization problem.
- See a contour line as the set of points for which a function takes on a single value.
- Recognize a pattern in the contour lines of a function.

KEY
Contour (20 meter interval)
0 .5 mi .8 km
N
1400
1500
1600
Mitre Peak
1500

Each contour line marks a 20-m change in height. What is it that is pictured here?

8.07 Getting Started

Have you ever seen a topographic map? A **topographic map** is a type of *contour plot* that usually depicts land elevations or sea depths. Curves or lines represent points of the same elevation.

> *Topograghy* is a precise detailed study of the surface features of a region. It comes from the Greek words *topos* (place) and *grafein* (to write).

Here is a map of a mountain. Each closed curve, or *contour line*, indicates a change of 200 feet. The lowest height marked on this map is 2000 feet.

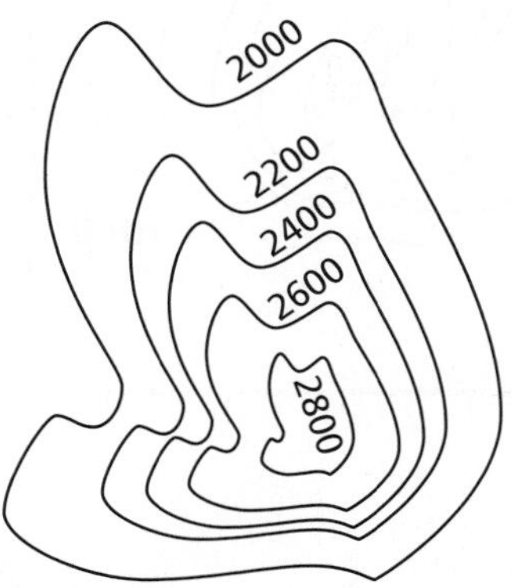

This diagram shows only closed curves. Other maps may include open (partial) curves. It depends on the size and scale of the map. For example, look at the following map that shows temperatures across Europe.

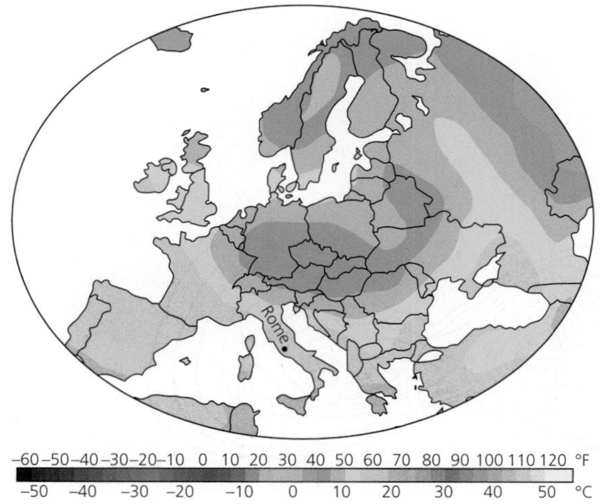

> Each color indicates an interval of temperatures. So, the temperature of Rome is between 55°F and 60°F.

For You to Explore

1. How high might the peak of the mountain in the Getting Started map be? What is its maximum possible height?

2. Here are two paths to get to the peak of the mountain.

   Suppose it is equally easy to get to the start of Path A and to the start of Path B at an altitude of 2000 feet. Which path would you choose? Explain.

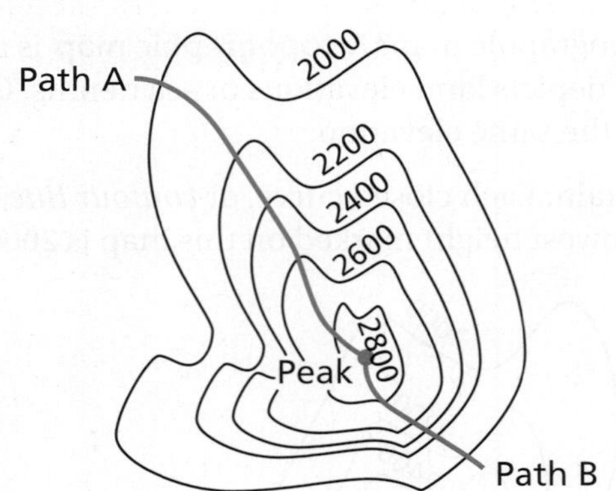

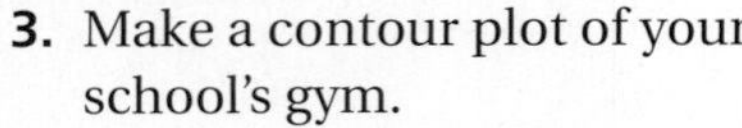

3. Make a contour plot of your school's gym.

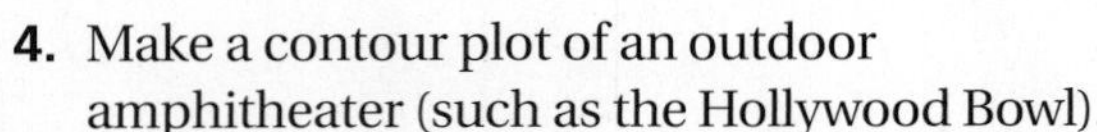

4. Make a contour plot of an outdoor amphitheater (such as the Hollywood Bowl).

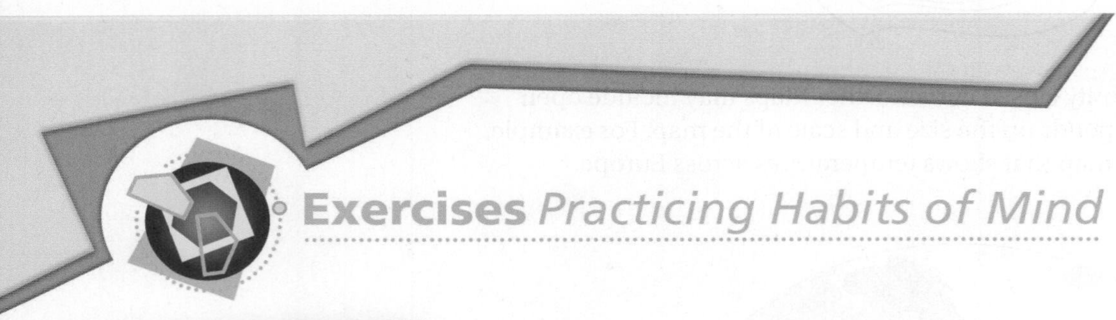

Exercises *Practicing Habits of Mind*

On Your Own

5. Here is the topographic map for two neighboring peaks. There is an increase of 100 feet between contour lines as you move in toward the peaks.

   a. The outermost line on the map represents points that are 1000 feet above sea level. Describe the areas on the map that are at least 1600 feet above sea level.

   b. The two summits are unmarked here. What is the maximum elevation that they could be? Which one must be higher? Explain.

   c. How can you find the steepest part of the mountains? Explain.

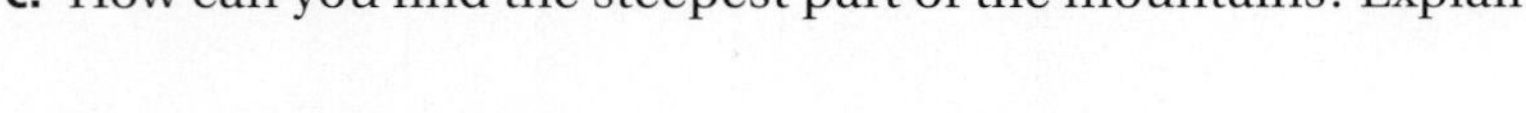

6. Make a contour plot of a local sports stadium (include the stands).

7. The map at the right is of a pond for which the outer contour line represents the edge of the water. Each contour line represents an increase in depth of 5 feet. A camp has rights to the property bounded by the quadrilateral. The director wants to rope off a swimming area with water no deeper than 7 feet. Trace the map and sketch a proposal for such a roped-off area.

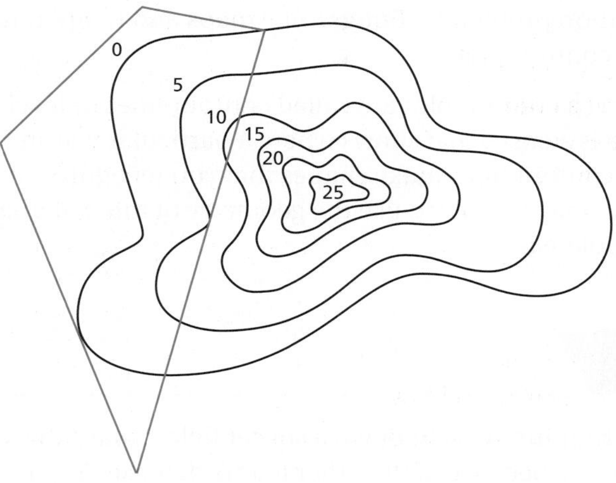

Maintain Your Skills

8. Use the contour plot of temperatures in the United States to answer the questions below.

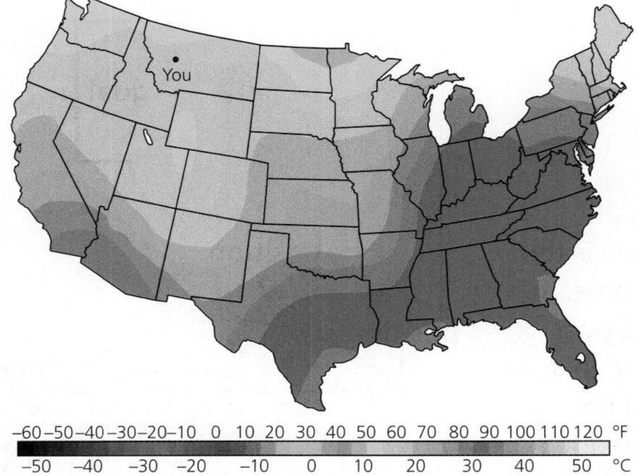

a. Which areas are the hottest? What is the range of their temperatures?

b. You are in Washington, D.C. You want to get to an area where the temperature is at most 80° F. In which direction should you go so that you travel the shortest distance? (Assume there are straight routes to any location.)

c. You are at the point on the map marked You, in Montana. You wish to get to an area where the temperature is at least 70° F. In which direction should you go so that you travel the shortest distance? (Assume there are straight routes to any location.)

8.08 Drawing Contour Plots

Contour plots provide a new way to visualize functions. They can often be used to solve optimization problems. Topographic maps and temperature maps are examples of contour plots.

The individual curves in a contour plot are called contour lines or level curves. A **contour line** is a curve that shows where a particular feature is invariant. Sometimes contour lines make shapes that you recognize such as circles or polygons. You may be able to use the geometry of those shapes to solve optimization problems.

Habits of Mind

Look for relationships. Why would people use the words *contour* and *level* to describe these paths?

Example

Problem Suppose you are running straight down a soccer field toward the goal. You are off to the side because of the other team's defense. As you run, you have various openings to score a goal. From what position should you shoot if you want the widest angle between the goal posts?

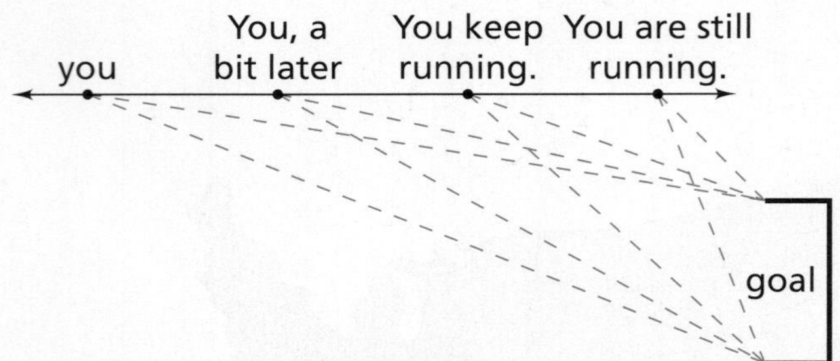

Habits of Mind

Experiment. Geometry software is an ideal tool for experimenting with this problem.

Solution The kicking angle is the angle from one goal post, to you, to the other goal post. You want to maximize this angle. To understand the situation, you might sketch a circle through the goal posts and you. (See the figure at the right.)

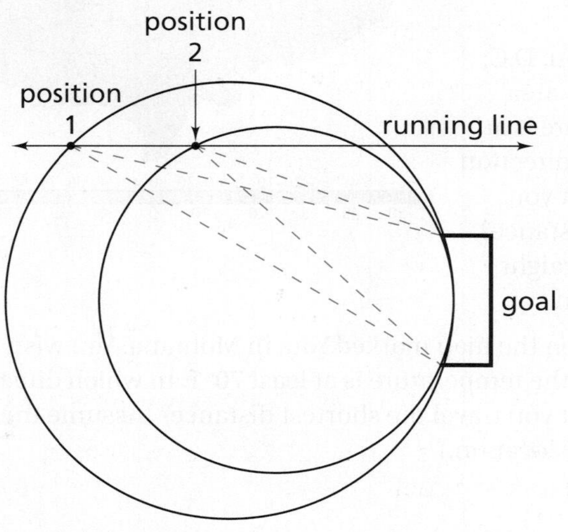

Recall from Chapter 5 that all angles inscribed in a circle with a given arc have the same degree measure. Therefore, each circle is a contour line that shows the set of points that have the same kicking angle.

As you try different kicking positions, the circle and angle change. The angle is greatest when the circle is tangent to the kicking line. This is because any other point on the kicking line is outside this tangent circle. It would make a lesser angle with the goal posts than the angle that has the tangent point as its vertex.

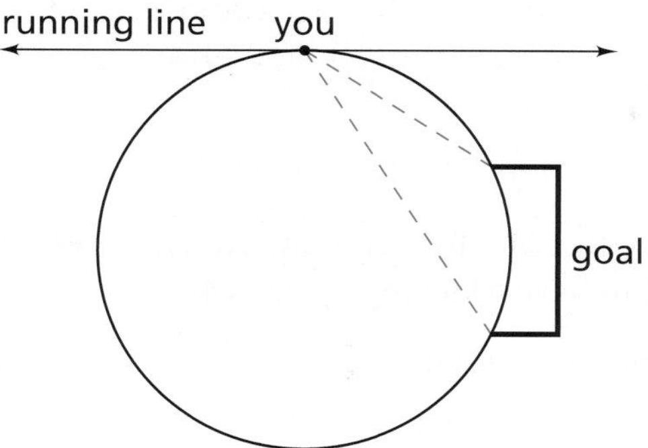

For You to Do

1. Imagine that you are running along a line parallel to the goal. You want to maximize your kicking angle. Where should you stop along that line to kick the ball?

Suppose your coach wants you to learn how to find the best kicking spots for scoring. This is a complicated skill, so first you look at some simple cases. Complete the following In-Class Experiment. Discuss your results with the class.

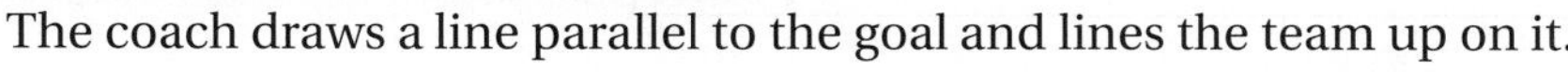

In-Class Experiment

The coach draws a line parallel to the goal and lines the team up on it.

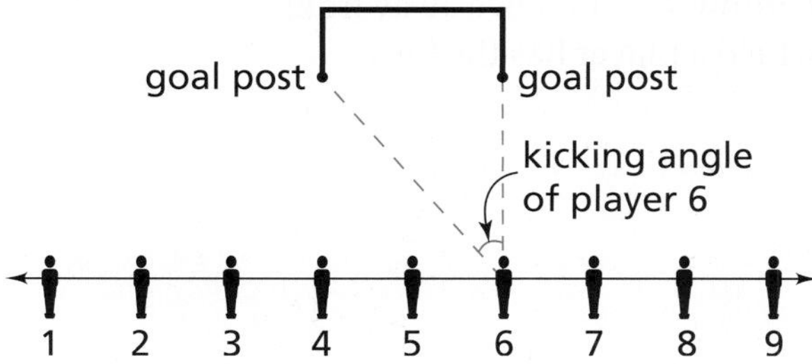

2. Which player has the maximum kicking angle?
3. How does the angle vary from player to player across the field?
4. Where would a player need to stand to have a kicking angle that is approximately 5° less than the maximum?
5. Are there any players on the line with a kicking angle of 1°? Approximately where are they?

The player's position is the vertex of the kicking angle and each goal post is on a side of the angle.

Exercises Practicing Habits of Mind

Check Your Understanding

1. Suppose you are on the soccer field from the In-Class Experiment. Sketch where the players should stand on the field to have a kicking angle of 40°.

Your sketch will show a contour line for a kicking angle of 40°.

2. Here is a contour map for the kicking angles in the penalty box of a soccer field.

   a. What shape are the contours? Explain.

   b. Copy the figure. Label the contour lines on your map with the measures of the kicking angles.

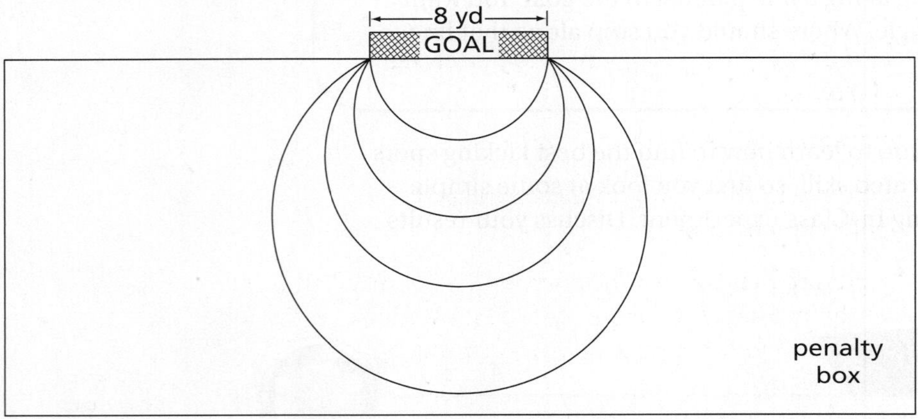

3. **Write About It** Describe the shape of the contour as you move away from the soccer goal. Explain from where on the field a player has the best chance to score.

On Your Own

4. You are driving through the country on a straight road. A building to your left has a beautiful façade that you wish to photograph. As shown in the diagram on the next page, you are currently as close to the building as it is possible to be while on this road. Because the building is not set parallel to the road, you think you will get a better angle farther along the road. What is the best viewing position along the road?

Façade is a French word that means the face or front of a building.

5. Write About It Find at least two ways in which weather forecasters use contour plots. You may have to contact a local weather service for help.

6. Write About It Are the constraints in this lesson's Example realistic? Explain.

In Exercises 7 and 8, a player with the ball is crossing the field in a straight line, but not parallel to the goal line.

7. Draw such a line on the contour map you made in Exercise 2.

8. Determine the spot on the line from which the player has the greatest kicking angle. Use the map in your explanation.

9. You are in a gallery looking at a picture that is 4 feet tall and 6 feet wide. Your eye level is 5 feet. The bottom of the picture is 5.5 feet above the ground. How far from the wall should you stand for the maximum viewing angle? Is this likely to be the best place to stand?

You have to think about the angle from the top of the picture, to you, to the bottom of the picture. You also have to think about the angle from the left side of the picture, to you, to the right side of the picture.

10. Standardized Test Prep A topographic map of a mountain contains contour lines labeled in 50-foot increments. What do the contour lines represent?

A. temperature **B.** elevation **C.** humidity **D.** air pressure

Maintain Your Skills

11. Which of the two marked angles is greater? Explain.

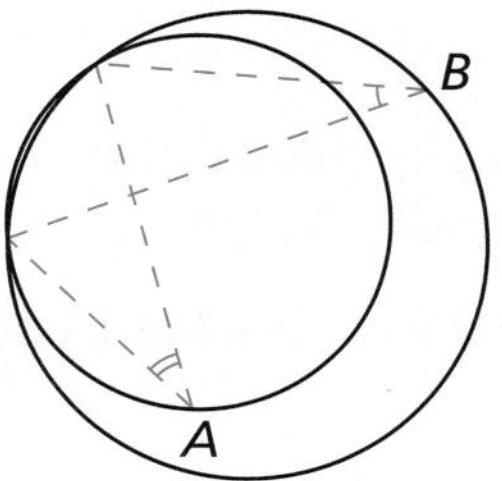

12. In the Example, you are running perpendicular to the goal. Now, suppose you are dribbling a soccer ball along a line that is *not* perpendicular to the goal. Describe how to locate the spot that maximizes your kicking angle.

8.09 Contour Lines and Functions

A contour plot assigns a number to each point on the plane. The number could represent any of the following.

- temperature
- barometric pressure
- height above sea level
- depth of water
- distance from a point to a pool's edge
- measure of a kicking angle

A contour line is a set of points (a curve of some type) with assigned values that are all the same. A contour plot is a collection of contour lines.

To understand a contour plot, you must be given information about the values of points that are between the lines.

Developing Habits of Mind

Visualize. The process of assigning a number to each point on a plane is an example of a function. In this new context, think of P moving around the plane carrying a little calculator on its back.

The calculator is programmed to do only one calculation, such as measure the kicking angle. The calculation is dependent on P's current location. As P travels along a contour line, the calculator produces the same value. A contour line is just the set of all points for which the calculator produces the same value.

Remember...

You met functions in first-year algebra. Many functions take in a number and output another number. The functions in this chapter take in a point and output a number.

In-Class Experiment

Use geometry software. Define three points A, B, and P. Consider the function f that calculates the sum $PA + PB$.

1. Measure $PA + PB$.
2. Drag P around. As the lengths change, the sum will change. In other words, the value of your function will change.
3. Tape a transparency over the screen. Mark enough points to draw in a few contour lines for f.

Now you are ready for a more formal presentation.

Facts and Notation

You can name functions. Let g be the function that determines $PA + PB$. The value of g for any P is written $g(P)$.

The notation $g(P)$ is pronounced "g of P" and means the "value of g at P." If you think of g as a calculating machine, $g(P)$ is the number produced by the machine when it is "fed" P. When P is the input, $g(P)$ is the output.

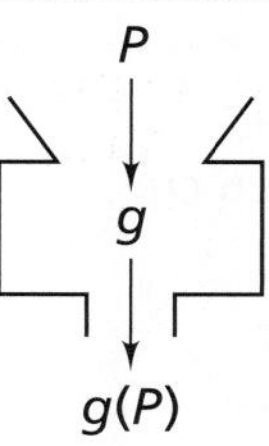

Minds in Action **episode 39**

Sasha decides to experiment with her drawing.

Sasha Look, Tony. I placed the cursor on P and dragged it around. I watched the value of $f(P)$ and tried to keep it equal to 5.8.

$f(P) = PA + PB$
$PA + PB = 5.80$ cm

A
B
P

Since Sasha's contour line was formed by dragging, there is some error. Not every point on the contour line has a value of f exactly equal to 5.8.

Tony Oh, I see.

Sasha Since $f(P)$ is 5.8 for any point on this contour line, I'll label the whole contour line 5.8.

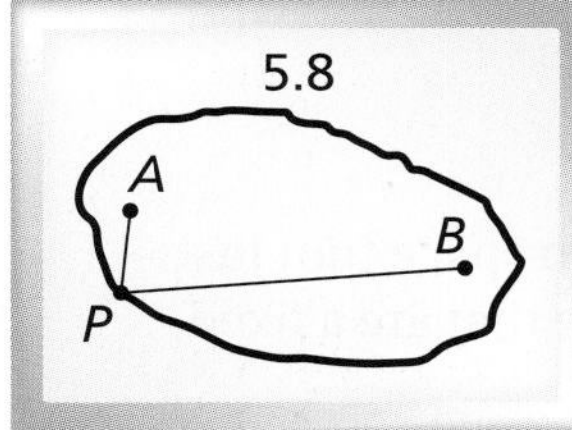

Tony Nice! Let me see what happens if A and B coincide. I'll use just one point, C. I'll define a new function h that determines the distance from C to any point P in the plane.

For Discussion

4. A contour line for Tony's function is below. Draw a few more contour lines for Tony's function. What shape is each contour line? Give a proof.

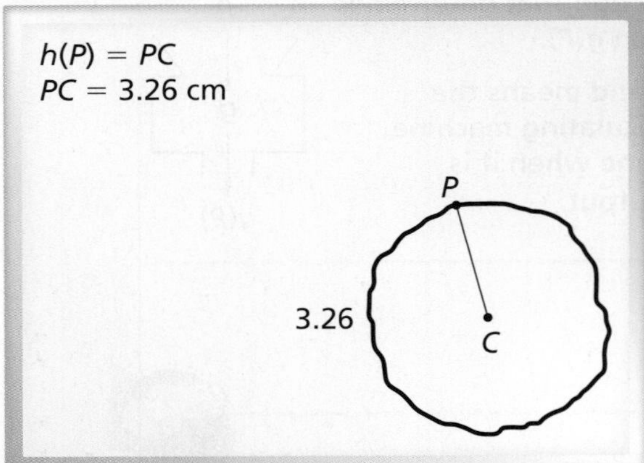

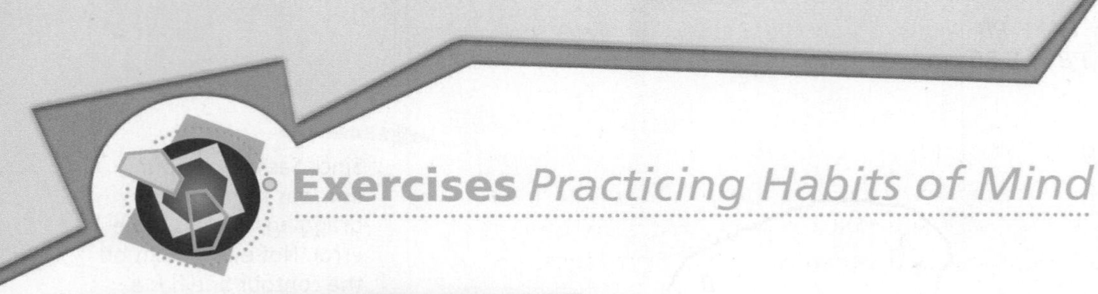

Check Your Understanding

Suppose ℓ is some fixed line in a plane. Suppose f is the function that determines the distance from ℓ to a point in the plane.

1. Make a contour plot for f.
2. What shape is each contour? Give a proof.
3. Label each contour line with the appropriate number.
4. What would the contours for f look like for all points in space (not just in the plane)? That is, what is the set of points in space that are a fixed distance from a given line ℓ?

On Your Own

5. Suppose E and F are fixed in the plane. Function f is defined so that $f(Z) = ZE + 2ZF$ for any point Z in the plane.

a. Make a contour plot for f. Label it appropriately.

b. Draw a straight line on your contour plot. Explain how to locate the point on the line that minimizes the value of f.

6. **Take It Further** Suppose A, B, and C are fixed in the plane. Function j is defined to measure the sum of the distances from P to A, B, and C.

$$j(P) = PA + PB + PC$$

Make a labeled contour plot for j.

Habits of Mind

Experiment. Try to invent a gadget using string that will help you draw the contour lines for j.

7. **Write About It** A function is defined on the points in a plane. Explain how to draw a contour plot for this function. Illustrate with examples.

Use a horizontal line $\overleftrightarrow{AB}$ for Exercises 8 and 9. Suppose A and B are fixed. P moves around the plane and can be on either side of $\overleftrightarrow{AB}$. Define h as follows.

$$h(P) = m\angle APB$$

8. **a.** Make a labeled contour plot for h.

b. Are any points in the plane on every contour line in your plot? Are there any points that could not be on any contour line in any contour plot for h? (That is, are there points on the plane for which h produces no number?) Explain.

Habits of Mind

Represent with color. You could use color coding to explain certain aspects of your map.

9. **a.** Place P above $\overleftrightarrow{AB}$ so that $m\angle APB = 90°$. Describe the contour line P traces.

b. Describe $m\angle APB$ if P is inside this contour line and still above $\overleftrightarrow{AB}$.

c. Describe $m\angle APB$ if P is outside this contour line.

10. **Take It Further** Suppose ℓ is a fixed line. E is a fixed point not on ℓ. Function f assigns a numerical value to each P as follows.

- f finds the distance from P to E.
- f finds the distance from P to ℓ.
- f adds the results and assigns that number to P.

Make a contour plot for f. Label your contour lines with the appropriate values determined by f.

11. **Take It Further** Define O as a fixed point in space. Suppose function g is defined in three-dimensional space. It determines the distance between any point in space and O.

a. Describe the shape formed by all P such that $g(P) = 1$.

b. Describe the three-dimensional picture (similar to a contour plot) formed by this function.

12. **Standardized Test Prep** Suppose P is a fixed point in the plane. Suppose f is the function that determines the distance between P and another point in the plane. What does the contour plot for f look like?

A. parallel lines

B. intersecting lines

C. concentric circles

D. intersecting circles

Maintain Your Skills

13. Place A, B, and X on a plane. The function f assigns $XA + XB$ to any X. Make a contour plot for f.

To find the value that f assigns to X, measure the distance from X to A and the distance from X to B. Then add.

a. Label each contour line with the appropriate number.

b. Your contour plot cannot show every contour line. Count your smallest contour line as the first. Picture a new contour line between your second and third contour lines. What range of numbers could belong to the new contour line?

c. Draw a line across your contour plot. Explain how to locate the point on that line for which f produces the least value.

d. On your contour plot, draw a circle that contains A and B in its interior. Explain how to locate the point or points on the circle for which f produces the least value.

e. Can any number be a value for some contour line? Explain your answer. If your answer is no, give an example of a number that could never be a value for f.

Go Online
Pearsonsuccessnet.com

Contour plowing prevents rain runoff from flowing directly downhill. Slowing runoff helps minimize soil erosion.

8.10 Revisiting the Burning Tent

Sometimes you can find patterns in incorrect answers. The patterns, in turn, may help you find the correct answer.

Minds in Action — episode 40

Tony explains how he used incorrect answers to reach the correct answer.

Tony Hey Derman, do you remember the burning tent problem from Lesson 8.2?

Derman Yes, we tried to find the best spot to fill the bucket in the river to minimize the total distance traveled.

Tony Well, I was thinking we could solve it by looking at some wrong answers, like this point *P*.

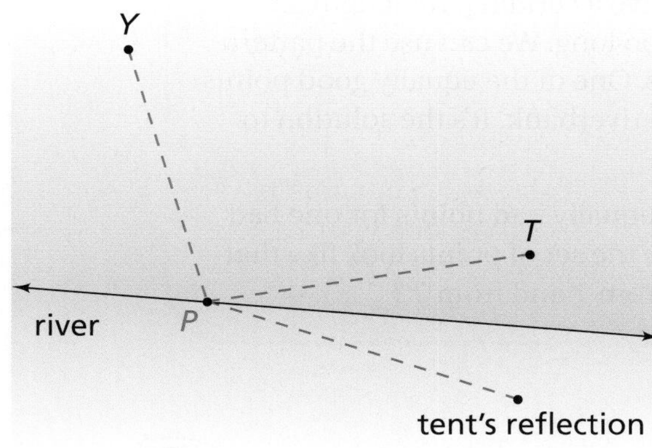

Why is point *P* not the best spot?

Derman Why would we do that?

Tony There are other points for which the length of the path is the same as the path above. We can call them equally bad points. To find them, I cut a piece of string equal to the total length above. I kept one end of the string at *T* and the other end at *Y*. The paths through *B* and *C* are equally bad paths.

Tony's Picture

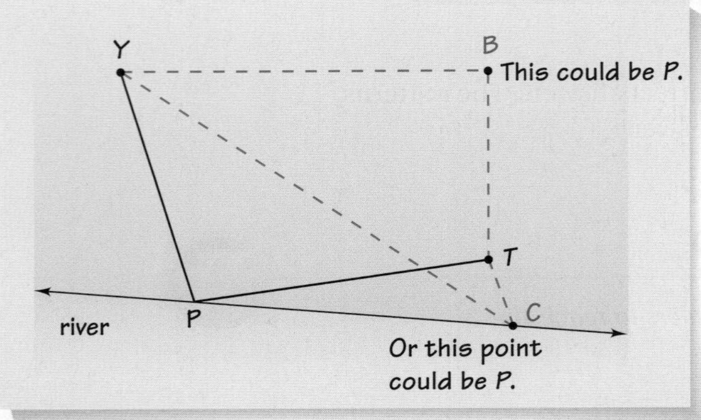

The three paths shown from you to the tent have the same length.

I think there's a pattern for the equally bad points. Many of the equally bad points are not on the riverbank, but the lengths from *Y* to *P* and then to *T* are equal. If we can find that pattern, I think we'll have a way to find the equally good points.

Derman Oh, I get it! All of the points that have a certain path length are equally bad if that path length is too long. We can use the pattern to find a set of equally good points. One of the equally good points is the point we want to find on the riverbank. It's the solution to the burning-tent problem.

Tony We have to start by finding all the equally bad points for one bad point on the river bank. What does the set of points look like that are some constant total distance from *Y* and from *T*?

In-Class Experiment

Help answer Tony's question. Pick a total path length, experiment, and determine the contour line. This contour line is the locus for all the points that share a given path length. You can use geometry software or a compass and ruler.

- Draw two points *A* and *B*.
- Construct a segment that has a path length greater than *AB*.
- Place *P* on the segment. This splits the segment into two parts d_1 and d_2. If you are using software, construct these two parts as separate segments.
- Construct a circle centered at *A* with radius d_1. Construct a circle centered at *B* with radius d_2.

You might want to hide the circles to neaten your sketch.

If you use software, do the following.

- Construct the intersections of these circles.
- Trace these points.
- You will get a contour line as you move P along the segment.

If you use a compass and ruler, do the following:

- Mark the intersections of these circles.
- Move P so that you have new lengths d_1 and d_2.
- Construct circles with these new radii. Mark their intersections.
- Repeat the last two steps for at least five points P. You should recognize the contour line that emerges.

1. Repeat the process with different path lengths. You should recognize a pattern to the contour lines.

The contour lines you have been drawing are called *ellipses.*

Definition

Begin with A and B and a positive number $k > AB$. The set of all P for which $PA + PB = k$ is called an ellipse. A and B are called the *foci* of the ellipse. A is one focus and B is the other focus.

Or you can define an ellipse as a contour line.

Definition

An ellipse with foci A and B is a contour line for the function f, which is defined by the following calculation.

$$f(P) = PA + PB, \text{ where } P \text{ is not on } \overline{AB}.$$

For Discussion

2. Are these two definitions of an ellipse equivalent? Explain.

Remember...

Two definitions A and B are equivalent if A implies B and B implies A.

Minds in Action episode 41

Tony is still trying to explain his idea to Derman.

Tony Look at the following figures. If there are points on the riverbank inside the ellipse, there is a shorter path. In the figure where $k = 3.7$, the runner never reaches the river, so that doesn't work, either. So we want to find the ellipse with only one point on the river. That will be the solution point.

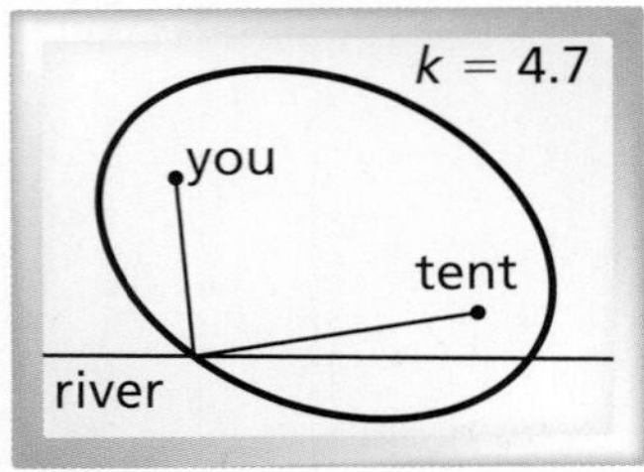

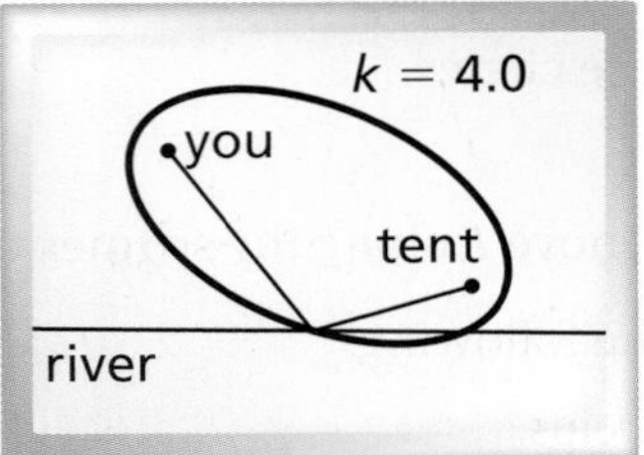

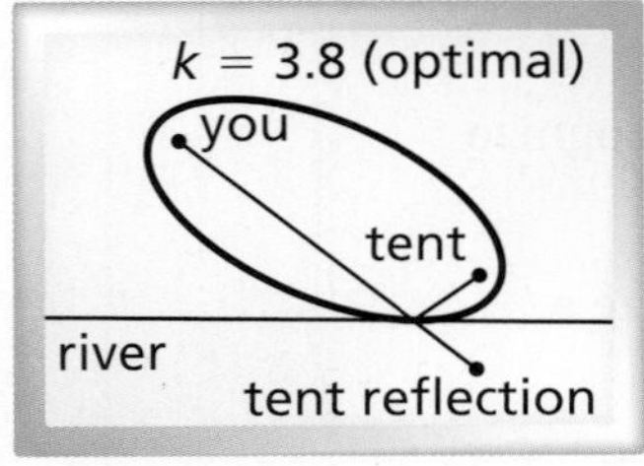

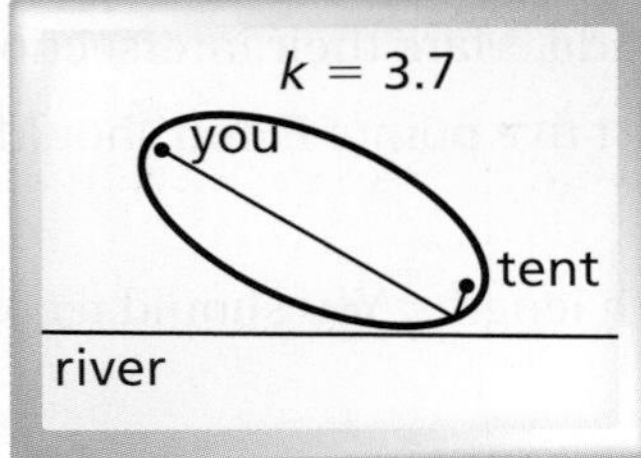

Derman Oh, now I see! The best path is the one that touches the river in exactly one point. We have to find an ellipse that is tangent to the river in a point. That happens when $k = 3.8$.

For Discussion

3. Do you see why the figure in which $k = 3.8$ is optimal? Describe its geometric characteristics.

Exercises *Practicing Habits of Mind*

Check Your Understanding

To construct elliptical shapes, builders can drive nails in at the two foci of the ellipse. Then they tie each end of a piece of string around the nails. With a pencil, they trace around the nails, keeping the string taut.

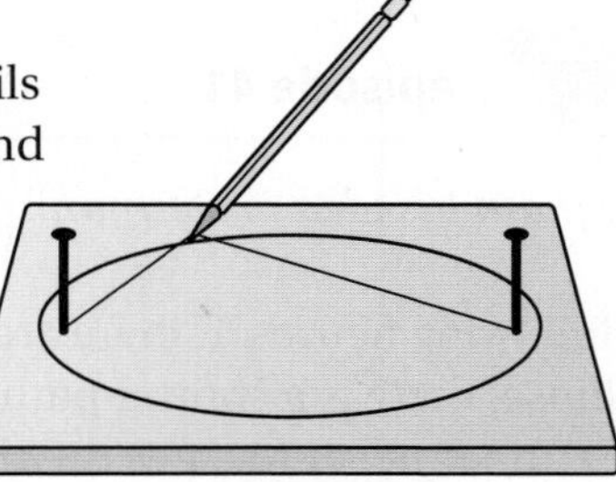

1. Explain how this setup guarantees that all of the points the pencil passes through are the same total distance from the two nails.

2. **Write About It** Draw a contour plot for the burning-tent problem. Explain how and why the contour lines are used to solve the problem.

3. Draw a circle and a line tangent to the circle. Which point on the tangent line is closest to the center of the circle? Draw a radius from the point of contact to the center of the circle. How are this radius and the tangent line related

On Your Own

4. Tony's little sister, Yeon, is celebrating her third birthday. This is a picture of her birthday cake. Each layer is 2 inches tall and the candles rise 3 inches above the top layer. Pretend you are looking at it from the top. Draw a contour plot of the cake.

5. Ellipses have some very interesting properties. One is the following tangent property.

   Suppose an ellipse has foci A and B and $\overline{ST}$ is tangent to the ellipse at P. Then $m\angle SPA = m\angle TPB$.

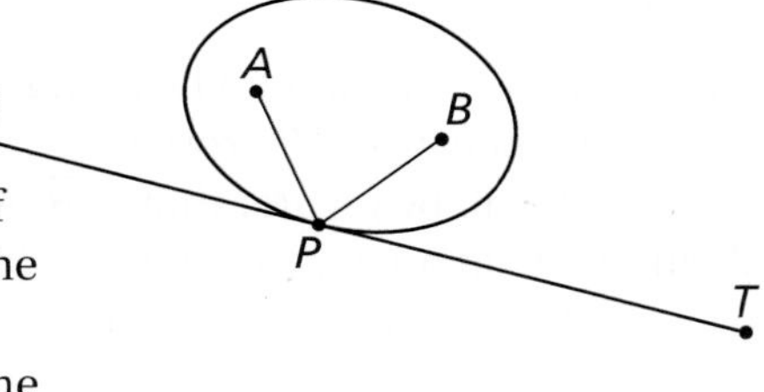

   Suppose you place a ball at each focus of an elliptical billiard table. Shoot one of the balls in any direction. If you use enough force, it will hit the other ball after just one bounce off the elliptical cushion. Within this context, prove that the above tangent property is true for any ellipse.

6. **Standardized Test Prep** In isosceles right triangle ABC, the coordinates of A, B, and C are (1, 0), (0, 1), and (0, 0), respectively. Which point on the bisector of the right angle minimizes the sum of the distances to the vertices of the triangle?

   A. (0.292893, 0.292893) **B.** (0.5, 0.5)

   C. (0.211325, 0.211325) **D.** (0, 0)

In mathematics, relief maps are called surface plots. Surface plots are supposed to be three-dimensional. In this lesson, you saw two-dimensional drawings of surface plots.

7. a. Write About It Investigate topographic maps and relief maps. Describe how they are different.

b. Suppose O is a fixed point and f is defined so that $f(X) = OX$. What would a relief map for f look like?

c. Let A and B be fixed. Let g be defined so that $g(X) = AX + BX$. Describe g's relief map.

8. Take It Further Review the burning-tent problem. This time, consider the fact that you run more slowly with a full bucket than with an empty bucket. Where should you fill the bucket to minimize the time it takes to reach the tent? Justify your answer.

9. Take It Further Here is a problem and a proposed solution. Read both carefully. Then critique the problem and support or refute the solution. There are some ambiguities in the problem and some weaknesses in the solution.

Problem Cities A and B are separated by a wildlife refuge. The taxpayers decide to pool their resources and build a recreation center. The new center cannot be located in the refuge. Traffic generated by the center cannot cross the refuge. New roads must be built. Where should the center be placed to minimize cost?

Solution To do the least road building, the road should be along $\overline{AB}$. However, that is not an option, because $\overline{AB}$ crosses the refuge. So, the total road length will be greater than $\overline{AB}$. All the locations that involve a certain road length lie on an ellipse. The best locations lie on the smallest ellipse that has foci at A and B and does not cross the refuge.

Maintain Your Skills

Equilateral $\triangle ABC$ is plotted on the coordinate plane. Vertices A and C have the coordinates indicated. In Exercises 10–12, what is the sum of the distances from P to each of the triangle's sides?

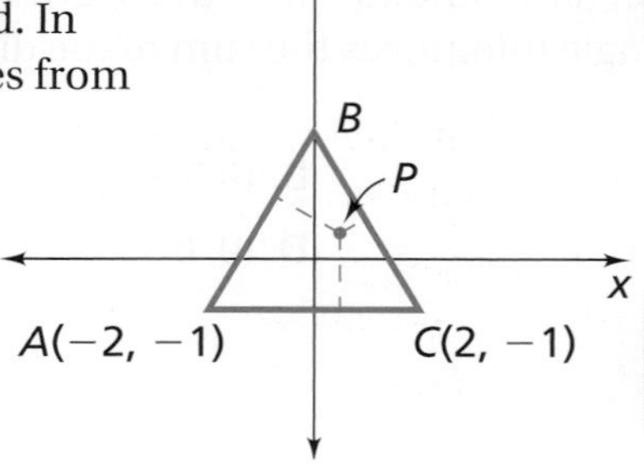

10. $P\left(\frac{1}{2}, \frac{1}{2}\right)$ **11.** $P(1, 0)$ **12.** $P\left(1, -\frac{1}{2}\right)$

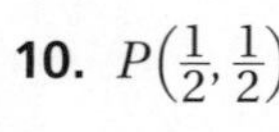

13. Compare your answers for Exercises 10–12. Which sum is the least? Can you find another point P for which the sum of the distances to the sides is even less? Explain.

In this investigation, you learned how to read topographic maps and how to interpret and draw contour plots. These questions will help you summarize what you have learned.

1. The contour plot at the right represents a mountain. You have to climb from the starting point to the peak on path A, B, or C. Which one is the shortest? Which one is the least steep?

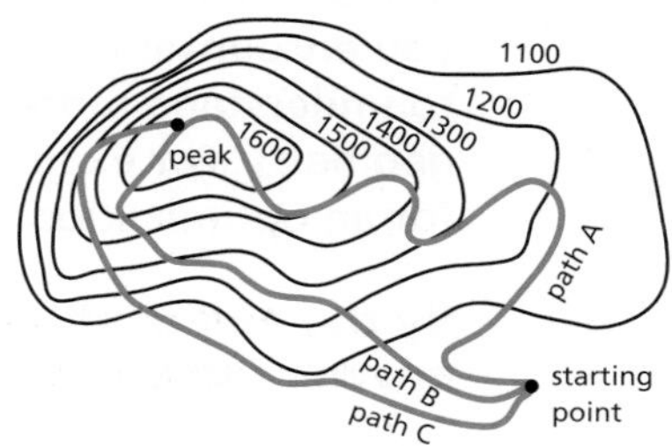

2. **a.** Graph the equation $2x - y = 0$. Label the graph ℓ.

   b. Find a function that gives the distance from any point to ℓ.

   c. Draw and label a contour plot for this function.

3. *P* falls in the interior of the rectangle. Write a function that calculates the sum of the distances from any point *P* to the sides of the rectangle.

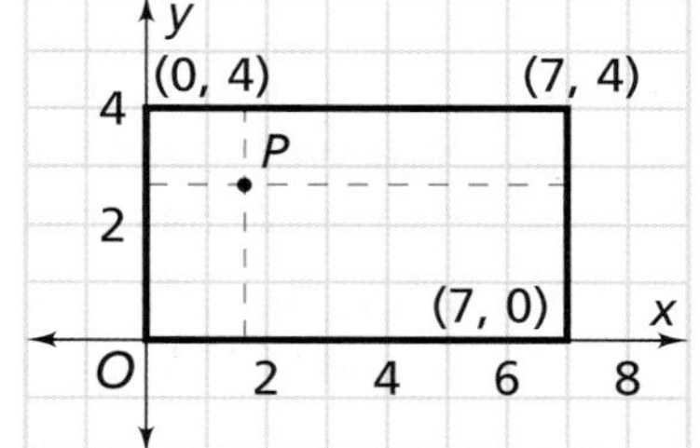

4. Write a function that determines the sum of the distances from point *P* to the vertices of the rectangle.

5. Consider two fixed points *A* and *B* on the plane. What shape are the contour lines that represent various values of $f(P) = PA + PB$?

6. Describe how a contour plot can help you solve the burning-tent problem.

7. Can two contour lines of a contour plot intersect? Explain.

8. At the right is a contour plot showing depth in feet of a lake. You drop your keys into the deepest part of the lake. How far down will you have to swim to get them?

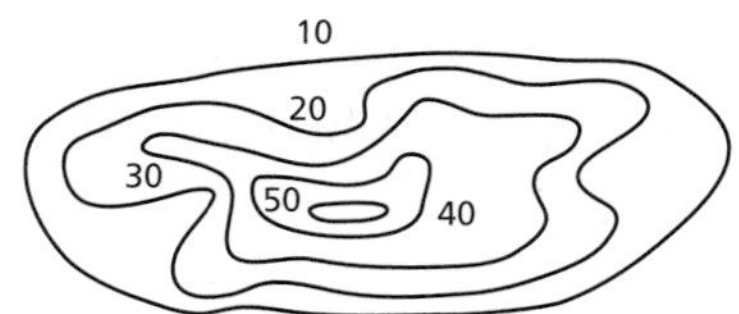

What might a contour map look like for Devils Tower in Wyoming?

Vocabulary

In this investigation, you learned these terms. Make sure you understand what each one means and how to use it.

- **contour line**
- **contour plot**
- **ellipse**
- **focus**
- **topographic map**

Advanced Optimization

In *Advanced Optimization*, you will work through proofs that at first seem fairly simple. By looking at the logical difficulties you encounter in proving these conjectures, you will come to understand more about the nature of optimization in geometry. For example, sometimes a maximum or minimum for an optimization problem does not exist.

By the end of this investigation, you will be able to answer questions like these.

1. For what point P is the sum of the distances from P to the sides of $\triangle ABC$ the least? Explain.
2. Give an example of an optimization problem that has no solution. Explain your reasoning.
3. What curve encloses the most area for a given perimeter? Explain.

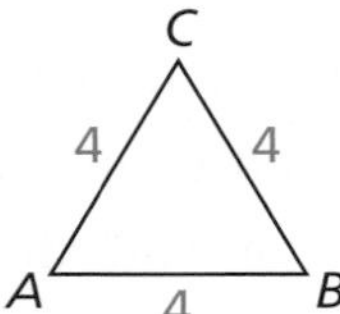

You will learn how to

- write functions and use them to solve optimization problems
- discuss the important variables of a problem, choose a subset of them, and find an optimal solution
- understand and explain a proof of the isoperimetric problem

You will develop these habits and skills:

- Reason by continuity.
- Use special cases and models to look for solutions of more general problems.
- Understand that a proof comes through careful thinking, experience, and the use of mathematical habits of mind.

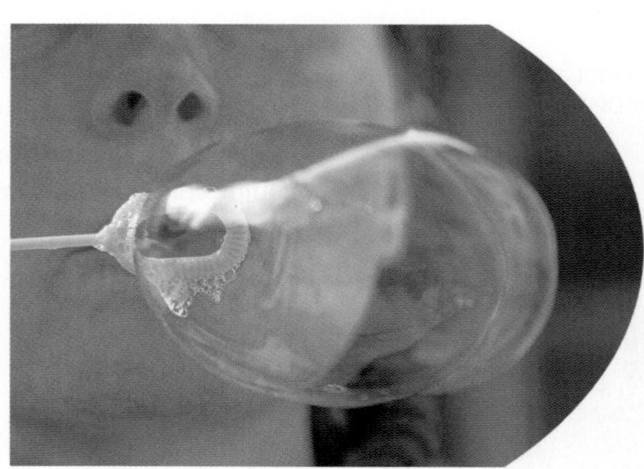

When the bubble floats free, surface tension minimizes the surface area needed to contain the air within. What shape is formed?

8.11 Getting Started

The distance from a point to a line is defined as the length of the perpendicular segment from the point to the line. The sum of the distances from *P*, a point inside a polygon, to the sides of the polygon depends on the location of *P*.

For You to Explore

Problems 1–4 refer to $\triangle ABC$, where $AB = 10$, $CB = 8$, $CA = 6$, $AH = 4$, $HB = 6$, and $PA = 5$.

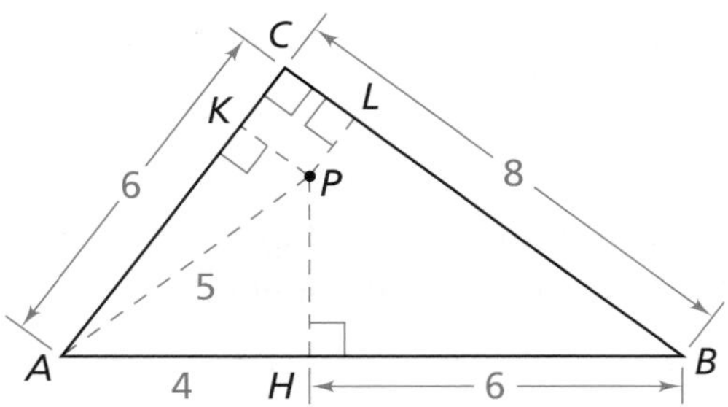

1. Find the sum of the distances from *P* to each side of the triangle. If you want an exact answer, use a system of two equations in *LP* and *KP*. For an approximate answer, draw a scaled copy of the triangle and the segments inside the triangle. Carefully measure the distances from *P* to the sides.

2. What is the sum of the distances from *P* to the vertices of $\triangle ABC$?

3. Find the sum of the distances from *P* to the vertices for each case.

a. *P* coincides with the vertex *C*.

b. *P* coincides with the vertex *A*.

c. *P* coincides with the vertex *B*.

4. Find a point for which the sum of the distances from the point to the vertices is less than 13.

Exercises *Practicing Habits of Mind*

On Your Own

5. M is the midpoint of $\overline{DE}$. Find the sum of the distances from M to the sides of $\triangle DEF$.

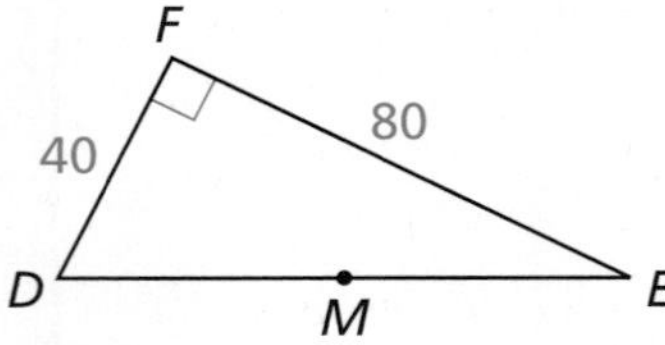

P is on a side of $\triangle DEF$. Find P where the sum of the distances from P to the sides of the triangle is less than the sum of the distances from M to the sides of the triangle.

For Exercises 6 and 7, you are given an equilateral triangle with side length 2 cm. P is inside the triangle.

6. Calculate (or measure) the sum of the distances from P to the sides of the triangle. If possible, find a point P that minimizes this sum.

7. Calculate (or measure) the sum of the distances from P to the vertices of the triangle. If possible, find a point P that minimizes this sum.

Maintain Your Skills

Find the sum of the distances from P to the sides of square $ABCD$.

8.

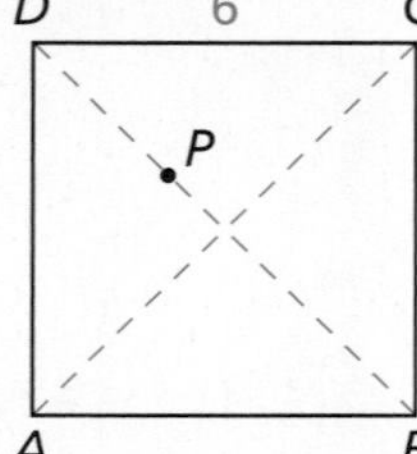

9.

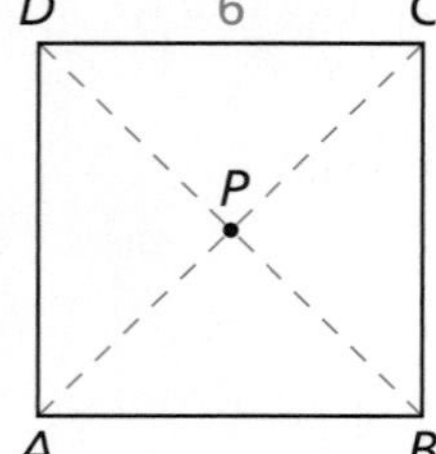

10.

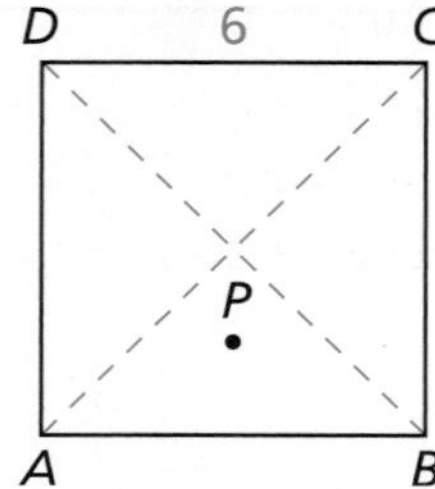

11. Does the placement of P within the square affect the sum? What is the sum if P is placed on a side of the square? Explain.

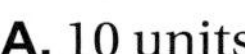

8.12 Reasoning by Continuity

Rich answered the following problem on a standardized multiple-choice test.

Given an equilateral triangle with side length 10 units, find $DR + DQ + DP$. This is the sum of the lengths of the distances from a point inside the triangle D to the sides of the triangle.

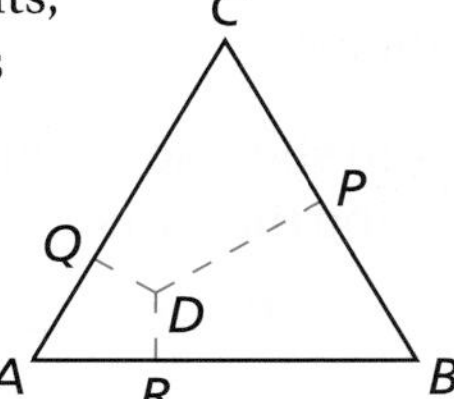

A. 10 units **B.** $5\sqrt{3}$ units

C. 30 units **D.** 8.6 units

For Discussion

1. Think about the problem above and find a strategy to solve it. Discuss your ideas with the rest of the class. Remember that the distance from a point to a line means the length of the shortest path. In the diagram, $\overline{DR} \perp \overline{AB}$, $\overline{DQ} \perp \overline{AC}$, and $\overline{DP} \perp \overline{BC}$.

Habits of Mind

Find another way. Rich had no ruler and no computer. See what you can do without those tools.

Rich developed a function that calculates the sum of the distances from an interior point to the sides of an equilateral triangle. In the spirit of professional mathematicians, the students in Rich's class referred to it as "Rich's Function."

Perhaps the writers of the test question above intended to find out if the students knew a particular theorem. Rich did not know it, but he demonstrated the ability to solve a problem through deduction, experimentation, and reasoning by continuity. Here is Rich's train of thought.

First, Rich decided that one of the four numbers listed had to be the right answer.

Then he imagined D at different spots inside the triangle and compared the sums of the distances. That is when Rich realized that the problem did not say anything specific about where D is located. Rich realized that no matter where D is placed inside the triangle, the sum of the distances from D to the sides must be the same.

Why is that a logical conclusion?

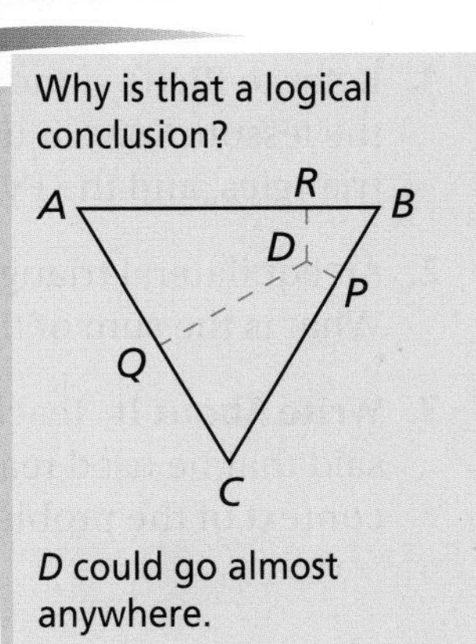

D could go almost anywhere.

After drawing this conclusion, Rich got another idea. He placed D very close to a vertex to see how that affects the three distances.

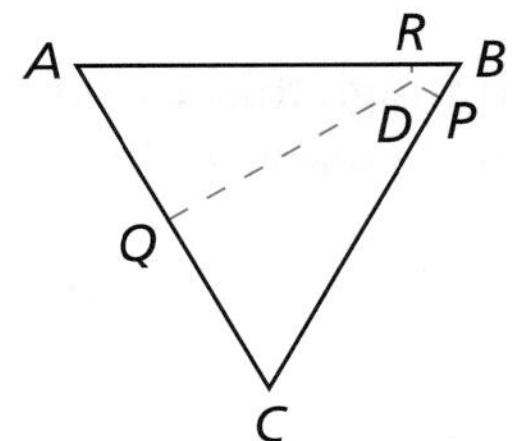

In-Class Experiment

Refer to the previous diagram.

2. With D close to vertex B, which two lengths are the least?
3. Can you make those two lengths even less? Explain.
4. What is the least you can make them?
5. You previously used notation $\rightarrow$ to show something getting very close to a value. Fill in these blanks to describe the situation as $D \rightarrow B$.

   a. $DP \rightarrow$ _?_ b. $DR \rightarrow$ _?_
6. As DP and DR decrease, what happens to DQ? DQ approaches the length of what part of the triangle?

Rich then made the following conjecture.

The sum of the distances from *any* point inside an equilateral triangle to the sides of the triangle is equal to the length of an altitude of the triangle. As a function, $f(P) = \frac{\sqrt{3}}{2}s$ where P is a point inside the triangle and s is the side length.

Exercises *Practicing Habits of Mind*

Check Your Understanding

1. Refer to Rich's standardized test question that is presented at the start of the lesson. Solve it using Rich's reasoning, your knowledge of equilateral triangles, and the Pythagorean Theorem.
2. An equilateral triangle has side length 8 cm, and G is inside the triangle. What is the sum of the distances from G to the sides of the triangle?
3. **Write About It** Teachers who followed Rich's reasoning through this lesson said that he used reasoning by continuity. Explain what this means in the context of the problem.

Remember...

The altitude of an equilateral triangle bisects the base.

On Your Own

4. Standardized Test Prep *EFGH* is a rectangle inscribed in a circle with radius *r*. Which of the following is NOT true?

   A. The area of *EFGH* is greatest when the length and width of *EFGH* are equal.

   B. The length of each diagonal of *EFGH* is $2r$.

   C. The perimeter of *EFGH* is greatest when the length of *EFGH* is twice its width.

   D. Each diagonal of *EFGH* is a diameter of the circle in which *EFGH* is inscribed.

5. An equilateral triangle with side length 2 is plotted on the coordinate plane. One vertex is $(-2, 1)$ and another is $(0, 1)$. What are possible coordinates of the third vertex? Choose the third vertex so that $P\left(-\frac{1}{2}, \frac{3}{2}\right)$ is inside the triangle. Calculate the sum of the distances from *P* to the sides of the triangle.

6. List as many facts as you can about equilateral triangles. Separate your list into facts that are true for all triangles, for some triangles, and just for equilateral triangles. Find a way to clearly present the information to other students.

7. The vertices of an isosceles triangle are $(-2, -1)$, $(1, -1)$, and $(-0.5, 3)$. Find the sum of the distances from $P(-1, 1)$ to each side of the triangle.

8. The term *function* has appeared many times in this course and in algebra 1. Since this term has not been officially defined in this course, write what you understand it to mean. If you can, give some examples. Write any questions or describe any confusion that you have about the term.

Maintain Your Skills

9. The circles have center *O*, chords $\overline{AP}$ and $\overline{PB}$, and radius $AO = 2$ cm. In the circle on the left, *P* is moved along the circle to draw the figure below. As you drag *P* clockwise, *AP* changes but the size of the circle does not.

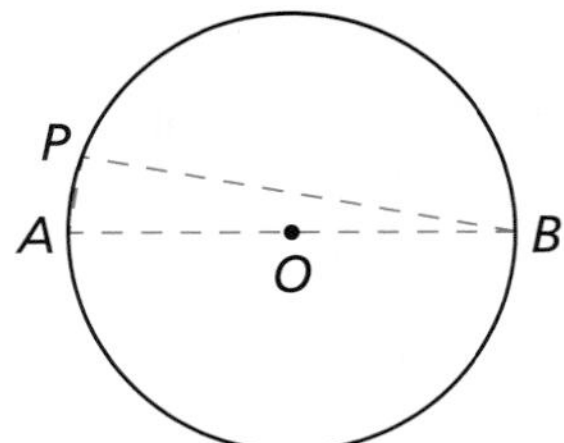

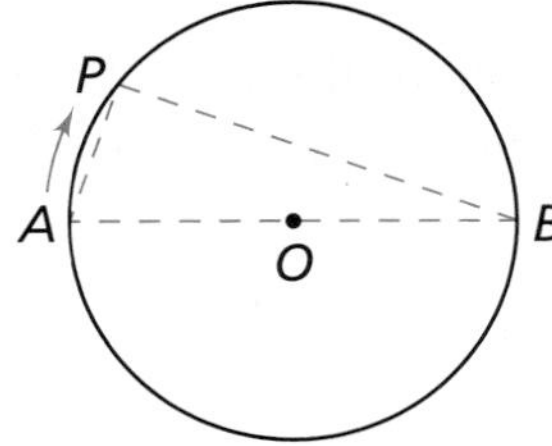

For (a)–(i) on the following page, determine whether the measure is *constant* or *changing* as *P* moves clockwise from *A* to *B*.

- For each measure that is constant, state what the constant value is or how it can be found.
- For each measure that is changing, explain how it is changing with a graph or a written explanation.

Measures:

a. $m\angle APB$

b. the distance from P to O

c. the perimeter of $\triangle APB$

d. the area of $\triangle APB$

e. the ratio of the circumference of the circle to the diameter of the circle

f. the sum of the distances $AP + PB$

g. the ratio of AP to BA

h. the ratio of AP to PB

i. MN, where M is the midpoint of $\overline{AP}$ and N is the midpoint of $\overline{PB}$

10. In $\triangle ABC$, $\angle A = 90°$, $AB = 12$, and $AC = 5$. Let $P(x, y)$ be inside $\triangle ABC$.

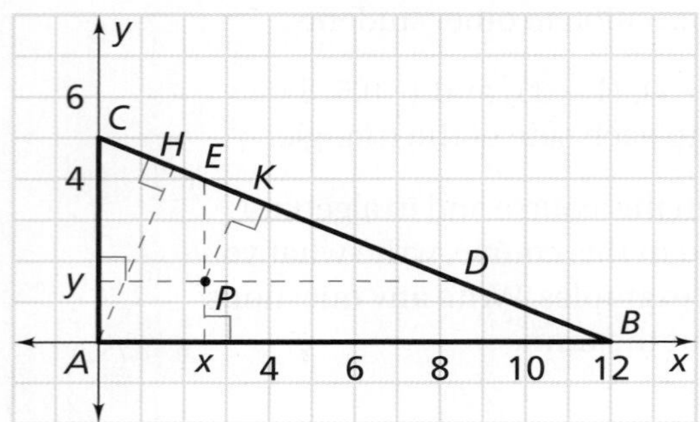

a. Find the height of $\triangle ABC$ relative to base $\overline{BC}$.

b. What are the side lengths of $\triangle PDE$ in terms of x and y? Compare corresponding side lengths to prove that $\triangle PDE$ is similar to $\triangle ABC$.

c. Find the length of $\overline{PK}$ as a function of x and y by solving the following proportion.

$$PD : AB = PK : AH$$

Why is the proportion true?

d. Write a function with inputs x and y that finds the sum of the distances from P to the sides of $\triangle ABC$. Call the function $f(x, y)$. Check your function with $P_1(5, 1)$ and $P_2(6, 2)$.

8.13 Proving Rich's Function Is Constant

Rich's conjecture about the altitudes of equilateral triangles was made during a test. He did not have time to prove it true.

One possible proof calculates the area of $\triangle ABC$ twice. First, it is calculated as one large triangle and then as the sum of the areas of three small triangles.

Before you read through the proof, make sure you understand the idea behind these two area formulas.

$$\text{area}(\triangle ABC) = \frac{1}{2}bh$$

$$\text{area}(\triangle ABC) = \text{area}(\triangle ADC) + \text{area}(\triangle CDB) + \text{area}(\triangle BDA)$$

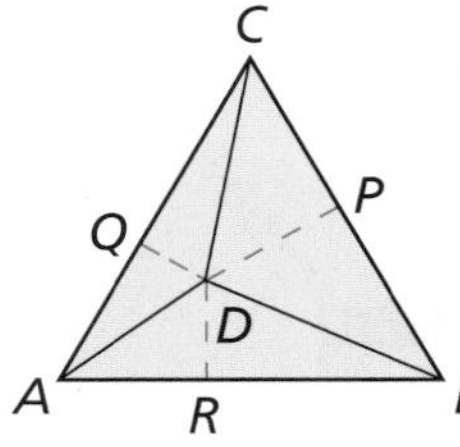

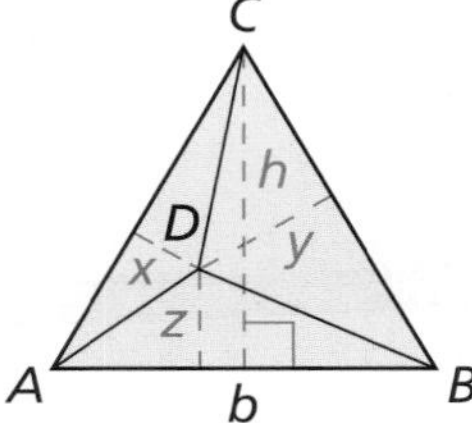

Here is the proof, using the diagrams above.

$$\begin{aligned}\frac{1}{2}bh &= \text{area}(\triangle ABC)\\ &= \text{area}(\triangle ADC) + \text{area}(\triangle CDB) + \text{area}(\triangle BDA)\\ &= \frac{1}{2}bx + \frac{1}{2}by + \frac{1}{2}bz\\ &= \frac{1}{2}b(x + y + z)\end{aligned}$$

Since $\frac{1}{2}bh = \frac{1}{2}b(x + y + z)$ and $b \neq 0$, then $h = x + y + z$.

> **Habits of Mind**
>
> **Find another way.** To calculate area in more than one way is a common geometric habit of mind.

> **Remember...**
>
> To divide both sides of the equation by *b*, you must be certain *b* is not zero. Because *b* is a triangle's side length, it cannot be zero.

For You to Do

1. Look back at the proof. Describe how you use the fact that the triangle is equilateral.

Now, rather than just a conjecture, Rich's class finally has a theorem.

Theorem 8.2 Rich's Theorem

The sum of the distances from any point inside an equilateral triangle to the sides of the triangle is equal to the length of the altitude of the triangle.

This theorem can be used to establish some inequalities.

For You to Do

2. Equilateral $\triangle EFG$ contains D and W, two points that do not coincide. $\overline{DA}$, $\overline{DB}$, and $\overline{DC}$ are perpendicular to the sides of the triangle. Show that the inequality $WA + WB + WC > DA + DB + DC$ is true.

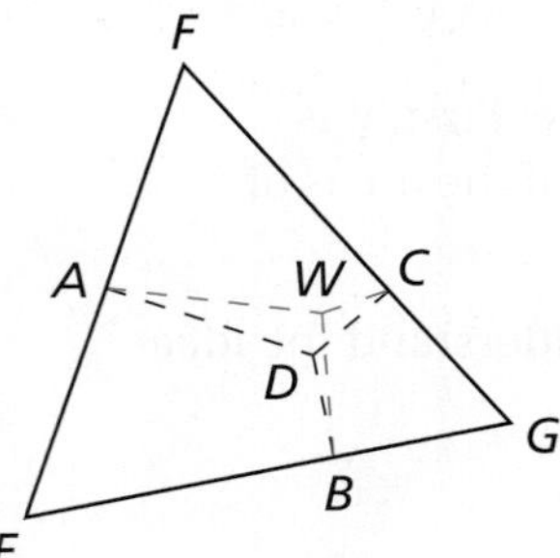

Hint: Draw perpendiculars to the sides from W, too.

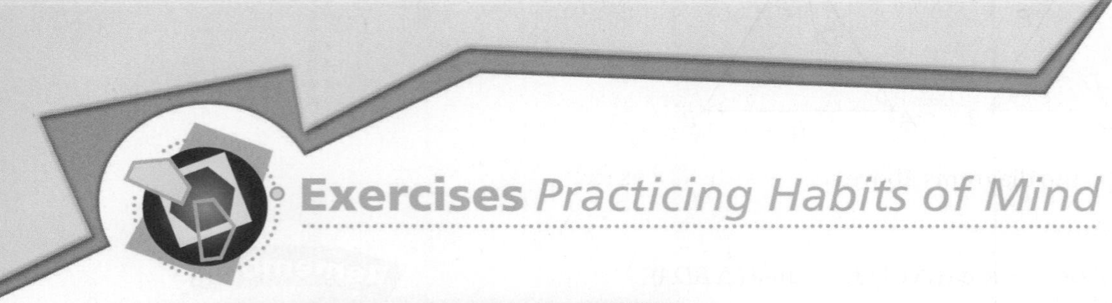

Check Your Understanding

1. Rewrite the proof of Rich's Theorem in your own words. Try not to refer back to the text.
2. There are other ways to prove Rich's Theorem. Study the following pictures and try to make sense of what is going on from one step to the next.

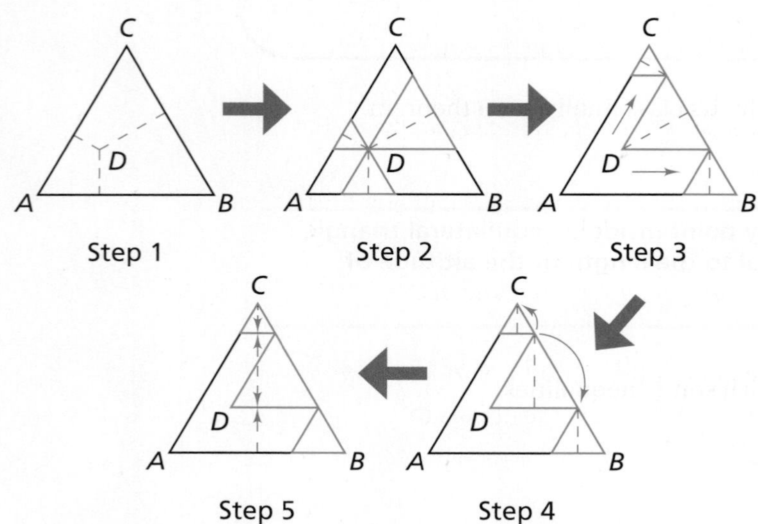

For each step, write down exactly what changed from the previous step. Supply reasons that explain why each step is valid. For Step 1, you might write the following: *ABC* is an equilateral triangle with *D* in the interior. Perpendiculars have been drawn from *D* to the sides of the triangle.

3. Look back at the two proofs of Rich's Theorem in Exercises 1 and 2. For each proof, describe where you use the fact that the triangle is equilateral.

On Your Own

4. Suppose a triangle is not equilateral. Will the sum of the distances from a point to the sides still be equal to the height of the triangle? To answer this question, look back at Exercises 1 and 2. What goes wrong in these proofs when the triangle is not equilateral?

There is a way that you can figure this out without any measuring at all.

5. If the triangle is not equilateral, Rich's function is no longer constant on the triangle's interior. Different points *P* produce different values.

Let *S* be the function that determines the sum of the distances from any *P* to the sides of a triangle.

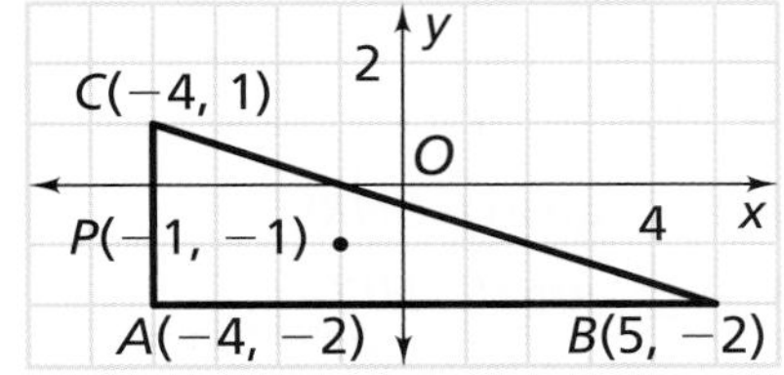

a. Calculate $S(P)$ for point $P(-1, -1)$ in the triangle.

b. If *P* can be in the interior or on the sides of the triangle, where is *S* the least?

c. If *P* can be in the interior or on the sides of the triangle, where is *S* the greatest?

d. If *P* is in the interior (but not on the sides) of the triangle, can you find a minimum value for *S*? Explain.

e. If *P* is in the interior (but not on the sides) of the triangle, can you find a maximum value for *S*? Explain.

6. In Exercise 5, you found the minimum and maximum value of *S* for the given triangle.

a. Build a sketch with geometry software that computes *S* for all triangles.

b. Describe the triangles in which the maximum value equals the minimum value.

c. What is the nature of the function for the subset of triangles with equal minimum and maximum values?

7. **Standardized Test Prep** In right triangle *GHI*, the coordinates of *G*, *H*, and *I* are (0, 0), (12, 0), and (0, 6), respectively. A rectangle is inscribed in $\triangle GHI$ so that one endpoint of one of the rectangle's diagonals is (0, 0). What are coordinates of the other endpoint of the diagonal when the area of the rectangle is maximized?

   A. (4, 4) **B.** (5, 3.5) **C.** (6, 3) **D.** (8, 2.5)

8. Triangle *FGH* is isosceles, with $GF = HF$. $\overline{GK}$ and $\overline{HJ}$ are medians.

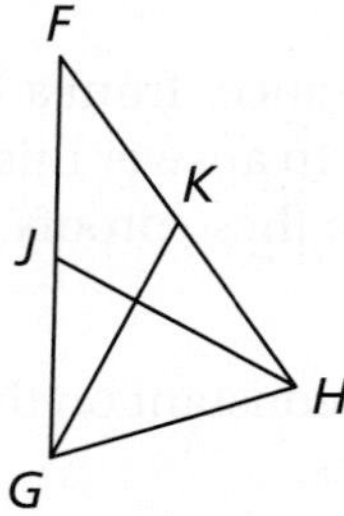

Choose the correct symbol to compare the relative measures of each pair of objects named. You may use =, >, ≥, <, ≤, or NG (not enough information given).

a. GJ ___?___ FJ **b.** GJ ___?___ GH **c.** KF ___?___ JF

d. $FJ + JH$ ___?___ $FK + KH$ **e.** area($\triangle GHJ$) ___?___ area($\triangle GHK$)

f. $m\angle KHG$ ___?___ $m\angle JGK$ **g.** area($\triangle FKG$) ___?___ area($\triangle HKG$)

h. distance from *G* to *K* ___?___ distance from *G* to $\overline{FH}$

i. JK ___?___ GH

9. Suppose $\triangle FGH$ is scalene with medians $\overline{GK}$ and $\overline{HJ}$. Which of the relationships in Exercise 8 would stay the same and which would change? Write *same* if the relationship stays the same, or choose the correct new symbol if the relationship changes.

   Try to do this exercise without drawing. Instead, visualize the scalene triangle. When you have finished, you can sketch or use geometry software to see if you are right.

10. **Take It Further** Find the length of $\overline{BN}$ if $AB = 5$ and $BC = 12$. Use the strategy of calculating area in more than one way.

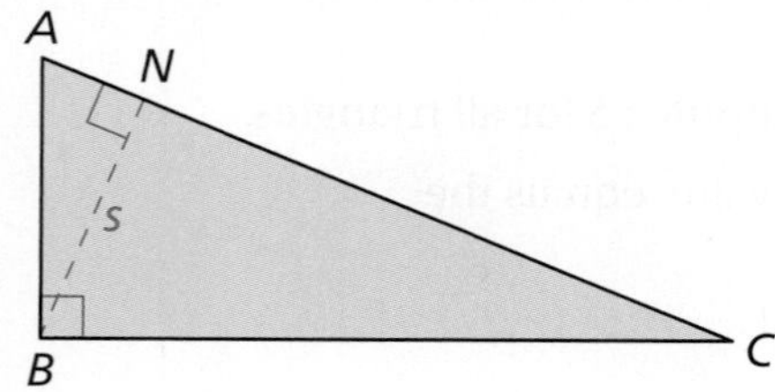

11. **Take It Further** Find the length of $\overline{ST}$ if $AB = 5$, $BC = 12$, and $SB = 4$. Use the strategy of calculating area in more than one way without using similar triangles. Recall that the area of a trapezoid is half the product of the height and the sum of the bases.

Do you know another way to find the length of $\overline{ST}$?

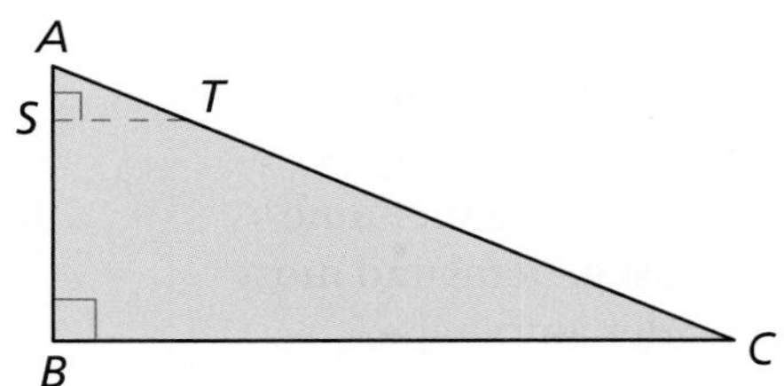

12. **Take It Further** Let P be any point on an equilateral triangle except for the vertices. Use a sketch to show that the sum of the lengths of the perpendiculars from P to the sides of the triangle is equal to the height of the triangle. Your sketch should be a proof without words.

Maintain Your Skills

13. You are given $\triangle ABC$ with $m\angle A > m\angle B$. Construct the altitudes $\overline{AD}$ and $\overline{BE}$, and show that $AD < BE$.

14. In $\triangle ABC$, D is somewhere on $\overline{AB}$. The distance from D to $\overline{AC}$ is a. The distance from D to $\overline{BC}$ is b. Assume $\triangle ABC$ is not obtuse. Answer the following questions.

C
a
b
A
D
B

a. What position for D maximizes $a + b$?

b. What is the maximum value of $a + b$?

c. What position for D minimizes $a + b$?

d. What is the minimum value of $a + b$?

15. D lies somewhere on $\overline{AB}$ of nonobtuse $\triangle ABC$. Perpendiculars are drawn from D to $\overline{AC}$ and $\overline{BC}$. Let c be the length of $\overline{QR}$.

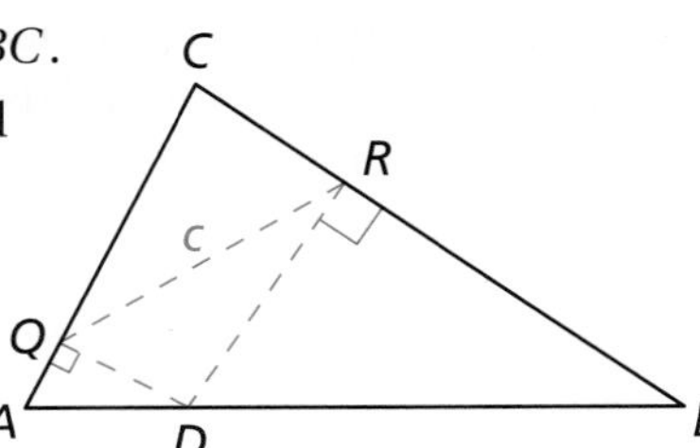

a. What position of D minimizes the value of c?

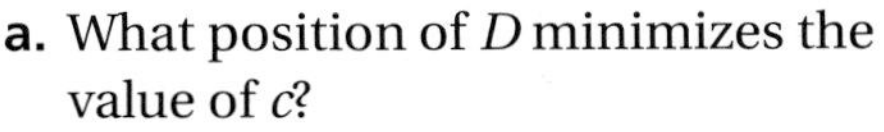

b. What is that minimum value?

c. What position of D maximizes the value of c?

d. What is that maximum value?

8.14 The Isoperimetric Problem

In Lesson 8.5, Sasha and Derman found the greatest floor area for a rectangular house with perimeter 128 feet. This is an isoperimetric problem. In general, **isoperimetric problems** involve geometric figures of a certain type with the same perimeter. You want to find the one that encloses the most area.

Remember...

The house with the greatest floor area was a square.

Suppose you have a rope of some fixed length, and you join the ends to make a loop. You can put the loop on the floor and form many shapes. The polygons, curves, and figure eights you can make all have the same perimeter. Which has the greatest area? This is the most general and most famous isoperimetric problem. It allows you to consider any shape.

The Isoperimetric Problem Of all closed curves with the same perimeter, which encloses the most area?

The word *isoperimetric* comes from three Greek words.

Iso- means "equal," as in *isosceles*, *isobars*, and *isometric*.

Peri- means "around," as in *pericardium* and *peripheral*.

Metri- means "measurement," as in *metric system*.

Theorem 8.1 from Lesson 8.6 is a good place to start. Even if the solution to the isoperimetric problem is not a polygon, proving the Regular Polygon Theorem will help.

Theorem 8.1 The Regular Polygon Theorem

Of all the polygons having a given perimeter and a given number of sides, the regular polygon has the greatest area.

For Discussion

1. You have already done some work that will contribute to the proof of this theorem. Explain how you know that the polygon that encloses the greatest area for a given perimeter must be convex and equilateral.

To prove the theorem, it is not enough to know that the polygon is convex and equilateral. You also need to show that the polygon is equiangular. One way to do this is to show that all the vertices of the polygon that encloses the greatest area must lie on a circle.

It turns out that it is much easier to do this if the polygon has an even number of sides. That case previews the key methods that you will use to solve the general isoperimetric problem, so it is the only one considered in this lesson.

For You to Do

2. Justify the following claim.

If all the vertices of an equilateral polygon lie on a circle, all the angles of the polygon are congruent. (The polygon is *regular*.)

Example 1

Problem You are given an octagon. It encloses the maximum possible area for a fixed perimeter. Show that all of its vertices must lie on a circle.

Solution First, show that if a line cuts the perimeter of the polygon in half, it must also cut the area in half. Draw a line that passes through two vertices and divides the octagon into two polygons, I and II. See the polygon below at the left.

This may seem like a strange place to start, but keep reading and it will make more sense.

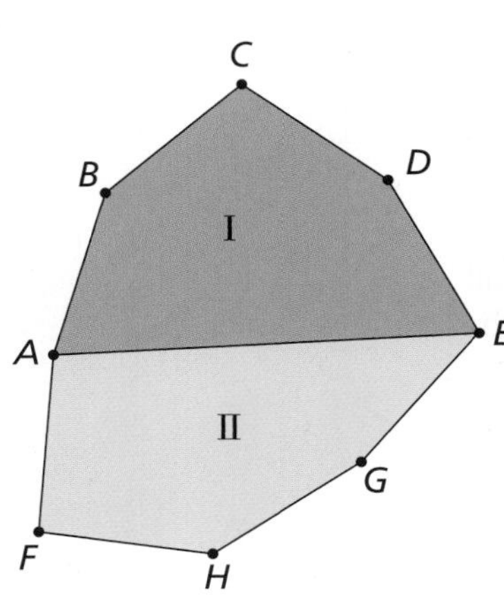

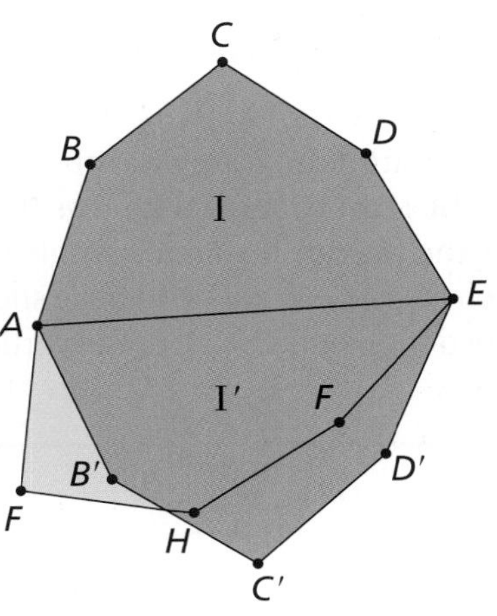

Both I and II have the same perimeter. Less obvious is that they also have the same area. To see this, suppose $\overline{AE}$ *does not* cut the area of the octagon in half—say, for example, that the area of I is greater than the area of II. You could reflect I over $\overline{AE}$ to create a new octagon with greater area and the same perimeter as shown above at the right.

But this contradicts the given fact that you started with an octagon of fixed perimeter that encloses the *maximum possible area* already. Therefore, $\overline{AE}$ must cut the area of the octagon in half.

Now work with a polygon that is half of the original octagon. If you can show that all of its vertices lie on a semicircle, you will be done.

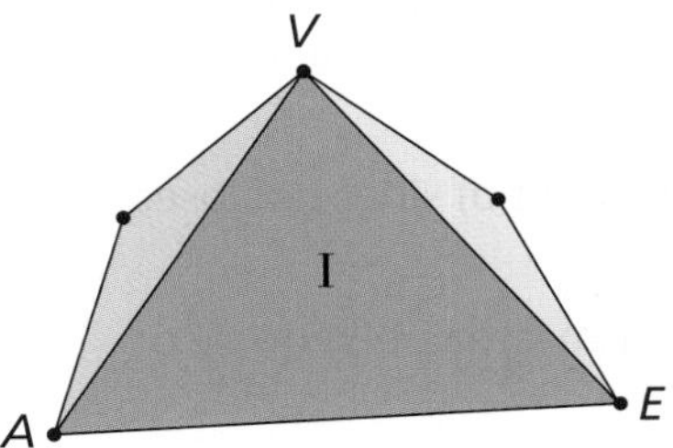

Look at $\angle AVE$, where V is any vertex of the half octagon except A or E. If $m\angle AVE = 90°$, then all V are on the semicircle with diameter $\overline{AE}$ and you are done. If $m\angle AVE$ does not equal 90°, then you have more work to do.

Imagine you are squeezing and stretching the polygon to find the measure for $\angle AVE$ that guarantees that the area of the polygon is maximized.

In the figures at the top of the next page, the shaded regions labeled α are congruent, and the shaded regions labeled β are congruent. The half octagons have been altered so that $\angle AVE$ is acute in the first figure and obtuse in the second.

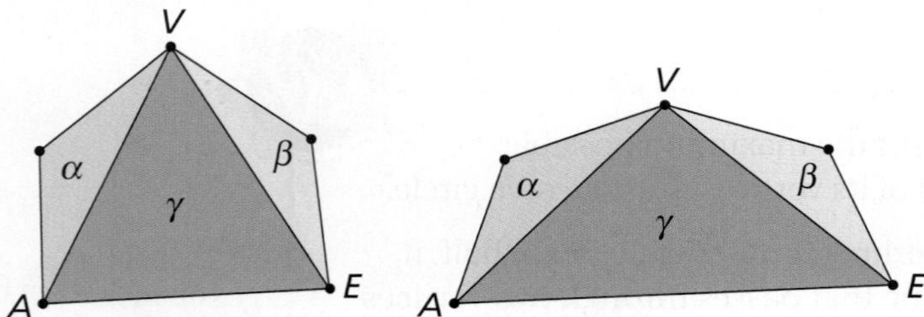

Remember that $\triangle AVE$ is part of the half octagon with maximized area. Therefore, the area of $\triangle AVE$ must be maximized as well. The lengths of $\overline{AV}$ and $\overline{VE}$ cannot change because that would alter the areas of the shaded regions.

Recall Exercise 7 in Lesson 8.5. You found the triangle with maximum area given two fixed side lengths. It is the right triangle with legs that measure the two given lengths. Therefore, the maximum-area triangle with sides $\overline{AV}$ and $\overline{VE}$ is the triangle in which $m\angle AVE = 90°$. You have shown that all vertices V of the half octagon lie on a semicircle. So all of the vertices V of the original octagon lie on a circle.

For You to Do

3. For the octagon, $\overline{AE}$ connected the "first" vertex A to the fifth vertex E. If the polygon had 10 sides, which vertex would be connected to A (if A is the first)? Which vertex would be connected to A if the polygon had 12 sides? If it had $2n$ sides?

4. Carry out the argument in the Example for a general polygon with an even number of sides (that is, for a $2n$-gon).

5. Explain how you know that if $m\angle AVB = 90°$ for some point V, it must lie on the same circle as any other point V for which that is true. In other words, explain why it cannot lie on a different circle.

You have now shown that Theorem 8.1 is true for polygons with an even number of sides.

- First, you showed that the polygon enclosing the maximum area must be convex and equilateral.
- Then, you showed that a polygon with an even number of sides encloses the most area when its vertices lie on a circle.
- You also explained why the vertices of this maximum-area polygon lie on the same circle.

The fact that the vertices all lie on a circle shows that the equilateral polygon is also equiangular. This is because you can divide the polygon into congruent triangles by connecting the center of the circle to each vertex. All the triangles formed are congruent and isosceles. The base angles are congruent, so when combined, they form congruent angles of the polygon.

You have shown that given a perimeter and number of sides of a polygon, the regular polygon encloses the greatest area. This is an important step on the path to solving the isoperimetric problem.

Exercises *Practicing Habits of Mind*

Check Your Understanding

1. When you were proving Theorem 8.1, you probably did not consider any self-intersecting polygons. Consider the one below.

   Explain why a self-intersecting polygon could not have maximum area for its perimeter. Describe a way to draw a simple polygon (one that does not cross itself) that has the same perimeter as the self-intersecting polygon but that encloses more area.

   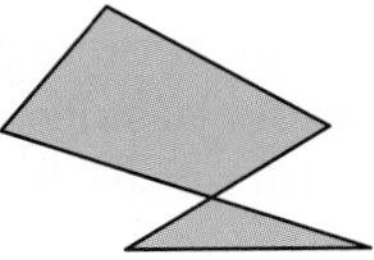

2. Find the maximum area of a 6-sided polygon with a perimeter of 36 inches. Then find another figure with a perimeter of 36 inches that encloses more area.

3. Find the least possible perimeter for a 5-sided polygon with area 30 square centimeters. Then find another figure that has area 30 square centimeters but a smaller perimeter.

On Your Own

4. **Write About It** Prove the even case of Theorem 8.1 in your own words. Explain how this theorem could affect a proof of the isoperimetric problem.

5. Work through the following sequence of steps. Develop a formula that will approximate the area of a regular polygon with n sides and perimeter p.

   a. Visualize your regular polygon inscribed in a circle. Draw segments connecting each vertex to the center of the circle. This process forms a number of congruent triangles. Sketch one of the triangles. Label the angle measures and side lengths you know in terms of n and p.

   b. Define h as the height of the triangle with respect to the triangle side that is also a side of the polygon. Use trigonometry to approximate h.

   c. Write an expression in terms of n and p for the area of a single triangle and for the total area of the polygon.

Remember...

The height h is the apothem of the polygon.

6. You want to build a five-sided dog run against a wall of your house. You have 84 feet of fence. From similar problems, you know that the best possibility will be half of some regular polygon. (You can see the whole polygon if you reflect your dog run over the line of the wall.)

   a. Reflect your five-sided dog run over the line of the wall. How many sides does the resulting polygon have? Consider all possible cases.

   b. For each of the possibilities, work out the area of the resulting best dog run.

7. **Standardized Test Prep** Sarah and Zoey want to build a pen for their puppy. They have 2 m of fencing, and they plan to use the side of the garage as one side of the pen. Which of the following possible pens has the greatest area?

A. an equilateral triangle **B.** a square with $\frac{2}{3}$-m sides

C. a 1 m-by-$\frac{1}{2}$ m rectangle **D.** a $\frac{3}{4}$ m-by-$\frac{1}{2}$ m rectangle

8. **What's Wrong Here?** Tony says, "I think I know where we are going with all this regular polygon stuff. Think about a regular polygon inscribed in a circle. If you double the number of sides, of course you increase the area. If you keep doubling, the area increases, but it cannot become greater than the area of the circumscribed circle."

Find the areas of the following regular polygons inscribed in a circle of radius 1.

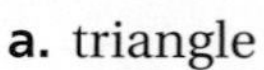

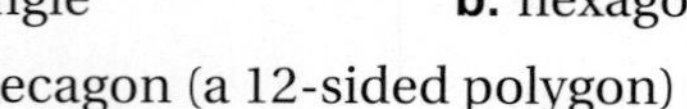

a. triangle **b.** hexagon

c. dodecagon (a 12-sided polygon)

d. Sasha says, "Hold on a minute! The perimeter isn't staying the same for all of your polygons. You're enclosing more area, but you're also increasing the perimeter." Is Sasha right?

9. Find the perimeter of Tony's polygons from Exercise 8.

10. Think about a regular polygon circumscribed about a circle. If you keep doubling the number of sides, what happens?

11. Think about a regular polygon with a fixed perimeter. If you keep doubling the number of sides, what happens?

12. Find the area of a regular triangle, hexagon, and dodecagon, each with perimeter 12 cm.

Maintain Your Skills

13. To prepare for Exercise 6 in Lesson 8.15, evaluate $x + \frac{1-x}{2}$ for the following values of x. Express your answer as an exact fraction.

a. $x = \frac{9}{10}$ **b.** $x = \frac{99}{100}$ **c.** $x = \frac{999}{1000}$ **d.** $x = \frac{9999}{10000}$

14. In Exercise 13, the values of x are all of the form $\frac{n-1}{n}$. As n increases, does $\frac{n-1}{n}$ increase or decrease? Is x approaching some value?

15. In Exercise 14, you describe the behavior of x as n increases. If x continues to change in this way, does the expression $x + \frac{1-x}{2}$ increase or decrease? Does it approach some value?

8.15 The Question of Existence

You have had some practice finding the polygon that encloses the most area for a given perimeter and number of sides. Now you can return to the isoperimetric problem.

Example

Problem Is the figure that encloses the most area for a given perimeter a polygon? Explain how you know.

Solution No, it is not. Consider a square of side length a. Cut off the lower right corner of the square. Call the lengths of the sides of the resulting triangle r, s, and t.

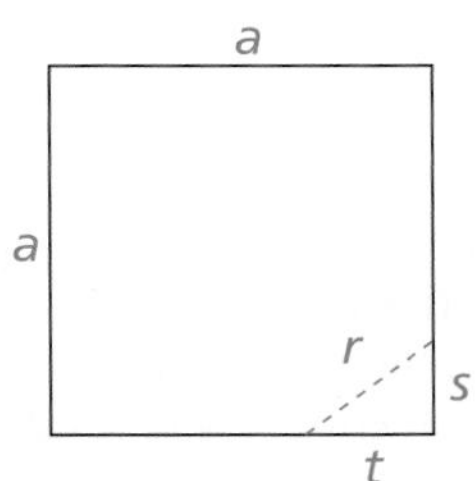

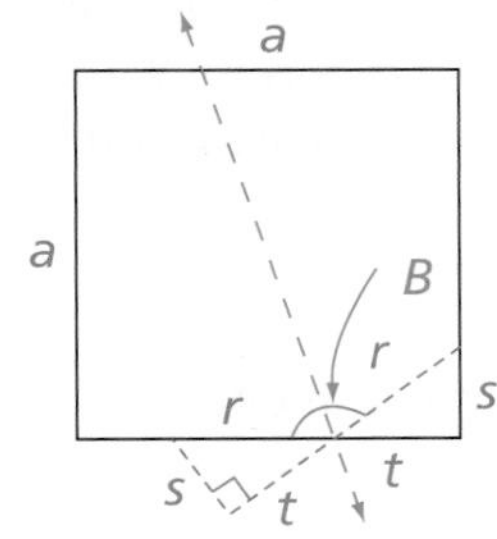

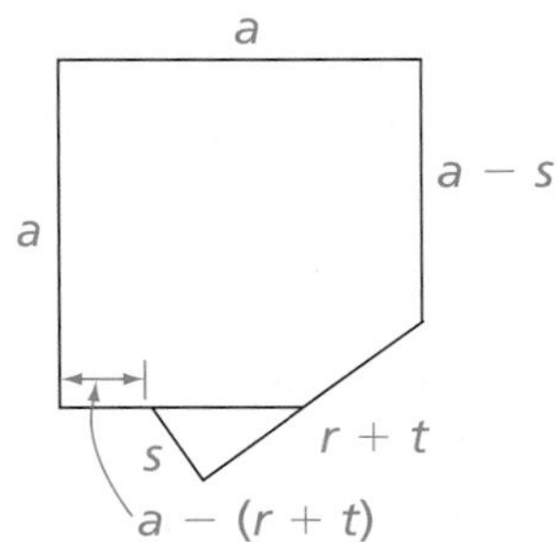

Now reflect the triangle about the angle bisector of $\angle B$. Line up its longest side r with the base of the square. You now have a hexagon with the same area and perimeter as the original square. The area is unchanged since you just cut off a piece of the square and taped it back on. To show that the perimeter is the same, add up the lengths of the six sides. Start at the top and proceed clockwise.

$$a + (a - s) + (r + t) + s + [a - (r + t)] + a = 4a$$

Call this new hexagon C for curve. The important fact about C is that it has the same area and perimeter as the original square, but it is concave. This means that there is another curve with the same perimeter as C that encloses more area. So the figure with this perimeter that encloses the maximum area is not a square.

Using this method, you can always draw a concave polygon with the same area and perimeter as any given polygon. You also can transform any concave polygon to increase its area without increasing its perimeter. Therefore, it is impossible that any polygon could be the solution to the isoperimetric problem.

Habits of Mind

Develop your understanding. This argument can be generalized to any polygon. The right angle that was cut off the square was not used in the proof, so you could cut off the corner of any polygon and reflect it this way.

For Discussion

1. Summarize everything you know about the curve that will eventually solve the isoperimetric problem. Share any conjectures you have made, and record any characteristics that the best curve must have.

Through experiments and visualization, you may know the solution to the isoperimetric problem. To make a conjecture about which shape solves the problem is a good start. Now, you must prove your conjecture.

From your experiments, you may have decided a circle is the best shape.

Conjecture 8.1 The Isoperimetric Conjecture

Of all closed curves with the same perimeter, the circle encloses the most area.

In this lesson and the next, you will study one plan for a proof. You will look at a sequence of partial results that imply the conjecture is a theorem. You will establish all but one of these partial results. Then you will have a good idea of how the Isoperimetric Conjecture is proven.

This particular plan follows the one described by Richard Courant and Herbert Robbins in *What is Mathematics?* (Oxford University Press, 1941).

Here are the main steps in the plan you will study.

Step 1 For a fixed perimeter, show that there is at least one curve that encloses the most area.

Step 2 You are given a curve that encloses the most area. Show that any line that cuts its perimeter in half must also bisect its area. Call such a line a diameter of the curve.

Step 3 You are given a curve that encloses the most area and one of its diameters. Pick any point P on the curve that is not on the diameter. Draw segments from P to the endpoints of the diameter. The angle formed at P is always a right angle.

Remember...

How do you define *diameter* in a circle?

For Discussion

2. How do the three steps above imply that a circle encloses the most area for a given perimeter?

As it turns out, the first step in this plan is the toughest. It cannot be proved using the methods developed in this text. In other words, you cannot prove that there is a curve of given perimeter that encloses the most area.

How could there not be a solution to an optimization problem? In the following exercises, you will see several examples of optimization problems that do not have solutions.

Exercises *Practicing Habits of Mind*

Check Your Understanding

1. **Write About It** The isoperimetric problem asks which curve encloses the most area. Could there be more than one best curve? Give an example of an optimization problem that has several solutions. That is, find a situation for which there is more than one way to maximize or minimize something.

2. Trace the figure below, including A and B. Take turns with a partner trying to draw the shortest path in the plane from A to B that does not touch the circle. Is there a shortest path? Explain.

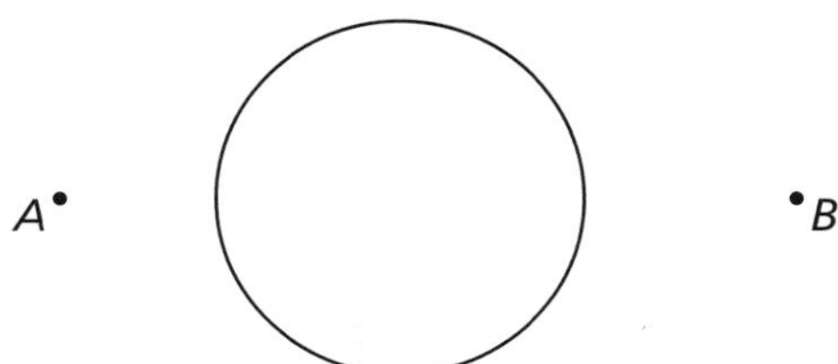

On Your Own

3. Describe how you would draw a regular polygon with n sides and perimeter p.

4. Look back at Steps 2 and 3 of the plan for establishing the Isoperimetric Conjecture. Point out the places where these steps assume that there is a best curve. Why is this assumption necessary?

5. **Standardized Test Prep** You cut an 80-cm wire into two pieces. You fold one piece into a square and the other piece into an equilateral triangle. Which wire lengths will produce the least total area of the square and equilateral triangle?

   A. square: 40 cm; triangle: 40 cm

   B. square: 45.7 cm; triangle: 34.3 cm

   C. square: 34.8 cm; triangle 45.2 cm

   D. square: 50 cm; triangle: 30 cm

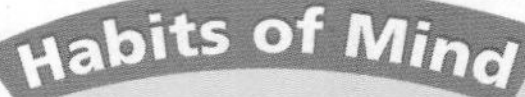

Use an indirect proof. This is one of those exercises where you have to read and understand a proof, so read carefully.

6. **Take It Further** Many positive numbers are less than 1. Examples include $\frac{1}{2}$, $\frac{3}{4}$, $\sqrt{2} - 1$, and 0.897. What is the greatest positive number less than 1? Here is an argument, a proof by contradiction, that shows such a number does not exist.

   Suppose there is a greatest number less than 1. Call it x.

   a. Explain how you know that $1 - x$ is a positive number.

   b. Begin with the assumption that x is the greatest number less than 1. What can you conclude about $\frac{1-x}{2}$? Give an argument that $x + \frac{1-x}{2}$ must be greater than or equal to 1.

   c. Draw a number line showing 0 and 1. Show possible locations for x and $x + \frac{1-x}{2}$.

   d. Use algebra to solve this inequality.

   $$x + \frac{1-x}{2} \geq 1$$

   Does your solution agree with your definition of x at the beginning of the exercise?

   e. How does this argument show that the optimization problem of finding the greatest number less than one does not have a solution?

If something exists, you can name it anything you like.

7. Explain why the following optimization problem has no solution.

   Find the polygon with perimeter 24 inches that encloses the greatest area.

Maintain Your Skills

8. Factor each of the following quadratic expressions.

   a. $-x^2 - 6x + 16$

   b. $-x^2 + 2x + 3$

   c. $x^2 - 3x - 10$

9. Use your factorizations from Exercise 8 to solve the following equations.

   a $-x^2 - 6x + 16 = 0$

   b. $-x^2 + 2x + 3 = 0$

   c. $x^2 - 3x - 10 = 0$

10. Use your solutions from Exercise 9 to sketch the graph of each function.

    a. $y = x^2 + 6x - 16$

    b. $y = x^2 - 2x - 3$

    c. $y = -x^2 + 3x + 10$

11. Find the maximum value for y in each graph in Exercise 10. If a maximum does not exist, explain why.

Go Online
Pearsonsuccessnet.com

8.16 Solving the Isoperimetric Problem

A plan for proving the Isoperimetric Conjecture is presented in Lesson 8.15. You learned you are unable to prove its first step. However, you can assume the first step is true and continue with the proof. This situation is fairly common in mathematics and can be addressed as follows.

Postulate 8.1 The Existence Hypothesis

For any given perimeter, there is a closed curve that encloses the greatest area.

You can assume the existence of a best-possible curve, which is Step 1 of the plan. That assumption can be used to prove Steps 2 and 3.

Developing Habits of Mind

Use a different process. Once you assume that there is a best possible curve, you can figure out some of its properties. You want to prove that the best possible curve must be a circle. Little by little, you will rule out curves that are not circles. You have already ruled out polygons, self-crossing curves, and concave curves. You are like a detective, on the hunt for a mystery curve. You will figure out what it is by nailing down its properties.

Maybe you will not prove the existence hypothesis today or even this year. It would be satisfying if you could prove it someday.

Even if you do not prove it now, it is important to note that it is possible to prove the existence hypothesis. Avoid assuming existence and then determining properties based on that assumption. It results in serious consequences in math and in other fields such as social sciences.

The solution of the isoperimetric problem that you are studying took centuries to evolve. When reading a plan like this, many people might say, "I'd never think of that." They might assume that mathematical ideas and proofs are only discovered by extremely gifted people. This is not true.

The truth is that mathematics is developed by a community of people. Each person contributes small insights and occasional breakthroughs. The three-step plan was not developed by one person. It emerged from the work of dozens of mathematicians over the centuries.

An important part of mathematics is reading and understanding discussions, such as this presentation of the isoperimetric problem. Think of the proof as a sophisticated machine that you can study.

Exercises *Practicing Habits of Mind*

Check Your Understanding

1. Prove Step 2 of the plan. Assume that curve C is the curve that encloses the greatest area for its perimeter. Show that any line that bisects the perimeter of C must also bisect its area.

2. Now that you have proved Step 2 of the plan, the Isoperimetric Conjecture has been reduced to the following.

Conjecture 8.2 The Reduced Isoperimetric Conjecture

Take line ℓ. Of all the curves that have two points on ℓ and have the same perimeter, the one that encloses the most area is a semicircle with diameter that lies along ℓ.

Explain why proving this restricted conjecture is enough to prove the Isoperimetric Conjecture.

3. Because of the Reduced Isoperimetric Conjecture, you now only have to consider half of a curve. Assume that any angle formed by a point on the half curve and the endpoints of a diameter is a right angle. (This is the condition for Step 3 of the plan.) Can you guarantee that the curve is a semicircle? Explain.

4. Curve C is your candidate for the best curve. Draw diameter $\overline{AB}$ and connect its endpoints to some point P on C. Why must $\angle APB$ be a right angle? Remember, C encloses the greatest area for its perimeter.

On Your Own

5. **Standardized Test Prep** Suppose you construct a semicircular fence with 2 m of curved fence. What is the radius r of the fence? What is the area enclosed by the fence?

A. $r = \frac{1}{2\pi}$ m; area $= 0.628$ m^2 **B.** $r = \frac{1}{\pi}$ m; area $= \frac{1}{\pi}$ m^2

C. $r = \frac{2}{\pi}$ m; area $= \frac{2}{\pi}$ m^2 **D.** $r = \frac{2}{\pi}$ m; area $= \frac{4}{\pi}$ m^2

6. In Exercise 1, you show that a line that cuts the perimeter of the curve in half must also cut the area in half. How do you know there is a line that cuts the perimeter of the best possible curve in half? Describe a method for constructing such a line.

7. **Write About It** State the existence hypothesis in your own words. Why do you need to assume it in order to establish the Isoperimetric Conjecture? Again, answer in your own words.

8. **Write About It** You used the detective method when you searched for a mystery curve by discovering its properties. It is a different approach than the one used to solve other optimization problems, such as the burning-tent problem. Describe the differences between the two approaches.

9. In the Developing Habits of Mind section of Lesson 8.5, you solved the rectangular-dog-run problem with a certain method. Can the same method be used to solve the reduced isoperimetric problem? Explain.

10. **Write About It** If you assume the existence hypothesis, you can now prove the Isoperimetric Conjecture. Write out a careful proof in your own words. Use examples and pictures and explain each step.

11. **Take It Further** The Isoperimetric Conjecture also can be proved with Theorem 8.1 and limits, a topic you will study in calculus. Think about a collection of regular polygons, each one having more vertices than the previous polygon. All the polygons have the same perimeter. What happens to the area of these polygons as the number of vertices increases? Sketch a proof of the Isoperimetric Conjecture using the idea of limits.

Maintain Your Skills

In Exercises 12–14, C is a closed curve of perimeter 4π cm that encloses the maximum area for that perimeter.

12. How much area does C enclose?

13. If C contains the points $(-1, 5)$, $(-3, 3)$, and $(1, 3)$, find an equation for C on the coordinate plane.

14. Give the coordinates of at least two other points on C.

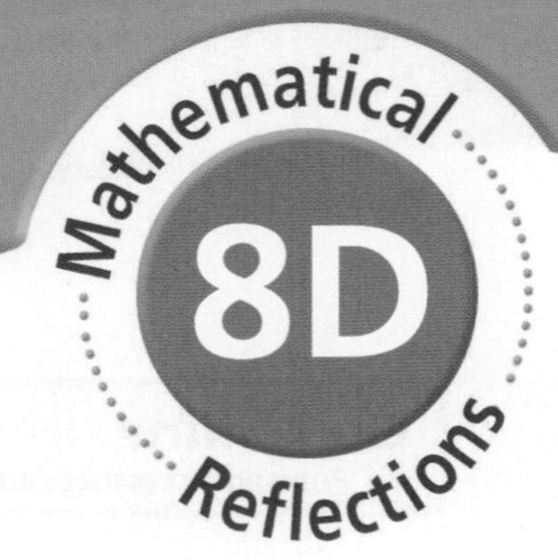

In this investigation, you learned how to write functions and use them to find an optimal solution, and you learned how to understand a proof of the Isoperimetric Conjecture. These questions will help you summarize what you have learned.

1. Let P be any point inside the square. Write a function $f(x, y)$ that finds the sum of the distances from P to the vertices of the square.

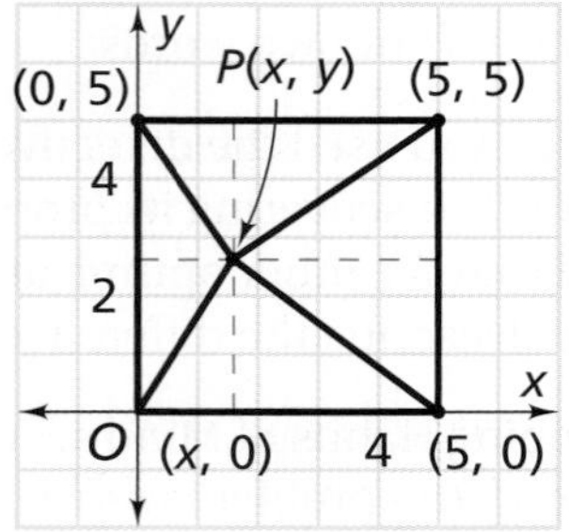

2. Use the function from Exercise 1 to calculate $f(2, 2)$, $f(1, 1)$, and $f(3, 3)$. Which P on a diagonal of the square gives the least value of f?

3. In the figure, $\triangle ABC$'s area is 45 and $AB = 5$. What is CH?

4. The centroid of an equilateral triangle divides each median into two segments. Use Rich's Theorem to prove that one of the segments is twice as long as the other.

5. There are many hexagons of perimeter 27 cm. Find the dimensions and area of the one that encloses the greatest possible area.

6. The interior of a triangle contains P. Consider the sum of the distances from P to each of the sides. Is this sum constant for any P or does it depend on the kind of triangle? Explain with examples.

7. For what point P is the sum of the distances from P to the sides of $\triangle ABC$ the least? Explain.

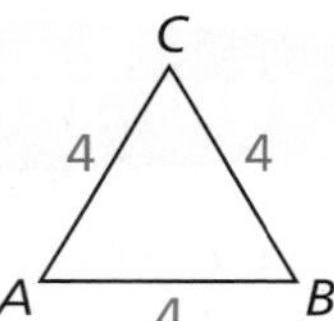

8. Give an example of an optimization problem that has no solution. Explain your reasoning.

9. What curve encloses the greatest area for a given perimeter? Explain.

Vocabulary

In this investigation, you learned this term. Make sure you understand what it means and how to use it.

- **isoperimetric problem**

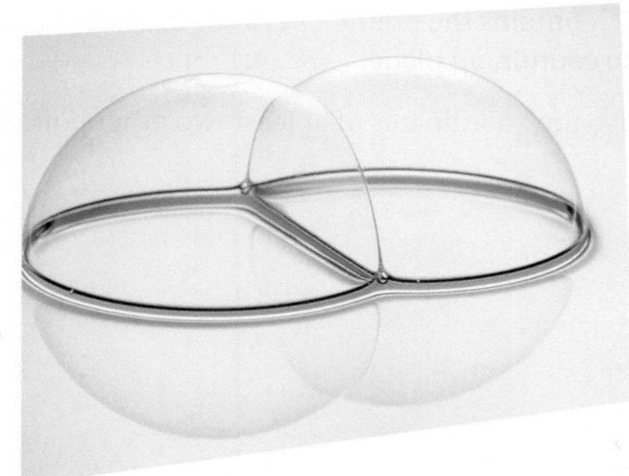

What shape do you think the joined bubbles had before they landed on this mirror?

Project: Using Mathematical Habits

The Airport Problem

Three neighboring cities, all about the same size, decide to share the cost of building a new airport. They hire your group as consultants to find a location for the airport.

The three cities decide that they want the location to be environmentally friendly and practical. They state their request to your group in the following way.

The Airport Problem Let A, B, and C be the locations of the cities. Let D be the location of the airport such that $DA + DB + DC$ is the least sum possible.

Models

Sometimes a model can help you experiment with a system. If you already have a conjecture, a model can help you test it. If you do not have a conjecture, a physical or computer model may help you come up with one.

Make a physical model to explore the airport problem. Take a flat piece of wood and pound nails into it, more or less in a circle.

Use a small metal ring to represent the airport and strong string to represent the roads to the cities. You will need twice as much string as the length of the roads because the string must be double-looped around the nails. The following sketch shows how the thread is passed through the ring and is looped around the nails.

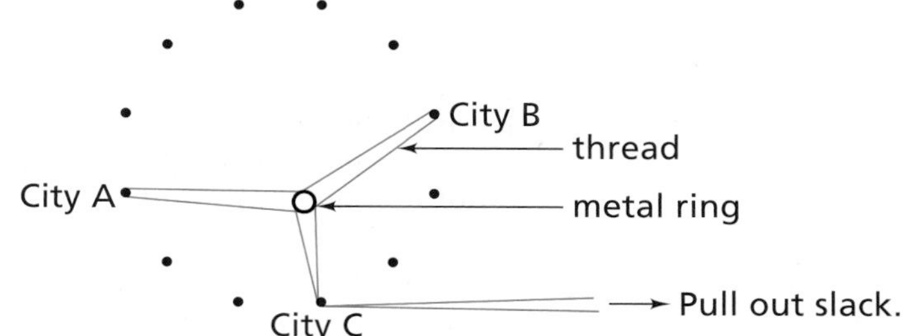

1. Explain how this device can be used to locate the best airport location for the three cities. Why does it work?
2. Use the model to explore several arrangements of the three cities. Place a piece of paper inside the circle of nails. Record each experiment by tracing out the roads to the best airport location for each arrangement.
3. For a given set of three cities, can there be more than one spot where the sum of the distances to the cities is the least possible? Explain.
4. Use the string, ring, and nails to make a contour plot for the sum of the distances from the airport to the cities. Use your contour plot to defend your answer to Exercise 3.

You can also use geometry software to model the airport problem. Construct a diagram, like the one on the next page, that lets you see the airport function both numerically and geometrically.

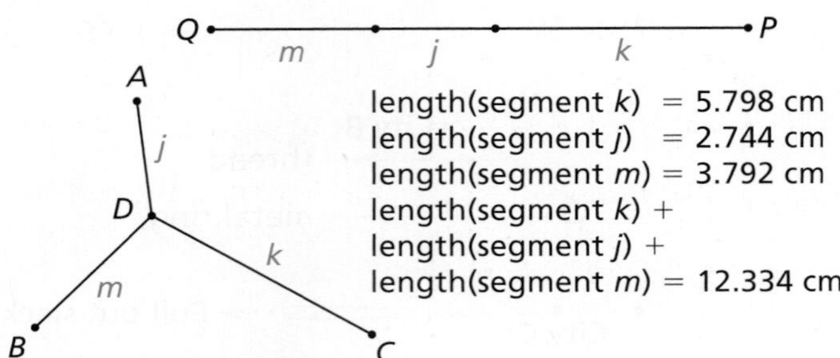

As you move D around, the total distance increases and decreases. The length QP is the value of the airport function for D. You are trying to minimize this length.

5. Have the software trace the locus of P. As you move D, what happens to P when you minimize the total distance?
6. Use your geometry software to draw the contour lines for the sum of the distances from the airport to the cities.
7. Use your computer to keep track of the angles in the airport problem. Make some conjectures about the patterns you find.

Hoffman's Construction

The Fermat point of a triangle is the point that forms three 120° angles when you connect it with the vertices of the triangle.

Since you have been thinking about the airport problem, the following conjecture may seem reasonable to you.

The Airport Conjecture Three cities form a triangle. If no angle of the triangle is too great, then the best place for the airport is where the roads form 120° angles with each other.

In 1929, the German mathematician J. E. Hoffman found an ingenious way to construct the Fermat point of a triangle.

Step 1 Start with $\triangle ABC$. Rotate $\overline{AB}$ 60° counterclockwise around B.

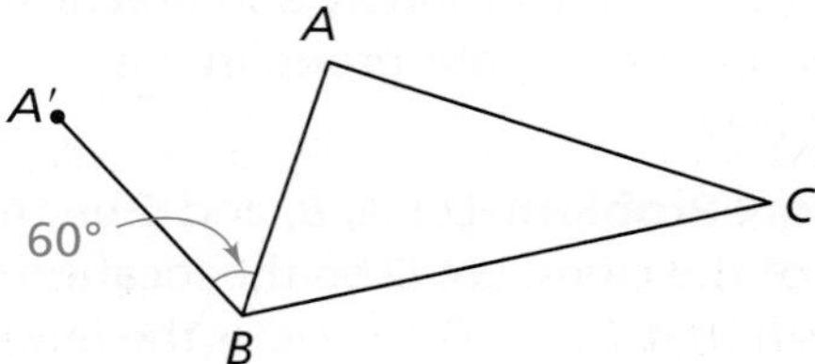

Step 2 Connect A' and C. Draw a line through B that intersects $\overline{A'C}$ in D so that $m\angle A'DB = 60°$. Then $m\angle BDC = 120°$.

So D is a good candidate for the Fermat point. For it to be the Fermat point, all you have to prove is that $m\angle ADB = 120°$.

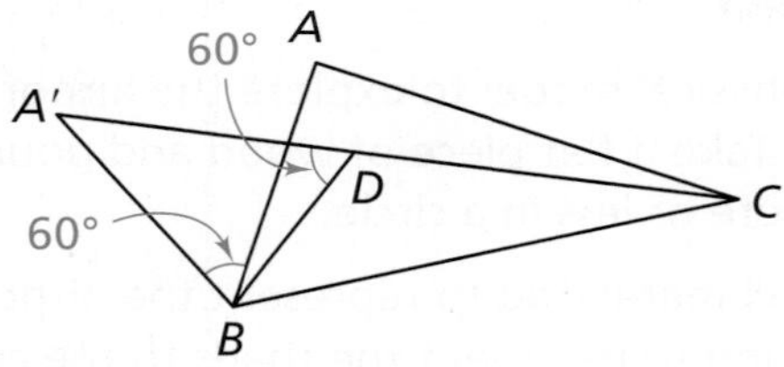

Step 3 Rotate $\overline{BD}$ 60° counterclockwise around B. Let D' be the image of D.

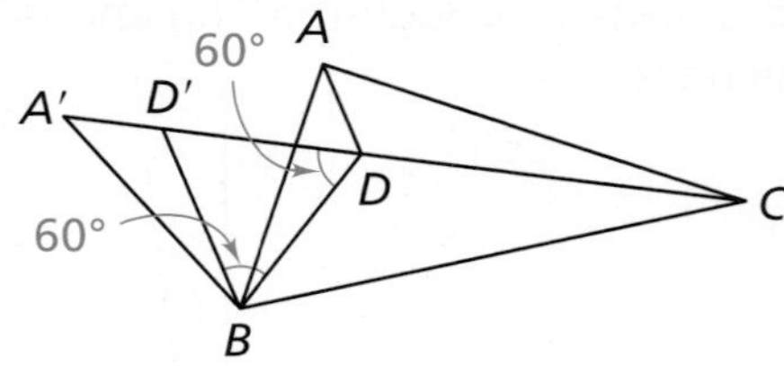

8. Prove that D' lies on $\overline{A'C}$.

Since A, D', and D are collinear, and $\triangle BDD'$ is equilateral, $m\angle A'D'B = 180° - m\angle BD'D = 180° - 60° = 120°$. You can show that $\triangle A'BD'$ is congruent to $\triangle ABD$, so $m\angle ADB = 120°$. This proves that D is the Fermat point of $\triangle ABC$.

Proving the Conjecture

To be sure that the Airport Conjecture is true, you need to think of a proof. There are different ways of proceeding. Start with a triangle and inside it, choose point D, which is not the Fermat point.

You will prove that the sum of the distances from any D to the vertices is greater than the sum from the Fermat point to the vertices.

9. Use Hoffman's construction to find the Fermat point F of $\triangle ABC$.

10. Draw the line perpendicular to $\overline{BF}$ through B, the line perpendicular to $\overline{FC}$ through C, and the line perpendicular to $\overline{AF}$ through A. Prove that $\triangle EGH$ is equilateral.

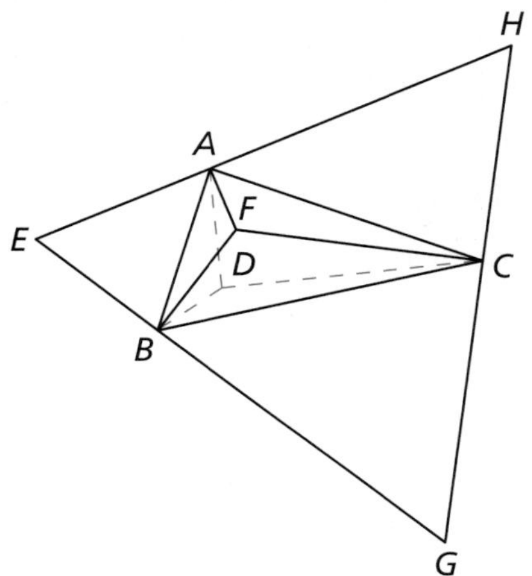

11. Prove that $DA + DB + DC > FA + FB + FC$. Use a result from Lesson 8.13.

You have proved the following theorem.

The best place to put the airport is where the roads make 120° angles with one another, unless there is no such place inside the triangle.

Review

In **Investigation 8A** you learned how to

- distinguish between distance and the length of a path
- use reflection to make a straight path from a segmented path
- find the shortest path between two points if you must pass through a third point

The following questions will help you check your understanding.

1.

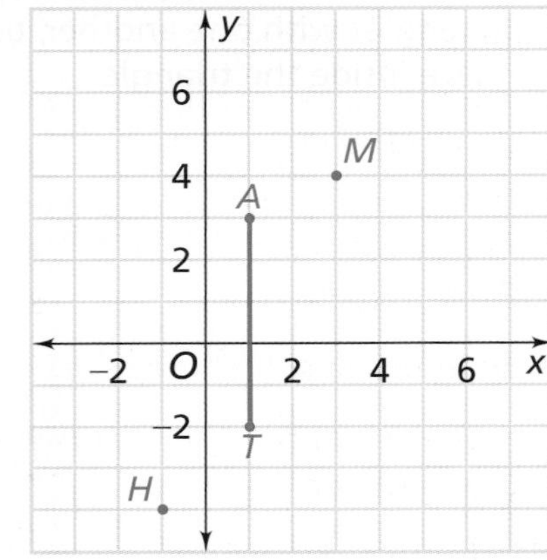

a. Find the distance from $M(3, 4)$ to $H(-1, -4)$.

b. Now find the shortest path from M to H if your path cannot intersect $\overline{AT}$.

2. Let A and B fall on opposite sides of a line. Explain how to find P on the line so that $AP + PB$ is a minimum. Include a sketch.

3. Let X and Y be on the same side of a line. Explain how to use reflection to find P on the line so that $XP + PY$ is a minimum. Include a sketch.

In **Investigation 8B** you learned how to

- find grid polygons with a given area or perimeter
- find the triangle or rectangle that maximizes area for a given perimeter
- find the polygon that maximizes area for a given perimeter

The following questions will help you check your understanding.

4. Use only grid lines on a sheet of graph paper. Find the maximum perimeter possible for a grid polygon with an area of 12 square units.

5. Find the maximum area for a triangle with perimeter 36 in.

6. The perimeter of a rectangle is 80 cm and its length is 32 cm. What is its area?

7. Find the area of each regular polygon, given that its perimeter is 52 in.

a. a triangle

b. a square

c. a hexagon

d. a dodecagon

8. You want to build a dog kennel along an outer wall of a barn. You have 200 feet of fencing. What is the maximum area of the dog kennel for each number of sides?

a. 4 sides

b. 5 sides

c. 6 sides

In **Investigation 8C** you learned how to

- draw and interpret contour plots
- define an ellipse
- use ellipses to solve optimization problems

The following questions will help you check your understanding.

9. This contour plot is of a hill where Tony and Sasha pick blueberries. The contour lines show height in feet. Since they carry a picnic basket and blueberry buckets, they are looking for the easiest hike up the hill. Copy the diagram and draw a path that you think Tony and Sasha might take. Explain why you think this is the easiest hike.

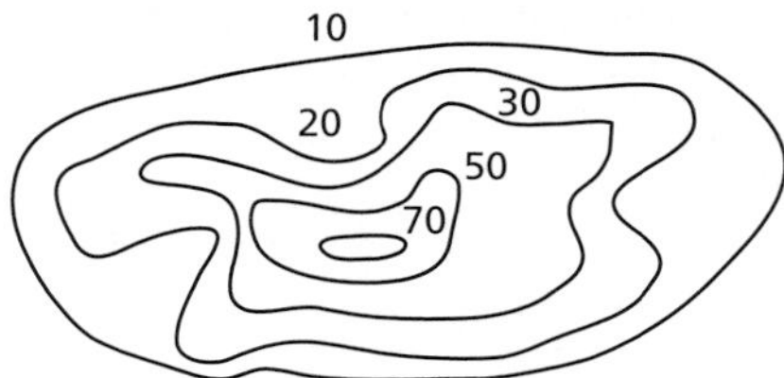

10. What is an ellipse? Mark A and B and draw an ellipse with those points as foci.

11. Solve Exercise 3 using contour lines.

12. Suppose points C and D are fixed points in a plane. Function f is defined so that $f(A) = 2AC + AD$. Make a contour plot for f. Label it appropriately.

In **Investigation 8D** you learned how to

- identify reasoning by continuity
- use Rich's Theorem
- state the isoperimetric problem and investigate related conjectures

The following questions will help you check your understanding.

13. State Rich's Theorem.

14. You have 24 cm of string to make different shapes.

a. What is the area of the equilateral triangle with this perimeter?

b. What is the area of the square with this perimeter?

c. What is the area of the regular hexagon with this perimeter?

d. Describe a shape that has a greater area than this triangle, square, and regular hexagon.

15. State the Isoperimetric Conjecture.

16. Explain why the following optimization problem has no solution.

Find the polygon with perimeter 60 inches that encloses the most area.

17. C is a closed curve that encloses the maximum area for each of the following perimeters. What is the area of C for each perimeter?

a. 9π m **b.** 24π in. **c.** π cm

Test

Multiple Choice

1. Suppose you want to enclose a rectangular garden with 50 feet of fencing. A stone wall will serve as the back of the garden. What are the dimensions of the rectangle that will maximize the area of the garden?

   A. 15 ft by 20 ft

   B. 17.5 ft by 15 ft

   C. 12.5 ft by 25 ft

   D. 7 ft by 18 ft

2. A company wants to minimize the costs associated with packaging a box of 30 markers. The length of each marker is 6.5 in., and the diameter of each marker is 0.5 in. What are the dimensions of the box that will minimize the costs?

   A. 0.5 in. by 15 in. by 6.5 in.

   B. 1 in. by 7.5 in. by 6.5 in.

   C. 1.5 in. by 5 in. by 6.5 in.

   D. 2.5 in. by 3 in. by 6.5 in.

Suppose you want to find the shortest path from $A(-2, 3)$ to any point P on the line $y = -1$ to $B(1, 2)$.

3. What point P on the line $y = -1$ should the path pass through?

   A. $(0, -1)$

   B. $\left(-\frac{2}{7}, -1\right)$

   C. $\left(-\frac{7}{3}, -1\right)$

   D. $\left(-\frac{5}{3}, -1\right)$

4. What is the length of the shortest path? Round your answer to the nearest hundredth.

   A. 7.62 **B.** 7.63

   C. 8.03 **D.** 8.50

A square and a rectangle have the same area. The rectangle has a perimeter of 212.

5. Suppose the length of the rectangle is 36. What is the perimeter of the square, rounded to the nearest tenth?

   A. 50.2

   B. 200.8

   C. 212

   D. 2520

6. Suppose you maximize the area of the rectangle. What is the perimeter of the square?

   A. 50.2

   B. 200.8

   C. 212

   D. 2520

Open Response

7. Which has the greatest area? Explain.

   - an equilateral triangle with perimeter 120 cm
   - a square with perimeter 120 cm
   - a nonsquare rectangle with perimeter 120 cm

8. This is a contour map for a pond at Camp Pascal. The greatest depth is 6.5 meters at the center of the pond. Each contour line represents a change of 1.5 meters in depth. Approximately how deep is the pond at X? At Y?

9. Below is a contour map for kicking angles on a soccer field. List the players in order from the player with the greatest kicking angle to the player with the least kicking angle.

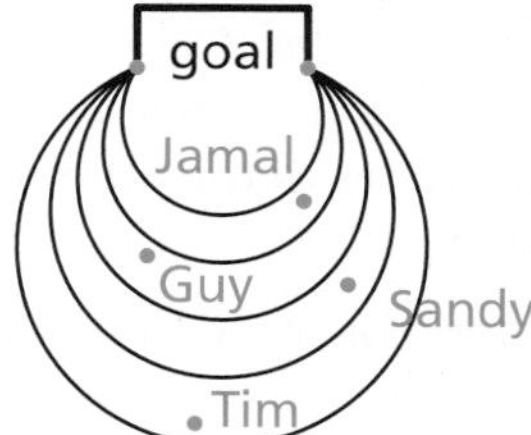

10. The equilateral triangle has side length 6 cm. Find $RH + IH + CH$.

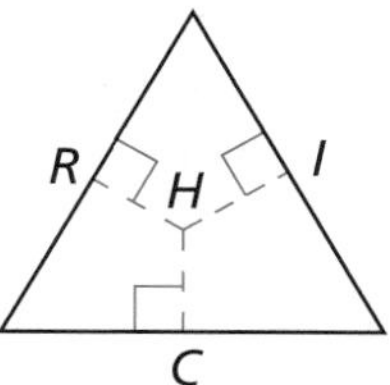

11. Given equilateral $\triangle PQR$ and altitude $\overline{PT}$, fill in each blank with $>$, $<$, or $=$.

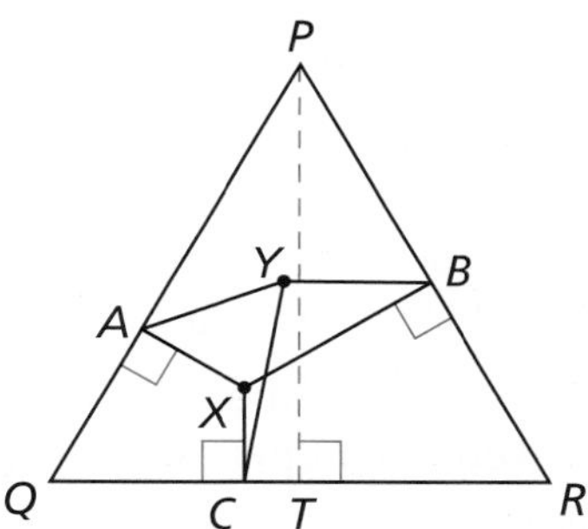

a. $AX + BX + CX$ __?__ $AY + BY + CY$

b. $AX + BX + CX$ __?__ PT

c. PT __?__ QR

d. $AY + BY + CY$ __?__ PT

12. Two cities want to build a park. The park must be built along an exisiting road. The amount of new road built to the park must be minimized. For each sketch below, determine where the park should be built. Explain your reasoning.

a. road

City B

City A

b. road

City B

City A

Chapter 8 Cumulative Review

1. In $\triangle ABC$, $A(1, 5)$, $B(-2, 3)$, and $C(4, 0)$.
   a. If you reflect $\triangle ABC$ over the line $y = -1$, what are the coordinates of the vertices of $\triangle A'B'C'$?
   b. If you reflect $\triangle A'B'C'$ over the line $x = 2$, what are the coordinates of the vertices of $\triangle A''B''C''$?

2. Copy each figure below. Draw all lines of symmetry.

a. 

b. c. 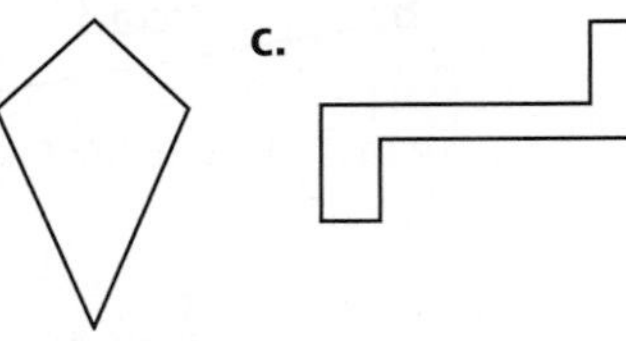

3. You are on another camping trip and your new tent catches on fire. This time, your bucket is with your supplies. You must get the bucket first and then get the water from the river and then put out the fire. What point along the river will minimize your path? Explain.

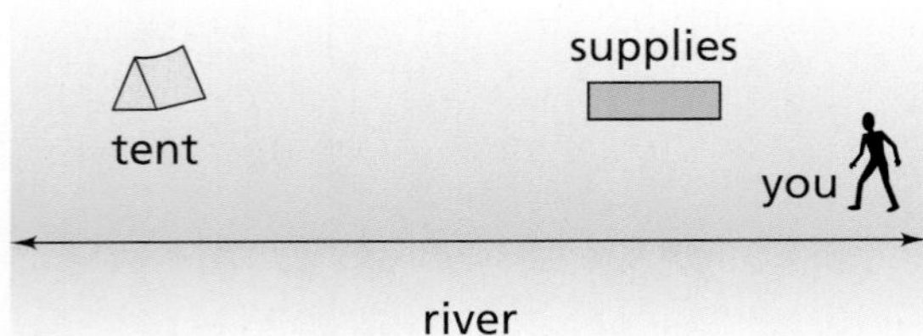

4. Copy each figure and point P on a separate piece of paper. Draw the image of each figure for the given rotation about P.

a. 60° b. 45° c. 150°

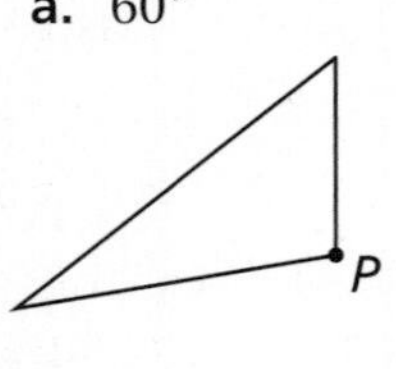

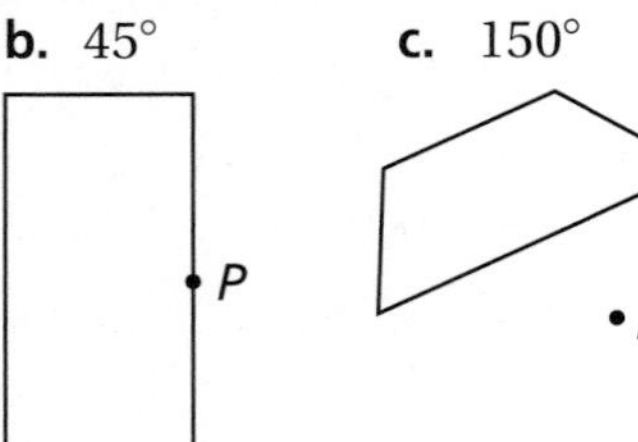

5. One endpoint of a circle's diameter is $(8, -2)$. If the center of the circle is $(5, -6)$, what are the coordinates of the other endpoint of the diameter?

6. The center of a certain equilateral triangle is $(5, 4)$. Give two sets of coordinates that could be the vertices of the triangle.

7. Find the coordinates of a point that is collinear with $J(5, -9)$ and $K(12, -3)$. Explain your reasoning.

8. The midpoint of a segment that is 7 units long is $(6, -3)$. For each condition below, give possible coordinates of the endpoints of this segment.
   a. The segment is horizontal.
   b. The segment is vertical.
   c. The segment is neither horizontal nor vertical.

9. Determine whether the following statements are *true* or *false*. If a statement is false, give a counterexample.
   a. If two nonvertical lines are parallel, then their slopes are equal.
   b. The product of the slopes of two nonvertical perpendicular lines is -1.

10. Write an equation of the line that is perpendicular to each line through the given point.
    a. $3x - 2y = 12$; $(0, 0)$
    b. $-x + 6y = 9$; $(2, 3)$

11. Find the following distances.
    a. from $(2, 0)$ to the line with equation $4x - 6y = 24$
    b. from $(-4, 5)$ to the line through $(6, 2)$ and $(-3, 5)$

12. Find a point that is collinear with $J(3, 5)$ and $K(5, 11)$.

13. A parallelogram has a base of 20 inches and a height of 12 inches. You dilate the parallelogram by the factor 2.5. What are the base and height of the resulting parallelogram?

14. Find the coordinates of the midpoint of each segment.

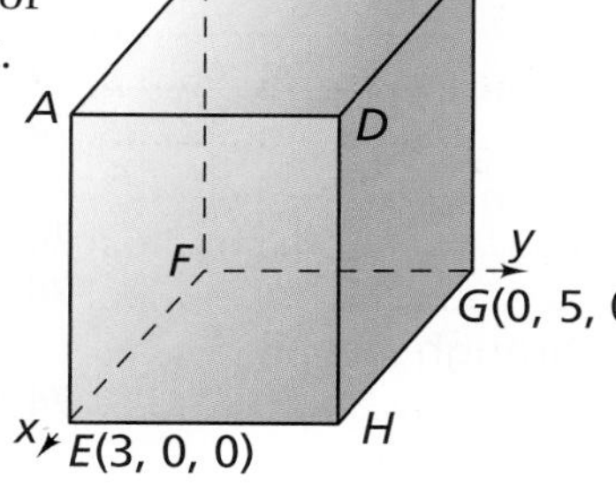

a. $\overline{AC}$

b. $\overline{DF}$

c. $\overline{BG}$

15. A cube has a side length of 8. One vertex of the cube is at the origin.

a. Draw a picture that illustrates this situation.

b. What is the length of a diagonal of the cube?

16. Given $A(2, 3)$ and $B(5, 10)$, find a vector that meets the following requirements.

- starts at the origin
- has the same direction as $\overrightarrow{AB}$
- is three times longer than $\overrightarrow{AB}$

17. Suppose that you have points $A(-5, 5)$ and $B(4, 8)$.

a. For what value of k does the head of $\overrightarrow{A(A + kB)}$ lie on the line $y = 3$?

b. For what value of k does the head of $\overrightarrow{A(A + kB)}$ lie on the line $x = -2$?

18. You are given points $J(2, 6)$ and $K(5, 9)$.

a. Calculate head minus tail for $\overrightarrow{JK}$. Draw a diagram that shows both $\overrightarrow{JK}$ and $\overrightarrow{O(K - J)}$. You have moved $\overrightarrow{JK}$ to the origin.

b. Move the tail of $\overrightarrow{O(K - J)}$ to $L(3, -1)$ by adding L to the head and to the tail. Draw this new vector. What are the coordinates of its head and tail?

19. Returning from a hike, you see that your tent is on fire. The stream is nearby, but you want to be sure you go to the point in the stream that minimizes the total distance you travel. Explain how you can use the reflection method to find this point.

20. Given: $\overline{AB} \parallel \overline{CD}$; $\overline{AB} \cong \overline{CD}$

Prove: E is the midpoint of $\overline{AD}$ and $\overline{BC}$.

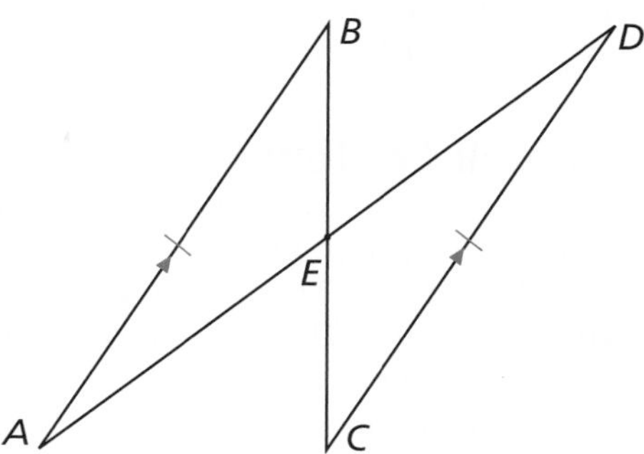

21. The vertices of $\triangle ABC$ are $A(-3, 5)$, $B(3, 5)$, and $C(0, 0)$.

a. Is $\triangle ABC$ equilateral, isosceles or scalene? Explain.

b. The coordinates of point P are $(1, 3)$. Find the sum of the distances from P to each *side* of the triangle.

c. Find the height of $\triangle ABC$ with respect to base $\overline{AB}$.

22. A path on the coordinate plane must go from $A(3, 4)$, to line ℓ with equation $x = 1$, to line m with equation $x = 6$, to $B(5, -4)$.

a. Graph the shortest path.

b. Suppose C is the point where the path intersects ℓ, and D is the point where the path intersects m. What are the coordinates of C and D?

23. a. Construct a square.

b. Construct a rectangle, such that the area of the rectangle is equal to the area of the square.

c. How does the perimeter of the square compare to the perimeter of the rectangle?

24. a. Describe a situation in which there is more than one way to maximize a certain area.

b. Describe a situation in which there is more than one way to minimize a certain area.

TI-Nspire Handbook

TI-Nspire™ Technology Handbook

Recognizing how to use technology to support your mathematics is an important habit of mind. Although the use of technology in this course is independent of any particular hardware or software, this handbook gives examples of how you can apply the TI-Nspire™ handheld technology.

Handbook Contents

Placing a Point on an Object, Lesson 1.11

1. Choose the **Point On** option in the **Points & Lines** menu.

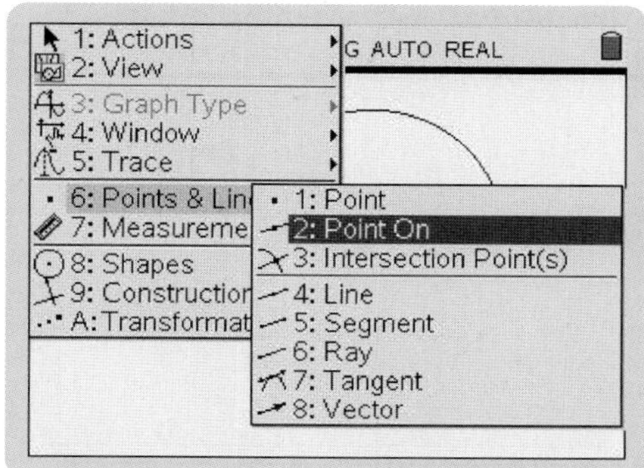

2. Position the pointer on the object. Press .

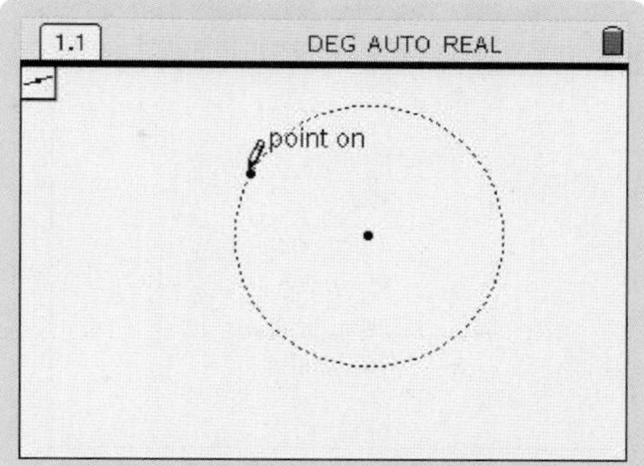

Constructing a Line Through Two Points, Lesson 1.07

1. Choose the **Line** option in the **Points & Lines** menu.

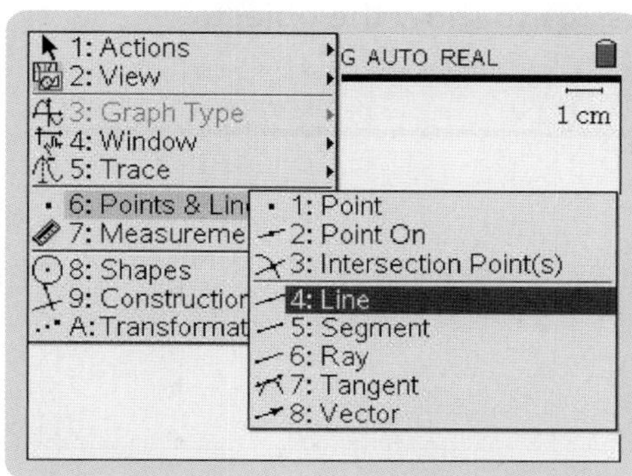

2. Position the pointer on a point. Press . Position the pointer on the other point. Press .

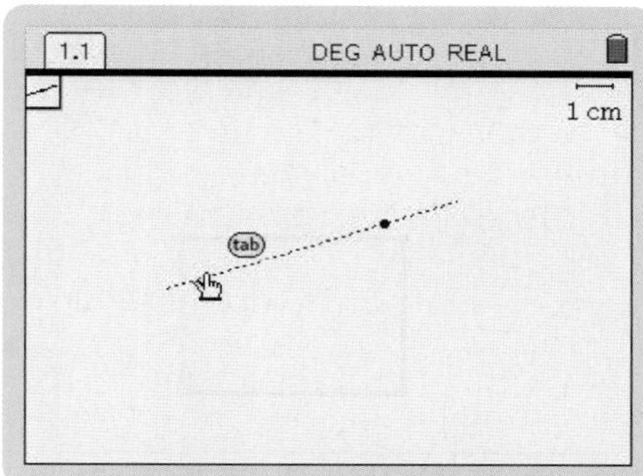

Constructing a Ray Through Two Points, Lesson 1.07

1. Choose the **Ray** option in the **Points & Lines** menu.

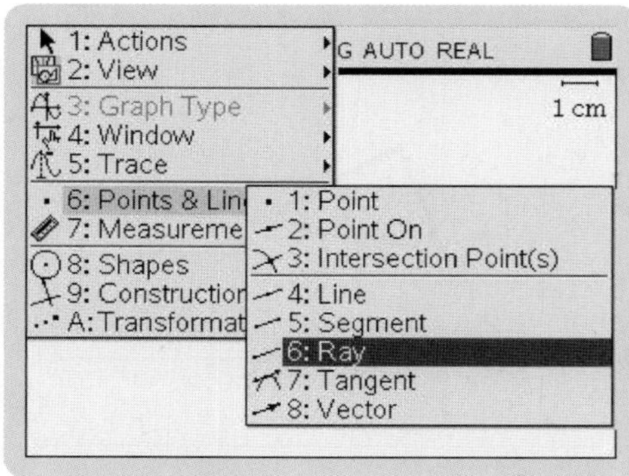

2. Position the pointer on the endpoint of the ray. Press . Position the pointer on the other point and press .

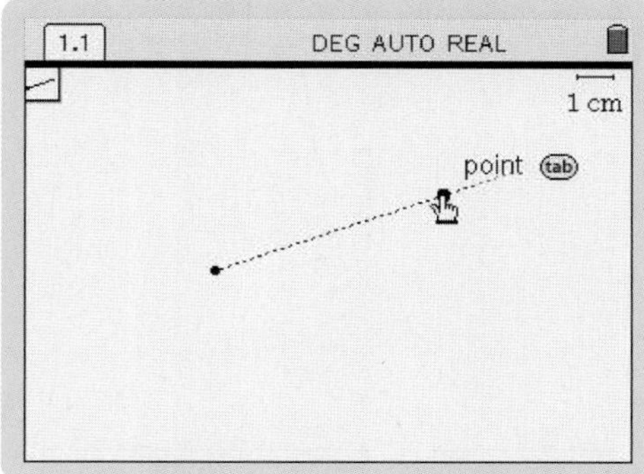

Dragging an Object, Lesson 1.09

1. Position the cursor on the object. Press ctrl ⊛.

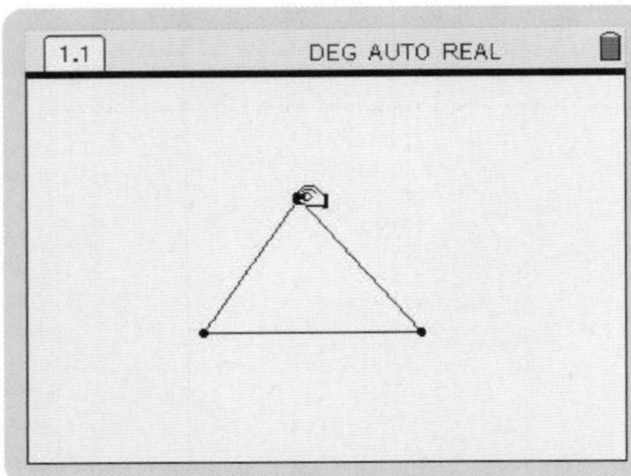

2. Drag the object to the desired location. Press ⊛.

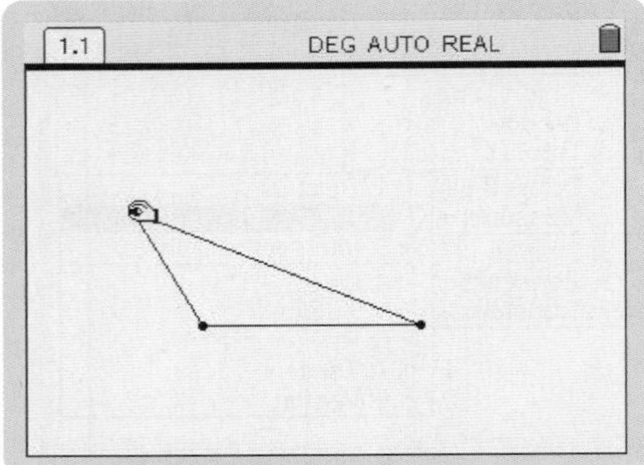

Hiding/Showing an Object, Lesson 1.08

1. Select **Hide/Show** from the **Actions** menu. Position the pointer on the object. Press ⊛ to hide the object.

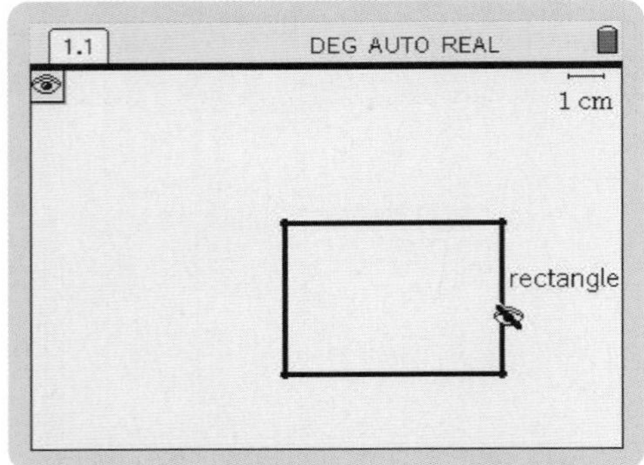

2. Select **Hide/Show** from the **Actions** menu. Position the pointer on the hidden object. Press ⊛ to show the object.

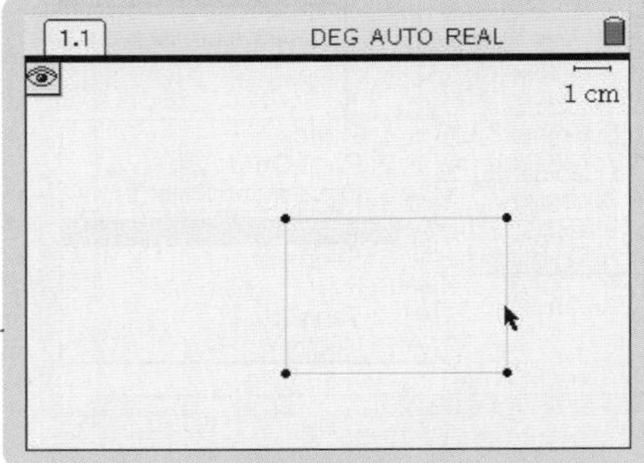

Deleting an Object, Lesson 1.08

1. Position the pointer anywhere on the object. Press ⊛ ⟵.

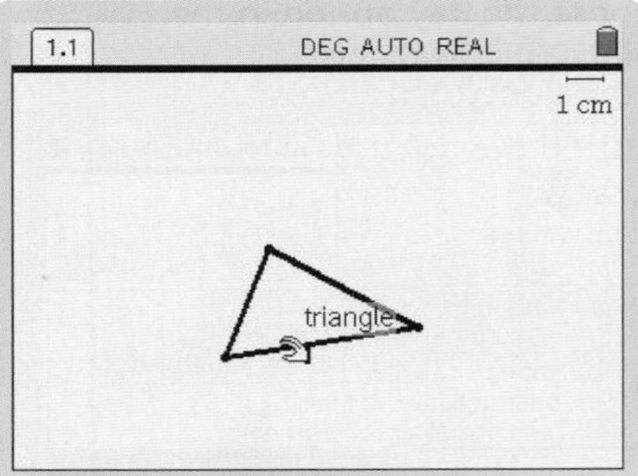

Constructing a Line Perpendicular to a Given Line Through a Given Point, Lessons 1.08, 2.05

1. Choose the **Perpendicular** option in the **Construction** menu.

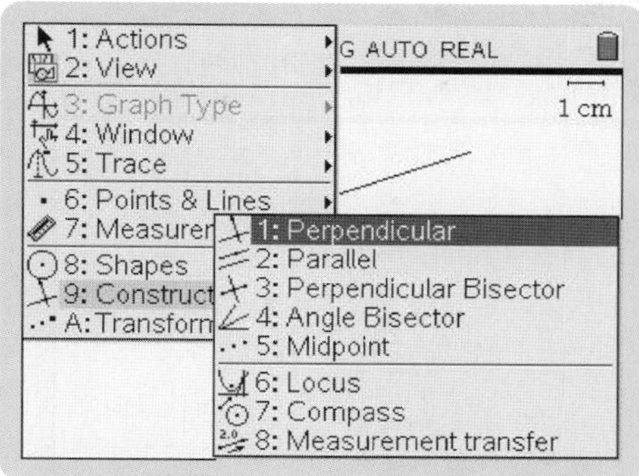

2. Position the pointer on the given line. Press . Position the pointer on the given point. Press .

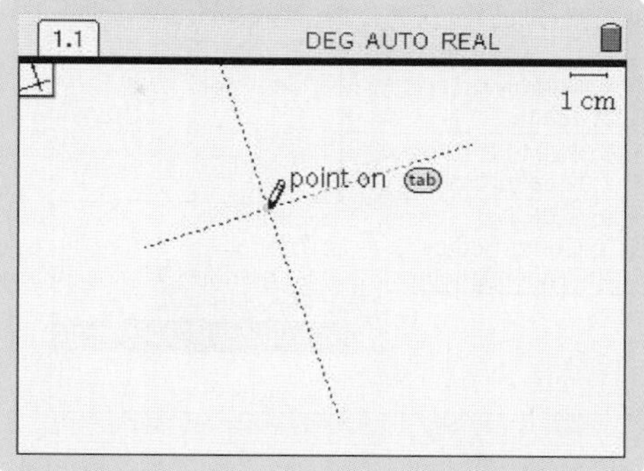

Constructing a Line Parallel to a Given Line Through a Given Point, Lessons 1.08, 2.05

1. Choose the **Parallel** option in the **Construction** menu.

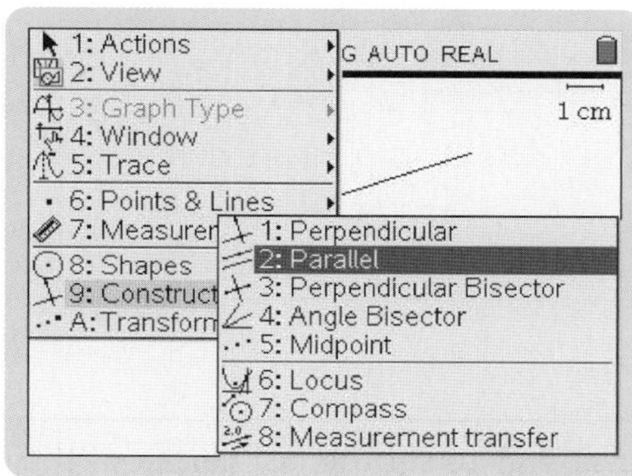

2. Position the pointer on the given line. Press . Position the pointer on the given point. Press .

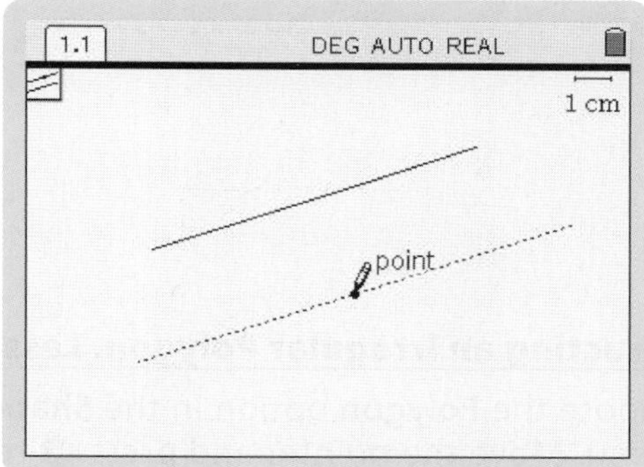

Constructing the Perpendicular Bisector of a Segment, Lesson 1.12

1. Choose the **Perpendicular Bisector** option in the **Construction** menu.
2. Position the pointer on the segment. Press .

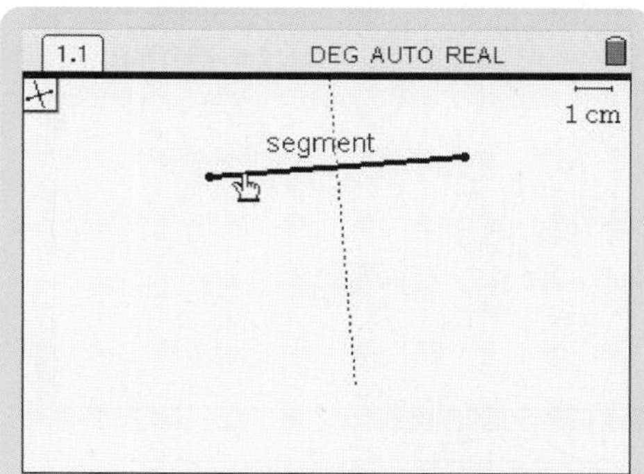

Constructing a Regular Polygon, Lesson 1.10

1. Choose the **Regular Polygon** option in the **Shapes** menu.

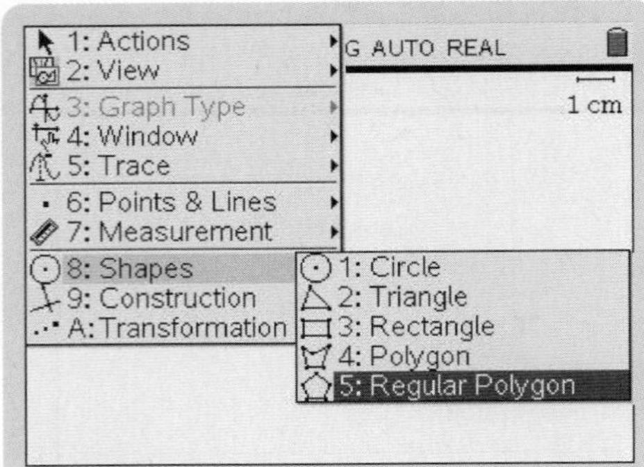

2. Press to set the center of the regular polygon. Move the pointer away from the center. Press to set a vertex.

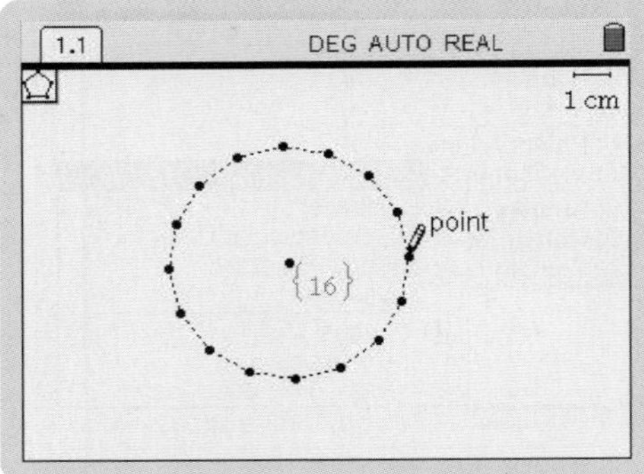

3. To reduce the number of sides, move the pointer clockwise around the polygon. When the polygon has the desired number of sides, press .

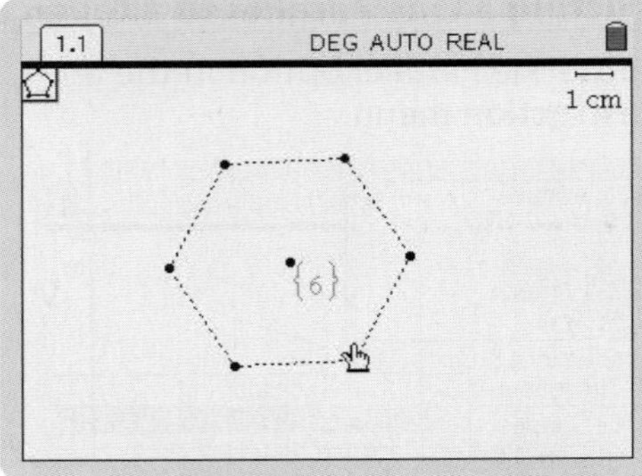

Constructing an Irregular Polygon, Lesson 1.12

1. Choose the **Polygon** option in the **Shapes** menu. Move the pointer and press to set each vertex.

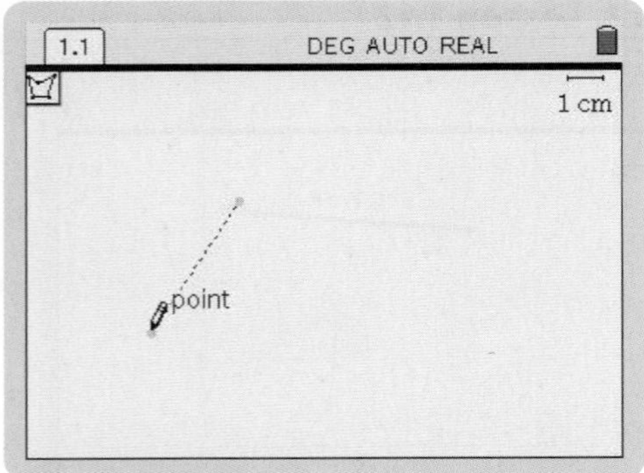

2. Press to set the last vertex of the polygon.

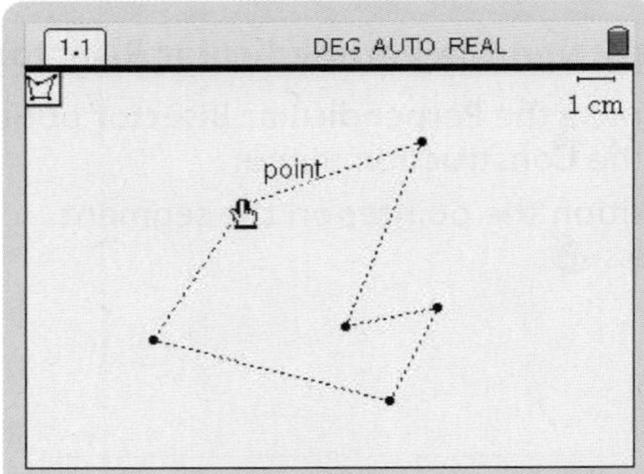

Constructing a Circle With a Given Center Through a Given Point, Lesson 1.09

1. Choose the **Circle** option in the **Shapes** menu.

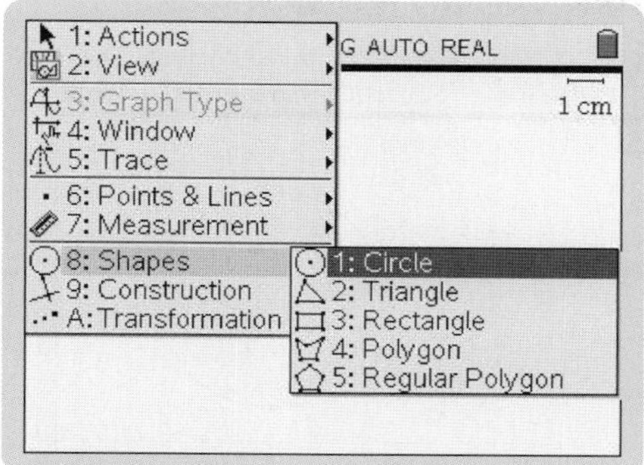

2. Position the pointer on the given center. Press [click]. Position the pointer on the given point. Press [click].

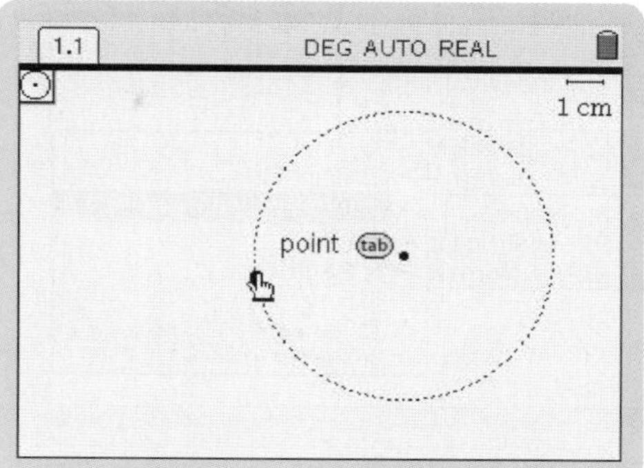

Constructing a Circle With a Given Center and Radius Length, Lesson 1.09

1. Use the **Text** tool in the **Actions** menu. Write the radius.

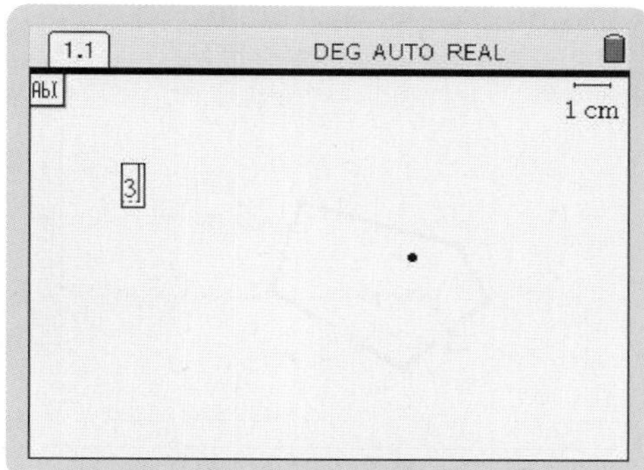

2. Choose the **Compass** option in the **Construction** menu.

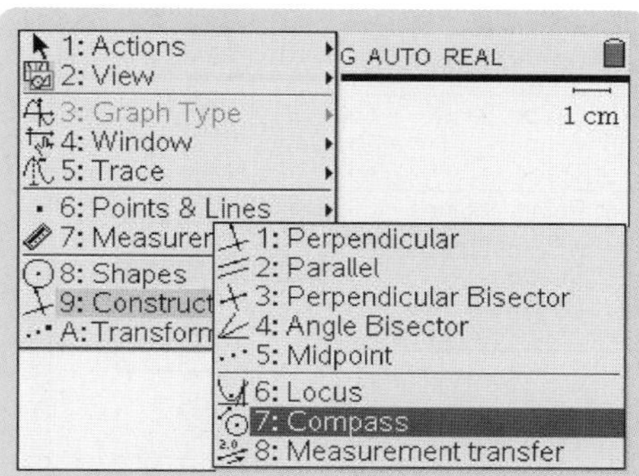

3. Position the pointer on the given center. Press [click].
4. Select the radius length on the screen. Press [click].

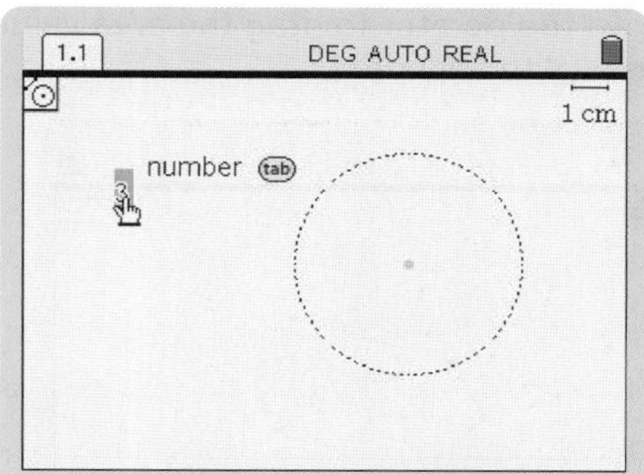

Finding the Intersection(s) of Two Objects, Lesson 5.08

1. Choose the **Intersection Point(s)** option in the **Points & Lines** menu.

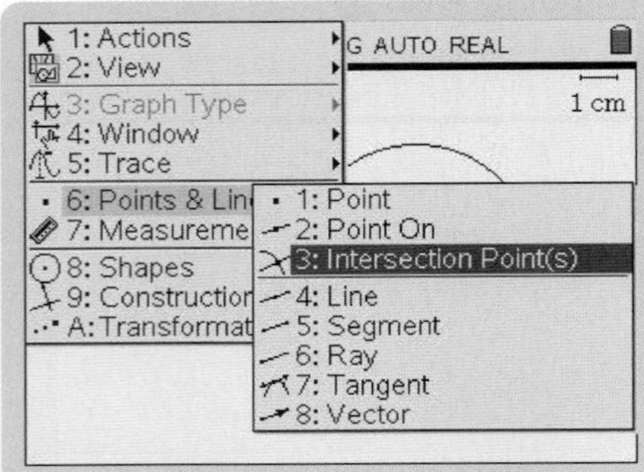

2. Position the pointer on the first object. Press ⊛. Position the pointer on the second object. Press ⊛.

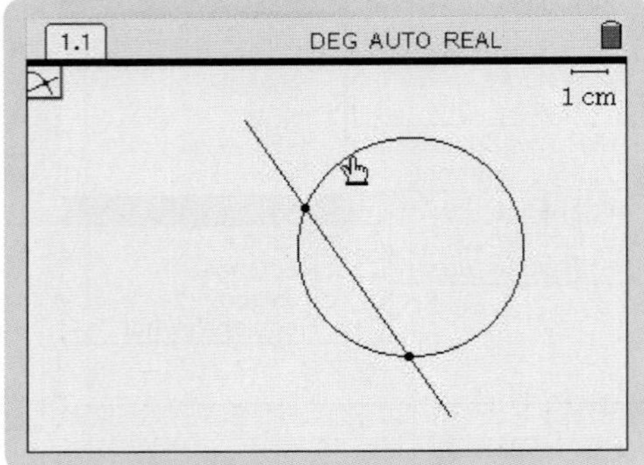

Finding the Area of a Polygon, Lessons 1.11, 4.06

1. Choose the **Area** option in the **Measurement** menu.

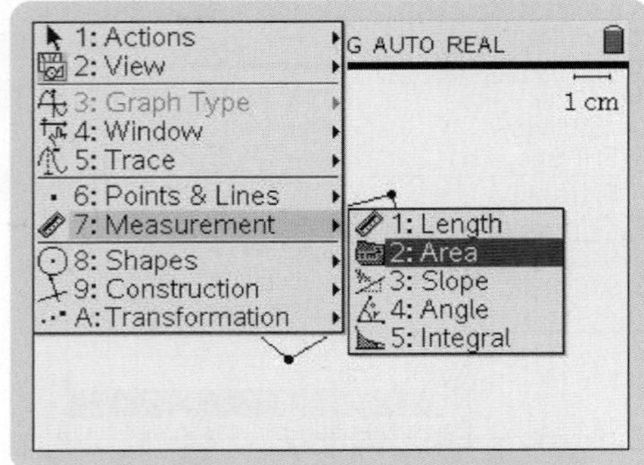

2. Place the pointer on the polygon. Press ⊛.

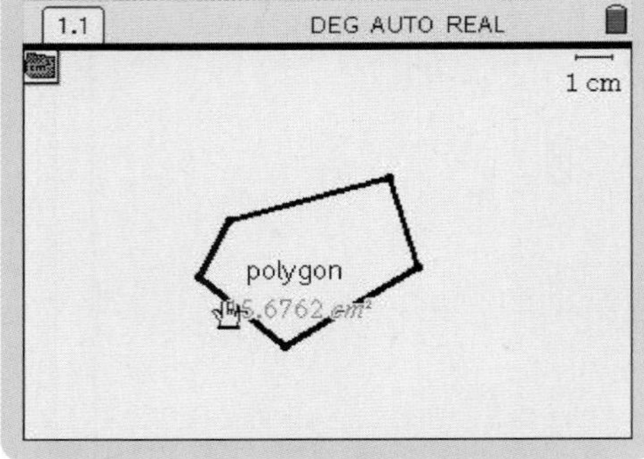

3. Move the pointer to drag the area value. Press ⊛ to anchor it.

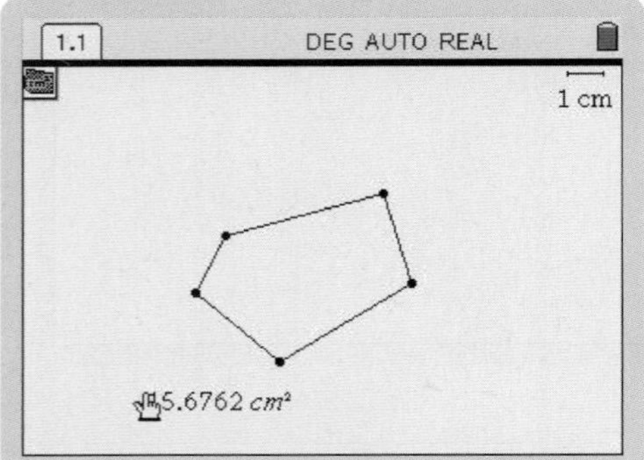

Measuring an Angle (in degrees), Lesson 2.05

1. Check that the system settings show degree mode.
2. Choose the **Angle** option in the **Measurement** menu.

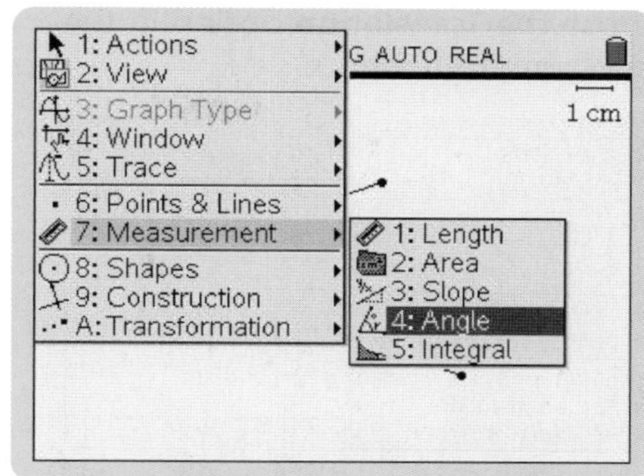

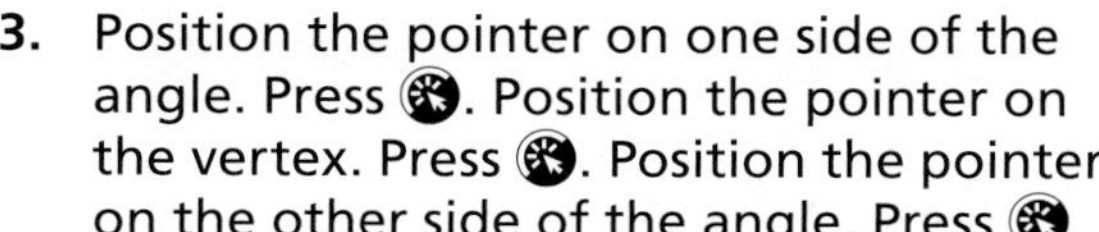

3. Position the pointer on one side of the angle. Press ⊛. Position the pointer on the vertex. Press ⊛. Position the pointer on the other side of the angle. Press ⊛.

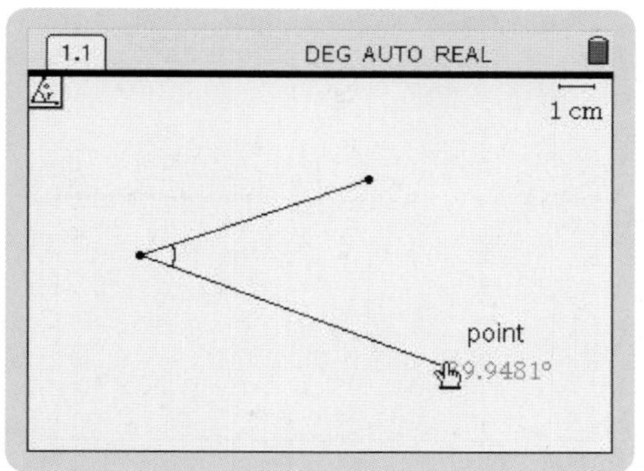

4. Move the pointer to drag the measurement. Press ⊛ to anchor it.

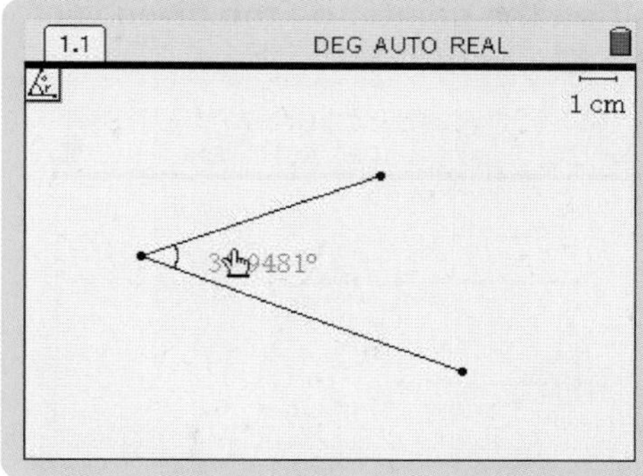

Measuring a Segment, Lesson 1.09

1. Choose the **Length** option in the **Measurement** menu. Position the pointer on the segment. Press ⊛.

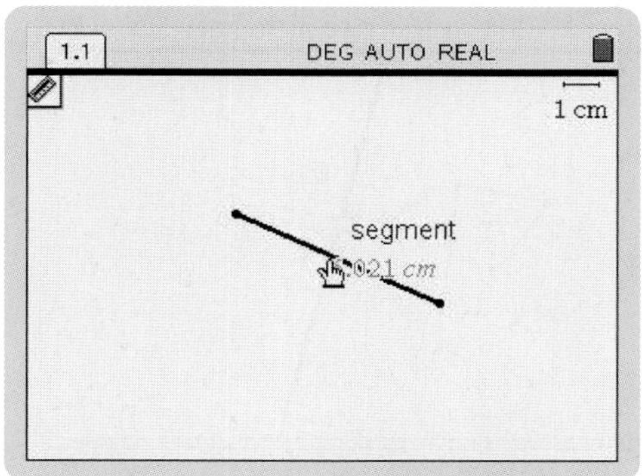

2. Move the pointer to drag the measurement. Press ⊛ to anchor it.

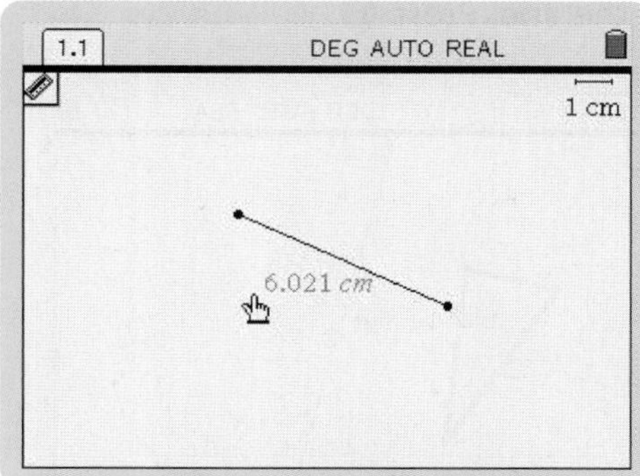

Translating an Object by a Given Vector, Lesson 7.03

1. Choose the **Translation** option in the **Transformation** menu.

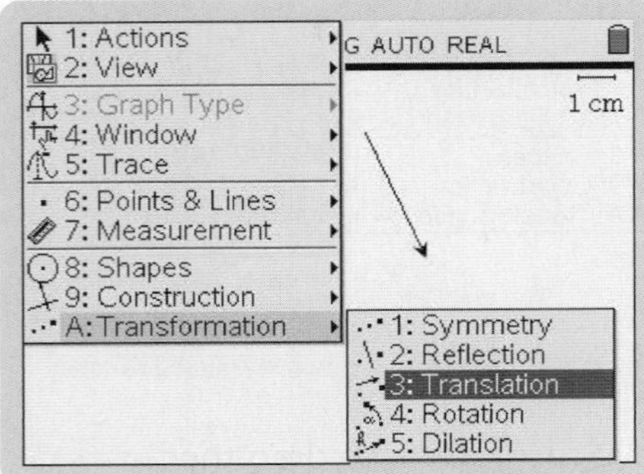

2. Position the pointer on the object. Press .

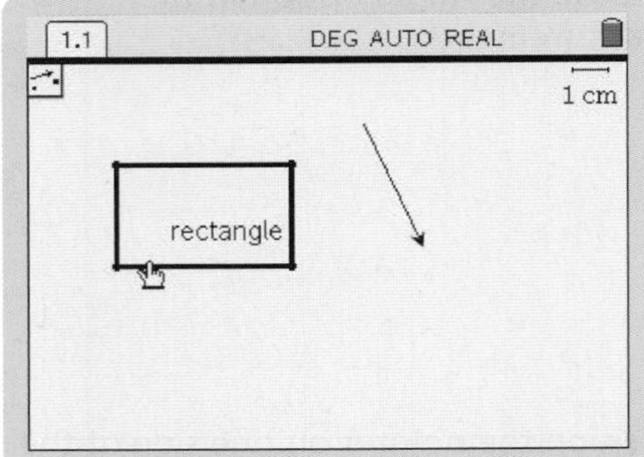

3. Position the pointer on the given vector. Press .

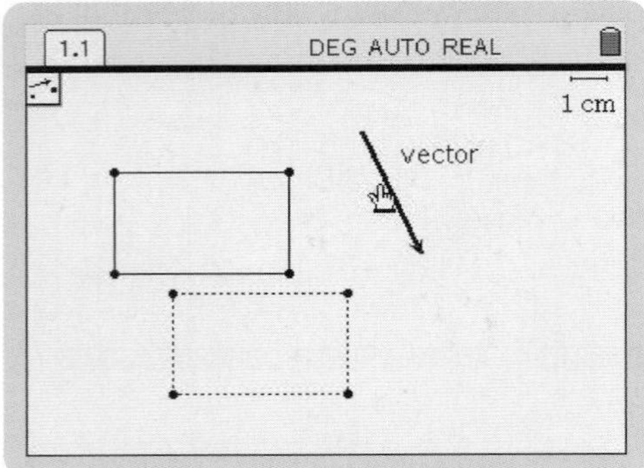

Reflecting an Object Over a Line, Lesson 7.02

1. Choose the **Reflection** option in the **Transformation** menu. Position the pointer on the line. Press .

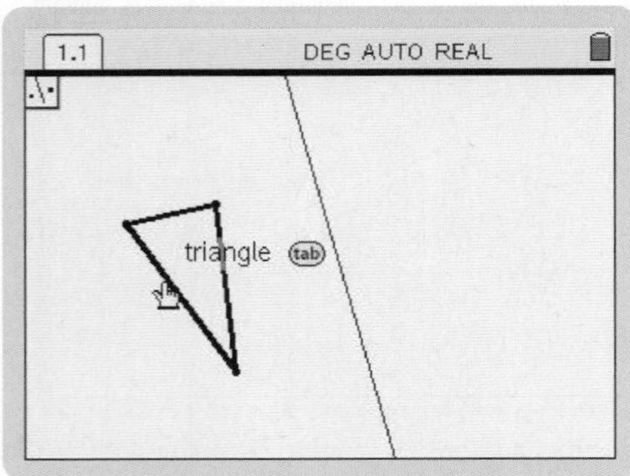

2. Position the pointer on the object. Press .

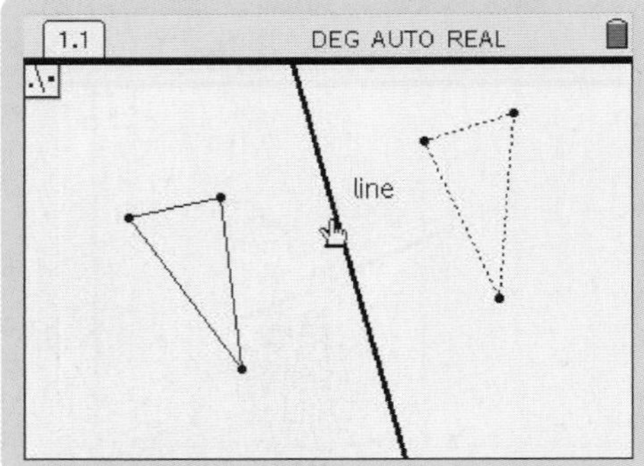

Rotating an Object About a Point by a Given Number of Degrees, Lesson 7.04

1. Check that the system settings show degree mode.
2. Use the **Text** tool in the **Tools** menu. Write the given number of degrees.

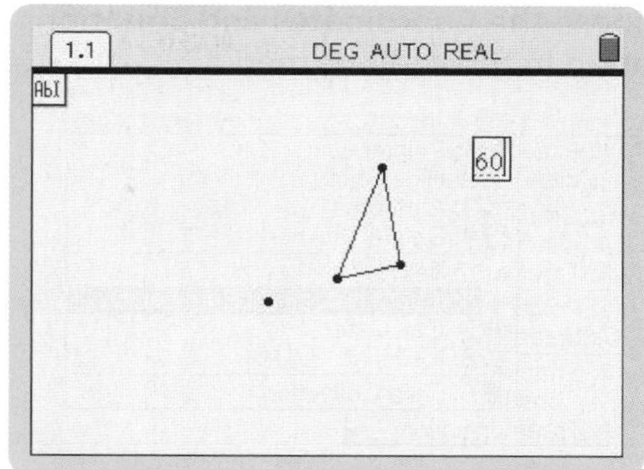

3. Choose the **Rotation** option in the **Transformation** menu.

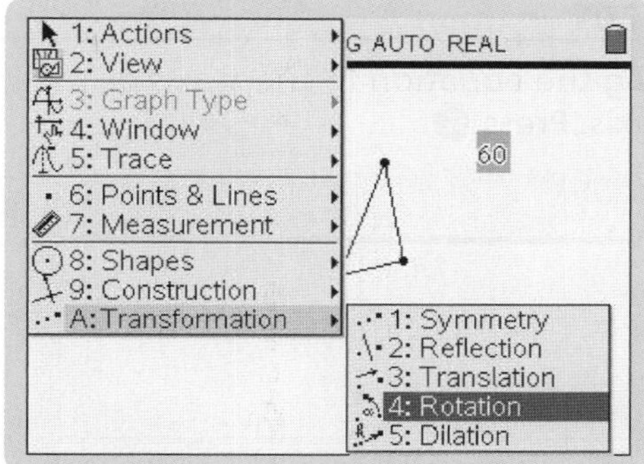

4. Place the pointer on the center of rotation. Press ⊛.

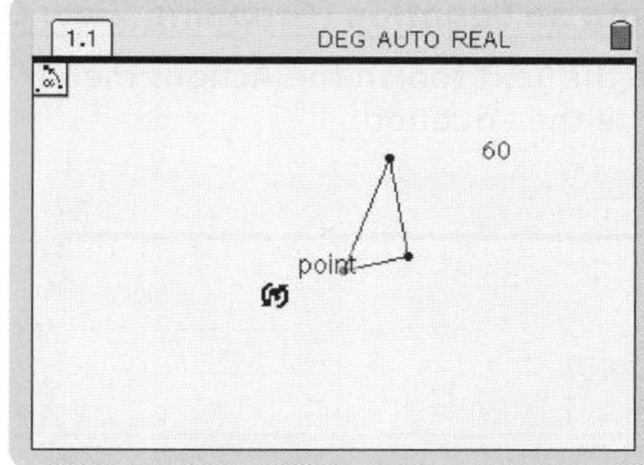

5. Place the pointer on the object. Press ⊛.

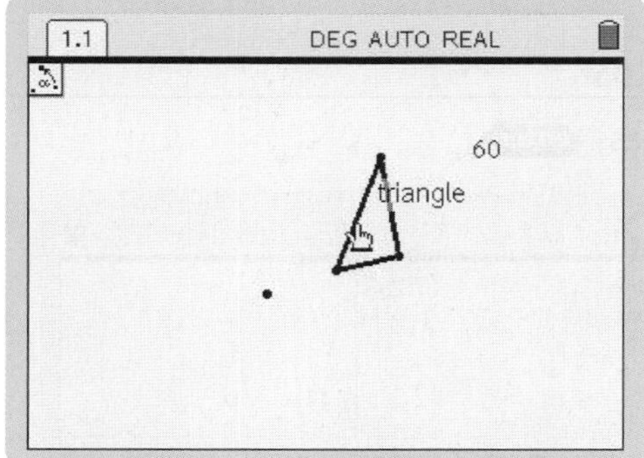

6. Select the angle of rotation on the screen. Press ⊛.

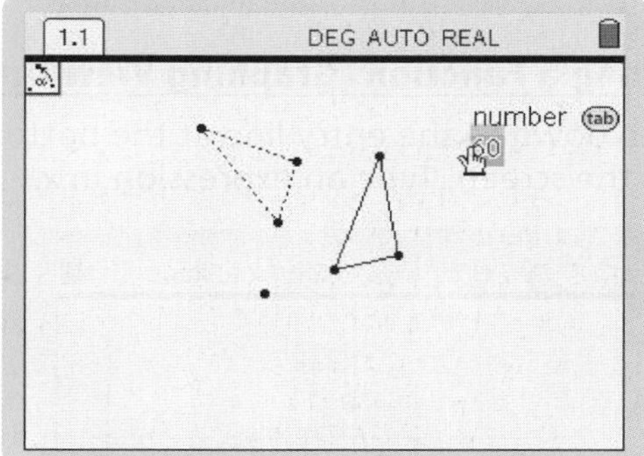

Finding the Coordinates of a Point (Graphing View Only), Lesson 7.03

1. Choose the **Coordinates and Equations** option in the **Actions** menu.

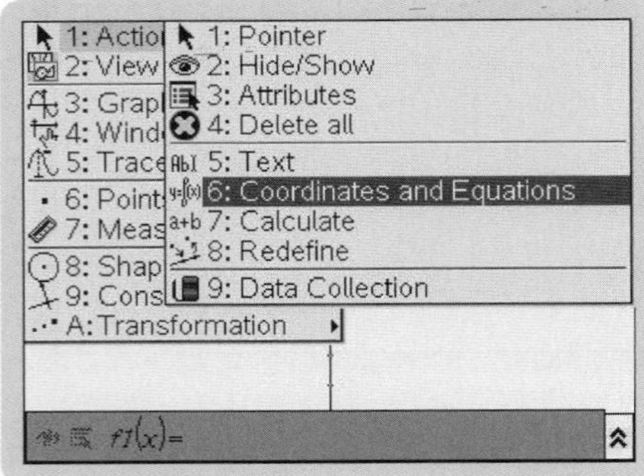

2. Position the pointer on the point. Press the click button. Press the click button to anchor the label.

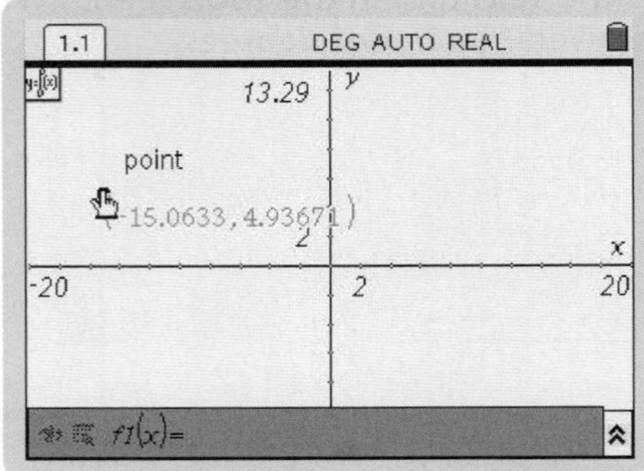

Graphing an Equation (Graphing View Only), Lesson 7.01

1. Use the **Text** tool in the **Actions** menu. Write the equation.

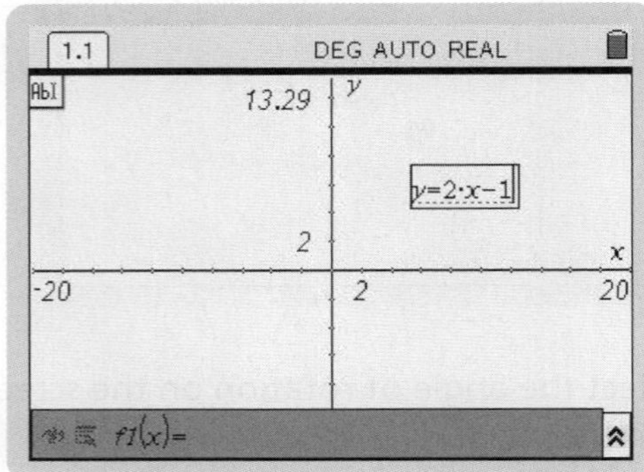

2. Drag the equation to the x-axis or the y-axis. Press the click button.

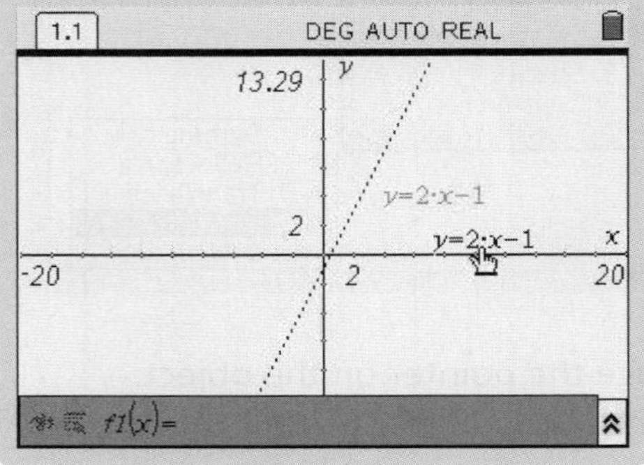

Graphing a Function (Graphing View Only), Lesson 8.05

1. Tab down to the entry line at the bottom of the screen. Type an expression in x.

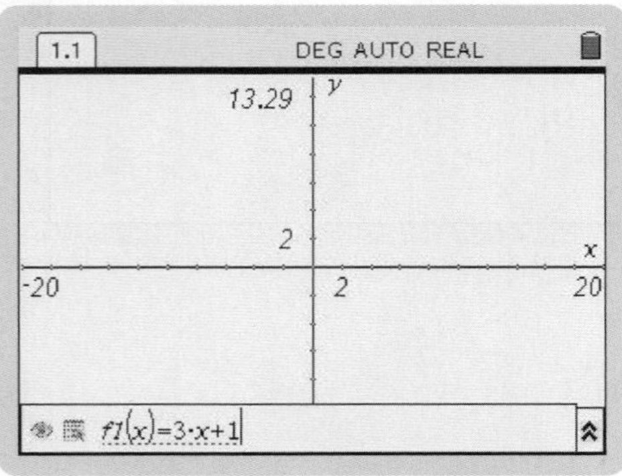

2. Press enter.

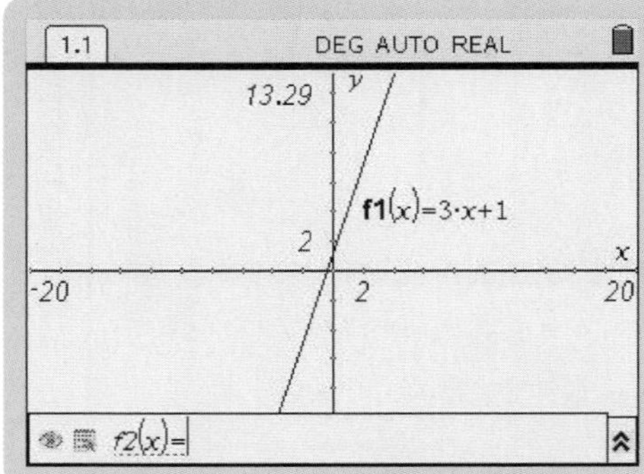

Scaling a Figure, Lesson 4.06

1. Use **Rectangle** in the **Shapes** menu. Construct a rectangle

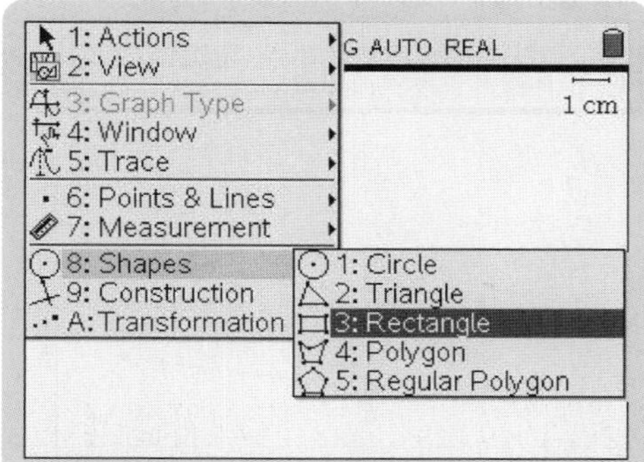

2. Use **Text** in the **Actions** menu. Label the rectangle.

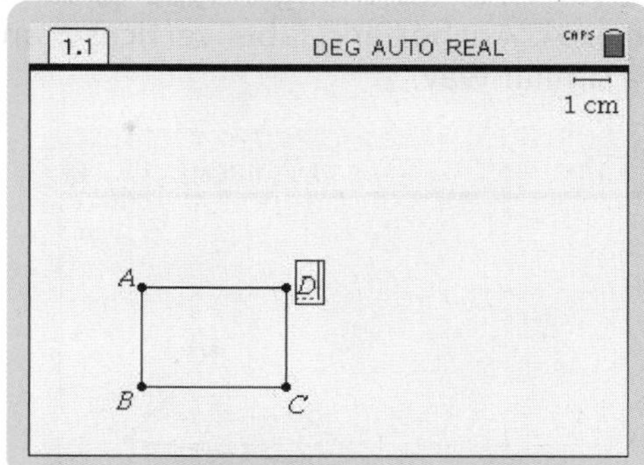

3. Use **Text** again. Write the scale factor on the screen.

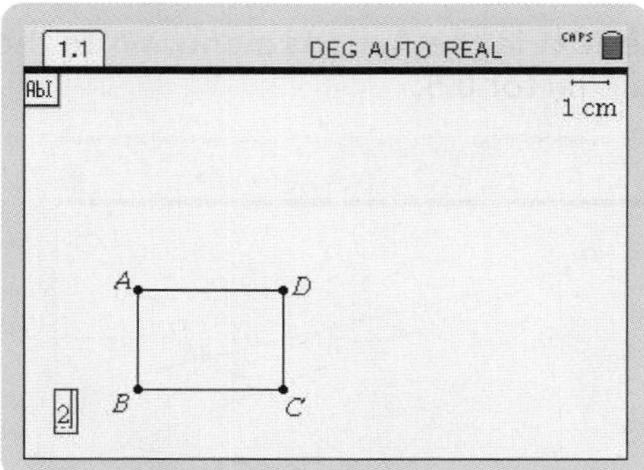

4. Choose **Dilation** in the **Transformation** menu.

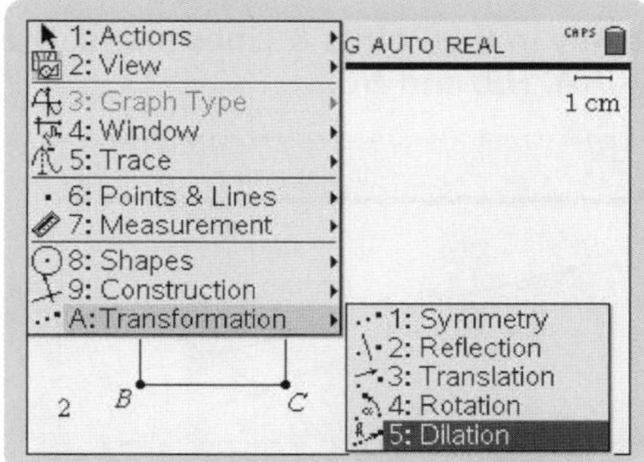

5. Select the scale factor on the screen. Press . Then select the rectangle to set the scaled rectangle. Press to anchor the scaled rectangle.

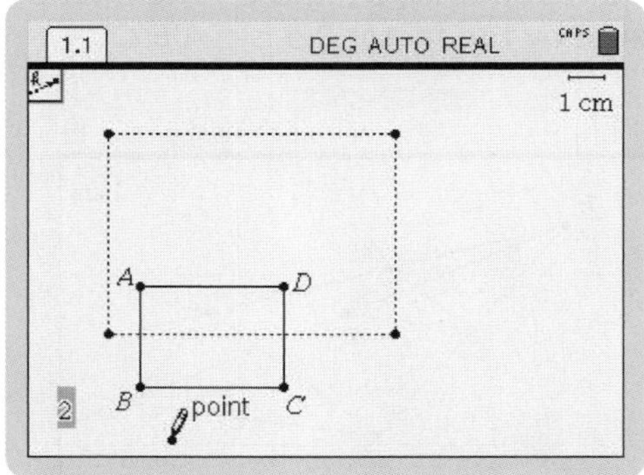

TI-Nspire Handbook

Finding a Dilation—The Ratio Method, Lesson 4.08

1. Choose **Triangle** from the **Shapes** menu. Position the pointer. Press [click] to anchor one vertex of the triangle. Type (A) to label vertex *A*. Anchor and label vertices *B* and *C* in a similar way.

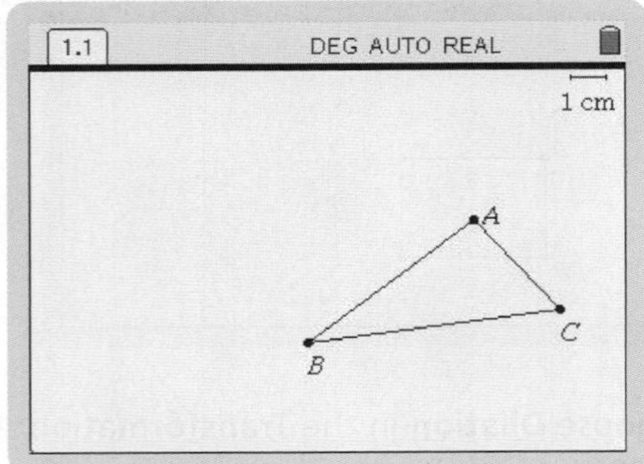

2. Choose **Point** in the **Points & Lines** menu. Position the pointer outside the triangle. Press [click]. Type (H) to label point *H*.

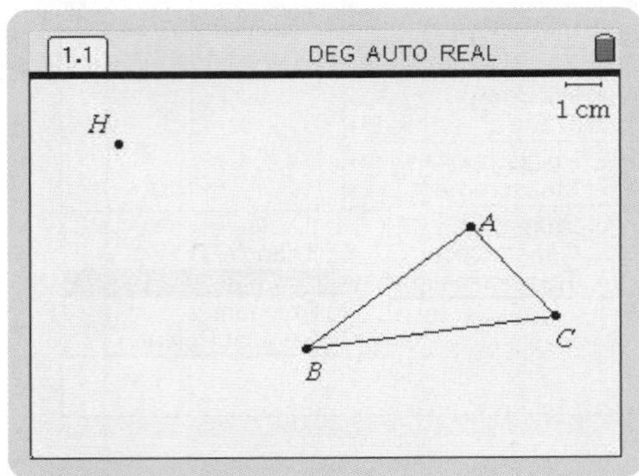

3. Use **Ray** in the **Points & Lines** menu. Draw rays *HA*, *HB*, and *HC*.

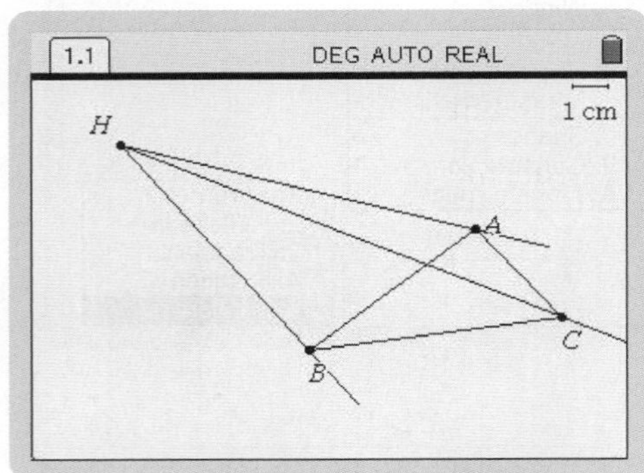

4. Use **Text** in the **Actions** menu. Write the scale factor 0.5.

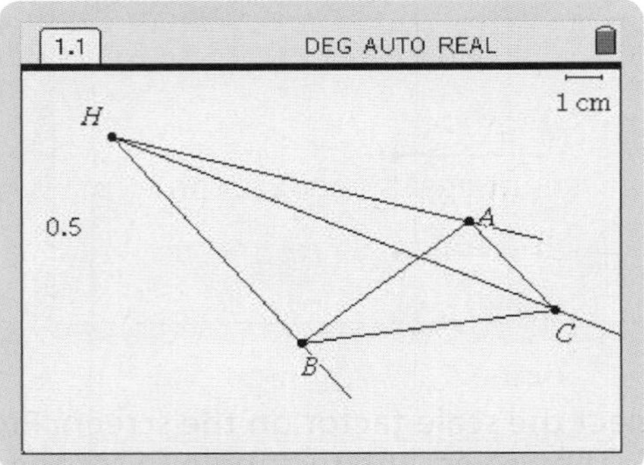

5. Choose **Dilation** in the **Transformation** menu. Click point *H*, point *A*, and the scale factor. The dilated point appears on ray *HA*. Label the dilated point *A′*. Scale points *B* and *C* in a similar way.

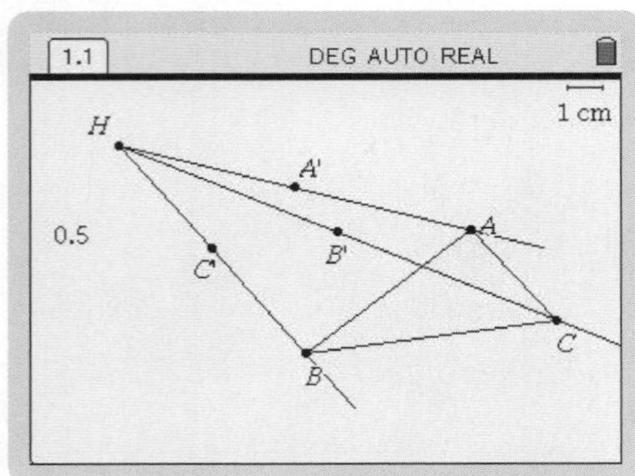

6. Use **Segment** in the **Points & Lines** menu to join points *A′*, *B′*, and *C′*. The dilation of $\triangle ABC$ by the factor 0.5 is $\triangle A'B'C'$.

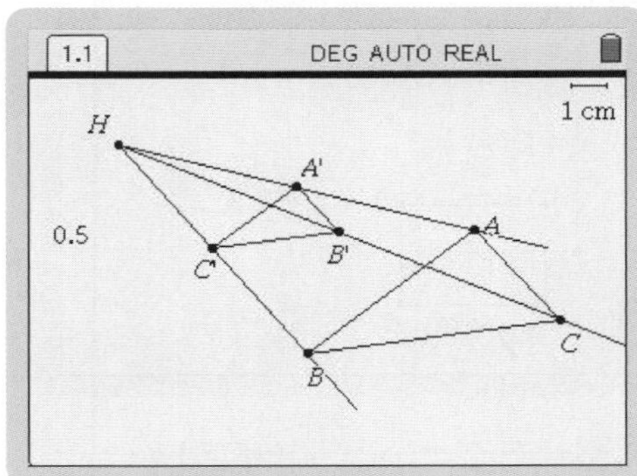

Tables

Table 1 Math Symbols

Symbol	Meaning
$\ldots$	and so on
$=$	is equal to
$\approx$	is approximately equal to
$\neq$	is not equal to
$>$	is greater than
$\geq$	is greater than or equal to
$<$	is less than
$\leq$	is less than or equal to
$\cdot, \times$	multiplication
$+$	addition
$-$	subtraction
$\pm$	plus or minus
$\mapsto$	which gives, leads to, maps to
$a_n \to r$	a_n approaches r
n^2	n squared
$\sqrt{x}$	nonnegative square root of x
Δ	difference (delta)
$\Leftrightarrow$	if and only if
A	point A
A'	image of A, A prime
$\overleftrightarrow{AB}$	line through A and B
$\overline{AB}$	segment with endpoints A and B
$\overrightarrow{AB}$	ray with endpoint A through B
$\overrightarrow{AB}$	vector with tail A and head B
AB	length of $\overline{AB}$
$\parallel$	is parallel to
$\perp$	is perpendicular to
$\cong$	is congruent to
$\sim$	is similar to
$\angle A$	angle A
$\angle ABC$	angle with sides $\overline{BA}$ and $\overline{BC}$
$m\angle A$	measure of angle A
$^\circ$	degree(s)
$\triangle ABC$	triangle with vertices A, B, and C
$\square ABCD$	parallelogram with vertices A, B, C, and D
n-gon	polygon with n sides
s	length of a side
b	base length
h	height, length of an altitude
a	apothem
P	perimeter
A	area
B	area of a base
L.A.	lateral surface area
S.A.	total surface area
ℓ	slant height
V	volume
d	diameter
r	radius
C	circumference
π	pi, the ratio of the circumference of a circle to its diameter
$\odot A$	circle with center A
$\widehat{AB}$	arc with endpoints A and B
$\widehat{ABC}$	arc with endpoints A and C and containing B
$m\widehat{AB}$	measure of $\widehat{AB}$
$a : b, \frac{a}{b}$	ratio of a to b
$\sin A$	sine of $\angle A$
$\cos A$	cosine of $\angle A$
$\tan A$	tangent of $\angle A$
$\sin^{-1} x$	inverse sine of x
$\Pi(P)$	power of point P

Table 2 Formulas

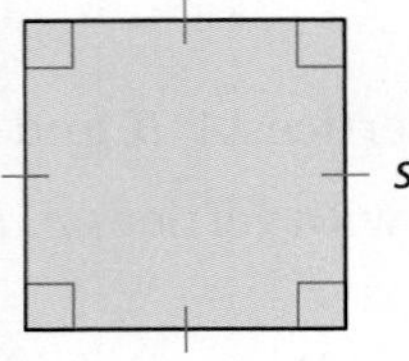

$P = 4s$
$A = s^2$

Square

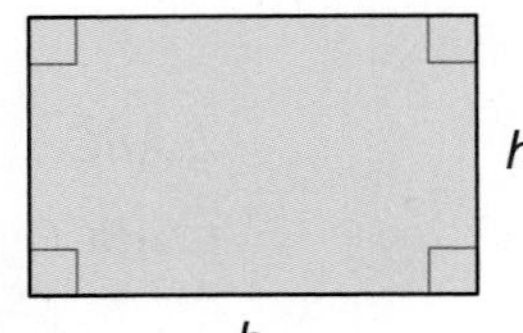

$P = 2b + 2h$
$A = bh$

Rectangle

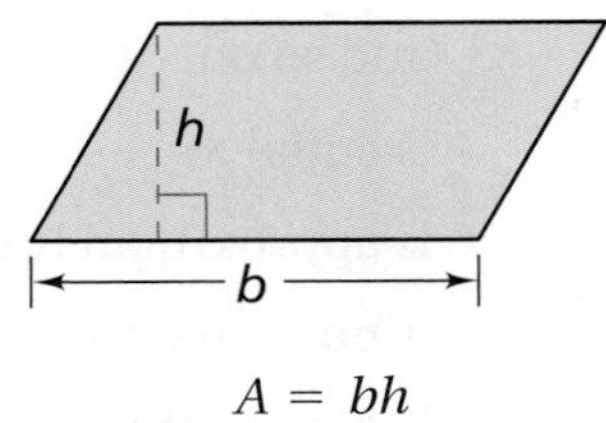

$A = bh$

Parallelogram

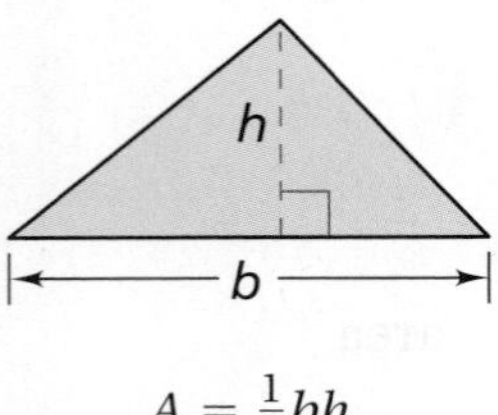

$A = \frac{1}{2}bh$

Triangle

b_1, h, b_2

$A = \frac{1}{2}h(b_1 + b_2)$

Trapezoid

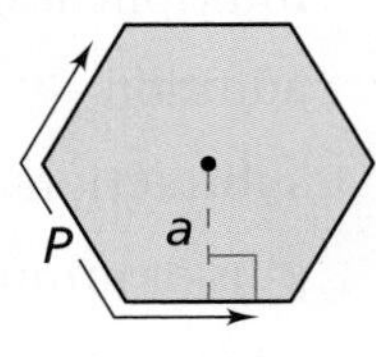

$A = \frac{1}{2}aP$

Regular Polygon

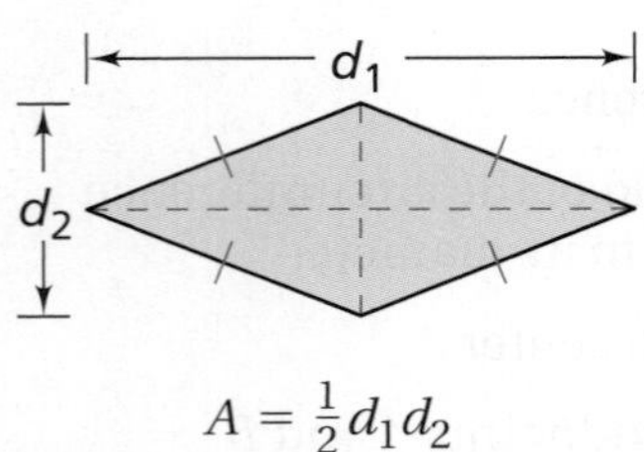

$A = \frac{1}{2}d_1d_2$

Rhombus

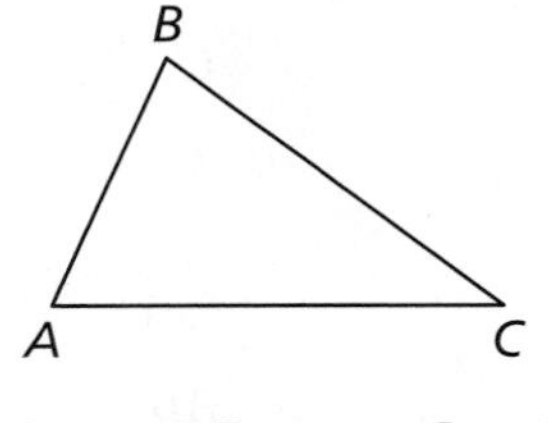

$m\angle A + m\angle B + m\angle C = 180°$

Triangle Angle Sum

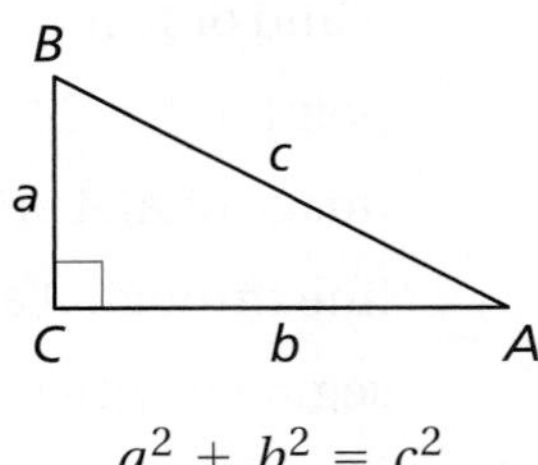

$a^2 + b^2 = c^2$

Pythagorean Theorem

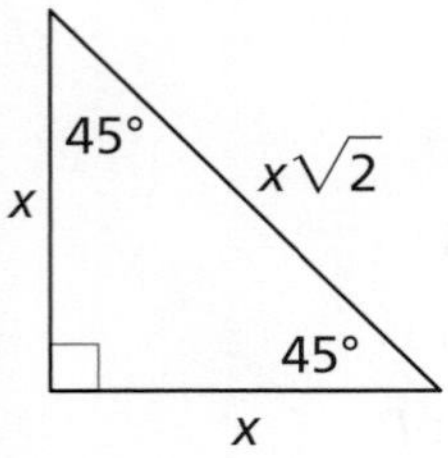

Ratio of sides $= 1 : 1 : \sqrt{2}$

45°-45°-90° Triangle

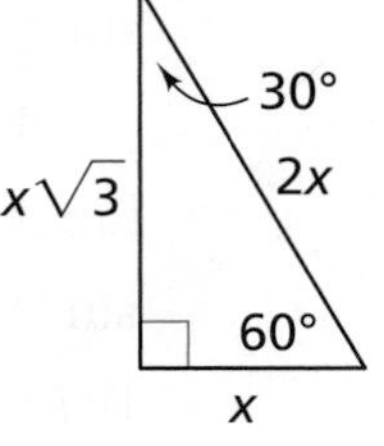

Ratio of sides $= 1 : \sqrt{3} : 2$

30°-60°-90° Triangle

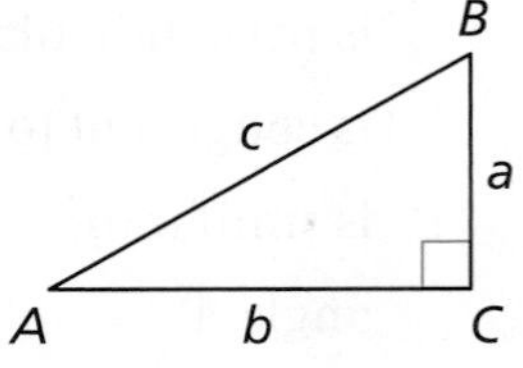

$\tan A = \frac{a}{b}$
$\sin A = \frac{a}{c} \quad \cos A = \frac{b}{c}$

Trigonometric Ratios

Table 2 Formulas (continued)

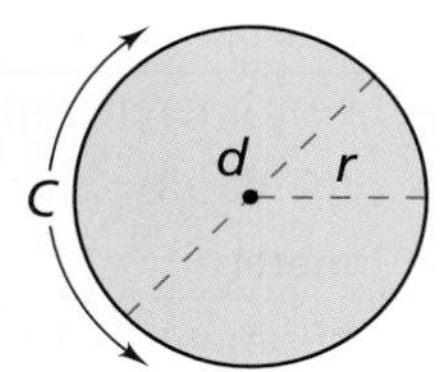

$C = \pi d$ or $C = 2\pi r$
$A = \pi r^2$

Circle

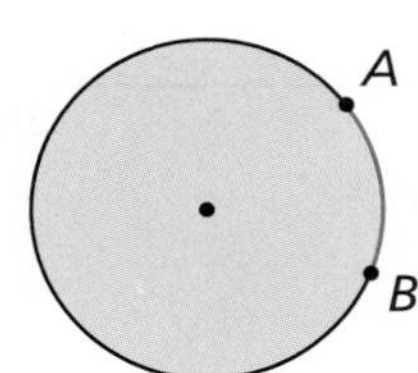

$\text{Length of } \widehat{AB} = \frac{m\widehat{AB}}{360} \cdot 2\pi r$

Arc

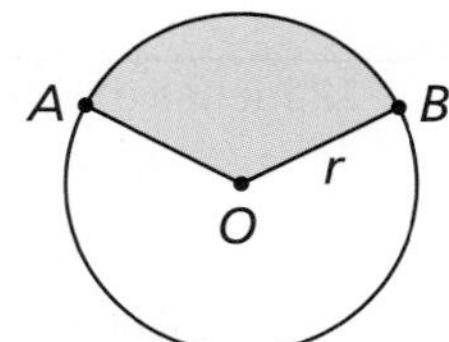

$\text{Area of sector } AOB = \frac{m\widehat{AB}}{360} \cdot \pi r^2$

Sector of a Circle

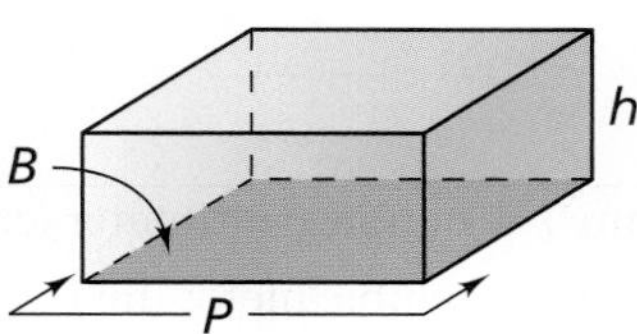

L.A. $= Ph$
S.A. $=$ L.A. $+ 2B$
$V = Bh$

Right Prism

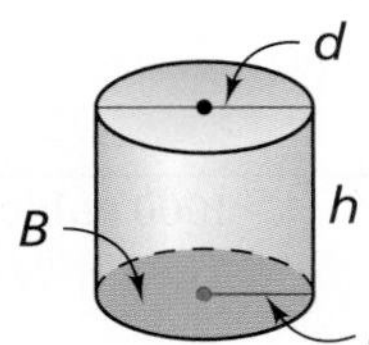

L.A. $= 2\pi rh$ or L.A. $= \pi dh$
S.A. $=$ L.A. $+ 2B$
$V = Bh$

Right Cylinder

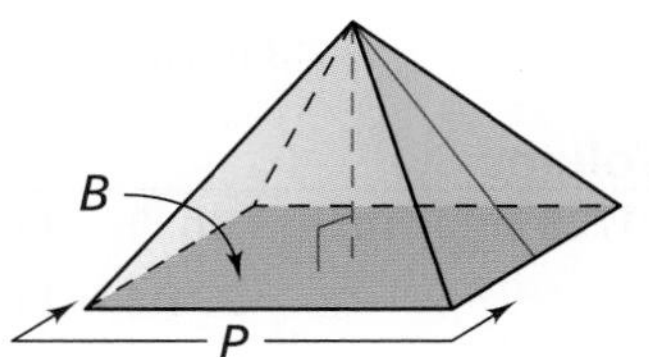

L.A. $= \frac{1}{2}P\ell$
S.A. $=$ L.A. $+ B$
$V = \frac{1}{3}Bh$

Regular Pyramid

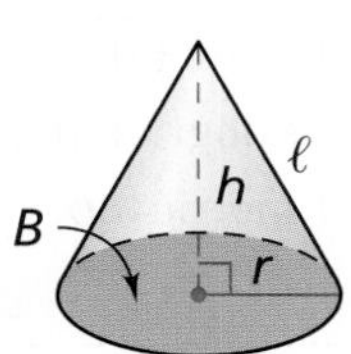

L.A. $= \pi r\ell$
S.A. $=$ L.A. $+ B$
$V = \frac{1}{3}Bh$ or $V = \frac{1}{3}\pi r^2 h$

Right Cone

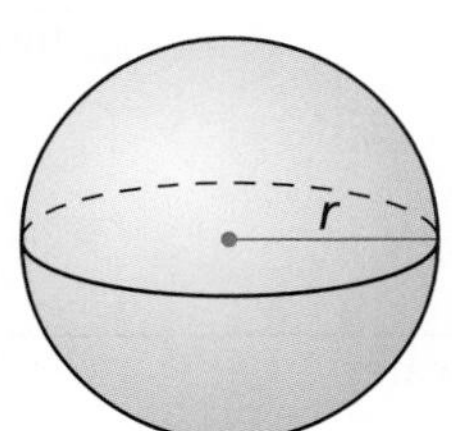

S.A. $= 4\pi r^2$
$V = \frac{4}{3}\pi r^3$

Sphere

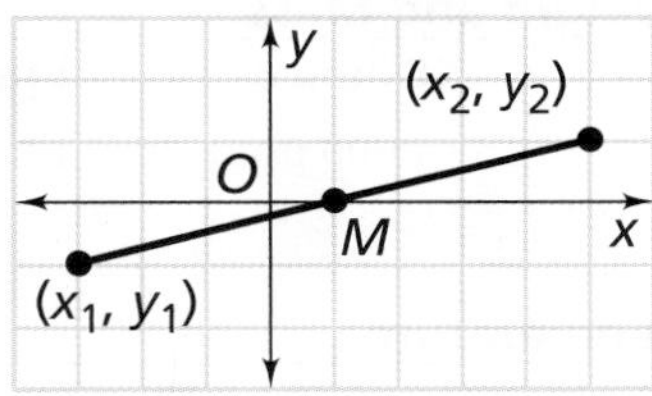

$d = \sqrt{(x_2 - x_1)^2 + (y_2 - y_1)^2}$
$M = \left(\frac{x_1 + x_2}{2}, \frac{y_1 + y_2}{2}\right)$

Distance and Midpoint

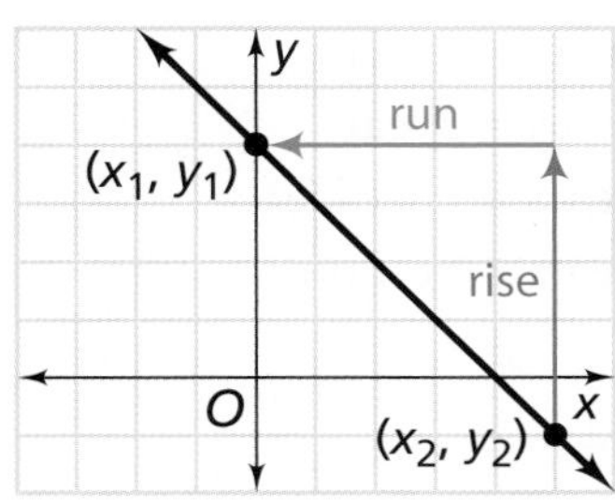
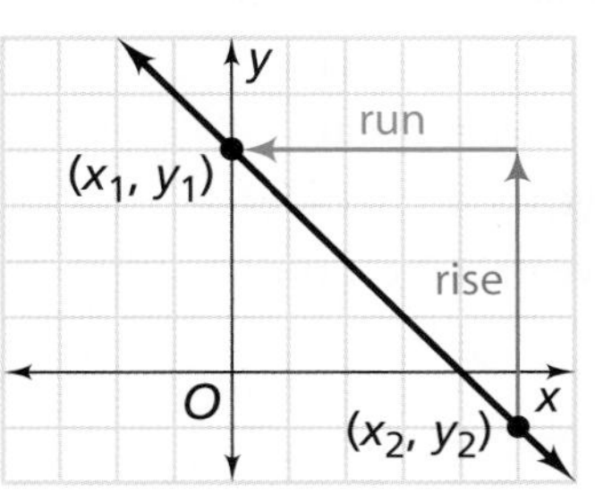

$m = \frac{\text{rise}}{\text{run}} = \frac{y_2 - y_1}{x_2 - x_1}$

Slope

Table 3 Measures

	United States Customary	Metric
Length		
	12 inches (in.) = 1 foot (ft)	10 millimeters (mm) = 1 centimeter (cm)
	36 in. = 1 yard (yd)	100 cm = 1 meter (m)
	3 ft = 1 yard	1000 mm = 1 meter
	5280 ft = 1 mile (mi)	1000 m = 1 kilometer (km)
	1760 yd = 1 mile	
Area		
	144 square inches (in.^{2}) = 1 square foot (ft^2)	100 square millimeters (mm^2) = 1 square centimeter (cm^2)
	9 ft^2 = 1 square yard (yd^2)	10,000 cm^2 = 1 square meter (m^2)
	43,560 ft^2 = 1 acre	10,000 m^2 = 1 hectare (ha)
	4840 yd^2 = 1 acre	
Volume		
	1728 cubic inches (in.^{3}) = 1 cubic foot (ft^3)	1000 cubic millimeters (mm^3) = 1 cubic centimeter (cm^3)
	27 ft^3 = 1 cubic yard (yd^3)	1,000,000 cm^3 = 1 cubic meter (m^3)
Liquid Capacity		
	8 fluid ounces (fl oz) = 1 cup (c)	1000 milliliters (mL) = 1 liter (L)
	2 c = 1 pint (pt)	1000 L = 1 kiloliter (kL)
	2 pt = 1 quart (qt)	
	4 qt = 1 gallon (gal)	
Weight and Mass		
	16 ounces (oz) = 1 pound (lb)	1000 milligrams (mg) = 1 gram (g)
	2000 pounds = 1 ton (t)	1000 g = 1 kilogram (kg)
		1000 kg = 1 metric ton
Temperature		
	32°F = freezing point of water	0°C = freezing point of water
	98.6°F = normal body temperature	37°C = normal body temperature
	212°F = boiling point of water	100°C = boiling point of water
Time		
	60 seconds (s) = 1 minute (min)	365 days = 1 year (yr)
	60 minutes = 1 hour (h)	52 weeks (approx.) = 1 year
	24 hours = 1 day (d)	12 months = 1 year
	7 days = 1 week (wk)	10 years = 1 decade
	4 weeks (approx.) = 1 month (mo)	100 years = 1 century

Table 4 Properties of Real Numbers

Unless otherwise stated, a, b, c, and d are real numbers.

Identity Properties

Addition	$a + 0 = a$ and $0 + a = a$
Multiplication	$a \cdot 1 = a$ and $1 \cdot a = a$

Commutative Properties

Addition	$a + b = b + a$
Multiplication	$a \cdot b = b \cdot a$

Associative Properties

Addition	$(a + b) + c = a + (b + c)$
Multiplication	$(a \cdot b) \cdot c = a \cdot (b \cdot c)$

Inverse Properties

Addition

The sum of a number and its *opposite*, or *additive inverse*, is zero.

$a + (-a) = 0 = -a + a = 0$

Multiplication

The reciprocal, or multiplicative inverse, of a rational number $\frac{a}{b}$ is $\frac{b}{a}$ $(a, b \neq 0)$.

$a \cdot \frac{1}{a} = 1$ and $\frac{1}{a} \cdot a = 1$ $(a \neq 0)$

Distributive Properties

$a(b + c) = ab + ac$	$(b + c)a = ba + ca$
$a(b - c) = ab - ac$	$(b - c)a = ba - ca$

Properties of Equality

Addition	If $a = b$, then $a + c = b + c$.
Subtraction	If $a = b$, then $a - c = b - c$.
Multiplication	If $a = b$, then $a \cdot c = b \cdot c$.
Division	If $a = b$ and $c \neq 0$, then $\frac{a}{c} = \frac{b}{c}$.
Substitution	If $a = b$, then b can replace a in any expression.
Reflexive	$a = a$
Symmetric	If $a = b$, then $b = a$.
Transitive	If $a = b$ and $b = c$, then $a = c$.

Properties of Proportions

$\frac{a}{b} = \frac{c}{d}$ ($a, b, c, d \neq 0$ is equivalent to

(1) $ad = bc$	(2) $\frac{b}{a} = \frac{d}{c}$
(3) $\frac{a}{c} = \frac{b}{d}$	(4) $\frac{a + b}{b} = \frac{c + d}{d}$

Zero-Product Property

If $ab = 0$, then $a = 0$ or $b = 0$.

Properties of Inequality

Addition	If $a > b$ and $c \geq d$, then $a + c > b + d$.
Multiplication	If $a > b$ and $c > 0$, then $ac > bc$. If $a > b$ and $c < 0$, then $ac < bc$.
Transitive	If $a > b$ and $b > c$, then $a > c$.
Comparison	If $a = b + c$ and $c > 0$, then $a > b$.

Properties of Exponents

For any nonzero numbers a and b, any positive number c, and any integers m and n,

Zero Exponent	$a^0 = 1$
Negative Exponent	$a^{-n} = \frac{1}{a^n}$
Product of Powers	$a^m \cdot a^n = a^{m+n}$
Quotient of Powers	$\frac{a^m}{a^n} = a^{m-n}$
Power to a Power	$(c^m)^n = c^{mn}$
Product to a Power	$(ab)^n = a^n b^n$
Quotient to a Power	$\left(\frac{a}{b}\right)^n = \frac{a^n}{b^n}$

Properties of Square Roots

For any nonnegative numbers a and b, and any positive number c,

Product of Square Roots	$\sqrt{a} \cdot \sqrt{b} = \sqrt{ab}$
Quotient of Square Roots	$\frac{\sqrt{a}}{\sqrt{c}} = \sqrt{\frac{a}{c}}$

Tables

Postulates and Theorems

Theorem 1.1
Perpendicular Bisector Theorem, pp. 29, 135
Each point on the perpendicular bisector of a segment is equidistant from the two endpoints of the segment.

Theorem 1.2
Concurrence of Perpendicular Bisectors, p. 60
In any triangle, the perpendicular bisectors of the sides are concurrent.

Theorem 1.3
Concurrence of Angle Bisectors, p. 60
In any triangle, the angle bisectors are concurrent.

Postulate 2.1
The Triangle Congruence Postulates, p. 84
If two triangles share the following triplets of congruent corresponding parts, the triangles are congruent.

- ASA
- SAS
- SSS

Exterior Angle Theorem, Version 1, p. 90
The measure of a triangle's exterior angle is greater than the measures of either of the triangle's two remote interior angles.

Theorem 2.1 The Vertical Angles Theorem, p. 93
Vertical angles are congruent.

Theorem 2.2 The AIP Theorem, p. 99
If two lines form congruent alternate interior angles with a transversal, then the two lines are parallel.

Postulate 2.2 The Parallel Postulate, p. 105
If a point P is not on line ℓ, exactly one line through P exists that is parallel to ℓ.

Theorem 2.3 The PAI Theorem, p. 105
If two parallel lines are cut by a transversal, then the alternate interior angles are congruent.

Theorem 2.4
The Triangle Angle-Sum Theorem, p. 107
The sum of the measures of the angles of a triangle is 180°.

Theorem 2.5
The Unique Perpendicular Theorem, p. 109
If a point P is not on a line ℓ, there is exactly one line through P that is perpendicular to ℓ.

Exterior Angle Theorem, Version 2, p. 110
The measure of an exterior angle of a triangle is equal to the sum of the measures of the two remote interior angles of the triangle.

Theorem 2.6 Isosceles Triangle Theorem, p. 136
The base angles of an isosceles triangle are congruent.

Triangle Inequality Theorem, p. 140
In a triangle, the length of one side is less than the sum of the lengths of the other two sides.

Theorem 2.7, p. 151
Each diagonal of a parallelogram divides the parallelogram into two congruent triangles.

Theorem 2.8, p. 152
The diagonals of a parallelogram bisect each other.

Theorem 2.9, p. 156
If two opposite sides of a quadrilateral are congruent and parallel, then the figure is a parallelogram.

Theorem 2.10 Midline Theorem, p. 156
The segment that joins the midpoints of two sides of a triangle is parallel to the third side and half the length of the third side.

Theorem 3.1, p. 178
The segment joining the midpoints of the legs of a trapezoid is parallel to the bases. Its length is the average (half the sum) of the lengths of the bases.

Postulate 3.1 The Congruence Postulate, p. 197
Congruent figures have the same area.

Postulate 3.2 The Additivity Postulate, p. 197
If two polygons P and Q do not intersect (except possibly at a point or along an edge), then the area of the union of P and Q is the sum of the areas of P and Q.

Postulate 3.3 The Rectangle Postulate, p. 199
The area of a rectangle with dimensions b and h (expressed in the same unit) is bh.

Postulate 3.4
The Scissors-Congruence Postulate, p. 199
Two figures that are scissors-congruent have the same area.

Theorem 3.2 Pythagorean Theorem, p. 217

In a right triangle, the square built on the longest side has area equal to the sum of the areas of the squares built on the other two sides.

Theorem 4.1
The Parallel Side-Splitter Theorem, p. 310

If a segment with endpoints on two sides of a triangle is parallel to the third side of the triangle, then

- the segment splits the sides it intersects proportionally
- the ratio of the length of the third side of the triangle to the length of the parallel segment is the common ratio

Theorem 4.2
The Proportional Side-Splitter Theorem, p. 311

If a segment with endpoints on two sides of a triangle splits those sides proportionally, then the segment is parallel to the third side.

Theorem 4.3 AAA Similarity Theorem, p. 331

If three angles of one triangle are congruent to three angles of another triangle, the triangles are similar.

Theorem 4.4 SAS Similarity Theorem, p. 332

If two triangles have two pairs of proportional side lengths and the included angles are congruent, the triangles are similar.

Theorem 4.5 SSS Similarity Theorem, p. 333

If two triangles have all three pairs of side lengths proportional, the triangles are similar.

Theorem 4.6, p. 340

If you scale a polygon by some positive number r, then the ratio of the area of the scaled copy to the area of the original polygon is r^2.

Theorem 5.1, p. 368

The area A of a regular polygon is equal to half of the product of its perimeter P and its apothem a.

$$A = \frac{1}{2}Pa$$

Theorem 5.2, p. 370

The area of a circle is one half its circumference times its radius.

$$A = \frac{1}{2}Cr$$

Theorem 5.3, p. 377

If a circle is scaled by a positive number s, then its area is scaled by s^2.

Theorem 5.4, p. 377

If the area of a circle with radius 1 is k, then the area of a circle with radius r is kr^2.

Theorem 5.5, p. 378

The area of a circle of radius r is π times the radius squared.

$$A = \pi r^2$$

Theorem 5.6, p. 382

The circumference of a circle of radius r is 2π times the radius.

$$C = 2\pi r$$

Theorem 5.7, p. 402

Two chords are congruent if and only if their corresponding arcs are congruent.

Theorem 5.8, p. 408

A line through the center of a circle bisects a chord if it is perpendicular to the chord.

Theorem 5.9, p. 409

If a line through the center of a circle bisects a chord, then it is perpendicular to the chord.

Theorem 5.10, p. 409

The center of a circle lies on the line perpendicular to a chord if and only if the line bisects the chord.

Theorem 5.11, p. 409

The measure of an inscribed angle is equal to half the measure of its intercepted arc.

Corollary 5.11.1, p. 410

Inscribed angles are congruent if and only if they intercept the same arc or congruent arcs.

Corollary 5.11.2, p. 410

Any triangle inscribed in a semicircle is a right triangle.

Theorem 5.12, p. 416

In a cyclic quadrilateral, opposite angles are supplementary.

Theorem 5.13, p. 421

If a line intersects a circle in one point (that is, the line is tangent to the circle), it is perpendicular to the radius r drawn to the point of contact.

Theorem 5.14, p. 422

A secant angle with vertex inside a circle is equal in measure to half of the sum of the measures of the arcs it intercepts.

Theorem 5.15, p. 423

A secant angle with vertex outside a circle is equal in measure to half of the difference of the measures of the arcs it intercepts.

Theorem 6.1, p. 468

In a right triangle, the length of either leg is the geometric mean of the length of its projection on the hypotenuse and the length of the whole hypotenuse.

Theorem 6.2, p. 468

In a right triangle, the length of the altitude relative to the hypotenuse is the geometric mean of the length of the two segments of the hypotenuse.

Postulate 6.1 Cavalieri's Principle, p. 518

Two solids of the same height are cut by a plane so that the resulting cross sections have the same areas. If the solids also have cross-sectional areas equal to each other when cut by any plane parallel to the first, then they have the same volume.

Theorem 6.3, p. 525

The volume of a prism is equal to the product of the area of its base and its height.

$$V_{\text{prism}} = A_{\text{base}} \cdot h$$

Theorem 6.4, p. 526

The volume of a cylinder is equal to the product of the area of its base (a circle) and its height.

$$V_{\text{cylinder}} = A_{\text{base}} \cdot h$$

Theorem 6.5, p. 528

The volume of a pyramid is equal to one third of the product of the area of its base and its height.

$$V_{\text{pyramid}} = \frac{A_{\text{base}} \cdot h}{3}$$

Theorem 6.6, p. 529

The volume of a cone is equal to one third of the product of the area of its base (a circle) and its height.

$$V_{\text{cone}} = \frac{A_{\text{base}} \cdot h}{3}$$

Theorem 6.7, p. 535

The volume of a sphere with radius r is $\frac{4}{3}\pi r^3$.

Theorem 6.8, p. 535

The surface area of a sphere with radius r is $4\pi r^2$.

Theorem 7.1, p. 572

The composition of two reflections over intersecting lines produces a rotation. Its center is the intersection of the lines. The measure of the angle of rotation is equal to twice the measure of the angle formed by the two lines.

Theorem 7.2 Distance Formula, p. 596

The distance between two points (x_1, y_1) and (x_2, y_2) can be found using the Pythagorean Theorem. It is the square root of the sum of the square of the difference in the x-coordinates and the square of difference in the y-coordinates.

Theorem 7.3 Midpoint Formula, p. 596

Each coordinate of the midpoint of a line segment is equal to the average of the corresponding coordinates of the endpoints of the line segment.

Theorem 7.4, p. 601

Two nonvertical lines are parallel if and only if they have the same slope.

Theorem 7.5, p. 602

Let A, B, and C be three points, no two of which are in line vertically. Points A, B, and C are collinear if and only if the slope between A and B, $m(A, B)$, is the same as the slope between B and C, $m(B, C)$.

Theorem 7.6, p. 607

Two nonvertical lines are perpendicular if and only if the product of their slopes is -1.

Theorem 7.7 The Head-Minus-Tail Test, p. 630

Two vectors are equivalent if and only if head minus tail for one vector gives the same result as head minus tail for the other.

$\overrightarrow{AB}$ is equivalent to $\overrightarrow{CD}$ if and only if $B - A = D - C$.

Corollary 7.7.1, p. 630

If A and B are points, the vector from O to $(B - A)$ is equivalent to the vector from A to B.

Theorem 7.8, p. 632

If $A = (a_1, a_2)$ and $B = (b_1, b_2)$, then $A + B$ is the fourth vertex of the parallelogram that has A, O, and B as three of its vertices and $\overline{OA}$ and $\overline{OB}$ as two of its sides.

Theorem 7.9, p. 633

Suppose A is a point, c is a number greater than or equal to 1, and $B = cA$. Then,

- B is collinear with A and the origin.
- B is c times as far from the origin as A.

Theorem 7.10, p. 634

Adding the same point to the tail and to the head of a vector produces an equivalent vector.

Theorem 7.11, p. 636

If A is a point different from the origin, the set of all multiples of A is the line through the origin and A.

Theorem 7.12, p. 638

Two vectors $\overrightarrow{AB}$ and $\overrightarrow{CD}$ are parallel if and only if there is a number k such that $B - A = k(D - C)$. If $k > 0$, the vectors have the same direction. If $k < 0$, the vectors have opposite directions. If $k = 1$, the vectors are equivalent.

Theorem 7.13, p. 639

If A and B are points, then the segment from O to $B - A$ is parallel and congruent to $\overline{AB}$.

Theorem 8.1 Regular Polygon Theorem, p. 681

Of all the polygons having a given perimeter and a given number of sides, the regular polygon has the greatest area.

Theorem 8.2 Rich's Theorem, p. 713

The sum of the distances from any point inside an equilateral triangle to the sides of the triangle is equal to the length of the altitude of the triangle.

Postulate 8.1 The Existence Hypothesis, p. 727

For any given perimeter, there is a closed curve that encloses the greatest area.

Glossary

A

acre (p. 671) An acre is a unit of area equal to 43,560 ft^2.

acute angle (p. 498) An acute angle is an angle whose measure is between 0° and 90°.

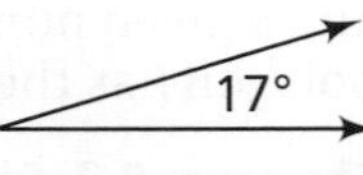

adjacent angles (p. 29) Adjacent angles are two coplanar angles that have a common side and a common vertex but no common interior points.

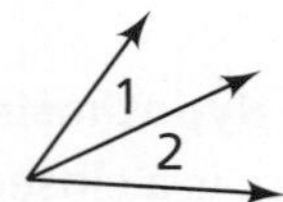

∠1 and ∠2 are adjacent.

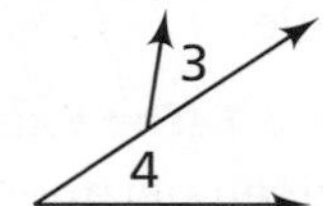

∠3 and ∠4 are *not* adjacent.

algorithm (p. 181) An algorithm is a set of steps to a completely determined result.

alternate exterior angles (p. 99) Alternate exterior angles are nonadjacent exterior angles that lie on opposite sides of a transversal.

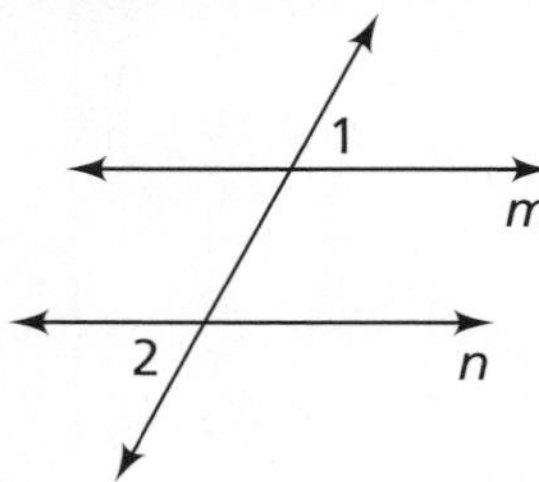

∠1 and ∠2 are alternate exterior angles.

alternate interior angles (p. 99) Alternate interior angles are nonadjacent interior angles that lie on opposite sides of a transversal.

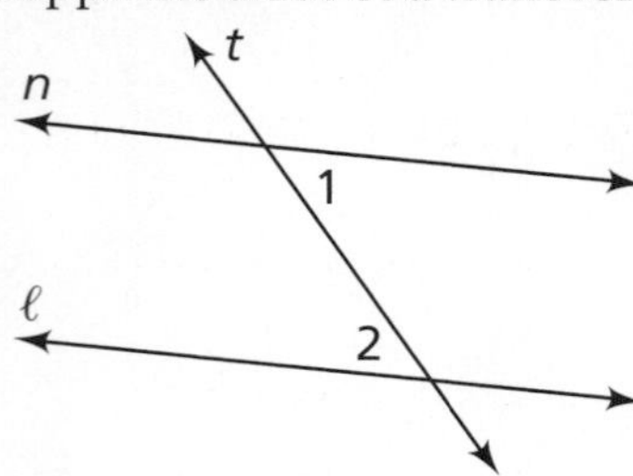

∠1 and ∠2 are alternate interior angles.

altitude *See* **cone; cylinder; prism; pyramid; triangle.**

angle bisector (p. 31) An angle bisector is a ray that divides an angle exactly in half, making two congruent angles.

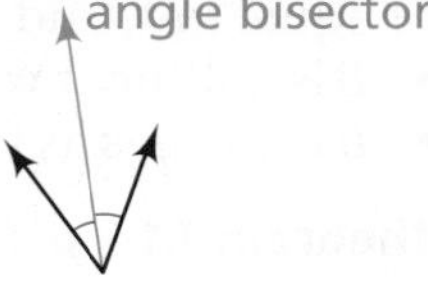

angle of incidence (p. 665) The angle of incidence is the angle between an incoming ray and the line perpendicular to the surface at the point of arrival.

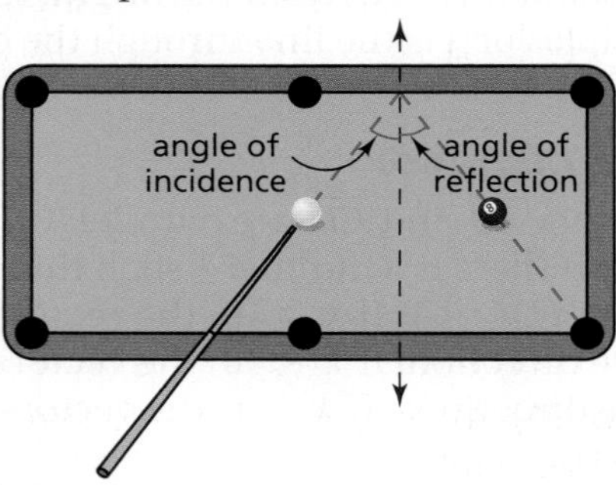

angle of reflection (p. 665) The angle of reflection is the angle between a reflected ray and the line perpendicular to the surface at the point of reflection.

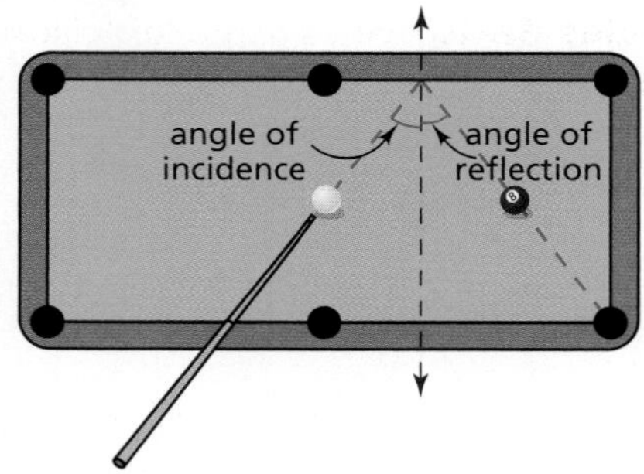

angle of rotation *See* **rotation.**

apex *See* **pyramid; cone.**

apothem (p. 367) An apothem of a regular polygon is the length of the perpendicular segment from the center point of the polygon to one of its sides.

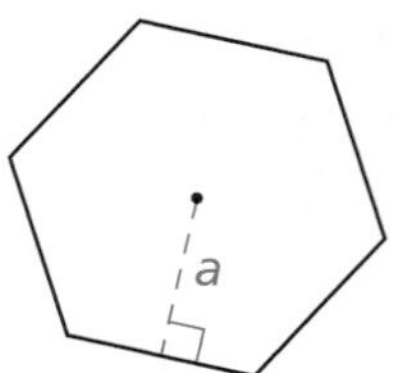

arc (p. 400) An arc is the set of points on a circle that lie in the interior of a particular central angle.

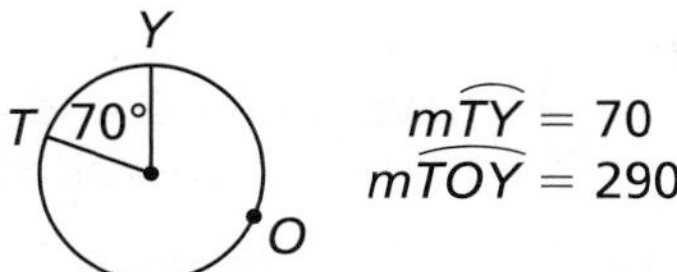

area (p. 197) Area is the number of square units contained within a figure.

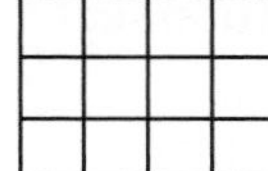

The area of the rectangle is 12 square units, or 12 units^2.

arithmetic mean (p. 462) The arithmetic mean of two numbers a and b is $\frac{a + b}{2}$. The arithmetic mean is commonly referred to as the average.

assumption (p. 84) An assumption is a statement accepted without proof.

axiom (p. 91) An axiom is a conclusion accepted without proof.

B

base(s) *See* **cone; prism; pyramid; cylinder; trapezoid; triangle; isosceles triangle.**

base angles *See* **isosceles trapezoid; isosceles triangle.**

bisection (p. 46) A bisection is a dissection that results in two congruent parts.

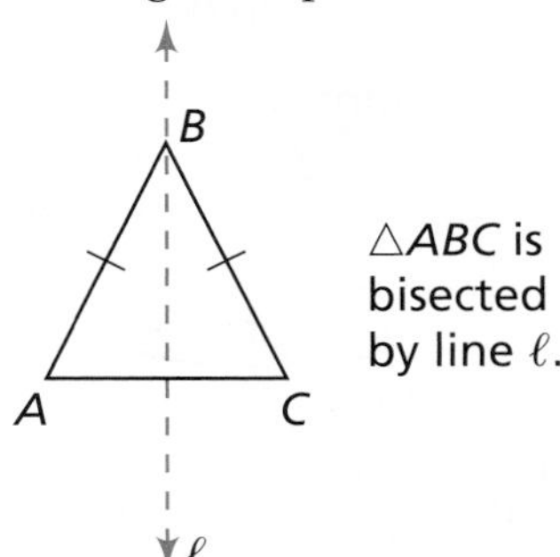

$\triangle ABC$ is bisected by line ℓ.

C

center of dilation *See* **dilation.**

center of rotation *See* **rotation.**

central angle (p. 400) A central angle is an angle that has its vertex at the center of a circle.

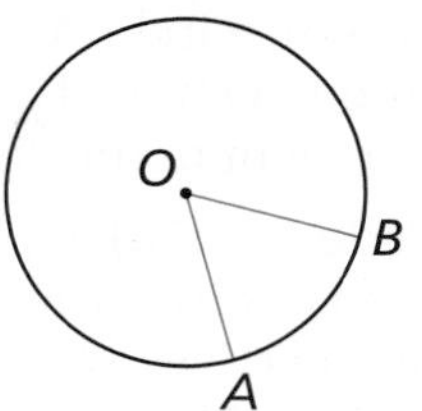

$\angle AOB$ is a central angle.

centroid (p. 472) A centroid is the point of concurrency of the three medians of a triangle.

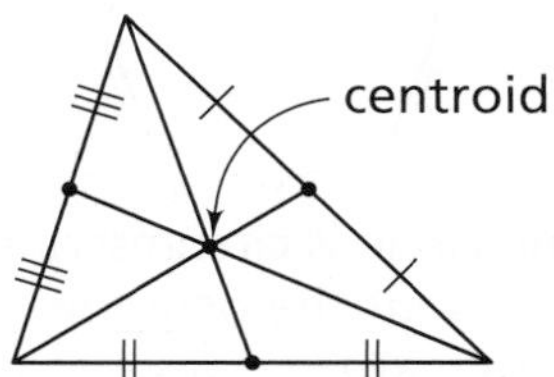

chord (p. 400) A chord is a segment that connects two points on a circle. Any chord through the center of a circle is a diameter.

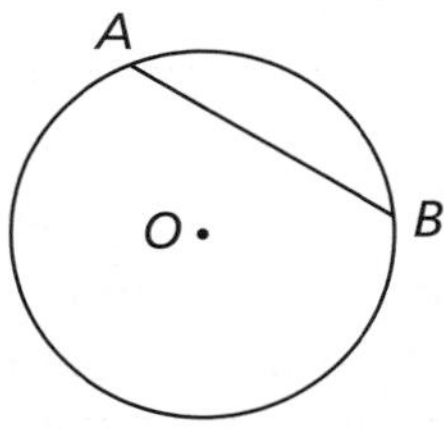

$\overline{AB}$ is a chord.

circle (p. 16) A circle is the set of all points that are a given distance, the radius, from a given point, the center.

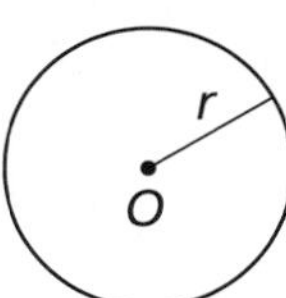

circumference (p. 241) The perimeter of a circle.

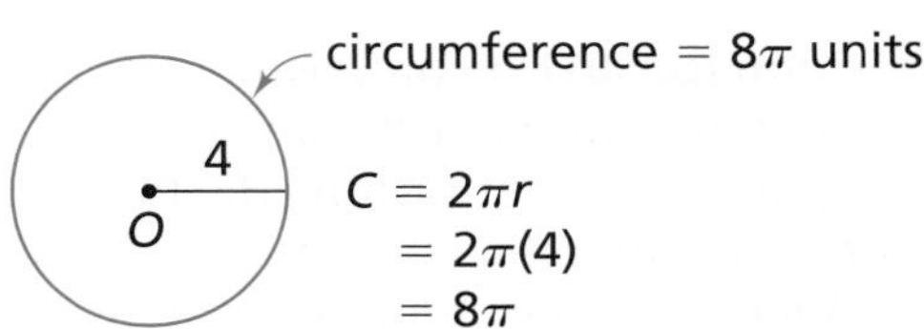

circumscribe (p. 361) A circle is circumscribed about a polygon if all of the vertices of the polygon are on the circle. A polygon is circumscribed about a circle if all of the sides of the polygon are tangent to the circle.

circumscribed circle (p. 428) A circumscribed circle of a polygon is a circle that passes through all of the polygon's vertices. The center of a circumscribed circle is the *circumcenter,* equidistant from the polygon's vertices.

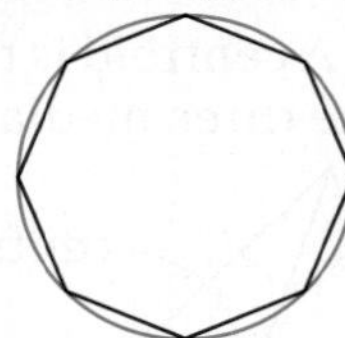

The circle is circumscribed about the octagon.

closed figure (p. 144) A figure is closed if you can "walk" its outer edges and get back to where you started.

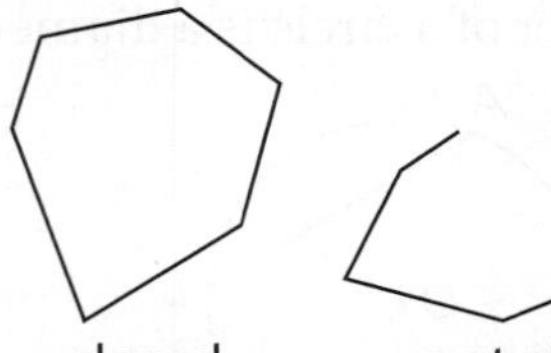

closed not closed

coincide (p. 281) Points or lines coincide if they take up the same place in space.

collinear points (p. 61) Collinear points exist on the same line.

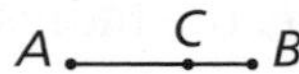

Points A, B, and C are collinear.

common ratio *See* **dilation, splits two sides proportionally.**

complementary angles Two angles are complementary angles if the sum of their measure is 90°.

composition (p. 561) A composition of two transformations is a transformation that is equivalent to performing the first transformation and then performing the second transformation on the image of the first.

concave polygon (p. 145) A concave polygon has at least one diagonal that contains points outside the polygon.

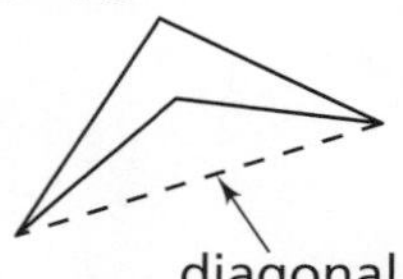

diagonal outside the quadrilateral

concentric circles (p. 412) Concentric circles are circles that have the same center but not necessarily the same radius.

The two circles both have center D and are therefore concentric.

conclusion (p. 123) The conclusion is the part of a statement that you need to prove.

concurrent lines (p. 59) Concurrent lines are three or more lines that meet or intersect at one point.

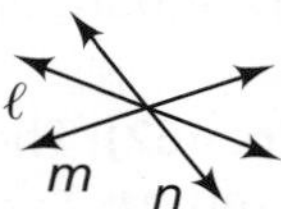

Lines ℓ, m, and n are concurrent lines.

cone (p. 242) A cone is a solid with a circular *base* and a smooth curved *lateral surface* that comes to a point, the *apex*. The distance from the edge of the base to the apex is the *slant height* of the cone. The *altitude* of the cone is a perpendicular segment from the apex of the cone to the plane of its base. The length of the altitude is the *height* of the cone.

congruent (p. 608) Two shapes are congruent if there is an isometry that maps one shape onto the other.

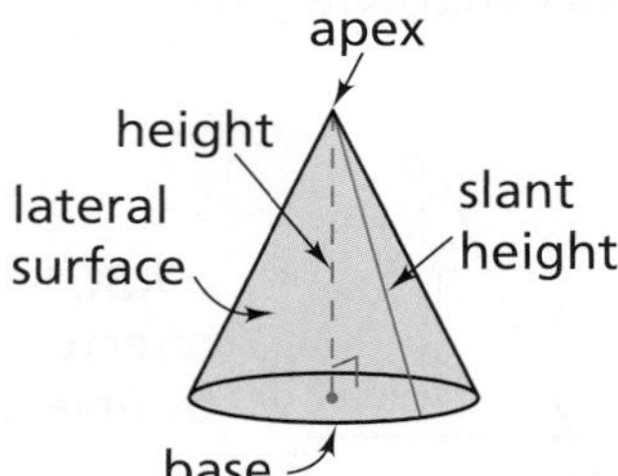

congruent figures (p. 73) Two figures are congruent if they have the same size and shape regardless of location or orientation.

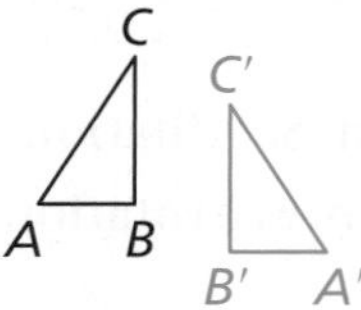

$\triangle ABC$ is congruent to $\triangle A'B'C'$.

congruent sides (p. 42) Congruent sides are sides that are equal in length.

conjecture (p. 22) A conjecture is a conclusion reached by using inductive reasoning.

consecutive angles (p. 99) Consecutive angles are the angles on the same side of a transversal and between the lines the transversal intersects.

constant (p. 51) A constant is a numerical invariant.

constant-area rectangle (p. 464) A constant-area rectangle is a construction of a rectangle in which the area of the rectangle remains the same as the dimensions are changed.

construction (p. 27) A construction is a guaranteed recipe for drawing a figure with a specified set of tools.

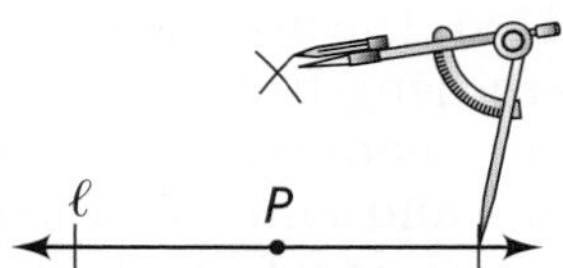

The diagram shows the construction (in progress) of a line perpendicular to a line ℓ through a point P on ℓ.

contour line (p. 690) A contour line is a curve that shows where a particular quantity is invariant.

contour plot (p. 690) A contour plot is a collection of contour lines.

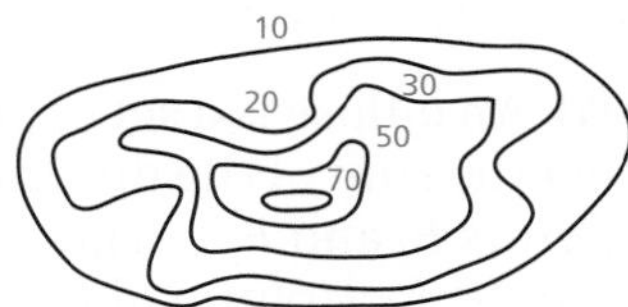

Contour plot showing height

converse (p. 105) The converse of the conditional "if *p*, then *q*" is the conditional "if *q*, then *p*."

convex polygon (p. 61) A polygon is convex if no diagonal of the polygon contains points outside the polygon.

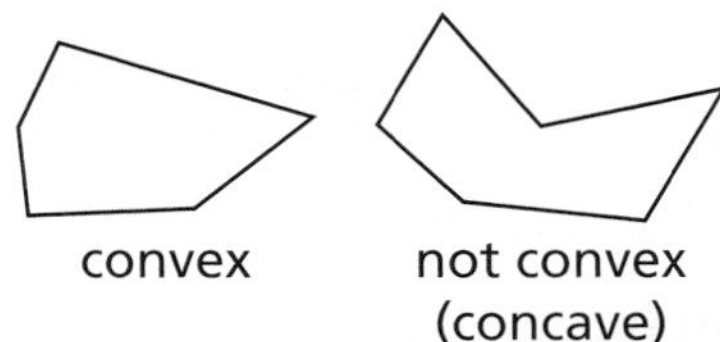

convex   not convex (concave)

corollary (p. 100) A corollary is a consequence that logically follows from a theorem.

corresponding angles (p. 99) Corresponding angles lie on the same side of a transversal and in corresponding positions relative to the two lines the transversal intersects.

corresponding parts (p. 45) Corresponding parts are in the same relative position in congruent figures.

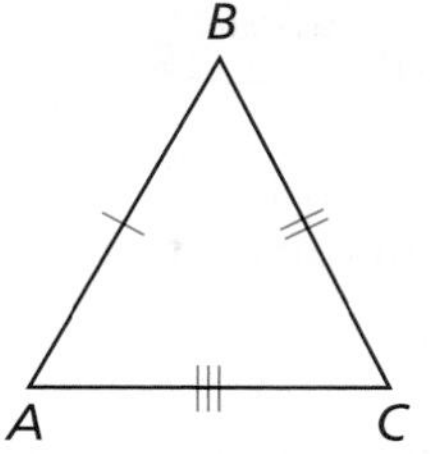

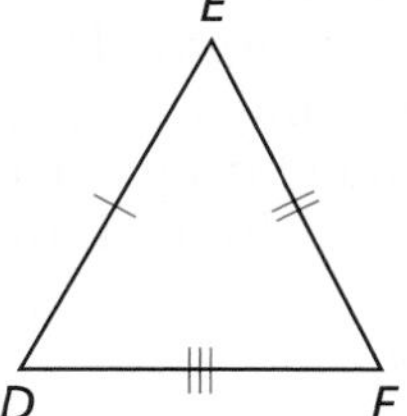

$\triangle ABC \cong \triangle DEF$
$\angle A$ and $\angle D$ are corresponding parts.
$\overline{BC}$ and $\overline{EF}$ are corresponding parts.

cosine *See* **trigonometric ratios.**

counterexample (p. 122) A counterexample is an example that proves that a statement is false.

CPCTC (p. 82) CPCTC is an abbreviation of "corresponding parts of congruent triangles are congruent."

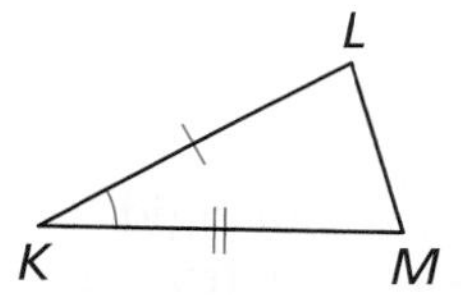

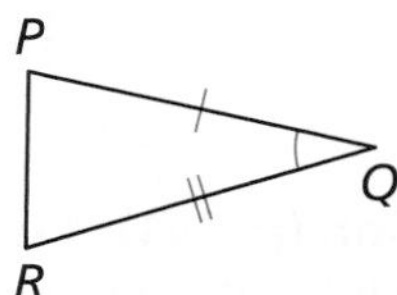

$\triangle KLM \cong \triangle QPR$ by *SAS*.
By CPCTC, you also know that $\angle L \cong \angle P$, $\angle M \cong \angle R$, and $\overline{LM} \cong \overline{PR}$.

cross section (p. 37) A cross section is the intersection of a solid and a plane.

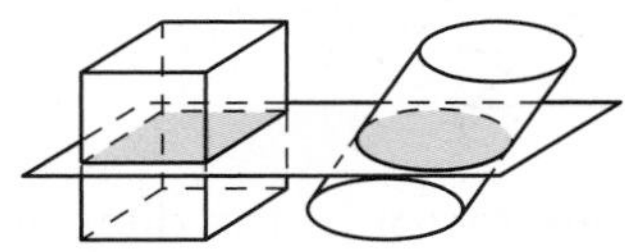

The blue regions are cross sections.

cube (p. 239) A cube is a polyhedron with six faces, each of which is a square.

cyclic quadrilateral (p. 476) A cyclic quadrilateral is a quadrilateral inscribed in a circle.

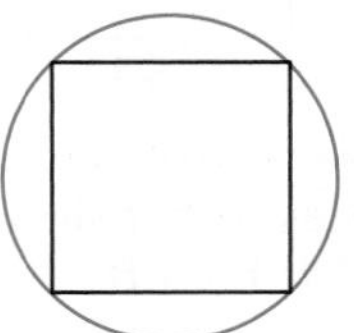

cylinder (p. 240) A cylinder is a solid with two congruent parallel circles as *bases,* joined by a curved smooth *lateral surface.* The *altitude* of the cylinder is a perpendicular segment from one base to the other. The *height* of the cylinder is the length of the altitude.

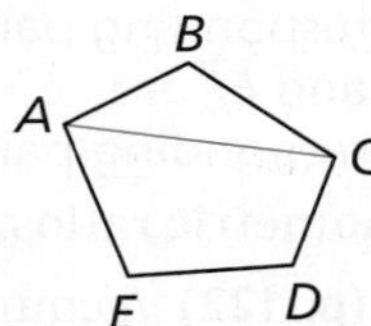

D

diagonal (p. 5) A diagonal is a segment that connects two nonconsecutive vertices of a polygon.

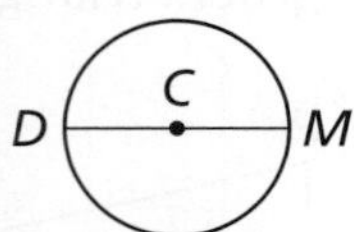

diameter (p. 400) A diameter is a chord that passes through the center of a circle.

$\overline{DM}$ is a diameter.

dilation (p. 291) A dilation is a nonrigid transformation that scales a figure from a *center of dilation* by a *scale factor.* The ratio of corresponding parts of the original figure to the scaled figure is the *common ratio.*

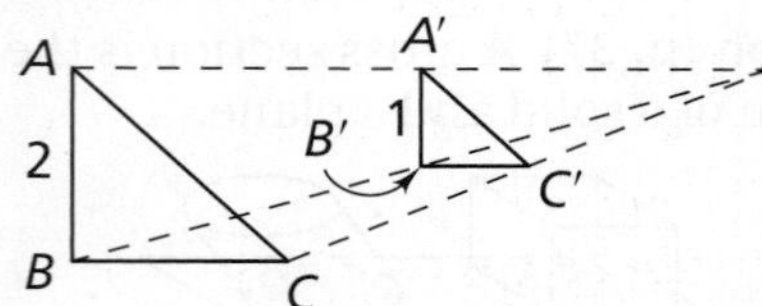

The scale factor of the dilation that maps $\triangle ABC$ to $\triangle A'B'C'$ is $\frac{1}{2}$.

dimensions (p. 265) The dimensions are measurements that indicate the size of a figure.

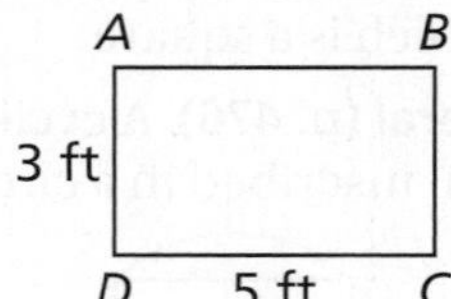

Rectangle *ABCD* has dimensions 3 ft by 5 ft.

direction *See* vector.

disc (p. 61) A disc is a circle and its interior points.

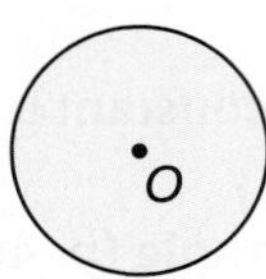

discrete case (p. 439) A discrete case deals with finite numbers.

dissection (p. 174) A dissection is a process of cutting a polygon into two or more polygons and rearranging them.

distance (p. 655) The distance between two points is the length of the segment that contains them as endpoints. The distance between a point and a line is the length of the perpendicular segment from the point to the line.

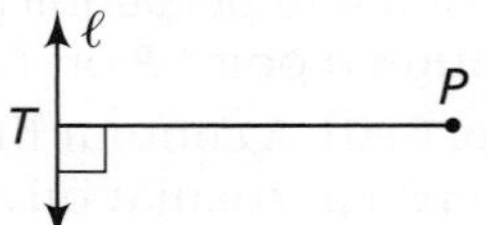

The distance from point *P* to line *ℓ* is *PT*.

E

ellipse (p. 701) An ellipse is a set of points *P* in a plane such that the sum of the distances from *P* to two fixed points F_1 and F_2 is a given constant *k*. F_1 and F_2 are the *foci* (plural of *focus*) of the ellipse.

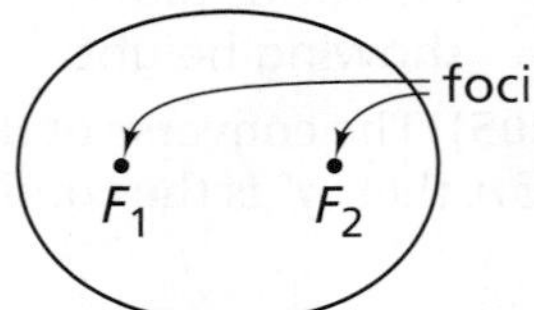

equiangular (p. 124) An equiangular polygon is a polygon with angles that are all congruent.

Each angle of the pentagon is a 108° angle.

equidistant (p. 29) Equidistant means "the same distance."

equilateral (p. 20) An equilateral figure has sides with equal lengths.

equilateral triangle (p. 20) An equilateral triangle is a triangle whose sides are all congruent. Each angle measures 60°.

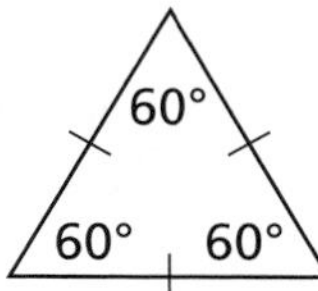

equivalent vectors (p. 628) Equivalent vectors are vectors that have the same size and direction, but different heads and tails.

exterior angle (p. 90) An exterior angle of a polygon is an angle formed by a side and an extension of an adjacent side.

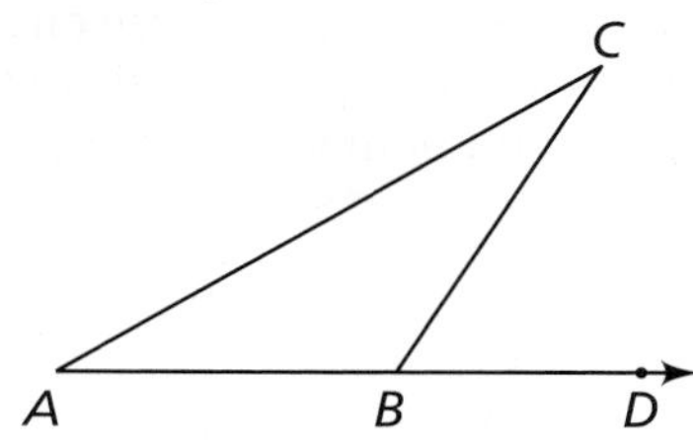

$\angle CBD$ is an exterior angle of $\triangle ABC$.

F

face (p. 235) The polygons that make up a polyhedron are the faces of the polyhedron.

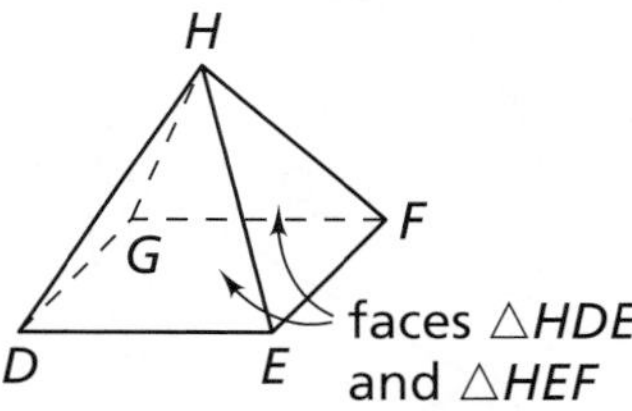

Fermat point (p. 732) When connected with the vertices of a triangle, the Fermat point forms three 120° angles.

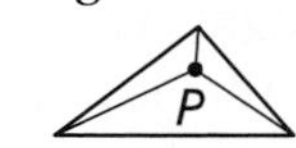

P is the Fermat point.

fixed point (p. 554) A fixed point is a point that is its own image after a transformation.

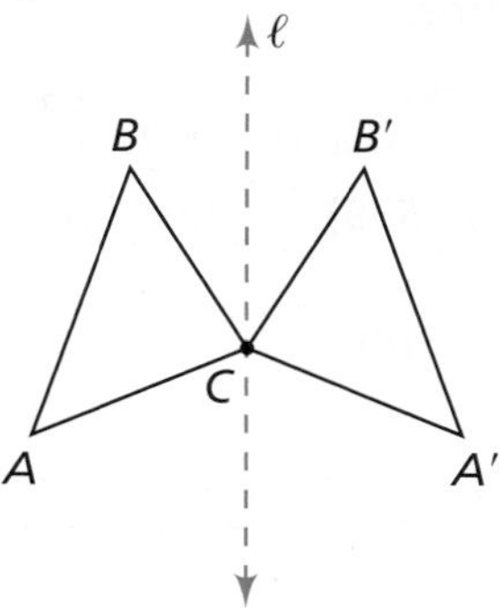

Point *C* is a fixed point for a reflection over line ℓ.

focus *See* **ellipse.**

frustum (p. 246) The frustum is the slice that remains when a smaller cone is cut from a cone.

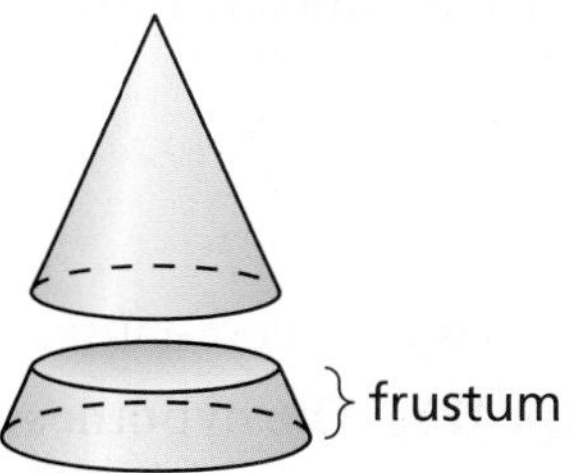

G

geometric mean (p. 461) The geometric mean of two numbers a and b is c if $c > 0$ and $c^2 = ab$. Equivalently, $c = \sqrt{ab}$. The geometric mean is midway between two numbers with respect to multiplication.

geometric probability (p. 438) Geometric probability is a probability that uses a geometric model in which points represent outcomes.

grid polygon (p. 11) A grid polygon is a polygon that has all of its sides on the grid lines of a rectangular coordinate system.

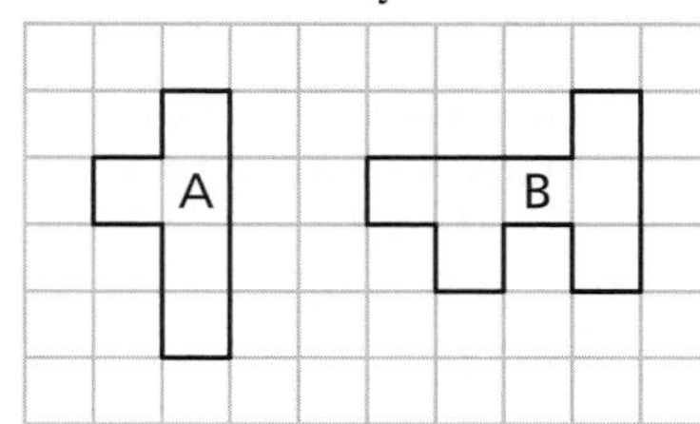

grid polygon (encloses 5 grid squares) grid polygon (encloses 7 grid squares)

H

head *See* **vector.**

height *See* **cone; cylinder; parallelogram; prism; pyramid; trapezoid; triangle.**

hemisphere (p. 539) A hemisphere is half of a sphere.

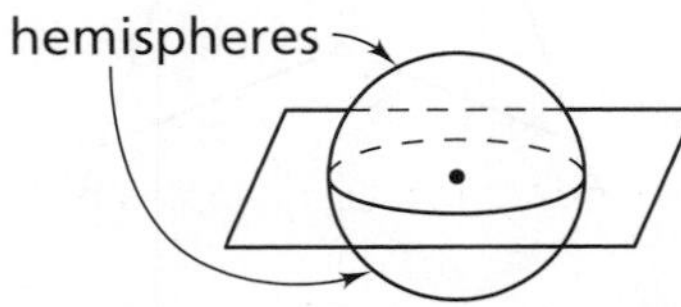

hexagon (p. 52) A hexagon is a polygon with six sides.

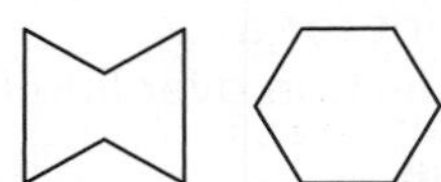

hypotenuse (p. 182) In a right triangle, the hypotenuse is the longest side of the triangle. The hypotenuse is opposite the right angle.

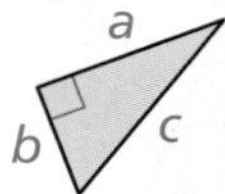

c is the hypotenuse.

hypothesis (p. 123) The hypothesis of a statement is what you are assuming to be true in order to prove the conclusion.

I

icosahedron (p. 239) An icosahedron is a solid figure with exactly twenty plane surfaces.

image (p. 551) An image is a figure obtained by a transformation of a preimage.

preimage image

X Y Y' X'

Z Z'

$\triangle XYZ \longrightarrow \triangle X'Y'Z'$

This transformation maps X to X', Y to Y' and Z to Z'.

included angle (p. 136) An included angle is an angle between two given sides of a triangle or polygon.

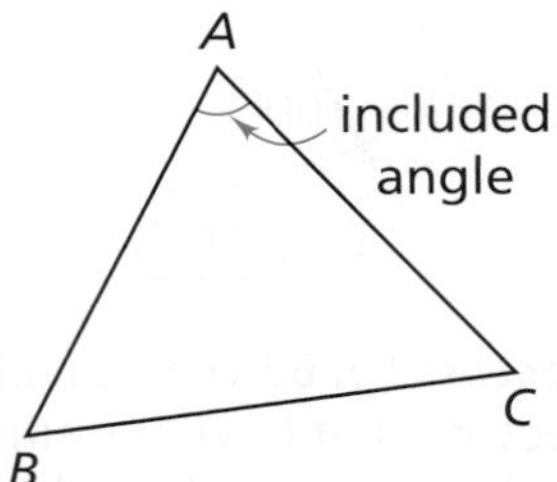

$\angle A$ is included between sides $\overline{AB}$ and $\overline{AC}$.

inscribe (p. 361) A polygon is inscribed in a circle if all of its vertices are on the circle. A circle is inscribed in a polygon if each side of the polygon is tangent to the circle.

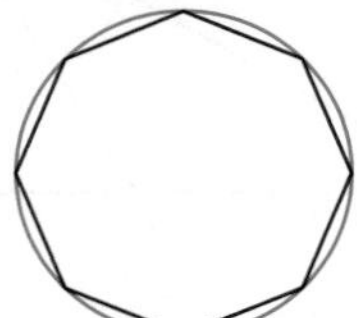

The octagon is inscribed in the circle.

inscribed angle (p. 408) An inscribed angle is an angle with its vertex on a circle and sides that are chords of the circle.

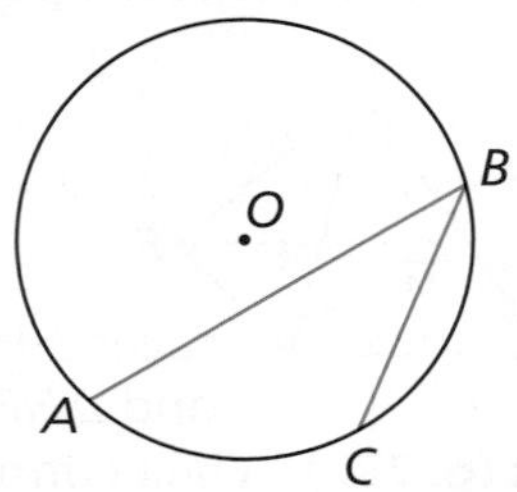

$\angle ABC$ is an inscribed angle.

inscribed circle (p. 428) An inscribed circle of a polygon is a circle that is tangent to all of the polygon's sides. The center of an inscribed circle is the *incenter*, equidistant from the polygon's sides.

invariant (p. 49) An invariant is something that is true for each member of a collection.

isometry (p. 607) An isometry, or rigid motion, is any composition of reflections, translations, and rotations.

isoperimetric problem (p. 718) Isoperimetric problems involve geometric figures of a certain type with the same perimeter.

isosceles trapezoid (p. 149) An isosceles trapezoid is a trapezoid with opposite nonparallel sides that are congruent. Each angle with vertices that are endpoints of the same base is a *base angle.*

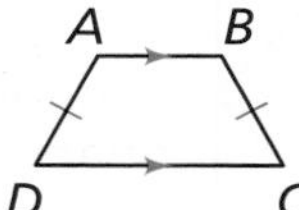

$\angle A$ and $\angle B$ are base angles.
$\angle D$ and $\angle C$ are base angles.

isosceles triangle (p. 120) An isosceles triangle is a triangle with at least two sides congruent. The third side is the *base.* The angles opposite the congruent sides are the *base angles.* The angle between two congruent sides is the *vertex angle.*

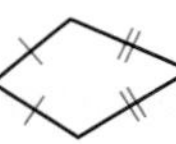

K

kite (p. 147) A kite is a quadrilateral in which a pair of adjacent sides are congruent, and the other pair of adjacent sides are congruent as well.

L

lateral face *See* **prism, pyramid.**

lateral surface *See* **cone; cylinder.**

lateral surface area (p. 237) The lateral surface area of a polyhedron is the sum of the areas of every lateral face of the polyhedron but not the areas of the bases.

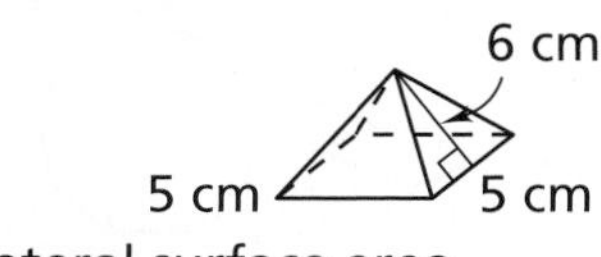

lateral surface area of pyramid $= 4 \cdot \frac{1}{2}(5)(6)\text{ cm}^2$
$= 4 \cdot 15\text{ cm}^2$
$= 60\text{ cm}^2$

Law of Cosines (p. 503) The Law of Cosines allows you to find the third side length in a triangle when given two side lengths and an included angle. The Law of Cosines also allows you to find the measure of an angle of a triangle when you know the three side lengths.

$$a^2 = b^2 + c^2 - 2bc\cos A$$
$$b^2 = a^2 + c^2 - 2ac\cos B$$
$$c^2 = a^2 + b^2 - 2ab\cos C$$

leg *See* **isosceles triangle; right triangle; trapezoid.**

level curves *See* **contour lines.**

limit (p. 359) A limit is the value a sequence of numbers gets increasingly close to.

light year (p. 459) A light year is the distance light travels in one year.

line (p. 30) In Euclidean geometry, a line is undefined. You can think of a line as a series of points that extends in two directions without end.

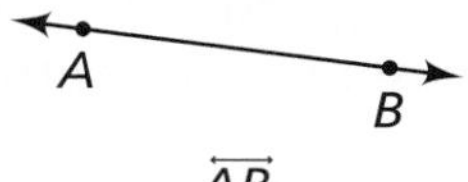

$\overleftrightarrow{AB}$

line of reflection *See* **reflection.**

line of symmetry (p. 9) If an object maps onto itself after reflection over a line, then the line is a line of symmetry for the object.

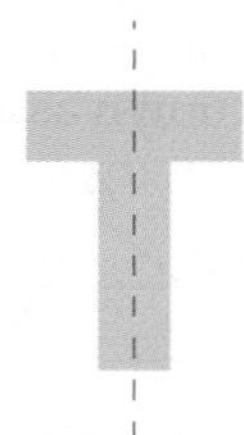

line segment (p. 12) A line segment is a part of a line that contains two endpoints and all the points between them.

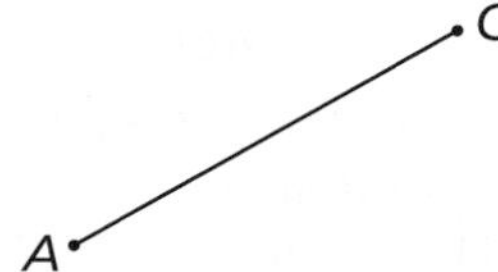

linear approximation (p. 361) Linear approximation is a process devised by Archimedes for approximating the length of a curve using line segments.

locus (p. 398) A locus is a set of points that satisfy a given property.

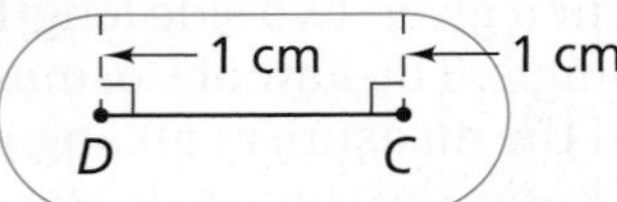

The points in blue are the locus of points in a plane 1 cm from $\overline{DC}$.

M

major arc (p. 402) A major arc of a circle is an arc that is larger than a semicircle.

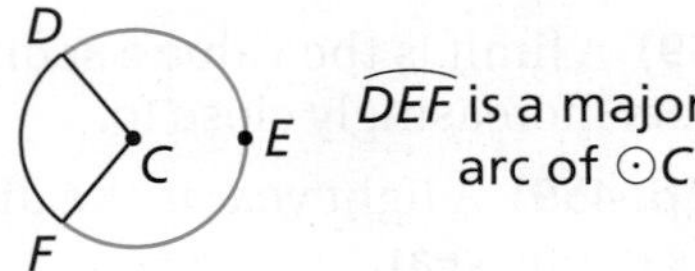

mapping (p. 562) *See* **transformation.**

maximize (p. 670) To maximize a quantity, you make the quantity as great as possible.

measure of an arc (p. 402) The measure of an arc is the measure of the central angle that intercepts it.

median (p. 31) A median is a segment that connects a vertex of a triangle to the midpoint of the opposite side.

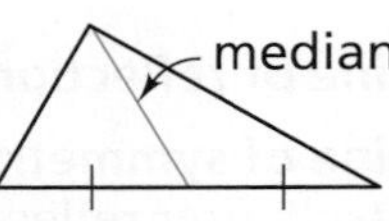

midline (p. 31) A midline is a segment that connects the midpoints of two sides of a triangle. The midline is also known as a midsegment.

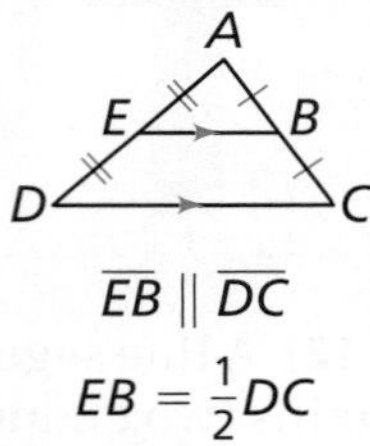

$\overline{EB} \parallel \overline{DC}$

$EB = \frac{1}{2}DC$

$\overline{EB}$ is a midline of $\triangle ACD$.

midpoint (p. 29) A midpoint is the point on a segment that is halfway between two endpoints. A midpoint on a coordinate grid is the average of the coordinates of the endpoints of the segment.

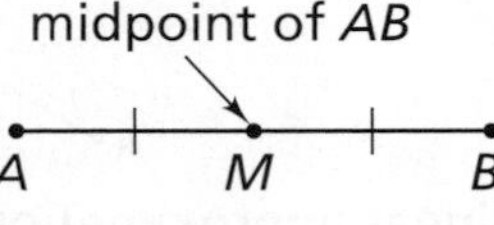

midpoint quadrilateral (p. 192) A midpoint quadrilateral is a quadrilateral formed by connecting the midpoints of the sides of a quadrilateral with segments.

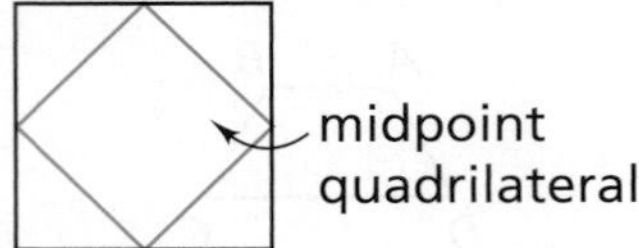

midsegment *See* **midline.**

minimize (p. 654) To minimize a quantity, you make the quantity as small as possible.

minor arc (p. 402) A minor arc is an arc that is smaller than a semicircle.

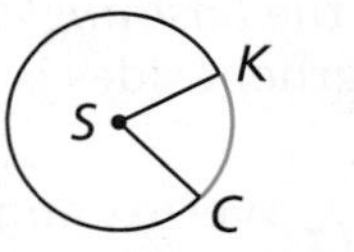

Monte Carlo Method (p. 439) The Monte Carlo Method is a statistical simulation method that utilizes sequences of random numbers to perform a simulation.

N

nested triangles (p. 307) One triangle is nested inside another triangle if the triangles share a vertex and the sides of the triangles opposite the shared vertex are parallel.

net (p. 6) A net is a figure that results from unfolding a three-dimensional solid.

***n*-gon (p. 119)** An *n*-gon is a polygon with *n* sides, where *n* is a whole number greater than or equal to 3.

nonagon (p. 21) A nonagon is a nine-sided polygon.

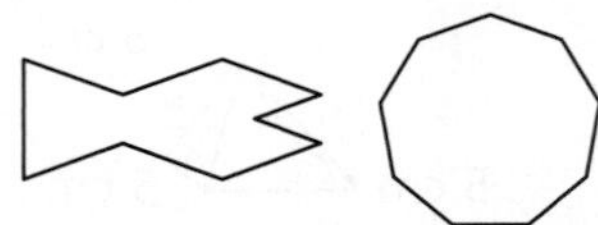

O

oblique prism (p. 236) An oblique prism is a prism with lateral edges that are not perpendicular to the bases.

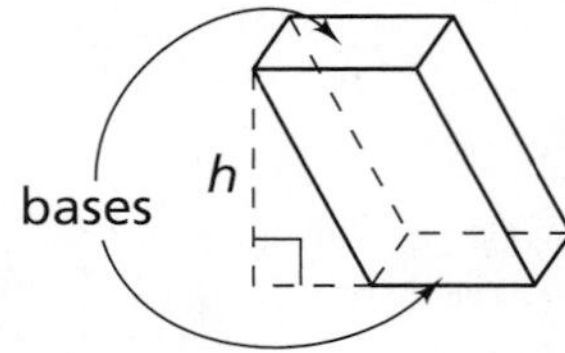

oblique pyramid (p. 237) An oblique pyramid is a pyramid in which the line through the apex and the center of the base is not perpendicular to the base.

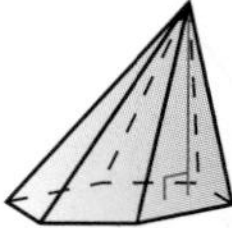

oblique hexagonal pyramid

octagon (p. 34) An octagon is a polygon with eight sides.

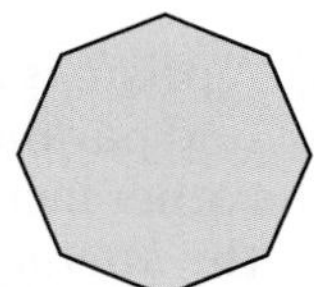

octahedron (p. 6) An octahedron is a polyhedron with exactly eight plane surfaces.

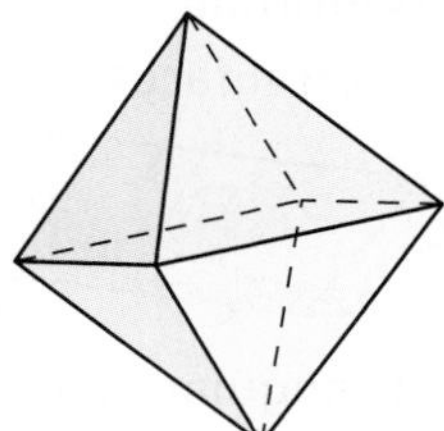

optimization (p. 653) Optimization is the process of evaluating alternatives to determine the best solutions to a problem.

ordered triple (p. 612) An ordered triple (x, y, z) describes the location of a point in three-dimensional space.

parallel lines (pp. 12, 98) Parallel lines are lines in the same plane that do not intersect.

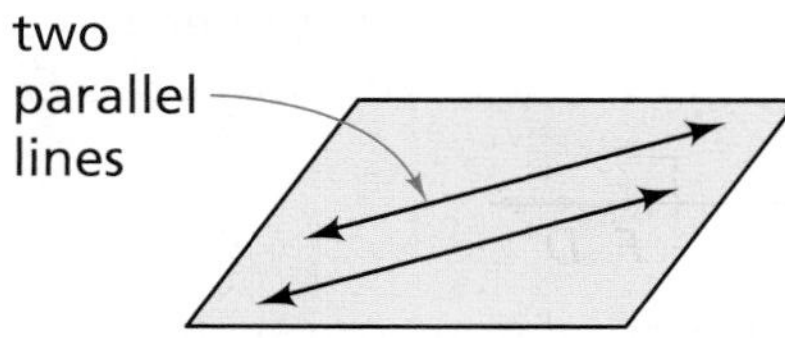

a plane (for example, a piece of paper)

parallel planes (p. 12) Parallel planes are planes in space that do not intersect.

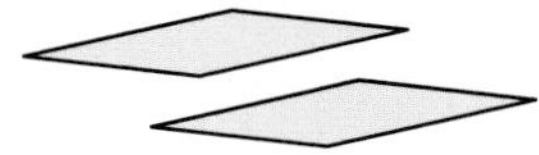

two parallel planes

parallelepiped (p. 232) A parallelepiped is a prism in which every pair of opposite faces are congruent parallelograms.

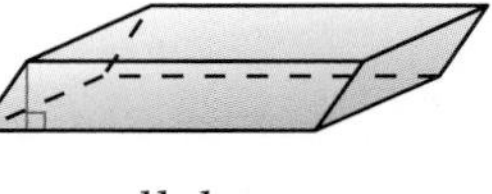

parallel method (p. 295) The parallel method is a process for dilating a figure by drawing parallel segments.

parallelogram (p. 151) A parallelogram is a quadrilateral with two pairs of parallel sides.

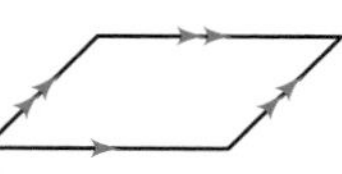

path (p. 655) A path is a continuous route from one point to another. A path between two points cannot be shorter than the distance between the points.

pentagon (p. 52) A pentagon is a polygon with exactly five sides.

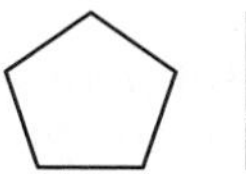

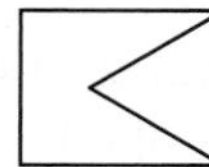

perimeter (p. 241) The perimeter is the length of the border of a two-dimensional figure.

4 in.
4 in.
3 in.
5 in.

$$P = 4 \text{ in.} + 4 \text{ in.} + 5 \text{ in.} + 3 \text{ in.}$$
$$= 16 \text{ in.}$$

perpendicular lines (p. 33) Perpendicular lines are lines that intersect to form right angles.

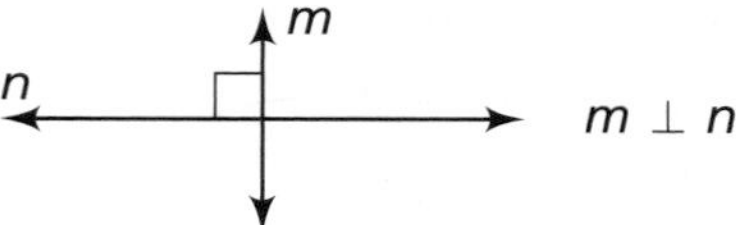

perpendicular bisector (p. 29) The perpendicular bisector of a segment is a line that is perpendicular to the segment at the segment's midpoint.

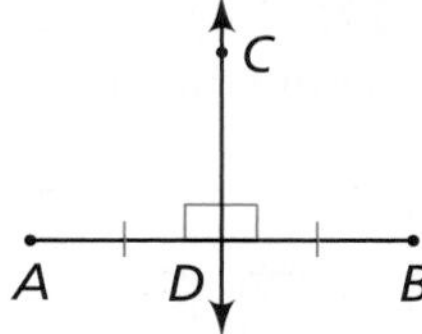

pi (p. 377) Pi (π) is the ratio of the circumference of any circle to its diameter. Pi is the numerical value of the area of a circle with radius 1. Pi is an infinite nonrepeating decimal constant that begins with 3.14159.

planar figure (p. 145) A planar figure is a figure with all of its points in the same plane.

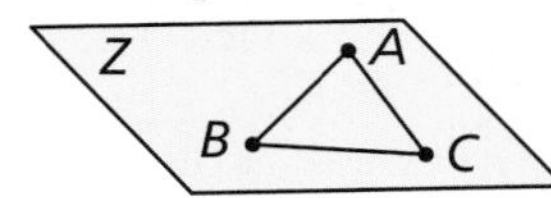

$\triangle ABC$ lies in plane Z.

plane (p. 12) A plane is a flat surface that has no thickness, contains many lines, and extends without end in the directions of its lines.

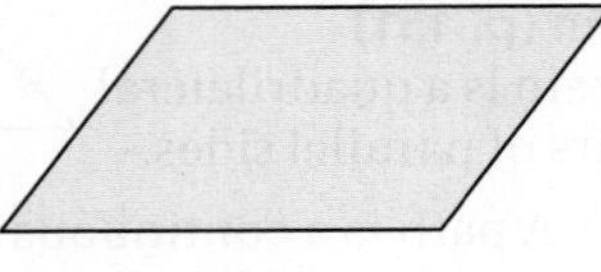

a plane

point (p. 12) A point is a location in space. It has no size.

point of tangency (p. 21) The point of tangency is the point of intersection of a tangent line and a circle.

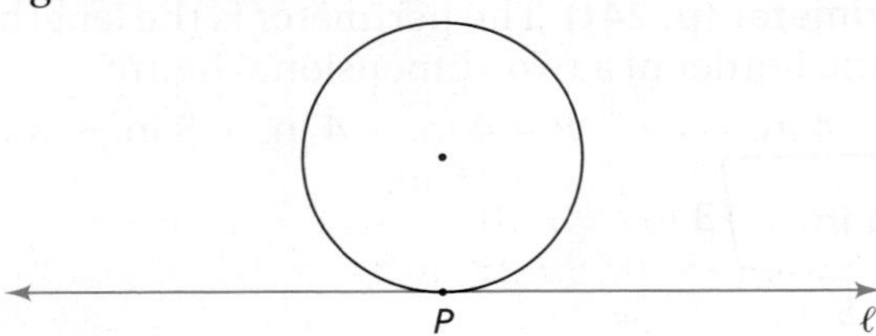

P is the point of tangency of line ℓ and the circle.

polygon (p. 49) A polygon is a closed plane figure with at least three sides.

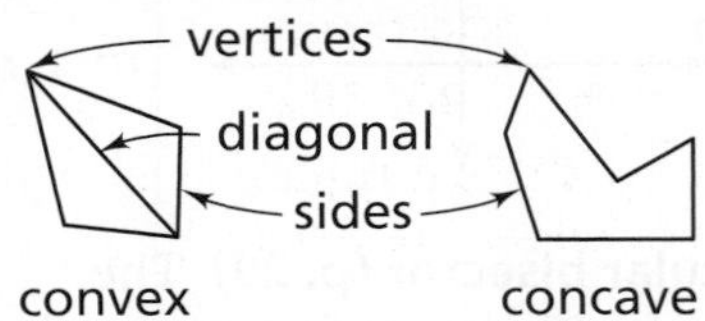

polyhedron (p. 235) A polyhedron is a solid with faces that are polygons.

polyominoes (p. 77) Polyominoes are shapes made up of congruent squares that meet edge to edge.

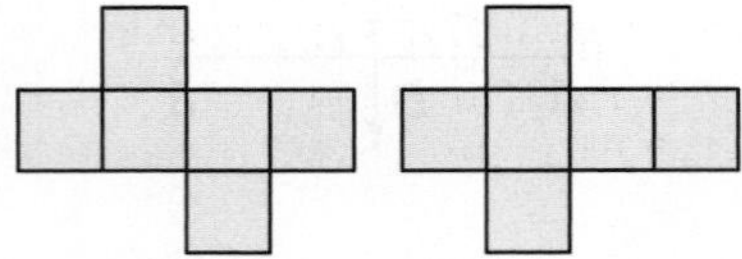

postulate (p. 84) A postulate is a statement accepted without proof.

power of a point (p. 432) The power of a point with respect to a circle is $(PA)(PB)$, where A and B are the points of intersection of a line through P and the circle.

preimage (p. 551) The preimage is the original figure before a transformation.

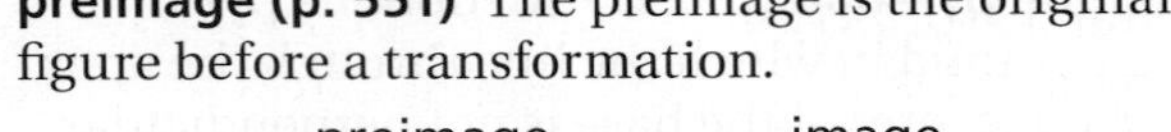

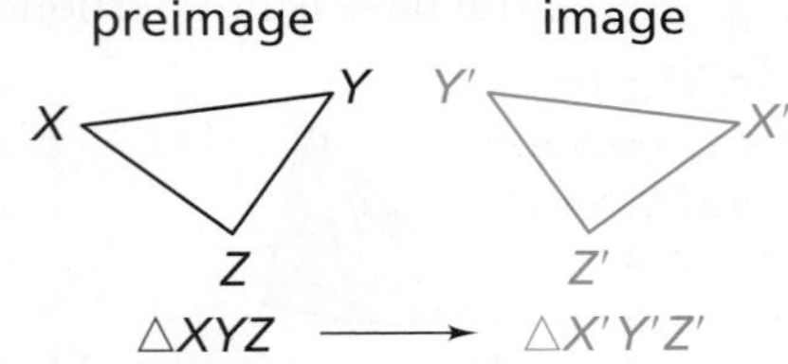

This transformation maps X to X', Y to Y' and Z to Z'.

prism (pp. 12, 235) A prism is a polyhedron with two congruent and parallel *faces*, called the *bases*. The other faces, which are parallelograms, are the *lateral faces*. An *altitude* of a prism is a perpendicular segment that joins the planes of the bases. The *height* of the prism is the length of its altitude.

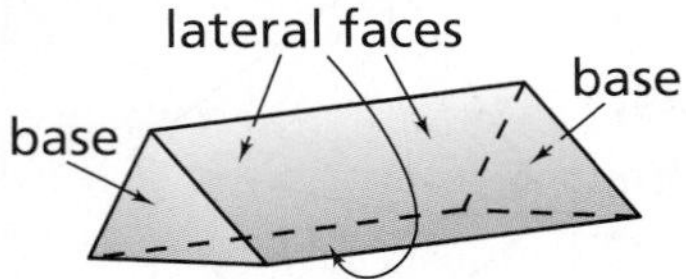

triangular prism

probability (p. 438) Probability is the likelihood than an event will occur.

projection (p. 468) A projection is the transformation of the points of a geometric figure onto the points of another figure. The projection of a point A onto a line ℓ is the intersection of ℓ with the line perpendicular to ℓ through A.

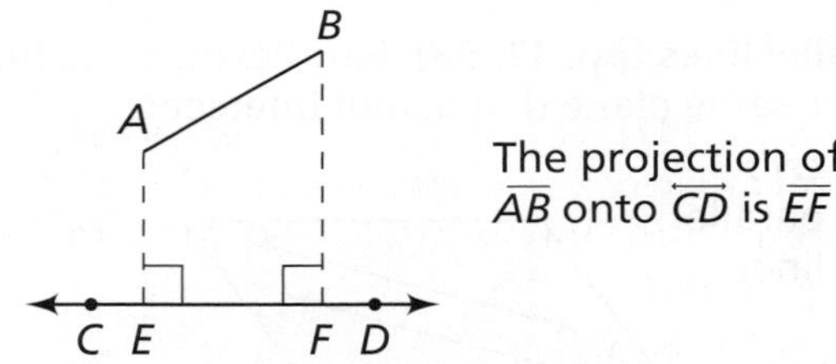

The projection of $\overline{AB}$ onto $\overleftrightarrow{CD}$ is $\overline{EF}$.

proof (p. 115) A proof is an argument in which every statement is supported with a reason.

pyramid (p. 237) A pyramid is a polyhedron with one *base*. The base can be any polygon. The *lateral faces* are triangles that have a common vertex, the *apex* of the pyramid. An *altitude* of the pyramid is the perpendicular segment from the apex to the plane of the base. The *height* of the pyramid is the length of the altitude. The *slant height* of the pyramid is the height of a triangular face.

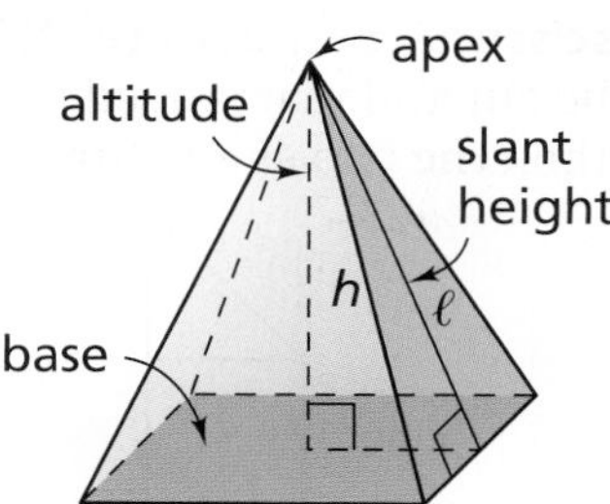
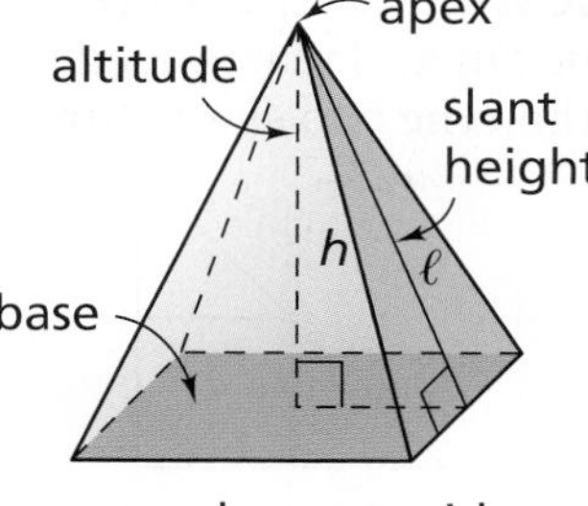

Pythagorean triple (p. 218) A Pythagorean triple is a set of three positive integers a, b, and c that satisfy the equation $a^2 + b^2 = c^2$.

Q

quadrilateral (p. 144) A quadrilateral is a polygon with exactly four sides.

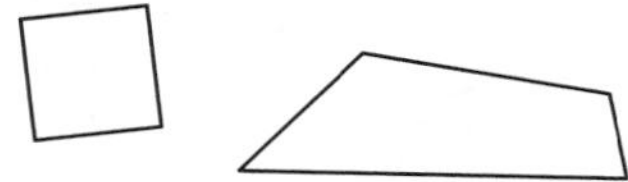

R

radius (p. 39) A radius of a circle is a segment from the center of the circle to a point on the circle. The radius of the circle may also refer to the length of the radius.

radian (p. 397) The measure in *radians* of a central angle of a circle is the ration L/r <stack fraction> of the intercepted arc length L to the circle's radius r.

ratio (p. 279) A ratio is the quotient of two numbers. If only one number is given, the second number is understood to be 1.

ratio method (p. 295) The ratio method is a process for dilating a figure.

rectangle (p. 157) A rectangle is a parallelogram with four right angles.

reflection (p. 555) A reflection, or flip, is a transformation that maps a point in the plane to its mirror image using a *line of reflection* as a mirror.

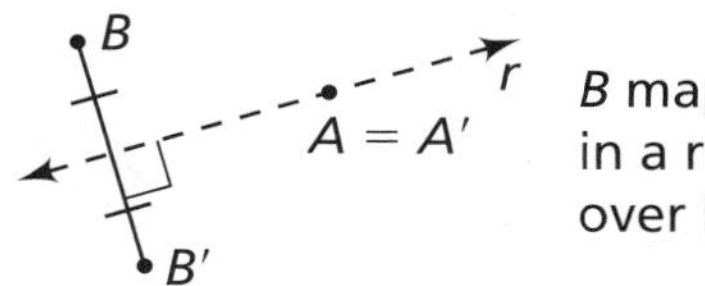

regular polygon (p. 5) A regular polygon is a polygon that is both equiangular and equilateral.

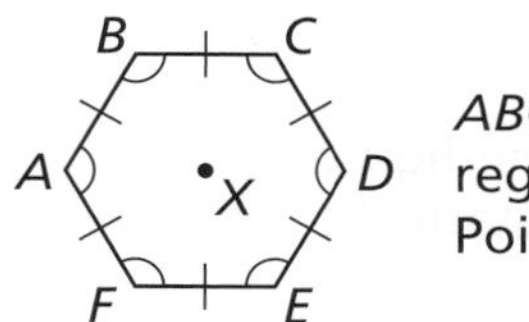

rhombus (p. 157) A rhombus is a parallelogram with four congruent sides.

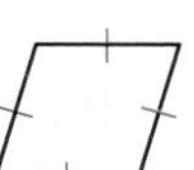

right angle (p. 76) A right angle is an angle that measures 90°.

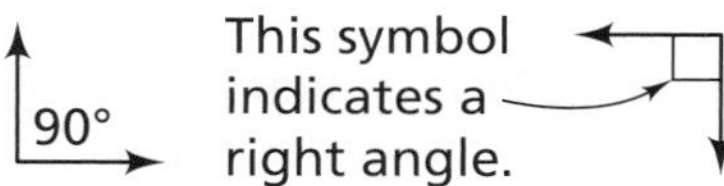

right prism (p. 236) A right prism is a prism whose lateral edges are perpendicular to its bases.

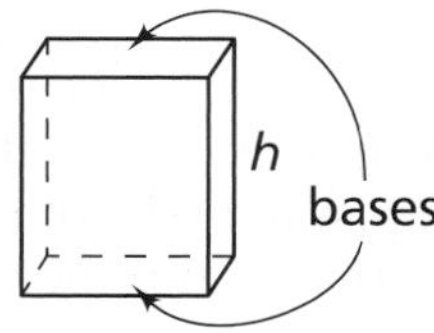

right pyramid (p. 237) A right pyramid is a pyramid in which the line through the apex and the center of the base is perpendicular to the base.

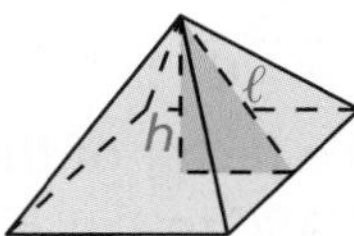

right triangle (p. 18) A right triangle is a triangle with a right angle. The *hypotenuse* is the side opposite the right angle. The other sides are the *legs* of the right triangle.

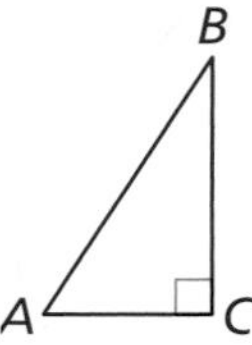

rigid motion *See* **isometry.**

rotation (p. 570) A rotation is a transformation that turns a figure about a fixed point, the *center of rotation.*

angle of rotation

R′ R V′ V

A rotation about *R* maps *V* to *V*′.

rotational symmetry (p. 560) Rotational symmetry is a type of symmetry for which there is a rotation of 180° or less that maps a figure onto itself.

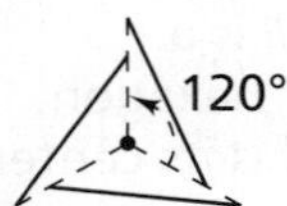

The figure has 120° rotational symmetry.

S

scale (p. 263) A scale is the ratio of any length in a scale drawing to the corresponding actual length. The lengths may be in different units. For example, on a map, 1 inch may represent 1 mile.

scale a figure (p. 267) When you scale a figure, you draw a new figure, called a *scaled figure,* that is the same shape as the given figure.

scaled figure (p. 267) In a scaled figure, each length is *r* times the corresponding length in the original figure.

scale factor (p. 266) A scale factor is a number that describes by how much you have reduced or enlarged a map, blueprint, or picture. The scale factor *r* can be any number, including a fraction.

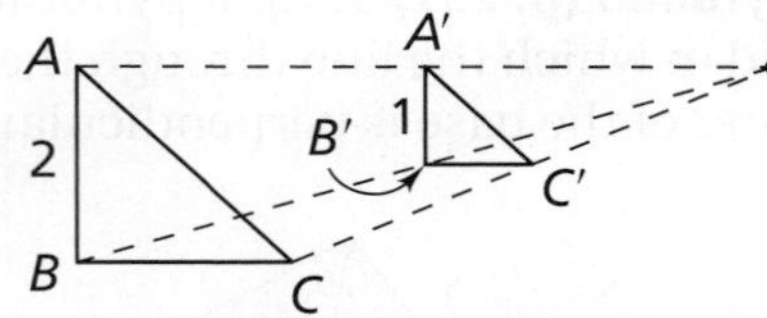

The scale factor of the dilation that maps $\triangle ABC$ to $\triangle A'B'C'$ is $\frac{1}{2}$.

scalene triangle (p. 136) A scalene triangle has no sides of equal length.

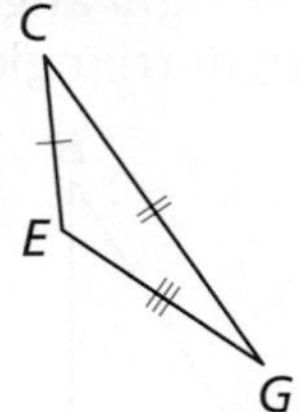

scissors-congruent (p. 172) If one shape can be cut and rearranged to form a second shape, then the two shapes are scissors-congruent.

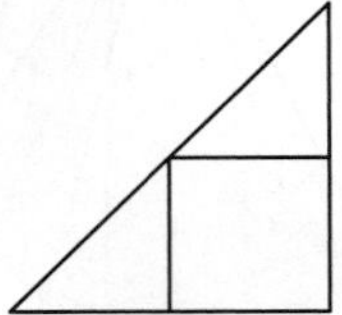

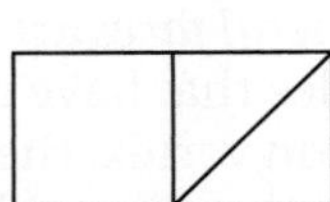

These figures are scissors-congruent.

secant (p. 420) A secant line is a line that has two intersections with a circle.

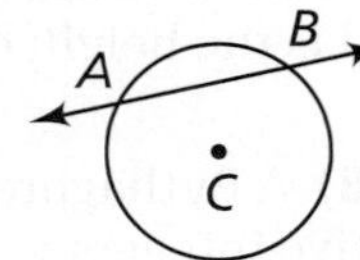

$\overleftrightarrow{AB}$ is a secant of ⊙*C*.

secant angle (p. 421) A secant angle is an angle with sides that are two secants of a circle. A secant angle's vertex can be inside or outside the circle.

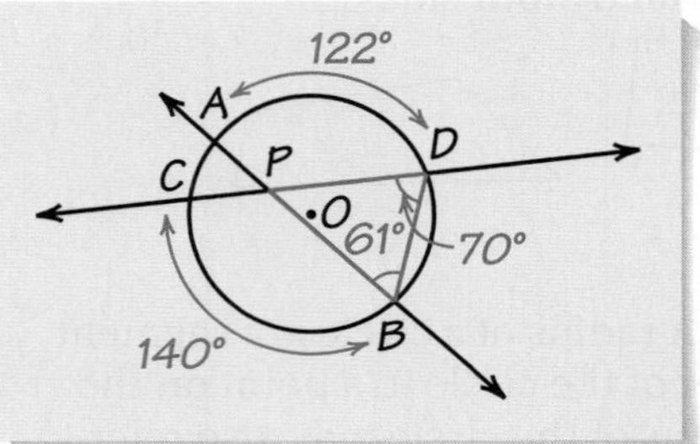

Secants $\overleftrightarrow{AB}$ and $\overleftrightarrow{CD}$ form angle $\angle DPB$.

sector (p. 379) A sector of a circle is a region bounded by two radii and the circle.

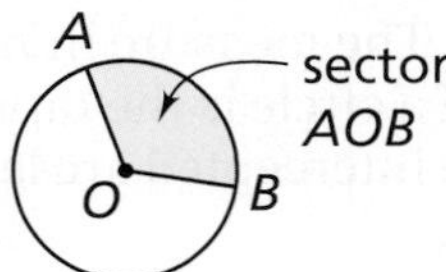

self-intersecting figure (p. 145) A figure is self-intersecting if you "walk" its outer edges and go through the same point more than once before you get back to where you started.

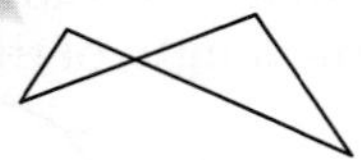

semicircle (p. 394) A semicircle is half of a circle.

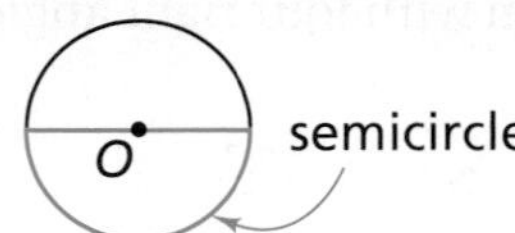

semi-cylinder (p. 523) A semi-cylinder is half of a right cylinder.

side *See* **quadrilateral.**

similar (p. 325) Two figures are similar if you can rotate and/or flip one of them so that you can dilate it onto the other. Two figures are similar if one is congruent to a dilation of the other.

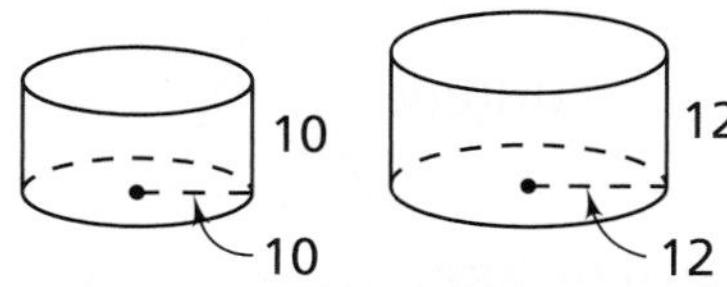

sine *See* **trigonometric ratios.**

skew quadrilateral (p. 145) A skew quadrilateral is a quadrilateral that does not lie completely in one plane.

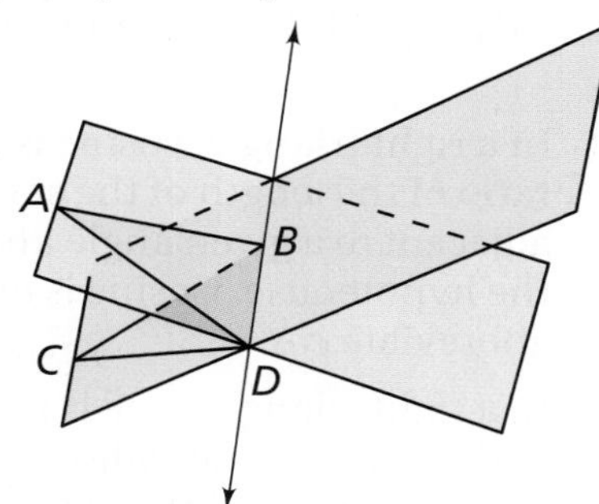

slant height *See* **cone; pyramid.**

sphere (p. 74) A sphere is the set of all points in space that are a given distance *r*, the radius, from a given point *C*, the center.

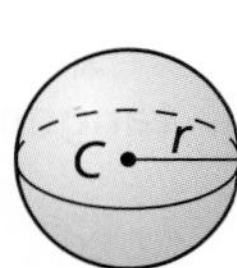

splits two sides proportionally (p. 310) In a $\triangle ABC$ with D on $\overline{AB}$ and E on $\overline{AC}$, the segment $\overline{DE}$ splits two sides $(\overline{AB}$ and $\overline{AC})$ proportionally if and only if $\frac{AB}{AD} = \frac{AC}{AE}$. The ratio $\frac{AB}{AD}$ is the common ratio.

square (p. 85) A square is a rectangle with four congruent sides.

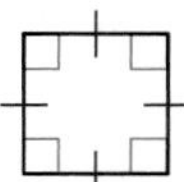

straight angle (p. 76) A straight angle measures 180°.

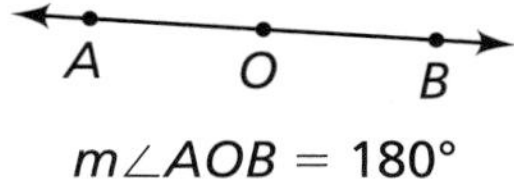

$m\angle AOB = 180°$

subscript (p. 594) A subscript is a character printed on a lower level than the other characters in a line of type. In a_n, n is a subscript.

supplementary angles (p. 102) Two angles are supplementary if the sum of their measures is 180°.

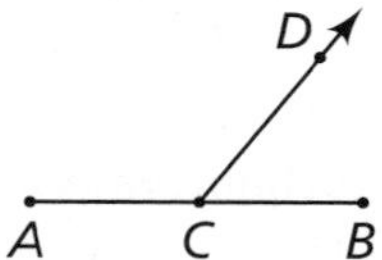

$\angle ACD$ and $\angle DCB$ are supplementary angles.

surface area (p. 231) The surface area of a polyhedron is the sum of the areas of all the faces of the polyhedron.

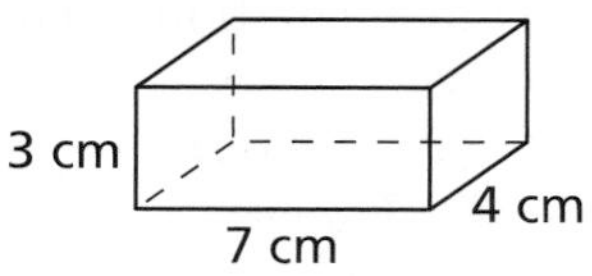

$$\begin{aligned}\text{surface area}&\\ \text{of prism} &= \text{L.A.} + 2B\\ &= 2 \cdot 3(4) + 2 \cdot 3(7) + 2 \cdot 7(4)\\ &= 122\ \text{cm}^2\end{aligned}$$

symmetric (p. 9) A figure is symmetric if you can fold it in half so that the two halves fit exactly on top of each other.

symmetry diagonal (p. 147) The symmetry diagonal is the diagonal of a kite that divides the kite into two congruent triangles.

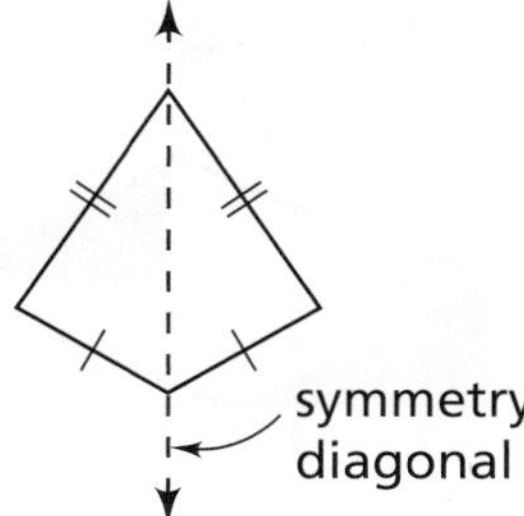

T

tail *See* **vector.**

tangent line (p. 420) A tangent line is a line that intersects a circle at exactly one point.

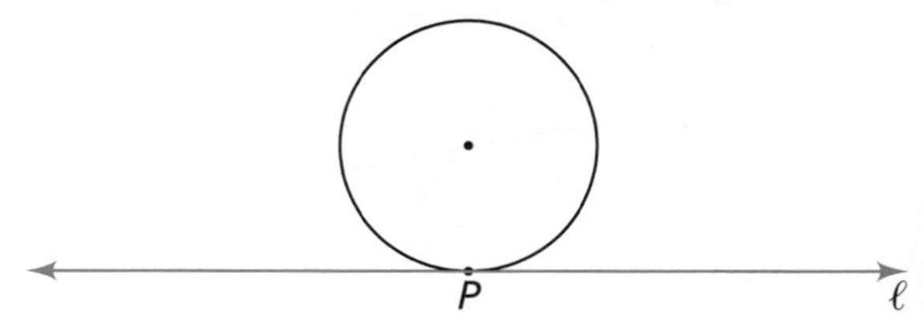

Line ℓ is tangent to the circle at P.

tangent (p. 489) *See* **trigonometric ratios.**

tetrahedron (p. 6) A tetrahedron is a solid with exactly four faces. All of the faces are congruent equilateral triangles.

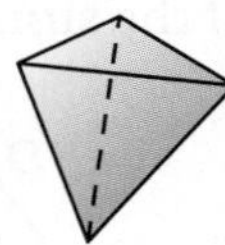

theorem (p. 29) A theorem is a statement that has been proven true.

topographic map (p. 687) A topographic map is a type of contour plot that depicts land elevations or sea depths.

transformation (p. 551) A transformation is a change in the position, size, or shape of a geometric figure. A transformation is a mapping of a figure onto its image.

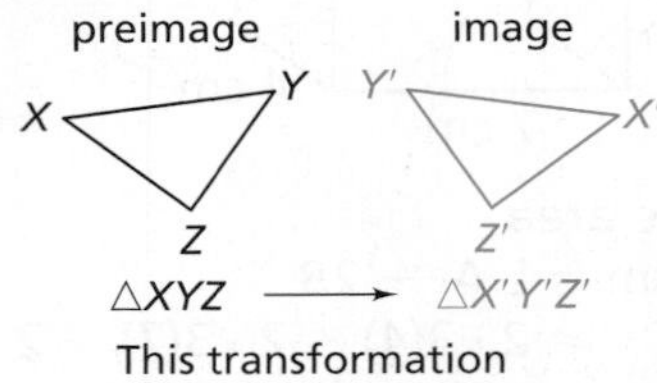

This transformation maps X to X', Y to Y' and Z to Z'.

translation (p. 561) A translation is a transformation that slides a graph or figure horizontally, vertically, or both without changing the size or shape of the graph. A translation on a coordinate plane is a transformation that adds a numeric value to each coordinate of the image.

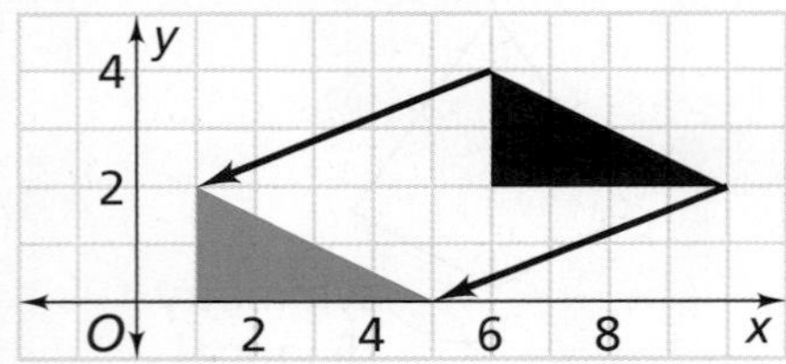

The blue triangle is the image of the black triangle under the translation (−5, −2).

transversal (p. 89) A transversal is a line that intersects two or more lines.

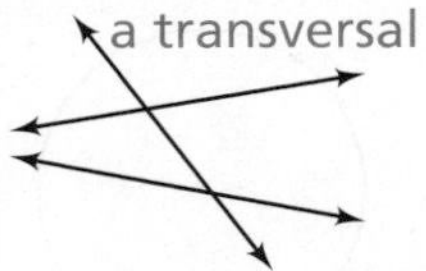

trapezoid (p. 147) A trapezoid is a quadrilateral with exactly one pair of parallel sides. The two parallel sides are the *bases* of the trapezoid. The other sides are the *legs* of the trapezoid. The *height* of a trapezoid is the length of a perpendicular segment between the lines containing the bases.

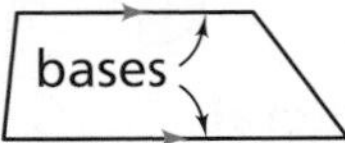

triangle (p. 11) A triangle is a polygon with exactly three sides. Any side of a triangle can be the *base* of the triangle. The *height* of the triangle is the length of the *altitude* drawn from a *vertex* to a line containing the base.

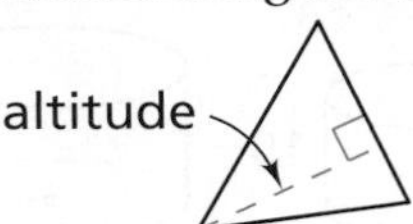

trigonometry (p. 488) Trigonometry is the study of triangles.

trigonometric ratios (p. 489) Trigonometric ratios are special ratios that compare the lengths of sides of right triangles. They are used to find missing side lengths and angle measures.

- **cosine** In a right triangle, cosine is the ratio of the length of the side adjacent to a given angle and the hypotenuse. Cosine is often abbreviate *cos.*
- **sine** In a right triangle, sine is the ratio of the length of the side opposite a given angle and the hypotenuse. Sine is often abbreviated *sin.*
- **tangent** In a right triangle, tangent is the ratio of the length of the side opposite a given angle to the side adjacent the given angle. Tangent is often abbreviated *tan.*

trisected (p. 155) A segment is trisected if it is divided into three congruent parts.

U

unit circle (p. 413) The unit circle has a radius of 1 unit and its center is at the origin of the coordinate plane.

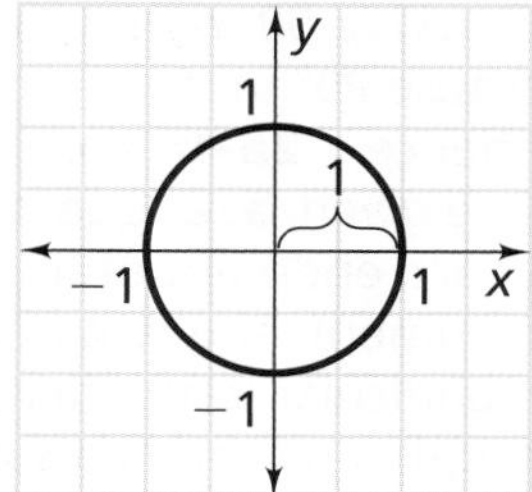

unit cube (p. 671) A unit cube is a cube with edge length one unit.

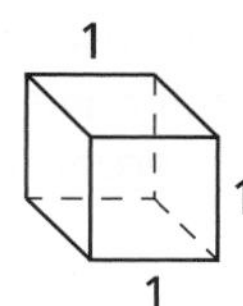

UnMessUpable Figure (p. 42) An UnMessUpable figure is a figure that remains unchanged when you move one point or other part of the figure.

V

vanishing point (p. 45) The vanishing point is the point where parallel lines that are receding from the observer seem to come together.

vector (p. 628) A vector is an arrow that starts at one point, the *tail*, and points to a second point, the *head*. Given two points A and B, the vector from A to B is the ordered pair of points (A, B).

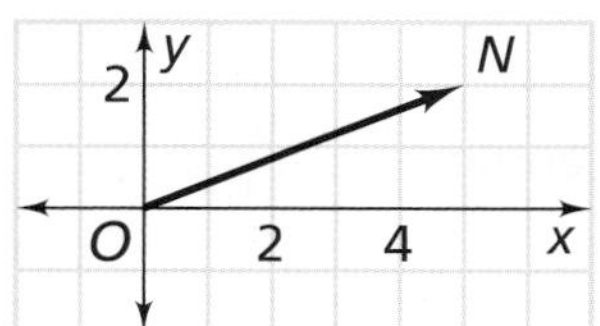

Vector *ON* has initial point *O* (tail) and terminal point *N* (head). The ordered pair notation for the vector is (5, 2).

Venn diagram (p. 159) A Venn diagram is a diagram using overlapping circles, often shaded, to show relationships between sets.

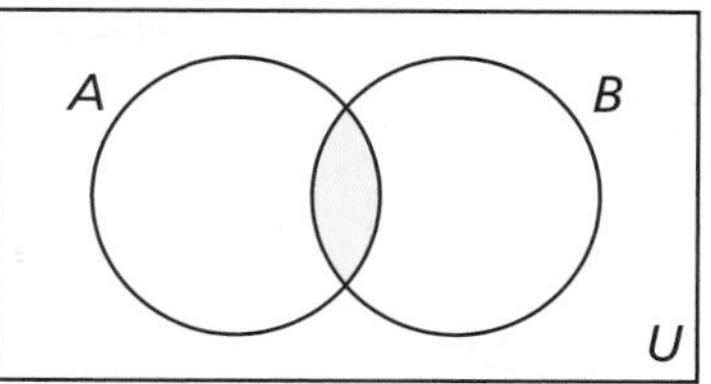

vertex (pp. 37, 144) The vertex is the point of intersection of two lines, segments, or rays.

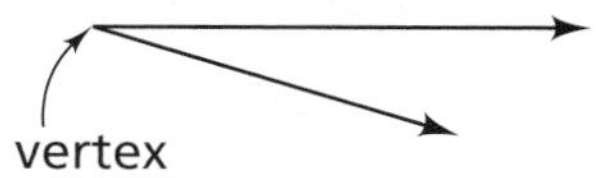

vertex angle (p. 120) The vertex angle of an isosceles triangle is formed by the two congruent sides of the triangle.

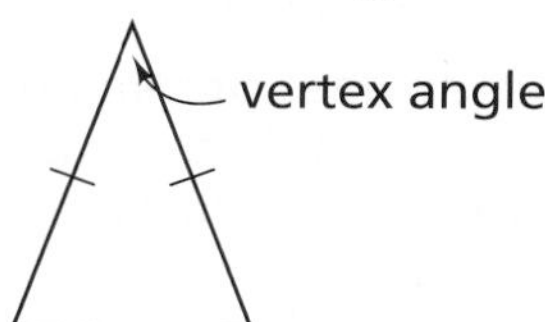

vertical angles (pp. 93, 99) Vertical angles are two angles with sides that form two intersecting rays. Vertical angles are congruent.

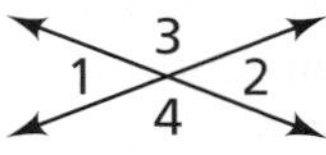

$\angle 1$ and $\angle 2$ are vertical angles, as are $\angle 3$ and $\angle 4$.

volume (p. 247) Volume is a measure of the space a figure occupies.

The volume of this prism is 24 cubic units, or 24 units^3.

Z

***z*-axis (p. 612)** The z-axis is a third coordinate axis that is perpendicular to the x-y plane. The z-axis allows you to locate points in three-dimensional space.

Selected Answers

Chapter 1

Lesson 1.01

On Your Own

6. 1 line of symmetry:

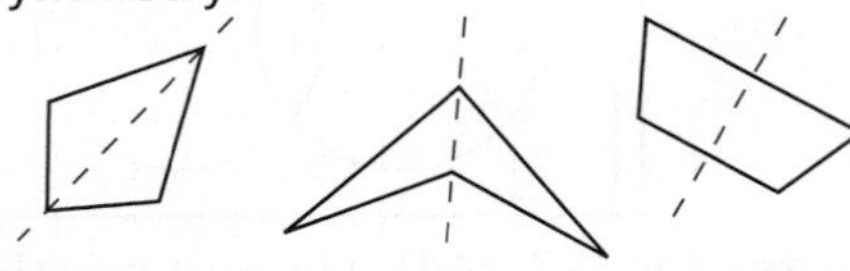

2 lines of symmetry:

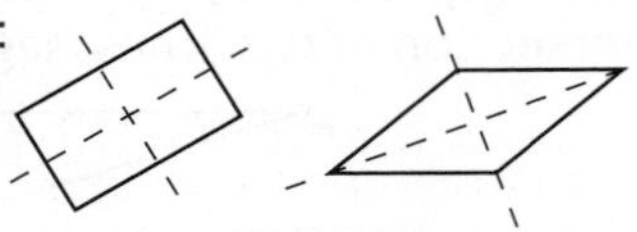

4 lines of symmetry:

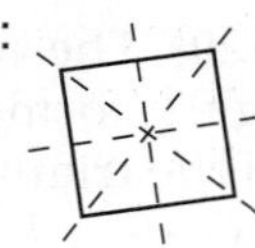

All others have no lines of symmetry.
7. The triangle and its shadow have the same shape, but the shadow is larger.

Lesson 1.02

Check Your Understanding

1. Answers may vary. Sample: Since the two bases are the same distance apart at all points, the connecting lines appear to be the same length. Since the points on the second base are translated in the same direction from the corresponding points on the first base, the connecting segments take on the same slope. This makes them parallel. **2a.** Faces with corresponding edges parallel in the block letter should be parallel. **b.** Light hits parallel faces at the same angle; answers may vary. Sample: Different shading on parallel faces would be necessary if other objects affect the light that the parallel faces receive. **3.** Answers may vary. Sample: The darkest regions sometimes appear to be upper parts of a three-dimensional figure. Then they suddenly switch to be right-hand parts of a different figure. **4.** Drawings may vary. The letter shape is the base of the prism.

On Your Own

6. 16 **10.** The area of the entire figure is $(a + b)^2$. The length of each side of the white square is $a - b$, so the area of the white square is $(a - b)^2$. Each shaded rectangle has area ab. The area of the entire figure equals the sum of the areas of the parts, so $(a + b)^2 = 4ab + (a - b)^2 = 4ab + a^2 - 2ab + b^2$, or $a^2 + 2ab + b^2$. **11.** Drawings may vary. Sample:

	c	f
d	dc	df

Lesson 1.03

Check Your Understanding

1a. a rectangle **b.** north **c.** The assumption is that the right turn is a 90° right turn. This is reasonable because 90° turns are common in everyday experience. **2a–b.** Answers may vary. Samples are given. **a.** a square **b.** Draw a segment. At each endpoint of this segment, draw another segment. The two new segments should be perpendicular to the first, should each be the same length, and should be on the same side of the original segment. Connect the other two endpoints of the two new segments to form a closed figure. **3a.** Answers may vary. Your figures should be rhombuses or squares. **b.** No; although the shape will have to be a rhombus, it can be a square if the segments drawn have the same length.

On Your Own

5a.

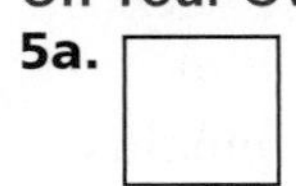

b. Yes; the figure must be a square, though the size of the square can vary. Squares are the only quadrilateral with horizontal, vertical, and diagonal lines of symmetry. **6.** a sphere

Lesson 1.04

Check Your Understanding

1.

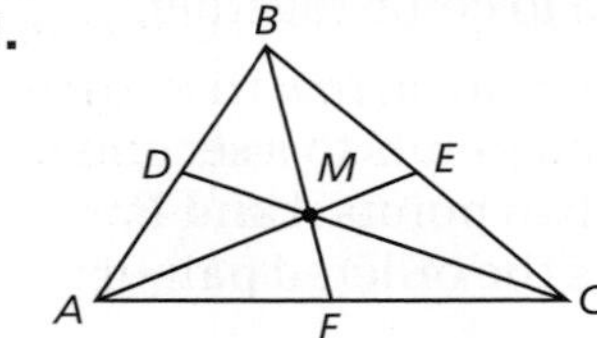

2. A **3.** S **4.** C

On Your Own

9a. square **b.** a right angle

Lesson 1.05

On Your Own

8. The 3 in.-8 in.-4 in. triangle in Problem 1 is impossible to construct because $3 + 4 < 8$. The 60°-70°-80° and 90°-90°-90° triangles in Problem 5 are impossible to construct because their angle sums would be greater than 180°. **9.** Comparing the results from Problem 6 shows that equal angle measures yield triangles that have the same shape, though the triangles may be different sizes. Comparing results from Problem 2 shows that equal side lengths yield triangles that are both the same shape and the same size. **10.** Triangles are possible for parts (b), (c), and (d) since the angle measures have a sum of 180°. No triangles are possible for parts (a) and (e) because the angle measures do not have a sum of 180°.

Lesson 1.06

Check Your Understanding

1a. Mark two points, A and B, on the given line. Construct the perpendicular bisector of $\overline{AB}$. **b.** Use the procedure from part (a) to construct a line perpendicular to the perpendicular bisector from part (a). **2.** Make a diagonal fold and crease the paper so that one corner of the sheet falls on the opposite long edge. Cut off the narrow rectangular strip of excess paper. **3a.** Fold the square to make the left side match the right side. Fold the resulting rectangle so that the top side matches the bottom side. **b.** Open the folded sheet from part (a). Fold the corners of the large square inward to meet at the point of intersection of the crease lines. The new crease lines form a square with half the area of the large square. **4.** Answers may vary. To construct the bisector of an angle, fold through the vertex so that the sides of the angle coincide. **5a.** Answers may vary. Sample: Construct a circle centered at one endpoint of the segment and having the segment as a radius. Draw another radius, not collinear with the first. Draw the segment that connects the endpoints on the circle. **b.** Answers may vary. Sample: Fold the segment in half so that its endpoints coincide. Mark a point on the crease line (but not the midpoint of the original segment), and draw segments from that point to the endpoints of the segment. **c.** Answers may vary. Sample: Open the compass to the length of the segment. Use that radius and construct the two circles that have centers at the endpoints of the segment. Select a point where the circles intersect and draw segments from that point to the endpoints of the segment. **d.** Answers may vary. Sample: Construct perpendicular lines through the endpoints of the given segment. Construct a circle, with one of the endpoints as its center, that passes through the other endpoint. Construct a line parallel to the original segment through one of the points of intersection of the circle and the line perpendicular to the original segment.

6b. 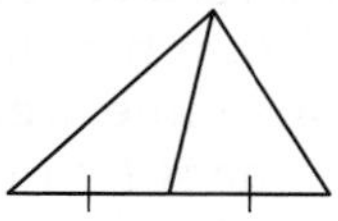 **c.**

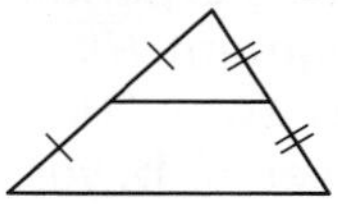

7a–c. Midpoints (the key to the constructions in parts (a) and (b) in the exercise) and angle bisectors have been constructed in earlier exercises. **d.** Answers may vary. Sample: Let the triangle be $\triangle ABC$. Construct a circle with center A that passes through B. If $\overline{BC}$ intersects the circle at another point, call this point D. If it does not, extend $\overline{BC}$ until it intersects the circle at D. Construct the midpoint of $\overline{BD}$ and call it E. The segment $\overline{AE}$ is an altitude of $\triangle ABC$. Construct the other two altitudes in a similar way. **e.** Answers may vary. **8.** Answers may vary. Sample: The diagonals of a square have the same length; each diagonal divides the square in half; the diagonals intersect at right angles; the diagonals cut the square into four right triangles that are the same size and shape. **9.** Answers may vary. Sample: Construct the perpendicular bisectors of two sides of the equilateral $\triangle ABC$. The perpendicular bisectors intersect at a point X. Construct the circle that has center X and radius XA.

On Your Own

13a. acute triangles **b.** right triangles **c.** obtuse triangles **15a.** Sketches may vary. **b.** Construct the perpendicular bisectors of two of the sides of the triangle that has the bases of the saplings as vertices. Place the sprinkler at the point of intersection of the perpendicular bisectors. **c.** Answers may vary. Sample: The point of intersection of the perpendicular bisectors of the triangle that the three saplings form is the center of the circle that passes through the three saplings. If you place the sprinkler at this point of intersection, the sprinkler is equidistant from the three saplings.

Lesson 1.07

On Your Own

5. Answers may vary. Sample: To construct the figure in Exercise 2, use the circle tool to construct a circle centered at A that passes through B. Then construct a circle with an arbitrary center that passes through a point on the first circle. To construct the figure in Exercise 3, draw a circle first using the circle tool. Place a point on the circle and construct a triangle with the segment tool using this point as one of the vertices. To construct the figure in Exercise 4, draw two lines and then place one point on one line and two points on the other line, using the point tool. Connect all three points using the segment tool. **7.** No; a line and a segment do not need to touch to be perpendicular. If the segment can be extended to intersect the line at a right angle, then the line and the segment are perpendicular.

Lesson 1.08

Check Your Understanding

1a. The other two segments rotate. One of them remains perpendicular to $\overline{BC}$ and the other parallel to $\overline{BC}$. The position of point A does not change. **b.** The segments that intersect at A also stretch or shrink. Their lengths are equal to BC. **2.** The four points trace paths that result in a figure that has rotational symmetry. **3.** Because the two segments have no constructed relationship to each other, they move independently. When you stretch or shrink one, the other does not change at all.

On Your Own

5. Drawing the line parallel to $\overline{BC}$ fails to link the behavior of the line to changes in $\overline{BC}$. As a result, the segments that intersect at A will not act like arms of a windmill. **6.** The circle keeps the arms of the windmill the same length as $\overline{BC}$.

Lesson 1.09

Check Your Understanding

1–5. Constructions may vary. **6.** Answers may vary. Sample: Method 1—Construct a circle with center C. Construct two noncollinear radii of the circle, $\overline{CX}$ and $\overline{CY}$. Construct a line through X parallel to $\overline{CY}$. Construct a line through Y parallel to $\overline{CX}$. Let P be the point where these two lines intersect. The required parallelogram is $CXPY$. Method 2—Construct $\overline{AB}$. Construct the perpendicular bisector of $\overline{AB}$. Construct a circle with its center at the midpoint of $\overline{AB}$. Mark the points D and E where the perpendicular bisector intersects the circle. The required parallelogram is $ADBE$. **7a.** Answers may vary. **b.** The ratios are equal. **8–9.** Constructions may vary.

On Your Own

12. There are infinitely many lines perpendicular to any given line or segment. Specifying a point makes it possible to tell the software which of these infinitely many lines you want.

Lesson 1.10

On Your Own

3. Answers may vary. Sample:

$\frac{z}{w} = 8$

w	z
2	16
3	24
4	32
5	40

$g + h = 8$

g	h
0	8
2	6
4	4
6	2

$m - n = 8$

m	n
10	2
20	12
30	22
40	32

4a. The figure formed by joining the midpoints has four vertices, no three of which are collinear, and when you connect the midpoints in order, the resulting figure will not cross itself. **b.** The quadrilaterals are parallelograms because each midline formed by connecting consecutive midpoints is parallel to a diagonal. Therefore, both pairs of opposite sides are parallel.

Lesson 1.11

Check Your Understanding

1. Call the endpoints of the diameter A and B. **a.** Answers may vary. Sample: $m\angle ADB$ is always 90°. In $\triangle ADB$, $\overline{AB}$ is the longest side and $\angle D$ is the largest angle. $m\angle A + m\angle B$ is always 90°. The length of $\overline{AB}$ does not change. $(AD)^2 + (BD)^2 = (AB)^2$ **b.** Answers may vary. Sample: $\angle D$ is the largest angle, and $\overline{AB}$ is the longest side. $m\angle D$ is 90°, as is $m\angle A + m\angle B$. The ratio of any two sides is constant. The ratio of the circumference of the circle to the diameter of the circle is constant. The ratio of the area of $\triangle ABD$ to the area of the circle is constant. **2.** b and d **3.** $AC + CB$, $m\angle ACD + m\angle DCB$ **4.** the area of $\triangle ABC$ **5.** opposite ways; $CE \cdot CD$ **6.** The product $CE \cdot CD$ is greatest when C is at the center of the circle because the diameter is the longest chord of a circle. **7.** Answers may vary. Sample: $\frac{AD}{DC} = \frac{AE}{EB}$, $\frac{\text{area}(\triangle ADE)}{\text{area}(\triangle ACB)} = \left(\frac{DE}{CB}\right)^2$; to support these observations, use the software to measure the lengths and areas, and calculate the quantities in the equations.

On Your Own

8. the circumference **9.** Construct the line through F perpendicular to $\overleftrightarrow{EG}$. Let H be the point where the perpendicular intersects $\overleftrightarrow{EG}$. Construct a segment $\overline{HK}$ on $\overleftrightarrow{EG}$ that has the same length as $\overline{EG}$. $\triangle FHK$ has the same area as $\triangle EFG$. **11a.** yes; $\frac{1}{2}$ **b.** yes; π (or about 3.14) **c.** no

Lesson 1.12
Check Your Understanding

1a. no **b.** yes **c.** yes **2.** yes **3.** Experimentation suggests that concurrence of perpendicular bisectors is an invariant for regular polygons. **4.** Experimentation suggests that concurrence of angle bisectors is an invariant for regular polygons. **5.** The five perpendicular bisectors are concurrent at the center of the circle. The five angle bisectors are not concurrent. **6.** The five angle bisectors are concurrent at the center of the circle. The five perpendicular bisectors are not concurrent.

On Your Own

7. Answers may vary. Sample: The medians are concurrent. Any midpoint is collinear with two vertices of the triangle.

Chapter 2

Lesson 2.01
On Your Own

6. Yes; if two segments have the same length, one will fit exactly on top of the other. You can ignore the widths of the segments because a line segment represents a one-dimensional object. **7.** Answers may vary. Sample: For spheres, cut through their centers with a straight slice and then compare the radii of the cross sections. For rectangular boxes, make a net that wraps perfectly around each box.

Lesson 2.02
Check Your Understanding

1a. numbers **b.** segments **c.** segments and numbers **d.** points and numbers **2a.** $\angle NPQ$ is a geometric object, and 56.6° is a numerical measure. **b.** $m\angle NPQ = 56.6°$ **3.** Yes; if two angles have equal measures, then you can place one angle on top of the other so that they fit exactly. **4.** Yes; if you can put one angle on top of another to get a perfect match, then the protractor positions can also be matched exactly when you measure them. **5.** Yes; if two triangles are congruent to the same triangle, then they can all be superimposed onto one another so that they fit exactly. **6a.** True; F and E are midpoints of segments that have the same length, so halves of those segments have the same length. **b.** Nonsensical; two segments cannot be equal. They can only be congruent. **c.** Nonsensical; a segment cannot equal a length. **d.** Nonsensical; an angle cannot equal a length. **e.** Nonsensical; triangles cannot be equal. They can only be congruent. **f.** True; $\overline{DC} \perp \overline{AB}$ and perpendicular segments form right angles. **g.** True; by part (a), $FA = BE$, therefore $\overline{FA} \cong \overline{BE}$. **h.** False; $FA = \frac{1}{2}DA = \frac{1}{2}BD$. **i.** Nonsensical; two angles cannot be equal. They can only have the same measure. **j.** True; if you fold along $\overline{DC}$, then $\overrightarrow{DA}$ and $\overrightarrow{DB}$ will coincide. **k.** Nonsensical; two measurements cannot be congruent. **l.** True; if you fold along $\overline{DC}$, the angles match perfectly. **m.** Nonsensical; a triangle cannot be congruent to an angle. **n.** Nonsensical; a triangle cannot be congruent to a segment.

On Your Own

9. No; equilateral triangles are not congruent if their side lengths are different. **11.** two

Lesson 2.03
Check Your Understanding

1. Explanations may vary. Samples are given. **a.** No; $\overline{DF} \cong \overline{EC}$, not $\overline{GC}$. **b.** No; $\overline{DF} \cong \overline{EC}$, not $\overline{EG}$. **c.** No; $\angle D \cong \angle E$, not $\angle C$. **d.** Yes; $\angle D \cong \angle E$, $\overline{DF} \cong \overline{EC}$, $\overline{FA} \cong \overline{CG}$, $\overline{DA} \cong \overline{EG}$. **e.** No; $\angle D \cong \angle E$, not $\angle G$. **f.** No; $\angle D \cong \angle E$, not $\angle C$. **2.** Answers may vary. Sample: $\triangle DAF \cong \triangle EGC$, $\triangle ADF \cong \triangle GEC$ **3.** Answers may vary. Sample: If you can place one figure on top of another so that they match perfectly, then the figures are congruent and the parts that match are the corresponding parts that are congruent. **4.** Answers may vary.

On Your Own

5. $\angle C \cong \angle D$, $\angle A \cong \angle O$, $\angle T \cong \angle G$, $\overline{CA} \cong \overline{DO}$, $\overline{AT} \cong \overline{OG}$, and $\overline{CT} \cong \overline{DG}$ **7.** $\triangle AFD \cong \triangle AEB$, $\triangle FBD \cong \triangle EDB$, $\triangle EGD \cong \triangle FGB$ **8a.** Yes; if two polygons are congruent, then one can be made to fit exactly on top of the other. What is inside the polygons will match, too, and area is a numerical measure of the inside. **b.** No; for example, a 4 in.-by-4 in. square has the same area as a 2 in.-by-8 in. rectangle, but they are not congruent.

Lesson 2.04
Check Your Understanding

1a. Constructions may vary. **b.** not necessarily **c.** one of the side lengths **2a.** Constructions may vary. **b.** not necessarily **c.** Answers may vary. Sample: the length of the third side **3.** yes; SSS **4.** yes, though you would need to first deduce that $\overline{AB} \cong \overline{AD}$; SAS **5.** Let the

square be $ABCD$, and choose the diagonal $\overline{BD}$. All sides of a square are congruent, and all angles of a square are right angles and hence congruent. The sides $\overline{BA}$ and $\overline{DA}$ and their included right angle in $\triangle BAD$ are congruent, respectively, to sides $\overline{BC}$ and $\overline{DC}$ and their included right angle in $\triangle BCD$. So $\triangle BAD \cong \triangle BCD$ by SAS. Also, $\overline{BD} \cong \overline{BD}$, so $\triangle BAD \cong \triangle BCD$ by SSS.
6. Answers may vary. Sample: SSA is not a valid test for congruence. **7.** Answers may vary. Sample: If SSA were a valid way to prove congruence, then $\triangle COA \cong \triangle COB$, implying that $m\angle COA = m\angle COB$. But $\angle COB$ is entirely contained within $\angle COA$, so these two angles cannot be equal in measure.

On Your Own

9a. yes **b.** $\triangle ABC \cong \triangle DEF$; SSS **11.** no
14. $\triangle ABD$ and $\triangle CBD$; since $\overline{BD}$ is the perpendicular bisector of $\overline{AC}$, $\overline{AD} \cong \overline{CD}$ and $\angle ADB \cong \angle CDB$. $\overline{BD}$ is common to the two triangles. Therefore, $\triangle ABD \cong \triangle CBD$ by SAS.

Lesson 2.05

On Your Own

3. Constructions and observations may vary. **a.** the length of the side that the midline does not intersect (twice the length of the midline) **b.** the area of each of the four triangles formed by the three midlines (one quarter of the area of the original triangle) **6a.** $m\angle BDA = 118°$, $m\angle ADQ = 62°$, $m\angle CDQ = 118°$ **b.** $m\angle BDA = 108°$, $m\angle ADQ = 72°$, $m\angle CDQ = 108°$
c. $m\angle BDA = 125°$, $m\angle ADQ = 55°$, $m\angle CDQ = 125°$ **d.** $m\angle BDA = 180° - x°$, $m\angle ADQ = x°$, $m\angle CDQ = 180° - x°$

Lesson 2.06

Check Your Understanding

1a. $m\angle COB = 65°$, $m\angle COD = 25°$
b. $m\angle BOA = 27°$, $m\angle COD = 27°$
c. $m\angle COB = 59°$, $m\angle BOA = 31°$
d. $m\angle DOA = 121°$ **e.** $m\angle COB = 90° - x°$, $m\angle COD = x°$ **2.** Because $m\angle COB + m\angle BOA = 90°$ and $m\angle DOC + m\angle COB = 90°$, $m\angle COB + m\angle BOA = m\angle DOC + m\angle COB$. Therefore $m\angle BOA = m\angle DOC$ (basic rules of algebra).

On Your Own

4b. given **c.** Every figure is congruent to itself. **d.** SAS **e.** CPCTC **6a.** Answers may vary. Sample: $m\angle FCA = m\angle FCB$
b. $\overline{FC} \perp \overline{ED}$ (given). $m\angle FCD = 90°$ and $m\angle FCE = 90°$ (definition of perpendicular lines). $m\angle ACE + m\angle FCA = m\angle FCE$ and $m\angle BCD + m\angle FCB = m\angle FCD$ (the measure of an angle is the sum of the measures of its parts). $m\angle ACE + m\angle FCA = m\angle BCD + m\angle FCB$ (properties of equality). But $m\angle ACE = m\angle DCB$ (given), so $m\angle FCA = m\angle FCB$ (basic rules of algebra).

Lesson 2.07

Check Your Understanding

1. Answers may vary. Samples are given:

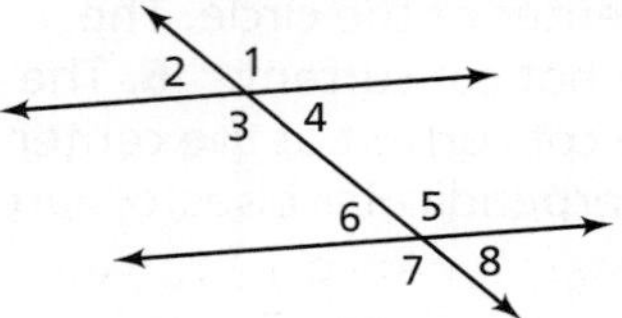

a. A pair of angles are alternate interior angles if they have different vertices, lie between the two lines cut by the transversal, and are on opposite sides of the transversal. $\angle 4$ and $\angle 6$ are alternate interior angles. **b.** A pair of angles are alternate exterior angles if they have different vertices, lie on opposite sides of the transversal, and are not between the two lines cut by the transversal. $\angle 2$ and $\angle 8$ are alternate exterior angles. **c.** A pair of angles are corresponding angles if they have different vertices and lie on the same side of the transversal, with exactly one of them lying between the two lines cut by the transversal. $\angle 1$ and $\angle 5$ are corresponding angles.
d. A pair of angles are consecutive angles if they have different vertices, lie on the same side of the transversal, and are both between the two lines cut by the transversal. $\angle 3$ and $\angle 6$ are consecutive angles.
2a. $\triangle PXU \cong \triangle UMP$; SSS

b.

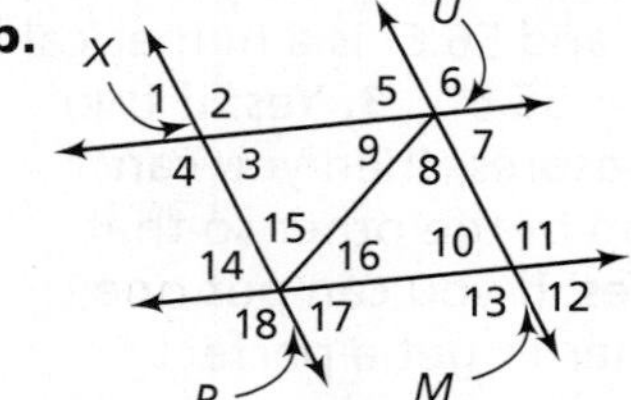

Angles congruent by CPCTC: $\angle 3 \cong \angle 10$, $\angle 9 \cong \angle 16$, $\angle 8 \cong \angle 15$; angles congruent because the parts of one are congruent to the parts of the other: $\angle XUM \cong \angle XPM$; vertical angles: $\angle 1 \cong \angle 3$, $\angle 2 \cong \angle 4$, $\angle 5 \cong \angle 7$, $\angle 6 \cong \angle XUM$, $\angle 10 \cong \angle 12$, $\angle 11 \cong \angle 13$, $\angle 14 \cong \angle 17$, $\angle 18 \cong \angle XPM$ **c.** $\overleftrightarrow{XU} \parallel \overleftrightarrow{PM}$ and $\overleftrightarrow{XP} \parallel \overleftrightarrow{UM}$; AIP Theorem **3a.** $\triangle XUP \cong \triangle MUP$; SSS **b.** Each pair of vertical angles is congruent. (There are two pairs of vertical angles at each of the points X, U, M, and P.) Also, $\angle XPU \cong \angle MPU$, $\angle XUP \cong \angle MUP$, and $\angle UXP \cong \angle UMP$ by CPCTC. **c.** None are necessarily parallel; the conditions that let you use the AIP Theorem are not present. **4.** Refer to the figure for parts (a), (b), and (e). Proofs may vary. Samples are given.

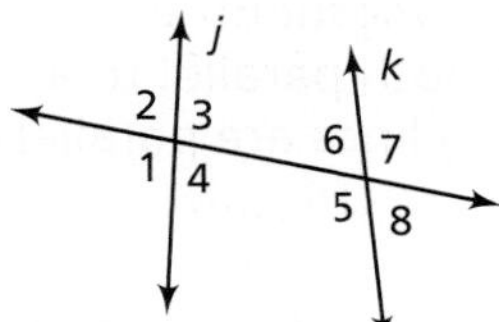

a. Yes; suppose $\angle 1 \cong \angle 5$. $\angle 1 \cong \angle 3$ (vertical angles). So $\angle 3 \cong \angle 5$ (angles congruent to the same angle are congruent). Hence $j \parallel k$ (AIP Theorem). **b.** Yes; suppose $\angle 1 \cong \angle 7$. Since $\angle 1 \cong \angle 3$ and $\angle 5 \cong \angle 7$ (vertical angles), it follows that $\angle 3 \cong \angle 5$. Hence $j \parallel k$ (AIP Theorem). **c.** No; answers may vary. Sample: Let $\triangle PAB$ be an isosceles triangle with $\overline{PA} \cong \overline{PB}$. If M is the midpoint of $\overline{AB}$, then $\triangle PMA \cong \triangle PMB$ by SSS. Hence $\angle A \cong \angle B$. But $\overleftrightarrow{AB}$ is a transversal of intersecting lines $\overleftrightarrow{PA}$ and $\overleftrightarrow{PB}$. **d.** No; answers may vary. Sample: Consider the situation described in the answer for part (c). For the transversal $\overleftrightarrow{AB}$ of $\overleftrightarrow{PA}$ and $\overleftrightarrow{PB}$, each pair of alternate exterior angles are supplementary, but $\overleftrightarrow{PA}$ and $\overleftrightarrow{PB}$ are not parallel. **e.** Yes; refer to the figure above the answer for part (a), and suppose $\angle 4$ and $\angle 5$ are supplementary. Since $\angle 4$ and $\angle 3$ are supplementary, it follows that $\angle 3 \cong \angle 5$. Hence $j \parallel k$ (AIP Theorem).

On Your Own

5. Yes; the two lines are parallel if they lie in the same plane. They are not parallel if they do not lie in the same plane. **7.** $\overline{MP} \parallel \overline{NQ}$; since O is the midpoint of $\overline{MQ}$ and $\overline{NP}$, $\overline{MO} \cong \overline{QO}$, and $\overline{NO} \cong \overline{PO}$. The vertical angles that have vertex O are congruent. Hence, $\triangle PMO \cong \triangle NQO$ by SAS, and $\angle N \cong \angle P$ by CPCTC. Therefore, $\overline{MP} \parallel \overline{NQ}$ by the AIP Theorem. **10.** $\overline{FI} \parallel \overline{EJ}$ and $\overline{DE} \parallel \overline{FH}$; it is given that $m\angle FGE = m\angle HFI$, so $\overline{FI} \parallel \overline{EJ}$ by the AIP Theorem. $\angle DEG$ is supplementary to $\angle HFI$ and hence is supplementary to the congruent angle $\angle FGE$. Using the corollary proved in Exercise 4e, it follows that $\overline{DE} \parallel \overline{FH}$.

Lesson 2.08

Check Your Understanding

1a. $m\angle 1 = 72°$, $m\angle 2 = 108°$, $m\angle 3 = 108°$, $m\angle 4 = 72°$, $m\angle 5 = 72°$, $m\angle 6 = 108°$, $m\angle 7 = 108°$, $m\angle 8 = 72°$ **b.** $m\angle 1 = 46°$, $m\angle 2 = 134°$, $m\angle 3 = 134°$, $m\angle 4 = 46°$, $m\angle 5 = 46°$, $m\angle 6 = 134°$, $m\angle 7 = 134°$, $m\angle 8 = 46°$ **c.** $m\angle 1 = x°$, $m\angle 2 = 180° - x°$, $m\angle 3 = 180° - x°$, $m\angle 4 = x°$, $m\angle 5 = x°$, $m\angle 6 = 180° - x°$, $m\angle 7 = 180° - x°$, $m\angle 8 = x°$ **d.** $m\angle 1 = 60°$, $m\angle 2 = 120°$, $m\angle 3 = 120°$, $m\angle 4 = 60°$, $m\angle 5 = 60°$, $m\angle 6 = 120°$, $m\angle 7 = 120°$, $m\angle 8 = 60°$ **e.** $m\angle 1 = 60°$, $m\angle 2 = 120°$, $m\angle 3 = 120°$, $m\angle 4 = 60°$, $m\angle 5 = 60°$, $m\angle 6 = 120°$, $m\angle 7 = 120°$, $m\angle 8 = 60°$ **2a.** Yes, $c \parallel d$; dependent on $\angle 2 \cong \angle 3$. **b.** $\angle 2 \cong \angle 3$ **c.** The relationships in parts (a) and (b) would not hold. **3.** Answers may vary. Sample: The measure of $\angle P$ is the sum of the measures of the acute angles at A and B. **4.** Suppose there are two lines perpendicular to ℓ through P, and that they intersect ℓ at M and N. The triangle MNP has two right angles at M and N. These together with the angle at P would give the triangle an angle sum greater than 180°. Therefore there is only one such perpendicular. **5.** Yes; a diagonal of a quadrilateral divides it into two triangles. The sum of the measures of the angles of the quadrilateral is equal to the sum of the angle measures of the triangles, which is 180° + 180°, or 360°. **6.** Answers may vary. Sample: One is the converse of the other. **7a.** Answers may vary. Sample: $\angle CBD \cong \angle CDB$ and $\angle DCE \cong \angle DEC$. **b.** No; suppose $\overline{BC} \parallel \overline{DE}$. Then $\angle ACB \cong \angle AED$ since they are corresponding angles. Since $\overline{BC} \cong \overline{DE}$ and $\angle A \cong \angle A$, you know that $\triangle ABC \cong \triangle ADE$ by AAS. Then $\overline{AC} \cong \overline{AE}$ by CPCTC. But this last statement is impossible given the way the diagram was drawn. Therefore, the assumption that $\overline{BC} \parallel \overline{DE}$ is wrong.

On Your Own

9a. PAI Theorem **b.** Vertical Angles Theorem **c.** $\angle 1 \cong \angle 2$ by part (a), and $\angle 2 \cong \angle 3$ by part (b), so $\angle 1 \cong \angle 3$. **12.** Suppose the exterior angle is at vertex C of $\triangle ABC$. Since the exterior angle is supplementary to $\angle BCA$, $m(\text{exterior angle}) + m\angle BCA = 180°$. But by the Triangle Angle-Sum Theorem, $m\angle A + m\angle B + m\angle BCA = 180°$. It follows by the base moves of algebra that $m(\text{exterior angle}) = m\angle A + m\angle B$.

Lesson 2.09

On Your Own

5. yes; SAS **6.** The pair of congruent angles is not an included pair.

Selected Answers

Selected Answers

Lesson 2.10

Check Your Understanding

1a. Answers may vary. Sample: Use geometry software to draw convex polygons with different numbers of sides. Use the measurement and calculate features of the software to find the sum of the measures of the angles of each polygon. Check that the sums are the ones predicted by the expression $(n - 2)180°$. **b.** Answers may vary. Sample: Suppose you start with an n-gon. If you select a vertex and draw all the diagonals from that vertex, you get $(n - 2)$ triangles. The sum of the angles of the n-gon is equal to the sum of the angles of all these triangles, or $(n - 2)180°$. **2.** $\angle ABD \cong \angle CBE$ by the Vertical Angles Theorem. Since $\overline{AB} \cong \overline{BC}$ and $\overline{BD} \cong \overline{BE}$, it follows by the SAS Postulate that $\triangle ABD \cong \triangle CBE$. **3.** It is given that $\overline{SV} \cong \overline{TU}$ and $\overline{ST} \cong \overline{VU}$. Since every segment is congruent to itself, $\overline{VT} \cong \overline{VT}$. Therefore, $\triangle STV \cong \triangle UVT$ by SSS. **4.** Since all sides of a square are congruent, $\overline{SW} \cong \overline{EB}$. $\overline{WB} \cong \overline{BW}$ since a segment is congruent to itself. The angles of a square are right angles and are congruent, so $\angle SWB \cong \angle EBW$. Therefore, $\triangle SWB \cong \triangle EBW$ by SAS.

On Your Own

7. Answers may vary. Sample: It is given that $\overline{XE}$ is a median of $\triangle XMY$. Hence E is the midpoint of $\overline{MY}$, and consequently $\overline{ME} \cong \overline{YE}$. It is given that $\overline{XY} \cong \overline{XM}$. A segment is congruent to itself, so $\overline{XE} \cong \overline{XE}$. Therefore, $\triangle XEM \cong \triangle XEY$ by SSS. **9a.** The configuration of the congruent corresponding parts is AAS not ASA. **b.** Yes; change the congruence test used in Timothy's proof from ASA to AAS. **11.** The angles marked in the diagram are given to be congruent. The segments that determine these angles are all congruent because they are radii of the same circle. Therefore, the three triangles are congruent by SAS.

Lesson 2.11

Check Your Understanding

1. The third statement is false; a right triangle with legs of length 1 and 4 has the same area as a right triangle with leg lengths 2 and 2, but they are not congruent. The fifth statement is false; there are people with large hands who do not have large feet. The sixth statement is false; you can keep things in mind even when they are not visible. **2a.** Hypothesis: Two lines form congruent alternate interior angles with a transversal; conclusion: the two lines are parallel. **b.** Hypothesis: n is a whole number; conclusion: $n^2 + n + 41$ is prime. **c.** Hypothesis: three sides of one triangle are congruent to three sides of another triangle; conclusion: the triangles are congruent. **d.** Hypothesis: two lines are both parallel to a third line; conclusion: the two lines are parallel to each other.

On Your Own

4. True; proofs may vary. Sample: Select two alternate interior angles formed by the two lines and the transversal to which they are perpendicular. These angles are congruent since all the angles formed by perpendicular lines are right angles. By AIP, the lines perpendicular to the transversal are parallel. **5.** False; the sketch of the hypothesis shown here provides a counterexample.

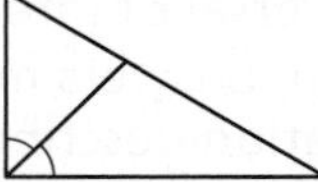

Lesson 2.12

Check Your Understanding

1a. The halves of $\overline{AC}$ may not be congruent to the halves of $\overline{BH}$. **b.** The original markings would allow you to conclude that $ABCH$ is a rectangle.

2.

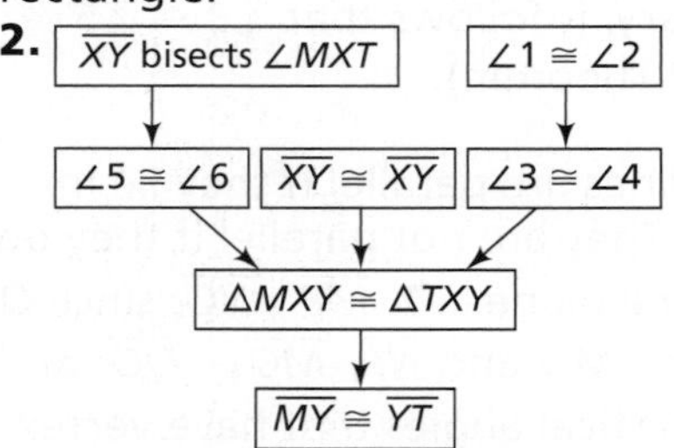

3a.

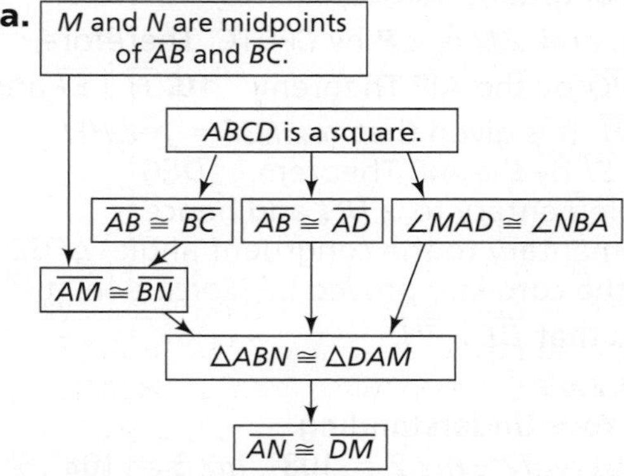

b. Because $ABCD$ is a square, all its sides are congruent. So $\overline{AB} \cong \overline{BC}$ and $\overline{AB} \cong \overline{DA}$. Also, all its angles are congruent. So $\angle MAD \cong \angle NBA$. Since $\overline{AB} \cong \overline{BC}$ and M and N are the midpoints of $\overline{AB}$ and $\overline{BC}$, respectively, it follows that $\overline{AM} \cong \overline{BN}$. Hence $\triangle ABN \cong \triangle DAM$ by SAS. By CPCTC, $\overline{AN} \cong \overline{DM}$.

On Your Own

6. Since $\overleftrightarrow{GF} \perp \overleftrightarrow{GH}$, $m\angle HGJ + m\angle JGF = 90°$. Since $\overleftrightarrow{GJ} \perp \overleftrightarrow{GK}$, $m\angle KGH + m\angle HGJ = 90°$. By the basic moves of algebra, it follows that $m\angle JGF = m\angle KGH$. Therefore, $\angle JGF \cong \angle KGH$. **8.** It follows from the Triangle Angle-Sum Theorem that each angle of an equilateral triangle has a measure of 60°. Therefore the parts of $\angle MLK$ are congruent to the parts of $\angle JLN$, which implies $\angle MLK \cong \angle JLN$. Sides of an equilateral triangle are congruent, so $\overline{ML} \cong \overline{JL}$ and $\overline{LK} \cong \overline{LN}$. So by SAS, $\triangle MLK \cong \triangle JLN$. Hence $\overline{MK} \cong \overline{JN}$ by CPCTC.

Lesson 2.13

Check Your Understanding

1a. Answers may vary. Sample: Let the intersection of the perpendicular bisector and $\overline{AB}$ be C. **Need:** $\triangle APB$ is isosceles.
Use: Isosceles triangles have two congruent sides. **Need:** $\overline{AP} \cong \overline{PB}$ **Use:** CPCTC
Need: $\triangle APC \cong \triangle BPC$ **Use:** SAS
Need: $\overline{PC} \cong \overline{PC}$ **Use:** The triangles share this side. **Need:** $\angle PCB \cong \angle PCA$ **Use:** Both are right angles because $\overrightarrow{PC}$ is a perpendicular bisector.
Need: $\overline{AC} \cong \overline{BC}$ **Use:** C is a midpoint because $\overrightarrow{PC}$ is a perpendicular bisector. **b.** Since $\overrightarrow{PC}$ is a perpendicular bisector of $\overline{AB}$, C is the midpoint of $\overline{AB}$ and hence $\overline{AC} \cong \overline{BC}$. Also, since $\overrightarrow{PC}$ is a perpendicular bisector of $\overline{AB}$, $m\angle PCB = m\angle PCA = 90°$. Since $\triangle ACP$ and $\triangle BCP$ share side $\overline{PC}$, these triangles are congruent by SAS. Also, by CPCTC, $\overline{AP} \cong \overline{PB}$. Thus $\triangle APB$ has two congruent sides and is isosceles. **2a.** $\triangle AFC$ and $\triangle AFB$ **b.** $\overline{CF} \cong \overline{BF}$ ($\overline{AD}$ bisects $\overline{BC}$). $\overline{AF} \cong \overline{AF}$ (every segment is congruent to itself). $\angle AFC \cong \angle AFB$ ($\overline{AD}$ and $\overline{BC}$ are perpendicular). Therefore, $\triangle AFC \cong \triangle AFB$ by SAS.

On Your Own

5. Let $\triangle ABC$ have altitudes $\overline{BE}$ and $\overline{CD}$, with $\overline{BE} \cong \overline{CD}$. If the triangle is acute, the altitudes lie inside the triangle. Since $\angle A \cong \angle A$, $\overline{BE} \cong \overline{CD}$, and $\angle ADC \cong \angle AEB$ (because all right angles are congruent), you can conclude that $\triangle ADC \cong \triangle AEB$ by AAS. Therefore $\overline{AC} \cong \overline{AB}$, and $\triangle ABC$ is isosceles. If the triangle is a right triangle, the altitudes coincide with two of the sides of the triangle. And since the altitudes are congruent, the sides are congruent as well. Therefore, the triangle is isosceles. If the triangle is obtuse, the altitudes $\overline{CD}$ and $\overline{BE}$ lie outside the triangle. $\angle AEB \cong \angle ADC$ (both are right angles) and $\angle EAB \cong \angle DAC$ (vertical angles). But $\overline{BE} \cong \overline{CD}$ (given). So $\triangle AEB \cong \triangle ADC$ (AAS). Hence $\overline{AB} \cong \overline{AC}$ (CPCTC), which means $\triangle ABC$ is isosceles.

Lesson 2.14

Check Your Understanding

1. Answers may vary. Sample: Since $\overleftrightarrow{ST}$ is the perpendicular bisector of $\overline{RQ}$, it follows from the Perpendicular Bisector Theorem that $\overline{SR} \cong \overline{SQ}$ and $\overline{TR} \cong \overline{TQ}$. Since $\overline{ST} \cong \overline{ST}$, $\triangle SRT \cong \triangle SQT$ (SSS). Therefore, $\angle SRT \cong \angle SQT$ (CPCTC). **2.** The side opposite the included angle for the first triangle is longer than the side opposite the included angle for the second triangle.

3. •

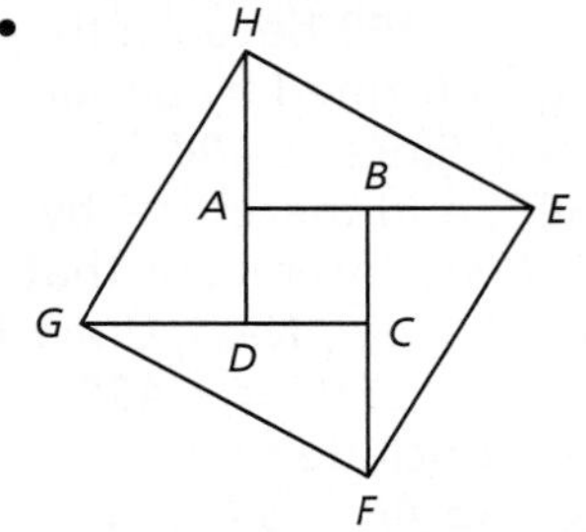

• $m\angle ABC = m\angle BCD = m\angle CDA = m\angle DAB = 90°$; $\overline{AB} \cong \overline{BC} \cong \overline{CD} \cong \overline{DA}$; $\overline{BE} \cong \overline{CF} \cong \overline{DG} \cong \overline{AH}$
• Conjectures may vary.
• Because they are all supplementary to right angles, $m\angle GDH = m\angle HAE = m\angle EBF = m\angle FCG = 90°$. Because $\overline{AB} \cong \overline{BC} \cong \overline{CD} \cong \overline{DA}$ and $\overline{BE} \cong \overline{CF} \cong \overline{DG} \cong \overline{AH}$, it is also true that $\overline{DH} \cong \overline{AE} \cong \overline{BF} \cong \overline{CG}$. Therefore, $\triangle HAE \cong \triangle EBF \cong \triangle FCG \cong \triangle GDH$ by SAS. This means that $\overline{GH} \cong \overline{HE} \cong \overline{EF} \cong \overline{FG}$ by CPCTC. Again by CPCTC, it follows that $\angle AHE \cong \angle BEF$, and hence that $m\angle AHE = m\angle BEF$. By the Triangle Angle-Sum Theorem, we know that $m\angle AHE + m\angle AEH = 90°$. Therefore, $m\angle HEF = m\angle BEF + m\angle AEH = m\angle AHE + m\angle AEH = 90°$. Similarly, $m\angle EFG = m\angle FGH = m\angle GHE = 90°$. Since the sides of $EFGH$ are all congruent, and all the angles of $EFGH$ are right angles, $EFGH$ is a square.

4. •

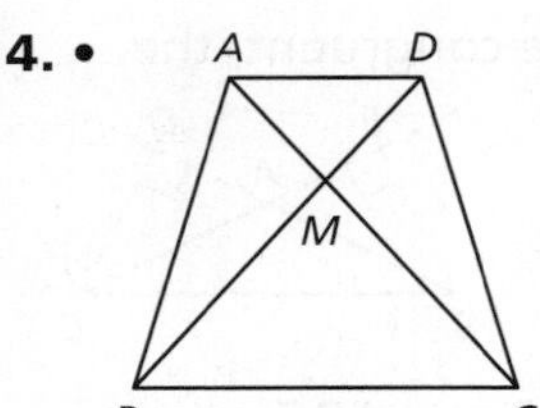

• $\overline{AC} \cong \overline{BD}$; $\overline{AB} \cong \overline{DC}$
• Conjectures may vary.
• $\triangle ABC \cong \triangle DCB$ by SSS. Therefore $\angle MBC \cong \angle MCB$ by CPCTC. It then follows that $\triangle MBC$ is isosceles.

5. •

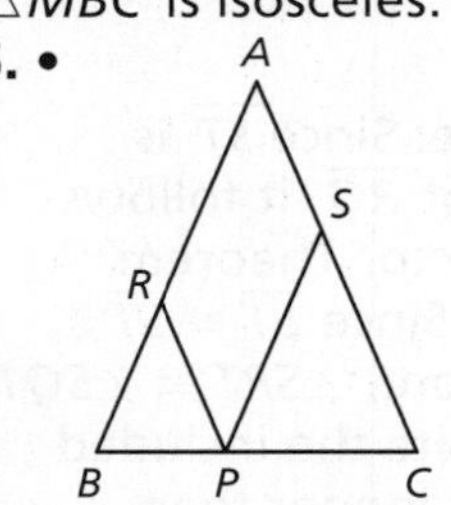

• $\overline{AB} \cong \overline{AC}$; $\overline{AB} \parallel \overline{SP}$, $\overline{AC} \parallel \overline{RP}$
• Conjectures may vary.
• First note that $\angle SCP \cong \angle RPB$ because they are corresponding angles formed by parallel lines cut by a transversal. Since $\triangle ABC$ is isosceles, $\angle RBP \cong \angle SCP$, and therefore, by transitivity, $\angle RBP \cong \angle RPB$. This means that $\triangle RBP$ is isosceles and $\overline{RB} \cong \overline{RP}$. Next, draw $\overline{RS}$. By PAI, $\angle RSP \cong \angle ARS$ and $\angle PRS \cong \angle ASR$. Since $\overline{RS} \cong \overline{RS}$, you can conclude that $\triangle SRA \cong \triangle RSP$ by ASA. So $PR = SA$ and $RA = PS$. It follows, by substitution, that perimeter $ARPS = PR + RA + AS + PS = BR + RA + BR + RA = 2(BR + RA) = 2BA$.

6. There are six proofs involved. For the first five, refer to the following figure.

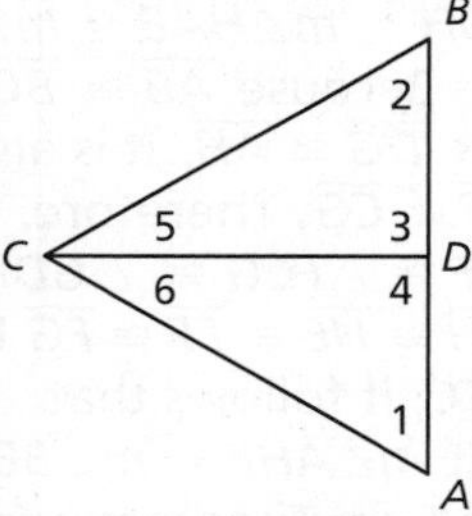

• Assume statements 1 and 2. Then $\overline{AC} \cong \overline{BC}$ and $\overline{DB} \cong \overline{DA}$. Since $\overline{CD} \cong \overline{CD}$, it follows that $\triangle ACD \cong \triangle BCD$. By CPCTC, $\angle 5 \cong \angle 6$. Hence $\overline{CD}$ bisects $\angle ACB$. Again by CPCTC, $\angle 3 \cong \angle 4$. Hence $\angle 3 \cong \angle 4$ (right angles), which implies $\overline{CD}$ is an altitude.
• Assume statements 1 and 3. Then $\overline{AC} \cong \overline{BC}$ and $\angle 3$ and $\angle 4$ are right angles. $\angle 1 \cong \angle 2$ by the Isosceles Triangle Theorem. Therefore, $\triangle ACD \cong \triangle BCD$ by AAS. By CPCTC, $\overline{DA} \cong \overline{DB}$. So $\overline{CD}$ is a median. Also by CPCTC, $\angle 5 \cong \angle 6$, and hence $\overline{CD}$ bisects $\angle ACB$.
• Assume statements 1 and 4. Then $\overline{BC} \cong \overline{AC}$ and $\angle 5 \cong \angle 6$. But $\overline{CD} \cong \overline{CD}$, so $\triangle ACD \cong \triangle BCD$ by SAS. By CPCTC, $\overline{DA} \cong \overline{DB}$. So $\overline{CD}$ is a median. Also by CPCTC, $\angle 3 \cong \angle 4$. Hence $\overline{CD}$ is an altitude.
• Assume statements 2 and 3. Then $\overline{DA} \cong \overline{DB}$ and $\overline{CD} \perp \overline{AB}$. It follows that $\overline{CD}$ is the perpendicular bisector of $\overline{AB}$ and hence, by the Perpendicular Bisector Theorem, $AC = BC$. Therefore $\triangle ABC$ is isosceles. Since $\overline{CD} \cong \overline{CD}$ and $\angle 3 \cong \angle 4$, $\triangle ACD \cong \triangle BCD$ by SAS. By CPCTC, $\angle 5 \cong \angle 6$. Thus $\overline{CD}$ bisects $\angle ACB$.
• Assume statements 3 and 4. Then $\angle 3 \cong \angle 4$ (right angles) and $\angle 5 \cong \angle 6$. Since $\overline{CD} \cong \overline{CD}$, it follows that $\triangle ACD \cong \triangle BCD$ (ASA). By CPCTC, $\overline{AC} \cong \overline{BC}$ and $\overline{DA} \cong \overline{DB}$. Therefore, $\triangle ABC$ is isosceles and $\overline{CD}$ is a median.
• Assume statements 2 and 4. Then $\overline{DB} \cong \overline{DA}$ and $\angle BCD \cong \angle ACD$. First we use an indirect proof that $\overline{AB} \perp \overline{CD}$. Suppose that $\overline{AB}$ is not perpendicular to $\overline{CD}$. Draw the line ℓ that is perpendicular to $\overline{CD}$ at D. Let M be the point where ℓ intersects $\overrightarrow{CB}$, and let N be the point where ℓ intersects $\overrightarrow{CA}$, as indicated in the figure below.

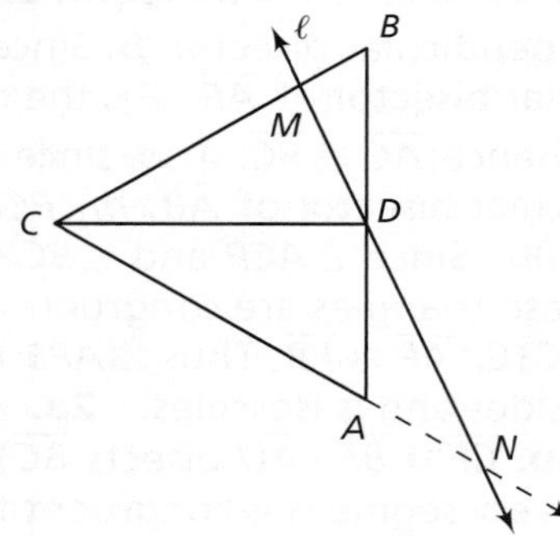

Since $\ell \perp \overline{CD}$, $\angle MDC$ and $\angle NDC$ are right angles and hence are congruent. But $\angle BCD \cong \angle ACD$ (given) and $\overline{CD} \cong \overline{CD}$. Hence $\triangle CMD \cong \triangle CND$ by AAS. By CPCTC, $\overline{DM} \cong \overline{DN}$. But $\overline{DB} \cong \overline{DA}$ (given) and $\angle BDM \cong \angle ADN$ (vertical angles). Hence $\triangle BMD \cong \triangle AND$ by SAS. By CPCTC, $\angle BMD \cong \angle AND$. However, these are alternate interior angles for lines CB and CA and the transversal ℓ. The AIP Theorem implies that lines CB and CA are parallel. This contradicts the fact that lines CB and CA intersect at C. Since the assumption that $\overline{AB}$ is not perpendicular to $\overline{CD}$ has led to a contradiction, these segments are perpendicular. Hence $\overline{CD}$ is an altitude and the perpendicular bisector of $\overline{AB}$. By the Perpendicular Bisector Theorem, $CA = CB$. So, $\overline{CA}$ and $\overline{CB}$ are legs of isosceles $\triangle ABC$ with base $\overline{AB}$.

On Your Own

9. Answers may vary. Sample: Mark three points A, B, and C on the circle. Draw $\overline{AB}$, $\overline{BC}$, and their perpendicular bisectors. The point of intersection of the bisectors is the center of the circle. **12.** Pick three points A, B, and C on the rim of the blade. Draw the perpendicular bisectors of $\overline{AB}$ and $\overline{BC}$. They will intersect at a point P. Measure $\overline{PA}$ to get the radius of the blade. Double the radius to find the diameter. **15.** Because of the way the folds were made, $\overline{CD}$ is perpendicular to $\overline{AB}$ at the midpoint of $\overline{AB}$. Thus $\overline{CD}$ is the perpendicular bisector of $\overline{AB}$, and it follows from the Perpendicular Bisector Theorem that each point on $\overline{CD}$ is equidistant from A and B.

Lesson 2.15

On Your Own

4. Drawings will vary; rhombus. **6.** Drawings will vary; yes. **8.** square

Lesson 2.16

Check Your Understanding

1. no **2.** yes **3.** Answers may vary. Samples are given. **a.** The four segments do not intersect at their endpoints. **b.** Some endpoints are not shared by exactly two segments.
c. There are only three segments in the figure.
d. Some endpoints are not shared by exactly two segments.

On Your Own

5. You can dissect a concave quadrilateral into two triangles just as you can a convex quadrilateral. The two triangles have angle sums of 180° each, and their combined angle sum is 360°. **7.** No; answers may vary. Sample: Consider the skew quadrilateral $ABCD$ shown at the bottom of p. 144. The four angles of this quadrilateral are $\angle DAB$, $\angle ABC$, $\angle BCD$, and $\angle CDA$. All four of these angles appear to measure less than 90° (and certainly the figure can be drawn so that they are), in which case, the sum of the measures of the angles of $ABCD$ is less than 360°.

Lesson 2.17

Check Your Understanding

1. A, B, C, G, H, I, and L; each of these figures is a quadrilateral with exactly one pair of sides that appears to be parallel. **2–8.** Justifications may vary. Samples are given. Figure references are to the figures in Exercise 1. **2.** always
3. sometimes; figures C and L **4.** sometimes; figures B and L **5.** sometimes; figures C and L **6.** sometimes; draw $\angle DAB$ with a ray bisecting it and then draw a parallel to $\overline{AB}$ through D. The point where this parallel intersects the angle bisector can be chosen as the fourth vertex of the trapezoid.
7. sometimes; figures L and C **8.** Never; if one angle of a trapezoid is a right angle, then an angle consecutive to it must also be a right angle, since consecutive angles of parallel lines are supplementary. So if a trapezoid has one right angle, it must in fact have two right angles. **9.** Answers may vary. Sample: The distance between two parallel lines is the length of any segment perpendicular to both lines and with one endpoint on each line.
10. Let $ABCD$ be an isosceles trapezoid with parallel bases $\overline{AB}$ and $\overline{CD}$ ($AB < DC$) and $\overline{BC} \cong \overline{AD}$. Draw lines through A and B perpendicular to the parallel bases. Let the intersection of $\overline{DC}$ and the perpendicular line through A be X, and let the intersection of $\overline{DC}$ and the perpendicular line through B be Y. $\overline{AX} \cong \overline{BY}$ (two segments perpendicular to the same parallel lines are congruent), so $\triangle ADX \cong \triangle CBY$ (HL). By CPCTC, $\angle ADX \cong \angle CBY$. Also $\angle CBY \cong \angle DAX$ by CPCTC, and $\angle YBA$ and $\angle XAB$ are right angles. So $m\angle CBY + m\angle YBA = m\angle DAX + m\angle XAB$. Therefore, $m\angle CBA \cong \angle DAB$. **11.** Let $ABCD$ be an isosceles trapezoid with parallel bases $\overline{AB}$ and $\overline{CD}$ and $\overline{BC} \cong \overline{AD}$. Draw diagonals $\overline{AC}$ and $\overline{BD}$. Sides $\overline{AD}$ and $\overline{DC}$ in $\triangle ADC$ are congruent to sides $\overline{BC}$ and $\overline{CD}$ in $\triangle BCD$. $\angle ADC \cong \angle BCD$ (by Exercise 10). Therefore $\triangle ADC \cong \triangle BCD$ by SAS, and $\overline{AC} \cong \overline{BD}$ by CPCTC.

On Your Own

12. All appear to be kites except Figure E. Each one appears to have two sets of adjacent congruent sides. **14.** always **16.** sometimes
19. Let $ABCD$ be a kite with $\overline{AB} \cong \overline{BC}$ and $\overline{CD} \cong \overline{DA}$. Draw the diagonal $\overline{BD}$. Since $\triangle DAB \cong \triangle DCB$ (SSS), the two parts of $\angle ABC$ are congruent, and the two parts of $\angle CDA$ are congruent (CPCTC). Therefore, the symmetry diagonal $\overline{BD}$ bisects these angles.

Selected Answers

Lesson 2.18
Check Your Understanding
1. If a quadrilateral has its opposite sides congruent, then it is a parallelogram; true; let $ABCD$ be a quadrilateral with $\overline{AB} \cong \overline{DC}$ and $\overline{AD} \cong \overline{BC}$. Draw diagonal $\overline{AC}$. By SSS, $\triangle ADC \cong \triangle CBA$. Use AIP to conclude $\overline{AB} \parallel \overline{DC}$ and $\overline{AD} \parallel \overline{BC}$. **2.** If a quadrilateral has each pair of consecutive angles supplementary, then it is a parallelogram; true; let $ABCD$ be a quadrilateral with each pair of consecutive angles supplementary. Since $\angle A$ and $\angle B$ are supplementary, $\overline{AD} \parallel \overline{BC}$. Since $\angle A$ and $\angle D$ are supplementary, $\overline{AB} \parallel \overline{DC}$. **3.** If a quadrilateral has both pairs of opposite angles congruent, then it is a parallelogram; true; let $ABCD$ be a quadrilateral with $\angle A \cong \angle C$ and $\angle B \cong \angle D$. Hence $m\angle A + m\angle B + m\angle C + m\angle D = 2(m\angle A + m\angle B) = 360°$, or $m\angle A + m\angle B = 180°$. Therefore, consecutive angles are supplementary, and, by Exercise 2, $ABCD$ is a parallelogram. **4.** If each diagonal of a quadrilateral divides it into two congruent triangles, then the quadrilateral is a parallelogram; true; match up any two congruent triangles along a congruent side. The opposite angles in the resulting quadrilateral are congruent, so, by Exercise 3, the quadrilateral is a parallelogram. **5.** If a quadrilateral has diagonals that bisect each other, then it is a parallelogram; true; the diagonals divide the parallelogram into four triangles. You can prove that pairs of these are congruent by SAS. Then you know that opposite sides of the quadrilateral are congruent. Therefore the quadrilateral is a parallelogram by Exercise 1. **6.** Answers may vary. Sample: If a pair of consecutive angles of a parallelogram are congruent, then the parallelogram is also a rectangle. To prove this, note that consecutive angles of a parallelogram are supplementary. Then each congruent angle must have measure 90°. The other two angles must then also have measure 90° since they are also consecutive with the first two angles considered. **7a.** Since a diagonal divides a parallelogram into two congruent triangles, opposite sides of the parallelogram are congruent by CPCTC.
b. Since a diagonal divides a parallelogram into two congruent triangles, opposite angles of the parallelogram are congruent by CPCTC.

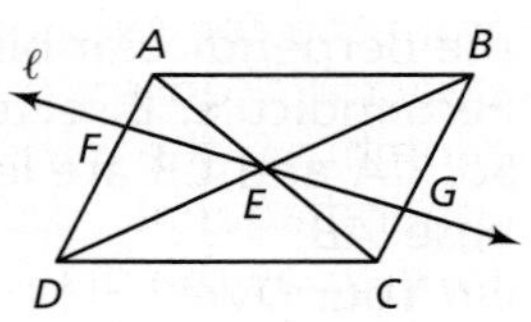

8. Let $ABCD$ be a parallelogram whose diagonals intersect at E, as shown in the diagram. Let ℓ be a line through E that does not contain a diagonal. (You can assume ℓ intersects $\overline{AD}$ and $\overline{BC}$, since you can easily modify the proof if ℓ intersects the other pair of parallel sides.) $\overline{AE} \cong \overline{CE}$ because the diagonals of a parallelogram bisect each other. $\angle EAF \cong \angle ECG$ because $\overline{AD}$ is parallel to $\overline{BC}$. Also, $\angle AEF \cong \angle CEG$ because they are vertical angles. Therefore, $\triangle AEF \cong \triangle CEG$ by ASA, and hence $\overline{EF} \cong \overline{EG}$.
On Your Own
9. always **11.** never **13.** sometimes **17.** sometimes **21.** never **23.** always
31. Draw $\overline{AC}$. $\angle DAC \cong \angle BCA$ by PAI, and $\overline{AC} \cong \overline{AC}$. So $\triangle ABC \cong \triangle CDA$ by SAS. Therefore $\angle BAC \cong \angle DCA$ by CPCTC, and $\overline{AB}$ is parallel to $\overline{CD}$ by AIP. Both pairs of opposite sides of $ABCD$ are parallel, so $ABCD$ is a parallelogram.

Lesson 2.19
Check Your Understanding
1. Let $ABCD$ be a rectangle. Opposite sides of $ABCD$ are congruent, so $\overline{AD} \cong \overline{BC}$. All angles of $ABCD$ are right angles, so $\angle DAB \cong \angle CBA$ by SAS. $\overline{AB}$ is congruent to itself. Hence $\triangle DAB \cong \triangle CBA$. Therefore, the diagonals $\overline{DB}$ and $\overline{CA}$ are congruent by CPCTC. **2.** Let $ABCD$ be a parallelogram with a pair of congruent adjacent sides. Opposite sides of a parallelogram are congruent, so all four sides of $ABCD$ are congruent. Therefore, $ABCD$ is a rhombus. **3.** sometimes **4.** always **5.** sometimes **6.** always **7.** always **8.** always **9.** sometimes **10.** sometimes **11.** sometimes **12.** sometimes **13.** always
On Your Own
15. If a parallelogram has a right angle, then all its angles are right angles (consecutive angles of a parallelogram are supplementary). A parallelogram with four right angles is a rectangle. **17.** Rhombus; let $ABCD$ be a rectangle with M, N, P, and Q as the midpoints of $\overline{AB}$, $\overline{BC}$, $\overline{CD}$, and $\overline{DA}$, respectively. $\triangle AMQ \cong \triangle MBN \cong \triangle PCN \cong \triangle PDQ$ by SAS, so $\overline{QM} \cong \overline{MN} \cong \overline{NP} \cong \overline{PQ}$ by CPCTC. Also, $MNPQ$ is a parallelogram because it has two pairs of congruent opposite sides. **19.** Since all sides of a rhombus are congruent, the two triangles formed by drawing a diagonal each have two congruent sides. **21.** It follows

from the converse of the Perpendicular Bisector Theorem that each diagonal of a rhombus is the perpendicular bisector of the other diagonal. **23.** By PAI, all four angles formed by the diagonal are congruent, so each triangle is isosceles. Moreover, the triangles are also congruent, so all four sides of the parallelogram are congruent by CPCTC.

Chapter 3

Lesson 3.01

On Your Own

6a. Answers may vary. Sample: Slide the triangle on the left side of the first figure to the right. **b.** Answers may vary. Sample: Rotate the top triangle in the first figure 180° about the top right vertex of the square. Then translate the other triangle to the right to fit. **c.** Answers may vary. Sample: Reflect the rightmost triangle in the first figure across the perpendicular bisector of the vertical segment. **7a.** Congruent; answers may vary. Sample: Reflect figure A about the horizontal line through the middle of the figure. Rotate the resulting figure 90° clockwise about the center point. Translate the resulting figure to the right. **b.** Not congruent; answers may vary. Sample: No side of figure B is as long as the longest side of figure A. **c.** Congruent; rotate figure A 90° clockwise. Reflect the resulting figure about a vertical line. Finally, translate the figure to the right.

Lesson 3.02

Check Your Understanding

1. Answers may vary. Sample: Opposite sides are parallel and congruent. Diagonals bisect each other and are congruent. **2a.** Opposite sides of a rectangle are congruent. **b.** Angles *A* and *C* are right angles, so they form a straight line when joined. **3.** No; diagonals of a rectangle are congruent. **4a.** Cut along a diagonal. Reflect one of the triangles along a horizontal line. Translate one of the triangles so that two congruent sides align. **b.** Find the midpoint of a side. Cut along the line from that midpoint to one of the endpoints of the opposite side. Rotate the resulting triangle 180° around the midpoint. **c.** Cut along a diagonal. Translate one of the triangles so that two congruent sides align. **d.** Use the procedure from part (b) to form a right triangle. The triangle is scalene unless one side of the rectangle is twice the length of the other. If so, choose the midpoint of the shorter side to start your dissection. **e.** Start with rectangle *ABCD*. Pick a point *E* on $\overline{BC}$ and a point *F* on $\overline{AD}$. Let *G* be the midpoint of $\overline{BE}$ and *H* be the midpoint of $\overline{EC}$. Draw $\overline{AG}$ and $\overline{FH}$. Rotate $\triangle ABG$ 180° about *G* and rotate trapezoid *FDCH* 180° about *H*. **5a.** $\triangle DCN \cong \triangle PBN$ follows by AAS, since $\angle C \cong \angle PBN$ and $\angle CDN \cong \angle P$ by PAI, and $\overline{CN} \cong \overline{BN}$. **b.** $\overline{CD} \cong \overline{BP}$ by CPCTC. **c.** $\overline{DN} \cong \overline{PN}$ by CPCTC, so $\overline{MN} \parallel \overline{AP}$ and $MN = \frac{1}{2}AP$ **d.** $MN = \frac{1}{2}(AB + CD)$ **e.** $MN < AB$; $MN > CD$ and $\overline{MN} \parallel \overline{CD}$

6.

7. Answers may vary. Sample: Suppose the original rectangle has side lengths *b* and *h*. Draw a segment connecting the midpoints of the sides of length *b*. Cut along this segment. Stack the pieces to get a rectangle with side lengths $2h$ and $\frac{b}{2}$. If $\frac{b}{2} \neq h$, you are done. If $\frac{b}{2} = h$, then go back to the original rectangle, and instead cut along the segment connecting the midpoints of the sides of length *h*. Stack the pieces to get a rectangle with side lengths $2b$ and $\frac{h}{2}$.

On Your Own

9. Use dissection methods from the lesson. Dissect the given triangle into a parallelogram. Dissect the parallelogram into a rectangle. Finally, dissect the rectangle into a right triangle. **10.** Cut along both diagonals of the square. Translate two adjacent triangles that result to form the desired rectangle.

14. Answers may vary. Sample: Cut and rearrange one shape and try to fit it inside the other. If it does not entirely cover the second shape, then the second shape has a greater area than the first.

Lesson 3.03

Check Your Understanding

1a. Answers may vary. Samples:

- parallelogram to rectangle

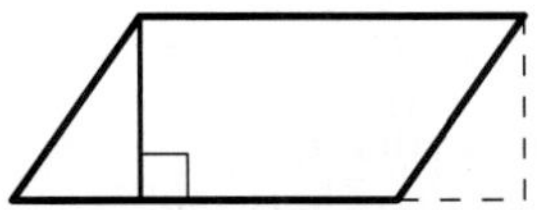

- triangle to rectangle

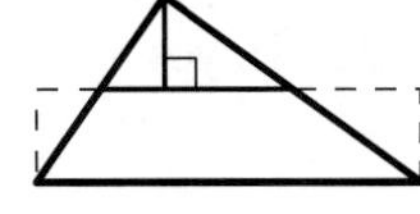

• trapezoid to rectangle

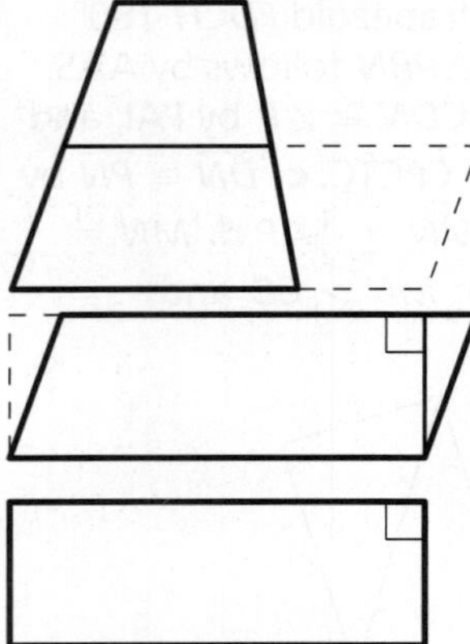

b. • Parallelogram to rectangle: Cut along an altitude that passes through a vertex of the parallelogram. Translate the resulting right triangle so that its hypotenuse aligns with the opposite side of the parallelogram.
• Triangle to rectangle: Cut along the midline parallel to the longest side of the triangle. Cut along the altitude to the longest side of the resulting smaller triangle. Rotate each of the smaller right triangles 180° about the midpoints of the sides of the original triangle.
• Trapezoid to rectangle: Cut along the midline parallel to the bases of the trapezoid. Rotate one of the resulting smaller trapezoids 180° about one of the endpoints of the midline. Dissect the resulting parallelogram into a rectangle using the technique described above. **2–3.** Answers may vary.

On Your Own

6. Answers may vary. Sample: Let *a*, *b*, and *c* be the digits (from left to right) of the three-digit number. Let *x* and *y* be the digits (from left to right) of the two-digit number. • Multiply *a* and *x* and append three zeros to the right side. • Multiply *a* and *y* and append two zeros to the right side. • Multiply *b* and *x* and append two zeros to the right side. • Multiply *b* and *y* and append one zero to the right side. • Multiply *c* and *x* and append one zero to the right side. • Multiply *c* and *y*. • Add all the sums to find the product.

Lesson 3.04

Check Your Understanding

1. Answers may vary. **2a.** It works for parallelograms with perpendicular diagonals. **b.** rhombuses and squares **3.** Answers may vary. **4a.** The pieces match because the cuts are through the midpoint of the sides. **b.** yes (because angles are supplementary) **c.** The upper angles of the quadrilateral are right angles because the vertical cut in Step 1 is perpendicular to the horizontal cut. The bottom two angles both have one acute angle of a right triangle meeting an angle congruent to the other acute angle of the same right triangle. **d.** The algorithm is general enough to use for any triangle if you can choose the longest side of the original triangle as the base of the final right triangle. If you need to choose the side at the "bottom" of the original triangle as the base, then this construction will not work for an obtuse triangle that is not resting on its longest side.

On Your Own

5. Answers may vary. Sample: Start with parallelogram *ABCD*. Let *M* be the midpoint of $\overline{BC}$. Draw $\overline{MD}$. Rotate $\triangle MCD$ 180° about *M*.
6. Answers may vary. Sample: $\overline{BM} \cong \overline{MC}$ since *M* is the midpoint of $\overline{BC}$. $\overline{AD'}$ (in the triangle) is straight because $\angle B$ and $\angle C$ are supplementary (in the parallelogram). $\overline{DD'}$ (in the triangle) is straight because $\angle DMB$ and $\angle DMC$ are supplementary (in the parallelogram).
9. Perform Jane's algorithm in reverse.
12a. the midpoint **b.** Yes; $\angle BFD$ and $\angle DFB'$ are supplementary because $\angle B'FD \cong \angle BFC$ (vertical angles). **c.** Yes; $\angle FDB' \cong \angle BCF$ by PAI, and $\angle BCF$ and $\angle FDA$ are supplementary.

Lesson 3.05

Check Your Understanding

1. $x = 3$, $y = 12$, $z = 90°$ **2.** By the Midline Theorem, $EF = \frac{1}{2}AC$ and $GH = \frac{1}{2}AC$. So $EF = GH$, which implies $\overline{EF} \cong \overline{GH}$. **3.** By the Midline Theorem, $EH = \frac{1}{2}BD$ and $FG = \frac{1}{2}BD$. So $EH = FG$, which implies $\overline{EH} \cong \overline{FG}$. **4.** *EFGH* is a parallelogram, since both pairs of opposite sides are congruent.

On Your Own

5a. 6 **b.** 5; 9; 9.5 **6.** The perimeter of the inner quadrilateral is 13, and all angles are right angles. **8.** rectangle

Lesson 3.06

On Your Own

4a. Answers may vary. **b.** The base and height of the parellelogram equal the length and width of the rectangle. **5a.** Answers may vary. **b.** The length of the rectangle equals the base of the triangle, and the width of the rectangle is half the height of the triangle.

Lesson 3.07

Check Your Understanding

1. • Midline Theorem • Definition of parallelogram • Definition of midpoint • Opposite sides of a parallelogram are congruent. • Segments congruent to the same segment are congruent to each other. • Parallel lines and a transversal form congruent corresponding angles. • Parallel lines and a transversal form congruent corresponding angles. • AAS • CPCTC **2a.** A, D, and E **b.** no

On Your Own

5. 125 **6.** 21.5 **10.** Equal to; all three triangles have the same height. $h = AX = BY$ and $AB = XC + XY$ so $\frac{1}{2}h(AB) = \frac{1}{2}h(XC) + \frac{1}{2}h(XY)$.

Lesson 3.08

Check Your Understanding

1a. 21 cm^2 **b.** 21 cm^2 **c.** 21 cm^2 **2a.** 6 **b.** 12 **c.** 18 **3a.** 98 **b.** 22.5 **c.** 98 **4a.** The bases of the trapezoids are equal and the heights are equal. **b.** The triangles are congruent and therefore have equal areas. **c.** The area of each trapezoid is the sum of the areas of its parts, and the triangular parts have equal areas. **5.** The trapezoids *BCGH* and *CDEH* have equal bases and equal heights and hence have equal areas. The area of each trapezoid is the sum of the areas of its parts, and $\triangle HCG$ is a common part for the trapezoids. So, area of $\triangle BCH =$ area of *EHGD*. **6.** The trapezoids *BCGH* and *BAEH* have equal bases and equal heights and hence have equal areas. The area of each trapezoid is the sum of the areas of its parts. Since $\triangle EAF$ and $\triangle CGH$ are congruent by SAS, the remaining parts $\triangle BCH$ and *EFBH* of the trapezoids have equal areas.

On Your Own

7a. Always true; since a median of a triangle always has a midpoint of a side as one of its endpoints, the two triangular parts of the original triangle have equal bases. The altitude from the other endpoint of the median is the same for both the triangular parts. Triangles with equal bases and equal altitudes have the same area. **b.** True for special cases; true for equilateral triangles or in an isosceles triangle. If you cut along the altitude from the vertex angle, then the statement is true, since that altitude is also a median. **c.** True for special cases; this is true only for the vertex angle of an isosceles triangle (or any angle in an equilateral triangle), since the angle bisector coincides with the median. **9a.** 4 cm **b.** 6 cm^2 **11.** $AC \cdot h = AB \cdot BC$ **13.** Since *M* is the midpoint of $\overline{AB}$, $AM = MB$. The altitude from *C* to $\overline{AM}$ in $\triangle ACM$ is the same as the altitude from *C* to $\overline{MB}$ in $\triangle MCB$. It follows that $\triangle ACM$ and $\triangle MCB$ have equal areas. By similar reasoning, $\triangle APM$ and $\triangle MPB$ have equal areas. But $\text{area}(\triangle ACM) = \text{area}(\triangle APC) + \text{area}(\triangle APM)$ and $\text{area}(\triangle MCB) = \text{area}(\triangle PBC) + \text{area}(\triangle MPB)$. Therefore, $\text{area}(\triangle APC) = \text{area}(\triangle PBC)$.

Lesson 3.09

On Your Own

2a. $\sqrt{2}$ ft **b.** $2\sqrt{2}$ ft **c.** $4\sqrt{2}$ ft **d.** $10\sqrt{2}$ ft **e.** $100\sqrt{2}$ ft **3.** If *x* is the length of a side of a square, then the length of a diagonal is $x\sqrt{2}$.

Lesson 3.10

Check Your Understanding

1a. Constructions may vary. **b.** The length of the hypotenuse is *c* by the Pythagorean Theorem. **c.** by SSS **d.** It is congruent to the right triangle from part (a). **2.** Construct a right triangle with legs of length *a* and *b*. By the Pythagorean Theorem, the hypotenuse must have length *c*, since you know that *c* is the number satisfying the equation $a^2 + b^2 = c^2$. The original triangle and the triangle you have just constructed are congruent by SSS, and therefore all the angles are congruent as well, by CPCTC. **3a.** 6 in.^2 **b.** 49 in.^2 **c.** 25 in.^2 **d.** yes **4.** 5 in.

On Your Own

6a. 36 ft^2 **b.** 6 ft, 8 ft, 10 ft **9a.** $\sqrt{10}$ **b.** 16 **c.** 16

Lesson 3.11

Check Your Understanding

1a. 64 **b.** 65 **c.** Answers may vary. Sample: The measures of the upper left and lower right angles of the 5-by-13 "rectangle" are about 88.8°. This is close enough to a right angle to fool the eye, but the figure is in fact not precisely a rectangle, and so you cannot use the formula for the area of a rectangle.

On Your Own

2a. $\frac{\sqrt{3}}{2}$ cm **b.** $\sqrt{3}$ cm **c.** $\frac{3\sqrt{3}}{2}$ cm **d.** $5\sqrt{3}$ cm **e.** $50\sqrt{3}$ cm **4.** $A = \frac{s^2\sqrt{3}}{4}$ **6.** $10\sqrt{3}$ in. **7.** about 750 miles **8.** Assume the figure is a trapezoid with one side perpendicular to the bases. The area is 70,000 ft^2. **10.** Answers may vary. Sample: (5, 12, 13), (8, 15, 17)

12. The sizes of the triangles are different, but each is a right triangle in which the ratio of the side lengths is 3 : 4 : 5.

Lesson 3.12
On Your Own
8a. $SA = 2(\ell w + wh + \ell h)$ **b.** $SA = 6s^2$ **c.** For a cube, ℓ, w, and h are all equal to s. Substitute in the formula from part (a). Simplify to get $SA = 6s^2$. **9a.** 6; 14; $2n - 2$ **b.** 18; 34; $4n + 2$ **c.** 4 more; 2 more **10a.** 26 in.^{2}

Lesson 3.13
Check Your Understanding
1a. 45 cm^2 **b.** 60 cm^2 **c.** 75 cm^2 **d.** $15n$ cm^2 **2.** Exercise 1a: $\left(45 + \frac{25\sqrt{3}}{2}\right)$ cm^2 Exercise 1b: 110 cm^2 **3a.** 36 cm^2 **b.** 48 cm^2 **c.** 60 cm^2 **4.** Exercise 3a: $(36 + 9\sqrt{3})$ cm^2; Exercise 3b: 84 cm^2; Exercise 3c: 96 cm^2
On Your Own
5a. $2\sqrt{4426}$ ft $\approx$ 133 ft **b.** $720\sqrt{4426}$ ft^2 $\approx$ 47,900 ft^2 **c.** $240\sqrt{4426} \approx 15{,}967$ **7a.** $\frac{3}{2}$ ft **b.** 4 cm by 4 cm by 8 cm **9a.** $SA = \sqrt{3}s^2$ **b.** $SA = 6s^2$ **10.** B

Lesson 3.14
Check Your Understanding
1a. 32 m^2; $16\sqrt{2}$ m^2; 8π m^2 **b.** Prism B; Prism A **c.** Cylinder C is inside Prism A. Prism B is inside Cylinder C; yes. **2.** $4\sqrt{17}$ m^2; $2\sqrt{33}$ m^2; $\pi\sqrt{17}$ m^2 **3a.** 168π cm^2; 84π cm^2; 96π cm^2 **b.** Cone B; Cylinder A
On Your Own
4a. 168π ft^2; 266π ft^2 **c.** 78π cm^2; 114π cm^2 **5.** shorter cylinder: $r = \frac{11}{2\pi}$ in., $h = 8.5$ in., $LA = 93.5$ in.^{2}, $SA = \left(93.5 + \frac{121}{2\pi}\right)$ in.^{2}; taller cylinder: $r = \frac{17}{4\pi}$ in., $h = 11$ in., $LA = 93.5$ in.^{2}, $SA = \left(93.5 + \frac{289}{8\pi}\right)$ in.^{2} **6.** 9.375 cm

Lesson 3.15
Check Your Understanding
1a. $40\sqrt{3}$ in.^{3} **b.** 4 ft^3 **c.** 1872π cm^3 **d.** 240π cm^3 **2.** The height of the prism is $\frac{13}{3}$ in. **3.** $9\sqrt{3}$ cm
On Your Own
4. $\frac{9}{16}$ in. **5.** $\frac{7}{\pi}$ cm **6.** 213 cans **8.** 192 in.^{3}

Chapter 4

Lesson 4.01
On Your Own
8a. 45 mi **b.** 22.5 mi **c.** about 5.6 mi **9.** Answers may vary. Samples are given. **a.** about 241.5 in. by 105 in. **b.** about 25,357.5 in.^{2} **c.** about 20 yd^2

Lesson 4.02
Check Your Understanding
1. Answers may vary. Samples: angle measures, congruence of sides, perpendicularity of diagonals **2a.** smaller **b.** same size **c.** larger **d.** smaller **3a.** No; the rectangles are not the same shape. **b.** Yes; the side lengths of the smaller triangle are half the corresponding side lengths of the larger triangle. **c.** No; the diameter of the smaller circle is not half the diameter of the larger circle. **4a.** about $\frac{6}{7}$ **b.** 1 **5.** about $\frac{7}{6}$; 1 **6.** They are reciprocals. **7a.** 4 copies **b.** 9 copies **8a.** 4 **b.** 324 **c.** 16
On Your Own
9a. 0.8, or $\frac{4}{5}$ **b.** 75% **10a.** different **b.** different **c.** same **d.** same **13a.** $\frac{1}{3}$; 3; they are reciprocals. **b.** $\frac{1}{5}$; 5; they are reciprocals. **c.** 6; $\frac{1}{6}$; they are reciprocals.

Lesson 4.03
Check Your Understanding
1. Compare ratios of corresponding distances, such as $\frac{AB}{EF}$ and $\frac{CD}{GH}$. **2.** The choice of unit does not affect the ratio. **3.** Answers may vary. Sample: the width of the bottom of each letter, the length of the horizontal bar in each letter, the height of each letter, the length of the "legs" of each letter.
On Your Own
6. The dimensions of the letters in the scaled copy should be twice the dimensions of the original letters.

Lesson 4.04
Check Your Understanding
1. 9 **2.** 5 **3.** These triangles are scaled copies. Explanations may vary. Sample: By measurement, the lengths of the corresponding sides are proportional, and the corresponding angles have equal measures. **4.** no
On Your Own
5. Yes; all the angles are right angles, and in each rectangle, the ratio $\frac{\text{length of short side}}{\text{length of long side}}$ is $\frac{1}{3}$. **6.** 3.2 in.

Lesson 4.05
Check Your Understanding
1. No; explanations may vary. Sample: All rectangles have 4 right angles, but not all rectangles are scaled copies of each other. **2.** no **3a.** yes **b.** No; explanations may vary. Sample: In both figures, the polygons have the same angle measures, but only the first pair has corresponding side lengths with equal ratios. **4.** Answers may vary. Sample: Draw

the diagonals and mark the point P where they intersect. Mark the midpoints of $\overline{PA}$, $\overline{PB}$, $\overline{PC}$, and $\overline{PD}$. Connect the midpoints, in order, to get the scaled trapezoid. **5a.** $\frac{3}{4}$ or $\frac{4}{3}$ **b.** 1
6. • No; corresponding sides must have the same ratio.
• No; corresponding angles must be congruent.

On Your Own

7. No. The angle measures for the first triangle are 28°, 31°, and 121°. The angle measures for the second triangle are 31°, 32°, and 117°.
10a. Sample counterexample: a 1-by-2 rectangle and a 1-by-3 rectangle **b.** All angles measure 90°, and ratios of corresponding sides are always equal. **d.** Sample counterexample: an equilateral triangle and a triangle that is not equilateral **f.** Both triangles have angles 45°, 45°, and 90°. If the legs of the triangles have measures m and n, then the hypotenuses have measures $m\sqrt{2}$ and $n\sqrt{2}$. Hence the ratio of corresponding sides is $\frac{m}{n}$ for all pairs of corresponding sides. **i.** Each polygon is equilateral, so the ratio of side lengths does not vary. If the polygons have n sides, then each angle measure is $\frac{(n-2)180^\circ}{n}$. **11a–l.** If no, a sample counterexample is given. **a.** no; a 1-by-2 rectangle and a 1-by-3 rectangle **c.** no; a trapezoid with bases of lengths 1 and 5 and a trapezoid with bases of lengths 2 and 4 **e.** yes; special case of Exercise 10i **g.** Yes; all radii of a circle are congruent, so the ratios of radii of two circles will always be equal. **i.** Yes; all radii of a sphere are congruent, so the ratios of radii of two spheres will always be equal. **l.** no; any cone and a cone with the same base, but different height

Lesson 4.06

On Your Own

5a–d. Drawings may vary. Each length in the scaled copy should have the given relationship to the corresponding length of the original hexagon. All angles should measure 120°. **a.** $\frac{1}{2}$ as long **b.** the same size **c.** $\frac{3}{2}$ as long **d.** $\frac{3}{4}$ as long **7.** The area A and the perimeter P of the original rectangle may vary. The areas and perimeters of the corresponding scaled copies are **a.** area $= 4A$, perimeter $= 2P$ **b.** area $= 9A$, perimeter $= 3P$ **c.** area $= \frac{1}{4}A$, perimeter $= \frac{1}{2}P$ **d.** area $= \frac{1}{9}A$, perimeter $= \frac{1}{3}P$ **9.** The area A and the perimeter P of the original triangle may vary. The areas and perimeters of the corresponding scaled copies are **a.** area $= 16A$, perimeter $= 4P$ **b.** area $= 0.01A$, perimeter $= 0.1P$ **c.** area $= \frac{9}{25}A$, perimeter $= \frac{3}{5}P$ **d.** area $= \frac{1}{49}A$, perimeter $= \frac{1}{7}P$

Lesson 4.07

Check Your Understanding

1a. Drawings may vary. **b.** The location of the center of dilation affects where the scaled copy is located in relation to the original circle.
2a. Drawings may vary. Each side of the scaled copy should be twice as long as the corresponding side of the original tilted square. **b.** They are the same. **c.** no
3. Answers may vary. Sample: To dilate a circle by the factor $\frac{1}{2}$ using point C as the center of dilation, select a point A on the circle. Draw $\overrightarrow{CA}$. Then mark point A' on $\overrightarrow{CA}$ such that $CA' = \frac{1}{2}CA$. Point A' will be on the scaled copy. Repeat this procedure for several other points of the original circle. Sketch the circle through all the resulting points for the scaled copy. The procedure for dilating the circle by the factor 3 is similar, except this time A' is a point such that $CA' = 3CA$. To dilate a square, find the points on the dilated square that correspond to the vertices of the original square. Connect these points in order to get the dilated square. **4.** Draw the line that passes through the top points of the two figures. Then draw the line that passes through the bottom points of the figures. The point where the two lines intersect is the center of dilation.

On Your Own

5. Choices may vary. The orientation of the two pictures should be the same, but each length in the scaled copy should be twice as long as the corresponding length in the original. **7.** No, the actual measurements on the face are about twice those of the mirror image. **8.** The image you see on "the other side" of the mirror appears the same distance behind the mirror that you are in front of the mirror. Imagine drawing lines from your eyes to the image on the other side of the mirror. Think of your eyes as the center of dilation. The mirror is halfway between, so the image on the mirror appears half the size of your actual face.

Lesson 4.08
Check Your Understanding
1–2. Drawings may vary.
3.

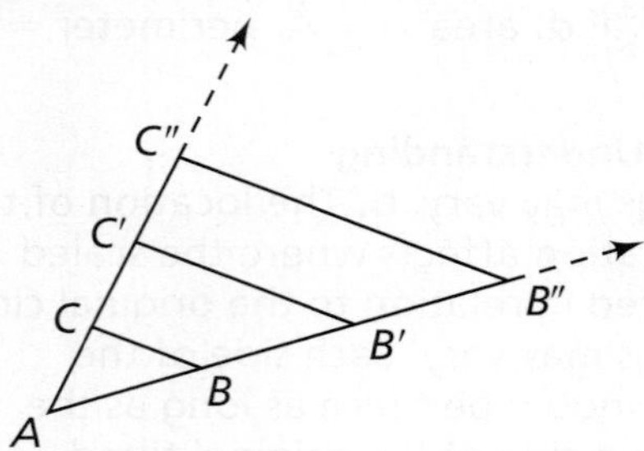

4. 3 times as long; he should have used $DA' = 2$, $DB' = 4$, and $DC' = 3$. **5.** The scale factor is about 1.4. **6a.** The scaled copy should be closer to *D* than the original, with lengths proportional to the original by the factor $\frac{3}{4}$. **b.** The scaled copy should be farther from *D* than the original, with lengths 1.5 times as big as those of the original.
7–8. Drawings may vary.
On Your Own
10. Drawings may vary. One of the polygons should have two of its sides contained in the corresponding sides of the other.
12a. $0 <$ scale factor < 1 **b.** scale factor > 1 **c.** scale factor $= 1$
Lesson 4.09
On Your Own
4. $PQ = 2\sqrt{13}$, $SR = 8$, $QR = 12$, $PR = 10$
6. All will have the same area; they have congruent bases ($\overline{RA}$ and $\overline{GM}$) and equal heights (the distance between $\overleftrightarrow{RA}$ and $\overleftrightarrow{GM}$).
Lesson 4.10
Check Your Understanding
1. 6 **2.** 16 **3.** 8 **4.** 12 **5.** $\frac{1}{4}$
On Your Own
8. Answers may vary. Sample: For the figure in Exercise 6, "whole is to part as whole is to part" means $\frac{AB}{AD} = \frac{AC}{AE}$, "part is to part as part is to part" means $\frac{AD}{DE} = \frac{AE}{DE}$, and "part is to whole as part is to whole" means $\frac{AD}{AB} = \frac{AE}{AC}$.
Lesson 4.11
Check Your Understanding
1. Reverse some of the steps in the proof of the Parallel Side-Splitter Theorem to show that $\frac{SV}{VR} = \frac{SW}{WT}$ implies $\frac{\text{area }(\triangle SVW)}{\text{area }(\triangle RVW)} = \frac{\text{area }(\triangle SVW)}{\text{area }(\triangle TVW)}$ and that this implies area $(\triangle RVW) =$ area$(\triangle TVW)$. Since area$(RVWT)$ is equal to both area$(\triangle RVW)$ + *area*$(\triangle RWT)$ and area$(\triangle TVW)$ + *area*$(\triangle RVT)$, it follows that area $(\triangle RVT) =$ area$(\triangle RWT)$. In $\triangle RVT$, draw the altitude $\overline{VM}$ from *V* to $\overline{RT}$, and in $\triangle RWT$, draw the altitude $\overline{WN}$ from *W* to $\overline{RT}$. Use the area formula with $\triangle RVT$ and $\triangle RWT$ to get $\frac{1}{2}(RT)(VM) = \frac{1}{2}(RT)(WN)$, from which it follows that $VM = WN$. Conclude that *MVWN* is a parallelogram (two sides parallel and congruent) and hence that $\overline{VM} \parallel \overline{RT}$. **2a.** $CD = 2$, $AD = 2$, $BC = 2$ **b.** $BC = 4.5$, $CE = 1.5$, $AC = 3$ **c.** $CD = 1$, $CE = 1$, $BC = 2$ **3a.** no **b.** yes **c.** yes
On Your Own
5. They cut $\overline{AB}$ and $\overline{BC}$ into four congruent segments. **7.** All the dashed lines are parallel to $\overline{AC}$.
Lesson 4.12
Check Your Understanding
1. $BE = 4$, $EC = 4$, $AD = 3$, $BD = 3$
2. $AD = 1$, $AB = 2$, $EC = 1$, $BC = 2$
3. $AB = 12$, $AD = 4$, $CE = 3$, $BE = 6$
On Your Own
5. Since $\overline{DE} \parallel \overline{BC}$, it follows that corresponding angles of the two triangles are congruent. Use the Parallel Side-Splitter Theorem to show that corresponding sides are proportional. Therefore, the triangles are scaled copies of each other.
Lesson 4.13
On Your Own
7. $\angle D \cong \angle M$, $\angle E \cong \angle A$, $\angle R \cong \angle N$, $\frac{DE}{MA} = \frac{DR}{MN} = \frac{ER}{AN}$, $\frac{DE}{ER} = \frac{MA}{AN}$, $\frac{DE}{DR} = \frac{MA}{MN}$, $\frac{DR}{ER} = \frac{MN}{AN}$
9. No; the sketch should feature two similar polygons that are reflected as well as dilated.
Lesson 4.14
Check Your Understanding
1a. Yes; corresponding angles are congruent, and corresponding sides are proportional.
b. No; corresponding angles are not congruent.
c. No; corresponding angles are not congruent.
2a. yes **b.** yes **c.** no **d.** yes **3.** Since $\triangle ABC \sim \triangle BDA$, $\angle B \cong \angle D$. Therefore $\overline{AB} \cong \overline{AD}$, and $\triangle BDA$ is isosceles. Any triangle similar to an isosceles triangle must itself be isosceles, so $\triangle ABC$ is isosceles. **4.** Answers may vary. Sample: By the Midline Theorem, the lengths of the sides of $\triangle GHF$ are half the lengths of the corresponding sides of $\triangle ABC$. Since a midline is parallel to the third side of its triangle, it follows that *AFGH*, *FGCH*, and *FBCH* are parallelograms. Opposite angles of a parallelogram are congruent, so the corresponding angles of $\triangle GHF$ and $\triangle ABG$ are

congruent. Therefore, $\triangle ABC \sim \triangle GHF$.
5. $m\angle BAC = 30°$, $m\angle DAC = 90°$, $m\angle BCA = 120°$, $m\angle ACD = 60°$, $m\angle ADB = 30°$, $BC = 2\sqrt{3}$, $CD = 4\sqrt{3}$, $BD = 6\sqrt{3}$, $AD = 6$

On Your Own

6a. incorrect **b.** correct **c.** incorrect **d.** correct **e.** incorrect **f.** incorrect **8a.** $\angle D$ **b.** $\angle DTO$ **c.** $\angle CTA$ **d.** $\angle O$ **e.** $\angle C$ **f.** $\angle A$

Lesson 4.15

Check Your Understanding

1a. Note that $\frac{KM}{KJ} = \frac{KN}{KL} = \frac{1}{4}$, and then use the Proportional Side-Splitter Theorem.
b. • Since $\overline{MN} \parallel \overline{JL}$, $\angle KMN \cong \angle KJL$ and $\angle KNM \cong \angle KLJ$. $\triangle MKN \sim \triangle JKL$ by the AA test.
• From part (a), $\frac{KM}{KJ} = \frac{KN}{KL}$. And since both triangles share a common angle, $\triangle MKN \sim \triangle JKL$ by the SAS Test.
• By the Parallel Side-Splitter Theorem, $\frac{KM}{KJ} = \frac{KN}{KL} = \frac{MN}{JL}$. By the SSS Theorem, $\triangle MKN \sim \triangle JKL$.
2a. 3; AA Similarity Theorem **b.** 3; AA Similarity Theorem **c.** 3; SAS Similarity Test
3. No; answers may vary. Sample: A square with sides of length 1 is not similar to a rectangle that has length 2 and width 1.
4. In quadrilaterals $ABCD$ and $EFGH$, let $\frac{AB}{EF} = \frac{AD}{EH} = \frac{CD}{GH}$, $\angle BAD \cong \angle FEH$, and $\angle ADC \cong \angle EHG$. By the SAS Similarity Theorem, $\triangle ABD \sim \triangle EFH$ and $\triangle CDA \sim \triangle GHE$. Therefore, $\angle CAD \cong \angle GEH$, and $\overline{AC}$ and $\overline{EG}$ are proportional. $\angle BAC \cong \angle FEG$ because each is the difference of congruent angles. By the SAS Similarity Theorem, $\triangle ABC \sim \triangle EFG$ and $\triangle BCD \sim \triangle FGH$. Therefore, BC and FG are proportional to AB and EF. Corresponding angles in similar triangles are congruent, so $\angle ABC \cong \angle EFG$ and $\angle BCD \cong \angle FGH$. All corresponding sides of $ABCD$ and $EFHG$ are proportional and all corresponding angles are congruent, so the quadrilaterals are similar.
5. For parallel lines cut by a transversal, corresponding angles are congruent, so $\angle HFG \cong \angle A$ and $\angle HGF \cong \angle C$. Therefore, $\triangle ABC \sim \triangle FHG$ by the AA Similarity Test. **6.** B

On Your Own

7. $\frac{15}{4}$ and 6; or $\frac{12}{5}$ and $\frac{24}{5}$; or $\frac{3}{2}$ and $\frac{15}{8}$; yes
9. AA Similarity test (since $\angle A \cong \angle A$ and $\angle ADE \cong \angle C$) **12.** $\frac{AC}{EC} = \frac{BC}{DC} = 2$, and $\angle C$ is common to the two triangles. Hence $\triangle ABC \sim \triangle EDC$ by the SAS Similarity Theorem; 2.

Lesson 4.16

Check Your Understanding

1. 540 **2.** He needed only 2 bags of seed for the small field. **3a.** about 31 cm^2 or 4.8 in.^{2} **b.** about 70 cm^2 or 11 in.^{2}

On Your Own

4a. $\sqrt{12}$ or $\frac{\sqrt{12}}{12}$ **b.** $\sqrt{12}$ or $\frac{\sqrt{12}}{12}$ **5.** The area of the scaled copy is $\frac{1}{16}$ times the area of the original. **7.** 68 in.^{2}

Chapter 5

Lesson 5.01

On Your Own

4a. There are 5 squares inside the figure.
b. Each square has an area of $\frac{1}{4}$ square inch. The area covered by the squares is $\frac{5}{4}$ square inches, which is definitely less than the area of the blob.

Lesson 5.02

Check Your Understanding

1. The following answers assume that two grid lines pass through the center of the circle.
a. Inner area = 1 in.^{2}; outer area = 4 in.^{2}; area of circle is between these measures.
b. Inner area = 2 in.^{2}; outer area = 3.75 in.^{2}; area of circle is between these measures.
c. Inner area = 2.56 in.^{2}; outer area = 3.5 in.^{2}; area of circle is between these measures.
d. Inner area = 2.86 in.^{2}; outer area = 3.34 in.^{2}; area of circle is between these measures.
2a. Answers may vary. Sample: Place a grid of squares over the shape. To get a low estimate, count grid squares that lie entirely inside the shape and multiply by the area of a grid square. To get a high estimate, count grid squares that lie inside or partially inside the shape and multiply by the area of a grid square. In most cases, the smaller the grid squares, the better the estimates will be.
b. 6 in.^{2} **c.** Answers may vary. Sample: inner area = 5.25 in.^{2}, outer area = 6.75 in.^{2} (You obtain these values by using a grid of $\frac{1}{4}$ in.-by-$\frac{1}{4}$ in. squares, with the perpendicular sides of the triangle lying along grid lines.)
3. ratio of area of smaller to area of larger = $\left(\frac{3.5}{4.5}\right)^2$, or about 0.605 **4a.** The area of the larger circle is 9 times the area of the smaller circle. **b.** The area of the smaller circle is $\frac{1}{4}$ the area of the larger circle. **5–7.** Answers may vary. Samples are given based on drawing a circle with radius 1 in. **5.** The circumference is

between 2 in. and 4 in. **6.** The circumference is between 2.8 in. and 3.3 in. **7.** The circumference is between 3.1 in. and 3.2 in. **8.** Tables may vary. The following table is based on measuring the figures shown in Exercises 5–7.

Number of Sides	Outer Perimeter	Inner Perimeter	Difference
4	20.4 cm	14.4 cm	6 cm
8	16.8 cm	15.2 cm	1.6 cm
16	16 cm	15.5 cm	0.5 cm

9. Answers may vary. Sample: 15.75 cm **10.** As the number of sides of the inscribed and circumscribed polygons increases, the polygons get to be more like the circle.

On Your Own

12a. s-by-$2s$ rectangles, where s is the length of a square of the original grid **b.** twice the area of a square of the original grid **c.** It doubles. **d.** No; in a scaled copy, all the lengths change by the same factor. **13.** The curve is approximately $7\frac{1}{8}$ inches long.

Lesson 5.03

Check Your Understanding

1. about 3.125 m^2 **2a.** $\sqrt{2}$ cm **b.** about 6.29 cm^2 **3.** Answers may vary. Sample: Suppose $ABCDEF$ is a regular hexagon and that point O is the center of the circumscribed circle. The sum of the angle measures of $ABCDEF$ is $4 \cdot 180°$, or $720°$. If you draw the radii from O to the vertices of $ABCDEF$, you divide the hexagon into six congruent isosceles triangles (congruent by SSS, isosceles because radii of the same circle are congruent). It follows that the angles of each triangle all have a measure of 60°. Therefore, the triangles are equilateral, and hence the radii are congruent to the sides of the hexagon. **4.** about 6.28 in.

On Your Own

5a. about 172.8 $in.^2$ **7.** about 7.9 cm

Lesson 5.04

On Your Own

4. about 5.57 cm **5.** about 9.1 cm^2

Lesson 5.05

Check Your Understanding

1a. 100π $in.^2$ **b.** 25π cm^2 **c.** $\frac{9}{4}\pi$ ft^2 **d.** 100π $in.^2$ **2a.** $\frac{1}{8}$ **b.** π **c.** $\frac{\pi}{8}$ **d.** Answers may vary. Sample: $\frac{11}{28}$ (using $\pi \approx \frac{22}{7}$), 0.3925 (using $\pi \approx 3.14$) **3a.** 25π **b.** $144\pi - 72$

On Your Own

4a. $\frac{25\pi}{6}$ **b.** 20π **6a.** shaded: 9π cm^2; white: $(36 - 9\pi)$ cm^2 **b.** shaded: 9π cm^2; white: $(36 - 9\pi)$ cm^2 **c.** The areas of the shaded regions are the same, and so are the areas of the white regions; if you cut the figure in part (a) vertically through the center and translate the part on the left 6 cm to the right, you get the figure in part (b), provided you ignore the segment down the middle.

Lesson 5.06

Check Your Understanding

1. small arc: $\frac{2\pi}{3}$ cm; large arc: $\frac{10\pi}{3}$ cm **2.** small arc: $\frac{\pi}{3}$ cm; large arc: $\frac{11\pi}{3}$ cm **3.** small arc: $\frac{\pi}{2}$ cm; large arc: $\frac{7\pi}{2}$ cm **4.** True; the formula $C = \pi d$ implies $\frac{C}{d} = \pi$.

On Your Own

6. circumference of canister ($C = 2\pi r$, $h = 6r$, and $2\pi > 6$) **7.** rectangle 5 in. tall and 3π in. wide

Lesson 5.07

Check Your Understanding

1. 2π; 360° **2a.** $2\pi/3$ <stack fraction> radians, or 120° **b.** $4\pi/9$ radians, or 80° **c.** 6/5 <stack fraction> radians, or $216/\pi$ <stack fraction> ≈ 68.8° **3a.** The central angle should take up a little less than one-third of the circle. **b.** 10 cm **c.** The radian measure of the central angle remains 2.

On Your Own

7. π; 180° **8a.** $2\pi/3$ <stack fraction> radians or 120° **b.** $2\pi/5$ <stack fraction> radians, or 72° **c.** $2\pi/9$ <stack fraction> radians, or 40° **d.** $\pi/2$ <stack fraction> radians, or 90° **e.** $\pi/180$ <stack fraction> radians, or 1° **9a.** 120 cm **b.** 72 cm **c.** 40 cm **d.** 90 cm **e.** 1 cm

Lesson 5.08

On Your Own

7a. right triangle **b.** $\overline{AB}$. (the hypotenuse), midpoint **c.** outside the circle (but not on $\overleftrightarrow{AB}$); inside the circle

Lesson 5.09

Check Your Understanding

1a. chord, diameter **b.** radius **c.** radius **d.** chord **e.** central angle **f.** central angle **g.** minor arc **h.** semicircle **2.** $m\angle MON = 60°$, $MN = 1$ in., $OH = \frac{\sqrt{3}}{2}$ in. **3a.** 60° **b.** 30° **c.** 45° **d.** 15° **e.** 15° **f.** 15° **g.** 75° **4.** Yes; given circle O with minor arc and points as described, assume $m\overset{\frown}{AC} = x$ and $m\overset{\frown}{CB} = y$. Then $m\angle AOC = x$ and $m\angle COB = y$. Therefore $m\angle AOC + m\angle COB = x + y$. And since $\angle AOC$ and $\angle COB$ are adjacent, we know that

$m\angle AOC + m\angle COB = m\angle AOB = x + y$. And since the arc associated with $\angle AOB$ is $\widehat{AB}$, we know that $m\widehat{AB} = m\angle AOB = x + y$ $= m\widehat{AC} + m\widehat{CB}$.

On Your Own

5. $\overline{OQ} \cong \overline{OR}$, since radii of the same circle are congruent. Hence $\triangle OQR$ is isosceles. But the bisector of the vertex angle of an isosceles triangle is a median. Thus *P* is the midpoint of $\overline{QR}$, and so $\overline{QP} \cong \overline{PR}$. **6.** The angles in question are base angles of congruent isosceles triangles $\triangle FOH$ and $\triangle IOJ$. Since the base angles of an isosceles triangle are congruent, it follows that all four of the angles are congruent.

Lesson 5.10

Check Your Understanding

1. 90° **2.** If *A* is at the center of the circle, then all chords through *A* will have the same length and hence the shortest possible length. If *A* is not at the center and the center is *O*, the shortest chord through *A* will be the chord $\overline{XY}$ perpendicular to $\overline{OA}$ at *A*. To see why, note that $\overline{XY}$ is shorter than a diameter. Suppose $\overline{PQ}$ is any chord other than $\overline{XY}$ that passes through *A*. In $\triangle POQ$, let $\overline{OR}$ be the altitude from *O*. Since $\triangle OAR$ is a right triangle with its right angle at *R*, it follows that $OA > OR$ (the hypotenuse of a right triangle is longer than each of the legs). $\triangle XOY$ and $\triangle POQ$ are isosceles triangles with legs that are radii of the circle. It follows from the Pythagorean Theorem that the triangle with the greater altitude from *O* has the shorter base. Hence $XY < PQ$. **3.** Sketches may vary. Sample:

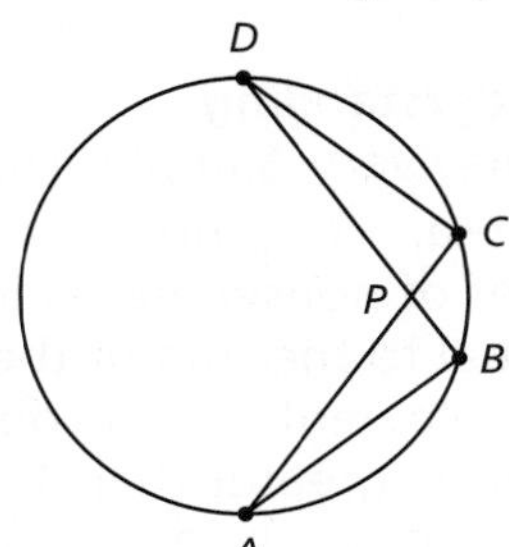

$\angle CAB \cong \angle BDC$, since they intercept the same arc. For the same reason, $\angle ABD \cong \angle DCA$. It is given that $\overline{AB} \cong \overline{CD}$, so $\triangle ABP \cong \triangle DCP$ by ASA. Since they are corresponding parts of congruent triangles, the two segments that form $\overline{AC}$ ($\overline{AP}$ and $\overline{PC}$) are congruent to the two segments that form $\overline{BD}$ ($\overline{DP}$ and $\overline{PB}$). Therefore, $\overline{AC} \cong \overline{BD}$. Similar reasoning applies for other possible diagrams. **4.** Suppose the adjacent chords are $\overline{AB}$ and $\overline{CB}$ and tha[t] ... is the radius with which they form congru[ent] angles. $\triangle AOB$ and $\triangle COB$ are isosceles (two sides of each are radii). It is given that $\angle ABO \cong \angle CBO$. So the base angles of $\triangle AOB$ are congruent to the base angles of $\triangle COB$. Since the triangles have $\overline{OB}$ as a common side, $\triangle AOB \cong \triangle COB$ (by AAS). Therefore, $\overline{AB} \cong \overline{BC}$ (by CPCTC). **5a.** 11.5° **b.** 23° **c.** 23° **d.** 78.5° **e.** 78.5°

On Your Own

7. a circle with the same center as the original circle and lying inside that circle **8.** 2 ways; $\frac{\sqrt{3}}{4} + \frac{\pi}{6}$, or $\frac{3\sqrt{3} + 2\pi}{12}$ **10a.** 90°, 90°, 90°, 90° **b.** 70° **c.** 140° **d.** 70° **e.** 40° **12a.** A diameter of a circle that is perpendicular to a chord bisects the chord (Theorem 5.8). $\overline{FZ}$ is perpendicular to $\overline{PQ}$ since it is perpendicular to $\overline{MN}$ and $\overline{MN} \parallel \overline{PQ}$. Hence $\overline{FZ}$ is the perpendicular bisector of $\overline{MN}$ and $\overline{PQ}$. **b.** 5 cm **c.** $5\sqrt{3}$ cm **d.** $\frac{5\sqrt{3}}{2}$ cm **e.** 90° **13.** 45°

Lesson 5.11

Check Your Understanding

1a. x = 106, y = 86 **b.** x = 91, y = 87 **c.** Not possible to determine x and y; at best, x = 180° − y, or y = 180° − x. **d.** not possible to determine x and y **2a.** 50 **b.** 50 π

On Your Own

7. $m\angle J = 101°$, $m\angle K = 112°$, $m\widehat{JK} = 58°$ $m\widehat{LK} = 78°$, $m\widehat{ML} = 124°$ **8.** In a cyclic quadrilateral, opposite angles are supplementary. In general, consecutive angles are not. James claimed that consecutive angles in ABCD are supplementary; $m\angle A = 110°$, $m\angle C = 70°$, $m\angle D = 85°$. **9.** All four angles are 90°; rectangle **10.** 18

Lesson 5.12

Check Your Understanding

1. The radius drawn to the point where a tangent line touches a circle is perpendicular to the tangent line, so $\triangle OPB$ and $\triangle OPA$ are right triangles. The triangles have a common hypotenuse and the legs $\overline{OB}$ and $\overline{OA}$ are congruent. It follows by the Pythagorean Theorem that $PA = PB$ and hence that $\overline{PA} \cong \overline{PB}$. **2.** $\overline{OB}$ and $\overline{OA}$ are radii, so $OB = OA$. From Exercise 1, $PA = PB$. Since *P* and *O* are equidistant from *A* and *B*, $\overline{PO}$ is the perpendicular bisector of $\overline{AB}$. **3.** Suppose the given circle has center *O*, and let the external point be *P*. Draw $\overline{OP}$. Construct the midpoint *M* of $\overline{OP}$. Draw the circle with center *M* and radius $\overline{MO}$. Let *C* and *D* be the points where

Selected Answers

this circle intersects the given circle. Draw *PCOD*. $\angle C$ and $\angle D$ both intercept a semicircle of the circle with center *M*. Therefore, $\angle C$ and $\angle D$ are right angles. Hence $\overline{PC}$ and $\overline{PD}$ are tangent to the original circle. **4a.** 57° **b.** 26° **c.** 65° **5a.** 14° **b.** 27.5° **c.** Answers may vary. From part (b), $m\angle CAD = 27.5°$. By Theorem 5.14, $m\angle ADC = \frac{1}{2}(m\widehat{CBF} - m\widehat{CE}) = \frac{1}{2}((180° + 14°) - 69°) = 62.5°$. So $m\angle ACD = 180° - 27.5° - 62.5° = 90°$.

On Your Own

6. If $m\angle POQ = 30°$, then $OQ = \frac{2\sqrt{3}}{3}$ in. and $PQ = \frac{\sqrt{3}}{3}$ in.; if $\angle POQ = 45°$, then $OQ = \sqrt{2}$ in. and $PQ = 1$ in.; if $m\angle POQ = 60°$, then $OQ = 2$ in. and $PQ = \sqrt{3}$ in. **9.** Drawings may vary. Sample:

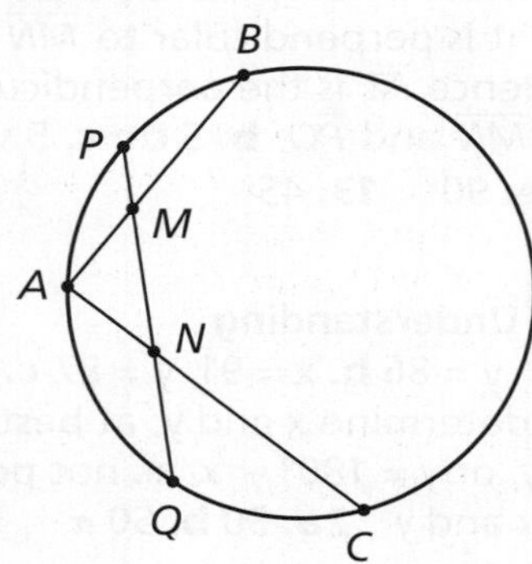

By Theorem 5.13, $m\angle AMN = \frac{1}{2}(m\widehat{BP} + m\widehat{AQ})$ and $m\angle ANM = \frac{1}{2}(m\widehat{AP} + m\widehat{CQ})$. But $\widehat{BP} \cong \widehat{AP}$ and $\widehat{AQ} \cong \widehat{CQ}$. Hence $m\angle AMN = m\angle ANM$. Therefore, $\triangle AMN$ is isosceles with legs $\overline{AM}$ and $\overline{AN}$, which means that $\overline{AM} \cong \overline{AN}$.

11a. Exercise 1 shows that $\overline{PA} \cong \overline{PB}$ and $\overline{PC} \cong \overline{PD}$. Radii of the same circle are congruent, so it follows that *PDOC* and *PBOA* are kites that have $\overline{PO}$ as a shared axis of symmetry. From this it follows easily that $\angle APC \cong \angle DPB$. **b.** Use the angle congruence proved in part (a) and the facts that $\overline{PA} \cong \overline{PB}$ and $\overline{PC} \cong \overline{PD}$ to conclude that $\triangle PAC \cong \triangle PBD$ (SAS). Hence $\overline{AC} \cong \overline{BD}$ by CPCTC. The diagonals of a kite are perpendicular and $\overline{PO}$ is a shared diagonal of *PDOC* and *PBOA*. Therefore $\overline{AB}$ and $\overline{CD}$ are both perpendicular to $\overline{PO}$. Hence $\overline{AB} \parallel \overline{CD}$.

Lesson 5.13

Check Your Understanding

1. Construct a circle and a point *P* inside it such that $\prod(P) = 12$. One such circle and point can be constructed by picking two numbers with a product of 12, such as 2 and 6. Draw a segment of length 8 (that is, 2 + 6). Mark its midpoint. Then draw the circle that has the segment as a diameter. Mark *P* on the segment so that *P* is 2 units from one endpoint. Then $\prod(P) = 12$. Select a stick and place it so that it goes through *P* and has one end on the circle. Mark the place on the stick that corresponds to *P*. Cut off any excess part of the stick that is outside the circle at the other end. Cut the stick in two at the point corresponding to *P*. Cut another two pieces of these same lengths from another stick. Use the four pieces to build one rectangle. Repeat the process to get rectangles with other dimensions. **2.** 35.5 in. **3.** $\prod(B) = \frac{3}{4}r^2$; $\prod(C) = \frac{7}{16}r^2$; $\prod(D) = \frac{15}{64}r^2$; define $\prod(E)$ to be 0.

On Your Own

6. $PB = 6$ cm, $CP = 7$ cm, $DP = 18$ cm (or $CP = 18$ cm, $DP = 7$ cm)

Lesson 5.14

On Your Own

8. Drawings may vary. The areas for the two colors should be approximately equal.

10. Drawings may vary. The area for one color should be 3 times the area for the other.

Lesson 5.15

Check Your Understanding

1. $\frac{\pi}{4}$ **2.** $\frac{3\pi}{16}$ **3.** $\frac{3\pi}{64}$

On Your Own

5. $\frac{39}{64} \approx 0.609$ **6.** Increase the side length of the squares to about 2.56 in., about 4.09 in., and 5.60 in., respectively.

Lesson 5.16

Check Your Understanding

1. 0; answers may vary. Sample: The squiggly lines have no area. **2.** $\frac{\pi}{9}$; no; $\frac{4\pi - 9}{18}$; the measure of a set of nonseparate elements is less than or equal to the sum of the measures of the separate elements. The probability of an event can never be greater than 1. **3.** $P_1 = 1$, $P_2 = \frac{1}{4}$, $P_3 = \frac{1}{16}$, $P_4 = \frac{1}{64}$, $P_5 = \frac{1}{256}$, $P_6 = \frac{1}{1024}$, $P_7 = \frac{1}{4096}$, . . . , $P_n = \frac{P_{n-1}}{4}$ (for $n \geq 2$); 0; the measure of the intersection of many elements, each contained in the previous one, is the measure of the smallest one; all of R_n is contained in R_{n-1}.

On Your Own

4a. $\frac{3}{4}$ **b.** $\frac{1}{4}$ **c.** The measure of a set of separate elements is the sum of the measures of the separate elements; there are only two kinds of small squares, white and black. **6.** $\frac{\pi r^2}{4\ell^2}$; 0, because the drop can be imagined as a circle of radius $r = 0$.

Chapter 6

Lesson 6.01

On Your Own

5a. Nancy; her shadow is longer. **b.** 68 in. **c.** about 60.24 in. **7.** about 4 in. **9.** about 8.08×10^{-9} in. **10.** about 6.19 million times

Lesson 6.02

Check Your Understanding

1a. 5; 4 **b.** 7.5; 6 **c.** 5; $2\sqrt{6}$ **d.** 5; 5 **2.** The largest angle with a vertex on the top semicircle intercepts the bottom semicircle and hence has measure $\frac{1}{2} \cdot 180°$, or $90°$. **3.** first figure: $AC = 5$, $BD = \sqrt{6}$, $AB = \sqrt{10}$, $BC = \sqrt{15}$; second figure: $AC = 4$, $AD = 3$, $AB = 2\sqrt{3}$, $BD = \sqrt{3}$ **4.** Drawing shows a circle of radius 2 in. with a diameter cut into segments of 1 in. and 3 in. A perpendicular to this diameter at the cut point intersects the circle, and the segment from the cut point to this intersection has length $\sqrt{3}$ in., the geometric mean of 1 and 3.

On Your Own

8a. The perimeters are equal. **b.** the square **9a.** No; c is too small. There is no way for the endpoint of c to stretch from P to the edge of the circle. **b.** The small size of the segment of length c makes the construction difficult. **c.** The circle would need to be larger than the circle in Minds in Action so that the chord $a + b$ would be far from the center of the circle such that a very small c would stretch between P and the edge of the circle.

Lesson 6.03

Check Your Understanding

1. Let $\triangle ABC$ be a right triangle with right angle at C. Let $\overline{CH}$ be the altitude from C to $\overline{AB}$. The AA Similarity test shows that $\triangle AHC \sim \triangle CHB$. So $\frac{AH}{CH} = \frac{CH}{BH}$. It follows that $CH^2 = AH \cdot BH$ and hence that $CH = \sqrt{AH \cdot BH}$. **2.** From the given proportion and the fact that the two angles with vertex H are right angles, it follows that $\triangle AHC \sim \triangle CHB$ (you can rotate $\triangle AHC$ so that it can be dilated onto the other triangle). This implies that $\angle A \cong \angle HCB$ and $\angle B \cong \angle ACH$. Since $\angle A$ and $\angle ACH$ are complementary angles, the two small angles with vertex C are complementary. Thus $\angle ACB$ is a right angle. Because $\angle ACB$ is a right angle, $\triangle ABC$ is a right triangle. **3.** If $\overline{CB}$ is the diameter through B, then $\angle CAB$ intercepts a semicircle and hence is a right angle. Theorem 6.1 implies that AB^2 is the product of CB and the length of the projection of $\overline{AB}$ on $\overline{CB}$. **4.** $\sqrt{rs}$

On Your Own

7. Let a and b be the lengths of the legs of a right triangle with hypotenuse of length c. The sum of the areas of the semicircles on the legs is $\frac{1}{2}\left(\frac{a}{2}\right)^2\pi + \frac{1}{2}\left(\frac{b}{2}\right)^2\pi$. Simplify to get $\frac{1}{8}\pi(a^2 + b^2)$, or $\frac{1}{8}\pi c^2$. But the area of the semicircle on the hypotenuse is $\frac{1}{2}\left(\frac{c}{2}\right)^2\pi$, or $\frac{1}{8}\pi c^2$. **9.** 6 **11.** $AB = 6$, $AC = 8$

Lesson 6.04

Check Your Understanding

1. P is the midpoint of $\overline{AG}$, so it cuts $\overline{AG}$ into two congruent pieces. Since $\triangle PQG \cong \triangle NMG$, you know that one of those pieces, $\overline{PG}$, is congruent to $\overline{NG}$. So $\overline{AG}$ is composed of two pieces, each congruent to $\overline{NG}$, and it must be twice as long. A similar argument shows that $BG = 2GM$. **2.** $\overline{PQ}$ and $\overline{MN}$ are both parallel to $\overline{AB}$ and hence are parallel to each other. Sasha's reasoning shows that $MN = PQ$. So $PQNM$ is a parallelogram. The diagonals of a parallelogram bisect each other. The desired result follows at once. **3.** Diagrams may vary. For every triangle, the angle bisectors are concurrent, the lines that contain the altitudes are concurrent, and the perpendicular bisectors of the sides of the triangle are concurrent.

On Your Own

7. Suppose that in $\triangle ABC$, the medians from C and A intersect at point P. From Exercise 6b, we know that $A_{\triangle APC} = A_{\triangle BPC}$ and $A_{\triangle APC} = A_{\triangle APB}$. Therefore $A_{\triangle BPC} = A_{\triangle APB}$, which implies, by Exercise 6d, that P is on the median from point B. Since P is on all three medians, the medians are concurrent.

Lesson 6.05

On Your Own

5. All the ramps are equally steep. The triangles formed by the ramps are similar. **7.** Ramp C with width 50.9 mm and height 18.5 mm is steepest. **9.** about 20.4 ft **10.** about 589 ft

Lesson 6.06

Check Your Understanding

1. A right triangle with legs of lengths a and b has a hypotenuse of length $\sqrt{a^2 + b^2}$. If $c^2 = a^2 + b^2$, this means the hypotenuse has length c. By SSS, a triangle with side lengths a, b, and c is congruent to the right triangle just described and hence is itself a right triangle. **2.** $DO = \sqrt{2}$ by the Pythagorean Theorem; $m\angle D = 45°$ because $\triangle DGO$ is isosceles. **3.** $m\angle T = 30°$, $m\angle A = 60°$, and $m\angle R = 90°$; the converse of the Pythagorean Theorem tells you that the triangle is a right triangle, and the ratios of the lengths of the sides tell you that its acute angles are 30° and 60°. The larger acute angle is opposite the longer leg. **4.** Such a triangle may be a 30-60-90 triangle, but it does not have to be. Sketches may vary. Sample:

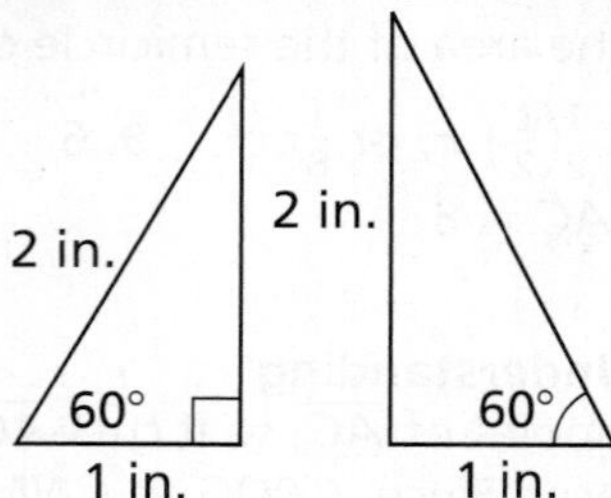

On Your Own

5. $m\angle T = 90°$, $AT = 17$, $AC = 17\sqrt{2}$; $\triangle CTA$ is a 45-45-90 triangle. **8.** $m\angle S = 60°$, $SI = \frac{4\sqrt{3}}{3}$, $SC = \frac{8\sqrt{3}}{3}$; $\triangle SIC$ is a 30-60-90 triangle.
13. $\frac{16\sqrt{6}}{3}$ cm

Lesson 6.07

Check Your Understanding

1a. $\sin 40° = 0.64$ **b.** $\cos 70° = 0.34$ **c.** $\tan 55° = 1.43$ **2a.** $\sin A = \frac{4}{5}$, $\cos A = \frac{3}{5}$, $\tan A = \frac{4}{3}$ **b.** $\sin B = \frac{3}{5}$, $\cos B = \frac{4}{5}$, $\tan B = \frac{3}{4}$ **c.** $\sin A = \cos B$, and $\cos A = \sin B$; leg adjacent and leg opposite switch roles when you switch from $\angle A$ to $\angle B$. **3a.** $\sin A = \frac{\sqrt{5}}{5}$, $\cos A = \frac{2\sqrt{5}}{5}$, $\tan A = \frac{1}{2}$ **b.** $\sin B = \frac{2\sqrt{5}}{5}$, $\cos B = \frac{\sqrt{5}}{5}$, $\tan B = 2$ **c.** $\cos A = \sin B$ and $\sin A = \cos B$; leg adjacent and leg opposite switch roles when you switch from $\angle A$ to $\angle B$. **4.** $\sin B = \frac{12}{13}$, $\cos B = \frac{5}{13}$ **5.** about 4226 ft

On Your Own

6. $m\angle B = 20°$, $UB \approx 23.39$ cm, $BT \approx 21.98$ cm
9. $\sin J = \frac{\sqrt{10}}{10}$, $\cos J = \frac{3\sqrt{10}}{10}$, $\tan J = \frac{1}{3}$, $\sin L = \frac{3\sqrt{10}}{10}$, $\cos L = \frac{\sqrt{10}}{10}$, $\tan L = 3$
13. $\sin\theta = \frac{c}{b}$, $\cos\theta = \frac{a}{b}$, $\tan\theta = \frac{c}{a}$
16. Yes; use the diagram from Exercise 14. $(\sin\theta)^2 + (\cos\theta)^2 = \left(\frac{c}{d}\right)^2 + \left(\frac{a}{b}\right)^2 = \frac{c^2 + a^2}{b^2} = \frac{b^2}{b^2} = 1$ **18a.** $\tan 40° \approx 0.84$ **b.** not possible **c.** $\sin 40° \approx 0.64$ **d.** not possible **e.** $\cos 40° \approx 0.77$ **f.** not possible **g.** $\tan 50° \approx 1.19$

Lesson 6.08

Check Your Understanding

1. $BC \approx 13.17$; $m\angle B \approx 22.98°$; $m\angle C \approx 17.02°$
2. $AB \approx 5.14$; $m\angle A \approx 48.57°$; $m\angle B \approx 91.43°$
3. $BC \approx 7.51$; $m\angle B \approx 71.62°$; $m\angle C \approx 45.38°$
4a. $A = \frac{1}{2}ab\sin\theta$ **b.** If you scale the given triangle by a factor of r, the lengths of the sides that form the given angle are ar and br. The angle of measure θ still has measure θ. The area of the scaled copy is $\frac{1}{2}(ar)(br)\sin\theta$, or $\left(\frac{1}{2}ab\sin\theta\right)\cdot r^2$. **5.** area$(ABCD) \approx 16.09$

On Your Own

6. $AB = 5$ cm; $BC = 3\sqrt{2}$ cm; $m\angle A \approx 36.87°$; $m\angle B \approx 98.13°$; $m\angle C = 45°$ **8.** $TR \approx 5.00$ in.; $m\angle R \approx 79.96°$; $m\angle T \approx 20.04°$; area$(\triangle RAT) \approx 4.28$ in.^{2} **11.** $(32 + 32\sqrt{2})$ in.^{2}, or about 77.25 in.^{2}; find the area of the square and then subtract the total area of the four triangles. **13.** $EG = 10$ in.; $m\angle E \approx 53.13°$; $m\angle G \approx 36.87°$ **16a.** definition of sin 25° (using $\triangle ABD$) and basic moves **b.** definition of sin 35° (using $\triangle BCD$) and basic moves **c.** From parts (a) and (b), $c(\sin 25°) = a(\sin 35°)$. Solve for c. **d.** definition of cos 25° (using $\triangle ABD$) and basic moves **e.** definition of cos 35° (using $\triangle BCD$) and basic moves **f.** $AC = x + y$ together with the equations in parts (d) and (e) **17.** $a \approx 4.39$ in., $c \approx 5.96$ in.

Lesson 6.09

Check Your Understanding

1. about 1.49 m **2.** about 20.66 cm **3.** about 62.72° **4.** about 93.82°

On Your Own

5. $m\angle A \approx 35.48°$; $m\angle C \approx 107.52°$; $AC \approx 14.51$ cm; area $(\triangle CAT) \approx 98.89$ cm^2 **8.** about 1.18 **12a.** about 0.165 **b.** about 0.165 **c.** about 0.165

Lesson 6.10

On Your Own

5a. about 2.31 cm **b.** about 1.44 cm **8a.** 135π cm^2 **b.** $2\sqrt{35}$ cm **10.** $\frac{5}{2}\sqrt{\pi}$ in.

Lesson 6.11

Check Your Understanding

1. There is not enough information given to tell how the volumes compare. **2.** No; the bases of the solids are congruent rectangles and hence have the same area. The right prism has a greater height than the new solid, so it has the greater volume. **3a.** 72 cm^3, 72 cm^3 **b.** Yes. Position the first figure so that the 4-cm edges of the two figures are parallel. The cross-sectional area of each prism is 12 cm^2.

On Your Own

4. Answers may vary. Sample: Use a sphere with radius 1 and a cylinder with radius 1 and height $\frac{4}{3}$. Both solids have a volume of $\frac{4\pi}{3}$. A plane that contains a diameter of the sphere has the same cross section as a plane parallel to the base of the cylinder. There are no other cross sections that have equal areas.

6. $3\sqrt{\pi}$ in. **10.** No; answers may vary. Sample: A right triangle with legs of length 1 and 2 has the same area as a square with side length 1, but there can only be one pair of cross sections of each figure that have the same area. **12.** $\frac{64 + \pi}{8\pi}$ in.

Lesson 6.12

Check Your Understanding

1. If r is the radius of the cross section between V and O, and R is the radius of the base, then $\frac{r}{R} = \frac{VO'}{VO}$. Thus $\frac{A_{\text{circle}}}{A_{\text{base}}} = \frac{\pi r^2}{\pi R^2} = \frac{r^2}{R^2} = \left(\frac{r}{R}\right)^2 = \left(\frac{VO'}{VO}\right)^2$. **2.** 96 in.^{3} **3a.** 20 cm^3 **b.** $\frac{2\sqrt{3\pi}}{\pi}$ cm

4a. Answers may vary. Sample: height π and base $2r^2$ **b.** Every pair of cross sections determined by a plane parallel to the bases of the cone and pyramid have the same area.

5. The cone and the pyramid are the same height and are cut by a plane, so the resulting cross sections have the same area. The cone and the pyramid also have cross-sectional areas that are equal to each other when cut by any plane parallel to the first, therefore the cone and pyramid have the same volume.

On Your Own

6. 8π ft^3 **8.** $\frac{128\sqrt{3}}{3}$ cm^3 **10.** 420

Lesson 6.13

Check Your Understanding

1. Yes; infinitely many ways; yes; infinitely many ways; if the sphere has radius r, then any two planes that are d units from the center of the sphere, where $0 < d < r$, will create two cross sections of equal area. **2.** $\frac{2000\pi}{3}$; 10; $\frac{2000\pi}{3}$

3. $\frac{45\sqrt{5\pi}}{2\pi}$ cm^3

On Your Own

7. $\frac{256\pi}{3}$ mm^3 **9.** $\frac{512\pi\sqrt{2}}{3}$ mm^3

11. about 902.3 in.^{3}

Chapter 7

Lesson 7.01

7a. $\overline{PQ}$: 1, $\overline{QR}$: $-\frac{1}{2}$, $\overline{RS}$: 1, $\overline{SP}$: $-\frac{1}{2}$; the slopes of opposite sides of $PQRS$ are equal. Hence $PQRS$ has its opposite sides parallel. Therefore, $PQRS$ is a parallelogram. **9.** $A(2, -5)$, $B(4, -2)$

10. $-2x + y = 6$

Lesson 7.02

Check Your Understanding

1a. Always; if you fold along the line of reflection, a segment in the preimage will coincide with the corresponding segment in the image. **b.** Always; if you fold along the line of reflection, an angle in the preimage will coincide with the corresponding angle in the image. **c.** Always; if you fold along the line of reflection, the image of a line is a line. **d.** Sometimes; answers may vary. Sample: Suppose the line of reflection is $y = x$. For $A(2, 4)$ and $B(5, 7)$, the image of $\overline{AB}$ is $\overline{A'B'}$ with $A'(4, 2)$ and $B'(7, 5)$. Both segments have slope 1. For $C(5, 9)$ and $C'(9, 5)$, the image of $\overline{AC}$ is $\overline{A'C'}$, but $\overline{AC}$ has slope $\frac{5}{3}$, and $\overline{A'C'}$ has slope $\frac{3}{5}$. **e.** Always; answers may vary. Sample: A transversal of two parallel segments in the preimage will form congruent corresponding angles with the segments. The angle measures will, by part (b), be preserved in the image. So the segments in the image will be parallel. **f.** Always; answers may vary. Sample: By part (b), angle measures are preserved. **2a.** $A' = (6, 5)$, $B' = (4, 2)$ **b.** $A'' = (10, 5)$, $B'' = (12, 2)$ **c.** a translation 8 units to the right (that is, in the positive direction, parallel to the x-axis) **3.** Draw $\overline{PP'}$. Label point S where PP' and ℓ intersect. Since P' is the reflection of P over ℓ, ℓ is the perpendicular bisector of PP'. $\overline{PS} \cong \overline{P'S}$ by definition of bisector. $\overline{OS} \cong \overline{OS}$ by the reflexive property. $\triangle OSP$ and $\triangle OSP'$ are right triangles. $\triangle OSP \cong \triangle OSP'$ by LL. $\angle POR \cong \angle P'OR$ by CPCTC. **4.** Suppose $\overline{AB} \parallel \ell$, and let $\overline{A'B'}$ be the image of $\overline{AB}$ for reflection over ℓ. Then ℓ is the perpendicular bisector of $\overline{AA'}$ and $\overline{BB'}$. If M is the midpoint of $\overline{AA'}$ and N is the midpoint of $\overline{BB'}$, then $ABNM$ and $A'B'NM$ are rectangles. It follows that $\overline{A'B'} \parallel \overline{MN}$ and hence that $\overline{A'B'} \parallel \ell$.

On Your Own

7a. $A'(1, -1)$, $B'(3, -2)$ **b.** $A''(1, -1)$, $B''(3, 0)$ **c.** a translation down 3 units **9.** $x - 3y = 6$

12. Yes, the y-axis; the point at (0, 0) is on the graph and on the y-axis. All other points of the graph are above the x-axis. For each $b > 0$, the line with equation $y = b$ intersects the graph of $y = x^2$ at $(-\sqrt{b}, b)$ and $(\sqrt{b}, b)$. These correspond to the endpoints of a segment whose midpoint is $(0, b)$. **15a.** yes **b.** no **c.** yes **d.** yes **e.** Answers may vary. Sample: If a figure is reflected over a line, the image over a second line, and so on, and if the number of reflections performed is even, then the final image can be obtained from the original figure by using a single rotation or a single translation.

Lesson 7.03
Check Your Understanding
1a. Answers may vary. Sample: You can slide the original figure straight from the original to the new position and all vertices will match. **b.** Answers may vary. Sample: It is the translation accomplished by sliding *AKLJ* to the right 8 units and up 6 units.
c. $(x, y) \mapsto (x + 8, y + 6)$ **2.** A triangle; the image is congruent to the original and is obtained by translating the original to the right 10 units and up 6 units. **3.** $2x + y = 22$
On Your Own
5. Answers may vary. Sample: $\overline{AA''}$ and $\overline{BB''}$ have slope 0 and hence are parallel. Also $AA'' = BB'' = 6$. Since $AA''B''B$ has a pair of opposite sides that are parallel and congruent, it is a parallelogram. **9.** Answers may vary. Sample: $(-3, 0)$, $(-1, 2)$, and $(1, 0)$
a. $(x + 1)^2 + (y + 2)^2 = 4$
b. $(x + 1)^2 + (y - 2)^2 = 4$
c. $(x - 2)^2 + y^2 = 4$ **d.** $x^2 + (y - 4)^2 = 4$
Lesson 7.04
Check Your Understanding
1a. $A'(4, 1)$, $B'(2, 3)$, $C'(4, 5)$, $D'(5, 2.5)$
b. $A''(4, -1)$, $B''(2, -3)$, $C''(4, -5)$, $D''(5, -2.5)$
c. Theorem 7.1 states that the composition of two reflections about intersecting lines produces a rotation. Its center is the intersection of the lines. The angle of rotation is equal to twice the measure of the angle formed by two lines.
On Your Own
7.

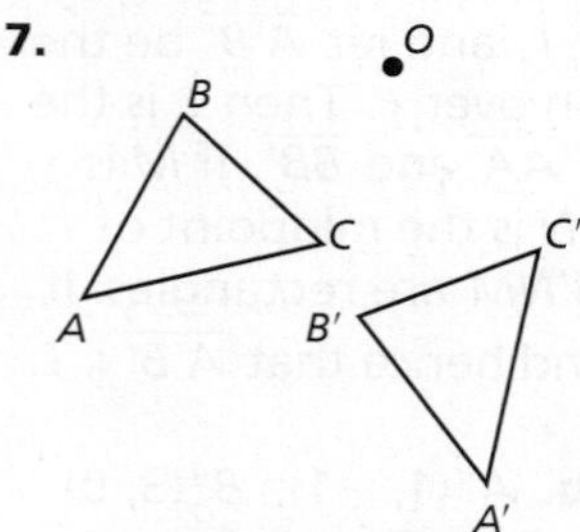

9. $CA = CB$, so A and B are on the circle with center C and radius CA; the measure of the angle of rotation is the same as $m\angle ACB$.
10.

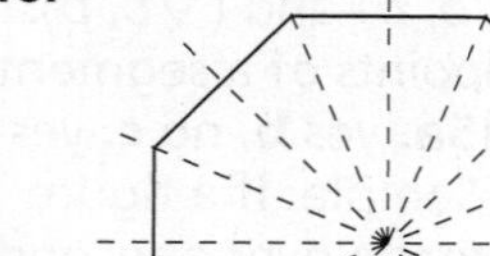

Lesson 7.05
Check Your Understanding
1. An isometry can be thought of as a function that maps points in the plane to points in the plane. Formally, an isometry is a function from $\mathbb{R}^2$ to $\mathbb{R}^2$. **2.** Answers may vary. Sample: You would need a description or ordered list of the transformations that make up the isometry.
3a. any point on the circle with the center *P* and radius *AB* **b.** Answers may vary. Sample: a description of the transformations that make up the isometry, including the order they were performed in
On Your Own
7. No; a transformation that takes one circle to the other does not preserve length. **8c.** Point *A* is a fixed distance from point *B* and a fixed distance from point *C*. Point A_1 is the same distance from point *B* and the same distance from point *C* as point *A*. Therefore, point A_1 coincides with point *A*.
Lesson 7.06
On Your Own
6a. 17 **b.** $(3.5, -7)$ **c.** 10 **d.** $(12, -2)$ **e.** $\sqrt{389}$
f. $(3.5, -2)$ **7a.** $A(5, 5)$, $B(5, 0)$ **b.** 5 **c.** $(5, 2.5)$
d. 12.5 **e.** $5\sqrt{2}$ **f.** $(2.5, 2.5)$ **9a.** 0 **b.** 2 **c.** 2 **d.** 3
Lesson 7.07
Check Your Understanding
1a. $(-33, 561)$ **b.** $\left(3x, \frac{y}{2}\right)$ **2.** $A(2, 4\sqrt{6})$, $B(5, 5\sqrt{3})$, $C(6, 8)$, $D(5\sqrt{2}, 5\sqrt{2})$, $E(10, 0)$, $F(0, -10)$, $G(-8, -6)$ **3a.** $AB = \sqrt{53}$, $BC = 2\sqrt{26}$, $AC = 5$ **b.** length of median from $A = \sqrt{13}$, length of median from $B = 8.5$, length of median from $C = \frac{\sqrt{205}}{2}$
4. $AB = A'B' = \sqrt{34}$, $BC = B'C' = \sqrt{29}$, $AC = A'C' = \sqrt{13}$, so $\triangle ABC \cong \triangle A'B'C'$ by SSS. **5.** $AB = \sqrt{960^2 + 512^2}$ and $A'B' = \sqrt{3840^2 + 2048^2}$, so $AB = \frac{1}{4}A'B'$ because $\sqrt{3840^2 + 2048^2} = \sqrt{(4 \cdot 960)^2 + (4 \cdot 512)^2}$. $BC = \sqrt{897^2 + 496^2}$ and $B'C' = \sqrt{3588^2 + 1984^2}$, so $BC = \frac{1}{4}B'C'$ because $\sqrt{3588^2 + 1984^2} = \sqrt{(4 \cdot 897)^2 + (4 \cdot 496^2)}$. $AC = \sqrt{63^2 + 16^2}$ and $A'C' = \sqrt{252^2 + 64^2}$, so $AC = \frac{1}{4}A'C'$ because $\sqrt{252^2 + 64^2} = \sqrt{(4 \cdot 63)^2 + (4 \cdot 16)^2}$. The lengths of the sides of $\triangle ABC$ are $\frac{1}{4}$ the lengths of the corresponding sides of $\triangle A'B'C'$, so the triangles are similar (SSS Similarity)
6. Answers may vary. Sample: Use the Distance Formula to calculate the side lengths of each

triangle. If the side lengths for the two triangles are the same, then the triangles are congruent by SSS. **7.** Answers may vary. Sample: Use the Distance Formula to calculate the side lengths of each triangle. If the side lengths of one triangle are proportional to those of the other triangle, then the triangles are similar by SSS Similarity. **8.** Answers may vary. Sample: Starting with $\overline{ST}$ and going clockwise, let the midpoints of the sides of *STAR* be *P, Q, V,* and *W.* Use the Midpoint Formula to show that these are the points $P(3, 5)$, $Q(4, 1)$, $V(-1, -2)$, and $W(-2, 4)$. Use the Distance Formula to show that $PW = VQ = \sqrt{26}$ and $PQ = WV = \sqrt{37}$. Since the opposite sides of *PQVW* are congruent, *PQVW* is a parallelogram.
9. Answers may vary. Sample: Quadrilateral *ABCD* has vertices $A(3, 1)$, $B(4,7)$, $C(11, 3)$, and $D(8, -5)$. The midpoint of $\overline{AB}$ is $E(3.5, 4)$, of $\overline{BC}$ is $F(7.5, 5)$, of $\overline{CD}$ is $G(9.5, -1)$, and of $\overline{DA}$ is $H(5.5, -2)$. *EFGH* is a parallelogram because the opposite sides are the same length. $EF = GH = \sqrt{17}$ and $EH = FG + 2\sqrt{10}$.

On Your Own

11a. $(-14, 14)$ **b.** $(86, -186)$ **13.** $E(113, 19)$, $D(116, 15)$ **16.** $(3, 5)$

Lesson 7.08

Check Your Understanding

1a. Parallel; the graphs of the lines are different and the ratios of corresponding coefficients are equal. **b.** Parallel; the graphs of the lines are different and the ratios of corresponding coefficients are equal. **c.** Not parallel; the lines are the same. **d.** Not parallel; the ratios of corresponding coefficients are not equal. **e.** Parallel; the graphs of the lines are different and the ratios of corresponding coefficients are equal. **2.** Answers may vary. Sample: $C(6.5, -1)$; find the coordinates of the midpoint of $\overline{AB}$. **3.** Answers may vary. Sample: Start with $B(8, -3)$. Add 3 to the *x*-coordinate and subtract 4 from the *y*-coordinate to get $(11, -7)$, the coordinates of a new point on $\overleftrightarrow{AB}$. Do the same with the new point, and continue in this fashion to get still more points.; the slope of $\overleftrightarrow{AB}$ is $\frac{-4}{3}$, and the procedure gives new points that are collinear with *A* and *B* by Theorem 7.5
4. No; answers may vary. Sample: The slope of $\overline{PR}$ is $\frac{4}{9}$, but the slope of $\overline{RS}$ is $\frac{5}{12}$. By Theorem 7.5, the points are not collinear.

On Your Own

5a. By the Midpoint Formula, the midpoint of each diagonal has coordinates $(5.5, 1)$.
b. By Theorem 2.8, *ABCD* is a parallelogram.
8. Yes; the segments joining two points at these locations all have slope $-\frac{1}{50}$. By Theorem 7.5, the points are collinear.

Lesson 7.09

Check Your Understanding

1. Answers may vary. Sample: $y = x$, $y = x + 1$; yes, infinitely many **2.** Answers may vary. Sample: $2x - y = 2$ **3.** $\frac{7}{5}$
4. Answers may vary. Sample: $(\sqrt{2})x + 4y = 3\sqrt{2}$ and $(\sqrt{2})x - 4y = 3\sqrt{2}$

On Your Own

6. a–d. Answers may vary. Samples are given.
a. $3x + 2y = 0$ **b.** $x - y = 3$
c. $x - 2y = 2$ **d.** $3x + 2y = 7$ **7a.** $\sqrt{10}$
b. $\frac{3\sqrt{26}}{13}$ **c.** $\frac{7}{5}$ **d.** $\frac{80}{29}$ **10.** Four; slope $\overline{AB} = \frac{1}{-3 + \sqrt{2}}$, slope $\overline{BC} = \frac{7}{3 + \sqrt{2}}$, slope $\overline{CD} = \frac{1}{-3 + \sqrt{2}}$, and slope $\overline{DA} = \frac{7}{3 + \sqrt{2}}$. Since opposite sides of *ABCD* have equal slopes, they are parallel. Hence *ABCD* is a parallelogram. (slope $\overline{AB}$) · (*slope* $\overline{BC}$) $= -1$, so $\overline{AB}$ and $\overline{BC}$ are perpendicular. Hence $\angle B$ is a right angle. Therefore *ABCD* is a rectangle and hence has four right angles.

Lesson 7.10

Check Your Understanding

1. Answers may vary. Samples are given. **a.** the corner of the room where the floor intersects the two walls shown in the diagram **b.** $(1, 0, 0)$, $(2, 0, 0)$, $(2, 0, 3)$, and $(1, 0, 3)$ **c.** $(0, 1, 2)$, $(0, 1, 3.5)$, $(0, 3, 3.5)$, and $(0, 3, 2)$ **d.** $(3, 1, 0)$, $(3, 4.5, 0)$, $(1, 4.5, 0)$, and $(1, 1, 0)$ **2a.** $(2, 2.5, 3)$ **b.** $(4, 0, 1.5)$ **c.** $(2, 0, 1.5)$ **d.** $(2, 2.5, 1.5)$
3a. right triangle **b.** 13 **c.** $\sqrt{178}$ **4a.** Answers may vary. Sample: $(0, \sqrt{5})$, $(-\sqrt{5}, 0)$, $(1, 2)$, $(2, 1)$, $(-2, -1)$, $(-2, 1)$, $(1, -2)$, and $\left(\frac{\sqrt{19}}{2}, \frac{1}{2}\right)$
b. a circle of radius $\sqrt{5}$ with center at the origin **c.** Answers may vary. Sample: $(0, \sqrt{13})$, $(\sqrt{13}, 0)$, $(3, 2)$, $(3, -2)$, $(-3, 2)$, $(-3, -2)$, $(2, 3)$, $(1, 2\sqrt{3})$ **d.** Answers may vary. Sample: $(0, 25)$, $(15, 20)$, $(-20, 15)$, $(5, 10\sqrt{6})$, $(5\sqrt{21}, 10)$, $(9, 4\sqrt{34})$, $(17, 4\sqrt{21})$, $(18, \sqrt{301})$
e. $(0, 10)$, $(0, -10)$, $(-10, 0)$, $(6, 8)$, $(-8, -6)$, $(2, 4\sqrt{6})$, $(2\sqrt{21}, 4)$, $(-5, 5\sqrt{3})$ **f.** $(0, 13)$, $(0, -13)$, $(12, 5)$ $(12, -5)$, $(-12, -5)$, $(-12, 5)$, $(8, \sqrt{105})$, $(3, 4\sqrt{10})$ **g.** $(0, 1)$, $(0, -1)$, $(0.6, 0.8)$, $(0.6, -0.8)$, $(-0.8, 0.6)$, $(0.2, 0.4\sqrt{6})$, $(-0.2, -0.4\sqrt{6})$,

$(0.5\sqrt{2}, 0.5\sqrt{2})$ **5a.** a circle of radius 13 with center at the origin **b.** Answers may vary. Sample: See the answer for Exercise 4c; find the sum of the squares of the coordinates of the point. **c.** a circle of radius 13 with center at $(4, -1)$ **d.** Answers may vary. Sample: $(4, 12)$, $(17, -1)$, $(4, -14)$, $(-9, -1)$, $(16, 4)$, $(-8, -6)$, $(16, -6)$, $(-8, 4)$; if the point has coordinates (a, b), calculate $(a - 4)^2 + (b + 1)^2$ to see if the sum is 169. **6a.** Answers may vary. Sample: $(0, 0, -9)$, $(4, 4, 7)$, $(-3, -6, -6)$, $(-3, 6\sqrt{2}, 0)$, $(-3, -5, \sqrt{47})$, $(3, 4, 2\sqrt{14})$, $(1, 2, \sqrt{76})$, and $(5, 6, \sqrt{20})$; a sphere of radius 9 with center at the origin **b.** A sphere of radius 7 with center at the origin; answers may vary. Sample: $(-2, -3, -6)$, $(2\sqrt{2}, 4, 5)$, and $(0, 0, 7)$

On Your Own

8a. 3 **b.** $3\sqrt{2}$ **c.** $3\sqrt{2}$ **d.** $3\sqrt{3}$ **10a.** $(0, 0, 0)$, $(1, 0, 0)$, $(0, 1, 0)$, $(1, 1, 0)$, $(0, 0, 1)$, $(1, 0, 1)$, $(1, 1, 1)$, $(0, 1, 1)$ **b.** $\sqrt{3}$ **14.** Answers may vary. Sample: $(30, 0, 0)$, $(15, 15, 0)$, $(0, 15, 15)$, $(10, 10, 10)$, $(20, 5, 5)$, $(10, 20, 0)$; a plane **16a.** $(1, 1, 1)$ **b.** $\sqrt{3}$

Lesson 7.11

On Your Own

9.

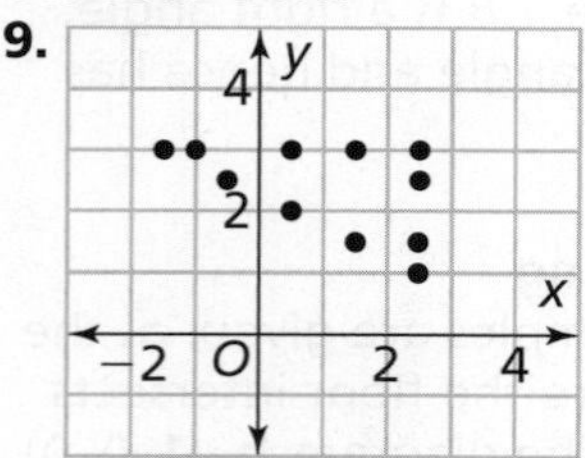

The original figure has been dilated with respect to the origin by a factor of $\frac{1}{2}$.
13a. Jorge: $A'(16.75, 1.5)$, $B'(18.25, 1.5)$, $C'(18.25, 0.75)$; Yutaka: $A'(4.75, 1.5)$, $B'(6.25, 1.5)$, $C'(6.25, 0.75)$ **b.** no **c.** Jorge used $(x, y) \mapsto \frac{1}{4}(x, y) + (16, 0)$, and Yutaka used $(x, y) \mapsto \frac{1}{4}(x + 16, y)$.

Lesson 7.12

Check Your Understanding

1. $\overrightarrow{OA}$, with $O = (0, 0)$ and $A = (6, 8)$ **2.** $(12, 1)$ **3.** True; if $A = (a_1, a_2)$ and $B = (b_1, b_2)$, then $B - O = (b_1, b_2)$ and $(A + B) - A = (a_1 + b_1, a_2 + b_2) - (a_1, a_2) = (b_1, b_2)$. Since $B - O = (A + B) - A$, it follows from Theorem 7.7 that the vector from O to B is equivalent to the vector from A to $A + B$.

4.

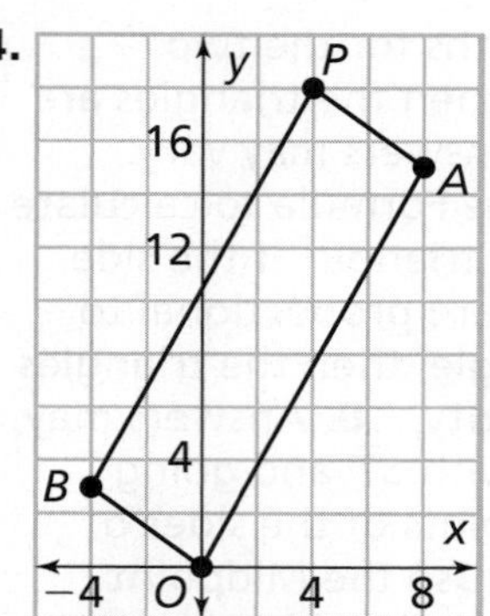

By the Distance Formula, $OA = 17$, $BP = 17$, $OB = 5$, and $AP = 5$. So $OA = BP$ and $OB = AP$.

5.

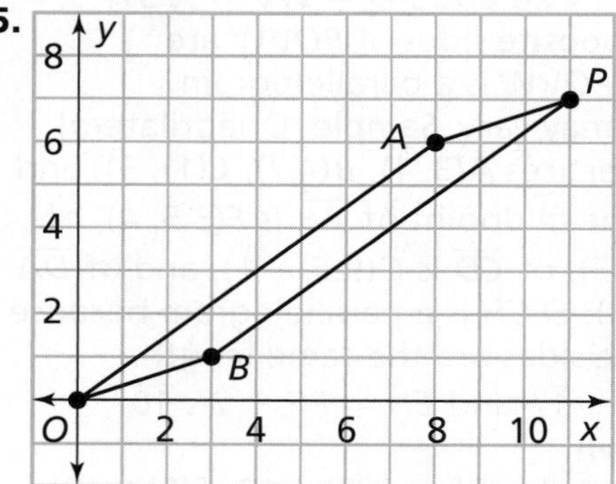

By the Distance Formula, $OA = 10$, $BP = 10$, $OB = \sqrt{10}$, and $AP = \sqrt{10}$. So $OA = BP$ and $OB = AP$. **6a.** $(7, 7)$ **b.** $(10, 9)$ **c.** $(13, 11)$ **d.** $(16, 13)$ **e.** $\left(\frac{11}{2}, 6\right)$ **f.** $\left(5, \frac{17}{3}\right)$ **g.** $\left(\frac{19}{4}, \frac{11}{2}\right)$

On Your Own

7. For $\overrightarrow{A(A + B)}$, $(A + B) - A = (11, 7) - (3, 5) = (8, 2)$. For $\overrightarrow{OB}$, $B - O = (8, 2) - (0, 0) = (8, 2)$. So $\overrightarrow{A(A + B)}$ is equivalent to $\overrightarrow{OB}$. For $\overrightarrow{OA}$, $A - O = (3, 5) - (0, 0) = (3, 5)$. For $\overrightarrow{B(A + B)}$, $(A + B) - B = (11, 7) - (8, 2) = (3, 5)$. So $\overrightarrow{OA}$ is equivalent to $\overrightarrow{B(A + B)}$. **15.** $\frac{1}{3}B + \frac{2}{3}A$; the point $\frac{1}{3}$ of the way from A to B is $A + \frac{1}{3}(B - A)$. Simplify $A + \frac{1}{3}(B - A)$ to obtain $\frac{1}{3}B + \frac{2}{3}A$.

Lesson 7.13

Check Your Understanding

1. Answers may vary. Sample: $B - A = (5, 4)$ and $D - C = (10, 8)$. Hence $D - C = 2(B - A)$. $\overrightarrow{AB}$ and $\overrightarrow{CD}$ are not collinear. It follows from Theorem 7.12 that $\overrightarrow{AB}$ and $\overrightarrow{CD}$ have the same direction and that $\overleftrightarrow{AB}$ and $\overleftrightarrow{CD}$ are parallel.

2. Assume $A \neq O$, $t \neq 0$, and O, A, and P are not collinear. By Theorems 7.8 and 7.11, it follows that O, P, tA, and $P + tA$ are the vertices of a parallelogram. $\overline{O(tA)}$ and $\overline{P(P + tA)}$ are opposite sides of the parallelogram and hence are parallel. Since $\overline{OA}$ and $\overline{O(tA)}$ are collinear, it follows that $\overline{OA}$ and $\overline{P(P + tA)}$ are parallel. **3.** The midpoint M of $\overline{OA}$ is $\frac{1}{2}(O + A) = (2, 2)$. The midpoint N of $\overline{OB}$ is $\frac{1}{2}(O + B) = (4, -2)$. The vectors $\overrightarrow{MN}$ and $\overrightarrow{AB}$ are noncollinear and $N - M = (2, -4) = \frac{1}{2}(B - A)$. By Theorem 7.12, it follows that $\overline{MN} \parallel \overline{AB}$. By the Distance Formula, $MN = 2\sqrt{5}$ and $AB = 4\sqrt{5}$. So $MN = \frac{1}{2}AB$. **4.** $B - A = (4, 4)$, so the segment from O to $B - A$ has slope 1 and length $4\sqrt{2}$. The segment from A to B also has slope 1 and length $4\sqrt{2}$. So $\overline{O(B - A)}$ is parallel to and congruent to $\overline{AB}$.

On Your Own

8. $X = (1, 5) + t(7, 2)$ **10.** $\frac{1}{4}B + \frac{3}{4}A$

Lesson 7.14

2. For $\overleftrightarrow{C_0M}$, an equation is $P = (4, 6) + t(-3, -\frac{11}{2})$. For $\overleftrightarrow{B_0K}$, an equation is $Q = (2, 1) + k(0, 2)$. You can see from the equations that $\overleftrightarrow{C_0M}$, is not vertical, that $\overleftrightarrow{B_0K}$ is vertical, and hence that the lines must intersect. The point of intersection is $(2, \frac{7}{3})$. **3.** $F = (0, 0) + q(3, \frac{7}{2})$; yes **4.** $t = \frac{2}{3}$, $k = \frac{2}{3}$, $q = \frac{2}{3}$; the point of intersection of the medians is two thirds of the way from each vertex to the corresponding midpoint.

On Your Own

5. Answers may vary. Sample: Interchange the coordinates of $(-3, 4)$ to get $(4, -3)$ and then change the sign of the second coordinate of $(4, -3)$ to get $(4, 3)$. Use $(4, 3)$ for B.
8. To define the "center of population," think of the cities as weights at three points. If each person (in each city) is a weight of the same size, the center of gravity lies at the point George describes.

Chapter 8

Lesson 8.01

On Your Own

5. Answers may vary. Sample: You can use a ruler or odometer readings on a car. On the coordinate plane, you can use the Distance Formula. **7a.** The following description uses L, R, U, and D for the words *left*, *right*, *up*, and *down*, respectively: D2L2D4R1U2R3D2R7D2L2U1. **b.** 28 units **c.** Answers may vary. Sample: R7D7 has length 14 units, D7R7 has length 14 units, and R1D8L1U1R7 has length 18 units. **d.** 14 units; to get from A to B with no backtracking, the horizontal moves must always be to the right, and the vertical moves must always be down. Since B is 7 units below and 7 units to the right of A, nothing less than 14 units will do. The first two sample paths in part (c) show that paths 14 units long are possible. **e.** No; see the answer for part (d). **8a.** $4\sqrt{2}$; 8 **b.** $3\sqrt{10}$; 12 **c.** $\sqrt{113}$; 15

Lesson 8.02

Check Your Understanding

1. $50(\sqrt{5} + \sqrt{29})$ ft ≈ 381 ft;
$(\sqrt{x^2 + 100^2} + \sqrt{(300 - x)^2 + 100^2})$ ft
2. Q is 200 ft downstream from P'. The side lengths are the same, so $DP = QF$ and $PF = DQ$. Q would be $(300 - 2x)$ ft downstream from P.
3.

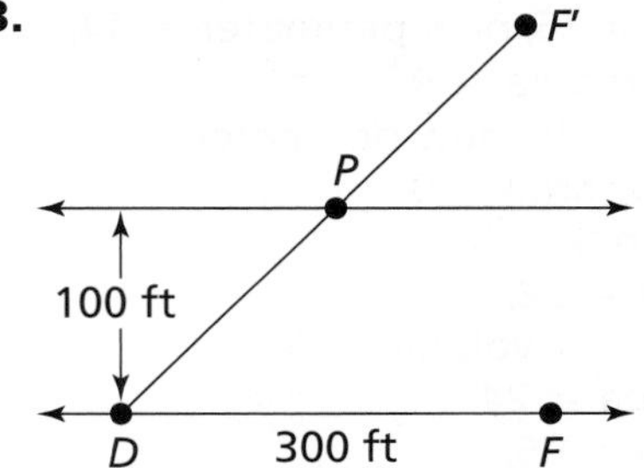

150 ft; no

On Your Own

5c. $4\sqrt{5} \approx 8.9$ **7.** $D = \sqrt{5}|x - 1|$; $x = 1$
9. The shortest path is the shortest perpendicular segment from M to a side; to a side.

Lesson 8.03

Check Your Understanding

1.

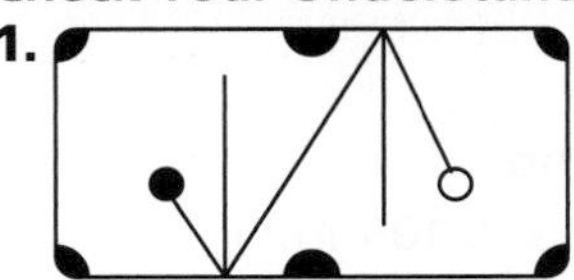

2. Answers may vary.
3. Refer to the following figure.

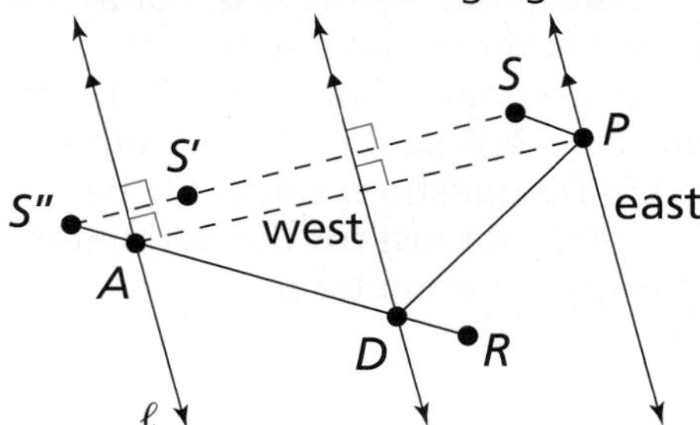

Line ℓ and S' result from reflecting east bank and S across west bank. S'' results from reflecting S' across line ℓ. Draw $\overline{S''R}$. Reflect A across west bank to get P. The points D and P are the drop-off and pickup points, respectively.

On Your Own

5. Answers may vary. Sample: Find the best place on each side of the pool and then measure each path to find the shortest one. **8.** Let d be the distance from the starting point to the finish point. The point for the left trough is $\frac{d}{4}$ units above the starting line. The point for the right trough is $\frac{d}{4}$ units below the finish line.

Lesson 8.04

On Your Own

6a. old perimeter = 12, new perimeter = 14, old area = 5, new area = 6
b. old perimeter = 12, new perimeter = 12, old area = 5, new area = 6
c. old perimeter = 16, new perimeter = 14, old area = 8, new area = 9
d. old perimeter = 16, new perimeter = 12, old area = 8, new area = 9
8a. old surface area = 18, new surface area = 22, old volume = 4, new volume = 5
b. old surface area = 24, new surface area = 26, old volume = 6, new volume = 7
c. old surface area = 32, new surface area = 32, old volume = 10, new volume = 11 **d.** old surface area = 42, new surface area = 40, old volume = 15, new volume = 16 **e.** old surface area = 46, new surface area = 42, old volume = 17, new volume = 18 **f.** old surface area = 60, new surface area = 54, old volume = 26, new volume = 27

Lesson 8.05

Check Your Understanding

1a. 10.247 in.^{2} (exact area: $\sqrt{105}$ in.^{2})
b. 10.825 in.^{2} (exact area: $\frac{25\sqrt{3}}{4}$ in.^{2})
c. 10.062 in.^{2} (exact area: $\frac{9\sqrt{5}}{2}$ in.^{2}) **d.** For a given triangular perimeter, an equilateral triangle encloses the maximum area. **2.** 13 cm and 13 cm; 60 cm^2 **3.** A square; the argument in the For You to Do questions can easily be generalized to work not just for the perimeter 128 but for any given perimeter p.

On Your Own

6. 13 m by 11.5 m
8a. $h^2 + (5 + a)^2 = (13 + b)^2$, $h^2 + (5 - a)^2 = (13 - b)^2$ **b.** $a = 2.6b$
c. $h = \sqrt{144 - 5.76b^2}$ **d.** h is greatest when $144 - 5.76b^2$ is greatest, and this occurs when $b = 0$. But when $b = 0$, both $13 + b$ and $13 - b$ equal 13, which means that the triangle is isosceles. **11.** $16\sqrt{3}$ in.^{2}; 36 in.^{2}; the area of the rectangle

Lesson 8.06

Check Your Understanding

1. The first polygon. Answers may vary. Sample: Cut up the second polygon and show that it fits inside the first polygon with some left over. **2.** Label the polygon $ABCDE$ starting with the bottom left vertex and ending with the bottom right vertex. Draw $\overleftrightarrow{BD}$ and reflect point C across $\overleftrightarrow{BD}$ to C'. Draw $ABC'DE$. **3.** A rectangle with side lengths 20, 30, 20, and 30; suppose $ABCD$ is a parallelogram with $AB = 20$ and $AD = 30$. Let h be the length of the perpendicular segment from B to $\overleftrightarrow{AD}$. If $\angle A$ is acute, then $h = 20 \sin A$; so $h < 20$ since $\sin A < 1$. If $\angle A$ is obtuse, then $h = 20 \sin (180° - m\angle A)$; so $h < 20$ since $\sin (180° - m\angle A) < 1$. If $\angle A$ is a right angle, then $h = AB = 20$. In this last case, h has its maximum possible value and the parallelogram has its maximum possible area.

On Your Own

8. A trapezoid formed by dividing a regular hexagon in half with a line through two opposite vertices gives the maximum area. The sides made with fencing will both be 280 ft long, and the side along the stone wall will be 560 ft long. **9.** Answers may vary. Sample: One reason is that the legs are perpendicular. The perpendicular is the shortest path from a point to a line, so any other path must be longer.

Lesson 8.07

On Your Own

5a. The areas around each peak on or inside the seventh contour line are at least 1600 ft. **b.** The peak on the left is at some elevation at least 2200 ft but less than 2300 ft above sea level. The peak on the right is at some elevation at least 1900 ft but less than 2000 ft above sea level. **c.** Answers may vary. Sample: The steepest areas are where contour lines are most closely packed together. **7.** The roped-off area can be anywhere within the shaded region shown below.

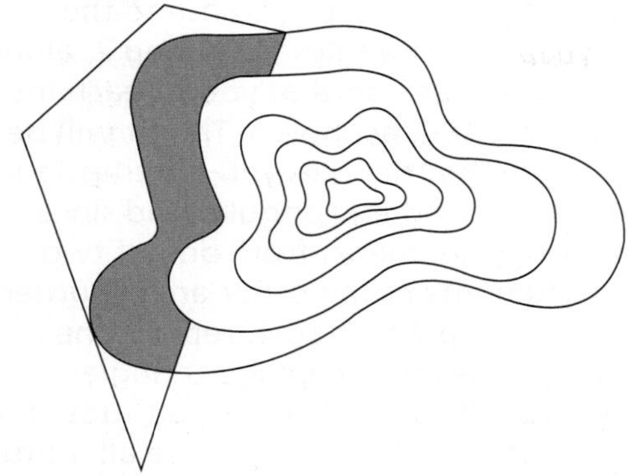

Lesson 8.08
Check Your Understanding

1. Players can be anywhere on the arc shown below.

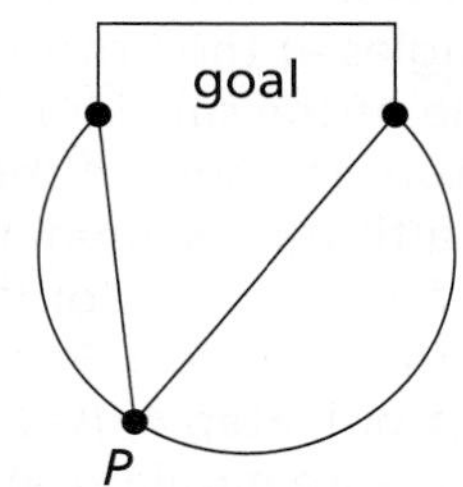

2a. circular arcs
b.

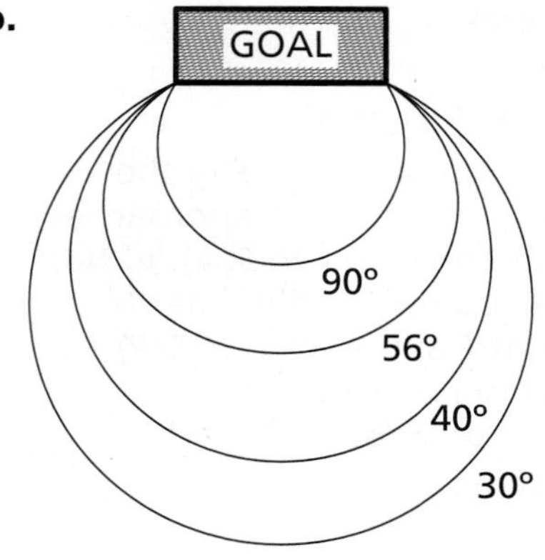

3. Answers may vary. Sample: More and more it resembles a full circle. A player is most likely to score if he or she is close to the goal posts and not too far from the perpendicular bisector of the segment that joins the base points of the goal posts.

On Your Own

4. Let A and B be the points at the front corners of the house, and let X be your location on the highway. Consider the circle through A, B, and X. The location of X that makes the circle tangent to your straight-line path is the best viewing position. **8.** The point where the line is tangent to a curve is the smallest contour line it will cross, which creates the maximum angle. **9.** about 1.5 ft from the wall; no, not if you face the wall directly, since you have a good view only of the bottom part of the picture

Lesson 8.09
Check Your Understanding

1.

2. Each contour is a pair of lines parallel to, and equidistant from, ℓ. To prove this, choose a coordinate system such that ℓ is the graph of the equation $y = 0$. For any point $P(x, y)$, the distance between P and ℓ is $|y|$. So the set of all points a distance c from ℓ is the graph of the equation $|y| = c$. The equation $|y| = c$ is equivalent to $y = c$ or $y = -c$, so the locus of points a distance c from ℓ is the two horizontal lines that pass through $(0, c)$ and $(0, -c)$.

3. Labels may vary. Sample:

4. The contour corresponding to the number 0 is the line ℓ. There are no contours for negative numbers. The contour for a positive number k is an infinitely long cylinder with line ℓ as its axis.

On Your Own

8b. No; yes, the points on $\overleftrightarrow{AB}$ that are not between A and B are excluded. **9a.** a semicircle minus its endpoints **b.** $m\angle APB$ will be greater than 90° but less than 180° **c.** $m\angle APB$ will be less than 90°. **11a.** a sphere with center O and radius 1 **b.** the point O and a set of concentric spheres with center O

Lesson 8.10
Check Your Understanding

1. The sum of the lengths of the segments from the pencil point to the nails is always equal to the length of the string.

2.

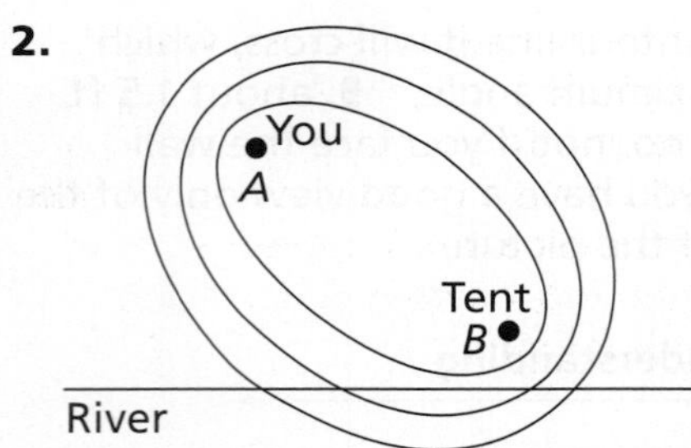

Only one contour line will be tangent to the river. The path from A to the point of tangency to B is the shortest. **3.** Drawings may vary; the point of tangency; perpendicular.

On Your Own

5. The point of tangency P is the point on $\overline{ST}$ for which the sum of the differences to A and B is least. This should be the same point that is found by using the reflection method to find the shortest path from A to B via $\overline{ST}$. With the reflection method, you could reflect B across $\overline{ST}$ and connect A to B'. $\overline{AB'}$ will intersect $\overline{ST}$ at P. But $\angle TPB \cong \angle TPB'$ since B' is the image of B across $\overline{ST}$, and $\angle TPB' \cong \angle SPA$ since these are vertical angles. Therefore, $\angle TPB \cong \angle SPA$. This implies that $m\angle SPA = m\angle TPB$.

Lesson 8.11

On Your Own

5. 60; answers may vary. Sample: point D
7. It appears that the sum is at its minimum $2\sqrt{3}$ when P is at the intersection of the medians.

Lesson 8.12

Check Your Understanding

1. B **2.** $4\sqrt{3}$ **3.** Answers may vary. Sample: If something, such as this distance sum, is the same for the entire interior of a triangle, then it will stay the same even when you get very close to a vertex.

On Your Own

5. $(-1, 1+\sqrt{3})$ or $(-1, 1-\sqrt{3})$; $(-1, 1+\sqrt{3})$, the sum is $\sqrt{3}$ **7.** $2 + \frac{12\sqrt{73}}{73}$

Lesson 8.13

Check Your Understanding

1. Answers may vary. **2.** In Step 1, draw the segments perpendicular to the sides of equilateral $\triangle ABC$ from a point D in the interior of $\triangle ABC$. In Step 2, draw segments through D parallel to the sides of $\triangle ABC$. Each of these segments should have its endpoints on the other two sides of the triangle. Three equilateral triangles will be formed, each having D as a vertex. The segments drawn in Step 1 will be altitudes of these triangles. To get the figure in Step 3, translate the small equilateral triangles from Step 2, along with their altitudes, so that you fit each into a corner of $\triangle ABC$, as shown. The fit will be perfect since the triangles you are translating are equilateral and equiangular and since perpendicular segments from one of two parallel segments to the other are congruent. To get from Step 3 to Step 4, replace the oblique altitudes of the image triangles with vertical altitudes. The new altitudes are congruent to the old ones because all altitudes of an equilateral triangle are congruent. To get from Step 4 to Step 5, use the fact that perpendicular segments from one of two parallel segments to the other are congruent. Translate the altitudes of the two small equilateral triangles at the bottom to align with the altitude of the small equilateral triangle at the top. The sum of the lengths of the three small altitudes is equal to the length of an altitude of $\triangle ABC$. **3.** For the first proof, see the answer for Exercise 1, For You to Do. For the second proof, Step 4 uses the fact that the small triangles are equilateral, and their being equilateral stems from the fact that $\triangle ABC$ is equilateral.

On Your Own

5a. $4 + \frac{3\sqrt{10}}{10}$ **b.** at A **c.** at B
d. No; $S(A) < S(P)$ for all points P in the interior of the triangle. But as P approaches A, $S(P)$ gets closer and closer to $S(A)$. **e.** No; $S(B) > S(P)$ for all points P in the interior of the triangle. But as P approaches B, $S(P)$ gets closer and closer to $S(B)$.
8a. = **b.** NG **c.** = **d.** > **e.** = **f.** > **g.** =
h. ≥ **i.** < **9a.** same

Lesson 8.14

Check Your Understanding

1. The given figure is not convex and so cannot enclose the maximum area for its perimeter. In the first diagram below, $ABCDEF$ is the original figure given in the text. Perform reflections across the dashed lines in the first diagram to get a figure with the same perimeter and a greater area that does not cross itself. Perform reflections across the dashed lines in the second diagram to get a convex polygon with the same perimeter and a yet-greater area.

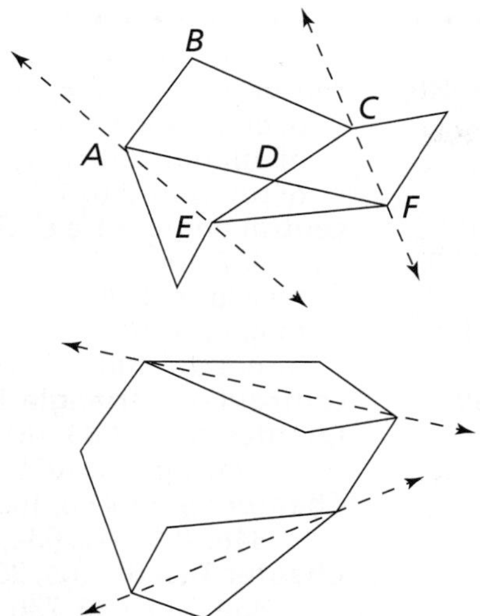

2. $54\sqrt{3}$ in.^{2}; answers may vary. Sample: a circle of radius $\frac{18}{\pi}$ in. **3.** ≈ 20.8788 cm (exact: $10\sqrt{6} \cdot \sqrt[4]{5 - 2\sqrt{5}}$ cm); answers may vary. Sample: a circle of radius $\frac{\sqrt{30\pi}}{\pi}$ cm

On Your Own

8a. $\frac{3}{4}\sqrt{3}$ unit^2 **b.** $\frac{3}{2}\sqrt{3}$ unit^2 **c.** 3 unit^2 **d.** yes **10.** The perimeter of the polygon increases, approaching the circumference of the circle. **12.** area of triangle $= 4\sqrt{3}$, area of hexagon $= 6\sqrt{3}$, area of dodecagon $= 6 + 3\sqrt{3}$

Lesson 8.15

Check Your Understanding

1. Answers may vary. Sample: Suppose a city has streets that run only north-south or east-west and that all blocks are the same length. Suppose you want to travel along the streets from a point A at one street intersection to a point B at an intersection 10 blocks east and 10 blocks south. There are many possible routes of minimum length even though the length of each such route will be 20 blocks. **2.** There is no shortest path. There are always points closer to the circle that are not on the circle.

On Your Own

4. The existence of a best curve is assumed in the opening words of each step: "Given a curve that encloses the most area." **7.** Answers may vary. Sample: We do not seem to have enough to give a proof of this result. However, the formula for the area of a regular n-gon of perimeter p (developed in Lesson 8.14, Exercise 5c) seems to produce a sequence of numbers that approach but never reach a limiting maximum value when $p = 24$ and n increases without limit.

Lesson 8.16

Check Your Understanding

1. Suppose a line ℓ cuts the perimeter in half. If the part of the area on one side of the line is greater than the part on the other side, you can reflect the part of the curve on the side with the greater area across ℓ to get a curve with the original perimeter but a greater area. This contradicts the assumption that the area of the original curve was the maximum possible area. **2.** If a closed curve with fixed perimeter encloses the maximum area, then a line ℓ that cuts the perimeter in half will also cut the area in half. So if you can prove that ℓ and the portion of the curve on one side of ℓ determine a semicircular region, the entire curve will be a circle. **3.** Yes; if the conclusion of Step 3 is true, then any point P not on a diameter $\overline{AB}$ of the curve is the vertex of a right angle whose sides pass through the endpoints of $\overline{AB}$. The midpoint of $\overline{AB}$ is equidistant from A, B, and P. So P is on a semicircle whose diameter is $\overline{AB}$. **4.** If this angle did not measure 90°, you could increase or decrease the angle to form a right triangle with larger area. This would create a new half-curve with the same perimeter as C, but enclosing more area, which would contradict your assumption that C is the best possible curve.

On Your Own

7. The existence hypothesis states that of all closed, non-self crossing curves that have a fixed perimeter, there is at least one that has the maximum possible area. You need this to proceed through Steps 2 and 3 of the proof plan. **9.** no, because the fence problem used the established fact that of all rectangles with a given perimeter, the one with maximum area is a square

Index

D

E

F

Index

Q

R

S

Index

Index

Acknowledgments

Staff Credits

The Pearson people on the CME Project team—representing design, editorial, editorial services, digital product development, publishing services, and technical operations—are listed below. Bold type denotes the core team members.

Ernest Albanese, Scott Andrews, Carolyn Artin, Michael Avidon, Margaret Banker, Suzanne Biron, Beth Blumberg, Stacie Cartwright, Carolyn Chappo, Casey Clark, Bob Craton, Jason Cuoco, Sheila DeFazio, Patty Fagan, **Frederick Fellows**, **Patti Fromkin**, Paul J. Gagnon, Cynthia Harvey, Gillian Kahn, Jonathan Kier, Jennifer King, Elizabeth Krieble, Sara Levendusky, Lisa Lin, Carolyn Lock, Clay Martin, **Carolyn McGuire**, Rich McMahon, Eve Melnechuk, Cynthia Metallides, **Hope Morley**, Jen Paley, Linda Punskovsky, Mairead Reddin, Marcy Rose, Rashid Ross, Carol Roy, Jewel Simmons, Ted Smykal, Laura Smyth, Kara Stokes, Richard Sullivan, Tiffany Taylor-Sullivan, Catherine Terwilliger, Mark Tricca, Lauren Van Wart, Paula Vergith, **Joe Will**, **Kristin Winters**, Allison Wyss

Additional Credits

Niki Birbilis, Gina Choe, Christine Nevola, Jill A. Ort, Lillian Pelaggi, Deborah Savona

Cover Design and Illustration

9 Surf Studios

Cover Photography

(BL) Jim Cummins/Corbis, © Irin-k/Shutterstock.

Illustration

Kerry Cashman, Rich McMahon, Jen Paley, Rashid Ross, Ted Smykal

Maps

XNR Productions, Inc.
p.686

Photography

Photo locators denoted as follows: Top (T), Center (C), Bottom (B), Left (L), Right (R), Background (Bkgd)

Front Matter: Pages iT, Irin-k/Shutterstock; **iB,** Jim Cummins/Corbis; **vi,** Brian Cahn/ZUMA Wire/Alamy; **viii,** Laurie Chamberlain/Corbis; **x,** Grigory Dukor/Reuters/Corbis; **xii,** Redmond Durrell/Alamy; **xviiTL,** David A. Parmenter Jr.; **xviiTR,** David A. Parmenter Jr.; **xviiB,** Redmond Durrell/Alamy.

Pages 2–3, Seventysix/123RF; **4,** Altrendo Images/Getty Images; **8,** Bill Ross/Corbis; **21,** David R. Frazier Photolibrary/Alamy; **23,** TS Corrigan/Alamy; **24,** Maskot/Alloy/Corbis; **48,** Brian Cahn/ZUMA Wire/Alamy; **64,** Brian Cahn/ZUMA Wire/Alamy; **65,** Terry Leung/Pearson Education; **70–71,** Altrendo travel/Getty Images; **72,** Gary Blakeley/Shutterstock; **74,** Lew Robertson/Corbis; **79,** Andrey Bayda/Shutterstock; **87,** Gary Blakeley/Shutterstock; **88,** Martin Shields/Alamy; **98,** Jim Cummins/Corbis; **112,** Martin Shields/Alamy; **114,** David Bergman/Corbis; **125,** Timothy D. Easley/AP Images; **132,** Georgette Douwma/Getty Images; **138T,** Elio Ciol/Corbis; **138B,** Mushy/Fotolia; **141,** David Bergman/Corbis; **142,** In Depth Imagery/Alamy; **160,** Rick Friedman/Corbis; **168–169,** Wolfgang Piefel/EyeEm/Getty Images; **189,** Steve Allen/Brand X/Corbis; **201T,** Michele Falzone/JAI/Corbis; **201B,** Buena Vista Images/Getty Images; **206,** Christian Hoehn/Getty Images; **216,** MAPS/Corbis; **225,** Robert Daly/Getty Images; **229Bkgd,** MAPS/Corbis; **229T,** Stephen Finn/Alamy; **229B,** Stephen Finn/Alamy; **230,** Scott Peterson/Getty Images; **237,** Larry Lee Photography/Corbis; **238,** Jose Fuste Raga/Corbis; **255,** Laurie Chamberlain/Corbis; **260–261,** JLImages/Alamy; **268L,** John Foxx Collection/Imagestate; **268R,** Racerunner/Fotolia; **271L,** Frontpage/Shutterstock; **271R,** Stephen Saks Photography/Alamy; **288,** Kavashkin Boris/ITAR-TASS/Corbis; **293,** Cusp/SuperStock; **314,** Lesley Ann Miller/WireImage/Getty Images; **319,** Enrique Algarra/AGE Fotostock; **352–353,** Pincasso/Shutterstock; **354,** Mark Wilson/AP Images; **366,** Big Cheese Photo LLC/Alamy; **373,** John Gaps III/AP Images; **374,** Krmelda/123RF; **385,** Matt Rourke/AP Images; **394,** Robert Harding Picture Library/Alamy; **396,** Allan Munsie/Alamy; **399,** Grigory Dukor/Reuters/Corbis; **407,** Ace stock limited/Alamy; **433,** Allan Munsie/Alamy; **434,** Torleif Svensson/Corbis; **443,** Jeffrey Coolidge/Getty Images; **447,** Richard S. Durrance/Getty Images; **454–455,** ER Productions/Corbis; **455,** Stockbyte/Getty Images; **456,** Artist painting a portrait over a grid for accurate proportion, printed Paris 1737 (engraving), Bosse, Abraham (1602-76) (after)/Private Collection/The Stapleton Collection/Bridgeman Images; **477,** Duerer, Albrecht (1471–1528) Oswold Krel. Center panel from a tryptich. 1499. Oil on wood, 49.7 x 38.9 cm. Inv. WAF 230./Art Resource, NY; **478,** Ted Pink/Alamy; **480,** David R. Frazier Photolibrary/Alamy; **510,** Ted Pink/Alamy; **538,** MacGregor and Gordon/Getty Images; **548–549,** David A. Parmenter Jr.; **549,** David A. Parmenter Jr.; **550,** WavebreakMediaMicro/Fotolia; **554,** WavebreakMediaMicro/Fotolia; **559,** Craig Tuttle/Corbis; **561,** Graciela Rossi/123RF; **589,** WavebreakMediaMicro/Fotolia; **597,** Adam Woolfitt/Corbis; **606,** Joel Day/Alamy; **611,** Bob Krist/Corbis; **615,** FB-StockPhoto/Alamy; **622,** Redmond Durrell/Alamy; **631,** 68/Ocean/Corbis; **645,** Frank Krahmer/Corbis; **647,** Karen A. Wyle/AGE Fotostock; **670,** Brett Roseman/Daily Southtown/AP Images; **684,** David McNew/Getty Images; **686,** XNR Productions; **698,** David R. Frazier Photolibrary/Alamy; **705,** Andreslebedev/Fotolia; **706,** Derek Mitchell/Alamy; **730,** Gusto/Science Source.

Note: Every effort has been made to locate the copyright owner of the material reprinted in this book. Omissions brought to our attention will be corrected in subsequent editions.

Additional Credits:

Chapter 1: Whole chapter taken from Chapter 1 of *CME Project: Geometry.*

Chapter 2: Whole chapter taken from Chapter 2 of *CME Project: Geometry.*

Chapter 3: Whole chapter taken from Chapter 3 of *CME Project: Geometry.*

Chapter 4: Whole chapter taken from Chapter 4 of *CME Project: Geometry.*

Chapter 5: Lessons 5.01 through 5.06, 5.08 through 5.10, and 5.12 through 5.16 taken from Chapter 5 of *CME Project: Geometry.* Lessons 5.07 and 5.11 taken from *CME Project: Geometry Common Core Additional Lessons.*

Chapter 6: Whole chapter taken from Chapter 6 of *CME Project: Geometry.*

Chapter 7: Lessons 7.01 through 7.03 and 7.06 through 7.14 taken from Chapter 7 of *CME Project: Geometry.* Lessons 7.04 and 7.05 taken from *CME Project: Geometry Common Core Additional Lessons.*

Chapter 8: Whole chapter taken from Chapter 8 of *CME Project: Geometry.*